THESAURUS

OF ENGLISH WORDS AND PHRASES

*Classified and Arranged so as to Facilitate the
Expression of Ideas and to Assist in Literary
Composition*

by

PETER MARK ROGET, M.D., F.R.S.

Enlarged by

JOHN LEWIS ROGET, M.A.

New Edition Revised and Enlarged by

SAMUEL ROMILLY ROGET, M.A.

1724

LONGMANS

LONGMANS, GREEN AND CO LTD
6 & 7 CLIFFORD STREET, LONDON W I
605-611 LONSDALE STREET, MELBOURNE C I
443 LOCKHART ROAD, HONG KONG
ACCRA, AUCKLAND, IBADAN
KINGSTON (JAMAICA), KUALA LUMPUR
LAHORE, NAIROBI, SALISBURY (RHODESIA)
LONGMANS SOUTHERN AFRICA (PTY) LTD
THIBAULT HOUSE, THIBAULT SQUARE, CAPE TOWN
LONGMANS, GREEN AND CO INC
119 WEST 40TH STREET, NEW YORK 18
LONGMANS, GREEN AND CO
137 BOND STREET, TORONTO 2
ORIENT LONGMANS PRIVATE LTD.
CALCUTTA, BOMBAY, MADRAS
DELHI, HYDERABAD, DACCA

AUTHORIZED COPYRIGHT EDITION
IN THE BERNE CONVENTION COUNTRIES

New Edition   .   .   .   July 1936
New Impressions August 1937, January
1939, May 1941, September 1941, February
1942, August 1942, January 1943, October
1944, January 1946, November 1946,
February 1949 (Reprint of 1941 Canadian
Revision), February 1952, August 1952, July
1953, January 1956, January 1958, November
1958, January 1959, May 1959

New Impressions by photolithography, April
1960, August 1960 and October 1960

Printed in Great Britain by
Lowe and Brydone (Printers) Limited, London, N.W.10

PREFACE
TO
1936 EDITION

In preparing the present edition, the Index (pp. 387–705) upon which the usefulness of the work so largely depends has been checked, line by line, from beginning to end. Not only have a considerable number of corrections been made but the opportunity has been taken to revise the index generally and to add further references. The editor should also acknowledge the kindness of many correspondents who, after expressing their appreciation of the value of the Thesaurus in their work and play, have helped to render it more nearly perfect by their suggestions both as regards the text and the index. After making these corrections in the type, a new set of plates has been made, and it is hoped that the edition now offered will prove of greater utility than any of its many predecessors.

S. R. R.

July 1936

PREFACE
TO
1933 EDITION

As explained in the author's original preface to the Thesaurus, Dr. P. M. Roget made a list in MS. of words classified according to the ideas that they express, for his own use, as long ago as 1805; and a facsimile of the first page of this interesting little notebook is given in the frontispiece of the present edition. It was not, however, until he was over seventy years of age that he could spare the time to undertake the colossal task of expanding this into the famous volume which was published by Messrs. Longmans, Brown, Green & Longman in 1852.

This was followed by a second edition in 1853, a ' third and cheaper edition, enlarged and improved ' two years later, a fourth edition in the same year, and a fifth edition in 1857. Since then edition has followed edition almost every year, and sometimes two or even three times in one year, until 76 printings have been called for, totalling some two hundred thousand books, and it is worthy of note that after eighty years the Thesaurus is still published by the same firm, and from the same address in Paternoster Row, now as when issued originally.

On Dr. Roget's death at an advanced age in 1869, the work passed into the hands of his son, John Lewis Roget, who completed the further comprehensive revision and enlargement on which Dr. Roget was engaged at the time of his death. This new edition, with its much more extensive index, appeared in 1879, and he continued to revise periodical reprints until his own death in 1908, when it devolved upon the undersigned to carry on the task initiated by his grandfather, and some further enlargement was made in 1925.

In the edition now presented a large number of further new words and phrases have been added throughout the book ; but in very few cases have words been removed, because archaic and even obsolete words are often sought for by authors. A few examples of alternative and obsolete spelling have however been removed, but no alteration whatever has been made in the general arrangement and classification of the categories. In its preparation advantage has been taken of a considerable number of suggestions from both sides of the Atlantic, and the editor wishes particularly to acknowledge the valuable assistance of Mr. Willard Jerome Heggen, to whom a substantial proportion of the additions are due, including some expressions in commoner use in America than in England, the presence of which in the Thesaurus will, it is hoped, extend its general usefulness.

S. R. ROGET

October 1933

PREFACE

TO

THE FIRST EDITION

(1852)

It is now nearly fifty years since I first projected a system of verbal classification similar to that on which the present Work is founded. Conceiving that such a compilation might help to supply my own deficiencies, I had, in the year 1805, completed a classed catalogue of words on a small scale, but on the same principle, and nearly in the same form, as the Thesaurus now published.* I had often during that long interval found this little collection, scanty and imperfect as it was, of much use to me in literary composition, and often contemplated its extension and improvement; but a sense of the magnitude of the task, amidst a multitude of other avocations, deterred me from the attempt. Since my retirement from the duties of Secretary of the Royal Society, however, finding myself possessed of more leisure, and believing that a repertory of which I had myself experienced the advantage might, when amplified, prove useful to others, I resolved to embark in an undertaking which, for the last three or four years, has given me incessant occupation, and has, indeed, imposed upon me an amount of labour very much greater than I had anticipated. Notwithstanding all the pains I have bestowed on its execution, I am fully aware of its numerous deficiencies and imperfections, and of its falling far short of the degree of excellence that might be attained. But, in a Work of this nature, where perfection is placed at so great a distance, I have thought it best to limit my ambition to that moderate share of merit which it may claim in its present form; trusting to the indulgence of those for whose benefit it is intended, and to the candour of critics who, while they find it easy to detect faults, can at the same time duly appreciate difficulties.

P. M. Roget

April 29th, 1852

* A facsimile of the first page of this little manuscript book which is the original form of the Thesaurus is given in the frontispiece.

EDITOR'S PREFACE

(1879)

(*Slightly Abridged*)

THE FIRST EDITION of Dr. Roget's Thesaurus was published in the year 1852, and a second in the ensuing spring. On the issue of the third, in 1855, the volume was stereotyped. Since that time until now, the work has been reprinted in the same form and with little alteration, in rapidly succeeding editions, the printing of which has worn out the original plates.

During the last years of the author's life, which closed, at a very advanced age, in the month of September, 1869, he was engaged in the task of collecting additional words and phrases, for an enlarged edition which he had long projected. This he did not live to complete, and it became my duty, as his son, to attempt to carry the design into execution.

The result of the author's labours was embodied in a copy of the Thesaurus, in which the margins and spaces about the letterpress were closely covered with written words and phrases, without any very precise indication of the places in the text where additions or alterations were intended to be made. On a careful examination of these *addenda*, I came to the conclusion that, in order to introduce them with advantage, it would be necessary to make some slight changes; without, however, interfering at all with the framework of the book, and but little with the details of its system. In this proceeding my course has been mainly determined by the following considerations.

Any attempt at a philosophical arrangement under categories of the words of our language must reveal the fact that it is impossible to separate and circumscribe the several groups by absolutely distinct boundary lines. Many words, originally employed to express simple conceptions, are found to be capable, with perhaps a very slight modification of meaning, of being applied in many varied associations. Connecting links, thus formed, induce an approach between the categories; and a danger arises that the outlines of our classification may, by their means, become confused and eventually merged. Were we to disengage these interwoven ramifications, and seek to confine every word to its main or original import, we should find some secondary meaning has become so firmly associated with many words and phrases, that to sever the alliance would be to deprive our language of the richness due to an infinity of natural adaptations.

Were we, on the other hand, to attempt to include, in each category of the Thesaurus, every word and phrase which could by any possibility be appropriately used in relation to the leading idea for which that category was designed, we should impair, if not destroy, the whole use and value of the book. For, in the endeavour to enrich our treasury of expression, we might easily allow ourselves to be led imperceptibly onward by the natural association of one word with another, and to add word after word, until group after group would successively be absorbed under some single heading, and the fundamental divisions of the system be effaced. The small cluster of nearly synonymous words, which had formed the nucleus of a category, would be lost in a sea of phrases, and it would become difficult to recognize those which were peculiarly adapted to express the leading ideas.

These considerations were material in dealing with the new and multitudinous store of words and phrases which the author had accumulated. Many of these were altogether new to the Thesaurus. Many were merely repetitions in new places of words already included in its pages. With reference to cases similar to the latter, the author had declared it to have been a general rule with him 'to place words and phrases which appertain more especially to one head, also under other heads to which they have a relation,' whenever it appeared to him 'that this repetition would suit the convenience of the inquirer and spare him the trouble of turning to other parts of the work.' But, with the now increased mass of words, it became a question, in many cases, whether such repetition would still prove convenient. Where categories might by that course be unduly swollen, or where they might, by reason of their being separated from each other by subtile distinctions or faint lines of demarcation, be thereby too nearly assimilated, I thought it would often be better to confine words of the kind referred to to their primary headings. The necessity of keeping the book within reasonable dimensions had also to be borne in mind.

Under these circumstances, the best method of ensuring the ready accessibility of the multitude of words now to be dealt with, and at the same time preserving unimpaired the unity of the several categories, appeared to me to lie in the copious use of references from one place in the book to another. Relying on this contrivance as a means of opening more widely the resources of the collection, by making the groups of words mutually suggestive, and thereby leading not only to more varied forms of expression, but to kindred ideas, I have added largely to the references already inserted by the author. I have also ventured occasionally to substitute a reference for a group of words, when the identical group existed in another place, and could thus be made immediately available.

In order, at the same time, to make the value of the references more appreciable, I have (whenever it has appeared to me to be necessary) inserted, in a parenthesis, a word indicating the nature of the group or category referred to. Any one using the book will thereby be enabled to judge whether it will be worth his while to turn to the place in question.

The cross references may also be looked upon as indicating in some degree the natural points of connection between the categories, and the ramification of the ideas which they embody. As would be the case under any classification of language, a large proportion of the expressions, to find which recourse is had to the Thesaurus, lie on an ill-defined border land between one category and another; and it is not always easy, even with the aid of a carefully compiled index, to determine under which of several allied headings they should be sought. In the present edition, when the inquirer has once started on his voyage of discovery, the references enable him to pass freely from one division to another without recurring to the Index.

Many new words have also been inserted which were not contained in the author's manuscript.

Except in a very few cases, where distinct ideas were obviously united under one head, I have not had the presumption to meddle with the author's division into categories; but, within each category, I have endeavoured to carry somewhat further the sorting of words according to the ideas which they convey.

With these objects in view, I have supplied the work with a new and elaborate Index, much more complete than that which was appended to the previous editions. Although, in the original design of his work, the author appears to have conceived the process of search for a required expression as one in which the system of classification would be first consulted, and the Index afterwards called in aid if necessary, I believe that almost everyone who uses the book finds it more convenient to have recourse to the Index first.

From the peculiar nature and use of the Thesaurus, its Index will be found to differ, in some of its essential functions, from an alphabetical table of contents. The present Index does not merely afford an indication of the place where every given word or topic occurs or is dealt with in the text; but it is intended as a guide to other expressions which may be found there. The word we look out in this Index is not that which we require, but that which we wish to avoid. It is, therefore, not necessary that every word there given should be a repetition of one in the text. It may even happen that the word selected as a guide, though suggestive of the group wanted, is wholly unfit to be comprised within it.

The new Index contains not only all the *words* in the book (without needless repetition of conjugate forms), but likewise the *phrases*, all of which had been excluded from the Index to the previous editions. It is hoped that these additions, although they increase the bulk of the book, will have the effect of extending its usefulness in at least a corresponding degree.

Some changes of detail have also been made, where the form of the work seemed susceptible of improvement, and there was no reason to suppose that the author would have disapproved of the alteration. In the previous editions, the *phrases* were in general placed in separate paragraphs, under the heading **Phr.**, in each of the subdivisions assigned to the different grammatical parts of speech. In the present edition, *words* and *phrases* are placed together, and the heading **Phr.** is only employed in the case of phrases which have no convenient place in such an arrangement. Much space has been saved, and many repetitions have been avoided, by the use of lines and hyphens, where words or phrases in the same group have syllables or parts in common, and by references from one part of speech to another. These abbreviations may be best explained by examples, of which the following are a few:—

'with -relation, - reference, - respect, - regard- to'; is meant to include the phrases 'with relation to,' 'with reference to,' 'with respect to,' 'with regard to.'

'root -, weed -, grub -, rake- -up, - out;' includes 'root up,' 'root out,' 'weed up,' 'weed out,' 'grub up,' 'grub out,' 'rake up,' 'rake out.'

'away from -, foreign to -, beside- the -purpose, - question, - transaction, - point;' includes 'away from the purpose,' 'foreign to the purpose,' 'beside the purpose,' 'away from the question,' 'foreign to the question,' 'foreign to the transaction,' 'beside the question,' 'away from the point,' 'beside the transaction,' 'foreign to the point,' 'away from the transaction,' 'beside the point.'

'raze - to the ground'; includes 'raze,' and 'raze to the ground.'

'campan-iform, -ulate, -iliform;' includes 'campaniform,' 'campanulate,' and 'campaniliform.'

'goodness &c. *adj.*'; 'badly &c. *adj.*'; 'hindred &c. *v.*'; include all words similarly formed from synonyms of 'good,' 'bad,' and 'hinder,' respectively, given under the headings **Adj.** and **V.** in the same categories where the abbreviations occur.

The participle 'to' before a verb has in all cases been rejected, the heading **V.** being thought sufficiently distinctive; the use of capitals for the initial letters of the first words of paragraphs has been abandoned, as giving those words undue importance; and the title of each category has been kept distinct from the collection of words under its heading.

I should be ungrateful were I not to acknowledge the assistance derived, both by my father and myself, from various suggestions made by well-wishers to the work, some of whom have been personally unknown to either of us; and also to record my thanks to several kind friends, and to Messrs. Spottiswoode and Co.'s careful reader, for valuable aid during the passage of the sheets through the press.

JOHN L. ROGET

March 17th, 1879.

INTRODUCTION

THE present Work is intended to supply, with respect to the English language, a desideratum hitherto unsupplied in any language; namely, a collection of the words it contains and of the idiomatic combinations peculiar to it, arranged, not in alphabetical order as they are in a Dictionary, but according to the *ideas* which they express.* The purpose of an ordinary dictionary is simply to explain the meaning of the words; and the problem of which it professes to furnish the solution may be stated thus:—The word being given, to find its signification, or the idea it is intended to convey. The object aimed at in the present undertaking is exactly the converse of this: namely,—The idea being given, to find the word, or words, by which that idea may be most fitly and aptly expressed. For this purpose, the words and phrases of the language are here classed, not according to their sound or their orthography, but strictly according to their *signification*.

The communication of our thoughts by means of language, whether spoken or written, like every other object of mental exertion, constitutes a peculiar art, which, like other arts, cannot be acquired in any perfection but by long and continued practice. Some, indeed, there are more highly gifted than others with a facility of expression, and naturally endowed with the power of eloquence; but to none is it at all times an easy process to embody, in exact and appropriate language, the various trains of ideas that are passing through the mind, or to depict in their true colours and proportions, the diversified and nicer shades of feeling which accompany them. To those who are unpractised in the art of composition, or unused to extempore speaking, these difficulties present themselves in their most formidable aspect. However distinct may be our views, however vivid our conceptions, or however fervent our emotions, we cannot but be often conscious that the phraseology we have at our command is inadequate to do them justice. We seek in vain the words we need, and strive ineffectually to devise forms of expression which shall faithfully portray our thoughts and sentiments. The appropriate terms, notwithstanding our utmost efforts, cannot be conjured up at will. Like 'spirits from the vasty deep,' they come not when we call; and we are driven to the employment of a set of words and phrases either too general or too

* See note in p. xxi.

limited, too strong or too feeble, which suit not the occasion, which hit not the mark we aim at; and the result of our prolonged exertion is a style at once laboured and obscure, vapid and redundant, or vitiated by the still graver faults of affectation or ambiguity.

It is to those who are thus painfully groping their way and struggling with the difficulties of composition, that this Work professes to hold out a helping hand. The assistance it gives is that of furnishing on every topic a copious store of words and phrases, adapted to express all the recognizable shades and modifications of the general idea under which those words and phrases are arranged. The inquirer can readily select, out of the ample collection spread out before his eyes in the following pages, those expressions which are best suited to his purpose, and which might not have occurred to him without such assistance. In order to make this selection, he scarcely ever need engage in any critical or elaborate study of the subtle distinction existing between synonymous terms; for if the materials set before him be sufficiently abundant, an instinctive tact will rarely fail to lead him to the proper choice. Even while glancing over the columns of this Work, his eye may chance to light upon a particular term, which may save the cost of a clumsy paraphrase, or spare the labour of a tortuous circumlocution. Some felicitous turn of expression thus introduced will frequently open to the mind of the reader a whole vista of collateral ideas, which could not, without an extended and obtrusive episode, have been unfolded to his view; and often will the judicious insertion of a happy epithet, like a beam of sunshine in a landscape, illumine and adorn the subject which it touches, imparting new grace and giving life and spirit to the picture.

Every workman in the exercise of his art should be provided with proper implements. For the fabrication of complicated and curious pieces of mechanism, the artisan requires a corresponding assortment of various tools and instruments. For giving proper effect to the fictions of the drama, the actor should have at his disposal a well-furnished wardrobe, supplying the costumes best suited to the personages he is to represent. For the perfect delineation of the beauties of nature, the painter should have within reach of his pencil every variety and combination of hues and tints. Now, the writer, as well as the orator, employs for the accomplishment of his purposes the instrumentality of words; it is in words that he clothes his thoughts; it is by means of words that he depicts his feelings. It is therefore essential to his success that he be provided with a copious vocabulary, and that he possess an entire command of all the resources and appliances of his language. To the acquisition of this power no procedure appears more directly conducive than the study of a methodized system such as that now offered to his use.

The utility of the present Work will be appreciated more especially by those who are engaged in the arduous process of translating into English a work written in another language. Simple as the operation may appear, on a superficial view, of rendering into English each of its sentences, the task of transfusing, with perfect exactness, the sense of the original, preserving at the same time the style and character of its composition, and reflecting with fidelity the mind and the spirit of the author, is a task of extreme difficulty. The cultivation of this useful department of literature was in ancient times strongly recommended both by Cicero and by Quintilian, as essential to the formation of a good writer and accomplished orator. Regarded simply as a mental exercise, the practice of translation is the best training for the attainment of that mastery of language and felicity of diction, which are the sources of the highest oratory, and are requisite for the possession of a graceful and persuasive eloquence. By rendering ourselves the faithful interpreters of the thoughts and feelings of others, we are rewarded with the acquisition of greater readiness and facility in correctly expressing our own; as he who has best learned to execute the orders of a commander, becomes himself best qualified to command.

In the earliest periods of civilization, translators have been the agents for propagating knowledge from nation to nation, and the value of their labours has been inestimable; but, in the present age, when so many different languages have become the depositories of the vast treasures of literature and of science which have been accumulating for centuries, the utility of accurate translations has greatly increased, and it has become a more important object to attain perfection in the art.

The use of language is not confined to its being the medium through which we communicate our ideas to one another; it fulfils a no less important function as an *instrument of thought*; not being merely its vehicle, but giving it wings for flight. Metaphysicians are agreed that scarcely any of our intellectual operations could be carried on to any considerable extent, without the agency of words. None but those who are conversant with the philosophy of mental phenomena, can be aware of the immense influence that is exercised by language in promoting the development of our ideas, in fixing them in the mind, and in detaining them for steady contemplation. Into every process of reasoning, language enters as an essential element. Words are the instruments by which we form all our abstractions, by which we fashion and embody our ideas, and by which we are enabled to glide along a series of premises and conclusions with a rapidity so great as to leave in the memory no trace of the successive steps of the process; and we remain unconscious how much we owe to this potent auxiliary of the reasoning faculty. It is on this ground, also, that the present Work founds a claim to utility. The review of a catalogue of words of analogous signification, will often suggest by association other trains of thought, which, presenting the subject under new and varied aspects, will vastly expand the sphere of our mental vision. Amidst the many objects thus brought within the range of our contemplation, some striking similitude or appropriate image, some ex-cursive flight or brilliant conception, may flash on the mind, giving point and force to our arguments, awakening a responsive chord in the imagination or sensibility of the reader, and procuring for our reasonings a more ready access both to his understanding and to his heart.

It is of the utmost consequence that strict accuracy should regulate our use of language, and that every one should acquire the power and the habit of expressing his thoughts with perspicuity and correctness. Few, indeed, can appreciate the real extent and importance of that influence which language has always exercised on human affairs, or can be aware how often these are determined by causes much slighter than are apparent to a superficial observer. False logic, disguised under specious phraseology, too often gains the assent of the unthinking multitude, disseminating far and wide the seeds of prejudice and error. Truisms pass current, and wear the semblance of profound wisdom, when dressed up in the tinsel garb of antithetical phrases, or set off by an imposing pomp of paradox. By a confused jargon of involved and mystical sentences, the imagination is easily inveigled into a transcendental region of clouds, and the understanding beguiled into the belief that it is acquiring knowledge and approaching truth. A misapplied or misapprehended term is sufficient to give rise to fierce and interminable disputes; a misnomer has turned the tide of popular opinion; a verbal sophism has decided a party question; an artful watchword, thrown among combustible materials, has kindled the flame of deadly warfare, and changed the destiny of an empire.

In constructing the following system of classification of the ideas which are expressible by language, my chief aim has been to obtain the greatest amount of practical utility. I have accordingly adopted such principles of arrangement as appeared to me to be the simplest and most natural, and which would not require, either for their comprehension or application, any disciplined acumen, or depth of metaphysical or antiquarian lore. Eschewing all needless refinements and subtleties, I have taken as my guide the more obvious characters of the ideas for which expressions were to be tabulated, arranging them under such classes and categories as reflection and experience had taught me would conduct the inquirer most readily and quickly to the object of his search. Commencing with the ideas expressing abstract relations, I proceeded to those which relate to space and to the phenomena of the material world, and lastly to those in which the mind is concerned, and which comprehend intellect, volition, and feeling; thus establishing six primary Classes of Categories.

1. The first of these classes comprehends ideas derived from the more general and ABSTRACT RELATIONS among things, such as *Existence, Resemblance, Quantity, Order, Number, Time, Power.*

2. The second class refers to SPACE and its various relations, including *Motion,* or change of place.

3. The third class includes all ideas that relate to the MATERIAL WORLD; namely, the *Properties of Matter*, such as *Solidity, Fluidity, Heat, Sound, Light*, and the *Phenomena* they present, as well as the simple *Perceptions* to which they give rise.

4. The fourth class embraces all ideas of phenomena relating to the INTELLECT and its operations; comprising the *Acquisition*, the *Retention*, and the *Communication of Ideas*.

5. The fifth class includes the ideas derived from the exercise of VOLITION; embracing the phenomena and results of our *Voluntary and Active Powers;* such as *Choice, Intention, Utility, Action, Antagonism, Authority, Compact, Property*, &c.

6. The sixth and last class comprehends all ideas derived from the operation of our SENTIENT AND MORAL POWERS; including our *Feelings, Emotions, Passions*, and *Moral and Religious Sentiments*.*

The further subdivisions and minuter details will be best understood from an inspection of the Tabular Synopsis of Categories prefixed to the Work, in which are specified the several *topics* or *heads of signification*, under which the words have been arranged. By the aid of this table the reader will, with a little practice, readily discover the place which the particular topic he is in search of occupies in the series; and on turning to the page in the body of the Work which contains it, he will find the group of expressions he requires, out of which he may cull those that are most appropriate to his purpose. For the convenience of reference, I have designated each separate group or heading by a particular number; so that if, during the search, any doubt or difficulty should occur, recourse may be had to the copious alphabetical Index of words at the end of the volume, which will at once indicate the number of the required group.†

---

* It must necessarily happen in every system of classification framed with this view, that ideas and expressions arranged under one class must include also ideas relating to another class; for the operations of the *Intellect* generally involve also those of the *Will*, and *vice versâ;* and our *Affections* and *Emotions*, in like manner, generally imply the agency both of the *Intellect* and of the *Will*. All that can be effected, therefore, is to arrange the words according to the principal or dominant idea they convey. *Teaching*, for example, although a Voluntary act, relates primarily to the Communication of Ideas, and is accordingly placed at No. 537, under Class IV Division (II). On the other hand, *Choice, Conduct, Skill*, &c., although implying the co-operation of Voluntary with Intellectual acts, relate principally to the former, and are therefore arranged under Class V.

† It often happens that the same word admits of various applications, or may be used in different senses. In consulting the Index the reader will be guided to the number of the heading under which that word, in each particular acceptation, will be found, by means of *supplementary words* printed in Italics; which words, however, are not to be understood as explaining the meaning of the word to which they are annexed, but only as assisting in the required reference. I have also, for shortness' sake, generally omitted words immediately derived from the primary one inserted, which sufficiently represents the whole group of correlative words referable to the same heading. Thus the number affixed to *Beauty* applies to all its derivatives, such as *Beautiful, Beauteous, Beautifulness, Beautifully*, &c., the insertion of which was therefore needless. [In compiling the new Index the editor has adopted this principle as a general rule, from which, however, he has not scrupled to depart where he has deemed it expedient to do so.]

The object I have proposed to myself in this Work would have been but imperfectly attained if I had confined myself to a mere catalogue of words, and had omitted the numerous phrases and forms of expression composed of several words, which are of such frequent use as to entitle them to rank among the constituent parts of the language.* Very few of these verbal combinations, so essential to the knowledge of our native tongue, and so profusely abounding in its daily use, are to be met with in ordinary dictionaries. These phrases and forms of expression I have endeavoured diligently to collect and to insert in their proper places, under the general ideas that they are designed to convey. Some of these conventional forms, indeed, partake of the nature of proverbial expressions; but actual proverbs, as such, being wholly of a didactic character, do not come within the scope of the present Work; and the reader must therefore not expect to find them here inserted.†

For the purpose of exhibiting with greater distinctness the relations between words expressing opposite and correlative ideas, I have, whenever the subject admitted of such an arrangement, placed them in two parallel columns in the same page, so that each group of expressions may be readily contrasted with those which occupy the adjacent column, and constitute their antithesis. By carrying the eye from the one to the other, the inquirer may often discover forms of expression, of which he may avail himself advantageously, to diversify and infuse vigour into his phraseology. Rhetoricians, indeed, are well aware of the power derived from the skilful introduction of antitheses in giving point to an argument, and imparting force and brilliancy to the diction. A too frequent and indiscreet employment of this figure of rhetoric may, it is true, give rise to a vicious and affected style; but it is unreasonable to condemn indiscriminately the occasional and moderate use of a practice on account of its possible abuse.

The study of correlative terms existing in a particular language, may often throw valuable light on the manners and customs of the nations using it. Thus, Hume has drawn important inferences with regard to the state of society among the ancient Romans, from certain deficiencies which he remarked in the Latin language.‡

---

* For example:—To take time by the forelock;—to turn over a new leaf;—to show the white feather;—to have a finger in the pie;—to let the cat out of the bag;—to take care of number one;—to kill two birds with one stone, &c., &c.

† See Trench, *On the Lessons in Proverbs.*

‡ 'It is an universal observation,' he remarks, 'which we may form upon language, that where two related parts of a whole bear any proportion to each other, in numbers, rank, or consideration, there are always correlative terms invented which answer to both the parts, and express their mutual relation. If they bear no proportion to each other, the term is only invented for the less, and marks its distinction from the whole. Thus, *man* and *woman*, *master* and *servant*, *father* and *son*, *prince* and *subject*, *stranger* and *citizen*, are correlative terms. But the words *seaman, carpenter, smith, tailor*, &c., have no correspondent terms, which express those who are no seamen, no carpenters, &c. Languages differ very much with regard to the particular words where this distinction obtains; and may thence afford very strong inferences concerning the manners and customs of different nations. The military government of the

In many cases, two ideas which are completely opposed to each other, admit of an intermediate or neutral idea, equidistant from both; all these being expressible by corresponding definite terms. Thus, in the following examples, the words in the first and third columns, which express opposite ideas, admit of the intermediate terms contained in the middle column, having a neutral sense with reference to the former.

Identity	*Difference*	*Contrariety*
Beginning	*Middle*	*End*
Past	*Present*	*Future*

In other cases, the intermediate word is simply the negative to each of two opposite positions; as, for example—

Convexity	*Flatness*	*Concavity*
Desire	*Indifference*	*Aversion*

Sometimes the intermediate word is properly the standard with which each of the extremes is compared; as in the case of

Insufficiency	*Sufficiency*	*Redundance*

for here the middle term, *Sufficiency*, is equally opposed, on the one hand to *Insufficiency*, and on the other to *Redundance*.*

These forms of correlative expressions would suggest the use of triple, instead of double, columns, for tabulating this threefold order of words; but the practical inconvenience attending such an arrangement would probably overbalance its advantages.

It often happens that the same word has several correlative terms, according to the different relations in which it is considered. Thus, to the word *Giving* are opposed both *Receiving* and *Taking*; the former

Roman emperors had exalted the soldiery so high that they balanced all the other orders of the state: hence *miles* and *paganus* became relative terms; a thing, till then, unknown to ancient, and still so to modern languages.'—'The term for a slave, born and bred in the family, was *verna*. As *servus* was the name of the genius, and *verna* of the species without any correlative, this forms a strong presumption that the latter were by far the least numerous: and from the same principles I infer that if the number of slaves brought by the Romans from foreign countries had not extremely exceeded those which were bred at home, *verna* would have had a correlative, which would have expressed the former species of slaves. But these, it would seem, composed the main body of the ancient slaves, and the latter were but a few exceptions'.— HUME, *Essay on the Populousness of Ancient Nations.*

The warlike propensity of the same nation may, in like manner, be inferred from the use of the word *hostis* to denote both *a foreigner* and *an enemy*.

* [In the following cases, the intermediate word signifies an imperfect degree of each of the qualities set in opposition—

Light	*Dimness*	*Darkness*
Transparency	*Semitransparency*	*Opacity*
Vision	*Dimsightedness*	*Blindness*]

correlation having reference to the *persons* concerned in the transfer, while the latter relates to the *mode* of transfer. *Old* has for opposite both *New* and *Young*, according as it is applied to *things* or to *livin͵ things*. *Attack* and *Defence* are correlative terms; as are also *Attack* and *Resistance*. *Resistance*, again, has for its other correlative *Submission*. *Truth in the abstract* is opposed to *Error*; but the opposite of *Truth communicated* is *Falsehood*. *Acquisition* is contrasted both with *Deprivation* and with *Loss*. *Refusal* is the counterpart both of *Offer* and of *Consent*. *Disuse* and *Misuse* may either of them be considered as the correlative of *Use*. *Teaching* with reference to what is taught, is opposed to *Misteaching*; but with reference to the act itself, its proper reciprocal is *Learning*.

Words contrasted in form do not always bear the same contrast in their meaning. The word *Malefactor*, for example, would, from its derivation, appear to be exactly the opposite of *Benefactor*: but the ideas attached to these two words are far from being directly opposed; for while the latter expresses one who confers a benefit, the former denotes one who has violated the laws.

Independently of the immediate practical uses derivable from the arrangement of words in double columns, many considerations, interesting in a philosophical point of view, are presented by the study of correlative expressions. It will be found, on strict examination, that there seldom exists an exact opposition between two words which may at first sight appear to be the counterparts of one another; for in general, the one will be found to possess in reality more force or extent of meaning than the other with which it is contrasted. The correlative term sometimes assumes the form of a mere negative, although it is really endowed with a considerable positive force. Thus *Disrespect* is not merely the absence of *Respect*; its signification trenches on the opposite idea, namely, *Contempt*. In like manner, *Untruth* is not merely the negative of *Truth*; it involves a degree of *Falsehood*. *Irreligion*, which is properly *the want of Religion*, is understood as being nearly synonymous with *Impiety*. For these reasons, the reader must not expect that all the words which stand side by side in the two columns shall be the precise correlatives of each other; for the nature of the subject, as well as the imperfections of language, renders it impossible always to preserve such an exactness of correlation.

There exist comparatively few words of a general character to which no correlative term, either of negation or of opposition, can be assigned, and which therefore require no corresponding second column. The correlative idea, especially that which constitutes a sense negative to the primary one, may, indeed, be formed or conceived; but, from its occurring rarely, no word has been framed to represent it; for, in language, as in other matters, the supply fails when there is no probability of a demand. Occasionally we find this deficiency provided for by the contrivance of prefixing the syllable *non*; as, for instance, the negatives of *existence, performance, payment*, &c., are expressed by the compound words, *non-existence, non-performance, non-payment*, &c. Functions of a similar kind are performed by the prefixes *dis-*, anti-, contra-, mis-, in-,* and *un-*.† With respect to all these, and especially the last, great latitude is allowed according to the necessities of the case; a latitude which is limited only by the taste and discretion of the writer.

On the other hand, it is hardly possible to find two words having in all respects the same meaning, and being therefore interchangeable; that is, admitting of being employed indiscriminately, the one or the other, in all their applications. The investigation of the distinctions to be drawn between words apparently synonymous, forms a separate branch of inquiry, which I have not presumed here to enter upon; for the subject has already occupied the attention of much abler critics than myself, and its complete exhaustion would require the devotion of a whole life The purpose of this Work, it must be borne in mind, is, not to explain the signification of words, but simply to classify and arrange them according to the sense in which they are now used, and which I presume to be already known to the reader. I enter into no inquiry into the changes of meaning they may have undergone in the course of time.‡ I am content to accept them at the value of their present currency, and have no concern with their etymologies, or with the history of their transformations; far less do I venture to thrid the mazes of the vast labyrinth into which I should be led by any attempt at a general discrimination of synonyms. The difficulties I have had to contend with have already been sufficiently great, without this addition to my labours.

The most cursory glance over the pages of a Dictionary will show that a great number of words are used in various senses, sometimes distinguished by slight shades of difference, but often diverging widely from their primary signification, and even, in some cases, bearing to it no perceptible relation. It may even happen that the very same word has two significations quite opposite to one another. This is the case with the verb *to cleave*, which means *to adhere tenaciously*, and also *to separate by a blow*. *To propugn* sometimes expressed *to attack*; at other times *to defend*. *To let* is *to hinder*, as well as *to permit*. *To*

---

* The words *disannul* and *dissever*, however, have the same meaning as *annul* and *sever; to unloose* is the same as *to loose*, and *inebriety* is synonymous with *ebriety*.

† In the case of adjectives, the addition to a substantive of the terminal syllable *less*, gives it a negative meaning: as *taste, tasteless; care, careless; hope, hopeless; friend, friendless; fault, faultless;* &c.

‡ Such changes are innumerable: for instance, the words *tyrant, parasite, sophist, churl, knave, villain*, anciently conveyed no opprobrious meaning. *Impertinent* merely expressed *irrelative*, and implied neither *rudeness* nor *intrusion*, as it does at present. *Indifferent* originally meant *impartial; extravagant* was simply *digressive;* and *to prevent* was properly *to precede* and *assist*. The old translations of the Scriptures furnish many striking examples of the alterations which time has brought in the signification of words. Much curious information on this subject is contained in Trench's *Lectures on the Study of Words.*

ravel means both *to entangle* and *to disentangle*. *Shameful* and *shameless* are nearly synonymous. *Priceless* may either mean *invaluable* or *of no value*. *Nervous* is used sometimes for *strong*, at other times for *weak*. The alphabetical Index at the end of this Work sufficiently shows the multiplicity of uses to which, by the elasticity of language, the meaning of words has been stretched, so as to adapt them to a great variety of modified significations in subservience to the nicer shades of thought, which, under peculiarity of circumstances, require corresponding expression. Words thus admitting of different meanings have therefore to be arranged under each of the respective heads corresponding to these various acceptations. There are many words, again, which express ideas compounded of two elementary ideas belonging to different classes. It is therefore necessary to place these words respectively under each of the generic heads to which they relate. The necessity of these repetitions is increased by the circumstance, that ideas included under one class are often connected by relations of the same kind as the ideas which belong to another class. Thus we find the same relations of *order* and of *quantity* existing among the ideas of *Time* as well as those of *Space*. Sequence in the one is denoted by the same terms as sequence in the other; and the measures of time also express the measures of space. The cause and the effect are often designated by the same word. The word *Sound*, for instance, denotes both the impression made upon the ear by sonorous vibrations, and also the vibrations themselves, which are the cause or source of that impression. *Mixture* is used for the act of mixing, as well as for the product of that operation. *Taste* and *Smell* express both the sensations and the qualities of material bodies giving rise to them *Thought* is the act of thinking; but the same word denotes also the idea resulting from that act. *Judgment* is the act of deciding, and also the decision come to. *Purchase* is the acquisition of a thing by payment, as well as the thing itself so acquired. *Speech* is both the act of speaking and the words spoken; and so on with regard to an endless multiplicity of words. Mind is essentially distinct from Matter; and yet, in all languages, the attributes of the one are metaphorically transferred to those of the other. Matter, in all its forms, is endowed by the figurative genius of every language with the functions which pertain to intellect; and we perpetually talk of its phenomena and of its powers, as if they resulted from the voluntary influence of one body on another, acting and reacting, impelling and being impelled, controlling and being controlled, as if animated by spontaneous energies and guided by specific intentions. On the other hand, expressions, of which the primary signification refers exclusively to the properties and actions of matter, are metaphorically applied to the phenomena of thought and volition, and even to the feelings and passions of the soul; and in speaking of a *ray of hope*, a *shade of doubt*, a *flight of fancy*, a *flash of wit*, the *warmth of emotion*, or the *ebullitions of anger,* we are scarcely conscious that we are employing metaphors which have this material origin.

As a general rule, I have deemed it incumbent on me to place words and phrases which appertain more especially to one head, also under the other heads to which they have a relation, whenever it appeared to me that this repetition would suit the convenience of the inquirer, and spare him the trouble of turning to other parts of the work; for I have always preferred to subject myself to the imputation of redundance, rather than incur the reproach of insufficiency.* When, however, the divergence of the associated from the primary idea is sufficiently marked, I have contented myself with making a reference to the place where the modified signification will be found.† But in order to prevent needless extension, I have, in general, omitted *conjugate words,* ‡ which are so obviously derivable from those that are given in the same place, that the reader may safely be left to form them for himself. This is the case with adverbs derived from adjectives by the simple addition of the terminal syllable *-ly*; such as *closely, carefully, safely,* &c., from *close, careful, safe,* &c., and also with adjectives or participles immediately derived from the verbs which are already given. In all such cases, an '&c.' indicates that reference is understood to be made to these roots.§ I have observed the same rule in compiling the Index; retaining only the primary or more simple word, and omitting the conjugate words obviously derived from them. Thus I assume the word *short* as the representative of its immediate derivatives *shortness, shorten, shortening, shortened, shorter, shortly,* which would have had the same references, and which the reader can readily supply. ||

The same verb is frequently used indiscriminately either in the active or transitive, or in the neuter or intransitive sense. In these cases, I have generally not thought it worth while to increase the bulk of the Work by the needless repetition of that word; for the reader, whom I suppose

* Frequent repetitions of the same series of expressions, accordingly, will be met with under various headings. For example, the word *Relinquishment* with its synonyms, occurs as a heading at No. 624, where it applies to *intention,* and also at No. 782, where it refers to *property.* The word *Chance* has two significations, distinct from one another: the one implying the *absence of an assignable cause;* in which case it comes under the category of the relation of Causation, and occupies the No. 156: the other, the *absence of design,* in which latter sense it ranks under the operations of the Will, and has assigned to it the place No. 621. I have, in like manner, distinguished *Sensibility, Pleasure, Pain, Taste,* &c., according as they relate to *Physical,* or to *Moral Affections;* the fomer being found at Nos. 375, 377, 378, 390, &c., and the latter at Nos. 822, 827, 828, 850, &c.

† [See Editor's Preface, p. x.]

‡ By '*conjugate* or *paronymous* words is meant, correctly speaking, different parts of speech from the same root, which exactly corresponds in point of meaning.'— *A Selection of English Synonyms,* edited by Archbishop Whately.

§ [The author's practice, in this respect, has been followed in the present edition, and a reference to the group of adjectives, verbs, or other roots, has been added. where such suggestion has been thought expedient.]

[See note in p. xvii.]

to understand the use of the words, must also be presumed to be competent to apply them correctly.

There are a multitude of words of a specific character which, although they properly occupy places in the columns of a dictionary, yet, having no relation to general ideas, do not come within the scope of this compilation, and are consequently omitted.* The names of objects in Natural History, and technical terms belonging exclusively to Science or to Art, or relating to particular operations, and of which the signification is restricted to those specific objects, come under this category. Exceptions must, however, be made in favor of such words as admit of metaphorical application to general subjects, with which custom has associated them, and of which they may be cited as being typical or illustrative. Thus, the word *Lion* will find a place under the head of *Courage,* of which it is regarded as the type. *Anchor,* being emblematic of *Hope,* is introduced among the words expressing that emotion; and in like manner, *butterfly* and *weathercock,* which are suggestive of fickleness, are included in the category of *Irresolution.*

With regard to the admission of many words and expressions, which the classical reader might be disposed to condemn as vulgarisms, or which he, perhaps, might stigmatize as pertaining rather to the slang than to the legitimate language of the day, I would beg to observe, that, having due regard to the uses to which this Work was to be adapted, I did not feel myself justified in excluding them solely on that ground, if they possessed an acknowledged currency in general intercourse. It is obvious that, with respect to degrees of conventionality, I could not have attempted to draw any strict lines of demarcation; and far less could I have presumed to erect any absolute standard of purity. My object, be it remembered, is not to regulate the use of words, but simply to supply and to suggest such as may be wanted on occasion, leaving the proper selection entirely to the discretion and taste of the employer.† If a novelist or a dramatist, for example, proposed to delineate some vulgar personage, he would wish to have the power of putting into the mouth of the speaker expressions that would accord with his character; just as the actor, to revert to a former comparison, who had to personate a peasant, would choose for his attire the most homely garb, and would have just reason to complain if the theatrical wardrobe furnished him with no suitable costume.

Words which have, in process of time, become obsolete, are of course

---

* [The author did not in all cases rigidly adhere to this rule; and the editors have thought themselves justified both in retaining and in adding some words of the specific character here mentioned, which may be occasionally in request by general writers, although in categories of this nature no attempt at completeness has been made.]

† [It may be added that the Thesaurus is an aid not only in the choice of appropriate forms of expression, but in the rejection of those which are unfit; and that a vulgar phrase may often furnish a convenient clue to the group of classic synonyms among which it is placed. Moreover, the slang expressions admitted into the work bear but a small proportion to those in constant use by English writers and speakers.]

rejected from this collection.* On the other hand, I have admitted a considerable number of words and phrases borrowed from other languages, chiefly the French and Latin, some of which may be considered as already naturalized; while others, though avowedly foreign, are frequently employed in English composition, particularly in familiar style, on account of their being peculiarly expressive, and because we have no corresponding words of equal force in our own language.† The rapid advances which are being made in scientific knowledge, and consequent improvement in all the arts of life, and the extension of those arts and sciences to so many new purposes and objects, create a continual demand for the formation of new terms to express new agencies, new wants, and new combinations. Such terms, from being at first merely technical, are rendered, by more general use, familiar to the multitude, and having a well-defined acceptation, are eventually incorporated into the language, which they contribute to enlarge and to enrich. *Neologies* of this kind are perfectly legitimate, and highly advantageous; and they necessarily introduce those gradual and progressive changes which every language is destined to undergo.‡ Some modern writers, however, have indulged in a habit of arbitrarily fabricating new words and a new-fangled phraseology, without any necessity, and with manifest injury to the purity of the language. This vicious practice, the offspring of indolence or conceit, implies an ignorance or neglect of the riches in which the English language already abounds, and which would have supplied them with words of recognized legitimacy, conveying precisely the same meaning as those they so recklessly coin in the illegal mint of their own fancy.

A work constructed on the plan of classification I have proposed might, if ably executed, be of great value, in tending to limit the fluctuations to which language has always been subject, by establishing an authoritative standard for its regulation. Future historians, philologists, and lexicographers, when investigating the period when new words were introduced, or discussing the import given at the present time to the old, might find their labours lightened by being enabled to appeal to such a standard, instead of having to search for data among the scattered writings of the

* [A few apparently obsolete words have nevertheless found their way into the Thesaurus. In justification of their admission, it may be contended that well-known words, though no longer current, give occasional point by an archaic form of expression, and are of value to the novelist or dramatist who has to depict a bygone age.]

† All these words and phrases are printed in Italics. [A few of these expressions, although widely used by writers of English, are of a form which is really incorrect or unusual in their own language, in some more extreme cases of this kind, the more widely used or incorrect form has been given.]

‡ Thus, in framing the present classification, I have frequently felt the want of substantive terms corresponding to abstract qualities or ideas denoted by certain adjectives, and have been often tempted to invent words that might express these abstractions; but I have yielded to this temptation only in the four following instances, having framed from the adjectives *irrelative, amorphous, sinistral,* and *gaseous,* the abstract nouns *irrelation, amorphism, sinistrality,* and *gaseity.* I have ventured also to introduce the adjective *intersocial* to express the active voluntary relations between man and man.

age. Nor would its utility be confined to a single language; for the principles of its construction are universally applicable to all languages, whether living or dead. On the same plan of classification there might be formed a French, a German, a Latin, or a Greek Thesaurus, possessing, in their respective spheres, the same advantages as those of the English model.* Still more useful would be a conjunction of these methodized compilations in two languages, the French and English, for instance; the columns of each being placed in parallel juxtaposition. No means yet devised would so greatly facilitate the acquisition of the one language, by those who are acquainted with the other: none would afford such ample assistance to the translator in either language; and none would supply such ready and effectual means of instituting an accurate comparison between them, and of fairly appreciating their respective merits and defects. In a still higher degree would all those advantages be combined and multiplied in a *Polyglot Lexicon* constructed on this system.

Metaphysicians engaged in the more profound investigation of the Philosophy of Language will be materially assisted by having the ground thus prepared for them, in a previous analysis and classification of our ideas; for such classification of ideas is the true basis on which words, which are their symbols, should be classified.† It is by such analysis alone that we can arrive at a clear perception of the relation which these

---

* [This suggestion has been followed, in French, in a *'Dictionnaire Idéologique'* by T. Robertson (Paris, 1859); and, in German, in a *'Deutscher Sprachschatz'* by D. Sanders (Hamburg, 1878), and *'Deutscher Wortschatz oder Der passende Ausdruck'* by A. Schelling (Stuttgart, 1829).]

† The principle by which I have been guided in framing my verbal classification is the same as that which is employed in the various departments of Natural History. Thus the sectional divisions I have formed, correspond to Natural Families in Botany and Zoology, and the filiation of words presents a network analogous to the natural filiation of plants or animals.

The following are the only publications that have come to my knowledge in which any attempt has been made to construct a systematic arrangement of ideas with a view to their expression. The earliest of these, supposed to be at least nine hundred years old, is the AMERA CÓSHA, or *Vocabulary of the Sanscrit Language*, by Amera Sinha, of which an English translation, by the late Henry T. Colebrooke, was printed at Serampoor, in the year 1808. The classification of words is there, as might be expected, exceedingly imperfect and confused, especially in all that relates to abstract ideas or mental operations. This will be apparent from the very title of the first section, which comprehends *'Heaven, Gods, Demons, Fire, Air, Velocity, Eternity, Much:'* while *Sin, Virtue, Happiness, Destiny, Cause, Nature, Intellect, Reasoning, Knowledge, Senses, Tastes, Odours, Colours*, are all included and jumbled together in the fourth section. A more logical order, however, pervades the sections relating to natural objects, such as *Seas, Earth, Towns, Plants*, and *Animals*, which form separate classes; exhibiting a remarkable effort at analysis at so remote a period of Indian literature.

The well-known work of Bishop Wilkins entitled *'An Essay towards a Real Character and a Philosophical Language,'* published in 1668, had for its object the formation of a system of symbols which might serve as a universal language. It professed to be founded on a 'scheme of analysis of the things or notions to which names were to be assigned'; but notwithstanding the immense labour and ingenuity expended in the construction of this system, it was soon found to be far too abstruse and recondite for practical application.

In the year 1797, there appeared in Paris an anonymous work, entitled 'PASI-GRAPHIE. ou Premiers Eléments du nouvel Art-Science d'écrire et d'imprimer une langue

symbols bear to their corresponding ideas, or can obtain a correct knowledge of the elements which enter into the formation of compound ideas, and of the exclusions by which we arrive at the abstractions so perpetually resorted to in the process of reasoning, and in the communication of our thoughts.

Lastly, such analysis alone can determine the principles on which a strictly *Philosophical Language* might be constructed. The probable result of the construction of such a language would be its eventual adoption by every civilized nation; thus realizing that splendid aspiration of philanthropists—the establishment of a Universal Language. However utopian such a project may appear to the present generation, and however abortive may have been the former endeavours of Bishop Wilkins and others to realize it,* its accomplishment is surely not beset with greater difficulties than have impeded the progress to many other beneficial objects, which in former times appeared to be no less visionary, and which yet were successfully achieved, in later ages, by the continued and persevering exertions of the human intellect. Is there at the present day, then, any ground for despair, that at some future stage of that higher civilization to which we trust the world is gradually tending, some new and bolder effort of genius towards the solution of this great problem may be crowned with success, and compass an object of such vast and paramount utility? Nothing, indeed, would conduce more directly to bring about a golden age of union and harmony among the several nations and races of mankind than the removal of that barrier to the interchange of thought and mutual good understanding between man and man, which is now interposed by the diversity of their respective languages.

---

de maniere a etre lu et entendu dans toute autre langue sans traduction,' of which an edition in German was also published. It contains a great number of tabular schemes of categories; all of which appear to be excessively arbitrary and artificial, and extremely difficult of application, as well as of apprehension. [Systems of grouping with relation to ideas are also adopted in an '*Analytical Dictionary of the English Language*' by David Booth (London, 1835), a '*Dictionnaire Analogique de la Langue Française*' by P. Boissière (Paris), and a '*Dictionnaire Logique de la Langue Française*' by L'Abbé Elie Blanc (Paris, 1882).]

* 'The Languages,' observes Horne Tooke, 'which are commonly used throughout the world, are much more simple and easy, convenient and philosophical, than Wilkins' scheme for a *real character;* or than any other scheme that has been at any other time imagined or proposed for the purpose.'—''Επεα Πτερόεντα, p. 125.

PLAN OF CLASSIFICATION

TABULAR SYNOPSIS OF CATEGORIES

Class I. ABSTRACT RELATIONS

I. EXISTENCE

1°. ABSTRACT...........	1. Existence.	2. Inexistence.
2°. CONCRETE..........	3. Substantiality.	4. Unsubstantiality.
	Internal.	*External.*
3°. FORMAL............	5. Intrinsicality.	6. Extrinsicality.
	Absolute.	*Relative.*
4°. MODAL.............	7. State.	8. Circumstance.

II. RELATION

	9. Relation.	10. Irrelation.
	11. Consanguinity.	
1°. ABSOLUTE.........	12. Correlation.	
	13. Identity.	14. Contrariety.
	15. Difference.	
2°. CONTINUOUS........	16. Uniformity.	16a. Non-uniformity.
	17. Similarity.	18. Dissimilarity.
	19. Imitation.	20. Non-imitation.
3°. PARTIAL...........	20a. Variation.	
	21. Copy.	22. Prototype.
4°. GENERAL..........	23. Agreement.	24. Disagreement.

III. QUANTITY

	Absolute.	*Relative.*
1°. SIMPLE............	25. Quantity.	26. Degree.
	27. Equality.	28. Inequality.

29. Mean.
30. Compensation.
By Comparison with a Standard.

2°. COMPARATIVE.......	31. Greatness.	32. Smallness.
	By Comparison with a similar Object.	
	33. Superiority.	34. Inferiority.
	Changes in Quantity.	
	35. Increase.	36. Decrease.
	37. Addition.	38. { Non-addition. / Subduction. }
	39. Adjunct.	40. Remainder.
		40a. Decrement.
3°. CONJUNCTIVE.......	41. Mixture.	42. Simpleness.
	43. Junction.	44. Disjunction.
	45. Vinculum.	
	46. Coherence.	47. Incoherence.
	48. Combination.	49. Decomposition.

[xxix]

4°. **With Reference to Direction**—*cont*...

305. Ascent.	306. Descent.
307. Elevation.	308. Depression.
309. Leap.	310. Plunge.
311. Circuition.	
312. Rotation.	313. Evolution.
314. Oscillation.	
315. Agitation.	

Class III. MATTER

I. MATTER IN GENERAL

316. Materiality.	317. Immateriality.
318. World.	
319. Gravity.	320. Levity.

II. INORGANIC MATTER

1°. **Solids**

321. Density.	322. Rarity.
323. Hardness.	324. Softness.
325. Elasticity.	326. Inelasticity.
327. Tenacity.	328. Brittleness.
329. Texture.	
330. Pulverulence.	
331. Friction.	332. Lubrication.

2°. **Fluids**

1. *In General*

333. Fluidity.	334. Gaseity.
335. Liquefaction.	336. Vaporization.
337. Water.	338. Air.
339. Moisture.	340. Dryness.

2. *Specific*

341. Ocean.	342. Land.
343. { Gulf. Lake. }	
	344. Plain.
345. Marsh.	346. Island.

3. *In motion*

347. Stream.	
348. River.	349. Wind.
350. Conduit.	351. Air-pipe.

3°. **Imperfect Fluids**

352. Semiliquidity.	353. Bubble.
354. Pulpiness.	355. Unctuousness.
	356. Oil.
	356a. Resin.

III. ORGANIC MATTER

1°. **Vitality**

1. *In General*

357. Organization.	358. Inorganization
359. Life.	360. Death.
	361. Killing.
	362. Corpse.
	363. Interment.

2. *Special*

364. Animality.	365. Vegetability.
366. Animal.	367. Vegetable.
368. Zoology.	369. Botany.
370. Cicuration.	371. Agriculture.
372. Mankind.	
373. Man.	374. Woman.

2. SENSATION

(1) General

375. Sensibility.	376. Insensibility.
377. Pleasure.	378. Pain.
379. Touch.	

1. Touch

380. Sensations of Touch.	381. Numbness.

2. Heat

382. Heat.	383. Cold.
384. Calefaction.	385. Refrigeration.
386. Furnace.	387. Refrigerator.
388. Fuel.	
389. Thermometer.	

3. Taste

390. Taste.	391. Insipidity.
392. Pungency.	
393. Condiment.	
394. Savouriness.	395. Unsavouriness.
396. Sweetness.	397. Sourness.

4. Odour

398. Odour.	399. Inodorousness.
400. Fragrance.	401. Fetor.

(2) Special

5. Sound

(i.) *Sound in General.*

402. Sound.	403. Silence.
404. Loudness.	405. Faintness.

(ii.) *Specific Sounds.*

406. Snap.	407. Roll.
408. Resonance.	408a. Non-resonance.
	409. Sibilation.
410. Stridor.	
411. Cry.	412. Ululation.

(iii.) *Musical Sounds.*

413. Melody. Concord.	414. Discord.
415. Music.	
416. Musician.	
417. Musical Instruments.	

(iv.) *Perception of Sound.*

418. Hearing.	419. Deafness.

6. Light

(i.) *Light in General.*

420. Light.	421. Darkness.
422. Dimness.	
423. Luminary.	424. Shade.
425. Transparency.	426. Opacity.
427. Semitransparency.	

(ii.) *Specific Light.*

428. Colour.	429. Achromatism.
430. Whiteness.	431. Blackness.
432. Gray.	433. Brown.
434. Redness.	435. Greenness.
436. Yellowness.	437. Purple.
438. Blueness.	439. Orange.
440. Variegation.	

(iii.) *Perceptions of Light.*

441. Vision.	442. Blindness.
443. Dimsightedness.	
444. Spectator.	
445. Optical Instruments.	
446. Visibility.	447. Invisibility.
448. Appearance.	449. Disappearance

Class IV. INTELLECT

Division (I.). FORMATION OF IDEAS

Division (II.). Communication of Ideas

I. Nature of Ideas Communicated

516. Meaning. 517. Unmeaningness.
518. Intelligibility. 519. Unintelligibility.
520. Equivocalness.
521. Metaphor.
522. Interpretation. 523. Misinterpretation.
524. Interpreter.
525. Manifestation. 526. Latency.
527. Information. 528. Concealment.
529. Disclosure. 530. Ambush.
531. Publication.
532. News. 533. Secret.
534. Messenger.

II. Modes of Communication

535. Affirmation. 536. Negation.
537. Teaching. 538. Misteaching.
539. Learning.
540. Teacher. 541. Learner.
542. School.
543. Veracity. 544. Falsehood.
545. Deception.
546. Untruth.
547. Dupe. 548. Deceiver.
549. Exaggeration.

III. Means of Communication

1°. Natural Means

550. Indication.
551. Record. 552. Obliteration.
553. Recorder.
554. Representation. 555. Misrepresentation.
556. Painting.
557. Sculpture.
558. Engraving.
559. Artist.

2°. Conventional Means

1. Language generally

560. Language.
561. Letter.
562. Word. 563. Neology.
564. Nomenclature. 565. Misnomer.
566. Phrase.
567. Grammar. 568. Solecism.
569. Style.

Qualities of Style.

570. Perspicuity. 571. Obscurity.
572. Conciseness. 573. Diffuseness.
574. Vigour. 575. Feebleness.
576. Plainness. 577. Ornament.
578. Elegance. 579. Inelegance.

2. Spoken Language

580. Voice. 581. Aphony.
582. Speech. 583. Stammering.
584. Loquacity. 585. Taciturnity.
586. Allocution. 587. Response.
588. Interlocution. 589. Soliloquy.

3. Written Language

590. Writing. 591. Printing.
592. Correspondence. 593. Book.
594. Description.
595. Dissertation.
596. Compendium.
597. Poetry. 598. Prose.
599. The Drama.

Class V. VOLITION

Division (I.). Individual Volition

I. Volition in General

1°. Acts....

600. Will.	601. Necessity.
602. Willingness.	603. Unwillingness.
604. Resolution.	605. Irresolution.
604a. Perseverance. }	
606. Obstinacy. }	607. Tergiversation.
	608. Caprice.
609. Choice.	609a. Absence of Choice.
	610. Rejection.
611. Predetermination.	612. Impulse.
613. Habit.	614. Desuetude.

2°. Causes..

615. Motive.	615a. Absence of Motive.
	616. Dissuasion.
617. Plea.	

3°. Objects..

618. Good.	619. Evil.

II. Prospective Volition........

1°. Conceptional..

620. Intention.	621. Chance.
622. Pursuit.	623. Avoidance.
	624. Relinquishment.
625. Business.	
626. Plan.	
627. Method.	
628. Mid-Course.	629. Circuit.
630. Requirement.	

2°. Subservience to Ends...

1. Actual Subservience.

631. Instrumentality.
632. Means.
633. Instrument.
634. Substitute.
635. Materials.
636. Store.

637. Provision.	638. Waste.

639. Sufficiency.

641. Redundance.	640. Insufficiency.

2. Degree of Subservience.

642. Importance.	643. Unimportance.
644. Utility.	645. Inutility.
646. Expedience.	647. Inexpedience.
648. Goodness.	649. Badness.
650. Perfection.	651. Imperfection.
652. Cleanness.	653. Uncleanness.
654. Health.	655. Disease.
656. Salubrity.	657. Insalubrity.
658. Improvement.	659. Deterioration.
660. Restoration.	661. Relapse.
662. Remedy.	663. Bane.

3. Contingent Subservience.

664. Safety.	665. Danger.
666. Refuge.	667. Pitfall.

668. Warning.
669. Alarm.
670. Preservation.
671. Escape.
672. Deliverance.

Class VI. AFFECTIONS

2°. Diffusive	906. Benevolence.	907. Malevolence.
		908. Malediction.
		909. Threat.
	910. Philanthropy.	911. Misanthropy.
	912. Benefactor.	913. Evil doer.
3°. Special	914. Pity.	914a. Pitilessness.
	915. Condolence.	
	916. Gratitude.	917. Ingratitude.
4°. Retrospective	918. Forgiveness.	919. Revenge.
		920. Jealousy.
		921. Envy.

IV. MORAL

1°. Obligations	922. Right.	923. Wrong.
	924. Dueness.	925. Undueness.
	926. Duty.	927. Dereliction.
		927a. Exemption.
	928. Respect.	929. Disrespect.
		930. Contempt.
2°. Sentiments	931. Approbation.	932. Disapprobation.
	933. Flattery.	934. Detraction.
	935. Flatterer.	936. Detractor.
	937. Vindication.	938. Accusation.
	939. Probity.	940. Improbity.
		941. Knave.
	942. Disinterestedness.	943. Selfishness.
3°. Conditions	944. Virtue.	945. Vice.
	946. Innocence.	947. Guilt.
	948. Good Man.	949. Bad Man.
	950. Penitence.	951. Impenitence.
	952. Atonement.	
	953. Temperance.	954. Intemperance.
		954a. Sensualist.
	955. Asceticism.	
4°. Practice	956. Fasting.	957. Gluttony.
	958. Sobriety.	959. Drunkenness.
	960. Purity.	961. Impurity.
		962. Libertine.
	963. Legality.	964. Illegality.
	965. Jurisprudence.	
	966. Tribunal.	
	967. Judge.	
5°. Institutions	968. Lawyer.	
	969. Lawsuit.	
	970. Acquittal.	971. Condemnation.
	973. Reward.	972. Punishment.
		974. Penalty.
		975. Scourge.

V. RELIGIOUS

1°. Superhuman Beings and Regions	976. Deity.	
	977. Angel.	978. Satan.
	979. Jupiter.	980. Demon.
	981. Heaven.	982. Hell.
2°. Doctrines	983. Theology.	
	983a. Orthodoxy.	984. Heterodoxy.
	985. Revelation.	986. Pseudo-revelation.
3°. Sentiments	987. Piety.	988. Impiety.
		989. Irreligion.

ABBREVIATIONS, &c.

Adj.	*adj.*	Adjectives, Participles, and Words having the power of Adjectives.
Adv.	*adv.*	Adverbs and Adverbial Expressions.
Int.	*int.*	Interjections.
Phr.	*phr.*	Phrases.
V.	*v.*	Verbs.

The numbers are those of the headings, or Categories.

Words in italics within parentheses are not intended to explain the meanings of the words which precede them, but to indicate the nature of allied group of words under the numbers which follow them.

See also the Editor's Preface, p. xi.

THESAURUS

OF

ENGLISH WORDS AND PHRASES

CLASS I

Words expressing ABSTRACT RELATIONS

Section I. EXISTENCE

1°. Being, in the Abstract

1. Existence.—**N.** existence, being, entity, *ens, esse,* subsistence, quiddity.

reality, realness, actuality; positiveness &c. *adj.*; fact, matter of fact, sober reality; truth &c. 494; actual existence.

presence &c. (*existence in space*) 186; coexistence &c. 120.

stubborn fact; not a -dream &c. 515; no joke.

substance, essence, prime constituent, hypostatis.

[Science of existence], ontology.

V. exist, be; have -being &c. *n.*; subsist, live, breathe, stand, obtain, be the case; occur &c. (*event*) 151; have place, rank, prevail; find oneself, pass the time, vegetate.

consist in, lie in, reside in, inhere in.

come into -existence &c. *n.*; arise &c. (*begin*) 66; come forth &c. (*appear*) 446.

become &c. (*be converted*) 144; bring into existence &c. 161; coexist, preexist, endure &c. 141.

Adj. existing &c. *v.*; existent, subsistent, under the sun; in -existence &c. *n.*; extant; afloat, on foot, current, prevalent, rife, in force, -vogue; undestroyed.

real, actual, positive, absolute; true &c. 494; substan-tial, -tive; self-existing, -ent.

2. Inexistence.—**N.** inexistence; non-existence, -subsistence; nonentity, *nil*; negativeness &c. *adj.*; nullity; nihil-ity, -ism; *tabula rasa,* blank; abeyance; absence &c. 187; no such thing &c. 4; nothingness, oblivion, *non esse.*

annihilation; extinction &c. (*destruction*) 162.

V. not -exist &c. 1; have no -existence &c. 1; be null and void; cease to -exist &c. 1; pass away, perish; be -, become- extinct &c. *adj.*; die out; disappear &c. 449; melt away, dissolve, leave not a rack behind, leave no trace; go, be no more; die &c. 360.

annihilate, render null, nullify; abrogate &c. 756; destroy &c. 162; take away; remove &c. (*displace*) 185.

Adj. inexistent, non-existent &c. 1; negative, blank, null and void; missing, omitted; absent &c. 187; visionary &c. 515.

unreal, potential, virtual; baseless, *in nubibus*; unsubstantial &c. 4; vain.

un-born, -created, -begotten, -conceived, -produced, -made.

perished, annihilated &c. *v.*; extinct, exhausted, gone, lost, departed; defunct &c. (*dead*) 360; *spurlos versenkt.*

fabulous, ideal &c. (*imaginary*) 515; supposititious &c. 514.

Adv. negatively, virtually, &c. *adj.*

well-founded, -grounded; un-ideal, -imagined; not -potential &c. 2.

Adv. actually &c. *adj.*; in -fact, – point of fact, – reality; indeed; *de –. ipso-facto.*

2°. BEING, IN THE CONCRETE

3. Substantiality.—N. substantiality, *hypostasis*; person, thing, object, article; something, a being, an existence; creature, body, substance, flesh and blood, stuff, *substratum*; matter &c. 316; physical nature.

[Totality of existences], world &c. 318; *plenum.*

Adj. substan-tive, -tial, concrete; hypostatic; personal, bodily; tangible &c. (*material*) 316; real, corporeal, evident.

Adv. substantially &c. *adj.*; bodily, essentially.

---

4. Unsubstantiality.—N. un-, in-substantiality; nothingness, nihility.

nothing, naught, *nil*, nullity, zero, cipher, no one, nobody; never –, ne'er -a one; no such thing, none in the world; nothing -whatever, – at all, – on earth; not a -particle &c. (*smallness*) 32; all -talk, – moonshine, – stuff and nonsense, matter of no import.

thing of naught, man of straw, John Doe and Richard Roe; *nominis umbra*, nonentity, figurehead, lay figure; flash in the pan, *vox et præterea nihil.*

shadow; phantasm, phantom &c. (*fallacy of vision*) 443; dream &c. (*imagination*) 515; *ignis fatuus* &c. (luminary) 423; 'such stuff as dreams are made on'; air, thin air; bubble &c. 353; 'baseless fabric of a vision'; mockery.

hollowness, blank; vacuity, void &c. (*absence*) 187.

inanity, fool's paradise, fatuity, stupidity, emptiness of mind.

V. vanish, evaporate, fade, sink, fly –, die –, melt- away, dissolve, disappear &c. 449, become extinct, become invisible.

Adj. unsubstantial; fleeting; base-, ground-less; ungrounded; without –, having no- foundation.

visionary &c. (*imaginary*) 515; immaterial &c. 317; spectral &c 980; dreamy; shadowy; ethereal, airy, imponderable, tenuous, vague.

vacant, vacuous; empty &c. 187; eviscerated; blank, hollow; nominal; null; inane.

Phr. there's nothing in it.

3°. FORMAL EXISTENCE

Internal conditions

5. Intrinsicality.—N. intrinsicality, inbeing, inherence, inhesion, immanence; subjectiveness; *ego*; essence; essentialness &c. *adj.*; essential part, essential stuff, substance, quintessence, incarnation, quiddity, gist, pith, core, kernel, marrow, sap, life-blood, backbone, heart, soul, life, flower; important part &c. (*importance*) 642.

principle, nature, constitution, character, ethos, type, quality, crasis, *diathesis.*

habit; temper, -ament; spirit, humour, grain, disposition, streak, tendency &c. 176.

External conditions

6. Extrinsicality.—N. extrinsicality, objectiveness, *non ego*; extraneousness &c. 57; accident; letter of the law.

Adj. derived from without; objective; extrin-sic, -sical; extraneous &c. (*foreign*) 57; modal, adventitious, additional, supervenient, fortuitous; a-, ad-scititious; incidental, casual, accidental, unessential, non-essential, accessory.

implanted, ingrafted, instilled, inculcated.

outward &c. (*external*) 220.

Adv. extrinsically &c. *adj.*

---

endowment, capacity; capability &c. (*power*) 157; moods, de-clensions, features, aspects; peculiarities &c. (*specialty*) 79; idiosyn-crasy; idiocrasy; diagnostics.

V. be –, run- in the blood; be born so; be -intrinsic &c. *adj.*

Adj. derived from within, subjective; idiocratic, idiosyncratic, intrin-sic, -sical; fundamental, cardinal, normal; inherent, essential, natural; in-nate, -born, -bred, -dwelling, -grained, -wrought; radi-cal, incarnate, thoroughbred, hereditary, inherited, immanent; congen-ital, -ite; connate, running in the blood; coeval with birth, genetic, ingenerate, -genite; indigenous; in the -grain &c. *n.*; bred in the bone, instinctive; inward, internal &c. 221; to the manner born; virtual.

characteristic &c. (*special*) 79, (*indicative*) 550; invariable, in-curable, ineradicable, fixed, settled, constant, unchanging.

Adv. intrinsically &c. *adj.*; at bottom, in the main, in effect, essentially, practically, virtually, substantially, *au fond*; fairly.

4°. Modal Existence

Absolute

7. State.—N. state, condition, cate-gory, estate, lot, case, trim, mood, pickle, plight &c. 735; temper; aspect &c. (*appearance*) 448.

constitution, habitude, *diathesis*; frame, fabric &c. 329; stamp, set, fit, mould.

mode, modality, schesis; fettle; form &c. (*shape*) 240.

tone, tenor, turn; trim, guise, fash-ion, light, complexion, style, character.

V. be in –, possess –, enjoy –, labour under- a -state &c. *n.*; be on a footing, do, fare; come to pass.

Adj. conditional, modal, formal; structural, organic.

Adv. conditionally &c. *adj.*; as -the matter stands, – things are; such being the case &c. 8.

Relative

8. Circumstance.—N. circumstance, situation, phase, position, posture, attitude, place, point; terms; *régime*; footing, standing, status.

occasion, juncture, conjuncture; con-tingency &c. (*event*) 151.

predicament; emergen-ce, -cy; exi-gency, crisis, pinch, pass, push; turning point; crossroads.

bearings, how the land lies.

Adj. circumstantial; given, condi-tional, provisional; critical; modal; contingent, incidental; adventitious &c. (*extrinsic*) 6.

Adv. in the circumstances &c. *n.*, under the conditions &c. 7; thus, in such wise.

accordingly; that –, such- being the case; that being so, since, seeing that. as matters stand; as -things, – times-go.

conditionally, provided, if, in case; if -so, – so be, – it be so; if it so -happen, – turn out; in the event of; in such a -contingency, – case, – event; provisionally, unless, without.

according to -circumstances, – the occasion; as it may -happen, – turn out, – be; as the -case may be, – wind blows; *pro re natâ*.

Section II.   RELATION

1°. Absolute Relation

9. Relation.—N. relation, bearing, reference, connection, apposition, in-terconnection, concern, cognation; ap-plicability, appositeness; correlation

10. [Want, or absence of relation.] Irrelation.—N. irrelation, dissociation; inapplicability; inconnection; multi-fariousness; disconnection &c. (*dis-*

&c. 12; analogy; similarity &c. 17; affinity intimacy, friendship; homology, alliance, homogeneity, association, rapport; approximation &c. (*nearness*) 197; filiation &c. (*consanguinity*) 11; interest; relevancy &c. 23; relationship, relative position; relativity; interrelation &c. 12.

comparison &c. 464; ratio, proportion.

link, tie, bond, bond of union.

V. be-related &c. *adj.*; have a relation &c. *n.*; relate –, refer- to; bear upon, regard, concern, touch, affect, have to do with; pertain –, belong –, appertain- to; have respect to; answer to; interest.

bring -into relation with, – to bear upon; connect, associate, draw a parallel; link &c. 43.

Adj. relative; correlative &c. 12; cognate; relating to &c. *v.*; relative to, in relation with, referable *or* referrible to; belonging to &c. *v.*; appurtenant to, in common with.

related, connected; implicated, associated, affiliated, akin, allied to; collateral, cognate, congenial, kindred, affinitive, *en rapport*, in touch with.

approxima-tive, -ting; approaching; proportion-al, -ate, -able; allusive, comparable.

in the same -category &c. 75; like &c. 17; relevant &c. (*apt*) 23.

Adv. relatively &c. *adj.*; pertinently &c. 23.

thereof; as -to, – for, – respects, – regards; about; concerning &c. *v.*; anent; relating –, as relates- to; with -relation, – reference, – respect, – regard- to; in respect of; while speaking –, *à propos-* of; in connection with; by the -way, – by; whereas; for –, in -as much as; in point of, as far as; on the -part, – score- of; *quoad hoc*; *pro re natâ*; under the -head &c. (*class*) 75- of; in the matter of, *in re*.

Phr. 'thereby hangs a tale.'

junction) 44; inconsequence, independence; incommensurability; irreconcilableness &c. (*disagreement*) 24; heterogeneity; unconformity &c. 83; irrelevancy, impertinence, *nihil ad rem*; intrusion &c. 24.

V. have no -relation &c. 9 to, – bearing upon, – concern &c. 9 with, – business with; not -concern &c. 9; have -nothing to do with, – no business there; intrude, &c. 24.

bring –, drag –, haul –, lug- in head and shoulders.

Adj. irrelative, irrespective, unrelated, irrelated; arbitrary; independent, unallied; un-, dis-connected; adrift, isolated, insular; extraneous, strange, alien, foreign, outlandish, exotic.

not comparable, incommensurable, heterogeneous; unconformable &c. 83.

irrelevant; rambling &c. 279; inapplicable; not -pertinent, – to the purpose; impertinent, inapposite, beside the mark, *à propos de bottes*; away from –, foreign to –, beside- the -purpose, – question, – transaction, – point; misplaced &c. (*intrusive*) 24.

remote, far fetched, out of the way, forced, neither here, nor there, quite another thing; detached, segregated, segregate.

multifarious; discordant &c. 24.

incidental, parenthetical, *obiter dictum*, episodic.

Adv. parenthetically &c. *adj.*; by the -way, – by; *en passant*, incidentally; irrespectively &c. *adj.*; without reference, – regard- to; in the abstract &c. 87; *a se*.

---

11. [Relations of kindred.] **Consanguinity.**—**N.** consanguinity, relationship, kindred, blood; parentage &c. (*paternity*) 166; filiation, affiliation; lineage, agnation, connection, cognation, alliance; family -connection, – tie; ties of blood; blood relationship; nepotism.

kins-man, -folk; people; kith and kin; rela-tion, -tive; connection; sib; next of kin; uncle, aunt, nephew, niece; cousin, -german; first –, second- cousin; cousin -once, – twice &c.- removed; near –, distant-relation; brother, sister, one's own flesh and blood.

family. patriarch, matriarch; fraternity; brother-, sister-, cousin-hood.
race, stock, generation: sept &c. 166; stirps, side; strain; breed,
clan, tribe.

V. be -related &c. *adj.* – to; claim -relationship &c. *n.*- with.

Adj. related, akin, consanguineous, matrilinear, patrilineal, of the
blood, family, allied, collateral; cog-, ag-, con-nate; kindred; affiliated,
affine; fraternal, avuncular.

intimately –, nearly –, closely –, remotely –, distantly- related, –
allied; german.

12. [Double or reciprocal relation.] **Correlation.—N.** reciprocalness
&c. *adj.*; recipro-city, -cality, -cation; mutuality, correlation, correspondence, interdependence; interchange &c. 148; exchange, barter;
interrelation, interconnection; alternation, see-saw.

V. reciprocate, alternate; interchange &c. 148; exchange; counter-
change; interact, correspond, mutualize, give and take.

Adj. reciprocal, mutual, commutual, correlative; alternate; interchangeable; international; correspondent, complementary, analogous.

Adv. *mutatis mutandis*; *vice versâ*; each other; by turns &c. 148;
reciprocally &c. *adj.*; to and fro &c. 314.

13. Identity.—N. identity, sameness,
oneness, ditto, homogeneity; unity, coincidence, coalescence; convertibility;
equality &c. 27; selfness, self, oneself;
identification.

monotony, tautology &c. (*repetition*)
104.

synonym.

fac-simile &c. (*copy*) 21; *alter ego*
&c. (*similar*) 17; *ipsissima verba* &c.
(*exactness*) 494; same; self –, very –,
one and the- same; very –, actual-
thing; no other.

V. be -identical &c. *adj.*; match, coincide, coalesce.

treat as –, render- -the same, –identical; identify; recognize the identity of.

Adj. identical; self, ilk; the -same
&c. *n.*; self same; synonymous; one
and the same.

coincid-, coalesc-ent, -ing; indistin-
guishable; one; equivalent &c. (*equal*)
27; much -the same, – of a muchness;
unaltered.

Adv. identically &c. *adj.*; on all
fours; *ibid*-, -*em*.

14. [Non-coincidence.] **Contrariety.**
—N. contrariety, contrast, foil, antithesis, oppositeness; counterpole; contradiction; antagonism &c. (*opposition*)
708; counteraction &c. 179.

inversion &c. 218; the -opposite, –
reverse. – inverse, – converse, – antipodes, – other extreme &c. 237.

antonym.

V. be -contrary &c. *adj.*; contrast
with, oppose; differ *toto cælo*.

invert, reverse, turn the tables &c.
218.

contra-dict, -vene; antagonize &c.
708.

Adj. contrar-y, -ious, -iant; opposite,
counter, dead against; ad-, con-, reverse; opposed, antithetical, contrasted, antipodean, antagonistic, opposing; conflicting, inconsistent, contradictory, at cross purposes; negative;
hostile &c. 708.

differing *toto cælo*; diametrically opposite; as opposite as -black and white,
– light and darkness, – fire and water,
– the poles, as different as chalk from
cheese; 'Hyperion to a satyr'; quite
the -contrary, – reverse; no such thing, just the other way, *tout
au contraire.*

Adv. contrarily &c. *adj.*; *contra*, contrariwise, *per contra*, on the
contrary, nay rather; topsy-turvy; *vice versâ*; on the other hand &c.
(*in compensation*) 30.

15. Difference.—N. difference, unlikeness; heterogeneity; vari-ance,
-ation, -ety; diversity, dissimilarity &c. 18; disagreement &c. 24; dis-

parity &c. (*inequality*) 28; distinction, contradistinction; distinctness; discrepancy, divergence, contrast &c. 18; nonconformity, incompatibility, antithesis.

discord &c. 713.

modification, moods and tenses.

nice -, fine -, delicate -, subtle- distinction; shade of difference, *nuance;* discrimination &c. 465; *differentia.*

different thing, something else, variant, apple off another tree, horse of another colour, another pair of shoes; this that or the other.

V. be -different &c. *adj.;* differ, vary, ablude, mismatch, contrast; diverge -, depart -, deviate- -from; divaricate; differ -*toto cœlo*, - *longo intervallo.*

disagree &c. 713.

vary, modify &c. (*change*) 140.

discriminate &c. 465.

Adj. differing &c. *v.;* different, diverse, divided, heterogeneous; distinguishable; varied, modified; divergent, incongruous, diversified, various; discrepant, dissentient, differential; divers, all manner of; variform &c. 81; discordant &c. 713.

other, another, not the same; unequal &c. 28; unmatched; widely apart.

distinctive, characteristic; discriminative; distinguishing.

Adv. differently &c. *adj.*

Phr. *il y a fagots et fagots; quot homines tot sententiæ;* one man's meat is another man's poison.

2°. Continuous Relation

16. Uniformity. — N. uniformity; homogene-ity, -ousness; continuity, stability, consistency; connatural-ity, -ness; homology; accordance; conformity &c. 82; agreement &c. 23.

regularity, constancy, even tenor, routine; monotony, evenness, sameness, dead level; steadiness, equability, unity.

V. be -uniform &c. *adj.;* accord with &c. 23; run through.

become -uniform &c. *adj.;* conform to &c. 82.

render uniform &c. *adj.;* assimilate, level, smooth, dress.

16a. [Absence or want of uniformity.] Non-uniformity.—N. diversity irregularity, unevenness; multiformity &c. 81; unconformity &c. 83; roughness &c. 256; heterogeneity, heteromorphism.

Adj. diversified, varied, irregular, uneven, rough &c. 256; multifarious; multiform &c. 81; of various kinds; all -manner, - sorts, - kinds- of.

Adv. in all manner of ways, here there and everywhere.

Adj. uniform; homo-geneous, -logous; of a piece, consistent, steady; connatural; monotonous, changeless, dreary, even, invariable, equable, level, regular, stereotyped, unchanged, unvarying; methodical &c. 60; habitual &c. 613.

Adv. uniformly &c. *adj.;* uniformly with &c. (*conformably*) 82; in harmony with &c. (*agreeing*) 23; in a -rut, - groove.

always, ever &c. 112; invariably, without exception, never otherwise; by clock-work; endlessly &c. 112.

Phr. *ab uno disce omnes.*

3°. Partial Relation

17. Similarity.—N. similarity, resemblance, likeness, similitude, sem-

18. Dissimilarity.—N. dissimil-arity. -itude; unlikeness, diversity, disparity,

blance; affinity, approximation, parallelism; parity; agreement &c. 23; ana-logy, -logicalness; correspondence, equality &c.

connatural-ness, -ity; brotherhood, family likeness.

alliteration, rhyme, pun.

repetition &c. 104; sameness &c. (*identity*) 13; uniformity &c. 16.

analogue; the like; match, *pendant*, fellow, companion, pair, mate, twin, double, counterpart, brother, sister; one's second self, *alter ego*, chip of the old block, *par nobile fratrum, Arcades ambo*, birds of a feather, *et hoc genus omne*.

parallel; simile; type &c. (*metaphor*) 521; image &c. (*representation*) 554; photograph; close -, striking -, speaking -, faithful &c. *adj.* - likeness, - resemblance.

V. be -similar &c. *adj.*; look like, resemble, bear resemblance, favour; savour -, smack- of; approximate; parallel, match, rhyme with; take after; imitate &c. 19; run in pairs.

render -similar &c. *adj.*; assimilate, approximate, bring near; connaturalize, make alike; rhyme, pun.

Adj. similar; resembling &c. *v.*; like, alike; twin.

analog-ous, -ical; parallel, of a piece; such as, so.

connatural, congeneric, allied to; corresponding, cognate; akin to &c. (*consanguineous*) 11.

approximate, much the same, near, close, something like, such like; a show of; mock, *pseudo*, simulating, representing.

exact &c. (*true*) 494; lifelike, faithful, realistic; true to -nature, - the life; the -very image - picture- of; for all the world like, *comme deux gouttes d'eau*; as like as -two peas, - it can stare; *instar omnium*, cast in the same mould, ridiculously like.

Adv. as if, so to speak; as -, as if- it were; *quasi*, just as, *veluti in speculum*.

dissemblance; divergence, inequality, difference &c. 15; novelty; variation, variety, originality, disguise.

V. be -unlike &c. *adj.*; vary &c. (*differ*) 15; bear no resemblance to, differ *toto cœlo*.

render -unlike &c. *adj.*; vary &c. (*diversify*) 140.

Adj. dissimilar, unlike, disparate; of a different kind &c. (*class*) 75; unmatched, unique; new, novel; unprecedented &c. 83; original.

nothing of the kind; no such -, quite another- thing; far from it, other than, cast in a different mould, *tertium quid*, as like a dock as a daisy, 'very like a whale'; as different as -chalk from cheese, - Macedon and Monmouth; *lucus a non lucendo*.

diversified &c. 16*a*.

Adv. otherwise, *alias*.

---

19. Imitation.—N. imitation; copying &c. *v.*; transcription; repetition, mimeograph, mimeotype, duplication, reduplication; quotation; reproduction.

mockery, mimicry, mime, simulation, impersonation; representation &c. 554; semblance, simulacrum; pretence; copy &c. 21; assimilation.

paraphrase, parody &c. 21.

plagiarism; forgery &c. (*falsehood*) 544.

imitator, echo, cuckoo, parrot, ape, monkey, mocking-bird, mimic, impersonator; copyist.

V. imitate, copy, mirror, reflect, reproduce, repeat, borrow; do like, echo, re-echo, catch; transcribe; match, parallel.

20. Non-Imitation.—N. no imitation, genuineness, originality; creativeness.

Adj. unimitated, uncopied; unmatched, unparalleled; inimitable &c. 33; *unique*, original, primordial, primary, pristine, underived, first-hand, archetypal, prototypal.

---

mock, take off, mimic, ape, simulate, personate, impersonate; forge; act &c. (*drama*) 599; represent &c. 554; counterfeit, duplicate; portray, parody, travesty, caricature, burlesque.

follow –, tread- in the- -steps, – footsteps, – wake- of; pattern after, take pattern by; follow -suit, – the example of; walk in the shoes of, take a leaf out of another's book, strike in with; take –, model -after; emulate.

Adj. imitated &c. *v.*; mock, mimic; counterfeit, false, pseudo; modelled after, moulded on, paraphrastic; literal; imitative, apish; second-hand; imitable; sham &c. 545.

Adv. literally, to the letter, strictly, precisely, *verbatim*, *literatim*, *sic*, *totidem verbis*, word for word, *mot à mot*.

Phr. like master like man.

20a. Variation.—N. variation; alteration &c. (*change*) 140.

modification, moods and tenses; modulation.

divergency &c. 291; deviation &c. 279; aberration; innovation.

V. vary &c. (*change*) 140; deviate &c. 279; diverge &c. 291.

Adj. varied &c. *v.*; modified; dissimilar &c. 18; diversified &c. 16*a*.

21. [Result of imitation.] Copy.—N. copy, fac-simile, counterpart, *effigies*, effigy, symbol, image, form, likeness, similitude, semblance, resemblance, cast, electrotype, stereotype, tracing, ectype; imitation &c. 19; model, representation, adumbration, study; counterfeit presentment, portrait &c. (*representment*) 554.

duplicate; transcript, -ion; reflex, -ion; shadow, echo; chip of the old block; reprint, reproduction, casting, engraving, replica; transfer; second edition &c. (*repetition*) 104; *réchauffé*; apograph, fair copy, revise.

22. [Thing copied.] Prototype.—N. prototype, original, model, pattern, founding, precedent, standard, scantling, type, arche-, anti-type; protoplast, copy-book, module, exemplar, example, ensample, specimen; paradigm; guide; templet; lay-figure.

text, copy, manuscript, MS., design; fugleman, keynote.

die, mould; matrix, engraving, last, plasm; pro-, proto-plasm; mint; seal, punch, *intaglio*, negative, stamp.

V. be –, set- an example; set a copy; standardize.

parody, caricature, cartoon, burlesque, travesty, paraphrase.

servile -copy, – imitation; counterfeit &c. (*deception*) 545; *pasticcio*.

Adj. faithful; lifelike &c. (*similar*) 17.

4°. GENERAL RELATION

23. Agreement. — N. agreement; ac-cord, -cordance; unison, harmony, syntony; concord &c. 714; concordance, concert, understanding, convention, *entente -cordiale, consortium*, consensus of opinion, pact, mutual understanding, unanimity.

conformity &c. 82; conformance; uniformity &c. 16; consonance, consentaneousness, consistency; congruity, -ence; keeping; congeniality; correspondence, concinnity, parallelism, apposition, union.

fitness, aptness &c. *adj.*; relevancy;

24. Disagreement. — N. disagreement; dis-cord, -cordance; disunion, dissonance, dissidence, discrepancy; unconformity &c. 83; incongru-ity, -ence; discongruity, *mésalliance*, *oxymoron*; jarring &c. *v.*; clash, collision, dissension &c. 713; conflict &c. (*opposition*) 708; controversy &c. 720; falling out, wrangle, argument.

disparity, mismatch, misfit, disproportion; disproportionateness &c. *adj.*; variance, divergence, repugnance.

unfitness &c. *adj.*; inaptitude, impropriety; inapplicability &c. *adj.*; in-

pertinen-ce, -cy; sortance; case in point; aptitude, coaptation, propriety, applicability, admissibility, commensurability, compatibility, suitability; cognation &c. (*relation*) 9.

adaptation, adjustment, arrangement, graduation, accommodation; reconcil-iation -ement; assimilation; attunement.

consent &c. (*assent*) 488; concurrence &c. 178; co-operation &c. 709.

right man in the right place, very thing; quite –, just- the thing.

V. be -accordant &c. *adj.*; agree, accord, harmonize; correspond, tally, respond; meet, suit, fit, befit, do, adapt itself to; fall in –, chime in –, square –, quadrate –, consort –, comport- with; dovetail, assimilate; fit like a glove; fit to a -tittle, – T; match &c. 17; become one.

consent &c. (*assent*) 488.

render -accordant &c. *adj.*; fit, suit, adapt, accommodate; graduate; adjust &c. (*render equal*) 27; dress, regulate, readjust; accord, harmonize, reconcile; fadge, dovetail, square.

Adj. agreeing, suiting &c. *v.*; in accord, accordant, concordant, consonant, congruous, consentaneous, correspondent, corresponding, homologous, congenial; becoming; harmonious, reconcilable, conformable; in -accordance, – harmony, – keeping, – unison, &c. *n.*- with; at one with, of one mind, of a piece; consistent, compatible, proportionate, answerable; commensurate; on all fours.

apt, apposite, pertinent, pat; to the -point, – purpose; happy, felicitous, germane, *ad rem*, in point, bearing upon, applicable, relevant, admissible.

fit, adapted, *in loco*, *à propos*, appropriate, seasonable, sortable, suitable, idoneous, deft; meet &c. (*expedient*) 646.

at home, in one's proper element.

Adv. *à propos of*; pertinently &c. *adj.*; *pro rata*.

Phr. *rem acu tetigisti*, the cap fits.

consistency, inconcinnity; irrelevancy &c. (*irrelation*) 10.

misjoin-ing, -der; syncretism, intrusion, interference; *concordia discors*.

fish out of water.

V. disagree; clash, quarrel, jar &c. (*discord*) 713; interfere, intrude, come amiss; not concern &c. 10; mismatch; *humano capiti cervicem jungere equinam.*

Adj. disagreeing &c. *v.*; discordant, discrepant; at -variance, – war; hostile, antagonistic, repugnant, factious, contradictory, dissentious, incompatible, irreconcilable, inconsistent with; unconformable, exceptional &c. 83; intrusive, incongruous; disproportionate, -ed; unharmonious; unconsonant; divergent, repugnant to.

inapt, unapt, inappropriate, inept, infelicitous, improper; unsuit-ed, -able; inapplicable; un-fit, -fitting, -befitting; unbecoming; ill-timed, ill-adapted, unseasonable, *mal à propos*, inadmissible; inapposite &c. (*irrelevant*) 10.

uncongenial; ill-assorted, -sorted, -matched; mis-matched, -mated, -joined, -placed; unaccommodating, irreducible, uncommensurable, unsympathetic.

out of -character, – keeping, – proportion, – joint, – tune, – place, – season, – its element; at -odds, – variance with.

Adv. in -defiance, – contempt, – spite-of; discordantly &c. *adj.*; *à tort et à travers.*

Section III. QUANTITY

1°. Simple Quantity

25. [Absolute quantity.] **Quantity.—** **N.** quantity, magnitude; size &c. (*dimensions*) 192; amplitude, mass,

26. [Relative quantity.] **Degree.—** **N.** degree, grade, extent, measure, proportion, amount, ratio, stint, standard

amount, *quantum*, measure, measurement, substance, strength.

[Science of quantity.] Mathematics, Mathesis.

[Definite or finite quantity] arm-, hand-, mouth-, spoon-, thimble-, capful; stock, batch, lot, dose, ration, quotum, quota, pittance, driblet, part, portion &c. 51.

Adj. quantitative,' some, any, more or less.

Adv. to the tune of.

----

height, pitch; reach, amplitude, range, scope, size, calibre; gradation, shade; tenor, compass; sphere, station, rank, standing; rate, way, sort.

point, mark, step, stage &c. (*term*) 71; intensity, strength &c. (*greatness*) 31.

V. compare, graduate, calibrate, measure.

Adj. comparative; gradual, shading off, gradational; within the bounds &c. (*limit*), 233.

Adv. by degrees, gradually, inasmuch, *pro tanto*; how-ever, -soever; step by step, bit by bit, little by little, inch by inch, drop by drop, gradatim; by -inches, - slow degrees, - little and little; in some -degree, - measure; to some extent; just a bit.

2°. COMPARATIVE QUANTITY

27. [Sameness of quantity or degree.] **Equality.—N.** equality, parity, co-extension, symmetry, balance, poise; evenness, monotony, level.

equivalence; equi-pollence, -poise, -librium, -ponderance; par, quits; not a pin to choose; distinction without a difference, six of one and half a dozen of the other; identity &c. 13; similarity &c. 17; isotropism; coequality.

equalization, equation; equilibration, co-ordination, adjustment, readjustment.

drawn -game, -battle, draw, stalemate; neck and neck race; tie, dead heat.

match, peer, compeer, equal, mate, fellow, brother; equivalent.

V. be -equal &c. *adj.*; equal, match, reach, keep pace with; run abreast; come -, amount -, come up-to; be -, lie- on a level with; balance; cope with; come to the same thing; level off.

render -equal &c. *adj.*; equalize, level, dress, balance, equate, handicap, give points, trim, adjust, poise; fit, accommodate; adapt &c. (*render accordant*) 23; strike a balance; establish -, restore-equality, - equilibrium; readjust; stretch on the bed of Procrustes.

Adj. equal, even, level, monotonous, coequal, symmetrical, co-ordinate; on a -par, - level, - footing- with; up to the mark; equiparent.

equivalent, tantamount; quits; homologous; synonymous &c. 522; resolvable into, convertible, much at one, as broad as long, neither more nor less; much the same -, the same thing -, as good-as; all -one, - the same; equi-pollent, -ponderant, -ponderous, -balanced; equalized &c. *v.*; drawn; half and half; isochronous; isoperimetrical.

28. [Difference of quantity or degree.] **Inequality.—N.** inequality; dis-, im-parity; odds; difference &c. 15; ill-balanced; unevenness; inclination of the balance, partiality; shortcoming; casting - make- weight; superiority &c. 33; inferiority &c. 34.

V. be -unequal &c. *adj.*; countervail; have -, give the advantage; turn the scale; kick the beam; topple, -over; over-match &c. 33; not come up to &c. 34.

Adj. unequal, uneven, disparate, partial; un-, over-balanced; top-heavy, lop-sided.

Adv. *haud passibus æquis.*

Adv. equally &c. *adj.*; *pari passu, ad eundem, cæteris paribus*; *in equilibrio*; to all intents and purposes.

Phr. it -comes, -adds up, – amounts- to the same thing.

29. Mean.—N. mean, medium, intermedium, average, run of the mill, normal, balance; mediocrity, generality, rule, ordinary -run, -ruck; golden mean &c. (*mid-course*) 628; middle &c. 68; compromise &c. 774; neutrality; middle point, middle course.

V. split the difference; take the -average &c. *n.*; reduce to a -mean &c. *n.*; strike a balance, pair off.

Adj. mean, intermediate; medial; middle &c. 68; average, normal, standard; neutral; middling, moderate.

mediocre, middle-class; *bourgeois*, commonplace &c. (*unimportant*) 643.

Adv. on an average, in the long run; taking -one with another, – all things together, – it for all in all; *communibus annis*, in round numbers.

30. Compensation.—N. compensation, equation; commutation; indemnification; compromise &c. 774; neutralization, nullification; counteraction &c. 179; reaction; measure for measure; retaliation &c. 718; equalization &c. 27; redemption, recoupment, recompense.

set-off, offset; make- casting-weight; counterpoise, equipoise, ballast; indemnity, reparation &c. 790; equivalent, *quid pro quo*; bribe, hush-money, tribute &c. 784; amends &c. (*atonement*) 952; counterclaim, counterbalance, equiponderance, countervail, cross demand.

V. make -amends, – compensation; com-pensate, -pense; indemnify; counter-act, -vail, -poise; equiponderate; balance; out-, over-, counterbalance; set off, offset, cancel; hedge, square, give and take; make up -for, – lee way; cover, fill up, neutralize, nullify; equalize &c. 27; make good; redeem &c. (*atone*) 952; recoup, pay &c. 973.

Adj. compensat-ing, -ory; amendatory, reparative, countervailing &c. *v.*; in the opposite scale; equivalent &c. (*equal*) 27.

Adv. in -return, – consideration; but, however, yet, still, notwithstanding; neverthe-, nath-less; although, though; al-, how-beit; in spite of, despite; maugre; at -all events, – any rate; be that as it may, for all that, even so, on the other hand, at the same time, *quoad minus, quand même*, however that may be; after all, – is said and done; taking one thing with another &c. (*average*) 29.

QUANTITY BY COMPARISON .WITH A STANDARD

31. Greatness.—N. greatness &c. *adj.*; magnitude; size &c. (*dimensions*) 192; multitude &c. (*number*) 102; immensity, enormity; infinity &c. 105; might, strength, intensity, fulness; importance &c. 642; fame &c. 873.

great quantity, quantity, deal, power, sight, pot, volume, world; mass, heap &c. (*assemblage*) 72; stock &c. (*store*) 636; peck, bushel, load, cargo; cart -, wagon -, car -, truck -, ship- load; flood, spring tide; abundance &c. (*sufficiency*) 639.

principal -, chief -, main -, greater -,

32. Smallness.—N. smallness &c. *adj.*; littleness &c. (*small size*) 193; tenuity; paucity; fewness &c. (*small number*) 103; meanness, insignificance &c. (*unimportance*) 643; mediocrity, moderation.

small quantity, *modicum, minimum*; vanishing point; material point, electron, atom, particle, molecule, corpuscle, point, dab, fleck, speck, dot, mote, jot, iota, ace; *minutiæ*, details; look, thought, idea, *soupçon*, whit, tittle, shade, shadow; spark, *scintilla*, gleam; touch, cast; grain. scruple,

major -, best -, essential- part; bulk, mass &c. (*whole*) 50.

V. be -great &c. *adj.*; run high, soar, loom up, tower, bulk large, transcend; rise -, carry- to a great height; know no bounds; scale, overtop, ascend.

enlarge &c. (*increase*) 35, (*expand*) 194.

Adj. great; greater &c. 33; large, considerable, fair, above par; big, massive, huge &c. (*large in size*) 192; ample; abundant &c. (*enough*) 639; Herculean &c. 159; full, intense, strong, sound, passing, heavy, plenary, deep, high; signal, at its height, in the zenith.

world-wide, wide-spread, extensive; wholesale; many &c. 102.

goodly, noble, precious, mighty; sad, grave, serious; far gone, arrant, downright; utter, -most; crass, gross, arch, profound, intense, consummate; rank, unmitigated, red-hot, desperate; glaring, flagrant, stark staring; thorough-paced, -going; roaring, thumping, thundering, strapping, whacking; extraordinary; important &c. 642; unsurpassed &c. (*supreme*) 33; complete &c. 52.

vast, immense, enormous, extreme; inordinate, excessive, extravagant, exorbitant, outrageous, preposterous, unconscionable, swingeing, monstrous, over-grown; towering, stupendous, prodigious, astonishing, incredible; terrific, frightful; marvellous &c. (*wonder*) 870; grand.

unlimited &c. (*infinite*) 105; unapproachable, unutterable, indescribable, ineffable, unspeakable, inexpressible, beyond expression, fabulous.

un-diminished, -abated, -reduced, -restricted.

absolute, positive, stark, decided, unequivocal, essential, perfect, finished.

remarkable, of mark, marked, pointed, veriest; noticeable, uncommon, noteworthy, eminent &c. 873.

Adv. [in a positive degree] truly &c. (*truth*) 494; decidedly, unequivocally, purely, absolutely, seriously, essentially, fundamentally, radically, downright, in all conscience; for the most part, in the main.

[in a complete degree] entirely &c. (*completely*) 52; abundantly, &c. (*suf-*

granule, globule, minim, sup, sip, sop, spice, drop, droplet, sprinkling, dash, smack, tinge, tincture; inch, patch, scantling, dole; scrap, shred, tag, splinter, rag, tatter, cantlet, flitter, gobbet, mite, bit, morsel, crumb, seed, fritter, shive; snip, -pet; snick, snack, snatch, slip, scrag; chip, -ping; shiver, sliver, driblet, clipping, paring, shaving, hair.

nutshell; thimble-, spoon-, hand-, cap-, mouth-ful; fragment; fraction &c. (*part*) 51; drop in the ocean, drop in the bucket.

animalcule &c. 193.

trifle &c. (*unimportant thing*) 643; mere -, next to- nothing; hardly anything; just enough to swear by; the shadow of a shade.

finiteness, finite quantity.

V. be -shall &c. *adj.*; lie in a nutshell.

diminish &c. (*decrease*) 36, (*contract*) 195.

Adj. small, little, tiny, weeny; diminutive &c. (*small in size*) 193; minute; minikin, fine, inconsiderable, dribbling, paltry &c. (*unimportant*) 643; faint &c. (*weak*) 160; slender, light, slight, scanty, scant, limited; meagre &c. (*insufficient*) 640; sparing; few &c. 103; low, so-so, middling, tolerable, no great shakes; below -, under-par, - the mark; at a low ebb; halfway; moderate, modest; tender, subtle; petty, shallow, skin-deep.

inappreciable, evanescent, infinitesimal, homœopathic, very small, atomic, molecular, ultra-, -microscopic.

petty, shallow &c. 499.

mere, simple, sheer, stark, bare; near run.

Adv. [in a small degree] to a small extent, on a small scale; a -little, - wee, - tiny bit; slightly &c. *adj.*; imperceptibly; miserably, wretchedly; insufficiently &c. 640; imperfectly; faintly &c. 160; passably, pretty well, well enough.

[in a certain or limited degree] partially, in part; in -, to a certain degree; to a certain extent; comparatively; some, rather; in some -degree, -measure; some-thing, -what; simply, only, purely, merely; at -, at the- -least,

ficiently) 639; widely, far and wide.

[in a great or high degree] greatly &c. *adj.*; much, muckle, well, indeed, very, very much, a deal, no end of, most, not a little; pretty, – well; enough, in a great measure, passing richly; to a -large, – great, – gigantic- extent; on a large scale; so; never –, ever- so; ever so much; by wholesale; mightily, mighty, powerfully; with a witness, *ultra*, in the extreme, ex- tremely, exceedingly, intensely, ex- quisitely, acutely, indefinitely, im- measurably; beyond -compare, – comparison, – measure, – all bounds; incalculably, infinitely.

[in a supreme degree] pre-eminently, superlatively &c. (*superiority*) 33.

[in a too great degree] immoderately, unduly, monstrously, grossly, prepos- terously, inordinately, exorbitantly, excessively, enormously, out of all proportion, with a vengeance.

[in a marked degree] particularly, remarkably, singularly, curi- ously, uncommonly, unusually, peculiarly, notably, signally, strikingly, pointedly, mainly, chiefly; famously, egregiously, prom- inently, glaringly, emphatically, strangely, wonderfully, amazingly, surprisingly, astonishingly, incredibly, marvellously, awfully, stupendously.

[in an exceptional degree] peculiarly &c. (*unconformity*) 83.

[in a violent degree] furiously &c. (*violence*) 173; severely, des- perately, tremendously, extravagantly, confoundedly, deucedly, devilishly, with a vengeance; *à –, à toute- outrance.*

[in a painful degree] painfully, sadly, grossly, sorely, bitterly, piteously, grievously, miserably, cruelly, woefully, lamentably, shockingly, frightfully, dreadfully, fearfully, terribly, horribly, distressingly, balefully.

– most; ever so little, as little as may be, *tant soit peu*, in ever so small a degree; thus far, *pro tanto*, within bounds, in a manner, after a fashion.

almost, nearly, well nigh, short of, not quite, all but; near –, close- upon; *peu s'en faut*, near the mark; within an ·ace, – inch- of; on the brink of; scarcely, hardly, barely, only just, no more than.

[in an uncertain degree] about, there- abouts, somewhere about, nearly, say; be the same -more, – little more- or less.

[in no degree] no- ways, – wise; not -at all, – in the least, – a bit, – a bit of it, – a whit, – a jot, – a shadow; in no -wise, – respect; by no -means, – man- ner of means; on no account, at no hand.

QUANTITY BY COMPARISON WITH A SIMILAR OBJECT

33. Superiority.—N. supremacy, superiority, majority; greatness &c. 31; advantage, odds, pull; preponder- ance, -ation; predominance, vantage ground, coign of vantage, prevalence, partiality; personal superiority; sover- eignty &c. 737; nobility &c. (*rank*) 875; Triton among the minnows, *primus inter pares, nulli secundus*, superman; captain &c. 745.

supremacy, pre-eminence; primacy, lead, *maximum*; record; climax, crest, top; culmination &c. (*summit*) 210; transcendence; *ne plus ultra*; lion's share, Benjamin's mess; excess; bisque,

34. Inferiority.—N. inferiority, mi- nority, subordinancy; shortcoming, de- ficiency; handicap; *minimum*; smallness &c. 32; imperfection, shabbiness.

[personal inferiority] commonalty &c. 876; subordinate, substitute, sub.

V. be -inferior &c. *adj.*; fall –, come- short of; not -pass, – come up to; want.

become –, render- smaller &c. (*decrease*) 36, (*contract*) 195; hide its diminished head, retire into the shade, yield the palm, play second fiddle, take a back seat; bow.

Adj. inferior, smaller; small &c. 32;

surplus &c. (*remainder*) 40, (*redundance*) 641.

V. be -superior &c. *adj.*; exceed, excel, transcend; out-do, -balance, -weigh, -rival, -Herod, outrank, pass, surpass, surmount, get ahead of; overtop, -ride, -pass, -balance, -weigh, -match; top, o'er-top, cap, beat, win out, cut out; beat hollow; outstrip &c. 303; eclipse, throw into the shade, take the shine out of, put one's nose out of joint; have the -upper hand, – whip hand of, – advantage; turn the scale, play first fiddle &c. (*importance*) 642; preponderate, predominate, prevail; precede, take precedence, come first; come to a head, culminate; beat &c. all others, bear the palm; break the record, take the cake.

minor, less, lesser, deficient, minus, lower, subordinate, secondary; second-rate &c. (*imperfect*) 651; sub, subaltern; thrown into the shade; weighed in the balance and found wanting; not fit to hold a candle to.

least, smallest &c. (*see* little, small &c. 193); lowest.

diminished &c. (*decreased*) 36; reduced &c. (*contracted*) 195; unimportant &c. 643.

Adv. less; under –, below- -the mark, – par; at -the bottom of the scale, – a low ebb, – a disadvantage; short of, under.

become –, render- -larger, &c. (*increase*) 35, (*expand*) 194.

Adj. superior, greater, major, higher; exceeding &c. *v.*; great &c. 31; distinguished, *ultra*; vaulting; more than a match for.

supreme, greatest, maximal, maximum, utmost, paramount, pre-eminent, foremost, crowning; first-rate &c. (*important*) 642, (*excellent*) 648; unrivalled; peer-, match-less; none such, second to none, *sans pareil*; un-paragoned, -paralleled, -equalled, -approached, -surpassed; superlative, inimitable, *facile princeps*, incomparable, sovereign, without parallel, *nulli secundus*, *ne plus ultra*; beyond -compare, – comparison; culminating &c. (*topmost*) 210; transcendent, -ental; *plus royaliste que le Roi*.

increased &c. (*added to*) 35; enlarged &c. (*expanded*) 194.

Adv. beyond, more, over; over –, above- the mark; above par; upwards –, in advance- of; over and above; at the top of the scale, on the crest, at its height.

[in a superior or supreme degree] eminently, egregiously, pre-eminently, surpassing, prominently, superlatively, supremely, above all, of all things, the most, to crown all, *par excellence*, principally, especially, particularly, peculiarly, *a fortiori*, even, yea, still more.

Phr. 'we shall not look upon his like again.'

CHANGES IN QUANTITY

35. Increase—N. increase, augmentation, addition, enlargement, extension; dilatation &c. (*expansion*) 194; multiplication; increment, accretion; accession &c. 37; production &c. 161; development, growth; aggrandizement, aggravation, intensification; rise; ascent &c. 305; anabasis; ex-aggeration, -acerbation; spread &c. (*dispersion*) 73; flood-, spring-, -tide; gain, produce, profit &c. 618; booty, plunder &c. 793.

V. increase, augment, add to, enlarge; dilate &c. (*expand*) 194; grow,

36. Non-Increase, Decrease.—N. decrease, diminution; lessening &c. *v.*; subtraction &c. 38; reduction, abatement, declension; shrinkage &c. (*contraction*) 195; coarctation; abridgment &c. (*shortening*) 201; extenuation.

subsidence, catabasis, wane, ebb-, neap-tide, decline; descent &c. 306; decrement, reflux, depreciation; erosion, wear and tear, deterioration &c. 659; anticlimax; mitigation &c. (*moderation*) 174.

V. decrease, diminish, lessen; abridge

wax, mount, swell, get ahead, gain strength; advance; run -, shoot- up; rise; ascend &c. 305; sprout &c. 194.

aggrandize; raise, exalt; deepen, heighten; lengthen; thicken; strengthen; intensify, enhance, inflate, magnify, double, redouble; multiply; aggravate, exaggerate; ex-asperate, -acerbate; add fuel to the flame, *oleum addere camino*, superadd &c. (*add*) 37; spread &c. (*disperse*) 73.

Adj. increased &c. *v.*; on the increase, undiminished; additional &c. (*added*) 37; increasing &c. *v.*; growing, crescent, intensive, cumulative.

Adv. *crescendo*, increasingly.

Phr. *vires acquirit eundo*.

&c. (*shorten*) 201; shrink &c. (*contract*) 195; drop -, fall -, tail- off, fall away, waste, wear, erode; wane, ebb, decline; descend &c. 306; subside; deliquesce, melt -, die -away; retire into the shade, hide its diminished head, fall to a low ebb, run low, languish, decay, crumble, consume away.

bate, abate, dequantitate; discount; depreciate; extenuate, lower, weaken, attenuate, fritter away; mitigate &c. (*moderate*) 174; belittle, minimize; dwarf, throw into the shade; keep down, reduce &c. 195; shorten &c. 201; subtract &c. 38.

Adj. unincreased &c. (*see* increase &c. 35); decreased &c. *v.*; decreasing &c. *v.*; on the -wane &c. *n.*; deliquescent.

Adv. *diminuendo*, *decrescendo*, decreasingly.

3°. CONJUNCTIVE QUANTITY

37. Addition.—N. addition, annexation, adjection; junction &c. 43; super-position, -addition, -junction, -fetation; accession, reinforcement; increase &c. 35; increment, supplement; accompaniment &c. 88; interposition &c. 228; insertion &c. 300; summation &c. 85; adjunct &c. 39.

V. add, annex, adject, affix, attach, superadd, subjoin, superpose; clap -, saddle- on; tack to, postfix, append, tag; ingraft; saddle with; sprinkle; introduce &c. (*interpose*) 228; insert &c. 300.

become added, accrue; ad-, supervene; add up &c. 85.

reinforce, strengthen, swell the ranks of; augment &c. 35.

Adj. added &c. *v.*; additional; supplement, -al, -ary; suppletory, subjunctive; adjec-, adsci-, asci-titious; additive, extra, spare, further, fresh, more, new, ulterior, other, auxiliary, supernumerary, accessory.

Adv. in addition, more, plus, extra; and, also, likewise, too, furthermore, further, item; and -also, - eke; else, besides, to boot, *et cætera*; &c.; and so -on, - forth; into the bargain, *cum multis aliis*, over and above, moreover.

with, withal; including, inclusive, as well as, not to mention, let

38. Non-Addition. Subduction.—N. sub-traction, -duction; deduction, retrenchment; removal; ab-, sub-lation; abstraction &c. (*taking*) 789; garbling &c. *v.*; mutilation, detruncation; amputation, severance; abs-, ex-, re-cision: curtailment &c. 201; minuend, subtrahend; decrease &c. 36; abrasion.

V. sub-tract, -duct; rebate, de-duct, -duce; bate, retrench; remove, withdraw; take -from, - away; detract.

garble, mutilate, amputate, sever, detruncate; cut -off, - away, - out; expurgate; abscind, excise; pare, thin, prune, decimate; abrade, scrape, file; geld, castrate, emasculate, unman, spay, caponize; eliminate.

diminish &c. 36; curtail &c. (*shorten*) 201; deprive of &c. (*take*) 789; weaken.

Adj. subtracted &c. *v.*; subtractive. tailless, acaudal.

Adv. in -deduction &c. *n.*; less; short of; minus, without, except, excepting, with the exception of, barring, bar, save, exclusive of, save and except, with a reservation.

alone; together –, along –, coupled –, in conjunction- with; conjointly; jointly &c. 43.

39. [Thing added.] **Adjunct.—N.** adjunct; addit-ion, -ament; *additum*, affix, appendage, annex; augment, -ation; increment, reinforcement, supernumerary, accessory, item; garnish, sauce; accompaniment &c. 88; adjective, *addendum*, accession, complement, supplement; continuation; extension, subscript, tag, appendix, postscript, interlineation, interpolation, insertion.

rider, codicil, off-shoot, episode, side issue, corollary; piece; flap, lapel, label, tab, strip, fold, lappet, apron, skirt, embroidery, trappings, *cortège*; tail, suffix &c. (*sequel*) 65; wing.

Adj. additional &c. 37.

Adv. in addition &c. 37.

40. [Thing remaining.] **Remainder·** **—N.** remainder, residue; remains, *remanet*, remnant, rest, relic, relict; leavings, heel-tap, odds and ends, cheese-parings, candle ends, orts; *residuum*; dottle, dregs &c. (*dirt*) 653; refuse &c. (*useless*) 645; stubble, result, educt; fag-end, stub; ruins, wreck, skeleton, stump; *alluvium*.

surplus, overplus, excess; balance, complement; superfluity &c. (*redundance*) 641; surviv-al, -ance; afterglow.

V. remain; be -left &c. *adj.*; exceed, survive; leave.

Adj. remaining, left; left -behind, – over; residu-al, -ary; over, odd; unconsumed, sedimentary; surviving; net; exceeding, over and above; outlying, -standing; cast off &c. 782; superfluous &c. (*redundant*) 641.

40a. [Thing deducted.] **Decrement.—N.** decrement, discount, rebate, defect, loss, deduction, eduction, tare; drawback; waste, wastage; reprise.

41. [Forming a whole without coherence.] **Mixture.—N.** mix-, admix-, commix-ture, -tion, mingling; commixion, immixture, interfusion, intermixture, alloyage, matrimony; junction &c. 43; combination &c. 48; entanglement, interlacing; miscegenation, interbreeding.

impregnation; in-, dif-, suf-, trans fusion; infiltration; seasoning, sprinkling, interlarding; interpolation &c. 228; adulteration, sophistication.

[Thing mixed] tinge, tincture, touch, dash, smack, sprinkling, spice, seasoning, infusion, *soupçon*.

[Compound resulting from mixture] alloy, brass, bronze, pewter &c.; amalgam, *magma*, blend, half-and-half, *mélange*, *tertium quid*, miscellany, *ambigu*, medley, mess, hash, hotchpotch, hodgepodge, *pasticcio*, patchwork, odds and ends, all sorts; jumble &c. (*disorder*) 59; salad, sauce, mash, *omnium*

42. [Freedom from mixture.] **Simpleness.—N.** simpleness &c. *adj.*; purity, homogeneity.

elimination; sifting &c. *v.*; purification &c. (*cleanness*) 652.

V. render -simple &c. *adj.*; simplify. sift, winnow, bolt, eliminate; narrow down; get rid of, exclude &c. 55; clear; purify &c. (*clean*) 652; disentangle &c. (*disjoin*) 44.

Adj. simple, uniform, of a piece, homogeneous, single, pure, clear, sheer, neat; Attic.

un-mixed, -mingled, -blended, -combined, -compounded; elementary, undecomposed; un-adulterated, -sophisticated, -alloyed, -tinged, -fortified; pure and simple.

free –, exempt- from; exclusive.

Adv. simply &c. *adj.*; only.

gatherum, gallimaufry, ragout, *olla podrida*, *olio*, salmagundi, *potpourri*, Noah's ark; texture, mingled yarn; mosaic &c. (*variegation*) 440.

half-blood, -caste, -breed, Eurasian; mulatto; terc-, quart-, quinteron &c.; quad-, octo-roon; *griffo*, *zambo*; cross, hybrid, mongrel &c. 83.

V. mix; join &c. 43; combine &c. 48; com-, im-, inter-mix; mix up with, mingle; com-, inter-, be-mingle; shuffle &c. (*derange*) 61; pound together; hash -, stir- up; knead, brew; impregnate with; interlard &c. (*interpolate*) 228; inter-twine, -weave &c. 219; associate with, miscegenate, interbreed.

be mixed &c.; get among, be entangled with.

instil, imbue; in-, suf-, trans-fuse; infiltrate, dash, tinge, tincture, season, sprinkle, besprinkle, attemper, medicate, blend, cross; alloy, amalgamate, compound, adulterate, sophisticate, infect.

Adj. mixed &c. *v.*; implex, composite, half-and-half, linsey-wolsey, hybrid, mongrel, heterogeneous; motley &c. (*variegated*) 440; miscellaneous, promiscuous, indiscriminate; miscible.

Adv. among, amongst, amid, amidst, with; in the midst of, in the crowd.

43. Junction.—N. junction; joining &c. *v.*; joinder, union; con-nection, -junction, -jugation, compendency, annex-ion, -ation, -ment; coalition; astriction, attachment, compagination, vincture, ligation, alligation; accouplement; marriage &c. (*wedlock*) 903; infibulation, inosculation, symphysis, anastomosis, confluence, communication, concatenation; concurrence, meeting, reunion; assemblage &c. 72.

copulation, coition, intercourse.

joint, joining, juncture, chiasma, pivot, hinge, articulation, commissure, seam, suture, gusset, stitch, splice; link &c. 45; mitre, mortise.

closeness, tightness &c. *adj.*; coherence &c. 46; combination &c. 48.

V. join, unite; con-join, -nect; associate; put -, lay -, clap -, hang -, lump -, hold -, piece -, tack -, fix -, bind up- together; embody, re-embody; roll into one.

attach, fix, affix, saddle on, fasten, bind, paste, secure, clinch, twist, make -fast &c. *adj.*; tie, pinion, string, strap, sew, lace, stitch, tack, baste, knit, button, buckle, hitch, lash, truss, bandage, braid, splice, swathe, gird, tether, moor, picket, harness, chain; fetter &c. (*restrain*) 751; lock, latch, belay, brace, hook, grapple, leash, couple, accouple, link, yoke, bracket; marry &c. (*wed*) 903; bridge over, span.

pin, nail, bolt, hasp, clasp, clamp, screw, rivet; impact, solder, braze, cement, set; weld -, fuse- together; wedge, rabbet, mortise, mitre, jam, dovetail, enchase; graft, ingraft, inosculate; en-, in-twine; inter-link, -lace,

44. Disjunction.—N. dis-junction, -connection, -unity, -union, -association, -engagement, -sociation; discontinuity &c. 70; inconnection; abstraction, -edness; isolation; insul-arity, -ation; oasis; separateness &c. *adj.*; severalty; *disjecta membra*; dispersion &c. 73; apportionment &c. 786.

separation; parting &c. *v.*; detachment, segregation; divorce, sejunction, seposition, diduction, diremption, discerption; elision; *cæsura*, division, subdivision, break, fracture, rupture; compartition; dis-memberment, -integration, -location; luxation; sever-, dis-sever-ance; scission; re-, ab-scission; circumcision; lacer-, dilacer-ation; dis-, ab-ruption; avulsion, divulsion; section, resection, cleavage; fission; separability; separatism.

fissure, breach, rent, split, rift, crack, slit, slot, incision.

dissection, anatomy; decomposition &c. 49; cutting instrument &c. (*sharpness*) 253; saw.

V. be -disjoined &c.; come -, fall- -off, - to pieces; peel off; get loose.

dis-join, -connect, -engage, -unite, -sociate, -pair; divorce, part, dispart, detach, uncouple, separate, cut off, rescind, segregate; set -, keep- apart; insulate, isolate; throw out of gear; cut adrift; loose; un-loose, -do, -bind, -tie, -hitch, -chain, -lock &c. (*fix*) 43, -pack, -ravel; disentangle; set free &c. (*liberate*) 750.

sunder, divide, subdivide, sectionalize, sever, dissever, abscind; cut; segment; in-cide, -cise; circumcise; saw, snip, nib, nip, cleave, rive, rend, slit,

-twine, -twist, -weave; entangle; twine round, belay; tighten; trice –, screw-up.

be -joined &c.; hang –, hold- together; cohere &c. 46.

Adj. joined &c. *v.*; joint; con-joint, -junct; corporate, compact; hand in hand.

firm, fast, close, tight, taut, taught, tense, secure, set, intervolved; in-separable, -dissoluble, -secable, -severable.

Adv. jointly &c. *adj.*; in conjunction with &c. (*in addition to*) 37; fast, firmly &c. *adj.*; intimately.

split, splinter, chip, crack, snap, break, tear, burst; rend &c. -asunder, – in twain; wrench, rupture, shatter, shiver, cranch, crunch, craunch, chop; rip up; hack, hew, slash; whittle; haggle, hackle, discind, lacerate, scamble, mangle, gash, hash, slice, shave.

cut up, carve, quarter, dissect, anat-omize; take –, pull –, pick –, tear- to pieces; tear to tatters, – piecemeal; divellicate; skin &c. 226; dis-integrate, -member, -branch, -band; disperse &c. 73; dis-locate, -joint; break up; mince; comminute &c. (*pulverize*) 330; distribute, apportion &c. 786.

part, – company; separate, leave; alienate, estrange.

Adj. disjoined &c. *v.*; discontinuous &c. 70; bipartite, multipartite, abstract; digitate; disjunctive; isolated &c. *v.*; insular, separate, disparate, discrete, apart, asunder, far between, loose, free; unattached, -annexed, -associated, -connected; distinct; adrift; straggling; rift, reft, cleft, split.

[capable of being divided] scissile, partible, divisible, separable, severable, detachable.

Adv. separately &c. *adj.*; one by one, severally, apart; adrift, asunder, in twain; in the abstract, abstractedly.

45. [Connecting medium.] **Vinculum.—N.** vinculum, link, *nexus*; connec-tive, -tion; junction &c. 43; bond of union, copula, intermedium, hyphen; bracket; bridge, stepping-stone, isthmus.

bond, tendon, tendril; fibre; cord, -age; riband, ribbon, rope, guy, cable, line, halser, hawser, painter, moorings, wire, chain; string &c. (*filament*) 205.

fastening, tie; liga-ment, -ture; strap; bowline, halliard, tackle, lanyard, rigging, shrouds; standing –, running- rigging; traces, harness; yoke; band, -age; brace, roller, fillet; with, withe, withy; thong, braid; girder, tie-beam; girt, cinch, girth, girdle, cestus, garter, braces, suspenders, halter, noose, lasso, lariat, surcingle, knot, hitch, running knot, frog.

pin, corking pin, nail, brad, tack, skewer, staple, cleat, clamp; cramp, screw, button, buckle, clasp, hasp, hinge, hank, catch, latch, bolt, ring, latchet, pawl, tag; tooth; stud; hook, – and eye; morse, lock, holdfast, padlock, rivet; anchor, grappling-iron, drawbar, coupler, drawhead, coupling, treenail, trennel, stake, pale, pile, post, bollard.

cement, glue, gum, paste, size, wafer, solder, lute, putty, bird-lime, mortar, stucco, plaster, grout.

shackle, rein &c. (*means of restraint*) 752; suspender &c. 214; prop &c. (*support*) 215.

V. bridge over, span; connect &c. 43; hang &c. 214.

46. Coherence.—N. co-, ad-herence, -hesion, -hesiveness; concretion, accretion; con-, ag-glutination, -glomeration; aggregation; consolidation, set, cementation; sticking, soldering &c. *v.*; connection.

47. [Want of adhesion, non-adhesion, immiscibility.] **Incoherence.—N.** non-adhesion; immiscibility; incoherence; looseness &c. *adj.*; laxity; relaxation; loosening &c. *v.*; freedom; disjunction &c. 44; rope of sand.

tenacity, toughness; stickiness &c. 352; insepara-bility, -bleness; bur, remora.

conglomerate, concrete &c. (*density*) 321.

V. cohere, adhere, stick, cling, cleave, hold, take hold of, hold fast, close with, embrace, clasp, hug; grow –, hang-together; twine round &c. (*join*) 43.

stick like -a leech, – wax; stick close; cling like -ivy, – a bur; adhere like -a remora, – Dejanira's shirt.

glue; ag-, con-glutinate; cement, lute, paste, gum; solder, weld; cake, coagulate, consolidate &c. (*solidify*) 321; agglomerate.

Adj. co-, ad-hesive, -hering &c. *v.*; tenacious, tough; sticky &c. 352.

united, unseparated, sessile, inseparable, inextricable, infrangible; compact &c. (*dense*) 321.

V. make -loose &c. *adj.*; loosen slacken, relax; un-glue &c. 46; detach &c. (*disjoin*) 44.

Adj. non-adhesive, immiscible; incoherent, detached, loose, slack, baggy, lax, relaxed, flapping, streaming; dishevelled; segregated, like grains of sand; un-consolidated &c. 321, -combined &c. 48; non-cohesive.

---

48. Combination.—N. combination;

mixture &c. 41; alloy; junction &c. 43; union, unification, synthesis, incorporation, amalgamation, embodiment, coalescence, crasis, fusion, blend, blending, absorption, centralization, federation.

compound, amalgam, composition, *tertium quid*; resultant, impregnation.

V. combine, unite, incorporate, alloy, intertwine &c. 41; amalgamate, embody, absorb, re-embody, blend, merge, fuse, melt into one, consolidate, coalesce, centralize, impregnate; put –, lump- together; federate, associate; fraternize; cement a union, marry, wed, couple, pair, ally.

Adj. combined &c. *v.*; conjunctive, conjugate, conjoint, allied, confederate; impregnated with, ingrained, inoculated.

49. Decomposition.—N. decomposition, analysis, diæresis, dissection, resolution, catalysis, electrolysis, hydrolysis, photolysis, dissolution; dispersion &c. 73; disjunction &c. 44; disintegration, decay, rot, putrefaction, putrescence, caries, necrosis, corruption &c. (*uncleanness*) 653.

V. decom-pose, -pound; analyze, disembody, dissolve; resolve –, separate-into its elements; electrolyze; dissect, decentralize, break up; disintegrate; disperse &c. 73; unravel &c. (*unroll*) 313; crumble into dust; decay &c. *n.*; deteriorate &c. 659.

Adj. decomposed &c. *v.*; catalytic, analytical.

4°. CONCRETE QUANTITY

50. Whole. [Principal part.]—N.

whole, totality, integrity; totalness &c. *adj.*; entirety, *ensemble*, collectiveness; unity &c. 87; completeness &c. 52; indivisibility, indiscerptibility; integration, embodiment; integer, integral.

all, the whole, total, aggregate, one and all, gross amount, sum, sum-total, *tout ensemble*, length and breadth of, Alpha and Omega, 'be all and end all,' lock, stock and barrel.

bulk, mass, lump, tissue, staple, body, torso, *compages*; trunk, bole, hull, hulk, skeleton; greater –, major

51. Part.—N. part, portion; dose;

item, particular; aught, any; division, ward; subdivision, section; chapter, verse; article, clause, count, paragraph, passage; phrase; number, volume, book, fascicule; sector, segment; fraction, fragment; cantle, -t; frustum; detachment, parcel, unit, class &c. 75.

piece, lump, bit; cut, -ting; chip, chunk, collop, slice, scale, shard; lamina &c. 204; moiety; small part; morsel, scrap, crumb; particle &c. (*smallness*) 32; instalment, dividend; share &c. (*allotment*) 786.

–, best –, principal –, main- part; essential part &c. (*importance*) 642; lion's share, Benjamin's mess; the long and the short; nearly –, almost- all.

V. form –, constitute- a whole; integrate, embody, amass; aggregate &c. (*assemble*) 72; amount to, come to.

Adj. whole, total, integral, entire; complete &c. 52; one, individual.

un-broken, -cut, -divided, -severed, -clipped, -cropped, -shorn; seamless; undiminished; un-demolished, -dissolved, -destroyed, -bruised.

in-divisible, -dissoluble, -dissolvable, -discerptible.

wholesale, sweeping, comprehensive.

Adv. wholly, altogether; totally &c. (*completely*) 52; entirely, all, all in all, considering all things, in a body, collectively, all put together; in the -aggregate, – lump, – mass, – gross, – main, – long run; *en masse*, on the whole, *in extenso*, throughout, every inch; substantially.

débris, odds and ends, oddments, *detritus*; *excerpta*; member, limb, lobe, lobule, arm, wing, scion, branch, bough, joint, link, offshoot, ramification, twig, stipule, tendril, bush, spray, sprig; runner; leaf, -let; stump; constituent, ingredient, component part &c. 56.

compartment; department &c. (*class*) 75; county &c. (*region*) 181.

V. part, divide, break &c. (*disjoin*) 44; partition &c. (*apportion*) 786.

Adj. fractional, fragmentary; sectional, aliquot; divided &c. *v.*; in compartments, multifid, incomplete, partial, divided &c. 44.

Adv. partly, in part, partially; piecemeal, part by part; by -instalments, – snatches, – inches, – driblets; bit by bit, inch by inch, foot by foot, drop by drop; in -detail, – lots.

as a whole, bodily, *en bloc*,

52. Completeness.—N. completeness &c. *adj.*; completion &c. 729; integration; integrality.

entirety; universality; totality; perfection &c. 650; solid-ity, -arity; unity; all; *ne plus ultra*, ideal, limit.

complement, supplement, make-weight; filling up &c. *v.*

impletion; satur-ation, -ity; high water; high –, flood –, spring- tide; fill, load, bumper, bellyful; brimmer; sufficiency &c. 639.

V. be -complete &c. *adj.*; come to a head.

render -complete &c. *adj.*; complete &c. (*accomplish*) 729; fill, charge, load, replenish; make-up, – good; piece –, eke- out; supply deficiencies; fill -up, – in, – to the brim, – the measure of; saturate &c. 869.

go the whole -hog, – length, go all lengths.

Adj. complete, entire; whole &c. 50; perfect &c. 650; full, good, absolute, thorough, plenary; solid, undivided; with all its parts.

exhaustive, radical, sweeping, thorough-going; dead.

regular, consummate, unmitigated, sheer, unqualified, unconditional, free; abundant &c. (*sufficient*) 639.

53. Incompleteness.—N. incompleteness &c. *adj.*; deficiency, short -measure, – weight; shortcoming &c. 304; insufficiency &c. 640; imperfection &c. 651; immaturity &c. (*non-preparation*) 674; half measures.

[part wanting] defect, deficit, shortage, ullage, defalcation, omission, *caret*; interval &c. 198; break &c. (*discontinuity*) 70; non-completion &c. 730; missing link.

V. be -incomplete &c. *adj.*; fall short of &c. 304; lack &c. (*be insufficient*) 640; neglect &c. 460.

Adj. incomplete; imperfect &c. 651; unfinished; uncompleted &c. (*see* complete &c. 729); defective, deficient, wanting; failing; in -default, – arrear; short, – of; hollow, meagre, lame, half-and-half, perfunctory, sketchy; crude &c. (*unprepared*) 674.

mutilated, garbled, mangled, docked, lopped, truncated; bobtailed, cropped, bobbed, shingled.

in -progress, – hand; going on, proceeding.

Adv. incompletely &c. *adj.*; by halves.

Phr. *cætera desunt*; *caret*.

brimming; brim-, top-ful; chock –, choke- full; as full as -an egg is of meat, – a vetch, – a tick; saturated, crammed; replete &c. (*redundant*) 641; fraught, laden; full-laden, -fraught, -charged; heavy laden.

completing &c. *v.*; supplement-al, -ary; ascititious.

Adv. completely &c. *adj.*; altogether, outright, wholly, totally, *in toto*, quite; over head and ears; effectually, for good and all, nicely, fully, through thick and thin, head and shoulders; neck and -heel, – crop; all out; in -all respects, – every respect; at all points, out and out, to all intents and purposes; *toto cœlo*; utterly, clean, – as a whistle; to the -full, – utmost, – backbone; hollow, stark; heart and soul, root and branch; down to the ground.

to the top of one's bent, as far as possible, *à outrance*.

throughout; from -first to last, – beginning to end, – end to end, – one end to the other, – Dan to Beersheba, – head to foot, – head to heels, – top to toe, – top to bottom; *de fond en comble*; *à fond, a capite ad calcem, ab ovo usque ad mala*, fore and aft; every -whit, – inch; *cap-à-pie*, to the end of the chapter; up to the -brim, – ears, – eyes; as . . . as can be.

on all accounts; *sous tous les rapports*; with a -vengeance, – witness.

---

54. Composition.—N. composition, constitution, crasis, synthesis; make-up; combination &c. 48; inclusion, admission, comprehension, reception; embodiment, formation, conformation, production.

compilation &c. 72; (*musical*) composition &c. 415; painting &c. 556; writing &c. 590; typography &c. 591.

V. be -composed, – made, – formed, – made up- of; consist of, be resolved into.

include &c. (*in a class*) 76; subsume; synthesize; contain, hold, comprehend, take in, admit, embrace, embody; involve; implicate, drag into.

compose, constitute, form, make; make –, fill –, build- up; weave, construct, fabricate; compile; write, draw; set up (*printing*); enter into the composition of &c. (*be a component*) 56.

Adj. containing, constituting &c. *v.*

---

56. Component.—N. component; component –, integral –, integrant-part; element, constituent, ingredient, leaven, part and parcel; contents; appurtenance; feature; member &c. (*part*) 51; personnel.

V. enter into, – the composition of; be a -component &c. *n.*; be –, form-part of; merge –, be merged- in; be

55. Exclusion.—N. exclusion, non admission, omission, exception, rejection, repudiation; exile &c. (*seclusion*) 893; preclusion, lock out, ostracism, prohibition; disbarment, expulsion, ban.

separation, segregation, seposition, elimination, coffer-dam.

V. be excluded from &c.

exclude, bar, ban; leave –, shut –, thrust –, bar- out; reject, repudiate, spurn, blackball; ostracize, boycott; lay –, put –, set -apart, – aside; relegate, segregate; throw overboard; strike -off, – out; neglect &c. 460; banish &c. (*seclude*) 893; separate &c. (*disjoin*) 44.

pass over, omit; garble; eliminate, weed, winnow.

Adj. excluding &c. *v.*; exclusive.

excluded &c. *v.*; unrecounted, not included in; inadmissible; preventive, interdictive.

Adv. exclusive of, barring; except; with the exception of; save, bating.

---

57. Extraneousness.—N. extraneousness &c. *adj.*; extrinsicality &c. 6; exteriority &c. 220; alienism.

foreign -body, – substance, – element; alien, stranger, intruder, interloper, foreigner, tramontane, *novus homo*, new comer, immi-, emi-grant; creole, Afrikander; outsider, outlander, tenderfoot.

implicated in; share in &c. (*participate*) 778; belong –, appertain- to.

form, make, constitute, compose.

Adj. forming &c. *v.*; inclusive; inherent &c. 5.

Adj. extraneous, foreign, alien, ulterior; exterior, external, outside, outlandish; oversea; tra-, ultra-montane.

excluded &c. 55; inadmissible; exceptional.

Adv. in foreign -parts, – lands; abroad, beyond seas, overseas.

Section IV.   ORDER

1°.   Order in General

58. Order.—N. order, regularity &c. 80; uniformity, symmetry, *lucidus ordo*; harmony, music of the spheres.

gradation, progression; series &c. (*continuity*) 69.

subordination; course, even tenor, routine; method, disposition, arrangement, array, system, economy, discipline; orderliness &c. *adj.*

rank, place, &c. (*term*) 71.

V. be –, become- in order &c. *adj.*; form, fall in, draw up; arrange –, range –, place- itself; adjust; fall into –, take- -one's place, – rank; rally round; arrange &c. 60.

Adj. orderly, regular; in -order, – trim, – apple-pie order, according to Cocker, – its proper place, neat, neat as a pin, tidy, *en règle*, well regulated, correct, methodical, uniform, symmetrical, ship-shape, business-like, systematic; habitual; unconfused &c. (*see* confuse &c. 61) arranged &c. 60.

Adv. in order; methodically &c. *adj.*; in -turn, – its turn; step by step; by regular -steps, – gradations, – stages, – intervals; *seriatim*, systematically, by clockwork, *gradatim*; at stated periods &c. (*periodically*) 138; O.K.

59. [Absence, or want of Order, &c.] **Disorder.—N.** disorder; derangement &c. 61; irregularity; anomaly &c. (*unconformity*) 83; anar-chy, -chism; want of method; dishevelment, untidiness &c. *adj.*; disunion; discord &c. 24.

confusion; confusedness &c. *adj.*; disarray, jumble, mix-up, huddle, litter, lumber; *cahotage*; farrago; mess, muss, mash, muddle, hash; hotchpotch; *imbroglio*, chaos, *omnium gatherum*, medley; mere -mixture &c. 41; fortuitous concourse of atoms, *disjecta membra*, *rudis indigestaque moles*.

complexity; complexness &c. *adj.*; com-, im-plication; intri-cacy, -cation; perplexity; network, maze, labyrinth; wilderness, jungle; involution, ravelling, entanglement; coil &c. (*convolution*) 248; sleave, tangled skein, knot, Gordian knot, kink, web; wheels within wheels.

turmoil; ferment, &c. (*agitation*) 315; to do, trouble, pudder, pother, row, disturbance, convulsion, tumult, pandemonium, uproar, riot, rumpus, stour, scramble, *fracas*, embroilment, *mêlée*, spill and pelt, rough and tumble; whirlwind &c. 349; bear garden, Babel, Saturnalia, Donnybrook Fair, confusion worse confounded, most admired disorder, *concordia discors*; Bedlam –,

hell- broke loose; bull in a china shop; all the fat in the fire, *diable à quatre*, Devil to pay; pretty kettle of fish; pretty piece of -work, – business.

slattern, slut, sloven, draggle-tail.

V. be -disorderly &c. *adj.*; ferment, play at cross purposes.

put out of order; derange &c. 61; ravel &c. 219; ruffle, rumple; bungle, botch.

Adj. disorderly, orderless; out of -order, – place, – gear, – whack; irregular, desultory; anomalous &c. (*unconformable*) 83; acephalous, disorganized, straggling; un-, im-methodical; unsymmetric; unsystematic; untidy, slovenly, bedraggled, messy; dislocated; out of sorts; promiscuous, indiscriminate; chaotic, anarchical, lawless; unarranged &c. 60; confused, tumultuous, turbulent, tempestuous; deranged &c. 61; topsy turvy &c. (*inverted*) 218; shapeless &c. 241; disjointed, out of joint.

com-plex, -plexed; intricate, complicated, perplexed, involved, ravelled, entangled, knotted, tangled, inextricable; irreducible.

troublous; riotous &c. (*violent*) 173.

Adv. irregularly &c. *adj.*; by fits and -snatches, – starts; pell-mell; higgledy-piggledy; helter-skelter, harum-scarum; in a ferment; at -sixes and sevens, – cross purposes; upside down &c. 218.

Phr. the cart before the horse, chaos is come again.

---

60. [Reduction to Order.] **Arrangement.**—**N.** arrangement; plan &c. 626; preparation &c. 673; dispos-al, -ition; col-, al-location; distribution; sorting &c. *v.*; assortment, allotment; grouping; apportionment, *taxis*, taxonomy, *syn-taxis*, graduation, organization, grading; re-organization, rationalization.

analysis, classification, division, digestion; systematism.

[Result of arrangement] order, orderliness, form, array; digest, synopsis &c. (*compendium*) 596; *syntagma*, table, atlas; register &c. (*record*) 551; score &c. 415; cosmos, organism, architecture.

[Instrument for sorting] sieve &c. 260; file, card index.

V. reduce to –, bring into- order; introduce order into; rally.

arrange, dispose, place, form; put –, set –, place- in order; straighten up, tidy up; set out, collocate, allocate, pack, marshal, range, size, rank, array, group, parcel out, allot, space, distribute, deal; cast –, assign- the parts; dispose of, assign places to; assort, sort; sift, riddle; put –, set- -to rights, – into shape, – in trim, – in array.

class, -ify; divide; file, string together, thread; register &c. (*record*) 551; list, catalogue, tabulate, index, alphabeticize, graduate, digest, grade, codify; orchestrate, score.

methodize, regulate, systematize, standardize, co-ordinate, organize, settle, fix, apportion.

unravel, disentangle, ravel, card; disembroil.

Adj. arranged &c. *v.*; embattled, in battle array; cut and dried; methodical. orderly, regular, systematic, tabular.

61. [Subversion of Order; bringing into disorder.] **Derangement.**—**N.** derangement &c. *v.*; disorder &c. 59; evection, discomposure, disturbance; dis-, de-organization; involvement; dislocation; perturbation, interruption; shuffling &c. *v.*; inversion &c. 218; corrugation &c. (*fold*) 258; insanity &c. 503.

V. derange; dis-, mis-arrange; dis-, mis-place; mislay, discompose, disorder, de-, dis-organize; embroil, unsettle, disturb, confuse, trouble, perturb, jumble, tumble; huddle, shuffle, muddle, toss, hustle, fumble, riot; bring –, put –, throw- into -disorder &c. 59; break the ranks, disconcert, convulse; break in upon.

unhinge, dislocate, put out of joint, throw out of gear.

turn topsy-turvy &c. (*invert*) 218; bedevil; complicate, involve, perplex, confound; im-, em-brangle; tangle, en-tangle, ravel, tousle, dishevel, ruffle, rumple &c. (*fold*) 258; dement.

litter, scatter; mix &c. 41.

Adj. deranged &c. *v.*; syncre-tic, -tistic.

2°. Consecutive Order

62. Precedence.—N. precedence; coming before &c. *v.*; the lead, *le pas*; superiority &c. 33; importance &c. 642; anteced-ence, -ency; anteriority &c. (*front*) 234; precursor &c. 64; priority &c. 116; precession ·&c. 280; anteposition, preference.

V. precede; come -before, – first; forerun, head, lead, take the lead; lead the -way, – dance; introduce, usher in; have the *pas*; set the fashion &c. (*influence*) 175; lead off, kick off, open the ball; take –, have- precedence; outrank; have the start &c. (*get before*) 280.

place before; prefix; premise, prelude, preface.

Adj. preceding &c. *v.*; pre-, antecedent; anterior; prior &c. 116; before; former, foregoing; before-, above-mentioned; aforesaid, said; precurs-ory, -ive; prevenient, preliminary, prefatory, introductory; prelus-ive, -ory; proemial, preparatory.

Adv. before; in advance &c. (*precession*) 280.

Phr. *seniores priores.*

63. Sequence.—N. sequence, coming after; going after &c. (*following*) 281; consecution, succession; posteriority &c. 117.

continuation; prolongation, order of succession; successiveness; Elijah's mantle.

secondariness; subordinancy &c. (*inferiority*) 34.

V. succeed; come -after, – on, – next; follow, ensue, step into the shoes of; alternate.

place after, suffix, append.

Adj. succeeding &c. *v.*; sequent; sub-, con-sequent; sequacious, proximate, next; consecutive &c. (*continuity*) 69; alternate, amœbæan.

latter; posterior &c. 117.

Adv. after, subsequently; behind &c. (*rear*) 235.

---

64. Precursor.—N. precursor, antecedent, precedent, predecessor; forerunner, van-courier, *avant-coureur*, pioneer, prodrome, *prodromos*, outrider; leader, bell-wether; herald, harbinger; dawn.

prelude, preamble, preface, prologue, foreword, *avant-propos*, *protasis*, prolusion, proem, *prolepsis*, *prolegomena*, prefix, introduction; lead, heading, frontispiece, groundwork; preparation &c. 673; overture, voluntary, *exordium*, symphony, *ritornello*; premises.

prefigurement &c. 511; omen &c. 512.

Adj. precursory; prelus-ive, -sory, -dious; proemial, introductory, prefatory, prodromous, inaugural, preliminary; precedent &c. (*prior*) 116.

65. Sequel.—N. sequel, suffix, successor; tail, queue, train, wake, trail, rear; retinue, suite; appendix, postscript, subscript; epilogue; conclusion; peroration; codicil; continuation, *sequela*; appendage &c. 39; tail –, heelpiece; tag, more last words; colophon, *feliciter explicit*.

follower, after-glow, -growth, -crop, -taste, -math.

after-part, -piece, -course, -thought, -game; *arrière pensée*, second thoughts.

---

66. Beginning.—N. beginning, commencement, opening, outset, incipience, inception, inchoation; introduction &c. (*precursor*) 64; *alpha*; initial; foundation; inauguration, *début*, *le premier pas*, embarcation, rising of the curtain; zero hour; exordium, curtain raiser; maiden speech; prelude; outbreak, onset, brunt; initiative, move, first move; gambit, narrow –, thin-

67. End.—N. end, close, termination; desinence, conclusion, *finis*, *finale*, period, term, *terminus*, last, *omega*; extreme, -tremity; gable –, butt –, fagend; tip, nib, point; tail &c. (*rear*) 235; verge &c. (*edge*) 231; tag, epilogue, peroration; *bonne bouche*; bitter end, tail end; terminal; *apodosis*; appendix.

consummation, *dénouement*; finish &c. (*completion*) 729; fate; doom, -sday;

end of the wedge; fresh start, new departure; forefront.

origin &c. (*cause*) 153; source, rise; bud, germ &c. 153; egg, rudiment; genesis, birth, nativity, cradle, infancy, incunabula; start, starting-point &c. 293; dawn &c. (*morning*) 125.

title-page; head, -ing, caption; van &c. (*front*) 234, *feliciter incipit*.

en-trance, -try; inlet, orifice, mouth, chops, lips, porch, portal, portico, *propylon*, door; gate, -way; postern, wicket, threshold, vestibule; skirts, border &c. (*edge*) 231; tee.

first -stage, – blush, – glance, – impression, – sight.

rudiments, elements, outlines, *principia*, grammar, *protasis*; alphabet, ABC.

V. begin, commence, inchoate, rise, arise, originate, institute, conceive, initiate, open, dawn, set in, take its rise, enter upon, start; enter; set out &c. (*depart*) 293; embark in.

usher in; lead -off, – the way; take the -lead, – initiative; inaugurate, head; stand -at the head, – first, – for; lay the foundations &c. (*prepare*) 673; found &c. (*cause*) 153; set -up, – on foot, – agoing, – abroach, – the ball in motion; apply the match to a train; launch, broach; open -up, – the door to; set -about, – to work; make a -beginning, – start; handsel; take the first step, lay the first stone, cut the first turf; break -ground, – the ice, – cover; pass –, cross- the Rubicon; open -fire, – the ball; ventilate, air; undertake &c. 676.

come into -existence, – the world; make one's *début*, take birth; burst forth, break out; spring –, crop- up.

begin -at the beginning, – *ab ovo*, – again, – *de novo*; start afresh, make a fresh start, shuffle the cards, resume, recommence.

Adj. beginning &c. *v.*; initi-al, -atory, -ative; inceptive, introductory, incipient; proemial, inaugural; incho-ate, -ative; embryonic, rudimental; primogenial; primeval &c. (*old*) 124; rudimentary, aboriginal; natal, nascent.

first, foremost, front, leading, head; maiden.

begun &c. *v.*; just -begun &c. *v.*

Adv. at –, in- the beginning &c. *n.*; first, in the first place, *imprimis*, first and foremost; *in limine*; in -the bud, – embryo, – its infancy; from -the beginning, – its birth; *ab -initio, – ovo, – incunabulis*, primarily, originally.

crack of doom, day of Judgement, fall of the curtain, wind-up; goal, destination; limit, stoppage, end all, determination; expiration, expiry; death &c. 360; end of all things; finality; eschatology.

break up, *commencement de la fin*, last stage, turning point; *coup de grâce*, death-blow; knock-out.

V. end, close, finish, terminate, conclude, be all over; expire; die &c. 360; come –, draw- to a -close &c. *n.*; have run its course; run out, pass away.

bring to an -end &c. *n.*; put an end to, make an end of; determine; get through; achieve &c. (*complete*) 729; stop &c. (*make to cease*) 142; shut up shop.

Adj. ending &c. *v.*; final, terminal, definitive, conclusive; crowning &c. (*completing*) 729; last, ultimate; hindermost; rear &c. 235; caudal.

contermin-ate, -ous, -able.

ended &c. *v.*; at an end; settled, decided, over, played out, set at rest.

penultimate; last but -one, – two, &c.

unbegun, uncommenced; fresh.

Adv. finally &c. *adj.*; in fine; at the last; once for all.

----

68. Middle.—N. middle, midst, mediety; mean &c. 29; medium, middle term; centre &c. 222, mid-course &c. 628; *mezzo termine*; *juste milieu* &c. 628; half-way house, nave, navel, omphalos; nucle-us, -olus.

equidistance, bisection, half-distance; middle-distance, equator, diaphragm, midriff; interjacence &c. 228.

Adj. middle, medial, mesial, mean, mid; middle-, mid-most; middling; mediate; intermediate &c. (*interjacent*) 228; equidistant; central &c. 222; mediterranean, equatorial.

Adv. in the middle; in the thick; mid-, half-way; midships, *in medias res.*

69. [Uninterrupted sequence.] **Continuity.**—**N.** continuity; consecu-tion, -tiveness &c. *adj.*; succession, round, suite, progression, series, train, chain; cat-, concat-enation; catena; scale; gradation, course, constant flow, perpetuity.

procession, column; retinue, *cortège*, cavalcade, rank and file, line of battle, array.

pedigree, genealogy, lineage, race &c. 166.

rank, file, line, row, range, tier, string, thread, team; suit; colonnade.

V. follow in –, form- a series &c. *n.*; fall in.

arrange in a -series &c. *n.*; string together, catenate, file, thread, graduate, tabulate.

Adj. continu-ous, -ed; consecutive; progressive, gradual; serial, successive; immediate, unbroken, entire; linear; in a -line, – row &c. *n.*; uninter-rupted, -mitting; unremitting; perennial, evergreen; constant.

Adv. continuously &c. *adj.*; *seriatim*; in a -line &c. *n.*; in -succession, – turn; running, gradually, step by step, *gradatim*, at a stretch; in -file, – column, – single file, – Indian file.

70. [Interrupted sequence.] **Discontinuity.**—**N.** discontinuity; disjunction &c. 44; anacoluthon, *non sequitur*; interruption, break, fracture, flaw, fault, split, crack, cut; gap &c. (*interval*) 198; solution of continuity, *cæsura*; broken thread; parenthesis, episode; rhapsody, patchwork; intermission; alternation &c. (*periodicity*) 138; dropping fire.

V. be -discontinuous &c. *adj.*; alternate, intermit.

discontinue, pause, interrupt; intervene; break, – in upon; interpose &c. 228; break –, snap- the thread; disconnect &c. (*disjoin*) 44.

Adj. discontinuous, unsuccessive, broken, interrupted, *décousu*; dis-, un-connected, discrete, disjunctive; fitful &c. (*irregular*) 139; spasmodic, desultory, intermit-ting &c. *v.*, -tent; alternate; recurrent &c. (*periodic*) 138; few and far between.

Adv. at intervals; by -snatches, – jerks, – skips, – catches, – fits and starts; skippingly, *per saltum*; *longo intervallo.*

---

71. Term.—**N.** term, rank, station, stage, step; degree &c. 26; scale, remove, grade, link, peg, round –, rung- of the ladder, *status*, position, place, point, mark, *pas*, period, pitch; stand, -ing; footing, range.

V. hold –, occupy –, fall into- a place &c. *n.*

3°. Collective Order

72. Assemblage.—**N.** assemblage; col-lection, -location, -ligation; compilation, levy, gathering, ingathering, mobilization, meet, foregathering, muster, *attroupement*; con-course, -flux, -gregation, -tesseration, -vergence &c. 290; meeting, *levée, réunion*, drawing room, at home; conversazione &c. (*social gathering*) 892; assembly, congress, eisteddfod; conven-tion, -ticle;

73. Non-assemblage. Dispersion.—**N.** dispersion; disjunction &c. 44; divergence &c. 291; scattering &c. *v.*; dissemination, broadcasting, diffusion, dissipation, distribution; apportionment &c. 786; spread, respersion, circumfusion, interspersion, spargefaction.

waifs and estrays, flotsam and jetsam, *disjecta membra.*

V. disperse, scatter, sow, dissemi-

gemote; conclave, &c. (*council*) 696; posse, *posse comitatûs*; Noah's ark.

miscellany, *collectanea*, symposium; museum, menagerie, &c. (*store*) 636.

crowd, throng, multitude; flood, rush, deluge; rout, rabble, mob, press, crush, *cohue*, jam, horde, body, tribe; crew, gang, knot, squad, band, party; swarm, shoal, school, covey, flock, herd, drove, kennel; array, bevy, galaxy; *corps*, company, troop, *troupe*; army, force, regiment, &c. (*combatants*) 726; host &c. (*multitude*) 102; populousness.

clan, brotherhood, association &c. (*party*) 712.

volley, shower, storm, cloud.

group, cluster, Pleiades, clump, pencil; set, batch, lot, pack; budget, *dossier*, assortment, bunch; parcel; pack-et, -age; bundle, *fasciculus*, fascine, bale; ser-on, -oon; faggot, wisp, truss, tuft; shock, rick, fardel, stack, sheaf, swath, gavel, haycock, stook.

accumulation &c. (*store*) 636; congeries, heap, lump, pile, *rouleau*, tissue, mass, pyramid; drift; snow-ball, -drift; acervation, cumulation; amassment, glom-, agglom-eration; conglobation; conglomeration, -ate; coacervation, coagmentation, aggregation, concentration, congestion, *omnium gatherum*, *spicilegium*, black hole of Calcutta; quantity &c. (*greatness*) 31.

collector, gatherer; whip, -per in.

V. [be or come together] assemble, collect, muster; meet, unite, join, rejoin; cluster, flock, swarm, surge, stream, herd, crowd, throng, associate; con-gregate, -glomerate, -centrate; centre round, *rendezvous*, resort; come –, flock –, get –, pig- together; forgather; huddle; reassemble.

[get or bring together] assemble, muster, mobilize; bring –, get –, put –, draw –, scrape –, lump- together; col-lect, -locate, -ligate; get –, whip- in; gather; hold a meeting; con-vene, -voke, -vocate; rake up, dredge; heap, mass, pile; pack, put up, truss, cram; acervate; ag-glomerate, -gregate; compile; group, aggroup, concentrate, unite; collect –, bring- into a focus; amass, accumulate &c. (*store*) 636; collect in a drag-net; heap Ossa upon Pelion.

Adj. assembled &c. *v.*; closely packed, dense, serried, crowded to suffocation, teeming, swarming, populous; as thick as hops; all of a heap, fasciculated; cumulative.

Phr. the plot thickens.

nate, radiate, diffuse, shed, spread, ted, bestrew, overspread, dispense, disband, disembody, demobilize, dismember, distribute; apportion &c. 786; blow off, let out, dispel, cast forth, draught off; strew, straw, strow; spirtle, cast, sprinkle, spatter; issue, deal out, retail, utter; re-, inter-sperse; set abroach, circumfuse.

turn –, cast- adrift; scatter to the winds; sow broadcast.

spread like wildfire, disperse themselves.

Adj. unassembled &c. (*see* assemble &c. 72); dispersed &c. *v.*; sparse, dispread, broadcast, sporadic, widespread; far-flung; epidemic &c. (*general*) 78; adrift, stray; dishevelled, streaming.

Adv. *sparsim*, here and there, *passim*.

---

74. [Place of meeting.] **Focus.**—**N.** focus; point of- convergence &c. 290; corradiation; centre &c. 222; gathering-place, resort; haunt; retreat; *venue*, *rendezvous*; rallying point, headquarters, home, club; *dépôt* &c. (*store*) 636; tryst, trysting-place; place of -meeting, – resort, – assignation; *point de –, lieu de- réunion*; issue.

V. bring to- a point, – a focus, – an issue; focus.

4°. DISTRIBUTIVE ORDER

75. Class.—N. class, category, *categorema*, head, order, section; division, subdivision; department, province, domain, sphere.

kind, sort, genus, species, variety, branch, family, race, tribe, caste, sept, clan, breed; *clique, coterie*; type, kit, sect, set; assortment; feather, kidney; suit; range; gender, sex, kin.

manner, description, denomination, persuasion, connection, designation, character, stamp; predicament; conviction &c. 484.

similarity &c. 17.

76. Inclusion. [Comprehension under, or reference to a class.]—**N.** inclusion, admission, incorporation, comprehension, reception.

composition &c. (*inclusion in a compound*) 54.

V. be -included in &c.; come –, fall –, range- under; belong –, pertain- to; range with; merge in.

include, compromise, comprehend, contain, admit, embrace, receive; enclose &c. (*circumscribe*) 229; incorporate, cover, embody, encircle.

reckon –, enumerate –, number- among; refer to; place –, arrange- under, – with; take into account.

Adj. includ-ed, -ing &c. *v.*; inclusive; comprehensive, all-embracing; congen-er, -erous: of the same -class &c. 75.

Phr. *et hoc genus omne,* &c.; *et cætera.*

77. Exclusion.*—**N.** exclusion &c. 55.

---

78. Generality. — **N.** general-ity, -ization; universality; catholic-ity, -ism; miscel-lany, -laneousness; drag-net.

every-one, -body; all hands, all the world and his wife; any body, N or M, all sorts; *tout le monde.*

prevalence, run.

V. be -general &c. *adj.*; prevail, obtain, be going about, stalk abroad.

render -general &c. *adj.*; generalize; spread, broadcast.

Adj. general, usual, current, generic, collective; broad, comprehensive, sweeping; encyclopedical, panoramic, widespread &c. (*dispersed*) 73.

universal; catho-lic, -lical; common, world-wide; œ-, e-cumenical; transcendental; prevalent, prevailing, rife, epidemic, besetting; all over, covered with.

every, all; indeterminate, indefinite, unspecified, impersonal.

customary &c. (*habitual*) 613.

Adv. what-ever, -soever; to a man, one and all, without exception.

generally &c. *adj.*; always, for better

79. Speciality.—**N.** speciality, *spécialité*; individ-uality, -uity; particularity, peculiarity; idiocrasy &c. (*tendency*) 176; personality, characteristic, mannerism, idiosyncrasy, attribute, specificness &c. *adj.*; singularity &c. (*unconformity*) 83; reading, version, lection; state; *trait*; distinctive feature; technicality; *differentia.*

particulars, details, minutiæ, items, counts.

I, self, I myself, *ego*; my-, him-, her-, it-self.

V. specify, particularize, individualize, realize, specialize, designate, differentiate, determine, define, denote, indicate, itemize, detail.

descend to particulars, enter into detail, come to the point.

Adj. special, particular, individual, specific, proper, personal, intimate, original, private, respective, definite, concrete, determinate, especial, certain, esoteric, endemic, partial, party, peculiar, marked, appropriate, several, characteristic, diagnostic, exact, exclusive; singular &c. (*exceptional*) 83;

---

* The same set of words is used to express *Exclusion from a class* and *Exclusion from a compound.* Reference is therefore made to the former at 55. This identity does not occur with regard to *Inclusion,* which therefore constitutes a separate category.

for worse; in general, generally speaking; speaking generally; for the most part; in the long run &c. (*on an average*) 29.

idiomatic; typical, representative, distinctive.

this, that; yon, -der.

Adv. specially &c. *adj.*; in particular, *in propriâ personâ*; *ad hominem*; for my part.

each, apiece, one by one; severally, respectively, each to each; *seriatim*, in detail, bit by bit; *pro hac vice, – re natâ.*

namely, that is to say, *videlicet*, viz.; to wit; i.e., e.g.

5°. ORDER AS REGARDS CATEGORIES

80. Rule.—N. regularity, uniformity &c. 16; clock-work precision; punctuality &c. (*exactness*) 494; routine &c. (*custom*) 613; formula; system; rut; canon, convention, maxim; rule &c. (*form, regulation*) 697; key-note, standard, model; precedent &c. (*prototype*) 22; conformity &c. 82.

nature, principle; law; order of things; normal –, natural –, ordinary –, model- -state, – condition; standing -dish, – order; normality; Procrustean law; law of the Medes and Persians; hard and fast rule.

Adj. regular, uniform, symmetrical, constant, steady; according to rule &c. 613; orderly &c. 58.

82. Conformity.—N. conform-ity, -ance; observance.

naturalization; conventionality &c. (*custom*) 613; agreement &c. 23.

example, instance, specimen, sample, quotation; exemplification, illustration, case in point; object lesson.

conventionalist, formalist, Philistine.

pattern &c. (*prototype*) 22.

V. conform to, – rule; accommodate –, adapt- oneself to; rub off corners.

be -regular &c. *adj.*; move in a groove; follow –, observe –, go by –, bend to –, obey- -rules, – precedents; comply –, tally –, chime in –, fall in with; be -guided, – regulated- by; fall into a -custom, – usage; follow the -fashion, – multitude; pass muster, do as others do, *hurler avec les loups*; do at Rome as the Romans do; go –, swim- with the -stream, – current, – tide; tread the beaten track &c. (*habit*) 613; rubber-stamp; keep one in countenance.

exemplify, illustrate, cite, quote, put

81. Multiformity.—N. multi-, omni-formity; variety, diversity; multi-fariousness &c. *adj.*

Adj. multi-form, -fold, -farious, -generous; multiplex, variform, manifold, many-sided, multiplicate; omni-form, -genous, -farious; polymorphic; protean; heterogeneous, motley, mosaic; epicene, indiscriminate, desultory, irregular, diversified, different, divers; all manner of; of -every description, – all sorts and kinds; *et hoc genus omne*; and what not? *de omnibus rebus et quibusdam aliis.*

(*conformable*) 82; customary

83. Unconformity.—N. non-conform-ity &c. 82; un-, dis-conformity; unconventionality, informality, abnormity, anomaly; anomalousness &c. *adj.*; exception, peculiarity, &c. 79; infraction –, breach –, violation –, infringement- of -law, – custom, – usage; eccentricity, *bizarrerie*, oddity, *je ne sais quoi*, monstrosity, rarity; freak of Nature.

individuality, idiosyncrasy, singularity, originality, mannerism.

aberration; irregularity; variety; singularity; exemption; *salvo* &c. (*qualification*) 469.

nonconformist; nondescript, character, original, nonsuch, monster, prodigy, wonder, miracle, curiosity, missing link, flying fish, black swan, *lusus naturæ*, *rara avis*, queer fish; mongrel; half-caste, -blood, -breed; *métis*, cross breed, hybrid, mule, mulatto, sacatra, marabou; *tertium quid*, hermaphrodite, gynander, androgyn.

phœnix, chimera, hydra, sphinx, minotaur; griff-in, -on; centaur; hippo-

a case; produce an- instance &c. *n.*

Adj. conformable to rule, adaptable, compliant, consistent, agreeable; regular &c. 80; according to -regulation, - rule, - Cocker; *en règle, selon les règles,* well regulated, orderly; symmetric &c. 242.

conventional, commonplace &c. (*customary*) 613; of -daily, - every day-occurrence; in the natural order of things; ordinary, common, - or garden, prosaic, habitual, usual.

in the order of the day; naturalized.

typical, normal, formal; canonical, orthodox, sound, strict, rigid, positive, uncompromising, Procrustean; point device.

secundum artem, ship-shape, technical.

exemplary, illustrative, in point.

Adv. conformably &c. *adj.*; by rule; agreeably to; in -conformity, - accordance, - keeping- with; according to; consistently with; as usual, *ad instar, instar omnium; more -solito, - majorum.*

for the sake of conformity; of -, as a matter of- course; *pro formâ,* for form's sake, by the card; according to plan.

invariably &c. (*uniformly*) 16.

for -example, - instance; *exempli gratiâ; e.g.; inter alia.*

Phr. *cela va sans dire; ex pede Herculem, noscitur a sociis.*

griff, -centaur; sagittary; kraken, cockatrice, wyvern, roc, liver, dragon, sea-serpent; mermaid; unicorn; Cyclops, 'men whose heads do grow beneath their shoulders'; Teratology.

fish out of water; neither -one thing nor another, - fish flesh nor fowl nor good red herring; one in a -way, - thousand; out-cast, -law; Ishmael, pariah; oasis.

V. be -unconformable &c. *adj.*; leave the beaten -track, - path; infringe -, break -, violate- a -law, - habit. - usage, - custom; drive a coach and six through; stretch a point; have no business there; baffle -, beggar- all description.

Adj. unconformable, exceptional; abnorm-al, -ous; anomal-ous, -istic; out of -order, - place, - keeping, - tune, - one's element; irregular, arbitrary; lawless, informal, aberrant, stray, wandering, wanton; peculiar, exclusive, unnatural, eccentric, crotchety, egregious; out of the -beaten track, - common, - common run, - pale of; misplaced; funny.

un-usual, -accustomed, -customary, -wonted, -common; rare, singular, unique, curious, odd, extraordinary, strange, monstrous; wonderful &c. 870; unexpected, unaccountable; *outré,* out of the way, remarkable, noteworthy; queer, quaint, nondescript, none such, *sui generis;* original, unconventional, Bohemian, unfashionable; un-described, -precedented, -paralleled, -exampled, -heard of, -familiar; fantastic, new-fangled, grotesque, *bizarre;* outlandish, exotic, *tombé des nues,* preternatural; denaturalized.

heterogeneous, heteroclite, amorphous, mongrel, amphibious, epicene, half-blood, hybrid; androgyn-ous, -al; unsymmetric &c. 243. qualified &c. 469.

Adv. unconformably &c. *adj.*; except, unless, save, barring, beside, without, save and except, let alone.

however, yet, but.

Int. what -on earth! - in the world!

Phr. never was -seen, - heard, - known- the like.

Section V.   NUMBER

1°. Number, in the Abstract

84. Number.—N. number, symbol, numeral, figure, cipher, digit, integer; counter; round number; formula; function; series.

sum, total, aggregate, difference, complement, subtrahend; product; multipli-cand, -er, -cator; coefficient, multiple; dividend, divisor, factor, quotient, sub-multiple, fraction; mixed number; numerator, denominator; decimal, circulating decimal, repetend; common measure, aliquot part; reciprocal; prime number; totitive, totient.

permutation, combination, variation; election.

ratio, proportion; progression; arithmetical –, geometrical –, harmonical- progression; percentage.

figurate –, pyramidal –, polygonal- numbers.

power, root, exponent, index, logarithm, antilogarithm; modulus. differential, integral, fluxion, fluent.

Adj. numeral, complementary, divisible, aliquot, reciprocal, prime, fractional, decimal, figurate, incommensurable.

proportional, exponential, logarithmic, logometric, differential, fluxional, integral.

positive, negative; rational, irrational; surd, radical, real, imaginary, impossible.

85. Numeration.—N. numeration; numbering &c. *v.*; pagination; tale, tally, recension, enumeration, summation, reckoning, computation, supputation; calcu-lation, -lus; algorithm, rhabdology, dactylonomy; measurement &c. 466; statistics.

arithmetic, analysis, algebra, fluxions; differential –, integral –, infinitesimal- calculus; calculus of differences.

[Statistics] dead reckoning, muster, poll, census, capitation, roll-call, recapitulation; account &c. (*list*) 86.

[Operations] notation, addition, subtraction, multiplication, division, proportion, rule of three, practice, equations, extraction of roots, reduction, involution, evolution, approximation, interpolation, differentiation, integration.

[Instruments] abacus, swan-pan, logometer, sliding –, slide- rule, tallies, Napier's bones, calculating –, adding- machine, difference engine; cash register.

arithmetician, calculator, abacist; mathematician, actuary, statistician, surveyor, geodesist.

V. number, count, tell; call –, run- over, take an account of, enumerate, call the roll, muster, poll, recite, recapitulate; sum; sum –, cast- up; tell off, score, cipher, compute, calculate, set a price, reckon, – up, estimate; suppute, add, subtract, multiply, divide, extract roots.

check, prove, demonstrate, balance, audit, overhaul, take stock; affix numbers to, page, foliate, paginate.

amount –, come- to.

Adj. numer-al, -ical; arithmetical, analytic, algebraic, statistical, numerable, computable, calculable; commensur-able, -ate; incommensur-able, -ate.

86. List.—N. list, catalogue, enumeration, inventory, schedule; register &c. (*record*) 551; account; bill, – of costs; syllabus; terrier, tally, file; almanac, calendar, index, table, atlas, contents, card index; rota, ticket; book, ledger; synopsis, *catalogue raisonné*; *tableau*; scroll, manifest, invoice, bill of lading; prospectus, *programme*; bill of fare, *menu, carte*; score, census, statistics, returns; Red –, Blue –, Domesday- book; *cadastre*; directory, gazetteer, dictionary, glossary, lexicon, thesaurus, gradus.

roll; check –, chequer –, bead- roll, – of honour; muster -roll, – book; roster, panel; cartulary, diptych.

V. list, enrol, schedule, register &c. *n.*; indent, post, docket; matriculate.

Adj. cadastral, listed &c. *v.*

2°. DETERMINATE NUMBER

87. Unity.—N. unity; oneness &c. *adj.*; individuality; solitude &c. (*seclusion*) 893; isolation &c. (*disjunction*) 44; unification &c. 48.

one, unit, ace; item; individual; solo, none else, no other, naught beside.

V. be -one, – alone &c. *adj.*; dine with Duke Humphrey.

isolate &c. (*disjoin*) 44.

render one; unite &c. (*join*) 43, (*combine*) 48.

Adj. one, sole, single, solitary, only-begotten; individual, apart, alone; kithless.

un-accompanied, -attended; *solus*, single-handed; singular, odd, unique, unrepeated, azygous, first and last; isolated &c. (*disjoined*) 44; insular; unitary.

lone; lone-ly, -some; desolate, dreary.

in-secable, -severable, -discerptible; compact, irresolvable.

Adv. singly &c. *adj.*; alone, by itself, *per se*, only, apart, in the singular number, in the abstract; one -by one, – at a time; simply; one and a half, *sesqui-*.

Phr. *natura il fece, e poi roppe la stampa.*

88. Accompaniment.—N. accompaniment; appurtenance, adjunct &c. 39; context.

coexistence, concomitance, company, association, companionship; part-, co-part-nership; coefficiency.

concomitant, accessory, coefficient; companion, attendant, fellow, associate, consort, spouse, colleague, *fidus Achates*; part-, co-part-ner; satellite, hanger on, shadow; escort, *entourage*, suite, *cortège*; convoy, follower &c. 65; attribute.

V. accompany, coexist, attend, convoy, chaperon; hang –, wait- on; go hand in hand with; synchronize &c. 120; bear –, keep- company; row in the same boat; bring in its train, associate –, couple- with.

Adj. accompanying &c. *v.*; concomitant, fellow, twin, joint; associated –, coupled- with; accessory, attendant, *obbligato*.

Adv. with, withal; together –, along –, in company- with; hand in hand, side by side; cheek by -jowl, – jole; arm in arm; there-, here-with; and &c. (*addition*) 37.

together, in a body, collectively.

---

89. Duality.—N. dual-ity, -ism; duplicity; bi-plicity, -formity; span, polarity.

two, deuce, couple, couplet, doublet, brace, pair, cheeks, twins, Castor and Pollux, *gemini*, Siamese twins; fellows; yoke, conjugation, dyad, distich.

V. [unite in pairs] pair, couple, bracket, yoke; conduplicate, mate.

Adj. two, twain; dual, -istic; binary, binomial; twin, biparous; dyadic; conduplicate; duplex &c. 90; *tête-à-tête*; paired; dihedral.

coupled &c. *v.*; conjugate.

both, – the one and the other.

90. Duplication.—N. duplication; doubling &c. *v.*; gemi-, ingemi-nation; reduplication; iteration &c. (*repetition*) 104; renewal.

V. double; re-double, -duplicate; geminate; repeat &c. 104; renew &c. 660; duplicate, copy &c. 21.

Adj. double; doubled &c. *v.*; bicameral, bicapital, bi-fold, -form, -lateral,

91. [Division into two parts.] **Bisection.—N.** bi-section, -partition; di-, subdi-chotomy; halving &c. *v.*; dimidiation; *hendiadys*.

bifurcation, forking, branching, furcation, ramification, divarication; fork, prong; fold.

half, moiety.

V. bisect, halve, divide, split, cut in

-farious, -facial; two-fold, -sided, -headed, -edged &c.; duplex; double-faced; twin, duplicate, ingeminate; second; dual &c. 89.

Adv. twice, once more; over again &c. (*repeatedly*) 104; as much again, twofold.

secondly, in the second place, again.

two, cleave, dimidiate, dichotomize divaricate.

go halves, divide with.

separate, fork, bifurcate; branch -off, ~ out; ramify.

Adj. bisected &c. *v.*; cloven, cleft; bipartite, biconjugate, bicuspid, bifid; bifur-cous, -cate, -cated; semi-, demi-hemi-.

92. Triality.—N. triality, trinity,* triplicity.

three, triad, triplet, trey, trio, ternion, trinomial, leash; tierce; tri-ennium; trefoil, triangle, trident, tripod, triumvirate, *troika*.

third power, cube.

Adj. three; tri-form, -nal, -nomial; tertiary; triune.

93. Triplication.—N. tripli-cation, ·-city; trebleness, trine, trilogy.

V. treble, triple, triplicate, cube.

Adj. treble, triple; tern, -ary; triplex, triplicate, threefold, trilogistic; third; trinal; trihedral.

Adv. three -times, – fold; thrice, in the third place, thirdly; trebly &c. *adj.*

94. [Division into three parts.] Tri-section. — N. tri-section, -partition, -chotomy; third, – part.

V. trisect, divide into three parts, trifurcate.

Adj. trifid; trisected &c. *v.*; tri partite, -chotomous, -sulcate.

95. Quaternity.—N. quaternity, four, tetrad, quartet, quaternion, square, quadrature, quarter, quadruplet; quadrilateral, quadrangle, quatrefoil; *quadriga*.

V. reduce to a square, square.

Adj. four; quat-ernary, -ernal; quadratic; quartile, quartic, tetractic. tetrad, tetrahedral; quadrennial; quadrivalent.

96. Quadruplication.—N. quadrupli-cation.

V. multiply by four, quadruplicate, biquadrate.

Adj. fourfold; quad-ruple, -ruplicate, -rible; quadruplex; fourth.

Adv. four times; in the fourth place, fourthly.

97. [Division into four parts.] Quad-risection.—N. quadri-section, -parti-tion; quartering &c. *v.*; fourth; quart, -er, -ern; farthing (*i.e.* fourthing); quarto.

V. quarter, divide into four parts, quadrisect.

Adj. quartered &c. *v.*; quadri-fid, -partite.

98. Five, &c.—N. five, cinque, quint, quincunx, quintuplet, quintet, penta-gon, pentameter, Pentateuch; six, half-a-dozen, sextet, hexagon, hexameter; seven, Heptarchy; eight, octet, octa-gon, octave; nine, three times three; ten, decade; eleven; twelve, dozen; thirteen; long –, baker's- dozen.

twenty, score; twenty-four, four and twenty, two dozen; twenty-five, five

99. Quinquesection, &c.—N. divi-sion by -five &c. 98; quinquesection &c.; fifth &c.; decimation.

V. decimate, quinquesect.

Adj. quinque-fid, -partite; quinquar-ticular; octifid; decimal, tenth, tithe, teind; duodecimal, twelfth; sexa-gesi-mal, -genary; hundredth, centesimal; millesimal &c.

and twenty, quarter of a hundred; forty, two score; fifty, half a hundred; sixty, three score, sexagenarian; seventy, three score and ten, septuagenarian; eighty, four score, octogenarian; ninety, four score and ten, nonagenarian.

* *Trinity* is hardly ever used except in a theological sense; *see* Deity 976.

hundred, centenary, hecatomb, century; hundredweight, cwt.;
one hundred and forty-four, gross; bicentenary, tercentenary &c.

thousand, chiliad; myriad, millennium, ten thousand; lac, lakh,
one hundred thousand, plum; million; thousand million, *milliard*.
billion, trillion &c.

V. centuriate.

Adj. five, quinary, quintuple; fifth; senary, sextuple; sixth;
seventh; octuple; eighth; ninefold, ninth; tenfold, decimal, denary,
decuple, tenth; eleventh; duo-denary, -denal; twelfth; in one's
'teens, thirteenth.

vices-, viges-imal; twentieth; twenty-fourth &c. *n.*

cent-uple, -uplicate, -ennial, -enary, -urial; secular, hundredth;
thousandth; millenary &c.

3°. INDETERMINATE NUMBER

100. [More than one.] **Plurality.—N.**
plurality; a -number, – certain number;
one or two, two or three &c.; a few,
several; multitude &c. 102.

Adj. plural, more than one, upwards
of, some, certain; not -alone &c. 87.

Adv. *et cætera*, &c., etc.

Phr. *non deficit alter.*

100a. [Less than one.] **Fraction.—N.**
fraction, fractional part, fragment;
part &c. 51.

Adj. fractional, fragmentary, partial.

101. Zero.—N. zero, nothing
naught, nought, duck's egg, goose egg;
cipher, none, nobody; not a soul; *âme
qui vive*; absence &c. 187; unsubstantiality &c. 4.

Adj. not -one, – any.

102. Multitude.—N. multitude;
numerousness &c. *adj.*; numer-osity,
-ality; multiplicity; profusion &c.
(*plenty*) 639; legion; host; great -,
large -, round -, enormous- number; a
quantity, numbers, array, sight, army,
sea, galaxy; scores, peck, bushel, school,
shoal, swarm, draft, bevy, cloud, flock,
herd, drove, flight, covey, hive, brood,
litter, farrow, fry, nest; mob, crowd
&c. (*assemblage*) 72; lots, loads, heaps;
all the world and his wife.

[Increase of number] greater number,
majority; multiplication, multiple.

V. be -numerous &c. *adj.*; swarm -,
teem -, crawl -, creep -with; crowd,
swarm, come thick upon; outnumber,
multiply; people; swarm like -locusts,
– bees; be alive with.

Adj. many, several, sundry, divers,
various, not a few; a -hundred, – thousand, – myriad, – million,
– thousand and one; some -ten or a dozen, – forty or fifty &c.;
half a -dozen, – hundred &c.; very -, full -, ever so- many;
numer-ous, -ose; profuse, in profusion; manifold, multiplied, multitudinous, multiferous, multiple, multinomial, teeming, crawling,
populous, peopled, crowded, thick, studded; galore.

thick coming, many more, more than one can tell, a world of; no
end -of, – to; *cum multis aliis*; thick as -hops, – hail; plenty as
blackberries; numerous as the -stars in the firmament, – sands on

103. Fewness.—N. fewness &c. *adj.*;
paucity, small number; small quantity
&c. 32; scarcity, sparsity; rarity; infrequency &c. 137; handful; maniple;
minority, exiguity.

[Diminution of number] reduction;
weeding &c. *v.*; elimination, sarcula-
tion, decimation.

V. be -few &c. *adj.*

render -few &c. *adj.*; reduce, dimin
ish the number, weed, eliminate, thin
decimate.

Adj. few; scarce; scant, -y; thin,
rare, thinly scattered, few and far
between; exiguous; infrequent &c.
137; *rari nantes*; hardly -, scarcely-
any; to be counted on one's fingers;
reduced &c. *v.*; unrepeated.

Adv. here and there.

the sea-shore, – hairs on the head; and -what not, – heaven knows what; endless &c. (*infinite*) 105.

Phr. their name is 'Legion.'

104. Repetition.—N. repetition, iteration, reiteration, duplication, ding-dong, alliteration; *epistrophe*; harping, recurrence, succession, run; batto-, tauto-logy; monotony, tautophony; rhythm &c. 138; pleonasm, redundancy, diffuseness.

chimes, repetend, echo, *ritornello*, burden of a song, *refrain*; rehearsal; encore; *réchauffé*, *rifacimento*, recapitulation.

cuckoo &c. (*imitation*) 19; reverberation &c. 408; drumming &c. (*roll*) 407; renewal &c. (*restoration*) 660.

twice-told tale; old -story, – song, chestnut; second –, new- edition; reprint, new impression; return game, return match, reappearance, reproduction; periodicity &c. 138.

V. repeat, iterate, reiterate, reproduce, parrot, echo, re-echo, drum, harp upon, battologize, hammer, redouble.

recur, revert, return, reappear; renew &c. (*restore*) 660.

rehearse; do –, say- over again; ring the changes on; harp on the same string; din –, drum- in the ear; conjugate in all its moods, tenses and inflexions, begin again, go over the same ground, go the same round, never hear the last of; resume, return to, recapitulate, reword.

Adj. repeated &c. *v.*; repetition-al, -ary; recur-rent, -ring; ever recurring, thick coming; frequent, incessant, redundant, pleonastic, tautological.

monotonous, harping, iterative; mocking, chiming; retold; aforesaid, -named; above-mentioned, said; habitual &c. 613; another.

Adv. repeatedly, often, again, afresh, anew, over again, once more; ditto, *encore, de novo, bis, da capo.*

again and again; over and over, – again; many times over; time-and again, – after time; year after year; day by day &c.; many –, several –, a number of- times; many –, full many- a time; times out of number, year in and year out, morning, noon and night; frequently &c. 136.

Phr. *ecce iterum Crispinus, toujours perdrix,* cut and come again; 'tomorrow and tomorrow.'

105. Infinity.—N. infini-ty, -tude, -teness &c. *adj.*; perpetuity &c. 112.

V. be -infinite &c. *adj.*; know –, have- no -limits, – bounds; go on for ever.

Adj. infinite; immense; number-, count-, sum-, measure-less; in-numer-, immeasur-, incalcul-, illimit-, intermin-, unfathom-, unapproach-able; exhaustless, inexhaustible, indefinite; without -number, – measure, – limit, – end; incomprehensible; limit-, end-, bound-, term-less; un-told, -numbered, -measured, -bounded, -limited; illimited; perpetual &c. 112.

Adv. infinitely &c. *adj.*; *ad infinitum.*

Section VI.   TIME

1°. Absolute Time

106. Time.—N. time, duration; period, term, stage, space, span, spell, season; the whole -time, – period; course &c. 109.

107. Neverness.*—N. 'neverness'; absence of time, no time; *dies non*; Tib's eve; Greek Kalends.

Adv. never; at no -time, – period;

* A term introduced by Bishop Wilkins.

intermediate time, while, *interim*, interval, bit, pendency; inter-vention, -mission, -mittence, -regnum, -lude; respite.

on no occasion, never in all one's born days, nevermore, *sine die*.

era, epoch, æon, cycle; time of life, age, year, date; decade &c. (*period*) 108; moment, &c. (*instant*) 113; reign &c. 737.

glass –, ravages –, whirligig –, noiseless foot- of time; scythe.

V. continue, last, endure, go on, hold out, remain, stay, persist, abide, run; intervene; elapse &c. 109.

take –, take up –, fill –, occupy- time.

pass –, pass away –, spend –, while away –, consume –, talk against –, kill- time; tide over; use –, employ- time; tarry &c. 110; seize an opportunity &c. 134; waste time &c. (*be inactive*) 683.

Adj. continuing &c. *v.*; on foot; permanent &c. (*durable*) 110.

Adv. while, whilst, during, pending; during the -time, – interval; in the course of; for the time being, day by day; in the time of, when; mean-time, -while; in the -meantime, – *interim*; *ad interim*, *pendente lite*; *de die in diem*; from -day to day, – hour to hour &c.; hourly, always; for a -time, – season; till, until, up to, yet; the whole –, all the- time; all along; throughout &c. (*completely*) 52; for good &c. (*diuturnity*) 110.

here-, there-, where-upon; then; *anno*, – *Domini*; A.D.; *ante Christum*; A.C.; before Christ; B.C.; *anno urbis conditæ*; A.U.C.; *anno regni*; A.R.; once upon a time, one fine morning.

Phr. time -runs, – runs against; *tempus fugit*.

---

108. [Definite duration, or portion of time.] **Period.**—**N.** period; second, minute, hour, day, week, sennight, octave, month, moon, quarter, semester, year, *lustrum*, *quinquennium*, decade, *decennium*, indiction, lifetime, generation, epoch, era, cycle.

century, age, *millennium*; *annus magnus*.

Adj. horary; hourly, annual &c. (*periodical*) 138.

108a. Contingent Duration.—**Adv.** during -pleasure, – good behaviour; *quamdiu se bene gesserit*.

Phr. *labitur et labetur*; *truditur dies die*; *fugaces labuntur anni*; 'tomorrow and tomorrow and tomorrow creeps in this petty pace from day to day.'

---

109. [Indefinite duration.] **Course.** —**N.** course –, progress –, process –, succession –, lapse –, flow –, flux –, effluxion, stream –, tract –, current –, sweep –, tide –, march –, step –, flight- of time; duration &c. 106.

[Indefinite time] aorist.

V. elapse, lapse, flow, run, proceed, advance, pass; roll –, wear –, press –, drag- on; flit, fly, slip, slide, glide, crawl; run -its course.

out; expire; go –, pass- by; be -past &c. 122.

Adj. elapsing &c. *v.*; aoristic; progressive, transient &c. 111.

Adv. in due -time, – season; in -course, – process, – the fulness- of time; in time.

---

110. [Long duration.] **Diuturnity.** —**N.** diuturnity; a -long –, length of- time; an age, a century, an eternity,

111. [Short duration.] **Transientness.** —**N.** transientness &c. *adj.*; evanescence, impermanence, fugacity, transi

æons; slowness &c. 275; perpetuity &c. 112; blue moon.

dura-bleness, -bility; persistence, lastingness &c. *adj.*; continuance, assiduity, endurance, standing; permanence &c. (*stability*) 150; survi-val, -vance; longevity &c. (*age*) 128; distance of time.

protraction –, prolongation –, extension- of time; delay &c. (*lateness*) 133.

V. last, endure, stand, remain, abide, continue, brave a thousand years.

tarry &c. (*be late*) 133; drag -on, – its slow length along, – a lengthening chain; protract, prolong; spin –, eke –, draw –, lengthen- out; temporize; gain –, make –, talk against- time.

out-last, -live; survive; live to fight again.

Adj. durable; perdurable; lasting &c. *v.*; of long -duration, – standing; permanent, chronic, long-standing; intransi-ent, -tive; intransmutable, persistent; life-, live-long; longeval, long-lived, macrobiotic, diuturnal, sempervirent, evergreen, perennial; unin-, ter-, unre-mitting; perpetual &c. 112.

lingering, protracted, prolonged, spun out &c. *v.*; long-pending, -winded; slow &c. 275.

Adv. long; for -a long time, – an age, – ages, – ever so long, – many a long day; long ago &c. (*in a past time*) 122; *longo intervallo.*

all the -day long, – year round; the livelong day, as the day is long, morning, noon and night; hour after hour, day after day, &c.; for good; permanently &c. *adj.*

112. [Endless duration.] **Perpetuity.**
—**N.** perpetuity, eternity, timelessness; everness,* aye, sempiternity, immortality, athanasia; everlastingness &c. *adj.*; perpetuation; infinite duration.

V. last –, endure –, go on- for ever; have no end.

eternize, eternify, perpetuate, immortalize.

Adj. perpetual, eternal, eterne; everlasting, -living, -flowing; continual, constant, sempiternal; co-eternal; endless, unending; ceaseless, incessant, uninterrupted, indesinent, unceasing; interminable, having no end; unfad-

toriness, volatility, caducity, mortality, span; flash in the pan, nine days' wonder, bubble, May-fly; spurt; temporary arrangement, interregnum.

velocity &c. 274; suddenness &c. 113; changeableness &c. 149.

V. be -transient &c. *adj.*; flit, pass away, fly, gallop, vanish, fade, fleet, melt away, evaporate; pass away like a -cloud, – summer cloud, – shadow, – dream.

Adj. transi-ent, -tory, -tive; passing, evanescent, fleeting; flying &c. *v.*; fug-acious, -itive; shifting, slippery; spasmodic.

tempor-al, -ary; provis-ional, -ory; cursory, short-lived, ephemeral, deciduous; perishable, mortal, precarious; impermanent.

brief, quick, brisk; cometary, meteoric, extemporaneous, summary; pressed for time &c. (*haste*) 684; sudden, momentary &c. (*instantaneous*) 113.

Adv. temporarily &c. *adj.*; *pro tempore*; for -the moment, – a time; awhile, *en passant, in transitu*; in a short time; soon &c. (*early*) 132; briefly &c. *adj.*; at short notice; on the -point, – eve -of; *in articulo*; between cup and lip.

Phr. one's days are numbered; the time is up; here to-day and gone to-morrow; *non semper erit æstas; eheu! fugaces labuntur anni; sic transit gloria mundi.*

---

113. [Point of time.] **Instantaneity.**
—**N.** instantane-ity, -ousness; sudden-, abrupt-ness.

moment, instant, second, minute; twinkling, trice, flash, breath, crack, jiffy, *coup*, burst, flash of lightning, stroke of time.

epoch, time; time of -day, – night; hour, minute; very -minute &c., – time, – hour; present –, right –, true –, exact –, correct- time.

V. be -instantaneous &c. *adj.*; twinkle, flash.

Adj. instantaneous, momentary, extempore, sudden, instant, abrupt;

*Bishop Wilkins.

ing, evergreen, amaranthine; never-ending, -dying, -fading; deathless, immortal, undying, imperishable.

Adv. perpetually &c. *adj.*; always, ever, evermore, aye; for -ever, – aye, – evermore, – ever and a day, – ever and ever; in all ages, from age to age; without end; world –, time- without end; *in sæcula sæculorum*; to the -end of time, – crack of doom, – 'last syllable of recorded time'; till doomsday; constantly &c. (*very frequently*) 136.

Phr. *esto perpetua!; labitur et labetur in omne volubilis ævum.*

subitaneous, hasty; quick as -thought,* – lightning, – a flash; rapid as electricity.

Adv. instantaneously &c. *adj.*; in –, in less than- no time; *presto, subito, instanter*, suddenly, at a stroke, like- a shot, – greased lightning; in a trice, in a moment &c. *n.*; eftsoons, in the twinkling of -an eye, – a bed post; at one jump, in the same breath, *per saltum, uno saltu*; at –, all at- once; in one's tracks; plump, slap; 'at one fell swoop'; at the same -instant &c. *n.*; immediately &c. (*early*) 132; extempore, on the -spot, – spur of the moment, – dot; just then; slap- dash &c. (*haste*) 684; before you could -turn round, – say -knife, – Jack Robinson.

Phr. touch and go; no sooner said than done.

114. [Estimation, measurement, and record of time.] **Chronometry.—N.** chrono-, horo-metry, -logy; date, epoch; style, era, age.

almanac, calendar, ephemeris; register, -try; chronicle, annals, journal, diary, chronogram.

[Instruments for the measurement of time] clock, watch; chrono-meter, -scope, -graph; repeater, alarum; time-keeper, -piece; dial, sun-dial, *gnomon, pendule*, horologe, pendulum, hourglass, water clock, clepsydra.

mean –, Greenwich –, solar –, sidereal –, local –, summer- time; daylight saving.

chrono-grapher, -loger, -logist; annalist.

V. fix –, mark- the time; date, register, chronicle; measure – beat –, mark- time; bear date.

Adj. chrono-logical, -metrical, -grammatical; isochronal.

Adv. o'clock; *a.m., p.m.*

115. [False estimate of time.] **Anachronism.—N.** ana-, meta-, para-, prochronism; *prolepsis*, misdate; anticipation, antichronism.

disregard –, neglect –, oblivion- of time.

intempestivity &c. 135.

V. mis-, ante-, post-, over-date; anticipate; take no note of time.

Adj. misdated &c. *v.*; undated; overdue; out of date; anachronous &c. *n.*

2°. Relative Time

1. *Time with reference to Succession*

116. Priority.—N. priority, antecedence, anteriority, pre-existence, precedence &c. 62; precession &c. 280; precursor &c. 64; the past &c. 122; premises.

V. precede, come before; forerun; antecede, go before &c. (*lead*) 280; pre-exist; dawn; premise, presage &c. 511.

be -beforehand &c. (*be early*) 132;

117. Posteriority.—N. posteriority; succession, sequence; following &c. 281; subsequence, supervention; futurity &c. 121; successor; sequel &c. 65; remainder, reversion.

V. follow &c. 281 –, come –, go-after; ensue, result; succeed, supervene; step into the shoes of.

Adj. subsequent, posterior, following, after, later, succeeding, postliminious,

* See note on 264.

steal a march upon, anticipate, forestall; have –, gain- the start.

Adj. prior, previous; preced-ing, -ent; anterior, antecedent; pre-existing, -existent; foresighted; former, foregoing; afore –, before-, above-mentioned; aforesaid, said; introductory &c. (*precursory*) 64; pre-war.

Adv. before, prior to; earlier; previously &c. *adj.*; afore, ere, theretofore, erewhile; ere –, before- -then, – now; erewhile, already, yet, beforehand; aforetime, on the eve of, in anticipation.

118. The Present Time.—N. the present -time, – day, – moment, – juncture, – occasion; the times, existing time, time being; twentieth century; nonce, crisis, epoch, day, hour.

age, time of life.

Adj. present, actual, instant, current, latest, existing, that is.

Adv. at this -time, – moment &c. 113; at the -present time &c. *n.*; now, at present.

at this time of day, to-day, now-a-days; already; even –, but –, just-now; on the present occasion; for the -time being, – nonce; *pro hâc vice*; on the -nail, – spot; on the spur of the -moment, – occasion.

until now; to -this, – the present day.

120. Synchronism.—N. synchronism; coexistence, coincidence; simultaneousness &c. *adj.*; concurrence, concomitance, unity of time, interim.

[Having equal times] isochronism, syntony.

contemporary, coetanian.

V. coexist, concur, accompany, go hand in hand, keep pace with; synchronize, isochronize.

Adj. synchron-ous, -al, -ical, -istical; simultaneous, coexisting, coincident, concomitant, concurrent; coev-al, -ous; contempora-ry, -neous; coetaneous; coterminous, coeternal; isochronous.

Adv. at the same time; simultaneously &c. *adj.*; together, in concert, during the same time; in the same breath; *pari passu*; in the interim.

at the -very moment &c. 113; just as, as soon as; meanwhile &c. (*while*) 106.

121. [Prospective time.] **Futurity.** **—N.** futur-ity, -ition; future, hereafter, time to come; approaching –, coming –, after- -time, – age, – days, – hours, – years, – ages, – life; morrow, to-morrow, by and by; millennium, doomsday, day of judgment, crack of doom, remote future.

postnate; successive &c. 63; postdiluvial, -an; *puisné*; posthumous; post-war, future &c. 121.

Adv. subsequently, after, afterwards, since, later; at a -subsequent, – later-period; next, in the sequel, close upon, thereafter, thereupon, upon which, eftsoons; from that -time, – moment; after a -while, – time; in process of time.

postcenal, postcibal, postprandial, after-dinner.

—— –

119. [Time different from the present.] **Different Time.—N.** different –, other- time.

[Indefinite time] aorist.

Adj. aoristic.

Adv. at that –, at which- -time, – moment, – instant; then, on that occasion, upon.

when; when-ever, -soever; upon which, on which occasion; at -another, – a different, – some other, – any- time; at various times; some –, one- -of these days, – fine morning, – day; sooner or later; some time or other; once upon a time, once.

——

122. [Retrospective time.] **Preterition.—N.** preterition; priority &c. 116; the past, past time; days –, times- -of yore, – of old, – past, – gone by; bygone days, good old days; old –, ancient –, former -times; fore time; yesterdays; the olden –, good old-time; auld lang syne; eld.

approach of time, advent, time drawing on, womb of time; destiny &c. 152; eventuality.

heritage, heirs. posterity, descendants.

prospect &c. (*expectation*) 507; foresight &c. 510.

V. look forwards; anticipate &c. (*expect*) 507, (*foresee*) 510; forestall &c. (*be early*) 132.

come –, draw- on; draw near; approach, await, threaten; impend &c. (*be destined*) 152.

Adj. future, to come; coming &c. (*impending*) 152; next, near; near –, close- at hand; eventual, ulterior; expectant, prospective, in prospect &c. (*expectation*) 507.

Adv. prospectively, hereafter, on the knees of the gods, in future; to-morrow, the day after to-morrow; in -course, – process, – the fulness- of time; eventually, ultimately, sooner or later; *proximo; paulo post futurum*; in after time; one of these days; after a -time, – while.

from this time; hence-forth, -forwards; thence; thence-forth, -forward; whereupon, upon which.

soon &c. (*early*) 132; on the -eve, – point, – brink- of; about to; close upon.

antiquity, antiqueness, *status quo*; time immemorial; distance of time; remote -age, – time; ancient history; remote past; rust of antiquity; ancientness.

pale-ontology, -ography, -ology; palætiology,* archæology; archaism, antiquarianism, mediævalism, pre-Raphaelitism; retrospection, looking back, memory &c. 505.

laudator temporis acti; mediævalist, pre-Raphaelite; antiqu-ary, -arian; archæologist &c.; Oldbuck, Dryasdust.

ancestry &c. (*paternity*) 166.

V. be -past &c. *adj.*; have -expired &c. *adj.*, – run its course, – had its day; pass; pass –, go- -by, – away, – off; lapse, blow over.

look –, trace –, cast the eyes- back; exhume.

Adj. past, gone, gone by, over, passed away, bygone, foregone; elapsed, lapsed, preterlapsed, expired, no more, run out, blown over, that has been, whilom, extinct, never to return, exploded, forgotten, irrecoverable; obsolete &c. (*old*) 124; extinct as the dodo.

former, pristine, *quondam, ci-devant*, late; ancestral.

foregoing; last, latter; recent, overnight; past, preterite, preter-perfect, -pluperfect, past perfect.

looking back &c. *v.*; retro-spective, -active; archæological &c. *n.*

Adv. formerly; of -old, – yore; erst, whilom, erewhile, time was, ago, over; in -the olden time &c. *n.*; anciently, long -ago, – since; a long -while, – time- ago; years –, ages- ago; some time -ago, – since, – back.

yesterday, the day before yesterday; last -year, – season, – month &c.; *ultimo*; lately &c. (*newly*) 123.

retrospectively; ere –, before –, till- now; hitherto, heretofore; no longer; once, – upon a time; from time immemorial; in the memory of man; time out of mind; already, yet, up to this time; *ex post facto*.

Phr. time was; the time -has, – hath- been.

2. Time with reference to a particular Period

123. Newness.—N. newness &c. *adj.*; neologism, neoterism; novelty, recency; immaturity; youth &c. 127; gloss of novelty.

124. Oldness.—N. oldness &c. *adj.*; age, antiquity; cobwebs of antiquity.

maturity, ripeness; decline, decay; senility &c. 128.

* Whewell.

innovation; renovation &c. (*restoration*) 660.

modernist, neologist, neoteric.

modernism, modernity; mushroom; latest fashion, *dernier cri*.

upstart, *parvenu, nouveau riche*.

V. renew &c. (*restore*) 660; modernize.

Adj. new, novel, recent, fresh, green; young &c. 127; evergreen; raw, immature; virgin; un-tried, -handseled, -used, -trodden, -beaten; fledgling.

late, modern, neoteric; new-born, -fashioned, -fangled, -fledged; of yesterday; just out, brand –, span-new, up to date, topical; vernal, renovated; innovatory.

fresh as -a rose, – a daisy, – paint; spick and span.

Adv. newly &c. *adj.*; afresh, anew, lately, just now, only yesterday, the other day; latterly, of late.

not long –, a short time- ago.

seniority, eldership, primogeniture.

archaism &c. (*the past*) 122; thing –, relic- of the past; megatherium.

tradition, prescription, custom, folklore, immemorial usage, common law.

V. be -old &c. *adj.*; have -had, – seen- its day; become -old &c. *adj.*; age, fade.

Adj. old, olden, ancient, antique; of long standing, time-honoured, venerable; eld-er, -est; first-born.

prime; prim-itive, -eval, -igenous; primordi-al, -nate; aboriginal &c. (*beginning*) 66; diluvian, antediluvian; pre-historic; patriarchal, preadamite; palæocrystic; fossil, paleozoic, preglacial, ante-mundane; archaic, classic, mediæval, pre-Raphaelite, ancestral, black-letter.

immemorial, traditional, prescriptive, customary, whereof the memory of man runneth not to the contrary; inveterate, rooted.

antiquated, of other times, rococo, of the old school, after-age, obsolete; fusty, moth-eaten; out of -date, – fashion; stale, old-fashioned, behind the -age, – times; exploded; gone out, – by; *passé*, outworn, run out; disused; senile &c. 128; time-worn; crumbling &c. (*deteriorated*) 659; second-hand.

old as -the hills, – Methuselah, – Adam, – history; Anno Domini.

Adv. since the -world was made, – year one, – days of Methuselah.

---

125. Morning. [Noon.]—N. morning, morn, matins, forenoon, *a.m.*, prime, dawn, daybreak, daylight, sun-up, peep –, break- of day; aurora, Eos; first blush –, prime- of the morning; twilight, crepuscule, sunrise, cockcrow.

spring; vernal equinox.

noon; mid-, noon-day; noontide, meridian, prime.

summer, midsummer; summer solstice.

Adj. matin, matutinal; vernal, æstival.

Adv. at -sunrise &c. *n.*; with the lark, when the morning dawns.

126. Evening. [Midnight.]—N. evening, eve; decline –, fall –, close- of day; eventide, evensong, vespers; candlelight; nightfall, curfew, dusk, twilight, blind man's holiday; eleventh hour; sun-set, -down; going down of the sun, cock-shut, dewy eve, gloaming, bed-time.

afternoon, *post meridiem, p.m.*

autumn; fall, – of the leaf; autumnal equinox, Indian summer, harvest-time.

midnight; dead –, witching time- of night; winter, – solstice.

Adj. vespertine, autumnal, nocturnal, wintry, brumal, hiemal.

127. Youth.—N. youth; juven- -ility, -escence; juniority; infancy; baby-, child-, boy-, girl-, youth-hood; *incunabula*; minority, immaturity, nonage, teens, tender age, bloom.

cradle, nursery, leading-strings, pupilage, puberty, *pucelage*.

128. Age.—N. age; oldness &c. *adj.*; old –, advanced- age; sen-ility, -escence; years, anility, grey hairs, climacteric, grand climacteric, declining years, decrepitude, hoary age, caducity, superannuation; second childhood, -ishness; dotage; vale of years

prime –, flower –, spring-tide –, seed-time –, golden season- of life; heyday of youth, school days; rising generation, younger generation.

Adj. young, youthful, juvenile, green, callow, budding, sappy, *puisné*, beardless, unfledged, unripe, under age, in one's teens; *in statu pupillari*; younger, junior.

decline of life, 'sear and yellow leaf'; three-score years and ten; green old age, ripe old age; longevity; time of life.

seniority, eldership; elders &c. (*veteran*) 130; firstling; *doyen*, dean, father; primogeniture; nostology.

V. be -aged &c. *a^dj.*; grow –, get-old &c. *adj.*; age; decline, wane.

Adj. aged; old &c. 124; elderly, senile; matronly, anile; in years; ripe, mellow, run to seed, declining, waning, past one's prime; grey, -headed; hoar, -y; venerable, time-worn, antiquated, *passé*, effete, doddering, decrepit, superannuated; advanced in -life, – years; stricken in years; wrinkled, marked with the crow's foot; having one foot in the grave; doting &c. (*imbecile*) 499.

old-, eld-er, -est; senior; first-born.

turned of, years old; of a certain age, no chicken, old as Methuselah; gerontic; ancestral; patriarchal &c. (*ancient*) 124.

---

129. Infant.—N. infant, babe, baby; nurse-, suck-, year-, wean-ling; *papoose*, *bambino*.

child, bairn, little- one, – tot, – mite, chick, brat, chit, pickaninny, kid, urchin; bant-, brat-ling; elf.

youth, boy, lad, slip, sprig, stripling, youngster, cub, unlicked cub, younker, callant, whipster, whipper-snapper, schoolboy, hobbledehoy, hopeful, cadet, minor, master.

scion; sap-, seed-ling; tendril, olive-branch, nestling, chicken, duckling; larva, caterpillar, chrysalis, cocoon; tadpole, whelp, cub, pullet, fry, callow; codlin, -g; *fœtus*, calf, colt, pup, foal, kitten; lamb, -kin.

girl; lass, -ie; wench, miss, damsel, *demoiselle*, damozel; maid, -en; virgin; nymph; colleen; minx, baggage, school-girl; tomboy, flapper, hoyden.

Adj. infant-ine, -ile; puerile; boy-, girl-, child-, baby-, kitten-ish; baby; new-born, unfledged, new-fledged, callow.

in -the cradle, – swaddling clothes, – long clothes, – arms, – leading strings; at the breast; in one's teens; young &c. 127.

130. Veteran.—N. veteran, old man, seer, patriarch, greybeard, dugout, grand-father, -sire; grandam, beldam; gaffer, gammer; hag, crone; pantaloon; sexage-, octoge-, nonage-, cente-narian; old stager; dotard &c. 501.

preadamite, Methuselah, Nestor, Rip van Winkle, old Parr; elders; forefathers &c. (*paternity*) 166.

---

131. Adolescence.—N. adolescence, pubescence, majority; adultness &c. *adj.*; manhood, virility, maturity; flower of age; prime –, meridian-of life.

man &c. 373; woman &c. 374; adult, no chicken.

V. come -of age, – to man's estate, – to years of discretion; attain majority, assume the *toga virilis*; have -cut one's eye-teeth, – sown one's wild oats, settle down.

Adj. adolescent, pubescent, of age; of -full, – ripe- age; out of one's teens, grown up, mature, full- blown, – grown, in one's prime, in full bloom, manly, virile, adult; womanly, matronly; marriageable, nubile.

3. *Time with reference to an Effect or Purpose*

132. Earliness.—**N.** earliness &c. *adj.*; morning &c. 125.

punctuality; promptitude &c. (*activity*) 682; haste &c. (*velocity*) 274; suddenness &c. (*instantaneity*) 113.

prematurity, precocity, precipitation, anticipation; prevenience, a stitch in time.

V. be -early &c. *adj.*, – beforehand &c. *adv.*; keep time, take time by the forelock, anticipate, forestall; have –, gain- the start; steal a march upon; gain time, draw on futurity; bespeak, secure, engage, pre-engage.

accelerate; expedite &c. (*quicken*) 274; make haste &c. (*hurry*) 684.

Adj. early, prime, timely, in time, punctual, forward; prompt &c. (*active*) 682; summary.

premature, precipitate, precocious; prevenient, anticipatory; rathe.

sudden &c. (*instantaneous*) 113; unexpected &c. 508; impending, imminent; near, – at hand; immediate.

Adv. early, soon, anon, betimes, rathe; eft, -soons; ere –, before- long; punctually &c. *adj.*; to the minute; in time; in -good, – military, – pudding, – due- time; time enough.

beforehand; prematurely &c. *adj.*; precipitately &c. (*hastily*) 684; too soon; before -its, – one's- time; in anticipation; unexpectedly &c. 508.

suddenly &c. (*instantaneously*) 113; before one can say 'Jack Robinson,' at short notice, extempore; on the spur of the -moment, – occasion; at once; on the -spot, – instant; at sight; off –, out of- hand; *à vue d'œil*; straight, -way, -forth; forthwith, incontinently, summarily, instanter, immediately, briefly, shortly, quickly, speedily, apace, before the ink is dry, almost immediately, presently, at the first opportunity, in no long time, by and by, in a while, directly.

Phr. touch and go, no sooner said than done.

134. Occasion.—**N.** occasion, opportunity, opening, room, scope, field; suitable –, proper- -time, – season; high time; opportuneness &c. *adj.*; tempestivity.

133. Lateness.—**N.** lateness &c. *adj.*; tardiness &c. (*slowness*) 275.

de-lay, -lation; cunctation, procrastination; detention; deferring &c. *v.*; filibuster, postponement, adjournment, prorogation, retardation, respite, reprieve, stay; protraction, prolongation, moratorium; contango; demurrage; remand; Fabian policy, *médecine expectante*, chancery suit; leeway; high time.

V. be -late &c. *adj.*; tarry, wait, stay, bide, take time; dawdle &c. (*be inactive*) 683; linger, loiter, saunter, lag behind; bide –, take- one's time; hang -about, – around, – back, – in the balance; gain time; hang fire; stand –, lie-over.

put off, defer, delay, lay over, suspend; shift –, stave- off; waive, retard, remand, postpone, adjourn; procrastinate; dally; prolong, protract; spin –, draw –, lengthen- out; prorogue; keep back; tide over; push –, drive- to the last; let the matter stand over; reserve &c. (*store*) 636; temporize; consult one's pillow, sleep upon it.

shelve, table, lay on the table.

lose an opportunity &c. 135; be kept waiting, dance attendance; kick –, cool- one's heels; *faire antichambre*; wait impatiently; await &c. (*expect*) 507; sit up, – at night.

Adj. late, tardy, slow, behindhand, belated, postliminious, posthumous, backward, unpunctual; dilatory &c. (*slow*), overdue 275; delayed &c. *v.*; in abeyance.

Adv. late; late-, back-ward; late in the day; at -sunset, – the eleventh hour, – length, – last, – long; ultimately; after –, behind- time; too late; too late for &c. 135.

slowly, leisurely, deliberately, at one's leisure; *ex post facto*; *sine die*.

Phr. *nonum prematur in annum.*

---

135. Intempestivity.—**N.** intempestivity; unseasonableness; unsuitable –, improper-time; unreasonableness &c. *adj.*; evil hour; *contretemps*; intrusion; anachronism &c. 115.

crisis, turn, juncture, emergency, conjuncture; turning point, given time.

nick of time; golden –, well-timed –, fine –, favourable- opportunity; clear stage, fair field; *mollia tempora*; *fata Morgana*; spare time &c. (*leisure*) 685.

V. seize &c. (*take*) 789 –, use &c. 677 –, give &c. 784- an -opportunity, – occasion; improve the occasion.

suit the occasion &c. (*be expedient*) 646.

strike the iron while it is hot, *battre le fer sur l'enclume*, make hay while the sun shines, take time by the forelock, *prendre la balle au bond*.

Adj. opportune, timely, well-timed, timeous, timeful, seasonable.

providential, lucky, fortunate, happy, favourable, propitious, auspicious, critical; suitable &c. 23; *obiter dicta*.

Adv. opportunely &c. *adj.*; in -proper, – due- -time, – course, – season; for the nonce; in the -nick, – fulness- of time; all in good time; just in time, at the eleventh hour, now or never.

by the -way, – by; *en passant, à propos*; pro -re natâ, – hac vice; *par parenthèse*, parenthetically, by way of parenthesis; while -speaking of, – on this subject; extempore; on the spur of the -moment, – occasion; on the spot &c. (*early*) 132.

Phr. *carpe diem; occasionem cognosce;* one's hour is come, the time is up; that reminds me.

V. be -ill timed &c. *adj.*; mistime, intrude, come amiss, break in upon; have other fish to fry; be -busy, – engaged, – tied up, – occupied.

lose –, throw away –, waste –, neglect &c. 460- an opportunity; allow –, suffer- the -opportunity, – occasion- to -pass, - slip, – go by, – escape, – lapse; waste time &c. (*be inactive*) 683; let slip through the fingers, lock the stable door when the steed is stolen.

Adj. ill-, mis-timed; untimely, intrusive, unseasonable; out of -date, – season; inopportune, timeless, untoward, *mal à propos*, unlucky, inauspicious, unpropitious, unfortunate, unfavourable; unsuited &c. 24; inexpedient &c. 647.

unpunctual &c. (*late*) 133; too late for; premature &c. (*early*) 132; too soon for; wise after the event.

Adv. inopportunely &c. *adj.*; as ill luck would have it, in an evil hour, the time having gone by, a day after the fair.

Phr. after meat mustard, after death the doctor.

3°. Recurrent Time

136. Frequency.—N. frequency, oftness; repetition, &c. 104.

V. recur &c. 104; do nothing but; keep, – on.

Adj. frequent, many times, not rare, thickcoming, incessant, perpetual, continual, constant, recurrent, repeated &c. 104; habitual &c. 613; hourly, &c. 138.

Adv. often, often to be met with, oft; oft-, often-times; frequently; repeatedly &c. 104; unseldom, not unfrequently; in -quick, – rapid- succession; many a time and oft; daily, hourly &c.; every -day, – hour, – moment &c.

perpetually, continually, constantly, incessantly, without ceasing, at all times, daily and hourly, night and day,

137. Infrequency.—N. infrequency, infrequence, rareness, rarity; fewness &c. 103; seldomness, uncommonness.

V. be -rare &c. *adj.*

Adj. un-, in-frequent; uncommon, sporadic, rare, – as a blue diamond; few &c. 103; scarce; almost unheard of, unprecedented, which has not occurred within the memory of the oldest inhabitant, not within one's previous experience.

Adv. seldom, rarely, scarcely, hardly; not often, unfrequently, infrequently, unoften; scarcely –, hardly- ever; once in a blue moon.

once; once -for all, – in a way; *pro hac vice*; like angels' visits, few and far between.

day and night, day after day, morning noon and night, ever and anon.

most often; commonly &c. (*habitually*) 613.

sometimes, occasionally, at times, now and then, from time to time, there being times when, *toties quoties*, often enough, again and again &c. 104.

138. Regularity of recurrence. **Periodicity.—N.** periodicity, intermittence; beat; oscillation &c. 314; pulse, pulsation; rhythm; alter-nation, -nateness, -nativeness, -nity.

bout, round, revolution, rotation, turn.

anniversary, birthday, jubilee, centenary, bi-, ter-centenary.

[Regularity of return] rota, cycle, period, stated time, routine; days of the week; Sunday, Monday &c.; months of the year; January &c.; feast, fast, saint's day &c.; Christmas, Easter, New Year's Day &c. 998; quarter-, Lady-, Midsummer-, Michaelmas-day; May Day, the King's Birthday; leap year; seasons.

punctuality, regularity, steadiness.

V. recur in regular -order, – succession; return, revolve, rotate; come -again, – in its turn; come round, – again; beat, pulsate; alternate; intermit.

Adj. periodic, -al; serial, recurrent, cyclic-, -al, rhythmic-, -al, even; recurring &c. *v.*; inter-, re-mittent; alternate, every other.

hourly; diurnal, daily; quotidian, tertian, weekly; hebdomad-al, -ary; bi-weekly, fortnightly; monthly, menstrual, catamenial; yearly, annual; biennial, triennial, &c.; bissextile; centennial, secular; paschal, lenten, &c.

regular, steady, punctual, constant, methodical, regular as clockwork.

Adv. periodically &c. *adj.*; at -regular intervals, – stated times; at -fixed, – established- periods; punctually &c. *adj.*; *de die in diem*; from day to day, day by day.

by turns; in -turn, – rotation; alternately, every other day, off and on, ride and tie, round and round.

139. Irregularity of recurrence.—**N.** irregularity, uncertainty, unpunctuality; fitfulness &c. *adj.*

Adj. irregular, uneven, uncertain, unpunctual, capricious, erratic, desultory, fitful, flickering; rambling, rhapsodical; spasmodic, unsystematic, unequal, variable, halting.

Adv. irregularly &c. *adj.*; by fits and starts &c. (*discontinuously*) 70.

Section VII. CHANGE

1°. Simple Change

140. [Difference at different times.] **Change.—N.** change, alteration, mutation, permutation, variation, modification, modulation, inflexion, mood, qualification, innovation, *metastasis*, deviation, shift, turn; diversion; break.

transformation, transfiguration; metamorphosis; metabolism; transmutation; transubstantiation; metagenesis, transanimation, transmigration, me-

141. [Absence of change.] **Permanence.—N.** stability &c. 150; quiescence &c. 265; obstinacy &c. 606.

permanence, -cy, persistence, fixity, fixity of purpose, endurance, durability; standing, *status quo*; maintenance, preservation, conservation; conservatism; *laissez-faire*; law of the Medes and Persians; standing dish.

V. let -alone, – be; persist, remain,

tempsychosis; version; metathesis; transmogrification; catalysis; *avatar*; alterative.

conversion &c. (*gradual change*) 144; revolution &c. (*sudden or radical change*) 146; inversion &c. (*reversal*) 218; displacement &c. 185; transference &c. 270.

changeableness &c. 149; tergiversation &c. (*change of mind*) 607.

V. change, alter, vary, wax and wane; modulate, diversify, qualify, tamper with; turn, shift, veer, jibe, tack, chop, shuffle, swerve, dodge, warp, deviate, turn aside, evert, intervert; pass to, take a turn, turn the corner, resume.

work a change, modify, vamp, revamp, superinduce; trans-form, –mute, –ume, -figure &c. *n.*; metamorphose, ring the changes; convert, resolve; revolutionize; chop and change; patch, re-shape.

innovate, introduce new blood, shuffle the cards, spin the wheel; give a -turn, – colour- to; influence, turn the scale; shift the scene, turn over a new leaf.

recast &c. 146; reverse &c. 218; disturb &c. 61; convert into &c. 144.

Adj. changed &c. *v.*; new-fangled; changeable &c. 149; transitional; modifiable; alterative.

Adv. *mutatis mutandis.*

Int. *quantum mutatus!*

Phr. 'a change came o'er the spirit of my dream'; *nous avons changé tout cela; tempora mutantur et nos mutamur in illis; non sum qualis eram.*

stay, tarry, rest; hold, – on; last, endure, bide, abide, aby, dwell, maintain, keep; stand, – still, – fast; subsist, live, outlive, survive; hold –, keep-one's -ground, – footing; hold good.

Adj. stable &c. 150; persisting &c. *v.*; permanent; established, fixed; durable; unchanged &c. (change &c. 140); unrenewed; intact, inviolate; persistent; monotonous, uncheckered; unfailing.

un-destroyed, -repealed, -suppressed; conservative, *qualis ab incepto*; prescriptive &c. (*old*) 124; stationary &c. 265.

Adv. *in statu quo*; for good, finally; at a stand, -still; *uti possidetis*; without a shadow of turning.

Phr. as you were!; *j'y suis j'y reste; esto perpetua; nolumus leges Angliæ mutari*; let sleeping dogs lie.

---

142. [Change from action to rest.] **Cessation.**—N. cessation, discontinuance, desistance, desinence.

inter-, re-mission; sus-pense, -pension; interruption, hitch; hartal; stop; stopping &c. *v.*; closure, stoppage, halt; arrival &c. 292.

pause, rest, lull, respite, truce, armistice, 'drop; interregnum, abeyance.

closure &c. 261.

dead -stop, – stand, – lock; checkmate; comma, colon, semicolon, period, full stop; end &c. 67; death &c. 360; *cæsura*.

V. cease, discontinue, desist, stay; break –, leave- off; hold, stop, pull up, stall, stop short, check; stick, deadlock, hang fire; halt; pause, rest.

have done with, give over, surcease,

143. Continuance in action.—N. continu-ance, -ation; run; extension, prolongation; maintenance, perpetuation; persistence &c. (*perseverance*) 604*a*; repetition &c. 104.

V. continue, persist; go –, jog –, keep –, carry –, run – hold- on; abide, keep, pursue, stick to; endure; take –, maintain- its course; keep up.

sustain, uphold, hold on, keep on foot; follow up, perpetuate, prolong; maintain; preserve &c. 604*a*; harp upon &c. (*repeat*) 104.

keep -going, – alive, – at it, – the pot boiling, – the ball rolling, – up the ball; plod-, plug- along; slog on; die in harness; hold on –, pursue- the even tenor of one's way.

let be; *stare super antiquas vias*;

shut up shop; give up &c. (*relinquish*) 624.

hold –, stay- one's hand; rest on one's oars, repose on one's laurels.

come to a -stand, – standstill, – dead lock, – full stop; arrive &c. 292; go out, die away, peter out; wear -away, – off; pass away &c. (*be past*) 122; be at an end.

intromit, interrupt, suspend, interpel; inter-, re-mit; put -an end, – a stop, – a period- to; bring to a stand, -still; stop, cut out, cut short, arrest, avast; stem the -tide, – torrent; pull the check string; switch off.

Int. halt! hold! stop! enough! avast! have done! a truce to! soft! leave off! shut up! give over! chuck it!

quieta non movere; let things take their course.

Adj. continuing &c. *v.*; uninterrupted, unintermitting, unremitting, unvarying, unshifting; unreversed, unstopped, unrevoked, unvaried; sustained; undying &c. (*perpetual*) 112; inconvertible.

follow-up.

Int. carry on! right away!

Phr. *vestigia nulla retrorsum*; *labitur et labetur.*

------

144. [Gradual change to something different.] **Conversion.**—**N.** conversion, reduction, transmutation, transformation, development, resolution, assimilation; assumption; naturalization.

chemistry, alchemy; progress, growth, lapse, flux.

passage; transit, -ion; transmigration, shifting &c. *v.*; conjugation; convertibility.

crucible, alembic, caldron, retort, test tube &c.

convert, neophyte, proselyte, pervert, renegade, deserter, apostate, turncoat.

V. be converted into; become, get, wax; come –, turn- -to, – into; turn out, lapse, shift; run –, fall –, pass –, slide –, glide –, grow –, ripen –, open –, resolve itself –, settle –, merge- into; melt, grow, come round to, mature, mellow; assume the -form, – shape, – state, – nature, – character- of; illapse; assume a new phase, undergo a change.

convert –, resolve- into; make, render; mould, form &c. 240; re-model, new model, refound, reform, reorganize; assimilate –, bring –, reduce- to; transform.

Adj. converted into &c. *v.*; convertible, resolvable into; transitional; naturalized.

Adv. gradually &c. (*slowly*) 275; *in transitu* &c. (*transference*) 270.

145. Reversion.—**N.** reversion, return; revulsion; reaction.

turning point, turn of the tide; *status quo ante bellum*; calm before a storm.

alternation &c. (*periodicity*) 138; inversion &c. 218; recoil &c. 277; regression &c. 283; restoration &c. 660; relapse &c. 661; vicinism, atavism, throwback.

V. revert, turn back, return; relapse &c. 661; recoil &c. 277; retreat &c. 283; restore &c. 660; undo, unmake; turn the -tide, – scale; escheat.

Adj. reverting &c. *v.*; revulsive, reactionary.

Adv. *à rebours*, wrong side out.

146. [Sudden or violent change.] **Revolution.**—**N.** revolution, *bouleversement*, subversion, break up; destruction &c. 162; sudden –, radical –, sweeping –, organic- change; clean sweep, *coup d'état*, overthrow, *débâcle*; counter-revolution, rebellion &c. 742.

transilience, jump, leap, plunge, jerk, start; explosion; spasm, convulsion, throe, revulsion; storm, earthquake, eruption, upheaval, cataclysm.

legerdemain &c. (*trick*) 545.

V. revolutionize; new model, remodel, recast; strike out something new, break with the past; change the face of, unsex; revert &c. 742.

Adj. unrecognizable.

Revolutionary, Bolshevik &c. 742.

---

147. [Change of one thing for another.] **Substitution.—N.** substitution, subrogation, commutation; supplanting &c. *v.*, supersession, metonymy &c. (*figure of speech*) 521.

[Thing substituted] substitute, *succedaneum*, make-shift, temporary expedient, shift, *pis aller*, stop-gap, jury-mast, *locum tenens*, warming-pan, dummy, goat, scape-goat; double; changeling; *quid pro quo*, alternative; remount; representative &c. (*deputy*) 759; palimpsest.

price, purchase-money, consideration, equivalent.

V. substitute, put in the place of, change for; make way for, give place to; supply –, take- the place of; supplant, supersede, replacè, cut out, serve as a substitute; step into –, stand in- the shoes of; make a shift –, put up- with; borrow of Peter to pay Paul; commute, redeem, compound for.

Adj. substituted &c. *v.*; vicarious, subdititious; substitutional.

Adv. instead; in -place, – lieu, – the stead, – the room- of; *faute de mieux*₁

148. [Double or mutual change.] **Interchange.—N.** inter-, ex-change; com-, per-, inter-mutation; reciprocation, transposal, transposition, shuffling; reciprocity, castling [at chess]; hocus-pocus.

interchange-ableness, -ability.

barter &c. 794; tit for tat &c. (*retaliation*) 718; cross fire, battledore and shuttlecock; *quid pro quo.*

V. inter-, ex-, counter-change; bandy, transpose, shuffle, change hands, swap, trade, permute, reciprocate, commute; give and take, return the compliment; play at -puss in the corner, – battledore and shuttlecock; retaliate &c. 718; barter &c. 794.

Adj. interchanged &c. *v.*; reciprocal, mutual, commutative, interchanged &c. *v.*; interchangeable, intercurrent.

Adv. in exchange, *vice versâ, mutatis mutandis*, backwards and forwards, by turns, turn and turn about, turn about; each –, every one- in his turn.

2°. COMPLEX CHANGE

149. Changeableness.—N. changeableness &c. *adj.*; mutability, inconstancy; versatility, mobility; instability, unstable equilibrium; vacillation &c. (*irresolution*) 605; fluctuation, vicissitude; alternation &c. (*oscillation*) 314.

restlessness &c. *adj.*; fidgets, disquiet; dis-, in-quietude; unrest; agitation &c. 315.

moon, Proteus, chameleon, kaleidoscope, quicksilver, shifting sands, weathercock, harlequin, Cynthia of the minute, April showers; wheel of Fortune; transientness &c. 111.

V. fluctuate, vary, waver, flounder, flicker, flitter, flit, flutter, shift, shuffle, shake, totter, tremble, vacillate, wamble, turn and turn about, ring the changes; sway –, shift- to and fro; change and change about; oscillate

150. Stability.—N. stability; immutability &c. *adj.*; unchangeableness &c. *adj.*; constancy; stable equilibrium, immobility, soundness, vitality, stabiliment, stabilization, stiffness, ankylosis, solidity, *aplomb*.

establishment, fixture; rock, pillar, tower, foundation, leopard's spots, Ethiopian's skin, law of the Medes and Persians.

stabilimeter, stabilizator.

permanence &c. 141; obstinacy &c. 606.

V. be -firm &c. *adj.*; stick fast; stand –, keep –, remain- firm; weather the storm.

settle, establish, stablish, ascertain, fix, set, stabilitate, stabilize; retain, stet, keep hold; make -good, – sure; fasten &c. (*join*) 43; set on its legs float; perpetuate.

&c. 314; vibrate –, oscillate- between two extremes; alternate; have as many phases as the moon.

Adj. change-able, -ful; changing &c. 140; mutable, variable, checkered, ever changing, kaleidoscopic, prote-an, -iform; versatile.

unstaid, inconstant; un-steady, -stable, -fixed, -settled; fluctuating &c. v.; restless; mercurial; agitated &c. 315; erratic, fickle; irresolute &c. 605; capricious &c. 608; touch-and-go; inconsonant, fitful, spasmodic; vibratory; vagrant, wayward, wavering; desultory; afloat; alternating; alterable, plastic, mobile; fleeting, transient &c. 111.

Adv. see-saw &c. (oscillation) 314; off and on.

_____

settle down; strike –, take- root; take up one's abode &c. 184; build one's house on a rock.

Adj. unchangeable, immutable; un-alter-ed, -able; not to be changed, constant; permanent &c. 141; invariable, undeviating; stable, durable; perennial &c. (diuturnal) 110.

fixed, steadfast, firm, fast, steady, balanced; confirmed, valid, fiducial, immovable, irremovable, riveted, rooted; settled, established &c. v.; vested; incontrovertible, stereotyped, indeclinable.

tethered, anchored, moored, at anchor, on a rock, firm as a rock; firmly -seated, – established &c. v.; deep-rooted, ineradicable; inveterate; obstinate &c. 606.

transfixed, stuck fast, aground, high and dry, stranded.

indefeasible, irretrievable, intransmutable, incommutable, irresoluble, irrevocable, irreversible, reverseless, inextinguishable, irreducible; indissol-uble, -vable; indestructible, undying, imperishable, indelible, indeciduous; insusceptible, – of change.

Int. stet.

_____

Present Events

151. Eventuality.—N. eventuality, event, occurrence, incident, affair, transaction, proceeding, fact; matter of –, naked- fact; phenomenon; advent.

business, concern; circumstance, particular, casualty, happening, accident, adventure, passage, crisis, pass, emergency, contingency, consequence &c. 154.

the world, life, things, doings, affairs, matters; things –, affairs- in general; the times, state of affairs, order of the day; course –, tide –, stream –, current –, run –, march- of -things, – events; ups and downs of life; chapter of accidents &c. (chance) 156; situation &c. (circumstances) 8.

V. happen, occur; take -place, – effect; come, become of; come -off, – about, – round, – into existence, – forth, – to pass, – on; pass, present itself; fall; fall –, turn- out; run, be on foot, fall in; be-fall, -tide, -chance; prove, eventuate, draw on; turn –, crop –, spring –, cast- up; super-, sur-vene; issue, emanate, arrive, ensue,

Future Events

152. Destiny.—N. destiny &c. (necessity) 601; hereafter, future –, post-existence; future state, next world, world to come, after life; futurity &c. 121; everlasting -life, – death; prospect &c. (expectation) 507.

V. impend; hang –, lie –, hover-over; threaten, loom, await, come on, approach, stare one in the face; fore-, pre-ordain; predestine, doom, fore-doom, foreshadow, have in store for.

Adj. impending &c. v.; destined; about to -be, – happen; coming, in store, to come, going to happen, instant, at hand, near; near –, close- at hand; overhanging, hanging over one's head, imminent; brewing, preparing, forthcoming; in the wind, on the cards, in reserve; that -will, – is to- be; in prospect &c. (expected) 507; looming in the -distance, – horizon, – future; unborn, in embryo; in the womb of -time; – futurity; on the knees of the gods; pregnant &c. (producing) 161.

Adv. in -time, – the long run; all in good time; eventually &c. 151; what-

arise, start, hold, take its course; pass off &c. (*be past*) 122.

meet with; experience; fall to the lot of; be one's -chance, – fortune, – lot; find; encounter, undergo; pass –, go-through; endure &c. (*feel*) 821.

Adj. happening &c. *v.*; going on, doing, current; in the wind, afloat; on -foot, – the *tapis*; at issue, in question; incidental.

eventful, momentous, signal; stirring, bustling, full of incident.

Adv. eventually, ultimately, in -the event of, – case; in the course of things; in the -natural, – ordinary- course of things; as -things, – times- go; as the world -goes, – wags; as the -tree falls, – cat jumps; as it may -turn out, – happen.

Phr. the plot thickens.

ever may happen &c. (*certainly*) 474; as -chance &c. 156- would have it.

———

SECTION VIII.   CAUSATION

1°. CONSTANCY OF SEQUENCE IN EVENTS

153. [Constant antecedent.] **Cause.**
—**N.** cause, origin, source, principle, element; occasioner, prime mover, engine, turbine, motor, *primum mobile*; *vera causa*; author &c. (*producer*) 164; main-spring, agent; dynamo, generator, battery (electric); leaven; groundwork, foundation &c. (*support*) 215.

spring, fountain, well, font; fountain –, spring- head; *fons et origo*, genesis; descent &c. (*paternity*) 166; remote cause; influence.

pivot, hinge, turning-point, lever; key; kernel, core; proximate cause, *causa causans*; last straw that breaks the camel's back.

ground; reason, – why; why and wherefore, rationale, occasion, derivation; final cause &c. (*intention*) 620; *le dessous des cartes*; undercurrents.

rudiment, egg, germ, embryo, fœtus bud, root, *radix*, radical, etymon, nucleus, seed, stem, stalk, stock, *stirps*, trunk, tap-root; latent organism.

nest, cradle, nursery, womb, *nidus*, birth-, breeding-place, hot-bed.

caus-ality, -ation; origination; production &c. 161.

V. be the -cause &c. *n.*- of; originate; give -origin, – rise, – occasion- to; cause, occasion, sow the seeds of, kindle, suscitate; bring -on, – to pass, – about; produce; create &c. 161; set -up, – afloat, – on foot; found, broach,

154. [Constant sequent.] **Effect.**—**N.** effect, consequence, sequela; derivative, -tion; result; result-ant, -ance; upshot, issue, *dénouement*; outcome; termination, end &c. 67; development, outgrowth, fruit, crop, harvest, product, bud, blossom, florescence, ear.

production, produce, product, finished product, work, handiwork, fabric, performance; creature, creation; offspring, -shoot; first-fruits, -lings; *prémices*.

V. be the -effect &c. *n.*- of; be -due, – owing- to; originate -in, – from; rise –, arise –, take its rise –, spring –, proceed –, emanate –, come –, grow –, bud –, sprout –, germinate –, issue –, flow –, result –, follow –, derive its origin –, accrue- from; come -to, – of, – out of; depend –, hang –, hinge –, turn- upon.

take the consequences, sow the wind and reap the whirlwind.

Adj. owing to; resulting from &c. *v.*; resultant; derivable from; due to; caused &c. by, 153; dependent upon; derived –, evolved- from; derivative; hereditary.

Adv. of course, it follows that, naturally, consequently; as a –, in- consequence; through all, all along of, necessarily, eventually.

Phr. *cela va sans dire*, thereby hangs a tale.

———

institute, lay the foundation of, inaugurate; lie at the root of.

procure, induce, draw°down, open the door to, superinduce, evoke, entail, operate; elicit, provoke.

conduce to &c. (*tend to*) 176; contribute; promote; have a -hand in, – finger in- the pie; determine, decide, turn the scale, give the casting vote; have a common origin; derive its origin &c. (*effect*) 154.

Adj. caused &c. *v.*; causal, original; prim-ary, -itive, -ordial; aboriginal; radical; inceptive, embry-onic, -otic; *in -embryo, – ovo*; seminal, germinal; formative, productive &c. 168; at the bottom of; connate, having a common origin.

Adv. because &c. 155; behind the scenes.

155. [Assignment of cause.] **Attribution.**—**N.** attribution, theory, etiology, ascription, reference to, rationale; accounting for &c. *v.*; palaetiology,* imputation, derivation from.

fil-, affil-iation; pedigree &c. (*pater-nity*) 166.

explanation &c. (*interpretation*) 522; reason why &c. (*cause*) 153.

V. attribute –, ascribe –, impute –, refer –, lay –, point –, trace –, bring home- to; put –, set- down- to; charge –, ground- on; invest with, assign as cause, charge with, blame, lay at the door of, father upon; saddle with; affiliate; account for, derive from, point out the -reason &c. 153; theorize; tell how it comes; put the saddle on the right horse.

Adj. attributed &c. *v.*; attributable &c. *v.*; refer-able, -rible; due to, derivable from; owing to &c. (*effect*) 154; putative.

Adv. hence, thence, therefore, for, since, on account of, because, owing to; on that account; from -this, – that- cause; thanks to, forasmuch as; whence, *propter hoc.*

why? wherefore? whence? how -comes, – is, – happens- it? how does it happen?

in -some, – some such- way; somehow, – or other.

Phr. that is why; *hinc illæ lachrymæ; cherchez la femme.*

156. [Absence of assignable cause.] **Chance.†**—**N.** chance, indetermination, accident, fortune, hazard, hap, haphazard, chance-medley, random, luck, *raccroc*, casualty, fortuity, contingence, coincidence, adventure, hit; fate &c. (*necessity*) 601; equal chance; lottery, raffle, tombola, sweepstake; toss up &c. 621; turn of the -table, – cards; hazard of the die, chapter of accidents; cast –, throw- of the dice; heads or tails, wheel of Fortune, whirligig of chance; *sortes, –Virgilianæ, -biblicæ.*

probability, possibility, contingency, odds, long odds, run of luck; main-chance.

theory of -probabilities, – chances; book-making; assurance; speculation, gamble, gaming &c. 621.

V. chance, hap, turn up; fall to one's lot; be one's -fate &c. 601; stumble on, light –, blunder –, hit- upon; take one's chance &c. 621.

Adj. casual, fortuitous, accidental, haphazard, random, stray, adventitious, adventive, causeless, incidental. contingent, uncaused, undetermined, indeterminate; possible &c. 470; unintentional &c. 621.

Adv. by -chance, – accident; casually; perchance &c. (*possibly*) 470; for aught one knows; as -good, – bad, – ill-luck &c. *n.*- would have it; as it may -be, – chance, – turn up, – happen; as the case may be.

2°. Connection between Cause and Effect

157. Power.—**N.** power; poten-cy, -tiality; puissance, might, force; energy &c. 171; dint; right -hand, – arm;

158. Impotence.—**N.** impotence; in-, dis-ability; disablement, impuissance, imbecility, caducity; incapa-city,

* Whewell, 'History of the Inductive Sciences,' book xviii, vol. iii., p. 397 (3rd edit.).

† The word *Chance* has two distinct meanings: the first, the absence of assignable *cause*, as above; and the second, the absence of *design*—for the latter see 621.

ascendency, sway, control; pre-potency, -pollence; almightiness, omnipotence; authority &c. 737; strength &c. 159.

ability; ableness &c. *adj.*; competency; effi-ciency, -cacy; validity, cogency; enablement; vantage ground; influence &c. 175; horse power; dynamometer.

pressure; elasticity; gravity, electricity, magnetism, galvanism, voltaic electricity, voltaism, electro-magnetism, electrostatics, electrification, electric current &c.; attraction, repulsion; *vis -inertiæ, – mortua, – viva*; potential –, dynamic –, kinetic –, electrical –, chemical –, atomic- energy; friction, suction.

capability, capacity; *quid valeant humeri quid ferre recusent*; faculty, quality, attribute, endowment, virtue, gift, property, qualification, susceptibility.

V. be -powerful &c. *adj.*; gain -power &c. *n.*

belong –, pertain- to; lie –, be- in one's power; can.

give –, confer –, exercise- power &c. *n.*; empower, enable, invest; in-, en-due; endow, arm; strengthen &c. 159; compel &c. 744.

Adj. powerful, puissant; potent, -ial; capable, able; equal –, up- to; cogent, valid; effect-ive, -ual; efficient, efficacious, adequate, competent; multi-, pleni-, omni-, armi- potent; mighty, ascendent; almighty.

electric, electrical &c.

forcible &c. *adj.* (*energetic*) 171; influential &c. 175; productive &c. 168.

Adv. powerfully &c. *adj.*; by -virtue, – dint- of.

-bility; inapt-, inept-itude; indocility; invalidity, inefficiency, incompetence, disqualification.

telum imbelle, brutum fulmen, blank cartridge, flash in the pan, *vox et præterea nihil*, dead letter, bit of waste paper, dummy; scrap of paper.

inefficacy &c. (*inutility*) 645; failure &c. 732.

helplessness &c. *adj.*; prostration, paralysis, palsy, ataxia, apoplexy, syncope, sideration, *deliquium*, collapse, exhaustion, softening of the brain, emasculation, inanition, senility &c. 128; castrato, eunuch.

cripple, old woman, muff, mollycoddle, milksop.

V. be -impotent &c. *adj.*; not have a leg to stand on.

vouloir -rompre l'anguille au genou, – prendre la lune avec les dents.

collapse, faint, swoon, fall into a swoon, drop; go by the board; end in smoke &c. (*fail*) 732.

render -powerless &c. *adj.*; deprive of power; decontrol; dis-able, -enable; disarm, incapacitate, disqualify, unfit, invalidate, undermine, deaden, cramp, tie the hands; double up, prostrate, paralyze, muzzle, cripple, becripple, maim, lame, hamstring, draw the teeth of; throttle, strangle, *garrotte*; ratten, silence, sprain, clip the wings of, render *hors de combat*, spike the guns; take the wind out of one's sails, scotch the snake, put a spoke in one's wheel; break the -neck, – back; un-hinge, -fit; put out of gear.

unman, unnerve, devitalize, attenuate, enervate; emasculate, spay, caponize, castrate, geld; effeminize.

shatter, exhaust; weaken &c. 160.

Adj. powerless, impotent, unable, incapable, incompetent; ineff-icient, -ective; inept; un-fit, -fitted; un-, dis-qualified; unendowed; in-, un-apt; crippled, decrepit, disabled &c. *v.*; armless.

harmless, unarmed, weaponless, defenceless, *sine ictu*, unfortified, indefensible, vincible, pregnable, untenable.

para-lytic, -lyzed; palsied, imbecile; nerve-, sinew-, marrow-, pith-, lust-less; emasculate, disjointed; out of -joint, – gear; un--nerved, -hinged; water-logged, on one's beam ends, rudderless; laid on one's back; done up, dead beat, exhausted, shattered, demoralized; gravelled &c. (*in difficulty*) 704; helpless, unfriended, fatherless; without a leg to stand on, *hors de combat*, laid on the shelf.

null and void, nugatory, inoperative, good for nothing; dud; invertebrate; ineffectual &c. (*failing*) 732; inadequate &c. 640; inefficacious &c. (*useless*) 645.

159. [Degree of power.] Strength.
—**N.** strength; power &c. 157; energy &c. 171; vigour, force; main –, physical –, brute- force; spring, elasticity, tone, tension, tonicity.

stoutness &c. *adj*; lustihood, stamina, nerve, muscle, sinew, thews and sinews, *physique*; pith, -iness; virility, vitality.

athlet-ics, -icism; gymnastics, feats of strength.

adamant, steel, iron, oak, heart of oak; iron grip; grit, bone.

athlete, gymnast, tumbler, acrobat; Atlas, Hercules, Antæus, Samson, Cyclops, Goliath, Titan; tower of strength; giant refreshed.

strengthening &c. *v.*; invigoration, refreshment, refocillation.

[Science of forces] dynamics, statics.

V. be -strong &c. *adj.*, – stronger; overmatch.

render -strong &c. *adj.*; give -strength &c. *n.*; strengthen, invigorate, brace, nerve, fortify, buttress, sustain, harden, case-harden, steel; gird; screw –, wind –, set- up; gird –, brace- up one's loins; recruit, set on one's legs; vivify; refresh &c. 689; refect; reinforce &c. (*restore*) 660.

Adj. strong, mighty, vigorous, forcible, hard, adamantine, stout, robust, sturdy, hardy, powerful, potent, puissant, valid.

resistless, irresistible, invincible, proof against, impregnable, unconquerable, indomitable, inextinguishable, unquenchable; incontestable; more than a match for; over-powering, -whelming; all-powerful; sovereign.

able-bodied; athletic, gymnastic; Herculean, Cyclopean, Atlantean; muscular, husky, brawny, wiry, well-knit, broad-shouldered, sinewy, strapping, stalwart, gigantic.

man-ly, -like, -ful; masculine, male, virile, in the prime of manhood.

un-weakened, -allayed, -withered, -shaken, -worn, -exhausted; in full -force, – swing; in the plenitude of power.

160. Weakness.—N. weakness &c. *adj.*; debility, atony, relaxation, languor, enervation; impotence &c. 158; infirmity; effeminancy, feminality; fragility, flaccidity; inactivity &c. 683.

declension –, loss –, failure- of strength; delicacy, invalidation, decrepitude, asthenia, adynamy, cachexy, *cachexia*, anæmia, bloodlessness, sprain, strain.

reed, thread, rope of sand, broken reed, house -of cards, – built on sand.

soft-, weak-ling; infant &c. 129; youth &c. 127.

V. be -weak &c. *adj.*; drop, crumble, give way, totter, tremble, shake, halt, limp, fade, languish, decline, flag, fail, have one foot in the grave.

render -weak &c. *adj.*; weaken, enfeeble, debilitate, shake, deprive of strength, relax, enervate; un-brace, -nerve; cripple, unman, &c. (*render powerless*) 158; cramp, reduce, sprain, strain, blunt the edge of; dilute, impoverish; decimate; extenuate; reduce -in strength, – the strength of; invalidate; *mettre de l'eau dans son vin.*

Adj. weak, feeble, debile; impotent &c. 158; relaxed, unnerved &c. *v.*; sap-, strength-, power-less; weakly, unstrung, flaccid, adynamic, asthenic; nervous.

soft, effeminate, feminate, womanish.

frail, fragile, shattery, frangible, brittle &c. 328; flimsy, unsubstantial, gimcrack, gingerbread; rickety, cranky; creachy; drooping, tottering &c. *v.*; broken, lame, halt, game, withered, shattered, shaken, crazy, shaky, tumble-down; palsied &c. 158; decrepit; C3.

languid, poor, poorly, infirm; faint, -ish; sickly &c. (*disease*) 655; dull, slack, evanid, spent, short-winded, effete; weatherbeaten; decayed, rotten, worn, seedy, languishing, wasted, washy, wishy-washy, laid low, pulled down, the worse for wear.

un-strengthened &c. 159, -supported, -aided, -assisted; aidless, defenceless &c. 158.

stubborn, thick-ribbed, made of iron, deep-rooted; strong as -a lion, – a horse, – brandy; sound as a roach; in -fine, – high- feather; in fine fettle; like a giant refreshed.

Adv. strongly &c. *adj.*; by -force &c. *n.*; by main force &c. (*by compulsion*) 744.

Phr. 'our withers are unwrung.'

on its last legs; weak as a -child, – baby, – chicken, – cat, – rat; weak as -water, – water gruel, – gingerbread, – milk and water; colourless &c. 429.

Phr. *non sum qualis eram.*

3°. POWER IN OPERATION

161. Production.—N. production, creation, construction, formation, fabrication, manufacture; building, architecture, erection, edification; coinage; organization; *nisus formativus*; putting together &c. *v.*; establishment; workmanship, performance; achievement &c. (*completion*) 729; effect &c. 154.

flowering, fructification, fruition.

bringing forth &c. *v.*; parturition, birth, birth-throe, child-birth, delivery, confinement, *accouchement*, travail, labour, midwifery, obstetrics; geniture; gestation &c. (*maturation*) 673; evolution, development, growth; genesis, fertilization, breeding, conception, germination, generation, *epigenesis*, pro-creation, -generation, -pagation; fecundation, impregnation; spontaneous generation; *arche-genesis, -biosis; bio-, abio-, homo-, xeno-genesis.* *

authorship, publication; works, *œuvre, opus.*

edifice, building, structure, fabric, erection, pile, tower, flower, fruit.

V. produce, perform, operate, do, make, gar. form, construct, fabricate, frame, contrive, manufacture; weave, forge, coin, carve, chisel; build, raise, edify, rear, erect, put together; set -, run- up; establish, constitute, compose, organize, institute, get up; achieve, accomplish &c. (*complete*) 729.

flower, sprout, blossom, burgeon, bear fruit, fructify, spawn, teem, ean, yean, farrow, drop, calf, pup, whelp, kitten, kindle; bear, lay, bring forth, give birth to, lie in, be brought to bed of, evolve, pullulate, usher into the world.

make productive &c. 168; create; beget, conceive, get, generate, fecun-

162. [Non-production.] Destruction. —N. destruction; waste, dissolution, breaking up; di-, dis-ruption; consumption; disorganization.

fall, downfall, ruin, perdition, crash, smash, havoc, *délabrement, débâcle;* break -down, – up; prostration; desolation, *bouleversement*, wreck, crack-up, crash, wrack, shipwreck, cataclysm; Caudine Forks, Sedan.

extinction, annihilation; destruction of life &c. 361; knock-out, knock-down blow; doom, crack of doom.

destroying &c. *v.*; demo-lition, -lishment; biblioclasm; overthrow, subversion, suppression; abolition &c. (*abrogation*) 756; sacrifice; ravage, devastation, *sabotage, razzia*; incendiarism; revolution &c. 146; extirpation &c. (*extraction*) 301; *commencement de la fin*, road to ruin; dilapidation &c. (*deterioration*) 659.

V. be -destroyed &c.; perish; fall, – to the ground; tumble, topple; go –, fall- to pieces; break up; crumble, – to dust; go to -the dogs, – the wall, – smash, – shivers, – wreck, – pot, – wrack and ruin; go -by the board, – all to smash, – to pieces, – under; be all -over, – up- with; totter to its fall.

destroy; do –, make- away with; nullify; annul &c. 756; sacrifice, demolish; tear up; over-turn, -throw, -whelm; upset, subvert, put an end to; seal the doom of, do for, dish, undo; break -, cut- up; break –, cut –, pull –, mow –, blow –, beat- down; suppress, quash, put down; cut short, take off, blot out; dispel, dissipate, dissolve; consume; abolish.

smash, – to smithereens, quell, squash, squelch, crumple up, shatter,

* Huxley.

date, impregnate; pro-create, -generate, -pagate; engender; bring -, call- into -being, - existence; breed, hatch, develop, bring up.

induce, superinduce; suscitate; cause &c. 153; acquire &c. 775.

Adj. produc-ed, -ing &c. *v.*; productive of; prolific &c. 168; creative; formative; gen-etic, -ial, -ital; fertile, pregnant; *enceinte*, big -, fraughtwith; with child, in the family way, teeming, parturient, in the straw, brought to bed of; puerper-al, -ous.

architectonic; constructive.

———

shiver; batter; tear -, crush -, cut -, shake -, pull -, pick- to pieces; nip; tear to -rags, - tatters; crush -, knockto atoms; pulverize; ruin; strike out; throw -, knock- -down, - over; lay by the heels; fell, sink, swamp, scuttle, wreck, crash, shipwreck, engulf, submerge; lay in -ashes, - ruins; sweep away, erase, expunge, strike out, delete, efface, raze; level, - with the -ground, - dust.

deal destruction, lay waste, ravage, gut; disorganize; dismantle &c. (*render useless*) 645; devour, swallow up, desolate, devastate, sap, mine, blast, confound; exterminate, extinguish, quench, annihilate; snuff -, put -, stamp -, trample- out; lay -, trample- in the dust; prostrate; tread -, crush -, trample- under foot; lay the axe to the root of; make -short work, - a clean sweep, - mincemeat- of; cut up root and branch; fling -, scatter- to the winds; throw overboard; strike at the root of, sap the foundations of, spring a mine, blow up; ravage with fire and sword; cast to the dogs; eradicate &c. 301.

Adj. destroyed &c. *v.*; perishing &c. *v.*; trembling -, nodding -, tottering- to its fall; in course of -destruction &c. *n.*; extinct.

destructive, subversive, ruinous, incendiary, deletory; destroying &c. *v.*; suicidal; deadly &c. (*killing*) 361.

Adv. with -crushing effect, - a sledge-hammer.

Phr. *delenda est Carthago.*

———

163. Reproduction.—N. reproduction, renovation; restoration &c. 660; renewal; new edition, reprint &c. 21; revival, regeneration, palingenesia, revivification; apotheosis; resuscitation, reanimation, resurrection, resurgence, reappearance, atavism; Phœnix; reincarnation.

generation &c. (*production*) 161; multiplication.

V. reproduce; restore &c. 660; revive, renovate, renew, regenerate, revivify, resuscitate, reanimate, refashion, stir the embers, put into the crucible; multiply, repeat, resurge.

crop up, spring up like mushrooms.

Adj. reproduced &c. *v.*; renascent, reappearing; reproductive; resurgent; progenitive; Hydra-headed.

---

164. Producer.—N. producer, creator, deviser, designer, originator, inventor, author, founder, generator, mover, architect; grower, constructor, maker &c. (*agent*) 690.

165. Destroyer.—N. destroyer &c. (destroy &c. 162); cankerworm &c. (*bane*) 663; iconoclast; assassin &c. (*killer*) 361; executioner &c. (*punish*) 975; Hun, Vandal, nihilist, anarchist.

166. Paternity.—N. paternity; parentage; fatherhood; consanguinity &c. 11.

parent, father, sire, dad, daddy, papa, governor, *pater*, *paterfamilias*, *abba*; genitor, progenitor, procreator, begetter; ancestor; grand-sire, -father; great-grandfather.

167. Posterity.—N. posterity, progeny, breed, issue, offspring, brood, litter, seed, farrow, spawn, spat; family, children, grandchildren, heirs; greatgrandchild.

child, son, daughter; kid; infant &c. 129; bantling, scion; shoot, sprout, olive branch, sprit, branch; off-shoot,

house, stem, trunk, tree, stock, *stirps*, pedigree, lineage, line, family, tribe, sept, race, clan; genealogy, descent, extraction, birth, ancestry; forefathers, forbears, patriarchs.

motherhood, maternity; mother, dam, mamma, *materfamilias*; grandmother; matriarch.

Adj. paternal, parental; maternal; matrilinear, patrilineal, patriarchal.

168. Productiveness.—N. productiveness &c. *adj.*; fecundity, fertility, luxuriance, uberty.

pregnancy, pullulation, fructification, multiplication, propagation, procreation; superfetation.

milch cow, rabbit, hydra, warren, seed-plot, land flowing with milk and honey; second crop, after-crop, -growth, -math; fertilization.

V. make -productive &c. *adj.*; fructify; procreate, generate, fertilize, spermatize, impregnate; fecund-ate, -ify; teem, pullulate, multiply; produce &c. 161; conceive.

Adj. productive, prolific; teem-ing, -ful; fertile, fruitful, frugiferous, fruit-bearing; fructiferous; fecund, luxuriant; pregnant, uberous.

procre-ant, -ative; generative, life-giving, spermatic; originative; multiparous; omnific; propagable.

parturient &c. (*producing*) 161; profitable &c. (*useful*) 644.

-set; ramification; descendant; heir, -ess; heir -apparent, – presumptive; chip of the old block; heredity; rising generation.

straight descent, sonship, line, lineage, filiation, primogeniture.

Adj. filial.

___

family, ancestral, linear,

169. Unproductiveness.—N. unproductiveness &c. *adj.*; infertility, steril; ity, infecundity; impotence &c. 158-unprofitableness &c. (*inutility*) 645.

waste, desert, Sahara, wild, wilderness, howling wilderness.

V. be -unproductive &c. *adj.*; hang fire, flash in the pan, come to nothing.

Adj. unproductive, inoperative, barren, addle, unfertile, unprolific, arid, sterile, unfruitful, acarpous, infecund; *sine prole*; fallow; teem-, issue-, fruitless; unprofitable &c. (*useless*) 645; null and void, of no effect.

___

170. Agency.—N. agency, operation, force, working, strain, function, office, maintenance, exercise, work, swing, play; inter-working, -action, procuration, procurement.

causation &c. 153; instrumentality &c. 631; influence &c. 175; action &c. (*voluntary*) 680; *modus operandi* &c. 627.

quickening –; maintaining- power; home stroke.

V. be -in action &c. *adj.*; operate, work; act, – upon; perform, play, support, sustain, strain, maintain, take effect, quicken, strike.

come –, bring- into -operation, – play; have -play, – free play; bring to bear upon.

Adj. operative, efficient, efficacious, practical, effectual.

at work, on foot; acting &c. (*doing*) 680; in -operation, – force, – action, – play, – exercise; acted –, wrought- upon.

Adv. by the -agency &c. *n.*- of; through &c. (*instrumentality*) 631; by means of &c. 632.

171. Physical Energy.—N. energy, physical energy, force; keenness &c. *adj.*; intensity, vigour, strength, elasticity; go; pep, live wire, high pressure; backbone, mettle, fire, vim.

acri-mony, -tude, -dity; causticity,

172. Physical Inertness.—N. inert-ness, dulness &c. *adj.*; inertia, *vis inertiæ*, inertion, inactivity, torpor, languor; dormancy, quiescence &c. 265; latency, inaction, passivity.

mental inertness; sloth &c. (*inac-

virulence, poignancy; harshness &c.
adj.; severity, edge, point; pungency
&c. 392.

cantharides; Spanish fly; seasoning
&c. (*condiment*) 393, stimulant, ex-
citant.

activity, agitation, effervescence;
ferment, -ation; ebullition, splutter,
perturbation, stir, bustle; voluntary
energy &c. 682; quicksilver.

resolution &c. (*mental energy*) 604;
exertion &c. (*effort*) 686; excitation &c.
(*mental*) 824.

V. give -energy &c. *n.*; energize,
stimulate, kindle, excite, activate,
exert; sharpen, pep up, intensify;
inflame &c. (*render violent*) 173; wind up &c. (*strengthen*) 159.

strike, – into, – hard, – home; make an impression.

Adj. strong, energetic, forcible, active; strenuous, forceful,
mettlesome, enterprising, go ahead; intense, deep-dyed, severe,
keen, vivid, sharp, acute, incisive, trenchant, brisk, vigorous, live.

rousing, irritating; poignant; virulent, caustic, corrosive, mordant,
harsh, stringent; double-edged, – shotted, – distilled; drastic,
escharotic; racy &c. (*pungent*) 392; sarcastic &c. 932; irenic.

potent &c. (*powerful*) 157; radio-active.

Adv. strongly &c. *adj.*; *fortiter in re*; with telling effect.

Phr. the steam is up; *vires acquirit eundo*.

---

173. Violence.—N. violence, inclemency, vehemence, might, impetuosity;
boisterousness &c. *adj.*; effervescence,
ebullition; turbulence, bluster; uproar,
riot, row, rumpus, *le diable à quatre*,
devil to pay, all the fat in the fire.

severity &c. 739; ferocity, rage,
berserk, fury; exacerbation, exasperation, malignity; fit, paroxysm, orgasm;
force, brute force; outrage; *coup de
main*; strain, shock, shog; spasm, convulsion, throe; hysterics, passion &c.
(*state of excitability*) 825.

out-break, -burst; burst, bounce,
dissilience, discharge, volley, explosion,
blow up, blast, detonation, rush, eruption, displosion, torrent.

turmoil &c. (*disorder*) 59; ferment
&c. (*agitation*) 315; storm, tempest,
rough weather; squall &c. (*wind*) 349;
earthquake, volcano, thunderstorm.

fury, dragon, demon, tiger, beldame,
Tisiphone, Megæra, Alecto, madcap,
wild beast; fire-eater &c. (*blusterer*) 887.

V. be -violent &c. *adj.*; run high;
ferment, effervesce; romp, rampage;
run -wild, – riot; break the peace;

tivity) 683; inexcitability &c. 826;
irresolution &c. 605; obstinacy &c.
606; permanence &c. 141.

V. be -inert &c. *adj.*; hang fire,
smoulder.

Adj. inert, inactive, passive, pacific;
torpid &c. 683; sluggish, stagnant, dull,
heavy, flat, slack, tame, slow, blunt;
lifeless, dead, uninfluential.

latent, dormant, smouldering, unex-
erted.

Adv. inactively &c. *adj.*; in -suspense,
-abeyance.

---

174. Moderation.—N. moderation,
lenity &c. 740; temperance, temper-
ateness, gentleness &c. *adj.*; sobriety;
quiet; mental calmness &c. (*inexcitability*) 826.

moderating &c. *v.*; relaxation, remission, mitigation &c. 834; tranquillization, alleviation, assuagement, ap-
peasement, contemperation, pacification.

measure, *juste milieu*, golden mean
&c. 29.

moderator; lullaby, sedative, lenitive, demulcent, rose-water, balm,
soothing syrup, poppy, opiate, anodyne, milk, opium, laudanum, 'poppy
or mandragora'; wet blanket; palliative, calmative.

V. be -moderate &c. *adj.*; keep within -bounds, – compass; sober -, settle-
down; keep the peace, remit, relent;
shorten sail.

moderate, soften, mitigate, temper,
accoy; at-, con-temper; mollify, lenify,
dull, take off the edge, blunt, obtund,
sheathe, subdue, chasten; sober -,
tone -, smooth- down; censor, blue-

rush, tear; rush head-long, -foremost; run amuck, raise a storm, make a riot; make –, kick up– a row, – a fuss; bluster, rage, roar, riot, storm; boil, – over; fume, foam, come in like a lion, wreak, bear down, ride rough-shod, out-Herod Herod; spread like wildfire.

break –, fly –, burst- out; bounce, shock, strain; break-, pry-, force-, prize- open.

render -violent &c. *adj.*; sharpen, stir up, quicken, excite, incite, urge, lash, stimulate; irritate, inflame, exacerbate, kindle, suscitate, foment; accelerate, aggravate, exasperate, convulse, infuriate, madden, lash into fury; fan –, add fuel to- the flame; *oleum addere camino.*

explode, go off, displode, fly, detonate, thunder, blow up, flash, flare, erupt, burst; let -off, – fly; discharge, detonize, fulminate.

Adj. violent, vehement, forcible; warm; acute, sharp; rough, rude, ungentle, bluff, boisterous, wild, vicious; brusque, abrupt, waspish; impetuous; rampant.

turbulent; disorderly; blustering, raging &c. *v.*; troublous, riotous; tumultu-ary, -ous; obstreperous, uproarious; extravagant, unmitigated; ravening, tameless; frenzied &c. (*insane*) 503; desperate &c. (*rash*) 863; infuriate, towering, furious, outrageous, frantic, hysteric, in hysterics.

fiery, flaming, scorching, hot, red-hot, ebullient.

savage, fierce, ferocious, fierce as a tiger.

excited &c. *v.*; un-quelled, -quenched, -extinguished, -repressed, -bridled, -ruly; headstrong; un-governable, -appeasable, -mitigable; un-, in-controllable; insup-, irre-pressible.

spasmodic, convulsive, explosive; detonating &c. *v.*; volcanic, meteoric; stormy &c. (*wind*) 349.

Adv. violently &c. *adj.*; amain; by -storm, – force, – main force; with might and main; tooth and nail, *vi et armis*, at the point of the -sword, – bayonet; at one fell swoop; with a high hand, through thick and thin; in desperation, with a vengeance; *à* –, *à toute-outrance*; head-long, -foremost, -first; like a bull at a gate.

pencil, weaken &c. 160; lessen &c. (*decrease*) 36; check; palliate.

tranquillize, assuage, appease, dulcify, swage, lull, soothe, compose, still, calm, cool, quiet, hush, quell, sober, pacify, tame, damp, lay, allay, rebate, slacken, smooth, alleviate, rock to sleep, deaden, smother; throw -cold water on, – a wet blanket over; slake; curb &c. (*restrain*) 751; tame &c. (*subjugate*) 749; smooth over; pour oil on the -waves, – troubled waters; pour balm into, *mettre de l'eau dans son vin.*

go out like a lamb, 'roar you as gently as any sucking dove.'

Adj. moderate; lenient &c. 740; gentle, mild; cool, sober, temperate, reasonable, measured; tempered &c. *v.*; calm, unruffled, quiet, tranquil, still; slow, smooth, untroubled; tame; peaceful, -able; pacific, halcyon.

un-exciting, -irritating; soft, bland, oily, demulcent, lenitive, anodyne; hypnotic &c. 683; sedative; assuaging.

mild as mother's milk; milk and water; gentle as a lamb.

Adv. moderately &c. *adj.*; gingerly; *piano*; under easy sail, at half speed; within -bounds, – compass; in reason.

Phr. *est modus in rebus.*

4°. INDIRECT POWER

175. Influence.—N. influence; importance &c. 642; weight, pressure, preponderance, prevalence, sway, pull; predomi-nance, -nancy; ascendency; control, dominance, reign; authority

175a. Absence of Influence.—N. impotence &c. 158; inertness &c. 172; irrelevancy &c. 10.

V. have no -influence &c. 175.

Adj. uninfluential; unconduc-ing,

&c. 737; capability &c. (*power*) 157; interest; spell, magic, magnetism.

footing; purchase &c. (*support*) 215; play, leverage, vantage ground.

tower of strength, host in himself; protection, patronage, auspices.

V. have -influence &c. *n.*; be -influential &c. *adj.*; carry weight, actuate, sway, bias, weigh, tell; have a hold upon, magnetize, bear upon, gain a footing, work upon; take -root, – hold; strike root in.

run through, pervade; prevail, dominate, predominate, subject; out-, over-weigh; over-ride, -bear, – come; gain head; rage; be -rife &c. *adj.*; spread like wildfire; have –, get –, gain- -the upper hand, – full play.

be -recognized, – listened to; make one's voice heard, gain a hearing; play a -part, – leading part- in; lead, control, rule, master; get the mastery over; make one's influence felt, cut ice with; take the lead, pull the strings; turn –, throw one's weight into- the scale; set the fashion, lead the dance.

Adj. influential; important &c. 642; weighty; prevailing &c. *v.*; prevalent, rife, rampant, dominant, regnant, predominant, in the ascendant, hegemonical; authoritative, recognized, telling, with authority.

Adv. with telling effect.

-ive, -ting to; powerless &c. 158; irrelevant &c. 10.

------

176. Tendency.—N. tendency; apt-ness, -itude; proneness, proclivity, bent, turn, tone, bias, set, warp, leaning to, predisposition, inclination, conatus, propensity, susceptibility; liability &c. 177; quality, nature, temperament; characteristic, idio-crasy, -syncrasy; cast, vein, grain; humour, mood; drift &c. (*direction*) 278; con-duciveness, -ducement; applicability &c. (*utility*) 644; subservience &c. (*instrumentality*) 631.

V. tend, contribute, conduce, lead, dispose, incline, verge, bend to, warp, turn, trend, affect, carry, redound to, bid fair to, gravitate towards; promote &c. (*aid*) 707.

Adj. tending &c. *v.*; conducive, working towards, in a fair way to, calculated to; liable &c. 177; subservient &c. (*instrumental*) 631; useful &c. 644; subsidiary &c. (*helping*) 707.

Adv. for, whither.

177. Liability.—N. lia-bility, -bleness; possibility, contingency; suscepti-vity, -bility.

V. be -liable &c. *adj.*; incur, lay oneself open to; run the –, stand a- chance; lie under, expose oneself to, open a door to.

Adj. liable, subject; in danger &c. 665; open –, exposed –, obnoxious- to; answerable, responsible, accountable, amenable; unexempt from; apt to; dependent on; incident to.

contingent, incidental, possible, on the cards, within range of, at the mercy of.

5°. COMBINATIONS OF CAUSES

178. Concurrence.—N. concurrence, co-operation, coagency; coincidence, consilience; union; agreement &c. 23; consent &c. (*assent*) 488; alliance; concert &c. 709; partnership &c. 712; collaboration, conformity.

V. con-cur, -duce, -spire, -tribute;

179. Counteraction.—N. counteraction, opposition; contrariety &c. 14; antagonism, polarity; clashing &c. *v.*; collision, interference, resistance, renitency, friction; reaction; retroaction; repercussion &c. (*recoil*) 277; counterblast; neutralization &c. (*compensa-*

agree, unite, harmonize; hang –, pull-together &c. (*co-operate*) 709; help to &c. (*aid*) 707.

keep pace with, run parallel to; go –, go along –, go hand in hand- with.

Adj. concurring &c. *v.*; concurrent, conformable, joint, co-operative, concordant, coincident, concomitant, harmonious; in alliance with, banded together, of one mind, at one with; parallel.

Adv. with one consent.

tion) 30; *vis inertiæ*; check &c. (*hindrance*) 706.

voluntary -opposition &c. 708, – resistance &c. 719; repression &c. (*restraint*) 751.

V. counteract; run counter, clash, cross; interfere –, conflict- with; jostle; go –, run –, beat –, militate- against; stultify; antagonize, frustrate, oppose &c. 708; withstand &c. (*resist*) 719; hinder &c. 706; repress &c. (*restrain*) 751; react &c. (*recoil*) 277.

undo, neutralize, cancel; counterpoise &c. (*compensate*) 30; overpoise.

Adj. counteracting &c. *v.*; antagonistic, conflicting, retroactive, renitent, reactionary; contrary &c. 14.

Adv. although &c. 30; in spite of &c. 708; *malgré*; against.

CLASS II

Words Relating to SPACE

Section I. SPACE IN GENERAL

1°. Abstract Space

180. [Indefinite space.] **Space.—N.** space, extension, extent, superficial extent, expanse, stretch; capacity, room, accommodation, scope, range, latitude, field, way, expansion, compass, sweep, play, swing, spread.

spare –, elbow –, house- room; stowage, roomage, margin; opening, sphere, arena; lee-, sea-, head-way.

open –, free- space; wide open spaces; void &c. (*absence*) 187; waste; wild-, wilder-ness; up-, bottom-, moor -land; *campagna, veld*, prairie, steppe.

abyss &c. (*interval*) 198; unlimited space; infinity &c. 105; world, wide world; ubiquity &c. (*presence*) 186; length and breadth of the land.

proportions, acreage; acres, – roods and perches; square -inches, – yards &c.

Adj. spacious, roomy, extensive, expansive, capacious, ample; wide-spread, vast, world-wide, uncircumscribed; boundless &c. (*infinite*) 105; shore-, track-, path-less; large &c. 192.

Adv. extensively &c. *adj.*; wherever; everywhere; far and -near, – wide; right and left, all over, all the world over; throughout the -world, – length and breadth of the land; under the sun, in every quarter; in all -quarters, – lands; here, there and everywhere; from -pole to pole, – China to Peru, – Indus to the pole, – Dan to Beersheba, – end to end; on the face of the earth, in the wide world, from all points of the compass; to the -four winds, – uttermost parts of the earth.

180a. Inextension.—N. in-, non-extension; point; atom &c. (*smallness*) 32; pinprick; limitation &c. 229.

181. [Definite space.] **Region.—N.** region, sphere, sphere of influence, corridor, ground, soil, area, realm, hemisphere, quarter, district, beat, orb, circuit, circle; pale &c. (*limit*) 233; com-, de-partment; domain, tract, territory, terrain, country, canton, county, shire, province, *arrondissement*, diocese, parish, township, borough, constituency, *commune*, ward, wapentake, hundred, riding, lathe, garth, soke, tithing, bailiwick; empire, kingdom, principality, duchy, grand –, arch- duchy, palatinate; republic, commonwealth, dominion, colony, state, island.

arena, precincts, *enceinte*, walk, march; patch, plot, enclosure, &c. 232; close, *enclave*, field, court; street &c. (*abode*) 189.

clime, climate, zone, meridian, latitude.

Adj. territorial, local, parochial, provincial, insular.

182. [Limited space.] **Place.—N.** place, lieu, spot, point, dot; niche, nook, &c. (*corner*) 244; hole; pigeon-hole &c. (*receptacle*) 191; compartment; premises, precinct, station, confine; area, court, yard, court-yard, quadrangle, square, compound; abode &c. 189; locality &c. (*situation*) 183.

ins and outs; every hole and corner.

Adv. somewhere, in some place, wherever it may be, here and there, in various places, *passim*.

2°. RELATIVE SPACE

183. Situation.—N. situation, position, locality, *locale*, *status*, latitude and longitude; footing, standing, standpoint, post; stage; aspect, attitude, posture, *pose*.

place, site, base, station, seat, *venue*, whereabouts, environment, neighbourhood; bearings &c. (*direction*) 278; spot &c. (*limited space*) 182.

top-, ge-, chor-ography; map &c. 554.

V. be -situated, – situate; lie; have its seat in.

Adj. situ-ate, -ated; local, topical, topographical &c. *n.*

Adv. *in -situ, – loco*; here and there, *passim*; here-, there-, whereabouts; in place, here, there.

in –, amidst- such and such- -surroundings, – *environs*, – *entourage*.

---

184. Location.—N. loca-tion, -liza-tion; lodgment; de-, re-position; stow-, pack-age; collocation; packing, lading; establishment, settlement, installation; fixation; insertion &c. 300.

anchorage, roadstead, mooring, mooring mast, encampment, camp, bivouac.

plantation, colony, settlement, cantonment, encampment, reservation; colonization, domestication, situation; habitation &c. (*abode*) 189; cohabitation; 'a local habitation and a name'; indenization, naturalization.

V. place, situate, locate, localize, make a place for, put, lay, set, seat, station, lodge, quarter, post, install; store, house, stow; establish, fix, pin, root; graft; plant &c. (*insert*) 300; shelve, pitch, camp, lay down, deposit, reposit; cradle; moor, tether, picket; pack, tuck in; embed; vest, invest in.

185. Displacement.—N. displacement, elocation, transposition.

ejectment &c. 297; exile &c. (*banishment*) 893; removal &c. (*transference*) 270; unshipment.

misplacement, dislocation &c. 61; fish out of water.

V. dis-place, -plant, -lodge, -nest, -establish; misplace, unseat, disturb; exile &c. (*seclude*) 893, ablegate, set aside, remove; take –, cart- away; take –, draft- off; lade &c. 184, unship.

unload, empty &c. (*eject*) 297; transfer &c. 270; dispel.

vacate; depart &c. 293.

Adj. displaced &c. *v.*; un-placed, -housed, -harboured, -established, -settled; house-, home-less; out of -place, – a situation.

misplaced, out of its element.

---

billet on, quarter upon, saddle with; load, lade, freight; pocket, put up, bag.

inhabit &c. (*be present*) 186; domesticate, colonize, populate, people; take –, strike- root; anchor; cast –, come to an- anchor; sit –, settle-down; settle; take up one's -abode, – quarters; plant –, establish –, locate- oneself; squat, perch, hive, *se nicher*, bivouac, burrow, get a footing; encamp, pitch one's tent; put up -at, – one's horses at; keep house.

indenizen, naturalize, adopt.

put back, replace &c. (*restore*) 660.

Adj. placed &c. *v.*; situate, posited, ensconced, embedded, embosomed, rooted; domesticated; vested in, unremoved.

moored &c. *v.*; at anchor.

3°. EXISTENCE IN SPACE

186. Presence.—N. presence; occupancy, -ation; attendance; whereness.

permeation, pervasion; diffusion &c. (*dispersion*) 73.

187. [Nullibiety.*] Absence. — N. absence; inexistence &c. 2; non-residence, absenteeism; non-attendance. *alibi.*

* Bishop Wilkins.

ubi-ety, -quity, -quitariness; omni-presence.

bystander &c. (*spectator*) 444.

V. exist in space, be -present &c. *adj.*; assist at; make one -of, – at; look on, attend, remain; find –, present- one-self; show one's face; fall in the way of, occur in a place; lie, stand; occupy.

people; inhabit, dwell, reside, stay, sojourn, live, room, abide, bunk, lodge, nestle, roost, perch; take up one's abode &c. (*be located*) 184; tenant, occupy.

resort to, frequent, haunt; revisit.

fill, pervade, permeate; be -diffused, – disseminated- through; over-spread, -run; run through; meet one at every turn.

Adj. present; occupying, inhabiting &c. *v.*; moored &c. 184; residential, resi-ant, -dent, -dentiary; domiciled.

ubiquit-ous, -ary; omnipresent.

peopled, populous, full of people, in-habited.

Adv. here, there, where, everywhere, aboard, on board, at home, afield; on the spot; here, there and everywhere &c. (*space*) 180; in presence of, before; under the -eyes, – nose- of; in the face of; *in propriâ personâ*.

emptiness &c. *adj.*; void, *vacuum*; vac-uity, -ancy; *tabula rasa*; exemp-tion; *hiatus* &c. (*interval*) 198; no man's land.

truant, absentee.

nobody; nobody -present, – on earth; no one; not a soul; *âme qui vive*.

V. be -absent &c. *adj.*; keep -away, – out of the way; play truant, absent oneself, stay away.

withdraw, make oneself scarce, va-cate; go away, slip out, slip away, retreat &c. 293.

Adj. absent, not present, away, non-resident, gone, from home; missing; lost; wanted, wanting; omitted; no-where to be found; inexistent &c. 2.

empty, void; blank, vac-ant, -uous; untenanted, -occupied, -inhabited; ten-antless; desert, -ed; devoid; un-, unin-habitable.

exempt from, not having.

Adv. without, *minus*, nowhere; else-where; neither here nor there; in de-fault of; *sans*; behind one's back.

Phr. the bird has flown, *non est inventus*.

---

188. Inhabitant. — N. inhabitant; habitant, resident, -iary; dweller, in-dweller; occup-ier, -ant, farmer, planter; householder, lodger, boarder, paying guest; inmate, tenant, renter, incum-bent, sojourner, *locum tenens*, com-morant; settler, squatter, backwoods-man, colonist; islander; denizen, citizen; burgher, oppidan, cockney, cit, towns-man, burgess; villager; cot-tager, -tier, -ter; compatriot.

native, indigene, aboriginal, aborig-ines, autochthones; Briton, English-man, John Bull; new comer &c. (*stranger*) 57.

garrison, crew; population; people &c. (*mankind*) 372; colony, settlement; household.

V. inhabit &c. (*be present*) 186; in-denizen &c. (*locate oneself*) 184.

Adj. indigenous; enchorial; national, nat-ive, -al; autochthonous; British, English; colonial; domestic; domicil-

189. [Place of habitation, or resort.] **Abode.—N.** abode, dwelling, lodging, -s; diggings, domicile, residence, ad-dress, habitation, where one's lot is cast, local habitation, berth, seat, lap, sojourn, housing, quarters, headquar-ters, resiance, tabernacle, throne, ark.

home, fatherland, mother country, country &c. 181; home-stead, -stall; fireside, chimney corner; hearth, – stone; household gods, *lares et penates*, roof, household, housing, *dulce domum*, paternal domicile; native -soil, – land, blighty.

nest, *nidus*, snuggery; arbour, bower &c. 191; lair, den, cave, hole, hiding-place, cache, cell, *sanctum sanctorum*, aerie, eyry, rookery, hive; *habitat*, haunt, covert, resort, retreat, perch; roost; nidification.

bivouac, camp, encampment, can-tonment, castrametation; barrack, casemate, casern.

iated, -ed; naturalized, vernacular, domesticated; domiciliary. in the occupation of; garrisoned –, occupied- by.

_____

tent &c. (*covering*) 223; building &c. (*construction*) 161; chamber &c. (*receptacle*) 191.

tenement, messuage, farm, farmhouse, grange, *hacienda*.

cot, cabin, log cabin, shack, hut, *châlet*, croft, shed, booth, stall, hovel, bothy, shanty, igloo, tepee, wigwam; pen &c. (*inclosure*) 232; barn, bawn; kennel, sty, dog-hole, cote, coop, hutch, byre; cowhouse, -shed; stable, dove-cote, shippen.

house, mansion, place, villa, cottage, box, lodge, hermitage, *rus in urbe*, folly, rotunda, tower, *château*, castle, pavilion, hotel, court, manor-house, capital messuage, hall, palace, alcazar; country seat; kiosk, bungalow; temple &c. 1000; home of rest, alms-, poor-, work-house, asylum; boarding-, lodging-house; flat, maisonette, duplex, penthouse, suite of rooms, apartments, rooms, room, building &c. 161; Mansion House, town hall, Capitol.

assembly-room, auditorium, coliseum, meeting-house, pump-room, spa, health resort, watering-place; club; theatre &c. 840; drill hall, gymnasium, church &c. 1000; Houses of Parliament &c. 696; school &c. 542; inn; hostel, -ry; hotel, tavern, caravansary, khan, hospice; public-, ale-, pot-, mug-house; gin-palace, gin-mill; coffee-, eating-house; canteen, *restaurant*, *rôtisserie*, cafeteria, grill-room, *buffet*, *café*, *estaminet*, *posada*, *bodega*; bar; saloon, speakeasy, shebeen.

hamlet, village, thorp, dorp, ham, kraal; borough, burgh, town, county-seat, – town, city, capital, metropolis; suburb, quarter. parish &c. 181; ghetto; province, country.

street, place, terrace, parade, esplanade, promenade, pier, embankment, road, villas, row, walk, lane, alley, court, quadrangle, quad, wynd, close, yard, passage, rents, mansions, buildings, mews.

square, polygon, circus, crescent, mall, *piazza*, arcade, colonnade, peristyle, cloister; gardens, grove, residences; block of buildings, market-place, *place*.

anchorage, roadstead, roads; dock, basin, wharf, quay, port. harbour; dry-, graving-, floating-dock.

garden, park, pleasure-ground, pleasance, demesne.

V. take up one's abode &c. (*locate oneself*) 184; inhabit &c. (*be present*) 186.

Adj. urban, oppidan, metropolitan; suburban; provincial, rural, rustic; countrified; regional, parochial, domestic; cosmopolitan, palatial.

190. [Things contained.] **Contents.—N.** contents; cargo, lading, freight, shipment, load, bale, burden; cart-, ship-load; cup –, basket –, &c. (*receptacle*) 191- of; inside &c. 221; stuffing, ullage.

V. load, lade, ship, charge, fill, stuff.

191. Receptacle.—N. receptacle, container; inclosure &c. 232; recipient, receiver, reservatory.

compartment; cell, -ule; follicle; hole, corner, niche, recess, nook; crypt, stall, pigeon-hole, cove, oriel; cave &c. (*concavity*) 252.

capsule, vesicle, cyst, pod, calyx, *cancelli*, utricle, bladder, udder.

stomach, paunch, *venter*, abdomen, ventricle, crop, craw, ingluvies, maw, gizzard, bread-basket, belly, little Mary; mouth.

pocket, pouch, fob, sheath, scabbard, socket, bag, vanity bag, compact, sac, sack, saccule, despatch –, attaché-, tachy- case, wallet, scrip, card-, note- case, billfold, poke, kit, knap-, haver-, ruck-sack, sachel, satchel, reticule, budget, net; ditty-, -box, -bag, kitbag; portfolio; saddlebags, holster; quiver &c. (*magazine*) 636.

chest, box, coffer, caddy, case, casket, pyx, pix, *caisson*, desk, *bureau*, reliquary, shrine; trunk, portmanteau, band-box, *valise*, suitcase, hand-, traveling-, overnight-, Gladstone-, carpet-bag, brief case; boot, imperial; *vache*; cage, manger, rack.

vessel, vase, bushel, barrel; canister, jar; pottle, basket, punnet, pannier, buck-basket, hopper, maund, creel, cran, crate, cradle, bassinet, wisket, whisket, *jardinière, corbeille*, hamper, wastepaper basket, dosser, dorser, tray, hod, scuttle, utensil, spittoon, cuspidor.

[For liquids] cistern &c. (*store*) 636; vat, caldron, barrel, cask, puncheon, keg, rundlet, tun, butt, firkin, hogshead, kilderkin, carboy, amphora, ampulla, bottle, jar, leather bottle, decanter, ewer, cruse, carafe, crock, kit, canteen, flagon; demijohn; flask, -et; stoup, noggin, vial, phial, *ampoule*, cruet, caster; gourd; urn, *épergne*, salver, *patella, tazza, patera*; pig-, big-gin; tea-, coffee-pot, percolator, *samovar*; tyg, nipperkin, pocket-pistol; tub, bucket, pail, skeel, pot, tankard, jug, pitcher, toby, mug, pipkin; gal-, gall-ipot, pannikin; matrass, receiver, retort, alembic, bolthead, can, kettle; bowl, basin, jorum, punch-bowl, cup, goblet, chalice, tumbler, glass, wineglass, rummer, beaker, tass, horn, saucepan, skillet, posnet, tureen, terrine, *casserole*, sauce-, gravy-boat.

plate, platter, paten, dish, vegetable –, *entrée-* dish, trencher, calabash, porringer, potager, saucer, pan, crucible.

shovel, trowel, spoon; table-, dessert-, tea-, egg-, salt-spoon; spatula, ladle; dipper; baler; watch-glass, thimble.

closet, commode, cupboard, cellaret, *chiffonnière*, locker, bin, bunker, *buffet*, press, safe, sideboard, drawer, chest of drawers, till, *scrutoire, secrétaire, éscritoire*, davenport, book-case, cabinet, canterbury; corner cupboard, wardrobe.

chamber, apartment, room, cabin; office, court, hall, atrium; suite of rooms, flat, story; saloon, *salon*, parlour; presence-chamber; sitting-, drawing-, reception-, state-, living-, work-room; gallery, cabinet, closet, cubicle; pew, box; *boudoir; adytum, sanctum*; bed-room, dormitory, dressing-room; refectory, dining-room, *salle-à-manger*; nursery, school-room; library, study; studio; billiard-, bath-, smoking-room; den, canteen, mess, officers' mess; gun-, ward-, mess-room.

attic, loft, garret, cockloft, clerestory; cellar, vault, hold, cockpit; *entresol*; mezzanine floor; ground-floor, *rez-de-chaussée*; basement, kitchen, cook-house, galley, pantry, scullery, offices; store-room &c. (*depository*) 636; lumber-room; dust-hole, -bin; dairy, laundry, coach-house; *garage; hangar*; out-, pent-house; lean-to.

portico, porch, piazza, verandah, lobby, court, hall, vestibule, corridor, passage; ante-room, -chamber; lounge; *foyer, loggia*.

conservatory, green-house, glass-house, vinery, bower, arbour, summer-house, alcove, grotto, hermitage, pergola.

lodging &c. (*abode*) 189; bed &c. (*support*) 215; carriage &c. (*vehicle*) 272.

Adj. capsular; saccu-lar, -lated; recipient; ventricular, cystic, vascular, vesicular, cellular, camerated, locular, multilocular, poly-gastric; marsupial; siliqu-ose, -ous.

Section II. DIMENSIONS

1°. General Dimensions

192. Size.—N. size, magnitude, dimension, bulk, volume; largeness &c. *adj.*; greatness &c. (*of quantity*) 31; expanse &c. (*space*) 180; amplitude, mass; proportions.

capacity; ton-, tun-nage; calibre, scantling.

turgidity &c. (*expansion*) 194; corpulence, obesity; plumpness, &c. *adj.*; *embonpoint*, corporation, flesh and blood, lustihood.

hugeness &c. *adj.*; enormity, immensity, monstrosity.

giant, Brobdingnagian, Antæus, Goliath, Gog and Magog, Gargantua, monster, mammoth, Cyclops; whale, porpoise, behemoth, leviathan, elephant, hippopotamus; colossus; tun, lump, bulk, block, loaf, mass, clod, nugget, bushel, thumper, whopper, spanker, strapper; Triton among the minnows.

mountain, mound; heap &c. (*assemblage*) 72.

largest portion &c. 50; full-, life-size.

V. be- large &c. *adj.*; become -large &c. (*expand*) 194.

Adj. large, big; great &c. (*in quantity*) 31; considerable, bulky, voluminous, ample, massive, massy; capacious, comprehensive; spacious &c. 180; mighty, towering, fine, magnificent.

corpulent, stout, fat, plump, squab, full, lusty, strapping, bouncing; portly, burly, well-fed, full-grown; stalwart, brawny, fleshy; goodly; in good -case, – condition; in condition; chopping, jolly; chub-, chubby-faced.

lubberly, hulky, unwieldy, lumpish, gaunt, spanking, whacking, whopping, thumping, thundering, hulking; overgrown; puffy &c. (*swollen*) 194.

huge, immense, enormous, mighty; vast, -y; amplitudinous, stupendous; monst-er, -rous; gigantic, elephantine;

193. Littleness.—N. littleness &c. *adj.*; smallness &c. (*of quantity*) 32; exiguity, inextension; parvi-tude, -ty; duodecimo; Elzevir edition, epitome, microcosm; rudiment; vanishing point; thinness &c. 203.

dwarf, pigmy, atomy, Liliputian, midget, chit, pigwidgeon, urchin, elf; doll, puppet; Tom Thumb, Hop-o'-my thumb, Humpty-dumpty; man-, mannikin; *homunculus*, dapperling, fingerling, dandiprat, cock-sparrow, scalawag.

animalcule, monad, mite, insect, emmet, fly, midge, gnat, shrimp, minnow, worm, maggot, entozoon; *bacillus*, microbe, micro-organism, *bacteria*; *infusoria*; microbe; grub; tit, tomtit, runt, mouse, small fry; millet-, mustard-seed; barley-corn; pebble, grain of sand; mole-hill, button, bubble.

point; atom &c. (*small quantity*) 32; fragment &c. (*small part*) 51; powder &c. 330; point of a pin, mathematical point; *minutiæ* &c. (*unimportance*) 643.

micro-graphy, -meter, -scope; vernier; scale.

V. be -little &c. *adj.*; lie in a nutshell; become small &c. (*decrease*) 36, (*contract*) 195.

Adj. little; small &c. (*in quantity*) 32; minute, diminutive, microscopic; inconsiderable &c. (*unimportant*) 643; exiguous, puny, tiny, wee, petty, minikin, miniature, pigmy, elfin; under sized; dwarf, -ed, -ish; spare, stunted, limited; cramp, -ed; pollard, Liliputian, dapper, pocket; port-ative, -able; duodecimo; dumpy, squat; compact, handy; short &c. 201.

impalpable, intangible, evanescent, imperceptible, invisible, inappreciable, infinitesimal, homœopathic; atomic, corpuscular, molecular; rudiment-ary, -al; embryonic.

weazen, scant, scraggy, scrubby;

giant, -like; colossal, Cyclopean, Brob-dingnagian, Gargantuan, Titanic; in-finite &c. 105.

large as life; plump as a -dumpling, – partridge; fat as -a pig, – a quail, – butter, – brawn, – bacon.

thin &c. (*narrow*) 203; granular &c. (*powdery*) 330; shrunk &c. 195.

Adv. in a -small compass, – nutshell; on a small scale.

---

194. Expansion. — N. expansion; increase &c. 35 -of size; enlargement, extension, augmentation; ampli-fica-tion, -ation; aggrandizement, spread, increment, growth, development, pullu-lation, swell, dilation, dilatation, rare-faction; turg-escence, -idness, -idity; obesity &c. (*size*) 192; dropsy, tume-faction, intumescence, swelling, tu-mour, *diastole*, distension; puff-ing, -iness; inflation; pandiculation.

dilatability, expansibility.

germination, growth, upgrowth; ac-cretion &c. 35.

over-growth, -distension; hyper-trophy, tympany.

bulb &c. (*convexity*) 250; plumper; superiority of size.

V. become -larger &c. (large &c. 192); expand, widen, enlarge, extend, grow, increase, incrassate, swell, gather; fill out; deploy, take open order, dilate, stretch, spread; mantle, wax; grow –, spring- up; bud, bourgeon, shoot, sprout, germinate, put forth, vegetate, pullulate, open, burst forth, flower, olow &c. 734; gain –, gather- flesh; outgrow; spread like wildfire, overrun.

be larger than; surpass &c. (*be supe-rior*) 33.

render -larger &c. (large &c. 192); expand, spread, extend, aggrandize, distend, develop. amplify, spread out, widen, magnify, rarefy, inflate, puff, puff out, blow up, stuff, pad, cram; exaggerate; fatten; bloat, augment.

Adj. expanded &c. *v.*; larger &c. (large &c. 192); swollen; expansive; wide-open, -spread; fan-shaped; fla-belliform; overgrown, exaggerated, bloated, fat, turgid, tumid, hyper-trophied, dropsical; pot-, swag-bellied; œdematous, obese, puffy, pursy, blowzy, distended; patulous; bulbous &c. (*convex*) 250; full-blown, -grown, -formed; big &c. 192.

195. Contraction.—N. contraction, reduction, diminution; decrease &c. 36- of size; defalcation, decrement; lessen-ing, shrinkage; collapse, emaciation, attenuation, tabefaction, consumption, marasmus, atrophy; systole, neck, hour-glass.

condensation, compression, con-straint, compactness; compendium &c. 596; squeezing &c. *v.*; strangulation; corrugation; astringency, constrin-gency; astringents, sclerotics; contrac-tility, compressibility; coarctation.

inferiority in size.

V. become -small, – smaller; lessen, decrease &c. 36; grow less, dwindle, shrink, contract, narrow, shrivel, col-lapse, wither, lose flesh, wizen, fall away, waste, wane, ebb; decay &c. (*deteriorate*) 659.

be smaller than, fall short of; not come up to &c. (*be inferior*) 34.

render smaller, lessen, diminish, con-tract, draw in, narrow, coarctate; con-strict, constringe; condense, compress, boil down, deflate, exhaust, empty; squeeze, corrugate, crush, crumple up, warp, purse up, pack, stow; pinch, tighten, strangle; cramp; dwarf, be-dwarf; shorten &c. 201; circumscribe &c. 229; restrain &c. 751; fold &c. 258.

pare, reduce, attenuate, rub down, scrape, file, grind, chip, shave, shear.

Adj. contracting &c. *v.*; astringent; shrunk, contracted &c. *v.*; strangulated, tabid, wizened, stunted; tabescent; marasmic; waning &c. *v.*; neap; com-pact.

unexpanded &c. (expand &c. 194); inswept; contractile; compressible; smaller &c. (small &c. 193).

---

196. Distance.—N. distance; space &c. 180; remoteness, farness; far- cry

197. Nearness.—N. nearness &c. *adj.*; proximity, propinquity; vicinity,

to; longinquity, elongation; offing, background; removedness; parallax; reach, span, stride; drift.

out-post, -skirt; horizon, sky-line; aphelion; foreign parts, *ultima Thule, ne plus ultra,* antipodes; long range, giant's stride.

dispersion &c. 73.

V. be -distant &c. *adj.*; extend –, stretch –, reach –, spread –, go –, get –, stretch away- to; range, outrange, outreach.

remain at a distance; keep –, stand- -away, – off, – aloof, – clear of.

Adj. distant; far -off, – away; remote, telescopic, distal, wide of; stretching to &c. *v.*; yon, -der; ulterior; trans-marine, -pontine, -atlantic, -alpine; tramon- tane; ultra-montane, -mundane; hyper- borean, antipodean; inaccessible, out of the way; unapproach-ed, -able; incontiguous.

Adv. far -off, – away; afar, -off; off; away; a -long, – great, – good- way off; wide away, aloof; wide –, clear- of; out of -the way, – reach; abroad, yonder, farther, further, beyond; *outre mer,* over the border, far and wide, over the hills and far away; from pole to pole &c. (*over great space*) 180; to the -uttermost parts, – ends- of the earth; out of -hearing, – range, nobody knows where, *à perte de vue,* out of the sphere of, wide of the mark; a far cry to.

apart, asunder; wide -apart, – asun- der; *longo intervallo*; at arm's length.

-age; neighbourhood, adjacency; con- tiguity &c. 199.

short -distance, – step, – cut; ear- shot, close quarters, stone's throw; bow –, gun –, pistol- shot; hair's breadth, span; close-up.

purlieus, neighbourhood, vicinage, *environs, alentours,* suburbs, confines, *banlieue,* borderland; whereabouts.

bystander; neighbour, borderer.

approach &c. 286; convergence &c. 290; perihelion.

V. be -near &c. *adj.*; adjoin, hang about, trench on; border –, verge upon; stand by, approximate, tread on the heels of, cling to, clasp, hug; cuddle huddle; hang upon the skirts of, hov over; burn; abut.

bring –, draw- -near &c. 286; con- verge &c. 290; crowd &c. 72; place -side by side &c. *adv.*

Adj. near, nigh; close –, near- at hand; close, neighbouring, propinquent, bordering upon; adjacent, adjoining, limitrophe; proxim-ate, -al; at hand, handy; near the mark, near run; home, intimate.

Adv. near, nigh; hard –, fast- by; close -to, – upon, – up; at the point of; next door to; within -reach, – call, – hearing, – earshot, – range; within an ace of; but a step, not far from, at no great distance; on the -verge, – brink, – skirts- of; in the -environs &c. *n.*; at one's -door, – feet, – elbow, – finger's end, – side; on the tip of one's tongue; under one's nose; within a -stone's throw &c. *n.*; in -sight, – presence- of; at close quarters; cheek by -jole, – jowl; beside, alongside, side by side, *tête-à-*

tête; in juxtaposition &c. (*touching*) 199; yard-arm to yard-arm; at the heels of; on the confines of, at the threshold, bordering upon, verging to; in the way.

about; here-, there-abouts; roughly, in round numbers; approxim- -ately, -atively; as good as, well nigh.

-----

198. Interval.—N. interval, inter- space; separation &c. 44; break, gap, opening; hole &c. 260; chasm, *hiatus,* cæsura; inter-ruption, -regnum; in- terstice, *lacuna,* cleft, mesh, crevice, chink, rime, creek, cranny, crack, chap, slit, slot, fissure, scissure, rift, flaw, breach, fracture, rent, gash, cut, leak, dike, ha-ha.

199. Contiguity.—N. contiguity, contact, proximity, apposition, juxta- position, touching &c. *v.*; abutment, osculation; meeting, appulse, appulsion, *rencontre,* rencounter, syzygy, coinci- dence, conjunction, coexistence; adhe- sion &c. 46.

border-land; frontier &c. (*limit*) 233; tangent.

gorge, defile, ravine, cañon, *crevasse*, abyss, abysm; gulf; inlet, frith, strait, gully, gulch, nullah; pass; notch; furrow &c. 259; yawning gulf; *hiatus -maxime, – valde- deflendus*; parenthesis &c. (*interjacence*) 228; void &c. (*absence*) 187; incompleteness &c. 530.

V. gape &c. (*open*) 260.

Adj. with an interval, far between.

Adv. at intervals &c. (*discontinuously*) 70; *longo intervallo*.

V. be -contiguous &c. *adj.*; join, adjoin, abut on, march with, border; tick, graze, touch, meet, osculate, kiss, come in contact, coincide; coexist; adhere &c. 46.

Adj. contiguous; touching &c. *v.*; in -contact &c. *n.*; conterminous, end to end, osculatory; pertingent; tangential.

hand to hand; close to &c. (*near*) 197; with no -interval &c. 198.

2°. Linear Dimensions

200. Length.—N. length, longitude, span, extent, mileage.

line, bar, rule, stripe, streak, spoke, radius.

lengthening &c. *v.*; pro-longation, -duction, -traction; ten-sion, -sure; extension.

[Measures of length] line, nail, inch, hand, palm, foot, cubit, yard, ell, fathom, rod, pole, perch, furlong, mile, league; chain, metre, kilo-, centi-, milli- &c. -metre.

pedometer, perambulator, odometer, odograph, speedometer, cyclometer, log, telemeter, range finder; scale &c. (*measurement*) 466.

V. be -long &c. *adj.*; stretch out, sprawl; extend –, reach –, stretch- to; make a long arm, 'drag its slow length along.'

render -long &c. *adj.*; lengthen, extend, elongate; stretch; pro-long, -duce, -tract; let –, pay –, draw –, spin- out; drawl.

enfilade, look along, view in perspective.

Adj. long, -some; lengthy, lank, wiredrawn, outstretched; lengthened &c. *v.*; sesquipedalian &c. (*words*) 577; interminable, no end of.

line-ar, -al; longitudinal, oblong.

as long as -my arm, – to-day and to-morrow; unshortened &c. (shorten &c. 201).

Adv. lengthwise, at length, longitudinally, endlong, along; *tandem*; in a line &c. (*continuously*) 69; in perspective.

from -end to end, – stem to stern, – head to foot, – the crown of the head to the sole of the foot, – top to toe, – head to heels; fore and aft.

201. Shortness.—N. shortness &c. *adj.*; brevity; littleness &c. 193; a span.

shortening &c. *v.*; abbrevia-tion, -ture; abridgment, concision, retrenchment, curtailment, decurtation; reduction &c. (*contraction*) 195; epitome &c. (*compendium*) 596.

abridger, abstractor, epitomiser.

elision, ellipsis; conciseness &c. (*in style*) 572.

V. be -short &c. *adj.*; render -short &c. *adj.*; shorten, curtail, abridge, abbreviate, take in, reduce; compress &c. (*contract*) 195; epitomize &c. 596.

retrench, cut short, obtruncate; scrimp, cut, chop up, hack, hew; cut –, pare- down; clip, snip, dock, lop, prune; shear, shave, mow, reap, crop; snub; truncate, pollard, stunt, nip, nip in the bud, check the growth of; [in drawing] foreshorten.

Adj. short, brief, curt; compendious, compact; stubby, scrimp; shorn, stubbed; stumpy, thickset, podgy, stocky, pug; squab, -by; squat, dumpy; little &c. 193; curtailed of its fair proportions; short by; oblate; concise &c. 572; summary.

Adv. shortly &c. *adj.*; in short &c. (*concisely*) 572.

----

202. Breadth. Thickness.—N.
breadth, width, latitude, amplitude;
diameter, bore, calibre, radius; superficial extent &c. (*space*) 180.

thickness, crassitude; corpulence &c.
(*size*) 192; dilatation &c. (*expansion*)
194.

V. be -broad &c. *adj.*; become –,
render- -broad &c. *adj.*; expand &c.
194; thicken, widen.

Adj. broad, wide, ample, extended;
discous; fan-like; out-spread, -stretched;
wide as a church-door.

thick, dumpy, squab, squat, thickset, tubby; thick as a rope, stubby &c.
201.

203. Narrowness. Thinness. —N.
narrowness &c. *adj.*; closeness, exility;
exiguity &c. (*little*) 193.

line; hair's –, finger's -breadth; strip,
streak, vein.

thinness &c. *adj.*; tenuity; emaciation, macilency, *marcor*.

shaving, slip &c. (*filament*) 205;
threadpaper, skeleton, shadow, scrag,
anatomy, spindle-shanks, barebones,
lantern jaws, mere skin and bone.

middle constriction, stricture, neck,
waist, isthmus, wasp, hour-glass; ridge,
ghaut, pass; ravine &c. 198.

narrowing, coarctation, angustation,
tapering; contraction &c. 195.

V. be -narrow &c. *adj.*; narrow, taper,
contract &c. 195; render -narrow &c.
adj.

Adj. narrow, close; slender, thin, fine; *svelte*; thread-like &c.
(*filament*) 205; finespun, taper, slim, gracile, slight, slight-made;
scant, -y; spare, delicate, incapacious; contracted &c. 195; unexpanded &c. (expand &c. 194); slender as a thread, capillary.

emaciated, lean, meagre, gaunt, macilent; lank, -y; weedy, skinny,
scrawny, scraggy; starv-ed, -eling; attenuated, shrivelled, wizened,
pinched, peaky, skeletal, spindling, spindle- -legged, -shanked;
extenuated, tabid, marcid, bare-bone, raw-boned; herring-gutted;
worn to a shadow, lean as a rake; thin as a -lath, – whipping post,
– wafer; hatchet-faced; lantern-jawed.

204. Layer.—N. layer, stratum,
course, bed, zone, *substratum*, floor,
flag, stage, story, tier, slab, escarpment,
table, tablet, panel, plaque; board,
plank; trencher, platter.

plate; lam-ina, -ella; sheet, flake,
foil, wafer, scale, coat, peel, pellicle,
ply, thickness, membrane, film, leaf,
slice, shive, cut, rasher, shaving, integument &c. (*covering*) 223.

stratification, lamination, scaliness,
nest of boxes, coats of an onion.

V. slice, shave, pare, peel; plate,
coat, veneer; cover &c. 223.

Adj. lamell-ar, -ated, -iform; lamin-
ated, -iferous; micaceous; schist-ose,
-ous; scaly, filmy, membranous, flaky,
squamous; folia-ted, -ceous; strati-
fied, -form; tabular, discoid, spathic.

205. Filament.—N. filament, line·
fibre, fibril; funicle, vein, hair, capilla-
ment, *cilium*, tendril, gossamer; hair-
stroke; harl.

wire, string, thread, packthread,
cotton, sewing-silk, twine, twist, whip-
cord, cord, rope, cable, yarn, hemp,
oakum, jute, wool, worsted.

strip, shred, slip, spill, list, band,
fillet, *fascia*, ribbon, riband, tape, roll,
lath, slat, strake, splinter, shiver,
shaving.

beard &c. (*roughness*) 256; ramification; strand.

Adj. fil-amentous, -aceous, -iform;
fibr-ous, -illous; thread-like, wiry,
stringy, ropy; capill-ary, -iform; funicular, wire-drawn; anguilliform; flagelliform; hairy &c. (*rough*) 256; ligulate.

206. Height.—N. height, altitude,
elevation, ceiling; eminence. pitch;
loftiness &c. *adj.*; sublimity.

tallness &c. *adj.*; stature, procerity;
prominence &c. 250.

207. Lowness.—N. lowness &c. *adj.*;
debasement, depression; prostration
&c. (*horizontal*) 213; depression &c.
(*concave*) 252.

molehill; lowlands; bottomlands;

colossus &c. (*size*) 192; giant, grenadier, giraffe.

mount, -ain; hill, butte, monticle, fell, knap; cape; head-, fore-land; promontory; ridge, hog's back, dune; rising -, vantage- ground; down; moor, -land; Alp; up-, high-lands; heights &c. (*summit*) 210; knoll, hummock, hillock, barrow, mound, mole, *kopje*; steeps, bluff, cliff, craig, tor, peak, pike, clough; escarpment, edge, ledge, brae; dizzy height.

tower, pillar, column, pylon, obelisk, monument, steeple, spire, minaret, *campanile*, belfry, turret, roof, dome, cupola, pagoda, pyramid; sky scraper; Eiffel tower.

pole, pikestaff, maypole, flagstaff; mast, top -, topgallant- mast.

ceiling &c. (*covering*) 223.

high water; high -, flood -, spring- tide.

altimetry &c. (*angle*) 244; altimeter, height-finder, hypsometer, barograph.

V. be -high &c. *adj.*; tower, soar. command; hover; cap, culminate; overhang, hang over, impend, beetle; bestride, ride, mount; perch, surmount; cover &c. 223; overtop &c. (*be superior*) 33; stand on tiptoe.

become -high &c. *adj.*; grow, - higher, - taller; upgrow; rise &c. (*ascend*) 305.

render -high &c. *adj.*; heighten &c. (*elevate*) 307.

Adj. high, elevated, eminent, exalted, lofty, supernal; tall; gigantic &c. (*big*) 192; Patagonian; towering, beetling, soaring, hanging [gardens]; elevated &c. 307; upper; highest &c. (*topmost*) 210; monticolous, perching, hill-dwelling.

up-, moor-land; hilly, mountainous, alpine, sub-alpine, heaven-kissing; cloud-topt, -capt, -touching; aerial.

overhanging &c. *v.*; incumbent, overlying; super-incumbent, -natant, -imposed; prominent &c. 250.

tall as a -maypole, - poplar, - steeple; lanky &c. (*thin*) 203.

Adv. on high, high up, aloft, up, above, aloof, overhead; up -, above- stairs; in the clouds; on -tiptoe, - stilts, - the shoulders of; over head and ears; breast high.

over, upwards; from top to bottom &c. (*completely*) 52.

basement, ground-floor; *rez-de-chaussée* &c. 211; hold; feet, heels.

low water; low -, ebb -, neap -, spring- tide.

V. be -low &c. *adj.*; lie -low, - flat; underlie; crouch, slouch, wallow, grovel; lower &c. (*dépress*) 308.

Adj. low, neap, debased; nether, -most; flat, level with the ground; lying low &c. *v.*; crouched, subjacent, squat, prostrate &c. (*horizontal*) 213.

Adv. under; be-, under-neath; below; down, -wards; adown, at the foot of; under-foot, -ground; down -, below-stairs; at a low ebb; below par.

208. **Depth.**—**N.** depth; deepness &c. *adj.*; profundity, depression &c. (*concavity*) 252.

hollow, pit, shaft, well, crater, abyss; gulf &c. 198; bowels of the earth, bottomless pit, hell.

soundings, depth of water, water, draught, submersion; plummet, sound, probe; sounding -rod, - line, - machine; lead; submarine, diving bell, bathysphere; diver.

V. be -deep &c. *adj.*; render -deep &c. *adj.*; deepen.

plunge &c. 310; sound, heave the lead, take soundings; dig &c. (*excavate*) 252.

209. **Shallowness.**—**N.** shallowness &c. *adj.*; shoals; mere scratch.

Adj. shallow, superficial; skin -ankle -, knee- deep; just enough to wet one's feet; shoal, -y

Adj. deep, -seated; profound, sunk, buried; submerged &c. 310; sub-aqueous, -marine, -terranean, -terrene; underground.

bottom-, sound-, fathom-less; unfathom-ed, -able; abysmal; deep as a well, deep-sea.

knee-, ankle-deep.

Adv. beyond –, out of- one's depth; over head and ears, over one's head.

210. Summit.—N. summit, -y; top, vertex, apex, zenith, pinnacle, acme, acropolis, culmination, meridian, utmost height, *ne plus ultra*, height, pitch, maximum, climax, apogee; culminating –, crowning –, turning- point; turn of the tide, fountain head; water-shed, -parting; sky, pole.

tip, -top; crest, crow's nest, cap, truck, peak, nib; end &c. 67; crown, brow; head, nob, noddle, pate.

high places, heights.

top-, top-gallant mast, sky scraper; quarter –, hurricane- deck.

architrave, frieze, cornice, coping, coping-stone, zoophorus, capital, headpiece, capstone, epistyle, sconce, pediment, entablature; tympanum; ceiling &c. (*covering*) 223.

attic, loft, garret, house-top, upper story, roof.

V. culminate, cap, crown, top; overtop &c. (*be superior to*) 33.

Adj. highest &c. (high &c. 206); top; top-, upper-most; tip-top; culminating &c. *v.*; meridi-an, -onal; capital, head, polar, supreme, supernal, top-gallant.

Adv. a-top, at the top of – the tree, – the heap.

211. Base.—N. base, -ment; plinth, dado, wainscot, baseboard; foundation &c. (*support*) 215; substructure, *substratum*, sump, ground, earth, pavement, floor, paving, flag, carpet, ground-floor, deck; footing, groundwork, basis; hold, bilge, orlop deck.

bottom, nadir, foot, sole, toe, hoof, keel, kelson, root.

Adj. bottom; under-, nether-most; fundamental; founded –, based –, grounded –, built- on.

212. Verticality. — N. verticality; erectness &c. *adj.*; perpendicularity; right angle, normal; azimuth circle.

wall, palisade, precipice, cliff, steep, bluff.

elevation, erection; square, plumb-line, plummet.

V. be -vertical &c. *adj.*; stand -up, – on end, – erect, – upright; stick –, cock-up.

render -vertical &c. *adj.*; set –, stick –, raise –, cock- up; erect, rear, raise, pitch, raise on its legs.

Adj. vertical, upright, erect, perpendicular, normal, plumb, straight, bolt upright; rampant; straight –, standing-up &c. *v.*; rectangular, orthogonal.

Adv. vertically &c. *adj.*; up, on end; up –, right- on end; *à plomb*, endwise; on one's legs; at right angles.

213. Horizontality.—N. horizontal-ity; flatness; level, plane; stratum &c. 204; dead -level, – flat; level plane.

recumbency; lying down &c. *v.*; reclination, decumbence; de-, discumbency; proneness &c. *adj.*; accubation, supination, resupination, prostration; azimuth.

plain, floor, platform, bowling-green; cricket-ground; court; gridiron; base-ball diamond; hockey rink; tennis-, croquet-ground, – lawn; billiard table; terrace, estrade, esplanade, *parterre*, table-land, *plateau*, ledge.

spirit-, level; T-square.

V. be -horizontal &c. *adj.*; lie, recline, couch; lie -down, – flat, – prostrate; sprawl, loll; sit down.

render -horizontal &c. *adj.*; lay, – down, – out; level, flatten, even, raze, equalize, smooth, align; prostrate, knock down, floor, fell, ground.

Adj. horizontal, level, even, plane;

flat &c. 251; flat as a -billiard table, – bowling green; alluvial; calm, – as a mill-pond; smooth, – as glass.

re-, de-, pro-, ac-cumbent; lying &c. *v.*; prone, supine, couchant, jacent, prostrate.

Adv. horizontally &c. *adj.*; on -one's back. – all fours, – its beam ends.

214. Pendency.—N. pend-, dependency; suspension, hanging &c. *v.*

pendant, drop, tippet, tassel, lobe, tail, train, flap, lappet, skirt, pig-tail, queue, pendulum.

peg, knob, button, hook, nail, stud, ring, staple, tenterhook; davit; fastening &c. 45; spar, horse.

chande-, gase-, electro-lier.

V. be -pendent &c. *adj.*; hang, depend, swing, dangle, droop, sag; swag; daggle, flap, trail, flow.

suspend, hang, sling, hook up, hitch, fasten to, append.

Adj. pend-ent, -ulous; pensile; hanging &c. *v.*; dependent; suspended &c. *v.*; lowering, overhanging, beetling, decumbent; loose, flowing.

having a -peduncle &c. *n.*; pedunculate, tailed, caudate.

215. Support.—N. support, ground, foundation, base, basis; *terra firma*; bearing, fulcrum, *point d'appui*, caudex, purchase, footing, hold, *-locus standi*; landing, – stage, – place; stage, platform; block; rest, resting-place; groundwork, *substratum*, sustentation, subvention; floor &c. (*basement*) 211.

supporter; aid &c. 707; prop, stand, anvil, fulciment; hod, stay, shore, skid, rib, sprag, truss, bandage; sleeper; stirrup, stilts, shoe, sole, heel, splint, lap; bar, rod, boom, sprit, outrigger.

staff, stick, crutch, alpenstock, bourdon; *bâton*, maulstick, colstaff, cowlstaff, staddle; stalk, ped-icel, -icle, – uncle.

post, pillar, shaft, column, pilaster; pediment, pedestal; plinth, shank, leg, socle, zocle; buttress, jamb, mullion, abutment; pile, baluster, banister, stanchion, king post; balustrade.

frame, -work, body, *chassis, fuselage*; scaffold, skeleton, beam, rafter, girder, lintel, joist, cantilever, travis, trave, corner-stone. summer, transom; rung, round, step, sill.

columella, back-bone; key-stone; axle, -tree; axis; arch, ogive, mainstay.

trunnion, pivot, rowlock; peg &c. (*pendency*) 214; tie-beam &c. (*fastening*) 45; thole pin.

board, ledge, shelf, hob, bracket, trevet, trivet, arbor, rack, hatrack; mantel, -piece, -shelf; slab, console; counter, dresser; flange, corbel; table, trestle, teapoy; shoulder; perch; horse; easel, desk; retable, predella.

seat, throne, dais; divan, musnud; chair, bench, form, stool, camp-stool, sofa, settee, davenport, stall, miserere, arm –, easy –, elbow –, rocking- chair; couch, day bed, *fauteuil*, woolsack, ottoman, settle, squab, bench, box, dicky; saddle, pannel, pillion; side –, pack- saddle; pommel.

bed, berth, pallet, tester, crib, cot, bassinet, hammock, shakedown, camp bed, bunk, truckle-bed, cradle, litter, stretcher, bedstead; four-poster, French bed; bedding, mattress, *paillasse*; pillow, bolster; mat, rug, cushion.

stool, footstool, hassock, faldstool, *prie-dieu*; tabouret; tripod. Atlas, Persides, Atlantes, Caryatides, Hercules.

V. be -supported &c.; lie –, sit –, recline –, lean –, loll –, rest – stand –, step –, repose –, abut –, bear –, be based &c.- on; have at one's back; be-stride, -straddle.

support, bear, carry, hold, sustain, shoulder; hold –, back –, bolster –, shore- up; up-hoid, -bear; prop; under-prop, -pin, -set; bandage, &c. 43; brace, truss; cradle, pillow.

give –, furnish –, afford –, supply –, lend- -support, – foundations; bottom, found, base, ground, embed.

maintain, keep on foot; aid &c. 707.

Adj. support-ing, -ed, &c. *v.*; atlantean, columellar; sustentative, fundamental, basal.

Adv. astride oṅ, astraddle; pick-a-back.

216. Parallelism.—N. parallelism; coextension, concentricity, collimation.

V. be –, lie- parallel to; collimate.

Adj. parallel; coextensive, collateral, concentric, concurrent.

Adv. alongside, abreast &c. (*laterally*) 236.

———

217. Obliquity.—N. obliquity, inclination, skew, slope, slant; crookedness &c. *adj.*; slopeness; leaning &c. *v.*; bevel, bezel, ramp, tilt; bias, list, twist, swag, cant, lurch; distortion &c. 243; bend &c. (*curve*) 245; tower of Pisa.

acclivity, rise, ascent, grade. gradient, *glacis*, rising ground, hill, bank, declivity, downhill, dip, fall, devexity; gentle –, rapid- slope; easy -ascent, – descent; shelving beach; *talus*; *montagne Russe*; *facilis descensus Averni*.

steepness &c. *adj.*; cliff, precipice &c. (*vertical*) 212; escarpment. scarp.

[Measure of inclination] clinometer, theodolite, level, sextant quadrant, protractor; angle, sine, cosine, tangent &c. hypothenuse. diagonal; zigzag, chevron.

V. be -oblique &c. *adj.*; slope, slant, lean, incline, shelve, stoop. decline, descend, bend, heel, cɪreen, sag, swag, seel, slouch, cant sidle.

render -oblique &c. *adj.*; sway, bias; slope, slant; incline, bend, crook; cant, tilt; distort &c. 243.

Adj. oblique, inclined; sloping &c. *v.*; tilted &c. *v.*; recumbent, clinal, skew, askew, slant, aslant, bias, plagiedral, indirect, wry, awry, ajee, crooked; knock-kneed &c. (*distorted*) 243; bevel, out of the perpendicular.

uphill, rising, ascending, acclivous; downhill, falling, descending; declining, declivous, devex, anticlinal; steep, abrupt, precipitous, break-neck.

diagonal; trans-verse, -versal; athwart, antiparallel; curved &c. 245.

Adv. obliquely &c. *adj.*; on –, all on- one side; askew, askant. askance, aslope, asquint, edgewise, at an angle; side-long, -ways; slopc-, slant-wise; by a side wind.

218. Inversion.—N. in-, e-, sub-, re-, retro-, intro-version; contraposition &c. 237; contrariety &c. 14; reversal; turn of the tide.

overturn; somer-sault, -set; summerset; *culbute*; revulsion; *pirouette.*

transposition, transposal, anastrophy, *metastasis, hyperbaton, ana-strophe, hysteron-proteron*, hypallage, *synchysis, tmesis*, parenthesis; *metathesis*; palindrome; Spoonerism.

pronation and supination.

V. be -inverted &c.; turn –, go –; wheel- -round, – about, – to ɔhe right about; turn –, go –, tilt –, topple-over; capsize, turn turtle.

in-, sub-, retro-, intro-vert; reverse; up-, over-turn, -set; turn -topsy turvy &c. *adj.*; *culbuter*; transpose, put the cart before the horse, turn the tables.

Adj. inverted &c. *v.*; wrong side -out, – up; inside out, upside down; bottom –, keel- upwards; supine, on one's head, topsy turvy, *sens dessus sens dessous.*

inverse; reverse &c. (*contrary*) 14; opposite &c. 237.

topheavy, unstable.

Adv. inversely &c. *adj.*; hirdie-girdie; heels over head, head over heels.

219. Crossing.—N. crossing &c. *v.*; inter-section, – lacement, – twine-ment, -digitation; decussation, transversion; convolution &c. 248.

reticulation, meshwork, network; inosculation, anastomosis, inter-texture, mortise.

net, *plexus*, web, mesh, twill, skein, sleeve, felt, lace; wicker; mat, -ting; plait, trellis, wattle, lattice, grating, *grille*, gridiron, tracery, fretwork, filigree, reticle; tissue, netting, mokes.

cross, crucifix, rood, crisscross, crux; chain, wreath, braid, cat's cradle, knot; entanglement &c. (*disorder*) 59.

[woven fabrics] cloth, linen, muslin, cambric, drill, homespun, tweed, broadcloth &c.

V. cross, decussate; inter-sect, -lace, -twine, -twist, -weave, -digitate, -link.

twine, entwine, weave, inweave, twist, wreathe; anastomose, inoscu-late, dovetail, splice, link.

mat, plait, plat, braid, felt, twill; tangle, entangle, ravel; net, knot; dishevel, raddle.

Adj. crossing &c. *v.*; crossed, matted &c. *v.*; transverse.

cross, cruciform, crucial; reti-form, -cular, -culated; areolar, cancel-lated, mullioned, latticed, grated, barred, streaked; textile, secant, plexal; interfretted.

Adv. across, thwart, athwart, transversely, crosswise.

3°. Centrical Dimensions*

1. *General*

220. Exteriority. — N. exteriority; outside, exterior; surface, superficies; skin &c. (*covering*) 223; *superstratum*; disk, disc; face, facet.

excentricity; circumjacence &c. 227.

V. be -exterior &c. *adj.*; lie around &c. 227.

place -exteriorly, – outwardly, – out-side; put –, turn- out.

Adj. exter-ior, -nal; extraneous, outer, -most; out-ward, -lying, -side, -door; round about &c. 227; extra-mural.

superficial, skin-deep; frontal, dis-coid.

extraregarding; eccentric; outstand-ing; extrinsic &c. 6.

Adv. externally &c. *adj.*; out, with-out, over, outwards, *ab extra*, out of doors; *extra muros.*

221. Interiority.—N. interiority; in-side, interior, endocrine; interspace, subsoil, *substratum.*

contents &c. 190; substance, pith, marrow; backbone &c. (*centre*) 222; heart, bosom, breast, abdomen; vitals, viscera, entrails, bowels, belly, intes-tines, guts, chitterlings, womb, lap; gland, cell; internal organs, *penetralia*, recesses, innermost recesses; cave &c. (*concavity*) 252.

inhabitant &c. 188.

V. be -inside &c. *adj.*, – within &c. *adv.*

place –, keep- within; enclose &c. (*circumscribe*) 229; intern; embed &c. (*insert*) 300.

Adj. inter-ior, -nal; inner, inside, intimate, inward, intraregarding; in-, inner-most; deep-seated; visceral, intes-

* That is. Dimensions having reference to a centre.

in the open air; *sub -Jove, — dio*; *à la belle étoile, al fresco*.

———

tine, -tinal; inland; subcutaneous; interstitial &c. (*interjacent*) 228; inwrought &c. (*intrinsic*) 5; enclosed &c. *v.*

home, domestic, indoor, intramural, vernacular; endemic.

Adv. internally &c. *adj.*; inwards, within, in, inly; here-, there-, where-in; *ab intra*, withinside; in –, within- doors; at home, in the bosom of one's family.

222. Centrality.—N. centrality, centricalness, centre; middle &c. 68; focus &c. 74.

core, kernel; nucleus, nucleolus; heart, pole, axis, pivot, fulcrum, bull's eye; hub, nave, navel; *umbilicus*, spine, backbone, marrow, pith; hot-bed; concentration &c. (*convergence*) 290; centralization; symmetry.

centre of -gravity, – pressure, – percussion, – oscillation, – buoyancy &c. metacentre.

V. be -central &c. *adj.*; converge &c. 290.

render central, centralize, concentrate; bring to a focus.

Adj. centr-al, -ical; middle &c. 68; axial, pivotal, focal, umbilical, concentric; middlemost, nuclear, centric, centraidal; spinal, vertebral.

Adv. middle; midst; centrally &c. *adj.*

223. Covering.—N. covering, cover; canopy, tilt, awning, baldachin, tent, marquee, *tente d'abri*, umbrella, parasol, sunshade; veil (*shade*) 424; shield &c. (*defence*) 717; pall.

roof, dome, cupola, mansard roof; ceiling; thatch, tile; pan-, pen-tile; tiling, shingles, slates, slating, leads; shed &c. (*abode*) 189.

224. Lining.—N. lining, inner coating; coating &c. (*covering*) 223; stalactite, -agmite.

filling, stuffing, wadding, padding, bushing.

wainscot, *parietes*, wall, brattice.

V. line, stuff, incrust, wad, pad, fill.

Adj. lined &c. *v.*

———

top, lid, covercle, door, *operculum*, eyelid, blind, curtain.

bandage, plaster, lint, wrapping, dossil, finger stall.

coverlet, counterpane, sheet, quilt, comforter, eiderdown; tarpaulin, blanket, rug, drugget, linoleum, oilcloth; housing.

in-, tegument; skin, pellicle, fleece, fell, fur, ermine, miniver, sable, sealskin &c.; leather, morocco, calf, pigskin, elk, kid, cowhide &c.; shagreen, hide; pelt, -ry; cuticle, *dermis*, scarf-skin, *epidermis*.

clothing &c. 225; mask &c. (*concealment*) 530.

peel, crust, bark, rind, *cortex*, husk, shell, coat.

capsule; ferrule; sheath, -ing; pod, cod; casing, case, theca, *elytron; involucrum*; wrapp-ing, -er, envelope, vesicle; dermatology, conchology.

armour, -plate, armouring; veneer, facing; pavement; scale &c. (*layer*) 204; coating, paint, stain; varnish &c. (*resin*) 356a; anointing &c. *v.*; inunction; incrustation, superposition, obduction, ground, enamel, whitewash, plaster, stucco, rough cast, pebble dash, compo; rendering; cerement; ointment &c. (*grease*) 356.

V. cover; super-pose, -impose; over-lay, -spread; wrap &c. 225; incase; face, case, veneer, pave, paper; tip, cap, bind, revet.

coat, paint, varnish, pay, incrust, stucco, cement, dab, plaster, tar; wash; be-, smear; be-, daub; anoint, do over; gild, plate, electroplate, japan, lacquer, lacker, enamel, whitewash; lay it on thick.

over-lie, -arch; conceal &c. 528.

Adj. covering &c. *v.*; cutaneous, dermal, cortical, cuticular, tegumentary, skinny, scaly, squamous; covered &c. *v.*; imbricated, loricated, armour-plated, iron-clad; under cover, hooded, cloaked, cowled.

225. Investment.—N. investment; covering &c. 223; dress, clothing, raiment, drapery, costume, attire, guise, toilet, *toilette*, trim; habiliment; vesture, -ment; garment, garb, palliament, apparel, wardrobe, wearing apparel, clothes, things.

array; tailoring, millinery; best bib and tucker; finery &c. (*ornament*) 847; full dress &c. (*show*) 882; garniture; theatrical properties.

outfit, equipment, *trousseau*; uniform, khaki, regimentals; academicals, canonicals &c. 999; livery, gear, harness, turn out, accoutrement, caparison, suit, rigging, trappings, traps, slops, togs, toggery; masquerade.

dishabille, morning dress, lounge suit, tea-gown, *kimono*, *négligé*, dressing-gown, *peignoir*, wrapper, undress; shooting-coat; smoking-jacket, mufti; rags, tatters, old clothes; mourning, weeds; duds; slippers.

robe, tunic, dolman, *paletot*, habit, gown, coat, coatee, frock, blouse, middy, sagum, *toga*, smock-frock; frock-, dress-, morning-, tail-coat; dress-suit, - clothes, swallow-tail coat, dinner-, Eton-jacket.

cloak, pall; mantle, mantlet, mantua, shawl, *pelisse*, veil, yashmak; cape, tippet, kirtle, plaid, muffler, comforter,

226. Divestment.—N. divestment; taking off &c. *v.*

nudity; bareness &c. *adj.*; undress; dishabille &c. 225, altogether; nu-, denu-dation; decortication, depilation, excoriation, desquamation; moulting; exfoliation.

baldness, alopecia, acomia.

V. divest; uncover &c. (*cover* &c. 223); denude, bare, strip; undress, unclothe, disrobe &c. (dress, enrobe, &c. 225); uncoif; dismantle; uncase; put −, take −, cast- off; shed, doff; husk, peel, pare, decorticate, desquamate, excoriate, skin, scalp, flay, bark, expose, lay open; exfoliate, moult, mew; cast the skin.

Adj. divested &c. *v.*; bare, naked, nude; un-dressed, -draped, -clad, -clothed, -appareled; exposed; in dishabille; *décolleté*; bald, threadbare, ragged, callow, roofless.

in -a state of nature, − nature's garb, − buff, − native buff, − birthday suit; *in puris naturalibus*; with nothing on, stark naked; bald as a coot, bare as the back of one's hand; out at elbows; barefoot; bareback; leaf-, nap-, hairless, shaved, clean shaven, tonsured, beardless, bald-headed, acomous.

Balaclava helmet, haik, huke, chlamys, mantilla, tabard, housing, horse-cloth, burnous, *roquelaure*; *houppelande*; sur-, top-, over-, great-coat; *surtout*, spencer, cardigan, sweater, blazer; mackintosh, waterproof, slicker, raincoat, oilskin, trench coat, ulster, monkey-, pea-, pilot-jacket, redingote; wraprascal, poncho, cardinal, pelerine, talma.

jacket, jumper, vest, jerkin, waistcoat, doublet, *camisole*, gabardine; stays, *corsage*, corset, corselet, bodice; stomacher; skirt, petticoat, slip, farthingale, kilt, jupe, crinoline, bustle, hobble skirt, *panier*, apron, pinafore; loin cloth.

trousers; breeches, trews, pantaloons, unmentionables, inexpressibles, overalls, pyjamas, smalls, small-clothes; tights, pants, shorts, drawers; knickerbockers, knickers, plus fours, bloomers, divided skirt; phil-, fill-ibeg.

head-dress, -gear; cap, *béret*, tam o' shanter, glengarry, topee, sombrero; hat; cocked –, high –, tall –, top –, silk –, opera –, crush -hat, *gibus*, beaver, castor, bonnet, tile, wideawake, billy-cock; bowler; soft felt –, straw –, leghorn -hat, panama; toque; wimple; night-, mob-, skull-cap, biretta; hood, cowl, coif; capote, calach; scull-cap; kerchief, snood; head, *coiffure*; crown &c. (*circle*) 247; *chignon*, pelt, wig, front, peruke, periwig; caftan, turban, fez, *tarboosh*, taj, shako, csako, busby; *képi*, forage cap, bearskin; helmet &c. 717; mask, domino.

body clothes; linen; shirt, sark, smock, shift, *chemise*, *lingerie*; night-gown, -shirt; bed-gown, *sac de nuit*; jersey, guernsey; underwear, undies, underclothing, -waistcoat.

neck-erchief, -cloth; tie, ruff, collar, cravat, stock, handkerchief, bandana, scarf; bib, tucker; dicky; boa; girdle &c. (*circle*) 247; cummerbund.

shoe, pump, brogue, boot, slipper, sandal, galoche, goloshes, arctics, rubber boots, overshoes, patten, clog, sabot; high-low; Blücher –, Wellington –, Hessian –, jack –, top- boot; Balmoral; legging, puttee, buskin, greave, galligaskin, moccasin, *gamache*, gambado, gaiter, spatter-dash, spat, antigropelos; stocking, hose, gaskins, trunk-hose, sock, hosiery.

glove, gauntlet, mitten, cuff, muffettee, wristband, sleeve.

swaddling cloth, baby-linen, *layette*; pocket-handkerchief.

shroud &c. 363.

clothier, tailor, milliner, *costumier*, sempstress, seamstress, snip; dress-, habit-, breeches-, shoe-maker; cordwainer, cobbler, Crispin, hosier, hatter; draper, linendraper, haberdasher, mercer.

V. invest; cover &c. 223; envelop, lap, involve; in-, en-wrap; wrap; fold –, wrap –, lap –, muffle- up; overlap; sheathe, swathe, swaddle, roll up in, shroud, circumvest.

vest, clothe, array, dress, dight, drape, robe, enrobe, attire, tire, garb, habilitate, apparel, accoutre, rig, fit out; bedizen, deck &c. (*ornament*) 847; perk; equip, harness, caparison; dress up.

wear; don; put –, huddle –, slip- on; mantle.

Adj. invested &c. *v.*; habited; dight, -ed; clad, *costumé*, shod, *chaussé*; *en grande tenue* &c. (*show*) 882.

sartorial.

---

227. Circumjacence.—N. circumjacence, -ambience; environment, encompassment; atmosphere, medium; surroundings, *entourage*.

outpost; border &c. (*edge*) 231; girdle &c. (*circumference*) 230; outskirts, *boulevards*, suburbs, purlieus, precincts, *faubourgs*, *environs*, *banlieue*, neighbourhood, vicinity.

V. lie -around &c. *adv.*; surround, beset, compass, encompass, environ, inclose, enclose, encircle, circle, embrace, circumvent, lap, gird; begird, girdle, engird; skirt, twine round; hem in &c. (*circumscribe*) 229; besiege, invest, blockade.

Adj. circum-jacent, -ambient, -fluent;

228. Interjacence.—N. inter-jacence, -currence, -venience, -location, -digitation, -penetration; permeation.

inter-jection, -polation, -lineation, -spersion, -calation; embolism.

inter-vention, -ference, -position; in-, ob-trusion; insinuation; insertion &c. 300; dovetailing; infiltration; intromission.

intermedi-um, -ary; go-between, agent, middleman, medium, bodkin, intruder, interloper; parenthesis, episode; fly-leaf.

partition, *septum*, diaphragm, midriff; party-wall, panel, vail, bulkhead, brattice, *cloison*; half-way house.

V. lie –, come –, get- between; inter-

ambient; surrounding &c. *v.*; circumferential, surburban.

Adv. around, about; without; on -every side, – all sides; right and left, all round, round about; in the neighbourhood.

vene, slide in, interpenetrate, permeate.

put between, introduce, intromit, import; throw –, wedge –, edge –, jam –, worm –, foist –, run –, plough –, work- in; inter-pose, -ject, -calate, -polate, -line, -leave, -sperse, -weave, -lard, -digitate; let in, dovetail, splice, mortise; insinuate, smuggle; infiltrate, ingrain.

interfere, put in an oar, thrust one's nose in; intrude, obtrude; have a finger in the pie; introduce the thin end of the wedge; thrust in &c. (*insert*) 300.

Adj. inter-jacent, -current, -venient, -vening &c. *v.*, -mediate, -mediary, -calary, -stitial, -costal, -mural, -planetary, -stellar; embolismal.

parenthetical, episodic; mediterranean; intrusive; embosomed; merged, mean, middle, medium, median.

Adv. between, betwixt; 'twixt; among, -st; amid, -st; 'mid, -st; in the thick of; betwixt and between; sandwich-wise; parenthetically, *obiter dictum*.

229. Circumscription.—N. circumscription, limitation, inclosure; confinement &c. (*restraint*) 751; circumvallation, encincture; envelope &c. 232.

V. circumscribe, limit, bound, confine, enclose; surround &c. 227; compass about; imprison &c. (*restrain*) 751; hedge –, wall –, rail- in; fence –, hedge- round; embar; picket, corral.

enfold, bury, incase, pack up, enshrine, inclasp; wrap up &c. (*invest*) 225; embosom.

Adj. circumscribed &c. *v.*; begirt, lapt; circumambient; buried –, immersed- in; embosomed, in the bosom of, imbedded, encysted, mewed up; imprisoned &c. 751; land-locked, in a ring fence.

230. Outline.—N. outline, circumference; peri-meter, -phery; ambit, circuit, lines, *tournure*, *contour*, profile, *silhouette*, lineaments; bounds, coastline.

zone, belt, girth, band, baldric, zodiac, girdle, tire, cingle, clasp, girt; *cordon* &c. (*inclosure*) 232; circlet &c. 247.

V. outline, delineate, *silhouette*, circumscribe &c. 229; profile, block out.

Adj. outlined &c. *v.*; circumferential, perimetric, peripheral.

231. Edge.—N. edge, verge, brink, brow, brim, margin, border, confines, skirt, rim, felloe, felly, flange, side, mouth; jaws, chops, chaps, *fauces*; lip, muzzle.

threshold, door, porch; portal &c. (*opening*) 260; coast, shore, strand, beach, bank, wharf, quay, dock.

frame, fringe, flounce, frill, list, trimming, edging, skirting, hem, selvedge, welt; furbelow, valance, exergue.

Adj. border, marginal, skirting; labial, labiated, marginated.

232. Inclosure.—N. inclosure, enclosure, envelope; case &c. (*receptacle*) 191; wrapper; girdle &c. 230.

pen, fold, croft, sty; pen-, in-, sheep-fold; paddock, pound, corral, kraal; yard, compound; net, seine net.

wall; hedge, -row; *espalier*; fence &c. (*defence*) 717; pale, paling,

balustrade, rail, railing, gunwale; quickset hedge, park paling, circumvallation, *enceinte*, ring fence.

barrier, barricade; gate, -way; door, hatch, *cordon*; prison &c. 752.
dike, dyke, ditch, fosse, moat, trench.

V. inclose; circumscribe &c. 229.

233. Limit.—N. limit, boundary, bounds, confine, *enclave*, term,
bourn, verge, kerb-stone, curbstone, but, pale; termin-ation, -us; stint,
frontier, precinct, marches.

boundary line, landmark, benchmark; line of -demarcation, – circumvallation; pillars of Hercules; Rubicon, turning-point; *ne plus ultra*;
sluice, flood-gate.

V. limit, bound, confine, define, circumscribe, demarcate, delimit,
encompass.

Adj. definite; contermin-ate, -able, terminable, limitable; terminal,
frontier, border, bordering, boundary.

Adv. thus far, – and no further.

2. *Special*

234. Front.—N. front; fore, – part;
foreground; forefront, face, disk, disc,
frontage, *façade*, *proscenium*, facia,
frontispiece; priority, anteriority; ob-
verse [of a medal].

fore –, front- rank, first line; van,
-guard; advanced guard; outpost,
scout.

brow, forehead, visage, physiognomy,
phiz, features, countenance, map, mug;
rostrum, beak, bow, stem, prow, prore,
jib, bowsprit; forecastle.

pioneer &c. (*precursor*) 64; metoposcopy.

V. be –, stand- in front &c. *adj.*;
front, face, confront, breast, brave;
bend forwards; come to the -front,
– fore.

Adj. fore, forward, anterior, front,
frontal.

Adv. before; in -front, – the van, –
advance; ahead, right ahead; fore-,
head-most; in the foreground; before
one's -face, – eyes; face to face, *vis-à-vis*.

236. Laterality.—N. laterality; side,
flank, beam, quarter, lee; hand; cheek,
jowl, jole, wing; profile; temple,
parietes, loin, haunch, hip.

gable, -end; broadside; lee side.

points of the compass; East, Orient,
Levant; West, occident; orientation.

V. be -on one side &c. *adv.*; flank,
outflank; sidle; skirt, border.

Adj. lateral, sidelong; collateral;

235. Rear.—N. rear, back, posteriority; rear -rank, – guard; background,
hinterland.

occiput, nape, scruff, chine; heels;
tail, rump, croup, buttock, posteriors,
bottom, seat, backside, scut, breech,
dorsum, loin; dorsal –, lumbar- region;
hind quarters.

stern, poop, after-part, counter;
postern, heel-, tail-piece, crupper.

wake; train &c. (*sequence*) 281.

reverse; other side of the shield.

V. be -behind &c. *adv.*; fall astern;
bend backwards; bring up the rear;
follow &c. 622; tail, shadow.

Adj. back, rear; hind, -er, -most,
-ermost; post-ern, -erior; dorsal, after;
caudal, lumbar; mizzen.

Adv. behind; in the -rear, – ruck, –
back-ground; behind one's back; at the
-heels, – tail, – back- of; back to back.

after, -most, aft, abaft, astern, stern-
most, aback, rear-, hind-, back-ward.

237. Contraposition.—N. contraposition, opposition; polarity; inversion &c.
218; opposite side; antithesis; reverse,
inverse; counterpart; antipodes; opposite poles, North and South.

V. be -opposite &c. *adj.*; subtend.

Adj. opposite; reverse, inverse; an-
tipodal, subcontrary; fronting, facing,
diametrically opposite.

Northern, Septentrional, Boreal, are

parietal, flanking, skirting; flanked; sideling.

many-sided; multi-, bi-, tri-, quadri-lateral.

East-ern, -ward, -erly; orient, -al, auroral, Levantine; West-ern, -ward, -erly; occidental, Hesperian; equatorial.

Adv. side-ways, -long; broadside on; on one side, abreast, abeam, alongside, beside, aside; by, – the side of; side by side; cheek by jowl &c. (*near*) 197; to -windward, – leeward; laterally &c. *adj.*; right and left; on her beam ends.

tic; Southern, Austral, antarctic, polar.

Adv. over, – the way, – against; against; face to face, *vis-à-vis*: as poles asunder.

------

238. Dextrality. — **N.** dextrality; right, – hand; dexter, offside, star-board.

Adj. dextral, right-handed; ambi-dextral, dexterous, dextrorsal &c.

239. Sinistrality.—**N.** sinistrality; left, – hand; *sinister*, nearside, lar-board, port.

Adj. sinistral, sinister, sinistrorsal &c., left-handed, sinistromanual, sinis-trous.

Section III.　FORM

1°. General Form

240. Form.—**N.** form, figure, shape; con-formation, -figuration; make, for-mation, frame, construction, design, cut, set, build, trim, cut of one's jib; stamp, type, cast, mould; fashion; contour &c. (*outline*) 230; structure &c. 329.

feature, lineament, outline, turn; phase &c. (*aspect*) 448; posture, atti-tude, *pose*.

[Science of form] morphology.

[Similarity of form] isomorphism.

forming &c. *v.*; form-, figur-, efform-ation; sculpture.

V. form, shape, figure, fashion, efform, carve, cut, chisel, hew, cast; rough-hew, -cast; sketch; block –, hammer- out; trim; lick –, put- into shape; model, knead, work up into, set, mould, sculpture; cast, stamp; build &c. (*construct*) 161.

Adj. formed &c. *v.*

[Receiving form] plastic, fictile, full-fashioned &c.

[Giving form] plasmic &c.

[Similar in form] isomorphous &c.

241. [Absence of form.] Amorphism. —**N.** amorphism, informity, uncouth-ness; unlicked cub, rough diamond; *rudis indigestaque moles*; disorder &c. 59; deformity &c. 243.

disfigure-, deface-ment, deformation; mutilation.

V. [Destroy form] deface, disfigure, deform, mutilate, truncate; derange &c. 61.

Adj. shapeless, amorphous, mal-formed, formless; un-formed, -hewn, -fashioned, -shapen; rough, rude, Goth-ic, barbarous, rugged, in the rough; misshapen &c. 243.

------

242. [Regularity of form.] Symmetry. —**N.** symmetry, shapeliness, finish; beauty &c. 845; proportion, eurythmy, eurythmic, uniformity, parallelism; bi-, tri-, multi-lateral symmetry; centrality &c. 222.

243. [Irregularity of form.] Distor-tion.—**N.** dis-, de-, con-tortion; knot, mop, warp, buckle, screw, twist; crookedness &c. (*obliquity*) 217; grim-ace; deformity; mal-, malcon-forma-tion; monstrosity, misproportion, want

arborescence, branching, ramification.

Adj. symmetrical, shapely, well set, finished; beautiful &c. 845; classic, chaste, severe.

regular, uniform, balanced; equal &c. 27; parallel, coextensive.

arbor-escent, -iform; dendr-iform, -oid; branching; ramous, ramose.

of symmetry, *anamorphosis*; ugliness &c. 846; teratology.

V. distort, contort, twist, warp &c. *n.*; wrest, writhe, make faces, deform, misshape.

Adj. distorted &c. *v.*; out of shape, irregular, unsymmetric, awry, wry, askew, crooked, sinuous; anamorphous; not -true, – straight; on one side, crump, deformed; mis-shapen, -begotten; mis-, ill-proportioned; ill-made;

grotesque, crooked as a ram's horn; hump-, hunch-, bunch-, crook-backed; bandy; bandy-, bow-legged; bow-, knock-kneed; splay-, club-footed; taliped; round-shouldered; snub-nosed; curtailed of one's fair proportions; scalene, stumpy &c. (*short*) 201; gaunt &c. (*thin*) 203; bloated &c. 194.

Adv. all manner of ways.

2°. SPECIAL FORM

244. Angularity.—N. angular-ity, -ness; aduncity; angle, cusp, bend; fold &c. 258; notch &c. 257; fork, bifurcation.

elbow, knee, knuckle, ankle, groin, crotch, crutch, crane, fluke, scythe, sickle, zigzag, kimbo.

corner, nook, recess, niche, oriel.

right angle &c. (*perpendicular*) 212; obliquity &c. 217; angle of 45°, mitre; acute –, obtuse –, salient –, re-entrant –, spherical –, solid –, dihedral- angle.

angular -measurement, – elevation, – distance, – velocity; trigon-, goni-ometry; altimetry; clin-, graph-, goni-ometer; theodolite; transit circle; sextant, quadrant; dichotomy.

triangle, trigon, wedge; rectangle, square, lozenge, diamond; rhomb, -us; quadr-angle, -ilateral; parallelogram; quadrature; poly-, penta-, hexa-, hepta-, octa-, deca-gon.

Platonic bodies; cube, rhomboid; tetra-, penta-, hexa-, octa-, dodeca-, icosa-hedron; prism, pyramid; parallelopiped.

V. bend, fork, bifurcate, crinkle, divaricate, branch, ramify.

Adj. angular, bent, crooked, aduncous, uncinated, aquiline, jagged, serrated; falc-iform, -ated; furcular, furcated, forked, bifurcate, crotched; zigzag; dovetailed; knock-kneed, crinkled, akimbo, kimbo, geniculated; oblique &c. 217.

fusiform, wedge-shaped, cuneiform; tri-angular, -gonal, -lateral; quadr-angular, -ilateral; rectangular, square, foursquare, multilateral; polygonal &c. *n.*; cubical, rhomboidal, pyramidal.

245. Curvature.—N. curv-ature, -ity, -ation; incurv-ity, -ation; bend; flex-ure, -ion; conflexure; crook, hook, bought, bending; de-, inflexion; arcuation, devexity, turn; deviation, *détour*, sweep; curl, -ing; bough; recurv-ity, -ation; sinuosity &c. 248; aduncity.

curve, arc, arch, arcade, vault, dome, bow, crescent, *meniscus*, half-moon, lunule, horse-shoe, loop, crane-neck;

246. Straightness.—N. straightness. rectilinearity, directness; inflexibility &c. (*stiffness*) 323; straight –, right –, direct-, bee- line; short cut.

V. be -straight &c. *adj.*; have no turning; not -incline, – bend, – turn, – deviate- to either side; go straight; steer for &c. (*direction*) 278.

render straight, straighten, rectify; set –, put- straight; un-bend, -fold,

para-, hyper-bola; catenary, festoon; conch-, cardi-oid; caustic, instep; tracery.

V. be -curved &c. *adj.*; sweep, swag, sag; deviate &c. 279; turn; re-enter.

render -curved &c. *adj.*; bend, curve, incurvate; de-, in-flect; crook; turn, round, arch, arcuate, arch over, loop the loop, concamerate; bow, coil, curl, recurve, frizzle.

Adj. curved &c. *v.*; curvi-form, -lineal, -linear; devex, devious; recurv-ed, -ous; *retroussé*; crump; bowed &c. *v.*; vaulted; hooked; falc-iform, -ated; semicircular, crescentic; lun-iform, -ular; semi-lunar, meniscal; conchoidal; cord-iform, -ated; cardioid; heart-, bell-, pear-, fig-shaped; reniform; lenti-form, -cular; bow-legged &c. (*distorted*) 243; oblique &c. 217; circular &c. 247.

-curl &c. 248, -ravel &c. 219, -wrap.

Adj. straight; rectiline-ar, -al; direct, even, right, true, in a line; unbent &c. *v.*; un-deviating, -turned, -distorted, -swerving; straight as an arrow &c. (*direct*) 278; inflexible &c. 323.

---

247. [Simple circularity.] **Circularity.**
—N. circularity, roundness; rotundity &c. 249.

circle, circlet, clasp, ring, washer, areola, hoop, roundlet, *annulus*, amulet, bracelet, armlet, armilla; ringlet; eye, loop, wheel; cycle, orb, orbit, rundle, zone, belt, *cordon*, band; sash, girdle, cestus, cincture, baldric, fillet, *fascia*, wreath, garland; crown, corona, coronet, chaplet, snood, necklace, collar; noose, lasso, lariat.

ellipse, oval, ovule; ellipsoid, cycloid; epi-cycloid, -cycle; semi-circle; quadrant, sextant, sector.

V. make -round &c. *adj.*; round.

go round; encircle &c. 227; describe -a circle &c. 311.

Adj. round, rounded, circular, annular, orbicular; oval, ovate; elliptic, -al; ovoid, egg-shaped; pear-shaped &c. 245; cycloidal &c. *n.*; spherical &c. 249.

248. [Complex circularity.] **Convolution.**—N. winding &c. *v.*; con-, in-circum-volution; wave, undulation. tortuosity, anfractuosity; sinu-osity, -ation, sinuousness; meandering, circuit, circumbendibus, twist, twirl, windings and turnings, *ambages*; torsion; inosculation; reticulation &c. (*crossing*) 219.

coil, roll, curl, buckle, spire, spiral, helix, corkscrew, worm, volute, whorl, rundle; tendril; scollop, scallop, escalop; kink.

serpent, snake, eel, maze, labyrinth.

V. be -convoluted &c. *adj.*; wind, twine, turn and twist, twirl; wave, undulate, meander; inosculate; en-twine, intwine; twist, coil, roll; wrinkle, curl, crisp, twill; frizz, -le; crimp, crape, indent, scollop, scallop; wring, intort; contort; wreathe &c. (*cross*) 219.

Adj. convoluted; winding, twisted &c. *v.*; tortile, tortive; wavy; und-ated, -ulatory; circling, snaky, snake-like,

serpentine; serpent-, anguill-, verm-iform; vermicular; mazy, tortuous, anfractuous, sinuous, flexuous, wavy, sigmoidal.

involved, intricate, complicated, perplexed; labyrinth-ic, -ian, -ine; circuitous; peristaltic; dædalian, curly.

wreathy, frizzly, crapy, buckled; ravelled &c. (*in disorder*) 59. spiral, coiled, helical, turbinated.

Adv. in and out, round and round.

---

249. Rotundity.—N. rotundity; roundness &c. *adj.*; cylindricity; spher-icity, -oidity; globosity.

cylin-der, -droid; barrel, drum; roll, -er; *rouleau*, column, rolling-pin, rundle; chimney-pot, drain-pipe.

cone, conoid; pear-, egg-, bell-shape.

sphere, globe, ball, boulder, bowlder; spher-, ellips-, ge-, glob-oid, oblong –, oblate- spheroid; drop, spherule, globule, vesicle, bulb, bullet, pellet, *pelote*, clew, pill, marble, pea, knob, pommel, knot.

V. render -spherical &c. *adj.*; form into a sphere, sphere, roll into a ball; give -rotundity &c. *n.*; round.

Adj. rotund; round &c. (*circular*) 247; cylindr-ic, -ical, -oid; columnar, lumbriciform; conic, -al; spher-ical, -oidal; glob-ular, -ated. -ous, -ose; egg-, bell-, pear-shaped; ov-oid, -iform; gibbous; campaniform, -ulate, -iliform; fungiform, bead-like, moniliform, pyriform, bulbous; *teres atque rotundus*; round as -an orange, – an apple, – a ball, – a billiard ball, – a cannon ball.

3°. SUPERFICIAL FORM

250. Convexity. — N. convexity, prominence, projection, swelling, gibbosity, bilge, bulge, protuberance, protrusion; excrescency, camber.

intumescence; tumour, tumor; tubercle, -osity; excrescence; hump, hunch, bunch, gnarl, lump.

tooth, knob, elbow, process, *apophysis*, condyle, bulb, node, nodule, nodosity, tongue, *dorsum*, boss, embossment, bump, clump; sugar-loaf &c. (*sharpness*) 253; bow; mamelon.

pimple, wen, wheal, *papula*, postule, pock, proud flesh, growth, goitre, *sarcoma*, carbuncle, corn, bunion, wart, furnuncle, polypus, adenoid, fungus, fungosity, *exostosis*, bleb, blister, blain; boil &c. (*disease*) 655; bubble, blob.

papilla, nipple, teat, pap, breast, dug, mammilla; proboscis, nose, neb, beak, snout, nozzle, snozzle; Adam's apple; belly, paunch, corporation; withers, back, shoulder, lip, flange.

peg, button, stud, ridge, rib, jutty, trunnion, snag.

cupola, dome, bee-hive; arch, balcony, caves; pilaster.

relief, relievo, *cameo*; *basso-, mezzo-, alto-rilievo*; low-, bas-, high-relief.

hill &c. (*height*) 206; cape, promontory, mull; fore-, head-land; point of land, naze, ness, mole, jetty, hummock, ledge, spur.

V. be -prominent &c. *adj.*; project, bulge, protrude, bag, belly, pout, bouge, bunch; jut –, stand –, stick –, poke- out; stick –, bristle –, start –, cock –, shoot- up; swell –, hang –, bend- over; beetle.

render -prominent &c. *adj.*; raise 307; emboss, chase

251. Flatness.—N. flatness &c. *adj.*; smoothness &c. 255.

plane; level &c. 213; plate, platter, table, tablet, slab.

V. render flat, flatten, squash; level &c. 213.

Adj. flat, plane, even, flush, scutiform, discoid; level &c. (*horizontal*) 213; smooth; flat as -a pancake, – a fluke, – a flounder, – a board, – my hand.

252. Concavity.—N. concavity, depression, dip; hollow, -ness; indentation, *intaglio*, cavity, antrum, dent, dint, dimple, follicle, pit, *sinus, alveolus. lacuna*; excavation, trench, sap, mine, tunnel, burrow; trough &c. (*furrow*) 259; honeycomb.

cup, basin, crater, punch-bowl; cell &c. (*receptacle*) 191; socket, faucet.

valley, vale, dale, dell, gap, dingle, combe, bottom, slade, strath, glade, grove, glen, cave, cavern, cove; grot, -to; alcove, *cul-de-sac*, blind alley; gully &c. 198; arch &c. (*curve*) 245; bay &c. (*of the sea*) 343.

excavator, sapper, miner.

V. be -concave &c. *adj.*; retire, cave in.

render -concave &c. *adj.*; depress, hollow; scoop, – out; gouge, dig, delve, excavate, dent, dint, mine, sap, undermine, burrow, tunnel, stave in.

Adj. depressed &c. *v.*; concave, hollow, stove in; dished; spoon-like; retiring; retreating; cavernous; porous &c. (*with holes*) 260; cellular, spongy, spongious; honeycombed, alveolar; infundibul-ar, -iform; funnel-, bell-shaped; campaniform, capsular; vaulted, arched. ———

Adj. convex, prominent, protuberant, underhung, undershot; projecting &c. *v.*; bossed, bossy, nodular, bunchy; clav-ate, -ated; hummocky, *moutonné*, mammiform; papul-ous, -ose; hemispheric, bulbous; bowed, arched; bold; bellied; tuber-ous, -culous; tumorous; cornute, knobby, odontoid; lenti-form, -cular; gibbous.

salient, in relief, raised, *repoussé*; bloated &c. (*expanded*) 194.

---

253. Sharpness.—N. sharpness &c. *adj.*; acuity, acumination; spinosity.

point, spike, spine, *spiculum*, tine; needle, pin; tack, nail; prick, -le; spur, rowel, barb; spit, cusp; horn, antler; snag; tag; thorn, bristle.

nib, tooth, incisor, tusk; spoke, cog, ratchet.

crag, crest, *arête*, cone, peak, sugar-loaf, pike, *aiguille*; spire, pyramid, steeple.

beard, *chevaux de frise*, porcupine, hedgehog, brier, bramble, thistle; comb, awn, bur.

wedge; knife-, cutting- edge; blade, edge-tool, cutlery, knife, penknife, whittle, razor; scalpel, bistoury, lancet; chisel; ploughshare, coulter; hatchet, axe, pick-axe, mattock, pick, adze, bill; bill-hook, cleaver, cutter; skiver; scythe, sickle, scissors, shears; sword &c. (*arms*) 727; bodkin &c. (*perforator*) 262.

sharpener, hone, strop; grind-, whet-stone; steel, emery.

V. be -sharp &c. *adj.*; taper to a point; bristle with.

render -sharp &c. *adj.*; sharpen, point, aculeate, acuminate, whet, barb, spiculate, set, strop, grind.

cut &c. (*sunder*) 44.

Adj. sharp, keen; acute; aci-cular, -form; acu-leated, -minated; pointed; tapering; conical, pyramidal; mucron-ate, -ated; spindle-, needle-shaped; spiked, spiky, ensiform, peaked, salient, cusp-ed; -idate, -idated; corn-ute, -uted, -iculate; prickly; spiny, spinous; thorny, bristling, muricated, pectinated, studded, thistly, briery; craggy &c. (*rough*) 256; snaggy; digitated, two-edged, fusiform; denti-form, -culated; toothed; odontoid; star-like; stell-ated, -iform; arrow-headed; arrowy, barbed, spurred, sagittal; spear-shaped, hastate; horned; conical.

cutting; sharp-, knife-edged; sharp -, keen- as a razor; sharp as a needle; sharpened &c. *v.*; set.

254. Bluntness.—N. bluntness &c. *adj.*

V. be -, render- blunt &c. *adj.*; obtund, dull; take off the -point, - edge; turn.

Adj. blunt, obtuse, dull, bluff.

---

255. Smoothness.—N. smoothness &c. *adj.*; polish, gloss; lubric-ity, -ation.

down, velvet, silk, satin; slide; bowling green &c. (*level*) 213; glass, ice; asphalt, pavement, flags.

roller, steam-roller; iron, flat-iron, tailor's goose; sand-, emery-paper; burnisher, turpentine and bees-wax.

V. smooth, -en; plane; file; mow, shave; level, roll; macadamize; polish, burnish, planish, levigate, calender, glaze; iron, hot-press, mangle; lubricate &c. (*oil*) 332.

256. Roughness.—N. roughness &c. *adj.*; tooth, grain, texture, ripple; asperity, rugosity, salebrosity, corrugation, nodosity; arborescence &c. 242.

brush, hair, beard, shag, mane, whisker, mutton-chops, *moustache*, *mustachio*, imperial, Van Dyke, tress, lock, curl, ringlet, *fimbriæ*, *cilia*, *villi*; eyelashes, eye-brows, love-lock.

plum-age, -osity; plume, *panache*, crest; feather, tuft, tussock, fringe, toupee.

wool, velvet, plush, nap, pile, floss,

Adj. smooth; polished &c. *v.*; even; level &c. 213; plane &c. (*flat*) 251; sleek, glossy; silken, silky; lanate, downy, velvety; glabrous, slippery, glassy, lubricous, oily, soft; unwrinkled; smooth as -glass, – ice, – velvet, – oil; slippery as an eel; woolly &c. (*feathery*) 256.

fluff, fur, down; byssus, moss, bur.

V. be -rough &c. *adj.*; go against the grain.

render -rough &c. *adj.*; roughen, rough cast, knurl; ruffle, crisp, crumple, crinkle, corrugate, engrail; set on edge, stroke –, rub- the wrong way, rumple.

Adj. rough, uneven; scabrous, knotted; nodular; rug-ged, -ose, -ous; asperous, crisp, salebrous, gnarled, unpolished, unsmooth, rough-hewn; knurled, cross-grained, crag-gy, -ged; crankling, scraggy, jagged, unkempt, prickly &c. (*sharp*) 253; arborescent &c. 242; leafy, well-wooded; feathery; plum-ose, -igerous; tufted, fimbriated, hairy, bristly, ciliated, filamentous, hirsute; crin-ose, -ite; bushy, hispid, villous, pappous, bearded, pilous, shaggy, shagged; fringed, befringed; set-ous, -ose, -aceous; 'like quills upon the fretful porcupine'; rough as a -nutmeg grater, – bear.

downy, velvety, flocculent, woolly; lan-ate, -ated; lanugin-ous. -ose; tomentous.

Adv. against the grain, in the rough, on edge.

257. Notch.—N. notch, dent, nick, cut; indent, -ation; serration; dimple.

embrasure, battlement, machicolation; saw, tooth, crenelle, scallop, scollop, vandyke.

V. notch, nick, cut, pink, mill, score, dent, indent, jag, scarify, scotch, crimp, scollop, crenulate, vandyke.

Adj. notched &c. *v.*; crenate, -d; dentate, -d; denticulate, -d; toothed, palmated, serrated.

258. Fold.—N. fold, plicature, pleat, plait, ply, crease; tuck, gather; flexion, flexure, joint, elbow, doubling, duplicature, wrinkle, rimple, crinkle, crankle, crumple, rumple, rivel, ruck, ruffle, dog's ear, corrugation, frounce, flounce, lapel; pucker, crow's feet.

V. fold, double, plicate, pleat, plait, crease, wrinkle, crinkle, crankle, curl, smock, cockle up, crocker, rimple, rumple, frizzle, frounce, rivel, twill, corrugate, ruffle, crimple, crumple, pucker; turn –, double- -down. – under; tuck, ruck, hem, gather.

Adj. folded &c. *v.*

259. Furrow.—N. furrow, groove, rut, *sulcus*, scratch, streak, *striæ*, crack, score, incision, slit; chamfer, fluting.

channel, gutter, trench, ditch, dike, dyke, moat, fosse, trough, kennel; ravine &c. (*interval*) 198.

V. furrow &c. *n.*; flute, groove, carve, corrugate, plough; incise, chase, enchase, grave, engrave, etch, bite in, cross-hatch.

Adj. furrowed &c. *v.*; ribbed, striated, sulcated, fluted, canaliculated; bisulc-ous, -ate; trisulcate; corduroy.

260. Opening.—N. hole, foramen; puncture, blow-out, perforation; pin-, key-, loop-, port-, peep-, mouse-, pigeon-hole; eye, – of a needle; eyelet; slot.

opening; apert-ure, -ness; hiation,

261. Closure.—N. closure, occlusion, blockade; shutting up &c. *v.*; obstruction &c. (*hindrance*) 706; gag; embolism; contraction &c. 195; infarction; con-, ob-stipation; blind -alley, – corner; *cul-de-sac*, *cæcum*; imper-foration,

yawning, oscitancy, dehiscence, patefaction, pandiculation; gap, chasm &c; (*interval*) 198.

embrasure, window, casement, light; sky-, fan-light; lattice; bay-, bow-window; oriel; dormer, lantern, *abat-jour*.

out-, in-let; vent, vomitory; *embouchure*; orifice, mouth, sucker, muzzle, throat, gullet, placket, weasand, wizen, nozzle, *œsophagus*.

portal, porch, gate, ostiary, postern, wicket, trap-door, hatch, door; arcade; gate-, door-, hatch-, gang-way; lichgate.

way, path &c. 627; thoroughfare; channel, passage, tube, pipe; water-pipe &c. 350; air-pipe &c. 351; vessel, tubule, canal, gut, fistula; adjutage, ajutage; chimney, smoke stack, flue, tap, funnel, gully, tunnel, main; mine, pit, adit, shaft; gallery.

alley, aisle, glade, lane, vista.

bore, calibre; pore; blind orifice.

por-ousness, -osity; sieve, cullender, colander; grater, shredder; cribble, riddle, screen; honeycomb.

apertion, perforation; piercing &c. *v.*; terebration, empalement, pertusion, puncture, acupuncture, penetration.

opener, key, master-key, *passe-partout*.

V. open, ope, gape, dehisce, yawn, bilge; fly open.

perforate, pierce, empierce, tap, bore, drill; mine &c. (*scoop out*) 252; tunnel; trans-pierce, -fix; enfilade, impale, spike, spear, gore, spit, stab, pink, puncture, lance, trepan, trephine, stick, prick, riddle, punch; stave in.

cut a passage through; make -way, – room- for.

un-cover, -close, -rip; lay –, cut –, rip –, throw- open.

Adj. open; perforated &c. *v.*; perforate; wide open, agape, ajar; un-closed, -stopped; oscitant, gaping, yawning; patent.

tubular, cannular, fistulous; per-vious, -meable; foraminous; vesi-, vas-cular; porous, follicular, cribriform, honeycombed, infundibular, riddled; tubul-ous, -ated, piped.

opening &c. *v.*; aperient.

Int. *open sesame!*

262. Perforator. — N. perforator, piercer, borer, auger, gimlet, stylet, drill, wimble, awl, bradawl, scoop, terrier, corkscrew, dibble, trocar, trepan, trephine, probe, bodkin, needle, stiletto, broach, reamer, rimer, warder, lancet; punch, -eon; spikebit, gouge; spear &c. (*weapon*) 727.

-viousness &c. *adj.*, -meability; stopper &c. 263; *operculum.*

V. close, occlude, plug; block –, stop –, fill –, bung –, cork –, button –, stuff –, shut –, dam- up, obturate; blockade; obstruct &c. (*hinder*) 706; bar, bolt, stop, seal, plumb; choke, throttle; ram down, tamp, dam, cram; trap, clinch; put to –, shut- the door; batten down the hatches.

Adj. closed &c. *v.*; shut, operculated; unopened.

unpierced, imporous, cæcal; imper-forate, -vious, -meable; impenetrable; un-, im-passable; invious; path-, way-less; untrodden.

unventilated; air-, water-tight; hermetically sealed; tight, snug.

263. Stopper.—N. stopper, stopple; plug, cork, bung, spike, spill, stop-cock, tap; rammer; ram, -rod; piston; stop-gap; wadding, stuffing, padding, stopping, dossil, pledget, tompion, tourni-quet. obturator; wad.

cover &c. 223; valve, slide valve; vent-peg, spigot.

janitor, door –, gate- keeper, porter, commissionaire, *concierge*, warder, beadle, Cerberus, usher, guard, sentry, sentinel; ostiary.

Section IV. MOTION

1°. Motion in General

264. [Successive change of place.*]
Motion.—N. motion, movement, move; motivity, motility, going &c. *v.*; unrest.

stream, current, flow, flux, run, course, stir; conduction, evolution; kinematics.

step, rate, pace, tread, stride, gait, clip, port, footfall, cadence, carriage, velocity, angular velocity; progress, locomotion; journey &c. 266; voyage &c. 267; transit &c. 270.

restlessness &c. (*changeableness*) 149; mobility; movableness, motive power; laws of motion; mobilization.

V. be -in motion &c. *adj.*; move, go, hie, gang, budge, stir, pass, flit; hover -round, – about; shift, slide, slither, glide; roll, – on; flow, stream, run, drift, sweep along; wander &c. (*deviate*) 279; walk &c. 266; change –, shift-one's -place, – quarters; dodge; keep -going, – moving.

put –, set- in motion; move; impel &c. 276; propel &c. 284; render mov-able, mobilize.

Adj. moving &c. *v.*;in motion;motile, transitional; motory, motive; shifting, movable, mobile, mercurial, unquiet; restless &c. (*changeable*) 149; nomadic &c. 266; erratic &c. 279.

Adv. under way; on the -move, – wing, – tramp, – march.

---

265. Quiescence.—N. rest; stillness &c. *adj.*; quiescence; stag-nation, -nancy; fixity, immobility, catalepsy; indisturbance; quietism.

quiet, tranquillity, calm; repose &c. 687; peace; dead calm, anticyclone; statue-like repose; silence &c. 403; not a -breath of air, – mouse stirring; sleep &c. (*inactivity*) 683.

pause, lull &c. (*cessation*) 142; stand, – still; standing still &c. *v.*; lock; dead -lock, – stop, – stand; full stop; fix; embargo.

resting-place; bivouac; home &c. (*abode*) 189; pillow &c. (*support*) 215; haven &c. (*refuge*) 666; goal &c. (*arrival*) 292.

V. be -quiescent &c. *adj.*; stand –, lie- still; keep quiet, repose, hold the breath.

remain, stay; stand, lie to, ride at anchor, remain *in situ*, mark time, tarry; bring –, heave –, lay- to; pull –, draw- up; hold, halt; stop, – short; rest, pause, anchor; cast –, come to an- anchor; rest on one's oars; repose on one's laurels, take breath; stop &c. (*discontinue*) 142.

stagnate, vegetate; *quieta non movere*; let -alone, – well alone; abide, rest and be thankful; keep within doors, stay at home, go to bed.

dwell &c. (*be present*) 186; settle &c. (*be located*) 184; alight &c. (*arrive*) 292.

stick, – fast; stand, – like a post; not stir a -peg, – step; be at a -stand &c. *n.*

quell, becalm, hush, stay, lull to sleep, lay an embargo on; put the brake on.

Adj. quiescent, still; motion-, move-less; fixed; stationary; at -rest, – a stand, – a stand-still, – anchor; stock-still; immotile; standing still &c. *v.*; sedentary, untravelled, stay-at-home; becalmed, stagnant, quiet; un-moved, -disturbed, -ruffled; calm, restful; cataleptic; immovable &c. (*stable*) 150; sleeping &c. (*inactive*) 683; silent &c. 403; still as -a statue, – a post, – a mouse, – death.

Adv. at a stand &c. *adj.*; *tout court*; at the halt.

Int. stop! stay! avast! halt! hold, – hard! whoa!

Phr. *requiescat in pace*.

---

* A thing cannot be said to *move* from one place to another, unless it passes in succession through every intermediate place; hence motion is only such a change of place as is *successive*. 'Rapid, swift, &c., as thought' are therefore incorrect expressions.

266. [Locomotion by land.] **Journey.**
—**N.** travel; travelling &c. *v.*; wayfaring, campaigning.

journey, excursion, expedition, tour, trip, grand tour, circuit, peregrination, discursion, ramble, pilgrimage, *trek*, course, ambulation, march, walk, hike, promenade, constitutional, stroll, saunter, tramp, jog-trot, turn, stalk, perambulation; noctambulation; somnambulism, sleep walking; outing, ride, drive, airing, jaunt.

equitation, horsemanship, riding, *manège*, ride and tie.

roving, vagrancy, pererration; marching and countermarching; nomadism; vagabond-ism, -age; gadding; flit, -ting; migration; e-, im-, de-, inter-migration.

plan, itinerary, guide; hand-, road-book; Baedeker, Murray, Bradshaw, time table.

procession, parade, cavalcade, caravan, file, *cortège*, column.

[Organs and instruments of locomotion] vehicle &c. 272; locomotive &c. 271; legs, feet, pegs, pins, trotters.

traveller &c. 268.

V. travel, journey, course; tour; take –, go- a journey; take –, go out for- -a walk &c. *n.*; have a run; take the air.

flit, take wing; migrate, emigrate, *trek*; rove, prowl, roam, range, patrol, pace up and down, traverse; scour –, traverse- the country; peragrate; per-, circum-ambulate; nomadize, wander, ramble, stroll, saunter, hover, go one's rounds, straggle; gad, – about; expatiate.

walk, march, step, tread, pace, plod, wend; promenade; trudge, tramp; stalk, stride, straddle, strut, foot it, stump, bundle, bowl along, toddle; paddle; tread –, follow –, pursue- a path.

267. [Locomotion by water, or air.] **Navigation.**—**N.** navigation; aquatics; boating, cruising, yachting; ship &c. 273; oar, scull, sweep, punt-pole, paddle, – wheel, screw, propeller, stern wheel, sail, canvas.

natation, swimming; fin, flipper- fish's tail.

aerial navigation, air service, airways, airmanship, aero-donetics, -dynamics, -mechanics, -station, -statics, -nautics; ballooning, balloonry; balloon &c. 273; flying, flight, aviation, volitation; wing, pinion, *aileron*.

voyage, sail, cruise, passage, circum-navigation, *periplus*; head-, stern-, lee-way.

mariner, aeronaut &c. 269.

V. sail; put to sea &c. (*depart*) 293; take ship, get under way; spread -sail, – canvas; gather way, have way on; make –, carry- sail; plough the -waves, – deep, – main, – ocean; walk the waters.

navigate, warp, luff, scud, boom, kedge; drift, course, cruise, coast; hug the -shore, – land; circumnavigate.

ply the oar, row, paddle, pull, scull, punt, steam.

swim, float; buffet the waves, ride the storm, skim, *effleurer*, dive, wade.

fly, aviate, be wafted, hover, soar, drift, glide, plane, sideslip, *volplane*, pique, dive, spin, roll, loop, flutter; take -wing, – a flight; wing one's -flight, – way.

Adj. sailing &c. *v.*; seafaring, nautical, maritime, naval; sea-going, coasting; afloat; navigable, aquatic, natatory.

volitant, volant, aerostatic, aerial, aeronautic; alar, alate, pennate.

Adv. under -way, – sail, – canvas, – steam; on the wing.

---

take horse, ride, drive, trot, amble, canter, prance, fisk, frisk, *caracoler*; gallop &c. (*move quickly*) 274; motor, cycle, taxi; go by -car, – train, – tram, – bus, – plane.

peg –, jog –, wag –, shuffle- on; stir one's stumps; bend one's -steps, – course; make –, find –, wend –, pick –, thread –, plough-one's way; coast, slide, glide, skim, skate, ski; march in procession, file off, defile.

go –, repair –, resort –, hie –, betake oneself- to.

Adj. travelling &c. *v.*; ambulatory, itinerant, peripatetic, perambulatory, roving, rambling, gadding, discursive, vagrant, migratory, nomadic; circumforane-an, -ous; somnambular, nocti-, mundi-vagant; locomotive, automotive, self-moving.

way-faring, -worn; travel-stained.

Adv. on -foot, – horseback, – Shanks's mare; by the Marrowbone stage; *in transitu* &c. 270; *en route* &c. 282.

Int. come along!

268. Traveller.—N. traveller, way-farer, voyager, itinerant, passenger.

tourist, excursionist, globe-trotter; explorer, adventurer, mountaineer, Alpine Club; peregrinator, wanderer, rover, straggler, rambler; bird of passage; gad-about, -ling; vagrant, scatterling, landloper, waifs and estrays, wastrel, stray; loafer; tramp, -er, hobo, beachcomber, vagabond, nomad, Bohemian, gipsy, Arab, Wandering Jew, Hadji, pilgrim, palmer; peripatetic; somnambulist, sleep walker, noctambulist; emigrant, fugitive, refugee, *émigré*.

runner, courier, King's messenger; Mercury, Iris, Ariel, comet.

pedestrian, walker, foot-passenger; cyclist; wheelman.

rider, horseman, equestrian, cavalier, jockey, rough rider, trainer, breaker, huntsman.

driver, coachman, whip, Jehu, charioteer, postilion, post-boy, carter, wagoner, drayman, truckman; cab-man, -driver; *voiturier*, *vetturino, condottiere*; engine-driver; stoker, fireman, guard, brakeman, conductor; chauffeur, automobilist, motorist, motor –, truck –, taxi- driver.

269. Mariner.—N. sailor, mariner, navigator, argonaut; sea-man, -farer; -faring man; yachtsman; tar, jack tar, salt, gob, sea-dog, shellback, able seaman, A.B.; man-of-war's man, bluejacket, marine, jolly; midshipman, middy, reefer; captain, commander, master mariner, skipper, mate; ship-, boat-, ferry-, water-, lighter-, barge-, longshore- man, hoveller; bargee, gondolier; oar-, -sman; rower; boat-, cock-swain; coxswain; steersman, helmsman, pilot; crew; lascar.

aerial navigator, aeronaut, balloonist, Icarus, aviator, pilot, observer, flyer, airman.

270. Transference.—N. transfer, -ence; trans-, e-location; displacement; *meta-stasis, -thesis*; removal; re-, a-motion; relegation; de-, as-portation; extradition, conveyance, draft; carrying, carriage; convection, -duction, -tagion, infection; transfusion; transfer &c. (*of property*) 783.

transit, transition; passage, ferry, gestation; portage, porterage, carting, cartage; shovelling &c. *v.*; vect-ion, -ure, -itation; shipment, freight, wafture; trans-mission, -port, -portation, -umption, -plantation, -lation; shift-, dodg-ing; dispersion &c. 73; transposition &c. (*interchange*) 148; traction &c. 285.

[Thing transferred] drift, alluvium, detritus, *moraine*; gift, legacy, bequest, lease; freight, mails, cargo, luggage, baggage, goods.

V. trans-fer, -mit, -port, -place, -plant; convey, assign, carry, bear, fetch and carry; carry –, ferry- over; hand, pass, forward; shift; conduct, convoy, bring, fetch, reach.

send, delegate, consign, mail, post, relegate, turn over to, pass the buck, deliver; ship, embark; waft; switch, shunt; transpose &c. (*interchange*) 148; displace &c. 185; throw &c. 284; drag &c. 285.

shovel, lade, dip, ladle, bale, decant, draft off, transfuse.

Adj. transferred &c. *v.*; drifted; movable; port-able, -ative; conductive; contagious, infectious.

transferable, assignable, conveyable, devisable, negotiable, transmissible.

Adv. from -hand to hand, – pillar to post.

on –, by- the way; on the -road, – wing; as one goes; *in transitu, en route, chemin faisant, en passant,* in mid-progress.

271. Carrier.—N. carrier, porter, red cap, bearer, messenger, postman, tranter, conveyer; stevedore; coolie; conductor, locomotive, tractor, caterpillar tractor, motor.

beast of burden, cattle, horse, steed, nag, palfrey, Arab, blood horse, thorough-bred, galloway, charger, courser, racer, hunter, jument, pony, filly, colt, foal, barb, roan, jade, hack, *bidet,* pad, cob, tit, punch, roadster, goer; race-, pack-, draft-, cart-, dray-, post-horse, mount; Shetland pony, sheltie; garran; jennet, genet, bayard, mare, stallion, gelding; stud.

Pegasus, Bucephalus, Rozinante.

ass, donkey, jackass, mule, hinny; sumpter -horse, – mule; reindeer; camel, dromedary, mehari, llama, elephant; carrier pigeon.

carriage &c. (*vehicle*) 272; ship &c. 273.

Adj. equine, asinine.

272. Vehicle.—N. vehicle, conveyance, carriage, car, caravan, van, furniture van, pantechnicon; wagon, wain, dray, cart, lorry.

carriole; sledge, sled, sleigh, bobsleigh, toboggan, *luge,* truck, tram; limber, tumbrel, pontoon; barrow; wheel-, hand- -barrow, – cart, trolley; perambulator; Bath –, wheel –, sedanchair, jinriksha, rickshaw; ekka; chaise; palan-keen, -quin; litter, horse-litter, brancard, crate, hurdle, stretcher, ambulance; velocipede, hobby-horse, coaster, scooter, go-cart; cycle; bi-, tri-, quadri-cycle; tandem, safety; skate, roller skate; ski, snow-shoe.

equipage, turn-out; coach, chariot, *quadriga,* chaise, phaëton, break, brake, mail-phaëton, wagonette, drag, curricle, tilbury, whisky, landau, *barouche,* victoria, brougham, clarence, calash, *calèche,* britzska, *araba,* kibitka; berlin; sulky, *désobligeant,* sociable, *vis-à-vis, dormeuse;* jaunting –, outside- car; *tarantass;* runabout; shay.

post-chaise; diligence, stage; stage –, mail –, hackney –, glass- coach; stage-wagon; car, omnibus, bus, fly, *cabriolet,* cab, hansom, shofle, four-wheeler, growler, *droshki,* drosky.

dog-cart, trap, gig, whitechapel, buggy, four-in-hand, unicorn, random, tandem; shandredhan, *char-à-banc.*

automobile, motor-, auto-, touring-, racing-, cycle-, side-, steam-, electric-

273. Ship.—N. ship, vessel, sail; craft, bottom.

navy, marine, fleet, flotilla, squadron; shipping.

man of war &c. (*combatant*) 726; transport, tender, store-ship; merchant ship, merchantman; packet, liner; whaler, slaver, collier, coaster, tanker, freighter, freight steamer, cargo boat, lighter; fishing-, pilot- boat; trawler, drifter; cable ship; hulk; yacht; floating palace, ocean greyhound.

ship, bark, barque, brig, snow, hermaphrodite brig; brigantine, barquentine; schooner; topsail –, fore and aft –, three masted- schooner; *chasse-marée;* sloop, cutter, corvette, clipper, foist, yawl, dandy, ketch, smack, lugger, barge, hoy, cat-, -boat, buss; sail-er, -ing vessel, wind-jammer; steam-er, -boat, -ship; mail –, paddle –, screw –, sternwheel- steamer; tug; train-ferry; line of steamers &c.

boat, pinnace, launch, motor-boat, picket-boat; hydroplane; life-, long-, jolly-, bum-, fly-, cock-, ferry-, canal-boat, dory, dugout, galliot; shallop, gig, funny, skiff, dingy, scow, cockleshell, wherry, coble, punt, cog, lerret; eight-, four-, pair- oar; randan; outrigger; float, raft, pontoon; prame, ice-yacht.

state barge, bucentaur.

catamaran, coracle, gondola, carvel, caravel; felucca, caique, canoe; trireme;

car; motor-, -omnibus, – bus, – cab, – cycle; limousine, landaulette, cabriolet, *coupé, voiturette,* runabout, electromobile, taxi, -cab.

train; passenger –, express –, freight –, subway –, special –, corridor –, parliamentary –, luggage –, goods-train, *train de luxe;* 1st-, 2nd-, 3rd-class- -train, – carriage, – compartment; Pullman –, sleeping-, club-, observation-, dining-, restaurant-car; mail-, luggage-, brake-van, coach, car, carriage; rolling stock; horse-box, cattle-truck.

tramcar, trolley-omnibus, trackless trolley.

shovel, spoon, spatula, ladle, hod, hoe; spade, spaddle, loy; spud; pitch-fork.

Adj. vehicular.

---

galley, – foist; bilander, dogger, hooker, howker; argosy, carack; galliass, galleon; galliot, polacca, polacre, corsair, tartane, junk, lorcha, praam, proa, prahu, saick, sampan, xebec, dhow; dahabeah; nuggar, cayak, pirogue.

submarine, submersible.

aircraft (*combatant*) &c. 726; flying machine, air mail, aero-, air-, mono-, bi-, tri-, hydroplane, plane, cabin plane, transport plane, *avion,* flying boat, glider, *aviette,* helicopter; balloon. air-, fire-, gas-, Mongolfier-, pilot-, captive-, free-, kite-, dirigible- balloon, air-ship, *Zeppelin,* blimp; kite, parachute.

nacelle, car, gondola, aileron; hangar, airport, landing field, airdrome; cat-walk, controls, rudder, tail.

Adj. marine, maritime, naval, nautical, seafaring, sea-, ocean ·going, seaworthy.

aerial, aeronautical, air-worthy, flying &c. *n.*

Adv. afloat, aboard; on -board, – ship board, – board ship.

2°. Degrees of Motion

274. Velocity.—N. velocity, speed, celerity; swiftness &c. *adj.;* rapidity, eagle speed; expedition &c. (*activity*) 682; pernicity; acceleration; haste &c. 684.

spurt, rush, dash, race, steeplechase; smart –, lively –, swift &c. *adj.* –, rattling –, spanking –, strapping- -rate, – pace; round pace; flying, flight.

gallop, canter, trot, round trot, run, scamper; hand –, full- gallop; swoop.

lightning, light, electricity, wind; cannon-ball, rocket, arrow, dart, quick-silver; telegraph, express train; torrent; swallow flight.

eagle, antelope, courser, race-horse, gazelle, greyhound, hare, doe, squirrel.

Mercury, Ariel, Camilla, Harlequin. [Measurement of velocity] speed-ometer, log, -line, tachometer.

V. move quickly, trip, fisk; speed, hie, hasten, sprint, spurt, post, spank, scuttle; scud, -dle, scurry; scour, – the plain; scamper; run, – like mad; fly, race, run a race, cut away, cut and run, shoot, tear, whisk, whiz, sweep, skim, brush; cut –, bowl- along; rush

---

275. Slowness.—N. slowness &c. *adj.;* languor &c. (*inactivity*) 683; drawl; creeping &c. *v.,* lentor.

retardation, slackening &c. *v.;* delay &c. (*lateness*) 133; claudication.

jog-, dog-trot, walk; mincing steps; slow -march, – time.

slow -goer, – coach, – back; lingerer, loiterer, sluggard, tortoise, snail; dawdle &c. (*inactive*) 683.

V. move -slowly, &c. *adv.;* creep, crawl, lag, slug, walk, drawl, linger, loiter, saunter; plod, trudge, stump along, lumber; trail; drag; dawdle &c. (*be inactive*) 683; grovel, worm one's way, steal along; jog –, rub –, bundle-on; toddle, waddle, wabble, slug: traipse, slouch, shuffle, halt, hobble, limp, claudicate, shamble; flag, falter, totter, stagger; mince, step short; march in -slow time, – funeral procession; take one's time; hang fire &c. (*be late*) 133.

retard, relax; slacken, check, moderate, rein in, curb; reef; strike –, shorten –, take in- sail; put on the drag, apply the brake; clip the wings; reduce the

&c. (*be violent*) 173; dash -on, – off, – forward; bolt; trot, gallop, bound, flit, spring, dart, boom; march in double-time; ride hard, get over the ground, scorch.

hurry &c. (*hasten*) 684; accelerate, put on; quicken; quicken –, mend- one's pace; clap spurs to one's horse; make -haste, – rapid strides, – forced marches, – the best of one's way; put one's best leg foremost, stir one's stumps, wing one's way, set off at a score; carry –, crowd- sail; go off like a shot, go ahead, gain ground; outstrip the wind, fly on the wings of the wind.

keep -up, – pace- with; outstrip &c. 303.

Adj. fast, speedy, swift, rapid, quick, fleet; nimble, agile, expeditious; express; active &c. 682; flying, galloping &c. *v.*; light-, nimble-footed; winged, eagle-winged, mercurial, electric, tele- graphic; light-legged, light of heel; swift as -an arrow &c. *n.*; quick as -lightning &c. *n.*, – thought.*

Adv. swiftly &c. *adj.*; with -speed &c. *n.*; apace; at -a great rate, – full speed, – railway speed; full -drive, – gallop; post-haste, in full sail, tantivy; trippingly; instantaneously &c. 113; like a shot.

under press of -sail, – canvas, – sail and steam; *velis et remis*, on eagle's wing, in double quick time; with -rapid, – giant- strides; *à pas de géant*; in seven league boots; whip and spur; *ventre à terre*; as fast as one's -legs, – heels- will carry one; as fast as one can lay feet to the ground, at the top of one's speed; by leaps and bounds; with haste &c. 684; in- high – gear, – speed.

Phr. *vires acquirit eundo.*

speed, decelerate; slacken -speed, – one's pace, lose ground; back -water, – pedal, put the engines astern, throttle down.

Adj. slow, slack; tardy; dilatory &c. (*inactive*) 683; gentle, easy; leisurely; deliberate, gradual; insensible, imper- ceptible; languid, sluggish, apathetic, phlegmatic, slow-paced, tardigrade, snail-like; creeping &c. *v.*

Adv. slowly &c. *adj.*; leisurely; *piano, adagio*; *largo, larghetto*; at half speed, under easy sail; at a -foot's, – snail's, – funeral- pace; slower than molasses in January; in slow time; with -mincing steps, – clipped wings; *haud passibus æquis*; in- low –, gear, – speed.

gradually &c. *adj.*; *gradatim*; by -degrees, – slow degrees, – inches, – little and little; step by step; inch by inch, bit by bit, little by little, *seriatim*; consecutively.

3°. Motion Conjoined with Force

276. Impulse.—**N.** impulse, impul- sion, impetus; momentum; push, pulsion, thrust, shove, jog, jolt, brunt, booming, boost, throw; explosion &c. (*violence*) 173; propulsion &c. 284.

percussion, concussion, collision, oc- cursion, clash, encounter, cannon, *carambole*, appulse, shock, crash, bump; impact; *élan*; charge &c. (*attack*) 716; beating &c. (*punishment*) 972.

blow, dint, stroke, knock, tap, rap, slap, smack, pat, dab; fillip; slam, bang; hit, whack, thwack, clout; cuff &c. 972; squash, dowse, whap, swap, punch, thump, swipe, jab, pelt, kick, punce, calcitration; *ruade*; arietation; cut, thrust, lunge, yerk.

277. Recoil.—**N.** recoil; re-, retro- action; revulsion; rebound, *ricochet*; re-percussion, -calcitration; kick, *contre- coup*; springing back &c. *v.*; elasticity &c. 325; reflection, reflex, reflux; rever- beration &c. (*resonance*) 408; rebuff, repulse; return.

ducks and drakes; boomerang; spring; reactionist, reactionary.

V. recoil, resile, react; spring –, fly –, bound- back; rebound, reverberate, repercuss, recalcitrate, echo, *ricochet*.

Adj. recoiling &c. *v.*; re-fluent, -percussive, -calcitrant, -actionary; retroactive.

Adv. on the -recoil &c. *n.*

---

* See note on 264.

hammer, sledge-hammer, mall, maul, mallet, flail; ram, -mer; bat-tering-ram, monkey, pile-driver, punch, bat, tamper, tamping iron; cudgel &c. (*weapon*) 727; axe &c. (*sharp*) 253.

[Science of mechanical forces] mechanics, dynamics &c.

V. give an -impetus &c. *n.*; impel, push; start, give a start to, set going; drive, urge, boom; thrust, prod, foin; cant; elbow, shoulder, jostle, justle, hustle, hurtle, shove, jog, jolt, bean, encounter; run –, bump –, butt- against; knock –, run- one's head against; impinge.

strike, knock, hit, bash, tap, rap, bat, slap, flap, dab, pat, thump, beat, bang, slam, dash; punch, thwack, whack; hit –, strike- hard; swap, batter, dowse, baste; pelt, patter, skelter, buffet, belabour, tamp; fetch one a blow, swat; poke at, pink, lunge, yerk; kick, calcitrate; butt; strike at &c. (*attack*) 716; whip &c. (*punish*) 972; propel &c. 284.

come –, enter- into collision; collide; foul; fall –, run- foul of. throw &c. (*propel*) 284.

Adj. impelling &c. *v.*; im-pulsive, -pellent; booming; dynamic, -al; impelled &c. *v.*

4°. MOTION WITH REFERENCE TO DIRECTION

278. Direction.—N. direction, bearing, course, set, drift, tenor; tendency &c. 176; incidence; bending, trending &c. *v.*; dip, tack, aim, collimation; steer-ing, -age.

point of the compass, cardinal –, half –, quarter- points; North, East, South, West; N by E, ENE, NE by N, NE &c.; rhumb, azimuth, line of collimation.

line, path, road, range, quarter, line of march; alignment; straight shot, bee-line.

V. tend –, bend –, point- towards; conduct –, go- to; point -to, – at; bend, trend, verge, incline, dip, determine.

steer –, make- -for, – towards; aim –, level- at; take aim; keep –, hold- a course; be bound for; bend one's steps towards; direct –, steer –, bend –, shape- one's course; align –, one's march; go straight, – to the point; march -on, – on a point.

ascertain one's -direction &c. *n.*; *s'orienter*, see which way the wind blows; box the compass.

Adj. directed &c. *v.*, – towards; pointing towards &c. *v.*; bound for; aligned –, alligned- with; direct, straight; un-deviating, -swerving; straightforward; North, -ern, -erly, &c. *n.*

directable &c. *v.*

Adv. towards; on the -road, – high

279. Deviation. — N. deviation; swerving &c. *v.*; obliquation, warp, refraction; flection, flexion; sweep; de-flection, -flexure; declination.

diversion, digression, departure from, aberration, drift, sheer; divergence &c. 291; zigzag; *détour* &c. (*circuit*) 629.

[Desultory motion] wandering &c. *v.*; vagrancy, evagation; by-paths and crooked ways.

[Motion sideways, oblique motion] sidling &c. *v.*; *échelon*, leeway; knight's move (at chess).

V. alter one's course, deviate, depart from, turn, trend; bend, curve &c. 245; swerve, heel, bear off.

intervert; deflect; divert, – from its course; put on a new scent, shift, shunt, switch, wear, draw aside, crook, warp short circuit.

stray, straggle; sidle, edge; diverge &c. 291; tralineate, digress, divagate, wander; wind, twist, meander, meander around Robin Hood's barn; veer, tack, sheer; turn -aside, – a corner, – away from; wheel, steer clear of; ramble, rove, drift; go -astray, – adrift; yaw, dodge; step aside, ease off, make way for, shy.

fly off at a tangent; glance off; turn, wheel –, face- about; turn –, face- to the right about; wabble &c. (*oscillate*) 314; go out of one's way &c. (*perform a circuit*) 629: lose one's way.

road- to; *versus*, to; hither, thither, whither; directly; straight, – forwards, – as an arrow; point blank; in a -direct, – straight- line -to, – for, – with; in a line with; full tilt at, as the crow flies.

before –, near –, close to –, against- the wind; windwards, in the wind's eye.

through, *via*, by way of; in all -directions, – manner of ways; *quaqua-versum*, from the four winds.

Adj. deviating &c. *v.*; aberrant, errant; ex-, dis-cursive; devious, de-sultory, loose; rambling; stray, erratic, vagrant, undirected; circuitous, indi-rect, zigzag; crab-like.

Adv. astray from, round about, wide of the mark; to the right about; all manner of ways; circuitously &c. 629.

obliquely, sideling, like the move of the knight on a chessboard.

---

280. [Going before.] **Precession.—N.** precession, leading, heading; preced-ence &c. 62; priority &c. 116; the lead, *le pas*; van &c. (*front*) 234; precursor &c. 64.

V. go -before, – ahead, – in the van, – in advance; precede, forerun; usher in, introduce, herald, head, take the lead; lead, – the way, – the dance; get –, have- the start; steal a march; get -before, – ahead, – in front of; outstrip &c. 303; take precedence &c. (*first in order*) 62.

Adj. foremost, first, leading &c. *v.*

Adv. in advance, before, ahead, in the van; fore-, head-most; in front.

Phr. *seniores priores.*

---

281. [Going after.] **Sequence.—N.** sequence, run; coming after &c. (*order*) 63; (*time*) 117; following; pursuit &c. 622.

follower, attendant, satellite, shad-ow, dangler, train.

V. follow; pursue &c. 622; go –, fly-after.

attend, beset, dance attendance on, dog, be-dog; tread -in the steps of, – close upon; be –, go –, follow- in the -wake, – trail. – rear- of; trail, follow as a shadow, hang on the skirts of; tread –, follow- on the heels of, tag after.

lag, get behind.

Adj. following &c. *v.*

Adv. behind; in the -rear &c. 235, – train of, wake of; after &c. (*order*) 63, (*time*) 117.

---

282. [Motion forwards; progressive motion.] **Progression.—N.** progress, -ion, -iveness; advancing &c. *v.*; ad-vance, -ment; ongoing; flood-tide, headway; march &c. 266; rise; improve-ment &c. 658.

V. advance; proceed, progress; get -on, – along, – over the ground; gain ground; jog –, rub –, wag- on; go with the stream; keep –, hold on- one's course; go –, move –, come –, get –, pass –, push –, press- -on, – forward, – forwards, – ahead; press onwards, step forward; make –, work –, carve –, push –, force –, edge –, elbow- one's way; make -progress, – head, – way, – headway, – advances, – strides, – rapid strides &c. (*velocity*) 274; go –, shoot-ahead; distance; make up leeway.

Adj. advancing &c. *v.*; pro-gressive, -fluent; advanced.

---

283. [Motion backwards.] **Regres-sion.—N.** regress, -ion; retro-cession, -gression, -gradation, -action; *reculade*; retreat, withdrawal, retirement, re-migration; recession &c. (*motion from*) 287; recess; crab-like motion.

re-fluence, -flux; backwater, regur-gitation, ebb, return; resilience; re-flexion (*recoil*) 277; *volte-face*.

counter -motion, – movement, ⌐ march; veering, tergiversation, re-cidivation, backsliding, fall, relapse; deterioration &c. 659.

turning-point &c. (*reversion*) 145.

V. re-cede, -grade, -turn, -vert, -treat, -tire; retro-grade, -cede; back, – down, – out, crawl; withdraw; rebound &c. 277; go –, come –, turn –, hark –, draw –, fall –, get –, put –, run- back; lose ground; fall –, drop- astern; back water, put about; veer, – round; double.

Adv. forward, onward; forth, on ahead, under way, *en route* for, on -one's way, – the way, – the road, – the high road- to; in -progress, – mid progress; *in transitu* &c. 270.

Int. Forward, march!

Phr. *vestigia nulla retrorsum.*

wheel, counter-march; ebb, regurgitate; jib, shrink, shy.

turn -tail, – round, – upon one's heel, – one's back upon; retrace one's steps, dance the back step; sound –, beat- a retreat; go home.

Adj. receding &c. *v.*; retro-grade, -gressive; re-gressive, -fluent, -flex, -cidivous, -silient; crab-like; reactionary &c. 277; counter-clockwise.

Adv. back, -wards; reflexively, to the right about; *à reculons, à rebours.*

Phr. *revenons à nos moutons,* as you were.

284. [Motion given to an object situated in front.] **Propulsion.—N.** pro-pulsion, -jection; *vis a tergo;* push &c. (*impulse*) 276; e-, jaculation; ejection &c. 297; throw, fling, toss, shot, discharge, shy.

[Science of propulsion] gunnery, ballistics, archery.

missile, projectile, ball, *discus,* javelin, hammer, quoit, brickbat, shot, bullet; arrow, shaft; gun &c. (*arms*) 727.

shooter, shot; gunner, gun-layer; archer, toxophilite; bow-, rifle-, marksman; good -, crack- shot; sharpshooter &c. (*combatant*) 726.

V. propel, project, throw, fling, cast, pitch, chuck, toss, jerk, heave, shy, hurl; flirt, fillip.

dart, lance, tilt; e-, jaculate; fulminate, bolt, drive, sling, pitchfork.

send; send -, let -, fire- off; discharge, shoot; launch, send forth, let fly; dash.

put -, set- in motion; set agoing, start; give -a start, – an impulse- to; push, impel &c. 276; trundle &c. (*set in rotation*) 312; expel &c. 297.

carry one off one's legs; put to flight.

Adj. propelled &c. *v.*; propelling &c. *v.*; pro-pulsive, -jectile.

285. [Motion given to an object situated behind.] **Traction.—N.** traction; drawing &c. *v.*; draught, pull, haul; rake; 'a long pull, a strong pull and a pull all together'; towage, haulage.

V. draw, pull, haul, lug, rake, drag, draggle, tug, tow, trail, trawl, train; take in tow.

wrench, jerk, twitch.

Adj. drawing &c. *v.*; tractive, tractile; ductile.

286. [Motion towards.] **Approach.—N.** approach, approximation, appropinquation; access; appulse; afflux, -ion; advent &c. (*approach of time*) 121; pursuit &c. 622; convergence &c. 290.

V. approach, approximate; near; get -, go -, draw- near; come, – near, – to close quarters; move -, set in- towards; drift; make up to; gain upon; pursue &c. 622; tread on the heels of; bear up; make the land; hug the -shore, -coast, – land.

Adj. approaching &c. *v.*; approximative; convergent; affluent; impending, imminent &c. (*destined*) 152.

287. [Motion from.] **Recession.—N.** re ession, retirement, withdrawal; retreat; retrocession &c. 283; departure &c. 293; recoil &c. 277; flight &c. (*avoidance*) 623.

V. recede, go, move from, retire, ebb, withdraw, shrink; come -, move -, go -, get -, drift- away; depart &c. 293; retreat &c. 283; move -, stand -, sheer- off; swerve from; fall back, stand aside; run away &c. (*avoid*) 623.

remove, shunt, side track, switch off

Adj. receding &c. *v.*

Adv. on the road.

Int. come hither! approach! here! come! come near!

288. [Motion towards, actively.] **Attraction.**—**N.** attract-ion, -iveness; pull; drawing to, pulling towards, adduction, magnetism, gravity, attraction of gravitation; lure, bait, decoy.

loadstone, -star; magnet, siderite, magnetite.

V. attract; draw –, pull –, drag- towards; adduce.

lure, bait, decoy.

Adj. attracting &c. *v.*; attrahent, attractive, adducent, adductive.

290. [Motion nearer to.] **Convergence.**—**N.** con-vergence, -fluence, -course, -flux, -gress, -currence, -centration; appulse, meeting; corradiation.

assemblage &c. 72; resort &c. (*focus*) 74; asymptote.

V. converge, concur; come together, unite, meet, fall in with; close -with, – in upon; centre -round, – in; enter in; pour in.

gather together, unite, concentrate, bring into a focus.

Adj. converging &c. *v.*; con-vergent, -fluent, -current; centripetal; asymptotical.

292. [Terminal motion at.] **Arrival.**—**N.** arrival, advent; landing; de-, disem-barkation; reception, welcome, *vin d'honneur*.

home, goal, bourn; landing-place, -stage; resting –, stopping -place; destination, harbour, haven, port; terminal, terminus, railway station, depot, airport; halt, halting -place, – ground; anchorage &c. (*refuge*) 666.

return, recursion, remigration; meeting; ren-, en-counter.

completion &c. 729.

V. arrive; get to, come to; come; reach, attain; come up, – with, – to; overtake; make, fetch; complete &c. 729; join, rejoin.

light, alight, dismount; land, go ashore; debark, disembark; put -in, – into; visit, cast anchor, pitch one's tent; sit down &c. (*be located*) 184; get to one's journey's end; make the

289. [Motion from, actively.] **Repulsion.**—**N.** repulsion; driving from &c. *v.*; repulse; abduction.

V. repel; push –, drive – &c. 276. from; chase, dispel; retrude; abduce, abduct; send away, repulse, dismiss.

keep at arm's length, turn one's back upon, give the cold shoulder; send packing; send -off, – away- with a flea in one's ear, – about one's business.

Adj. repelling &c. *v.*; repellant, repulsive; abducent, abductive.

291. [Motion further off.] **Divergence.**—**N.** diverg-ence, -ency; divarication, ramification, radiation; separation &c. (*disjunction*) 44; dispersion &c. 73; deviation &c. 279; aberration, declination.

V. diverge, divaricate, radiate; ramify; branch –, glance –, file- off; fly off, – at a tangent; spread, scatter, disperse &c. 73; deviate &c. 279; part &c. (*separate*) 44; splay apart.

Adj. diverging &c. *v.*; divergent, radiant, centrifugal; aberrant.

---

293. [Initial motion from.] **Departure.**—**N.** departure, decession, decampment; embarkation; take-off; outset, start; removal; exit &c. (*egress*) 295; exodus, Hejira, flight.

leave-taking, *congé*, valediction, valedictory, adieu, farewell, good-bye, stirrup-cup.

starting -point, – post; point –, place- of -departure, – embarkation; port of embarkation.

V. depart; go, – away; take one's departure, set out; set –, march –, put –, start –, be –, move –, get –, whip –, pack –, go –, take oneself- off; start, issue, march out, debouch; go –, sally- forth; sally, set forward; be gone.

leave a place, quit, vacate, evacuate, abandon; go off the stage, make one's exit; retire, withdraw, remove; go -one's way, – along, – from home; take -flight, – wing; spring, fly, flit, wing

land; be in at the death; come –, get- -back, – home; return; come in &c. (*ingress*) 294; make one's appearance &c. (*appear*) 446; drop in; detrain; outspan.

come to hand; come -at, – across; hit; come –, light –, pop –, bounce –, plump –, burst –, pitch- upon; meet; en- ren-counter; come in contact.

Adj. arriving &c. *v.*; homeward-bound; terminal.

Adv. here, hither.

Int. welcome! hail! all hail! good-day, – morrow; greetings! hullo! well!

one's flight; fly –, whip- away; take off, hop off; embark; go -on board, – aboard; set sail; put –, go- to sea; sail, take ship; hoist blue Peter; get under way, weigh anchor; strike tents, break camp, decamp; walk one's chalks, make tracks, cut one's stick; cut and run; take leave; say –, bid- -good-bye &c. *n.*; disappear &c. 449; abscond &c. (*avoid*) 623; entrain, saddle –, harness –, hitch- up; inspan.

Adj. departing &c. *v.*; valedictory; outward bound.

Adv. whence, hence, thence; with a foot in the stirrup; on the -wing, – move.

Int. begone! &c. (*ejection*) 297; to horse! all aboard! farewell! adieu! good-bye, – day! *au revoir! auf Wiedersehen!* fare you well! so long! God -bless you, – speed! *bon voyage!*

---

294. [Motion into.] **Ingress.—N.** ingress; entrance, entry; introgression; influx; intrusion, inroad, incursion, invasion, irruption; pene-, interpenetration; illapse, import, importation, infiltration; immigration; admission &c. (*reception*) 296; insinuation &c. (*interjacence*) 228; insertion &c. 300.

inlet; way in; mouth, door &c. (*opening*) 260; path &c. (*way*) 627; conduit &c. 350; immigrant, visitor, incomer, newcomer, colonist.

V. have the *entrée*; enter; go –, come –, pour –, flow –, creep –, slip –, pop –, break –, burst- -into, – in; set foot on; burst –, break- in upon; invade, intrude, butt in, horn in, crash; insinuate itself; inter-, penetrate; infiltrate; find one's way –, wriggle –, worm oneself- into.

give entrance to &c. (*receive*) 296; insert &c. 300.

Adj. incoming, ingressive &c. *n.*; inward bound.

Adv. inward.

295. [Motion out of.] **Egress.—N.** egress, exit, issue; emer-sion, -gence; disemboguement; out-break, -burst; e-, pro-ruption; emanation; evacuation; ex-, trans-udation; extravasation, perspiration, sweating, leakage, percolation, distillation, oozing; gush &c. (*water in motion*) 348; outpour, -ing; effluence, effusion; efflux, -ion; drain; dribbling &c. *v.*; defluxion; drainage; out-come, -put; discharge &c. (*excretion*) 299.

export; expatriation; e-, re-migration; *débouche*; exodus &c. (*departure*) 293; emigrant, migrant, *émigré*, colonist.

outlet, vent, spout, tap, sluice, floodgate; pore; vomitory, out-gate, sallyport; way out; mouth, door &c. (*opening*) 260; path &c. (*way*) 627; conduit &c. 350; air-pipe &c. 351.

V. emerge, emanate, issue; go –, come –, move –, pass –, pour –, flow-out of; pass off, evacuate; migrate.

ex-, trans-ude; leak; run, – out, – through; per-, trans-colate; seep; strain, distil; perspire, sweat, drain, ooze; filter, filtrate; dribble, gush, spout, flow out; well, – out; pour, trickle &c. (*water in motion*) 348; effuse, extravasate, disembogue, discharge itself, debouch; come –, break- forth; burst- out, – through; find vent, escape &c. 671.

Adj. effused &c. *v.*; outgoing, outward bound.

Adv. outward.

296. [Motion into, actively.] **Reception.—N.** reception; admission, admittance, *entrée*, importation; initiation; intro-duction, -mission, -ception; im-mission, ingestion, imbibition, absorption, ingurgitation, inhalation; suction, sucking; eating, drinking &c. (*food*) 298; insertion &c. 300; interjection &c. 228.

V. give -entrance to, – admittance to, – the *entrée*; intro-duce, -mit; usher, admit, receive, import, initiate, bring in, open the door to, throw open, in-gest, absorb, imbibe, inhale, infiltrate; let –, take –, suck- in; re-admit, -sorb, -absorb; snuff up; swallow, ingurgitate; engulf, engorge; gulp; eat, drink &c. (*food*) 298.

Adj. admit-ting &c. *v.*, -ted &c. *v.*; admissible; absorbent; introductory, introceptive, intromittent, initiatory.

297. [Motion out of, actively.] **Ejection.—N.** ejection, emission, effusion, rejection, expulsion, eviction, extrusion, trajection; discharge.

egestion, evacuation, vomition, disgorgement, voidance, eruption, eruptiveness; ruc-, eruc-tation, blood-letting, venesection, phlebotomy, paracentesis; tapping, drainage; clear-ance, -age, voidance; vomiting, excretion &c. 299.

deportation; banishment &c. (*punishment*) 972; rogue's march; relegation, extradition; dislodgment.

V. give -exit, – vent- to; let –, give -, pour –, send- out; des-, dis-patch; exhale, excern, excrete, disembogue, secrete, secern; extravasate, shed, void, evacuate, egest, emit; open the -sluices, – floodgates; turn on the tap; extrude, detrude; effuse, spend, expend; pour forth; squirt, spirt, spill, slop; perspire &c. (*exude*) 295; breathe, blow &c. (*wind*) 349.

tap, draw off; bale –, lade- out; let blood, broach.

eject, reject; expel, discard; cut, send to Coventry, boycott, ostracize; *chasser*; banish &c. (*punish*) 972; throw &c. 284 -out, – up, – off, – away, – aside; push &c. 276 -out, – off, – away, – aside; shovel –, sweep- -out, – away; brush –, whisk –, turn –, send- -off, – away; discharge; send –, turn –, cast- adrift; turn –, bundle- out; throw overboard; give the sack to; send -packing, – about one's business, – to the right about; strike off the roll &c. (*abrogate*) 756; turn out- neck and heels, – head and shoulders, – neck and crop; pack off; send away with a flea in the ear; send to Jericho; bow out, show the door to, dismiss, fire, sack.

turn out of -doors, – house and home; evict, oust; exorcise, un-house, -kennel; dislodge; un-, dis-people; depopulate; relegate, deport.

empty; drain, – to the dregs; sweep off; clear, – off, – out, – away; suck, draw off, extract; clean out, make a clean sweep of, clear decks, purge.

em-, dis-, disem-bowel; eviscerate, gut; unearth, root -out, – up; averruncate; weed –, get out; eliminate, get rid of, do away with, shake off; exenterate.

vomit, spew, puke, keck, retch; belch, – out, eruct, eructate; cast –, bring- up; disgorge; expectorate, salivate, clear the throat, hawk, spit, sputter, splutter, slobber, drool, drivel, slaver, slabber.

unpack, unlade, unload, unship; break bulk.

be let out; ooze &c. (*emerge*) 295.

Adj. emitt-ing, -ed &c. *v.*

Int. begone! get you gone! get –, go- -away, – along, – along with you! go your way! away, – with! off with you! go, – about your business! be off! avaunt! aroynt! get out! beat it!

298. [Eating.] Food.—N. eating &c. *v.*; deglutition, gulp, epulation, mastication, manducation, rumination, gastronomy, gastrology; panto-, hippo-, ichthyo-phagy &c.; gluttony &c. 957; carnivorousness, vegetarianism.

mouth, jaws, mandible, mazard, chops.

drinking &c. *v.*; potation, draught, libation; carousal &c. (*amusement*) 840; drunkenness &c. 959.

food, *pabulum*; aliment, nourishment, nutriment; susten-ance, -tation; nurture, subsistence, provender, feed, fodder, provision, ration, keep, commons, board; commissariat &c. (*provision*) 637; prey, forage, pasture, pasturage; fare, cheer; diet, -ary; regimen; belly timber, staff of life; bread, -and cheese; proteins, carbohydrates, vitamines.

299. Excretion.—N. excretion, discharge, emanation; ejection &c. 297; exhalation, extrusion, secretion, effusion, extravasation, *ecchymosis*, evacuation, cacation, defecation, dysentery, dejection, *fæces*, excrement; perspiration, sweat; sud-, exud-ation; *diaphoresis*; sewage.

saliva, spittle, rheum; ptyalism, salivation, catarrh, diarrhœa; *ejecta*, *egesta*, *sputum*, *sputa*; *excreta*; lava; *exuviæ* &c. (*uncleanness*) 653.

hemorrhage, bleeding; catamenia, menses; outpouring &c. (*egress*) 295; leucorrhea.

V. excrete &c. (*eject*) 297; emanate &c. (*come out*) 295.

Adj. excretory, fæcal, secretory; ejective, eliminant.

comestibles, eatables, victuals, edibles, *ingesta*; grub, prog, tack, hard tack, meat; bread, -stuffs; cereals; viands, cates, delicacy, dainty, creature comforts, contents of the larder, flesh-pots; festal board; ambrosia; good -cheer; — living.

hors-d'œuvre; soup, pottage, *potage*, broth, *bouillon, consommé, purée, borsch*, stock, skilly, gumbo; fish, – cakes, – pie; joint, *rôti, pièce de résistance, relevé*, hash, *réchauffé*, stew, *ragoût*, fricassee, mince, *salmi, goulash, bouillabaisse*, remove, *entrée, croquette, rissole*, sausage, curry, bubble and squeak; haggis, collops, giblets; poultry, game &c.; biscuit, bun, scone, rusk, pancake, pie, pastry, pasty, patty, *patisserie*, tart, turnover, *vol-au-vent, soufflé*, dumpling, pudding, duff, *compote*, fritters, cake, napoleon, *blancmange*, custard, jelly, jam, sweets &c. 396; *entremet*; oatmeal, porridge, hasty pudding, gruel; eggs, omelet, cheese, matzoon, savoury; vegetable, salad, *mayonnaise*, fruit; sauce, condiment &c. 393; kickshaws.

table, *cuisine*, bill of fare, *menu, prix fixe*, ordinary, *à la carte*; cover.

meal, repast, feed, spread; mess; dish, plate, course, side dish; regale; regale-, refresh-, entertain-ment; refection, collation, picnic, feast, banquet, junket; breakfast; lunch, -eon; *déjeuner*, bever, tiffin, tea, dinner, supper, snack, whet, bait, dessert; pot-luck, *table d'hôte, déjeuner à la fourchette*; hearty –, square –, substantial –, full- -meal; blow out; light refreshment; pemmican.

mouthful, bolus, gobbet, tit-bit, morsel, sop, sippet.

drink, beverage, liquor, broth, soup; potion, dram, draught, drench, swill; nip, peg, sip, sup, gulp.

wine, champagne, spirits, *liqueur*, beer, porter, stout, ale, malt liquor, julep, Sir John Barleycorn, stingo, heavy wet, bitter, lager-beer, cider; grog, toddy, flip, purl, punch, negus, cup, bishop, posset, wassail; bitters, *apéritif*, high-ball, cocktail; whisky, rum, absinthe; gin &c. (*intoxicating liquor*) 959; coffee, chocolate, cocoa, tea, *maté*, the cup that cheers but not inebriates.

eating-house &c. 189.

V. eat, feed, fare, devour, swallow, take; gulp, bolt, snap; fall to; despatch, dispatch; discuss; take –, get –, gulp-down; lay –, tuck- in; lick, pick, peck; gormandize &c. 957; bite, champ, munch, cranch, craunch, crunch, chew, masticate, nibble, gnaw, mumble.

live on; feed –, batten –, fatten –, feast- upon; browse, graze, crop, regale; carouse &c. (*make merry*) 840; eat heartily, do justice to, play a good knife and fork, banquet.

break -bread, – one's fast; breakfast, lunch, dine, take tea, sup.

drink, – in, – up, – one's fill; quaff, sip, sup; suck, – up; lap; swig; swill, tipple &c. (*be drunken*) 959; empty one's glass, drain the cup; toss -off, – one's glass; wash down, crack a bottle, wet one's whistle.

cater, purvey &c. 637.

Adj. eatable, edible, esculent, comestible, alimentary; cereal, cibarious; dietetic; culinary; nutri-tive, -tious; succulent; drinkable, pot-able, -ulent; bibulous.

omn-, carn-, herb-, frug-, gran-, gramin-, phyt-ivorus; ichthyoph-agous.

prandial.

300. [Forcible ingress.] **Insertion.—**
N. insertion, implantation, intercalation, embolism, introduction; interpolation, insinuation &c. (*intervention*) 228; planting &c. *v.*; injection, inoculation, importation, infusion; forcible -ingress &c. 294; immersion; submersion, -gence; dip, plunge; bath &c. (*water*) 337; interment &c. 363.

V. insert; intro-duce, -mit; put –, run- into; import; inject; interject &c. 228; infuse, instil, inoculate, impregnate, imbue, imbrue.

graft, ingraft, bud, plant, implant; dovetail.

obtrude; thrust –, stick –, ram –, stuff –, tuck –, press –, drive –, pop –, whip –, drop –, put- in; impact; empierce &c. (*make a hole*) 260.

embed; immerse, immerge, merge; bathe, soak &c. (*water*) 337; dip, plunge &c. 310.

bury &c. (*inter*) 363.

insert &c.- itself; plunge *in medias res.*
Adj. inserted &c. *v.*

301. [Forcible egress.] **Extraction.—**
N. extraction; extracting &c. *v.*; removal, elimination, extrication, eradication, evolution.

evulsion, avulsion; wrench; expression, squeezing; extirpation, extermination; ejection &c. 297; export &c. (*egress*) 295; distillation.

extractor, corkscrew, forceps, pliers.

V. extract, draw, pit; take –, draw –, pull –, tear –, pluck –, pick –, get- out; wring from, wrench; extort; root –, weed –, grub –, rake- up, – out; eradicate; pull –, pluck- up by the roots; averruncate; unroot; uproot, pull up, extirpate, dredge.

remove; educe, elicit; evolve, extricate; eliminate &c. (*eject*) 297; eviscerate &c. 297.

express, squeeze –, press- out; distil.
Adj. extracted &c. *v.*

302. [Motion through.] **Passage.—N.** passage, transmission; permeation; pene-, interpene-tration; transudation, infiltration; *osmosis*, osmose, endos-, exos-mose; intercurrence; ingress &c. 294; egress &c. 295; path &c. 627; conduit &c. 350; opening &c. 260; journey &c. 266; voyage &c. 267.

V. pass, – through; perforate &c. (*hole*) 260; penetrate, permeate, thread, thrid, enfilade; go -through, – across; go –, pass- over; cut across; ford, cross; pass and repass, work; make –, thread –, worm –, force- one's way; make –, force- a passage; cut one's way through;

find its -way, – vent; transmit, make way, clear the course; traverse, go over the ground.

Adj. passing &c. *v.*; intercurrent; osmotic &c. *n.*

Adv. *en passant* &c. (*transit*) 270.

---

303. [Motion beyond.] **Overstep.—**

N. trans-cursion, -ilience, -gression; infraction, intrusion; trespass; encroach-, infringe-ment; extravagation, transcendence; redundance &c. 641; ingress &c. 294.

V. transgress, surpass, pass; go- beyond, – by; show in –, come to the-front; shoot ahead of; steal a march –, gain- upon.

over-step, -pass, -reach, -go, -ride, -leap, -jump, -skip, -lap, -shoot the mark; out-strip, -leap, -jump, -go, -step, -run, -ride, -rival, -do; beat, – hollow; distance; leave in the -lurch, – rear; go one better, throw into the shade; exceed, transcend, surmount; soar &c. (*rise*) 305.

encroach, intrude, trespass, infringe, invade, trench upon, intrench on; strain; stretch –, strain- a point; pass the Rubicon.

Adj. surpassing &c. *v.*

Adv. beyond the mark, ahead.

---

304. [Motion short of.] **Shortcoming.**

—N. shortcoming, failure; delinquency; falling short &c. *v.*; de-fault, -falcation; leeway; labour in vain, no go.

incompleteness &c. 53; imperfection &c. 651; insufficiency &c. 640; non-completion &c. 730; failure &c. 732.

V. come –, fall –, stop- -short, – short of; not reach; want; keep within -bounds, – the mark, – compass.

break down, stick in the mud, collapse, come to nothing; fall -through, – to the ground, – down; cave in, end in smoke, fizzle out, miss the mark, fail; lose ground; miss stays, slump.

Adj. unreached; deficient; short, – of; *minus*; out of depth; perfunctory &c. (*neglect*) 460.

Adv. within -the mark, – compass, – bounds; behindhand; *re infectâ*; to no purpose; far from it.

Phr. the bubble burst.

---

305. [Motion upwards.] **Ascent.—N.** ascent, ascension; rising &c. *v.*; rise, upgrowth; leap &c. 309; acclivity, hill &c. 217; stair, stairs, stair-case, -way, flight of -steps, – stairs; ladder, companion, – way; lift, elevator &c. 307.

rocket, lark; sky-rocket, -lark; Alpine Club.

V. ascend, rise, mount, arise, uprise; go –, get –, work one's way –, start –, spring –, shoot- up; zoom; aspire.

climb, clamber, ramp, scramble, swarm, *escalade*, surmount; scale, – the heights.

tower, soar, hover, spire, plane, swim, float, surge; leap &c. 309.

Adj. rising &c. *v.*; scandent, buoyant; super-natant, -fluitant; excelsior.

Adv. uphill.

---

306. [Motion downwards.] **Descent.**

—N. descent, descension, declension, declination; fall; falling &c. *v.*; drop, cadence; subsidence, lapse; come-down, downfall, tumble, slip, tilt, trip, lurch; cropper, *culbute*; titubation, stumble; fate of Icarus; dive, nose-dive, *volplane*.

avalanche, *débâcle*, land-slip, -slide.

declivity, dip, hill; decline, drop.

V. descend; go –, drop –, come-down; fall, gravitate, drop, slip, slide, glissade, dive, plunge, settle; decline, slump, set, sink, droop, come down a peg.

dismount, alight, light, get down; swoop; stoop &c. 308; fall prostrate, precipitate oneself; let fall &c. 308.

tumble, trip, stumble, titubate, lurch, pitch, swag, topple; topple –, tumble- -down, – over; tilt, sprawl, plump down, come a cropper.

Adj. descending &c. *v.*; descendent, declivitous; downcast; decur-rent, -sive; labent, deciduous; nodding to its fall.

Adv. down, -hill, -wards.

307. Elevation.—N. elevation; raising &c. *v.*; erection, lift; sublevation, upheaval; sublimation, exaltation; prominence &c. (*convexity*) 250.

lever &c. 633; crane, derrick, windlass, capstan, winch, dredger, lift, elevator, escalator, dumb waiter.

V. heighten, elevate, raise, lift, erect; set –, stick –, perch –, perk –, tilt- up; rear, hoist, heave; up-lift, -raise, -rear, -bear, -cast, -hoist, -heave; buoy, weigh, mount, give a lift; exalt, sublimate; place –, set- on a pedestal.

take –, drag –, fish- up; dredge.

stand –, rise –, get –, jump- up; spring to one's feet; hold -oneself, – one's head- up; draw oneself up to his full height.

Adj. elevated &c. *v.*; standing up; stilted, attollent, rampant.

Adv. on -stilts, – the shoulders of, one's legs, – one's hind legs.

―――――

308. Depression.—N. lowering &c. *v.*; depression; dip &c. (*concavity*) 252; abasement; detrusion; reduction.

over-throw, -set, -turn; upset; prostration, subversion, precipitation.

bow; courtesy, curtsy; genuflexion, *kowtow*, obeisance, *salaam*.

V. depress, lower; let –, take- -down, – down a peg; cast; let -drop, – fall; sink, debase, bring low, abase, slash, reduce, detrude, pitch, precipitate.

over-throw, -turn, -set; upset, subvert, prostrate, level, fell; cast –, take –, throw –, fling –, dash –, pull –, cut –, knock –, hew- down; raze, – to the ground; humiliate, trample in the dust, pull about one's ears.

sit, – down; couch, squat, crouch, stoop, bend, bow, courtsey, curtsy; bob, duck, dip, genuflect, kneel; *kowtow*, *salaam*, make obeisance, prostrate oneself; bend, bow- the -head, – knee; incline the head; bow down; cower; recline &c. (*be horizontal*) 213.

Adj. depressed &c. *v.*; at a low ebb; prostrate &c. (*horizontal*) 213; detrusive.

―――――

309. Leap.—N. leap, jump, hop, spring, bound, vault, saltation.

dance, caper, gambol; curvet, caracole; *gam-bade, -bado*; capriole, demivolt; buck, – jump; hop, skip and jump.

kangaroo, jerboa, chamois, goat, frog, grasshopper, flea.

V. leap; jump -up, – over the moon; hop, spring, bound, vault, ramp, cut capers, gambol, trip, skip, dance, caper; curvet, *caracole*; foot it, bob, bounce, flounce, start, frisk &c. (*amusement*) 840; jump about &c. (*agitation*) 315; trip it on the light fantastic toe, dance oneself off one's legs.

Adj. leaping &c. *v.*; saltatory, frisky.
Adv. on the light fantastic toe.

310. Plunge.—N. plunge, dip, dive, header; ducking &c. *v.*; submergence, immersion, diver.

V. plunge, dip, souse, duck; dive, plump; take a -plunge, – header, make a plunge; bathe &c. (*water*) 337.

sub-merge, -merse; immerse, douse, sink, engulf, send to -the bottom, – Davy Jones' locker.

get out of one's depth; go -to the bottom, – down like a stone; founder, welter, wallow.

―――――

311. [Curvilinear motion.] **Circuition.—N.** circuition, circulation; turn, curvet; excursion; circum-vention, -navigation, -ambulation; north-west passage; ambit, gyre, lap, circuit &c. 629.

turning &c. *v.*; wrench; evolution; coil, helix, spiral; corkscrew.

V. turn, bend, wheel; go –, put- about; heel; go –, turn -round, – to the right about; turn on one's heel; make –, describe- a -circle, – complete circle; encircle; go –, pass- through -180°, – 360°.

circum-navigate, -aviate, -ambulate, -vent; put a girdle round the earth, go the round, make the round of.

turn –, round- a corner; double a point.

wind, circulate, meander; whisk, twirl; twist &c. (*convolution*) 248; make a *détour* &c. (*circuit*) 629.

Adj. turning &c. *v.*; circuitous; circum-foraneous, -fluent; devious, roundabout, circum-ambient, -flex, -navigable.

Adv. round about.

312. [Motion in a continued circle.] **Rotation.—N.** rotation, revolution, gyration, circulation, roll; circum-rotation, -volution, -gyration; volutation, circination, turbination, *pirouette*, convolution.

verticity; whir, whirl, swirl, eddy, vortex, whirlpool, gurge; cyclone, tornado; surge; *vertigo*, dizzy round; Maelstrom, Charybdis; Ixion; wheel of Fortune.

313. [Motion in a reverse circle.] **Evolution.—N.** evolution, unfolding, development; eversion &c. (*inversion*) 218.

V. evolve; un-fold, -roll, -wind, -coil, -twist, -furl, -twine, -ravel; disentangle; develop.

Adj. evolving &c. *v.*; evolved &c. *v.*

wheel, screw, propeller, whirligig, rolling stone, windmill; top, teetotum, merry-go-round; roller; cog-, fly-wheel, spit; jack; caster.

axis, axle, spindle, spool, pivot, pin, hinge, pole, swivel, gimbals, arbor, bobbin, mandrel, shaft.

[Science of rotatory motion] trochilics, gyrostatics.

V. rotate; roll, – along; revolve, spin; turn, – round; circumvolve; circulate, gyre, gyrate, wheel, whirl, swirl, twirl, trundle, troll, bowl; slew round.

roll up, furl; wallow, welter; box the compass; spin like a -top, – teetotum.

Adj. rotating &c. *v.*; rota-tory, -ry; circumrotatory, trochilic, vertiginous, gyratory; vortic-al, -ose.

Adv. head over heels, round and round, like a horse in a mill.

314. [Reciprocating motion, motion to and fro.] **Oscillation.—N.** oscillation; vibration, libration; motion of a pendulum; nutation; undulation; pulsation; pulse; throb; seismic disturbance.

alternation; coming and going &c. *v.*; ebb and flow, flux and reflux, ups and downs; wave, vibratiuncle, swing, beat, shake, wag, see-saw, dance, lurch, dodge; fluctuation; vacillation &c. (*irresolution*) 605.

seismometer, vibroscope, seismograph.

V. oscillate; vi-, li-brate; alternate, undulate, wave; sway, rock, swing; pulsate, beat; wag, -gle; nod, bob, courtesy, curtsy; tick; play; chatter, wamble, wabble; teeter, dangle, swag.

fluctuate, dance, curvet, reel, quake; quiver, quaver, shake, flicker; wriggle; roll, toss, pitch; flounder, stagger, totter, waddle; move –, bob- up and down &c. *adv.*; pass and repass, ebb and flow, come and go, shuttle; vacillate &c. 605.

brandish, shake, flourish.

Adj. oscillating &c. *v.*; oscill-, undul-, puls-, libr-atory; vibrat-ory, -ile; pendulous, shutterwise, seismic.

Adv. to and fro, up and down, backwards and forwards, see-saw, zigzag, wibble-wabble, in and out, from side to side, like buckets in a well.

315. [Irregular motion.] **Agitation.—N.** agitation, stir, tremor, shake, ripple, jog, jolt, jar, jerk, shock, succussion, trepidation, quiver, quaver, dance; jactit-ation, -ance; shuffling &c. *v.*; twitter, flicker, flutter.

disquiet, perturbation, commotion, turmoil, turbulence; tumult, -uation; hubbub, rout, bustle, fuss, racket, *subsultus*, staggers, megrims, epilepsy, fits, twitching, vellication, St. Vitus' dance.

spasm, throe, throb, palpitation, convulsion, paroxysm; tetanus.

disturbance &c. (*disorder*) 59; restlessness &c. (*changeableness*) 149.

ferment, -ation; ebullition, effervescence, hurly-burly, *cahotage*; tempest, storm, ground swell, heavy sea, whirlpool, vortex &c. 312, whirlwind &c. (*wind*) 349.

V. be -agitated &c.; shake; tremble, – like an aspen leaf; quiver, quaver, quake, shiver, twitter, twire, dither, dodder; twitch, writhe, toss, shuffle, tumble, stagger, bob, reel, sway; wag, -gle, wiggle; wriggle, – like an eel; squirm; dance, stumble, shamble, flounder, totter, flounce, flop, curvet, prance.

throb, pulsate, beat, palpitate, go pit-a-pat; flutter, flitter, flicker, bicker; bustle.

ferment, effervesce, foam; boil, – over; bubble, – up; simmer.

toss –, jump- about; jump like a parched pea; shake to its -centre, – foundations; be the sport of the winds and waves; reel to and fro like a drunken man; move –, drive- from post to pillar and from pillar to post; keep between hawk and buzzard.

agitate, shake, convulse, toss, tumble, bandy, wield, brandish, flap, flourish, whisk, jerk, hitch, jolt; jog, -gle; jostle, buffet, hustle, disturb, stir, shake up, churn, jounce, wallop, whip, vellicate.

Adj. shaking &c. *v.*; agitated, tremulous; de-, sub-sultory; shambling; giddy-paced, saltatory, convulsive, jerky, unquiet, restless, all of a twitter.

Adv. by fits and starts; subsultorily &c. *adj.*; *per saltum*; hop, skip and jump; in -convulsions, – fits, pit-a-pat.

CLASS III

WORDS RELATING TO MATTER

SECTION I. MATTER IN GENERAL

316. Materiality.—N. material-ity, -ness; materialization; corpor-eity, -ality; substantiality, material existence, incarnation, flesh and blood, *plenum*; physical condition.

matter, body, substance, brute matter, stuff, element, principle, protoplasm, plasma, *parenchyma*, material, *substratum*, hyle, *corpus*, *pabulum*; frame.

object, article, thing, something; still life; stocks and stones; materials &c. 635.

[Science of matter] physics; somatology, -ics; natural –, experimental-philosophy; physical science, *philosophie positive*, materialism, hylism; materialist, physicist.

V. materialize, incorporate, incarnate, substantiate, embody.

Adj. material, bodily; corpor-eal, -al; physical; somat-ic, -oscopic; sensible, tangible, ponderable, palpable, substantial; fleshly incarnate.

objective, impersonal, neuter, unspiritual, materialistic.

317. Immateriality.—N. immateriality, -ness; incorporeity, dematerialization, unsubstantiality, spirituality; inextension; astral plane.

personality; I, myself, me; *ego*, spirit &c. (*soul*) 450; astral body; immaterialism; spiritual-ism, -ist; subliminal –, subconscious- self.

V. disembody, spiritualize, dematerialize.

Adj. immateri-al, -ate; incorpor-eal, -al; asomatous, unextended; un-, disembodied; extramundane, supersensible, unearthly; pneumatoscopic; spiritual &c. (*psychical*) 450; aery.

personal, subjective.

---

318. World.—N. world, creation, nature, universe; earth, globe, wide world; *cosmos*; terraqueous globe, sphere; macro-, mega-cosm; music of the spheres.

heavens, sky, welkin, empyrean; starry -heaven, – host; firmament; vault –, canopy- of heaven; celestial spaces.

heavenly bodies, stars, luminaries, nebulæ; galaxy, milky way, galactic circle, *via lactea*.

sun, orb of day, Apollo, Phœbus; photo-, chromo-sphere; solar system; planet, -oid, asteroid; comet; satellite; moon, orb of night, Diana, Luna; aerolite, meteor; falling –, shooting- star; meteorite.

constellation. zodiac, signs of the zodiac, Charles's wain, Great Bear, Southern Cross, Orion's belt, Cassiopeia's chair, Pleiades &c.

colures, equator, ecliptic, orbit.

[Science of heavenly bodies] astronomy; urano-graphy, -logy; cosmo-logy, -graphy, -gony; *eidouranion*, orrery; geography; geodesy

&c. (*measurement*) 466; star-gazing, -gazer; astronomer; cosmogonist, geodesist, geographer; observatory.

Adj. cosmic, cosmical, mundane; terr-estrial, -estrious, -aqueous, -ene, -eous; telluric, earthly, geotic, geodetic, cosmogonal, under the sun; sub-lunary, -astral.

solar, heliacal; lunar; celestial, heavenly, empyreal, sphery; starry, stellar; sider-eal, -al; astral; nebular.

Adv. in all creation, on the face of the globe, here below, under the sun.

319. Gravity.—N. gravi-ty, -tation; weight; heaviness &c. *adj.*; specific gravity; ponderosity, pressure, load; bur-den, -then; ballast, counterpoise; lump –, mass –, weight- of.

lead, millstone, mountain, Ossa on Pelion.

weighing, ponderation, trutination; weights; avoirdupois –, troy –, apothecaries'- weight; grain, scruple, drachm, ounce, pound, lb., load, stone, hundredweight, cwt., ton, quintal, carat, pennyweight, tod, gramme, kilogramme &c.

[Weighing instrument] balance, scales, steelyard, beam, weighbridge, spring balance, weighing machine.

[Science of gravity] statics.

V. be -heavy &c. *adj.*; gravitate, weigh, press, cumber, load.

[Measure the weight of] weigh, poise.

Adj. weighty; weighing &c. *v.*; heavy, – as lead; ponder-ous, -able; lump-ish, -y; cumber-, burden-some; cumbrous, unwieldy, massive.

in-, superin-cumbent.

320. Levity.—N. levity; lightness &c; *adj.*; imponderability, imponderableness, buoyancy, volatility.

feather, dust, mote, down, thistledown, flue, cobweb, gossamer, straw, cork, bubble; float, buoy; ether, air.

leaven, ferment, barm, yeast, enzyme.

V. be -light &c. *adj.*; float, swim, be buoyed up.

render -light &c. *adj.*; lighten, levitate; leaven.

Adj. light, subtile, subtle, airy; imponder-ous, -able; astatic, weightless, ethereal, sublimated; uncompressed, volatile; buoyant, floating &c. *v.*; barmy, frothy; portable.

light as -a feather, – thistle down, – air.

fermenting &c. *n.*

Section II.   INORGANIC MATTER

1°. Solid Matter

321. Density.—N. density, solidity; solidness &c. *adj.*; impenetra-, impermea-bility; incompressibility; imporosity; cohesion &c. 46; constipation, consistence, spissitude.

specific gravity; hydro-, areo-meter.

condensation; solid-ation, -ification; consolidation; concretion, caseation, coagulation; petrifaction &c. (*hardening*) 323; crystallization, precipitation; deposit, precipitate, silt; inspissation; thickening &c. *v.*

indivisibility, indiscerptibility, indissolvableness.

solid body, mass, block, knot, lump; con-cretion, -crete, -glomerate; cake,

322. Rarity.—N. rarity; tenuity; absence of -solidity &c. 321; subtility; sponginess, compressibility.

rarefaction, expansion, dilatation, inflation, subtilization.

ether &c. (*gas*) 334.

V. rarefy, expand, dilate, subtilize, attenuate, thin.

Adj. rare, subtile, thin, fine, tenuous, compressible, flimsy, slight; light &c. 320; cavernous, spongy &c. (*hollow*) 252.

rarefied &c. *v.*; unsubstantial; un-com-pact, -pressed.

---

clot, stone, curd, coagulum, grume; bone, gristle, cartilage.
V. be -dense &c. *adj.*; become –, render- solid &c. *adj.*; solid-ify,
-ate; concrete, set, take a set, consolidate, congeal, coagulate; curd,
-le; fix, clot, cake, candy, precipitate, deposit, cohere, crystallize;
petrify &c. (*harden*) 323.

condense, thicken, inspissate, incrassate; compress, squeeze, ram
down, constipate.

Adj. dense, solid; solidified &c. *v.*; cohe-rent, -sive &c. 46; compact,
close, serried, thickset; substantial, massive, lumpish; impenetrable,
impermeable, imporous; incompressible; constipated; concrete &c.
(*hard*) 323; knot-ted, -ty; gnarled; crystal-line, -lizable; thick,
grumous, stuffy.

un-dissolved, -melted, -liquefied, -thawed.

in-divisible, -discerptible, -frangible, -dissolvable, -dissoluble,
-soluble, -fusible.

323. Hardness.—N. hardness &c.
adj.; rigidity, renitence, inflexibility,
temper, callosity, durity.

induration, petrifaction; lapid-ifica-
tion, -escence; vitri-, ossi-, corni-fica-
tion; crystallization.

stone, pebble, flint, marble, rock,
fossil, crag, crystal, quartz, granite,
adamant; bone, cartilage; heart of oak,
block, board, deal board; iron. steel;
cast –, wrought- iron; nail; brick, concrete; cement.

V. render -hard &c. *adj.*; harden,
stiffen, indurate, petrify, temper, ossify,
vitrify.

Adj. hard, rigid, stubborn, stiff, firm;
starch, -ed; stark, unbending, unlim-
ber, unyielding; inflexible, tense; indurate, -d; gritty, proof.

adamant-ine, -ean; concrete, stony,
rocky, lithic, granitic, vitreous; crystalline; horny, corneous; bony; oss-eous,
-ific; cartilaginous; hard as a -stone
&c. *n.*; stiff as -buckram, – a poker.

325. Elasticity. — N. elasticity,
springiness, spring, resilience, renitency, buoyancy.

india-rubber, caoutchouc, gutta-
percha, whalebone, gum elastic.

V. be -elastic &c. *adj.*; spring back
&c. (*recoil*) 277.

Adj. elastic, tensile, springy, ductile, resilient, renitent, buoyant.

327. Tenacity.—N. tenacity, tough-
ness, strength; cohesion &c. 46; sequacity; stubbornness &c. (*obstinacy*)
606; viscidity &c. 352.

leather; gristle, cartilage.

324. Softness.—N. softness, pliable-
ness &c. *adj.*; flexibility; pli-ancy,
-ability; sequacity, malleability; flabbi-
ness; duct-, tract-ility; extend-, extens-
ibility; plasticity; inelasticity, flaccidity, laxity.

clay, wax, butter, dough, pudding;
cushion, pillow, feather-bed, pad, down,
padding, wadding.

mollification; softening &c. *v.*

V. render -soft &c. *adj.*; soften, mollify, mellow, relax, temper; mash,
knead, squash, *massage*.

bend, yield, relent, relax, give.

Adj. soft, tender, supple; pli-ant,
-able; flex-ible, -ile; lithe, -some; lis-
som, limber, plastic; ductile; tract-ile,
-able; malleable, extensile, sequacious,
inelastic, mollient.

yielding &c. *v.*; flabby, limp, flimsy.

flaccid, flocculent, downy; spongy,
œdematous, medullary, doughy, argil-
laceous, mellow.

soft as -butter, – down, – silk; yielding as wax; tender as a chicken.

326. Inelasticity.—N. want of –,
absence of- elasticity &c. 325; inelasticity &c. (*softness*) 324.

Adj. inelastic &c. (*soft*) 324.

328. Brittleness.—N. brittleness &c.
adj.; frag-, friab-, frangib-, fiss-ility;
frailty; house of -cards, – glass.

V. be -brittle &c. *adj.*; live in a glass
house.

V. be -tenacious &c. *adj.*; resist fracture.

Adj. tenacious, tough, cohesive, adhesive, strong, resisting, sequacious, stringy, gristly, cartilaginous, leathery, coriaceous, tough as whit-leather; stubborn &c. (*obstinate*) 606.

break, crack, snap, split, shiver, splinter, crumble, break short, burst, fly, give way; fall to pieces; crumble -to, – into- dust.

Adj. breakable, brittle, frangible, fragile, frail, friable, delicate, gimcrack, shivery, fissile; splitting &c. *v.*; lacerable, splintery, crisp, crimp, short, brittle as glass.

329. [Structure.] **Texture.**—**N.** structure, organization, anatomy, frame, mould, fabric, construction; frame-work, carcass, architecture; stratification, cleavage.

substance, stuff, *compages, parenchyma*; constitution, staple, organism.

[Science of structures] organ-, oste-, my-, splanchn-, neur , angi-, aden-ology; angi-, aden-ography.

texture; inter-, con-texture; tissue, grain, web, surface; warp and -woof, – weft; tooth, nap &c. (*roughness*) 256; fineness –, coarseness- of grain.

[Science of tissues] histology.

Adj. structural, organic; anatomic, -al.

text-ural, -ile; fine-, coarse-grained; fine, delicate, subtile, gossamery, filmy; coarse; home-spun; linsey-woolsey.

330. Pulverulence.—**N.** [State of powder.] pulverulence; sandiness &c. *adj.*; efflorescence; friability.

powder, dust, sand, shingle; sawdust; grit; attrition; meal, bran, flour, *farina*, spore, sporule; crumb, seed, grain; particle &c. (*smallness*) 32; thermion; limature, filings, *débris, detritus*, scobs, magistery, fine powder; *flocculi*.

smoke; cloud of -dust, – sand, – smoke; puff –, volume -of smoke; sand –, dust- storm.

[Reduction to powder] pulverization, comminution, attenuation, granulation, disintegration, subaction, contusion, trituration, levigation, abrasion, detrition, multure; limation; filing &c. *v.*

[Instruments for pulverization] mill, millstone, grater, rasp, file, pestle and mortar, nutmeg-grater, teeth, molar, grinder, chopper, grindstone, kern, quern, muller.

V. come to dust; be -disintegrated, – reduced to powder &c.

reduce –, grind- to powder; pulverize, comminute, granulate, triturate, levigate; scrape, file, abrade, rub down, grind, grate, rasp, pound, bray, bruise; con-tuse, -tund; beat, crush, cranch, craunch, crunch, muller, scranch, crumble, disintegrate; attenuate &c. 195.

Adj. powdery, pulverulent, granular, mealy, floury, farinaceous, branny, furfuraceous, flocculent, dusty, sandy, sabulous; aren-ose, -arious, -aceous; gritty; efflorescent, impalpable.

pulverizable; friable, crumbly, shivery; pulverized &c. *v.*; attrite; in pieces.

331. Friction.—**N.** friction, attrition; rubbing &c. *v.*; erasure; con-frication, -trition; affriction, abrasion, arrosion, limature, frication, rub; elbow-grease; rosin; massage.

V. rub, scratch, abrade, scrape, scrub,

332. [Absence of friction. Prevention of friction.] **Lubrication.**—**N.** smoothness &c. 255; unctuousness &c. 355.

lubri-cation, -fication; anointment; oiling &c. *v.*

fray, rasp, graze, curry, scour, polish, rub out, erase, gnaw; file, grind &c. (*reduce to powder*) 330; *massage.*

set one's teeth on edge; rosin.

Adj. anatriptic, abrasive.

synovia; lubricant, graphite, glycerine, oil &c. 356; saliva; lather.

V. lubri-cate, -citate; oil, grease, lather, soap; wax.

Adj. lubricated &c. *v.*

2°. FLUID MATTER

1. *Fluids in General*

333. Fluidity.—N. fluidity, liquidity; liquidness &c. *adj.*; gaseity &c. 334; liquefaction &c. 334.

fluid, inelastic fluid; liquid, liquor; lymph, humour, juice, sap, serum, blood, serosity, gravy, rheum, ichor, sanies.

solu-bility, -bleness.

[Science of liquids] hydro-logy, -statics, -dynamics, hydraulics &c.

V. be -fluid &c. *adj.*; flow &c. (*water in motion*) 348; liquefy &c. 335.

Adj. liquid, fluid, serous, juicy, succulent, sappy; fluent &c. (*flowing*) 348.

liquefied &c. 335; uncongealed; soluble, hydrostatic &c. *n.*

334. Gaseity.—N. gaseity, gaseousness; vapourousness &c. *adj.*; flatulence, -lency; volatility, aeration, gasification.

elastic fluid, gas, air, vapour, ether, steam, fume, reek, *effluvium, flatus*; cloud &c. 353.

[Science of elastic fluids] pneumat-ics, -ostatics; aero-statics, -dynamics &c.

gas-, gaso-meter.

V. gassify, aerate, aerify; emit vapour &c. 336.

Adj. gaseous, aeriform, ethereal, aerial, airy, vaporous, volatile, evaporable; flatulent; aerostatic &c. *n.*

335. Liquefaction.—N. liquefaction; liquescen-ce, -cy, deliquescence; melting &c. (*heat*) 384; colliqu-ation, -efaction; thaw; de-, liquation; lixiviation, dissolution.

solution, apozem, lixivium, infusion, decoction, flux.

solvent, diluent, menstruum, alkahest, *aqua fortis.*

V. render -liquid &c. 333; liquefy, run, deliquesce; melt &c. (*heat*) 384; solve; dissolve, resolve; liquate; hold in solution; leach, lixiviate.

Adj. lique-fied &c. *v.*, -scent, -fiable; deliquescent, soluble, colliquative; solvent.

336. Vaporization. — N. vapor-, volatil-ization; gasification; e-, vaporation; distillation, cohobation, sublimation, exhalation; volatility.

vaporizer, still, retort, spray, atomizer; fumigation, steaming.

V. render -gaseous &c. 334; vaporize, volatilize; distil, sublime; evaporate, exhale, smoke, transpire, emit vapour, fume, reek, steam, fumigate.

Adj. volatilized &c. *v.*; reeking &c. *v.*; volatile; evaporable, vaporizable.

---

2. *Specific Fluids*

337. Water.—N. water; serum, serosity; lymph; rheum; diluent.

dilution, maceration, lotion; washing &c. *v.*; im-, mersion; humectation, infiltration, spargefaction, affusion, irrigation, *douche*, balneation, bath.

deluge &c. (*water in motion*) 348; high water, flood-, spring-tide.

338. Air.—N. air &c. (*gas*) 334; common -, atmospheric- air; atmosphere, stratosphere, isothermal layer, troposphere, Heaviside layer.

open, - air; sky, welkin; blue, - sky; cloud &c. 353.

weather, climate, rise and fall of the barometer, isobar.

V. be -watery &c. *adj.*; reek.

add water, water, wet; moisten &c. 339; dilute, dip, immerse; merge; im-, sub-merge; plunge, souse, duck, drown; soak, steep, macerate, pickle, wash, sprinkle, sparge, lave, bathe, affuse, splash, swash, douse, slosh, drench; dabble, slop, slobber, irrigate, inundate, deluge; syringe, inject, gargle; infiltrate, percolate.

Adj. watery, aqueous, aquatic, lymphatic; balneal, diluent; drenching &c. *v.*; diluted &c. *v.*; weak; wet &c. (*moist*) 339.

Phr. the waters are out.

339. Moisture.—N. moisture; moistness &c. *adj.*; hum-idity, -ectation; madefaction, dew; *serein*; marsh &c. 345; Hygromet-ry, -er.

V. moisten, wet; humect, -ate; sponge, damp, dampen, bedew; imbue, imbrue, infiltrate, saturate; seethe, sop; soak, drench &c. (*water*) 337.

be -moist &c. *adj.*; not have a dry thread; perspire &c. (*exude*) 295.

Adj. moist, damp; watery &c. 337; undried, humid, wet, dank, muggy, dewy; roric; roscid; juicy.

wringing wet; wet -through, – to the skin; saturated &c. *v.*

swashy, soggy, dabbled; reeking, seething, dripping, soaking, soft, sodden, sloppy, muddy; swampy &c. (*marshy*) 345; irriguous.

341. Ocean.—N. sea, ocean, main, deep, brine, salt water, waters, waves, billows, high seas, offing, great waters, watery waste, 'vasty deep,' briny ocean, herring pond, steamer track, the seven seas; wave, tide &c. (*water in motion*) 348.

hydrograph-y, -er, oceanography; Neptune, Thetis, Triton, Naiad, Nereid; sea-nymph, Siren, mer-maid, -man; trident, dolphin.

Adj. oceanic; mar-ine, -itime; pelagic, -ian; sea-going, -worthy; hydrographic.

Adv. at –, on- sea; afloat, on the high seas.

[Science of air] pneumatics, aero-logy, -scopy, -graphy; meteorology, climatology; eudio-, baro-, aero-meter; aneroid, baro-graph, -scope; weather-gauge, -glass, -cock.

exposure to the -air, – weather; ventilation; aero-station, -nautics, -naut &c. 267 and 269.

V. air, ventilate; fan &c. (*wind*) 349.

Adj. containing air, flatulent, effervescent; windy &c. 349.

atmospheric, airy; aeri-al, -form; pneumatic; meteorological; weatherwise.

Adv. in the open air, out of doors, *à la belle étoile, al fresco; sub -Jove, – dio.*

340. Dryness.—N. dryness &c. *adj.*; siccity, aridity, drought, ebb-, neaptide, low water.

drying, ex-, de-siccation; evaporation; dehydration; arefaction, dephlegmation, drainage.

drier, desiccator.

V. be -dry &c. *adj.*; render -dry &c. *adj.*; dry; dry –, soak- up; sponge, swab, wipe; ex-, de-siccate, dehydrate, anhydrate; drain, parch.

be fine, hold up.

Adj. dry, anhydrous, arid, waterless; dried &c. *v.*; undamped; juice-, sapless; sear; husky; rainless, without rain, fine; dry as -a bone, – dust, – a stick, – a mummy, – a biscuit; desiccated; dehydrated; water-proof, -tight.

342. Land.—N. land, earth, ground, dry land, *terra firma*.

continent, mainland, peninsula, delta; tongue –, neck- of land; isthmus, oasis; promontory &c. (*projection*) 250; highland &c. (*height*) 206.

coast, shore, scar, strand, beach; bank, lea; sea- board, -side, -shore, -bank, -coast, -beach; rock-, ironbound coast; loom of the land; derelict; innings; *alluvium*, alluvion.

soil, glebe, clay, loam, marl, cledge, chalk, gravel, mould, subsoil, clod, clot; rock, crag, cliff.

acres; real estate &c. (*property*) 780; landsman, land-lubber, farmer.

geography &c. 318; agriculture &c. 371.

V. land, come to land; set foot on -the soil, - dry land; come -, go- ashore.

Adj. earthy; continental, midland; littoral, riparian, ripuarian; alluvial; terrene &c. (*world*) 318; landed, predial, territorial.

Adv. ashore; on -shore, - land.

343. Gulf. Lake.—N. land covered with water, gulf, gulph, bay, inlet, bight, estuary, arm of the sea, fiord, armlet; frith, firth, ostiary, mouth; lagune, lagoon; indraught; cove, creek; natural harbour; roads; strait, narrows; Euripus; sound, belt, gut, kyles.

lake, loch, lough, mere, tarn, plash, broad, pond, pool, lin, puddle, well, artesian well, tank, sump; standing -, dead -, sheet of- water; fish -, millpond; race; ditch, dike, dyke, dam; reservoir &c. (*store*) 636.

Adj. lacustrine; land locked.

344. Plain.—N. plain, table land, mesa, face of the country; open -, country; basin, downs, waste, weary waste, desert, tundra, wild, steppe, pampas, savanna, prairie, champaign, heath, common, wold, veld; moor, -land, uplands, fell; bush; *plateau* &c. (*level*) 213; *campagna*.

meadow, mead, haugh, pasturage, park, field, lawn, green, plat, plot, grass-plat, greensward, sward, grass, turf, sod, heather; lea, ley, lay; grounds.

Adj. campestrian, champaign, alluvial.

345. Marsh.—N. marsh, swamp, morass, marish, moss, fen, bog, quagmire, slough, sump, wash; mud, squash, slush.

Adj. marsh, -y; swampy, boggy, plashy, poachy, quaggy, soft; muddy, sloppy, squashy, spongy; paludal; moor-ish, -y; fenny.

346. Island.—N. island, isle, islet, eyot, ait, holm, reef, atoll, breaker; archipelago; islander.

Adj. insular, sea-girt.

———

3. *Fluids in Motion*

347. [Fluid in motion.] Stream.—N. stream &c. (*of water*) 348, (*of air*) 349.

V. flow &c. 348; blow &c. 349.

348. [Water in motion.] River.—N. running water.

jet, spirt, squirt, spout, splash, swash, rush, gush, *jet d'eau*; sluice, chute.

water-spout, -fall: fall, cascade, force, foss; lin, -n; ghyll, Niagara; cata-ract, -dupe, -clysm; *débâcle*, inundation, deluge.

rain, -fall; *serein*; shower, scud; downpour, cloud burst; driving -, pouring -, drenching- rain; hyeto-logy, -graphy; rainy season, monsoon; predominance of Aquarius, reign of St. Swithin; mizzle, drizzle, *stillicidium*, plash; dropping &c. *v.*

stream, course, flux, flow, profluence; effluence &c. (*egress*) 295; defluxion; flowing &c. *v.*; current, tide, race.

spring; fount, -ain; rill, rivulet, gill,

349. [Air in motion.] Wind.—N. wind, draught, *flatus, afflatus,* air; breath, - of air; puff, whiff, zephyr; blow, drift; *aura*; stream, current; under-current.

gust, blast, breeze, squall, gale, half a gale, storm, tempest, hurricane, whirlwind, tornado, samiel, cyclone, typhoon; simoom; harmattan, monsoon, trade wind, sirocco, *mistral, bise, föhn,* tramontane, levanter; capful of wind; fresh -, stiff- breeze; keen blast; blizzard.

windiness &c. *adj.*; ventosity; rough -, dirty -, ugly -, stress of- weather; dirty-, windy-, mackerel- sky; mare's tail; thick -, black -, white- squall.

anemography, aerodynamics; wind-gauge, anemometer, weather-cock, vane.

gullet, rillet; stream-, brook-let; runnel, sike, burn, beck, brook, stream, river; reach; tributary.

body of water, torrent, rapids, flush, flood, swash, spate; spring -, high -, full-tide; bore; eagre, *hygre*; fresh, -et; undertow, indraught, reflux, under-current, eddy, vortex, gurge, whirlpool, Maelstrom, regurgitation, overflow; confluence, corrivation.

wave, billow, surge, swell, ripple; roller, ground swell, surf, breaker, white horses; comber, beach-comber; rough -, heavy -, cross -, long -, short -, chopping -, choppy- sea, choppiness; tidal wave.

[Science of fluids in motion] Hydro-dynamics; Hydraul-ics &c.; rain-gauge &c.

water-bearer, - carrier, Aquarius.

irrigation &c. (*water*) 337; pump; watering-pot, - cart; hydrant, stand-pipe, hose, sprinkler, drencher; fire-engine, squirt, syringe.

V. flow, run; meander; gush, pour, spout, roll, jet, well, issue; drop, drip, dribble, plash, squirt, spurt, spirtle, trill, trickle, distil, percolate; stream, overflow, inundate, deluge, flow over, splash, swash; guggle, murmur, babble, bubble, purl, gurgle, sputter, regurgitate; ooze, flow out &c. (*egress*) 295.

rain, - hard, - in torrents, - cats and dogs, - pitchforks; come down in sheets; pour with rain, drizzle, mizzle, spit, sprinkle, set in.

flow -, fall -, open -, drain- into; discharge itself, disembogue.

[Cause a flow] pour; pour out &c. (*discharge*) 297; shower down; irrigate, drench &c. (*wet*) 337; spill, splash.

[Stop a flow] stanch; dam, -up &c. (*close*) 261; obstruct &c. 706.

Adj. fluent; dif-, pro-, af-fluent; tidal; flowing &c. *v.*; meand-ering, -ry, -rous; fluvi-al, -atile; streamy, showery, rainy; drizzly, drizzling, pluvial, pluviose, stillicidous.

suf-, insuf-, per-, in-, af-flation; blowing, fanning &c. *v.*; ventilation.

sneezing &c. *v.*; sternutation; hic-cup, -cough; catching of the breath; breathing &c.

Eolus, Eurus, Boreas, Zephyr, cave of Eolus.

air-pump, lungs, bellows, blow-pipe, fan, blower; pulmotor, ventilator, punkah, aspirator, exhauster, ejector.

V. blow, waft; blow -hard, - great guns, - a hurricane &c. *n.*; whistle, roar, howl, ring in the shrouds; stream, issue.

respire, breathe, in-, ex-hale, puff; whif, -fle; gasp, wheeze; snuff, -le; sniff, -le; sneeze, cough, belch.

fan, ventilate; in-, per-flate; blow -, pump- up.

Adj. blowing &c. *v.*; windy, airy, æolian, flatulent; breezy, gusty, squally; stormy, tempestuous, blustering; bois-terous &c. (*violent*) 173.

pulmon-ic, -ary.

---

350. [Channel for the passage of water.] Conduit.—N. conduit, channel, duct, watercourse, race; head -, tail-race; adit, aqueduct, canal, trough, flume, gutter, pantile; dike, canyon, ravine, gorge, hollow, main, gully, moat, ditch, drain, sewer, culvert, *cloaca*, sough, kennel, siphon, *piscina*; pipe &c. (*tube*) 260; funnel; tunnel &c. (*passage*) 627; water -, waste- pipe; emunctory, gully-hole, artery, aorta, vein, blood vessel; lymphatic; throat, alimentary canal, intestine; pore, spout, scupper; ad-, a-jutage;

351. [Channel for the passage of air.] Air-pipe.—N. air-pipe, - shaft, - way, - passage, - tube; shaft, flue, chimney, funnel, vent, blow-hole, nostril, nozzle, throat, weasand, *trachea*; bronch-us, -ia; larynx, tonsils, wind-pipe, spiracle; venti-duct, -lator; louvre, blow-pipe &c. (*wind*) 349; pipe &c. (*tube*) 260.

---

hose; gar-, gur-goyle; penstock, weir; flood-, water-gate; sluice, lock, valve; rose; waterworks.

Adj. vascular &c. (*with holes*) 260.

3°. IMPERFECT FLUIDS

352. Semiliquidity.—N. semiliquidity; stickiness &c. *adj.*; visc-idity, -osity; gumm-, glutin-, muc-osity; spiss-, crass-itude; lentor; adhesiveness &c. (*cohesion*) 46.

inspiss-, incrass-ation; thickening, coagulation.

jelly, aspic, mucilage, gelatin, isinglass; colloid, mucus, phlegm; pituite, lava; glair, starch, gluten, albumen, milk, cream, protein; syrup, treacle; gum, size, glue, paste; wax, bee's-wax; emulsoid, emulsion, soup; squash, mud, slush, slime, ooze; moisture &c. 339; marsh &c. 345.

V. inspiss-, incrass-ate; coagulate, gelatinize, gelatinify, gel, jell, emulsify, thicken; mash, squash, churn, beat up.

Adj. semi-fluid, -liquid; half-melted, -frozen; milky, muddy &c. *n.*; lact-eal, -ean, -eous, -escent, -iferous; emulsive, curdled, thick, succulent, uliginous.

gelat-, album-, mucilag-, glut-inous; gelatine, mastic, amylaceous, ropy, clammy, clotted; vis-cid, -cous; sticky, tacky; slab, -by; lentous, pituitous; mu-cid, -culent, -cous.

353. [Mixture of air and water.] Bubble. [Cloud.]—N. bubble; foam, froth, head, fume, spume, lather, suds, spray, surf, yeast, barm, spindrift.

cloud, vapour, fog, mist, haze, steam; scud, rack, *nimbus; cumulus,* woolpack, *cirrus, stratus; cirro-, cumulostratus; cirro-cumulus;* mackerel sky, mare's tail, dirty sky.

[Science of clouds] nephelognosy, nephology.

effervescence, fermentation; bubbling &c. *v.*

nebula; cloudiness &c. (*opacity*) 426; nebulosity &c. (*dimness*) 422.

V. bubble, boil, foam, froth, spume, mantle, sparkle, guggle, gurgle; effervesce, ferment, fizzle; aerate; cloud, overcast, befog.

Adj. bubbling &c. *v.*; frothy, nappy, effervescent, sparkling, *mousseux,* up, fizzy, with a head on.

cloudy &c. *n.*; vaporous, nebulous, overcast; nubiferous, nephological; foggy, brumous.

354. Pulpiness.—N. pulpiness &c. *adj.*; pulp, paste, dough, sponge, curd, pap, rob, jam, pudding, mush, fool, poultice, grume, *papier mâché.*

Adj. pulpy &c. *n.*; pultaceous, grumous.

V. pulp, pulpify, mash.

355. Unctuousness.—N. unctuousness &c. *adj.*; unctuosity, lubricity; ointment &c. (*oil*) 356; anointment; lubrication &c. 332.

V. oil &c. (*lubricate*) 332.

Adj. unctuous, oily, oleaginous, adipose, sebaceous; fat, -ty; greasy; waxy. butyraceous, soapy, saponaceous, pinguid, lardaceous; slippery.

356. Oil.—N. oil, fat, butter, cream, grease, tallow, suet, lard, dripping, margarine, oleomargarine, exunge, blubber; glycerine, stearine, elaine, oleagine; soap; soft soap, wax, cerement; paraffin, spermaceti, adipocere; petroleum, mineral –, rock –, crystal- oil, kerosene, vegetable –, colza –, olive –, linseed –, cotton seed –, rape –, nut –, fusel- oil; animal –, neat's foot –, signal –, train- oil; ointment, unguent, liniment, salve, pomade, pomatum, brilliantine, spike –, nard.

356a. Resin.—N. resin, rosin, colophony; gum; lac, shellac, sealing-wax; amber, -gris; bitumen, pitch, tar, asphalt, -e, -um; varnish, copal, mastic, magilp, lacquer, japan.

V. varnish &c. (*overlay*) 223.

Adj. resinous, bituminous, pitchy, tarry.

Section III. ORGANIC MATTER

1°: Vitality

1. *Vitality in general*

357. Organization.—N. organized -world, − nature; living −, animated-nature; living beings; organic remains, organism; fossils; animal and vegetable kingdom, *fauna* and *flora*, biota.

prot-oplasm, -ein; albumen; structure &c. 329; organ-ization, -ism.

[Science of living beings] biology; natural history,* organic −, bio-chemistry, anatomy, physiology, embryology, morphology, evolution, Darwinism, Lamarkism, zoology &c. 368; botany &c. 369; naturalist, biologist &c.

Adj. organ-ic, -ized.

358. Inorganization. — N. mineral -world, − kingdom; unorganized −, inorganic −, brute −, inanimate- matter.

[Science of the mineral kingdom] mineralogy; geo-logy, -gnosy, -scopy; metall-urgy, -ography; lithology; orycto-logy, -graphy.

V. turn to dust, pulverize.

Adj. in-organic, -animate; unorganized; azoic; mineral.

---

359. Life.—N. life; vi-tality, -ability; animation; vital -spark, − flame, − force.

respiration, wind; breath -of life, − of one's nostrils; life-blood; Archeus; existence &c. 1.

vivification, vitalization; revivification &c. 163; Prometheus; life to come &c. (*destiny*) 152.

[Science of life] physiology, etiology, embryology, biology; animal economy.

nourishment, staff of life &c. (*food*) 298.

V. be -alive &c. *adj.*; live, breathe, respire; subsist &c. (*exist*) 1; walk the earth; strut and fret one's hour upon a stage; be spared.

see the light, be born, come into the world; fetch −, draw- -breath, − the breath of life; quicken; revive; come to, − life.

give birth to &c. (*produce*) 161; bring to life, put life into, vitalize; vivi-fy, -ficate; reanimate &c. (*restore*) 660; keep -alive, − body and soul together, − the wolf from the door; support life.

have nine lives like a cat.

360. Death.—N. death, dying &c. *v.*; de-cease, -mise; dissolution, departure, *obit*, release, rest, *quietus*, fall; loss, bereavement.

end &c. 67 −, cessation &c. 142 −, loss −, extinction −, ebb- of -life &c. 359.

death-warrant, -watch, -rattle, -bed; stroke −, agonies −, shades −, valley of the shadow −, jaws −, hand- of death; last -breath, − gasp, − agonies; dying -day, − breath, − agonies; swan song, *chant du cygne*; *rigor mortis*; Stygian shore; crossing the bar, the great adventure.

King -of terrors, − Death; Death, Angel of Death; mortality; doom &c. (*necessity*) 601.

euthanasia; happy release; break up of the system; natural -death, − decay; sudden −, violent- death; untimely end, watery grave; suffocation, *asphyxia*; heart failure; fatal disease &c. (*disease*) 655; death-blow &c. (*killing*) 361.

necrology, bills of mortality, obituary; death-song &c. (*lamentation*) 839.

V. die, expire, perish; meet one's -death, − end; pass away, be taken; yield −, resign- one's breath; resign

---

* The term *Natural History* is also used as relating to all the objects in Nature whether organic or inorganic, and including therefore *Mineralogy, Geology Meteorology,* &c.

Adj. living, alive; in -life, – the flesh, – the land of the living; on this side of the grave, above ground, breathing, quick, animated, viable; lively &c. (*active*) 682; alive and kicking; tenacious of life.

vital; vivi-fying, -fied &c. *v.*; Promethean.

Adv. *vivendi causâ.*

one's -being, – life; end one's -days, – life, – earthly career; breathe one's last; cease to -live, – breathe; depart this life; be -no more &c. *adj.*; go –, drop –, pop -off; lose –, lay down –, relinquish –, surrender- one's life; drop –, sink- into the grave; close one's eyes; fall –, drop- dead, – down dead; break one's neck; give –, yield- up the ghost; be all over with one.

pay the debt to nature, shuffle off this mortal coil, take one's last sleep; go the way of all flesh; join the -greater number, – majority, – choir invisible; awake to life immortal; come –, turn- to dust; cross the Stygian ferry; go to -one's long account, – one's last home, – Davy Jones's locker, – the wall; receive one's death warrant, make one's will, die a natural death, go out like the snuff of a candle; come to an untimely end; catch one's death; go off the hooks, kick the bucket, peg out; go West; hop the twig, turn up one's toes; die a violent death &c. (*be killed*) 361; make the supreme sacrifice.

Adj. dead, lifeless; deceased, demised, departed, defunct; late, gone, no more; ex-, in-animate; out of the world, taken off, released; departed this life &c. *v.*; dead and gone; bereft of life, stone dead, dead as -a door nail, – a door post, – mutton, – a herring, – nits; launched into eternity, gathered to one's fathers, numbered with the dead, gone to a better land, behind the veil, beyond the grave, – mortal ken.

dying &c. *v.*; mori-bund, -ent, Acherontic; hippocratic; *in -articulo, – extremis*; in the -jaws, – agony- of death; going, – off; *aux abois*; on one's -last legs, – death bed; at -the point of death, – death's door, – the last gasp; near one's end, given over, booked, fey; with one foot in –, tottering on the brink of- the grave.

still-born; mortuary; deadly &c. (*killing*) 361.

Adv. *post -obit, – mortem.*

Phr. life -ebbs, – fails, – hangs by a thread; one's -days are numbered, – hour is come, – race is run, – doom is sealed; Death -knocks at the door, – stares one in the face; the breath is out of the body; the grave closes over one; *sic itur ad astra.*

---

361. [Destruction of life; violent death.] **Killing.—N.** killing &c. *v.*; homicide, manslaughter, murder, assassination, trucidation, occision; lynching, effusion of blood; blood, -shed; gore, slaughter, carnage, butchery; *battue*, gladiatorial combat:

massacre; *fusillade, noyade, pogrom*; Thuggee, thuggism.

death blow, finishing stroke, *coup de grâce, quietus*; execution &c: (*capital punishment*) 972; judicial murder; martyrdom.

butcher, slayer, murderer, Cain, assassin. cut-throat, garrotter, *bravo,* thug, racketeer, gunman, mobster, gangster, Moloch, *matador, sabreur; guet-à-pens*; gallows, executioner &c. (*punishment*) 975; man-eater.

regicide, parricide, fratricide, infanticide, aborticide &c.

suicide, *felo-de-se, suttee, hara-kiri*, Juggernaut; immolation, holocaust.

suffocation, strangulation, garrotte; hanging &c. *v.*

deadly weapon &c. (*arms*) 727; Aceldama; the potter's field, the field of blood.

fatal accident, violent death, casualty.

[Destruction of animals] slaughtering; phthiozoics;* sport, -ing; the chase, venery; hunting, coursing, shooting, fishing; pig-sticking; sports-, hunts-, fisher-man; hunter, Nimrod; slaughterer, knacker, slaughter-house, shambles, *abattoir.*

V. kill, put to death, slay, shed blood; murder, assassinate, butcher, slaughter; victimize, immolate; massacre; take away –, deprive of- life; make away with, put an end to; despatch, decimate; burke, settle do, – to death, – for.

strangle, garrotte, hang, lynch, throttle, choke, stifle, suffocate, stop the breath, smother, asphyxiate, drown.

sabre; cut -down, – to pieces, – the throat; jugulate; stab, run through the body, bayonet; put to the -sword, – edge of the sword.

shoot, -- dead; blow one's brains out; brain, knock on the head; stone, lapidate; give –, deal- a death blow; give a -*quietus,* – *coup de grâce.*

behead, bowstring &c. (*execute*) 972.

hunt, shoot &c. *n.*

cut off, nip in the bud, launch into eternity, send to one's last account. bump off, rub out, sign one's death warrant, strike the death knell of.

give no quarter, pour out blood like water; run amuck, wade knee-deep –, imbrue one's hands- in blood.

die a violent death, welter in one's blood; dash –, blow- out one's brains; commit suicide; kill –, -make away with –, put an end to- oneself.

Adj. killing &c. *v.*; murd-, slaught-erous; sanguin-ary, -olent; blood-stained, -thirsty; homicidal, red-handed; bloody, -minded; ensanguined, gory, sanguineous.

mortal, fatal, lethal; dead-, death-ly; mort-, leth-iferous; unhealthy &c. 657; internecine; suicidal.

sporting; piscator-ial, -y:

Adv. in at the death.

362. Corpse.—N. corpse, corse, carcass, bones, skeleton, dry-bones; defunct, relics, *reliquiæ,* remains, mortal remains, dust, ashes, earth, clay; mummy; carrion; food for- worms, – fishes; tenement of clay, this mortal coil.

shade, ghost, *manes,* apparition &c. 980.

organic remains, fossils.

Adj. cadaverous, corpse-like; unburied &c. 363.

363. Interment.—N. interment, burial, sepulture, entombment; in-, humation; obs-, ex-equies; funeral, wake, pyre, funeral pile; crema-tion.

funeral -rite, – solemnity; knell, passing bell, tolling; dirge &c. (*lamentation*) 839; cypress; *obit,* dead march, muffled drum; coroner, mortician, undertaker, mute, mourner, professional mourner, pall-bearer; elegy; funeral -oration, – sermon; epitaph.

grave clothes, shroud, winding-sheet, cere-cloth; cerement.

coffin, shell, sarcophagus, urn, pall, bier, hearse, catafalque, cinerary urn.

grave, pit, sepulchre, tomb, vault, crypt, catacomb, mausoleum, *Gol-gotha,* house of death, narrow house, long home; cemetery, necropolis, boneyard; burial-place, -ground; grave-, church-yard; God's acre; mortuary, tope, cromlech, dolmen, menhir, barrow, tumulus, cairn;

* Bentham, 'Chrestomathia.'

ossuary; bone-, charnel-, dead-house; *morgue*; lich-gate; crematorium.
sexton, grave-digger.

monument, memorial, cenotaph, shrine; grave-, head-, tomb-stone;
memento mori; hatchment, stone, cross.

exhumation, disinterment; necropsy, autopsy, *post-mortem* examination.

V. inter, bury; lay in –, consign to- the -grave, – tomb; en-, in-tomb;
inhume; lay out, prepare for burial, embalm, mummify; conduct a
funeral, hold services; toll the knell; put to bed with a shovel.

exhume, disinter, unearth.

Adj. buried &c. *v.*; burial; fune-real, -brial; mortuary, sepulchral,
cinerary; elegiac; necroscopic.

Adv. *in memoriam*; *post-obit*, *-mortem*; beneath –, under- the sod.

Phr. *hic jacet, ci-gît, requiescat in pace.*

2. *Special Vitality*

364. Animality.—N. animal life;
anima-tion, -lity, -lization; breath.

flesh, – and blood; corporeal nature;
physique; strength &c. 159.

V. animalize, incorporate.

Adj. fleshly, incarnate, **carnal**, corporeal, human.

366. Animal.*—N. animal, – kingdom; *fauna*; brute creation.

beast, brute, creature, created being;
creeping –, living- thing; dumb -animal,
– creature.

flocks and herds, live stock; domestic –, wild- animals; game, *feræ naturæ*;
beasts of the field, fowls of the air,
denizens of the day.

vertebrate, bi-, quadru-ped, mammal, marsupial, bird, reptile, batrachian, amphibian, fish, crustacean,
shell fish, articulate, mollusc, worm,
insect, zoophyte; protozoon, animalcule &c. 193.

horse &c. (*beast of burden*) 271;
cattle, kine, ox; bull, -ock; steer, stot;
cow, milch cow, calf, heifer, shorthorn;
sheep; lamb, -kin; ewe –, pet- lamb;
ewe, ram, tup; pig, swine, boar, hog,
shoat, sow; tag, teg, wether.

dog, bitch, hound; pup, -py; whelp,
cur, mutt, mongrel; house-, watch-,
sheep-, shepherd's-, sporting-, fancy-,
lap-, toy-, bull-, badger-dog; mastiff;
blood-, grey-, stag-, deer-, fox-, otter-
hound; harrier, beagle, spaniel, pointer,

365. Vegetability.—N. vegetable life;
vegeta-tion, -bility; herbage.

V. vegetate, germinate, sprout,
shoot; cultivate.

Adj. vegetable &c. 367; rank, lush.

367. Vegetable.*— N. vegetable
– kingdom; *flora*, verdure.

plant; tree, shrub, bush; creeper;
vine; herb, -age; grass.

annual; per-, bi-, tri-ennial; exotic.

timber; primeval –, virgin- forest;
wood, -lands; hurst, frith, holt, weald,
park, chase, greenwood, brake, grove,
copse, coppice, *bocage, tope*, clump of
trees, thicket, spinet, spinney; under-
brush-wood; boscage, scrub; the oak
and the ash and the bonny ivy tree.

bush, jungle, prairie; heath, -er;
fern, bracken; furze, gorse, whin,
broom; grass, turf, grassland, greensward, green, lawn, meadow; pas-ture,
-turage; turbary; sedge, rush, weed;
fungus, mushroom, toadstool; lichen,
moss, conferva, mould; seaweed &c.;
growth, crop.

foliage, leafage, branch, bough, ramage; spray &c. 51; leaf, frond, flag,
petal, shoot, tendril.

flower, blossom, bud, bloom, bine;
flowering plant; tree, sapling, pollard;
timber-, fruit-tree; palm-, gum-tree;
pulse, legume.

* Extended lists of names of specific varieties of animals, vegetables, &c., are
beyond the scope of this work; see Introduction, p. xxv.

setter, retriever; Newfoundland; water -dog, – spaniel; pug, poodle; dachshund; Pinscher; turnspit; terrier; fox –, Skye-terrier; Dandie Dinmont; collie.

cat; puss, -y; kitten; grimalkin; gib-, tom-cat; mouser; fox, Reynard, vixen, stag, deer, hart, buck, doe, roe, antelope.

bird; poultry, fowl, cock, hen, chicken, chanticleer, partlet, rooster, dunghill cock, barn-door fowl; feathered -tribes, – songster; singing –, dicky- bird; canary; finch; auk, dodo, moa, roc, phœnix.

snake, serpent, viper, adder; newt, eft; asp, vermin.

Adj. animal, zoological.

equine, bovine, vaccine, canine, feline; fishy; piscator-y, -ial; molluscous, porcine, vermicular.

Adj. veget-able, -ous; herb-aceous, -al; botanic; sylvan, silvan; arbor- ary, -eous, -escent, -ical; dendritic, dendri-form; woody, grassy; ver-dant, -durous; floral, mossy; lign-ous, -eous; wooden, leguminous; end-, ex-ogenous.

---

368. [The science of animals.] **Zoology.**—N. zoo-logy, -nomy, -graphy, -tomy; anatomy; comparative anatomy; animal –, comparative- physiology; morphology.

anthrop-, ornith-, ichthy-, herpet-, ophi-, malac-, helminth-, entom-, oryct-, paleont-ology; ichthy- &c. -otomy; taxidermy.

zo- &c. -ologist.

Adj. zoological &c. n.

369. [The science of plants.] **Botany.** —N. botany; phyto-graphy, -logy, -tomy; vegetable physiology, herbori-zation, dendr-, myc-, fung-, alg-ology; flora, pomona; botanist &c.; botanic garden &c. (*garden*) 371; *hortus siccus, herbarium*, herbal.

herb-ist, -arist, -alist, -orist, -arian &c.

V. botanize, herborize.

Adj. botanical &c. n.

370. [The economy or management of animals.] **Cicuration.**—N. taming &c. *v.*; cicuration, zoohygiantics; domestic-ation, -ity; *manège*; veterinary art; breeding, pisciculture, apiculture &c.

menagery, vivarium, zoological garden, zoo; bear-pit; aviary, apiary, hive; aquarium, fishery, fish hatchery; duck-, fish-pond; stud-farm; stock farm, dairy.

[Destruction of animals] phthisozo-ics* &c. (*killing*) 361.

neat-, cow-, shep-herd, shepherdess; grazier, drover, cowboy, cowkeeper; trainer, breeder, groom, ostler &c. 746; veterinary surgeon, vet, horse doctor; farrier; keeper; gamekeeper.

cage &c. (*prison*) 752; hen-coop, bird-cage, cauf; sheep-fold &c. (*inclosure*) 232.

V. tame, domesticate, acclimatize, breed, tend, break in, train, corral, round up; cage, bridle &c. (*restrain*) 751; ride &c. 266.

drive, yoke, harness, hitch; groom,

371. [The economy or management of plants.] **Agriculture.**—N. agricul-ture, cultivation, husbandry, farming; georgics, geoponics; tillage, tilth, agron-omy, gardening, spade husbandry, vintage; hort-, arbor-, silv-, citr-, vit-, flor-iculture; intensive culture; land-scape gardening; forestry, afforesta-tion.

husbandman, horticulturist, citri-culturist, gardener, florist; agricult-or, -urist; yeoman, farmer, cultivator, tiller of the soil, ploughman, sower, reaper; woodcutter, backwoodsman, forester; vine grower, vintager; Boer; Triptolemus.

field, meadow, garden; botanic –, winter –, ornamental –, flower –, kit-chen –, truck –, market –, hop- garden; nursery; green-, hot-, glass-house; conservatory, cucumber frame, *cloche*, bed, border, seed-plot; grass-plat, lawn; park &c. (*pleasure ground*) 840; *parterre*, shrubbery, plantation, avenue,

---

* Bentham.

curry-comb; milk; shear; hatch; in-cubate.

Adj. pastoral, bucolic; tame, domestic, domesticated, broken in, gentle, docile.

————

arboretum, pinery, *pinetum*, orchard; vineyard, vinery; orangery; farm &c. (*abode*) 189.

V. cultivate; till, – the soil; farm, garden; sow, plant; reap, mow, cut; manure, dress the ground, dig, delve, dibble, hoe, plough, plow, harrow, rake, weed, lop and top, force, transplant, thin out, bed out, prune, graft.

Adj. agr-icultural, -arian, -estic.

arable; predial, rural, rustic, country, bucolic, Bœotian; horticultural.

372. Mankind.—N. man, -kind; human -race, – species, – nature; humanity, mortality, flesh, generation.

[Science of man] anthropo-logy, -graphy, -sophy; ethno-logy, -graphy; humanitarianism.

human being; person, -age; individual, creature, fellow creature, mortal, body, somebody, one; such a –, some- one; soul, living soul; earthling; party, head, hand; *dramatis personæ*.

people, persons, folk, public, society, world; community, – at large; general public; nation, -ality; state, realm; common-weal, -wealth; republic, body politic; million &c. (*commonalty*) 876; population &c. (*inhabitant*) 188.

cosmopolite; lords of the creation; ourselves.

Adj. human, mortal, personal, individual, national, civic, public, cosmopolitan; anthropoid.

373. Man.—N. man, male, he; man-hood &c. (*adolescence*) 131; gentleman, sir, master; yeoman, wight, swain, fellow, guy, blade, *beau*, chap, gaffer, goodman; husband &c. (*married man*) 903; Mr., mister, *monsieur, sahib, Herr, señor, signor*; boy &c. (*youth*) 129; Adonis.

[Male animal] cock, drake, gander, dog, boar, stag, hart, buck, horse, entire horse, stallion; gib-, tom-cat; he-, Billy-goat; ram, tup; bull, -ock; capon, ox, gelding; steer, stot.

Adj. male, he, masculine; manly, virile; un-womanly, -feminine.

————

374. Woman.—N. woman, she, female, petticoat, skirt, moll, broad.

feminality, feminity, muliebrity; womanhood &c. (*adolescence*) 131; feminism; gynecology, gyniatrics, gynics.

womankind; the -sex, – fair; fair –, softer- sex; weaker vessel; the distaff side.

dame, madam, *madame*, mistress, Mrs., lady, *mem-sahib, Frau, señora, signora, donna, belle*, matron, dowager, goody, gammer; good -woman, – wife; squaw; wife &c. (*marriage*) 903; matron-age, -hood.

Venus, nymph, wench, *grisette*; little bit of fluff; girl &c. (*youth*) 129.

inamorata (love) &c. 897; courtesan &c. 962.

spinster, old maid, virgin, bachelor girl, new woman, Amazon.

[Female animal] hen, slut, bitch, sow, doe, roe, mare; she-, Nanny-goat; ewe, cow; lioness, tigress; vixen.

gynecæum, harem, *seraglio, zenana, purdah*.

Adj. female, she; feminine, womanly, ladylike, matronly, maidenly; womanish, effeminate, unmanly, gynecic.

2°. SENSATION

(1.) *Sensation in general*

375. Physical Sensibility.—N. sensibility; sensitiveness &c. *adj.*; physical sensibility, feeling, perceptivity, anaphylaxis, susceptibility, æsthetics; moral sensibility &c. 822.

sensation, impression, effect; consciousness &c. (*knowledge*) 490.

external senses.

V. be -sensible &c. *adj.* -of; feel, perceive.

render, -sensible &c. *adj.*; excite, stir, sharpen, cultivate, tutor.

cause sensation, impress; excite -, produce- an impression.

Adj. sens-ible, -itive, -uous; æsthetic, perceptive, sentient; conscious &c. (*aware*) 490; impressionable, responsive, alive to.

acute, sharp, keen, vivid, lively, impressive, thin-skinned.

Adv. to the quick.

376. Physical Insensibility.—N. insensibility, physical insensibility; obtuseness &c. *adj.*; palsy, paralysis, *anæsthesia, analgesia, narcosis, hypnosis,* twilight sleep, stupor, coma, trance, catalepsy; sleep &c. (*inactivity*) 683; moral insensibility &c. 823; numbness &c. 381.

anæsthetic agent, general -, local-anæsthetic, opium, ether, chloroform, cocaine, novocaine, chloral; nitrous oxide, laughing gas; refrigeration.

V. be -insensible &c. *adj.*; have a -thick skin, - rhinoceros hide.

render -insensible &c. *adj.*; blunt. pall, obtund, benumb, deaden, paralyze; anæsthetize, drug, dope; put under the influence of -chloroform &c. *n.*; hypnotize; stupefy, stun, narcotize.

Adj. insensible, unfeeling, senseless, comatose, dazed, impercipient, callous, thick-skinned, pachydermatous; hard, -ened; case-hardened; proof; obtuse, dull; anæsthetic; paralytic, palsied, numb, dead.

377. Physical Pleasure.—N. pleasure; physical -, sensual -, sensuous-pleasure; bodily enjoyment, animal gratification, sensuality; hedonism, luxuriousness &c. *adj.*; dissipation, round of pleasure; titillation, *gusto,* creature comforts, comfort, ease; pillow &c. (*support*) 215; luxury, lap of luxury; purple and fine linen; bed of -down, - roses; velvet, clover; cup of Circe &c. (*intemperance*) 954.

treat; diversion, divertisement, entertainment; refreshment, regale; feast; *délice;* dainty &c. 394; *bonne bouche.*

source of pleasure &c. 829; happiness &c. (*mental enjoyment*) 827.

V. feel -, experience -, receive-pleasure; enjoy, relish; luxuriate -, revel -, riot -, bask -, swim -, wallow-in; feast on; gloat -over, - on; smack the lips.

live -on the fat of the land, - in comfort &c. *adv.*; bask in the sunshine, *faire ses choux gras.*

give pleasure &c. 829.

378. Physical Pain.—N. pain; suffering, -ance; bodily - physical- -pain, - suffering; mental suffering &c. 828; dolour, ache; aching &c. *v.*; smart; shoot, -ing; twinge, twitch, gripe, head-, ear-, tooth-ache; *migraine,* neuralgia, neuritis, lumbago, gout, sciatica; hurt, cut; sore, -ness; discomfort, *malaise; tic douloureux.*

spasm, cramp; nightmare, *ephialtes;* crick, stitch, kink; thrill, convulsion, throe; throb &c. (*agitation*) 315; pang.

sharp -, piercing -, throbbing -, shooting -, gnawing -, burning- pain; anguish, agony.

torment, torture; rack; cruci-ation, -fixion; martyrdom; martyr, toad under a harrow, vivisection.

V. feel -, experience -, suffer -, undergo- pain &c. *n.*; suffer, ache, smart, bleed; tingle, shoot; twinge, twitch, lancinate; writhe, wince, make a wry face; sit on -thorns, - pins and needles.

give -, inflict- pain; pain, hurt, chafe, sting, bite, gnaw, gripe, stab, grind;

Adj. enjoying &c. *v.*; luxurious, voluptuous, sensual, hedonistic, comfortable, cosy, snug, in comfort, at ease.

agreeable &c. 829; grateful, refreshing, comforting, cordial, genial; sensuous; palatable &c. 394; sweet &c. (*sugar*) 396; fragrant &c. 400; melodious &c. 413; lovely &c. (*beautiful*) 845.

Adv. in -comfort &c. *n.*; on -a bed of roses &c. *n.*; at one's ease.

pinch, tweak; grate, gall, fret, prick, pierce, wring, convulse; torment, torture; rack, agonize; crucify; excruciate; break on the wheel, put to the rack; flog &c. (*punish*) 972; grate on the ear &c. (*harsh sound*) 410.

Adj. in -pain &c. *n.*, — a state of pain; pained &c. *v.*

painful; aching &c. *v.*; biting, poignant; sore, raw, tender, with exposed nerve.

(2.) *Special Sensation*

1. *Touch*

379. [Sensation of pressure.] **Touch.**—**N.** touch; tact, -ion, -ility; feeling; palp-ation, -ability; manipulation; brush, tick, graze, contact &c. 199.

[Organ of touch] hand, finger, fore-finger, thumb, paw, feeler, *antenna*.

V. touch, feel, handle, finger, thumb, paw, fumble, grope, grabble; twiddle, tweedle; pass -, run- the fingers over, massage, rub, knead; palpate, stroke, manipulate, wield; throw out a feeler.

Adj. tact-ual, -ile; tangible, palpable; lambent.

380. Sensations of Touch.—**N.** itching &c. *v.*; titillation, formication, *aura*.

V. itch, tingle, creep, thrill, sting; prick, -le; tickle, titillate.

Adj. itching &c. *v.*

381. [Insensibility to touch.] **Numbness.**—**N.** numbness &c. (*physical insensibility*) 376; pins and needles.

local anæsthetic, cocaine, novocaine &c.; morphia.

V. benumb &c. 376; freeze, dull, deaden.

Adj. numb; benumbed &c. *v.*; intangible, impalpable.

2. *Heat*

382. Heat.—**N.** heat, caloric; temperature, warmth, fervour, calidity; incal-, incand-, recal-, decal-escence; glow, flush, blush; fever, hectic.

phlogiston; fire, spark, scintillation, flash, flame, blaze; arc; bonfire; firework, pyrotechny; wild-fire; sheet of fire, lambent flame; devouring element; conflagration.

summer, dog-days, canicule; baking &c. 384 -, white -, tropical -, Afric -, Bengal -, summer -, blood- heat; heat wave, sirocco, simoon; broiling sun; isolation; warming &c. 384.

sun &c. (*luminary*) 423; fire worshipper &c. 991; furnace &c. 386.

geyser, hot spring, volcano.

[Science of heat] pyrology; therm-

383. Cold.—**N.** cold, -ness &c. *adj.*; frigidity, gelidity, algidity, inclemency, *fresco*.

winter; depth of -, hard- winter; Siberia, Nova Zembla; Ant-, arctic, North -, South- Pole.

ice; snow, - flake, - crystal, - drift; sleet; hail, -stone; rime, frost; hoar -, white -, hard -, sharp- frost; icicle, thick-ribbed ice; fall of snow, snow storm, heavy fall, *avalanche*; ice-berg, -floe; floe, berg; *glacier*; *névé*, *serac*.

[Sensation of cold] chilliness &c. *adj.*; chill; shivering &c. *v.*; gooseskin, -flesh; *rigor*, horripilation, chattering of teeth; frostbite, chilblain.

V. be -cold &c. *adj.*; shiver, starve, quake, shake, tremble, shudder, didder,

ology, -otics; thermometer &c. 389.

V. be -hot &c. *adj.*; glow, incandesce, flush, sweat, swelter, bask, smoke, reek, stew, simmer, seethe, boil, burn, singe, scorch, scald, grill, broil, blaze, flame; smoulder; parch, fume, pant.

heat &c. (*make hot*) 384; thaw, fuse, melt, give.

Adj. hot, heated, warm, mild, genial, tepid, lukewarm, unfrozen; therm-al, -ic; calorific; ferv-ent, -id; ardent; aglow.

sunny, torrid, tropical, estival, canicular; close, sultry, stifling, stuffy, suffocating, oppressive; reeking &c. *v.*; baking &c. 384.

red -, white -, smoking -, burning &c. *v.* -, piping- hot; like -a furnace, - an oven; hot as -fire, - pepper; hot enough to roast an ox.

fiery; incand-, incal-escent; candent, ebullient, glowing, smoking; on fire; blazing &c. *v.*; in -flames, - a blaze; alight, afire, ablaze; un-quenched, -extinguished; smouldering; in a -heat, - glow, - fever, - perspiration, - sweat; sudorific; swelter-ing, -ed; blood-hot, -warm; warm as -a toast, - wool; recalescent, thermogenic, pyrotechnic, feverish, febrile, inflamed.

volcanic, plutonic, igneous; isother-mal, -mic, -al.

Phr. Not a breath of air.

384. Calefaction.—N. increase of temperature; heating &c. *v.*; cale-, tepe-, torre-faction; melting, fusion; liquefaction &c. 335; burning &c. *v.*; kindling, combustion; in-, ac-cension; con-, cremation; scorification; cauter-y, -ization; ustulation, calcination; in-, cineration; cupellation; carbonization.

ignition, inflammation, adustion, flagration; de-, con-flagration; empyrosis, incendiarism; arson; *auto-dafé*; suttee.

boiling &c. *v.*; coction, ebullition, estuation, elixation, decoction.

furnace &c. 386; blanket, flannel, fur, muffler, wrap; wadding &c. (*lining*) 224; clothing &c. 225.

match &c. (*fuel*) 388; incendiary, pyromaniac; *pétroleur, pétroleuse*; cauterant, caustic, lunar caustic, apozem, moxa.

sunstroke, *coup de soleil*; insolation, sunburn.

pottery, ceramics, crockery, porcelain, china; earthen-, stone-ware; pot.

quiver; perish with cold; chill &c. (*render cold*) 385.

Adj. cold, cool; chill, -y; gelid, frigid, algid; fresh, keen, bleak, raw, inclement, bitter, biting, niveous, cutting, nipping, piercing, pinching; clay-cold; starved &c. (*made cold*) 385; shivering &c. *v.*; aguish, *transi de froid*; frostbitten, -bound, -nipped.

cold as -a stone, - marble, - lead, - iron, - a frog, - charity, - Christmas; cool as -a cucumber, - custard.

icy, glacial, frosty, freezing, wintry, brumal, hibernal, boreal, arctic, antarctic, polar, Siberian, hyemal; hyperbore-an, -al; ice-bound; frozen out.

un-warmed, -thawed, -heated; isocheimal, -chimenal.

Adv. coldly, bitterly &c. *adj.*; *à pierre fendre.*

---

385. Refrigeration.—N. refrigeration, infrigidation, reduction of temperature; cooling &c. *v.*; con-gelation, -glaciation; ice &c. 383; solidification &c. (*density*) 321; refrigerator &c. 387.

V. cool, fan, refrigerate, refresh, ice; congeal, freeze, glaciate; benumb, starve, pinch, chill, petrify, chill to the marrow, nip, cut, pierce, bite, make one's teeth chatter; damp.

Adj. cooled &c. *v.*; frozen out; cooling &c. *v.*; frigorific.

Extinction.—N. *extincteur*; fire, - engine, - extinguisher, - annihilator, - brigade, - man; sprinkler, hose, hydrant, standpipe.

incombusti-bility, -bleness &c. *adj.*

V. Quench; damp; blow-, put-, stamp - out; extinguish.

go -, burn-out.

Adj. incombustible; un-, unin-flammable; fire-proof.

mug, *terra-cotta*, brick, clinker; cinder, ash, *scoriæ*; embers, dross, slag, products of combustion, coke, carbon, charcoal.

inflamma-, combusti-bility.

[Transmission of heat] diathermancy, transcalency.

V. heat, warm, chafe, stive, foment; make -hot &c. 382; sun oneself, bask in the sun.

fire; set -fire to, – on fire; kindle, enkindle, light, ignite, strike a light; apply the -match, – torch- to; re-kindle, -lume; fan –, add fuel to- the flame; poke –, stir –, blow- the fire; make a bonfire of; burn at the stake.

melt, thaw, fuse; liquefy &c. 335.

burn, inflame, roast, toast, fry, grill, singe, parch, bake, torrefy, scorch; brand, cauterize, sear, burn in; corrode, char, carbonize, calcine, incinerate; smelt, cupel, scorify; reduce to ashes; burn to a cinder; commit –, consign- to the flames.

boil, digest, stew, cook, seethe, scald, parboil, simmer; do to rags.

take –, catch- fire; blaze &c. (*flame*) 382.

Adj. heated &c. *v.*; molten, sodden; *réchauffé*; heating &c. *v.*

inflammable, burnable, inflammatory, combustible; diatherm-al -anous; burnt &c. *v.*; volcanic.

---

386. Furnace.—N. furnace, blast furnace, fire-box, stove, incinerator, destructor, crematorium, crematory, kiln, oven, oast-house; hot-, bake-, wash-house; laundry; conservatory; hearth, focus; athanor, hypocaust, reverberatory; volcano; forge, fiery furnace; *tuyère*, brasier, salamander,

387. Refrigerator.—N. refrigerator, -y; *frigidarium*; cold storage; refrigerating-plant, – machine; ice-house, -pail, -bag, -chest, -pack; cooler, damper; wine-cooler, freezing mixture.

See 385.

---

heater, warming-pan, foot-warmer, hot-water bottle; radiator; boiler, geyser, caldron, seething caldron, pot; urn, kettle; chafing-dish; retort, crucible, alembic, still; saggar.

fire-place, -dog, -irons; hearth, ingle, grate, range, kitchener; kitchen range; oil-, gas-, electric, -cooker, -stove; fireless cooker; fire; galley; ca-, cam-boose; poker, tongs, shovel, hob, trivet; and-, grid-iron; frying-, stew-pan &c.

hot –, Turkish –, Russian –, vapour –, shower –, warm- bath; *calidarium, tepidarium, sudatorium*, sudatory; *hammam*.

388. Fuel.—N. fuel, firing, combustible, coal, wallsend, anthracite, bituminous coal, slack, culm, cannel coal, lignite, briquette, coke, carbon, charcoal; turf, peat, fire-wood, bobbing, faggot, log, Yule log, ember, cinder &c. (*products of combustion*) 384; kindling wood, tinder, touch-wood; fumigator, sulphur, brimstone; incense; port-fire; fire-barrel, -ball, -brand.

fuel oil, gas, gasoline.

brand, torch, fuse; wick; spill, match, safety match, light, lucifer, congreve, vesuvian, vesta, fusee, locofoco; linstock; illuminant.

candle &c. (*luminary*) 423; oil &c. (*grease*), 356; petrol, gasoline, methylated –, spirit; gas, acetylene.

Adj. carbonaceous; combustible, inflammable.

V. stoke, fire, feed, add fuel to the flames.

389. Thermometer.—N. thermo-meter, -scope, -stat, -pile, differential thermometer; pyro-, calori-meter; radio micrometer &c.

3. *Taste*

390. Taste.—N. taste, flavour, gust, *gusto*, relish, savour; sapor, sapidity; twang, smack, smatch; after-taste, tang.

tasting; de-, gustation.

palate, tongue, tooth, stomach.

V. taste, savour, smatch, smack, flavour, twang; tickle the palate &c. (*savoury*) 394; smack the lips.

Adj. sapid, saporific; gusta-ble, -tory; strong; flavoured, spiced, savoury; palatable &c. 394.

391. Insipidity.—N. insipidity; taste-lessness &c. *adj.*

V. be -tasteless &c. *adj.*

Adj. void of -taste &c. 390; insipid; jejune; taste-, gust-, savour-less; in-gustible, mawkish, milk and water, weak, stale, flat, vapid, *fade*, wishy-washy, mild; untasted.

---

392. Pungency.—N. pungency, piquancy, poignancy, *haut-goût*, strong taste, twang, race, tang.

sharpness &c. *adj.*; acrimony, acridity; roughness &c. (*sour*) 397; unsavouriness &c. 395.

nitre, saltpetre; mustard, cayenne, caviare; seasoning &c. (*condiment*) 393; brine.

dram, cordial, nip, pick-me-up, bracer, potion.

nicotine, tobacco, snuff, quid; segar; cigar, -ette, gasper, fag; cheroot; weed; fragrant –, Indian- weed; pipe, clay pipe, churchwarden, brier, meerschaum, hookah, hubble-bubble.

V. be -pungent &c. *adj.*; bite the tongue.

render -pungent &c. *adj.*; season, spice, salt, pepper, pickle, brine, devil, curry.

smoke, chew, take snuff.

Adj. pungent, strong; high-, full-flavoured; high-tasted, -seasoned; gamy; sharp, stinging, rough, *piquant*, racy; biting, mordant; spicy; seasoned &c. *v.*; hot, – as pepper; peppery, vellicating, escharotic, meracious; acrid, acrimonious; bitter; rough &c. (*sour*) 397; unsavoury &c. 395.

salt, saline, brackish, briny; salt as -brine, – a herring, – Lot's wife.

---

393. Condiment.—N. condiment, flavouring, salt, mustard, pepper, cayenne, curry, seasoning, sauce, spice, cinnamon, chillies, relish, *sauce piquante*, caviare, pot-herbs, onion, garlic, pickle, chutney, nutmeg &c.

V. season &c. (*render pungent*) 392.

---

394. Savouriness.—N. savouriness &c. *adj.*; relish, zest.

tit-bit, dainty, delicacy, ambrosia, nectar, *bonne bouche*; game, turtle, venison.

V. taste good, be -savoury &c. *adj.*; tickle the -palate, – appetite; flatter the palate.

render -palatable &c. *adj.*

relish, like, smack the lips.

Adj. savoury, well-tasted, to one's taste, tasty, good, palatable, nice, dainty, delectable; tooth-ful, -some;

395. Unsavouriness.—N. unsavouriness &c. *adj.*; amaritude; acri-mony, -tude; roughness &c. (*sour*) 397; acerbity, austerity; gall and worm-wood, rue, quassia, aloes; sickener.

V. be -unpalatable &c. *adj.*; sicken, disgust, nauseate, pall, turn the stomach.

Adj. un-savoury, -palatable, -sweet: ill-flavoured, un-appetizing, -eatable, inedible; bitter, – as gall; acrid, acri-monious; rough.

offensive, repulsive, nasty; sickening

gustful, appetizing, lickerish, delicate, delicious, exquisite, rich, luscious, ambrosial.

Adv. *per amusare la bocca.*

Phr. *cela se laisse manger.*

396. Sweetness.—N. sweetness, dulcitude, saccharinity.

sugar, cane-, beet-sugar; saccharine, glucose, syrup, treacle, molasses, honey, manna; confection, -ery; sweets, grocery, conserve, preserve, *confiture*, jam, marmalade, julep; sugar-candy, -plum; licorice, liquorice, plum, lollipop, *bonbon*, *jujube*, comfit, sweetmeat, caramel, toffee, butterscotch.

nectar; hydromel, mead, metheglin, honeysuckle, *liqueur*, sweet wine.

pastry, pie, tart, puff, pudding, cake.

dulc-ification, -oration.

V. be -sweet &c. *adj.*

render -sweet &c. *adj.*; sugar, saccharize, sweeten; edulcorate; dulc-orate, -ify; candy; mull.

Adj. sweet, sugary; sacchar-ine, -iferous; dulcet, honied, candied, luscious, nectarious, melliferous; sweetened &c. *v.*

sweet as -a nut, – sugar, – honey.

&c. *v.*; nauseous; loath-, ful-some; unpleasant &c. 830.

397. Sourness.—N. sourness &c. *adj.*; acid, -ity; acetous fermentation; acerbity.

vinegar, verjuice, crab, alum.

V. be –, turn- -sour &c. *adj.*; set the teeth on edge.

render -sour &c. *adj.*; acid-ify, -ulate.

Adj. sour; acid, -ulous, -ulated; acerb; tart, crabbed; acet-ous, -ose; sour as vinegar, sourish, acescent, sub-acid; styptic, hard, rough; unripe, green.

---

4. Odour

398. Odour.—N. odour, smell, odorament, scent, effluvium; eman-, exhal-ation; fume, essence, trail, nidor, redolence.

sense of smell; scent; act of -smelling &c. *v.*

V. have an -odour &c. *n.*; smell, – of, – strong of; exhale; give out a -smell &c. *n.*; scent.

smell, scent; snuff, – up; sniff, nose, inhale.

Adj. odor-ous, -iferous; smelling, graveolent, nidorous, pungent.

[Relating to the sense of smell] olfactory, quick-scented.

399. Inodorousness.—N. inodorousness; absence –, want- of smell.

V. be -inodorous &c. *adj.*; not smell. deodorize.

Adj. inodor-ous, -ate; scentless; without –, wanting- smell &c. 398.

deodoriz-ed, -ing.

strong-scented; redolent,

400. Fragrance. — N. fragrance, aroma, redolence, perfume, *bouquet*; sweet smell, aromatic perfume.

perfumery; incense; musk, frankincense; pastil, -le; myrrh, perfumes of Arabia, chypre; otto, ottar, attar; bergamot, balm, civet, *pot-pourri*, pulvil; nosegay, *boutonnière*; scent, -bag; *sachet*, scent-bottle, smelling bottle, *vinaigrette*; toilet water, *eau de Cologne*; thurible, censer, thurification.

perfumer; incense bearer.

401. Fetor.—N. fetor, fetidness; bad &c. *adj.*; -smell, – odour; stench, stink; mephitis, foul –, mal- odour; *empyreuma*; mustiness &c. *adj.*; rancidity; foulness &c. (*uncleanness*) 653.

stoat, polecat, skunk; assafœtida; fungus, garlic; stink-pot, -bomb.

V. have a -bad smell &c. *n.*; smell; stink, – in the nostrils, – like a polecat; smell -strong &c. *adj.*, – offensively.

Adj. fetid; strong-smelling; high, bad, strong, fulsome, offensive, noisome, rank, rancid, reasty, tainted, musty,

V. be -fragrant &c. *adj.*; have a -perfume &c. *n.*; smell sweet, scent, perfume, thurify, embalm.

Adj. fragrant, aromatic, redolent, spicy, balmy, scented; sweet-smelling, -scented; perfum-ed, -atory; thuriferous; fragrant as a rose, muscadine, ambrosial.

fusty, frouzy; olid, -ous; nidorous; smelling, stinking; putrid &c. 653; suffocating, mephitic; empyreumatic.

---

5. Sound

(i.) SOUND IN GENERAL

402. Sound.—N. sound, noise, strain; accent, twang, intonation, tone, tune; cadence; sonority, sonorousness &c. *adj.*; audibility; resonance &c. 408; voice &c. 580.

[Science of sound] acou-, acu-stics; catacoustics, cataphonics; phon-ics, -etics, -ology, -ography; dia-coustics, -phonics.

telephone, phonograph &c. 418.

V. produce sound; sound, make a noise; give out -, emit- sound; phonetize, phonate; resound &c. 408.

Adj. sounding; soniferous; sonorific; resonant, audible, acoustic, auditory, distinct; stertorous; phonic, sonant; phonetic.

---

403. Silence.—N. silence; stillness &c. (*quiet*) 265; peace, hush, lull, rest; muteness &c. 581; solemn -, awful -, dead -, deathlike- silence.

V. be -silent &c. *adj.*; hold one's tongue &c. (*not speak*) 585.

render -silent &c. *adj.*; silence, still, hush; stifle, muffle, gag, stop; muzzle, put to silence &c. (*render mute*) 581.

Adj. silent; still, -y; calm, quiet; noise-, sound-, speech-less; hushed &c. *v.*; mute &c. 581; aphonic.

soft, solemn, awful, deathlike, silent as the grave; inaudible &c. (*faint*) 405.

Adv. silently &c. *adj.*; *sub silentio*; in perfect silence.

Int. hush! 'sh! silence! soft! whist! tush! chut! tut! *pax!* mum's the word! hold your tongue! shut up! be silent! be quiet! stop that noise! hold your row! dry up! peace, be still!

Phr. one might hear a -feather, - pin- drop.

---

404. Loudness.—N. loudness, power; loud noise, din; clang, -or; clatter, noise, bombilation, roar, uproar, racket, static, grinders, hubbub, *fracas, charivari*, trumpet blast, blare, flourish of trumpets, fanfare, *tintamarre*, peal, swell, blast, alarum, boom; resonance &c. 408.

vociferation; pandemonium, hullaballoo &c. 411; lungs; Stentor; megaphone; siren.

artillery, cannon, gunfire, shellburst, bomb; thunder.

V. be -loud &c. *adj.*; peal, swell, clang, boom, thunder, fulminate, roar; resound &c. 408; speak up, shout &c. (*vociferate*) 411; bellow &c. (*cry as an animal*) 412; give tongue.

rend the -air, - skies; fill the air; din -, ring -, thunder- in the ear;

---

405. Faintness.—N. faintness &c. *adj.*; faint sound, whisper, breath; under-tone, -breath; murmur, hum, rustle, buzz, purr; plash; sough, moan, sigh, susurration; tinkle; 'still small voice.'

hoarseness &c. *adj.*; raucity.

silencer, soft pedal, damper, mute, *sourdine*.

V. whisper, breathe, murmur, purl, hum, gurgle, ripple, babble, flow; tinkle; mutter &c. (*speak imperfectly*) 583.

steal on the ear; melt in -, float on- the air.

muffle, mute, deaden, damp, stifle.

Adj. inaudible; scarcely -, justaudible; low, dull; stifled, muffled; hoarse, husky; gentle, soft, faint; floating; purling, flowing &c. *v.*;

pierce –, split –, rend- the -ears, – head; deafen, stun; *faire le diable à quatre;* make one's windows shake; awaken –, startle- the echoes; make the welkin ring.

Adj. loud, sonorous; high-, big-sounding; blatant; deep, full, powerful, noisy, clangorous, multisonous, *fortissimo;* thundering, deafening &c. *v.;* trumpet-tongued; ear-splitting, -rending, -deafening; piercing; obstreperous, rackety, uproarious; enough to wake the -dead, – seven sleepers.

shrill &c. 410; clamorous &c. (*vociferous*) 411; stentor-ian, -ophonic;

Adv. loudly &c. *adj.;* aloud; at the top of one's voice, lustily, in full cry.

Phr. the air rings with.

whispered &c. *v.;* liquid; soothing; dulcet &c. (*melodious*) 413.

Adv. in a whisper, with bated breath, *sotto voce,* between the teeth, aside; *pian-o, -issimo; à la sourdine; con sordine;* out of earshot, inaudibly &c. *adj.*

(ii.) SPECIFIC SOUNDS*

406. [Sudden and violent sounds.] **Snap.—N.** snap &c. *v.;* rapping &c. *v.;* de-, crepitation; smack, clap, report; thud; burst, explosion, discharge, detonation, blow-out, back-fire, firing, salvo, volley, pistol-shot.

squib, cracker, gun, rifle, pop-gun.

V. rap, snap, tap, knock; click; clash; crack, -le; crash; pop; slam, bang, clap, thump, plump; toot; back-fire, explode, burst on the ear.

Adj. rapping &c. *v.*

Int. crash! bang!

Adj. rolling &c. *v.;* monotonous &c. (*repeated*), 104; like a bee in a bottle.

407. [Repeated and protracted sounds.] **Roll.—N.** roll &c. *v.;* drumming &c. *v.;* tattoo; ding-dong; tantara; rataplan; whirr; rat-a-tat; rub-a-dub; pit-a-pat; quaver, clutter, *charivari,* racket; cuckoo; repetition &c. 104; peal of bells, devil's tattoo; reverberation &c. 408.

drumfire, barrage.

machine gun.

V. roll, drum, rumble, rattle, clatter, rustle, roar, drone, patter, clack.

hum, trill, shake; chime, peal, toll; tick, beat.

drum –, din- in the ear.

---

408. Resonance.—N. resonance; ring &c. *v.;* ringing &c. *v.;* tintinnabulation; reflection, reverberation, clangor.

low –, base –, bass –, flat –, grave –, deep –, pedal- note; bass; *basso, – profondo;* bari-, bary-tone; *contralto.*

V. re-sound, -verberate, -echo; ring, ding, sing, jingle, gingle, chink, clink; tink, -le; chime; gurgle &c. 405; plash, guggle, echo, ring in the ear.

Adj. resounding &c. *v.;* resonant, tinnient, tintinnabulary; deep-toned, -sounding, -mouthed; hollow, sepulchral; gruff &c. (*harsh*) 410.

408a. Non-resonance. — N. thud, thump, dead sound; non-resonance; muffled drums, cracked bell; silencer, damper; mute, *sourdine.*

V. sound dead; stop –, damp- the -sound, – reverberations; deaden, muffle.

Adj. non-resonant, dead, muted, muffled.

---

409. [Hissing sounds.] **Sibilation.—N.** sibilation; hiss &c. *v.;* sternutation; high note &c. 410.

goose, serpent, snake.

* [The author's classification of 'sounds has been retained, though it does not entirely accord with the theories of modern science.—ED.]

V. hiss, buzz, whiz, rustle; fizz, -le, sizzle, swish; wheeze, whistle, snuffle; squash; sneeze.

Adj. sibilant; hissing &c. *v.*; wheezy.

410. [Harsh sounds.] **Stridor.—N.** creak &c. *v.*; creaking &c. *v.*; discord &c. 414; stridor; harshness, roughness, sharpness &c. *adj.*; cacophony.

acute –, high- note; *soprano*, treble, tenor, *alto*, falsetto, *voce di testa*; shriek, cry &c. 411.

piccolo, fife, penny -whistle, – trumpet.

V. creak, grate, jar, burr, pipe, twang, jangle, clank, clink; scream &c. (*cry*) 411; yelp &c. (*animal sound*) 412; buzz &c. (*hiss*) 409.

set the teeth on edge, *écorcher les oreilles*; pierce –, split- the -ears, – head; offend –, grate upon –, jar upon- the ear.

Adj. creaking &c. *v.*; strident, stridulous, harsh, coarse, hoarse, horrisonous, raucous, metallic, rough, gruff, grum, sepulchral.

sharp, high, acute, shrill, high-pitched; trumpet-toned; piercing, ear-piercing; cracked; discordant &c. 414; cacophonous.

411. Cry.—N. cry &c. *v.*; voice &c. (*human*) 580; bark &c. (*animal*) 412.

vociferation, outcry, hullaballoo, chorus, clamour, hue and cry, plaint; lungs; stentor.

V. cry, roar, shout, bawl, brawl, halloo, halloa, hail, hoop, whoop, yell, bellow, howl, scream, screech, screak, shriek, shrill, squeak, squeal, squall, whine, whinny, pule, pipe, yaup.

cheer, hurrah; hoot; grumble, moan, groan.

snore, snort; grunt &c. (*animal sounds*) 412.

vociferate; raise –, lift up- the voice; call –, sing –, cry- out; exclaim; rend the air; thunder –, shout- at the -top of one's voice, – pitch of one's breath; *s'égosiller*; strain the -throat, – voice, – lungs; give a -cry &c.

Adj. crying &c. *v.*; clam-ant, -orous; vociferous; stentorian &c. (*loud*) 404; open-mouthed.

412. [Animal sounds.] **Ululation.—N.** cry &c. *v.*; crying &c. *v.*; ululation, latration, belling; reboation; call, note; bark, howl, yelp; twittering, woodnote; insect cry, fritinancy, drone; screech; cuckoo.

V. cry, ululate, howl, roar, bellow, blare, rebellow, bark, yelp; bay, – the moon; yap, growl, yarr, yawl, snarl, howl; grunt, -le; snort, squeak; neigh, bray; mew, mewl; purr, caterwaul, pule; bleat, low, moo; troat, croak, crow, screech, caw, coo, gobble, quack, cackle, gaggle, guggle; chuck, -le; cluck; clack; cheep, chirp, chirrup, twitter, sing, cuckoo; pout, wail, hum, buzz; hiss, blatter; hoot.

Adj. crying &c. *v.*; blatant, latrant; re-, mugient; deep-, full-mouthed.

Adv. in full cry.

(iii.) MUSICAL SOUNDS

413. Melody. Concord.—N. melody, rhythm, measure; rhyme &c. (*poetry*) 597.

pitch, *timbre*, intonation, tone, over-tone.

scale, gamut; diapason; diatonic –, chromatic –, enharmonic- scale; key, clef, chords,

modulation, temperament, syncope, syncopation, preparation, suspension, resolution.

414. Discord.—N. discord, -ance; dissonance, cacophony, caterwauling; harshness &c. 410; consecutive fifths.

[Confused sounds] Babel, pande-monium; Dutch –, cat's- concert, marrow-bones and cleavers.

V. be -discordant &c. *adj.*; jar &c (*sound harshly*) 410.

Adj. discordant; dis-, ab-sonant; out of tune, tuneless; un-musical, -tunable, un-, im-melodious; un-, in-harmonious;

staff, stave, line, space, brace; bar, rest; *appogia-to, -tura; acciaccatura,* shake, *arpeggio.*

sing-song; cacophonous; jarring, harsh &c. 410.

note, musical note, notes of a scale; sharp, flat, natural; high note &c. (*shrillness*) 410; low note &c. 408; interval; semitone; second, third, fourth &c.; diatessaron.

breve, semibreve, minim, crotchet, quaver; semi-, demisemi-quaver; sustained note, drone, burden.

tonic; key-, leading-, fundamental- note; supertonic, mediant, dominant; sub-mediant, -dominant, organ-, pedal-point; octave, tetrachord; major −, minor- -mode, − scale, − key; Doric mode, passage, phrase.

concord, harmony; unison, -ance; chime, homophony; euphon-y, -ism; tonality; consonance; concent; part.

orchestration, harmonization, − phrasing.

[Science of harmony] harmon-y, -ics; thorough-, fundamental-bass; counterpoint; faburden.

piece of music &c. 415; composer, harmonist, contrapuntist.

V. be -harmonious &c. *adj.*; harmonize, chime, symphonize, transpose; put in tune, tune, accord, string; score, arrange, orchestrate.

Adj. harmoni-ous, -cal; in -concord &c. *n.*, − tune, − concert; unisonant, concentual, symphonizing, isotonic, homophonous, assonant, consonant.

measured, rhythmical, diatonic, chromatic, enharmonic.

melodious, musical; tuneful, tunable; sweet, dulcet, canorous; mell-ow, -ifluous; soft; clear, − as a bell; silvery; euphon-ious, -ic, -ical; symphonious; enchanting &c. (*pleasure-giving*) 829; fine-, full-, silver-toned.

Adv. harmoniously &c. *adj.*

---

415. Music.—N. music, classical −, modern −, descriptive- music; concert, recital; strain, tune, air, *motif*; melody &c. 413; *aria, arietta*; piece of music, *sonata; rond-o, -eau; pastorale, cavatina,* roulade, *fantasia, toccata, concerto,* overture, symphony, symphonic poem, tone poem, prelude, voluntary, *intermezzo,* variations, *cadenza*; cadence; fugue, canon, serenade, *nocturne, notturno,* rhapsody, romance, *aubade,* dithyramb; opera, operetta; oratorio; composition, movement; stave.

instrumental music; full-, orchestral- score; minstrelsy, tweedle-dum and tweedledee, band, orchestra &c. 416; concerted piece, *pot-pourri,* medley, *capriccio,* incidental music; improvisation; peal.

vocal music, vocalism; chaunt, chant; psalm, -ody; hymn; song &c. (*poem*) 597; canticle, canzonet, *cantata, bravura, coloratura*; lay, ballad, ditty, carol, barcarolle, pastoral, recitative, *recitativo, solfeggio,* tonic sol-fa.

Lydian measures; slow -music, − movement; *adagio* &c. *adv.*; minuet; siren strains, soft music, lullaby; *berceuse,* cradle song, dump; dirge &c. (*lament*) 839; pibroch; martial music, march, funeral-, dead- march; dance music; waltz &c. (*dance*) 840; rag-time, syncopation, jazz.

solo, duet, *duo, trio*; quartet; quintet, sextet, septet; part song, descant, glee, madrigal, catch, round, chorus, *chorale*; antiphon, -y; accompaniment, second −, alto −, tenor −, bass- part; score, thorough bass; counterpoint.

composer &c. 413; musician &c. 416.

V. compose, perform &c. 416; attune.

Adj. musical; instrumental, orchestral, vocal, choral, lyric, operatic; harmonious &c. 413.

Adv. *adagio; largo, larghetto, andan-te, -tino; alla capella; maestoso, moderato; allegr-o, -etto; spiritoso, vivace, veloce; prest-o, -issimo; pian-o, -issimo, fort-e, -issimo, sforzando; con brio; capriccioso; scherz-o, -ando; legato, sostenuto, staccato, crescendo, diminuendo, rallentando, affettuoso, arioso; parlante, cantabile; obbligato; pizzicato, tremolo, vibrato.*

416. Musician. [Performance of Music.]—**N.** musician, *artiste, virtuoso,* performer, player, minstrel; bard &c. *(poet)* 597; instrumental-, organ-, accompan-, pian-, violin-, flaut-, harp-ist; harper, fiddler, fifer, trumpeter, piper, drummer; catgut scraper.

band, orchestra, waits.

vocal-, melod-ist; singer, warbler; songst-, chaunt-er, -ress; *diva, cantatrice,* coloratura, soprano, mezzo-soprano, alto, contralto, tenor, baritone, bass, *basso, -profondo.*

choir, quire, chorister; chorus, – singer; choral society, festival, *eisteddfod.*

nightingale, philomel, thrush; siren; Orpheus, Apollo, the Muses, Erato, Euterpe, Terpsichore; tuneful -nine, – quire.

composer &c. 413.

performance, virtuosity, execution, touch, expression, solmization.

V. play, pipe, strike –, tune- up, sweep the chords, tickle –, paw- the ivories, vamp, tweedle, fiddle; strike the lyre, beat the drum; blow –, sound –, wind- the horn; grind the organ; touch the -guitar &c. *(instruments)* 417; thrum, strum, twang, drum, beat –, keep- time, conduct.

execute, perform; accompany; sing –, play- a second; compose, write music, set to music, arrange, harmonize, orchestrate.

sing, chaunt, chant, hum, warble, carol, chirp, chirrup, lilt, purl, quaver, trill, shake, twitter, whistle; sol-fa; intone.

have -an ear for music, – a musical ear, – a correct ear, – absolute pitch.

Adj. playing &c. *v.*; musical, lyric.

Adv. *adagio, andante* &c. *(music)* 415.

417. Musical Instruments.—**N.** musical instruments; band; string-, brass-, drum and fife-, military-, bugle-, German-, dance-, jazz-band: orchestra, string quartet; orchestrion, orchestrelle.

[Stringed instruments] mono-, poly-chord; harp, lyre, lute, archlute, theorbo; mandol-a, -in, -ine; guitar; *ukulele*; psaltery, zither; bandore, cither, -n; gittern, rebeck, *bandurria,* banjo, zither banjo, *balalaika, samisen*; plectrum.

viol, -in, Cremona, Stradivarius; fiddle, kit; *vielle, viola, – d'amore, – di gamba*; tenor, *violoncello,* cello; bass, bass-, base-viol; double-bass, *contrabasso, violone,* hurdy-gurdy; strings, catgut; bow, fiddlestick.

piano, -forte; grand –, concert grand –, baby –, upright –, cottage-piano; pianino, pianette; harpsi-, clavi-, clari-, mani-chord; *clavier,* spinet, virginals; dulcimer, *cymbalo*; Eolian harp; piano-organ, -player, electric piano, player-piano, pianola.

[Wind instruments] organ, church –, pipe –, American- organ; harmoni-um, -phon; accordion, seraphina, concertina; melodeon; barrel-organ; humming top.

flute, fife, piccolo, flageolet, penny-whistle, reed instrument; clari-net, -onet; bass clarionet; saxophone; basset horn, *corno di bassetto*; musette, shawm, oboe, hautboy, *cor Anglais, corno Inglese*, bassoon, double bassoon, *contrafagotto*; bag-, union-pipes; ocarina, Pandean pipes; calliope; sirene, pipe, pitch-pipe; sourdet; whistle, catcall.

horn, bugle, key bugle, cornet, *cornet-à-pistons*, cornopean, clarion, trumpet, trombone, ophicleide, serpent; English-, French-, bugle-, sax-, flugel-, alt-, helicon-, post-horn; sackbut, euphonium, bombardon, tuba, bass tuba.

[Vibrating surfaces] cymbal, bell, gong, peal of bells, *carillon*; tambour, -ine; drum, tom-tom, tab-or, -ret, -ourine, -orin; *sistrum*; *grande caisse*, bass-, big-, side-, kettle-drum; *tympani*; war drums; tymbal, timbrel, castanet, bones; musical-glasses, -stones; harmonica, sounding-board, rattle; gramophone, phonograph.

[Vibrating bars] reed, tuning-fork, triangle, Jew's harp, musical box, harmonicon, xylophone, marimba, *celeste*.

sord-ine, -et; *sourd-ine, -et*; mute.

(iv.) Perception of Sound

418. [Sense of sound.] **Hearing.—N.** hearing &c. *v.*; audition, auscultation; eavesdropping; audibility; acoustics &c. 402.

acute –, nice –, delicate –, quick –, sharp –, correct –, musical -ear; ear for music.

ear, auricle, lug, acoustic organs, auditory apparatus, ear-drum, tympanum; ear-, speaking-trumpet, megaphone; telephone, radiophone, stethoscope, phonograph, gramophone, microphone.

hearer, auditor, listener, eavesdropper; audi-tory, -ence.

V. hear, overhear; hark, -en; list, -en; give –, lend –, bend- an ear; give attention; catch a sound, prick up one's ears; give -a hearing, – audience- to.

hang upon the lips of, be all ear, listen with both ears.

become audible; meet –, fall upon –, catch –, reach- the ear; be heard; ring in the ear &c. (*resound*) 408.

Adj. hearing &c. *v.*; auditory, auricular, aural, auditive, acoustic.

Adv. *arrectis auribus.*

Int. hark, – ye! hear! list, -en! *Oyez!* attention! lend me your ears!

419. Deafness.—N. deafness, hardness of hearing, surdity; inaudibility.

V. be -deaf &c. *adj.*; have no ear; shut –, stop –, close- one's ears; turn a deaf ear to.

render deaf, stun, deafen.

Adj. deaf, earless, surd; hard –, dull- of hearing; deaf-mute, stunned, deafened; stone deaf; deaf as -a post, – an adder, – a beetle, – a trunk-maker.

inaudible &c. 405; out of hearing.

6. *Light*

(i.) Light in General

420. Light.—N. light, ray, beam, stream, gleam, streak, pencil; sun-, moon-beam; dawn, aurora.

day; sunshine; light of -day, – heaven; sun &c. (*luminary*) 423, day-, broad day-, noontide- light; noon-tide, -day; glare.

421. Darkness.—N. darkness &c. *adj.*; blackness &c. (*dark colour*) 431; obscurity, gloom, murk; dusk &c. (*dimness*) 422; tenebrosity, umbrageousness.

Cimmerian –, Stygian –, Egyptian-darkness: night; midnight; dead of –,

glow &c. *v.*; afterglow, sunset; glimmering &c. *v.*; glint; play –, flood- of light; phosphorescence, lambent flame.

flush, halo, glory, nimbus, aureole, *aureola.*

spark, *scintilla; facula*; sparkling &c. *v.*; emication, scintillation, flash, blaze, coruscation, fulguration; flame &c. (*fire*) 382; lightning, *ignis fatuus,* &c. (*luminary*) 423, radio-activity.

lustre, sheen, shimmer, reflection; gloss, tinsel, spangle, brightness, brilliancy, splendour; ef-, re-fulgence; ful-gor, -gidity; dazzlement, resplendence, transplendency; luminousness &c. *adj.*; luminosity; lucidity; renitency; radi-ance, -ation; irradiation, illumination, phosphorescence, luminescence.

radiation, radiant heat, infra-red rays, visible radiation, ultra-violet –, actinic- rays, actinism; X –, Roentgenrays; phot-, heli-ography; optical instruments &c. 445.

[Science of light] optics; photo-logy, -metry; di-, cat-optrics.

[Distribution of light] *chiaroscuro, clair-obscur,* clear-obscure, breadth, light and shade, black and white, tonality, half-tone, mezzotint.

reflection, refraction, dispersion, double refraction, polarization, diffraction, interference.

illuminant &c. 423.

V. shine, glow, glitter, phosphoresce; glis-ter, -ten; twinkle, gleam; flare, – up; glare, beam, shimmer, glimmer, flicker, sparkle, scintillate, coruscate, flash, fulgurate, blaze; be -bright &c. *adj.*; reflect light, daze, dazzle, bedazzle, radiate, shoot out beams.

clear up, brighten.

lighten, enlighten; light, – up; irradiate, shine upon; give –, hang out- a light; cast –, throw –, shed- -lustre, – light- upon; illum-e, -ine, -inate; relume, strike a light; kindle &c. (*set fire to*) 384.

Adj. shining &c. *v.*; lumin-ous, -iferous; luc-id, -ent, -ulent, -ific, -iferous; illuminating, light, -some; bright, vivid, splendent, nitid, lustrous, shiny, brilliant, beamy, scintillant, radiant, lambent; sheen, -y; glossy,

witching time of- night; blind man's holiday; darkness -visible, – that can be felt; palpable, obscure; Erebus.

shade, shadow, umbra, penumbra; sciagraphy; *silhouette*; radiograph, skiagraph.

obscuration; ad-, ob-umbration; obtenebration, offuscation, caligation; extinction; eclipse, total eclipse; gathering of the clouds.

shading; distribution of shade; *chiaroscuro* &c. (*light*) 420.

noctivagation, noctograph, noctuary. obscurantist.

V. be -dark &c. *adj.*

darken, obscure, shade; dim; tone down, lower; over-cast, -shadow; cloud, eclipse; ob-, of-fuscate; ob-, ad-umbrate, cast into the shade; be-cloud, -dim, -darken; cast –, throw –, spread- a -shade, – shadow, – gloom.

extinguish; put –, blow –, snuff- out; doubt.

Adj. dark, -some, -ling; obscure, tenebrous, tenebrious, sombrous, pitch dark, pitchy; caliginous; black &c. (*in colour*) 431.

sunless, lightless &c. (*see* sun, light, &c. 423); sombre, dusky; unilluminated &c. (*see* illuminate &c. 420); nocturnal; dingy, lurid, gloomy; murk-y, -some; shady, umbrageous; overcast &c. (*dim*) 422; cloudy &c. (*opaque*) 426; darkened &c. *v.*

dark as -pitch, – a pit, – Erebus.

benighted; noctivag-ant, -ous.

Adv. in the -dark, – shade; at night.

422. Dimness.—N. dimness &c. *adj.*; darkness &c. 421; paleness &c. (*light colour*) 429.

half-light, *demi-jour*; partial -shadow, – eclipse; shadow of a shade; glimmer, -ing; nebulosity; cloud &c. 353; eclipse.

aurora, dusk, twilight, gloaming, blind man's holiday, shades of evening, crepuscule, cockshut time; break of day, daybreak, dawn.

moon-light, -beam, -shine; star-, owl's-, candle-, rush-, fire-light; farthing candle.

V. be –, grow- -dim &c. *adj.*; flicker, twinkle, glimmer; loom, lower; fade; darken; pale, – its ineffectual fire.

burnished, glassy, sunny, orient, meridian; noon-day, -tide; cloudless, clear; un-clouded, -obscured.

garish; re-, tran-splendent; re-, effulgent; ful-gid, -gent; relucent, splendid, blazing, in a blaze, ablaze, rutilant, meteoric, phosphorescent; aglow.

bright as silver; light –, bright- as -day, – noonday, – the sun at noonday.

optical, actinic; photo-genic, -graphic; heliographic, radioactive.

423. [Source of light &c.] **Luminary.** —N. luminary; light &c. 420; flame &c. (*fire*) 382.

spark, *scintilla*; phosphorescence.

sun, orb of day, day star, Phœbus, Apollo, Helios, Phaethon, Hyperion, Ra, Aurora; star, orb, meteor; falling –, shooting- star; blazing –, dog- star; Sirius, canicula, Aldebaran; morning star, Lucifer, Phosphor, evening star; Hesperus, Venus, planet, moon &c. 318; constellation, galaxy; northern light, *aurora -borealis*, – *australis*, zodiacal light; mock sun, parhelion.

lightning; fork –, sheet –, summer- lightning, St. Elmo's fire; phosphorus; *ignis fatuus*; Jack o' –, Friar's- lantern; Will o' the wisp, fire-drake, *Fata Morgana*.

glow-worm, fire-fly.

radium, luminous paint.

[Artificial light] gas; gas –, lime –, electric –, head –, search –, spot –, flash –, flood –, foot-light; lamp, oil –, gas –, arc –, incandescent- lamp; flare; lant-ern, -horn; dark lantern, bull's eye, projector; candle, *bougie*, tallow –, wax- candle; dip, farthing dip; taper, rush-light; oil &c. (*grease*) 356; wick, burner; Argand, moderator, duplex; torch, *flambeau*, link, brand; cresset; gase-, chande-, electro-lier; candelabrum, *girandole*, sconce, lustre, candle-stick.

firework, fizgig; pyrotechnics; Roman candle, Véry light, star shell, parachute light; rocket, lighthouse &c. (*signal*) 550.

V. illuminate &c. (*light*) 420.

Adj. self-luminous, incandescent; phosphor-ic, -escent; luminescent, fluorescent, radiant &c. (*light*) 420.

425. Transparency. — N. transparen-ce, -cy; translucen-ce, -cy; diaphaneity; luc-, pelluc-, limp-idity.

transparent medium, glass, crystal, mica; lymph, water.

V. be -transparent &c. *adj.*; transmit light.

Adj. transparent, pellucid, lucid, diaphanous; trans-, tra-lucent; limpid, clear, serene, crystalline, clear as crys-

render -dim &c. *adj.*; dim, bedim, obscure.

Adj. dim, dull, lack-lustre, dingy, darkish, shorn of its beams; dark 421.

faint, shadowed forth; glassy; bleary; cloudy; misty &c. (*opaque*) 426; muggy, fuliginous; nebul-ous, -ar; obnubilated, overcast, crepuscular, twilight, muddy, lurid, leaden, dun, dirty; looming &c. *v.*

pale &c. (*colourless*) 429; confused &c. (*invisible*) 447.

424. Shade.—N. shade; awning &c. (*cover*) 223; parasol, sunshade, umbrella; screen, curtain, shutter, blind, gauze, veil, mantle, mask; cloud, mist, gathering of clouds; smoke screen; smoked glasses, coloured spectacles; blinkers, blinders.

umbrage, glade; shadow &c. 421.

V. draw a curtain; put up –, close- a shutter; veil &c. *v.*; cast a shadow &c. (*darken*) 421; screen, obstruct the view.

Adj. shady, umbrageous, bowery.

426. Opacity.—N. opacity; opaqueness &c. *adj.*

film; cloud &c. 353.

V. be -opaque &c. *adj.*; obstruct the passage of light; ob-, of-fuscate.

Adj. opaque, impervious to light.

dim &c. 422; turbid, thick, muddy, opacous, obfuscated, fuliginous, cloudy, hazy, foggy, vaporous, nubiferous, muggy.

tal, vitreous, transpicuous, glassy, hyaline.

smoky, fumid, murky, dirty.

_____

427. Semitransparency.—N. semitransparency, opalescence, milkiness, pearliness; gauze, muslin; film; mist &c. (cloud) 353; frosted glass.

Adj. semi-transparent, -pellucid, -diaphanous, -opacous, -opaque; opal-escent, -ine; pearly, milky, frosted, mat; misty.

(ii.) Specific Light

428. Colour.—N. colour, hue, tint, tinge, dye, complexion, shade, tincture, cast, livery, coloration, chromatism, glow, flush; tone, key.

pure –, positive –, primary –, primitive –, complementary- colour; three primaries; spectrum, chromatic dispersion; broken –, secondary –, tertiary-colour.

local colour, colouring, keeping, tone, value, aerial perspective.

[Science of colour] chromatics, spectrum analysis; prism, spectroscope.

pigment, colouring matter, paint, dye, wash, distemper, stain; medium; mordant; oil-paint &c. (painting) 556.

V. colour, dye, tinge, stain, tint, tinct, tone, paint, wash, ingrain, grain, illuminate, emblazon, imbue; paint &c. (fine art) 556; daub.

Adj. coloured &c. v.; colorific, tingent, tinctorial; chromatic, prismatic; full-, high-, deep-coloured; doubly-dyed; polychromatic.

bright, vivid, intense, deep; fresh, unfaded; rich, gorgeous; highly coloured; gay; variegated &c. 440.

gaudy, florid; garish; showy, flaunting, flashy; raw, crude; glaring, flaring; discordant, inharmonious.

mellow, harmonious, pearly, sweet, delicate, tender, refined.

429. [Absence of colour.] Achromatism.—N. achromatism; de-, discoloration; pall-or, -idity; paleness &c. adj.; etiolation; neutral tint, monochrome, black-and-white.

V. lose -colour &c. 428; fade, fly, go; become -colourless &c. adj.; turn pale, pale, whiten.

deprive of colour, decolorize, bleach, tarnish, achromatize, blanch, etiolate, wash out, tone down.

Adj. uncoloured &c. (see colour &c. 428); colourless, achromatic, hueless, pale, pallid; pale-, tallow-faced; faint, dull, cold, muddy, leaden, dun, wan, sallow, dead, dingy, ashy, ashen, ghastly, cadaverous, glassy, lack-lustre; discoloured &c. v.

light-coloured, fair, blond; white &c. 430.

pale as -death, – ashes, – a witch, – a ghost, – a corpse.

_____

430. Whiteness.—N. whiteness &c. adj.; argent.

albification, albescence, albinism, etiolation.

snow, paper, chalk, milk, lily, ivory, silver, alabaster; white lead, chinese –, flake –, ivory –, zinc- white, white-wash, -ning, whiting.

V. be -white &c. adj.

render -white &c. adj.; whiten-bleach, blanch, etiolate, whitewash, silver, frost.

Adj. white; milky, milk-, snow-white; snowy, niveous, candid, chalky; hoar,

431. Blackness.—N. blackness &c. adj.; darkness &c. (want of light) 421; swarthness, lividity, dark colour, tone, colour; chiaroscuro &c. 420.

nigrification, infuscation, denigration.

jet, ink, ebony, coal, pitch, soot, smudge, charcoal, sloe, raven, crow; negro, blackamoor, man of colour, nigger, darky, Ethiopian, black.

[Pigments] lamp –, ivory –, blue-black; writing –, printing –, printer's –, Indian- ink.

V. be -black &c. adj.

-y; frosted, silvery; argent, -ine; canescent.

whitish, creamy, pearly, ivory, fair, *blond*, ash-blond, platinum blond; blanched &c. *v.*; high in tone, light.

white as -a sheet, – driven snow, – a lilv – silver; like -ivory &c. *n.*

render -black &c. *adj.*; blacken, infuscate, denigrate; blot, -ch; smutch; smirch; darken &c. 421.

Adj. black, sable, swarthy, sombre, dark, inky, ebon, atramentous, jetty; coal-, jet-black; fuliginous, pitchy, sooty, swart, dusky, dingy, murky, Ethiopic; low-toned, low in tone; of the deepest dye.

black as -jet &c. *n.*, – my hat, – a shoe, – a tinker's pot, – November, – thunder, – midnight; nocturnal &c. (*dark*) 421; nigrescent; gray &c. 432; obscure &c. 421.

Adv. in mourning.

432. Gray.—N. gray &c. *adj.*; neutral tint, silver, pepper and salt, *chiaroscuro, grisaille,* grayness.

[Pigments] Payne's gray; black &c. 431.

Adj. gray, grey; steel –, iron- gray, dun, drab, dingy, leaden, livid, sombre, sad, pearly; silver, -y, -ed; ash-en, -y; ciner-eous, -itious; grizzl-y, -ed; dove-, slate-, stone-, mouse-, ash-coloured; mole; cool.

433. Brown.—N. brown &c. *adj.*
[Pigments] bistre, ochre, sepia, Vandyke brown.

Adj. brown, adust, bay, dapple, auburn, chestnut, nutbrown, cinnamon, hazel, fawn, puce, *écru,* russet, tawny, fuscous, chocolate, maroon, foxy, tan, brunette, whitey-brown; snuff-, liver-coloured; brown as -a berry, – mahogany; reddish brown; copper-, rust- coloured; henna, bronze, khaki; roan, sorrel.

sun-burnt; tanned &c. *v.*

V. render -brown &c. *adj.*; tan, embrown, bronze.

*Primitive Colours**

434. Redness.—N. red, scarlet, vermilion, cardinal, Post Office red, carmine, crimson, pink, lake, *cerise,* cherry red, maroon, carnation, *couleur de rose, rose du Barry;* magenta, damask; flesh -colour, – tint; colour; fresh –, highcolour; warmth; gules.

ruby, garnet, carbuncle; rose; rust, iron-mould.

[Dyes and pigments] cinnabar, cochineal; fuchsine; ruddle, madder, redlead; Indian –, light –, Venetian- red; red ink, annotto.

redness &c. *adj.*; rub-escence, -icundity, -ification; erubescence, blush.

V. be –, become- -red &c. *adj.*; blush, flush, colour up, mantle, redden.

render -red &c. *adj.*; redden, rouge; rub-ify, -ricate; incarnadine; ruddle.

Adj. red &c. *n.*, -dish; rufous, ruddy, florid, incarnadine, sanguine, bloody, gory; ros-y, -eate; blowz-y, -ed; burnt; rubi-cund, -form;

Complementary Colours

435. Greenness.—N. green &c. *adj.*; blue and yellow; vert.

emerald, verd antique, verdigris, malachite, beryl, aquamarine, reseda.

[Pigments] *terre verte,* verditer, bice, chlorophyl.

greenness, verdure, verdancy; viridity, -escence.

Adj. green, verdant; glaucous, olive; porraceous; green as grass.

emerald –, pea –, grass –, apple –, sea –, olive –, bottle –, leaf- green.

greenish; vir-ent, -escent.

* The author's classification of colours has been retained, though it does not entirely accord with the theories of modern science: Complete lists of shades or pigments are beyond the scope of this work.

lurid, stammel, blood-red; russet, murrey, carroty, sorrel, lateritious.

rose-, ruby-, cherry-, claret-, wine-, plum-, flame-, flesh-, peach-, salmon-, brick-, brickdust-coloured, reddish brown &c. 433.

blushing &c. *v.*; erubescent; reddened &c. *v.*

red as -fire, – blood, – scarlet, – a turkeycock, – a lobster; warm, hot; foxy.

436. Yellowness.—**N.** yellow &c. *adj.*; or.

[Pigments] gamboge; cadmium –, chrome –, Indian –, lemon- yellow; orpiment, yellow ochre, Claude tint, aureolin.

crocus, saffron, topaz, gold.

jaundice; London fog; yellowness &c. *adj.*

Adj. yellow, aureate, gold, golden, gilt, gilded, flavous, citrine, fallow; fulv-ous, -id; sallow, luteous, tawny, creamy, sandy; xanth-ic, -ous; jaundiced.

gold-, citron-, saffron-, lemon-, sulphur-, amber-, straw-, primrose-, cream-coloured; flaxen, yellowish, buff.

yellow as a -quince, – guinea, – crow's foot.

437. Purple.—**N.** purple &c. *adj.*; blue and red, bishop's purple; aniline dyes, gridelin, amethyst; purpure.

livid-ness, -ity.

V. empurple.

Adj. purple, violet, plum-coloured, lavender, lilac, puce, *mauve*; livid.

---

438. Blueness.—**N.** blue &c. *adj.*; garter-blue; watchet.

[Pigments] ultramarine, smalt, cobalt, cyanogen; Prussian –, syenite-blue; bice, indigo, woad.

lapis lazuli, sapphire, turquoise.

blue-, bluish-ness; bloom.

Adj. blue, azure, cerulean; sky-blue, -coloured, -dyed; navy-blue, aquamarine, electric blue, royal blue, cyanic; bluish; atmospheric, retiring; cold.

439. Orange.—**N.** orange, red and yellow; gold; or; flame &c. colour, *adj.*

[Pigments] ochre, Mars orange, cadmium.

V. gild, warm.

Adj. orange; ochreous; orange-, gold-, flame-, copper-, brass-, apricot-coloured; warm, hot, glowing.

---

440. Variegation.—**N.** variegation; di-, tri-chroism; iridescence, irisation, play of colours, polychrome, maculation, spottiness, striæ.

spectrum, rainbow, iris, tulip, peacock, chameleon, butterfly, tortoise-shell; mackerel, – sky; zebra, leopard, mother-of-pearl, nacre, opal, marble, batik.

check, plaid, tartan, patchwork; mar-, par-quetry; mosaic, *tesseræ*, tesselation, chess-board, checkers, chequers; harlequin; Joseph's coat; tricolour; patches, bands, stripes, spots &c. of colour.

V. be -variegated &c. *adj.*; variegate, stripe, streak, checker, chequer; be-, speckle, fleck; be-, sprinkle; stipple, maculate, dot, bespot; tattoo, inlay, tesselate, damascene; embroider, braid, quilt.

Adj. variegated &c. *v.*; many-coloured, -hued; divers-, parti-coloured; di-, poly-chromatic; bi-, tri-, versi-colour; of all -the colours of the rainbow, – manner of colours; kaleidoscopic.

iridescent; opal-ine, -escent; prismatic, nacreous, pearly, shot, *gorge de pigeon*, *chatoyant*, irisated.

pied, piebald, skewbald; motley; mottled, marbled; pepper and salt, paned, dappled, clouded, cymophanous.

mosaic, tesselated, chequered, plaid; tortoiseshell &c. *n.*

spott-ed, -y; punctated, powdered; speckled &c. *v.*; freckled, flea-bitten, studded; fleck-ed, -ered; striated, barred, veined; brind-ed, -led; tabby; watered; grizzled; listed; embroidered &c. *v.*; dædal.

(iii.) PERCEPTIONS OF LIGHT

441. Vision.—N. vision, sight, optics, eye-sight.

view, look, espial, glance, ken, *coup d'œil*; glimpse, peep, glint; gaze, stare, leer; perlustration, contemplation; conspect-ion, -uity; regard, survey; in-, intro-spection; *reconnaissance*, speculation, watch, espionage, *espionnage*, autopsy; ocular -inspection, - demonstration; sight-seeing.

macrography, micrography.

point of view; view-, stand-point; gazebo, loop-hole, *belvedere*, watchtower.

field of view; theatre, amphitheatre, arena, vista, horizon; commanding -, bird's eye -, panoramic- view; periscope.

visual organ, organ of vision; eye; naked -, unassisted- eye; eye-ball, retina, pupil, iris, cornea, white; optics, orbs; saucer -, goggle -, gooseberry-eyes.

short sight &c. 443; clear -, sharp -, quick -, eagle -, piercing -, penetrating--sight, - glance, - eye; perspicacity, discernment; catopsis.

eagle, hawk; cat, lynx; Argus.

evil eye; basilisk, cockatrice.

spectacles, telescope &c. 445.

442. Blindness.—N. blindness, anopsia, cecity, excecation, *amaurosis*, cataract, ablepsy, prestriction; dim-sightedness &c. 443.

V. be -blind &c. *adj.*; not see; lose sight of; have the eyes bandaged; grope in the dark.

not look; close -, shut -, turn away -, avert- the eyes; look another way; wink &c. (*limited vision*) 443; shut the eyes -, be blind- to; wink -, blink- at.

render -blind &c. *adj.*; blind, -fold; hoodwink, dazzle; put one's eyes out; throw dust into one's eyes; *jeter de la poudre aux yeux*; screen from sight &c. (*hide*) 528.

Adj. blind; eye-, sight-, vision-less; dark; stone-, sand-, stark-blind; undiscerning; dim-sighted &c. 443.

blind as -a bat, - a buzzard, - a beetle, - a mole, - an owl; wall-eyed.

blinded &c. *v.*

Adv. blind-ly, -fold; darkly.

V. see, behold, discern, perceive, have in sight, descry, sight, make out, discover, distinguish recognize, spy, espy, ken; get -, have -, catch- a -sight, - glimpse- of; command a view of; witness, contemplate, speculate; cast -, set- the eyes on; be a -spectator &c. 444- of; look on &c. (*be present*) 186; see sights &c. (*curiosity*) 455; see at a glance &c. (*intelligence*) 498.

look, view, eye; lift up the eyes, open one's eye; look -at, - on, - upon, - over, - about one, - round; survey, scan, inspect; run the eye -over, - through; reconnoitre, glance -round, - on, - over; turn -, bend- one's looks upon; direct the eyes to, turn the eyes on, cast a glance, make eyes at.

observe &c. (*attend to*) 457; watch &c. (*care*) 459; see with one's own eyes; watch for &c. (*expect*) 507; peek, peep, peer, pry, take a peep; play at bo-peep.

look -full in the face, - hard at, - intently; strain one's eyes; fix -, rivet- the eyes upon; stare, gaze; pore over, gloat -over, - on; leer, ogle, glare; goggle; cock the eye, squint, gloat, look askance; give the glad eye.

Adj. seeing &c. *v.*; visual, ocular, -al; ophthalmic.

far-, clear-sighted &c. *n.*; eagle-, hawk-, lynx-, keen-, Argus-eyed.

visible &c. 446.

Adv. visibly &c. 446; in sight of, with one's eyes open.

at -sight, – first sight, – a glance, – the first blush; *primâ facie.*

Int. look! &c. (*attention*) 457.

Phr. the scales falling from one's eyes.

443. [Imperfect vision.] **Dim-sightedness.** [Fallacies of vision.]—**N.**
dim –, dull –, half –, short –, near –, long –, double –, astigmatic –,
failing- sight; dim &c. -sightedness; snow blindness; purblindness,
lippitude; my-, presby-opia; confusion of vision; astigmatism, nystag-
mus; colour-blindness, dichromism, chromato-pseudo-blepsis, Dalton-
ism; nyctalopy; *strabismus*, strabism, squint, cast in the eye, swivel
eye, goggle eyes; obliquity of vision.

winking &c. *v.*; nictitation; blinkard, albino.

dizziness, swimming, scotomy; cataract; ophthalmia.

[Limitation of vision] eye shade, blinker, blinder; screen &c. (*hider*)
530.

[Fallacies of vision] *deceptio visûs*; refraction, distortion, illusion,
false light, *anamorphosis*, virtual image, *spectrum*, *mirage*, looming,
phasma; phant-asm, -asma, -om; vision; spectre, apparition, ghost;
ignis fatuus &c. (*luminary*) 423; spectre of the Brocken; magic mirror;
magic lantern &c. (*show*) 448; mirror, lens &c. (*instrument*) 445.

V. be -dim-sighted &c. *n.*; see double; have a -mote in the eye, –
mist before the eyes, – film over the eyes; see through a -prism, – glass
darkly; wink, blink, nictitate; squint; look ask-ant, -ance; screw up
the eyes, glare, glower.

dazzle, glare, blur, swim, loom.

Adj. dim-sighted &c. *n.*; my-, presby-opic; astigmatic; moon-, mope-,
blear-, goggle-, gooseberry-, one-eyed; blind of one eye, monoculous;
half-, pur-, colour-blind; dichromatic.

blind as a bat &c. (*blind*) 442; winking &c. *v.*

444. Spectator.—N. spectator, beholder, observer, inspector, viewer,
looker-on, onlooker, witness, eye-witness, bystander, passer by;
sight-seer.

spy, scout; sentinel &c. (*warning*) 668.

V. witness, behold &c. (*see*) 441; look on &c. (*be present*) 186.

445. Optical Instruments.—N. optical instruments; lens, meniscus,
magnifier, reading –, burning- glass; micro-, mega-, teino-scope; spectacles, glasses, barnacles, goggles, giglamps, eyeglass, *pince-nez*, monocle;
periscopic lens; telescope, glass, lorgnette, binocular; spy-, opera-,
field-glass, periscope, range finder.

mirror, reflector, speculum; looking-, pier-, cheval-, hand-glass.

prism; camera, *camera-lucida*, -*obscura*; projector, stereopticon,
magic lantern &c. (*show*) 448; chro-, thau-matrope; stereo-, pseudo-,
poly-, kaleido-scope.

photo-, opto-, erio-, actino-, luci-, radio-, spectro-meter; polari-,
polemo-, spectro-scope, diffraction grating.

optics, optician, optometry, optometrist; microscop-y, -ist; photom-
etry, photography; photographer.

446. Visibility.—N. visibility, per-
ceptibility; conspicuousness, distinctness &c. *adj.*; conspicuity; appearance
&c. 448; exposure; manifestation &c.
525; ocular -proof, – evidence, – demonstration; field of view &c. (*vision*) 441.

447. Invisibility.—N. invisibility,
non-appearance, imperceptibility; indistinctness &c. *adj.*; mystery, delitescence.

concealment &c. 528; latency &c.
526.

V. be –, become- -visible &c. *adj.*; appear, emerge, open to the view; meet –, catch- the eye; present –, show –, manifest –, produce –, discover –, reveal –, expose –, betray-itself; stand -forth, – out; show; arise; peep –, peer –, crop- out; start –, spring –, show –, turn –, crop- up; glimmer, glitter, glow, loom; glare; burst forth, scintillate; burst upon the -view, – sight; heave in sight; come -in sight, – into view, – out, – forth, – forward; see the light of day; break through the clouds; make its appearance, show its face, materialize, appear to one's eyes, come upon the stage, enter; float before the eyes, speak for itself &c. (*manifest*) 525; attract the attention &c. 457; reappear; live in a glass house.

expose to view &c. 525.

Adj. visible, perceptible, perceivable, discernible, apparent; in -view, – full view, – sight; exposed to view, *en évidence*; unclouded.

obvious &c. (*manifest*) 525; plain, clear, distinct, definite; well-defined, -marked; in focus; recognizable, palpable, autoptical; glaring, staring, conspicuous; stereoscopic; in -bold, – strong, – high- relief.

periscopic, panoramic.

before –, under- one's eyes; before one, *à vue d'œil*, in one's eye, *oculis subjecta fidelibus*.

Adv. visibly &c. *adj.*; in sight of; before one's eyes &c. *adj.*; *veluti in speculum.*

V. be -invisible &c. *adj.*; be hidden &c. (*hide*) 528; lurk &c. (*lie hidden*) 526; escape notice.

render -invisible &c. *adj.*; conceal &c. 528; put out of sight.

not see &c. (*be blind*) 442; lose sight of.

Adj. invisible, imperceptible; un-, in-discernible; un-, non-apparent; out of –, not in- sight; *à perte de vue*; behind the -scenes, – curtain; view-, sight-less; in-, un-conspicuous; unseen &c. (*see* see &c. 441); covert &c. (*latent*) 526; eclipsed, under an eclipse.

dim &c. (*faint*) 422; mysterious, dark, obscure, confused; indistin-ct, -guishable; shadowy, indefinite, undefined; ill-defined, -marked; blurred, fuzzy, out of focus; misty &c. (*opaque*) 426; veiled &c. (*concealed*) 528; delitescent.

---

448. Appearance.—N. appearance, phenomenon, sight, spectacle, show, premonstration, scene, species, view, *coup d'œil*; look-out, out-look, prospect, vista, perspective, bird's-eye view, scenery, landscape, picture, *tableau*; display, exposure, *mise en scène*; scenery, *décor*; rising of the curtain.

phant-asm, -om &c. (*fallacy of vision*) 443.

pageant, *spectacle*; peep-, raree-, gallanty-show; *ombres chinoises*; projector, optical –, magic- lantern, phantasmagoria, dissolving views; cinema, -tograph; bio-scope. -graph; moving pictures, movies, film, screen &c.; pan-, di-, cosm-, ge-orama; *coup –, jeu- de théâtre*; pageantry &c. (*ostentation*) 882; insignia &c. (*indication*) 550.

aspect, phase, *phasis*, seeming; shape &c. (*form*) 240; guise, look,

449. Disappearance.—N. disappearance, evanescence, eclipse, occultation.

departure &c. 293; exit, vanishing point; dissolving views.

V. disappear, vanish, dissolve, fade, melt away, pass, go, avaunt; be -gone &c. *adj.*; leave -no trace, – 'not a rack behind'; go off the stage &c. (*depart*) 293; suffer –, undergo- an eclipse; be lost to –, retire from- -sight, – view.

lose sight of.

efface &c. 552.

Adj. disappearing &c. *v.*; evanescent; missing, lost; lost to -sight, – view; gone; *spurlos versenkt*.

Int. vanish! disappear! avaunt! &c. (*ejection*) 297.

---

complexion, colour, image, mien, air, cast, carriage, port, demeanour; presence, expression, first blush, face of the thing; point of view, light.

lineament, feature, trait, lines; out-line, -side; contour, *silhouette*, face, countenance, physiognomy, visage, phiz, mug, cast of countenance, profile, *tournure*, cut of one's jib, metoposcopy; outside &c. 220.

V. appear; be –, become- visible &c. 446; seem, look, show; present –, wear –, carry –, have –, bear –, exhibit –, take –, take on –, assume- the -appearance, – semblance- of; look like; cut a figure, figure; present to the view; show &c. (*make manifest*) 525.

Adj. apparent, seeming, ostensible; on view.

Adv. apparently; to all -seeming, – appearance; ostensibly, seemingly, as it seems, on the face of it, *primâ facie*; at the first blush, at first sight; in the eyes of; to the eye.

CLASS IV

Words relating to the INTELLECTUAL FACULTIES

Division (I.) FORMATION OF IDEAS

Section I. Operations of Intellect in General

450. Intellect.—N. intellect, mind, understanding, reason, thinking principle; rationality; cogitative –, cognitive –, intellectual- faculties; faculties, senses, consciousness, observation, percipience, apperception, mentality, intelligence, intellection, intuition, association of ideas, instinct, flair, conception, judgement, wits, parts, capacity, intellectuality, reasoning power, brains, genius; wit &c. 498; ability &c. (*skill*) 698; wisdom &c. 498.

soul, spirit, ghost, inner man, heart, breast, bosom, *penetralia mentis, divina particula auræ,* heart's core; ego, psyche, pneuma, subconsciousness, subconscious, subliminal self; dual personality.

organ –, seat- of thought; *sensorium,* sensory, brain, gray matter; head, -piece; pate, noddle, skull, scull, *pericranium, cerebrum, cranium,* brain-pan, -box; sconce, upper story.

[Science of mind] metaphysics; psychics, psycho-logy, -metry, -genesis, -analysis, -physics, psychi-atry, -cal research, thought reading &c. 992; ideology; mental –, moral- philosophy; philosophy of the mind; pneumat-, phren-ology; no –, cranio-logy, -scopy.

ideal-ity, -ism; transcendental-, spiritual-ism; immateriality &c. 317.

metaphysician, psychologist &c.

V. note, notice, mark; take -notice, – cognizance- of; be -aware, – conscious- of; realize; appreciate; ruminate &c. (*think*) 451; fancy &c. (*imagine*) 515; conceive, reason, understand.

Adj. [Relating to intellect] intellectual, mental, rational, subjective, metaphysical, nooscopic, spiritual; ghostly; psych-ical, -ological; cerebral.

immaterial &c. 317; endowed with reason.

Adv. *in petto.*

450a. Absence or want of Intellect.—N. absence –, want- of -intellect &c. 450; imbecility &c. 499; brutality; brute -instinct, – force.

Adj. unendowed with reason.

---

451. Thought.—N. thought; exercitation –, exercise- of the intellect; reflection, cogitation, consideration, meditation, study, lucubration, speculation, deliberation, pondering; head-,

452. [Absence or want of thought.] Incogitancy.—N. incogitancy, vacancy, inunderstanding; inanity, fatuity &c. 499; thoughtlessness &c. (*inattention*) 458.

brain-work; cerebration; mentation, deep reflection; close study, application &c. (*attention*) 457.

abstract thought, abstraction, contemplation, musing; brown study &c. (*inattention*) 458; reverie, Platonism; depth of thought, workings of the mind, thoughts, inmost thoughts; self-counsel, -communing, -consultation.

association -, succession -, flow -, train -, current- of -thought, - ideas.

after -, mature- thought; reconsideration, second thoughts; retrospection &c. (*memory*) 505; excogitation; examination &c. (*inquiry*) 461; invention &c. (*imagination*) 515.

thoughtfulness &c. *adj.*

V. think, reflect, reason, cogitate, excogitate, consider, deliberate; bestow -thought, - consideration- upon; speculate, contemplate, meditate, ponder, muse, dream, ruminate; brood -, con- over; animadvert, study; bend -, apply- the mind &c. (*attend*) 457; digest, discuss, hammer at, weigh, perpend; realize, appreciate; fancy &c. (*imagine*) 515; trow.

take into consideration; take counsel &c. (*be advised*) 695; commune with -, bethink- oneself; collect one's thoughts; revolve -, turn over -, run over- in the mind; chew the cud -, sleep- upon; take counsel of -, advise with- one's pillow.

rack -, ransack -, crack -, beat -, cudgel- one's brains; set one's -brain, - wits- to work.

harbour -, entertain -, cherish -, nurture- an -idea &c. 453; take into one's head; bear in mind; reconsider.

occur; present -, suggest- itself; come -, get- into one's head; strike one, flit across the view, come uppermost, run in one's head; enter -, pass in -, cross -, flash on -, flash across -, float in -, fasten itself on -, be uppermost in -, occupy- the mind; have in one's mind.

make an impression; sink -, penetrate- into the mind; engross the thoughts.

Adj. thinking &c. *v.*; thoughtful, pensive, meditative, reflective, cogitative, museful, wistful, contemplative, speculative, deliberative, studious, sedate, introspective, Platonic, philosophical.

lost -, engrossed -, rapt -, absorbed- in thought &c. (*inattentive*) 458; deep musing &c. (*intent*) 457.

in the mind, under consideration, in contemplation.

Adv. all things considered; taking everything into account.

Phr. the mind being on the stretch; the -mind, - head- -turning, - running- upon.

V. not -think &c. 451; not think of; dismiss from the -mind, - thoughts &c. 451.

indulge in reverie &c. (*be inattentive*) 458.

put away thought; unbend -, relax -, divert- the mind.

Adj. vacant, unintellectual, unideal, unoccupied, unthinking, inconsiderate, thoughtless; absent &c. (*inattentive*) 458; diverted; irrational &c. 499; narrow-minded &c. 481.

un-thought of, -dreamt of, -considered; off one's mind; incogitable, not to be thought of, inconceivable.

---

453. [Object of thought.] **Idea.—N.** idea, notion, conception, thought, apprehension, impression, perception, image, sentiment, reflection, observation, consideration; abstract idea, principle; archetype.

view &c. (*opinion*) 484; theory &c.

454. [Subject of thought.] **Topic.— N.** subject of -, material for- thought; food for the mind, mental *pabulum*.

subject, -matter; matter, theme, topic, what it is about, *thesis*, text, business, affair, matter in hand, argument; motion, resolution; head, chap-

514; conceit, fancy; phantasy &c.
(*imagination*) 515.

point of view &c. (*aspect*) 448; field
of view.

———

ter; case, point; proposition, theorem;
field of inquiry; moot point, problem,
&c. (*question*) 461.

V. float –, pass- in the mind &c. 451.

Adj. thought of; uppermost in the
mind; *in petto*.

Adv. under -discussion, – consideration, – advisement; in -question,
– the mind; on -foot, – the carpet, – the *tapis*; before the house,
relative to &c. 9.

Section II. Precursory Conditions and Operations

455. [The desire of knowledge.]
Curiosity. — N. interest, thirst for
knowledge; curi-osity, -ousness; inquiring mind; inquisitiveness.

sight-seer, quidnunc, newsmonger,
Paul Pry, peeping Tom, eavesdropper;
gossip &c. (*news*) 532; questioner,
enfant terrible.

V. be -curious &c. *adj.*; take an
interest in, stare, gape; prick up the
ears, see sights, lionize; pry, speer;
dig up.

Adj. curious, inquisitive, burning with curiosity, overcurious,
nosey; inquiring &c. 461; prying; inquisitorial; agape &c. (*expectant*)
507; attentive &c. 457.

Phr. what's the matter? what next?

457. Attention.—N. attention; mindfulness &c. *adj.*; intent-ness, -iveness;
thought &c. 451; adverten-ce, -cy;
observ-ance, -ation; consideration, reflection, perpension; heed; particularity; notice, regard &c. *v.*; circumspection &c. (*care*) 459; study, scrutiny,
once-over; in-, intro-spection; revision,
-al.

active –, diligent –, exclusive –,
minute –, close –, intense –, deep –,
profound –, abstract –, laboured –,
deliberate- -thought, – attention, –
application, – study.

minuteness, attention to detail &c.
459.

absorption of mind &c. (*abstraction*)
458.

indication, calling attention to &c. *v.*

V. be -attentive &c. *adj.*; attend,
advert to, observe, look, see, view,
remark, notice, regard, take notice,
mark; give –, pay- -attention, – heed-
to; listen in, incline –, lend- an ear to;
trouble one's head about; give a

456. [Absence of curiosity.] **Incuriosity.—N.** incuriosity; incuriousness &c.
adj.; *insouciance* &c. 866; indifference,
apathy.

V. be -incurious &c. *adj.*; have no
-curiosity &c. 455; take no interest in
&c. 823; mind one's own business.

Adj. incurious, uninquisitive, uninterested, indifferent, bored; impassive
&c. 823.

———

458. Inattention.—N. in-attention,
-consideration; inconsiderateness &c.
adj.; oversight; inadverten-ce, -cy;
non-observance, disregard.

supineness &c. (*inactivity*) 683; *étourderie*; want of thought; heedlessness
&c. (*neglect*) 460; *insouciance* &c. (*indifference*) 866.

abstraction; absence –, absorption-
of mind; preoccupation, distraction,
reverie, brown study, deep musing, fit
of abstraction, woolgathering.

V. be -inattentive &c. *adj.*; overlook,
disregard; pass by &c. (*neglect*) 460;
not -observe &c. 457; think little of.

close –, shut- one's eyes to; wink at;
pay no attention to; dismiss –, discard
–, discharge- from one's -thoughts, –
mind; drop the subject, think no more
of; set –, turn –, put- aside; turn -away
from, – one's attention from, – a deaf
ear to, – one's back upon.

abstract oneself, dream, indulge in
reverie.

escape -notice, – attention; come in

thought –, animadvert- to; occupy oneself with; contemplate &c. (*think of*) 451; look -at, – to, – after, – into, – over; see to; turn –, bend –, apply –, direct –, give- the -mind, – eye, – attention- to; have -an eye to, – in one's eye; bear in mind; take into -account, – consideration; keep in -sight, – view; have regard to, heed, mind, take cognizance of, be engaged in, entertain, recognize; make –, take-note of; note.

examine cursorily; glance -at, – upon, – over; cast –, pass- the eyes over; run over, turn over the leaves, dip into, perstringe; skim &c. (*neglect*) 460; take a cursory view of.

examine, – closely, – intently; scan, scrutinize, consider; give –, bend- one's mind to; overhaul, revise, pore over; inspect, review, pass under review; take stock of; fix –, rivet –, focus –, devote- the -eye, – mind, – thoughts, – attention- on *or* to; hear –, think- out; mind one's business.

revert –, hark back- to; watch &c. (*expect*) 507, (*take care of*) 459; hearken –, listen- to; prick up the ears; have –, keep- the eyes open; come to the point.

meet with attention; fall under one's -notice, – observation; be -under consideration &c. (*topic*) 454.

catch –, strike- the eye; attract notice; catch –, awaken –, wake –, invite –, solicit –, attract –, claim –, excite –, engage –, occupy –, strike –, arrest –, fix –, engross –, absorb –, rivet- the- attention, – mind, – thoughts; be -present to, – uppermost in- the mind.

bring under one's notice; point -out, – to, – at, – the finger at; lay the finger on, indigitate, indicate; direct –, call- attention to; show; put a -mark &c. (*sign*) 550- upon; call soldiers to 'attention'; bring forward &c. (*make manifest*) 525.

at one ear and go out at the other; forget &c. (*have no remembrance*) 506.

call off –, draw off –, call away –, divert –, distract- the -attention, – thoughts, – mind; put out of one's head; dis-concert, -compose; put out, confuse, perplex, bewilder, moider, fluster, muddle, dazzle; throw a sop to Cerberus.

Adj. inattentive; un-observant, -mindful, -heeding, -discerning; inadvertent; mind-, regard-, respect-less; listless &c. (*indifferent*) 866; blind, deaf; flighty, hand over head; cur-, percur-sory; giddy-, scatter-, hare-brained; unreflecting, écervelé, inconsiderate, off-hand, thoughtless, dizzy, muzzy, brainsick; giddy, – as a goose; wild, harum-scarum, rantipole, highflying; heed-, care-less &c. (*neglectful*) 460.

absent, absent-minded, abstracted, *distrait*; lost; lost –, wrapped- in thought, woolgathering; rapt, in the clouds, bemused; dreaming –, musing-on other things; pre-occupied; engrossed &c. (*attentive*) 457; in a -reverie &c. *n.*; off one's guard &c. (*inexpectant*) 508; napping; dreamy.

disconcerted, put out &c. *v.*; rattled.

Adv. inattentively, inadvertently &c. *adj.*; per incuriam, sub silentio.

Int. stand -at ease, – easy!

Phr. the attention wanders; one's wits gone a -woolgathering, – bird's nesting; it never entered into one's head; the mind running on other things; one's thoughts being elsewhere; had it been a bear it would have bitten you.

_____

Adj. attentive, mindful, heedful, observant, regardful; alive –, awake- to, alert; observing &c. *v.*; taken up –, occupied- with; engaged –, engrossed –, interested –, wrapped- in; absorbed, rapt; breathless; pre-occupied &c. (*inattentive*) 458; watchful &c. (*careful*) 459; intent on, open-eyed, undistracted, upon the stretch; on the watch &c. (*expectant*) 507.

steadfast.

Int. see! look, – here, – out, – alive, – you, – to it, mark! lo!

behold! soho! hark, – ye! mind! halloo! observe! lo and behold! attention! *nota bene*; N.B.; *, †; I'd have you to know; notice! take notice! O yes! *Oyez!*

Phr. this is -, these are- to give notice.

459. Care. [Vigilance.]—**N.** care, solicitude, heed; heedfulness &c. *adj.*; scruple &c. (*conscientiousness*) 939.

watchfulness &c. *adj.*; vigilance, *surveillance*, eyes of Argus, watch, vigil, look out, watch and ward, *l'œil du maître.*

alertness &c. (*activity*) 682; attention &c. 457; prudence &c., circumspection &c. (*caution*) 864; forethought &c. 510; precaution &c. (*preparation*) 673; tidiness &c. (*order*) 58, (*cleanliness*) 652; accuracy &c. (*exactness*) 494; minuteness, attention to detail; meticulousness, nicety, circumstantiality.

V. be -careful &c. *adj.*; reck; take care &c. (*be cautious*) 864; pay attention to &c. 457; take care of; look -, see- -to, - after; keep -an eye, - a sharp eye- upon; keep -watch, – watch and ward; mount guard, set watch, watch; keep in -sight, – view; chaperon, play gooseberry; mind, – one's business.

look -sharp, -- about one; look with one's own eyes; keep a -good, – sharp-look-out; have all one's -wits, – eyes-about one; watch for &c. (*expect*) 507; stand to; keep one's eyes -, have the eyes -, sleep with one eye- open.

take precautions &c. 673; protect &c. (*render safe*) 664.

do one's best &c. 682; mind one's Ps and Qs, speak by the card, pick one's steps.

Adj. care-, regard-, heed-ful; taking care &c. *v.*; particular; prudent &c. (*cautious*) 864; considerate; thoughtful &c. (*deliberative*) 451; provident &c. (*prepared*) 673; alert &c. (*active*) 682; sure-footed.

guarded, on one's guard; on the -*qui vive*, – alert, – watch, – look-out; awake, broad awake, vigilant; watch-, wake-, wist-ful; Argus-, lynx- eyed; wide awake &c. (*intelligent*) 498; on the watch for &c. (*expectant*) 507.

tidy &c. (*orderly*) 58, (*clean*) 652; accurate &c. (*exact*) 494; scrupulous

460. Neglect.—**N.** neglect; carelessness &c. *adj.*; trifling &c. *v.*; negligence; omission, laches, default; remissness, slackness, procrastination; supineness &c. (*inactivity*) 683; inattention &c. 458; nonchalance &c. (*insensibility*) 823; imprudence, recklessness &c. 863; slovenliness &c. (*disorder*) 59, (*dirt*) 653; improvidence &c. 674; non-completion &c. 730; inexactness &c. (*error*) 495.

paraleipsis [in rhetoric].

trifler, slacker, waster, waiter on Providence; Micawber.

V. be -negligent &c. *adj.*; take no care of &c. (take care of &c. 459); neglect; let -slip, – go; lay -, set -, cast -, put- aside; keep -, leave- out of sight; lose sight of.

overlook, disregard; pass -over, – by; let pass; blink; wink -, connive- at; gloss over; take no -note, – notice, – thought, – account- of; pay no regard to; *laisser aller*; allow to lie on the table.

scamp; trifle, fribble; do by halves; skimp; cut; slight &c. (*despise*) 930; play -, trifle- with; slur; skim, – the surface; *effleurer*; take a cursory view of &c. 457.

slur -, slip -, skip -, jump- over; pretermit, miss, skip, jump, omit, give the go-by to, push aside, throw into the background, shelve, sink; ignore, shut one's eyes to, refuse to hear, turn a deaf ear to; leave out of one's calculation; not -attend to &c. 457, – mind; not trouble -oneself, – one's head- -with, – about; forget &c. 506; be caught napping &c. 508; leave a loose thread; let the grass grow under one's feet.

render -neglectful &c. *adj.*; put -, throw- off one's guard.

Adj. neglecting &c. *v.*; unmindful, negligent, neglectful; heedless, careless, thoughtless; perfunctory; remiss, slack.

inconsiderate; un-, in-circumspect;

&c. (*conscientious*) 939; *cavendo tutus*
&c. (*safe*) 664.

Adv. carefully &c. *adj.*; with care,
gingerly.

Phr. *quis custodiet ipsos custodes?*

off one's guard; un-wary, -watchful,
-guarded; offhand.

supine &c. (*inactive*) 683; inattentive
&c. 458; insouciant &c. (*indifferent*)
823; imprudent, reckless &c. 863;
slovenly &c. (*disorderly*) 59, (*dirty*)
653; inexact &c. (*erroneous*) 495; improvident &c. 674.

neglected &c. *v.*; un-heeded, -cared
for, -perceived, -seen, -observed, -no-
ticed, -noted, -marked, -attended to, -thought of, -regarded, -re-
marked, -missed; shunted, shelved.

un-examined, -studied, -searched, -scanned, -weighed, -sifted,
-explored.

abandoned; buried in a napkin, hid under a bushel.

Adv. negligently &c. *adj.*; hand over head, anyhow; in an unguarded moment &c. (*unexpectedly*) 508; *per incuriam*.

Int. never mind, no matter, let it pass; it will be all the same a
hundred years hence.

---

461. Inquiry. [Subject of Inquiry.
Question.]—**N.** inquiry; request &c.
765; search, research, quest; pursuit
&c. 622.

examination, review, scrutiny, investigation, indagation; per-quisition,
-scrutation, -vestigation; inqu-est,
-isition; exploration; *exploitation*,
ventilation.

sifting; calculation, analysis, dissection, resolution, induction; Baconian
method.

strict –, close –, searching –, ex-
haustive- inquiry; narrow –, strict-
search; study &c. (*consideration*) 451.
scire facias, ad referendum; trial.

questioning &c. *v.*; interroga-tion,
-tory; third degree; interpellation; challenge, examination, cross-examination,
catechism; feeler, Socratic method,
zetetic philosophy; leading question;
discussion &c. (*reasoning*) 476; ques-
tionnaire, questionary.

reconnoitering, *reconnaissance*; prying &c. *v.*; espionage, *espionnage*;
domiciliary visit, peep behind the
curtain; lantern of Diogenes.

462. Answer.—**N.** answer, response,
reply, replication, *riposte*, rejoinder,
surrejoinder, rebutter, surrebutter,
counter-evidence &c. 468, countercharge, defence, plea; retort, repartee;
contradiction &c. 536; rescript, -ion;
antiphon, -y; acknowledgment; pass-
word; echo.

discovery &c. 480a; solution &c.
(*explanation*) 522; rationale &c. (*cause*)
153; clue &c. (*indication*) 550.

Œdipus; oracle &c. 513; return &c.
(*record*) 551.

V. answer, respond, reply, rebut,
retort, rejoin; give –, return for-
answer; acknowledge, echo.

explain &c. (*interpret*) 522; solve &c.
(*unriddle*) 522; discover &c. 480a;
fathom, hunt out &c. (*inquire*) 461;
satisfy, set at rest, determine.

Adj. answering &c. *v.*; respon-sive,
-dent; oracular; antiphonal; conclusive.

Adv. because &c. (*cause*) 153; on
the -scent, – right scent.

Int. *eureka!*

---

question, query, problem, *desideratum*, point to be solved, porism;
subject –, field- of -inquiry, – controversy; point –, matter- in
dispute; moot-point; issue, question at issue; bone of contention
&c. (*discord*) 713; plain –, fair –, open- question; enigma &c. (*secret*)
533; knotty point &c. (*difficulty*) 704; *quodlibet*; threshold of an
inquiry.

inquirer, investigator, experimenter, inquisitor, inspector, querist, examiner, catechist; scrut-ator, -ineer; analyst; quidnunc &c. (*curiosity*) 455.

V. make -inquiry &c. *n.*; inquire, seek, search, frisk, speer, look -for, – about for, – out for; scan, reconnoitre, explore, sound, rummage, ransack, pry, peer, look round; look –, go- -over, – through; spy, over-haul.

scratch the head, slap the forehead.

look –, peer –, pry- into every hole and corner; look behind the scenes; trace up; hunt –, fish –, dig –, ferret- out; unearth; leave no stone unturned.

seek a -clue, – clew; hunt, track, trail, shadow, mouse, dodge, trace; follow the -trail, – scent; pursue &c. 622; beat up one's quarters; fish for; feel for &c. (*experiment*) 463.

investigate; take up –, institute –, pursue –, follow up –, con-duct –, carry on –, prosecute- -an inquiry &c. *n.*; look -at, – into; pre-examine; discuss, canvass, agitate.

examine, study, consider, calculate; dip –, dive –, delve –, go deep- into; make sure of, probe, sound, fathom; probe to the -bottom, – quick; scrutinize, analyze, anatomize, dissect, parse, resolve, sift, winnow; view –, try- in all its phases; thresh out.

bring in question, subject to examination; put to the proof &c. (*experiment*) 463; audit, tax, pass in review; take into consideration &c. (*think over*) 451; take counsel &c. 695.

ask, question, demand; put –, pop –, propose –, propound –, moot –, start –, raise –, stir –, suggest –, put forth –, ventilate –, grapple with –, go into- a question.

put to the question, interrogate, catechize, pump, grill; cross-question, -examine; dodge; require an answer; pick –, suck- the brains of; feel the pulse.

be -in question &c. *adj.*; undergo examination.

Adj. inquiring &c. *v.*; inquisitive &c. (*curious*) 455; requisit-ive, -ory; catechetical, inquisitorial, analytic; in -search, – quest- of; on the look-out for, interrogative, zetetic; all-searching.

un-determined, -tried, -decided; in -question, – dispute, – issue, – course of inquiry; under -discussion, – consideration, – investiga-tion &c. *n.*, *sub judice*, moot, proposed; doubtful &c. (*uncertain*) 475.

Adv. what? why? wherefore? whence? whither? where? *quare?* how -comes, – happens, – is- it? what is the reason? what's -the matter, – up, – in the wind? what on earth? when? who?

463. Experiment.—N. experiment; essay &c. (*attempt*) 675; research &c. (*investigation*) 461; trial, tentative method, *tâtonnement*.

verification, probation, *experimentum crucis*, proof, criterion, diag-nostic, test, tryout, crucial test, acid test.

crucible, reagent, check, touchstone, pix; assay, ordeal; ring.

empiricism, rule of thumb.

feeler; pilot –, messenger- balloon, *ballon d'essai*; pilot engine; scout; straw to show the wind.

speculation, random shot, leap in the dark.

analy-zer, -st; adventurer, explorer, sourdough, prospector; experi-ment-er, -ist, -alist; assayer.

V. experiment; essay &c. (*endeavour*) 675; try, assay, sample; make -an experiment, – trial of; give a trial to; put upon –, subject to- trial; experiment upon; rehearse; put –, bring –, submit- to the -test, – proof; prove, verify, test, touch, practise upon, try one's strength.

grope; feel –, grope- -for, – one's way; fumble; *tâtonner, aller à tâtons*; put –, throw- out a feeler; send up a pilot balloon; see how the -land lies, – wind blows; consult the barometer; feel the pulse; fish –, bob- for; cast –, beat- about for; angle, trawl, cast one's net, beat the bushes.

venture, try one's fortune &c. (*adventure*) 675; explore &c. (*inquire*) 461.

Adj. experimental; probat-ive, -ory, -ionary; analytic, docimastic; tentative; empirical; speculative.

under probation, on one's trial, on trial, on approval.

464. Comparison.—**N.** comparison, collation, contrast; identification. sim-ile, -ilitude; allegory &c. (*metaphor*) 521.

V. compare -to, – with; collate, confront; place side by side &c. (*near*) 197; set –, pit- against one another; contrast, balance.

identify, draw a parallel, parallel.

compare notes; institute a comparison; *parva componere magnis*.

Adj. comparative, relative; metaphorical &c. 521.

compared with &c. *v.*; comparable.

Adv. relatively &c. (*relation*) 9; as compared with &c. *v.*

465. Discrimination.—**N.** discrimina-tion, distinction, differentiation, diagnosis, diorism; nice perception; per-ception –, appreciation- of difference; acuteness; estimation &c. 466; nicety, refinement; taste &c. 850; *critique*, judgement, tact; insight, discernment &c. (*intelligence*) 498; *nuances*.

V. discriminate, distinguish, differentiate, severalize; separate; draw the line, sift; separate –, winnow- the chaff from the wheat; split hairs.

estimate &c. (*measure*) 466; know -which is which, – one's stuff, – one's way about, – what is what, – 'a hawk from a handsaw.'

take into -account, – consideration; give –, allow- due weight to; weigh carefully.

Adj. discriminating &c. *v.*; dioristic, discriminative, critical, distinctive; nice.

Phr. *il y a fagots et fagots; rem acu tetigisti.*

465a. Indiscrimination.—**N.** indiscrimination; promiscuity; indistinctness, -ion; uncertainty &c. (*doubt*) 475; obtuseness.

V. not -indiscriminate &c. 465; overlook &c. (*neglect*) 460- a distinction; con-found, -fuse, jumble; swallow whole.

Adj. indiscriminate, undiscriminating, promiscuous; undistinguish-ed, -able, -ing; unmeasured.

466. Measurement.—**N.** measurement, admeasurement, mensuration, survey, valuation, appraisement, assessment, assize; estim-ate, -ation; dead reckoning; reckoning &c. (*numeration*) 85; gauging &c. *v.*

metrology, weights and measures, compound arithmetic.

measure, yard measure, standard, rule, foot-rule, chain, tape, staff, compass, callipers; dividers; gage, gauge, planimeter; meter, line, rod, check.

volt, kilowatt, ampere, candle power; horse power; axle load; foot pound.

flood –, high water- mark; Plimsoll mark; index &c. 550.

scale; gradu-ation, -ated scale; nonius; vernier &c. (*minuteness*) 193; pedo (*length*)- 200, sounding line &c. (*depth*)- 208, thermo (*heat* &c. 389)-, baro (*air* &c. 338)-, dynamo (*power*)- 276, anemo (*wind* 349)-, gonio (*angle* 244)- meter; landmark &c. (*limit*) 233; balance &c. (*weight*) 319; optical instruments &c. 445.

co-ordinates, ordinate and abscissa, polar co-ordinates, latitude and longitude, declination and right ascension, altitude and azimuth.

geo-, stereo-, hypso-metry; metage; surveying, land surveying; geo-desy, -detics, -desia; ortho-, alti-metry; *cadastre.*

astrolabe, armillary sphere.

land, -surveyor; geometer, topographer, cartographer, hydrographer.

V. measure, meter, mete; value, assess, rate, appraise, estimate, form an estimate, set a value on; appreciate; standardize.

span, pace, step; apply the -compass &c. *n.*; gauge, plumb, probe, calliper, sound, fathom &c. 208; heave the -log, - lead; weigh &c. 319; survey.

take an average &c. 29; graduate.

Adj. measuring &c. *v.*; metric, -al; measurable; geodetical, cadastral, topographical.

Section III. MATERIALS FOR REASONING

467. Evidence [on one side.]—**N.** evidence; facts, premises, *data, præcognita,* grounds.

indication &c. 550; criterion &c. (*test*) 463.

testi-mony, -fication; attestation; deposition &c. (*affirmation*) 535; examination.

admission &c. (*assent*) 488; authority, warrant, credential, diploma, voucher, certificate, docket; record &c. 551; document, muniments; *pièce justificative*; deed, warranty &c. (*security*) 771; signature, seal &c. (*identification*) 550; exhibit, citation, reference.

witness, indicator; eye-, ear-witness; deponent; sponsor.

oral -, documentary -, hearsay -, external -, extrinsic -, internal -, intrinsic -, circumstantial -, cumulative -, *ex parte* -, presumptive -, collateral -, constructive- evidence; proof &c. (*demonstration*) 478; evidence in chief; finger prints, dactylogram.

secondary evidence; confirmation, corroboration, adminicle, support; ratification &c. (*assent*) 488; authentication, verification; compurgation, wager of law, comprobation.

citation, reference.

V. be -evidence &c. *n.*; evince, show, betoken, tell of; indicate &c. (*denote*) 550; imply, involve, argue, bespeak, breathe.

have -, carry- weight; tell, speak

468. [Evidence on the other side, on the other hand.] **Counter-evidence.**— **N.** counter-evidence; evidence on the other -side, - hand; disproof; refutation &c. 479; negation &c. 536; conflicting evidence.

plea &c. 617; vindication &c. 937; counter-protest; *tu quoque* argument; other side -, reverse- of the shield.

V. countervail, oppose; run counter; rebut &c. (*refute*) 479; subvert &c. (*destroy*) 162; check, weaken; contravene; contradict &c. (*deny*) 536; tell another story, turn the -tables, - scale; alter the case; cut both ways; prove a negative.

audire alteram partem.

Adj. countervailing &c. *v.*; contradictory, in rebuttal.

un-attested, -authenticated, -supported by evidence; supposititious, trumped up.

Adv. *per contra,* conversely, on the other hand.

469. Qualification.—**N.** qualification, limitation, modification, colouring.

allowance, grains of allowance, consideration, extenuating circumstances.

condition, proviso, exception; exemption; salvo, saving clause; discount &c. 813.

V. qualify, limit, modify, affect, temper, leaven, give a colour to, introduce new conditions.

allow -, make allowance- for; ad-

volumes; speak for itself &c. (*manifest*) 525.

rest -, depend- upon; repose on.

bear -witness &c. *n.*; give -evidence &c. *n.*; testify, depose, witness, vouch for; sign, seal, undersign, set one's hand and seal, sign and seal, deliver as one's act and deed, certify, attest; acknowledge &c. (*assent*) 488.

make absolute, confirm, ratify, corroborate, endorse, countersign, support, bear out, vindicate, uphold, warrant.

adduce, attest, cite, quote; refer -, appeal- to; call, - to witness; bring -forward, - into court; allege, plead; produce -, confront- witnesses; collect -, bring together -, rake up- evidence.

have -, make out- a case; establish, circumstantiate, authenticate, substantiate, verify, make good, quote chapter and verse; bring -home to, - to book.

Adj. showing &c. *v.*; evidential, indica-tive, -tory; deducible &c. 478; grounded -, founded -, based- on; first hand, authentic, verifiable; corroborative, confirmatory; significant, conclusive.

Adv. by inference; according to, witness, *a fortiori*; still -more, - less; *raison de plus*; in corroboration &c. *n.* of; *valeat quantum*; under -seal, - one's hand and seal.

mit exceptions, take into account. take exception, object.

Adj. qualifying &c. *v.*; conditional; extenuatory; exceptional &c. (*unconformable*) 83.

hypothetical &c. (*supposed*) 514; contingent &c. (*uncertain*) 475.

Adv. provided, - always; if, unless, but, yet; according as; conditionally, admitting, supposing; on the supposition of &c. (*theoretically*) 514; with the understanding, even, although, though, for all that, after all, at all events.

with grains of allowance, *cum grano salis*; *exceptis excipiendis*; wind and weather permitting; if possible &c. 470.

subject to; with this -proviso &c. *n.*

Degrees of Evidence

470. Possibility.—N. possibility, potentiality; what -may be, - is possible &c. *adj.*; compatibility &c. (*agreement*) 23.

practicability, feasibility; practicableness &c. *adj.*

contingency, chance &c. 156.

V. be -possible &c. *adj.*; stand a chance, have a leg to stand on; admit of, bear.

render -possible &c. *adj.*; put in the way of.

Adj. possible; on the -cards, - dice; *in posse*, within the bounds of possibility, conceivable, credible, imaginable; compatible &c. 23.

practicable, feasible, workable, performable, achievable; within -reach, - measurable distance; accessible, superable, surmountable; at-, ob-tainable; contingent &c. (*doubtful*) 475.

Adv. possibly, by possibility; perhaps, -chance, -adventure; may be, haply, mayhap.

471. Impossibility.—N. impossibility &c. *adj.*; what -cannot, - can never- be; sour grapes; infeasibility, impracticability, hopelessness &c. 859.

V. be -impossible &c. *adj.*; have no chance whatever.

attempt impossibilities; square the circle; discover the -philosopher's stone, - elixir of life, - secret of perpetual motion; wash a blackamoor white; skin a flint; make -a silk purse out of a sow's ear, - bricks without straw; have nothing to go upon; weave a rope of sand, build castles in the air, *prendre la lune avec les dents*, extract sunbeams from cucumbers, set the Thames on fire, milk a he-goat into a sieve, catch a weasel asleep, *rompre l'anguille au genou*, be in two places at once.

Adj. impossible; not -possible &c. 470; absurd, contrary to reason; unlikely, at variance with facts; unreasonable &c. 477; incredible &c. 485; beyond the bounds of -reason, - possi-

if possible, wind and weather permitting, God willing, *Deo volente*, D.V.

---

impracticable, unachievable; un-, in-feasible; insuperable; un-, in-surmountable; unat-, unob-tainable; out of -reach, – the question; not to be -had, – thought of; beyond control; desperate &c. (*hopeless*) 859; incompatible &c. 24; inaccessible, uncomeatable, impassable impervious, innavigable, inextricable.

out of –, beyond- one's -power, – depth, – reach, – grasp; too much for; *ultra crepidam*.

Phr. the grapes are sour; *non possumus*; *non nostrum tantas componere lites*.

bility; from which reason recoils; visionary; inconceivable &c. (*improbable*) 473; prodigious &c. (*wonderful*) 870; un-, in-imaginable, unthinkable, not a Chinaman's chance.

472. Probability.—N. probability, likelihood; likeliness &c. *adj.*

vraisemblance, verisimilitude, plausibility; colour, semblance, show of; presumption; presumptive –, circumstantial- evidence; credibility.

reasonable –, fair –, good –, favourable- -chance, – prospect; prospect, well-grounded hope; chance &c. 156.

V. be -probable &c. *adj.*; give –, lend- colour to; point to; imply &c. (*evidence*) 467; bid fair &c. (*promise*) 511; stand fair for; stand –, run- a good chance.

presume, infer, suppose, take for granted.

think likely, dare say, flatter oneself; expect &c. 507; count upon &c. (*believe*) 484.

473. Improbability.—N. improbability, unlikelihood; unfavourable –, bad –, little –, small –, poor –, scarcely any –, no –, not a ghost of a- chance; bare possibility; long odds; incredibility &c. 485.

V. be -improbable &c. *adj.*; have a -small chance &c. *n.*

Adj. improbable, unlikely, contrary to all reasonable expectation, implausible.

rare &c. (*infrequent*) 137; unheard of, inconceivable; un-, in-imaginable; incredible &c. 485; more than doubtful.

Int. not likely! no fear!

Phr. the chances are against.

Adj. probable, likely, hopeful, to be expected, in a fair way.

plausible, specious, ostensible, colourable, *ben trovato*, well-founded, reasonable, credible, easy of belief, presumable, presumptive, apparent.

Adv. probably &c. *adj.*; belike; in all -probability, – likelihood; very –, most- likely; as likely as not; like enough; ten &c. to one; apparently, seemingly, according to every reasonable expectation; *primâ facie*; to all appearance &c. (*to the eye*) 448.

Phr. the -chances, – odds- are; appearances –, chances- are in favour of; there is reason to -believe, – think, – expect; I dare say; all Lombard Street to a China orange.

474. Certainty.—N. certainty; necessity &c. 601; certitude, certainness, surety, assurance, sureness; dead –, moral- certainty; infallibleness &c. *adj.*; infallibility, reliability.

gospel, scripture, church, pope, court of final appeal; *res judicata, ultimatum.*

positiveness; dogmat-ism, -ist, -izer; *doctrinaire*, know-all, bigot, -ry; opin-

475. Uncertainty.—N. uncertainty, incertitude, doubt; doubtfulness &c. *adj.*; dubi-ety, -tation, -tancy, -ousness.

hesitation, suspense; perplexity, embarrassment, dilemma, quandary, Morton's fork, bewilderment; timidity &c. (*fear*) 860; indecision, vacillation &c. 605; *diaporesis*, indetermination.

vagueness &c. *adj.*; haze, fog; ob-

ionist, Sir Oracle; *ipse dixit*; zealot.

fact; positive -, matter of- fact; *fait accompli*.

V. be -certain &c. *adj.*; stand to reason.

render -certain &c. *adj.*; in-, en-, assure; clinch, make sure; determine, decide, set at rest, 'make assurance double sure'; know &c. (*believe*) 484; dismiss all doubt.

dogmatize, lay down the law.

Adj. certain, sure; assured &c. *v.*; solid, well-founded.

unqualified, absolute, positive, determinate, definite, clear, unequivocal, categorical, unmistakable, decisive, decided, ascertained.

inevitable, unavoidable, ineluctable, avoidless.

unerring, infallible; unchangeable &c. 150; to be depended on, trustworthy, reliable, bound.

un-impeachable, -deniable, -questionable; in-disputable, -contestable, -controvertible, -defeasible, -dubitable; irrefutable &c. (*proven*) 478; conclusive, without power of appeal, final.

indubious; without -, beyond a -, without a shade or shadow of- -doubt - question; past dispute; beyond all -question, - dispute; un-doubted, -contested, -questioned, -disputed; question-, doubt-less.

bigoted, fanatical, dogmatic, opinionat-ed, -ive, *doctrinaire*.

authoritative, authentic, official.

sure as -fate, - death and taxes, - a gun.

evident, self-evident, axiomatic; clear, - as day, - as the sun at noonday; obvious.

Adv. certainly &c. *adj.*; for certain, certes, sure, no doubt, doubtless, and no mistake, *flagrante delicto*, sure enough, to be sure, of course, as a matter of course, *à coup sur*, to a certainty, undoubtedly; in truth &c. (*truly*) 494; at -any rate, - all events; without fail; *coûte que coûte*; whatever may happen, if the worst come to the worst; come -, happen- what -may, - will; sink or swim; rain or shine.

Phr. *cela va sans dire*; there is ·no question, - not a shadow of doubt;

scurity &c. (*darkness*) 421; ambiguity &c. (*double meaning*) 520; contingency, double contingency, possibility upon a possibility; conjecture; open question &c. (*question*) 461; *onus probandi*; blind bargain, pig in a poke, leap in the dark, something or other; needle in a bottle of hay; roving commission.

fallibility, unreliability, untrustworthiness, precariousness.

V. be -uncertain &c. *adj.*; wonder whether.

lose the -clue, - clew, - scent; miss one's way.

not know -what to make of &c. (*unintelligibility*) 519, - which way to turn, - whether one stands on one's head or one's heels; float in a sea of doubt, hesitate, flounder; lose -oneself, - one's head, - one's way, wander aimlessly; muddle one's brains.

render -uncertain &c. *adj.*; put out, pose, puzzle, perplex, embarrass; confuse, -found; bewilder, mystify, bother, moider, nonplus, addle the wits, throw off the scent; *spargere voces in vulgum ambiguas*; keep in suspense.

doubt &c. (*disbelieve*) 485; hang -, tremble- in the balance; depend.

Adj. uncertain; casual; random &c. (*aimless*) 621; changeable &c. 149.

doubtful, dubious; indecisive; unsettled, -decided, -determined; in suspense, open to discussion; controvertible; in question &c. (*inquiry*) 461; insecure, unstable.

vague; in-determinate, -definite; ambiguous, equivocal; undefin-ed, -able; confused &c. (*indistinct*) 447; mystic, mysterious, veiled, obscure, cryptic, oracular.

perplexing &c. *v.*; enigmatic, paradoxical, apocryphal, problematical, hypothetical; experimental &c. 463.

fallible, questionable, precarious, slippery, ticklish, debatable, disputable; un-reliable, -trustworthy.

contingent, - on, dependent on; subject to; dependent on circumstances; occasional; provisional.

unauth-entic, -enticated, -oritative; un-ascertained, -confirmed; undemonstrated; un-told, -counted.

in a -state of uncertainty, - cloud,

the die is cast &c. (*necessity*) 601.

_____

- maze; ignorant &c. 491; on the horns of a dilemma; afraid to say; out of one's reckoning, astray, adrift; at -sea,

- fault, - a loss, - one's wit's end, - a *nonplus*; puzzled &c. *v.*; lost, abroad, *désorienté*; dis-tracted, -traught.

Adv. *pendente lite*; *sub spe rati*.

Phr. Heaven knows; who can tell? who shall decide when doctors disagree?

Section IV. REASONING PROCESSES

476. Reasoning. — N. reasoning; ratio-cination, -nalism; dialectics, induction, generalization.

discussion, comment; ventilation; inquiry &c. 461.

argumentation, controversy, debate; polemics, wrangling; contention &c. 720; logomachy; dis-putation, -ceptation; paper war.

art of reasoning, logic.

process -, train -, chain- of reasoning; de-, in-duction; synthesis, analysis.

argument; case, plea, *plaidoyer*, opening; *lemma*, proposition, terms, premises, postulate, *data*, starting point, principle; inference &c. (*judgment*) 480.

pro-, syllogism; enthymeme, sorites, dilemma, *perilepsis*, a priori reasoning, *reductio ad absurdum*, horns of a dilemma, *argumentum ad hominem*, comprehensive argument.

reasoner, logician, dialectician; disputant; controver-sialist, -tist; wrangler, arguer, debater, polemic, casuist, rationalist; scientist.

logical sequence; good case; correct -, just -, sound -, valid -, cogent -, logical -, forcible -, persuasive -, persuasory -, consectary -, conclusive &c. 478 -, subtle- reasoning; force of argument; strong -point, - argument.

arguments, reasons, pros and cons.

V. reason, argue, discuss, debate, dispute, wrangle; bandy -words, - arguments; chop logic; hold -, carry on- an argument; controvert &c. (*deny*) 536; canvass; comment -, moralize- upon; consider &c. (*examine*) 461.

open a -discussion, - case; join -, be at- issue; moot; come to the point; stir -, agitate -, ventilate -, torture- a question; try conclusions; take up a -side, - case.

477. [The absence of reasoning.] Intuition. [False or vicious reasoning; show of reason.] **Sophistry.—N.** intuition, instinct, association; presentiment; rule of thumb.

sophistry, paralogy, perversion, casuistry, jesuitry, equivocation, evasion, mental reservation; chicane, -ry; quiddit, quiddity; mystification; special pleading; speciousness &c. *adj.*; nonsense &c. 497; word-, tongue-fence.

false -, vicious- reasoning; *petitio principii, ignoratio elenchi*; *post hoc ergo propter hoc*; *non sequitur, ignotum per ignotius*.

misjudgment &c. 481; false teaching &c. 538.

sophism, solecism, paralogism; quibble, quirk, *elenchus*, elench, fallacy, *quodlibet*, subterfuge, subtlety, quillet; inconsistency, antilogy; 'a mockery, a delusion and a snare'; claptrap, mere words; 'lame and impotent conclusion.'

meshes -, cobwebs- of sophistry; flaw in an argument; weak point, bad case.

over-refinement; hair-splitting &c. *v.* sophist, casuist, paralogist.

V. judge -intuitively, - by intuition; hazard a proposition, talk at random.

reason -ill, - falsely &c. *adj.*; paralogize; misjudge &c. 481.

pervert, quibble; equivocate, mystify, evade, elude; gloss over, varnish; misteach &c. 538; mislead &c. (*error*) 495; cavil, refine, subtilize, split hairs; misrepresent &c. (*lie*) 544.

beg the question, reason in a circle, cut blocks with a razor, beat about the bush, play fast and loose, blow hot and cold, prove that black is white and white black, travel out of the record, *parler à tort et à travers*, put oneself out of court, not have a leg to stand on.

Adj. intuitive, instinctive, impulsive;

contend, take one's stand upon, insist, lay stress on; infer &c. 480.

follow from &c. (*demonstration*) 478.

Adj. rational; reasoning &c. *v.*; rationalistic; argumentative, controversial, dialectic, polemical; discursory, -ive; disputatious.

debatable, controvertible.

logical; in-, de-ductive; synthetic, analytic; relevant &c. 23.

Adv. for, because, hence, whence, seeing that, since, sith, then, thence, so; for -that, – this, – which- reason; for-, inasmuch as; whereas, *ex concesso*, considering, in consideration of; there-, where-fore; consequently, *ergo*, thus, accordingly; *a fortiori*.

in -conclusion, – fine; finally, after all, *au bout du compte*, on the whole, taking one thing with another.

rationally &c. *adj.*

---

478. Demonstration.—N. demonstration, proof; conclusiveness &c. *adj.*; *apodixis*, probation, comprobation.

logic of facts &c. (*evidence*) 467; *experimentum crucis* &c. (*test*) 463; argument &c. 476; irrefragability.

V. demonstrate, prove, establish, make good; show; evince &c. (*be evidence of*) 467; verify &c. 467; settle the question, reduce to demonstration, set the question at rest.

make out, – a case; prove one's point, have the best of the argument; draw a conclusion &c. (*judge*) 480.

follow, – of course; stand to reason; hold -good, – water.

Adj. demonstra-ting &c. *v.*, -tive, -ble; probative, unanswerable, conclusive; apodictic, -al; irre-sistible, -futable, -fragable, undeniable.

categorical, decisive, crucial.

demonstrated &c. *v.*; proven; un-confuted, -answered, -refuted; evident &c. 474.

deducible, consequential, consectary, inferential, following.

Adv. of course, in consequence, consequently, as a matter of course.

Phr. *probatum est*; there is nothing more to be said, Q.E.D., it must follow.

independent of –, anterior to- reason; gratuitous, hazarded; unconnected.

unreasonable, illogical, false, unsound, invalid; unwarranted, not following; inconsequent, -ial; inconsistent, incongruous; abson-ous, -ant; unscientific; untenable, inconclusive, incorrect; fall-acious, -ible; groundless, unproved.

deceptive, sophistical, sophisticated, casuistical, jesuitical; illus-ive, -ory; specious, hollow, plausible, *ad captandum*, evasive; irrelevant &c. 10.

weak, feeble, poor, flimsy, loose, vague, irrational; nonsensical &c. (*absurd*) 497; foolish &c. (*imbecile*) 499; frivolous, pettifogging, quibbling; finespun, over-refined.

at the end of one's tether, *au bout de son latin*.

Adv. intuitively &c. *adj.*; by intuition; illogically &c. *adj.*

Phr. *non constat*; that goes for nothing.

---

479. Confutation.—N. con-, re-futation; answer, complete answer; disproof, conviction, redargution, invalidation; expos-ure, -ition; clincher; retort; *reductio ad absurdum*; knock down –, *tu quoque*- argument.

V. con-, re-fute; parry, negative, disprove, redargue, expose, show the fallacy of, rebut, defeat; demolish &c. (*destroy*) 162; over-throw, -turn; scatter to the winds, explode, invalidate; silence; put –, reduce- to silence; clinch -an argument, – a question; give one a set down, stop the mouth, shut up; have, – on the hip; get the better of; confound, convince.

not leave a leg to stand on, cut the ground from under one's feet.

be confuted &c.; fail; expose –, show- one's weak point.

Adj. confut-ing, -ed &c. *v.*; capable of refutation; re-, con-futable.

condemned -on one's own showing, – out of one's own mouth.

Phr. the argument falls to the ground, *cadit quæstio*, it does not hold water, '*suo sibi gladio hunc jugulo.*'

Section V. Results of Reasoning

480. Judgement. [Conclusion.]—N. result, conclusion, upshot; deduction, inference, ergotism, illation; corollary, porism; moral.

estimation, valuation, appreciation, judication; di-, ad-judication; arbitrament, -ement, -ation; assessment, ponderation.

award, estimate; review, criticism, *critique*, notice, report.

decision, determination, judgment, finding, verdict, sentence, decree, – nisi, – absolute, – interlocutory; *dictum*; *res judicata*.

plébiscite, referendum, voice, casting vote; vote &c. (*choice*) 609; opinion &c. (*belief*) 484; good judgment &c. (*wisdom*) 498.

judge, jurist, umpire; arbi-ter, -trator; assessor, referee; censor, reviewer, critic; *connoisseur*; commentator &c. 524; inspector, inspecting officer.

V. judge, conclude; come to –, draw –, arrive at- a conclusion; ascertain, determine, make up one's mind.

deduce, derive, gather, collect, draw an inference, make a deduction, weet, ween.

form an estimate, estimate, size up, appreciate, value, count, assess, rate, rank, account; regard, consider, think of; look upon &c. (*believe*) 484.

settle; pass –, give- an opinion; decide, try, pronounce, rule; pass -judgment, – sentence; sentence, doom; find; give –, deliver- judgment; adjud-ge, -icate; arbitrate, award, report; bring in a verdict; make absolute, set a question at rest; confirm &c. (*assent*) 488.

comment, criticize; review, pass under review &c. (*examine*) 457; investigate &c. (*inquire*) 461.

hold the scales, sit in judgment; try –, hear- a cause.

Adj. judging &c. *v.*; judicious &c. (*wise*) 498; determinate, conclusive, censorious, critical &c. 932.

Adv. on the whole, all things considered.

481. Misjudgment. — N. misjudgment, obliquity of –, warped- judgment; mis-calculation, -computation, -conception &c. (*error*) 495; hasty conclusion.

prejud-gment, -ication, -ice; foregone conclusion; pre-notion, -vention, -conception, -dilection, -possession, -apprehension, -sumption, -sentiment; fixed –, preconceived- idea; *idée fixe*; *mentis gratissimus error*; fool's paradise.

esprit de corps, party spirit, race –, class- prejudice, partisanship, clannishness, *prestige*.

bias, warp, twist; hobby, fad, whim, craze, quirk, crotchet, partiality, infatuation, blind side, mote in the eye.

one-sided –, partial –, narrow –, confined –, superficial- -views, – ideas, – conceptions, – notions; narrow mind; bigotry &c. (*obstinacy*) 606; *odium theologicum*; pedantry; hypercriticism. *doctrinaire* &c. (*positive*) 474.

V. mis-judge, -estimate, -think, -conjecture, -conceive &c. (*error*) 495; fly in the face of facts; mis-calculate, -reckon, -compute.

overestimate &c. 482; underestimate &c. 483.

pre-, fore-judge; pre-suppose, -sume, -judicate; dogmatize; have a -bias &c. *n.*; have only one idea; *jurare in verba magistri*, run away with the notion; jump –, rush- to a conclusion; look only at one side of the shield; view -with jaundiced eye, – through distorting spectacles; not see beyond one's nose; *dare pondus fumo*; get the wrong sow by the ear &c. (*blunder*) 699.

give a -bias, – twist; bias, warp, twist; pre-judice, -possess.

Adj. misjudging &c. *v.*; ill-judging, wrong-headed; prejudiced, prejudicial, &c. *v.*; jaundiced; short-sighted, purblind; partial, one-sided, superficial.

narrow-minded; confined, insular, provincial, parochial, illiberal, intolerant, narrow, besotted, infatuated, fanatical, cracked, warped, *entêté*, positive, dogmatic, dictatorial; conceited; opin-, opini-ative; opinion-ed, -ate, -ative, -ated; self-opinioned, wedded to an opinion, *opiniâtre*; bigoted &c. (*obstinate*) 606; crotchety, fussy, impracticable; unreason-able, -ing; stupid &c. 499; credulous &c. 486.

misjudged &c. *v.*

Adv. *ex parte.*

Phr. nothing like leather; the wish the father to the thought.

480a. [Result of search or inquiry.] **Discovery.—N.** discovery, invention, detection, disenchantment, disclosure, find, ascertainment, revelation.

trover &c. 775.

V. discover, find, determine, evolve; fix upon; find -, trace -, make -, hunt -, fish -, worm -, ferret -, root- out; fathom; bring -, draw- out; educe, elicit, bring to light, invent; dig -, grub -, fish- up; unearth, disinter.

solve, resolve; un-riddle, -ravel, -lock; pick -, open- the lock; find a -clue, - clew- to; interpret &c. 522; disclose &c. 529.

trace, get at; hit it, have it; lay one's -finger, - hands- upon; spot; get -, arrive- at the -truth &c. 494; put the saddle on the right horse, hit the right nail on the head.

be near the truth. burn; smoke, scent, sniff, smell a rat.

open the eyes to; see -through, - daylight, - in its true colours, - the cloven foot; detect; catch, - tripping.

pitch -, fall -, light -, hit -, stumble -, pop- upon; come across; meet -, fall in- with.

recognize, realize, verify, make certain of, identify.

Int. *eureka!*

482. Overestimation.—N. overestimation &c. *v.*; exaggeration &c. 549; vanity &c. 880; optim-, pessim-ism, -ist; megalomania.

much -cry and little wool, - ado about nothing; storm in a teacup; fine talking, rodomontade, gush, hot air, gas, bombast.

egotism &c. 880; boasting &c. 884.

V. over-estimate, -rate, -value, -prize, -weigh, -reckon, -strain, -praise; estimate too highly, attach too much importance to, make mountains of molehills, catch at straws; strain, magnify; exaggerate &c. 549; set too high a value upon; think -, make- -much, - too much- of; outreckon.

extol, - to the skies; make the -most, - best, -worst- of, eulogize, panegyrize, gush, puff, boost; make two bites of a cherry.

have too high an opinion of oneself &c. (*vanity*) 880.

Adj. overestimated &c. *v.*; oversensitive &c. (*sensibility*) 822; inflated, puffed up, exaggerated &c. 549.

Phr. all his geese are swans; *parturiunt montes.*

483. Underestimation.—N. underestimation; depreciation &c. (*detraction*) 934; pessim-ism, -ist; undervaluing &c. *v.*; modesty &c. 881.

V. under-rate, -estimate, -value, -reckon; depreciate; disparage &c. (*detract*) 934; not do justice to; mis-, dis-prize; ridicule &c. 856; slight &c. (*despise*) 930; neglect &c. 460; slur over, under-state.

make -light, - little, - nothing, - no account- of; minimize, belittle, run down, think nothing of; set -no store by, - at naught; shake off as dew-drops from the lion's mane.

Adj. depreciat-ing, -ed, -ive, -ory, &c. *v.*; un-appreciated, -valued, -prized; pejorative.

484. Belief.—N. belief; credence; credit; assurance; faith, trust, troth, confidence, presumption, sanguine expectation &c. (*hope*) 858; dependence on, reliance on.

persuasion, conviction, convincement, plerophory, self-conviction; certainty &c. 474; opinion, mind, view; conception, thinking; impression &c. (*idea*) 453; surmise &c. 514; conclusion &c. (*judgment*) 480.

tenet, dogma, principle, way of thinking; popular belief &c. (*assent*) 488.

firm -, implicit -, settled -, fixed -, rooted -, deep-rooted -, staunch -, unshaken -, steadfast -, inveterate -, calm -, sober -, dispassionate -, impartial -, well-founded- -belief, - opinion &c.; *uberrima fides*.

system of opinions, school, doctrine, articles, canons; declaration -, profession- of faith; tenets, *credenda*, creed; thirty-nine articles &c. (*orthodoxy*) 983a; catechism; assent &c. 488; *propaganda* &c. (*teaching*) 537.

credibility &c. (*probability*) 472.

V. believe, credit; give -faith, - credit, - credence- to; see, realize; assume, receive; set down -, take- for; have -, take- it; consider, esteem, presume.

count -, depend -, calculate -, pin one's faith -, reckon -, lean -, build -, rely -, rest- upon; lay one's account for; make sure of.

make oneself easy -about, - on that score; take on -trust, - credit; take for -granted, -gospel; allow -, attach-some weight to.

know, - for certain; have -, make-no doubt; doubt not; be - rest- -assured &c. *adj.*; persuade -, assure -, satisfy-oneself; make up one's mind.

give one credit for; confide -, believe -, put one's trust- in; place -, repose- implicit confidence in; take -one's word for, - at one's word; place reliance on, rely upon, swear by, pay regard to.

think, hold; take, - it; opine, be of opinion, conceive, trow, ween, fancy, apprehend; have -, hold -, possess -, entertain -, adopt -, imbibe -, embrace

485. Unbelief. Doubt.—N. un-, dis-. mis-belief; discredit, miscreance; infidelity &c. (*irreligion*) 989; dissent &c. 489; change of -opinion &c. 484; retraction &c. 607.

doubt &c. (*uncertainty*) 475; skepticism, misgiving, demur; dis-, mis-trust; misdoubt, suspicion, jealousy, scruple, qualm; *onus probandi*.

incredib-ility, -leness; incredulity; unbeliever &c. 487.

V. dis-believe, -credit; not -believe &c. 484; misbelieve; refuse to admit &c. (*dissent*) 489; refuse to believe &c. (*incredulity*) 487.

doubt; be -doubtful &c. (*uncertain*) 475; doubt the truth of; be -skeptical as to &c. *adj.*; diffide; dis-, mis-trust; suspect, smoke, scent, smell a rat; have -, harbour -, entertain- -doubts, - suspicions; have one's doubts.

demur, stick at, pause, hesitate, scruple, waver, stop and consider.

hang in -suspense, - doubt.

throw doubt upon, raise a question; bring -, call- in question; question, challenge, query; dispute; deny &c. 536; cavil; cause -, raise -, start -, suggest -, awake- a -doubt, - suspicion; ergotize.

startle, stagger; shake -, stagger-one's faith, - belief.

Adj. unbelieving; incredulous -, skeptical- as to; distrustful -, shy -, suspicious- of; doubting &c. *v.*

doubtful &c. (*uncertain*) 475; disputable; unworthy -, undeserving- of -belief &c. 484; questionable; sus-pect, -picious; open to -suspicion, - doubt; staggering, hard to believe, incredible, not to be believed, inconceivable.

fallible &c. (*uncertain*) 475; undemonstrable; controvertible &c. (*untrue*) 495.

Adv. *cum grano salis.*

Phr. *fronti nulla fides*; *nimium ne crede colori*; '*timeo Danaos et dona ferentes*'; *credat Judæus Apella*; let those believe who may.

–, get hold of –, hazard –, foster –, nurture –, cherish- -a belief, – an opinion &c. *n.*

view –, consider –, take –, hold –, conceive –, regard –, esteem –, deem –, look upon –, account –, set down- as; surmise &c. 514.

get –, take- it into one's head; come round to an opinion; swallow &c. (*credulity*) 486.

cause to -be believed &c. *v.*; satisfy, persuade, have the ear of, gain the confidence of, assure; con-vince, -vict, -vert; put across, sell; wean, bring round; bring –, put –, win- over; indoctrinate &c. (*teach*) 537; cram down the throat; produce –, carry- conviction; bring –, drive- home to.

go down, find credence, pass current; be -received &c. *v.*, – current &c. *adj.*; possess –, take hold of –, take possession of- the mind.

Adj. believing &c. *v.*; certain, sure, assured, positive, cocksure, satisfied, confident, unhesitating, convinced, secure.

under the impression; impressed –, imbued –, penetrated- with.

confiding, trustful, suspectless; unsusp-ecting, -icious; void of suspicion; credulous &c. 486; wedded to.

believed &c. *v.*; accredited, putative; unsuspected.

worthy of –, deserving of –, commanding- -belief, – confidence; credible, reliable, trusted, trustworthy, to be depended on, un-doubted; satisfactory; probable &c. 472; fiduci-al, -ary; persuasive, impressive.

relating to belief, doctrinal.

Adv. in the -opinion, – eyes- of; *me judice*; me-seems, -thinks; to the best of one's belief; I -dare say, – doubt not, – have no doubt, – am sure; in my opinion; sure enough &c. (*certainty*) 474; depend –, rely- upon it; be –, rest- assured; I'll warrant you &c. (*affirmation*) 535.

---

486. Credulity.—N. credul-ity, -ous-ness &c. *adj.*; gull-, cull-ibility; gross credulity, infatuation; self-delusion, -deception; blind reasoning; supersti-tion; one's blind side; bigotry &c. (*obstinacy*) 606; hyper-orthodoxy &c. 984; misjudgment &c. 481.

credulous person &c. (*dupe*) 547.

V. be -credulous &c. *adj.*; *jurare in verba magistri*; follow implicitly; swal-low, – whole, gulp down; take on trust; take for -granted, – gospel; run away with -a notion, – an idea; jump –, rush- to a conclusion; think the moon is made of green cheese; take –, grasp- the shadow for the substance; catch at straws.

impose upon &c. (*deceive*) 545.

Adj. credulous, gullible; easily -de-ceived &c. 545; simple, green, soft, childish, silly, stupid; over-credulous, -confident; infatuated, superstitious; confiding &c. (*believing*) 484.

Phr. the wish the father to the thought; *credo quia impossibile*.

487. Incredulity.—N. incredul-ous-ness, -ity; skepticism, pyrrhonism; want of faith &c. (*irreligion*) 989.

suspiciousness &c. *adj.*; scrupulosity; suspicion &c. (*unbelief*) 485; dissent &c. 489.

unbeliever, skeptic, aporetic; atheist, agnostic, infidel, disbeliever, misbe-liever, pyrrhonist &c. 989; heretic &c. (*heterodox*) 984.

V. be -incredulous &c. *adj.*; distrust &c. (*disbelieve*) 485; refuse to believe; shut one's -eyes, – ears- to; turn a deaf ear to; hold aloof; ignore; *nullius jurare in verba magistri.*

Adj. incredulous, skeptical, unbeliev-ing, inconvincible; hard –, shy- of belief; suspicious, scrupulous, distrust-ful, heterodox &c. 984.

488. Assent.—N. assent, -ment; acquiescence, admission; nod; ac-, con-cord, -cordance; agreement &c. 23; affirm-ance, -ation; recognition, acknowledgment, avowal; confession, – of faith.

unanimity, common consent, *consensus*, acclamation, chorus, *vox populi*; popular –, current- -belief; – opinion; public opinion; concurrence &c. (*of causes*) 178; co-operation &c. (*voluntary*) 709.

ratification, confirmation, corroboration, approval, acceptance, *visa*; indorsement, &c. (*record*) 551; O.K.

consent &c. (*compliance*) 762.

affirmant, consenter, covenanter, subscriber, endorser, upholder.

V. assent; give –, yield –, nod- assent; acquiesce; agree &c. 23; receive, accept, accede, accord, concur, lend oneself to, consent, coincide, reciprocate, go with; be -at one with &c. *adj.*; **go** along –, chime in –, strike in –, **close**- with; echo, enter into one's **views**, agree in opinion; vote –, give **one's** voice- for; recognize; subscribe –, **conform** –, defer- to; say -yes, – ditto, **–** amen, – aye- to; to O.K.

acknowledge, own, admit, allow, **avow**, confess; concede &c. (*yield*) 762; **come** round to; abide by; permit &c. 760.

come to –, arrive at- -an understanding, – terms, – an agreement.

con-, af-firm; ratify, approve, endorse, countersign; visa; corroborate &c. 467.

go –, swim- with the stream, float with the current; be in the fashion, join in the chorus; be in every mouth.

Adj. assenting &c. *v.*; of one -accord, – mind; of the same mind, at one with, **agreed**, acquiescent, content; willing &c. 602.

un-contradicted, -challenged, -questioned, -controverted.

carried –, agreed- -*nem. con.* &c. *adv.*; unanimous; agreed on all hands, carried by acclamation.

affirmative &c. 535.

Adv. yes, yea, ay, aye, true; good; well; very -well, – true; well and good; granted; *placet*; even –, just- so; to be sure, surely, 'thou hast sa¹d'; truly, exactly, precisely,

489. Dissent.—N. dissent; discordance &c. (*disagreement*) 24; difference –, diversity- of opinion.

non-conformity &c. (*heterodoxy*) 984; protestantism, recusancy, schism; disaffection; secession &c. 624; recantation &c. 607.

dissension &c. (*discord*) 713; discontent &c. 832; cavilling.

protest; contradiction &c. (*denial*) 536; non-compliance &c. (*rejection*) 764; disapprobation &c. 932; hartal.

dissent-ient, -er; non-juror, -content; recusant, sectary, schismatic, protestant, non-conformist, separatist, non-co-operator, conscientious objector, passive resister.

V. dissent, demur; call in question &c. (*doubt*) 485; differ in opinion, disagree; say -no &c. 536; refuse -assent, – to admit; cavil, protest, raise one's voice against, make bold to differ; repudiate; contradict &c. (*deny*) 536; agree to differ.

have no notion of, differ *toto cælo*; revolt -at, – from the idea.

shake the head, shrug the shoulders; look -askance, – askant.

secede; recant &c. 607.

Adj. dissenting &c. *v.*; negative &c. 536; diss-ident, -entient; unconsenting &c. (*refusing*) 764; non-content, -juring; protestant, recusant; uncon-vinced, -verted.

unavowed, unacknowledged; out of the question.

discontented &c. 832; unwilling &c. 603; extorted.

sectarian, denominational, schismatic, heterodox, intolerant.

Adv. no &c. 536; at -variance, – issue- with; under protest; *non placet*.

Int. God forbid! not for the world; not on your life; I beg to differ; I'll be hanged if; never tell me; your humble servant, pardon me; tell that to the marines.

Phr. many men many minds; *quot homines tot sententiæ*; *tant s'en faut*; *il s'en faut bien.*

that's just it, indeed, certainly, certes, *ex concesso*; of course, un-questionably, assuredly, no doubt, doubtless, undoubtedly.

be it so; so -be it, – let it be, so mote it be; amen; with all my heart; willingly &c. 602.

affirmatively, in the affirmative.

with one -consent, – voice, – accord; unanimously, *unâ voce*, by common consent, in chorus, to a man, *nem. con.*; *nemine -contradi-cente, – dissentiente*; without a dissentient voice; as one man, one and all, on all hands.

---

490. Knowledge.—N. knowledge; cogn-izance, -ition, -oscence; acquaint-ance, experience, ken, privity, insight, familiarity; com-, ap-prehension; re-cognition; appreciation &c. (*judgment*) 480; intuition; consci-ence, -ousness; perception, precognition; acroamatics.

light, enlightenment; glimpse, ink-ling; side light; glimmer, -ing; dawn; scent, suspicion; impression &c. (*idea*) 453; discovery &c. 480a.

system –, body- of knowledge; science, philosophy, pansophy; theory, etiology; circle of the sciences; pan-dect, doctrine, body of doctrine; cy-, ency-clopædia; school &c. (*system of opinions*) 484.

tree of knowledge; republic of letters &c. (*language*) 560.

erudition, learning, lore, scholarship, reading, letters; literature; book-learning, bookishness; biblio-mania, -latry; information, general informa-tion; store of -knowledge &c.; educa-tion &c. (*teaching*) 537; culture, attain-ments; acqui-rements, -sitions; ac-complishments, proficiency; practical knowledge &c. (*skill*) 698; higher edu-cation, liberal education; dilettantism; rudiments &c. (*beginning*) 66.

deep –, profound –, solid –, accurate –, acroatic –, acroamatic –, vast –, ex-tensive –, encyclopædical- -knowledge, – learning; omniscience, pantology.

march of intellect; progress –, ad-vance- of -science, – learning; school-master abroad.

V. know, ken, scan, wot; wot –, be aware &c. adj.- of; ween, weet, trow, have, possess.

conceive; ap-, com-prehend; take, realize, understand, appreciate; fathom, make out; recognize, discern, perceive, see, get a sight of, experience.

491. Ignorance. — N. ignorance, nescience, *tabula rasa*, crass ignorance, *ignorance crasse*; unacquaintance; un-consciousness &c. *adj.*; dark-, blind-ness; incomprehension, inexperience, simplicity.

unknown quantities, x, y, z.

sealed book, *terra incognita*, virgin soil, unexplored ground; dark ages.

[Imperfect knowledge] smattering, superficiality, half-learning, sciolism, glimmering; bewilderment &c. (*uncer-tainty*) 475; incapacity.

[Affectation of knowledge] pedantry; charlatan-ry, -ism.

V. be -ignorant &c. *adj.*; not -know &c. 490; know -not, – not what, – no-thing of; have no -idea, – notion, – conception; not have the remotest idea; not know chalk from cheese.

ignore, be blind to; keep in ignorance &c. (*conceal*) 528.

see through a glass darkly; have a -film over the eyes, – glimmering &c. *n.*; wonder whether; not know what to make of &c. (*unintelligibility*) 519; not pretend –, not take upon oneself- to say.

Adj. ignorant, nescient; un-knowing, -aware, -acquainted, -apprized, -wit-ting, -weeting, -conscious; wit-, weet-less; a stranger to; unconversant.

un-informed, -cultivated, -versed, -instructed, -taught, -initiated, -tu-tored, -schooled, -guided, -enlightened; Philistine; behind the age.

shallow, superficial, green, rude, empty, half-learned, illiterate; un-read, -informed, -educated, -learned, -let-tered, -bookish; empty-headed; low-brow; pedantic.

in the dark; be-nighted, -lated; blind-ed, -fold; hoodwinked; misin-formed; *au bout de son latin*, at the

know full well; have –, possess- some knowledge of; be -*au courant* &c. *adj.*; have -in one's head, – at one's fingers' ends; know by -heart, – rote; be master of; *connaître le dessous des cartes*, know what's what &c. 698.

see one's way; learn, discover &c. 480*a*.

come to one's knowledge &c. (*information*) 527.

Adj. knowing &c. *v.*; cognitive; acroamatic.

aware –, cognizant –, conscious- of; acquainted –, made acquainted- with; privy –, no stranger- to; *au -fait, – courant*; in the secret; up –, alive- to; sensible of; behind the -scenes, – curtain; let into; apprised –, informed- of; undeceived.

proficient –, versed –, read –, forward –, strong –, at home- in; conversant –, familiar- with.

erudite, instructed, learned, lettered, educated; high-brow; well-conned, -informed, -read, -grounded, -educated; enlightened, shrewd, insightful, *savant*, blue, bookish, scholastic, solid, profound, deep-read, book-learned; accomplished &c. (*skilful*) 698; omniscient; self-taught, -educated.

known &c. *v.*; ascertained, well-known, recognized, received, notorious, noted; proverbial; familiar, – as household words, to every schoolboy; hackneyed, trite, commonplace.

knowable, cogn-oscible, -izable.

Adv. to –, to the best of- one's knowledge.

Phr. one's eyes being opened &c. (*disclosure*) 529.

end of his tether; at fault; at sea &c. (*uncertain*) 475; caught tripping.

un-known, -apprehended, -explained, -ascertained, -investigated, -explored, -heard of, -perceived; concealed &c. 528; novel.

Adv. ignorantly &c. *adj.*; unawares; for -anything, – aught- one knows; not that one knows.

Int. God –, Heaven –, the Lord –, nobody- knows.

Phr. a little learning is a dangerous thing.

---

492. Scholar—N. scholar, *connoisseur*, *savant*, pundit, schoolman, professor, graduate, wrangler, moonshee; academ-ician, -ist; fellow, don, post graduate, advanced student; master –, bachelor- of arts; doctor, licentiate, gownsman; philo-sopher, -math; scientist, clerk; soph, -ist, -ister; linguist, classicist; glosso-, etymo-, philologist; philologer; lexico-, glosso-grapher; scholiast, commentator, annotator, grammarian; *littérateur, literati, dilettanti, illuminati*; Mezzofanti, admirable Crichton, Mæcenas.

book-worm, *helluo librorum*, biblio-phile, -maniac; blue-stocking, *bas-bleu*; big-wig, learned Theban.

learned –, literary- man; *homo multarum literarum*; man of -learning, – letters, – education; high-brow, intelligentsia.

antiquar-ian, -y; archæologist; sage &c. (*wise man*) 500.

pedant, *doctrinaire*; pedagogue, Dr. Pangloss; pantologist.

teacher &c. 540; schoolboy &c. (*learner*) 541.

Adj. learned &c. 490; brought up at the feet of Gamaliel.

493. Ignoramus.—N. ignoramus, illiterate, moron, dunce, numskull; wooden spoon; no scholar.

sciolist, smatterer, dabbler, half-scholar; *charlatan*; wiseacre.

novice, griffin; greenhorn &c. (*dupe*) 547; tyro &c. (*learner*) 541.

lubber &c. (*bungler*) 701; fool &c. 501; pedant &c. 492.

Adj. bookless, shallow, simple, dense, dumb, thick, dull, ignorant &c. 491.

494. [Object of knowledge.] Truth.
—**N.** fact, reality &c. (*existence*) 1;
plain matter of fact; nature &c. (*principle*) 5; truth, verity; gospel; orthodoxy &c. 983a; authenticity; veracity
&c. 543.

accuracy, exactitude; exact-, precise-ness &c. *adj.*; precision, delicacy;
rigour, mathematical precision, punctuality; clockwork precision &c. (*regularity*) 80.

orthology; *ipsissima verba*; letter of
the law, realism.

plain -, honest -, sober -, naked -,
unalloyed -, unqualified -, stern -,
exact -, intrinsic- truth; *nuda veritas*;
the very thing; not an -illusion &c.
495; real Simon Pure; unvarnished
tale; the truth, the whole truth and
nothing but the truth; just the thing.

V. be -true &c. *adj.*, – the case; stand
the test; have the true ring; hold
-good, – true, – water; conform to rule.

render -, prove- -true &c. *adj.*; substantiate &c. (*evidence*) 467.

get at the truth &c. (*discover*) 480a.

Adj. real, actual &c. (*existing*) 1;
veritable, true; certain &c. 474; substantially -, categorically- true &c.;
true -to the letter, – to life, – to scale,
– the facts, – as gospel; unimpeachable;
veracious &c. 543; unre-, uncon-futed;
un-ideal, -imagined; realistic.

exact, accurate, definite, precise. well
defined, just, right, correct, strict,
severe; close &c. (*similar*) 17; literal;
rigid, rigorous; scrupulous &c. (*conscientious*) 939; religiously exact, punctual, mathematical, scientific; faithful,
constant, unerring; curious, particular,
punctilious, meticulous, nice, delicate,
fine.

genuine, authentic, legitimate, pukka; orthodox &c. 983a; official, *ex officio*.

pure, natural, sound, sterling; unsophisticated, -adulterated, -varnished,
-coloured; in its true colours.

well-grounded, -founded; solid, substantial, tangible, valid; undis-torted,
-guised; un-affected, -exaggerated, -romantic, -flattering.

Adv. truly &c. *adj.*; verily, indeed,
in reality; as a matter of fact; beyond

495. Error.—**N.** error, fallacy; misconception, -apprehension, -understanding; inexactness &c. *adj.*; laxity;
misconstruction &c. (*misinterpretation*)
523; miscomputation &c. (*misjudgment*) 481; *non-sequitur* &c. 477; misstatement, -report; anachronism; malapropism.

mistake; miss, fault, blunder, boner,
bloomer, howler, *quid pro quo*, cross
purposes, oversight, misprint, *erratum*,
corrigendum, slip, blot, flaw, loose
thread; trip, stumble &c. (*failure*) 732;
botchery &c. (*want of skill*) 699; slip
of the -tongue, – pen; *lapsus -linguæ*,
– *calami*, clerical error; bull &c. (*absurdity*) 497.

il-, de-lusion; false -impression, –
idea; bubble; self-deceit, -deception;
warped notion; mists of error; superstition, exploded notion.

heresy &c. (*heterodoxy*) 984; hallucination &c. (*insanity*) 503; false light
&c. (*fallacy of vision*) 443; dream &c;
(*fancy*) 515; fable &c. (*untruth*) 546;
bias &c. (*misjudgment*) 481; misleading
&c. *v.*

V. be -erroneous &c. *adj.*

cause error; mis-lead, -guide; lead
-astray, – into error; beguile, misinform &c. (*misteach*) 538; delude; give
a false -impression, – idea; falsify,
garble, misstate; deceive &c. 545; lie
&c. 544.

err; be -in error &c. *adj.*, – mistaken
&c. *v.*; be deceived &c. (*duped*) 547;
mistake, receive a false impression, deceive oneself; fall into -, lie under -,
labour under- -an error &c. *n.*; be in
the wrong, blunder; mis-apprehend,
-conceive, -understand, -reckon, -count,
-calculate &c. (*misjudge*) 481.

play -, be- at cross purposes &c.
(*misinterpret*) 523.

trip, stumble; lose oneself &c. (*uncertainty*) 475; go astray; fail &c. 732;
take the wrong sow by the ear &c.
(*mismanage*) 699; put the saddle on
the wrong horse; reckon without one's
host; take the shadow for the substance &c. (*credulity*) 486; dream &c.
(*imagine*) 515.

Adj. erroneous, untrue, false, devoid
of truth, fallacious, faulty, apocryphal,

-doubt, – question; with truth &c. (*veracity*) 543; certainly &c. (*certain*) 474; actually &c. (*existence*) 1; in effect &c. (*intrinsically*) 5.

exactly &c. *adj.*; *ad amussim*; *verbatim*, – *et literatim*; word for word, literally, *literatim, totidem verbis, sic,* to the letter, chapter and verse, *ipsissimis verbis*; *ad unguem*; to an inch; to a -nicety, – hair, – tittle, – turn, – T; *au pied de la lettre*; neither more nor less; in -every respect, – all respects; *sous tous les rapports*; at -any rate, – all events; strictly speaking.

Phr. the -truth, – fact- is; *rem acu tetigisti.*

unreal, ungrounded, groundless; unsubstantial &c. 4; heretical &c. (*heterodox*) 984; unsound; illogical &c. 477; wrong.

in-, un-exact; in-accurate, -correct; indefinite &c. (*uncertain*) 475.

illus-ive, -ory; delusive; mock; ideal &c. (*imaginary*) 515; spurious &c. 545; deceitful &c. 544; perverted.

controvertible, unsustain-able, -ed; unauthenticated, untrustworthy.

exploded, refuted, discarded.

in –, under an- error &c. *n.*; mistaken &c. *v.*; tripping &c. *v.*; out, – in one's reckoning; aberrant; beside –, wide of the- -mark, – truth; astray &c. (*at fault*) 475; on -a false, – the wrong- at cross purposes, all in the wrong, all

scent; in the wrong box; all abroad, at sea.

Adv. more or less.

---

496. Maxim.—**N.** maxim, aphorism; apo-, apoph-thegm; *dictum,* saying, gnome, adage, saw, proverb, epigram; sentence, *mot,* motto, word, by-word, precept, moral, phylactery, *protasis,* brocard.

axiom, postulate, theorem, *scholium,* truism.

reflection &c. (*idea*) 453; conclusion &c. (*judgment*) 480; golden rule &c. (*precept*) 697; principle, *principia*; profession of faith &c. (*belief*) 484; formula.

wise –, sage –, received –, admitted –, recognized- maxim &c.; true –, common –, hackneyed –, trite –, commonplace- saying &c.

Adj. aphoristic, proverbial, phylacteric; axiomatic, gnomic.

Adv. as -the saying is, – they say.

---

497. Absurdity.—**N.** absurd-ity, -ness &c. *adj.*; imbecility &c. 499; alogy, nonsense, paradox, inconsistency; stultiloqu-y, -ence, futility.

blunder, muddle, bull; Irish-, Hibernic-ism; slip-slop; anticlimax, bathos; sophism &c. 477.

farce, burlesque, *galimatias, amphigouri,* rhapsody; farrago &c. (*disorder*) 59; extravagance, romance; sciomachy.

joke, catch, sell, pun, verbal quibble, macaronic.

jargon, fustian, twaddle &c. (*no meaning*) 517; exaggeration &c. 549; moonshine, stuff; mare's nest.

vagary, tomfoolery, mummery, monkey trick, practical joke, *boutade, escapade.*

V. play the fool &c. 499; stultify, blunder, muddle; joke; talk nonsense, *parler à tort et à travers*; *battre la campagne*; be -absurd &c. *adj.*

Adj. absurd, nonsensical, preposterous, egregious, senseless, farcical, inconsistent, ridiculous, extravagant, quibbling, futile; macaronic, punning, paradoxical.

foolish &c. 499; sophistical &c. 477; unmeaning &c. 517; without rhyme or reason; fantastic.

Int. fiddle-de-dee! pish! pish and tush! pho! stuff and nonsense! rubbish! rot! bosh! in the name of the Prophet—figs!

Phr. *credat Judæus Apella*; tell it to the marines.

Faculties

498. Intelligence. Wisdom.—**N.** intelligence, capacity, comprehension,

499. Imbecility. Folly.—**N.** want of -intelligence &c. 498, – intellect &c.

understanding; intellect &c. 450; nous, parts, sagacity, mother wit, wit, *esprit*, gumption, quick parts, grasp of intellect; acuteness &c. *adj.*; acumen, subtlety, penetration; perspica-cy, -city; discernment, long-headedness, due sense of, good judgement; discrimination &c. 465; craftiness, cunning &c. 702; refinement &c. (*taste*) 850.

head, brains, gray matter, headpiece, upper story, long head; eagle -eye, – glance; eye of a -lynx, – hawk.

wisdom, sapience, sense; good –, common –, plain –, horse- sense; clear thinking; rationality, reason; reasonableness &c. *adj.*; judgement; solidity, depth, profundity, calibre; enlarged views; reach –, compass- of thought; enlargement of mind.

genius, inspiration, *Geist*, fire of genius, heaven-born genius, soul; talent &c. (*aptitude*) 698.

[Wisdom in action] prudence &c. 864; vigilance &c. 459; tact &c. 698; foresight &c. 510; sobriety, self-possession, *aplomb*, ballast, mental -poise, – balance.

a bright thought, inspiration, brainwave, not a bad idea.

V. be -intelligent &c. *adj.*; have all one's wits about one; understand &c. (*intelligible*) 518; catch –, take in- an idea; take a -joke, – hint.

see -through, – at a glance, – with half an eye, – far into, – through a millstone; penetrate; discern &c. (*descry*) 441; foresee &c. 510.

discriminate &c. 465; know what's what &c. 698; listen to reason.

Adj. [Applied to persons] intelligent, quick of apprehension, keen, acute, alive, brainy, awake, bright, quick, sharp; quick-, keen-, clear-, sharp- -eyed, -sighted, -witted; wide awake; canny, shrewd, astute; clear-headed; far-sighted &c. 510; discerning, perspicacious, penetrating, piercing; argute; nimble-, needle-witted; sharp as a needle; alive to &c. (*cognizant*) 490; clever &c. (*apt*) 698; arch &c. (*cunning*) 702; *pas si bête* &c. 682.

wise, sage, sapient, sagacious, reasonable, rational, sound, in one's right

450; shallow-, silli-, foolish-ness &c. *adj.*; imbecility, incapacity, vacancy of mind, poverty of intellect, clouded perception, poor head, apartments to let; stup-, stol-idity; hebetude, dull understanding, meanest capacity; short-sightedness; incompetence &c. (*unskilfulness*) 699.

one's weak side; bias &c. 481; infatuation &c. (*insanity*) 503.

simplicity, puerility, babyhood; dotage, anility, second childishness, senile dementia, fatuity; idio-cy, -tism; drivelling.

folly, frivolity, desipience, irrationality, trifling, ineptitude, nugacity, inconsistency, lip-wisdom, conceit; sophistry &c. 477; giddiness &c. (*inattention*) 458; eccentricity &c. 503; extravagance &c. (*absurdity*) 497; rashness &c. 863.

act of folly &c. 699.

V. be -imbecile &c. *adj.*; have no -brains, – sense &c. 498.

trifle, drivel, *radoter*, dote; ramble &c. (*madness*) 503; play the -fool, – monkey, – goat, take leave of one's senses; not see an inch beyond one's nose; stultify oneself &c. 699; talk nonsense &c. 497.

Adj. [Applied to persons] un-intelligent, -intellectual, -reasoning; mind-, wit-, reason-, brain-less; having no -head &c. 498; not -bright &c. 498; inapprehensible.

weak-, addle-, puzzle-, blunder-, muddle-, muddy-, pig-, beetle-, maggoty-, gross-headed; beef-, fat- -witted, -headed.

weak-, feeble-minded; dull-, shallow-, rattle-, lack-brained; half-, nit-, short-, dull-, blunt-witted; shallow-, clod-, addle-pated; dim-, short-sighted; thick-skulled; weak in the upper story.

shallow, *borné*, weak, wanting, soft, nutty, sappy, spoony; dull, – as a beetle; stupid, heavy, insulse, obtuse. blunt, stolid, doltish, asinine; inapt &c. 699; prosaic &c. 843.

child-ish, -like; infant-ine, -ile; baby-bab-ish; puerile, anile; simple &c (*credulous*) 486.

fatuous, idiotic, imbecile, moronic

mind, sensible, *abnormis sapiens*, judicious, strong-minded.

un-prejudiced, -biassed, -bigoted, -prepossessed; un-dazzled, -perplexed; of unwarped judgment, impartial, equitable, fair, broad-minded.

cool; cool-, long-, hard-, strong-headed; long-sighted, calculating, thoughtful, reflecting; solid, deep, profound.

oracular; heaven-directed, -born.

prudent &c. (*cautious*) 864; sober, staid, solid; considerate, politic, wise in one's generation; watchful &c. 459; provident &c. (*prepared*) 673; in advance of one's age; wise as -a serpent, – Solomon, – Solon.

[Applied to actions] wise, sensible, reasonable, judicious; well-judged, -advised; prudent, politic; expedient &c. 646.

---

500. Sage.—N. sage, wise man; pundit; master -mind, – spirit of the age; longhead, thinker, philosopher.

authority, oracle, mentor, luminary, shining light, *esprit fort, magnus Apollo*, Solon, Solomon, Nestor, Magi, 'second Daniel.'

man of learning &c. 492; expert &c. 700; wizard &c. 994.

[Ironically] wiseacre, bigwig.

Adj. wise, learned; authoritative, oracular; erudite &c. 490; venerable, reverenced, revered, *emeritus*.

---

drivelling; blatant, babbling; vacant; sottish; bewildered &c. 475.

blockish, unteachable; Bœot-ian, -ic; bovine; un-gifted, -discerning, -enlightened, -wise, -philosophical; apish.

foolish, silly, senseless, irrational, insensate, nonsensical, inept; maudlin.

narrow-minded &c. 481; bigoted &c. (*obstinate*) 606; giddy &c. (*thoughtless*) 458; rash &c. 863; eccentric &c. (*crazed*) 503.

[Applied to actions] foolish, unwise, indiscreet, injudicious, improper, unreasonable, without reason, ridiculous, silly, stupid, asinine; ill-imagined, -advised, -judged, -devised; inconsistent, irrational, unphilosophical; extravagant &c. (*nonsensical*) 497; sleeveless, idle; useless &c. 645; inexpedient &c. 647; frivolous &c. (*trivial*) 643; absurd &c. 497.

Phr. *Davus sum non Œdipus.*

501. Fool.—N. fool, idiot, tomfool, wiseacre, simpleton, Simple Simon, nit-wit, witling, dizzard, donkey, ass; ninny, -hammer; moron, dolt, booby, Tom Noddy, looby, hoddy-doddy, noddy, nonny, noodle, nizy, owl; goose, -cap; *imbécile*; gaby, *radoteur*, nincompoop, *badaud*, zany; trifler, babbler; pretty fellow; natural, *niais*.

child, baby, infant, innocent, milk-sop, sop.

oaf, lout, loon, lown, dullard, doodle, calf, colt, buzzard, block, put, stick, stock, numps, tony.

bull-, dunder-, addle-, block-, dull-, logger-, jolt-, jolter-, beetle-, gross-, thick-, giddy-head; num-, thick-skull; lack-, shallow-brain; half-, lack-wit; dunder-pate; fat-head, poor stick.

sawney, gowk; clod, -hopper; clod-, clot-poll, -pate; bull-calf; men of Bœotia, wise men of Gotham.

un sot à triple étage, sot; jobbernowl, changeling, mooncalf, *gobemouche.*

dotard, driveller; old -fogey, – woman; crone, grandmother.

greenhorn &c. (*dupe*) 547; dunce &c. (*ignoramus*) 493; lubber &c. (*bungler*) 701; madman &c. 504.

one who -will not set the Thames on fire, – did not invent gunpowder; *qui n'a pas inventé la poudre*; no conjuror.

502. Sanity.—N. sanity; soundness &c. *adj.*; rationality, normality, sobriety, lucidity, lucid interval; senses, sober senses, sound mind, *mens sana.*

503. Insanity.—N. disordered -reason, – intellect; diseased –, unsound –, abnormal- mind; derangement, unsoundness.

V. be -sane &c. *adj.*; retain one's senses, – reason.

become -sane &c. *adj.*; come to one's senses, sober down.

render -sane &c. *adj.*; bring to one's senses, sober.

Adj. sane, rational, reasonable, *compos mentis*, of sound mind; sound, -minded.

self-possessed; sober, -minded.

in one's -sober senses, – right mind; in possession of one's faculties.

Adv. sanely &c. *adj.*

---

insanity, lunacy; madness &c. *adj.*; mania, *rabies, furor*, mental alienation, paranoia, aberration; *amentia*, dementation, -tia, -cy; *dementia præcox*; *morosis*, idiocy, phrenitis, frenzy, raving, incoherence, wandering, delirium, calenture of the brain, delusion, hallucination; lycanthropy, brain storm, *delirium tremens*, D.T's.

vertigo, dizziness, swimming; sunstroke, *coup de soleil*, siriasis.

fanaticism, infatuation, craze; oddity, eccentricity, twist, monomania; klepto-, dipso-mania; hypochondriasis &c. (*low spirits*) 837; *melancholia*, hysteria.

screw –, †ile –, slate- loose; bee in one's bonnet, rats in the upper story.

dotage &c. (*imbecility*) 499.

V. be –, become- -insane &c. *adj.*; lose one's senses, – reason, – faculties, – wits; go –, run- mad, run amuck; rave, dote, ramble, wander; drivel &c. (*be imbecile*) 499; have a -screw loose &c. *n.*, – devil; *avoir le diable au corps*; lose one's head &c. (*be uncertain*) 475.

derange, render –, drive- -mad &c. *adj.*; madden, dementate, addle the wits, derange the head, infatuate, befool; turn -the brain, – one's head.

Adj. insane, mad, lunatic; crazy, crazed, *aliéné, non compos mentis*; not right, cracked, touched; bereft of reason; unhinged, deranged, unsettled in one's mind; insensate, reasonless, beside oneself, demented, daft; phren-, fren-zied, -etic; possessed, – with a devil; far gone, maddened, moonstruck; shatterpated; barmy; mad-, scatter-, shatter-, crack-brained; off one's head; bug-house, *loco*.

maniacal; manic, manic-depressive; delirious, light-headed, incoherent, rambling, doting, wandering; frantic, raving, stark staring mad, amok, amuck, berserk.

corybantic, dithyrambic; rabid, giddy, vertiginous, dizzy, wild, haggard, mazed; flighty; distr-acted, -aught; bewildered &c. (*uncertain*) 475.

mad as a -March hare, – hatter; of -unsound mind &c. *n.*; touched -, wrong -, not right- in one's -head, – mind, – wits, – upper story; out of one's -mind, – senses, – wits; not in one's right mind.

fanatical, infatuated, odd, eccentric; hipp-ed, -ish.

imbecile, silly &c. 499.

Adv. like one possessed.

Phr. the mind having lost its balance; the reason under a cloud; *tête -exaltée, -montée.*

---

504. Madman.—N. madman, lunatic, maniac, bedlamite, candidate for Bedlam, raver, madcap; energumen; paranoiac; auto-, mono-, pyro-, megalo-, dipso-, klepto-maniac; hypochondriac &c. (*low spirits*) 837.

dreamer &c. 515; rhapsodist, seer, high-flier, enthusiast, crank, eccentric, nut, fanatic, *fanatico*; *exalté*; knight errant, Don Quixote.

idiot &c. 501.

Section VI. Extension of Thought

1°. *To the Past*

505. Memory.—N. memory, remembrance; reten-tion, -tiveness; tenacity; *veteris vestigia flammæ*; tablets of the memory; readiness.

reminiscence, recognition, recurrence, recollection, rememoration; retrospect, -ion; after-thought.

suggestion &c. (*information*) 527; prompting &c. *v.*; hint, reminder, token of remembrance, *memento, souvenir,* keepsake, relic, *memorandum*; remembrancer, flapper; memorial &c. (*record*) 551; commemoration &c. (*celebration*) 883.

things to be remembered, *memorabilia.*

art of -, artificial- memory; *memoria technica*; mnemo-nics, -technics; phrenotypics; Mnemosyne; memorandum-, note-, engagement-, prompt-book.

retentive -, tenacious -, green -, trustworthy -, capacious -, faithful -, correct -, exact -, ready -, prompt-memory.

V. remember, mind; retain the -memory, - remembrance- of; keep in view.

have -, hold -, bear -, carry -, keep -, retain- in *or* in the -thoughts, - mind, - memory, - remembrance; be in -, live in -, remain in -, dwell in -, haunt -, impress- one's -memory, - thoughts, - mind.

sink in the mind; run in the head; not be able to get it out of one's head; be deeply impressed with; rankle &c. (*revenge*) 919.

506. Oblivion.—N. oblivion; forgetfulness &c. *adj.*; obliteration &c. 552, of -, insensibility &c. 823 to- the past.

short -, treacherous -, loose -, slippery -, failing- memory; decay -, failure -, lapse- of memory; memory like a sieve; waters of -Lethe, - oblivion, *amnesia.*

pardon, acquittal, amnesty, oblivion; absolution.

V. forget; be -forgetful &c. *adj.*; fall -, sink- into oblivion; have -a short memory &c. *n.*, - no head.

forget one's own name, have on the tip of one's tongue, come in at one ear and go out at the other.

slip -, escape -, fade from -, die away from- the memory; lose, - sight of.

unlearn; efface &c. 552 -, discharge-from the memory; consign to -oblivion, - the tomb of the Capulets; think no more of &c. (*turn the attention from*) 458; cast behind one's back, wean one's thoughts from; let bygones be bygones &c. (*forgive*) 918.

Adj. forgotten &c. *v.*; unremembered, past recollection, bygone, out of mind; buried -, sunk- in oblivion; clean forgotten; gone out of one's -head, - recollection.

forgetful, oblivious, mindless, heedless, Lethean; insensible &c. 823- to the past.

Phr. *non mi ricordo*; the memory -failing, - deserting one, - being at (*or* in) fault.

————

recur to the mind; flash -on the mind, - across the memory.

recognize, recollect, bethink oneself, recall, call up, conjure up, retrace; look -, trace- -back, - backwards; think -, look back- upon; review; call -, recall -, bring- to mind; remembrance; carry one's thoughts back; rake up the past.

suggest &c. (*inform*) 527; prompt; put -, keep- in mind; remind; fan the embers; call -, summon -, rip- up; renew; *infandum renovare dolorem*; task -, tax -, jog -, flap -, refresh -, rub up -, awaken-the memory; pull by the sleeve; bring back to the memory, put in remembrance, memorialize.

get -, have -, learn -, know -, say -, repeat- by -heart - rote; drive -, get- into -one's head; say one's lesson; repeat, - as a parrot; have at one's fingers' ends.

commit to memory; memorize; con, – over; fix –, rivet –, imprint –, impress –, stamp –, grave –, engrave –, store –, treasure up –, bottle up –, embalm –, enshrine- in the memory; load –, store –, stuff –, burden- the memory with.

redeem from oblivion; keep the memory -alive, – green; *tangere ulcus*; keep up the memory of; commemorate &c. (*celebrate*) 883.

make a note of &c. (*record*) 551.

Adj. remember-ing, -ed &c. *v.*; mindful, reminiscential; retained in the memory &c. *v.*; pent up in one's memory; fresh; green, – in remembrance, still vivid; unforgotten, present to the mind; within one's -memory &c. *n.*; indelible; not to be forgotten, unforgettable, enduring; uppermost in one's thoughts; memorable &c. (*important*) 642.

Adv. by -heart, – rote; without book, *memoriter*.

in memory of; *in memoriam*; suggestive.

Phr. *manet altâ mente repostum; forsan et hæc olim meminisse juvabit.*

2°. *To the Future*

507. Expectation.—N. expect-ation, -ance, -ancy; anticipation, reckoning, calculation; contingency; foresight &c. 510.

contemplation, prospection, look out; prospect, perspective, horizon, vista; destiny &c. 152.

suspense, waiting, abeyance; curiosity &c. 455; anxious –, ardent –, eager –, breathless –, sanguine- expectation; torment of Tantalus.

presumption, hope &c. 858; trust &c. (*belief*) 484; prognostication, auspices &c. (*prediction*) 511.

V. expect; look -for, – out for, – forward to; hope for, anticipate; have in -prospect, – contemplation; keep in view; contemplate, promise oneself; not -wonder &c. 870 -at, – if.

wait –, tarry –, lie in wait –, watch –, bargain- for; keep a -good, – sharp- look-out for; await; stand at 'attention,' abide, bide one's –, mark- time, watch.

foresee &c. 510; prepare for &c. 673; forestall &c. (*be early*) 132; count upon &c. (*believe in*) 484; think likely &c. (*probability*) 472; make one's mouth water.

lead one to expect &c. (*predict*) 511; have in store for &c. (*destiny*) 152.

prick up one's ears, hold one's breath.

Adj. expectant; expecting &c. *v.*; in -expectation &c. *n.*; on the watch &c. (*vigilant*) 459; open -eyed, -mouthed;

508. Inexpectation.—N. in-, non-expectation; false expectation &c. (*disappointment*) 509; miscalculation &c. 481; unforeseen contingency, the unforeseen, the unexpected.

surprise, sudden burst, thunderclap, blow, shock; bolt out of the blue; eye-opener; wonder &c. 870.

V. not -expect &c. 507; be taken by surprise; start; miscalculate &c. 481; not bargain for; come –, fall- upon.

be -unexpected &c. *adj.*; come -unawares &c. *adv.*; turn up, pop, drop from the clouds; come –, burst –, flash –, bounce –, steal –, creep- upon one; come –, burst- like a thunderclap, -bolt; take –, catch- -by surprise, – unawares, – napping.

pounce –, spring a mine- upon.

surprise, startle, take aback, electrify, stun, stagger, take away one's breath, throw off one's guard; astonish &c. (*strike with wonder*) 870.

Adj. non-expectant; surprised &c. *v.*; un-warned, -aware; off one's guard; inattentive &c. 458.

un-expected, -anticipated, -prepared for, -looked for, -foreseen, -hoped for; dropped from the clouds; beyond –, contrary to –, against- expectation; out of one's reckoning; unheard of &c. (*exceptional*) 83; startling; sudden &c. (*instantaneous*) 113.

Adv. abruptly, unexpectedly, plump, pop, *à l'improviste*, unawares; without

agape, gaping, all agog; on -tenter-hooks, – tiptoe, – the tiptoe of expectation; *aux aguets*; ready; curious &c. 455; looking forward to; prepared for; on the rack.

expected &c. *v.*; long expected, foreseen; in prospect &c. *n.*; prospective; iñ -one's eye, – view, – the horizon; impending &c. (*destiny*) 152.

Adv. expectantly; in the event of; on the watch &c. *adj.*; with -breathless expectation &c. *n.*, – bated breath, – eyes, – ears strained; *arrectis auribus*; on edge.

Phr. we shall see; *nous verrons.*

-notice, – warning, – saying 'by your leave'; like a -thief in the night, – thunderbolt; in an unguarded moment; suddenly &c. (*instantaneously*) 113.

Int. heyday! &c. (*wonder*) 870.

Phr. little did one -think, – expect; nobody would ever -suppose, – think, – expect; who would have thought?

---

509. [Failure of expectation.] **Disappointment.—N.** disappointment, disillusionment; blighted hope, balk; blow; slip 'twixt cup and lip; non-fulfilment of one's hopes; sad –, bitter- disappointment; trick of fortune; afterclap; false –, vain- expectation; miscalculation &c. 481; fool's paradise; much cry and little wool.

V. be disappointed; look -blank, – blue; look –, stand- -aghast &c. (*wonder*) 870; find to one's cost; laugh on the wrong side of one's mouth; find one a false prophet.

disappoint; crush –, dash –, balk –, disappoint –, blight –, falsify –, defeat –, not realize- one's -hope, – expectation; balk, jilt, bilk; play one -false, – a trick; dash the cup from the lips; tantalize; dumb-found, -founder; disillusion, -ize; dissatisfy, disgruntle.

Adj. disappointed &c. *v.*; disconcerted, aghast; out of one's reckoning; disgruntled.

Phr. the mountain brought forth a mouse; *nascitur ridiculus mus*; *parturiunt montes*; *dis aliter visum*, the bubble burst; one's countenance falling.

---

510. Foresight.—N. foresight, prospicience, prevision, longsightedness; anticipation; providence &c. (*preparation*) 673.

fore-thought, -cast; pre-deliberation, -surmise; foregone conclusion &c. (*prejudgment*) 481; prudence &c. (*caution*) 864.

foreknowledge; *prognosis*; pre-cognition, -science, -notion, -sentiment; second sight; sagacity &c. (*intelligence*) 498.

prospect &c. (*expectation*) 507; foretaste; prospectus &c. (*plan*) 626.

V. foresee; look -forwards to, – ahead, – beyond; scent from afar; feel in one's bones; look –, pry –, peep- into the future.

see one's way; see how the -land lies, – wind blows, – cat jumps.

anticipate; expect &c. 507; be beforehand &c. (*early*) 132; predict &c. 511; fore-know, -judge, -cast; surmise; have an eye to the -future, – main chance; *respicere finem*; keep a sharp look-out &c. (*vigilance*) 459; forewarn &c. 668.

Adj. foreseeing &c. *v.*; prescient; anticipatory; far-seeing, -sighted; sagacious &c. (*intelligent*) 498; weather-wise; provident &c. (*prepared*) 673; prospective &c. 507.

Adv. against the time when.

---

511. Prediction.—N. prediction, announcement; program, programme &c. (*plan*) 626; premonition &c. (*warning*) 668; *prognosis*, prophecy, vaticination, mantology, prognostication, premonstration, augur-y, -ation; a-, ha-riolation; fore-, a-boding; bode-, abode-ment; omin-ation,

-ousness; auspices, forecast; sign, presage, prognostic; omen &c. 512; horoscope, nativity; sooth, -saying; fortune-telling; divination; crystal gazing, necromancy &c. 992; prophet &c. 512.

[Divination by the stars] astrology, horoscopy, astromancy, judicial astrology.*

[Place of prediction] *adytum.*

prefigur-ation, -ement; prototype, type.

V. predict, prognosticate, prophesy, vaticinate, divine, foretell, sooth-say, augurate, tell fortunes; cast a -horoscope, – nativity; advise; forewarn &c. 668.

presage, augur, bode; a-, fore-bode, -cast; fore-, be-token; pre-figure, -show; portend; fore-show, -shadow, shadow forth, typify, ominate, signify, point to, precurse.

usher in, herald, premise, announce; lower.

hold out –, raise –, excite- -expectation, – hope; bid fair, promise, lead one to expect; be the -precursor &c. 64.

Adj. predicting &c. *v.*; predictive, prophetic, fatidical, vaticinal, oracular, Sibylline, haruspical, weatherwise.

ominous, presageful, portentous; augur-ous, -al, -ial; auspici-al, -ous; prescious, monitory, extispicious, premonitory, precursory, significant of, pregnant with, big with the fate of.

Phr. 'coming events cast their shadows before.'

512. Omen.—N. omen, portent, presage, prognostic, augury, auspice; sign &c. (*indication*) 550; herald, forerunner, harbinger &c. (*precursor*) 64.

bird of ill omen; signs of the times; gathering clouds; warning &c. 668.

prefigurement &c. 511.

513. Oracle.—N. oracle; prophet, -ess; seer, soothsayer, augur, fortune-teller, palmist, medium, clairvoyant, crystal gazer, witch, geomancer, *aruspex*; a-, ha-ruspice; Sibyl; Python, -ess; Pythia; Pythian –, Delphian- oracle; Monitor, Sphinx, Tiresias, Cassandra, Sibylline leaves; Zadkiel, Old Moore; sorcerer &c. 994; interpreter &c. 524.

Section VII. Creative Thought

514. Supposition.—N. supposition, assumption, postulation, condition, pre-supposition, hypothesis, postulate, *postulatum*, theory, *data*; ' pro-, position; *thesis*, theorem; proposal &c. (*plan*) 626.

* The following terms, expressive of different forms of divination, have been col-lected from various sources, and are here given as a curious illustration of bygone superstitions:

Divination *by oracles*, Theomancy; *by the Bible*, Bibliomancy; *by ghosts*, Psycho-mancy; *by spirits seen in a magic lens*, Cristallomantia; *by shadows or manes*, Scio-mancy; *by appearances in the air*, Aeromancy, Chaomancy; *by the stars at birth*, Genethliacs; *by meteors*, Meteoromancy; *by winds*, Austromancy; *by sacrificial ap-pearances*, Aruspicy (*or* Haruspicy), Hieromancy, Hieroscopy; *by the entrails of animals sacrificed*, Hieromancy; *by the entrails of a human sacrifice*, Anthropomancy; *by the entrails of fishes*, Ichthyomancy; *by sacrificial fire*, Pyromancy; *by red-hot iron*, Sidero-mancy; *by smoke from the altar*, Capnomancy; *by mice*, Myomancy; *by birds*, Orniscopy, Ornithomancy; *by a cock picking up grains*, Alectryomancy (*or* Alectoromancy); *by fishes*, Ophiomancy; *by herbs*, Botanomancy; *by water*, Hydromancy; *by fountains*,

bare –, vague –, loose- -supposition, – suggestion; conceit; conjecture; guess, – work; rough guess, shot; conjecturality; surmise, suspicion, inkling, suggestion, suggestiveness, association of ideas, hint; presumption &c. (*belief*) 484; divination, speculation.

theorist, speculator, doctrinarian, hypothesist.

V. suppose, conjecture, surmise, suspect, guess, divine; theorize; pre-sume, -surmise, -suppose; assume, fancy, wis, take it; give a guess, speculate, believe, dare say, take it into one's head, take for granted.

put forth; pro-pound, -pose; moot; hypothesize; start, put a case, submit, move, make a motion; hazard –, throw out –, put forward- a -suggestion, – conjecture.

allude to, suggest, hint, put it into one's head.

suggest itself &c. (*thought*) 451; run in the head &c. (*memory*) 505; marvel –, wonder- -if, – whether.

Adj. supposing &c. *v.*; given, mooted, postulatory; assumed &c. *v.* supposit-ive, -itious; gratuitous, speculative, conjectural, hypothetical, suppositional, theoretical, academic, supposable, presumptive, putative.

suggestive, allusive, stimulating.

Adv. if, – so be; an; on the -supposition &c. *n.*; *ex hypothesi*; in -case, – the event of; *quasi*, as if, provided; perhaps &c. (*by possibility*) 470; for aught one knows.

515. Imagination.—**N.** imagination; originality; invention; fancy; inspiration; *verve*; empathy.

warm –, heated –, excited –, sanguine –, ardent –, fiery –, boiling –, wild –, bold –, daring –, playful –, lively –, fertile- -imagination, – fancy. 'mind's eye'; 'such stuff as dreams are made of.'

ideal-ity, -ism; romanticism, utopianism, castle-building; dreaming; frenzy; ecs-, ex-tasy; calenture &c. (*delirium*) 503; reverie, brown study, trance; somnambulism.

conception, *vorstellung*, excogitation, 'a fine frenzy,' poetic frenzy, divine afflatus; cloud-, dream-land; flight –, fumes- of fancy; 'thick-coming fancies'; creation –, coinage- of the brain; imagery, word painting.

conceit, maggot, figment, myth, dream, vision, shadow, chimera; phan-tasm, -tasy; fantasy, fancy; whim, -sey; vagary, rhapsody, romance, *extravaganza*; air-drawn dagger, bugbear, nightmare; flying Dutchman, great sea-serpent, man in the moon, castle in the air, *châteaux en Espagne*; Utopia, Atlantis, happy valley, millennium, fairy land; land of Prester John, kingdom of Micomicon; work of fiction &c. (*novel*) 594; poetry &c. 597; drama &c. 599; Arabian nights; *le pot au lait*; dream of Alnaschar &c. (*hope*) 858; day –, golden- dream.

illusion &c. (*error*) 495; phantom &c. (*fallacy of vision*) 443; *Fata*

Pegomancy; *by a wand*, Rhabdomancy; *by dough of cakes*, Crithomancy; *by meal*, Aleuromancy, Alphitomancy; *by salt*, Halomancy; *by dice*, Cleromancy; *by arrows*, Belomancy; *by a balanced hatchet*, Axinomancy; *by a balanced sieve*, Coscinomancy; *by a suspended ring*, Dactyliomancy; *by dots made at random on paper*, Geomancy; *by precious stones*, Lithomancy; *by pebbles*, Pessomancy; *by pebbles drawn from a heap*, Psephomancy; *by mirrors*, Catoptromancy; *by writings in ashes*, Tephramancy; *by dreams*, Oneiromancy; *by the hand*, Palmistry, Chiromancy; *by nails reflecting the sun's rays*, Onychomancy; *by finger rings*, Dactylomancy; *by numbers*, Arithmancy; *by drawing lots*, Sortilege; *by passages in books*, Stichomancy; *by the letters forming the name of the person*, Onomancy, Nomancy; *by the features*, Anthroposcopy; *by the mode of laughing*, Geloscopy; *by ventriloquism*, Gastromancy; *by walking in a circle*, Gyromancy; *by dropping melted wax into water*, Ceromancy; *by currents*, Bletonism.

Morgana &c. (*ignis fatuus*) 423; vapour &c. (*cloud*) 353; stretch of the imagination &c. (*exaggeration*) 549.

idealist, romanticist, visionary; mopus; romancer, dreamer; somnambulist; rhapsodist &c. (*fanatic*) 504.

V. imagine, fancy, conceive; ideal-, real-ize; dream, – of; 'give to airy nothing a local habitation and a name.'

create, originate, devise, invent, coin, fabricate; improvise, strike out something new.

set one's wits to work; strain –, crack- one's invention; rack –, ransack –, cudgel- one's brains; excogitate.

give -play, – the reins, – a loose- to the -imagination, – fancy; empathize; indulge in reverie.

conjure up a vision; fancy –, represent –, picture –, figure- to oneself; envisage.

float in the mind; suggest itself &c. (*thought*) 451.

Adj. imagined &c. *v.*; *ben trovato*; air-drawn, -built.

imagin-ing &c. *v.*, -ative; original, inventive, creative, fertile, productive; ingenious.

romantic, high-flown, flighty, extravagant, fanatic, enthusiastic, Utopian, Quixotic; preposterous, rhapsodical.

ideal, unreal; in the clouds, *in nubibus*; unsubstantial &c. 4; illusory &c. (*fallacious*) 495; fictitious, theoretical, hypothetical.

fabulous, legendary; myth-ic, -ological; chimerical; imagin-, visionary; notional; fan-cy, -ciful, -tastic, -tastical; whimsical; fairy, -like.

dreamy, entranced, vaporous.

DIVISION (II.) COMMUNICATION OF IDEAS
Section I. NATURE OF IDEAS COMMUNICATED

516. [Idea to be conveyed.] **Meaning.** [Thing signified.]—**N.** meaning; signific-ation, -ance; sense, expression; im-, pur-port; drift, tenor, implication, connotation, essence, force, spirit, bearing, colouring; scope.

matter; subject, -matter; argument, text, sum and substance; gist &c. 5.

general –, broad –, substantial –, colloquial –, literal –, plain –, simple –, accepted –, natural –, unstrained –, true &c. (*exact*) 494 –, honest &c. 543 –, *primâ facie* &c. (*manifest*) 525- meaning.

literality; literal interpretation; after acceptation; allusion &c. (*latency*) 526; suggestion &c. (*information*) 527; synonym; figure of speech &c. 521; acceptation &c. (*interpretation*) 522.

V. mean, signify, express, connote, denote; im-, pur-port; convey, imply, breathe, indicate, bespeak, bear a sense; tell –, speak- of; touch on; point –, allude- to; drive at; involve &c. (*latency*) 526; declare &c. (*affirm*) 535.

517. [Absence of meaning.] **Unmeaningness.**—**N.** unmeaningness &c. *adj.*; scrabble, scribble, scrawl, daub, (*painting*), strumming (*music*).

empty sound, dead letter, *vox et præterea nihil*; 'a tale told by an idiot, full of sound and fury, signifying nothing'; 'sounding brass and a tinkling cymbal.'

nonsense, jargon, gibberish, jabber, mere words, hocus-pocus, fustian, rant, bombast, balderdash, palaver, patter, flummery, verbiage, babble, *bavardage*, *baragouin*, platitude, *niaiserie*; inanity; rigmarole, rodomontade; truism; *nugæ canoræ*; twaddle, twattle, fudge, trash; stuff, – and nonsense; bosh, rubbish, rot, drivel, moonshine, wish-wash, fiddle-faddle, flapdoodle; absurdity &c. 497; vagueness &c. (*unintelligibility*) 519.

V. mean nothing; be -unmeaning &c. *adj.*; twaddle, quibble, rant, gabble, scrabble &c. *n.*

Adj. unmeaning; meaning-, sense-less;

understand by &c. (*interpret*) 522.

Adj. meaning &c. *v.*; expressive, suggestive, meaningful, allusive; signific-ant, -ative, -atory; pithy; full of –, pregnant with- meaning.

declaratory &c. 535; intelligible &c. 518; literal, metaphrastic; synonymous; tantamount &c. (*equivalent*) 27; implied &c. (*latent*) 526; explicit &c. 525; literal &c. 562.

Adv. to that effect; that is to say &c. (*being interpreted*) 522.

literally; evidently, from the context.

518. Intelligibility.—N. intelligibility, clearness, clarity, explicitness &c. *adj.*; lucidity, perspicuity; legibility, plain speaking &c. (*manifestation*) 525; precision &c. 494; a word to the wise.

V. be -intelligible &c. *adj.*; speak -for itself, – volumes; tell its own tale, lie on the surface.

render -intelligible &c. *adj.*; popularize, simplify, clear up; elucidate &c. (*explain*) 522.

understand, comprehend; take, – in; catch, grasp, recognize, follow, collect, master, make out; see -with half an eye, – daylight, – one's way; enter into the ideas of; come to an understanding.

Adj. intelligible; clear, – as -day, – crystal, – noonday; lucid; per-, transpicuous; luminous, transparent; comprehensible.

easily understood, easy to understand, for the million, intelligible to the meanest capacity, popularized.

plain, distinct, explicit, clear-cut; positive; definite &c. (*precise*) 494.

graphic, vivid, telling; expressive &c. (*meaning*) 516; illustrative &c. (*explanatory*) 522.

un-ambiguous, -equivocal, -mistakable &c. (*manifest*) 525, -confused; legible, recognizable; obvious &c. 525.

Adv. in plain -terms, – words, – English.

Phr. he that runs may read &c. (*manifest*) 525.

nonsensical; void of -sense &c. 516.

in-, un-expressive; vacant, fatuous; not significant; insignificant.

trashy, waṣhy, inane, vague, trumpery, trivial, fiddle-faddle, twaddling, quibbling.

unmeant, not expressed; tacit &c. (*latent*) 526.

inexpressible, undefinable, incommunicable.

Int. rubbish! &c. 497.

---

519. Unintelligibility.—N. unintelligibility, incomprehensibility, imperspicuity; inconceivableness, vagueness &c. *adj.*; obscurity; ambiguity &c. 520; doubtful meaning; uncertainty &c. 475; perplexity &c. (*confusion*) 59; spinosity; *obscurum per obscurius*; mystification &c. (*concealment*) 528; latency &c. 526; transcendentalism.

paradox; enigma, riddle &c. (*secret*) 533; *dignus vindice nodus*; sealed book; steganography, Freemasonry.

pons asinorum, asses' bridge; double –, high- Dutch, Greek, Hebrew; jargon &c. (*unmeaning*) 517.

obscurantist.

V. be -unintelligible &c. *adj.*; require -explanation &c. 522; have a doubtful meaning, pass comprehension.

render -unintelligible &c. *adj.*; conceal &c. 528; darken &c. 421; confuse &c. (*derange*) 61; perplex &c. (*bewilder*) 475.

not -understand &c. 518; lose, – the clue; miss; not know what to make of, be able to make nothing of, give it up; not be able to -account for, – make either head or tail of; be at sea &c. (*uncertain*) 475; wonder &c. 870; see through a glass darkly &c. (*ignorance*) 491.

not understand one another; play at cross purposes &c. (*misinterpret*) 523.

Adj. un-intelligible, -accountable, -decipherable, -discoverable, -knowable, -fathomable; in-cognizable, -explicable, -scrutable; inap-, incomprehensible; insol-vable, -uble; impenetrable.

illegible, indecipherable, as Greek to one, unexplained, paradoxical; enigmatic, -al; puzzling, baffling.

obscure, dark, muddy, clear as mud, seen through a mist, dim, nebulous, shrouded in mystery; undiscernible &c. (*invisible*) 447; misty &c. (*opaque*) 426; hidden &c. 528; latent &c. 526.

indefinite &c. (*indistinct*) 447; perplexed &c. (*confused*) 59; undetermined, vague, loose, ambiguous; mysterious; mystic, -al; transcendental; occult, recondite, esoteric, abstruse, crabbed.

incon-ceivable, -ceptible; searchless; above –, beyond –, past-comprehension; beyond one's depth; unconceived.

inexpressible, undefinable, incommunicable, unutterable, ineffable, unpronounceable.

520. [Having a double sense.] Equivocalness.—N. equivocalness &c. *adj.*; double -meaning &c. 516; ambiguity, *double entendre*, pun, paragram, *calembour*, quibble, *équivoque*, anagram; conundrum &c. (*riddle*) 533; word-play &c. (*wit*) 842; homonym, -y; amphibo-ly, -logy; ambiloquy.

Sphinx, Delphic oracle.

equivocation &c. (*duplicity*) 544; white lie, mental reservation &c. (*concealment*) 528.

V. be -equivocal &c. *adj.*; have two -meanings &c. 516; equivocate &c. (*palter*) 544.

Adj. equivocal, ambiguous, amphibolous, homonymous; double-tongued &c. (*lying*) 544.

521. Metaphor.—N. figure of speech; *façon de parler*, way of speaking, colloquialism.

phrase &c. 566; figure, trope, metaphor, tralatition, metonymy, enallage, *catachresis*, *synecdoche*, *antonomasia*; irony, satire, figurativeness &c. *adj.*; image, -ry; *metalepsis*, type, anagoge, simile, personification, *prosopopæia*, allegory, apologue, parable, fable; allusion, adumbration; application; euphemism; euphuism.

V. employ -metaphor &c. *n.*; personify, allegorize, adumbrate, shadow forth, apply, allude –, refer- to.

Adj. metaphorical &c. *n.*; figurative, catachrestical, typical, tralatitious, parabolic, allegorical, allusive, anagogical; ironical; colloquial.

Adv. so to -speak, – say, – express oneself; as it were.

Phr. *mutato nomine de te fabula narratur.*

522. Interpretation.—N. interpretation, definition; explan-, explic-ation; solution, answer; rationale; plain –, simple –, strict- interpretation; meaning &c. 516.

translation; rend-ering, -ition; reddition; literal –, free- translation; key, crib; secret; clew &c. (*indication*) 550; Rosetta stone.

exegesis; ex-pounding, -position; Hermeneutics; comment, -ary; inference &c. (*deduction*) 480; illustration, exemplification; gloss, annotation, *scholium*, note; e-, di-lucidation, enucleation; *éclaircissement*, *mot de l'énigme*.

symptomat-, semei-ology; metoposcopy, physiognomy; diagnosis, prog-

523. Misinterpretation. — N. misinterpretation, -apprehension, -understanding, -acceptation, -construction, -application; *catachresis*; cross -reading, – purposes; mistake &c. 495.

misrepresentation, perversion, exaggeration &c. 549; false -colouring, – construction; abuse of terms; parody, travesty; falsification &c. (*lying*) 544.

V. mis-interpret, -apprehend, -understand, -conceive, -judge, -doubt, -spell, -translate, -construe, -apply; mistake &c. 495.

misrepresent, pervert; garble &c. (*falsify*) 544; distort, detort; travesty, play upon words; stretch –, strain –, wrest- the -sense, – meaning; explain

nosis; paleography &c. (*philology*) 560.

accept-ion, -ation, -ance; light, reading, lection, construction, version.

equivalent, – meaning &c. 516; synonym; para-, meta-phrase; convertible terms, apposition; dictionary &c. 562; polyglot.

V. interpret, explain, define, construe, translate, render; do –, turninto; transfuse the sense of.

find out &c. 480a- -the meaning &c. 516- of; read; spell –, figure –, make- out; decipher, decode, unravel, disentangle, puzzle out; find the key of, enucleate, resolve, solve; read between the lines.

account for; find –, tell- the cause &c. 153- of; throw –, shed--light, – new light, – a fresh light- upon; clear up, elucidate.

illustrate, exemplify; unfold, expound, comment upon, annotate; popularize &c. (*render intelligible*) 518.

take –, understand –, receive –, accept- in a particular sense; understand by, put a construction on, be given to understand.

Adj. explanatory, expository; explica-tive, -tory; exegetical; hermeneutic, interpretive, illustrative, elucidative, annotative, scholiastic.

polyglot; literal; para-, meta-phrastic; cosignificative, synonymous; equivalent &c. 27.

Adv. in -explanation &c. *n.*; that is to say, *id est*, *videlicet*, to wit, namely, in other words.

literally, strictly speaking; in -plain, – plainer- -terms, – words, – English; more simply.

away; put a -bad, – false- construction on; give a false colouring, look through -rose coloured –, – dark – spectacles.

be –, play- at cross purposes.

Adj. misinterpreted &c. *v.*; untranslat-ed, -able.

Adv. at cross purposes.

---

524. Interpreter.—N. interpreter, translator, ex-positor, -pounder, -ponent, -plainer; demonstrator.

scholiast, commentator, annotator; meta-, para-phrast.

spokesman, speaker, mouthpiece, prolocutor; diplomat &c. 758.

guide, courier, dragoman, *valet de place*, *cicerone*, showman; oneirocritic; Œdipus; oracle &c. 513.

Section II. Modes of Communication

525. Manifestation.—N. manifestation; unfolding; plainness &c. *adj.*; plain speaking; expression; showing &c. *v.*; exposition, demonstration, *séance*; exhibition, production; display, showing off &c. 882, premonstration. [Thing shown] exhibit, show.

indication &c. (*calling attention to*) 457; publicity &c. 531; disclosure &c. 529; openness &c. (*honesty*) 543, (*artlessness*) 703; *épanchement*, prominence.

V. make –, render- -manifest &c. *adj.*; bring -forth, – forward, – to the front, – into view; give notice; express; represent, set forth, exhibit; show, – up; expose; produce; hold up –, expose- to view; set –, place –, lay-

526. Latency.—N. latency, inexpression; hidden –, occult- meaning; occultness, occultism, mysticism, mystery, cabala, symbolism, anagoge; silence &c. (*taciturnity*) 585; concealment &c. 528; more than meets the -eye, – ear; Delphic oracle; *le dessous des cartes*, undercurrent.

allusion, insinuation, implication; innuendo &c. 527; adumbration; 'something rotten in the state of Denmark.'

snake in the grass &c. (*pitfall*) 667; secret &c. 533.

darkness, invisibility, imperceptibility.

latent influence, power behind the throne; friend at court, wire puller.

before -one, – one's eyes; tell to one's face; trot out, put through one's paces, unfold, show off, show forth, unveil, bring to light, display, demonstrate, unroll; lay open; draw –, bring- out; bring out in strong relief; call –, bring- into notice; hold up the mirror; wear one's heart upon his sleeve; show one's -face, – colours; manifest oneself; speak out; make no -mystery, – secret- of; unfurl the flag; proclaim &c. (*publish*) 531.

indicate &c. (*direct attention to*) 457; disclose &c. 529; elicit &c. 480a; interpret &c. 522.

be -manifest &c. *adj.*; appear &c. (*be visible*) 446; transpire &c. (*be disclosed*) 529; speak for itself, stand to reason; stare one in the face; loom large, appear on the horizon, rear its head; give -token, – sign, – indication of; tell its own tale &c. (*intelligible*) 518; go without saying.

Adj. manifest, apparent; salient, striking, demonstrative, prominent, in the foreground, notable, pronounced.

flagrant; notorious &c. (*public*) 531; arrant; stark staring; unshaded, glaring.

defin-ed, -ite; distinct, conspicuous &c. (*visible*) 446; obvious, evident, incontestable, unmistakable, not to be mistaken, plain, clear, palpable, self-evident, autoptical; intelligible &c. 518; clear as -day, – daylight, – noonday; plain as -a pikestaff, – the sun at noonday, – the nose on one's face, – the way to the parish church.

ostensible; open, – as day; overt, patent, express, explicit; naked, bare, literal, downright, undisguised, exoteric.

V. be -latent &c. *adj.*; lurk, smoulder, underlie, make no sign; escape -observation, – detection, – recognition; lie hid &c. 528.

laugh in one's sleeve; keep back &c: (*conceal*) 528.

involve, imply, implicate, connote, import, understand, allude to, infer, leave an inference; symbolize; whisper &c. (*conceal*) 528.

Adj. latent; lurking &c. *v.*; secret &c. 528; occult, symbolic, mystic; implied &c. *v.*; dormant.

un-apparent, -known, -seen &c. 441; in the background; invisible &c. 447; indiscoverable, dark; impenetrable &c. (*unintelligible*) 519; un-spied, -suspected.

un - said, - written, - published, -breathed, -talked of, -told &c. 527, -sung, -exposed, -proclaimed, -disclosed &c. 529, -pronounced, -mentioned, -expressed; not expressed, tacit.

un-developed, -solved, -explained, -traced, -discovered &c. 480a, -tracked, -explored, -invented.

indirect, crooked, inferential; by -inference, – implication; implicit; constructive; allusive, covert, muffled; steganographic; under-stood, -hand, -ground; concealed &c. 528; delitescent.

Adv. by a side wind; *sub silentio*; in the background; behind -the scenes, – one's back, – the veil; below the surface; on the tip of one's tongue; secretly &c. 528; between the lines; by a mutual understanding.

Phr. 'thereby hangs a tale.' 'that is another story.'

---

unreserved; frank, plain spoken &c. (*artless*) 703; barefaced, brazen, bold, shameless, daring, flaunting, loud.

manifested &c. *v.*; disclosed &c. 529; expressible, capable of being shown, producible; in-, un-concealable.

Adv. manifestly, openly &c. *adj.*; before one's eyes, under one's nose, to one's face, face to face, above board, *cartes sur table*, on the stage, in plain sight, in open court, in the open, – streets; at the cross roads; in market overt; in the face of -day, – heaven; in -broad –, open- daylight; without reserve; at first blush, *primâ facie*, on the face of; in set terms.

Phr. *cela saute aux yeux*; he that runs may read; you can see it with half an eye; it needs no ghost to tell us; the meaning lies on the surface; *cela va sans dire*; *res ipsa loquitur*.

527. Information.—N. information, enlightenment, acquaintance, knowledge &c. 490; publicity &c. 531.

communication, intimation; not-ice, -ification; e-, an-nunciation; announcement; representation, round robin, presentment.

case, estimate, specification, report, advice, monition; news &c. 532; return &c. (*record*) 551; account &c. (*description*) 594; statement &c. (*affirmation*) 535.

mention; acquainting &c. *v.*; instruction &c. (*teaching*) 537; outpouring; intercommunication, communicativeness.

informant, authority, teller, announcer, annunciator, harbinger, herald, intelligencer, commentator, columnist, reporter, exponent, mouthpiece; informer, keek, eavesdropper, delator, detective, sleuth; *mouchard*, spy, stool pigeon, newsmonger; messenger &c. 534; *amicus curiæ.*

valet de place, cicerone, pilot, guide; guide-, hand-book; *vade mecum*; manual; map, plan, chart, gazetteer; itinerary &c. (*journey*) 266.

hint, suggestion, wrinkle, innuendo, inkling, whisper, passing word, word in the ear, subaudition, cue, by-play; gesture &c. (*indication*) 550; gentle – broad- hint; *verbum sapienti*; word to the wise; insinuation &c. (*latency*) 526.

V. tell; inform, – of; acquaint, – with; impart, – to; make acquainted with, bring to the ears of, apprise, advise, enlighten, awaken.

let fall, mention, express, intimate, represent, communicate, make known; publish &c. 531; notify, signify, specify, convey the knowledge of.

let one –, have one to- know; serve notice, give one to understand; give notice; set –, lay –, put- before; point out, put into one's head; put one in possession of; instruct &c. (*teach*) 537; direct the attention to &c. 457.

an-nounce, -nunciate; report, – progress; bring –, send –, leave –, writeword; tele-graph, -phone; ring –, callup; wire; retail, render an account; give an account &c. (*describe*) 594; state &c. (*affirm*) 535.

528. Concealment.—N. concealment; hiding &c. *v.*; occultation, mystification.

seal of secrecy; screen &c. 530; disguise &c. 530; masquerade; masked battery; hiding place &c. 530; cipher, code, crypt-, stegan-ography; invisible –, sympathetic- ink; palimpsest; Freemasonry.

stealth, -iness; obreption; slyness &c. (*cunning*) 702.

latit-ancy, -ation; seclusion &c. 893; privacy, secrecy, secretness; *incognita.*

reticence; reserve; mental –, reservation, aside; *arrière pensée*, suppression, evasion, white lie, misprision; silence &c. (*taciturnity*) 585; suppression of truth &c. 544; underhand dealing; close-, secretive-ness &c. *adj.*; mystery.

latency &c. 526; snake in the grass; secret &c. 533.

V. conceal, hide, secrete, stow away, put out of sight; lock –, seal –, bottle-up.

cover, screen, cloak, veil, shroud; screen from -sight, – observation; draw the veil; draw –, close- the curtain; curtain, shade, eclipse, throw a veil over; be-cloud, -fog, -mask; mask, disguise; ensconce, muffle, smother; whisper.

keep -from, – back, – to oneself; keep -snug, – close, – secret, – dark; bury; sink, suppress; keep -from, – out of- -view, – sight; keep in –, throw into- the -shade, – background; cover up one's tracks; stifle, hush up, withhold, reserve; fence with a question; ignore &c. 460.

code, codify, use a cipher.

keep -a secret, – one's own counsel; hold one's tongue &c. (*silence*) 585; make no sign, not let it go further; not breathe a -word, – syllable- about; not let the right hand know what the left is doing; hide one's light under a bushel, bury one's talent in a napkin.

keep –, leave- in -the dark, – ignorance; blind, – the eyes; blindfold, hoodwink, mystify; puzzle &c. (*render uncertain*) 475; bamboozle &c. (*deceive*) 545.

be -concealed &c. *v.*; suffer an eclipse;

disclose &c. 529; show cause; explain &c. (*interpret*) 522.

hint; give an inkling of; give –, drop –, throw out- a hint; insinuate; allude –, make allusion- to; glance at; tip off, tip the wink &c. (*indicate*) 550; suggest, prompt, give the cue, breathe; whisper, – in the ear.

give a bit of one's mind; tell one plainly, – once for all; speak volumes.

un-deceive, -beguile; set right, correct, open the eyes of, disabuse.

be -informed of &c.; know &c. 490; learn &c. 539; get scent of, gather from; awaken –, open one's eyes- to; become -alive, – awake- to; keep posted; hear, overhear, understand.

come to one's -ears, – knowledge; reach one's ears.

Adj. informed &c. *v.*; *communiqué*; reported &c. *v.*; published &c. 531; advisory.

expressive &c. 516; explicit &c. (*open*) 525, (*clear*) 518; plain-spoken &c. (*artless*) 703.

declara-, nuncupa-, exposi-tory; de-clarative, enunciative, communicat-ive, -ory; oral.

Adv. from information received; according to -rumour, – report; in the air; from what one can gather.

Phr. a little bird told me.

---

retire from sight, couch; hide oneself; lie -hid, – in ambush, – low, – *perdu*, – snug, – close; seclude oneself &c. 893; lurk, sneak, skulk, slink, pussy-foot, prowl; steal -into, – out of, – by, – along; play at -bopeep, – hide and seek; hide in holes and corners.

Adj. concealed &c. *v.*; hidden; veiled, secret, recondite, mystic, cabalistic, occult, dark; cryptic, -al; private, privy, *in petto*, auricular, clandestine, close, inviolate.

behind a -screen &c. 530; under -cover, – an eclipse; in -ambush, – hiding, – disguise; in a -cloud, – fog, – mist, – haze, – dark corner; in the -shade, – dark; clouded, wrapt in clouds; invisible &c. 447; buried, under-ground, *perdu*; incommunicado; se-cluded &c. 893.

un-disclosed &c. 529, -told &c. 527; covert &c. (*latent*) 526; mysterious &c. (*unintelligible*) 519.

irrevealable, inviolable; confidential; esoteric; not to be spoken of.

obreptitious, furtive, stealthy, feline; skulking &c. *v.*; surreptitious, under-hand, hole and corner; sly &c. (*cunning*) 702; secretive, evasive, non-com-mittal, reserved, reticent, uncommuni-cative, buttoned up; close, – as wax; taciturn &c. 585.

Adv. secretly &c. *adj.*; in -secret, – private, – one's sleeve, – holes and corners; in the dark &c. *adj.*

januis clausis, with closed doors, *à huis clos*; hugger-mugger, *à la dérobée*; under the -cloak of, – rose, – table; *sub rosâ, en tapinois*, in the background, aside, on the sly, with bated breath, *sotto voce*, in a whisper, without beat of drum, *à la sourdine*.

in –, strict- confidence; confidentially &c. *adj.*; between -our-selves, – you and me; *entre nous, inter nos*, under the seal of secrecy; in -code, – cipher.

underhand, by stealth, like a thief in the night; stealthily &c. *adj.*; behind -the scenes, – the curtain, – one's back, – a screen &c. 530; *incognito; in camerâ*.

Phr. it -must, – will- go no further; 'tell it not in Gath,' nobody the wiser.

529. Disclosure.—N. disclosure; re-tection; unveiling &c. *v.*; deterration, revealment, revelation; divulgence, expos-ition, -ure; *exposé*; whole truth; tell-tale &c. (*news*) 532.

acknowledgment, avowal; confes-sion, -al; shrift.

530. Ambush. [Means of conceal-ment.]**—N.** hiding-place; secret -place, – drawer; recess, hole, funk hole, holes and corners; closet, crypt, *adytum*, ab-ditory, *oubliette*, safe, – deposit; cache.

am-bush, -buscade; stalking horse; lurking-hole, -place; secret path,

bursting of a bubble; *dénouement.*

V. dis-close, -cover, -mask; draw –, draw aside –, lift –, raise –, lift up –, remove –, tear- the -veil, – curtain; un-mask, -veil, -fold, -cover, -seal, -kennel; take off –, break- the seal; lay -open, – bare; expose; open, – up; bare, bring to light; evidence; make - clear, – evident, – manifest; evince.

divulge, reveal, break; let into the secret; reveal the secrets of the prison-house; tell &c. (*inform*) 527; breathe,

backstairs; retreat &c. (*refuge*) 666.

screen, cover, shade, blinker; veil, curtain, blind, *purdah*, cloak, cloud.

mask, vizor, visor, disguise, masquerade dress, domino; *camouflage.*

pitfall &c. (*source of danger*) 667; trap &c. (*snare*) 545.

V. ambush, ambuscade, lie in ambush &c. (*hide oneself*) 528; lie in wait for; set a trap for &c. (*deceive*) 545.

Adv. *aux aguets.*

utter, blab, peach; let -out, – fall, – drop, – the cat out of the bag; betray; tell tales, – out of school; come out with; give -vent, – utterance- to; open the lips, blurt out, vent, whisper about; speak out &c. (*make manifest*) 525; make public &c. 531; unriddle &c. (*find out*) 480a; split; blow the gaff; break the news.

acknowledge, allow, concede, grant, admit, own, confess, avow, throw off all disguise, turn inside out, make a clean breast; show one's -hand, – cards; unburden –, disburden- one's -mind, – conscience, – heart; open –, lay bare –, tell a piece of- one's mind; unbosom oneself, own to the soft impeachment; say –, speak- the truth; turn -King's, –Queen's, –State's- evidence.

raise –, drop –, lift –, remove –, throw off- the mask; expose; debunk; lay open; un-deceive, -beguile; disabuse, set right, correct, open the eyes of; *désillusionner.*

be -disclosed &c.; transpire, come to light; come in sight &c. (*be visible*) 446; become known, escape the lips; come –, ooze –, creep –, leak –, peep –, crop- out; show its -face, – colours; discover &c. itself; break through the clouds, flash on the mind.

Adj. disclosed &c. *v.*

Int. out with it!

Phr. the murder is out; a light breaks in upon one; the scales fall from one's eyes; the eyes are opened.

531. Publication.—N. publication; public -announcement &c. 527; promulgation, propagation, proclamation, pronouncement, encyclical, *pronunciamento*; circulation, indiction, edition, imprint, impression, printing; hue and cry.

publicity, notoriety, currency, flagrancy, cry, *bruit*; *vox populi*; report &c. (*news*) 532.

the Press, fourth estate, public press, newspaper, periodical, journal, gazette; house organ, trade publication, tabloid; daily, weekly, monthly, quarterly, annual, magazine, monograph, book; review; news sheet, special edition, supplement, feature, rotogravure, comic strips; leaflet, pamphlet; telegraphy; publisher &c. *v.*

circular, – letter; manifesto, advertisement, puff, placard, bill, *affiche,* broadside, poster; notice &c. 527; programme.

V. publish; make -public, – known &c. (*information*) 527; speak –, talk- of; broach, utter; put forward; circulate, propagate, promulgate; spread –, abroad; rumour, diffuse, disseminate, evulgate; put –, give –, send- forth; emit, edit, get out; issue; cover, report; bring –, lay –, drag- before the public; give -out, – to the world; put –, bandy –, hawk –, buzz –, whisper –, bruit –, blaze- about; drag into the -open day, – limelight; voice.

proclaim, herald, blazon; blaze –, noise- abroad; sound a trumpet; trumpet –, thunder- forth; give tongue; announce with -beat of drum, – flourish of trumpets; proclaim -from the housetops, – at Charing Cross, at the cross roads; declare, declaim.

advertise, placard; post, – up; *afficher*, publish in the Gazette, send round the crier.

raise a -cry, – hue and cry, – report; set news afloat.

telegraph, cable, wireless, broadcast.

be -published &c.; be –, become- public &c. *adj.*; come out; go –, fly –, buzz –, blow- about; get -about, – abroad, – afloat, – wind; find vent; see the light; go forth, take air, acquire currency, pass current; go -the rounds, – the round of the newspapers, – through the length and breadth of the land; *virum volitare per ora*; pass from mouth to mouth; spread; run –, spread- like wildfire.

Adj. published &c. *v.*; current &c. (*news*) 532; in circulation, public; notorious; flagrant, arrant; open &c. 525; trumpet-tongued; encyclical, promulgatory; exoteric.

Adv. publicly &c. *adj.*; in open court, with open doors; in the limelight.

Int. *Oyez!* O yes! notice!

Phr. notice is hereby given; this is –, these are- to give notice.

---

532. News.—N. news; information &c. 527; piece –, budget- of -news, – information; report, story, yarn, copy, filler, intelligence, tidings; stop press news.

word, advice, *aviso*, message; dis-, des-patch; radio, telegram, cablegram, wireless telegram, radiogram, marconi-gram, communication, errand, em-bassy; *bulletin, petit bleu.*

rumour, hearsay, *on dit*, flying rumour, news stirring, cry, buzz, *bruit*, fame; talk, *ouï-dire*, scandal, eaves-dropping; town –, table- talk; tittle-tattle; *canard*, topic of the day, idea afloat.

fresh –, stirring –, old –, stale- news; glad tidings; old –, stale- story.

narrator &c. (*describe*) 594; news-, scandal-monger; tale-bearer; tell-tale, gossip, tattler, busy-body, chatterer; informer.

V. transpire &c. (*be disclosed*) 529; rumour &c. (*publish*) 531.

Adj. many-tongued; rumoured; publicly –, currently- -rumoured, – reported; rife, current, floating, afloat, going about, in circulation, in everyone's mouth, all over the town.

Adv. as the story -goes, – runs; as they say, it is said.

533. Secret.—N. secret; dead –, profound- secret; *arcanum*, mystery; latency &c. 526; Asian mystery; sealed book, secrets of the prison-house; *le dessous des cartes.*

enigma, riddle, puzzle, nut to crack, conundrum, charade, rebus, logogriph; mono-, ana-gram; acrostic, cross-word puzzle; Sphinx; *crux criticorum.*

maze, labyrinth, Hyrcynian wood.

problem &c. (*question*) 461; paradox &c. (*difficulty*) 704; unintelligibility &c. 519; *terra incognita* &c. (*ignorance*) 491.

Adj. secret &c. (*concealed*) 528.

---

534. Messenger.—N. messenger, envoy, emissary, legate; nuncio, internuncio; intermediary; ambassador &c. (*diplomatist*) 758.

marshal, flag-bearer, herald, crier, trumpeter, bellman, pursuivant, *parlementaire, apparitor.*

courier, runner, dawk, *estafette*; Hermes, Mercury, Iris, Ariel.

postman, letter carrier, telegraph boy, messenger boy, district mes-senger; despatch rider, commissionaire, errand-boy.

mail; post, -office; letter-bag; mail -boat, – train, – coach, – van, air mail; tele-graph, -phone; cable, wire; carrier-pigeon; wireless tele-graph, -phone; radiotele-graph, -phone.

journalist, newspaperman, reporter; gentleman –, representative- of the press; sob sister; penny-a-liner; special –, war –, own- correspondent; spy, scout; informer &c. 527.

535. Affirmation.—N.

affirm-ance, -ation; statement, allegation, assertion, predication, declaration, word, averment.

asseveration, adjuration, swearing, oath, affidavit; deposition &c. (*record*) 551; avouchment, assurance; protest, -ation; profession; acknowledgment &c. (*assent*) 488; pledge.

vote, voice, suffrage, ballot.

remark, observation; position &c. (*proposition*) 514; saying, *dictum*, sentence, *ipse dixit*.

emphasis, positiveness, peremptoriness; dogmatism &c. (*certainty*) 474; dogmatist &c. 887.

V. assert; make -an assertion &c. *n.*; have one's say; say, affirm, predicate, declare, state, represent; protest, profess.

put -forth, – forward; advance, allege, propose, propound, enunciate, enounce, broach, set forth, hold out, maintain, contend, pronounce, pretend.

depose, depone, aver, avow, avouch, asseverate, swear; make –, take one's-oath; make –, swear –, put in- an affidavit; take one's Bible oath, kiss the book, vow, *vitam impendere vero*; swear till -one is black in the face, – all's blue; be sworn, call Heaven to witness; vouch, warrant, certify, assure, swear by bell, book and candle.

swear by &c. (*believe*) 484; insist –, take one's stand- upon; emphasize, lay stress on; assert -roundly, – positively; lay down, – the law; raise one's voice, dogmatize, have the last word; rap out; repeat; re-assert, -affirm.

announce &c. (*information*) 527; acknowledge &c. (*assent*) 488; attest &c. (*evidence*) 467; adjure &c. (*put to one's oath*) 768.

536. Negation.—N.

ne-, abne-gation; denial; dis-avowal, -claimer; abjuration; contra-diction, -vention; recusation, protest; rebuttal; recusancy &c. (*dissent*) 489; flat –, emphatic- -contradiction, – denial; *démenti*.

qualification &c. 469; repudiation &c. 610; retractation &c. 607; confutation &c. 479; refusal &c. 764; prohibition &c. 761.

V. deny; contra-dict, -vene; controvert, give denial to, gainsay, negative, shake the head.

dis-own, -affirm, -claim, -avow; recant &c. 607; revoke &c. (*abrogate*) 756.

dispute, impugn, traverse, rebut, join issue upon; bring –, call- in question &c. (*doubt*) 485.

deny -flatly, – peremptorily, – emphatically, – absolutely, – wholly, – entirely; give the lie to, belie.

repudiate &c. 610; set aside, ignore &c. 460; rebut &c. (*confute*) 479; qualify &c. 469; refuse &c. 764.

Adj. denying &c. *v.*; denied &c. *v.*; contradictory; negat-ive, -ory; revocatory; recusant &c. (*dissenting*) 489; at issue upon.

Adv. no, nay, not, nowise; not a -bit, – whit, – jot; not -at all, – in the least, – so;. no such thing; nothing of the -kind, – sort; quite the contrary, *tout au contraire*, far from it; *tant s'en faut*; on no account, in no respect; by -no, – no manner of- means; negatively.

Phr. there never was a greater mistake; I know better; *non hæc in fœdera*.

Adj. asserting &c. *v.*; declaratory, predicatory, pronunciative, affirmative, *soi-disant*; positive; certain &c. 474; express, explicit &c. (*patent*) 525; absolute, emphatic, flat, broad, round, pointed, marked, distinct, decided, confident, assertive, insistent, trenchant, dogmatic, definitive, formal, solemn, categorical, peremptory; unretracted; predicable, affirmable.

Adv. affirmatively &c. *adj.*; in the affirmative.

with emphasis, *ex cathedrâ*, without fear of contradiction.

I must say, indeed, i' faith, let me tell you, why, give me leave to say, marry, you may be sure, I'd have you to know; upon my -word, – honour; by my troth, egad, I assure you; by -jingo, – Jove, – George, – &c.; troth, seriously, sadly; in –, in sober- -sadness, – truth, – earnest; of a truth, truly, pardi, perdy; in all conscience, upon oath; be assured &c. *(belief)* 484; yes &c. *(assent)* 488; I'll -warrant, – warrant you, – engage, – answer for it, – be bound, – venture to say, – take my oath; in fact, as a matter of fact, forsooth, joking apart; so help me God; not to mince the matter.

Phr. quoth he; *dixi.*

537. Teaching.—**N.** teaching &c. *v.*; instruction; edification; education; pedagogy; tuition; tutor-, tutel-age; direction, guidance.

qualification, preparation; train-, school-ing &c. *v.*; discipline; exer-cise, -citation; drill, practice.

persuasion, proselytism, propagandism, *propaganda*; in-doctrination, -culcation, -oculation.

explanation &c. *(interpretation)* 522; lesson, lecture, sermon, homily; apologue, parable; discourse, prelection, preachment, disquisition.

exercise, task; *curriculum*; course, – of study; grammar, three R's, initiation, A. B. C. &c. *(beginning)* 66.

elementary –, primary –, secondary –, grammar school –, high school –, college –, university –, technical –, liberal –, classical –, religious –, denominational –, moral –, secular- education; technical –, vocational- training; university extension lectures; propædeutics, moral tuition; evening classes, correspondence course.

physical education, gymnastics, calisthenics, eurythmics; *sloyd.*

V. teach, instruct, edify, school, tutor; cram, prime, coach; enlighten &c. *(inform)* 527.

in-culcate, -doctrinate, -oculate, -fuse, -stil, -fix, -graft, -filtrate; imbue, -pregnate, -plant; graft, sow the seeds of, disseminate, propagandize.

give an idea of; put -up to, – in the way of; set right.

sharpen the wits, enlarge the mind; give new ideas, open the eyes, bring forward, 'teach the young idea how to shoot'; improve &c. 658.

538. Misteaching.—**N.** mis-teaching, -information, -intelligence, -guidance, -direction, -persuasion, -instruction, -leading &c. *v.*; perversion, false teaching; sophistry &c. 477; college of Laputa; the blind leading the blind.

V. mis-inform, -teach, -direct, -guide, -instruct, -correct; pervert; put on a false –, throw off the- scent; deceive &c. 545; mislead &c. *(error)* 495; misrepresent; lie &c. 544; *spargere voces in vulgum ambiguas*, preach to the wise, teach one's grandmother to suck eggs.

render unintelligible &c. 519; bewilder &c. *(uncertainty)* 475; mystify &c. *(conceal)* 528; unteach.

Adj. misteaching &c. *v.*; unedifying.

Phr. *piscem natare doces.*

539. Learning.—**N.** learning; acquisition of -knowledge &c. 490, – skill &c. 698; acquirement, attainment; edification, scholarship, erudition; lore; information; self-instruction; study, reading, perusal; inquiry &c. 461.

ap-, prenticeship; pupil-age, -arity; tutelage, novitiate, matriculation.

docility &c. *(willingness)* 602; aptitude &c. 698.

V. learn; acquire –, gain –, receive –, take in –, drink in –, imbibe –, pick up –, gather –, get –, obtain –, collect – glean- -knowledge, – information, - learning.

acquaint oneself with, master; make oneself -master of, – acquainted with; grind, cram; get –, coach- up; learn by -heart, - rote.

read, spell, peruse; con –, pore –, thumb- over; wade through; dip into;

expound &c. (*interpret*) 522; lecture; prelect; read –, give- a -lesson, – lecture, – sermon, – discourse; hold forth, preach; sermon-, moral-ize; point a moral.

train, discipline; bring up, – to; educate, form, ground, prepare, qualify, drill, exercise, practice, habituate, familiarize with, nurture, dry-nurse, breed, rear, take in hand; break, – in; tame; pre-instruct; initiate; inure &c. (*habituate*) 613.

put to nurse, send to school.

direct, guide; direct attention to &c. (*attention*) 457; impress upon the -mind, – memory; beat into, – the head; convince &c. (*belief*) 484.

Adj. teaching &c. *v.*; taught &c. *v.*; educational; scholastic, academic, doctrinal; disciplinal; instructive, didactic, hortative, pedagogic, tutorial.

Phr. the schoolmaster abroad.

540. Teacher.—N. teacher, trainer, instructor, institutor, master, tutor, don, director, Corypheus, dry nurse, coach, grinder, crammer; governor, bear-leader; governess, duenna; disciplinarian.

professor, lecturer, reader, prelector, prolocutor, preacher; Boanerges; pastor &c. (*clergy*) 996; schoolmaster, dominie, usher, pedagogue, abecedarian; schoolmistress, dame, monitor, proctor, pupil-teacher.

expositor &c. 524; preceptor, guide; mentor &c. (*adviser*) 695; pioneer, apostle, missionary, propagandist, moonshee; example &c. (*model for imitation*) 22.

professorship &c. (*school*) 542.

tutelage &c. (*teaching*) 537.

Adj. professorial, tutorial &c. 537.

run the eye -over, – through; turn over the leaves.

study; be -studious &c. *adj.*; consume the midnight oil, mind one's book.

go to -school, – college, – the university; serve -an (*or* one's) apprenticeship, – one's time; learn one's trade; be -informed &c. 527; be -taught &c. 537.

Adj. studious; schol-astic, -arly; teachable; docile &c. (*willing*) 602; apt &c. 698, industrious &c. 682; learned, erudite.

Adv. at one's books; *in statu pupillari* &c. (*learner*) 541.

541. Learner.—N. learner, scholar, student, *alumnus, élève*, pupil; ap-, prentice; articled clerk; school-boy, -girl, beginner, tyro, abecedarian, alphabetarian.

recruit, novice, neophyte, tenderfoot, inceptor, *débutant*, catechumen, probationer; undergraduate; freshman, frosh; sophomore, junior, senior; junior –, senior- soph; sophister, questionist, fellow-, commoner, pensioner, exhibitioner, sizar, scholar, fellow, advanced –, post graduate –, research- student.

class, form, grade, standard, remove; pupilage &c. (*learning*) 539.

disciple, follower, apostle, proselyte; fellow student, school-mate, -fellow, class mate, condisciple.

Adj. *in statu pupillari*, in leading strings, sophomoric.

542. School.—N. school, academy, university, *alma mater*, college, seminary, Lyceum; instit-ute, -ution, *conservatoire; palæstra, gymnasium*.

day –. boarding –, public –, preparatory –, elementary –, primary –, infant –, dame's –, grammar –, middle class –, Board –, County –, Council –, parochial –, denominational –, Sunday –, National –, British and Foreign –, collegiate –, secondary –, continuation –, night –, correspondence –, secretarial –, military –, law –, medical –, business –, technical- school; technical –, training- college; Polytechnic; training ship; *Kindergarten*, nursery, *crèche*, reformatory.

pulpit, desk, reading desk, ambo, class-, lecture-room, theatre, amphitheatre, forum, stage, rostrum, platform, hustings, tribune.

school –, horn –, text- book; grammar, primer, abecedary, rudiments, manual, *vade mecum*, Lindley Murray, Cocker.

professor-, lecture-, reader-ship; chair; schoolmaster &c. 540.

School Board, Council of Education; *propaganda*.

Adj. scholastic, academic, collegiate; educational.

Adv. *ex cathedrâ*.

---

543. Veracity.—N. veracity; truthfulness, frankness &c. *adj.*; truth, sooth, sincerity, candour, honesty, fidelity; plain dealing, *bona fides*; love of truth; probity &c. 939; ingenuousness &c. (*artlessness*) 703.

the truth the whole truth and nothing but the truth; honest –, sober-truth &c. (*fact*) 494; unvarnished tale; light of truth.

V. speak –, tell- the truth; speak by the card; paint in its –, show oneself in one's-true colours; make a clean breast &c. (*disclose*) 529; speak one's mind &c. (*be blunt*) 703; not -lie &c. 544, – deceive &c. 545.

Adj. truthful, true; ver-acious, -edical; scrupulous &c. (*honourable*) 939; sincere, candid, frank, open, straightforward, unreserved; open-, true-, simple- hearted; honest, trustworthy; undissembling &c. (dissemble &c. 544); guileless, pure; unperjured, true blue, as good as one's word; unaffected, unfeigned, *bonâ fide*; outspoken, ingenuous &c. (*artless*) 703; undisguised &c. (*real*) 494.

Adv. truly &c. (*really*) 494; on oath; in plain words &c. 703; in –, with –, of a –, in good –, very- truth; as the -dial to the sun, – needle to the pole; honour bright; troth; in good -sooth, – earnest; unfeignedly, with no nonsense, in sooth, sooth to say, *bonâ fide*, *in foro conscientiæ*; without equivocation; *cartes sur table*, from the bottom of one's heart; by my troth &c. (*affirmation*) 535.

544. Falsehood. — N. false-hood, -ness; fals-ity, -ification; misrepresentation; deception &c. 545; untruth &c. 546; guile; bad faith; lying &c. *v.*; misrepresentation; mendacity, perjury, false swearing; forgery, invention, fabrication; subreption; covin.

perversion –, suppression- of truth; *suppressio veri*; perversion, distortion, false colouring; exaggeration &c. 549; prevarication, equivocation, shuffling, fencing, evasion, fraud; *suggestio falsi* &c. (*lie*) 546; mystification &c. (*concealment*) 528; simulation &c. (*imitation*) 19; dis-simulation, -sembling; deceit.

sham; pretence, pretending, malingering.

lip -homage, – service; mouth honour; hollowness; mere -show, – outside, eye-wash, window dressing; duplicity, double dealing, insincerity, hypocrisy, cant, humbug, casuistry; jesuit-ism, -ry; pharisaism; Machiavellism, 'organized hypocrisy'; crocodile tears, mealy-mouthedness, quackery; charlatan-ism, -ry; gammon; bun-kum, -come; flam, bam, flim-flam, cajolery, flattery; Judas kiss; perfidy &c. (*bad faith*) 940; *il volto sciolto i pensieri stretti*.

unfairness &c. (*dishonesty*) 940; artfulness &c. (*cunning*) 702; misstatement &c. (*error*) 495.

V. be -false &c. *adj.*, – a liar &c. 548; speak -falsely &c. *adv.*; tell -a lie &c. 546; lie, fib; lie like a trooper; swear falsely, forswear, perjure oneself, bear false witness.

mis-state, -quote, -cite, -report, -represent; belie, falsify, pervert, distort; put a false construction upon &c. (*misinterpret*) 523.

prevaricate, equivocate, quibble; palter, – to the understanding; *répondre en Normand*; trim, shuffle, fence, mince the truth, beat about the bush, blow hot and cold, play fast and loose.

garble, gloss over, disguise, give a colour to; give –, put- a -gloss, – false colouring- upon; colour, varnish, cook, dress up, embroider; varnish right and puzzle wrong, exaggerate &c. 549.

invent, fabricate; trump –, get- up; forge, hatch, concoct; romance &c. (*imagine*) 515; cry 'wolf!'

dis-semble, -simulate; feign, assume, put on, pretend, make believe; play -false, – a double game; coquet; act –, play- a part; affect &c. 855; simulate, pass off for; counterfeit, fake, sham, make a show of; malinger; swing the lead; say the grapes are sour.

cant, play the hypocrite, sham Abraham, *faire pattes de velours*, put on the mask, clean the outside of the platter, lie like a conjuror; hang out –, hold out –, sail under- false colours; 'commend the poisoned chalice to the lips'; *spargere voces in vulgum ambiguas*; deceive &c. 545.

Adj. false, deceitful, mendacious, unveracious, fraudulent, untruthful, dishonest; faith-, truth-, troth-less; un-fair, -candid; evasive; un-, dis-ingenuous; hollow, insincere, *Parthis mendacior*; forsworn.

canting; hypocrit-, jesuit-, pharisa-ical; tartuffish; Machiavelian; double-tongued, -faced, -handed, -minded, -hearted, -dealing; two-faced; bare-faced; Janus-faced; smooth-faced, -spoken, -tongued; plausible; mealy-mouthed; affected &c. 855.

collus-ive, -ory; artful &c. (*cunning*) 702; perfidious &c. 940, spurious &c. (*deceptive*) 545; untrue &c. 546; falsified &c. *v.*; covinous.

Adv. falsely &c. *adj.*; *à la Tartufe*, with a double tongue; out of whole cloth; slily &c. (*cunning*) 702.

545. Deception.—**N.** deception; falseness &c. 544; untruth &c. 546; impos-ition, -ture; fraud, deceit, guile; fraudulen-ce, -cy; covin; knavery &c. (*cunning*) 702; misrepresentation &c. (*falsehood*) 544.

delusion, gullery, bluff, spoof, *blague*; juggl-ing, -ery; sleight of hand, legerdemain; presti-giation, -digitation; magic &c. 992; conjur-ing, -ation; hocus-pocus, jockeyship; trickery, coggery, hanky-panky, chicanery, pettifogging, sharp practice; *supercherie*, cozenage, circumvention, ingannation, collusion; treachery &c. 940; practical joke.

trick, cheat, wile, ruse, blind, feint, plant, bubble, fetch, catch, chicane, juggle, reach, hocus, bite; thimble-rig, card-sharping, artful dodge, machination, swindle, hoax; tricks upon travellers; confidence trick; stratagem &c. (*artifice*) 702; theft &c. 791.

snare, trap, pitfall, decoy, gin; sprin-ge, -gle; noose, hook; bait, decoy-duck, tub to the whale, baited trap, *guet-à-pens*; cobweb, net, meshes, toils, mouse-trap, bird-lime; ambush &c. 530; trap-door, sliding panel, false bottom; spring-net, -gun; mask, -ed battery; mine; booby trap.

Cornish hug; wolf in sheep's clothing &c. (*deceiver*) 548; disguise, -ment; false colours, masquerade, mummery, borrowed plumes; *pattes de velours*.

mockery &c. (*imitation*) 19; copy &c. 21; counterfeit, sham, Brummagem, make-believe, forgery, fraud, fake; lie &c. 546; 'a mockery, a delusion, and a snare,' hollow mockery.

whited –, painted- sepulchre; tinsel, paste, false jewellery, scagliola, ormolu, German silver, Britannia metal, paint; jerry building; man of straw.

illusion &c. (*error*) 495; *ignis fatuus* &c. 423; *mirage* &c. 443.

V. deceive, take in; defraud, cheat, jockey, do, cozen, diddle, nab, gyp, chouse, double cross, play one false, bilk, cully, jilt, bite, pluck, swindle, victimize; abuse; mystify; blind one's eyes; blindfold, hoodwink, spoof, bluff; throw dust into the eyes, 'keep the word of promise to the ear and break it to the hope,' 'draw a herring across the trail.'

impose -, practise -, play -, put -, palm -, foist- upon; snatch a verdict.

circumvent, overreach; out-reach, -wit, -manœuvre; steal a march upon, give the go-by to, leave in the lurch.

set -, lay- a -trap, - snare- for; bait the hook, forelay, spread the toils, lime; decoy, waylay, lure, beguile, delude, inveigle; tra-, tre-pan; kidnap; let-, hook-in; trick; en-, in-trap, -snare, entoil, benet; nick, springe; catch, - in a trap; sniggle, entangle, illaqueate, hocus, practise on one's credulity, dupe, gull, hoax, fool, befool, bamboozle; hum, -bug; gammon, stuff up, dope, sell; play a -trick, - practical joke- upon one; balk, trip up, throw a tub to a whale; fool to the top of one's bent, send on -a wild goose chase, - a fool's errand; make -game, - a fool, - an April fool, - an ass- of; trifle with, cajole, flatter; come over &c. (*influence*) 615; gild the pill, make things pleasant, divert, put a good face upon; dissemble &c. 544.

cog, - the dice, play with marked cards; live by one's wits, play at hide and seek; obtain money under false pretences &c. (*steal*) 791; conjure, juggle, practise chicanery; gerrymander.

play -, palm -, foist -, fob- off.

lie &c. 544; misinform &c. 538; mislead &c. (*error*) 495; betray &c. 940; be -deceived &c. 547.

Adj. deceived &c. *v.*; deceiving &c. *v.*; cunning &c. 702; prestigi-ous, -atory; decept-ive, -ious; deceitful, covinous; delus-ive, -ory; illus-ive, -ory; elusive, insidious, *ad captandum vulgus*.

untrue &c. 546; mock, sham, make-believe, counterfeit, faked, pseudo, spurious, so-called, pretended, feigned, trumped up, bogus, scamped, fraudulent, tricky, factitious, artificial, bastard; surreptitious, illegitimate, contraband, adulterated, sophisticated; unsound, rotten at the core; colourable; disguised; meretricious; tinsel, pinchbeck, plated; catch-penny; Brummagem; simulated &c. 544.

Adv. under -false colours, - the garb of, - cover of; over the left.
Phr. *fronti nulla fides.*

546. Untruth.—N. untruth, falsehood, lie, story, thing that is not, fib, bounce, crammer, taradiddle, whopper.

forgery, fabrication, invention; mis-statement, -representation; per-version, falsification, gloss, *suggestio falsi*; exaggeration &c. 549.

fiction; fable, nursery tale; romance &c. (*imagination*) 515; untrue -, false -, trumped up- -story, - statement; thing devised by the enemy; *canard*; shave, sell, hum, yarn, traveller's tale, Canterbury tale, cock and bull story, fairy tale, clap-trap.

myth, moonshine, bosh, all my eye, -and Betty Martin, mare's nest, farce.

irony; half truth, white lie, pious fraud; mental reservation &c. (*concealment*) 528.

pretence, pretext; false -plea &c. 617; subterfuge, evasion, shift, shuffle, make-believe; sham &c. (*deception*) 545.

profession, empty words; Judas kiss &c. (*hypocrisy*) 544; disguise &c. (*mask*) 530.

V. have a false meaning; not ring true.

pretend, sham, feign, counterfeit, make believe.

Adj. untrue, false, trumped up; void of -, without- foundation; far from the truth, false as dicer's oaths; unfounded, *ben trovato*, invented, fabulous, fabricated, forged; fict-, fact-, supposit-, surrept-itious; e-, il-lusory; ironical; satirical; evasive; *soi-disant* &c. (*misnamed*) 565.

Phr. *se non è vero è ben trovato.*

547. Dupe.— N. dupe, gull, gudgeon, *gobemouche*, cull, cully, victim, sucker, pigeon, April fool; laughing stock &c. 857; Cyclops, simple Simon, flat, mug, greenhorn; fool &c. 501; puppet, cat's paw.

V. be -deceived &c. 545, – the dupe of; fall into a trap; swallow –, nibble at- the bait; bite; catch a Tartar.

Adj. credulous &c. 486; mistaken &c. (*error*) 495.

548. Deceiver.—N. deceiver &c. (deceive &c. 545); dissembler, hypocrite; sophist, Pharisee, Jesuit, Mawworm, Pecksniff, Joseph Surface, Tartufe, Janus; serpent, snake in the grass, cockatrice, Judas, wolf in sheep's clothing; Molly Maguire; jilt; shuffler.

liar &c. (lie &c. 544); story-teller, perjurer, false-witness, *menteur, -à triple étage, -à payer patente*; Scapin.

impostor, pretender, capper, decoy, fraud, *soi-disant*, humbug; adventurer; Cagliostro, Fernam Mendez Pinto; ass in lion's skin &c. (*bungler*) 701; actor &c. (*stage player*) 599.

quack, *charlatan*, mountebank, saltimbanco, *saltimbanque*, empiric, quacksalver, medicaster.

conjuror, juggler, magician, necromancer, trickster, prestidigitator, medium, jockey; crimp; decoy-duck, stool pigeon; rogue, knave, cheat; swindler &c. (*thief*) 792; jobber.

549. Exaggeration.—N. exaggeration; expansion &c. 194; hyperbole, stretch, strain, colouring; high colouring, caricature, *caricatura*; extravagance &c. (*nonsense*) 497; Baron Munchausen; men in buckram, yarn, fringe, embroidery, traveller's tale; Ossa upon Pelion.

storm in a teacup; much ado about nothing &c. (*over-estimation*) 482; puffery &c. (*boasting*) 884; rant &c. (*turgescence*) 577.

figure of speech, *façon de parler*; stretch of -fancy, – the imagination; flight of fancy &c. (*imagination*) 515.

false colouring &c. (*falsehood*) 544; aggravation &c. 835.

V. exaggerate, magnify, pile up, aggravate; amplify &c. (*expand*) 194; overestimate &c. 482; hyperbolize; over-charge, -state, -draw, -lay, -shoot the mark, -praise; make -much, – the most- of; strain, – a point; stretch, – a point; go great lengths; spin a long yarn; draw –, shoot with- a long-bow; deal in the marvellous.

out-Herod Herod, run riot, talk at random.

heighten, overcolour; colour -highly, – too highly; embroider, *broder*; flourish; colour &c. (*misrepresent*) 544; puff &c. (*boast*) 884.

Adj. exaggerated &c. *v.*; overwrought; bombastic &c. (*magniloquent*) 577; hyperbolical, on stilts; fabulous, extravagant, preposterous, egregious, *outré*, high-flying.

Adv. hyperbolically &c. *adj.*

Section III. MEANS OF COMMUNICATING IDEAS
1.° *Natural Means*

550. Indication.—N. indication; symbol-ism, -ization; semeio-logy, -tics; sign of the times.

lineament, feature, *trait*, characteristic, trick, diagnostic; divining-rod; cloven hoof; footfall; means of recognition; earmark.

sign, symbol; ind-ex, -ice, -icator; point, -er; marker; exponent, note, token, symptom.

type, figure, emblem, cipher, device; representation &c. 554; epigraph, motto, posy.

gest-ure, -iculation; pantomime; wink, glance, leer; nod, shrug, beck; touch, nudge; grip; dactylo-logy, -nomy; Freemasonry, telegraphy, chirology, by-play, dumb-show; cue; hint &c. 527; clue, clew, key, scent, track &c. 551.

signal, -post; rocket, blue light; watch-fire, -tower; telegraph, semaphore, flag-staff; cresset, fiery cross; calumet; heliograph, signal-, flash-lamp.

mark, line, stroke, dash, score, stripe, streak, scratch, tick, dot, point, notch, nick, blaze; asterisk, red letter, italics, heavy type, inverted commas, quotation marks, sublineation, underlining, jotting; print; impr-int, -ess, -ession; note, annotation, mark of exclamation.

[For identification] badge, criterion; counter-check, -mark, -sign, -foil; duplicate, tally; label, tab, ticket, stub, billet, letter, counter, *tessera*, card, bill, check; witness, voucher; stamp; *cachet*; trade -, hall- mark; broad arrow; signature; address -, visiting- card; *carte de visite*; credentials &c. (*evidence*) 467; passport, indentity book, *carte d' identité*; attestation; hand, - writing, sign-manual; cipher; monogram, - mark, seal, sigil, signet; autograph, -y; paraph, brand; superscription; in-, en-dorsement; title, heading, rubric, docket; *mot -de passe, - du guet; passe-parole*; shibboleth; watch-, catch-, pass-word; *open sesame!*

insignia; banner, -et, -ol; bandrol; flag, colours, streamer, standard, eagle, labarum, oriflamb, *oriflamme*; figure-head; ensign; pen-non, -nant, -dant; burgee, blue Peter, jack, ancient, gonfalon, Union jack; tricolour, stars and stripes; bunting, Jolly Roger, *drapeau, pavillon*.

heraldry, crest; coat of -, arms; armorial bearings, hatchment; e-, scutcheon; shield, supporters; livery, uniform; cockade, *epaulette*, brassard, chevron; garland, chaplet, love-knot, fillet, favour.

[Of locality] beacon, cairn, post, staff, flagstaff, hand, pointer, vane, cock, weathercock; guide-, hand-, finger-, directing-, sign-post; pillars of Hercules, pharos, signal fire; bench-, land-, sea-mark; lighthouse, balize; pole-, load-, lode-star; cynosure, guide; address, direction, name; sign, -board.

[Of the future] warning &c. 668; omen &c. 512; prefigurement &c. 511. [Of the past] trace record &c. 551. [Of danger] warning &c. 668; alarm &c. 669. [Of authority] sceptre &c. 747. [Of triumph] trophy &c. 733. [Of quantity] gauge &c. 466. [Of distance] mile-stone, -post. [Of disgrace] brand, fool's cap, stigma, mark of Cain.. [For detection] check, tell-tale; test &c. (*experiment*) 463.

notification &c. (*information*) 527; advertisement &c. (*publication*) 531.

word of command, call; bugle-, trumpet-call; reveille, taps; bell, alarum, cry; battle -, rallying- cry.

church, bell, angelus, sacring bell; muezzin.

exposition &c. (*explanation*) 522; proof &c. (*evidence*) 467; pattern &c. (*prototype*) 22.

V. indicate; be the -sign &c. *n.*- of; denote, betoken; argue, testify &c. (*evidence*) 467; bear the -impress &c. *n.*- of; con-note, -notate.

represent, stand for; typify &c. (*prefigure*) 511; symbolize.

put -an indication, - a mark, - &c. *n.*; note, mark, tick, blaze, stamp, **earmark**; set one's seal upon; label, ticket, docket; dot, spot, score, dash, trace, chalk; print; im-print, -press, surprint; engrave, stereotype, electrotype.

make a -sign &c. *n.*; signalize; give –, hang out- a signal; beck, -on; gesture; nod; wink, glance, leer, nudge, shrug, tip the wink; gesticulate; raise –, hold up- the -finger, – hand; saw the air, suit the action to the word.

wave –, unfurl –, hoist –, hang out- a banner &c. *n.*; wave -the hand, – a kerchief; give the cue &c. (*inform*) 527; show one's colours; give –, sound- an alarm; beat the drum, sound the trumpets, raise a cry.

sign, seal, attest &c. (*evidence*) 467; underline &c. (*give importance to*) 642; call attention to &c. (*attention*) 457; give notice &c. (*inform*) 527.

Adj. indicat-ing &c. *v.*, -ive, -ory; de-, con-notative; diacritical, representative, typical, symbolic, pantomimic, pathognomonic, symptomatic, ominous, characteristic, demonstrative, diagnostic, exponential, emblematic, armorial; individual &c. (*special*) 79.

known –, recognizable- by; indicated &c. *v.*; pointed, marked.

[Capable of being denoted] denotable; indelible.

Adv. in token of; symbolically &c. *adj.*; in dumb show.

Phr. *ecce signum; ex ungue leonem, ex pede Herculem.*

---

551. Record.—**N.** trace, vestige, relic, remains; scar, *cicatrix*; foot-step, -mark, -print; track, mark, wake, trail, spoor, scent, *piste*.

monument, hatchment, escutcheon, slab, tablet, trophy, achievement; obelisk, pillar, column, monolith, cromlech, dolmen; memorial; *memento* &c. (*memory*) 505; testimonial, medal, ribbon, order; commemoration &c. (*celebration*) 883.

record, note, minute; *dossier*; register, -try; census, roll &c. (*list*) 86; cartulary, diptych, Domesday book; entry, memorandum, indorsement, inscription, copy, duplicate, docket; notch &c. (*mark*) 550; muniment, deed &c. (*security*) 771; document; deposition, *procès-verbal*; affidavit; certificate &c. (*evidence*) 467.

552. [Suppression of sign.] **Obliteration.**—**N.** obliteration; erasure, rasure; effacement; cancel, -lation; cassation; circumduction; deletion, blot; *tabula rasa.*

V. efface, obliterate, erase, rase, expunge, cancel; blot –, take –, rub –, scratch –, strike –, wipe –, wash –, sponge- out; wipe –, rub- off; wipe away; deface, render illegible; draw the pen through, apply the sponge.

be -effaced &c.; leave no -trace &c. 449; 'leave not a rack behind.'

Adj. obliterated &c. *v.*; out of print; printless; leaving no trace; intestate; un-recorded, -registered, -written.

Int. *dele*; out with it!

---

note-, memorandum-, pocket-, commonplace-book; portfolio; scoring-board, -sheet; bulletin board; card index, file; pigeon-holes, *excerpta, adversaria*, jottings, dottings.

gazette, -er; newspaper, magazine &c. 531; alman-ac, -ack; calendar, ephemeris, noctuary, diary, log, journal, account-, cash-, day-book, ledger.

archive, scroll, state-paper, Congressional Record, return, blue-book; statistics &c. 86; *compte rendu*; Acts –, Transactions –, Proceedings- of; Hansard's Debates; chronicle, annals; legend; history, biography &c. 594.

registration; en-, in-rolment; tabulation; entry, booking; signature &c. (*identification*) 550; recorder &c. 553; journalism.

drawing, photograph &c. 554; phonograph –, gramophone-record; music roll.

V. record; put –, place- upon record; go on record; chronicle, calendar, hand down to posterity; keep up the memory of &c. (*remember*) 505; commemorate &c. (*celebrate*) 883; report &c. (*inform*) 527; commit to –, reduce to- writing; put –, set down- -in writing, – in black and white; put –, jot –, take –, write –, note –, set- down; note, minute, put on paper; take –, make- a -note, – minute, – memorandum; make a return.

mark &c. (*indicate*) 550; sign &c. (*attest*) 467.

enter, book; post, – up; insert, make an entry of; mark –, tick- off; register, list, docket, enroll, inscroll; file &c. (*store*) 636.

Adv. on record.

553. Recorder.—N. recorder, notary, clerk; regis-trar, -trary, -ter; prothonotary; amanuensis, secretary, scribe, stenographer, remem-brancer, book-keeper, *custos rotulorum*, Master of the Rolls.

annalist; histori-an, -ographer; chronicler, journalist, reporter, col-umnist; biographer &c. (*narrator*) 594; antiquary &c. (*antiquity*) 122; memorialist.

draughtsman &c. 559; engraver 558; photographer, cinematographer, camera man.

Recording instrument, recorder, camera, phonograph, gramophone, dictaphone, telegraphone, telautograph, printing telegraph, tape ma-chine, ticker, time recorder, cash register, turnstile, speedometer, voting machine, seismograph, photostat.

554. Representation.—N. represent- -ation, -ment; imitation &c. 19; illus-tration, delineation, depictment, por-trayal; imagery, portraiture, iconog-raphy; design, -ing; art, fine arts; painting &c. 556; sculpture &c. 557; engraving &c. 558; photography, radi-ography, skiagraphy.

person-ation, -ification; impersona-tion; drama &c. 599.

555. Misrepresentation.—N. mis-representation, distortion, exaggera-tion; daubing &c. *v.*; bad likeness, daub, sign-painting; scratch, carica-ture; *anamorphosis*.

V. misrepresent, distort, overdraw, travesty, parody, burlesque, exagger-ate, caricature, daub.

Adj. misrepresented &c. *v.*

picture, drawing, sketch, draught, draft; tracing; copy &c. 21; photo-, helio-graph; daguerreo-, talbo-, calo-, helio-type; cabinet, *carte-de-visite*, snapshot; X-ray photo-graph; radio-gram, -graph, skia-graph, -gram.

image, likeness, icon, portrait; striking –, speaking- likeness; very image; effigy, fac-simile.

figure, – head; puppet, doll, *figurine*, aglet, manikin, lay-figure, model, *marionnette*, *fantoccini*, bust; waxwork, statue, -tte, auto-maton, Robot.

hieroglyphic, anaglyph; dia-, mono-gram, -graph.

map, plan, chart; ground plan, projection, elevation; ichno-, carto-graphy; atlas; outline, scheme; view &c. (*painting*) 556.

artist, draughtsman &c. 559.

V. represent, delineate; depict, -ure; portray; picture; take –, catch- a likeness &c. *n.*; hit off, photograph, daguerreotype; figure; shadow -forth, – out; adumbrate; body forth; describe &c. 594; trace, copy; mould.

dress up; illustrate, symbolize.

paint &c. 556; carve &c. 557; engrave &c. 558.

person-ate, -ify; impersonate; assume a character; pose as; act;

play &c. (*drama*) 599; mimic &c. (*imitate*) 19; hold the mirror up to nature.

Adj. represent-ing &c. *v.*, -ative; illustrative; represented &c. *v.*; imitative, figurative.

like &c. 17; graphic &c. (*descriptive*) 594.

556. Painting.—**N.** painting; depicting; drawing &c. *v.*; design; perspective, skiagraphy; *chiaroscuro* &c. (*light*) 420; composition; treatment, values, atmosphere, tone, technique.

historical -, portrait -, miniature -, battle -, *genre* -, landscape -, marine -, fruit and flower -, scene- painting; scenography.

school, style; the grand style, high art, *genre*, portraiture; ornamental art &c. 847.

mono-, poly-chrome; *grisaille*.

pallet, palette; easel; brush, pencil, stump; blacklead, charcoal, crayons, chalk, pastel; paint &c. (*colouring matter*) 428; water-, body-, oil-colour; oils, oil-paint; varnish &c. 356a; *gouache*, tempera, distemper, fresco; enamel; encaustic painting; *graffito, gesso*; mosaic; tapestry.

picture, painting, piece, *tableau*, canvas; oil &c.- painting; cartoon; easel -, cabinet- picture; drawing, draught, draft; pencil &c. -, water-colour- drawing; sketch, outline; study.

portrait &c. (*representation*) 554; whole -, full -, half- length; kitcat, head; miniature; shade, *silhouette*; profile.

landscape, sea-piece, -scape; view, scene, prospect; interior; bird's-eye view; pan-, di-orama; still life.

picture -, art- gallery; studio, *atelier*.

V. paint, design, limn, draw, sketch, pencil, scratch, shade, stipple, hatch, dash off, chalk out, square up; colour, dead-colour, wash, varnish; draw in -pencil &c. *n.*; paint in -oils &c. *n.*; stencil; depict &c. (*represent*) 554.

Adj. painted &c. *v.*; pictorial, graphic, picturesque, decorative; classical, romantic, pre-Raphaelite, modern, cubist, futurist, vorticist, post-, impressionist.

pencil, oil &c. *n.*

Adv. in -pencil &c. *n.*

Phr. *fecit, delineavit, pinxit.*

557. Sculpture.—**N.** sculpture, insculpture; carving &c. *v.*; statuary, ceramics, plastic arts.

high -, low -, bas- relief; relievo; *basso-, alto-, mezzo-rilievo; intaglio,* anaglyph; medal, -lion; *cameo.*

marble, bronze, terracotta; ceramic ware, pottery, porcelain, china, earthenware, faïence, enamel, *cloisonné.*

statue &c. (*image*) 554; cast &c. (*copy*) 21; glyptotheca.

V. sculpture, carve, cut, chisel, model, mould; cast.

Adj. sculptured &c. *v.*; in relief, anaglyptic, ceroplastic, ceramic; parian; marble &c. *n.* **Phr.** *sculpsit.*

558. Engraving.—**N.** engraving, chalcography; line -, mezzotint -, stipple -, chalk- engraving; dry-point, bur; etching, aquatinta; plate -, copper-plate -, steel -, wood-, process-, photo-engraving; xylo-, ligno-, glypto-, cero-, litho-, chromolitho-, photolitho-, zinco-, glypho- -graphy, -graph.

impression, print, engraving, plate; steel-, copper-plate; etching; mezzo-, aqua-, litho-tint; cut, woodcut, block; stereo-, grapho-, auto-, helio-type; half-tone; *photogravure, rotogravure.*

graver, *burin*, etching-point, style; plate, stone, wood-block, negative; die, punch, stamp.

printing; plate –, copper-plate –, intaglio –, anastatic –, lithographic –, colour –, three or four colour- printing; type-printing &c. 591.

illustr-, illumin-ation; *vignette*, initial letter, *cul de lampe*, tail-piece.

V. engrave, grave, stipple, scrape, etch; bite, – in; lithograph &c. *n.*; print.

Adj. insculptured; engraved &c. *v.*

Phr. *fecit, sculpsit, imprimit, incisit.*

559. Artist.—N. artist; painter, limner, drawer, sketcher, delineator; cartoon-, caricatur-ist, designer, engraver; draughtsman; copyist; enamel-ler, -list.

historical –, landscape –, battle-, *genre* –, marine –, fruit and flower –, portrait –, miniature –, scene –, sign- painter; engraver; Apelles; sculptor, carver, chaser, modeller, lapidary, *figuriste*, statuary; Phidias, Praxiteles; Royal Academician.

photographer, retoucher.

2°. *Conventional Means*
1. *Language generally*

560. Language.—N. language; phraseology &c. 569; speech &c. 582; tongue, lingo, vernacular, slang; mother –, vulgar –, native- tongue; household words; King's *or* Queen's English; idiom; dialect &c. 563.

Volapuk, Esperanto, Ido, occidental, Ro.

confusion of tongues, Babel, *pasigraphie*; pantomime &c. (*signs*) 550; *onomatopœia.*

phil-, gloss-, glott-ology; linguistics, chrestomathy; paleo-logy; -graphy; comparative grammar.

literature, letters, polite literature, *belles lettres*, muses, humanities, *literæ humaniores*, republic of letters, dead languages, classics; genius of a language; scholarship &c. (*knowledge*) 490.

linguist &c. (*scholar*) 492.

V. speak, say, express by words &c. 566.

Adj. lingu-al, -istic; dialectic; vernacular, current, colloquial, slangy; bilingual, polyglot; literary.

561. Letter.—N. letter; character; hieroglyphic &c. (*writing*) 590; type &c. (*printing*) 591; capitals; majus-, minus-cule; alphabet, ABC, abecedary, Christ-cross-row.

consonant, vowel, diphthong; mute, surd; sonant, liquid, labial, dental, palatal, guttural.

syllable; mono-, dis-, poly-syllable; affix, prefix, suffix.

spelling, orthography; phon-ography, -etic spelling; ana-, meta-grammatism.

cipher, monogram, anagram; double –, acrostic.

V. spell.

Adj. literal; alphabetical, abecedarian; syllabic; uncial &c. (*writing*) 590; phonetic, voiced, mute &c. *n.*

562. Word.—N. word, term, vocable; name &c. 564; phrase &c. 566; root, etymon; derivative; part of speech &c. (*grammar*) 567.

dictionary, vocabulary, word book,

563. Neology.—N. neolo-gy, -gism; new-fangled expression; barbarism; caconym; archaism, black letter, monkish Latin; corruption; missaying, antiphrasis.

lexicon, index, glossary, thesaurus, *gradus, delectus,* concordance.

etymology, lexicology, derivation; phonology, orthoepy; gloss-, termin-, orism-ology; paleology &c. (*philology*) 560; comparative philology.

lexicograph-er, -y; glossographer &c. (*scholar*) 492; etymologist; logolept.

verbosity, verbiage, loquacity &c. 584.

Adj. verbal, literal; titular, nominal. [Similarly derived] conjugate, paronymous; derivative.

Adv. verbally &c. *adj.*; *verbatim* &c. (*exactly*) 494.

---

paronomasia, play upon words; word-play &c. (*wit*) 842; pun; *double-entendre* &c. (*ambiguity*) 520; palindrome, paragram, clinch; abuse of -language, – terms.

dialect, brogue, *patois,* provincialism, broken English, *lingua franca;* Brit-, Gall-, Scott-, Hibern-icism; Americanism; Gipsy lingo, Romany, pidgin English.

dog Latin, macaronics, gibberish, confusion of tongues, Babel; jargon.

colloquialism &c. (*figure of speech*) 521; by-word; technicality, lingo, slang, cant, *argot,* St. Giles's Greek, thieves' Latin, peddler's French, flash tongue, Billingsgate, Wall Street slang.

pseudonym &c. (*misnomer*) 565; Mr. So-and-so; what d'ye call 'em, what's his name; N. N.; *Monsieur Un Tel;* thingum-my, -bob; gadget, dooflicker, do-funny, *oo-ja-ka-pi-vi; je ne sais quoi.*

neologist, coiner of words.

V. coin words.

Adj. neologic, -al; rare; archaic; obsolete &c. (*old*) 124; colloquial, dialectic, slang, cant.

Phr. *Il a passé par Marseille.*

---

564. Nomenclature. — N. nomenclature; naming &c. *v.;* nuncupation, nomination, baptism; orismology; *onomatopæia;* antonomasia.

name; appella-tion, -tive; designation; title; head, -ing, caption; denomination; by-name, epithet.

style, proper name; præ-, ag-, cognomen; patronymic, surname; cognomination; compellation, description; empty -title, – name; handle to one's name; namesake, eponym.

synonym, antonym.

term, expression, noun; by-word; convertible terms &c. 522; technical term; cant &c. 563.

V. name, call, term, denominate, designate, style, entitle, intitule, clepe, dub, christen, baptize, nickname, characterize, specify, define, distinguish by the name of; label &c. (*mark*) 550.

be -called &c. *v.;* take –, bear –, go (*or* be known) by –, go (*or* pass) under –, rejoice in- the name of.

Adj. named &c. *v.;* hight, yclept, known as; what one may -well, – fairly, – properly, – fitly- call.

nuncupa-tory, -tive; cognominal, titular, nominal; orismological.

---

565. Misnomer.—N. misnomer; *lucus a non lucendo;* Mrs. Malaprop; what d'ye call 'em &c. (*neologism*) 563.

nickname, *sobriquet,* by-name, handle, moniker; assumed -name, – title; *alias; nom de -guerre, – plume, – théâtre;* pseudonym, pen name, stage name.

V. mis-name, -call, -term; nickname; assume -a name, – an alias.

Adj. misnamed &c. *v.;* pseudonymous; *soi-disant;* self-called, -styled, -christened; so-called.

nameless, anonymous; without a –, having no- name; innominate, unnamed.

Adv. in no sense.

---

566. Phrase.—N. phrase, expression, set phrase; sentence, paragraph; figure of speech &c. 521; idi-om, -otism; turn of expression.

paraphrase &c. (*synonym*) 522; periphrase &c. (*circumlocution*) 573; motto &c. (*proverb*) 496; phraseology &c. 569.

V. express, phrase; word, – it; give -words, – expression- to; voice; arrange in –, clothe in –, put into –, express by- words; couch in terms; find words to express; speak by the card.

Adj. expressed &c. *v.*; idiomatic.

Adv. in -round, – set, – good, set- terms; in set phrases.

567. Grammar.—N. grammar, accidence, syntax, *praxis*, analysis, paradigm, punctuation; parts of speech; inflexion, case, declension, conjugation; *jus et norma loquendi*; Lindley Murray &c. (*school-book*) 542; correct style; philology &c. (*language*) 560.

V. parse, analyze; decline, conjugate; punctuate.

Adj. grammatical; syntactic; inflexional.

568. Solecism.—N. solecism; bad –, false –, faulty- grammar; slip, error; slip of the -pen, – tongue; *lapsus calami-, – linguæ; faux pas*; slip-slop; bull.

V. use -bad, – faulty- grammar; solecize, commit a solecism; murder the -King's, – Queen's- English; break Priscian's head.

Adj. ungrammatical; in-correct, -accurate; faulty, improper, incongruous, abnormal.

569. Style.—N. style, diction, phraseology, wording; manner, strain; composition; mode of expression, choice of words, literary power, ready pen, pen of a ready writer; command of language &c. (*eloquence*) 582; authorship; *la morgue littéraire*.

V. express by words &c. 566; write.

Various Qualities of Style

570. Perspicuity.—N. perspicuity &c. (*intelligibility*) 518; plain speaking &c. (*manifestation*) 525; defin-iteness, -ition; exactness &c. 494; perspicuousness, logical acuteness.

Adj. lucid &c. (*intelligible*) 518; explicit &c. (*manifest*) 525; exact &c. 494.

571. Obscurity.—N. obscurity &c. (*unintelligibility*) 519; involution; hard words; ambiguity &c. 520; vagueness &c. 475, inexactness &c. 495; what d'ye call 'em &c. (*neologism*) 563; cloudiness, confusion.

Adj. obscure &c. *n.*; crabbed, involved, confused.

572. Conciseness.—N. conciseness &c. *adj.*; brevity, 'the soul of wit,' laconism; Tacitus; ellipsis; syncope; abridgment &c. (*shortening*) 201; compression &c. 195; epitome &c. 596; monostitch; portmanteau word, telescope word, protogram.

V. be -concise &c. *adj.*; condense &c. 195; abridge &c. 201; abstract &c. 596; come to the point.

Adj. concise, brief, short, terse, close; to the point, exact; neat, compact, condensed, pointed; laconic, curt, pithy, trenchant, summary; pregnant; compendious &c. (*compendium*) 596; succinct; elliptical, epigrammatic, crisp, sententious.

Adv. concisely &c. *adj.*; briefly,

573. Diffuseness.—N. diffuseness &c. *adj.*; amplification &c. *v.*; dilating &c. *v.*; verbosity, verbiage, wordiness, cloud of words, *copia verborum*; flow of words &c. (*loquacity*) 584.

poly-, tauto-, batto-, perisso-logy; pleonasm, exuberance, redundance; thrice-told tale; prolixity; circumlocution, *ambages*; periphra-se, -sis; roundabout phrases; episode; expletive; penny-a-lining; padding, drivel, twaddle, rigmarole; richness &c. 577.

V. be -diffuse &c. *adj.*; run out on, descant, expatiate, enlarge, dilate, amplify, expand, inflate, pad; launch –, branch- out; rant.

maunder, prose; harp upon &c. (*repeat*) 104; dwell on, insist upon.

summarily; in -brief, – short, – a word, – few words, – a nutshell; for shortness sake; to -come to the point, – make a long story short, – cut the matter short, – be brief; it comes to this, the long and the short of it is.

-winded, -spun, -drawn out; prosing, maundering; roundabout; digressive; dis-, ex-cursive; rambling, episodic; flatulent, frothy.

Adv. diffusely &c. *adj.*; at large, *in extenso*; about it and about it;

digress, ramble, *battre la campagne*, beat about the bush, perorate, spin a long yarn, protract; spin –, swell –, draw- out, drivel.

Adj. dif-, pro-fuse; wordy, verbose, largiloquent, copious, exuberant, effusive, pleonastic, lengthy; long, -some; diffusive, spun out, protracted, prolix, circumlocutory, periphrastic, ambagious,

---

574. Vigour.—N. vigour, power, force; boldness, raciness &c. *adj.*; spirit, point, antithesis, piquancy; *verve*, glow, fire, warmth, ardour, enthusiasm; 'thoughts that breathe and words that burn'; strong language; punch; gravity, sententiousness; elevation, loftiness, sublimity.

eloquence; command of -words, – language.

Adj. vigorous, nervous, powerful, forcible, trenchant, mordant, biting, incisive, impressive; sensational.

spirited, lively, glowing, sparkling, racy, bold, slashing; pungent, *piquant*, full of point, pointed, pithy, antithetical; sententious.

lofty, elevated, sublime, grand, weighty, ponderous; eloquent; vehement, petulant, impassioned; poetic.

Adv. in -glowing, – good set, – no measured- terms.

575. Feebleness.—N. feebleness &c. *adj.*

Adj. feeble, bald, tame, meagre, insipid, nerveless, jejune, vapid, trashy, cold, frigid, poor, dull, dry, languid; pros-ing, -y, -aic; unvaried, monotonous, weak, frail, washy, wishy-washy, sloppy; sketchy, slight; careless, slovenly, loose, lax; slip-shod, -slop; inexact; dis-jointed, -connected; puerile, childish; flatulent; rambling &c. (*diffuse*) 573.

---

576. Plainness.—N. plainness &c. *adj.*; simplicity, severity; plain -terms, – English; Saxon English; household words.

V. speak plainly; call a spade 'a spade'; plunge *in medias res*; come to the point.

Adj. plain, simple; un-ornamented, -adorned, -varnished; home-ly, -spun; neat; severe, chaste, pure, Saxon; commonplace, matter of fact, natural, prosaic, sober, unimaginative.

dry, unvaried, monotonous &c. 575.

Adv. in plain -terms, – words, – English, – common parlance; point blank.

577. Ornament. — N. ornament; floridness &c. *adj.*; turg-idity, -escence; altiloquence &c. *adj.*; orotundity; declamation, teratology; well-rounded periods; elegance &c. 578.

inversion, antithesis, alliteration, *paronomasia*; figurativeness &c. (*metaphor*) 521.

flourish; flowers of -speech, – rhetoric; euph-uism, -emism.

big-, high-sounding words; macrology, *sesquipedalia verba*, sesquipedalianism; Alexandrine; inflation, pretension; rant, bombast, fustian, bunkum, balderdash, prose run mad; fine writing; Minerva press.

phrasemonger; euph-uist, -emist.

V. ornament, overlay with ornament, overcharge; smell of the lamp.

Adj. ornamented &c. *v.*; beautified &c. 847; ornate, florid, rich, flowery; euph-uistic, -emistic; sonorous; high-, big-sounding; inflated, swelling, tumid; turg-id, -escent; pedantic, pompous, stilted;

high-flown, -flowing; sententious, rhetorical, declamatory; grandiose; grand-, magn-, alt-iloquent; sesquipedal, -ian; Johnsonian, mouthy; bombastic; fustian; frothy, flashy, flaming, flamboyant.

antithetical, alliterative; figurative &c. 521; artificial &c. (*inelegant*) 579.

Adv. *ore rotundo*; with rounded phrase.

578. Elegance.—N. elegance, purity, grace, ease, felicity, distinction, gracefulness, refinement, readiness &c. *adj.*; concinnity, euphony, numerosity, balance, rhythm, symmetry, proportion; restraint; good taste, propriety.

well rounded –, well turned –, flowing- periods; the right word in the right place; antithesis &c. 577.

purist, stylist.

V. point an antithesis, round a period.

Adj. elegant, polished, classical, Attic, correct, Ciceronian, artistic; chaste, pure, Saxon, academical.

graceful, easy, readable, fluent, flowing, tripping; unaffected, natural, unlaboured; mellifluous; euph-onious, -emistic; rhythmical, balanced, symmetrical.

felicitous, happy, neat; well –, neatly- -put, – expressed.

579. Inelegance. — N. inelegance; vulgarity, bad taste; stiffness &c. *adj.*; unlettered Muse; barbarism; slang &c. 563; solecism &c. 568; mannerism &c. (*affectation*) 855; euphuism; fustian &c. 577; cacophony; want of balance; words that -break the teeth, – dislocate the jaw.

V. be -inelegant &c. *adj.*

Adj. inelegant, graceless, ungraceful, unpolished; harsh, abrupt; dry, stiff, cramped, formal, *guindé*; forced, laboured, awkward; artificial, mannered, ponderous; turgid &c. 577; affected, euphuistic; barbarous, uncouth, grotesque, rude, crude, halting; vulgar, offensive to ears polite.

---

2. *Spoken Language*

580. Voice.—N. voice; vocality; organ, lungs, bellows; good –, fine –, powerful &c. (*loud*) 404 –, musical &c. 413- voice; intonation; tone &c. (*sound*) 402- of voice.

vocalization; cry &c. 411; strain, utterance, prolation; exclam-, ejacul-, vocifer-ation; enunci-, articul-ation; articulate sound, distinctness; clearness, – of articulation; stage whisper; delivery; attack.

accent, -uation; emphasis, stress; broad –, strong –, pure –, native –, foreign- accent; pronunciation.

[Word similarly pronounced] homonym.

orthoepy; euphony &c. (*melody*) 413.

gastri-, ventri-loquism; ventriloquist; polyphon-ism, -ist.

[Science of voice] phonology &c. (*sound*) 402.

V. sing, speak, utter, breathe, voice; give -utterance, – tongue; cry &c.

581. Aphony.—N. aphony, *aphonia*; dumbness &c. *adj.*; obmutescence; absence –, want- of voice; dysphony; silence &c. (*taciturnity*) 585; raucity; harsh &c. 410 –, unmusical &c. 414- voice; *falsetto*, 'childish treble'; mute, dummy, deaf mute.

V. keep silence &c. 585; speak -low, – softly; whisper &c. (*faintness*) 405.

silence; render -mute, – silent &c. 403; muzzle, muffle, suppress, smother, gag, strike dumb, dumb-found, -founder; drown the voice, put to silence, stop one's mouth, cut one short, stick in the throat.

Adj. aphon-ous, -ic, dumb, mute; deaf-mute, – and dumb; mum; tonguetied; breath-, tongue-, voice-, speech-, word-less; mute as a -fish, – stockfish, – mackerel; silent &c. (*taciturn*) 585; muzzled; in-articulate, -audible.

croaking, raucous, hoarse, husky,

(*shout*) 411; ejaculate, rap out; vocalize, prolate, articulate, enunciate, enounce, pronounce, accentuate, aspirate, deliver, mouth; emit, murmur, whisper, – in the ear, croon, yodel.

Adj. vocal, phonetic, oral; ejaculatory, articulate, distinct, stertorous; enunciative; accentuated, aspirated; euphonious &c. (*melodious*) 413.

582. Speech.—**N.** speech, faculty of speech; locution, talk, parlance, verbal intercourse, prolation, oral communication, word of mouth, *parole*, palaver, prattle; effusion.

oration, recitation, delivery, say, address, speech, lecture, harangue, sermon, *tirade*, screed, formal speech, salutatory, peroration; prelection; speechifying; soliloquy &c. 589; allocution &c. 586; interlocution &c. 588.

oratory; elo-cution, -quence; rhetoric, declamation; grandi-, multiloquence; burst of eloquence; facundity; talkativeness; flow –, command- of -words, – language; *copia verborum*; power of speech, gift of the gab; *usus loquendi*.

speaker &c. *v.*; spokesman; pro-, inter-locutor; mouthpiece, Hermes; ora-tor, -trix, -tress; Demosthenes, Cicero; rhetorician; stump –, platform-orator, tub-thumper; elocutionist; speech-maker, patterer, *improvisatore*.

V. speak, – of; say, utter, pronounce, deliver, give utterance to; utter –, pour- forth; breathe, let fall, come out with; rap –, blurt- out; have on one's lips; have at the -end, – tip- of one's tongue.

break silence; open one's -lips, – mouth; lift –, raise- one's voice; give –, wag the- tongue; talk, outspeak; put in a word or two.

hold forth; make –, deliver- -a speech &c. *n.*; speechify, harangue, declaim, stump, flourish, spout, rant, recite, lecture, preach, sermonize, discourse, be on one's legs; have –, say- one's say; expatiate &c. (*speak at length*) 573; speak one's mind.

soliloquize &c. 589; tell &c. (*inform*) 527; speak to &c. 586; talk together &c. 588.

be -eloquent &c. *adj.*; have -a tongue in one's head, – the gift of the gab &c. *n.*

pass –, escape- one's lips; fall from the -lips, – mouth.

Adj. speaking &c., spoken &c. *v.*; oral, lingual, phonetic, not written, unwritten, outspoken; elo-quent, -cutionary; orat-, rhet-orical; declamatory; grandiloquent &c. 577; talkative &c. 584.

dry, hollow, sepulchral, hoarse as a raven.

Adv. with -bated breath, – the finger on the lips; *sotto voce*; in a -low tone, – cracked voice, – broken voice; in an aside.

Phr. *vox faucibus hæsit.*

———

583. [Imperfect Speech.] **Stammering.**—**N.** inarticulateness; stammering &c. *v.*; hesitation &c. *v.*; impediment in one's speech; aphasia, titubancy, traulism; whisper &c. (*faint sound*) 405; lisp, drawl, tardiloquence; nasal -tone, – accent; twang; *falsetto* &c. (*want of voice*) 581; broken -voice, – accents, – sentences.

brogue &c. 563; slip of the tongue, *lapsus linguæ.*

V. stammer, stutter, hesitate, falter, hammer; balbu-tiate, -cinate; haw hum and haw, be unable to put two words together.

mumble, mutter; maund, -er; whisper &c. 405; mince, lisp; jabber, gabble. gibber; sp-, spl-utter; muffle, mump; drawl, mouth; croak; speak -thick, – through the nose; snuffle, clip one's words; murder the -language, – King's (*or* Queen's) English; mis-pronounce, -say.

Adj. stammering &c. *v.*; inarticulate, guttural, nasal; tremulous.

Adv. *sotto voce* &c. (*faintly*) 405.

———

Adv. orally &c. *adj.*; by word of mouth, *vivâ voce*, from the lips of.
Phr. quoth –, said- he &c.

584. Loquacity. — N. loquac-ity,
-iousness; talkativeness &c. *adj.*; garrulity; multiloquence, much speaking,
effusion, wordiness.

jaw; gab, -ble; jabber, chatter; prate,
prattle, cackle, clack; twaddle, twattle,
rattle; *caquet, -terie*; blabber, *bavardage*,
bibble-babble, gibble-gabble; small talk
&c. (*converse*) 588.

fluency, flippancy, volubility, flowing tongue; flow, – of words; *flux de
-bouche, – mots, – paroles; copia verborum, cacoëthes loquendi*; verbosity &c.
(*diffuseness*) 573; gift of the gab &c.
(*eloquence*) 582.

talker; chatter-er, -box; babbler &c.
v.; rattle; ranter; sermonizer, proser,
driveller; windbag; gossip &c. (*converse*) 588; magpie, jay, parrot, poll,
Babel; *moulin à paroles*.

V. be -loquacious &c. *adj.*; talk
glibly, pour forth, patter; prate,
palaver, prose, chatter, prattle, clack,
jabber, jaw; rattle, – on; twaddle,
twattle; babble, gabble; out-talk; talk
oneself -out of breath, – hoarse;
maunder, gush, blather; talk a donkey's hind leg off; expatiate &c. (*speak
at length*) 573; gossip &c. (*converse*) 588;
din in the ears &c. (*repeat*) 104; talk
-at random, – nonsense &c. 497; be hoarse with talking.

Adj. loquacious, talkative, conversational, garrulous, linguacious,
multiloquous; chattering &c. *v.*; chatty &c. (*sociable*) 892; declamatory &c. 582; open-mouthed.

fluent, voluble, glib, flippant; long-tongued, -winded &c. (*diffuse*) 573.

Adv. trippingly on the tongue; glibly &c. *adj.*
Phr. the tongue running -fast, – loose, – on wheels.

585. Taciturnity.—N. silence, muteness, obmutescence; taciturnity, paucil-
oquy, costiveness, curtness; reserve,
reticence &c. (*concealment*) 528; *aposiopesis.*

man of few words.

V. be -silent &c. *adj.*; keep silence;
hold one's -tongue, – peace, – jaw; not
speak &c. 582; say nothing; seal –,
close –, put a padlock on- the -lips,
– mouth; put a bridle on one's tongue;
keep one's tongue between one's teeth;
make no sign, not let a word escape
one; keep a secret &c. 528; not have a
word to say; lay –, place- the finger on
the lips; render mute &c. 581.

stick in one's throat.

Adj. silent, mute, mum; silent as
-a post, – a stone, – the grave &c. (*still*)
403; dumb &c. 581.

taciturn, sparing of words; close,
– mouthed, – tongued; laconic, costive,
inconversable, curt; reserved; reticent
&c. (*concealing*) 528.

Int. tush! silence! mum! hush! *chut!*
hist! tut! &c. 403.

---

586. Allocution. — N. allocution,
alloquy, address; speech &c. 582;
apostrophe, interpellation, appeal, invocation, salutation; word in the ear.

[Feigned dialogue] dialogism.

platform &c. 542; audience &c. (*interview*) 588.

V. speak to, address, accost, make up to, apostrophize, appeal to,
invoke; hail, salute; call to, halloo.

take -aside, – by the button, button-hole; talk to in private.

lecture &c. (*make a speech*) 582.

Int. soho! halloo! hey! hist! hi!

587. Response &c., *see* Answer 462.

---

588. Interlocution.—N. interlocution; collocution, colloquy, converse, conversation, confabulation, talk, discourse, verbal intercourse; communion, oral communication, commerce; dia-, duo-, tria-logue.

causerie, chat, chit-chat; small –, table –, tea-table –, town –, village –, idle- talk; tattle, gossip, tittle-tattle; babble, -ment; *tripotage*, cackle, prittle-prattle, *on dit*; talk of the -town, – village.

conference, parley, interview, audience, *pourparler*; *tête-à-tête*; reception, *conversazione*; congress &c. (*council*) 696; pow-wow.

hall of audience, *durbar*, coliseum, assembly hall, auditorium.

palaver, debate, logomachy, war of words, controversy.

talker, gossip, tattler; Paul Pry; tabby; chatterer &c. (*loquacity*) 584; interlocutor &c. (*spokesman*) 582; conversation-ist, -alist; dialogist.

'the feast of reason and the flow of soul'; *mollia tempora fandi*.

V. talk together, converse, confabulate; hold –, carry on –, join in –, engage in- a conversation; put in a word; shine in conversation; bandy words; parley; palaver; chat, gossip, tattle; prate &c. (*loquacity*) 584.

discourse –, confer –, commune –, commerce- with; hold -converse, – conference, – intercourse; talk it over; be closeted with; talk with one -in private, – *tête-à-tête*.

Adj. conversing &c. *v.*; interlocutory; convers-ational, -able; discursive, -coursive; chatty &c. (*sociable*) 892; colloquial, *tête-à-tête*, confabulatory.

589. Soliloquy.—N. soliloquy, monologue, apostrophe.

solilo-quist, -quizer, monologist.

V. soliloquize; say –, talk- to oneself; say aside, think aloud, apostrophize.

Adj. soliloquizing &c. *v.*

Adv. aside.

---

3. *Written Language*

590. Writing.—N. writing &c. *v.*; chiro-, stelo-, cero-graphy, graphology; stylography; pen-craft, -script, -manship; quill-driving; typewriting.

writing, manuscript, MS., *literæ scriptæ*; these presents.

stroke –, dash- of the pen; *coup de plume*; line; pen and ink.

letter &c. 561; uncial writing, cuneiform character, arrow-head, Ogham, Runes, futhorc; hieroglyphic, hieratic, demotic; script; contraction.

short-hand; steno-, brachy-, tachy-graphy; secret writing, writing in cipher; crypt-, stegan-ography; phono-, pasi-, poly-, logo-graphy.

copy; tran-, re-script; draft, rough –, fair- copy; handwriting; signature, sign-manual; auto-, mono-, holo-graph; hand, fist; mark.

calligraphy; good –, running –,

591. Printing.—N. printing; block –, type- printing, lino-, mono-type; plate printing &c. (*engraving*) 558; the press &c. (*publication*) 531; composition.

print, letterpress, text, matter, standing type; context, note, page, column; over-running; head-, foot-line; title.

typography; stereo-, electro-, apro-type; type, black letter, heavy type, font, fount; pi, pie; capitals &c. (*letters*) 561; diamond, pearl, nonpareil, minion, brevier, bourgeois, long primer, small pica, pica, english, great primer.

folio &c. (*book*) 593; copy, impression, pull, proof, galley –, author's –, page- proof, revise.

printer, compositor, reader; printer's devil.

V. print; compose; put –, go- to press; pass –, see- through the press;

flowing –, cursive –, legible –, copper-plate –, round –, bold- hand.

cacography, *griffonage, barbouillage*; bad –, cramped –, crabbed –, illegible-hand; scribble &c. *v.; pattes de mouche*; ill-formed letters; pot-hooks and hangers.

publish &c. 531; bring out; appear in –, rush into- print.

Adj. printed &c. *v.*; in type; typo-graphical &c. *n.*

stationery; pen, quill, goose-quill, reed; stylographic-, fountain-pen; pencil, style, stylus; paper, foolscap, parchment, vellum, papyrus, pad, tablet, block, note-book, slate, marble, pillar, table, black board.

ink-bottle, -pot, -stand, -well, -horn; typewriter.

transcription &c. (*copy*) 21; inscription &c. (*record*) 551; super-scription &c. (*indication*) 550.

composition, authorship; *cacoëthes scribendi*.

writer, scribe, amanuensis, scrivener, secretary, clerk, penman, copyist, transcriber, quill-driver; writer for the press &c. (*author*) 593.

shorthand writer, stenographer; typewriter, typist.

V. write, pen; copy, engross; write out, – fair; transcribe; scribble, scrawl, scrabble, scratch; interline; stain paper; write down &c. (*record*) 551; sign &c. (*attest*) 467; take down, – in shorthand; typewrite, type.

compose, indite, draw up, redact, draft, formulate; dictate; in-scribe, throw on paper, dash off; concoct.

take -up the pen, – pen in hand; shed –, spill –, dip one's pen in- ink.

Adj. writing &c. *v.*; written &c. *v.*; in -writing, – black and white; under one's hand.

uncial, Runic, cuneiform, hieroglyphical &c. *n.*

Adv. *currente calamo*; pen in hand.

592. Correspondence. — N. corre-spondence, letter, epistle, note, *billet*, post-, letter-card, missive, circular, form letter; favour, *billet-doux*; des-, dis-patch; *bulletin*, communication &c. 532; these presents; rescript, -ion; post &c. (*messenger*) 534; letter writer, correspondent.

V. correspond, – with; write –, send a letter- to; keep up a correspondence; drop a line to; despatch; communicate with; circularize.

Adj. epistolary.

593. Book.—N. book, -let; writing, work, volume, tome, opuscule; tract, -ate; *livret*; brochure, *libretto*, hand-book, treatise, text-book, codex, man-ual, pamphlet, monograph, enchiridion, circular, publication; book of poems; novel; chap-book.

part, issue, number, *livraison*; album, portfolio; periodical, serial, magazine, ephemeris, annual, journal.

paper, bill, sheet, broadsheet, screed; leaf, -let; fly-leaf, page; quire, ream.

chapter, section, head, article, para-graph, passage, clause, supplement, appendix; *feuilleton*.

folio, quarto, octavo; duo-, sexto-, octo-decimo.

en-, cyclopædia, dictionary, lexicon, thesaurus, concordance, an-thology, bibliography; compilation, compendium, catalogue &c. 86; library, bibliotheca; the press &c. (*publication*) 531.

writer, author, *littérateur, homme de lettres*, essayist, journalist, publicist; scribe, penman, war –, special –, correspondent; pen, scribbler, the scribbling race; ghost, hack, literary hack, Grub-street writer; writer for –, gentleman of –, representative of- the press; reporter, penny-a-liner; editor, sub-editor; literary agent; playwright &c. 599; poet &c. 597.

bookseller, publisher; biblio-pole, -polist, -grapher; librarian; book -collector, – worm.

book -shop, – club, circulating –, lending –, public- library; publishing house.

knowledge of books, bibliography; book-learning &c. (*knowledge*) 490.

594. Description.—N. description, account, statement, report; *exposé* &c. (*disclosure*) 529; specification, particulars, scenario, plot; state –, summary- of facts; brief &c. (*abstract*) 596; return &c. (*record*) 551; *catalogue raisonné* &c. (*list*) 86; guide-book &c. (*information*) 527.

delineation &c. (*representation*) 554; sketch, vignette; monograph; minute –, detailed –, particular –, circumstantial –, graphic- account; narration, recital, rehearsal, relation.

histori-, chron-ography; historic Muse, Clio; history; bi-, autobi-ography; necrology, obituary.

narrative, history; memoir, memorials; annals &c. (*chronicle*) 551; tradition, legend, saga, epic, epos, story, tale, historiette; personal narrative, journal, letters, life, adventures, fortunes, experiences, confessions; anecdote, ana, *trait*.

work of fiction, short story, novelette, novel, romance, penny dreadful, shilling shocker, Minerva press; fairy –, nursery- tale; fable, allegory, parable, apologue.

relator &c. *v.*; *raconteur*; historian &c. (*recorder*) 553; biographer, fabulist, novelist, story teller, romancer, teller of tales, spinner of yarns, anecdotist.

V. describe; set forth &c. (*state*) 535; draw a picture, picture; portray &c. (*represent*) 554; characterize, particularize; narrate, relate, recite, recount, sum up, run over, recapitulate, rehearse, fight one's battles over again.

unfold &c. (*disclose*) 529- a tale; tell; give –, render- an account of; report, make a report, draw up a statement.

detail; enter into –, descend to- -particulars, – details.

Adj. descriptive, graphic, narrative, epic, suggestive, well-drawn; historic; auto-, biographical, realistic, expository, tradition-al, -ary; legendary; fabulous, mythical; anecdotic, storied; described &c. *v.*

595. Dissertation.—N. dissertation, treatise, essay; *thesis*, theme; tract, -ate, -ation, excursus; discourse, memoir, disquisition, lecture, sermon, homily, pandect.

commentary, review, *critique*, criticism, article; lead-er, -ing article, editorial; argument, running commentary.

investigation &c. (*inquiry*) 461; study &c. (*consideration*) 451; discussion &c. (*reasoning*) 476; exposition &c. (*explanation*) 522.

commentator, critic, essayist, pamphleteer; publicist, reviewer, leader writer, editor, annotator.

V. dissert –, descant –, write –, touch- upon a subject; dissertate; treat of –, take up –, ventilate –, discuss –, deal with –, go into –, canvass –, handle –, do justice to- a subject; comment, criticize, interpret &c. 522; argue.

Adj. dis-cursive, -coursive; disquisitional, disquisitionary; expository, critical.

596. Compendium.—N. compend, -ium; abstract, *précis*, epitome, *multum in parvo*, analysis, pandect, digest, sum and substance, brief, abridgment, summary, *aperçu*, draft, minute, note; synopsis, textbook, *conspectus*, outlines, syllabus, contents, heads, prospectus.

album; scrap -, note -, memorandum -, commonplace- book; extracts, *excerpta*, cuttings; fugitive -pieces, - writings; *spicilegium*, flowers, anthology, miscellany, *collectanea, analecta*; compilation.

recapitulation, *résumé*, review.

abbrevia-tion, -ture; contraction; shortening &c. 201; compression &c. 195.

V. abridge, abstract, epitomize, summarize; make -, prepare -, draw -, compile- an abstract &c. *n.*

recapitulate, review, skim, run over, sum up.

abbreviate &c. (*shorten*) 201; condense &c. (*compress*) 195; compile &c. (*collect*) 72; edit, blue pencil.

Adj. compendious, synoptic, analectic, analytical; abridged &c. *v.*

Adv. in -short, - epitome, - substance, - few words.

Phr. it lies in a nutshell.

---

597. Poetry.—N. poetry, poetics, poesy, Muse, Calliope, tuneful Nine, Parnassus, Helicon, Pierides, Pierian spring, afflatus, inspiration.

versification, rhyming, making verses; prosody, scansion, orthometry.

poem; epic, - poem; epopee, *epopæa*, ode, epode, idyl, lyric, eclogue, pastoral, bucolic, georgic, dithyramb, anacreontic, sonnet, roundelay, *rondel, rondoletto, rondeau, rondo,* triolet; madrigal, canzonet, *cento*, monody, elegy, palinode; rhapsody.

dramatic -, lyric- poetry; opera; posy, anthology.

song, ballad, lay; love -, drinking -, war -, folk -, sea- song; lullaby; music &c. 415; nursery rhymes.

[Bad poetry] doggerel, Hudibrastic verse, prose run mad; macaronics; macaronic -, leonine- verse; runes.

canto, stanza, distich, verse, line, couplet, triplet, quatrain, sestet; *strophe, antistrophe,* refrain, chorus, burden.

verse, rhyme, assonance, crambo, metre, measure, foot, numbers, strain, rhythm; accentuation &c. (*voice*) 580; iambus, dactyl, spondee, trochee, anapæst &c.; hex-, pent-ameter; Alexandrine; blank verse, alliteration.

elegiacs &c. *adj.*; elegiac &c. *adj.* -verse, - metre, - poetry.

poet, - laureate; laureate; minor poet, bard, lyrist, scald, troubadour, *trouvère*; minstrel; minne-, meister-singer; *improvisatore*; versifier, sonneteer; ballad monger; rhym-er, -ist, -ester; poetaster.

V. poetize, sing, versify, make verses, rhyme, scan.

Adj. poetic, -al; lyric, -al; tuneful; epic; dithyrambic &c. *n.*; metrical; a-, catalectic; elegiac, iambic, trochaic, spondaic, dactylic, anapæstic; Ionic, Sapphic, Alcaic, Pindaric.

598. Prose.—N. prose, - writer pros-aism, -aist, -er.

V. prose, write prose.

write -prose, - in prose.

Adj. pros-y, -aic; unpoetical.

rhymeless, unrhymed, in prose, not in verse.

---

599. The Drama.—N. the -drama, - stage, - theatre, - play; theatricals, dramaturgy, histrionic art, buskin, sock, *cothurnus,* Melpomene and Thalia, Thespis.

play, drama, stage-play, piece, five-act play, tragedy, comedy, opera, comic opera, *vaudeville, comedietta, lever de rideau,* curtain raiser, interlude, afterpiece, exode, farce, *divertissement, extravaganza,* burletta, harlequinade, pantomime, mimodrama, burlesque, *opéra bouffe*, musical comedy, review, revue, intimate revue, variety, cabaret entertainment, *ballet*, *spectacle*, masque, *drame*, *comédie drame*; melo-drama, -drame; *comédie larmoyante*, emotional drama, sensation drama, tragi-, farcical-comedy; mono-drame, -logue; duologue; trilogy; charade, *proverbe*; mystery, miracle –, morality- play.

act, scene, *tableau*; in-, intro-duction; pro-, epi-logue, curtain; *libretto*, book, script.

performance, representation, show, *mise en scène*, stagery, *jeu de théâtre*, stage-craft; acting; gesture &c. 550; impersonation &c. 554; stage business, gag, patter, buffoonery.

theatre; play-, opera-house; house; music hall; *cabaret*; amphi-theatre, circus, hippodrome; puppet-show, *fantoccini*; *marionnettes*, Punch and Judy.

cinema, -tograph-, picture –, theatre, the pictures, the movies, the talkies.

auditory, *auditorium*, front of the house, stalls, boxes, balcony, dress –, upper- -circle, – boxes, amphitheatre, pit, gallery; *foyer*; green-room; dressing rooms, *coulisses*.

flat; drop, – scene; wing, screen, side-scene; transformation scene, curtain, act-drop, safety –, fire- curtain; *proscenium*, forestage.

stage, revolving stage, scene, the boards; star –, grave –, trap, mezzanine floor; flies; gridiron, floats, battens, footlights; lime –, spot –, flood –, bunch-lights; scenery, set, *décor*; orchestra.

theatrical -costume, – properties, props.

part, *rôle*, character, cast, *dramatis personæ*; *répertoire*.

actor, player; stage –, strolling- player; old –, stager, performer; mime, -r; *artiste*; com-, trag-edian, straight man; *tragédienne*, Thespian, Roscius, star.

pantomimist, clown, harlequin, *buffo*, buffoon, *farceur*, *grimacier*, pantaloon, columbine; *Pierrot*, *Pierrette*; punch, -inello; *pulcinell-o*, ·*a*; mute, *figurante*, general utility; super, -numerary, extra.

mummer, guiser, guisard, gysart, masque.

mountebank, Jack Pudding; tumbler, posture-master, acrobat, equilibrist, juggler, contortionist; *danseuse*, *ballerina*, ballet -dancer, - girl, *coryphée*; *bayadère*, *geisha*; chorus -singer, – girl.

company; first tragedian, *prima donna*, lead, leading lady, pro-tagonist; *jeune premier*; juvenile lead, *débutant*, -*e*; light –, genteel –, low- -comedy, – comedian; *soubrette*, walking gentleman, *amoroso*, heavy, heavy father, *ingénue*, *jeune veuve*, *commère*, *compère*.

property man, *costumier*, machinist, stage hand, electrician, prompter, call-boy; director, manager; stage –, business- manager; *entrepreneur*, *impresario*, producer, press agent.

dramatic -author, – writer; play-writer, -wright; dramatist, mimo-grapher; dramatic critic.

V. act, play, perform; stage, produce, put on the stage; personate &c. 554; mimic &c. (*imitate*) 19; enact; play –, act –, go through –, perform- a part; rehearse, spout, gag, rant; 'strut and fret one's hour upon a stage'; tread the -stage, – boards; come out; star.

Adj. dramatic; theatric, -al; scenic, histrionic, comic, tragic, bus-kined, farcical, tragi-comic, melodramatic, operatic; stagey, spectacular; stagestruck.

Adv. on the -stage, – boards; before -the floats, – an audience; in the limelight, behind the footlights; behind the scenes.

CLASS V

Words relating to THE VOLUNTARY POWERS*

Division (I.) INDIVIDUAL VOLITION

Section I. Volition in General

1°. *Acts of Volition*

600. Will.—N. will, volition, co-nation†, velleity; will and pleasure, free-will; freedom &c. 748; discretion; choice, inclination, intent, purpose, option &c. (*choice*) 609; voluntariness; spontane-ity, -ousness; originality.

pleasure, wish, desire, mind; frame of mind &c. (*inclination*) 602; intention &c. 620; predetermination &c. 611; self-control &c. determination &c. (*resolution*) 604; will-power.

V. will, list; see –, think- fit; determine &c. (*resolve*) 604; settle &c. (*choose*) 609; volunteer.

have a will of one's own; do what one chooses &c. (*freedom*) 748; have it all one's own way; have one's -will, – own way.

use –, exercise- one's discretion; take -upon oneself, – one's own course, – the law into one's own hands; do -of one's own accord, – upon one's own -responsibility, – authority; take the bit between one's teeth; take responsibility; originate &c. (*cause*) 153.

Adj. voluntary, volitive, volitional, wilful; free &c. 748; optional; discretion-al, -ary; volitient; dictatorial.

minded &c. (*willing*) 602; prepense &c. (*predetermined*) 611; intended &c. 620; autocratic; unbidden &c. (bid &c. 741); spontaneous; original &c. (*causal*) 153.

Adv. voluntarily &c. *adj.*; at -will, – pleasure; *à -volonté, – discrétion; al piacere; ad -libitum, – arbitrium*; as -one thinks proper, – it seems good to.

601. Necessity.—N. involuntariness; instinct, blind –, natural- impulse; inborn –, innate- proclivity; the force of circumstances.

necessi-ty, -tation, necessarianism; obligation; compulsion &c. 744; subjection &c. 749; stern –, hard –, dire –, imperious –, inexorable –, iron –, adverse- -necessity, – fate; what must be.

desti-ny, -nation; fatality, fate, *kismet*, doom, foredoom, election, predestination; pre-, fore-ordination; lot, fortune; fatalism, determinism; inevitableness &c. *adj.*; spell &c. 993.

star, -s; planet, -s; astral influence; sky, Fates, Norns, *Parcæ*, Sisters three, Clotho, Lachesis, Atropos; book of fate; God's will, will of Heaven; wheel of Fortune, Ides of March, Hobson's choice.

last -shift, – resort; *dernier ressort; pis aller* &c. (*substitute*) 147; necessaries &c. (*requirement*) 630.

necess-arian, -itarian; fatalist, determinist; automaton.

V. lie under a necessity; be -fated, – doomed, – destined &c., – in for, – under the necessity of; have no -choice, – alternative; be- obliged –, forced –, driven –, one's -fate &c. *n.*-to; be -pushed to the wall, – driven into a corner, – unable to help, – drawn irresistibly.

destine, doom, foredoom, devote; pre-destine, -ordain; cast a spell &c. 992; necessitate; compel &c. 744.

* Conative powers or faculties (Hamilton).   †Hamilton.

of one's own -accord, – free will; *proprio* –, *suo* –, *ex mero- motu*; out of one's own head; by choice &c. 609; purposely &c. (*intentionally*) 620; deliberately &c. 611.

Phr. *stet pro ratione voluntas*; *sic volo sic jubeo*.

Adj. necessary; needful &c. (*requisite*) 630.

fated; destined &c. *v.*; fateful; elect; spell-bound.

compulsory &c. (*compel*) 744; uncontrollable, inevitable, unavoidable, irresistible, irrevocable, inexorable, binding; avoid-, resist-less; written in the book of fate.

involuntary, instinctive, automatic, blind, mechanical; un-conscious, -witting, -thinking; unintentional &c. (*undesigned*) 621; impulsive &c. 612.

Adv. necessarily &c. *adv.*; of -necessity, – course; *ex necessitate rei*; needs must; perforce &c. 744; *nolens volens*; will he nil he, willy nilly, *bon gré mal gré*, willing or unwilling, *coûte que coûte*, forcefully. *faute de mieux*; by stress of; if need be.

Phr. it cannot be helped; there is no- help for, – helping- it; it -will, – must, – must needs- be, – be so, – have its way; the die is cast; *jacta est alea*; *che sarà sarà*; 'it is written'; one's- days are numbered, – fate is sealed; *Fata obstant*; *dis aliter visum*.

---

602. Willingness.—N. willingness, voluntariness &c. *adj.*; willing mind, heart.

disposition, inclination, leaning, *animus*; frame of mind, humour, mood, vein; bent &c. (*turn of mind*) 820; *penchant* &c. (*desire*) 865; aptitude &c. 698.

doc-ility, -ibleness, tractability; persuasi-bleness, -bility; pliability &c. (*softness*) 324.

geniality, cordiality; goodwill; alacrity, readiness, earnestness, forwardness, enthusiasm; zeal, eagerness &c. (*desire*) 865.

assent &c. 488; compliance &c. 762; pleasure &c. (*will*) 600.

labour of love, self-appointed task; volunteer, -ing, gratuitous service; unpaid worker, amateur.

V. be -willing &c. *adj.*; incline, lean to, mind, propend; had as lief; lend –, give –, turn- a willing ear; have -a, – half a, – a great- mind to; hold –, cling- to; desire &c. 865.

see –, think- -good, – fit, – proper; acquiescence &c. (*assent*) 488; comply with &c. 762.

swallow –, nibble at- the bait; gorge the hook; swallow hook, line and sinker; have –, make- no scruple of; make no bones of; jump –, catch- at; meet half way; volunteer, offer oneself &c. 763.

---

603. Unwillingness.—N. unwillingness &c. *adj.*; indispos-ition, -edness; disinclination, aversation, aversion; nolleity, nolition; renitence; reluctance; indifference &c. 866; backwardness &c. *adj.*; slowness &c. 275; want of -alacrity, – readiness; indocility &c. (*obstinacy*) 606.

scrupul-ousness, -osity; qualms of conscience, delicacy, demur, scruple, qualm, shrinking, recoil; hesitation &c. (*irresolution*) 605; fastidiousness &c. 868.

averseness &c. (*dislike*) 867; dissent &c. 489; refusal &c. 764.

slacker, scrimshanker, *embusqué*, unwilling worker, forced labour.

V. be -unwilling &c. *adj.*; nill; dislike &c. 867; grudge, begrudge; not be able to find it in one's heart to, not have the stomach to.

demur, stick at, scruple, stickle; hang fire, run rusty, slack, shirk, scamp, give up, fight shy of, not pull fair; recoil, shrink, swerve; hesitate &c. 605; avoid &c. 623.

oppose &c. 708; dissent &c. 489; refuse &c. 764.

Adj. unwilling; not in the vein, loth, shy of, disinclined, indisposed, averse, reluctant, not content; adverse &c. (*opposed*) 708; laggard, backward, remiss, slack, slow to; renitent; indifferent &c. 866; scrupulous; squeamish

Adj. willing, minded, fain, disposed, inclined, favourable; favourably-minded, -inclined, -disposed; nothing loth; in the -vein, – mood, – humour, – mind.

ready, forward, enthusiastic, earnest, eager; bent upon &c. (*desirous*) 865; predisposed, propense.

docile; persua-dable, -sible; suasible, easily persuaded, facile, easy-going; amenable; tractable &c. (*pliant*) 324; genial, gracious, cordial, hearty; content &c. (*assenting*) 488.

voluntary, gratuitous, spontaneous; unasked &c. (ask &c. 765); unforced &c. (*free*) 748.

Adv. willingly &c. *adj.*; fain, freely, as lief, heart and soul; with -pleasure, – all one's heart, – open arms; with -good, – right good- will; *de bonne volonté, ex animo; con amore*, heart in hand, nothing loth, without reluctance, of one's own accord, graciously, with a good grace, without demur.

à la bonne heure; by all -means, – manner of means; to one's heart's content; yes &c. (*assent*) 488.

Int. sure, -ly! of course!

&c. (*fastidious*) 868; repugnant &c. (*dislike*) 867; rest-iff, -ive; demurring &c. *v.*; unconsenting &c. (*refusing*) 764; involuntary &c. 601; grudging, irreconcilable.

Adv. unwillingly &c. *adj.*; grudgingly, with a heavy heart; with -a bad, – an ill- grace; against –, sore against- -one's wishes, – one's will, – the grain; *invitâ Minervâ; à contre cœur; malgré soi*; in spite of -one's teeth, – oneself; *nolens volens* &c. (*necessity*) 601; perforce &c. 744; under protest; no &c. 536; not for the world, far be it from me; not if I can help it; if I must I must.

---

604. Resolution.—**N.** determination, will; iron –, unconquerable- will; will of one's own, decision, resolution, backbone, grit; strength of -mind, – will; resolve &c. (*intent*) 620; intransigeance; firmness &c. (*stability*) 150; energy, manliness, vigour; game, pluck; resoluteness &c. (*courage*) 861; zeal &c. 682; aplomb; desperation; devot-ion, -edness.

mastery over self; self-control, -command, -mastery, -possession, -reliance, -government, -restraint, -conquest, -denial; moral -courage, – strength, – fibre; persèverance &c. 604a; tenacity; obstinacy &c. 606; bull-dog; British lion.

V. have -determination &c. *n.*; know one's own mind; be -resolved &c. *adj.*; make up one's mind, will, resolve, determine; decide &c. (*judgment*) 480; form –, come to- a -determination, – resolution, – resolve; conclude, fix, seal, determine once for all, bring to a crisis, drive matters to an extremity; take a decisive step &c. (*choice*) 609; take upon oneself &c. (*undertake*) 676.

devote oneself –, give oneself up- to; throw away the scabbard, kick down

605. Irresolution.—**N.** irresolution, infirmity of purpose, indecision; in-, un-determination, loss of will power; unsettlement; uncertainty &c. 475; demur, suspense; hesi-tating &c. *v.*, -tation, -tancy; vacillation; ambivalence; changeableness &c. 149; fluctuation; alternation &c. (*oscillation*) 314; caprice &c. 608; lukewarmness.

fickleness, levity, *légèreté*; pliancy &c. (*softness*) 324; weakness; timidity &c. 860; cowardice &c. 862; half measures.

waverer, ass between two bundles of hay; shuttlecock, butterfly; timeserver, opportunist, turn coat.

V. be -irresolute &c. *adj.*; hang –, keep- in suspense; leave '*ad referendum*'; think twice about, pause; dawdle &c. (*inactivity*) 683; remain neuter; dilly-dally, hesitate, boggle, hover, wobble, shilly-shally, hum and haw, demur, not know one's own mind; debate, balance; dally –, coquet- with; will and will not, *chasser-balancer*; go half-way, compromise, make a compromise; be thrown off one's balance, stagger like a drunken man; be afraid &c. 860; let 'I dare not' wait upon 'I would'; falter, waver.

the ladder, nail one's colours to the mast, set one's back against the wall, set one's teeth, put one's foot down, burn one's bridges, take one's stand; stand firm &c. (*stability*) 150; steel oneself; stand no nonsense, not listen to the voice of the charmer.

buckle to; put –, lay –, set- one's shoulder to the wheel; put one's heart into; run the gauntlet, make a dash at, take the bull by the horns; beard the lion in his den; rush –, plunge- *in medias res*; go in for; insist upon, make a point of; set one's heart, – mind- upon.

stick at nothing; make short work of &c. (*activity*) 682; not stick at trifles; go -all lengths, – the whole hog; persist &c. (*persevere*) 604a; go down with colours flying, die game; go through fire and water, ride in the whirlwind and direct the storm.

Adj. resolved &c. *v.*; determined; strong-willed, -minded; resolute &c. (*brave*) 861; self-possessed, plucky, tenacious; decided, definitive, peremptory; un-hesitating, -flinching, -shrinking; firm, cast iron, indomitable, game to the backbone; inexorable, relentless, not to be -shaken, – put down; *tenax propositi*; inflexible &c. (*hard*) 323; obstinate &c. 606; steady &c. (*persevering*) 604a; unbending, unyielding, irrevocable; firm as a rock; grim.

earnest, serious; set –, bent –, intent- upon.

steeled –, proof- against; *in utrumque paratus*.

Adv. resolutely &c. *adj.*; in –, in good- earnest; seriously, joking apart, earnestly, heart and soul; on one's metal; manfully, like a man, with a high hand; with a strong hand &c. (*exertion*) 686.

at any -rate, – risk, – hazard, – price, – cost, – sacrifice; at all -hazards, – risks, – events; cost what it may; *coûte que coûte*; *à tort et à travers*; once for all; neck or nothing; rain or shine; with colours nailed to the mast.

Phr. *spes sibi quisque.*

vacillate &c. 149; change &c. 140; retract &c. 607; fluctuate; alternate &c. (*oscillate*) 314; keep off and on, play fast and loose; blow hot and cold &c. (*caprice*) 608.

shuffle, palter, blink; trim.

Adj. irresolute, infirm of purpose, double-minded, half-hearted; un-decided, -resolved, -determined; drifting; shilly-shally; fidgety, tremulous; wobbly; hesitating &c. *v.*; off one's balance; at a loss &c. (*uncertain*) 475.

vacillating &c. *v.*; unsteady &c. (*changeable*) 149; unsteadfast, fickle, unreliable, irresponsible, unstable, without ballast; capricious &c. 608; volatile, frothy; light, -some, -minded; giddy; fast and loose.

weak, feeble-minded, frail; timid &c. 860; cowardly &c. 862; facile; pliant &c. (*soft*) 324; unable to say 'no,' easy-going.

revocable, reversible.

Adv. irresolutely &c. *adj.*; irresolvedly; in faltering accents; off and on; from pillar to post; see-saw &c. 314.

Int. 'how happy could I be with either!'

604a. Perseverance.—N. perseverance; continuance &c. (*inaction*) 143; permanence &c. (*absence of change*) 141; firmness &c. (*stability*) 150.

constancy, steadiness; singleness –, tenacity- of purpose; persistence, plodding, patience; sedulity &c. (*industry*) 682; pertina-cy, -city, -ciousness; iteration &c. 104.

bottom, game, pluck, stamina, backbone, grit; indefatiga-bility, -bleness; bulldog courage.

V. persevere, persist; hold -on, – out; die in the last ditch, be in at the death; stick –, cling –, adhere- to; stick to one's text, keep on; keep to –, maintain- one's -course, – ground; bear –, keep –, hold-up; plod; stick to work &c. (*work*) 686; continue &c. 143; follow up; die -in harness, – at one's post.

Adj. persevering, constant; stead-y, -fast; un-deviating, -wavering, -faltering, -swerving, -flinching, -sleeping, -flagging, -drooping; steady as time; uninter-, un-remitting; plodding; industrious &c. 682; strenuous &c. 686; pertinacious; persist-ing, -ent.

solid, sturdy, staunch, stanch, true to oneself; unchangeable &c. 150; unconquerable &c. (*strong*) 159; indomitable, game to the last, indefatigable, untiring, unwearied, never tiring.

Adv. through -evil report and good report, – thick and thin, – fire and water; *per fas et nefas*; without fail, sink or swim, at any price, *vogue la galère*; in sickness and in health.

Phr. never say die; *vestigia nulla retrorsum*.

---

606. Obstinacy.—N. obstinateness &c. *adj.*; obstinacy, tenacity; perseverance &c. 604a; immovability; old school; inflexibility &c. (*hardness*) 323; obdur-acy, -ation; dogged resolution; resolution &c. 604; ruling passion; blind side.

self-will, contumacy, perversity; pervica-cy, -city; indocility.

bigotry, intolerance, dogmatism; opinia-try, -tiveness; fixed idea &c.; intractability, incorrigibility; (*prejudgment*) 481; fanaticism, zealotry, infatuation, monomania, opinionativeness.

mule; opin-ionist, -ionatist, -iator, -ator; stickler, dogmatist, die-hard, bitter-ender; bigot; zealot, enthusiast, fanatic.

V. be -obstinate &c. *adj.*; stickle, take no denial, fly in the face of facts; opinionate, be wedded to an opinion, hug a belief; have one's own way &c. (*will*) 600; persist &c. (*persevere*) 604a; have –, insist on having- the last word.

die -hard, – fighting, fight -against destiny, – to the last ditch; not yield an inch, stand out.

Adj. obstinate, tenacious, stubborn, obdurate, case-hardened; inflexible &c. (*hard*) 323; immovable, not to be moved; inert &c. 172; unchangeable &c. 150; inexorable &c. (*determined*) 604; mulish, obstinate as a mule, pig-headed.

dogged; sullen, sulky; un-moved, -influenced, -affected.

wilful, self-willed, perverse; res-ty, -tive, -tiff; pervicacious, wayward, refractory, unruly; head-y, -strong; *entêté*; contumacious; cross-grained.

---

607. Tergiversation.—N. change of -mind, – intention, – purpose; afterthought.

tergiversation, recantation; palinode, -ody; renunciation; abjur-ation, -ement; defection &c. (*relinquishment*) 624; going over &c. *v.*; apostasy; retract-ion, -ation; withdrawal, disavowal &c. (*negation*) 536; revo-cation, -kement; reversal; repentance &c. 950; *redintegratio amoris*.

coquetry, flirtation; vacillation &c. 605; back-sliding, recidivation.

turn-coat, -tippet; rat, apostate, renegade, mugwump; con-, per-vert; proselyte, deserter; backslider, recidivist; black leg.

time-server, -pleaser; timist, Vicar of Bray, trimmer, ambidexter; weathercock &c. (*changeable*) 149; Janus.

V. change one's -mind, – intention, – purpose, – note; abjure, renounce; withdraw from &c. (*relinquish*) 624; wheel –, turn –, veer- round; turn a *pirouette*; go over –, pass –, change –, skip- from one side to another; go to the right about; box the compass, shift one's ground, go upon another tack; back down, crawl, crawfish.

apostatize, change sides, go over, rat; recant, retract; revoke; rescind &c. (*abrogate*) 756; recall, forswear, abjure, unsay; come -over, – round- to an opinion.

draw in one's horns, eat one's words; eat –, swallow- the leek; swerve, flinch, back out of, retrace one's steps, think better of it; come back –, return- to one's first love; turn over a new leaf &c. (*repent*) 950.

arbitrary, dogmatic, opinionated, positive, bigoted; prejudiced &c. 481; prepossessed, infatuated; stiff-backed, -necked, -hearted; hard-mouthed, hidebound; unyielding; im-pervious, -practicable, -persuasible; unpersuadable; in-, un-tractable; incorrigible, deaf to advice, impervious to reason; crotchety &c. 608.

Adv. obstinately &c. *adj.*

Phr. *non possumus*; no surrender.

———

trim, shuffle, play fast and loose, blow hot and cold, coquet, flirt, hold with the hare but run with the hounds; straddle; *nager entre deux eaux*; wait to see how the -cat jumps, – wind blows.

Adj. changeful &c. 149; irresolute &c. 605; ductile, slippery as an eel, trimming, ambidextrous, timeserving; coquetting &c. *v.*

revocatory, reactionary.

Phr. 'a change came o'er the spirit of my dream.'

———

608. Caprice.—N. caprice, fancy, humour; whim, -sey, -wham; crotchet, *capriccio*, quirk, freak, maggot, fad, vagary, prank, fit, flim-flam, *escapade, boutade,* wild-goose chase; capriciousness &c. *adj.*; kink.

V. be -capricious &c. *adj.*; have a maggot in the brain; take it into one's head, strain at a gnat and swallow a camel; blow hot and cold; play -fast and loose, – fantastic tricks.

Adj. capricious; erratic, eccentric, fitful, hysterical; full of -whims &c. *n.*; maggoty; inconsistent, fanciful, fantastic, whimsical, crotchety, particular, humoursome, freakish, skittish, wanton, wayward; contrary; captious; arbitrary; unrestrained, undisciplined; not amenable to reason; uncomfortable &c. 83; penny wise and pound foolish; fickle &c. (*irresolute*) 605; frivolous, sleeveless, giddy, volatile.

Adv. by fits and starts, without rhyme or reason, at one's own sweet will.

Phr. *nil fuit unquam sic impar sibi*; the deuce is in him.

———

609. Choice.—N. choice, option; discretion &c. (*volition*) 600; preoption; alternative; dilemma; *embarras de choix*; adoption, co-optation; novation; decision &c. (*judgment*) 480.

election, poll, ballot, vote, voice, suffrage, plumper, cumulative vote; *plebiscitum, plébiscite, vox populi; referendum,* electioneering; voting &c. *v.*; franchise; ballot box; slate, ticket.

selection, excerption, gleaning, eclecticism; *excerpta,* gleanings, cuttings, scissors and paste; pick &c. (*best*) 650.

preference, prelation; predilection &c. (*desire*) 865.

V. offer for one's choice, set before; hold out –, present –, offer- the alternative; put to the vote.

use –, exercise –, one's- -discretion, – option; adopt, take up, embrace, espouse; choose, elect, co-opt; take –, make- one's choice; make choice of, fix upon.

vote, poll, hold up one's hand; divide.

settle; decide &c. (*adjudge*) 480; list

609a. Absence of Choice.—N. no –, Hobson's- choice; first come, first served; necessity &c. 601; not a pin to choose &c. (*equality*) 27; any, the first that comes.

neutrality, indifference; indecision &c. (*irresolution*) 605.

V. be -neutral &c. *adj.*; have no choice; waive, not vote; abstain –, refrain- from voting; leave undecided; make a virtue of necessity.

Adj. neu-tral, -ter; indifferent; un-decided &c. (*irresolute*) 605.

Adv. either &c. (*choice*) 609.

———

610. Rejection.—N. rejection, repudiation, exclusion; declination; refusal &c. 764.

V. reject; set –, lay- aside; give up; decline &c. (*refuse*) 764; exclude, except, eliminate; pluck, spin; cast.

repudiate, scout, set at naught; fling –, cast –, thrown –, toss- -to the winds, – to the dogs, – overboard, – away; send to the right about; dis-

&c. (*will*) 600; make up one's mind &c. (*resolve*) 604.

select; pick, – and choose; pick –, single- out, excerpt; cull, glean, winnow; sift –, separate –, winnow- the chaff from the wheat; pick up, pitch upon; pick one's way; indulge one's fancy.

set apart, reserve, mark out for; mark &c. 550.

prefer; have -rather, – as lief; fancy &c. (*desire*) 865; be persuaded &c. 615.

take a -decided, – decisive- step; commit oneself to a course; pass –, cross- the Rubicon; cast in one's lot with; take for better or for worse.

Adj. optional; co-optative; discretional &c. (*voluntary*) 600; on approval.

eclectic; choosing &c. *v.*; preferential; chosen &c. *v.*; choice &c. (*good*) 648.

Adv. optionally &c. *adj.*; at pleasure &c. (*will*) 600; either, – the one or the other; or; at the option of; whether or not; once for all; for one's money.

by -choice, – preference; in preference; rather, before.

claim &c. (*deny*) 536; discard &c. (*eject*) 297, (*have done with*) 678.

Adj. rejected &c. *v.*; reject-aneous, -itious; not -chosen &c. 609, – to be thought of; out of the question.

Adv. neither, – the one nor the other; no &c. 536.

Phr. *non hæc in fœdera.*

---

611. Predetermination. — N. premeditation, -deliberation, -determination, -destination; foreordination; foregone conclusion; *parti pris*; resolve, propendency; intention &c. 620; project &c. 626.

V. pre-determine, -destine, -meditate, -resolve, -concert; foreordain; resolve beforehand.

Adj. pre-pense, -meditated &c. *v.*, -designed; advised, studied, designed, calculated; aforethought; intended &c. 620; foregone.

well-laid, -devised, -weighed; maturely considered; cut and dried; cunning.

Adv. advisedly &c. *adj.*; with premeditation, deliberately, all things considered, with eyes open, in cold blood; intentionally &c. 620.

613. Habit.—N. habit, -ude; assuetude, -faction; wont; run, way.

common –, general –, natural –, ordinary –, habitual- -course, – run, – state- of things; matter of course; beaten -path, – track, – ground.

prescription, custom, use, usage, immemorial usage, practice; tradition; prevalence, observance: conventional-

612. Impulse.—N. impulse, sudden thought; *impromptu*, improvisation; inspiration, hunch, flash, spurt.

improvisatore, *improvisatrice*, improviser, extemporizer; creature of impulse.

V. flash on the mind.

say what comes uppermost; improvise, extemporize; rise to the occasion; spurt.

Adj. extemporaneous, impulsive, indeliberate; improvis-ed, -ate, -atory; un-, unpre-meditated; *improvisé*; unprompted, -guided; natural, unguarded; spontaneous &c. (*voluntary*) 600; instinctive &c. 601.

Adv. extem-pore, -poraneously; offhand, *impromptu, à l'improviste*; improviso; on the spur of the -moment, – occasion.

614. Desuetude.—N. desuetude, disusage; disuse &c. 678; want of -habit, – practice; insitation; newness to; new brooms.

infraction of usage &c. (*unconformity*) 83; non-prevalence; 'a custom more honoured in the breach than the observance.'

V. be -unaccustomed &c. *adj.*; leave

ism, -ity; mode, fashion, vogue; *éti-quette* &c. (*gentility*) 852; order of the day, cry; conformity &c. 82.

habitué, addict.

one's old way, old school, consue-tude, *veteris vestigia flammæ; laudator temporis acti*.

rule, standing order, precedent, routine; red-tape, -tapism; pipe-clay; rut, groove.

cacoëthes; bad -, confirmed -, in-veterate -, intrinsic &c. 5- habit; addiction, trick.

training &c. (*education*) 537; season-ing, hardening, inurement; radication; second nature, acclimatization; knack &c. (*skill*) 698.

V. be -wont &c. *adj.*

fall into a custom &c. (*conform to*) 82; tread -, follow- the beaten -track, - path; *stare super antiquas vias*; move in a rut, run on in a groove, go round like a horse in a mill, go on in the old jog-trot way.

habituate, inure, harden, season, caseharden; accustom, familiar-ize; naturalize, acclimatize; keep one's hand in; train &c. (*educate*) 537.

get into the -way, - knack- of; learn &c. 539; cling -, adhere- to; repeat &c. 104; acquire -, contract -, fall into- a -habit, - trick; addict oneself -, take- to; accustom oneself to.

be -habitual &c. *adj.*; prevail; come into use, become a habit, take root; gain -, grow- upon one.

Adj. habitual; ac-, customary; prescriptive; accustomed &c. *v.*; traditional; of -daily, - every-day- occurrence; wonted, usual, gen-eral, ordinary, common, frequent, every-day, household, jog-trot; well-trodden, -known; familiar, vernacular, trite, commonplace, banal, bromidic, conventional, regular, set, stock, officinal, estab-lished, stereotyped; pre-vailing, -valent; current, received, acknowl-edged, recognized, accredited; of course, admitted, understood.

conformable &c. 82; according to -use, - custom, - routine; in -vogue, - fashion; fashionable &c. (*genteel*) 852.

wont; used - given - addicted -, attuned -, habituated &c. *v.*- to; in the habit of; *habitué*; at home in &c. (*skilful*) 698; seasoned; per-meated -, imbued- with; devoted -, wedded- to; never free from.

hackneyed, fixed, rooted, deep-rooted, ingrafted, permanent, in-veterate, besetting; naturalized; ingrained &c. (*intrinsic*) 5.

Adv. habitually &c. *adj.*; always &c. (*uniformly*) 16.

as -usual, - is one's wont, - things go, - the world goes, - the sparks fly upwards; *more -suo, - solito*.

as a rule, for the most part; generally &c. *adj.*; most often, - fre-quently.

Phr. *cela s'entend.*

off -, cast off -, break off -, wean one-self of -, violate -, break through -, infringe- -a habit, - a custom, - a usage; break one's fetters; disuse &c. 678; wear off.

Adj. un-accustomed, -used, -wonted, -seasoned, -inured, -habituated, -train-ed; new; green &c. (*unskilled*) 699; fresh, original, unhackneyed.

unusual &c. (*unconformable*) 83; un-conventional, non-observant; disused &c. 678.

Adv. just for once.

2°. *Causes of Volition*

615. Motive.—N. motive, springs of action.

reason, ground, call, principle; main-

615a. Absence of Motive.—N. ab-sence of motive; caprice &c. 608; chance &c. (*absence of design*) 621.

spring, *primum mobile*, key-stone; the why and the wherefore; *pro* and *con*, reason why; secret –, ulterior- motive, *arrière-pensée*; intention &c. 620.

inducement, consideration; attraction &c. 288; loadstone; magnet, -ism, -ic force; allect-ation, -ive; temptation, enticement, *agacerie*, allurement, witchery; bewitch-ment, -ery; charm; spell &c. 993; fascination, blandishment, cajolery; seduc-tion, -ement; honeyed words, voice of the tempter, song of the Sirens; forbidden fruit, golden apple.

persuasi-bility, -bleness; attractability; impress-, suscept-ibility; softness; persuas-, attract-iveness; tantalization.

influence, prompting, dictate, instance; impuls-e, -ion; incit-ement, -ation; press, instigation; provocation &c. (*excitation of feeling*) 824; inspiration; per-, suasion; encouragement, advocacy; exhortation, advice &c. 695; solicitation &c. (*request*) 765; lobbying.

incentive, stimulus, spur, fillip, whip, goad, rowel, provocative, whet, dram.

bribe, lure, decoy, – duck; bait, trail of a red herring; bribery and corruption; sop, – for Cerberus.

prompter, tempter; seduc-er, -tor; suggester, coaxer, wheedler; instigator, firebrand, incendiary; Siren, Circe; *agent provocateur*; lobbyist.

V. induce, move; draw, – on; bring in its train, give an -impulse &c. *n.*- to; inspire; put up to, prompt, call up; attract, beckon.

stimulate &c. (*excite*) 824; spirit up, inspirit; a-, rouse; ecphorize; animate, incite, provoke, instigate, set on, actuate; act –, work –, operate- upon; encourage; pat –, clap- on the -back, – shoulder.

influence, weigh with, bias, sway, incline, dispose, predispose, turn the scale, inoculate; lead, – by the nose; have –, exercise-influence- -with, – over, – upon; go –, come- round one; turn the head, magnetize.

persuade; prevail -with, – upon; overcome, carry; bring -round, – to one's senses; draw –, win –, gain –, come –, talk- over; procure, enlist, engage; invite, court.

tempt, seduce, overpersuade, entice, allure, captivate, fascinate, intrigue, bewitch, carry away, charm, conciliate, wheedle, coax, lure, suggest; inveigle; tantalize; cajole &c. (*deceive*) 545.

tamper with, bribe, suborn, grease the palm, bait with a silver hook, gild the pill, make things pleasant, put a sop into the pan, throw a sop to, bait the hook.

V. have no motive; scruple &c. (*be unwilling*) 603.

Adj. without rhyme or reason; aimless &c. (*chance*) 621.

Adv. capriciously; out of mere caprice.

616. Dissuasion.—N. dissuasion, dehortation, expostulation, remonstrance: deprecation &c. 766.

discouragement, damper, wet blanket; warning.

cohibition &c. (*restraint*) 751; curb &c. (*means of restraint*) 752; check &c. (*hindrance*) 706.

reluctance &c. (*unwillingness*) 603; contraindication.

V. dissuade, dehort, cry out against, remonstrate, expostulate, warn, contraindicate.

disincline, indispose, shake, stagger; dispirit; dis-courage, -hearten, -enchant; deter; hold –, keep- back &c. (*restrain*) 751: render -averse &c. 603; repel; turn aside &c. (*deviation*) 279; wean from; act as a drag &c. (*hinder*) 706; throw cold water on, damp, cool, chill, blunt, calm, quiet, quench; deprecate &c. 766.

Adj. dissuading &c. *v.*; dissuasive; dehortatory, expostulatory; monit-ive, -ory.

dissuaded &c. *v.*; uninduced &c. (induce &c. 615); unpersuadable &c. (*obstinate*) 606; averse &c. (*unwilling*) 603; repugnant &c. (*dislike*) 867.

enforce, force; impel &c. (*push*) 276; propel &c. 284; whip, lash, goad, spur, prick, urge; egg –, hound –, hurry- on; drag &c. 285; exhort; advise &c. 695; call upon &c., press &c. (*request*) 765; advocate.

set -an example, – the fashion; keep in countenance; back up.

be -persuaded &c.; yield to temptation, come round; concede &c. (*consent*) 762; obey a call; follow -advice, – the bent, – the dictates of; act on principle.

Adj. impulsive, motive; suas-, persuas-, hortat-ive, -ory; protreptical; inviting, tempting &c. *v.*; seductive, attractive, irresistible; fascinating &c. (*pleasing*) 829; provocative &c. (*exciting*) 824.

induced &c. *v.*; disposed; persuadable &c. (*docile*) 602; spellbound; instinct –, smitten- with; inspired &c. *v.*- by.

Adv. because, therefore &c. (*cause*) 155; from -this, – thatmotive; for -this, – that- reason; for; by reason –, for the sake –, on the score –, on account- of; out of, from, as, forasmuch as.

for all the world; on principle.

617. [Ostensible motive, ground, or reason assigned.] Plea.—N. plea, pretext; allegation, advocation; ostensible -motive, – ground, – reason; excuse &c. (*vindication*) 937; colour; gloss, guise.

loop-, starting-hole; how to creep out of, salvo, come off.

handle, peg to hang on, room, *locus standi*; stalking-horse, *cheval de bataille*, cue.

pretence &c. (*untruth*) 546; put off, subterfuge, dust thrown in the eyes; blind; moonshine; mere –, shallow- pretext; lame -excuse, – apology; tub to a whale; false plea, sour grapes; makeshift, shift, white lie; special pleading &c. (*sophistry*) 477; soft sawder &c. (*flattery*) 933.

V. plead, allege; shelter oneself under the plea of; excuse &c. (*vindicate*) 937; gloss over; lend a colour to; furnish a -handle &c. *n.*; make a -pretext, – handle- of; use as a plea &c. *n.*; take one's stand upon, make capital out of; pretend &c. (*lie*) 544.

Adj. ostensible &c. (*manifest*) 525; excusing; alleged, apologetic; pretended &c. 545.

Adv. ostensibly; under -colour, – the plea, – the pretence- of.

3°. *Objects of Volition*

618. Good.—N. good, benefit, advantage; improvement &c. 658; interest, service, behoof, behalf; weal; main chance, *summum bonum*, common weal; 'consummation devoutly to be wished'; gain, boot; profit, harvest.

boon &c. (*gift*) 784; good turn; blessing, benison; world of good; piece of good -luck, – fortune; nuts, prize, windfall, godsend, waif, treasure trove.

good fortune &c. (*prosperity*) 734; happiness &c. 827.

[Source of good] goodness &c. 648; utility &c. 644; remedy &c. 662; pleasure-giving &c. 829.

Adj. commendable &c. 931; useful &c. 644; good &c., beneficial &c. 648.

619. Evil.—N. evil, ill, harm, hurt, mischief, nuisance; machinations of the devil, Pandora's box, ills that flesh is heir to.

blow, buffet, stroke, scratch, bruise, wound, gash, mutilation; mortal -blow, – wound; *immedicabile vulnus*; damage, loss &c. (*deterioration*) 659.

disadvantage, prejudice, drawback; disaster, accident, casualty; mishap &c. (*misfortune*) 735; bad job, devil to pay; calamity, bale, woe, catastrophe, tragedy; ruin &c. (*destruction*) 162; adversity &c. 735.

mental suffering &c. 828. [Evil spirit] demon &c. 980. [Cause of evil] bane &c. 663. [Production of evil]

V. benefit, profit, advantage, serve, help, avail; do good to, gain, prosper, flourish.

Adv. well, aright, satisfactorily, favourably, not amiss; all for the best; to one's -advantage &c. *n.*; in one's -favour, – interest &c. *n.*

Phr. so far so good.

---

badness &c. 649; painfulness &c. 830; evil doer &c. 913.

outrage, wrong, injury, foul play; bad -, ill- turn; disservice; spoliation &c. 791; grievance, crying evil.

V. be in trouble &c. (*adversity*) 735; harm, injure, hurt, do disservice to.

Adj. disastrous, bad &c. 649; awry, out of joint; disadvantageous, injurious, harmful.

Adv. amiss, wrong, ill, to one's cost.

Section II. PROSPECTIVE VOLITION*
1°. *Conceptional Volition*

620. Intention.—**N.** intent, -ion, -ionality; purpose; *quo animo*; project &c. 626; undertaking &c. 676; predetermination &c. 611; design, ambition.

contemplation, mind, *animus*, view, purview, proposal; study; look out.

final cause; *raison d'être*; *cui bono*; object, aim, end; 'the be all and the end all'; drift &c. (*meaning*) 516; tendency &c. 176; destination, mark, point, butt, goal, target, bull's-eye, quintain; prey, quarry, game.

decision, determination, resolve; set -, settled- purpose; *ultimatum*; resolution &c. 604; wish &c. 865; *arrière-pensée*; motive &c. 615.

[Study of final causes] teleology.

V. intend, purpose, design, mean; have to; propose to oneself; harbour a design; have in -view, – contemplation, – one's eye, – *petto*; have an eye to.

bid -, labour- for; be -, aspire -, endeavour- after; be -, aim -, drive -, point-, level - at; take aim; set before oneself; study to.

take upon oneself &c (*undertake*) 676; take into one's head; meditate, contemplate; think – dream -, talk-of; premeditate &c. 611; compass, calculate; dest-ine, -inate: propose.

project &c. (*plan*) 626; have a mind to &c. (*be willing*) 602; desire &c. 865; pursue &c. 622.

Adj. intended &c. *v.*; intentional, advised, express, determinate; prepense &c. 611; bound for; intending &c. *v.*; minded, disposed, inclined;

621. [Absence of purpose in the succession of events.] **Chance.†**—**N.** chance &c. 156; lot, fate &c. (*necessity*) 601; luck; good luck &c. (*good*) 618; bad luck &c. 735; wheel of fortune; mascot; swastika.

speculation, venture, stake, flutter, flier, gamble, game of chance; mere -, random- shot; blind bargain, leap in the dark; pig in a poke &c. (*uncertainty*) 475; fluke, pot-luck.

drawing lots; sorti-legy, -tion; *sortes, – Virgilianæ, -biblicæ; rouge et noir,* hazard, *roulette,* pitch and toss, chuck-farthing, cup-tossing, heads or tails, cross and pile, wager; bet, -ting; risk, stake, plunge; gambling; the turf.

stock exchange, bourse, board of trade (U.S.A.), curb exchange.

gaming-, gambling-, betting-house; hell; betting ring, totalisator; dice, – box; dicer; gam-bler, -ester, plunger, stock operator, manipulator, punter; man of the turf; adventurer, speculator; bookmaker, layer, backer.

V. chance &c. (*hap*) 156; stand a chance &c. (*be possible*) 470.

toss up; cast -, draw- lots; leave -, trust- -to chance, – to the chapter of accidents; tempt fortune; chance it, take one's chance; run -, incur -, encounter- the -risk, – chance; stand the hazard of the die.

speculate, try one's luck, set on a cast, raffle, put into a lottery, buy a pig in a poke, shuffle the cards.

risk, venture, hazard, stake; lay, – a wager; make a bet, wager, bet, gamble,

---

* That is, volition having reference to a future object.   † See note on 156.

bent upon &c. (*earnest*) 604; at stake, on the -anvil, – *tapis*; in -view; – prospect, – the breast of; *in petto*; teleological.

Adv. intentionally &c. *adj.*; advisedly, wittingly, knowingly, designedly, purposely, on purpose, by design, studiously, pointedly; with -intent &c. *n.*; deliberately &c. (*with premeditation*) 611; with one's eyes open, in cold blood.

for; with -a view, – an eye- to; in order -to, – that; to the end –, with the intent- that; for the purpose –, with the view –, in contemplation –, on account- of.

in pursuance of, pursuant to; *quo animo*; to all intents and purposes.

622. [Purpose in action.] **Pursuit.**— N. pursuit; pursuing &c. *v.*; prosecution; pursuance; enterprise &c. (*undertaking*) 676; business &c. 625; adventure &c. (*essay*) 675; quest &c. (*search*) 461; scramble, hue and cry, game; hobby.

chase, hunt, *battue*, race, steeplechase, hunting, coursing; ven-ation, -ery; fox-chase; sport, -ing; shooting, angling, fishing, hawking.

pursuer; hunt-er, -sman; sportsman, Nimrod, the field; hound &c. 366.

V. pursue, prosecute, follow; run –, make –, be –, hunt –, prowl- after; shadow; carry on &c. (*do*) 680; engage in &c. (*undertake*) 676; set about &c. (*begin*) 66; endeavour &c. 675; court &c. (*request*) 765; seek &c. (*search*) 461; aim at &c. (*intention*) 620; follow the trail &c. (*trace*) 461; fish for &c. (*experiment*) 463; press on &c. (*haste*) 684; run a race &c. (*velocity*) 274.

chase, give chase, course, dog, hunt, hound, stalk; tread –, follow- on the heels of &c. (*sequence*) 281.

rush upon; rush headlong &c. (*violence*) 173; ride –, run- full tilt at; make a leap –, jump –, snatch- at; run down; start game.

tread a path; take –, hold- a course; shape –, direct –, bend- one's -steps, – course; play a game; fight –, elbow- one's way; follow up; take -to, – up; go in for; ride one's hobby.

Adj. pursuing &c. *v.*; in quest of &c.

game, play for; play at chuck-farthing.

Adj. fortuitous &c. 156; unintentional, -ded; accidental; not meant; un-designed, -purposed; unpremeditated &c. 612; never thought of.

indiscriminate, promiscuous; undirected, random; aim-, drift-, design-, purpose-, cause-less; without purpose. possible &c. 470.

Adv. casually &c. 156; unintentionally &c. *adj.*; unwittingly.

en passant, by the way, incidentally; as it may happen; at -random, – a venture, – haphazard; as luck would have it, by -chance, – good fortune; un-, -luckily.

---

623. [Absence of pursuit.] **Avoidance.** —N. abst-ention, -inence; forbearance; refraining &c. *v.*; inaction &c. 681; neutrality.

avoidance, evasion, elusion; seclusion &c. 893.

avolation, flight; escape &c. 671; retreat &c. 287; recoil &c. 277; departure &c. 293; rejection &c. 610.

shirker &c. *v.*; slacker; truant; fugitive, refugee; runa-way, -gate; renegade; deserter.

V. abstain, refrain, spare, not attempt; not do &c. 681; maintain the even tenor of one's way.

eschew, keep from, let alone, have nothing to do with; keep –, stand –, hold- -aloof, – off; take no part in, have no hand in.

avoid, shun, steer –, keep- clear of; fight shy of; keep -one's, – at a respectful- distance; keep –, get- out of the way; evade, elude, turn away from; set one's face against &c. (*oppose*) 708; deny oneself.

shrink; hang –, hold –, draw- back; recoil &c. 277; retire &c. (*recede*) 287; flinch, blink, blench, shy, shirk, dodge, parry, make way for, give place to.

beat a retreat; turn -tail, – one's back; take to one's heels; run, -away, – for one's life; cut and run; be off, – like a shot; fly, flee; fly –, flee –, run away- from; take –, take to- flight; desert, elope; make –, scamper –, sneak –, shuffle –, sheer- off; break –,

(inquiry) 461; in -pursuit, – full cry, – hot pursuit; on the scent.

Adv. in pursuance of &c. *(intention)* 620; after.

Int. tally-ho! yoicks! so-ho!

———

burst –, tear oneself –, slip –, slink –, steal- -away, – away from; slip cable, part company, turn on one's heel; sneak out of, play truant, give one the go by, give leg bail, take French leave, slope, decamp, flit, bolt, abscond, levant, skedaddle, absquatulate, cut one's stick, walk one's chalks, show a light pair of heels, make oneself scarce; escape &c. 671; go away &c. *(depart)* 293; abandon &c. 624; reject &c. 610.

lead one a -dance, – a merry chase, – pretty dance; throw off the scent, play at hide and seek.

Adj. unsought, unattempted; avoiding &c. *v.*; neutral; shy of &c. *(unwilling)* 603; elusive, evasive, distant; fugitive, runaway; shy, wild.

Adj. lest, in order to avoid.

Int. forbear! keep –, hands- off! *sauve qui peut!* devil take the hindmost!

624. Relinquishment.—N. relinquish-, abandon-ment; desertion, defection, secession, withdrawal; cave of Adullam; *nolle prosequi.*

discontinuance &c. *(cessation)* 142; renunciation &c. *(recantation)* 607; abrogation &c. 756; resignation &c. *(retirement)* 757; desuetude &c. 614; cession &c. *(of property)* 782.

V. relinquish, give up, abandon, desert, forsake, leave in the lurch; depart –, secede –, withdraw- from; back – out of, – down from, leave, go back on one's word, quit, take leave of, bid a long farewell; vacate &c. *(resign)* 757.

renounce &c. *(abjure)* 607; forego, have done with, drop; write off; disuse &c. 678; discard &c. 782; wash one's hands of; drop all idea of; *nolle-pros.*; lose interest in.

break –, leave- off; desist; stop &c. *(cease)* 142; hold –, stay- one's hand; quit one's hold; give over, shut up shop.

throw up the -game, – cards; give up the -point, – argument; pass to the order of the day, move the previous question, table the motion.

Adj. unpursued; relinquished &c. *v.*; relinquishing &c. *v.*

Int. avast &c.! *(stop)* 142.

625. Business.—N. business, occupation, employment; pursuit &c. 622; what one is doing-, – about; affair, concern, matter, case, undertaking.

matter in hand, irons in the fire; thing to do, *agendum*, task, work, job, chore, errand, transaction, commission, mission, charge, care; duty &c. 926.

part, *rôle*, cue; province, function, look-out, department, capacity, sphere, orb, field, line; walk, – of life; beat, round, routine; race, career.

office, place, post, incumbency, living; situation, appointment, billet, berth, employ; service &c. *(servitude)* 749; engagement; undertaking &c. 676.

vocation, calling, profession, *métier*, cloth, faculty; industry, art; industrial arts; craft, mystery, handicraft; trade &c. *(commerce)* 794.

exercise; work &c. *(action)* 680; avocation; press of business &c. *(activity)* 682.

V. pass –, employ –, spend- one's time in; employ oneself -in, – upon;

occupy –, concern- oneself with; make it one's -business &c. *n*.; undertake &c. 676; enter a profession; betake oneself to, turn one's hand to; have to do with &c. (*do*) 680.

drive a trade; carry on –, do –, transact- -business, – a trade &c. *n*.; keep a shop; ply one's task, – trade; labour in one's vocation; pursue the even tenor of one's way; attend to -business, – one's work.

officiate, serve, act; act –, play- one's part; do duty; serve –, discharge –, perform- the -office, – duties, – functions- of; hold –, fill- -an office, – a place, – a situation; hold a portfolio.

be -about, – doing, – engaged in, – employed in, – occupied with, – at work on; have one's hands in, have in hand; have on one's -hands, – shoulders; bear the burden; have one's hands full &c. (*activity*) 682.

be -in the hands of, – on the stocks, – on the anvil; pass through one's hands.

Adj. business-like; work-a-day; professional; official, functional; busy &c. (*actively employed*) 682; on –, in- -hand, – one's hands; afoot; on -foot, – the anvil; going on; acting.

Adv. in the course of business, all in a day's work; professionally &c. *adj.*

626. Plan.—N. plan, scheme, design, project; propos-al, -ition; suggestion; resolution, motion; precaution &c. (*provision*) 673; deep-laid &c. (*premeditated*) 611- plan &c.; racket.

system &c. (order) 58; organization &c. (*arrangement*) 60; germ &c. (*cause*) 153; Five Year Plan.

sketch, skeleton, outline, draught, draft, *ébauche*, *brouillon*; rough -cast, – draft, – draught, – copy; copy; proof, revise.

forecast, *programme*, prospectus, scenario; *carte du pays*; card; bill, protocol; order of the day, list of agenda, *memorandum*; bill of fare &c. (*food*) 298; base of operations; platform, plank.

rôle; policy &c. (*line of conduct*) 692.

contrivance, invention, expedient, receipt, nostrum, artifice, device, gadget; stratagem &c. (*cunning*) 702; trick &c. (*deception*) 545; alternative, loophole, shift &c. (*substitute*) 147; last shift &c. (*necessity*) 601.

measure, step; stroke, – of policy; master stroke; trump-, court-card; *cheval de bataille*, great gun; *coup*, – *d'état*; clever –, bold –, good- -move, – hit, – stroke; bright -thought, – idea, great idea.

intrigue, cabal, plot, frame-up, conspiracy, complot, machination; under-, counter-plot.

schem-ist, -atist; strategist, machinator, schemer; projector, author, builder, artist, promoter, designer &c. *v*.; conspirator; *intrigant* &c. (*cunning*) 702.

V. plan, scheme, design, frame, contrive, project, forecast, sketch; conceive, devise, invent &c. (*imagine*) 515; set one's wits to work &c. 515; spring a project; fall –, hit- upon; strike –, chalk –, cut –, lay –, map-out; lay down a plan; shape –, mark- out a course; predetermine &c. 611; concert, preconcert, preestablish; prepare &c. 673; hatch, – a plot; concoct; take -steps, – measures.

cast, recast, systematize, organize; arrange &c. 60; digest, mature.

plot; counter-plot, -mine; dig a mine; lay a train; intrigue &c. (*cunning*) 702.

Adj. planned &c. *v*.; strategic, -al; planning &c. *v*.; in course of preparation &c. 673; under consideration; on the -*tapis*, – carpet, – table.

627. Method. [Path.]—**N.** method, way, manner, wise, gait, form, mode, fashion, tone, guise; *modus operandi*; procedure &c. (*line of conduct*) 692.

path, road, route, course; line of -way, – road; trajectory, orbit, track, beat, tack.

steps; stair, -case; flight of stairs, ladder, stile.

bridge, viaduct, gauntry, pontoon, stepping stone, plank, gangway, catwalk, drawbridge; pass, ford, ferry, tunnel, subway, elevated; pipe &c. 260.

door; gateway &c. (*opening*) 260; channel, passage, avenue, means of access, approach, perron, adit, entrance; artery, lane, alley, aisle, lobby, corridor, cloister; back- door, -stairs; secret passage; covert-way.

road-, path-, stair-way; thoroughfare; highway, pike, turnpike, trail, parkway, *boulevard*; turnpike –, royal –, coach- road; broad –, King's –, Queen's- highway; beaten -track, – path; horse –, bridle- road, – track, – path; pathway; walk, *trottoir*, foot-path, pavement, flags, side-walk; by –, cross- -road, – path, – way; cut; short -cut &c. (*mid-course*) 628; *carrefour*; private –, occupation- road; highways and byways; rail-, tram-road, -way; funicular, ropeway, causeway; defile, cutting; canal &c. (*conduit*) 350; street &c. (*abode*) 189.

Adv. how; in what -way, – manner; by what mode; so, in this way, after this fashion, on these lines.

one way or another, anyhow; somehow or other &c. (*instrumentality*) 631; by way of; *viâ*; *in transitu* &c. 270; on the high road to.

Phr. *hæ tibi erunt artes.*

---

628. Mid-course.—N. middle-, mid-course; moderation, mean &c. 29: middle &c. 68; *juste milieu*, *mezzo termine*, golden mean, *aurea mediocritas*.

straight &c. (*direct*) 278 -course, – path; short –, cross- cut; short-circuit; great circle sailing.

neutrality; half –, half and half-measures; compromise.

V. keep in –, steer –, preserve- -a middle, – an even- course; go straight &c. (*direct*) 278.

go half way, compromise, make a compromise.

Adj. neutral, average, even, impartial, moderate, straight &c. (*direct*) 278.

629. Circuit.—N. circuit, round-about way, digression, divagation, *détour*, circum-ambience, -ambulation, -bendibus, *ambages*, loop; winding &c. (*circuition*) 311; zigzag &c. (*deviation*) 279.

V. perform –, make- a circuit; go -round about, – out of one's way; make a *détour*; meander &c. (*deviate*) 279; circumambulate.

lead a pretty dance; beat about, – the bush; make two bites of a cherry.

Adj. circuitous, indirect, round-about; zig-zag &c. (*deviating*) 279; circum-ambient, -ambulatory.

Adv. by -a side wind, – an indirect course; in a roundabout way; from pillar to post.

---

630. Requirement.—N. requirement, need, wants, necessities; neces-saries, – of life; stress, exigency, pinch, *sine quâ non*, matter of necessity; case of -need, – life or death.

needfulness, essentiality, necessity, indispensability, urgency, pre-requisite.

requisition &c. (*request*) 765, (*exaction*) 741; run upon; demand –, call- for.

desideratum &c. (*desire*) 865; want &c. (*deficiency*) 640.

charge, claim, command, injunction, requisition, mandate, order, *ultimatum.*

V. require, need, want, have occasion for, entail; not be able to -do without, – dispense with; prerequire.

render necessary, necessitate, create a necessity for, call for, put in requisition; make a requisition &c. (*ask for*) 765, (*demand*) 741.

stand in need of; lack &c. 640; desiderate; desire &c. 865; be -necessary &c. *adj.*

Adj. required &c. *v.*; requisite, needful, necessary, imperative, essential, indispensable, prerequisite; called for; in -demand, – request.

urgent, exigent, pressing, instant, crying, absorbing.

in want of; destitute of &c. 640.

Adv. *ex necessitate rei* &c. (*necessarily*) 601; of –, out of stern- necessity; at a pinch.

Phr. there is no time to lose; it cannot be -spared, – dispensed with.

2° *Subservience to Ends*
1. *Actual Subservience*

631. Instrumentality.—**N.** instrumentality; aid &c. 707; subservien-ce, -cy; mediation, inter-vention, -mediacy, medium, inter-medium, -mediary, vehicle, hand; agency &c. 170.

minister, handmaid, servant, slave, maid, valet; midwife, *accoucheur*, obstetrician; go-between; cat's paw; stepping-stone.

key; master –, pass –, latch- key; 'open sesame'; passport, *passepartout*, safe-conduct; influence.

instrument &c. 633; expedient &c. (*plan*) 626; means &c. 632.

V. subserve, minister, tend, mediate, intervene; come –, go- between, interpose; pull the strings; be -instrumental &c. *adj.*; pander to.

Adj. instrumental; useful &c. 644; ministerial, subservient, mediatorial; inter-mediate, -vening; conducive.

Adv. through, by, *per*; where-, there-, here-by; by the -agency &c. 170- of; by dint of; by –, in- virtue of; through the -medium &c. *n.*-of; along with; on the shoulders of; by means of &c. 622; by –, with- -the aid &c. (*assistance*) 707- of.

per fas et nefas. by fair means or foul; somehow, – or other; by hook or by crook.

632. Means.—**N.** means, resources, revenue, wherewithal, ways and means, income; capital &c. (*money*) 800; stock in trade &c. 636; provision &c. 637; a shot in the locker; appliances &c. (*machinery*) 633; means and appliances; conveniences; cards to play; expedients &c. (*measures*) 626; two strings to one's bow; sheet anchor &c. (*safety*) 666; aid &c. 707; medium &c. 631.

V. find –, have –, possess- means &c. *n.*; provide the wherewithal.

Adj. instrumental &c. 631; mechanical &c. 633.

Adv. by means of, with; by -what, – all, – any, – some- means; where-, here-, there-with; wherewithal.

how &c. (*in what manner*) 627; through &c. (*by the instrumentality of*) 631; with –, by- the aid &c. (*assistance*) 707- of; by the -agency &c. 170- of.

633. Instrument.—**N.** machinery, mechanism, engineering.

instrument, organ, tool, implement, utensil, contrivance, machine, motor, engine, lathe, gin, mill, pump.

gear; tack-le, -ling, trice, rigging, gear, apparatus, appliances; plant, *matériel*; harness, trappings, fittings, accoutrements; equip-ment. -age;

appointments, furniture, upholstery; chattels; paraphernalia &c. (*belongings*) 780; *impedimenta*.

mechanical powers; lever, -age; mechanical advantage; crow, -bar; handspike, gavelock, jemmy, arm, limb, wing; oar, paddle; pulley, sheave; parbuckle; wheel and axle; wheel-, clock-work; wheels within wheels; pinion, gear wheel, spur –, bevel- gearing, chains, belting, crank, winch, capstan, windlass, crane, derrick, hoist, lift &c. 307; cam; pedal; wheel &c. (*rotation*) 312; inclined plane; wedge; screw; jack; spring, mainspring.

handle, hilt, haft, shaft, heft, shank, blade, trigger, tiller, helm, treadle, key; turnscrew, screwdriver, spanner, wrench.

hammer &c. (*impulse*) 276; edge tool &c. (*cut*) 253; borer &c. 262; vice, teeth &c. (*hold*) 781; nail, rope &c. (*join*) 45; peg &c. (*hang*) 214; support &c. 215; spoon &c. (*vehicle*) 272; arms &c. 727; oar &c. (*navigation*) 267.

Adj. instrumental &c. 631; mechanical, machinal, automatic, self-acting; brachial.

634. Substitute.—N. substitute &c. 147; deputy &c. 759; proxy, alternative, understudy.

635. Materials.—N. material, raw material, stuff, stock, staple; building materials, bricks and mortar; metal; stone; clay, brick; crockery &c. 384; compo, -sition; reinforced –, ferro-, concrete; cement; wood, ore, timber; gravel, cobbles, macadam, asphalt, tarmac.

materials; supplies, munition, fuel, grist, household stuff; *pabulum* &c. (*food*) 298; ammunition &c. (*arms*) 727; contingents; relay, reinforcement; baggage &c. (*personal property*) 780; means &c. 632.

Adj. raw &c. (*unprepared*) 674; wooden &c. *n.*

636. Store.—N. stock, fund, mine, vein, lode, quarry; spring; fount, -ain; well, -spring; milch cow.

stock in trade, supply; heap &c. (*collection*) 72; treasure; reserve, *corps de réserve*, reserve fund, nest-egg, savings, *bonne bouche*.

crop, harvest, mow, vintage; yield, product, gleanings.

store, accumulation, hoard, rick, stack; lumber; relay &c. (*provision*) 637.

store-house, -room, -closet; depository, depot, *cache*, safe deposit, vault, pantechnicon, re-pository, -servatory, -pertory; *repertorium*; promptuary, warehouse, *entrepôt*, magazine, dump, buttery, larder, pantry, panary, lanary, still-room, spence; crib, garner, granary, silo, barn; bunker; thesaurus; bank &c. (*treasury*) 802; armoury; arsenal; dock; gallery, museum, library, conservatory, hot-house; menag-ery, -erie, aquarium, zoological gardens.

reservoir, cistern, tank, sump, pond, mill-pond; gasometer.

budget, quiver, bandolier, portfolio; coffer &c. (*receptacle*) 191.

conservation; storing &c. *v.*; storage.

dictionary &c. 562; list &c. 86.

V. store; put –, lay –, set- by; stow away; set –, lay- apart; store –, hoard –, treasure –, lay –, heap –, put –, garner –, save- up; *cacher*; accumulate, amass, hoard, fund, garner, save, bank.

conserve, reserve; keep –, hold- back; husband, – one's resources.

deposit; stow, stack, load, dump; harvest; heap, collect &c. 72; lay -in, – down, – by, store &c. *adj.*; keep, file [papers]; lay in &c. (*provide*) 637; preserve &c. 670; put by for a rainy day.

Adj. stored &c. *v.*; in -store, – reserve, – ordinary; spare, supernumerary.

637. Provision.—N. provision, supply; grist, – to the mill; subvention &c. (*aid*) 707; resources &c. (*means*) 632.

providing &c. *v.*; purveyance; reinforcement; commissary, commissariat.

rations; iron -, emergency- rations; provender &c. (*food*) 298; *viaticum*; ensilage.

caterer, purveyor, commissary, quartermaster, steward, housekeeper, manciple, feeder, batman, victualler, storekeeper, provision merchant, green-, grocer, *comprador*, *restaurateur*; sutler &c. (*merchant*) 797; innkeeper, publican, confectioner, baker, butcher, wine merchant, vintner.

V. provide; make -provision, – due provision for; lay in, – a stock, – a store.

sup-ply, -peditate; furnish; find, – one in; arm.

cater, victual, provision, purvey, forage; beat up for; stock, – with; make good, replenish; fill, – up; recruit, feed, ration.

have in -store, – reserve; keep, – by one, – on foot; have to fall back upon; store &c. 636; provide against a rainy day &c. (*economy*) 817.

638. Waste.—N. consumption, expenditure, exhaustion; dispersion &c. 73; ebb; leakage &c. (*exudation*) 295; loss &c. 776; wear and tear; waste; prodigality &c. 818; misuse &c. 679; wasting &c. *v.*; rubbish &c. (*useless*) 645.

mountain in labour.

V. spend, expend, use, consume, swallow up, exhaust, deplete; impoverish; spill, drain, empty; disperse &c. 73.

cast -, throw -, fling -, fritter- away; burn the candle at both ends, waste; squander &c. 818.

'waste its sweetness on the desert air'; cast -one's bread upon the waters, – pearls before swine; employ a steam hammer to crack a nut, waste powder and shot, break a butterfly on a wheel; labour in vain &c. (*useless*) 645; cut a whetstone with a razor, pour water into a sieve; tilt at windmills.

leak &c. (*run out*) 295; run to waste; ebb; melt away, run dry, dry up.

Adj. wasted &c. *v.*; at a low ebb.

wasteful &c. (*prodigal*) 818; penny wise and pound foolish.

Phr. *magno conatu magnas nugas; le jeu n'en vaut pas la chandelle.*

639. Sufficiency.—N. sufficiency, adequacy, enough, withal, *quantum sufficit*, satisfaction, competence; no less.

mediocrity &c. (*average*) 29.

fill; fulness &c. (*completeness*) 52; plen-itude, -ty; abundance; copiousness &c. *adj.*; amplitude, galore, lots, profusion; full measure; 'good measure pressed down, shaken together and running over.'

luxuriance &c. (*fertility*) 168; affluence &c. (*wealth*) 803; fat of the land; 'a land flowing with milk and honey'; cornucopia; horn of -plenty, – Amalthæa; mine &c. (*stock*) 636.

outpouring; flood &c. (*great quantity*) 31; tide &c. (*river*) 348; repletion &c. (*redundance*) 641; satiety &c. 869; rich man &c. 803.

640. Insufficiency.—N. insufficiency; inadequa-cy, -teress; incompetence &c. (*impotence*) 158; deficiency &c. (*incompleteness*) 53; imperfection &c. 651; shortcoming &c. 304; paucity; stint; scantiness &c. (*smallness*) 32; none to spare; bare subsistence.

scarcity, dearth; want, need, lack, poverty, exigency; inanition, starvation, famine, drought.

dole, pittance, mite; short -allowance, – commons; half-rations; banyan -, fast- day. Lent.

emptiness, poorness &c. *adj.*; depletion, vacancy, flaccidity; ebb-tide; low water; 'a beggarly account of empty boxes'; indigence &c. (*poverty*) 804; insolvency &c. (*non-payment*) 808; poor man &c. 804; bankrupt &c. 808.

V. be -insufficient &c. *adj.*; not -suf-

V. be -sufficient &c. *adj.*; suffice, do, just do, satisfy, pass muster; have -enough &c. *n.*; eat –, drink –, have- one's fill; roll –, swim- in; wallow in &c. (*superabundance*) 641.

abound, exuberate, teem, flow, stream, rain, shower down; pour, – in; swarm; bristle with.

render -sufficient &c. *adj.*; replenish &c. (*fill*) 52.

Adj. sufficient, enough, adequate, up to the mark, commensurate, compe- tent, satisfactory, valid, tangible.

measured; moderate &c. (*temperate*) 953.

full &c. (*complete*) 52; ample; plen-ty, -tiful, -teous; plenty as blackberries; copious, abundant; abounding &c. *v.*; replete, enough and to spare, flush; choke-full; well-stocked, -provided; lib- eral; unstint-ed, -ing; stintless; without stint; un-sparing, -measured; lavish &c. 641; wholesale.

rich; luxuriant &c. (*fertile*) 168; afflu- ent &c. (*wealthy*) 803; wantless; big with &c. (*pregnant*) 161.

un -exhausted, -wasted; exhaustless, inexhaustible.

Adv. sufficiently, amply &c. *adj.*; full; in -abundance &c. *n.*; with no sparing hand; to one's heart's content, *ad libitum*, without stint.

Phr. cut and come again.

fice &c. 639; come short of &c. 304; run dry.

want, lack, need, require; *caret*; be in want &c. (*poor*) 804; live from hand to mouth.

render- insufficient &c. *adj.*; drain of resources; impoverish &c. (*waste*) 638; stint &c. (*begrudge*) 819; put on short -commons, – allowance.

do -insufficiently &c. *adv.*; scotch the snake.

Adj. insufficient, inadequate; too -little &c. 32; not -enough &c. 639; unequal to; incompetent &c. (*impotent*) 158; 'weighed in the balance and found wanting'; perfunctory &c. (*neglect*) 460; deficient &c. (*incomplete*) 53; wanting &c. *v.*; imperfect &c. 651; ill-furnished, -provided, -stored, -off.

slack, at a low ebb; empty, vacant, bare; short –, out –, destitute –, de- void –, bereft &c. 776 –, denuded- of; dry, drained.

un -provided, -supplied, -furnished; un-replenished, -fed; un-stored, -treas- ured; empty-handed.

meagre, poor, thin, scrimp, sparing, spare, stinted, stunted; skimpy; starv-ed, -eling; half-starved, emaci- ated, famine-stricken, famished, under- fed, undernourished; jejune.

scant &c. (*small*) 32; scarce; not to be had, – for love or money, – at any price; scurvy; stingy &c. 819; at the end of one's tether; without -resources &c. 632; in want &c. (*poor*) 804; in debt &c. 806.

Adv. insufficiently &c. *adj.*; in default –, for want- of; failing.

641. Redundance.—N. redundance; too -much, – many; super- abundance, -fluity, -fluence, -saturation; nimiety, transcendency, ex- uberance, profuseness; profusion &c. (*plenty*) 639; repletion, enough in all conscience, *satis superque*, lion's share; more than -enough &c. 639; plethora, engorgement, congestion, load, surfeit, sickener; turges- cence &c. (*expansion*) 194; over-dose, -measure, -supply, -flow; inun- dation &c. (*water*) 348; avalanche.

accumulation &c. (*store*) 636; heap &c. 72; drug, – in the market, glut; crowd; burden.

excess; sur-, over-plus, epact; margin; remainder &c. 40; duplicate; surplusage, expletive; work of –, supererogation; *bonus, bonanza*.

luxury; intemperance &c. 954; extravagance &c. (*prodigality*) 818; exorbitance, lavishment.

pleonasm &c. (*diffuseness*) 573; too many irons in the fire; embar- rassment of riches; money to burn.

V. super-, over-abound; know no bounds, swarm; meet one at every turn; creep –, bristle- with; overflow; run –, flow –, well –, brim-over; run riot; over-run, -stock, -lay, -charge, -dose, -feed, -burden, -load, -do, -whelm, -shoot the mark &c. (*go beyond*) 303; surcharge, supersaturate, gorge, glut, load, drench, whelm, inundate, deluge, flood; drug, – the market.

choke, cloy, accloy, suffocate; pile up, lay it on, – with a trowel, lay on thick; impregnate with; lavish &c. (*squander*) 818.

send –, carry- coals to Newcastle, – owls to Athens; teach one's grandmother to suck eggs; *pisces natare docere*; kill the slain, 'gild refined gold,' 'paint the lily'; butter one's bread on both sides, put butter upon bacon; employ a steam-hammer to crack a nut &c. (*waste*) 638.

exaggerate &c. 549; wallow in; roll in &c. (*plenty*) 639; remain on one's hands, hang heavy on hand, go a begging.

Adj. redundant; too -much, – many; exuberant, inordinate, superabundant, excessive, overmuch, replete, profuse, lavish; prodigal &c: 818; exorbitant; overweening; extravagant; overcharged &c. *v.*; supersaturated, drenched, overflowing; running -over, – to waste, – down.

crammed –, filled- to overflowing; gorged, stuffed, ready to burst; dropsical, turgid, plethoric, full-blooded; obese &c. 194; voluminous.

superfluous, unnecessary, needless, supervacaneous, uncalled for, to spare, in excess; over and above &c. (*remainder*) 40; *de trop*; adscititious &c. (*additional*) 37; supernumerary &c. (*reserve*) 636; on one's hands, spare, duplicate, supererogatory, expletive; *un peu fort*.

Adv. over, too, over and above; over –, too- much; too far; without –, beyond –, out of- measure; with . . . to spare; over head and ears; up to one's -eyes, – ears; *extra*; beyond the mark &c. (*transcursion*) 303; over one's head.

Phr. it never rains but it pours.

2. *Degree of Subservience*

642. Importance.—N. importance, consequence, moment, prominence, consideration, mark, materialness.

import, significance, concern; emphasis, interest.

greatness &c. 31; superiority &c. 33; notability &c. (*repute*) 873; weight &c. (*influence*) 175; value &c. (*goodness*) 648; usefulness &c. 644.

gravity, seriousness, solemnity; no -joke, – laughing matter; pressure, urgency, stress; matter of life and death. *memorabilia, notabilia*, great doings; red-letter day.

great -thing, – point; main chance, 'the be all and end all,' cardinal point, outstanding feature; substance, gist &c. (*essence*) 5; sum and substance, *gravamen*, head and front; important –, principal –, prominent –, essential-part; half the battle; *sine quâ non*; breath of one's nostrils &c. (*life*) 359; cream, salt, core, kernel, heart, nucleus;

643. Unimportance.—N. unimportance, insignificance, nothingness, immateriality.

triviality, trivia, fribble, levity, frivolity; paltriness &c. *adj.*; poverty; smallness &c. 32; vanity &c. (*uselessness*) 645; matter of -indifference &c. 866; no object; side issue.

nothing, – to signify, – worth speaking of, – particular, – to boast of, – to speak of; small –, no great –, trifling &c. *adj.* -matter; mere -joke, – nothing; hardly –, scarcely- anything; nonentity, cipher, figurehead; no great shakes, *peu de chose*; child's play; small beer.

toy, plaything, popgun, paper pellet, gimcrack, gewgaw, bauble, trinket, *bagatelle*, kickshaw, knicknack, whimwham, trifle, 'trifles light as air.'

trumpery, trash, rubbish, stuff, *fatras*, frippery; 'leather or prunello'; chaff, drug, froth, bubble, smoke, cob-

key, -note, -stone; corner stone; trump-card &c. (*device*) 626; salient points.

top-sawyer, first fiddle, *prima donna*, chief, big-wig; triton among the minnows.

V. be -important &c. *adj.*, – somebody, – something; import, signify, matter, be an object; carry weight &c. (*influence*) 175; make a figure &c. (*repute*) 873; be in the ascendant, come to the front, lead the way, take the lead, play first fiddle, throw all else into the shade; lie at the root of; deserve –, merit –, be worthy- -of notice, – regard, – consideration.

attach –, ascribe –, give- importance &c. *n.*- to; value, care for; set store -upon, – by; mark &c. 550; mark with a white stone, underline; write –, put –, print- in -italics, – capitals, – large letters, – large type, – letters of gold; accentuate, emphasize, lay stress on.

make -a fuss, – a stir, – a piece of work, – much ado- about; make -of, – much of.

Adj. important; of -importance &c. *n.*; momentous, material; to the point; not to be -overlooked, – despised, – sneezed at; egregious; weighty &c. (*influential*) 175; of note &c. (*repute*) 873; notable, prominent, salient, signal; memorable, remarkable; worthy of -remark, – notice; never to be forgotten; stirring, eventful.

grave, serious, earnest, noble, grand, solemn, impressive, commanding, imposing.

urgent, pressing, critical, instant.

paramount, essential, vital, all-absorbing, radical, cardinal, chief, main, prime, primary, principal, leading, capital, foremost, overruling; of vital &c. importance.

in the front rank, first-rate, A1; superior &c. 33; considerable &c. (*great*) 31; marked &c. *v.*; rare &c. 137.

significant, telling, trenchant, emphatic, pregnant; *tanti*.

Adv. materially &c. *adj.*; in the main; above all, *par excellence*, to crown all.

web; weed; refuse &c. (*inutility*) 645; scum &c. (*dirt*) 653.

joke, jest, snap of the fingers; fudge &c. (*unmeaning*) 517; fiddlestick, – end; pack of nonsense, mere farce.

straw, pin, fig, continental, button, rush; bulrush, feather, halfpenny, farthing, brass farthing, doit, peppercorn, jot, rap, pinch of snuff, old song.

minutiæ, details, minor details, small fry; dust in the balance, feather in the scale, drop in the ocean, flea-bite, molehill; fingle-fangle.

nine days' wonder, *ridiculus mus*; flash in the pan &c. (*impotence*) 158; much ado about nothing &c. (*overestimation*) 482; storm in a teacup.

V. be -unimportant &c. *adj.*; not -matter &c. 642; go for –, matter –, signify- -little, – nothing, – little or nothing; not matter a -straw &c. *n.*

make light of &c. (*underestimate*) 483; catch at straws &c. (*overestimate*) 482.

Adj. unimportant; of -little, – small, – no- -account, – importance &c. 642; immaterial; un-, non-essential; not vital; irrelevant, incidental, indifferent.

subordinate &c. (*inferior*) 34; mediocre &c. (*average*) 29; passable, fair, respectable, tolerable, commonplace; uneventful, mere, common; ordinary &c. (*habitual*) 613; inconsiderable, so-so, insignificant, inappreciable, nugatory.

trifling, trivial; slight, slender, light, flimsy, frothy, idle; puerile &c. (*foolish*) 499; airy, shallow; weak &c. 160; powerless &c. 158; frivolous, petty, niggling; pid-, ped-dling; fribble, inane, ridiculous, farcical; fini-cal, -kin; fiddle-faddle, namby-pamby, wishy-washy, milk and water.

poor, paltry, pitiful; contemptible &c. (*contempt*) 930; sorry, mean, meagre, shabby, miserable, wretched, vile, scrubby, scrannel, weedy, niggardly, scurvy, putid, beggarly, worthless, twopenny-halfpenny, cheap, trashy, catchpenny, gimcrack, trumpery, one-horse; toy.

not worth -the pains, – while, – mentioning, – speaking of, – a thought, – a curse, – a straw, – rap &c. *n.*; beneath –, unworthy of- -notice, – regard, – consideration, – contempt; *de lanâ caprinâ*; vain &c. (*useless*) 645.

Adv. slightly &c. *adj.*; rather, somewhat, pretty well, fairly well, tolerably.

for aught one cares.

Int. no matter! pish! tush! tut! pshaw! pugh! pooh, -pooh! fudge! bosh! humbug! fiddle-stick, – end! fiddlededee! never mind! *n'importe!* what -signifies, – matter, – boots it, – of that, –'s the odds! a fig for! stuff! nonsense! stuff and nonsense!

Phr. *magno conatu magnas nugas*; *le jeu n'en vaut pas la chandelle*; it -matters not, – does not signify; it is of no -consequence, – importance.

---

644. Utility.—N. utility; usefulness &c. *adj.*; efficacy, efficiency, adequacy; service, use, stead, avail; help &c. (*aid*) 707; applicability &c. *adj.*; subservience &c. (*instrumentality*) 631; function &c. (*business*) 625; value; worth &c. (*goodness*) 648; money's worth; productiveness &c. 168; *cui bono* &c. (*intention*) 620; utilization &c. (*use*) 677; step in the right direction.

common weal, public good; utilitarianism &c. (*philanthropy*) 910.

V. be -useful &c. *adj.*; avail, serve; subserve &c. (*be instrumental to*) 631; conduce &c. (*tend*) 176; answer –, serve- -one's turn, – a purpose.

act a part &c. (*action*) 680; perform –, discharge- -a function &c. 625; do –, render- -a service, – good service, – yeoman's service; bestead, stand one in good stead; be the making of; help &c. 707.

bear fruit &c. (*produce*) 161; bring grist to the mill; profit, remunerate; benefit &c. (*do good*) 648.

find one's -account, – advantage- in; reap the benefit of &c. (*be better for*) 658.

render useful &c. (*use*) 677.

Adj. useful; of -use &c. *n.*; serviceable, usable, proficuous, good for; subservient &c. (*instrumental*) 631; conducive &c. (*tending*) 176; subsidiary &c. (*helping*) 707.

advantageous &c. (*beneficial*) 648; profitable, gainful, remunerative, worth one's salt; in-, valuable; prolific &c. (*productive*) 168.

adequate; ef-ficient, -ficacious; effect-ive, -ual; practicable, expedient &c. 646.

645. Inutility.—N. inutility; uselessness &c. *adj.*; inefficacy, futility; inep-, inap-titude; unsubservience; inadequacy &c. (*insufficiency*) 640; inefficiency &c. (*incompetence*) 158; unskilfulness &c. 699; disservice; unfruitfulness &c. (*unproductiveness*) 169; labour -in vain, – lost, – of Sisyphus; lost -trouble, – labour; work of Penelope; sleeveless errand, wild goose chase, mere farce.

tautology &c. (*repetition*) 104; supererogation &c. (*redundance*) 641.

vanitas vanitatum, vanity, inanity, worthlessness, nugacity; triviality &c. (*unimportance*) 643.

caput mortuum, waste paper, dead letter; blunt tool.

litter, rubbish, lumber, odds and ends, cast-off clothes; button-top; shoddy; rags, orts, trash, refuse, sweepings, scourings, off-scourings, dross, slag, waste, rubble, dottle, drast, *débris*; stubble, leavings; broken meat; dregs &c. (*dirt*) 653; weeds, tares; rubbish heap, dust hole; *rudera*, deads.

fruges consumere natus &c. (*drone*) 683.

V. be -useless &c. *adj.*; go a begging &c. (*redundant*) 641; fail &c. 732.

seek –, strive- after impossibilities; use vain efforts, labour in vain, roll the stone of Sisyphus, beat the air, lash the waves, *battre l'eau avec un bâton, donner un coup d'épée dans l'eau*, fish in the air, milk the ram, drop a bucket into an empty well, sow the sand; bay the moon; preach –, speak- to the winds; whistle jigs to a milestone; kick against the pricks, *se battre contre des moulins*; lock the stable door

applicable, available, ready, handy, at hand, tangible; commodious, adaptable; of all work.

Adv. usefully &c. *adj.*; *pro bono publico.*

---

when the steed is stolen &c. (*too late*) 135; hold a farthing candle to the sun; cast pearls before swine &c. (*waste*) 638; carry coals to Newcastle &c. (*redundance*) 641; wash a blackamoor white &c. (*impossible*) 471.

render -useless &c. *adj.*; dis-mantle, -mast, -mount, -qualify, -able; unrig; cripple, lame &c. (*injure*) 659; spike guns, clip the wings; put out of gear.

Adj. useless, inutile, inefficacious, futile, unavailing, bootless; inoperative &c. 158; inadequate &c. (*insufficient*) 640; in-, un-sub-servient; inept, inefficient &c. (*impotent*) 158; of no -avail &c. (*use*) 644; ineffectual &c. (*failure*) 732; incompetent &c. (*unskilful*) 699; 'stale, flat and unprofitable'; superfluous &c. (*redundant*) 641; dispensable; thrown away &c. (*wasted*) 638; abortive &c. (*immature*) 674.

worth-, value-less; unsaleable; not worth a straw &c. (*trifling*) 643; dear at any price.

vain, empty, inane; gain-, profit-, fruit-less; un-serviceable, -profitable; ill-spent; unproductive &c. 169; *hors de combat*; barren, sterile, impotent, unproductive; effete, past work &c. (*impaired*) 659; obsolete &c. (*old*) 124; fit for the -dust-hole, - wastepaper basket; good for nothing; of no earthly use; not worth -having, - powder and shot; leading to no end, uncalled for; un-necessary, -needed, superfluous.

Adv. uselessly &c. *adj.*; to -little, - no, - little or no- purpose. **Int.** *cui bono?* what's the good!

---

646. [Specific subservience.] **Expedience.—N.** expedien-ce, -cy; desirableness, -bility &c. *adj.*; fitness &c. (*agreement*) 23; utility &c. 644; propriety; advantage; opportunism, pragmatism.

high time &c. (*occasion*) 134.

V. be -expedient &c. *adj.*; suit &c. (*agree*) 23; befit; suit -, befit- the -time, - season, - occasion.

conform &c. 82.

Adj. expedient; desir-, advis-, acceptable; convenient; worth while, meet; fit, -ting; due, proper, eligible, seemly, becoming; befitting &c. *v.*; opportune &c. (*in season*) 134; *in loco*; suitable &c. (*accordant*) 23; applicable &c. (*useful*) 644; practical, effective, pragmatical; suitable, handy; appropriate.

Adv. in the right place; conveniently &c. *adj.*; in the nick of time.

Phr. *operæ pretium est.*

647. Inexpedience.—N. inexpedien-ce, -cy; undesira-bleness, -bility &c. *adj.*; discommodity, impropriety; unfitness &c. (*disagreement*) 24; in-utility &c. 645; inconvenience, in-advisability; disadvantage.

V. be -inexpedient &c. *adj.*; come amiss &c. (*disagree*) 24; embarrass &c. (*hinder*) 706; put to inconvenience; pay too dear for one's whistle.

Adj. inexpedient, undesirable; un-, in-advisable; objectionable; troublesome, in-apt, -eligible, -admissible, -convenient; in-, dis-commodious; disadvantageous; inappropriate, unsuitable, unfit &c. (*inconsonant*) 24.

ill-contrived, -advised; unsatisfactory; unprofitable &c., unsubservient &c. (*useless*) 645; inopportune &c. (*unseasonable*) 135; out of -, in the wrong-place; improper, unseemly.

clumsy, awkward; cum-brous, -bersome; lumbering, unwieldy, hulky; un-manageable &c. (*impracticable*) 704; impedient &c. (*in the way*) 706, unnecessary &c. (*redundant*) 641.

Phr. it will never do.

648. [Capability of producing good. Good qualities.] **Goodness.—N.** goodness &c. *adj.*; excellence, merit; virtue &c. 944; value, worth, price.

super-excellence, -eminence; superiority &c. 33; perfection &c. 650; *coup de maître*; master-piece, *chef d'œuvre*, prime, flower, cream, *élite*, pick, A1, none such, *nonpareil*, *crème de la crème*, flower of the flock, cock of the roost, salt of the earth; champion.

tid-bit; gem, – of the first water; *bijou*, precious stone, jewel, pearl, diamond, ruby, brilliant, treasure; good thing; *rara avis*, one in a thousand.

beneficence &c. 906; good man &c. 948.

V. be -beneficial &c. *adj.*; produce –, do- -good &c. 618; profit &c. (*be of use*) 644; benefit; confer a -benefit &c. 618.

be the making of, do a world of good, make a man of.

produce a good effect; do a good turn, confer an obligation; improve &c. 658.

do no harm, break no bones.

be -good &c. *adj.*; excel, transcend &c. (*be superior*) 33; bear away the bell.

stand the -proof, – test; pass -muster, – an examination.

challenge comparison, vie, emulate, rival.

Adj. harm-, hurt-less; unobnoxious; in-nocuous, -nocent, -offensive.

beneficial, valuable, of value; serviceable &c. (*useful*) 644; advantageous, profitable, edifying; salutary &c. (*healthful*) 656.

favourable; propitious &c. (*hope-giving*) 858; fair.

good, – as gold; excellent; better; superior &c. 33; above par; nice, fine; genuine &c. (*true*) 494.

best, choice, select, picked, elect, eximious, *recherché*, rare, priceless; unpara-goned, -lleled &c. (*supreme*) 33; superlatively &c. 33; good; superfine, -excellent; bonzer; of the first water; first-rate, -class; high-wrought; exquisite, very best, crack, prime, tip-top, gilt-edged, capital, cardinal; standard &c. (*perfect*) 650; inimitable.

admirable, estimable; praiseworthy &c. (*approve*) 931; pleasing &c. 829; *couleur de rose*, precious, of great price;

649. [Capability of producing evil. Bad qualities.] **Badness.—N.** hurtfulness &c. *adj.*; virulence.

evil doer &c. 913; bane &c. 663; plague-spot &c. (*insalubrity*) 657; evil star, ill wind; snake in the grass, skeleton in the closet; *amari aliquid*, thorn in the side; Jonah, jinx, hoodoo.

malignity; malevolence &c. 907; tender mercies [ironically].

ill-treatment, annoyance, molestation, abuse, oppression, persecution, outrage; misusage &c. 679; injury &c. (*damage*) 659.

badness &c. *adj.*; peccancy, abomination; painfulness &c. 830; pestilence &c. (*disease*) 655; guilt &c. 947; depravity &c. 945.

V. be -hurtful &c. *adj.*; cause –, produce –, inflict –, work –, do- evil &c. 619; damnify, endamage, hurt, harm, scathe; injure &c. (*damage*) 659; pain &c. 830.

wrong, aggrieve, oppress, persecute; trample –, tread –, bear hard –, put-upon; overburden; weigh -down, – heavy on; victimize; run down; molest &c. 830.

maltreat, abuse; ill-use, -treat; thwart, buffet, bruise, scratch, maul; smite &c. (*scourge*) 972; do -violence, – harm, – a mischief; stab, pierce, outrage.

do –, make- mischief; bring –, get-into trouble.

destroy &c. 162.

Adj. hurt-, harm-, scath-, bane-, baleful; injurious, deleterious, detrimental, noxious, pernicious, mischievous, full of mischief, mischief-making, malefic, malignant, nocuous, noisome; prejudicial; dis-serviceable, -advantageous; wide-wasting.

unlucky, sinister; obnoxious, untoward, disastrous.

oppressive, burdensome, onerous; malign &c. (*malevolent*) 907.

corrupting &c. (corrupt &c. 659); virulent, venomous, envenomed, corrosive; poisonous &c. (*morbific*) 657; deadly &c. (*killing*) 361; destructive &c. (*destroying*) 162; inauspicious &c. 859.

bad, ill, arrant, as bad as bad can be, dreadful; hor-rid, -rible; dire; rank,

costly &c. (*dear*) 814; worth -its weight in gold, - a Jew's eye, - a king's ransom; matchless, peerless, invaluable, inestimable, precious as the apple of the eye.

tolerable &c. (*not very good*) 651; up to the mark, un-exceptionable, -objectionable; satisfactory, tidy.

in -good, - fair- condition; fresh; unspoiled; sound &c. (*perfect*) 650.

Adv. beneficially &c. *adj.*; well &c. 618.

---

peccant, foul, fulsome; rotten, - at the core.

vile, base, villainous; mean &c. (*paltry*) 643; injured &c., deteriorated &c. 659; unsatisfactory, exception, -able, indifferent; below par &c. (*imperfect*) 651; ill-contrived, -conditioned; wretched, sad, grievous, deplorable, lamentable; piti-ful, -able, woeful &c. (*painful*) 830.

evil, wrong; depraved &c. 945; shocking; reprehensible &c. (*disapprove*) 932.

hateful, - as a toad; abominable, detestable, execrable, cursed, accursed, confounded; damn-ed, -able; infernal; diabolic &c. (*malevolent*) 907.

inadvisable &c. (*inexpedient*) 647; unprofitable &c. (*useless*) 645; incompetent &c. (*unskilful*) 699; irremediable &c. (*hopeless*) 859.

Adv. badly &c. *adj.*; wrong, ill; to one's cost; where the shoe pinches.

Phr. bad is the best; the worst come to the worst.

---

650. Perfection. — N. perfection; perfectness &c. *adj.*; indefectibility; impecc-ancy, -ability.

pink, *beau idéal*, phœnix, paragon; pink -, acme- of perfection; *ne plus ultra*; summit &c. 210.

cygne noir; philosopher's stone; chrysolite, Koh-i-noor, black tulip.

model, standard, pattern, mirror, admirable Crichton; trump; very prince of.

master-piece, -stroke, super-excellence &c. (*goodness*) 648; transcendence &c. (*superiority*) 33.

V. be -perfect &c. *adj.*; transcend &c. (*be supreme*) 33.

bring to perfection, perfect, ripen, mature; consummate, complete &c. 729; put in trim &c. (*prepare*) 673; put the finishing touch to.

Adj. perfect, faultless, ideal; indefective, -ficient, -fectible; immaculate, spotless, impeccable; free from -imperfection &c. 651; un-blemished, -injured &c. 659; sound, - as a roach; in perfect condition; scathless, intact, harmless; seaworthy &c. (*safe*) 644; right as a trivet; *in seipso totus teres atque rotundus*; consummate &c. (*complete*) 52; finished &c. 729; complete in itself.

best &c. (*good*) 648; model, standard; inimitable, unparagoned, unparalleled &c. (*supreme*) 33; superhuman, divine;

651. Imperfection.—N. imperfection; imperfectness &c. *adj.*; deficiency; inadequacy &c. (*insufficiency*) 640; peccancy &c. (*badness*) 649; immaturity &c. 674.

fault, defect, weak point; screw loose; rift within the lute; fly in the ointment; flaw &c. (*break*) 70; gap &c. 198; twist &c. 243; taint, attainder; bar sinister, hole in one's coat; blemish &c. 848; weakness &c. 160; half-blood, touch of the tar brush; shortcoming &c. 304; drawback; seamy side.

mediocrity; no great -shakes, - catch; not much to boast of.

V. be -imperfect &c. *adj.*; have a -defect &c. *n.*; lie under a disadvantage; spring a leak.

not -, barely- pass muster; fall short &c. 304.

Adj. imperfect; not -perfect &c. 650; de-ficient, -fective; faulty, unsound, mutilated, tainted; out of -order, - tune; cracked, leaky; sprung; warped &c. (*distort*) 243; lame; injured &c. (*deteriorated*) 659; peccant &c. (*bad*) 649; frail &c. (*weak*) 160; inadequate &c. (*insufficient*) 640; crude &c. (*unprepared*) 674; incomplete &c. 53; found wanting; below par; shorthanded; below -, under- its full -strength, - complement.

indifferent, middling, ordinary, medi-

beyond all praise &c. (*approbation*) 931;
sans peur et sans reproche.

Adv. to perfection, to the limit;
perfectly &c. *adj.*; *ad unguem*; clean,
– as a whistle.

ocre; average &c. 29; so-so; *così-così*,
milk and water; tolerable, fair, passable; pretty -well, – good; rather –,
moderately- good; good –, well- enough;
decent; not -bad, – amiss; unobjectionable, admissible, bearable, only better
than nothing.

secondary, inferior; second-rate, -best, one-horse.

Adv. almost &c.; to a limited extent, rather &c. 32; pretty,
moderately; only; considering, all things considered, enough.

Phr. *surgit amari aliquid.*

---

652. Cleanness.—N. cleanness &c.
adj.; purity; cleaning &c. *v.*; purification, defecation &c. *v.*; purgation, lustration; de-, abs-tersion; epuration,
mundation, ablution, lavation, colature; disinfection &c. *v.*; drain-, sewerage.

lavatory, bath, -room; swimming
pool, natatorium; public baths; hot –,
cold –, Turkish –, Swedish –, Russian –,
vapour- bath; *hammam*, laundry, washhouse; washerwoman, laundress, laundryman; scavenger, cleaner, sweeper,
goody; crossing sweeper, white wings,
dustman, sweep.

brush; broom, besom, carpet-sweeper,
vacuum-cleaner, mop, squilgee, rake,
shovel, sieve, riddle, screen, filter;
scraper, strigil.

napkin, *serviette*, cloth, table-, carving-cloth, table-linen, napery, maukin,
handkerchief, towel, sudary; doyley,
doily, duster, sponge, mop, swab.

cover, drugget, mat, doormat.

soap, wash, lotion, detergent, cathartic, purgative; purifier &c. *v.*; dentifrice, tooth-powder, -paste; mouth
wash; disinfectant.

V. be –, render- clean &c. *adj.*

clean, -se; mundify, rinse, wring,
flush, full, wipe, mop, sponge, scour,
swab, scrub, holystone, brush up.

wash, shampoo, lave, launder, buck;
abs-, de-terge; clear, purify; de-purate,
-spumate, -fecate; purge, expurgate;
Bowdlerize; elutriate, lixiviate, edulcorate, clarify, refine, rack; fil-ter,
-trate; drain, strain.

disinfect, sterilize, pasteurize, fumigate, ventilate, deodorize; whitewash.

sift, winnow, screen, riddle, pick,
weed, comb, rake, brush, sweep.

653. Uncleanness.—N. uncleanness
&c. *adj.*; impurity; immundi-ty, -city;
impurity &c. [of mind] 961.

defilement, contamination &c. *v.*;
defœdation; soil-ure, -iness; abomination; leaven; taint, -ure; fetor &c. 401.

decay; putre-scence, -faction; corruption; mould, must, mildew, dry-rot,
mucor, rubigo, caries.

slovenry; slovenliness &c. *adj.*;
squalor.

dowdy, drab, slut, malkin, slattern,
sloven, slammerkin, scrub, draggletail,
mudlark, dustman, sweep; beast.

dirt, filth, soil, slop; dust, cobweb,
flue; smoke, soot, smudge, smut, grime,
raff.

sordes, dregs, grounds, lees; sedi-,
settle-ment; heel-tap; dross, -iness;
mother, precipitate, *scoriæ*, ashes, cinders, recrement, slag; scum, froth.

hog-wash, swill, ditch-, dish-, bilgewater; rinsings, cheese-parings; sweepings &c. (*useless refuse*) 645; off-, outscourings; off-scum; *caput mortuum*,
residuum, sprue, feculence, clinker,
draff; scurf, -iness; *exuviæ*, morphew;
fur, -fur; dandruff; tartar.

riffraff; vermin, louse, cootie, flea,
bug.

mud, mire, quagmire, *alluvium*, silt,
sludge, slime, slush, slosh.

spawn, offal, garbage, carrion; *excreta* &c. 299; slough, peccant humour,
pus, matter, suppuration, *lienteria*;
fæces, excrement, ordure, dung; sew-,
sewer-age; muck, coprolite; guano,
manure, compost.

dunghill, *coluvies*, mixen, midden,
bog, laystall, sink, w.c., water-, earthcloset, latrine, privy, jakes, John's;
cess, -pool; sump, sough, *cloaca*, drain,

rout –, clear –, sweep &c.- out; make a clean sweep of.

Adj. clean, -ly; pure; immaculate; spot-, stain-, taint-less; without a stain, un-stained, -spotted, -soiled, -sullied, -tainted, -infected, -adulterated; aseptic; sweet, – as a nut.

neat, spruce, tidy, trim, gimp, clean as a new penny, like a cat in pattens; cleaned &c. *v.*; kempt.

Adv. neatly &c. *adj.*; clean as a whistle.

———

sewer, common sewer; Cloacina; dust-hole.

sty, pig-sty, lair, den, Augean stable, sink of corruption; slum, rookery.

V. be –, become- unclean &c. *adj.*; rot, putrefy, fester, rankle, reek; stink &c. 401; mould, -er; go -bad &c. *adj.*

render -unclean &c. *adj.*; dirt, -y; soil, smoke, tarnish, slaver, spot, smear, daub, blot, blur, smudge, smutch, smirch; d-, dr-abble, -aggle; spatter, slubber; be-smear &c., -mire, -slime, -grime, -foul; splash, stain, distain, maculate, sully, pollute, defile, debase, corrupt &c. (*injure*) 659; cover with -dust &c. *n.*; drabble in the mud.

contaminate, taint, leaven; wallow in the mire; slob-, slab-ber.

Adj. unclean, dirty, filthy, grimy; soiled &c. *v.*; not to be handled with kid gloves; dusty, snuffy, smutty, sooty, smoky; thick, turbid, dreggy; slimy.

uncleanly, slovenly, untidy, sluttish, dowdy, slatternly, draggle-tailed; un-combed, -kempt, -scoured, -swept, -wiped, -washed, -strained, -purified; squalid.

nasty, coarse, foul, impure, offensive, abominable, beastly, reeky, reechy; fetid &c. 401;

mouldy, lentiginous, musty, mildewed, rusty, moth-eaten, mucid, rancid, bad, gone bad, touched, fusty, reasty, rotten, corrupt, tainted, high, fly-blown, maggoty; putr-id, -escent, -efied; purulent, carious, peccant, fec-al, -ulent; stercoraceous, excrementitious; scurfy, impetiginous; gory, bloody; rotting &c. *v.*; rotten as -a pear, – cheese.

crapulous &c. (*intemperate*) 954; gross &c. (*impure in mind*) 961;

654. Health.—N. health, sanity; soundness &c. *adj.*; vigour; good –, perfect –, excellent –, rude –, robust-health; bloom, *mens sana in corpore sano*; Hygeia; incorrupti-on, -bility; good state –, clean bill- of health, eupepsia.

V. be in health &c. *adj.*; bloom, flourish.

keep -body and soul together, – on one's legs; enjoy -good, – a good state of- health; have a clean bill of health.

return to health; recover &c. 660; get better &c. (*improve*) 658; take a -new, – fresh- lease of life; convalesce, be convalescent, recruit; restore to health; cure &c. (*restore*) 660.

Adj. health-y, -ful; in -health &c. *n.*; well, sound, strong, fit, hearty, hale, fresh, blooming, green, whole; florid, flush, hardy, stanch, staunch,

655. Disease.*—N. disease; illness, sickness &c. *adj.*; ailing &c. *v.*; 'the ills that flesh is heir to'; morb-idity, -osity; infirmity, ailment, indisposition; complaint, disorder, malady; distemper, -ature.

visitation, attack, seizure, stroke, fit, epilepsy, apoplexy, shock, shell-shock.

delicacy, loss of health, valetudinarianism, invalidism, cachexy; *cachexia*, atrophy, *marasmus*; indigestion, *dyspepsia*; decay &c. (*deterioration*) 659; malnutrition, decline, consumption, palsy, paralysis, prostration; occupational diseases.

taint, pollution, infection, contagion, septicity, septicæmia, blood poisoning, pyæmia, epi-, en-demic; murrain, plague, pestilence, virus, pox.

sore, ulcer, abscess, fester, boil; pimple &c. (*swelling*) 250; carbuncle,

* Extended lists of different diseases are beyond the scope of this work.

brave, robust, vigorous, weather-proof; convalescent.

un-scathed, -injured, -maimed, -marred, -tainted; sound of wind and limb, safe and sound; without a scratch.

on one's legs; sound as a -roach, – bell; fresh as -a daisy, – a rose, – April; picture of health; bursting with health; fit as a fiddle; hearty as a buck; in -fine, – high- feather; in -good case, – full bloom; in fine fettle; pretty bobbish, tolerably well, as well as can be expected.

sanitary &c. (health-giving) 656; sanatory &c. (remedial) 662.

gathering, whitlow, imposthume, peccant humour, issue; rot, canker, cancer, *carcinoma, caries*, mortification, corruption, gangrene, *sphacelus*, leprosy, eruption, rash, breaking out, venereal disease.

fever, calenture; inflammation.

fatal &c. (hopeless) 859- -disease &c.; dangerous illness, galloping consumption, churchyard cough; general breaking up, break up of the system.

[Disease of mind] neurasthenia; idiocy &c. 499; insanity &c. 503.

martyr to disease; cripple; 'the halt, the lame and the blind'; valetudinar-y, -ian; invalid, patient, case; sick-room, -chamber, hospital &c. 662.

[Science of disease] path-, eti-, nos-ology, therapeutics, diagnosis, prognosis.

V. be -ill &c. *adj.*; ail, suffer, labour under, be affected with, complain of; droop, flag, languish, halt; sicken, peak, pine, waste away, fail, lose strength; gasp.

keep one's bed; feign sickness &c. (falsehood) 544, malinger.

lay -by, – up; take –, catch- -a disease &c. *n.*, – an infection; be stricken by; break out.

Adj. diseased; ailing &c. *v.*; ill, – of; taken ill, seized with; indisposed, unwell, sick, squeamish, poorly, seedy; affected –, afflicted- with illness; laid up, confined, bed-ridden, invalided, in hospital, on the sick list; out of -health, – sorts; valetudinary.

un-sound, -healthy; sickly, morbose, healthless, infirm, chlorotic, unbraced, drooping, flagging, lame, halt, crippled, halting.

morbid, tainted, vitiated, peccant, contaminated, poisoned, septic, tabid, mangy, leprous, cankered; rotten, – to, – at- the core; withered, palsied, paralytic, tuberculous; dyspeptic.

touched in the wind, broken-winded, spavined, gasping; *hors de combat* &c. (useless) 645.

weak-ly, -ened &c. (weak) 160; decrepit; decayed &c. (deteriorated) 659; incurable &c. (hopeless) 859; in declining health; cranky; in a bad way, in danger, prostrate; moribund &c. (death) 360.

morbific, epidemic &c. 657.

---

656. Salubrity.—N. salubrity, salubriousness; healthiness &c. *adj.*

fine -air, – climate; eudiometer.

[Preservation of health] *hygiène*; valetudinarian, -ism, preventorium, sanitarian; *sanitarium, sanitorium*, immunity.

V. be -salubrious &c. *adj.*; agree with, be good for; assimilate &c. 23.

Adj. salu-brious, -tary, -tiferous, wholesome; health-y, -ful; sanitary, prophylactic, benign, bracing, tonic,

657. Insalubrity.—N. insalubrity; unhealthiness &c. *adj.*; non-naturals; plague spot; malaria &c. (poison) 663; death in the pot, contagion.

Adj. insalubrious; un-healthy, -wholesome; noxious, noisome, foul; morbi-fic, -ferous; mephitic, septic, azotic, deleterious; pesti-lent, -ferous, -lential; virulent, venomous, envenomed, poisonous, toxic, narcotic.

contagious, infectious, catching, taking, communicable, epidemic, zymotic;

invigorating, **good for,** nutritious, hyg-eian, -ienic.

in-noxious, -nocuous, -nocent; harmless, uninjurious, uninfectious; immune.

sanative &c. (*remedial*) 662; restorative &c. (*reinstate*) 660; useful &c. 644.

658. Improvement.—N. improvement; a-, melioration; betterment; mend, amendment, emendation; mending &c. *v.*; advancement; advance &c. (*progress*) 282; ascent &c. 305; promotion, preferment; elevation &c. 307; increase &c. 35.

cultiv-, civiliz-ation; menticulture, culture, march of intellect; eugenics, euthenics, meliorism, telesis.

reform, -ation; revision, radical reform; second thoughts, correction, *limæ labor,* refinement, elaboration; purification &c. 652; repair &c. (*restoration*) 660; recovery &c. 660.

revise; revised –, new- edition.

reformer, radical, progressive.

V. improve; be –, become –, get-better; mend, amend.

advance &c. (*progress*) 282; ascend &c. 305; increase &c. 35; fructify, ripen, mature; pick up, come about, rally, take a favourable turn; turn -over a new leaf, – the corner; raise one's head, sow one's wild oats; recover &c. 660.

be -better &c. *adj.*, – improved by; turn to -right, – good, – best- account; profit by, reap the benefit of; make -good use of, – capital out of; place to good account; take advantage of.

render better, improve, emend, make over, better; a–, meliorate; correct.

improve –, refine- upon; rectify; enrich, mellow, elaborate, fatten.

promote, cultivate, advance, forward, enhance; bring -forward, – on; foster &c. 707; invigorate &c. (*strengthen*) 159.

touch –, rub –, brush –, furbish –, bolster –, vamp –, brighten –, warm-up; polish, cook, make the most of, set off to advantage; prune; repair &c. (*restore*) 660; put in order &c. (*arrange*) 60.

review, revise, edit, redact; make -corrections, – improvements &c. *n.*; doctor &c. (*remedy*) 662; purify &c. 652.

sporadic, endemic, pandemic, epizoötic.

innutritious, indigestible, ungenial; uncongenial &c. (*disagreeing*) 24.

deadly &c. (*killing*) 361.

---

659. Deterioration.—N. deterioration, debasement; want, ebb; recession &c. 287; retrogradation &c. 283; decrease &c. 36.

degenera-cy, -tion, -teness; degradation; deprav-ation, -ement; depravity &c. 945; demoralization, retrogression.

impairment, inquination, injury, damage, loss, detriment, delaceration, outrage, havoc, inroad, ravage, scath; perversion, prostitution, vitiation, discoloration, oxidation, pollution, defœdation, poisoning, venenation, leaven, contamination, canker, corruption, adulteration, alloy.

decl-ine, -ension, -ination; decadence, -cy; falling off &c. *v.*; caducity, decrepitude, senility.

decay, dilapidation, ravages of time, wear and tear; cor-, e-rosion; mouldi-, rotten-ness; moth and rust, dry-rot, blight, marasmus, atrophy, collapse; disorganization; *délabrement* &c. (*destruction*) 162.

wreck, mere wreck, honeycomb, *magni nominis umbra.*

V. be –, become--worse,–deteriorated &c. *adj.*; have seen better days, deteriorate, degenerate, fall off; wane &c. (*decrease*) 36; ebb; retrograde &c. 283; decline, droop; go down &c. (*sink*) 306; go -downhill, – on from bad to worse, – farther and fare worse; jump out of the frying pan into the fire.

run to -seed, – waste; swale, sweal; lapse, be the worse for; break, – down; spring a leak, crack, start; shrivel &c. (*contract*) 195; fade, go off, wither, moulder, rot, rankle, decay, go bad; go to –, fall into- decay; 'fall into the sear and yellow leaf,' rust, crumble, shake; totter, – to its fall; perish &c. 162; die &c. 360.

[Render less good] deteriorate; weaken &c. 160; put back; taint, infect, contaminate, poison, empoison,

relieve, refresh, revive, infuse new blood into, recruit, re-invigorate, re-new, revivify, freshen, build -afresh, – anew; uplift, inspire.

re-form, -model, -organise; new model, civilize.

view in a new light, think better of, appeal from Philip drunk to Philip sober.

palliate, mitigate; lessen &c. 36- an evil.

Adj. improving &c. *v.*; progressive, improved &c. *v.*; better, – off, – for; all the better for; better advised.

reform-, emend-atory; reparatory &c. (*restorative*) 660; remedial &c. 662.

corrigible, improvable, curable, ac-cultural.

Adv. on -consideration, – reconsider-ation, – second thoughts, – better advice; *ad melius inquirendum*; on the -mend, – up grade.

envenom, canker, corrupt, exulcerate, pollute, vitiate, inquinate; de-, em-base; denaturalize, leaven; de-flower, -bauch, -file, -prave, -grade; stain &c. (*dirt*) 653; discolour; alloy, adulterate, sophisticate, tamper with, prejudice.

pervert, prostitute, demoralize, bru-talize; render vicious &c. 945; compro-mise.

embitter, ex-, acerbate, aggravate.

injure, impair, labefy, damage, harm, hurt, shend, scathe, spoil, mar, despoil, dilapidate, waste; overrun; ravage; pillage &c. 791.

wound, stab, pierce, maim, lame, surbate, cripple, hough, hamstring, hit between wind and water, scotch, mangle, mutilate, disfigure, blemish, deface, warp.

blight, rot; cor-, e-rode, eat away; wear -away, – out; gnaw, – at the root of; sap, mine, undermine, shake, sap the foundations of, break up; dis-organ-ize, -mantle, -mast; destroy &c. 162.

damnify &c. (*aggrieve*) 649; do one's worst; knock down; deal a blow to; play -havoc, – sad havoc, – the mischief, – the deuce, – the very devil- -with, – among; decimate.

Adj. unimproved &c. (improve &c. 658); deteriorated &c. *v.*; altered, – for the worse; injured &c. *v.*; sprung; withering, spoiling, &c. *v.*; on the -wane, – decline; tabid; degenerate; worse; the –, all the- worse for; out of -repair, – tune; imperfect &c. 651; the worse for wear; battered; weather-ed, -beaten; stale, *passé*, shaken, dilapidated, frayed, faded, wilted, shabby, second-hand, second-rate, threadbare; worn, – to- -a thread, – a shadow, – the stump, rags; reduced, – to a skeleton, skeletonized; far gone.

decayed &c. *v.*; moth-, worm-eaten; mildewed, rusty, mouldy, spotted, seedy, time-worn, moss-grown; discoloured; effete, wasted, crumbling, mouldering, rotten, cankered, blighted, tainted; depraved &c. (*vicious*) 945; decrep-id, -it; broken down; done, – for, – up; worn out, used up; fit for the -dust-hole, – wastepaper basket; past work &c. (*useless*) 645.

at a low ebb, in a bad way, on one's last legs, washed -up, – out; undermined, deciduous; nodding to its fall &c. (*destruction*) 162; tottering &c. (*dangerous*) 665; past cure &c. (*hopeless*) 859; fatigued &c. 688; backward, retrograde &c. (*retrogressive*) 283; deleterious &c. 649; behind the times.

Adv. on the down grade; beyond hope.

Phr. out of the frying pan into the fire; *ægrescit medendo*.

---

660. Restoration.—**N.** restor-ation, -al; re-instatement, -placement, -habi-litation, -establishment, -construction; reproduction &c. 163; re-novation, -newal; reviv-al, -escence; refreshment

661. Relapse.—**N.** relapse, lapse; falling back &c. *v.*; retrogradation &c. (*retrogression*) 283; deterioration &c. 659.

[Return to, or recurrence of a bad

&c. 689; re-suscitation, -animation, -vivification, -viction; Phœnix; reorganization.

renaissance, renascence, rebirth, second youth, rejuvenation, rejuvenescence, new birth; regenera-tion, -cy, -teness; palingenesis, reconversion, resurgence, resurrection.

redress, retrieval, reclamation, recovery; convalescence; resumption, résumption.

recurrence &c. (repetition) 104; réchauffé, rifacimento.

cure, recure, sanation; healing &c. v.; redintegration; rectification, instauration.

repair, reparation, mending; recruiting &c. v.; cicatrization; disinfection; tinkering.

reaction; redemption &c. (deliverance) 672; restitution &c. 790; relief &c. 834.

mender, repairer, renewer; tinker, cobbler; doctor &c. 662; vis medicatrix &c. (remedy) 662.

curableness.

V. return to the original state; recover, rally, revive; come -to, - round, - to oneself; pull through, weather the storm, be oneself again; get -well, - round, - the better of, - over, - about; rise from -one's ashes, - the grave; resurge, resurrect; survive &c. (outlive) 110; resume, reappear; come to, - life again; live -, rise- again; relive.

heal, skin over, cicatrize; right itself.

restore, put back, place in statu quo; re-instate, -place, -seat, -habilitate, -establish, -estate, -install.

re-construct, -build, -organize, -constitute; reconvert; re-new, -novate; recondition; regenerate; rejuvenate.

re-deem, -claim, -cover, -trieve; rescue &c. (deliver) 672.

redress, recure; cure, heal, remedy, doctor, physic, medicate; break of; bring round, set on one's legs.

re-suscitate, -vive, -animate, -vivify, -call to life; reproduce &c. 163; warm up; reinvigorate, refresh &c. 689.

redintegrate, make whole; recoup &c. 790; make -good, - all square; rectify; put -, set- -right, - to rights, - straight; set up, correct; put in order &c. (arrange) 60; refit, recruit; fill up, - the ranks; reinforce.

repair, mend; put in -repair, - thorough repair, - complete repair; retouch, botch, vamp, tinker, doctor, cobble; do -, patch -, plaster -, vamp- up; darn, fine-draw, heel-piece; stop a gap, stanch, staunch, caulk, calk, careen, splice, bind up wounds.

Adj. restored &c. v.; redivivus, convalescent; in a fair way; none the worse; rejuvenated, renascent.

restoring &c. v.; restorative, recuperative; sana-, repara-tive, -tory; curative, remedial.

restor-, recover-, san-, remedi-, retriev-, cur-able.

Adv. in statu quo; as you were.

Phr. revenons à nos moutons.

state] backsliding, recidivation, recrudescence.

V. relapse, lapse; fall -, slide -, sink-back; have a relapse; return; retrograde &c. 283; recidivate; fall off &c. 659 again.

————

662. Remedy.—N. remedy, help, redress; antidote, anti-toxin, anti-,

663. Bane.—N. bane, curse, thorn in the -side, -flesh, bugbear, bête noire;

counter-poison, prophylactic, antiseptic, germicide, bactericide, corrective, restorative, stimulant, pick-me-up, tonic; sedative &c. 174; palliative; febrifuge; alter-ant, -ative; specific; emetic, carminative; narcotic &c. *adj.*; Nepenthe, Mithridate.

cure; radical –, perfect –, certain-cure; sovereign remedy.

physic, medicine, patent medicine, Galenicals, simples, drug, potion, draught, dose, pill, bolus, lozenge, tablet, tabloid, capsule; electuary; linct-us, -ure; medicament.

nostrum, receipt, recipe, prescription; catholicon, panacea, elixir, *elixir vitæ*, philosopher's stone; balm, balsam, cordial, theriac, ptisan.

salve, ointment, cerate, oil, lenitive, lotion, cosmetic; plaster; epithem, embrocation, liniment, cataplasm, sinapism, arquebusade, traumatic, vulnerary, pepastic, poultice, collyrium, depilatory.

compress, pledget; bandage &c. (*support*) 215.

treatment, medical treatment, regimen; diet-ary, -etics; *vis medicatrix, naturæ; medicine expectante;* seton,

evil &c. 619; hurtfulness &c. (*badness*) 649; painfulness &c. (*cause of pain*) 830; scourge &c. (*punishment*) 975; *damnosa hereditas;* white elephant.

sting, fang. thorn, tang, bramble, brier, nettle.

poison, leaven, virus, venom; intoxicant; arsenic, Prussic acid, antimony, tartar emetic, strychnine, nicotine, cyanide of potassium, corrosive sublimate; curare; hyoscine &c.; poison-, mustard-, tear-gas; carbon di-, monoxide; ptomaine poisoning, botulism; miasm, mephitis, malaria, azote, sewer gas; pest, stench &c. 401.

rust, worm, moth, moth and rust, fungus, mildew; dry-rot; canker, -worm; cancer; torpedo; viper &c. (*evil-doer*) 913; demon &c. 980.

hemlock, hellebore, nightshade, *belladonna,* henbane, aconite; Upas tree.

drugs, dope, opium, morphia, morphine, cocaine, heroin, hashish, bhang.

[Science of poisons] Toxicology.

Adj. baneful &c. (*bad*) 649; poisonous &c. (*unwholesome*) 657.

blood-letting, bleeding, venesection, phlebotomy, cupping, leeches; operation, surgical operation; tonsillectomy, appendectomy; injection, electrolysis, massage.

pharma-cy, -cology, -ceutics; acology; materia medica, pharmacopœia, therapeutics, therapy, posology, pathology &c. 655; homœ-, heter-, all-, hydr-opathy; cold water –, open air- cure; dietetics; sur-, chirur-gery, osteopathy; healing art, leechcraft, practice of medicine; ortho-pædy, -praxy; dentistry, midwifery, obstetrics, gynæcology.

faith -cure, – healing; psycho-therapy, -analysis, psychiatry.

hospital, infirmary, clinic; pest-, lazar-house; lazaretto, lazaret; lock hospital; *maison de santé; ambulance;* dispensary; *sanatorium, sanitarium,* spa, baths, pump-room, well; *hospice;* Red Cross; nursing home; asylum.

doctor, physician, surgeon; medical –, general- practitioner, consultant, specialist; medical attendant; medical student, medico; chemist, apothecary, pharmacopolist, druggist; leech; Æsculapius, Hippocrates, Galen; *accoucheur,* gynæcologist, midwife, oculist, aurist, dentist; operator; osteopath, bonesetter; nurse, monthly nurse, sister; dresser; *masseur, masseuse.*

V. apply a -remedy &c. *n.;* doctor, dose, physic, nurse, minister to, attend, dress the wounds, plaster, bandage, poultice; heal, cure, work a cure, kill or cure, remedy, stay (disease), snatch from the jaws of death; prevent &c. 706; relieve &c. 834; palliate &c. 658:

restore &c. 660; drench with physic; consult, operate, extract, deliver; bleed, cup, let blood, transfuse; electrolyse; psycho-analyse.

Adj. remedial; restorative &c. 660; corrective, palliative, healing; sana-tory, -tive; prophylactic; salutiferous &c. (*salutary*) 656; medic-al, -inal; therapeutic, surgical, chirurgical, orthopedic, epulotic, paregoric, tonic, corroborant, analeptic, balsamic, anodyne, hypnotic, neurotic, narcotic, sedative, lenitive, demulcent, emollient; depuratory; deter-sive, -gent; abstersive, disinfectant, febrifugal, alternative; traumatic, vulnerary.

dietetic, alimentary; nutrit-ious, -ive; peptic; alexi-pharmic, -teric; remedi-, cur-able.

3. *Contingent Subservience*

664. Safety.—N. safety, security, impregnability; invulnera-bility, -ble-ness &c. *adj.*; danger -past, – over; storm blown over; coast clear; escape &c. 671; means of escape, safety-valve; safeguard, palladium, sheet anchor, rock, tower of strength.

guardian-, ward-, warden-ship; tutelage, custody, safe keeping; preservation &c. 670; protection, auspices.

safe-conduct, escort, convoy; guard, shield &c. (*defence*) 717; guardian angel, tutelary -god, – deity, – saint; *genius loci*.

protector, guardian; ward-en, -er; preserver, custodian, *duenna*, *chaperon*, third person.

watch-, ban-dog; Cerberus; watch-, patrol-, police-man, constable, peeler, bobby, copper, cop, bull, flat-foot, detective, armed guard; sentinel, sentry, scout &c. (*warning*) 668; garrison; guard-ship.

[Means of safety] refuge &c., anchor &c. 666; precaution &c. (*preparation*) 673; quarantine, *cordon sanitaire*. [Sense of security] confidence &c. 858.

V. be -safe &c. *adj.*; keep one's head above water, tide over, save one's bacon; ride out –, weather- the storm; light upon one's feet; bear a charmed life; escape &c. 671; possess nine lives.

make –, render- -safe &c. *adj.*; protect, watch over; take care of &c. (*care*) 459; preserve &c. 670; cover, screen, shelter, shroud, flank, ward; guard &c. (*defend*) 717; secure &c. (*restrain*) 751; intrench, fence round &c. (*circumscribe*) 229; house, nestle, ensconce; take charge of.

665. Danger.—N. danger, peril, insecurity, jeopardy, risk, hazard, venture, precariousness, slipperiness; instability &c. 149; defencelessness &c. *adj.*

exposure &c. (*liability*) 177; vulner-ability; vulnerable point, heel of Achilles; forlorn hope &c. (*hopelessness*) 859.

[Dangerous course] leap in the dark &c. (*rashness*) 863; road to ruin, *facilis descensus Averni*, hair-breadth escape.

cause for alarm; source of danger &c. 667. [Approach of danger] rock –, breakers- ahead; storm brewing; clouds -in the horizon, – gathering; warning &c. 668; alarm &c. 669. [Sense of danger] apprehension &c. 860.

V. be -in danger &c. *adj.*; be exposed to –, run into –, incur –, encounter--danger &c. *n.*; run a risk; lay oneself open to &c. (*liability*) 177; lean on –, trust to- a broken reed; feel the ground sliding from under one, have to run for it; have the -chances, – odds- against one.

hang by a thread, totter; tremble on the -verge, – brink; sleep –, stand -on a volcano; sit on a barrel of gunpowder, live in a glass house.

bring –, place –, put- in -danger &c. *n.*; endanger, expose to danger, imperil; jeopard, -ize, compromise; sail too near the wind &c. (*rash*) 863; put one's head in the lion's mouth.

adventure, risk, hazard, venture, stake, set at hazard; run the gauntlet &c. (*dare*) 861; engage in a forlorn hope.

threaten &c. 909- danger; run one

escort, convoy; garrison; watch, mount guard, patrol, scout, spy.

make assurance double sure &c. (*caution*) 864; take up a loose thread; take precautions &c. (*prepare for*) 673; take in a reef; double reef topsails.

seek safety; take –, find- shelter &c. 666; run into port.

Adj. safe, secure, sure; in -safety, – security; have an anchor to windward; on the safe side; under the -shield of, – shade of, – wing of, – shadow of one's wing; under -cover, – lock and key; out of -danger, – the meshes, – harm's way; in -harbour, – port; on sure ground, at anchor, high and dry, above water, on *terra firma*; unthreatened, -molested; protected &c. *v.*; *cavendo tutus*; panoplied &c. (*defended*) 717.

snug, sea-, air-worthy; weather-, water-, fire-, bomb-proof.

defensible, tenable, proof against, invulnerable; un-assailable, -attackable; im-pregnable, -perdible; founded on a rock; inexpugnable.

safe and sound &c. (*preserved*) 670; harmless; scathless &c. (*perfect*) 650; unhazarded; not -dangerous &c. 665.

protecting &c. *v.*; guardian, tutelary; preservative &c. 670; trustworthy &c. 939.

Adv. *ex abundanti cautelâ*; with impunity.

Phr. all's well; all clear; *salva res est*; *suave mari magno*; safety first.

---

hard; lay a trap for &c. (*deceive*) 545.

Adj. in -danger &c. *n.*; endangered &c. *v.*; fraught with danger; danger-, hazard-, peril-, parl-, pericul-ous; unsafe, unprotected &c. (safe, protect &c. 664); insecure, untrustworthy, unreliable; built upon sand, on a sandy basis.

defence-, fence-, guard-, harbourless; unshielded; vulnerable, expugnable, unsheltered, exposed; open to &c. (*liable*) 177.

aux abois, at bay; on -the wrong side of the wall, – a lee shore, – the rocks.

at stake, in question; precarious, aleatory, critical, ticklish; slip-pery, -py; hanging by a thread &c. *v.*; with a halter round one's neck; between -the hammer and the anvil, – Scylla and Charybdis, – two fires; on the -edge, – brink, – verge of a- -precipice, – volcano; in the lion's den, on slippery ground, under fire; not out of the wood.

un-warned, -admonished, -advised; unprepared &c. 674; off one's guard &c. (*inexpectant*) 508.

tottering; un-stable, -steady; shaky, top-heavy, tumble-down, ramshackle, crumbling, waterlogged; help-, guideless; in a bad way; reduced to –, at the last extremity; trembling in the balance; nodding to its fall &c. (*destruction*) 162.

threatening &c. 909; ominous, ill-omened; alarming &c. (*fear*) 860; explosive; poisonous &c. 657.

adventurous &c. (*rash*) 863, (*bold*) 861.

Int. stop! look out! beware! take care!

Phr. *incidit in Scyllam qui vult vitare Charybdim; nam tua res agitur paries dum proximus ardet.*

---

666. [Means of safety.] **Refuge.**—**N.** refuge, sanctuary, retreat, fastness; stronghold, keep, last resort; ward; prison &c. 752; asylum, ark, home, almshouse, refuge for the destitute; hiding-place &c. (*ambush*) 530; *sanctum sanctorum* &c. (*privacy*) 893; cache.

roadstead, anchorage; breakwater, mole, port, haven; harbour, – of refuge; sea-port; pier, jetty, embankment, quay.

667. [Source of danger.] **Pitfall.**—**N.** rocks, reefs, coral reef, sunken rocks, snags; sands, quicksands, Goodwin sands, sandy foundation; slippery ground; breakers, shoals, shallows, bank, shelf, flat, lee shore, iron-bound coast; rock –, breakers- ahead; derelict.

precipice; abyss, chasm, pit, crevasse; maelstrom, whirlpool, eddy, vortex, rapids, current, bore, tidal wave; storm, squall, hurricane, whirl-

covert, shelter, abri, screen, lee-wall, wing, shield, umbrella; splash-, dash-board, mudguard.

wall &c. (*inclosure*) 232; fort &c. (*defence*) 717.

anchor, kedge; grap-nel, -pling iron; sheet-, mushroom-anchor, main-stay; support &c. 215; check &c. 706; ballast.

jury-mast; vent-peg; safety -valve, - lamp; lightning conductor.

means of escape &c. (*escape*) 671; life-boat, swimming belt, cork jacket; life preserver, breeches buoy; parachute, plank, stepping-stone.

safeguard &c. (*protection*) 664.

V. seek -, take -, find- refuge &c. *n.*; seek -, find- safety &c. 664; throw oneself into the arms of; claim sanctuary; take to the -hills, - woods; make port, reach shelter, bar -, bolt -, lock -the door, - gate; let the portcullis down; raise the drawbridge.

wind; volcano; ambush &c. 530; pit-fall, trap-door; trap &c. (*snare*) 545.

sword of Damocles; wolf at the door, snake in the grass, viper in one's bosom, death in the pot; latency &c. 526.

ugly customer, dangerous person, *le chat qui dort*; firebrand, hornet's nest.

Phr. *latet anguis in herbâ; proximus ardet Ucalegon.*

---

668. Warning.—**N.** warning, caution, *caveat*; notice &c. (*information*) 527; premoni-tion, -shment; prediction &c. 511; contraindication; symptom; lesson, dehortation; admonition, monition; alarm &c. 669.

handwriting on the wall, *tekel upharsin*, yellow flag; fog-signal, -horn; siren; monitor, warning voice, Cassandra, signs of the times, Mother Carey's chickens, stormy petrel, bird of ill omen, gathering clouds, clouds in the horizon, cloud no bigger than a man's hand, death-watch.

watch-tower, beacon, signal-post; light-house &c. (*indication of locality*) 550.

sent-inel, -ry; watch, -man; watch and ward; watch-, ban-, house-dog; patrol, vedette, picket, bivouac, scout, spy, spial; advanced -, rear-guard, lookout, flagman.

cautiousness &c. 864.

V. warn, caution; fore-, pre-warn; ad-, pre-monish; give -notice, - warning; menace &c. (*threaten*) 909; put on one's guard; sound the alarm &c. 669; croak.

beware, ware; take -warning, - heed at one's peril; watch out for; keep watch and ward &c. (*care*) 459.

Adj. warning &c. *v.*; premonitory, monitory, cautionary; admoni-tory, -tive; ominous, threatening, lowering, minatory, symptomatic.

warned &c. *v.*; on one's guard &c. (*careful*) 459, (*cautious*) 864.

Adv. *in terrorem* &c. (*threat*) 909.

Int. beware! ware! take care! mind -, take care-what you are about; mind! look out!

Phr. *ne reveillez pas le chat qui dort; fœnum habet in cornu.*

669. [Indication of danger.] **Alarm.**—**N.** alarm; alarum, larum, alarm bell, tocsin, *alerte*, beat of drum, sound of trumpet, note of alarm, hue and cry, signal of distress, S.O.S.; blue-lights; war-cry, -whoop; warning &c. 668; fog-signal, -horn; siren; yellow flag; danger signal; red -light, - flag; fire -bell, - alarm; burglar alarm, police whistle, watchman's rattle.

false alarm, cry of wolf; bugbear, -aboo.

V. give -, raise -, sound -, beat- the *or* an -alarm &c. *n.*; alarm; warn &c. 668; ring the tocsin; *battre la générale*; cry wolf.

Adj. alarming &c. *v.*

Int. *sauve qui peut! qui vive?* who goes there?

670. Preservation.—N. preservation; safe keeping; conservation &c. (*storage*) 636; maintenance, upkeep, support, sustentation, conservatism; *vis conservatrix*; salvation &c. (*deliverance*) 672; drying &c. *v.*

[Means of preservation] prophylaxis; preserv-er, -ative; canned goods; cold pack; hygi-astics, -antics; cover, drugget; *cordon sanitaire.* [Superstitious remedies] charm &c. 993.

V. preserve, maintain, keep, sustain, support; keep -up, – alive; not willingly let die; shore –, bank- up; nurse; save, rescue; be –, make- -safe &c. 664; take care of &c. (*care*) 459; guard &c. (*defend*) 717.

stare super antiquas vias; hold one's own; hold –, stand- -one's ground &c. (*resist*) 719.

embalm, dry, cure, smoke, salt, pickle, season, kyanize, bottle, pot, tin, can; husband &c. (*store*) 636.

Adj. preserving &c. *v.*; conservative; prophylactic; preserva-tory, -tive; hygienic.

preserved &c. *v.*; un-impaired, -broken, -injured, -hurt, -singed, -marred; safe, – and sound; intact, with a whole skin, without a scratch.

Phr. *nolumus leges Angliæ mutari.*

671. Escape.—N. escape, scape; avolation, elopement, flight, getaway; evasion &c. (*avoidance*) 623; retreat; narrow –, hairbreadthescape; close –, near- shave; come off, impunity.

[Means of escape] loophole &c. (*opening*) 260; path &c. 627; secret -door, – passage; refuge &c. 666; vent, – peg; safety-valve; drawbridge, fire-escape.

reprieve &c. (*deliverance*) 672; liberation &c. 750.

refugee &c. (*fugitive*) 623.

V. escape, scape; make –, effect –, make good- one's escape, make a get-away; get -off, – clear off, – well out of; *échapper belle*, save one's bacon; weather the storm &c. (*safe*) 664; escape scot-free.

elude &c., make off &c. (*avoid*) 623; march off &c. (*go away*) 293; give one the slip; slip through the -hands, – fingers; slip the collar, wriggle out of; break -loose, – from prison; break –, slip –, get- away; find -vent, – a hole to creep out of.

Adj. escap-ing, -ed &c. *v.*; stolen away, fled.

Phr. the bird has flown.

672. Deliverance.—N. deliverance, extrication, rescue; repriev-e, -al; respite; ransom; liberation &c. 750; truce, armistice; redemption, salvation; riddance; gaol delivery; exemption, day of grace; redeemableness.

V. deliver, extricate, rescue, save, redeem, ransom, free, liberate, release, set free, redeem, emancipate; bring -off, – through; *tirer d'affaire*, get the wheel out of the rut; snatch from the jaws of death, come to the rescue; rid; retrieve &c. (*restore*) 660; be –, get- rid of.

Adj. saved &c. *v.*; extric-, redeem-, rescu-able.

Phr. to the rescue!

3°. *Precursory Measures*

673. Preparation.—N. preparation; providing &c. *v.*; provi-sion, -dence; anticipation &c. (*foresight*) 510; precaution, -concertation, -disposition;

674. Non-Preparation. — N. non-absence of –, want of- preparation; unpreparedness; inculture, inconcoction, improvidence.

forecast &c. (*plan*) 626; rehearsal, note of preparation.

[Putting in order] arrangement &c. 60; clearance; adjustment &c. 23; tuning; equipment, outfit, accoutrement, armament, array.

ripening &c. *v.*; maturation, evolution; elaboration, concoction, digestion; gestation, hatching, incubation, sitting.

groundwork, datum, first stone, cradle, stepping-stone; foundation, scaffold &c. (*support*) 215; scaffolding, *échafaudage*.

[Preparation -of men] training &c. (*education*) 537; inurement &c. (*habit*) 613; novitiate; [– of food] cook-ing, -ery; brewing, culinary art; [– of the soil] till-, plough-, sow-ing; semination, cultivation.

[State of being prepared] prepared-, readi-, ripe-, mellow-ness; maturity; *un impromptu fait à loisir*.

[Preparer] preparer, teacher, coach, trainer, pioneer; *avant-courrier*, *-coureur*; sappers and miners, paviour, navvy; packer, stevedore; warming-pan; precursor &c. 64.

V. prepare; get –, make- ready; make preparations, settle preliminaries, get up, sound the note of preparation; address oneself to.

set –, put- in order &c. (*arrange*) 60; forecast &c. (*plan*) 626; prepare –, plough –, dress- the ground; till –, cultivate- the soil; predispose, sow the seed, lay a train, dig a mine; lay –, fix- the -foundations, – basis, -groundwork; dig the foundations, erect the scaffolding; lay the first stone &c. (*begin*) 66.

rough-hew; cut out work; block –, hammer- out; lick into shape &c. (*form*) 240.

elaborate, mature, ripen, mellow, season, bring to maturity; nurture &c. (*aid*) 707; hatch, cook, brew; temper; anneal, smelt; dry, cure &c. 670.

equip, arm, man; fit-out, -up; furnish, rig, dress, garnish, betrim, accoutre, array, fettle, fledge; dress –, furbish –, brush –, vamp- up; refurbish; sharpen one's tools, trim one's foils, set, prime, attune; whet the -knife, – sword; wind –, screw- up; adjust &c. (*fit*) 27; put in -trim, – train, – gear, – working order, – tune, – a groove for, – harness; pack, stow away, store.

immaturity, crudity; rawness &c. *adj.*; abortion; disqualification.

[Absence of art] nature, state of nature; virgin soil, unweeded garden; rough diamond, neglect &c. 460.

rough copy &c. (*plan*) 626; germ &c. 153; raw material &c. 635.

improvisation &c. (*impulse*) 612.

V. be -unprepared &c. *adj.*; want –, lack- preparation; lie fallow; *s'embarquer sans biscuits*; live from hand to mouth.

[Render unprepared] dismantle &c. (*render useless*) 645; undress &c. 226.

extemporize, improvise.

surprise, pay a surprise visit, take by surprise, drop in upon, take unawares; take pot-luck.

Adj. un-prepared &c. [prepare &c. 673]; without -preparation &c. 673; incomplete &c. 53; rudimental, embryonic, abortive; immature, unripe, raw, green, crude; coarse; rough, -cast, -hewn; in the rough; un-hewn, -formed, -fashioned, -wrought, -laboured, -blown, -cooked, -boiled, -concocted, -cut -polished.

callow, un-hatched, -fledged, -nurtured, -licked, -taught, -educated, -cultivated, -trained, -tutored, -drilled, -exercised; precocious, premature; un-, in-digested; un-mellowed, -seasoned, -leavened.

fallow; un-sown, -tilled; natural, in a state of nature; undressed; in dishabille, *en déshabille*, *en négligé*.

un-, dis-qualified; unfitted; ill-digested; un-begun, -ready, -arranged, -organized, -furnished, -provided, -equipped, -trimmed; out of -gear, – order; dismantled &c. *v.*

shiftless, improvident, unthrifty, thoughtless, unguarded; happy-go-lucky; caught napping &c. (*inexpectant*) 508; unpremeditated &c. 612.

Adv. extempore &c. 612.

————

train &c. (*teach*) 537; inure &c. (*habituate*) 613; breed; prepare &c.- for; rehearse; make provision for; take -steps, – measures, – precautions; provide, – against; beat up for recruits; open the door to &c. (*faciliate*) 705.

set one's house in order, make all snug; clear -decks, – for action; close one's ranks; shuffle the cards.

prepare oneself; serve an apprenticeship &c. (*learn*) 539; lay oneself out for, get into harness, gird up one's loins, buckle on one's armour, *reculer pour mieux sauter*, prime and load, shoulder arms, get the steam up, put the horses to.

guard –, make sure- against; forearm, make sure, prepare for the evil day, have a rod in pickle, provide against a rainy day, feather one's nest; lay in provisions &c. 637; make investments; keep on foot.

be -prepared, – ready &c. *adj.*; hold oneself in readiness, watch and pray, keep one's powder dry; lie in wait for &c. (*expect*) 507; anticipate &c. (*foresee*) 510; *principiis obstare*; *veniente occurrere morbo*.

Adj. preparing &c. *v.*; in -preparation, – course of preparation, – agitation, – embryo, – hand, – train; afoot, afloat; on -foot, – the stocks, – the anvil; under consideration &c. (*plan*) 626; brewing, hatching, forthcoming, brooding; in -store for, – reserve.

precautionary, provident; prepara-tive, -tory; provisional, inchoate, under revision; preliminary &c. (*precedent*) 62.

prepared &c. *v.*; in readiness; ready, – to one's hand, – made, cut and dried; ready for use, reach me down; made to one's hand, handy, on the table, made to order; in gear; in working -order, – gear; snug; in practice.

ripe, mature, mellow; practised &c. (*skilled*) 698; laboured, elaborate, highly-wrought, smelling of the lamp, worked up.

in -full feather, – best bib and tucker; in –, at- harness; in – the saddle, – arms, – battle array, – war paint; up in arms; armed -at all points, – to the teeth, – *cap-à-pie*; sword in hand; booted and spurred.

in utrumque –, *semper- paratus*; on the alert &c. (*vigilant*) 459; at one's post.

Adv. in -preparation, – anticipation of; afoot, astir, abroad; abroach.

675. Essay.—N. essay, trial, endeavour, aim, attempt; venture, adventure, speculation, *coup d'essai*, *début*; probation &c. (*experiment*) 463.

V. try, essay; experiment &c. 463; endeavour, strive; tempt, tackle, take on, attempt, make an attempt; venture, adventure, speculate, take one's chance, tempt fortune; try one's -fortune, – luck, – hand; use one's endeavour; feel –, grope –, pick- one's way.

try hard, push, make a bold push, use one's best endeavour; do one's best &c. (*exertion*) 686.

Adj. essaying &c. *v.*; experimental &c. 463; tentative, empirical, probationary.

Adv. experimentally &c. *adj.*; on trial, at a venture; by rule of thumb. if one may be so bold.

676. Undertaking.—N. undertaking; compact &c. 769; engagement &c. (*promise*) 768; enter-, em-prise; venture &c. 675; pilgrimage; matter in hand &c. (*business*) 625; move; first move &c. (*beginning*) 66.

V. undertake; engage –, embark- in; launch –, plunge- into; volunteer; apprentice oneself to; engage &c. (*promise*) 768; contract &c. 769; take upon -oneself, – one's shoulders; devote oneself to &c. (*determination*) 604.

take -up, – in hand; tackle; set –, go- about; set –, fall- -to, – to work; launch forth; set up shop; put in -hand, – execution; set forward; break the neck of a business, be in for; put one's hand to; betake oneself to, turn one's hand to, go to do; begin &c. 66; broach, institute, &c. (*originate*) 153; put –, lay- one's -hand to the plough, – shoulder to the wheel.

have in hand &c. (*business*) 625; have many irons in the fire &c. (*activity*) 682.

Adj. undertaking &c. *v.*; on the anvil &c. 625; adventurous, venturesome.

Int. here goes!

677. Use.—**N.** use; employ, -ment; exer-cise, -citation; appli-cation, -ance; adhibition, disposal; consumption; agency &c. (*physical*) 170; usufruct; usefulness &c. 644; recourse, resort, avail, pragmatism.

[Conversion to use] utilization, service, wear.

[Way of using] usage.

V. use, make use of, employ, put to use; apply, put in -action, – operation, – practice; set -in motion, – to work.

ply, work, wield, handle, manipulate; play, – off; exert, exercise, practise, avail oneself of, profit by; resort –, have recourse –, recur –, take –, betake oneself- to; take -up with, – advantage of; lay one's hands on, try.

render useful &c. 644; mould; turn to -account, – use; convert to use, utilize, administer; work up; call –, bring- into play; put into requisition; call –, draw- forth; press –, enlist- into the service; bring to bear upon, devote, dedicate, consecrate, apply, adhibit, dispose of; make a -handle, – cat's paw- of.

fall back upon, make a shift with; make the -most, – best- of.

use –, swallow- up; consume, absorb, expend; tax, task, wear, put to task.

Adj. in use; used &c. *v.*; well-worn, -trodden.

useful &c. 644; subservient &c. (*instrumental*) 631; utilitarian; pragmatical.

678. Disuse.—**N.** forbearance, abstinence; disuse; relinquishment &c. 782; desuetude &c. (*want of habit*) 614.

V. not use; do without, dispense with, let alone, not touch, forbear, abstain, spare, waive, neglect; keep back, reserve.

lay -up, – by, – on the shelf, – up in a napkin; shelve; set –, put –, lay-aside; disuse, leave off, have done with; supersede; discard &c. (*eject*) 297; dismiss, give warning.

throw aside &c. (*relinquish*) 782; make away with &c. (*destroy*) 162; cast –, heave –, throw- overboard; cast to the -dogs, – winds; dismantle &c. (*render useless*) 645.

lie –, remain- unemployed &c. *adj.*

Adj. not used &c. *v.*; un-employed, -applied, -disposed of, -spent, -exercised, -touched, -trodden, -essayed, -gathered, -culled; uncalled for, not required.

disused &c. *v.*; done with; run down, used up, cast off.

679. Misuse.—**N.** mis-use, -usage, -employment, -application, -appropriation.

abuse, profanation, prostitution, desecration; waste &c. 638.

V. mis-use, -employ, -apply, -appropriate.

desecrate, abuse, profane, prostitute; waste &c. 638; over-task, -tax, -work; squander &c. 818.

cut a whetstone with a razor, employ a steam-engine to crack a nut; catch at a straw.

Adj. misused &c. *v.*

Section III. VOLUNTARY ACTION

1°. *Simple Voluntary Action*

680. Action.—N. action, performance; doing &c. *v.*; perpetration; exercise, -citation; movement, operation, evolution, work; labour &c. (*exertion*) 686; *praxis*, execution; procedure &c. (*conduct*) 692; handicraft; business &c. 625; agency &c. (*power at work*) 170.

deed, act, overt act, stitch, touch, gest; transaction, job, doings, dealings, proceeding, measure, step, manœuvre, bout, passage, move, stroke, blow; *coup*, – *de main*, – *d'état*; *tour de force* &c. (*display*) 882; feat, exploit, stunt; achievement &c. (*completion*) 729; handiwork, workmanship, craftsmanship; manufacture; stroke of policy &c. (*plan*) 626.

actor &c. (*doer*) 690.

V. do, perform, execute; achieve &c. (*complete*) 729; transact, enact; commit, perpetrate, inflict; exercise, prosecute, carry on, work, practise, play.

employ oneself, ply one's task; officiate, have in hand &c. (*business*) 625; labour &c. 686; be at work; pursue a course; shape one's course &c. (*conduct*) 692.

act, operate; take -action, – steps; strike a blow, lift a finger, stretch forth one's hand; take in hand &c. (*undertake*) 676; put oneself in motion; put in practice; carry into execution &c. (*complete*) 729; act upon.

be -an actor &c. 690; take –, act –, play –, perform- a part in; participate in; have a -hand in, – finger in the pie; have to do with; be a -party to, – participator in; bear –, lend- a hand; pull an oar, run in a race; mix oneself up with &c. (*meddle*) 682.

be in action; come into operation &c. (*power at work*) 170.

Adj. doing &c. *v.*; acting; in action; in harness; on duty; at work; in operation &c. 170; up to one's ears in work, in the midst of things.

Adv. in the -act, – midst of, – thick of; red-handed, *in flagrante delicto*; while one's hand is in.

681. Inaction.—N. inaction, passiveness, abstinence from action; noninterference; Fabian –, conservative-policy; neglect &c. 460; stagnation, vegetation; loafing.

inactivity &c. 683; rest &c. (*repose*) 687; quiescence &c. 265; want of –, in- occupation; unemployment; idle hours, time hanging on one's hands, *dolce far niente*; sinecure.

V. not -do, – act, – attempt; be -inactive &c. 683; abstain from doing, do nothing, hold, spare; not -stir, – move, – lift- a -finger, – foot, – peg; fold one's -arms, – hands; leave –, let- alone; let -be, – pass, – things take their course, – it have its way, – well alone; *quieta non movere*; *stare super antiquas vias*; rest and be thankful, live and let live; lie –, rest- upon one's oars; *laisser -aller*, – *faire*; stand aloof; refrain &c. (*avoid*) 623; keep oneself from doing; remit –, relax- one's efforts; desist &c. (*relinquish*) 624; stop &c. (*cease*) 142; pause &c. (*be quiet*) 265.

wait, lie in wait, bide one's time, take time, tide it over.

cool –, kick- one's heels; loaf, while away the -time, – tedious hours; pass –, fill up –, beguile- the time; talk against time; waste time &c. (*inactive*) 683.

lie -by, – on the shelf, – in ordinary, – idle, – to, – fallow; keep quiet, slug; have nothing to do, whistle for want of thought; twiddle one's thumbs.

undo, do away with; take -down, – to pieces; destroy &c. 162.

Adj. not doing &c. *v.*; not done &c. *v.*; undone; passive; un-occupied, -employed; out of -employ, – work, – a job; fallow; *désœuvré*.

Adv. *re infectâ*, at a stand, *les bras croisés*, with folded arms; with the hands -in the pockets, – behind one's back; *pour passer le temps*.

Int. so let it be! stop! &c. 142; hands off!

Phr. nothing doing; *cunctando restituit rem*.

682. Activity.— N. activity; brisk-ness, liveliness &c. *adj.*; animation, life, vivacity, spirit, verve, dash, energy, go⸱

nimbleness, agility; smartness, quick-ness &c. *adj.*; velocity &c. 274; alacrity, promptitude; des-, dis-patch; expedi-tion; haste &c. 684; punctuality &c. (*early*) 132.

eagerness, zeal, ardour, *perfervidum ingenium*, *empressement*, earnestness, intentness; *abandon*; vigour &c. (*physi-cal energy*) 171; devotion &c. (*resolu-tion*) 604; exertion &c. 686.

industry, assiduity; assiduousness &c. *adj.*; sedulity; laboriousness; drudg-ery &c. (*labour*) 686; painstaking, diligence; perseverance &c. 604*a*; in-defatigation; habits of business.

vigilance &c. 459; wakefulness; sleep-, rest-lessness; *pervigilium, in-somnia*; racketing.

movement, bustle, hustle, stir, fuss, ado, bother, pottering; fidgets, -iness; flurry &c. (*haste*) 684.

officiousness; dabbling, meddling; inter-ference, -position, -meddling, but-ting in, intrusiveness; tampering with, intrigue⸱

press of business, no sinecure, plenty to do, many irons in the fire, great doings, busy hum of men, battle of life, thick of -things, – the action; the mad-ding crowd.

housewife, busy bee; new brooms; sharp fellow, blade; hustler, devotee, enthusiast, fan, zealot, fanatic; med-dler, intermeddler, intriguer, busybody, kibitzer, pickthank.

V. be -active &c. *adj.*; busy oneself in; stir, -about, – one's stumps; bestir –, rouse- oneself; speed, hasten, peg away, lay about one, bustle, fuss; raise –, kick up- a dust; push; make a -push, – fuss, – stir; go ahead, push forward; fight –, elbow- one's way; make prog-ress &c. 282; toil &c. (*labour*) 686; drudge, plod, persist &c. (*persevere*) 604*a*; keep -up the ball, – the pot boiling.

look sharp; have all one's eyes about one &c. (*vigilance*) 459; rise, arouse oneself, get up early, hustle, push; be about, keep moving, steal a march, kill two birds with one stone; seize the opportunity &c. 134: lose no time, not

683. Inactivity.—N. inactivity; in-action &c. 681; inertness, inertia &c. 172; obstinacy &c. 606.

lull &c. (*cessation*) 142; quiescence &c. 265; rust, -iness.

idle-, remiss-ness &c. *adj.*; sloth, indolence, indiligence; otiosity, daw-dling &c. *v.*

dullness &c. *adj.*; languor; segni-ty, -tude; lentor; sluggishness &c. (*slow-ness*) 275; procrastination &c. (*delay*) 133; torp-or, -idity, -escence; stupor &c. (*insensibility*) 823; somnolence; drowsiness &c. *adj.*; nodding &c. *v.*; oscit-ation, -ancy; pandiculation, hyp-notism, lethargy; heaviness, heavy eye-lids, sand in the eyes.

sleep, slumber; sound –, heavy –, balmy- sleep; Morpheus, dreamland; coma, trance, catalepsy, hypnosis, *ecstasis*, dream, hibernation, nap, doze, snooze, *siesta*, wink of sleep, forty winks, snore; Hypnology.

dull work; pottering; relaxation &c. (*loosening*) 47; Castle of Indolence.

[Cause of inactivity] lullaby, *ber-ceuse*; anæsthetic, sedative &c. 174; torpedo.

idler, drone, droil, dawdle, mopus; do-little, *fainéant*, dummy, sleeping partner; afternoon farmer; truant &c. (*runaway*) 623; lounger, *lazzarone*, floater, loafer, tramp, beggar, cadger; lub-ber, -bard; slow-coach &c. (*slow*) 275; opium –, lotus- eater; slug; lag-, slug-gard; lie-abed; slumberer, dor-mouse, marmot; waiter on Providence, *fruges consumere natus*.

V. be -inactive &c. *adj.*; do nothing &c. 681; move slowly &c. 275; let the grass grow under one's feet; take one's time, dawdle, poke, drawl, droil, lag, hang back, slouch; loll, -op; lounge, loaf, loiter; go to sleep over; sleep at one's post, *ne battre que d'une aile.*

take -it easy, – things as they come; lead an easy life, vegetate, swim with the stream, eat the bread of idleness; loll in the lap of -luxury, – indolence; waste –, consume –, kill –, lose- time; burn daylight, waste the precious hours.

idle –, trifle –, fritter –, fool- away time; spend –, take- time in; ped-, pid-dle; potter, putter, dabble, faddle,

lose a moment, make the most of one's time, not suffer the grass to grow under one's feet, improve the shining hour, make short work of; dash off; make haste &c. 684; do one's best, take pains &c. (*exert oneself*) 686; do –, work- wonders.

have -many irons in the fire, – one's hands full, – much on one's hands; have other -things to do, – fish to fry; be busy; not have a moment -to spare, – that one can call one's own.

have one's fling, run the round of; go all lengths, stick at nothing, run riot.

outdo; over-do, -act, -lay, -shoot the mark; make a toil of a pleasure.

have a hand in &c. (*act in*) 680; take an active part, put in one's oar, have a finger in the pie, mix oneself up with, trouble one's head about, intrigue; agitate.

tamper with, meddle, moil; inter-meddle, -fere, -pose; obtrude; poke –, thrust- one's nose in, butt in.

Adj. active; brisk, – as a lark, – as a bee; lively, animated, vivacious; alive, – and kicking; frisky, spirited, stirring.

nimble, – as a squirrel; agile; light-, nimble-footed; featly, tripping.

quick, prompt, yare, instant, ready, alert, spry, sharp, smart, slick, go-ahead; fast &c. (*swift*) 274; quick as a lamplighter, expeditious; awake, broad awake; wide awake &c. (*intelligent*) 498.

forward, eager, ardent, strenuous, zealous, enterprising, pushing, in earnest; resolute &c. 604.

industrious, assiduous, diligent, sedulous, notable, painstaking; intent &c. (*attention*) 457; indefatigable &c. (*persevering*) 604a; unwearied; unsleeping, sleepless, never tired; plodding, hardworking &c. 686; business-like, workaday.

bustling; restless, – as a hyæna; fussy, fidgety, pottering; busy, – as a hen with one chicken.

working, labouring, at work, on duty, in harness; up in arms; on one's legs, at call; up and -doing, – stirring.

busy, occupied; hard at -work, – it; up to one's ears in, full of business, busy as a bee.

meddling &c. *v.*; meddlesome, pushing, officious, overofficious, *intrigant.*

astir, stirring; a-going, -foot; on foot; in full swing; eventful; on the alert &c. (*vigilant*) 459.

fribble, fiddle-faddle; dally, dilly-dally.

sleep, slumber, be asleep; hibernate; oversleep; sleep like a -top, – log, – dormouse; sleep -soundly, – heavily; doze, drowze, snooze, nap; take a -nap &c. *n.*; dream; snore; settle –, go –, go off- to sleep; drop off; fall –, drop-asleep; close –, seal up- -the -eyes, – eyelids; weigh down the eyelids; get sleepy, nod, yawn; go to bed, turn in.

languish, expend itself, flag, hang fire; relax.

render -idle &c. *adj.*; sluggardize; mitigate &c. 174.

Adj. inactive; motionless &c. 265; unoccupied &c. (*doing nothing*) 681.

indolent, lazy, slothful, idle, otiose, lusk, remiss, slack, inert, torpid, sluggish, languid, supine, heavy, dull, leaden, lumpish; exanimate, soulless; listless; dron-y, -ish; lazy as Ludlam's dog.

dilatory, laggard; lagging &c. *v.*; slow &c. 275; rusty, flagging; lackadaisical, maudlin, fiddle-faddle; pottering &c. *v.*; shilly-shally &c. (*irresolute*) 605.

sleeping &c. *v.*; asleep; fast –, dead –, sound- asleep; in a sound sleep; sound as a top, dormant, comatose; in the -arms, – lap- of Morpheus.

sleep-y, -ful; dozy, drowsy, somnolent, torpescent; lethargic, -al; heavy, – with sleep; napping; somni-fic, -ferous; sopor-ous, -ific, -iferous; hypnotic; balmy, dreamy; un-, una-wakened.

sedative &c. 174.

Adv. inactively &c. *adj.*; at leisure &c. 685.

Phr. the eyes begin to draw straws.

Adv. actively &c. *adj.*; with -life and spirit, – might and main &c. 686, – haste &c. 684, – wings; full tilt, *in mediis rebus.*

Int. be –, look- -alive, – sharp! move –, push- on! keep moving! go ahead! stir your stumps! *age quod agis!*

Phr. *carpe diem* &c. (*opportunity*) 134; *nulla dies sine lineâ*; *nec mora nec requies*; no sooner said than done &c. (*early*) 132; catch a weasel asleep.

---

684. Haste.—N. haste, urgency; des-, dis-patch; acceleration, spurt, spirt, forced march, rush, dash; velocity &c. 274; precipit-ancy, -ation, -ousness &c. *adj.*; impetuosity; *brusquerie*; hurry, scurry, scuttle, drive, scramble, push, hustle, bustle, fuss, fidgets, flurry, flutter, splutter.

V. haste, hasten; make -haste, – a dash &c. *n.*; hurry –, dash –, whip –, push –, press- -on, – forward; hurry, skurry, scuttle along, bundle on, dart to and fro, bustle, flutter, scramble; plunge, – headlong; run, race, speed; dash off; rush &c. (*violence*) 173.

bestir oneself &c. (*be active*) 682; lose -no time, – not a moment, – not an instant; make short work of; make the best of one's -time, – way.

be -precipitate &c. *adj.*; jump at; be in -haste, – a hurry &c. *n.*; have -no time, – not a moment- -to lose, – to spare; work -under pressure, – against time.

quicken &c. 274; accelerate, expedite, put on, precipitate, urge, whip, spur, flog, goad.

Adj. hasty, hurried, *brusque*; scrambling, cursory, precipitate, headlong, furious, boisterous, impetuous, hot-headed; feverish, fussy; pushing.

in -haste, – a hurry &c. *n.*; in -hot, – all- haste; breathless, pressed for time, hard pressed, urgent.

Adv. with -haste, – all haste, – breathless speed; in haste &c. *adj.*; apace &c. (*swiftly*) 274; amain; all at once &c. (*instantaneously*) 113; at short notice &c., immediately &c. (*early*) 132; posthaste; by -express, – telegraph, – wire, – wireless, – air mail.

hastily, precipitately &c. *adj.*; helter-skelter, hurry-skurry, holus-bolus; slap-dash, -bang; full-tilt, -drive; heels over head, head and shoulders, headlong, *à corps perdu.*

by -fits and starts, – spurts; hop, skip and jump.

Phr. *sauve qui peut*, devil take the hindmost, no time to be lost; no sooner said than done &c. (*early*) 132; a word and a blow.

Int. hurry up! look alive! get a move on! buck up! double march! rush! urgent!

---

685. Leisure.—N. leisure; spare -time, – hours, – moments; vacant hour; time, – to spare, – on one's hands; holiday &c. (*rest*) 687; *otium cum dignitate*, ease.

V. have -leisure &c. *n.*; take one's -time, – leisure, – ease; repose &c. 687; move slowly &c. 275; while away the time &c. (*inaction*) 681; be -master of one's time, – an idle man; *desipere in loco.*

Adj. leisurely; slow &c. 275; deliberate, quiet, calm, undisturbed; at -leisure, – one's ease, – a loose end.

Phr. time hanging heavy on one's hands.

---

686. Exertion.—N. exertion, effort, strain, tug, pull, stress, force, pressure, throw, stretch, struggle, spell, spurt, spirt; stroke –, stitch- of work.

687. Repose.—N. repose, rest, silken repose; sleep &c. 683.

relaxation, breathing time; halt. pause &c. (*cessation*) 142; respite.

'a strong pull, a long pull and a pull all together'; dead lift; heft; gymnastics, sports; exer-cise, -citation; wear and tear; ado; toil and trouble; uphill -, hard -, warm- work; harvest time.

labour, work, toil, travail, manual labour, sweat of one's brow, swink, operoseness, drudgery, slavery, fagging, hammering; *limæ labor*.

trouble, pains, duty; resolution &c. 604; energy &c. (*physical*) 171.

V. exert oneself; exert -, tax- one's energies; use exertion.

labour, work, toil, moil, sweat, fag, drudge, slave, drag a lengthened chain, wade through, strive, strain; make -, stretch- a long arm; pull, tug, ply; ply -, tug at- the oar; do the work; take the labouring oar.

bestir oneself (*be active*) 682; take trouble, trouble oneself.

work hard; rough it; put forth -one's strength, - a strong arm; fall to work, bend the bow; buckle to, set one's shoulder to the wheel &c. (*resolution*) 604; work like a -Briton, - horse, - carthorse, - galley-slave, - coalheaver; labour -, work- day and night; redouble one's efforts; do double duty; work double -hours, - tides; sit up, burn the -midnight oil, - candle at both ends; stick to &c. (*persevere*) 604a; work -, fight- one's way; lay about one, hammer at.

take pains; do one's -best, - level best, - utmost; do -the best one can, - all one can, - all in one's power, - as much as in one lies, - what lies in one's power; use one's -best, - utmost- endeavour; try one's -best, - utmost; play one's best card; put one's -best, - right- leg foremost; have one's whole soul in one's work, put all one's strength into, strain every nerve; spare no -efforts, - pains; go all lengths; go through fire and water &c. (*resolution*) 604; move heaven and earth, leave no stone unturned.

Adj. labouring &c. *v.*

laborious, operose, elaborate; strained; toil-, trouble-, burden-, weari-some; uphill; herculean, gymnastic, athletic, palestric.

hardworking, painstaking, strenuous, energetic.

hard at work, on the stretch.

Adv. laboriously &c. *adj.*; lustily; with -might and main, - all one's might, - a strong hand, - sledge-hammer, - much ado; to the best of one's abilities, *totis viribus, vi et armis, manibus pedibusque,* tooth and nail, *unguibus et rostro,* hammer and tongs, heart and soul; through thick and thin &c. (*perseverance*) 604a.

by the sweat of one's brow, *suo Marte.*

day of rest, *dies non*, Sabbath, Lord's day, holiday, red-letter day, vacation, recess.

V. repose; rest, - and be thankful; take -rest, - one's ease.

relax, unbend, slacken; take breath &c. (*refresh*) 689; rest upon one's oars· pause &c. (*cease*) 142; stay one's hand.

lie down; recline, - on a bed of down, - on an easy chair; go to -rest, - bed, - sleep &c. 683.

take a holiday, shut up shop; lie fallow &c. (*inaction*) 681.

Adj. reposing &c. *v.*; unstrained.

Adv. at rest.

———

688. Fatigue.—N. fatigue; weariness &c. 841; yawning, drowsiness &c. 683; lassitude, tiredness, fatigation, exhaustion; sweat.

anhelation, shortness of breath, panting; faintness; collapse, prostration,

689. Refreshment.—N. bracing &c. *v.*; recovery of -strength &c. 159; restoration, revival &c. 660; repair, refection, refocillation, refreshment, regalement, bait; relief &c. 834.

V. brace &c. (*strengthen*) 159; rein-

swoon, fainting, *deliquium*, syncope, lipothymy.

V. be -fatigued &c. *adj.*; yawn &c. (*get sleepy*) 683; droop, sink, flag; lose -breath, – wind; gasp, pant, puff, blow, drop, swoon, faint, succumb.

fatigue, tire, weary, bore, irk, fag, jade, harass, exhaust, knock up, wear out, prostrate.

tax, task, strain; over-task, -work, -burden, -tax, -strain.

Adj. fatigued &c. *v.*; weary &c. 841; drowsy &c. 683; drooping &c. *v.*; haggard; toil-, way-worn; footsore, surbated, weatherbeaten; faint; done –, used –, knocked- up; exhausted, prostrate, spent; over-tired, -spent, -fatigued; forspent; unre-freshed, -stored.

worn, – out; battered, shattered, pulled down, seedy, altered.

breath-, wind-less; short of –, out of -breath, – wind; blown, puffing and blowing; short-breathed; anhelous; broken-, short-winded.

ready to drop, more dead than alive, dog -tired, – weary, walked off one's legs, tired to death, on one's last legs, played out, *hors de combat*.

fatiguing &c. *v.*; tire-, irk-, weari-some; weary; trying.

vigorate; air, freshen up, refresh, recruit; repair &c. (*restore*) 660; fan, refocillate.

breathe, respire; draw –, take –, gather –, take a long –, regain –, recover- breath; get better, raise one's head; recover –, regain –, renew- one's strength &c. 159; perk up.

come to oneself &c. (*revive*) 660; feel like a giant refreshed.

Adj. refreshing &c. *v.*; recuperative &c. 660.

refreshed &c. *v.*; un-tired, -wearied.

---

690. Agent.—**N.** doer, actor, agent, performer, perpetrator, operator; execu-tor, -trix; practitioner, worker, stager.

bee, ant, working bee, labouring oar, shaft horse, servant –, maid-of all work, general servant, factotum.

workman, artisan; crafts-, handicrafts-man; mechanic, operative; working –, labouring- man; hewers of wood and drawers of water, labourer, navvy; hand, man, day labourer, journeyman, hack; mere -tool &c. ˜33; porter, docker, stevedore, beast of burden, drudge, fag.

maker, artificer, artist, wright, manufacturer, architect, contractor, builder, mason, bricklayer, smith, forger, Vulcan; black-, tin-smith; carpenter; ganger, platelayer.

machinist, mechanician, engineer, electrician, plumber, gasfitter &c.

semp-, sem-, seam-stress; needle-, char-, work-woman; tailor, cord-wainer.

minister &c. (*instrument*) 631; servant &c. 746; representative &c; (*commissioner*) 758, (*deputy*) 759.

co-worker, fellow-worker, party to, participator in, co-operator, colleague, associate, collaborator, *particeps criminis, dramatis personæ; personnel.*

Phr. '*quorum pars magna fui.*'

---

691. Workshop.—**N.** work-shop, -house; laboratory; manufactory, mill, factory, armoury, arsenal, mint, forge, loom; cabinet, studio, *bureau, atelier;* hive, – of industry; nursery; hot-house, -bed; kitchen, kitchenette; dock, -yard; slip, yard, wharf; found-ry, -ery; furnace; vineyard, orchard, farm, kitchen garden.

melting pot, crucible, alembic, caldron, mortar, *matrix*.

2°. *Complex Voluntary Action*

692. Conduct.—N. dealing, transaction &c. (*action*) 680; business &c. 625.

tactics, game, policy, polity; general-, statesman-, seaman-ship; strate-gy, -gics; plan &c. 626.

husbandry; house-keeping, -wifery; stewardship; *ménage*; regimen, *régime*; econom-y, -ics; political economy; management; government &c. (*direction*) 693.

execution, manipulation, treatment, campaign, career, life, course, walk, race.

conduct; behaviour; de-, com-portment; carriage, *maintien*, de-meanour, guise, bearing, manner, mien, air, observance.

course -, line- of -conduct, - action, - proceeding; *rôle*; process, ways, practice, procedure, *modus operandi*; method &c., path &c. 627.

V. transact, execute; des-, dis-patch; proceed with, discharge; carry -on, - through, - out, - into effect; work out; go -, get- through; enact; put into practice; officiate &c. 625.

behave -, comport -, demean -, carry -, bear -, conduct -, acquit-oneself.

run a race, lead a life, play a game; take -, adopt- a course; steer -, shape- one's course; play one's- -part, - cards; shift for oneself; paddle one's own canoe.

conduct; manage &c. (*direct*) 693.

deal -, have to do- with; treat, handle a case; take -steps, - measures.

Adj. conducting &c. *v.*; strategical, business-like, practical, economic, executive.

693. Direction.—N. direction; manage-ment, -ry; government, guber-nation, conduct, legislation, regulation, guidance; steer-, pilot-age; reins, - of government; helm, rudder, controls, joy stick, needle, com-pass, binnacle; guiding -, load -, lode -, pole- star; cynosure.

super-vision, -intendence; *surveillance*, oversight; eye of the master; control, charge, auspices; board of control &c. (*council*) 696; command &c. (*authority*) 737.

premier-, senator-ship; director &c. 694; chair, seat, portfolio.

statesmanship; state-, king-craft.

minis-try, -tration; administration; steward-, proctor-ship; agency.

V. direct, manage, govern, conduct; order, prescribe, cut out work for; head, lead; lead -, show- the way; take the lead, lead on; regulate, guide, steer, pilot; take -, be at- the helm; have -, handle -, hold -, take- the reins, handle the ribbons; drive, tool; tackle.

super-intend, -vise; overlook, control, keep in order, look after, see to, oversee, legislate for; administer, ministrate; patronize; have the -care, - charge- of; have -, take- the direction; pull the -strings, - wires; rule &c. (*command*) 737; have -, hold- -office, - the portfolio; preside, - at the board; take -, occupy -, be in- the chair; pull the stroke oar.

Adj. directing &c. *v.*; executive, supervisory, hegemonic.

Adv. at the -helm, - head of, in charge of; under the auspices of.

694. Director.—N. director, manager, governor, rector, comptroller; super-intendent, -visor; intendant; over-seer, -looker; foreman, boss, straw boss; supercargo, husband, inspector, visitor, ranger, surveyor, ædile, moderator, monitor, taskmaster; master &c. 745; leader, ring-leader, demagogue, corypheus, conductor, fugleman, precentor, bell-wether, agitator.

guiding star &c. (*guidance*) 693; adviser &c. 695; guide &c. (*information*) 527; pilot; helmsman; steers-man, -mate; man at the wheel; wire-puller.

driver, whip, Jehu, charioteer; coach-, car-, cab-man, jarvey; postilion, *vetturino*, muleteer, teamster; whipper in; engineer, engine driver, motorman, *chauffeur*.

head, – man; principal, president, speaker; chair, -man; captain &c. (*master*) 745; superior; dean; mayor &c. (*civil authority*) 745; vice-president, prime minister, premier, vizier, grand vizier; dictator.

officer, functionary, minister, official, red-tapist, bureaucrat; man –, Jack- in office; office-bearer; person in authority &c. 745.

statesman, strategist, legislator, lawgiver, politician, administrator, statist, statemonger; Minos, Draco; arbiter &c. (*judge*) 967; king maker, power behind the throne.

board &c. (*council*) 696.

secretary, – of state; Reis Effendi; vicar &c. (*deputy*) 759; steward, factor; agent &c. 758; bailiff, middleman; ganger, clerk of works; landreeve; factotum, major-domo, seneschal, housekeeper, shepherd, *croupier*; proctor, procurator, curator, librarian.

Adv. *ex officio*.

695. Advice.—N. advice, counsel, adhortation; word to the wise; suggestion, submonition, recommendation, advocacy, consultation.

exhortation &c. (*persuasion*) 615; expostulation &c. (*dissuasion*) 616; admonition &c. (*warning*) 668; guidance &c. (*direction*) 693.

instruction, charge, injunction.

adviser, prompter; counsel, -lor; monitor, mentor, Nestor, *magnus Apollo*, senator; teacher &c. 540.

guide, manual, chart &c. (*information*) 527.

physician, leech, archiater; arbiter &c. (*judge*) 967.

refer-ence, -ment; consultation, conference, parley, *pourparler* &c. 696.

V. advise, counsel; give -advice, – counsel, – a piece of advice; suggest, prompt, submonish, recommend, prescribe, advocate; exhort &c. (*persuade*) 615.

enjoin, enforce, charge, instruct, call; call upon &c. (*request*) 765; dictate.

expostulate &c. (*dissuade*) 616; admonish &c. (*warn*) 668.

advise with; lay heads –, consult- together; compare notes; hold a council, deliberate, be closeted with.

confer, consult, refer to, call in; take –, follow- advice; follow implicitly; be advised by, have at one's elbow, take one's cue from.

Adj. recommendatory; hortative &c. (*persuasive*) 615; dehortatory &c. (*dissuasive*) 616; admonitory &c. (*warning*) 668; consultative.

Int. go to!

696. Council.—N. council, committee, subcommittee, *comitia*, court, chamber, cabinet, board, bench, staff; consultation.

senate, *senatus*, parliament, House, – of Lords, – Peers, – Commons, legislature, legislative assembly, federal council, chamber of deputies, directory, *Reichsrath*, *rigsdag*, *cortes*, storthing, witenagemote, *junta*, divan, *musnud*, *sanhedrim*, Amphictyonic council; *duma*, *zemstvo*, *soviet*, *cheka*, *ogpu*; *Dail Eireann*; caput, consistory, chapter, syndicate; court of appeal &c. (*tribunal*) 966; board of -control, – works; vestry; county –, borough –, district –, parish –, town- council, local board.

cabinet –, privy- council, royal commission; cockpit, convocation, synod, congress, congregation, convention, diet, states-general, aulic council.

League of Nations, assembly, *caucus*, conclave, *clique*, conventicle; meeting, sitting, *séance*, conference, session, hearing, palaver, *pourparler*, *durbar*, pow-wow, house; *quorum*.

senator; member, – of parliament; councillor, M.P., representative of the people.

Adj. senatorial, curule, parliamentary.

697. Precept.—N. precept, direction, instruction, charge; prescript, -ion; *recipe*, receipt; golden rule; maxim &c. 496.

commandment, rule, ruling, canon, law, code, *corpus juris*, *lex scripta*, common –, unwritten –, canon-law; the Ten Commandments; act, statute, convention, rubric, stage direction, regulation; form, -ula, -ulary; technicality; nice point.

order &c. (*command*) 741.

698. Skill.—N. skill, skilfulness, ad-dress; dexter-ity, -ousness; adroitness, expertness &c. *adj.*; proficiency, competence, craft, callidity, facility, knack, trick, sleight; master-y, -ship; excellence, panurgy; ambidext-erity, -rousness; sleight of hand &c. (*deception*) 545.

sea-, air-, marks-, horse-manship; tight-, rope-dancing.

accomplish-, acquire-, attain-ment; **art**, science; techn-icality, -ology, -ique; practical –, technical- knowledge; technocracy; finish, technic.

knowledge of the world, world wisdom, *savoir-faire*; tact; mother wit &c. (*sagacity*) 498; discretion &c. (*caution*) 864; *finesse*; craftiness &c. (*cunning*) 702; management &c. (*conduct*) 692; *ars celare artem*; self-help.

cleverness, talent, ability, ingenuity, capacity, parts, talents, faculty, endowment, *forte*, turn, gift, genius, flair, feeling; intelligence &c. 498; sharpness, readiness &c. (*activity*) 682; invention &c. 515; apt-ness, -itude; turn –, capacity –, genius- for; felicity, capability, *curiosa felicitas*, qualification, habilitation.

proficient &c. 700.

masterpiece, *coup de maître*, *chef-d'œuvre*, *tour de force*; good stroke &c. (*plan*) 626.

V. be -skilful &c. *adj.*; excel in, be master of; have -a turn for &c. *n.*

know -what's what, – a hawk from a handsaw, – what one is about, – on

699. Unskilfulness.—N. unskilfulness &c. *adj.*; want of -skill &c. 698; incompeten-ce, -cy; in-ability, -felicity, -dexterity, -experience; clumsiness; disqualification, unproficiency; quackery.

folly, stupidity &c. 499; indiscretion &c. (*rashness*) 863; thoughtlessness &c. (*inattention*) 458, (*neglect*) 460.

mis-management, -conduct; impolicy; maladministration; mis-rule, -government, -application, -direction, -feasance.

absence of rule, rule of thumb; bungling &c. *v.*; failure &c. 732; screw loose; too many cooks.

blunder &c. (*mistake*) 495; *étourderie*, *gaucherie*, act of folly, *balourdise*; botch, -ery; bad job, sad work.

sprat sent out to catch a whale, much ado about nothing, wildgoose chase.

bungler &c. 701; fool &c. 501.

layman, amateur.

V. be -unskilful &c. *adj.*; not see an inch beyond one's nose; blunder, bungle, boggle, fumble, muff, botch, bitch, flounder, loppet, stumble, trip; hobble &c. 275; put one's foot in it; make a -mess, – hash, – sad work- of; overshoot the mark.

play -tricks with, – Puck; mis-manage, -conduct, -direct, -apply, -send.

stultify –, make a fool of –, commit-oneself; act foolishly; play the fool; put oneself out of court; lose one's -head, – cunning.

begin at the wrong end; do things

which side one's bread is buttered, – what's o'clock, – a thing or two; have cut one's -eye, – wisdom- teeth.

see -one's way, – where the wind lies, – which way the wind blows; have -all one's wits about one, – one's hand in; *savoir-vivre*; *scire quid valeant humeri quid ferre recusent*.

look after the main chance; cut one's coat according to one's cloth; live by one's wits; exercise one's discretion, feather the oar, sail near the wind; stoop to conquer &c. (*cunning*) 702; play one's -cards well, – best card; hit the right nail on the head, put the saddle on the right horse.

take advantage of, make the most of; profit by &c. (*use*) 677; make a hit &c. (*succeed*) 731; make a virtue of necessity; make hay while the sun shines &c. (*occasion*) 134.

Adj. skilful, dexterous, adroit, expert, apt, slick, handy, quick, deft, ready, resourceful, gain; smart &c. (*active*) 682; proficient, good at, up to, at home in, master of, a good hand at, *au fait*, thoroughbred, masterly, crack, accomplished; conversant &c. (*knowing*) 490.

experienced, practised, skilled; up -, well up- in; in -practice, – proper cue; competent, efficient, qualified, capable, fitted, fit for, up to the mark, trained, initiated, prepared, primed, finished.

clever, able, ingenious, felicitous, gifted, talented, endowed, cute, inventive &c. 515; shrewd, sharp &c. (*intelligent*) 498; cunning &c. 702; alive to, up to snuff, not to be caught with chaff; discreet.

neat-handed, fine-fingered, ambidextrous, sure-footed; cut out -, fitted- for.

technical, artistic, scientific, dædalian, shipshape; workman-, business-, statesman-like.

Adv. skillfully &c. *adj.*; well &c. 618; artistically; with -skill, – consummate skill; *secundum .artem, suo Marte*; to the best of one's abilities &c. (*exertion*) 686; like a machine.

---

by halves &c. (*not complete*) 730; make two bites of a cherry; play at cross purposes; strain at a gnat and swallow a camel &c. (*caprice*) 608; put the cart before the horse; lock the stable door when the horse is stolen &c. (*too late*) 135.

not know -what one is about, – one's own interest, – on which side one's bread is buttered; stand in one's own light, quarrel with one's bread and butter, throw a stone in one's own garden, kill the goose which lays the golden eggs, pay dear for one's whistle, cut one's own throat, burn one's fingers; knock -, run- one's head against a stone wall; fall into a trap, catch a Tartar, bring the house about one's ears; have too many -eggs in one basket (*imprudent*) 863, – irons in the fire.

mistake &c. 495; take the shadow for the substance &c. (*credulity*) 486; be in the wrong box, aim at a pigeon and kill a crow; take -, get- the wrong sow by the ear, – the dirty end of the stick; put -the saddle on the wrong horse, – a square peg into a round hole, – new wine into old bottles.

cut a whetstone with a razor; hold a farthing candle to the sun &c. (*useless*) 645; fight with -, grasp at- a shadow; catch at straws, lean on a broken reed, reckon without one's host, pursue a wildgoose chase; go on a fool's -, sleeveless- errand; go further and fare worse; loose -, miss- one's way; fail &c. 732.

Adj. un-skilful &c. 698; unskilled, inexpert; bungling &c. *v.*; awkward, clumsy, unhandy, lubberly, *gauche*, *maladroit*; left-, heavy-handed; slovenly, slatternly; gawky.

adrift, at fault.

in-, un-apt; inhabile; un-tractable. -teachable; giddy &c. (*inattentive*) 458; inconsiderate &c. (*neglectful*) 460; stupid &c. 499; inactive &c. 683; incompetent; un-, dis-, ill-qualified; unfit; quackish; raw, green, inexperienced, rusty, out of practice.

un-accustomed, -used, -trained &c. 537, -initiated, -conversant &c. (*ignorant*) 491; shiftless; unbusinesslike, unpractical; unstatesmanlike.

un-, ill-, mis-advised; ill-devised, -imagined, -judged, -contrived, -conducted; un-, mis-guided; misconducted, foolish, wild; infelicitous; penny wise and pound foolish &c. (*inconsistent*) 608.

Phr. one's fingers being all thumbs; the right hand forgets its cunning.

il se noyerait dans une goutte d'eau.

incidit in Scyllam qui vult vitare Charybdim; out of the frying pan into the fire.

700. Proficient.—N. proficient, expert, adept, dab; *connoisseur* &c. (*scholar*) 492; master, -hand; topsawyer, *prima donna*, first fiddle, *cordon bleu*; protagonist; past master; profess-or, -ional, specialist.

picked man; medallist, prizeman.

veteran; old -stager, – campaigner, – soldier, – file, – hand; man of -business, – the world.

nice –, good –, clean- hand; practised –, experienced- -eye, – hand; marksman; good –, dead –, crack- shot; rope-dancer, funambulist, acrobat, contortionist; cunning man; conjuror &c. (*deceiver*) 548; wizard &c. 994.

genius; master-mind, – head, – spirit;

cunning –, sharp -blade, – fellow; jobber; cracksman &c. (*thief*) 792; politician, tactician, diplomat, -ist, strategist.

pantologist, admirable Crichton, Jack of all trades; prodigy of learning; walking encyclopædia; mine of information.

701. Bungler.—N. bungler; blunderer, -head; marplot, fumbler, lubber, lout, oaf, duffer, stick, clown; bad –, poor- -hand, – shot; butter-fingers.

no conjuror, flat, muff, slow coach, looby, lubber, swab; clod, yokel, hick, awkward squad, novice, greenhorn, jaywalker, *blanc-bec*.

land lubber; fresh water –, fair weather- sailor; horse-marine; fish out of water, ass in lion's skin, jackdaw in peacock's feathers; quack &c. (*deceiver*) 548; Lord of Misrule.

sloven, slattern, trapes.

Phr. *il n'a pas inventé la poudre*; h will never set the Thames on fire.

---

702. Cunning.—N. cunning, craft; cunningness, craftiness &c. *adj.*; subtlety, artificiality; manœuvring &c. *v.*; temporization; circumvention.

chicane, -ry; sharp practice, knavery, jugglery; concealment &c. 528; nigger in the woodpile; guile, duplicity &c. (*falsehood*) 544; foul play.

diplomacy, politics; Machiavellism; jobbery, back-stairs influence, gerrymandering.

art, -ifice; device, machination; plot &c. (*plan*) 626; manœuvre, stratagem, dodge, artful dodge, wile; trick, -ery &c. (*deception*) 545; *ruse*, – *de guerre*; *finesse*, side-blow, thin end of the wedge, shift, go by, subterfuge, evasion; white lie &c. (*untruth*) 546; juggle, *tour de force*; tricks -of the trade, – upon travellers; imposture, deception; *espièglerie*; net, trap &c. 545.

Ulysses, Machiavel, sly boots, fox,

703. Artlessness.—N. artlessness &c. *adj.*; nature, simplicity; innocence &c. 946; *bonhomie, naïveté, abandon*, candour, sincerity; singleness of -purpose, – heart; honesty &c. 939; plain speaking; *épanchement*.

rough diamond, matter of fact man; *le palais de vérité; enfant terrible*.

V. be -artless &c. *adj.*; look one in the face; wear one's heart upon his sleeve for daws to peck at; think aloud; speak -out, – one's mind; be free with one, call a spade a spade.

Adj. artless, natural, pure, native, simple, plain, inartificial, untutored, unsophisticated, *ingénue*, unaffected, *naïve*; sincere, frank; open, – as day; candid, ingenuous, guileless, unsuspicious, childlike; honest &c. 939; innocent &c. 946; Arcadian; undesigning, straightforward, unreserved, unvarnished, above-board; simple-, single-

reynard; Scotch-, Yorkshire-man; Jew, Greek, Yankee; intriguer, *intrigant,* schemer, trickster.

V. be -cunning &c. *adj.*; have cut one's eye-teeth; contrive &c. *(plan)* 626; live by one's wits; manœuvre; intrigue, gerrymander, *finesse,* double, temporize, stoop to conquer, *reculer pour mieux sauter,* circumvent, steal a march upon; overreach &c. 545; throw off one's guard; surprise &c. 508; out-do, get the better of, snatch from under one's nose; snatch a verdict; waylay, undermine, introduce the thin end of the wedge; play -a deep game, – tricks with; have an axe to grind; *spargere voces in vulgum ambiguas;* flatter, make things pleasant.

Adj. cunning, crafty, artful; skilful &c. 698; subtle, feline, vulpine; cunning as a -fox, – serpent; deep, – laid; profound; designing, contriving; intriguing &c. *v.*; strategic, diplomatic, politic, Machia-vellian, time-serving; artificial; trick-y, -sy; wily, sly, slim, insidious, stealthy, foxy; underhand &c. *(hidden)* 528; subdolous; deceitful &c. 545; double-tongued, -faced; shifty; crooked; arch, pawky, shrewd, acute; sharp, – as a needle; canny, astute, leery, knowing, up to snuff, too clever by half, not to be caught with chaff.

Adv. cunningly &c. *adj.*; slily, on the sly, by a side wind.

Phr. diamond cut diamond.

minded; frank-, open-, single-, simple-hearted; open and above-board.

free-, plain-, out-spoken; blunt, downright, direct, matter of fact, un-poetical; unflattering.

Adv. in plain -words, – English; without mincing the matter; not to mince the matter &c. *(affirmation)* 535.

Phr. *Davus sum non Œdipus; liberavi animam meam.*

Section IV. ANTAGONISM

1°. *Conditional Antagonism*

704. Difficulty.—N. difficulty; hard-ness &c. *adj.*; impracticability &c. *(impossibility)* 471; tough -, hard -, uphill- work; hard -, Herculean -, Augean- task; task of Sisyphus, Sisy-phean labour, tough job, teaser, rasper, dead lift.

dilemma, embarrassment; perplexity &c. *(uncertainty)* 475; involvement; in-tricacy; entanglement &c. 59; cross fire; awkwardness, delicacy, ticklish card to play, deadlock, knot, Gordian knot, *dignus vindice nodus,* net, meshes, maze; coil &c. *(convolution)* 248; crooked path.

nice -, delicate -, subtle -, knotty-point; vexed question, *vexata quæstio* poser; puzzle &c. *(riddle)* 533; para-dox; hard -, nut to crack; bone to pick, *crux, pons asinorum,* where the shoe pinches.

nonplus, quandary, strait, pass, pinch, pretty pass, stress, brunt; criti-

705. Facility. — N. facility, ease; easiness &c. *adj.*; capability; feasibility &c. *(practicability)* 470; flexibility, pli-ancy &c. 324; smoothness &c. 255; convenience.

plain -, smooth -, straight- sailing; mere child's play, holiday task.

smooth water, fair wind; smooth – royal- road; clear -coast, – stage; *tabula rasa;* full play &c. *(freedom)* 748.

disen-cumbrance, -tanglement; de-oppilation; permission &c. 760.

V. be -easy &c. *adj.*; go on -, run-smoothly; have -full play &c. *n.*; go -, run- on all fours; obey the helm, work well.

flow -, swim -, drift -, go- with the--stream, – tide; see one's way; have -it all one's own way, – the game in one's own hands; walk over the course, win -at a canter, – hands down; make -light of, – nothing of; be at home in &c. *(skilful)* 698.

cal situation, crisis; trial, rub, emergency, exigency, scramble.

scrape, hobble, slough, quagmire, hot water, hornet's nest; sea –, peck- of troubles; pretty kettle of fish; pickle, stew, *imbroglio*, mess, muddle, botch, fuss, bustle, ado; false position; set fast, stand; dead -lock, – set; fix, horns of a dilemma, *cul de sac*; hitch; stumbling block &c. (*hindrance*) 706.

V. be -difficult &c. *adj.*; run one hard, go against the grain, try one's patience, put one out; put to one's -shifts, – wit's end; go hard with –, try- one; pose, perplex &c. (*uncertain*) 475; bother, nonplus, gravel, bring to a dead lock; be -impossible &c. 471; be in the way of &c. (*hinder*) 706.

meet with –, labour under –, get into –, plunge into –, struggle with –, contend with –, grapple with- difficulties; labour under a disadvantage; be -in difficulty &c. *adj.*

fish in troubled waters, buffet the waves, swim against the stream, scud under bare poles.

have -much ado with, – a hard time of it; come to the -push, – pinch; bear the brunt.

grope in the dark, lose one's way, weave a tangled web, walk among eggs.

get into a -scrape &c. *n.*; bring a hornet's nest about one's ears; be put to one's shifts; flounder, boggle, struggle; not know which way to turn &c. (*uncertain*) 475; get -tangled up, – wound up; *perdre son latin*; stick - at, – in the mud, – fast; come to a -stand, – dead lock; hold the wolf by the ears.

render -easy &c. *adj.*; facilitate, smooth, ease; popularize; lighten, – the labour; free, clear; dis-encumber, -embarrass, -entangle, -engage; deobstruct, unclog, extricate, unravel; untie –, cut- the knot; disburden, unload, exonerate, emancipate, free from, deoppilate; humour &c. (*aid*) 707; lubricate &c. 332; relieve &c. 834.

leave -a hole to creep out of, – a loophole, – the matter open; give -the reins to, – full play, – full swing; make way for; open the -door to, – way; prepare –, smooth –, clear- the -ground, – way, – path, – road; pave the way, bridge over; permit &c. 760.

Adj. easy, facile; feasible &c. (*practicable*) 470; easily -managed, – accomplished; within reach, accessible, easy of access, for the million, open to.

manageable, wieldy; towardly, tractable; submissive; yielding, ductile; pliant &c. (*soft*) 324; glib, slippery; smooth &c. 255; on -friction wheels, – velvet; convenient.

un-, dis-burdened, -encumbered, -embarrassed; exonerated; un-loaded, -obstructed, -trammelled, - impeded, -restrained &c. (*free*) 748; at ease, light.

at -, quite at- home; in -one's element, – smooth water.

Adv. easily &c. *adj.*; readily, smoothly, swimmingly, *ad lib.*, on easy terms, single-handed.

Phr. touch and go.

Int. all clear!

_____

render -difficult &c. *adj.*; encumber, embarrass, ravel, entangle; put a spoke in the wheel &c. (*hinder*) 706; lead a pretty dance.

Adj. difficult, not easy, hard, tough; trouble-, toil-, irk-some; operose, laborious, onerous, arduous, Herculean, formidable; sooner –, more easily- said than done; difficult –, hard- to deal with; ill-conditioned, crabbed; not -to be handled with kid gloves, – made with rosewater.

awkward, unwieldy, unmanageable; intractable, stubborn &c. (*obstinate*) 606; perverse, refractory, plaguy, trying, thorny, rugged; knot-ted, -ty; invious; path-, track-less; labyrinthine &c. (*convoluted*) 248; intricate, complicated &c. (*tangled*) 59; impracticable &c. (*impossible*) 471; not -feasible &c. 470; desperate &c. (*hopeless*) 859.

embarrassing, perplexing &c. (*uncertain*) 475; delicate, ticklish, critical; beset with –, full of –, surrounded by –, entangled by –, encompassed with- difficulties.

under a difficulty; in -difficulty, – hot water, – the suds, – a cleft stick, – a fix, – the wrong box, – a scrape &c. *n.*, – deep water, – a fine pickle; *in extremis*; between -two stools, – Scylla and Charybdis; surrounded by -shoals, – breakers, – quicksands; at cross purposes; not out of the wood.

reduced to straits; hard –, sorely- pressed; run hard; pinched, put to it, straitened; hard -up, – put to it, – set; put to one's shifts; puzzled, at a loss &c. (*uncertain*) 475; at -the end of one's tether, – one's wit's end, – a nonplus, – a standstill; gravelled, nonplussed, stranded, aground; stuck –, set- fast; up a tree, at bay, *aux abois*, driven -into a corner, – from post to pillar, – to extremity, – to one's wit's end, – to the wall; *au bout de son latin*; out of one's -depth, – reckoning; put –, thrown -out.

accomplished with difficulty; hard-fought, -earned.

Adv. with -difficulty, – much ado; hardly &c. *adj.*; uphill; against the -stream, – grain; *à rebours*; *invitâ Minervâ*; in the teeth of; at –, upon- a pinch; at long odds.

Phr. ay there's the rub; *hic labor hoc opus*; things are come to a pretty pass.

2°. *Active Antagonism*

706. Hindrance. — N. prevention, preclusion, obstruction, stoppage; prohibition; inter-ruption, -ception, -clusion; hindrance, impedition; retardment, -ation; constriction; embarrassment, oppilation; coarctation, stricture, restriction; anchor &c. 666; restraint &c. 751 & 752; inhibition &c. 761; blockade &c. (*closure*) 261; picketing.

inter-ference, -position; obtrusion; dis-couragement, -countenance, -approval, -approbation; opposition &c. 708.

impediment, let, obstacle, obstruction, knot, knag; check, hitch, *contretemps*, *impasse*, screw loose, grit in the oil.

bar, stile, barrier; turn-stile, -pike; gate, portcullis; bulwark, parapet, barricade &c. (*defence*) 717; wall, dead wall, breakwater, groyne; bulkhead, block, buffer; stopper &c. 263; boom, dam, weir, burrock.

drawback, objection; stumbling-block, -stone; lion in the path; snag; snags and sawyers.

en-, in-cumbrance; clog, skid, shoe, spoke; brake, drag, – chain, – weight; stay, stop; preventive, prophylactic; contraception; load, burden, fardel,

707. Aid.—N. aid, -ance; assistance, help, opitulation, succour; support, lift, advance, furtherance, promotion; coadjuvancy &c. (*co-operation*) 709.

patronage, championship, countenance, favour, interest, advocacy, auspices.

sustentation, subvention, subsidy, bounty, alimentation, nutrition, nourishment, maintenance; manna in the wilderness; food &c. 298; means &c. 632.

ministr-y, -ation; subministration; accommodation.

relief, rescue; help at a dead lift; supernatural aid; *deus ex machinâ*.

supplies, reinforcements, succours, contingents, recruits; support &c. (*physical*) 215; adjunct, ally &c. (*helper*) 711.

V. aid, assist, help, succour, lend one's aid; come to the aid &c. *n.*- of; contribute, subscribe to; bring –, give –, furnish –, afford –, supply- -aid &c. *n.*; render assistance; give –, stretch –, lend –, bear –, hold out- a -hand, – helping hand; give one a -lift, – cast, – turn; take -by the hand, – in tow; help a lame dog over a stile, lend wings to.

onus, millstone round one's neck, *impedimenta*; dead weight; lumber, pack; nightmare, Ephialtes, incubus, old man of the sea; remora.

difficulty &c. 704; insuperable &c. 471- obstacle; estoppel; ill wind; head wind &c. (*opposition*) 708; trammel, tether &c. (*means of restraint*) 752; hold back, counterpoise; damper, wet blanket, hinderer, marplot, kill-joy, dog in the manger, interloper; trail of a red herring; opponent &c. 710.

V. hinder, impede, impedite, embarrass.

keep -, stave -, ward- off; picket; obviate; a-, ante-vert; turn aside, draw off, prevent, forefend, nip in the bud; retard, slacken, check, let; counter-act, -check; preclude, debar, foreclose, estop; inhibit &c. 761; shackle &c. (*restrain*) 751; restrict, restrain, cohibit.

obstruct, filibuster, stop, stay, bar, bolt, lock; block, - up; belay, barricade; block -, stop- the way; dam up &c. (*close*) 261; put on the -brake &c. *n*.; scotch -, lock -, put a spoke in- the wheel; put a stop to &c. 142; traverse, contravene; inter-rupt, -cept; oppose &c. 708; hedge -in, - round; cut off; interclude.

inter-pose, -fere, -meddle &c. 682.

cramp, hamper; clog, - the wheels; cumber; en-, in-cumber; handicap; choke; saddle -, load- with; over-load, -lay; lumber, trammel, tie one's hands, put to inconvenience; in-, discommode; discompose; hustle, drive into a corner; choke off.

run -, fall- foul of; cross the path of, break in upon.

thwart, frustrate, disconcert, balk, foil, baffle, snub, override, circumvent; defeat &c. 731; spike guns &c. (*render useless*) 645; spoil, mar, clip the wings of; cripple &c. (*injure*) 659; put an extinguisher on; damp; dishearten &c. (*dissuade*) 616; discountenance, throw cold water on, spoil sport; lay -, throw- a wet blanket on; cut the ground from under one, take the wind out of one's sails, undermine; be -, stand- in the way of; act as a drag; hang like a millstone round one's neck.

relieve, rescue; set -up, - agoing, - on one's legs; bear -, pull- through; give new life to, be the making of; reinforce, recruit; set -, put -, push- forward; give -a lift, - a shove, - an impulse- to; promote, further, forward, advance; speed, expedite, quicken, hasten.

support, sustain, uphold, prop, hold up, bolster.

cradle, nourish; nurture, nurse, dry nurse, suckle, put out to nurse; manure, cultivate, force; foster, cherish, foment; feed -, fan- the flame.

serve; do service to, tender to, pander to; ad-, sub-, minister to; tend, attend, wait on; take care of &c. 459; entertain; smooth the bed of death.

oblige, accommodate, consult the wishes of; humour, cheer, encourage.

second, stand by; back, - up; pay the piper, abet; work -, make interest -, stick up -, take up the cudgels- for; take up -, espouse -, adopt- the cause of; advocate, beat up for recruits, press into the service; squire, give moral support to, keep in countenance, countenance, patronize; lend -oneself, - one's countenance- to; smile -, shine- upon; favour, befriend, take up, take in hand, enlist under the banners of; side with &c. (*co-operate*) 709.

be of use to; subserve &c. (*instrument*) 631; benefit &c. 648; render a service &c. (*utility*) 644; conduce &c. (*tend*) 176.

Adj. aiding &c. *v*.; auxiliary, adjuvant, helpful; coadjuvant &c. 709; subservient, ministrant, ancillary, accessory, subsidiary.

at one's beck; friendly, amicable, favourable, propitious, well-disposed; neighbourly; obliging &c. (*benevolent*) 906.

Adv. with -, by- -the aid &c. *n*.- of; on -, in- behalf of; in -aid, - the service, - the name, - favour, - furtherance- of; on account of; for the sake of, on the part of; *non obstante*.

Int. help! save us! to the rescue! SOS! *à moi!*

Adj. hindering &c. *v.*; obstr-uctive, -uent; impedi-tive, -ent; intercipient; prophylactic &c. (*remedial*) 662.

in the way of, unfavourable; onerous, burdensome; cumb-rous, -ersome; obtrusive.

hindered &c. *v.*; wind-bound, water-logged, heavy laden; hard pressed.

unassisted &c. (*see* assist &c. 707); single-handed, alone; deserted &c. 624.

---

708. Opposition.—N. opposition, antagonism; oppug-nancy, -nation; impugnation; contravention; counteraction &c. 179; counterplot, obstacle.

cross-fire, under-current, head-wind.

clashing, collision, conflict, lack of harmony, contest.

competition, two of a trade, rivalry, emulation, race; war to the knife.

absence of -aid &c. 707; resistance &c. 719; restraint &c. 751; hindrance &c. 706.

V. oppose, counteract, run counter to; withstand &c. (*resist*) 719; control &c. (*restrain*) 751; hinder &c. 706; antagonize, oppugn, fly in the face of, go dead against, kick against, fall foul of; set -, pit- against; face, confront, cope with; make a -stand, - dead set-against; set -oneself, one's face- against; protest -, vote -, raise one's voice-against; disfavour, turn one's back upon; set at naught, slap in the face, slam the door in one's face.

be -, play- at cross purposes; counter-work, -mine; thwart, overthwart.

stem, breast, encounter; stem -, breast- the -tide, - current, - flood; buffet the waves; beat up -, make head- against; grapple with; kick against the pricks &c. (*resist*) 719; contend &c. 720 -, do battle &c. (*warfare*) 722- -with, - against.

contra-dict, -vene; belie; go -, run -, beat -, militate- against; come in conflict with.

emulate &c. (*compete*) 720; rival, spoil one's trade.

Adj. oppos-ing, -ed &c. *v.*; adverse, antagonistic; ambivalent; contrary &c. 14; at variance &c. 24; at issue, at war with; in opposition; 'agin the Government.'

un-favourable, -friendly; hostile, inimical, cross, unpropitious.

709. Co-operation.—N. co-operation; coadju-vancy, -tancy; coagency, co-efficiency; concert, concurrence, complicity, participation; union &c. 43; amalgamation, combination &c. 48; collusion.

association, alliance, colleagueship, jointstock, copartnership, trust, cartel, pool, ring, combine, interlocking directorate; confederation &c. (*party*) 712; federation, coalition, fusion; a long pull, a strong pull and a pull all together; log-rolling, Freemasonry.

unanimity &c. (*assent*) 488; *esprit de corps*, party spirit; clan-, partisan-ship; reciprocity, concord &c. 714.

V. co-operate, co-adjute, concur; conduce &c. 178; combine, cartelize, unite one's efforts; keep -, draw -, pull -, club -, hang -, hold -, league -, band -, be banded- together; stand -, put-shoulder to shoulder; act in concert, join forces, fraternize, cling to one another, conspire, concert, lay one's heads together; confederate, be in league with; collude, understand one another, play into the hands of, hunt in couples.

side -, take side -, go along -, go hand in hand -, join hands -, make common cause -, strike in -, unite -, join -, mix oneself up -, take part -, play along -, cast in one's lot- with; join -, enter into- partnership with; rally round, follow the lead of; come to, pass over to, come into the views of; be -, row -, sail- in the same boat; sail on the same tack.

be a party to, lend oneself to; participate; have a -hand in, - finger in the pie; take -, bear- part in; second &c. (*aid*) 707; take the part of, play the game of; espouse a -cause, - quarrel.

Adj. co-operating &c. *v.*; in -co-operation &c. *n.*, - league &c. (*party*) 712;

in hostile array, front to front, with crossed bayonets, at daggers drawn; up in arms; resistant &c. 719.
competitive, emulous.

Adv. against, *versus*, counter to, in conflict with, at cross purposes.

against the -grain, – current, – stream, – wind, – tide; with a head-wind; with the wind -ahead, – in one's teeth.

in spite, in despite, in defiance; in the -way, – teeth, – face- of; across; a-, over-thwart; where the shoe pinches.

though &c. 30; even; *quand même*; *per contra*.

Phr. *nitor in adversum.*

coadju-vant, -tant; hand and glove with.

favourable &c. 707- to; un-opposed &c. 708.

Adv. as one man &c. (*unanimously*) 488; shoulder to shoulder; in co-operation with.

_____

710. Opponent.—N. opponent, antagonist, adversary; adverse party, opposition; enemy &c. 891; assailant.

oppositionist, obstructive; obscurantist; brawler, wrangler, brangler, disputant, extremist, irreconcilable, die-hard, bitter-ender.

malcontent; Jacobin, Fenian &c. 742; demagogue, reactionist.

passive resister, conscientious objector.

rival, competitor, contestant.

_____

711. Auxiliary.—N. auxiliary; recruit; assistant; adju-vant, -tant; adjunct; help, -er, -mate, -ing hand; midwife; colleague, partner, mate, *confrère*, co-operator; coadju-tor, -trix; collaborator.

ally; friend &c. 890, confidant, *fidus Achates*, pal, chum, buddy, *alter ego*.

confederate; ac-, complice; accessory, – after the fact; *particeps criminis*.

aide-de-camp, secretary, clerk, associate, marshal; right-hand; candle-, bottle-holder; hand-maid; servant &c. 746; puppet, cat's-paw, stooge, dependent, creature, jackal; tool, *âme damnée*; satellite, adherent, parasite.

votary, disciple; secta-rian, -ry; seconder, backer, upholder, supporter, abettor, advocate, partisan, champion, patron, friend at court, mediator.

friend in need, Jack at a pinch, *deus ex machinâ*, guardian angel, fairy godmother; special providence, tutelary genius.

712. Party.—N. party, faction, side, denomination, class, communion, set, crowd, crew, band, horde, posse, phalanx; regiment &c. 726; family, clan &c. 166.

Tories, Conservatives, Unionists, Whigs, Liberals, Radicals, Labour party, Socialists, Communists &c.; Republicans, Democrats, Farmer-Labor; *Fascisti*, Revolutionaries &c. 742.

community, body, fellowship, sodality, solidarity; con-, fraternity; sorority; brother-, sister-hood.

Freemasons, Knights Templars, Odd Fellows, Ku Klux Klan, Rosicrucians; knot, gang, *clique*, ring, circle; *coterie*, club, *casino*.

corporation, corporate body, guild; establishment, company; co-partnership; firm, house; joint concern, joint-stock company, trust, investment trust, combine &c. 709.

society, association; instit-ute, -ution; union; trade-union; league, syndicate, alliance, *Verein*, *Bund*, *Zollverein*, combination; league –, alliance- offensive and defensive; coalition; federation; confedera -tion, -cy; junto, cabal, *camarilla*, *Camorra*, *brigue*; Freemasonry; party spirit &c. (*co-operation*) 709.

staff; cast, *dramatis personæ.*

V. unite, join; club together &c. (*co-operate*) 709; cement –, form- a party &c. *n.*; associate &c. (*assemble*) 72.

Adj. in -league, – partnership, – alliance &c. *n.*

bonded –, banded –, linked &c. (*joined*) 43- together; embattled; confederated, federative, joint, corporate, leagued, fraternal, Masonic, cliquish.

Adv. hand in hand, side by side, shoulder to shoulder, *en masse,* in the same boat.

---

713. Discord.—N. disagreement &c. 24; dis-cord, -accord, -sidence, -sonance; jar, clash, shock; jarring, jostling &c. *v.*; screw loose.

variance, difference, dissension, misunderstanding, cross purposes, odds, *brouillerie*; division, split, rupture, disruption, division in the camp, house divided against itself, rift within the lute; disunion, breach; schism &c. (*dissent*) 489; feud, faction.

quarrel, dispute, rippet, spat, tiff, *tracasserie,* squabble, altercation, words, high words; wrangling &c. *v.*; jangle, brabble, cross questions and crooked answers, snip-snap; family jars.

polemics; litigation; strife &c. (*contention*) 720; warfare &c. 722; outbreak, open rupture; breaking off of negotiations, recall of ambassadors; declaration of war.

broil, brawl, row, racket, hubbub, rixation; embroilment, embranglement, *imbroglio, fracas,* breach of the peace, piece of work, scrimmage, rumpus; breeze, squall; riot, disturbance &c. (*disorder*) 59; commotion &c. (*agitation*) 315; bear garden, Donnybrook Fair.

subject of dispute, ground of quarrel, battle ground, disputed point; bone -of contention, – to pick; apple of discord, *casus belli*; question at issue &c. (*subject of inquiry*) 461; vexed question, *vexata quæstio,* brand of discord.

troublous times; cat-and-dog life; contentiousness &c. *adj.*; enmity &c. 889; hate &c. 898; Kilkenny cats; disputant &c. 710; strange bedfellows.

V. be -discordant &c. *adj.*; disagree, come amiss &c. 24; clash, jar, jostle, pull different ways, conflict, have no

714. Concord.—N. concord, accord, harmony, symphony, homology; agreement &c. 23; sympathy &c. (*love*) 897; response; union, unison, unity; bonds of harmony; peace &c. 721; unanimity &c. (*assent*) 488; league &c. 712; happy family.

rapprochement; réunion; amity &c. (*friendship*) 888; reciprocity; alliance, *entente cordiale,* good understanding, conciliation, arbitration, peacemaker &c. 724.

V. agree &c. 23; accord, harmonize with; fraternize; be -concordant &c. *adj.*; go hand in hand; blend –, tone in- with; run parallel &c. (*concur*) 178; understand one another; pull together &c. (*co-operate*) 709; put up one's horses together, sing in chorus.

side –, sympathize –, go –, chime in –, fall in- with; come round; be pacified &c. 723; assent &c. 488; enter into the -ideas, – feelings- of; reciprocate.

hurler avec les loups; go –, swim- with the stream.

pour oil on troubled waters, keep in good humour, render accordant, put in tune; come to an understanding, meet half-way; keep the –, remain at- peace.

Adj. concordant, congenial; agreeing &c. *v.*; in- accord &c. *n.*; harmonious, united, cemented; banded together &c. 712; allied; friendly &c. 888; fraternal; conciliatory; at one with; of one mind &c. (*assent*) 488.

at peace, in still water; tranquil &c. (*pacific*) 721.

Adv. with one voice &c. (*assent*) 488; in concert with, hand in hand; on one's side, unanimously.

---

measures with, misunderstand one another; live like cat and dog; differ; dissent &c. 489; have a -bone to pick, – crow to pluck- with.

fall out, quarrel, dispute; litigate; controvert &c. (*deny*) 536;

squabble, wrangle, jangle, brangle, bicker, nag; spar &c. (*contend*) 720; have -words &c. *n.* with; fall foul of.

split; break -, break squares -, part company- with; declare war, try conclusions; join -, put in- issue; pick a quarrel, fasten a quarrel on; sow -, stir up- -dissension &c. *n.*; embroil, estrange, entangle, disunite, widen the breach; set -at odds, - together by the ears; set -, pit- against; rub up the wrong way.

get into hot water, fish in troubled waters, brawl; kick up a -row, - dust; turn the house out of window.

Adj. discordant; disagreeing &c. *v.*; out of tune, dissonant, inharmonious, harsh, grating, jangling, ajar, on bad terms; dissentient &c. 489; inconsistent, contradictory, incongruous, discrepant; un--reconciled, -pacified.

quarrelsome, unpacific; gladiatorial, controversial, polemic, disputatious; factious; liti-gious, -gant; pettifogging.

at odds, at loggerheads, at daggers drawn, at variance, at issue, at cross purposes, at sixes and sevens, at feud, at high words; up in arms, together by the ears, in hot water, embroiled.

torn, disunited.

Phr. *quot homines tot sententiæ*; no love lost between them, *non nostrum tantas componere lites.*

715. Defiance.—N. defiance; daring &c. *v.*; dare, challenge, *cartel*; threat &c. 909; war-cry, -whoop.

V. defy, dare, beard; brave &c. (*courage*) 861; bid defiance to; set at -defiance, - naught; hurl defiance at; dance the war dance; snap the fingers at, laugh to scorn; disobey &c. 742.

show -fight, - one's teeth, - a bold front; bluster, look big, stand akimbo; double -, shake- the fist; threaten &c. 909.

challenge, call out; throw -, fling- down the -gauntlet, - gage, - glove.

Adj. defiant; defying &c. *v.*; with arms akimbo; rebellious, insolent; reckless, greatly daring.

Adv. in -defiance, - the teeth- of; under one's very nose.

Int. do your worst! come if you dare! come on! marry come up! hoity toity!

Phr. *noli me tangere; nemo me impune lacessit.*

716. Attack.—N. attack; assault, - and battery; onset, onslaught, charge.

aggression, drive, offence; incursion, inroad, invasion; irruption; outbreak; *estrapade, ruade; coup de main*, sally, *sortie, camisade*, raid, foray; run -at, - against; dead set at.

storm, -ing; boarding, *escalade*; siege, investment, obsession, bombardment, cannonade; air raid.

fire, volley; platoon -, file -, rapid-fire; *fusillade*; sharp-shooting, sniping; broadside; raking -, cross -, machine gun- fire; volley of grapeshot, *feu d'enfer*; salvo.

cut, thrust, lunge, pass, *passado*, *carte* and *tierce*, home thrust; *coup de pied*; kick, punch &c. (*impulse*) 276.

717. Defence.—N. defence, protection. guard, ward; shielding &c. *v.*; propugnation; preservation &c. 670; guardianship.

self-defence, -preservation; resistance &c. 719.

safeguard &c. (*safety*) 664; screen &c. (*shelter*) 666, (*concealment*) 530; barrage; fortification; muni-tion, -ment; bulwark, fosse, moat, ditch, intrenchment, trench, dugout, gas mask; dike, dyke; parapet, parados, sunk fence, embankment, mound, mole, bank; earth- field-work, gabions; fence, wall, dead wall, contravallation; paling &c. (*inclosure*) 232; palisade, ha-ha, stockade, *stoccado, laager, sangar*; barri-er, -cade; boom; portcullis, *chevaux de*

battue, razzia, Jacquerie, dragonnade; devastation &c. 162.

assailant, aggressor, invader.

base of operations, point of attack.

V. attack, assault, assail; set –, fall-upon; charge, impugn, break a lance with, enter the lists.

assume –, take- the offensive; be –, become- the aggressor; strike the first blow, fire the first shot, throw the first stone at; lift a hand –, draw the sword-against; take up the cudgels; advance –, march- against; march upon, invade, harry; come on, show fight.

strike at, poke at, thrust at; aim –, deal- a blow at; give –, fetch- one a -blow; – kick; have a -cut, – shot, – fling, – shy- at; be down –, pounce-upon; fall foul of, pitch into, launch out against; bait, slap on the face; make a -thrust, – pass, – set, – dead set- at; dunt; bear down upon.

close with, come to close quarters, bring to bay.

ride full tilt against; let fly at, dash at, run a tilt at, rush at, tilt at, run at, fly at, hawk at, have at, let out at; make a -dash, – rush at; attack tooth and nail; strike home; drive –, press-one hard; be hard upon, run down, strike at the root of.

lay about one, run amuck.

fire -upon, – at, – a shot at; shoot at, pop at, level at, let off a gun at; open fire, pepper, bombard, shell, pour a broadside into; fire -a volley, – red-hot shot; spring a mine.

throw -a stone, – stones- at; stone, lapidate, pelt; hurl -at, – against, – at the head of.

beset, besiege, beleaguer; lay siege to, invest, open the trenches, plant a battery, sap, mine; storm, board, scale the walls.

cut and thrust, bayonet, butt; kick, strike &c. (*impulse*) 276; whip &c. (*punish*) 972.

Adj. attacking &c. *v.*; aggressive, offensive, obsidional.

up in arms; on the warpath; over the top.

Adv. on the offensive.

Int. 'up and at them!'

---

frise; aba-, abat-, abba-tis; *vallum,* circumvallation, battlement, rampart, scarp; e–, counter-scarp; glacis, case-mate, obstacle.

mine, countermine.

buttress, abutment; shore &c. (*support*) 215.

breastwork, *banquette,* curtain, mant-let, bastion, demilune, redan, ravelin; advanced –, horn –, out- work, lunette; barb-acan, -ican; redoubt; fort-elage, -alice; lines; coast defence.

loop-hole, machicolation; sally-port, postern gate.

hold, stronghold, fastness; asylum &c. (*refuge*) 666; keep, donjon, fort-ress, citadel; capitol, castle; tower, – of strength; fort, barracoon, pah, sconce, martello tower, peel-house, block-house, rath; wooden walls; turret, barbette.

buffer, corner-stone, fender, apron, mask, gauntlet, thimble, carapace, armour, shield, buckler; target, targe, ægis, breastplate, cuirass, plastron, habergeon, mail, coat of mail, brigan-dine, hauberk, lorication, helmet, helm, basinet, sallet, salade, heaume, morion, murrion, armet, cabaset, vizor, cas-quetel, siege-cap, head-piece, casque, steel helmet, tin hat; *Pickelhaube,* csako; shako &c. (*dress*) 225; bearskin; panoply; truncheon &c. (*weapon*) 727.

garrison, picket, piquet; defender, protector; guardian &c. (*safety*) 664; trabant, body guard, champion; knight-errant, Paladin; propugner.

V. defend, forfend, fend; shield, screen, shroud; fence round &c. (*cir-cumscribe*) 229; fence, intrench; guard &c. (*keep safe*) 664; guard against; take care of &c. (*vigilance*) 459; bear harm-less; keep –, ward –, beat- off; hinder &c. 706.

parry, repel, propugn, put to flight; give a warm reception to [*ironical*]; hold –, keep- at -bay, – arm's length.

stand –, act- on the defensive; show fight; maintain –, stand- one's ground; stand by; hold one's own; bear –, stand- the brunt; fall back upon, hold, stand in the gap.

Adj. defending &c. *v.*; defensive; mural; armed, – at all points, – *cap-à-pie,* – to the teeth; panoplied, accou-

tred, harnessed; iron-plated, -clad; loop-holed, castellated, machic-
olated, casemated; defended &c. *v.*; proof against, bomb-, bullet-
proof; protective.

Adv. defensively; on the -defence, – defensive; in defence; at
bay, *pro aris et focis.*

Int. no surrender! *ils ne passeront pas!*

Phr. defence not defiance.

718. Retaliation. — N. retaliation,
reprisal, retort; counter-stroke, -blast,
-plot, -project; retribution, *lex talionis*;
reciprocation &c. (*reciprocity*) 12.

requital, desert, tit for tat, give and
take, blow for blow, *quid pro quo*, a
Roland for an Oliver, measure for
measure, an eye for an eye, diamond
cut diamond, the biter bit, a game at
which two can play; boomerang.

recrimination &c. (*accusation*) 938;
revenge &c. 919; compensation &c. 30;
reaction &c. (*recoil*) 277.

V. retaliate, retort, turn upon; pay
-off, – back; pay in -one's own, – the
same- coin; cap; reciprocate &c. 148;
turn the tables upon, return the compliment; give -a *quid pro quo* &c. *n.*,
– as much as one takes; give and take,
exchange -blows, – fisticuffs; be -quits,
– even- with; pay off old scores.

serve one right, be hoist on one's own
petard, throw a stone in one's own
garden, catch a Tartar.

Adj. retaliating &c. *v.*; retalia-tory,
-tive; retributive, recriminatory, reciprocal.

Adv. in retaliation; *en revanche.*

Phr. *mutato nomine de te fabula narratur; par pari refero; tu quoque*; you're
another; *suo sibi gladio hunc jugulo.*

719. Resistance. — N. resistance,
stand, front, oppugnation; opposition
&c. 708; renitence, reluctation, recal-
citration, recalcitrance; repugnance;
kicking &c. *v.*

repulse, rebuff.

insurrection &c. (*disobedience*) 742;
strike; turn –, lock –, barring- out;
levée en masse, Jacquerie; riot &c. (*disorder*) 59.

V. resist; not -submit &c. 725; re-
pugn, reluctate, withstand; stand up
–, strive –, bear up –, be proof –, make
head- against; stand, – firm, – one's
ground, – the brunt of, – out; hold
-one's ground, – one's own, – out.

breast the -wave, – current; stem
the -tide, – torrent; face, confront,
grapple with; show a bold front &c.
(*courage*) 861; present a front; make
a –, take one's- stand.

kick, – against; recalcitrate, kick
against the pricks; oppose &c. 708;
fly in the face of; lift the hand against
&c. (*attack*) 716; rise up in arms &c.
(*war*) 722; strike, turn out; draw up a
round robin &c. (*remonstrate*) 932; revolt &c. (*disobey*) 742; make a riot.

prendre le mors aux dents; take the
bit between the teeth; sell one's life
dearly, die hard, keep at bay; repel
repulse.

Adj. resisting &c. *v.*; resist-ive, -ant; refractory &c. (*disobedient*)
742; recalcitrant, re-nitent, -pulsive, -pellant; up in arms.

proof against; unconquerable &c. (*strong*) 159; stubborn, uncon-
quered; indomitable &c. (*persevering*) 604a; unyielding &c. (*obstinate*) 606.

Int. hands off! keep off!

720. Contention. — N. contention,
strife; contest, -ation; struggle; bel-
ligerency; opposition &c. 708.

controversy, polemics; debate &c.
(*discussion*) 476; war of words, logomachy, litigation; paper war, ink slinging; high words &c. (*quarrel*) 713;
sparring &c. *v.*

721. Peace.—N. peace; amity &c.
(*friendship*) 888; harmony &c. (*concord*) 714; tranquillity &c. (*quiescence*)
265; truce &c. (*pacification*) 723;
pacificism; pipe –, calumet- of peace.

piping time of peace, quiet life; neutrality.

V. be at peace; keep the peace &c.

competition, rivalry; corrival-ry, -ship; agonism, *concours*, match, race, horse-racing, heat, steeple chase, point-to-point race, handicap; boat race, regatta; field-day; sham fight, Derby day; turf, sporting, bull-fight, tauro-machy, *gymkhana*, rodeo, Olympiad.

wrestling, *ju-jitsu*, pugilism, boxing, fisticuffs, spar, mill, set-to, scrap, round, bout, event; prize-fighting; quarter-staff, single stick; gladiatorship, gymnastics; athletic-s, – sports; games of skill &c. 840.

shindy; *fracas* &c. (*discord*) 713; clash of arms; tussle, scuffle, broil, fray; affray, -ment; velitation; col-, luctation; brabble, *brigue*, scramble, *mêlée*, scrimmage, stramash, bush-fighting.

free –, stand up –, hand to hand –, running- fight.

conflict, skirmish; ren-, en-counter; *rencontre*, collision, affair, brush, fight; battle, – royal; combat, action, engagement, joust, tournament; tilt, -ing; tourney, list; pitched battle, guerilla warfare.

death-struggle, struggle for life or death, Armageddon; hard knocks, sharp contest, tug of war.

naval -engagement, – battle; *naumachia*, sea-fight.

duel, -lo; single combat, monomachy, satisfaction, *passage d'armes*, passage of arms, affair of honour; triangular duel; hostile meeting, digladiation; appeal to arms &c. (*warfare*) 722.

deeds –, feats- of arms; pugnacity; combativeness &c. *adj.*; bone of contention &c. 713.

V. contend; contest, strive, struggle, scramble, wrestle; spar, square; exchange -blows, – fisticuffs; scrap, mix with, fib, justle, tussle, tilt, box, stave, fence; skirmish; fight &c. (*war*) 722; wrangle &c. (*quarrel*) 713.

contend &c. –, grapple –, engage –, close –, buckle –, bandy –, try conclusions –, have a brush &c. *n.* –, tilt- with; encounter, fall foul of, pitch into, clapperclaw, run a tilt at; oppose &c. 708; reluct.

join issue, come to blows, be at loggerheads, set-to, come to the scratch, exchange shots, measure swords, meet hand to hand; take up the -cudgels, – glove, – gauntlet; enter the lists; couch one's lance; give satisfaction; appeal to arms &c. (*warfare*) 722.

lay about one; break the peace.

compete –, cope –, vie –, race- with; outvie, emulate, rival; run a race; contend &c: –, stipulate –, stickle- for; insist upon, make a point of.

Adj. contending &c. *v.*; together by the ears, at loggerheads, at war, at issue.

competitive, rival; belligerent; contentious, combative, bellicose, unpeaceful; warlike &c. 722; quarrelsome &c. 901; pugnacious; pugilistic, gladiatorial; palestric, -al; irenic.

Phr. *a verbis ad verbera*; a word and a blow

(*concord*) 714; make peace &c. 723.

Adj. pacific; peace-able, -ful; calm, tranquil, untroubled, halcyon; blood-less; neutral.

Phr. the storm blown over; the lion lies down with the lamb.

———

722. Warfare.—N. warfare; fighting &c. *v.*; hostilities; war, arms, the sword; Mars, Bellona, grim visaged war, *horrida bella*, Armageddon.

appeal to -arms, – the sword; ordeal

723. Pacification.—N. pacification, conciliation; reconcil-iation, -ement; shaking of hands, accommodation, arrangement, adjustment; terms, compromise; amnesty, deed of release.

-, wager- of battle; *ultima ratio regum,* arbitrament of the sword.

battle array, campaign, crusade, expedition; mobilization; state of siege; battle-field &c. (*arena*) 728; warpath.

art of war, tactics, strategy, castrametation; general-, soldier-ship; aerial-, submarine -, naval -, chemical- warfare; military evolutions, ballistics, gunnery; chivalry; poison gas; gunpowder, shot, - and shell.

battle, tug of war &c. (*contention*) 720; service, campaigning, active service, tented field; fiery cross, trumpet, clarion, bugle, pibroch, slogan; warcry, -whoop; battle cry, beat of drum, rappel, tom-tom; word of command; pass-, watch-word.

war to the -death, - knife; *guerre à -mort, - outrance;* open -, internecine -, civil- war.

V. arm; raise -, mobilize- troops; rise up in arms; take up the cudgels &c. 720; take up -, fly to -, appeal to--arms, - the sword; draw -, unsheathe-the sword; dig up the hatchet; go to -, declare -, wage -, let slip the dogs of-war; cry havoc; kindle -, light- the torch of war; raise one's banner, send round the fiery cross; hoist the black flag; throw -, fling- away the scabbard; enrol, enlist, join up; take the field; take the law into one's own hands; do -, give -, join -, engage in -, go to- battle; flesh one's sword; set to, fall to, engage, measure swords with, draw the trigger, cross swords; come to -blows, - close quarters; fight; combat; contend &c. 720; battle -, break a lance- with.

serve; see -, be on- -service, - active service; campaign; wield the sword, shoulder a musket, smell powder, be under the fire; spill -, imbrue the hands in- blood; be on the warpath.

carry on -war, - hostilities; keep the field; fight the good fight; go over the top; cut one's way through; fight -it out, - like devils, - one's way, - hand to hand; sell one's life dearly.

Adj. conten-ding, -tious &c. 720; armed, - to the teeth, - cap-à-pie; sword in hand; in -, under -, up in- arms; at war with; bristling with arms; in -battle array, - open arms, - the field; embat-tled.

unpacific, unpeaceful; belligerent, combative, armigerous, belli-cose, martial, warlike; mili-tary, -tant; soldier-like, -ly; chivalrous; strategical, internecine.

Adv. *flagrante bello,* in the -thick of the fray, - cannon's mouth; at the -sword's point, - point of the bayonet.

Int. *væ victis!* to arms! to your tents O Israel!

Phr. the battle rages.

peace-offering; olive-branch; overtures; pipe -, calumet -, preliminaries-of peace.

truce, armistice; suspension of -arms, - hostilities; breathing-time; convention; *modus vivendi;* flag of truce, white flag, *parlementaire, cartel.*

hollow truce, *pax in bello;* drawn battle.

V. pacify, tranquillize, compose; allay &c. (*moderate*) 174; reconcile, propiti-ate, placate, conciliate, meet half-way, hold out the olive-branch, heal the breach, make peace, restore harmony, bring to terms.

settle -, arrange -, accommodate--matters, - differences; set straight; make up a quarrel, *tantas componere lites;* come to -an understanding, - terms; bridge over, hush up; make -it, - matters- up; shake hands.

raise a siege; put up -, sheathe- the sword; bury the hatchet, lay down one's arms, turn swords into plough-shares; smoke the calumet of peace, close the temple of Janus; keep the peace &c. (*concord*) 714; be -pacified &c.; come round.

Adj. conciliatory, pacificatory; composing &c. *v.;* pacified &c. *v.*

Phr. *requiescat in pace.*

---

724. Mediation.—**N.** media-tion, -torship, -tization; inter-vention, -position, -ference, -meddling, -cession; parley, negotiation, arbitration; flag of truce &c. 723; good offices, peace-offering; diploma-tics, -cy; compromise &c. 774.

mediator, intercessor, peacemaker, make-peace, negotiator, go-between; diplomatist &c. (*consignee*) 758; moderator, propitiator, umpire, arbitrator.

V. media-te, -tize; inter-cede, -pose, -fere, -vene; step in, negotiate; meet half-way; arbitrate; *magnas componere lites*.

Adj. mediatory, propitiatory, diplomatic.

725. Submission.—**N.** submission, yielding, acquiescence, compliance; non-resistance; obedience &c. 743; submissiveness, deference.

surrender, cession, capitulation, resignation.

obeisance, homage, kneeling, genuflexion, courtesy, curtsy, *salaam*, *kowtow*, prostration.

V. succumb, submit, yield, bend, resign, defer to, accede.

lay down –, deliver up- one's arms; hand over one's sword; lower –, haul down –, strike- one's flag, – colours; deliver the keys of the city.

surrender, – at discretion; cede, capitulate, come to terms, retreat, beat a retreat; draw in one's horns &c. (*humility*) 879; give -way, – ground, – in, – up; cave in; suffer judgment by default; bend, – to one's yoke, – before the storm; reel back; bend –, knuckle- -down, – to, – under; knock under.

humble oneself; eat -dirt, – the leek, – humble pie; bite –, lick- the dust; be –, fall- at one's feet; craven; crouch before, throw oneself at the feet of; swallow the -leek, – pill; kiss the rod; turn the other cheek; *avaler des couleuvres*, gulp down.

obey &c. 743; kneel to, bow to, pay homage to, cringe to, truckle to; bend the -neck, – knee; kneel, fall on one's knees, bow submission, courtesy, curtsy, *kowtow*; make obeisance.

pocket the affront; make -the best of, – a virtue of necessity; grin and abide, shrug the shoulders, resign oneself; submit with a good grace &c. (*bear with*) 826.

Adj. surrendering &c. *v.*; submissive, resigned, crouching; down-trodden; down on one's marrow bones; on one's bended knee; weak-kneed, un-, non-resisting; pliant &c. (*soft*) 324; undefended.

untenable, indefensible; humble &c. 879.

Phr. have it your own way; it can't be helped; amen &c. (*assent*) 488.

726. Combatant.—**N.** combatant; disputant, controversialist, polemic, litigant, belligerent; competitor, rival, corrival; fighter, assailant, aggressor; champion, Paladin; moss-trooper, swashbuckler, fire-eater, duellist, bully, bludgeon-man, rough, fighter, fighting-man, prize-fighter, pugilist, pug, boxer, bruiser, the fancy, gladiator, athlete, wrestler; fighting-, game-cock; swordsman, *sabreur*.

warrior, soldier, Amazon, man-at-arms, armigerent; campaigner, veteran; red-coat, military man, *rajpoot*, brave.

armed force, troops, soldiery, military, forces, sabaoth, the army, standing army, regulars, the line, troops of the line, militia, territorials, yeomanry, volunteers, trainband, fencible; auxiliary –, reserve- forces; reserves, *posse comitatus*, national guard, *gendarme*, beefeater; guards, -man; yeoman of the guard, life guards, household troops.

janissary; myrmidon; Mama-, Mame-luke; spahee, *spahi*, Cossack

Croat, Pandour; irregular, free lance, *franc-tireur, bashi-bazouk, guerilla, condottiere;* mercenary.

levy, draught, commando; *Land-wehr, -sturm;* conscript, recruit, rookie, cadet, raw levies.

private, – soldier; Tommy Atkins, rank and file, peon, trooper, doughboy, sepoy, *askari, légionnaire,* legionary, food for powder, cannon fodder; officer &c. (*commander*) 745; subaltern, ensign, shave-tail, standard bearer, non-com; spear-, pike-man; halberdier, lancer; musketeer, carabineer, rifleman, sharpshooter, yager, skirmisher; grenadier, fusileer; archer, bowman.

horse and foot; horse –, foot- soldier; cavalry, horse, artillery, horse –, field –, heavy –, mountain- artillery, infantry, light horse, *voltigeur, Uhlan,* mounted rifles, dragoon, hussar, trooper; light –, heavy-dragoon; heavy; *cuirassier;* gunner, cannoneer, bombardier, artilleryman, matross; sapper, – and miner; engineer; light infantry, rifles, *chasseur, zouave;* military train, supply and transport, coolie.

army, – corps, *corps d'armée,* host, division, column, wing, detachment, *escadrille,* garrison, flying column, brigade, regiment, *corps,* battalion, squadron, company, platoon, battery, subdivision, section, squad; piquet, picket, guard, rank, file; legion, phalanx, cohort; cloud of skirmishers; impi.

war-horse, charger, *destrier.*

armoured -train, – car; tank.

marine, man of war's·man &c. (*sailor*) 269; navy, first line of defence, wooden walls; naval forces, fleet, flotilla, armada, squadron.

man-of-war, warship; H.M.S., U.S.S.; capital ship; line-of-battle ship, battle ship; super-, dreadnought, battle –, armoured –, protected – light- cruiser; scout, flotilla leader; destroyer, torpedo boat; submarine, submersible, U-boat; submarine chaser, eagle boat, mystery ship, Q-boat; mine-layer, -sweeper; ship of the line, iron-clad, turret-ship, ram, Monitor, floating battery; first-rate, frigate, sloop of war, corvette, gunboat, bomb-vessel, fire-boat; flag ship, guard ship, cruiser; aircraft carrier; privateer; tender; depot –, parent- ship; store –, troop- ship; transport, catamaran.

aircraft &c. 273, air force, scout, fighter, bomber, troop carrier, aerial patrol, seaplane, flying boat, torpedo plane; airship, Zeppelin; rigid –, semi-rigid –, non-rigid- airship; dirigible –, free –, captive –, kite –, observation- balloon.

anti-aircraft guns, searchlights, sound locators; catapult.

727. Arms.—N. arm, -s; weapon, deadly weapon; arma-ment, -ture; panoply, stand of arms; armour &c. (*defence*) 717; armoury &c. (*store*) 636.

ammunition; powder, – and shot; explosive; propellant; gun-powder, -cotton; dynam-, melin-, cord-, lydd-ite; trinitrotoluene, T.N.T., ammonal; cartridge; ball cartridge, *cartouche,* fire-ball; dud, black Maria; 'villainous saltpetre'; poison –, mustard –, lachrymatory –, tear- gas.

sword, sabre, broadsword, cutlass, falchion, scimitar, cimeter, brand, whinyard, bilbo, glaive, glave, rapier, skean, Toledo, Ferrara, tuck, claymore, creese, kris, *kukri,* dagger, dirk, hanger, poniard, stiletto, stylet, dudgeon, bayonet; sword-bayonet, -stick; side arms, foil, blade, steel; axe, bill; pole-, battle-axe; gisarm, halberd, partisan, tomahawk, bowie-knife; at-, att-, yat-aghan; yatachan; good –, trusty –, naked-sword; cold –, naked- steel.

club, mace, truncheon, staff, bludgeon, cudgel, life-preserver, shillelagh, sprig; hand-, quarter-staff; bat, cane, stick, knuckle-duster,
sand bag.

gun, piece; fire-arms; artillery, ordnance; siege –, battering-train;
park, battery; cannon, gun of position, heavy –, siege –, field –, mountain –, anti-aircraft –, breech loading –, quick firing- gun; field piece,
mortar, trench mortar, mine thrower, howitzer, carronade, culverin,
basilisk; falconet, jingal, swivel, *pederero, bouche à feu*; smooth bore,
rifled cannon; Armstrong –, Lancaster –, Paixhan –, Whitworth –,
Parrott –, Krupp –, Gatling –, Maxim –, Vickers –, Hotchkiss –,
Lewis –, machine- gun; tommy gun, Thompson submachine gun;
mitrailleu-r, -se; pom-pom; blow pipe.

small arms; musket, -ry, firelock, flintlock, fowling-piece, shot gun,
rifle, *fusil*, caliver, carbine, blunderbuss, musketoon, Brown Bess,
matchlock, harquebuss, *arquebuse*, haguebut; petronel; smallbore;
breech-, muzzle-loader; Miniè –, Enfield –, Westley Richards –, Snider –,
Springfield –, Martini-Henry –, Lee-Metford –, Lee-Enfield –, Mauser –,
Männlicher –, magazine –, repeating- rifle; needle-gun, *chassepot*; pistol, -et; revolver, automatic pistol, automatic; wind-, air-gun; flame –,
gas-projector.

bow, cross-bow, arbalest, balister, catapult, sling; battering-ram &c.
(*impulse*) 276; gunnery; ballistics &c. (*propulsion*) 284.

missile, bolt, projectile, shot, pellet, ball; grape; grape –, canister –,
bar –, cannon –, langrel –, langrage –, round –, chain- shot; explosive;
incendiary –, expanding –, soft-nosed –, dum-dum- bullet; slug, stone,
brickbat; hand –, rifle- grenade; high explosive –, incendiary –, star –,
gas- shell; depth –, gas –, incendiary –, stink- bomb; petard, torpedo,
carcass, rocket; congreve, – rocket; shrapnel, *mitraille*; thunderbolt;
mine, land mine, infernal machine.

pike, lance, spear, spontoon, javelin, assagai, throwing stick, dart,
djerrid, arrow, reed, shaft, bolt, boomerang, harpoon, gaff.

728. Arena.—N. arena, field, platform; scene of action, theatre;
walk, course; hustings; stage, boards &c. (*playhouse*) 599; amphitheatre; Coli-, Colos-seum; Flavian amphitheatre, hippodrome, circus,
race-course, track, *stadium, corso*, turf, cockpit, bear-garden, play-
ground, playing fields, *gymnasium, palæstra*, ring, lists; tilt-yard, -ing
ground; *Campus Martius, Champ de Mars*; aerodrome, airport, air
base, flying field.

theatre –, seat- of war; battle-field, -ground; field of -battle, –
slaughter; no man's land; Aceldan.a, camp; the enemy's camp; trysting-
place &c. (*place of meeting*) 74.

Section V. Results of Voluntary Action

729. Completion.—N. completion;
accomplish-, achieve-, fulfil-ment; performance, execution; des-, dis-patch;
consummation, culmination, climax;
finish, conclusion, effectuation; close
&c. (*end*) 67; terminus &c. (*arrival*)
292; winding up; *finale, dénouement*,
catastrophe, issue, upshot, result; final
–, last –, crowning –, finishing- -touch,
– stroke; last finish, *coup de grâce*;

730. Non-Completion.—N. non-completion, -fulfilment; shortcoming &c.
304; incompleteness &c. 53; drawn
-battle, – game; work of Penelope, task
of Sisyphus.

non-performance, inexecution; neglect &c. 460.

V. not -complete &c. 729; leave
-unfinished &c. *adj.*, – undone; neglect
&c. 460; let -alone, – slip; lose sight of.

crowning of the edifice; coping-, key-stone; missing link &c. 53; superstruc-ture, *ne plus ultra*, work done, *fait accompli.*

elaboration; finality; completeness &c. 52.

V. effect, -uate; accomplish, achieve, compass, consummate, hammer out; bring to -maturity; – perfection; per-fect, complete; elaborate.

do, execute, make; go –, get- through; work out, enact; bring -about, – to bear, – to pass, – through, – to a head.

des-, dis-patch; knock –, finish –, polish- off; make short work of; dis-pose of, set at rest; perform, discharge, fulfil, realize; put in -practice, – force; – into execution; make good; be as good as one's word.

do thoroughly, not do by halves, go the whole hog; drive home; be in at the death &c. (*persevere*) 604*a*; carry through, play out, exhaust, deliver the goods, fill the bill.

finish, bring to a close &c. (*end*) 67; wind up, stamp, clinch, seal, set the seal on, put the seal to; give the -final touch &c. *n.* to; put the -last, – finishing- hand to; crown, – all; cap.

ripen, culminate; come to a -head, – crisis; come to its end; die -a natural death, – of old age; run -its course, – one's race; touch –, reach –, attain- the goal; reach &c. (*arrive*) 292; get in the harvest.

Adj. completing, final; conclu-ding, -sive; crowning &c. *v.*; ex-haustive, complete, mature, perfect, consummate.

done, completed &c. *v.*; done for, sped, wrought out; highly wrought &c. (*preparation*) 673; thorough &c. 52; ripe &c. (*ready*) 673.

Adv. completely &c. (*thoroughly*) 52; to crown all, out of hand.

Phr. the race is run; *actum est; finis coronat opus; consummatum est; c'en est fait;* it is all over; the game is played out, the bubble has burst.

fall short of &c. 304; do things by halves; scotch the snake, not kill it; hang fire; be slow to; collapse &c. 304.

Adj. not completed &c. *v.*; incom-plete &c. 53; uncompleted, unfinished, unaccomplished, unperformed, unexe-cuted; sketchy, addle.

in progress, in hand; going on, pro-ceeding; on one's hands; on the fire; on the stocks; in preparation; lacking the finishing touch.

Adv. *re infectâ.*

---

731. Success.—N. success, -fulness; speed; advance &c. (*progress*) 282.

trump card; hit, stroke; lucky –, fortunate –, good- -hit, – stroke; bold –, master- stroke; *coup de maître*, check-mate; half the battle, prize; profit &c. (*acquisition*) 775; best seller.

continued success; good fortune &c. (*prosperity*) 734; time well spent.

advantage over; edge; upper-, whip-hand; ascendancy, mastery; expugna-tion, conquest, victory, subdual; sub-jugation &c. (*subjection*) 749.

triumph &c. (*exultation*) 884; profi-ciency &c. (*skill*) 698; conqueror, victor, winner, champion; master of the -situation; – position.

V. succeed; be -successful &c. *adj.*;

732. Failure. — N. failure; non-success, -fulfilment; dead failure, suc-cesslessness; abortion, miscarriage; *brutum fulmen* &c. 158; labour in vain &c. (*inutility*) 645; no go; inefficacy; inefficaciousness &c. *adj.*; vain –, inef-fectual –, abortive- -attempt, – efforts; flash in the pan, 'lame and impotent conclusion'; frustration; slip 'twixt cup and lip &c. (*disappointment*) 509.

blunder &c. (*mistake*) 495; fault, omission, miss, oversight, slip, trip, stumble, claudication, footfall; false –, wrong- step; *faux pas*, titubation, *bévue, faute,* lurch; botchery &c. (*want of skill*) 699; scrape, jam, mess, muddle, foozle, *fiasco*, breakdown.

mishap &c. (*misfortune*) 735; split,

gain one's -end, - ends; crown with success.

gain -, attain -, carry -, secure -, win- -a point, - an object; put over; make a go of; manage to, contrive to; accomplish &c. (*effect, complete*) 729; do -, work- wonders.

come off -well, - successfully, - with flying colours; make short work of; take -, carry- by storm; bear away the bell; win -one's spurs, - the battle; win -, carry -, gain- the -day, - prize, - palm; climb on the bandwagon; have -the best of it, - it all one's own way, - the game in one's own hands, - the ball at one's feet, - one on the hip; walk over the course; carry all before one, remain in possession of the field; score a success, win hands down.

speed; make progress &c. (*advance*) 282; win -, make -, work -, find- one's way; strive to some purpose; prosper &c. 734; drive a roaring trade; make profit &c. (*acquire*) 775; reap -, gather- the -fruits, - benefit of, - harvest; make one's fortune, get in the harvest, turn to good account; turn to account &c. (*use*) 677.

triumph, be triumphant; gain -, obtain- -a victory, - an advantage; chain victory to one's car.

surmount -, overcome -, get over- -a difficulty, - an obstacle &c. 706; *se tirer d'affaire*; make head against; stem the -torrent, - tide, - current; weather -the storm, - a point; turn a corner, keep one's head above water, tide over; master; get -, have -, gain- the -better of, - best of, - upper hand, - ascendancy, - whip hand, - start of; distance; surpass &c. (*superiority*) 33.

defeat, conquer, vanquish, discomfit; over-come, throw, -power, -master, -match, -set, -ride, -reach; out-wit, -do, -flank, -manœuvre, -general, -vote; take the wind out of one's adversary's sails; beat, - hollow; rout, lick, drub, floor, worst; put -down, - to flight, - to the rout, - *hors de combat*, - out of court.

silence, quell, nonsuit, checkmate, upset, confound, nonplus, trump; baffle &c. (*hinder*) 706; circumvent, elude; trip up, - the heels of; drive

collapse, smash, blow, explosion.

repulse, rebuff, defeat, rout, over-throw, discomfiture; beating, drubbing; *quietus*, nonsuit, subjugation; check-, fool's-mate.

fall, downfall, ruin, perdition; wreck &c. (*destruction*) 162; death-blow; bankruptcy &c. (*non-payment*) 808.

losing game, *affaire flambée*.

victim, prey; bankrupt.

V. fail; be -unsuccessful &c. *adj.*; not -succeed &c. 731; make -vain efforts &c. *n.*; do -, labour -, toil- in vain; lose one's labour, take nothing by one's motion; bring to naught, make nothing of; wash a blackamoor white &c. (*impossible*) 471; roll the stone of Sisyphus &c. (*useless*) 645; do by halves &c. (*not complete*) 730; lose ground &c. (*recede*) 283; flunk; fall short of &c. 304.

miss, - one's aim, - the mark, - one's footing, - stays; slip, trip, stumble; make a -slip &c. *n.*, - blunder &c. 495, - mess of, - botch of; bitch it, mis-carry, abort, go up like a rocket and come down like the stick, reckon with-out one's host; get the wrong sow by the ear &c. (*blunder, mismanage*) 699.

limp, halt, hobble, titubate; fall, tumble; lose one's balance; fall -to the ground, - between two stools; flounder, falter, stick in the mud, run aground, split upon a rock; run -, knock -, dash-one's head against a stone wall; break one's back; break down, sink, drown, founder, have the ground cut from under one; get into -trouble, - a mess, - a scrape; come to grief &c. (*adversity*) 735; go to -the wall, - the dogs, - pot; lick -, bite- the dust; be -defeated &c. 731; have the worst of it, lose the day, come off second best, lose; fall a prey to; succumb &c. (*submit*) 725; not have a leg to stand on.

come to nothing, end in smoke; fall -to the ground, - through, - dead, - still-born, - flat; slip through one's fingers; hang -, miss- fire; flash in the pan, collapse; topple down &c. (*descent*) 305; go to wrack and ruin &c. (*destruction*) 162.

go amiss, go wrong, go cross, go hard with, go on a wrong tack; go on -,

-into a corner, – to the wall; run hard, put one's nose out of joint.

settle, do for; break the -neck of, – back of; capsize, sink, shipwreck, drown, swamp; subdue; subjugate &c. (*subject*) 749; reduce; make the enemy bite the dust; victimize, roll in the dust, trample under foot, put an extinguisher upon.

answer, – the purpose; avail, prevail, take effect, do, turn out well, work well, take, tell, bear fruit; hit -it, – the mark, – the right nail on the head; nick it; turn up trumps, make a hit; find one's account in.

Adj. succeeding &c. *v.*; successful; prosperous &c. 734; triumphant; flushed –, crowned- with success; victorious; set up; in the ascendant; unbeaten &c. (*see* beat &c. *v.*); well-spent; felicitous, effective, in full swing.

Adv. successfully &c. *adj.*; with flying colours, in triumph, swimmingly; *à merveille*, beyond all hope; to some –, good- purpose; to one's heart's content.

Phr. *veni vidi vici*, the day being one's own, one's star in the ascendant; *omne tulit punctum*.

come off –, turn out –, work- ill; take -a wrong, – an ugly- turn; gang agley.

be all -over with, – up with; explode; dash one's hopes &c. (*disappoint*) 509; defeat the purpose; upset the apple cart; sow the wind and reap the whirlwind, jump out of the frying pan into the fire.

Adj. unsuccessful, successless; failing, tripping &c. *v.*; at fault; unfortunate &c. 735.

abortive, addle, still-born; fruitless, sterile, bootless; ineffect-ual, -ive; inefficient &c. (*impotent*) 158; inefficacious; lame, hobbling, *décousu*; insufficient &c. 640; unavailing &c. (*useless*) 645; of no effect.

aground, grounded, swamped, stranded, cast away, wrecked, foundered, capsized, shipwrecked, nonsuited; foiled; defeated &c. 731; struck –, borne –, broken- down; down-trodden; over-borne, -whelmed; all up with; beaten to a frazzle.

lost, undone, ruined, broken; bankrupt &c. (*not paying*) 808; played out; done -up, – for; dead beat, ruined root and branch, *flambé*, knocked on the head; destroyed &c. 162.

frustrated, thwarted, crossed, unhinged, disconcerted, dashed; thrown -off one's balance, – on one's back, – on one's beam ends; unhorsed, in a sorry plight; hard hit.

stultified, befooled, dished, hoist on one's own petard; victimized, sacrificed.

wide of the mark &c. (*error*) 495; out of one's reckoning &c. (*inexpectation*) 508; left in the lurch; thrown away &c. (*wasted*) 638; unattained; uncompleted &c. 730.

Adv. unsuccessfully &c. *adj.*; to little or no purpose, in vain, *re infectâ*.

Phr. the bubble has burst, the game is up, all is lost; the devil to pay; *parturiunt montes* &c. (*disappointment*) 509.

---

733. Trophy.—N. trophy; medal, prize, palm; ribbon, blue ribbon, *cordon bleu*; citation; cup; laurel, -s; bays, crown, chaplet, wreath, civic crown; Victoria Cross, V.C., *Croix de Guerre*, Iron Cross; Distinguished Service Cross, Medal of Honor, Congressional Medal; insignia &c. 550; feather in one's cap &c. (*honour*) 873; decoration &c. 877; garland, triumphal arch.

triumph &c. (*celebration*) 883; flying colours &c. (*show*) 882.
monumentum ære perennius.

---

734. Prosperity.—N. prosperity, welfare, well-being; affluence &c. (*wealth*) 803; success &c. 731; thrift, roaring

735. Adversity.—N. adversity, evil &c. 619; failure &c. 732; bad –, ill –, evil –, adverse –, hard- -fortune, – hap,

trade; chicken in every pot, the full dinner pail; good –, smiles of- fortune; blessings, godsend.

luck; good –, run of- luck; sunshine; fair -weather, – wind; palmy –, bright –, halcyon- days; piping times, tide, flood, high tide.

Saturnia regna, Saturnian age; golden ·time, – age; bed of roses; fat of the land, milk and honey, loaves and fishes, fleshpots of Egypt.

made man, lucky dog, *enfant gâté*, spoiled child of fortune.

upstart, *parvenu*, *nouveau riche*, profiteer, skipjack, mushroom.

V. prosper, thrive, flourish; be -prosperous &c. *adj.*; drive a roaring trade; go on -well, – smoothly, – swimmingly; sail before the wind, swim with the tide; run -smooth, – smoothly, – on all fours.

rise –, get on- in the world; work –, make- one's way; look up; lift –, raise- one's head, make one's -fortune, – pile, feather one's nest.

flower, blow, blossom, bloom, fructify, bear fruit, fatten, batten.

keep oneself afloat; keep –, hold- one's head above water; light –, fall- on one's -legs, – feet; drop into a good thing; bear a charmed life; bask in the sunshine; have a -good, – fine- time of it; have a run, – of luck; have the -good fortune &c. *n.* to; take a favourable turn; live -on the fat of the land, – in clover.

Adj. prosperous; thriving &c. *v.*; in a fair way, buoyant; well -off, – to do, – to do in the world; set up, at one's ease; rich &c. 803; in good case; in -full, – high- feather; fortunate, lucky, in luck; born -with a silver spoon in one's mouth, – under a lucky star; on the sunny side of the hedge.

auspicious, propitious, providential.

palmy, halcyon; agreeable &c. 829; *couleur de rose.*

Adv. prosperously &c. *adj.*; swimmingly; as good luck would have it; beyond all -expectation, – hope, – one's wildest dreams.

Phr. one's star in the ascendant, all for the best, one's course runs smooth.

– luck, – lot; frowns of fortune; evil -dispensation, – star, – genius; ups and downs of life, broken fortunes; hard -case, – lines, – life; sea –, peck- of troubles; hell upon earth; slough of despond; jinx.

trouble, humiliation, hardship, curse, blight, blast, load, pressure, plight.

pressure of the times, iron age, evil day, time out of joint; hard –, bad –, sad- times; rainy day, cloud, dark cloud, gathering clouds, ill wind; visitation, infliction; affliction &c. (*painfulness*) 830; bitter -pill, – cup; care, trial; the sport of fortune.

mis-hap, -chance, -adventure, -fortune; disaster, calamity, catastrophe; accident, casualty, cross, reverse, check, *contretemps*, rub, pinch, setback.

losing game; falling &c. *v.*; fall, down-fall, come-down; ruin-ation, -ousness; undoing; extremity; ruin &c. (*destruction*) 162.

V. be -ill off &c. *adj.*; go hard with; fall on evil, – days; go on ill; not -prosper &c. 734.

go -downhill, – to rack and ruin &c. (*destruction*) 162, – to the dogs; fall, – from one's high estate; decay, sink, decline, go down in the world; have seen better days; bring down one's grey hairs with sorrow to the grave; come to grief; be all -over, – up- with; bring a -wasp's, – hornet's- nest about one's ears.

Adj. unfortunate, unblest, unhappy, unlucky; im-, un- prosperous; luck-, hap-less; out of luck; in trouble, in a bad way, in an evil plight; under a cloud; clouded; ill –, badly- off; in adverse circumstances; poor &c. 804; behindhand, down in the world, decayed, undone; on the road to ruin, on its last legs, on the wane; in one's utmost need.

planet-struck, devoted; born -under an evil star, – with a wooden ladle in one's mouth; ill-fated, -starred, -omened; inconspicuous, ominous, doomed, unpropitious.

adverse, untoward; disastrous, calamitous, ruinous, dire, deplorable.

Adv. if the worst come to the worst, as ill luck would have it, from bad to worse, out of the frying pan into the fire.

Phr. one's star is on the wane; one's luck -turns, – fails; the game is up, one's doom is sealed, the ground crumbles under one's feet, *sic transit gloria mundi, tant va la cruche à l'eau qu'à la fin elle se casse.*

736. Mediocrity.—N. moderate –, average- circumstances; respectability; middle classes, *bourgeoisie*; mediocrity; golden mean &c. (*midcourse*) 628, (*moderation*) 174.

V. jog on; go –, get on- -fairly, – quietly, – peaceably, – tolerably, – respectably; steer a middle course &c. 628.

Adj. middling, so-so, fair, medium, moderate, mediocre, second-, third- &c. -rate.

Division (II). INTERSOCIAL VOLITION*

Section I. General Intersocial Volition

737. Authority.—N. authority; influence, patronage, power, preponderance, credit, *prestige*, prerogative, jurisdiction; right &c. (*title*) 924.

divine right, dynastic rights, authoritativeness; absolut-eness, -ism; despotism, tyranny; *jus nocendi.*

command, empire, sway, rule; domin-ion, -ation; sovereignty, supremacy, suzerainty; lord-, head-ship; chiefdom; seignior-y, -ity, hegemony, patriarchate, patriarchy; master-y, -ship, -dom; government &c. (*direction*) 693; dictation, control.

hold, grasp; grip, -e; reach; iron sway &c. (*severity*) 739; fangs, clutches, talons; rod of empire &c. (*sceptre*) 747.

reign, regnancy, *régime*, dynasty; director-, dictator-ship; protector-ate, -ship; caliphate, pashalic, electorate; presiden-cy, -tship; administration; pro-, consulship; prefecture; seneschalship; magistra-ture, -cy; raj.

empire; monarchy; king-hood, -ship; royalty, regality, autocracy, monocracy, arist-archy, -ocracy; oligarchy, democracy, demogogy; republic, -anism, federalism; socialism, collectivism; communism, bolshevism, syndicalism; mob law, mobocracy, ochlocracy, ergatocracy; *vox populi, imperium in imperio*; bureaucracy; beadle-, bumble-dom; stratocracy; martial law, military -power, – government; feodality, feudal system, feudalism.

Thearchy, dinarchy, diarchy; du-, tri-, heter-archy; du-, tri-umvirate; auto-cracy, -nomy; limited monarchy; constitutional -government, – monarchy; home rule, self-government, -determination; representative government; Soviet government.

738. [Absence of authority.] Laxity. —N. laxity; lax-, loose-, slack-ness; toleration &c. (*lenity*) 740; freedom &c. 748.

anarchy, interregnum; relaxation; loosening &c. *v.*; remission; dead letter, *brutum fulmen*, misrule; licence, licentiousness; insubordination &c. (*disobedience*) 742; lynch law &c. (*illegality*) 964; nihilism.

[Deprivation of power] dethronement, deposition, usurpation, abdication.

V. be -lax &c. *adj.*; *laisser -faire, – aller*; hold a loose rein; give -the reins to, – rope enough, – a loose to; tolerate; relax; misrule.

go beyond the length of one's tether; have one's -swing, – fling; act without -instructions, – authority; act on one's own responsibility, usurp authority.

dethrone, depose; abdicate.

Adj. lax, loose; slack; remiss &c. (*careless*) 460; weak.

relaxed; licensed; reinless, unbridled; anarchical; unauthorized &c. (*unwarranted*) 925.

---

*Implying the action of the will of one mind over the will of another.

gyn-archy, -ocracy, -æocracy; petticoat government, matri-archate, matriarchy.

[Vicarious authority] commission &c. 755; deputy &c. 759; per-mission &c. 760.

country, state, realm, commonwealth, canton, constituency, toparchy, municipality, polity, body politic, *posse comitatus.*

person in authority &c. (*master*) 745; judicature &c. 965; cabinet &c. (*council*) 696; usurper; seat of -government, – authority; headquarters.

[Acquisition of authority] accession; installation &c. 755; usur-pation.

V. authorize &c. (*permit*) 760; warrant &c. (*right*) 924; dictate &c. (*order*) 741; have –, hold –, possess –, exercise –, exert –, wield--authority &c. *n.*

be -at the head of &c. *adj.*; hold –, be in –, fill an- office; hold –, occupy- a post; be -master &c. 745.

rule, sway, command, control, administer; govern &c. (*direct*) 693; lead, preside over, reign; possess –, be seated on –, occupy-the throne; sway –, wield- the sceptre; wear the crown.

have –, get- the -upper, – whip- hand; gain a hold upon, pre-ponderate, dominate, boss, rule the roost; over-ride, -rule, -awe; lord it over, hold in hand, keep under, make a puppet of, lead by the nose, hold in the hollow of one's hand, turn round one's little finger, bend to one's will, hold one's own, wear the breeches; have -the ball at one's feet, – it all one's own way, – the game in one's own hand, – on the hip, – under one's thumb; be master of the situation; take the lead, play first fiddle, set the fashion; give the law to; carry with a high hand; lay down the law; 'ride in the whirl-wind and direct the storm'; rule with a rod of iron &c. (*severity*) 739.

ascend –, mount- the throne, take the reins, – into one's hand; assume -authority &c. *n.*, – the reins of government; take –, assume the- command.

be -governed by, – in the power of; be under -the rule of, – the domination of.

Adj. ruling &c. *v.*; regnant, at the head, dominant, paramount, supreme, predominant, preponderant, in the ascendant, influential; gubernatorial; imperious; authoritative, executive, administrative, clothed with authority, official, *ex officio*, ministerial, bureaucratic, departmental, imperative, peremptory, overruling, absolute; hege-monic, -al; arbitrary; compulsory &c. 744; stringent.

regal, sovereign; royal, -ist; monarchical, kingly; imperial, -istic; princely; feudal; aristo-, auto-cratic; oligarchic &c. *n.*; democratic, republican, dynastic.

at one's command; in one's -power, – grasp; under control; authorized &c. (*due*) 924.

Adv. in the name of, by the authority of, *de par le Roi*, in virtue of; under the auspices of, in the hands of.

at one's pleasure; by a -dash, – stroke- of the pen; *ex mero motu*; *ex cathedrâ.*

Phr. the grey mare the better horse; 'every inch a king.'

---

739. Severity.—N. severity; strict-ness, formalism, harshness &c. *adj.*; rigour, stringency, austerity; inclem-

740. Lenity. — N. leni-ty, -ence, -ency; moderation &c. 174; toler-ance, -ation; mildness, gentleness; favour;

ency &c. (*pitilessness*) 914*a*; arrogance &c. 885.

arbitrary power; absolut-, despotism; dictatorship, autocracy, tyranny, domineering, oppression; assumption, usurpation; inquisition, reign of terror, martial law; iron -heel, – rule, – hand, – sway; tight grasp; brute -force, – strength; coercion &c. 744; strong –, tight- hand.

hard -lines, – measure; tender mercies [ironical]; sharp practice; bureaucracy, red tape; pipe-clay, officialism.

tyrant, disciplinarian, martinet, stickler, formalist, bashaw, despot, hard master, Draco, oppressor, inquisitor, extortioner, harpy, vulture, bird of prey.

V. be -severe &c. *adj.*

assume, usurp, arrogate, take liberties; domineer, bully &c. 885; tyrannize, inflict, wreak, stretch a point, put on the screw; be hard upon; bear –, lay- a heavy hand on; be –, come- down upon; illtreat; deal -hardly with, – hard measure to; rule with a rod of iron, chastise with scorpions; dye with blood; oppress, override; trample –, tread- -down, – upon, – under foot; crush under an iron heel, ride roughshod over; rivet the yoke; hold –, keep- a tight hand; force down the throat; coerce &c. 744; give no quarter &c. (*pitiless*) 914*a*.

Adj. severe; strict, hard, harsh, dour, rigid, stiff, stern, rigorous, uncompromising, exacting, exigent, *exigeant*, inexorable, inflexible, obdurate, austere, relentless, Spartan, Draconian, stringent, straitlaced, puritanical, prudish, searching, unsparing, ironhanded, hardheaded, peremptory, absolute, positive, arbitrary, imperative; coercive &c. 744; tyrannical, despotic, masterful, extortionate, grinding, withering, oppressive, inquisitorial; inclement &c. (*ruthless*) 914*a*; cruel &c. (*malevolent*) 907; haughty, arrogant &c. 885.

Adv. severely &c. *adj.*; with a -high, – strong, – tight, – heavy-hand.

at the point of the -sword, – bayonet.

Phr. *Delirant reges plectuntur Achivi.*

indulgen-ce, -cy; clemency, mercy, forbearance, quarter; compassion &c. 914.

V. be -lenient &c. *adj.*; tolerate, bear with; *parcere subjectis*, give quarter.

indulge, allow one to have his own way, spoil.

Adj. lenient; mild, – as milk; gentle. soft; tolerant, indulgent, easy-going; clement &c. (*compassionate*) 914; forbearing; complaisant, long-suffering.

---

741. Command.—**N.** command, order, ordinance, act, *fiat*, bidding, *dictum*, hest, behest, call, beck, nod.

des-, dis-patch; message, direction, injunction, charge, instructions; appointment, fixture.

demand, exaction, imposition, requisition, claim, reclamation, revendication; *ultimatum* &c. (*terms*) 770; request &c. 765; requirement.

dictation; dict-, mand-ate; *caveat*, decree, decree -nisi, – absolute, *senatus consultum*; precept; pre-, re-script; writ, ordination, bull, edict, decretal, dispensation, prescription, brevet, placet, ukase, *firman*, hattisheriff, warrant, passport, *mittimus*, *mandamus*, summons; subpœna, –*duces tecum*, *nisi prius*, interpellation, citation; word, – of command; *mot d'ordre*; bugle –, trumpet- call; beat of drum, tattoo; order of the day; enactment &c. (*law*) 963; *plebiscite* &c. (*choice*) 609.

V. command, order, decree, enact, ordain, dictate, direct, give orders.

prescribe, set, appoint, mark out; set –, prescribe –, impose- a task; set to work, put in requisition &c. 926.

bid, enjoin, charge, call upon, instruct; require, – at the hands of; exact, impose, tax, task; demand; insist on &c. (*compel*) 744.

claim, lay claim to, revendicate, reclaim.

cite, summon; call –, send- for; subpœna; beckon.

issue a command; make –, issue –, promulgate- -a requisition, – a decree, – an order &c. *n.*; give the -word of command, – word, – signal; call to order; give –, lay down- the law; assume the command &c. (*authority*) 737; remand.

be -ordered &c.; receive an order &c. *n.*

Adj. commanding &c. *v.*; authoritative &c. 737; decret-ory, -ive, -al: imperative, jussive, decisive, final.

Adv. in a commanding tone; by a -stroke, – dash- of the pen; by order, at beat of drum, on the first summons; at the word of command.

Phr. the decree is gone forth; *sic volo sic jubeo*; *le Roi le veut*.

---

742. Disobedience.—N. disobedience, insubordination, contumacy; infraction, -fringement; violation, non-compliance; non-observance &c. 773.

revolt, rebellion, mutiny, outbreak, rising, uprising, putsch, insurrection, *émeute*; riot, tumult &c. (*disorder*) 59; strike &c. (*resistance*) 719; barring out; defiance &c. 715.

mutinousness &c. *adj.*; mutineering; sedition, treason; high –, petty –, misprision of- treason; *premunire*; *lèse-majesté*; violation of law &c. 964; defection, secession, revolution, *sabotage*, bolshevism, *Sinn Fein*.

insurgent, mutineer, rebel, revolter, rioter, traitor, *carbonaro*, *sansculottes*, red republican, communist, Fenian, chartist, *frondeur*; seceder, runagate, brawler, anarchist, demagogue; suffragette; Spartacus, Masaniello, Wat Tyler, Jack Cade; bolshevist, bolshevik, maximalist, ringleader.

V. disobey, violate, infringe; shirk; set at defiance &c. (*defy*) 715; set authority at naught, run riot, fly in the face of, bolt, take the law into one's own hands; kick over the traces.

turn –, run- restive; champ the bit; strike &c. (*resist*) 719; rise, – in arms; secede; mutiny, rebel.

Adj. disobedient; uncompl-ying, -iant; unsubmissive, unruly, ungovernable; insubordinate, impatient of control; rest-iff, -ive; refractory, contumacious; recusant &c. (refuse) 764; recalcitrant; resisting &c. 719; lawless, mutinous, seditious, insurgent, riotous, revolutionary.

disobeyed, unobeyed; unbidden.

743. Obedience.—N. obedience; observance &c. 772; compliance; submission &c. 725; subjection &c. 749; non-resistance; passiveness, passivity, resignation.

allegiance, loyalty, fealty, homage, deference, devotion, fidelity, constancy.

submiss-ness, -iveness; ductility &c. (*softness*) 324; obsequiousness &c. (*servility*) 886.

V. be -obedient &c. *adj.*; obey, bear obedience to; submit &c. 725; comply, answer the helm, come at one's call; do -one's bidding, – what one is told, – suit and service; attend to orders, serve -devotedly, – loyally, – faithfully.

follow, – the lead of, – to the world's end; serve &c. 746; play second fiddle.

Adj. obedient; compl-ying, -iant; law-abiding, loyal, faithful, leal, devoted; at one's -call, – command, – orders, – beck and call; under -beck and call, – control.

restrainable; resigned, passive; submissive &c. 725; henpecked; pliant &c. (*soft*) 324.

unresist-ed, -ing.

Adv. obediently &c. *adj.*; in compliance with, in obedience to.

Phr. to hear is to obey; as –, if- you please; at your service.

744. Compulsion.—N. compulsion, coercion, coaction, constraint, eminent domain, duress, enforcement, press, conscription.

force; brute –, main –, physical- force; the sword, *ultima ratio*; club –, mob –, lynch- law; *argumentum ad baculum, le droit du plus fort,* martial law.

restraint &c. 751; necessity &c. 601; *force majeure*; Hobson's choice; the spur of necessity.

V. compel, force, make, drive, coerce, constrain, enforce, necessitate, oblige.

force upon, press; cram –, thrust –, force- down the throat; say it must be done, make a point of, insist upon, take no denial; put down, dragoon.

extort, wring from; put –, turn- on the screw; drag into; bind, – over; pin –, tie- down; require, tax, put in force; commandeer; restrain &c. 751.

Adj. compelling &c. *v.*; coercive, coactive; inexorable &c. 739; compuls-ory, -atory; obligatory, stringent, peremptory, binding.

forcible, not to be trifled with; irresistible &c. 601; compelled &c. *v.*; fain to.

Adv. by -force &c. *n.,* – force of arms; on compulsion, perforce; *vi et armis,* under the lash; at the point of the -sword, – bayonet; forcibly; by a strong arm.

under protest, in spite of one's teeth; against one's will &c. 603; *nolens volens* &c. (*of necessity*) 601; by stress of -circumstances, – weather; under press of; *de rigueur.*

745. Master.—N. master, *padrone*; lord, – paramount; command-er, -ant; captain; chief, -tain; *sahib,* sirdar, sachem, sheik, head, senior, governor, *duce,* ruler, dictator; leader &c. (*director*) 694.

lord of the ascendant; cock of the -walk, – roost; grey mare; mistress.

potentate; liege, – lord; suzerain, sovereign, monarch, autocrat, despot, tyrant, oligarch, overlord.

crowned head, emperor, king, anointed king, majesty, *imperator,* protector, president, stadtholder, judge:

cæsar, kaiser, czar, sultan, grand Turk, caliph, imaum, shah, padishah, sophi, mogul, great mogul, khan, cham; lama, tycoon, mikado, inca, cazique; domn; vaivode; wai-, way-wode; landamman; seyyid, cacique.

prince, duke &c. (*nobility*) 875; archduke, doge, elector; seignior; mar-, land-grave; rajah, emir, nizam, nawab, negus.

empress, queen, sultana, czarina, princess, infanta, duchess, margravine, begum, maharani.

regent, viceroy, exarch, palatine,

746. Servant.—N. subject, liegeman; servant, retainer, follower, henchman, servitor, domestic, menial, help, lady help, *employé, attaché*; official.

retinue, suite, *cortège,* staff, court.

attendant, squire, usher, page, buttons, donzel, footboy; dog robber; train-, cup-bearer; waiter, busboy, tapster, butler, livery servant, lackey, footman, flunkey, valet, *valet de` chambre*; boots; scout, gyp; equerry, groom; jockey, hostler, ostler, tiger, orderly, messenger, cad, gillie, caddie; *wallah*; journeyman, herdsman, swineherd.

bailiff, castellan, seneschal, chamberlain, *major-domo,* groom of the chambers.

secretary; under –, assistant- secretary; clerk; clerical staff, stenographer, subsidiary; agent &c. 758; subaltern: under-ling, -strapper; man.

maid, -servant, waitress; handmaid; *confidente,* lady's maid, abigail, *soubrette*; nurse, *bonne, ayah*; nurse-, nursery-, house-, parlour-, waiting-, chamber-, kitchen-, scullery-, between –, laundry –, dairy-maid; *femme –, fille-de chambre*; *camarista*; *chef de cuisine,*

khedive, hospodar, beglerbeg, three-tailed bashaw, pasha, pashaw, bashaw, bey, beg, dey, scherif, tetrarch, satrap, mandarin, subahdar, Nabob, maharajah; burgrave; laird &c. (*proprietor*) 779; High Commissioner.

the -authorities, – powers that be, – government; staff, *état major*, aga, official, man in office, person in authority.

[Naval authorities] admiral, -ty, – of the fleet; rear-, vice-, port-admiral; senior-, naval officer, S.N.O., commodore, captain, commander, lieutenant-commander, lieutenant, sub-lieutenant, midshipman, warrant –, petty- officer, leading seaman; skipper, mate, master.

[Military authorities] marshal, field-marshal, *maréchal*; general, -issimo; commander-in-chief, *seraskier, hetman*; lieutenant-, major-general; commandant; colonel, lieutenant-colonel, major, captain, centurion, skipper, lieutenant, second-lieutenant, officer, staff-officer, aide-de-camp, brigadier, brigade-major, adjutant, *jemidar*, ensign, cornet, cadet, subaltern, warrant officer, quartermaster, noncommissioned officer, N.C.O.; sergeant, -major; top-sergeant, troop-sergeant, colour sergeant; corporal, -major; lance-, acting-corporal; drum major; shavetail.

[Air authorities] air -marshal, – commodore; group captain, squadron leader, wing commander, flight lieutenant, flying –, pilot-officer.

[Civil authorities] judge &c. 967; mayor, -alty; prefect, chancellor, archon, provost, magistrate, syndic; alcalde, alcaid; burgomaster, *corregidor*, seneschal, alderman, warden, constable, portreeve; lord mayor, sheriff; officer &c. (*executive*) 965.

cordon bleu, cook, scullion, Cinderella; maid –, servant- of all work, tweeny, general servant, girl, slavey; laundress, bed-maker, goody, char-woman &c. (*worker*) 690.

serf, vassal, slave, negro, helot; bondsman, -woman; bondslave; *âme damnée, odalisque*, ryot, *adscriptus glebæ*; vill-ain, -ein; bead-, bede-sman; sizar; pension-er, -ary; client; dependant, -ent; hanger on, stooge, satellite; parasite &c. (*servility*) 886; led captain; *protégé*, ward, hireling, mercenary, puppet, creature.

badge of slavery; bonds &c. 752.

V. serve; minister to, wait –, attend –, dance attendance –, pin oneself-upon; squire, tend, hang on the sleeve of, char, do for; fag; valet.

Adj. in the train of; in one's -pay, – employ; at one's call &c. (*obedient*) 743; in bonds.

---

747. [Insignia of authority.] **Sceptre.—N.** sceptre, regalia, rod of empire, sword of state, mace, *fasces*, wand; staff, – of office; *bâton*, truncheon; flag &c. (*insignia*) 550; ensign –, emblem –, badge –, insignia- of authority, rank marks, brassard, badge, sash; cocked –, brass- hat.

epaulette, *aiguillette*, crown, star, eagle, bar, double bar, pip, stripe, chevron, curl, ring, anchor, shoulder-strap, tab.

throne, chair, musnud, divan, dais, woolsack.

toga, pall, mantle, robes of state, ermine, purple.

crown, coronet, diadem, tiara, triple crown, mitre, crozier, cardinal's hat &c.; cap of maintenance; decoration; title &c. 877; portfolio.

key, signet, seals, talisman; helm; reins &c. (*means of restraint*) 752.

---

748. Freedom.—N. freedom, liberty, independence; licence &c. (*permission*) 760; facility &c. 705.

scope, range, latitude, play; free –, full- -play, – scope; free stage and no

749. Subjection. — N. subjection; depend-ence, -ance, -ency; subordination; thrall, thraldom, enthralment, subjugation, bondage, serfdom; feudal--ism, -ity; vassalage, villenage; slavery,

favour; swing, full swing, elbow-room, margin, rope, wide berth; Liberty Hall.

franchise, denization; free –, freed-, livery- man; denizen.

autonomy, self-government, home-rule, self-determination, liberalism, free trade; non-interference &c. 706.

immunity, exemption; emancipation &c. (*liberation*) 750; en-, af-franchise-ment; rights, privileges.

free land, freehold; allodium; frank-almoigne, mortmain.

independent, free-lance, -thinker, -trader.

V. be -free &c. *adj.*; have -scope &c. *n.*, – the run of, – one's own way, – a will of one's own, – one's fling; do what one -likes, – wishes, – pleases, – chooses; go at large, feel at home, paddle one's own canoe; stand on one's -legs, – rights; shift for oneself.

take a liberty; make -free with, – oneself quite at home; use a freedom; take -leave, – French leave.

set free &c. (*liberate*) 750; give the reins to &c. (*permit*) 760; allow –, give-scope &c. *n.* to; give a horse his head.

make free of; give the -freedom of, – franchise; en-, af-franchise.

laisser -faire, – *aller*; live and let live; leave to oneself; leave –, let- alone; mind one's own business.

Adj. free, – as air; out of harness, independent, at large, loose, scot free; left -alone, – to oneself.

in full swing; uncaught, uncon-strained, unbuttoned, unconfined, un-restrained, unchecked, unprevented, unhindered, unobstructed, unbound, uncontrolled, untrammelled.

unsubject, ungoverned, unenslaved, unenthralled, unchained, unshackled, unfettered, unreined, unbridled, un-curbed, unmuzzled, unimpeded.

unrestricted, unlimited, unconditional; absolute; discretionary &c. (*optional*) 600.

unassailed, unforced, uncompelled.

unbiassed, unprejudiced, uninfluenced, spontaneous.

free and easy; at –, at one's- ease; *dégagé*, quite at home; wanton, rampant, irrepressible, unvanquished.

exempt; freed &c. 750; freeborn; autonomous, freehold, allodial; *gratis* &c. 815.

unclaimed, going a begging.

Adv. freely &c. *adj.*; *ad libitum* &c. (*at will*) 600.

enslavement, involuntary servitude.

service; servi-tude, -torship; ten-dence, employ, tutelage, clientship; liability &c. 177; constraint &c. 751; oppression &c. (*severity*) 739; yoke &c. (*means of restraint*) 752; submission &c. 725; obedience &c. 743.

V. be -subject &c. *adj.*; be –, lie- at the mercy of; depend –, lean –, hang-upon; fall -a prey to, – under; play second fiddle.

be a -mere machine, – puppet, – foot-ball; not dare to say one's soul is his own; drag a chain.

serve &c. 746; obey &c. 743; submit &c. 725.

break in, tame; subject, subjugate; master &c. 731; tread -down, – under foot; weigh down; drag at one's chariot wheels; reduce to -subjection, – slavery; en-, in-, be-thral; enslave, lead captive; take into custody &c. (*restrain*) 751; rule &c. 737; drive into a corner, hold at the sword's point; keep under; hold in -bondage, – leading strings, – swad-dling clothes.

Adj. subject, dependent, subordi-nate; feud-al, -atory; in subjection to, under control; in -leading strings, – harness; subjected, enslaved &c. *v.*; constrained &c. 751; subservient, ser-vile, fawning, slavish, obsequious, cringing; down-trodden; over-borne, -whelmed; under the' lash, on the hip, led by the nose, henpecked; the -pup-pet, – sport, – plaything- of; under one's -orders, – command, – thumb; like dirt under one's feet; a slave to; at the mercy of; in the -power, – hands, – clutches- of; at the feet of; at one's beck and call &c. (*obedient*) 743; liable &c. 177; parasitical; stipendiary.

Adv. under.

[280]

750. Liberation.—N. liberation, disengagement, release, disenthrallment, enlargement, emancipation; af-, enfranchisement; manumission; discharge, dismissal.

deliverance &c. 672; redemption, extrication, acquittance, absolution; acquittal &c. 970; escape &c. 671.

V. liberate, free; set -free, – clear, – at liberty; render free, emancipate, release; en-, af-franchise; manumit; enlarge; dis-band, -charge, -miss, -enthral; let -go, – loose, – out, – slip; cast –, turn- adrift; deliver &c. 672; absolve &c. (*acquit*) 970; reprieve.

unfetter &c. 751; untie &c. 44; loose &c. (*disjoin*) 44; loosen, relax; un-bolt, -bar, -close, -cork, -clog, -hand, -bind, -latch, -chain, -harness; dis-engage, -entangle; clear, extricate, unloose.

gain –, obtain –, acquire- one's -liberty &c. 748; get -rid, – clear- of; deliver oneself from; shake off the yoke, slip the collar; break -loose, – prison; tear asunder one's bonds, cast off trammels; escape &c. 671.

Adj. at -liberty, – large, free, liberated &c. *v.*; out of harness &c. 748; adrift.

Int. unhand me! let me go!

---

751. Restraint.—N. restraint; hindrance &c. 706; coercion &c. (*compulsion*) 744; cohibition, constraint, repression; discipline, control, self-restraint &c. 604.

confinement; durance, duress; im-, prisonment; incarceration, coarctation, entombment, mancipation, durance vile, thrall, limbo, captivity; blockade; quarantine; detention.

arrest, -ation; custody, keep, care, charge, ward, restringency.

curb &c. (*means of restraint*) 752; *lettre de cachet*.

limitation, restriction, protection, monopoly; prohibition &c. 761; economic pressure.

prisoner &c. 754.

V. restrain, check; put -, lay- under restraint; en-, in-, be-thral; restrict; debar &c. (*hinder*) 706; constrain; coerce &c. (*compel*) 744; curb, control; hold –, keep- -back, – from, – in, – in check, – within bounds; hold in -leash, – leading strings; withhold.

keep under; repress, suppress; smother; pull in, rein in; hold, – fast; keep a tight hand on; prohibit &c. 761; in-, co-hibit.

enchain; fasten &c. (*join*) 43; fetter, shackle; en-, trammel; bridle, muzzle, gag, pinion, manacle, handcuff, tie one's hands, hobble, bind hand and foot; swathe, swaddle; pin –, peg- down; tether, picket; tie, – up, – down; secure; forge fetters; belay.

confine; shut –, clap –, lock –, box –, mew –, bottle –, cork –, seal –, button- up; shut –, hem –, bolt –, wall –, rail- in; impound, pen, coop; enclose &c. (*circumscribe*) 229; cage; in-, en-cage; close the door upon, cloister; imprison, immure; incarcerate, entomb; clap –, lay- under hatches; put in -irons, – a strait waistcoat; throw –, cast- into prison; put into bilboes.

arrest; take -up, – charge of, – into custody; take –, make- -prisoner, – captive; captivate; lead -captive, – into captivity; send –, commit- to prison; commit; give in -charge, – custody; subjugate &c. 749.

Adj. re-, con-strained; imprisoned &c. *v.*; pent up; jammed in, wedged in; under -restraint, – lock and key, – hatches; serving –, doing- time; in swaddling clothes; on *parole*; in custody &c. (*prisoner*) 754; cohibitive; coactive &c. (*compulsory*) 744.

stiff, restringent, straitlaced, hide-bound.

ice-, wind-, weather-bound; 'cabined, cribbed, confined'; in Lob's pound, laid by the heels.

Adv. in captivity, under arrest, behind the bars, in -prison, – jail, – durance vile.

752. [Means of restraint.] **Prison.**—**N.** prison, -house; jail, gaol, cage, coop, den, death house, condemned –, cell; stronghold, fortress, keep, donjon, dungeon, *Bastille, oubliette,* bridewell, house of correction, hulks, toll-booth, panopticon, penitentiary, guard-room, clink, can, stir, tronk, jug, lock-up, hold; round –, watch –, station –, sponging-house; station; house of detention, black hole, pen, fold, pound; enclosure &c. 232; penal settlement; chain gang; debtors' prison; reformatory; federal penitentiary, state prison; criminal lunatic asylum; bilboes, stocks, limbo, quod.

Dartmoor, Newgate, Fleet, Marshalsea; King's (*or* Queen's) Bench; Sing Sing, Dannemora.

bond; strap, bandage, splint, tourniquet; irons, pinion, gyve, fetter, shackle, trammel, manacle, handcuff, bracelets, darbies, strait waistcoat, strait-jacket.

yoke, collar, halter, harness; muzzle, gag, bit, brake, curb, snaffle, bridle; rein, -s; ribbons, lines, bearing-rein; martingale, leading string; tether, picket, band, guy, chain; cord &c. (*fastening*) 45.

bolt, bar, lock, padlock, rail, wall; paling, palisade; fence; barrier, barricade.

brake, drag &c. (*hindrance*) 706.

---

753. Keeper.—**N.** keeper, custodian, *custos,* ranger, warder, jailer, gaoler, turnkey, castellan, guard; watch, -dog, -man; Charley; sen-try, -tinel; watch and ward; *concierge,* coast-guard, *guarda costa,* gamekeeper.

escort, body guard, convoy.

protector, governor, duenna; guardian; governess &c. (*teacher*) 540; nurse, *bonne, ayah, amah.*

---

754. Prisoner.—**N.** prisoner, captive, *détenu,* close prisoner.

jail-bird, ticket-of-leave man.

V. stand committed; be -imprisoned &c. 751.

Adj. imprisoned &c. 751; in -prison, – quod, – durance vile, – limbo, – custody, – charge, – chains; under -lock and key, – hatches; on *parole;* detained at his Majesty's pleasure.

---

755. [Vicarious authority.] **Commission.**—**N.** commission, delegation; con-, as-signment; procuration; deputation, legation, mission, embassy; agency, agentship; power of attorney, proxy; clerkship.

errand, charge, *brevet,* diploma, *exequatur,* permit &c. (*permission*) 760.

appointment, nomination, return; charter; ordination; installation, inauguration, investiture; accession, coronation, enthronement.

vicegerency; regency, regentship.

viceroy &c. 745; consignee &c. 758; deputy &c. 759.

V. commission, delegate, depute; consign, assign; charge; in-, en-trust; turn over to; commit, – to the hands of; authorize &c. (*permit*) 760.

put in commission, accredit, engage, hire, bespeak, appoint, name, nominate, return, ordain; install, induct,

---

756. Abrogation.—**N.** abrogation, annulment, nullification; cancelling &c. *v.*; cancel; revo-cation, -kement; repeal, rescission, defeasance.

dismissal, *congé,* demission; depos-al, -ition; sack, dethronement; disestablish-, disendow-ment; deconsecration.

aboli-tion, -shment; dissolution.

counter-order, -mand; repudiation, retractation; recantation &c. (*tergiversation*) 607.

V. abrogate, annul, cancel; destroy &c. 162; abolish; revoke, repeal, rescind, reverse, retract, recall; over-rule, -ride; set aside; disannul, dissolve, quash, nullify, declare null and void; dis-establish, -endow; deconsecrate.

disclaim &c. (*deny*) 536; ignore, repudiate; recant &c. 607; divest oneself, break off.

counter-mand, -order; do away with; sweep –, brush- away; throw -over-

inaugurate, invest, crown; en-roll, -list.

employ, empower; give power of attorney to; set -, place- over; send out.

be commissioned, be accredited; represent, stand for; stand in the -stead, - place, - shoes- of.

Adj. commissioned &c. *v.*

Adv. *per procuratione.*

————

board, - to the dogs; scatter to the winds, cast behind.

dismiss, discard; cast -, turn- -off, - out, - adrift, - out of doors, - aside, - away; send -off, - away, - about one's business; discharge, get rid of, fire out, fire &c. (*eject*) 297; jilt.

cashier; break; oust; set down, unseat, -saddle; un-, de-, disen-throne; depose, uncrown; unfrock, strike off the roll; dis-bar, -bench.

be -abrogated &c.; receive its quietus.

Adj. abrogated &c. *v.; functus officio.*

Int. get along with you! begone! go about your business! away with!

757. Resignation.—N. resignation, retirement, abdication, renunciation, abjuration, disclaimer, abandonment, relinquishment.

V. resign; give -, throw- up; lay down, throw up the cards, wash one's hands of, abjure, renounce, forego, disclaim, abandon, relinquish, retract, demit; deny &c. 536.

abrogate &c. 756; desert &c. (*relinquish*) 624; get rid of &c. 782.

abdicate; vacate, - one's seat; apply for -, accept- the stewardship of the Chiltern Hundreds; retire; tender -, send in -, hand in- one's resignation.

Adj. abdicant, renunciatory &c. *v.* **Phr.** 'Othello's occupation's gone.'

758. Consignee.—N. consignee, trustee, nominee, committee.

delegate; commiss-ary, -ioner; emissary, envoy, commissionaire; messenger &c. 534.

diplomatist, diplomat, *corps diplomatique*, embassy; am-, em-bassador; representative, resident, consul, legate, nuncio, internuncio, *chargé d'affaires, attaché.*

vicegerent &c. (*deputy*) 759; plenipotentiary.

functionary, placeman, curator; treasurer &c. 801; agent, factor, bailiff, steward, clerk, secretary, attorney, solicitor, proctor, broker, underwriter, commission agent, auctioneer, one's man of business; factotum &c. (*director*) 694; caretaker.

negotiator, go between; middleman; under agent, *employé*; servant &c. 746.

salesman; commercial, - traveller; bagman, *commis-voyageur*, touter.

newspaper -, own -, war -, special- correspondent; reporter.

759. Deputy.—N. deputy, substitute, vice, proxy, *locum tenens*, delegate, representative, next friend, surrogate, secondary.

regent, vicegerent, vizier, minister, vicar; premier &c. (*director*) 694; chancellor, prefect, provost, warden, lieutenant, archon, consul, proconsul; viceroy &c. (*governor*) 745; commissioner &c. 758; plenipotentiary, *alter ego.*

team, eight, eleven; champion.

V. be -deputy &c. *n.*; stand -, appear -, hold a brief -, answer- for; represent; stand -, walk- in the shoes of; stand in the stead of.

substitute, ablegate, accredit; commission, empower, delegate &c. 755.

Adj. acting; vice, -regal; accredited to.

Adv. in behalf of, by proxy.

Section II. Special Intersocial Volition

760. Permission.—N. permission, leave; allow-, suffer-ance; toler-ance, -ation; liberty, law, licence, concession, grace; indulgence &c. (*lenity*) 740; favour, dispensation, exemption, release; connivance; vouchsafement.

authorization, warranty, accordance, admission.

permit, warrant, *brevet*, precept, sanction, authority, *firman*; pass, -port; furlough, licence, *carte blanche*, ticket of leave; grant, charter, patent.

V. permit; give -permission &c. *n.*, – power; let, allow, admit; suffer, bear with, tolerate, recognize; concede &c. 762; accord, vouchsafe, favour, humour, gratify, indulge, stretch a point; wink at, connive at; shut one's eyes to.

grant, empower, charter, enfranchise, privilege, confer a privilege, license, authorize, warrant; sanction; entrust &c. (*commission*) 755.

give -*carte blanche*, – the reins to, – scope to &c. (*freedom*) 748; leave -alone, – it to one, – the door open; open the -door to, – floodgates; give a loose to.

let off; absolve &c. (*acquit*) 970; release, exonerate, dispense with.

ask –, beg –, request- -leave, – permission.

761. Prohibition.—N. pro-, in-hibition; *veto*, disallowance; interdict, -ion; injunction; embargo, ban, *verboten*, taboo, proscription; *index expurgatorius*; restriction &c. (*restraint*) 751; hindrance &c. 706; forbidden fruit.

V. pro-, in-hibit; forbid, put one's *veto* upon, disallow; bar; debar &c. (*hinder*) 706, forefend.

keep -in, – within bounds; restrain &c. 751; cohibit, withhold, limit, circumscribe, clip the wings of, restrict, narrow; interdict, taboo; put –, place-under -an interdiction, – the ban; proscribe, censor; exclude, shut out; shut –, bolt –, show- the door; warn off; dash the cup from one's lips; forbid the banns.

Adj. prohibit-ive, -ory; interdictive; proscriptive; restrictive, exclusive; forbidding &c. *v.*

prohibited &c. *v.*; not -permitted &c. 760; unlicensed, contraband, under the ban of; illegal &c. 964; unauthorized, not to be thought of.

Adv. on no account &c. (*no*) 536.

Int. forbid it heaven! &c. (*deprecation*) 766.

hands –, keep- off! hold! stop! avast!

Phr. that will never do.

Adj. permitting &c. *v.*; permissive, indulgent; permitted &c. *v.*; patent, chartered, permissible, allowable, lawful, legitimate, legal; legalized &c. (*law*) 963; licit; unforbid, -den; unconditional.

Adv. permissibly; by –, with –, on- -leave &c. *n.*; *speciali gratiâ*; under favour of; *pace*; *ad libitum* &c. (*freely*) 748, (*at will*) 600; by all means &c. (*willingly*) 602; yes &c. (*assent*) 488.

---

762. Consent.—N. consent; assent &c. 488; acquiescence; approval &c. 931; compliance, agreement, concession; yield-ance, -ingness; accession, acknowledgment, acceptance, agnition.

settlement, ratification, confirmation, adjustment.

permit &c. (*permission*) 760; promise &c. 768.

V. consent; assent &c. 488; yield assent, admit, allow, concede, grant, yield; come -over, – round; give in to, acknowledge, agnize, give consent, comply with, acquiesce, agree to, fall in with, accede, accept, embrace an offer, close with, take at one's word, have no objection.

satisfy, meet one's wishes, settle, come to terms &c. 488; not -refuse &c. 764; turn a willing ear &c. (*willingness*) 602; jump at; deign, vouchsafe; promise &c. 768.

Adj. consenting &c. *v.*; agreeable, compliant; agreed &c. (*assent*) 488; unconditional.

Adv. yes &c. (*assent*) 488; by all means &c. (*willingly*) 602; if –, as-you please; be it so, so be it, well and good, of course.

763. Offer.—**N.** offer, proffer, presentation, tender, bid, overture; propos-al, -ition; motion, invitation; candidature; offering &c. (*gift*) 784.

V. offer, proffer, present, tender; bid; propose, move; make -a motion, – advances; start; invite, hold out, place- at one's disposal, – in one's way, put forward.

hawk about; offer for sale &c. 796; press &c. (*request*) 765; lay at one's feet.

offer –, present- oneself; volunteer, come forward, be a candidate; stand –, bid- for; seek; be at one's service; go a begging; bribe &c. (*give*) 784.

Adj. offer-ing, -ed &c. *v.*; in the market, for sale, to let, disengaged, on hire.

764. Refusal.—**N.** refusal, rejection; non-, in-compliance; denial; declining &c. *v.*; declension; peremptory –, flat –, point blank- refusal; repulse, rebuff; discountenance.

recusancy, renunciation, abnegation, negation, protest, disclaimer; dissent &c. 489; revocation &c. 756.

V. refuse, reject, deny, decline; nill, negative; refuse –, withhold- one's assent; shake the head; close the -hand, – purse; grudge, begrudge, be slow to, hang fire.

be deaf to; turn -a deaf ear to, – one's back upon; set one's face against, discountenance, not hear of, have nothing to do with, wash one's hands of, stand aloof, forswear, set aside, cast behind one; not yield an inch &c. (*obstinacy*) 606.

resist, cross; not -grant &c. 762; repel, repulse; shut –, slam- the door in one's face; rebuff; send -back, – to the right about, – away with a flea in the ear; deny oneself, not be at home to; discard &c. (*repudiate*) 610; rescind &c. (*revoke*) 756; disclaim, protest; dissent &c. 489.

Adj. refusing &c. *v.*; rest-ive, -iff; recusant; uncomplying, non-compliant, unconsenting, uncomplaisant, protestant; not willing to hear of, deaf to.

refused &c. *v.*; ungranted, out of the question, not to be thought of, impossible.

Adv. no &c. 536; on no account, not for the world; no thank you.

Phr. *non possumus*; [ironically] your humble servant; *bien obligé*.

765. Request.—**N.** requ-est, -isition; claim &c. (*demand*) 741; petition, suit, prayer; begging letter, round-robin.

motion, overture, application, canvass, address, appeal, apostrophe; imprecation; rogation; proposal, proposition.

orison &c. (*worship*) 990; incantation &c. (*spell*) 993.

mendicancy; asking, panhandling, begging &c. *v.*; postulation, solicitation, invitation, entreaty, importunity, supplication, instance, impetration, imploration, obsecration, obtestation, invocation, interpellation.

V. request, ask; beg, crave, sue, pray, petition, solicit, invite, pop the question, make bold to ask; beg -leave, – a boon; apply to, call to, put to; call -upon, – for; make –, address –, prefer –, put up- a -request, – prayer, – petition;

766. [Negative request.] **Deprecation.**—**N.** deprecation, expostulation; remonstrance; intercession, mediation.

V. deprecate, protest, expostulate, enter a protest, intercede for.

Adj. deprecatory, expostulatory, intercessory, mediatorial.

deprecated, protested.

un-, unbe-sought; unasked &c. (*see* ask &c. 765).

Int. cry you mercy! God forbid! forbid it Heaven! Heaven -forefend, – forbid! far be it from! hands off! &c. (*prohibition*) 761.

make -application, – a requisition; ask –, trouble- one for; claim &c. (*demand*) 741; offer up prayers &c. (*worship*) 990; whistle for.

beg hard, entreat, beseech, plead, supplicate, implore, apostrophize; conjure, adjure; obtest; cry to, kneel to, appeal to; invoke, evoke; impetrate, imprecate, ply, press, urge, beset, importune, dun, tax, clamour for; cry -aloud, – for help; fall on one's knees; throw oneself at the feet of; come down on one's marrow-bones.

beg from door to door, send the hat round, go a begging; mendicate, mump, cadge, panhandle, beg one's bread.

dance attendance on, besiege, knock at the door.

bespeak, canvass, tout, make interest, court; seek, bid for &c. (*offer*) 763; publish the banns.

Adj. requesting &c. *v.*; precatory; suppli-ant, -cant, -catory; invoc-, imprec-, rog-atory; postulant, mendicant.

importunate, clamorous, urgent; solicitous; cap in hand; on one's -knees, – bended knees, – marrow-bones.

Adv. prithee, do, please, pray; be so good as, be good enough; have the goodness, vouchsafe, will you, I pray thee, if you please.

Int. for -God's, – heaven's, – goodness', – mercy's- sake.

767. Petitioner.—N. petitioner, solicitor, applicant; suppli-ant, -cant; suitor, candidate, claimant, postulant, aspirant, competitor, bidder; place –, pot –, mug- hunter; prizer.

beggar, mendicant, mumper, sturdy beggar, cadger, panhandler.

canvasser, barker, touter &c. 758.

sycophant, parasite &c. 886.

Section III. Conditional Intersocial Volition

768. Promise.—N. promise, undertaking, word, troth, plight, pledge, *parole*, word of honour, vow; oath &c. (*affirmation*) 535; profession, assurance, warranty, guarantee, insurance, obligation; contract &c. 769.

768a. Release from engagement.— **N.** release &c. (*liberation*) 750.

Adj. absolute; unconditional &c. (*free*) 748.

engagement, pre-engagement: affiance; betroth, -al, -ment; marriage -compact, – vow.

V. promise; give a -promise &c. *n.*; undertake, engage; make –, form- an engagement; enter -into, – on- an engagement; bind –, tie –, pledge –, commit –, take upon- oneself; vow; swear &c. (*affirm*) 535, give –, pass –, pledge –, plight- one's -word, – honour, – credit, – troth; betroth, plight faith; take the vows.

assure, warrant, guarantee, vouch for, avouch, covenant &c. 769; attest &c. (*bear witness*) 467.

hold out an expectation; contract an obligation; become -bound to, – sponsor for; answer –, be answerable- for; secure; give security &c. 771; underwrite.

adjure, administer an oath, put to one's oath, swear a witness.

Adj. promising &c. *v.*; promissory; votive; under hand and seal; upon -oath, – affirmation.

promised &c. *v.*; affianced, pledged, bound; committed, compromised; in for it.

Adv. as one's head shall answer for; upon my honour.

Phr. in for a penny, in for a pound.

769. Compact.—N. compact, contract, agreement, bargain, deal, transaction; affidation; pact, -ion; bond, covenant, indenture.

stipulation, settlement, convention; compromise, *cartel.*

protocol, treaty, *concordat, Zollverein, Sonderbund,* charter, *Magna Charta,* Pragmatic Sanction.

negotiation &c. (*bargaining*) 794; diplomacy &c. (*mediation*) 724; negotiator &c. (*agent*) 758.

ratification, completion, signature, seal, sigil, signet.

V. contract, covenant, agree for, engage &c. (*promise*) 768.

treat, negotiate, stipulate, make terms; bargain &c. (*barter*) 794.

make –, strike- a bargain; come to -terms, – an understanding; compromise &c. 774; set at rest; close, – with; conclude, complete, settle; confirm, ratify, clench, subscribe, underwrite; en-, in-dorse; put the seal to; sign, seal &c. (*attest*) 467; indent.

take one at one's word, bargain by inch of candle.

Adj. contractual, agreed &c. *v.*; conventional; under hand and seal; signed, sealed and delivered.

Phr. *caveat emptor.*

770. Conditions.—N. conditions, terms; articles, – of agreement.

clauses, provisions; proviso &c. (*qualification*) 469; covenant, stipulation, obligation, *ultimatum, sine quâ non; casus fœderis.*

V. make –, come to- -terms &c. (*contract*) 769; make it a condition, stipulate, insist upon, make a point of; bind, tie up.

Adj. conditional, provisional, guarded, fenced, hedged in.

Adv. conditionally &c. (*with qualification*) 469; provisionally, *pro re natâ*; on condition; with a reservation.

771. Security.—N. security; guaran-ty, -tee; gage, warranty, bond, tie, pledge, plight, mortgage, debenture, hypothecation, bill of sale, lien, pignus, pawn, pignoration; real security; bottomry; collateral, vadium.

stake, deposit, earnest, handsel, caution.

promissory note; bill, – of exchange; I.O.U.; personal security, covenant, specialty; *parole* &c. (*promise*) 768.

acceptance, indorsement, signature, execution, stamp, seal.

spon-sor, -sion, -sorship; surety, bail; mainpernor, hostage.

recognizance; deed –, covenant- of indemnity.

authentication, verification, warrant, certificate, voucher, docket, doquet; record &c. 551; probate, attested copy.

receipt; ac-, quittance; discharge, release.

muniment, title-deed, instrument; deed, – poll; assurance, insurance, indenture; charter &c. (*compact*) 769; charter-poll; paper, parchment, settlement, will, testament, last will and testament, codicil.

V. give -security, – bail, – substantial bail; go bail; pawn, impawn, hock, spout, mortgage, hypothecate, impignorate.

guarantee, warrant, assure; accept, indorse, underwrite, insure.

execute, stamp; sign, seal &c. (*evidence*) 467.

let, sett; grant –, take –, hold- a lease; hold in pledge; lend on security &c. 787.

Adj. secure, -ed; pledged &c. *v.*; in pawn, on deposit.

772. Observance.—N. observance, performance, compliance; obedience

773. Non-observance. — N. non-observance &c. 772; evasion, inob-

&c. 743; fulfilment, satisfaction, discharge; acquit-tance, -tal.

adhesion, acknowledgment; fidelity &c. (*probity*) 939; exact &c. 494- observance.

V. observe, comply with, respect, acknowledge, abide by; cling to, adhere to, to be faithful to, act up to; meet, fulfil; carry -out, – into execution; execute, perform, keep, satisfy, discharge; do one's office.

perform –, fulfill –, discharge –, acquit oneself of- an obligation; make good; make good –, keep- one's -word, – promise; redeem one's pledge; keep faith with, stand to one's engagement.

Adj. observant, faithful, true, loyal; honourable &c. 939; true as the -dial to the sun, – needle to the pole; punct-ual, -ilious; meticulous; literal &c. (*exact*) 494; as good as one's word.

Adv. faithfully &c. *adj.*

servance, failure, omission, neglect, laches, laxity, informality.

infringement, infraction; violation, transgression.

retractation, repudiation, nullification; protest; forfeiture.

lawlessness; disobedience &c. 742; bad faith &c. 940.

V. fail, neglect, omit, elude, evade, give the go by to, cut, set aside, ignore; shut –, close- one's eyes to, avoid.

infringe, transgress, pirate, violate, break, trample under foot, do violence to, drive a coach and six through.

discard, protest, repudiate, fling to the winds, set at naught, nullify, declare null and void; cancel &c. (*wipe off*) 552.

retract, go back from, be off, forfeit, go from one's word, palter; stretch –, strain- a point.

Adj. violating &c. *v.*; lawless, transgressive; elusive, evasive; lax, casual; non-observant.

unfulfilled &c. (*see* fulfil &c. 772).

774. Compromise.—N. com-promise, -mutation, -position; middle term, *mezzo termine*; compensation &c. 30; adjustment, mutual concession.

V. com-promise, -mute, -pound; take the mean; split the difference, meet one half way; give and take; come to terms &c. (*contract*) 769; submit to –, abide by- arbitration; patch up, bridge over, fix up, arrange; adjust, – differences; agree; make -the best of, – a virtue of necessity; take the will for the deed.

Section IV. POSSESSIVE RELATIONS*

1°. *Property in general*

775. Acquisition.—N. acquisition; gaining &c. *v.*; obtainment; procuration, -ement; purchase, descent, inheritance; gift &c. 784.

recovery, retrieval, revendication, replevin; redemption, salvage, trover; find, *trouvaille*, foundling.

gain, thrift; money-making, -grubbing; lucre, filthy lucre, loaves and fishes, the main chance, pelf; emolument &c. 973; wealth &c. 803.

profit, earnings, winnings, innings, clean-up, pickings, perquisite, net profit; income &c. (*receipt*) 810; proceeds, -duce, -duct; out-come, -put;

776. Loss.—N. loss; de-, perdition; forfeiture, lapse.

privation, bereavement; deprivation &c. (*dispossession*) 789; riddance.

V. lose; incur –, experience –, meet with- a loss; miss; mislay, let slip, allow to slip through the fingers, squander; be without &c. (*exempt*) 777a; forfeit.

get rid of &c. 782; waste &c. 638.

be lost, lapse.

Adj. losing &c. *v.*; not having &c. 777a.

shorn of, deprived of; denuded, bereaved, bereft, *minus*, cut off; dispos-

* That is, relations which concern property.

return, fruit, crop, harvest, tilth; second crop, aftermath; benefit &c. (*good*) 618.

sweepstakes, trick, prize, pool.

[Fraudulent acquisition] subreption· theft, stealing &c. 791.

V. acquire, get, gain, win, earn, obtain, procure, gather, annex; collect &c. 72; pick, – up; glean, take &c. 789.

find; come –, pitch –, light- upon; scrape -up, – together; get in, reap and carry, net, bag, sack, bring home, secure, come across, derive, draw, get in the harvest.

profit; make –, draw- profit; turn to -profit, – account; make -capital out of, – money by; obtain a return, reap the fruits of; reap –, gain- an advantage; turn -a penny, – an honest penny; make the pot boil, bring grist to the mill; make –, coin –, raise- money; raise -funds, – the wind; fill one's pocket &c. (*wealth*) 803.

treasure up &c. (*store*) 636; realize, clear; produce &c. 161; take &c. 789.

get back, recover, regain, retrieve, revendicate, replevy, redeem, come by one's own.

come -by, – in for; receive &c. 785; inherit; step into, – a fortune, – the shoes of; succeed to.

get -hold of, – between one's finger and thumb, – into one's hand, – at; take –, come into –, enter into- possession.

be -profitable &c. *adj.*; pay, answer.

accrue &c. (*be received*) 785.

Adj. acquir-ing, -ed &c. *v.*; acquisitive; productive, profitable, advantageous, gainful, remunerative, paying, lucrative.

sessed &c. 789; rid of, quit of; out of pocket.

lost &c. *v.*; long lost; irretrievable &c. (*hopeless*) 859; irredentist; off one's hands.

Int. farewell to! adieu to! good riddance!

---

777. Possession.—N. possession, seisin; ownership &c. 780; occupancy; hold, -ing; tenure, tenancy, feodality, dependency; villenage; socage, chivalry, knight service.

exclusive possession, impropriation, monopoly, corner; retention &c. 781; pre-possession, -occupancy; nine points of the law.

future possession, heritage, inheritance, heirship, reversion, fee, seigniority, feud, fief.

bird in hand, *uti possidetis*, *chose* in possession.

V. possess, have, hold, occupy, enjoy; be -possessed of &c. *adj.*; have -in hand &c. *adj.*; own &c. 780; command.

inherit; come -to, – in for.

engross, monopolize, forestall, regrate, impropriate, have all to oneself, corner; have a firm hold of &c. (*retain*) 781; get into one's hand &c. (*acquire*) 775.

belong to, appertain to, pertain to; be -in one's possession &c. *adj.*; vest in.

Adj. possessing &c. *v.*; worth; possessed of, seized of, master of, in possession of; endowed –, blest –, instinct –, fraught –, laden –, charged –, instilled –, with.

possessed &c. *v.*; on hand, by one; in hand, in store, in stock; in one's -hands, – grasp, – possession; at one's -command, – disposal; one's own &c. (*property*) 780.

unsold; unshared.

777a. Exemption.—N. exemption; exception, immunity, privilege, release &c. 927a; absence &c. 187.

V. not -have &c. 777; be -without &c. *adj.*

Adj. exempt from, devoid of, without, unpossessed of, unblest with, immune from.

not -having &c. 777; unpossessed; untenanted &c. (*vacant*) 187; without an owner.

unobtained, unacquired.

778. [Joint possession.] **Participation.—N.** participation; co-, joint-tenancy; possession -, tenancy- in common; joint -, common- stock; co-, partnership; communion; community of -possessions, - goods; communalism, communism, socialism, collectivism; co-operation &c. 709; profit sharing.

snacks, co-portion, picnic, hotchpotch; co-heirship, -parceny, -parcenary; gavelkind.

participator, sharer; co-, partner; shareholder; co-, joint-tenant; tenants in common; co-heir, -parcener.

communist, socialist.

V. par-ticipate, -take; share, - in; come in for a share; go -shares, - snacks, - halves; share and share alike.

have -, possess -, be seized- -in common, - as joint tenants &c. *n.* join in; have a hand in &c. (*co-operate*) 709.

Adj. partaking &c. *v.*; communistic, socialistic, co-operative, profit sharing.

Adv. share and share alike.

779. Possessor.—N. possessor, holder; occup-ant, -ier; tenant; person -, man- -in possession &c. 777; renter, lodger, lessee, under-lessee; zemindar, ryot; tenant -on sufferance, - at will, - from year to year, - for years, - for life.

owner; propriet-or, -ress, -ary; impropriator, master, mistress, lord.

land-holder, -owner, -lord, -lady; lord -of the manor, - paramount; heritor, laird, vavasour, landed gentry, mesne lord.

cestui-que-trust, beneficiary, mortgagor.

grantee, feoffee, relessee, devisee; legat-ee, -ary.

trustee; holder &c.- of the legal estate; mortgagee.

right -, rightful- owner.

[Future possessor] heir, - apparent; - presumptive; heiress; inherit-or, -ress, -rix; reversioner, remainder-man.

780. Property.—N. property, possession, *suum cuique, meum et tuum.*

owner-, proprietor-, lord-ship; seignority; empire &c. (*dominion*) 737.

interest, stake, estate, right, title, claim, demand, holding; tenure &c. (*possession*) 777; vested -, contingent -, beneficial -, equitable-interest; use, trust, benefit; legal -, equitable- estate; seisin.

absolute interest, paramount estate, freehold; fee, - simple, - tail; estate -in fee, - in tail, - tail; estate in tail -male, - female, - general.

limitation, term, lease, settlement, strict settlement, particular estate; estate -for life, - for years, - *pur autre vie*; remainder, reversion, expectancy, possibility.

dower, dowry, *dot,* jointure, marriage portion, appanage, inheritance, heritage, patrimony, alimony; legacy &c. (*gift*) 784.

assets, belongings, means, resources, circumstances; wealth &c. 803; money &c. 800; what one -is worth, - will cut up for; estate and effects.

landed -, real- -estate, - property; realty; land, -s; subdivision; plot, site; tenements; hereditaments; corporeal -, incorporeal- hereditaments; acres; ground &c. (*earth*) 342; acquest; messuage.

territory, state, kingdom, principality, realm, empire, protectorate, margravate, dependancy, colony, sphere of influence, mandate.

manor, honour, domain, demesne; farm, ranch, plantation, *hacienda*; allodium &c. (*free*) 748; fief, feoff, feud, zemindary, dependency.

free-, copy-, lease-holds; chattels real; fixtures, plant, heirloom easement; folkland; right of -common, - user.

personal -property, - estate, - effects; personalty, chattels, goods, effects, movables; stock, - in trade; things, traps, rattle-traps, paraphernalia; equipage &c. 633.

parcels, appurtenances.

impedimenta; lug-, bag-gage; bag and baggage; pelf; cargo, lading. rent-roll; income &c. (*receipts*) 810.

patent, copyright; *chose* in action; credit &c. 805; debt &c. 806.

V. possess &c. 777; be the -possessor &c. 779- of· own; have for one's own, - very own; come in for, inherit; enfeoff.

savour of the realty.

be one's -property &c. *n.*; belong to; ap-, pertain to.

Adj. one's own; landed, predial, manorial, allodial, seigniorial; free-, copy-, lease-hold; feu-, feo-dal; hereditary, entailed, personal.

Adv. to one's -credit, - account; to the good.

to one and -his heirs for ever, - the heirs of his body, - his heirs and assigns, - his executors, administrators and assigns.

---

781. Retention.—N. retention; retaining &c. *v.*; keep, detention, custody; tenacity, firm hold, grasp, gripe, grip, iron grip.

fangs, teeth, claws, talons, nail, hook, tentacle, *tenaculum*; bond &c. (*vinculum*) 45.

clutches, tongs, forceps, pincers, nippers, pliers, tweezers, vice.

paw, hand, finger, wrist, fist, neaf, neif.

bird in hand; captive &c. 754.

V. retain, keep; hold, - fast, - tight, - one's own, - one's ground; clinch, clench, clutch, grasp, gripe, hug, have a firm hold of.

secure, withold, detain; hold -, keep-back; keep close; husband &c. (*store*) 636; reserve; have -, keep- in stock &c. (*possess*) 777; entail, tie up, settle.

Adj. retaining &c. *v.*; retentive, tenacious.

unforfeited, undeprived, undisposed, uncommunicated.

incommunicable, inalienable; in mortmain; in strict settlement.

Phr. *uti possidetis.*

---

782. Relinquishment. — N. relinquishment, abandonment &c. (*of a course*) 624; renunciation, expropriation, dereliction; cession, surrender, dispensation; resignation &c. 757; riddance.

derelict &c. *adj.*; jetsam; waif, foundling, orphan.

V. relinquish, give up, surrender, yield, cede; let -go, - slip; spare, drop, resign, forego, renounce, abjure, abandon, expropriate, give away, dispose of, part with; lay -aside, - apart, - down, - on the shelf &c. (*disuse*) 678; set -, put- aside; make away with, cast behind; discard, cast off, dismiss; maroon;

give -notice to quit, - warning; supersede; be -, get- -rid of, - quit of; eject &c. 297.

rid -, disburden -, divest -, dispossess- oneself of; wash one's hands of; divorce, desert; disinherit, cut off.

cast -, throw -, pitch -, fling- -away, - aside, - overboard, - to the dogs; cast -, throw -, sweep- to the winds;· put -, turn -, sweep- away; jettison; quit one's hold.

Adj. relinquished &c. *v.*; cast off, derelict; unowned, unappropriated, unculled; left &c. (*residuary*) 40; divorced; disinherited.

Int. away with!

2°. *Transfer of Property*

783. Transfer.—N. transfer, conveyance, assignment, alienation, abalienation; demise, limitation; conveyancing; transmission &c. (*transference*) 270; enfeoffment, bargain and sale, lease and release; exchange &c. (*interchange*) 148; barter &c. 794; substitution &c. 147.

succession, reversion; shifting -use, – trust; devolution.

V. transfer, convey; alien, -ate; assign; grant &c. (*confer*) 784; consign; make –, hand- over; pass, hand, transmit, negotiate; hand down; exchange &c. (*interchange*) 148.

change -hands, – from one to another; devolve, succeed; come into possession &c. (*acquire*) 775; take over.

abalienate; disinherit; dispossess &c. 789; substitute &c. 147.

Adj. alienable, negotiable, transferable, reversional.

Phr. estate coming into possession.

784. Giving.—N. giving &c. *v.*; bestowal, donation; present-ation, -ment; accordance; con-, cession; delivery, consignment, dispensation, communication, endowment; invest-ment,-iture; award.

almsgiving, charity, liberality, generosity; philanthropy &c. 910.

[Thing given] gift, donation, present, *cadeau*; fairing; free gift, boon, favour, benefaction, grant, offering, oblation, sacrifice, immolation.

grace, act of grace, *bonus, bonanza*.

allowance, contribution, subscription, subsidy, tribute, subvention.

bequest, legacy, devise, will, dotation, appanage; dowry; voluntary -settlement, – conveyance &c. 783; amortization.

alms, largess, bounty, dole, sportule, donative, help, oblation, offertory, Peter's pence, *honorarium*, gratuity, Maundy money, Christmas box, Easter offering, vail, tip, *douceur*, drink money, *pourboire, Trinkgeld, backsheesh*; fee &c. (*recompense*) 973; consideration.

bribe, bait, ground-bait; peace-offering, handsel.

giver, grantor &c. *v.*; donor, feoffer, settlor; almoner; testator; investor, subscriber, contributor; fairy godmother; Santa Claus, benefactor &c. 816.

V. deliver, hand, pass, put into the hands of; hand –, make –, deliver –, pass –, turn- over.

present, give away, dispense, dispose of; give –, deal –, dole –, mete –, fork –, shell –, squeeze- out.

pay &c. 807; render, impart, communicate.

785. Receiving.—N. receiving &c. *v.*; acquisition &c. 775; reception &c. (*introduction*) 296; suscipiency, acceptance, admission.

re-, ac-cipient; assignee, devisee; lega-tee, -tary; grantee, feoffee, donee, relessee, lessee.

sportulary, stipendiary; beneficiary; pension-er, -ary; almsman.

income &c. (*receipt*) 810.

V. receive; take &c. 789; acquire &c. 775; admit.

take in, catch, touch; pocket; put into one's -pocket, – purse; accept; take off one's hands.

be received; come -in, – to hand; pass –, fall- into one's hand; go into one's pocket; fall to one's -lot, – share; come –, fall- to one; accrue; have -given &c. 784 to one.

Adj. receiving &c. *v.*; re-, suscipient.

received &c. *v.*; given &c. 784; second-hand.

not given, unbestowed &c. (*see give, bestow* &c. 734).

concede, cede, yield, part with, shed cast; spend &c. 809.

give, bestow, confer, grant, accord, award, assign.

entrust, consign, vest in.

make a present; allow, contribute, subscribe, donate, furnish its quota.

invest, endow, settle upon; bequeath, leave, devise.

furnish, supply, help; ad-, minister to; afford, spare; accommodate -, indulge -, favour- with; shower down upon; lavish, pour on, thrust upon; tip, bribe; tickle -, grease- the palm; offer &c. 763; sacrifice, immolate.

Adj. giving &c. *v.*; given &c. *v.*; allow-ed, -able; concessional; communicable; charitable, eleemosynary, sportulary, tributary; *gratis* &c. 815.

786. Apportionment.—**N.** apportion-, allot-, consign-, assign-, appointment; appropriation; dis-pensation, -tribution; allocation, division, deal; repartition; administration.

dividend, portion, contingent, share, allotment, lot, cut, split, measure, dose; dole, meed, pittance; *quantum*, ration; ratio, proportion, quota, *modicum*, mess, allowance.

V. apportion, divide; cut, split, divvy; distribute, administer, dispense; billet, allot, detail, cast, share, mete; portion -, parcel -, dole-out; deal, carve.

partition, assign, appropriate, appoint.

come in for one's share &c. (*participate*) 778.

Adj. apportioning &c. *v.*; respective.

Adv. respectively, each to each.

787. Lending.—**N.** lending &c. *v.*; loan, advance, accommodation, feneration; mortgage &c. (*security*) 771; investment.

mont-de-piété, pawnshop, hock shop, spout, my uncle's.

lender, pawnbroker, money-lender, usurer, Jew, Shylock.

V. lend, advance, loan, accommodate with; lend on security; pawn &c. (*security*) 771.

intrust, invest; place -, put- out to interest; sink, risk.

let, demise, lease, sett, under-, sublet.

Adj. lending &c. *v.*; lent &c. *v.*; unborrowed &c. (*see* borrowed &c. 788).

Adv. in advance; on -loan, - security.

788. Borrowing. — N. borrowing pledging, pawning.

borrowed plumes; plagiarism &c. (*thieving*) 791.

replevin.

V. borrow, desume; pawn.

hire, rent, farm; take a -lease, - demise; take -, hire- by the -hour, - mile, - year &c.

raise -, take up- money; float bonds; raise the wind; fly a kite, borrow of Peter to pay Paul; run into debt &c. (*debt*) 806.

make use of, plagiarize, pirate.

replevy.

---

789. Taking.—**N.** taking &c. *v.*; reception &c. (*taking in*) 296; deglutition &c. (*taking food*) 298; appropriation, prehension, prensation; capture, caption; ap-, de-prehension; abreption, seizure; ab-duction, -lation; subtraction &c. (*subduction*) 38; abstraction, a-demption.

790. Restitution.—**N.** restitution, return; ren-, red-dition; reinstatement, restoration; reinvestment, recuperation; repatriation; rehabilitation &c. (*reconstruction*) 660; reparation, atonement, indemnity, compensation, recompense.

release, replevin, redemption; recov-

dispossession; depriv-ation, -ement; bereavement; divestment; disherison; distraint, distress; sequestration, confiscation, attachment, execution; eviction &c. 297.

rapacity, extortion, vampirism, predacity, blood-sucking; theft &c. 791.

resumption; repris-e, -al; recovery &c. 775.

clutch, swoop, wrench; grip &c. (*retention*) 781; haul, take, catch; scramble.

taker, captor, capturer; vampire; extortioner.

V. take, catch, hook, nab, bag, sack, pocket, put into one's pocket, scrounge; receive; accept.

reap, crop, cull, pluck; gather &c. (*get*) 775; draw.

ap-, im-propriate; assume, possess oneself of; take possession of; commandeer; lay -, clap- one's hands on; help oneself to; make free with, dip one's hands into, lay under contribution; intercept; scramble for; deprive of.

take -, carry -, bear- -away, - off; abstract; hurry off -, run away- with; abduct; steal &c. 791; ravish; seize; pounce -, spring- upon; swoop -to, - down upon; take by -storm, - assault; snatch, reave.

snap up, nip up, whip up, catch up; kidnap, crimp, capture, lay violent hands on.

get -, lay -, take -, catch -, lay fast -, take firm- hold of; lay by the heels, take prisoner; fasten upon, grip, grapple, embrace, gripe, clasp, grab, clutch, collar, throttle, take by the throat, claw, clinch, clench, make sure of; apprehend.

catch at, jump at, make a grab at, snap at, snatch at; reach, make a long arm, stretch forth one's hand.

take -from, - away from; deduct &c. 38; retrench &c. (*curtail*) 201; dispossess, ease one of, snatch from one's grasp; tear -, tear away -, wrench -, wrest -, wring- from; extort; deprive of, bereave; disinherit, cut off with a shilling.

oust &c. (*eject*) 297; divest; levy, distrain, confiscate; sequest-er, -rate, accroach; usurp; despoil, strip, fleece, shear, displume, impoverish, eat out of house and home; drain, - to the dregs; gut, dry, exhaust, swallow up; absorb &c. (*suck in*) 296; draw off; suck, - like a leech, - the blood of.

retake, resume; recover &c. 775.

Adj. taking &c. *v.*; privative, prehensile; pred-aceous, -al, -atory, -atorial; rap-acious, -torial; ravenous: parasitic; all-devouring, -engulfing.

bereft &c. 776.

Adv. at one fell swoop.

Phr. give an inch and take an ell.

ery &c. (*getting back*) 775; remitter, reversion.

V. return, restore; recondition; give -, carry -, bring- back; render, - up; give up; let go, unclutch; dis-, re-gorge; regurgitate; recoup, reimburse, repay, indemnify, reinvest, remit, rehabilitate; repair &c. (*make good*) 660.

redeem, recover &c. (*get back*) 775; take back again; revest, revert.

Adj. restoring &c. *v.*; recuperative &c. 660; in full restitution, to compensate for.

Phr. *suum cuique.*

---

791. Stealing.—N. stealing &c. *v.*; theft, thievery, robbery, latrociny, direption; abstraction, appropriation; plagiar-y, -ism; rape, kidnapping, depredation; **raid, hold up.**

spoliation, plunder, pillage; sack, -age; rapine, *brigandage*, highway robbery, foray, *razzia*; black-mail; piracy, privateering, buccaneering; filibuster-ing, -ism; burglary; house-breaking; cattle-stealing, -rustling, -lifting.

peculation, embezzlement; fraud &c. 545; larceny, petty larceny, pilfering, shop-lifting.

thievishness, rapacity, kleptomania, Alsatia; den of -Cacus, – thieves.

licence to plunder, letters of marque.

V. steal, thieve, rob, purloin, pilfer, filch, lift, prig, bag, nim, crib, cabbage, palm; abstract; appropriate, plagiarize.

convey away, carry off, abduct, kidnap, shanghai, impress, crimp; make –, walk –, run- off with; run away with; spirit away; seize &c. (*lay violent hands on*) 789.

plunder, pillage, rifle, sack, loot, ransack, spoil, spoliate, despoil, strip, sweep, gut, forage, levy black-mail, pirate, pickeer, maraud, lift cattle, rustle, poach, smuggle, run.

stick –, hold- up.

swindle, peculate, embezzle; sponge, mulct, rook, bilk, pluck, pigeon, skin, fleece, diddle; defraud &c. 545; obtain under false pretences; live by one's wits.

rob –, borrow of- Peter to pay Paul; set a thief to catch a thief.

disregard the distinction between *meum* and *tuum*.

Adj. thieving &c. *v.*; thievish, light-fingered; fur-acious, -tive; pirati-cal; pred-aceous, -al, -atory, -atorial; raptorial &c. (*rapacious*) 789.

stolen &c. *v.*

Phr. *sic vos non vobis.*

792. Thief.—N. thief, robber, *homo trium literarum*, pilferer, rifler, filcher, plagiarist.

spoiler, depredator, pillager, marauder; harpy, shark, land-shark, falcon, moss-trooper, bushranger, Bedouin, brigand, freebooter, bandit, thug, dacoit, pirate, corsair, viking, Paul Jones; buccan-eer, -ier; piqu-, pick-eerer; rover, ranger, privateer, filibuster; rapparee, wrecker, picaroon; smuggler, poacher, plunderer; racketeer.

highwayman, Dick Turpin, Claude Duval, Macheath, knight of the road, footpad, sturdy beggar; abductor, kidnapper.

cut-, pick-purse; pick-pocket, light-fingered gentry; sharper; card-, skittle-sharper; crook; thimble-rigger; rook, Greek, blackleg, leg, welsher, defaulter; Autolycus, Cacus, Barabbas, Jeremy Diddler, Robert Macaire, artful dodger, trickster; swell mob, *chevalier d'industrie*; shop-lifter.

swindler, peculator; forger, coiner, counterfeiter, shoful; fence, re-ceiver of stolen goods, duffer; smasher.

burglar, housebreaker; cracks-, mags-man; Bill Sikes, Jack Sheppard, Jonathan Wild, Raffles, cat burglar.

793. Booty.—N. booty, spoil, plunder, prize, loot, graft, swag, pick-ings, boodle; *spolia opima*, prey; blackmail; stolen goods.

Adj. looting &c. *n.*; manubial, spoliative.

3°. *Interchange of Property*

794. Barter.—N. barter, exchange, scorse, truck system; interchange &c. 148.

a Roland for an Oliver; *quid pro quo*; com-mutation, -position.

trade, commerce, mercature, buying and selling, bargain and sale; traffic, business, nundination, custom, shopping; commercial enterprise, speculation, jobbing, stock-jobbing, *agiotage*, brokery, arbitrage.

dealing, transaction, negotiation, bargain.

free trade.

V. barter, exchange, truck, scorse, swop; interchange &c. 148; commutate &c. (*substitute*) 147; compound for.

trade, traffic, buy and sell, give and take, nundinate; carry on –, ply –, drive- a trade; be in -business, – the city; keep a shop, deal in, employ one's capital in.

trade –, deal –, have dealings- with; transact –, do- business with; open –, keep- an account with.

bargain; drive –, make- a bargain; negotiate, bid for; dicker, haggle, higgle; chaffer, huckster, cheapen, beat down; stickle, – for; out-, under-bid; ask, charge; strike a bargain &c. (*contract*) 769.

speculate, give a sprat to catch a herring; buy in the cheapest and sell in the dearest market; rig the market.

Adj. commercial, mercantile, trading; interchangeable, marketable, staple, in the market, for sale.

wholesale, retail.

Adv. across the counter; on 'change.

---

795. Purchase.—N. purchase, emption; buying, purchasing, shopping; pre-emption, refusal.

coemption, bribery; slave trade.

buyer, purchaser, *emptor*, vendee; patron, employer, client, customer, *clientèle*.

V. buy, purchase, invest in, procure; rent &c. (*hire*) 788; repurchase, buy in.

keep in one's pay, bribe, suborn; pay &c. 807; spend &c. 809.

make –, complete- a purchase; buy over the counter; pay cash for.

shop, market, go a shopping.

Adj. purchased &c. *v.*

Phr. *caveat emptor.*

---

796. Sale.—N. sale, vent, disposal; auction, roup, Dutch auction; custom &c. (*traffic*) 794.

vendi-bility, -bleness.

seller, salesman; peddler, smous; vender, vendor, consignor; merchant &c. 797; auctioneer.

V. sell, vend, dispose of, effect a sale; sell -over the counter, – by auction &c. *n.*; dispense, retail; deal in &c. 794; sell -off, – out; turn into money; realize; bring -to, – under- the hammer; put up to auction; auction, offer –, put up- for sale; hawk, peddle, bring to market; offer &c. 763; undersell; dump, unload.

let; mortgage &c. (*security*) 771.

Adj. under the hammer, in the market, for sale.

saleable, marketable, vendible, in demand, having a ready sale; unsaleable &c., unpurchased, unbought; on one's hands.

---

797. Merchant.—N. merchant, trader, dealer, monger, chandler, salesman; changer; regrater; shop-keeper, -man; trades-man, -people, -folk.

retailer; chapman, hawker, huckster, higgler; peddler, smous, pedlar, *colporteur*, cadger, Autolycus; sutler, *vivandière*; coster-man, -monger; market woman; cheap jack; caterer &c. 637; tallyman.

money-broker, -changer, -lender; stock-broker, -jobber; cambist, usurer, moneyer, banker.

jobber; broker &c. (*agent*) 758; buyer &c. 795; seller &c. 796.

concern; firm &c. (*partnership*) 712.

798. Merchandise. — N. merchandise, ware, commodity, effects, goods, article, stock, produce, staple commodity; stock in trade &c. (*store*) 636; cargo &c. (*contents*) 190.

799. Mart.—N. mart; market, -place, *forum*; fair, bazaar, staple; stock –, exchange; 'change, *bourse*, Wall Street, Rialto, hall, guildhall; toll-booth, custom-house; Tattersalls.

shop, stall, booth; wharf; office, chambers, counting-house, *bureau*; coun-, comp-ter.

ware-house, -room; depot, interposit, *entrepôt, emporium*, establishment; store &c. 636.

open market, market-overt.

4°. *Monetary Relations*

800. Money.—N. money -matters, – market; finance; accounts &c. 811; funds, treasure; capital, stock; assets &c. (*property*) 780; wealth &c. 803; supplies, ways and means, wherewithal, sinews of war, almighty dollar, needful, cash.

sum, amount; balance, -sheet; sum total; proceeds &c. (*receipts*) 810.

currency, circulating medium, specie; coin, – of the realm; piece, hard cash, dollar, sterling coin; pounds shillings and pence; £ s. d., guineas; pocket, breeches pocket, purse; money in hand; the best, ready, – money; filthy lucre, shekels, roll, jack, rhino, blunt, dust, bawbees, brass, dibs, dough, mopus, tin, salt, chink, oof, spondulics, pile, wads.

precious metals, gold, silver, copper, nickel; bullion, bar, ingot, nugget.

petty cash; pocket-, pin-money; small –, change; small coin, loose cash; doit, stiver, rap, mite, farthing, *sou*, penny, shilling, bob, tanner, tester, groat, guinea, ducat; *rouleau*; *wampum*; good –, round –, lump-sum; power –, mint –, tons- of money; plum, lac of rupees, millions, money-bags, miser's hoard, stocking, mine of wealth &c. 803.

[Science of coins] numismatics, chrysology.

paper-money; money –, postal –, Post Office- order; note, – of hand; bank –, treasury- note; Bradbury; promissory note; I O U., bond; bill, – of exchange; draft, cheque, order, warrant, coupon, debenture, exchequer bill, *assignat*, greenback, gold –, silver- certificate.

copper, nickel, dime, quarter, two bits, half a dollar, dollar, buck, simoleon, fiver, tenner, a twenty, a sawbuck, a century, a grand; eagle, double eagle.

gold standard, bimetallism, fiat money; rate of –, exchange; in-, de-flation.

remittance &c. (*payment*) 807; credit &c. 805; liability &c. 806; solvency &c. 803.

draw-er, -ee; oblig-or, -ee; moneyer, coiner, counterfeiter, forger.

false –, bad- money; base –, counterfeit- coin, flash note, slip, kite; Bank of Elegance.

argumentum ad crumenam.

V. amount to, come to, mount up to; touch the pocket; draw, – upon; endorse &c. (*security*) 771; issue, utter, circulate; discount &c. 813.

forge, counterfeit, coin, circulate –, pass- bad money.

Adj. monetary, pecuniary, crumenal, fiscal, financial, sumptuary, numismatical; sterling; solvent &c. 803.

801. Treasurer.—**N.** treasurer; bursar, -y; purser, purse-bearer; cash-keeper, banker; depositary; questor, receiver, steward, trustee, chartered -, accountant; Accountant-General, almoner, liquidator, paymaster, cashier, teller; cambist; money-changer &c. (*merchant*) 797.

financier, Chancellor of the Exchequer, minister of finance; Secretary of the Treasury, Director of the Budget, Controller of Currency.

802. Treasury.—**N.** treasury, thesaurus, bank, exchequer, almonry, fisc, hanaper, bursary; safe; strong-box, -hold, -room; coffer; chest &c. (*receptacle*) 191; depository &c. 636; till, -er; cash-box, -register, purse, pocket-book, wallet; money-bag, -belt, -box; *porte-monnaie*.

purse-strings; pocket, breeches pocket.

sinking fund; stocks; government -, public -, parliamentary- -stocks, - funds, - securities, bonds; gilt-edged securities; Consols, Liberty bonds, government bonds, *crédit mobilier*.

803. Wealth.—**N.** wealth, riches, fortune, handsome fortune, opulence, affluence; good -, easy- circumstances; independence; competence &c. (*sufficiency*) 639; solvency, soundness, solidity.

provision, livelihood, maintenance; alimony, dowry; means, resources, substance; property &c. 780; command of money.

income &c. 810; capital, money; round sum &c. (*treasure*) 800; mint of money, mine of wealth, El Dorado, Pactolus, Golconda, Potosi, *bonanza*; philosopher's stone.

long -, full -, well lined -, heavy-purse; purse of Fortunatus.

pelf, Mammon, lucre, filthy lucre; loaves and fishes; fleshpots of Egypt.

rich -, moneyed -, warm- man; man of substance; capitalist, millionaire, Nabob, Crœsus, Midas, Plutus, Dives, Timon of Athens; Timo-, Pluto-cracy; Danaë.

V. be -rich &c. *adj.*; roll -, wallow-in -wealth, - riches; have money to burn.

afford, well afford; command -money, - a sum; make both ends meet, hold one's head above water.

become -rich &c. *adj.*; fill one's -pocket &c. (*treasury*) 802; feather one's nest, clean up -, make- a fortune; make money &c. (*acquire*) 775.

enrich, imburse.

worship -Mammon, - the golden calf.

Adj. wealthy, rich, affluent, opulent, moneyed, monied, worth -a great deal,

804. Poverty.—**N.** poverty, indigence, penury, pauperism, destitution, want; need, -iness; lack, necessity, privation, distress, difficulties, wolf at the door.

bad -, poor -, needy -, embarrassed -, reduced -, straitened- circumstances; slender -, narrow- means; straits; hand to mouth existence, *res angusta domi*, low water, impecuniosity.

beggary; mendi-cancy, -city; broken -, loss of- fortune; insolvency &c. (*non-payment*) 808.

empty -purse, - pocket; light purse; beggarly account of empty boxes.

poor man, pauper, mendicant, mumper, beggar, starveling; *pauvre diable*.

V. be -poor &c. *adj.*; want, lack, starve, live from hand to mouth, have seen better days, go down in the world, be on one's uppers, come upon the parish; go to -the dogs, - wrack and ruin; not have a -penny &c. (*money*) 800, - shot in one's locker; beg one's bread; *tirer le diable par la queue*; run into debt &c. (*debt*) 806.

render -poor &c. *adj.*; impoverish; reduce, - to poverty; pauperize, fleece, ruin, bring to the parish.

Adj. poor, indigent; poverty -stricken; badly -, poorly -, ill- off; poor as -a rat, - a church mouse, - Job's turkey, - Job; fortune-, dower-, money-, penni-less; unportioned, unmoneyed; impecunious; broke, flat; out -, short-of -money, - cash; without -, not worth- a rap &c. (*money*) 800; *qui n'a pas le sou*, out of pocket, hard up; out at

– much; well -to do, – off; warm; well –, provided for.

made of money; rich as Crœsus; rolling in -riches, – wealth.

flush, – of -cash, – money, – tin; in -funds, – cash, – full feather; solvent, solid, sound, pecunious, out of debt, all straight; able to pay 20s in the £.

Phr. one's ship coming in.

_____

elbows, down at heels; seedy, bare-foot; beggar-ly, -ed; destitute; fleeced, strapped, stripped; bereft, bereaved; reduced.

in -want &c. *n.*; needy, necessitous, distressed, pinched, straitened; put to one's -shifts, – last shifts; unable to -keep the wolf from the door, – make both ends meet; embarrassed, under hatches; involved &c. (*in debt*) 806; insolvent &c. (*not paying*) 808.

Adv. in formâ pauperis.
Phr. zonam perdidit.

805. Credit.—N. credit, trust, tick, score, tally, account.

letter of credit, circular note; duplicate; mortgage, lien, debenture, paper credit, floating capital; draft; securities.

creditor, lender, lessor, mortgagee; dun; usurer.

V. keep –, run up- an account with; entrust, credit, accredit.

place to one's -credit, – account; give –, take- credit; fly a kite.

Adj. credit-ing, -ed; accredited.

Adv. on -credit &c. *n.*; to the -account, – credit- of.

806. Debt.—N. debt, obligation, liability, indebtment, debit, score.

arrears, deferred payment, deficit, default; insolvency &c. (*non-payment*) 808; bad debt.

interest; usance, usury; premium; floating -debt, – capital.

debtor, debitor; mortgagor; defaulter &c. 808; borrower.

V. be -in debt &c. *adj.*; owe; incur –, contract- a debt &c. *n.*; run up -a bill, – a score, – an account; go on tick, put on the cuff; borrow &c. 788; run –, get- into debt; outrun the constable.

answer –, go bail- for; back one's note.

Adj. indebted; liable, chargeable, answerable for.

in -debt, – embarrassed circumstances, – difficulties; incumbered, involved; involved –, plunged –, deep –, over head and ears- in debt; deeply involved; fast tied up; insolvent &c. (*not paying*) 808; *minus*, out of pocket.

unpaid; unrequited, unrewarded; owing, due, in arrear, outstanding.

_____

807. Payment.—N. pay-, defrayment; discharge; ac-, quittance; settlement, clearance, liquidation, satisfaction, reckoning, arrangement.

acknowledgment, release; receipt, – in full, – in full of all demands; voucher.

repayment, reimbursement, retribution; pay &c. (*reward*) 973; money paid &c. (*expenditure*) 809.

ready money &c. (*cash*) 800; stake, remittance, instalment.

payer, liquidator &c. 801.

V. pay, defray, make payment; pay -down, – on the nail, – ready money, – at sight, – in advance; cash, honour a bill, acknowledge; redeem; pay in kind.

808. Non-payment.—N. non-payment; default, defalcation; protest, repudiation; application of the sponge; whitewashing.

insolvency, bankruptcy, failure; overdraft, overdrawn account; insufficiency &c. 640; run upon a bank.

waste paper bonds; dishonoured –, protested- bills; bogus cheque.

bankrupt, insolvent debtor, lame duck, man of straw, welsher, stag, defaulter, absconder, levanter.

V. not -pay &c. 807; fail, break, stop payment; become -insolvent, – bankrupt; be gazetted; abscond.

protest, dishonour, repudiate, nullify. pay under protest; button up one's

pay one's -way, – shot, – footing; pay -the piper, – sauce for all, – costs; do the needful; come across; shell –, fork- out; come down with, – the dust; tickle –, grease- the palm; expend &c. 809; put –, lay- down.

discharge, settle, quit, acquit one-self of; account –, reckon –, settle –, be even –, be quits- with; strike a balance; settle –, balance –, square-accounts with; quit scores; foot the bill; wipe –, clear- off old scores; satisfy; pay in full; satisfy –, pay in full of- all demands; clear, liquidate; pay -up, – old debts.

disgorge, make repayment; repay, refund, reimburse, retribute; make compensation &c. 30.

Adj. paying &c., paid &c. *v.*; owing nothing, out of debt, all straight, clear of -debt, – encumbrance; unowed, never indebted.

Adv. to the tune of; on the nail; money –, cash- down; cash on delivery.

pockets, draw the purse strings; apply the sponge; pay over the left shoulder, get whitewashed; swindle &c. 791; run up bills, fly kites.

Adj. not paying; in debt &c. 806; behindhand, in arrear; beggared &c. (*poor*) 804; unable to make both ends meet; *minus*; worse than nothing.

insolvent, bankrupt, in the gazette, gazetted, ruined.

unpaid &c. (*outstanding*) 806; *gratis* &c. 815; unremunerated.

---

809. Expenditure.—N. expenditure, money going out; out-goings, -lay; expenses, disbursement; prime cost &c. (*price*) 812; circulation; run upon a bank.

[Money paid] payment &c. 807; pay &c. (*remuneration*) 973; bribe &c. 973; fee, footing, garnish; subsidy; tribute, Peter's pence; contingent, quota; dona-tion &c. 784.

pay in advance, earnest, handsel, deposit, instalment.

investment; purchase &c. 795.

V. expend, spend; run –, get-through; pay, disburse; open –, loose –, untie- the purse strings; lay –, shell –, fork- out; bleed; make up a sum, invest, sink money.

fee &c. (*reward*) 973; pay one's way &c. (*pay*) 807; subscribe &c. (*give*) 784; subsidize, bribe.

810. Receipt.—N. receipt, accountable –, conditional –, binding –, return-receipt; value received, money coming in; income, incomings, innings, reve-nue, return, proceeds; gross receipts; net profit; earnings &c. (*gain*) 775.

rent, – roll; rent-al, -age; rack-rent.

premium, *bonus*; sweepstakes, ton-tine, prize, drawing.

pension, annuity; jointure &c. (*prop-erty*) 780; alimony, pittance; emolu-ment &c. (*remuneration*) 973.

V. receive &c. 785; take money; draw –, derive- from; get, be in receipt of, acquire &c. 775; take &c. 789.

bring in, yield, afford, pay, return; accrue &c. (*be received from*) 785.

Adj. receiv-ing, -ed &c. *v.*; profitable &c. (*gainful*) 775.

Adj. expend-ing, -ed &c. *v.*; sumptuary, liberal &c. 816; open-handed, lavish &c. 818; expensive &c. 814.

811. Accounts.—N. accounts, accompts; commercial –, monetary-arithmetic; statistics &c. (*numeration*) 85; money matters, finance, budget, bill, score, reckoning, account.

books, account book, ledger; day –, cash –, pass- book; journal; debtor and creditor –, cash –, petty cash –, running- account; account-current; balance, – sheet; *compte rendu*, account settled.

book-keeping, audit; double –, single- entry; reckoning &c. 85.

chartered –, certified public –, accountant; auditor, actuary, book-keeper; financier &c. 801; accounting party.

V. keep accounts, enter, post, book, credit, debit, carry over; take stock; balance –, make up –, square –, settle –, wind up –, cast up –, add up –, tot up- accounts; make accounts square.

bring to book, audit, tax, surcharge and falsify.

falsify –, garble –, cook –, doctor- an account.

Adj. monetary &c. 800; account-able, -ing; statistical.

812. Price.—**N.** price, amount, cost, expense, prime cost, charge, figure, demand, fare, hire; wages &c. (*remuneration*) 973.

dues, duty, toll, tax, impost, cess, sess, tallage, levy, capitation-, poll-, income-, sur-, sales-, super-tax; gabel, *gabelle*; gavel, *octroi*, custom, tariff, excise, assessment, taxation, benevolence, tithe, tenths, exactment, ransom, salvage; broker-, wharf-, lighter-, ton-, freight-age.

worth, rate, value, valuation, appraisement, money's worth, par value; penny &c. -worth; price current, market price, quotation; what it will -fetch &c. *v.*

bill &c. (*account*) 811; shot.

V. bear –, set –, fix- a price; appraise, assess, price, charge, demand, ask, require, exact, run up; distrain; run up a bill &c. (*debt*) 806; have one's price; liquidate.

amount to, come to, mount up to; stand one in.

fetch, sell for, cost, bring in, yield, afford.

Adj. priced &c. *v.*; to the tune of, *ad valorem*; mercenary, venal.

Phr. no penny, no paternoster; *point d'argent, point de Suisse*; no longer pipe, no longer dance; no song, no supper.

one may have it for.

813. Discount.—**N.** discount, abatement, concession, reduction, depreciation, allowance, qualification, set off, drawback, poundage, *agio*, percentage; rebate, -ment; backwardation, contango; salvage; tare and tret.

V. discount, bate; a-, re-bate; deduct, reduce, mark down, take off, allow, give, make allowance; tax, depreciate.

Adj. discounting &c. *v.*

Adv. at a discount, below par.

---

814. Dearness. — N. dearness &c. *adj.*; high –, famine –, fancy- price; overcharge; extravagance; exorbitance, extortion; heavy pull upon the purse; Pyrrhic victory.

V. be -dear &c. *adj.*; cost -much, – a pretty penny; rise in price, look up.

overcharge, bleed, fleece, skin, extort.

pay -too much, – through the nose, – too dear for one's whistle.

Adj. dear; high, -priced; of great price, expensive, costly, precious, worth a Jew's eye, dear bought; unreasonable, extravagant, exorbitant, extortionate.

at a premium; not to be had, – for love or money; beyond –, above- price; priceless, of priceless value.

Adv. dear, -ly; at great –, heavy- cost; *à grands frais*.

Phr. prices looking up; *le jeu n'en vaut pas la chandelle*.

---

815. Cheapness.—**N.** cheapness, low price; depreciation; bargain; good penny &c.- worth, *bon marché*.

[Absence of charge] gratuity; free -quarters, – seats, – admission, – warren; pass, Annie Oakley; run of one's teeth; nominal price, peppercorn rent; labour of love.

drug in the market.

V. be -cheap &c. *adj.*; cost little; come down –, fall- in price.

buy for -a mere nothing, – an old song; have one's money's worth; cheapen, beat down.

Adj. cheap; low, – priced; moderate, reasonable; in-, un-expensive; well –, worth the money; *magnifique et pas cher*; good –, cheap- at the price; dirt –, dog- cheap; cheap, -as dirt, – and nasty; catchpenny.

reduced, marked down, half-price, depreciated, unsaleable.

gratuitous, *gratis*, free, for love,

– nothing; cost-, expense-less; without charge, not charged, un-taxed; scot –, shot –, rent- free; free of -cost, – expense; honor-ary, unbought, unpaid, complimentary.

Adv. for a mere song; at -cost price, – prime cost, – a reduction, – a bargain; on the cheap.

---

816. Liberality.—N. liberality, gener-osity, munificence; bount-y, -eousness, -ifulness; hospitality; charity &c. (*beneficence*) 906.

benefactor, free giver, Lady Bounti-ful.

V. be -liberal &c. *adj.*; spend –, bleed- freely; shower down upon; open one's purse strings &c. (*disburse*) 809; spare no expense, give -with both hands, – *carte blanche.*

Adj. liberal, free, generous; charit-able &c. (*beneficent*) 906; hospitable; bount-iful, -eous; handsome; unspar-ing, ungrudging; open-, free-, full-handed; open-, large-, free-hearted; munificent, princely, unstinting.

overpaid.

Adv. liberally, ungrudgingly, with open hand.

---

818. Prodigality.—N. prodi-gality, -gence; unthriftiness, waste, -fulness; profus-ion, -eness; extravagance; squan-dering &c. *v.*; lavishness; malversation.

prodigal; spend-, waste-thrift; losel, play-boy, spender, squanderer, locust.

V. be -prodigal &c. *adj.*; squander, lavish, sow broadcast; pour forth like water; pay through the nose &c. (*dear*) 814; spill, waste, dissipate, exhaust, drain, eat out of house and home, overdraw, outrun the constable; run -out, – through; misspend; throw -good money after bad, – the helve after the hatchet; burn the candle at both ends; make ducks and drakes of one's money; squander one's substance, spend money like water; fool –, potter –, muddle –, fritter –, throw- away one's money; pour water into a sieve, kill the goose that lays the golden eggs; *manger son blé en herbe.*

Adj. prodigal, profuse, thriftless, un-thrifty, improvident, wasteful, losel,

817. Economy.—N. economy, fru-gality; thrift, -iness; prudence, care, husbandry, good housewifery, saving-ness, retrenchment.

savings; prevention of waste, save-all; cheese parings and candle ends; parsimony &c. 819.

V. be -economical &c. *adj.*; econo-mize, save; retrench; cut- down ex-penses, – one's coat according to one's cloth, make both ends meet, keep within compass, meet one's expenses, pay one's way; keep one's head above water; husband &c. (*lay by*) 636; save –, invest- money; put out to interest; provide –, save- -for, – against- a rainy day; feather one's nest; look after the main chance.

Adj. economical, frugal, careful, thrifty, saving, chary, spare, sparing; parsimonious &c. 819.

underpaid.

Adv. sparingly &c. *adj.*; *ne quid nimis.*

---

819. Parsimony. — N. parsimony, parcity; parsimoniousness, stinginess &c. *adj.*; stint; illiberality, avarice, tenacity, avidity, rapacity, extortion, venality, cupidity; selfishness &c. 943; *auri sacra fames.*

miser, niggard, churl, screw, tight-wad, skinflint, crib, codger, muckworm, money-grubber, pinchfist, scrimp, lick-penny, hunks, curmudgeon, *Harpagon,* Silas Marner, harpy, extortioner, Jew, usurer.

V. be -parsimonious &c. *adj.*; grudge, begrudge, stint, skimp, pinch, gripe, screw, dole out, hold back, withhold, starve, famish, live upon nothing, skin a flint.

drive a -bargain, – hard bargain; cheapen, beat down; stop one hole in a sieve; have an itching palm, grasp, grab.

Adj. parsimonious, penurious, stingy, miserly, mean, shabby, peddling, scrubby, pennywise, near, niggardly,

extravagant, lavish, dissipated, over liberal; full-handed &c. (*liberal*) 816.

penny wise and pound foolish.

Adv. with an unsparing hand; money burning one's pocket; recklessly profuse.

Int. hang the expense!

---

frugal to excess; close; fast-, close-, strait-handed; close-, hard-, tight-fisted; tight, sparing; chary; grudging, griping &c. *v.*; illiberal ungenerous, churlish, hidebound, sordid, mercenary, venal, covetous, usurious, avaricious, greedy, extortionate, rapacious.

Adv. with a sparing hand.

CLASS VI

Words relating to the SENTIENT and MORAL POWERS.

~~~~~~~~~~

Section I. AFFECTIONS IN GENERAL

820. Affections.—N. affections, character, qualities, disposition, nature, spirit, tone; temper, -ament; *diathesis*, idiosyncrasy; cast –, habit –, frame- of -mind, – soul; predilection, turn; natural –, turn of mind; bent, bias, predisposition, proneness, proclivity; propen-sity, -sedness, -sion, -dency; vein, humour, mood, grain, mettle; sympathy &c. (*love*) 897.

soul, heart, breast, bosom, inner man; heart's -core, – strings, – blood; heart of hearts, *penetralia mentis*; secret and inmost recesses of the –, cockles of one's- heart; inmost -heart, – soul; back-bone.

passion, pervading spirit; ruling –, master- passion; *furore*; fulness of the heart, heyday of the blood, flesh and blood, flow of soul, force of character.

V. have –, possess- -affections &c. *n.*; be of a -character &c. *n.*; be -affected &c. *adj.*; breathe.

Adj. affected, characterized, formed, moulded, cast; at-, tempered; framed; pre-, disposed; prone, inclined; having a -bias &c. *n.*; tinctured –, imbued –, penetrated –, eaten up- with.

inborn, inbred, ingrained, in the grain, congenital, inherent, bred in the bone; deep-rooted, ineffaceable, inveterate; pathoscopic.

Adv. in one's -heart &c. *n.*; at heart; heart and soul &c. 821; in the -vein, – mood.

821. Feeling.—N. feeling; suffering &c. *v.*; endurance, tolerance, sufferance, supportance, experience, response; sympathy &c. (*love*) 897; impression, inspiration, affection, sensation, emotion, pathos, deep sense.

fire, warmth, glow, unction, *gusto*, vehemence; ferv-our, -ency; heartiness, cordiality; earnestness, eagerness; *empressement*, ardour, zeal, passion, enthusiasm, *verve*, *furore*, fanaticism; excitation of feeling &c. 824; fulness of the heart &c. (*disposition*) 820; passion &c. (*state of excitability*) 825; ecstasy &c. (*pleasure*) 827.

blush, suffusion, flush; hectic; tingling, thrill, kick, turn, shock; agitation &c. (*irregular motion*) 315; quiver, heaving, flutter, flurry, fluster, twitter, tremor; throb, -bing; pulsation, palpitation, panting; trepid-, perturb-ation; ruffle, hurry of spirits, pother, stew, ferment.

V. feel; receive an -impression &c. *n.*; be -impressed with &c. *adj.*; entertain –, harbour –, cherish- -feeling &c. *n.*

respond; catch the -flame, – infection; enter the spirit of.

bear, suffer, support, sustain, endure, brook, thole, aby; abide &c.

(*be composed*) 826; experience &c. (*meet with*) 151; taste, prove; labour
–, smart- under; bear the brunt of, brave, stand.

swell, glow, warm, flush, blush, change colour, mantle; turn -colour,
– pale, – red, – black in the face; blench, crimson, whiten, pale, tingle,
thrill, heave, pant, throb, palpitate, go pit-a-pat, tremble, quiver,
flutter, twitter; stagger, reel; shake &c. 315; be -agitated, – excited
&c. 824; look -blue, – black; wince, draw a deep breath.

impress &c. (*excite the feelings*) 824.

Adj. feeling &c. *v.*; sentient; sensuous; sensor-ial, -y; emo-tive,
-tional; of –, with- feeling &c. *n.*

warm, quick, lively, smart, strong, sharp, acute, cutting, piercing,
incisive; keen, – as a razor; trenchant, pungent, racy, *piquant*, poignant, caustic.

impressive, deep, profound, indelible; deep-, home-, heart-felt;
swelling, soul-stirring, deep-mouthed, heart-expanding, electric, thrilling, rapturous, ecstatic.

earnest, wistful, eager, breathless; fer-vent, -vid; gushing, passionate, warmhearted, hearty, cordial, sincere, zealous, enthusiastic, glowing, ardent, burning, red-hot, fiery, flaming; boiling, – over.

pervading, penetrating, absorbing; rabid, raving, feverish, fanatical,
hysterical; impetuous &c. (*excitable*) 825; overmastering.

impressed –, moved –, touched –, affected –, penetrated –, seized –,
imbued &c. 820- with; devoured by; wrought up &c. (*excited*) 824;
struck all of a heap; rapt; in a -quiver &c. *n.*; enraptured &c. 829.

Adv. heart and soul, from the bottom of one's heart, *ab imo pectore*,
de profundis, at heart, *con amore*, heartily, devoutly, over head and ears.

Phr. the heart -big, – full, – swelling, – beating, – pulsating, – throb-
bing, – thumping, – beating high, – melting, – overflowing, – bursting,
– breaking.

---

822. Sensibility. — N. sensi-bility,
-bleness, -tiveness; moral sensibility;
impress-, affect-ibility; suscepti-ble-
ness, -bility, -vity; mobility; viva-city,
-ciousness; tender-, soft-ness; senti-
mental-ity, -ism.

excitability &c. 825; fastidiousness
&c. 868; physical sensibility &c. 375.

sore -point, – place; where the shoe
pinches.

V. be -sensible &c. *adj.*; have a
-tender, – warm, – sensitive- heart.

take to –, treasure up in the- heart;
shrink.

'die of a rose in aromatic pain';
touch to the quick.

Adj. sensi-ble, -tive; impressi-ble,
-onable; suscepti-ve, -ble; alive to,
impassion-able, -ed; gushing; warm-,
tender-, soft-hearted; tender –, as a
chicken; soft, sentimental, romantic;
enthusiastic, highflying, spirited, mettlesome, vivacious, lively, expressive,
mobile, tremblingly alive; excitable

823. Insensibility.—N. insensi-bility,
-bleness; moral insensibility; inertness,
inertia, *vis inertiæ*; impassi-bility,
-bleness; inappetency, apathy, phlegm,
dulness, hebetude, supineness, lukewarmness, insusceptibility, unimpress-
ibility.

cold -fit, – blood, – heart; cold-,
cool-ness; frigidity, *sang-froid*; stoicism,
imperturbation &c. (*inexcitability*) 826;
nonchalance, unconcern, dry eyes;
insouciance &c. (*indifference*) 866;
recklessness &c. 863; callousness; heart
of stone, stock and stone, marble,
deadness.

torp-or, -idity; obstupefaction, lethargy, coma, trance; sleep &c. 683;
suspended animation; stup-or, -efac-
tion; paralysis, palsy; numbness &c.
(*physical insensibility*) 376.

neutrality; quietism, vegetation.

V. be -insensible &c. *adj.*; have a
rhinoceros hide; show -insensibility
&c. *n.*; not -mind, – care, – be affected

&c. 825; over-sensitive, without skin, thin-skinned; fastidious &c. 868.

Adv. sensibly &c. *adj.*; to the -quick, - inmost core.

by; have no desire for &c. 866; have -, feel -, take- no interest in; *nil admirari*; not care a -straw &c. (*unimportance*) 643 for; disregard &c. (*neglect*) 460; set at naught &c. (*make light of*) 483; turn a deaf ear to &c. (*inattention*) 458; vegetate.

render -insensible, - callous; blunt, obtund, numb, benumb, paralyze, chloroform, deaden, hebetate, stun, stupefy; brut-ify, -alize.

inure; harden, - the heart; steel, case-harden, sear.

Adj. insensible, unconscious; impassi-ve, -ble; blind to, deaf to, dead to; un-, in-susceptible; unimpress-ionable, -ible; passion-, spirit-, heart-, soul-less; unfeeling, unmoral.

apathetic; leuco-, phlegmatic; dull, frigid; cold, -blooded, -hearted; unemotional; cold as charity; flat, obtuse, inert, supine, sluggish, torpid; sleepy &c. (*inactive*) 683; languid, half-hearted, tame; numb, -ed; comatose; anæsthetic &c. 376; stupefied, chloroformed, palsy-stricken.

indifferent, lukewarm; Laodicean; careless, mindless, regardless; inattentive &c. 458; neglectful &c. 460; disregarding.

unconcerned, *nonchalant, pococurante, insouciant, sans souci*; un-ambitious &c. 866.

un-affected, -ruffled, -impressed, -inspired, -excited, -moved, -stirred, -touched, -shocked, -struck; unblushing &c. (*shameless*) 885; unanimated; vegetative.

callous, thick-skinned, pachydermatous, impervious; hard, -ened; inured, case-hardened; steeled -, proof- against; imperturbable &c. (*inexcitable*) 826; unfelt.

Adv. insensibly &c. *adj.*; *æquo animo*; without being -moved, - touched, - impressed; in cold blood; with -dry eyes, - withers unwrung.

Phr. never mind; it is of no consequence &c. (*unimportant*) 643; it cannot be helped; nothing coming amiss; it is all -the same, - one- to.

824. Excitation.—N. excitation of feeling; mental -, excitement; suscitation, galvanism, stimulation, piquancy, provocation, inspiration, calling forth, infection; interest, animation, agitation, perturbation; subjugation, fascination, intoxication; en-, ravishment; entrancement, high pressure.

unction, impressiveness &c. *adj.*; emotional appeal; melodrama; psychological moment, crisis; sensationalism.

trial of temper, *casus belli*; irritation &c. (*anger*) 900; passion &c. (*state of excitability*) 825; thrill &c. (*feeling*) 821; repression of feeling &c. 826.

V. excite, affect, touch, move, impress, strike, interest, intrigue, animate, inspire, impassion, smite, infect; stir -, fire -, warm- the blood; set astir; a-, wake; a-, waken; call forth; e-, pro-voke; raise up, summon up, call up, wake up, blow up, get up, light up; raise; get up steam, rouse, arouse, stir, fire, kindle, enkindle, apply the torch, set on fire, inflame, illuminate.

stimulate; ex-, suscitate; inspirit; spirit up, stir up, work up; infuse life into, give new life to; bring -, introduce- new blood; quicken;

sharpen, whet; work upon &c. (*incite*) 615; hurry on, give a fillip, put on one's mettle.

fan the -fire, – flame; blow the coals, stir the embers; fan, – into a flame; foster, heat, warm, foment, raise to a fever heat; keep -up, – the pot boiling; revive, rekindle; rake up, rip up.

stir –, play on –, come home to- the feelings; touch -a string, – a chord, – the soul, – the heart; go to one's heart, penetrate, pierce, go through one, touch to the quick, open the wound; possess –, pervade –, penetrate –, imbrue –, absorb –, affect –, disturb- the soul.

absorb, rivet the attention; sink into the -mind, – heart; prey on the mind; intoxicate; over-whelm, -power; *bouleverser*, upset, turn one's head.

fascinate; enrapture &c. (*give pleasure*) 829.

agitate, perturb, ruffle, fluster, flutter, shake, disturb, faze, startle, shock, stagger; give one a -shock, – turn; strike -dumb, – all of a heap; stun, astound, electrify, galvanize, petrify.

irritate, sting; cut, – to the -heart, – quick; try one's temper; fool to the top of one's bent, pique; infuriate, madden, make one's blood boil; lash into fury &c. (*wrath*) 900.

be -excited &c. *adj.*; flash up, flare up; catch the infection; thrill &c. (*feel*) 821; mantle; work oneself up; seethe, boil, simmer, foam, fume, flame, rage, rave; run mad &c. (*passion*) 825.

Adj. excited &c. *v.*; wrought up, on the *qui vive*, astir, sparkling; in a -quiver &c. 821, – fever, – ferment, – blaze, – state of excitement; in hysterics; black in the face, over-wrought; hot, red-hot, flushed, feverish; all -of a twitter, – of a flutter, – of a dither, – in a pucker; with -quivering lips, – tears in one's eyes.

flaming; boiling, – over; ebullient, seething; foaming, – at the mouth; fuming, raging, carried away by passion, wild, raving, frantic, mad, distracted, distraught, beside oneself, out of one's wits, amuck, ready to burst, *bouleversé*, demoniacal.

lost, *éperdu*, tempest-tossed; haggard; ready to sink.

stung to the quick, up, on one's high ropes.

exciting &c. *v.*; impressive, warm, glowing, fervid, swelling, impos-ing, spirit-stirring, thrilling; high-wrought; soul-stirring, -subduing; heart-swelling, -thrilling; agonizing &c. (*painful*) 830; telling, sensa-tional, melodramatic, hysterical; over-powering, -whelming; more than flesh and blood can bear.

piquant &c. (*pungent*) 392; spicy, appetizing, provocative, *provoquant*, tantalizing.

Adv. till one is black in the face.

Phr. the heart -beating high, – going pit-a-pat, – leaping into one's mouth; the blood -being up, – boiling in one's veins; the eye -glisten-ing, – 'in a fine frenzy rolling'; the head turned.

---

825. [Excess of sensitiveness.] **Excit-ability.—N.** excitability, impetuosity, vehemence; boisterousness &c. *adj.*; turbulence; impatience, intolerance, non-endurance; irritability &c. (*irasci-bility*) 901; itching &c. (*desire*) 865; wincing; disquiet, -ude; restlessness; fidgets, fidgetiness; agitation &c. (*ir-regular motion*) 315.

826. [Absence of excitability, or of excitement.] **Inexcitability.—N.** inex-cit-, imperturb-, inirrit-ability; even temper, tranquil mind, dispassion; tol-erance, toleration, patience.

passiveness &c. (*physical inertness*) 172; hebet-ude, -ation; impassibility &c. (*insensibility*) 823; stupefaction.

coolness, calmness &c. *adj.*; compo-

trepidation, perturbation, ruffle, hurry, -skurry, fuss, flurry; fluster, flutter; pother, stew, ferment; whirl; thrill &c. (*feeling*) 821; state -, fever- of excitement; transport.

passion, excitement, flush, heat; fever, -heat; fire, flame, fume, blood boiling; tumult; effervescence, ebulli- tion; boiling, – over; whiff, gust, storm, tempest; scene, breaking out, burst, fit, paroxysm, explosion; out-break, -burst; agony.

violence &c. 173; fierceness &c. *adj.*; rage, fury, *furor, furore,* desperation, madness, distraction, raving, delirium, brain storm; frenzy, hysterics; intoxi- cation; tearing –, raging- passion, towering rage; anger &c. 900.

fascination, infatuation, fanaticism; Quixot-ism, -ry; *tête montée.*

V. be -impatient &c. *adj.*; not be able to -bear &c. 826; bear ill, wince, chafe, champ the bit; be in a -stew &c. *n.*; be out of all patience, fidget, fuss, not have a wink of sleep; toss, – on one's pillow.

lose one's temper &c. 900; break –, burst –, fly- out; go –, fly- -off, – off the handle, – off at a tangent; explode; flare up, flame up, fire up, burst into a flame, take fire, fire, burn; boil, – over; foam, fume, rage, rave, rant, tear; go –, run- -wild, – mad; go into hysterics; run -riot, – amuck; *battre la campagne, faire le diable à quatre,* play the deuce; raise -Cain, – the devil.

Adj. excitable, easily excited, in an excitable state; highly strung; irritable &c. (*irascible*) 901; impatient, intol- erant.

feverish, febrile, hysterical; delirious, mad, moody, maggoty-headed.

unquiet, mercurial, electric, galvanic, hasty, hurried, restless, fidgety, fussy; chafing &c. *v.*

startlish, mettlesome, high mettled, skittish.

vehement, demonstrative, violent, wild, furious, fierce, fiery, hot-headed, mad-cap.

over-zealous, enthusiastic, impas- sioned, fanatical; rabid &c. (*eager*) 865.

rampant, clamorous, uproarious, tur-

sure, placidity, indisturbance, imper- turbation, *sang-froid,* tranquillity, se- renity; quiet, -ude; peace of mind, mental calmness.

staidness &c. *adj.*; gravity, sobriety, Quakerism; philosophy, equanimity, stoicism, command of temper; self- possession, -control, -command, -re- straint; presence of mind.

submission &c. 725; resignation; suffer-, support-, endur-, long-suffer-, forbear-ance; longanimity; fortitude; patience -of Job, – 'on a monument,' – 'sovereign o'er transmuted ill'; moder- ation; repression –, subjugation- of feeling; restraint &c. 751.

tranquillization &c. (*moderation*) 174.

V. be -composed &c. *adj.*

laisser -faire, – aller; take things -easily, – as they come; take it easy, run on, live and let live; take -easily, – coolly, – in good part; *æquam ser- vare mentem.*

bear, – well, – the brunt; go through, support, endure, brave, disregard.

tolerate, suffer, stand, bide; abide, aby; bear –, put up –, abide- with; acquiesce; submit &c. (*yield*) 725; submit with a good grace; resign –, reconcile- oneself to; brook, digest, eat, swallow, pocket, stomach; make -light of, – the best of, – a virtue of necessity; put a good face on, keep one's countenance; carry -on, – through; check &c. 751- oneself.

compose, appease &c. (*moderate*) 174; propitiate; repress &c. (*restrain*) 751; render insensible &c. 823; over- come –, allay –, repress- one's -excit- ability &c. 825; master one's feelings.

make -oneself, – one's mind- easy; set one's mind at -ease, – rest.

calm –, cool- down; thaw, grow cool.

be -borne, – endured; go down.

Adj. in-, un-excitable; imperturbable; unsusceptible &c. (*insensible*) 823; un-, dis-passionate; cold-blooded, inirri- table; enduring &c. *v.*; stoical, Platonic, philosophic, staid, stayed; sober, – minded; grave; sober –, grave- as a judge; sedate, demure, cool-, level- headed; steady.

easy-going, peaceful, placid, calm; quiet, – as a mouse; tranquil, serene;

bulent, tempestuous, tumultuary, bois-terous.

impulsive, impetuous, passionate; uncontroll-ed, -able; ungovernable, irrepressible, stanchless, inextinguishable, burning, simmering, volcanic, ready to burst forth.

excit-ed, -ing &c. 824.

Int. pish! pshaw!

Phr. noli me tangere.

cool, – as -a cucumber, – custard; undemonstrative.

temperate &c. (moderate) 174; composed, collected; un-excited, -stirred, -ruffled, -disturbed, -perturbed, -impassioned; unoffended; unresisting.

meek, tolerant; patient, – as Job; submissive &c. 725; tame; content, resigned, chastened, subdued, lamb-like; gentle, – as a lamb; suaviter in modo; mild, – as mother's milk; soft as peppermint; armed with patience, bearing with, clement, forbearant, long-suffering.

Adv. 'like patience on a monument smiling at grief'; æquo animo, in cold blood &c. 823; more in sorrow than in anger.

Int. patience! and shuffle the cards.

Section II. PERSONAL AFFECTIONS*

1°. Passive Affections

827. Pleasure.—N. pleasure, gratification, enjoyment, fruition; ob-, delectation; relish, zest; gusto &c. (physical pleasure) 377; satisfaction &c. (content) 831; complacency.

well-being; good &c. 618; snugness, comfort, ease; cushion &c. 215; sans souci, mind at ease.

joy, gladness, delight, glee, cheer, sunshine; cheerfulness &c. 836.

treat, refreshment; frolic, fun, lark, gambol, merry-making; amusement &c. 840; luxury &c. 377; hedonism.

mens sana in corpore sano.

happiness, felicity, bliss; beati-tude, -fication; enchantment, transport, rapture, ravishment, ecstasy; summum bonum; paradise, elysium &c. (heaven) 981; third –, seventh- heaven; unalloyed -happiness &c.

honeymoon; palmy –, halcyon- days; golden -age, – time; Saturnia regna, Eden, Arcadia, happy valley, Agapemone; Cockaigne.

V. be pleased &c. 829; feel –, experience- pleasure &c. n.; joy; enjoy –, hug- oneself; be in -clover &c. 377, – elysium &c. 981; tread on enchanted ground; fall –, go- into raptures.

feel at home, breathe freely, bask in the sunshine.

be -pleased &c. 829- with; receive –, derive- pleasure &c. n.- from; take -pleasure &c. n.- in; delight in, rejoice

828. Pain. — N. mental suffering, pain, dolour; suffer-ing, -ance; ache, smart &c. (physical pain) 378; passion.

displeasure, dissatisfaction, discomfort, discomposure, disquiet; malaise; inquietude, uneasiness, vexation of spirit; taking; discontent &c. 832.

dejection &c. 837; weariness &c. 841.

annoyance, irritation, worry, infliction, visitation; plague, bore; bother, -ation; stew, vexation, mortification, chagrin, esclandre; mauvais quart d'heure.

care, anxiety, solicitude, trouble, trial, ordeal, fiery ordeal, shock, blow, cark, dole, fret, burden, load.

concern, grief, sorrow, distress, affliction, woe, bitterness, gloom, heartache; heavy –, aching –, bleeding –, broken-heart; heavy affliction, gnawing grief.

unhappiness, infelicity, misery, tribulation, wretchedness, desolation; despair &c. 859; extremity, prostration, depth of misery.

nightmare, ephialtes, incubus.

anguish, agony; throe, tor-ture, -ment; crucifixion, martyrdom; pang, twinge, stab; the rack, the stake; purgatory &c. (hell) 982.

hell upon earth; iron age, reign of terror; slough of despond &c. (adversity) 735; peck –, sea- of troubles; ills that flesh is heir to &c. (evil) 619;

* Or those which concern one's own state of feeling.

in, indulge in, luxuriate in; gloat over &c. (*physical pleasure*) 377; enjoy, relish, like; love &c. 897; take -to, – a fancy to; have a liking for; enter into the spirit of.

take in good part.

treat oneself to, solace oneself with.

Adj. pleased &c. 829; not sorry; glad, -some; pleased as Punch.

happy, blest, blessed, blissful, beatified; happy as -a king, – the day is long; thrice happy, *ter quaterque beatus*; enjoying &c. *v.*; joyful &c. (*in spirits*) 836; hedonic.

in -a blissful state, – paradise &c. 981, – raptures, – ecstasies, – a transport of delight; rapturous.

comfortable &c. (*physical pleasure*) 377; at ease; content &c. 831; *sans souci*, in clover.

overjoyed, entranced, enchanted; enraptured; en-, ravished; transported; fascinated, captivated.

with -a joyful face, – sparkling eyes.

pleasing &c. 829; ecstatic, beat-ic, -ific; painless, unalloyed, without alloy, cloudless.

Adv. happily &c. *adj.*; with pleasure &c. (*willingly*) 602; with -glee &c. *n.*

Phr. one's heart leaping with joy.

———

miseries of human life; unkindest cut of all.

sufferer, victim, prey, martyr, object of compassion, wretch, shorn lamb.

V. feel –, suffer –, experience –, undergo –, bear –, endure- pain &c. *n.*; smart, ache &c. (*physical pain*) 378; suffer, bleed, ail; be the victim of; bear –, take up- the cross.

labour under afflictions; quaff the bitter cup, have a bad time of it; fall on evil days &c. (*adversity*) 735; go hard with, come to grief, fall a sacrifice to, drain the cup of misery to the dregs, sup full of horrors.

sit on thorns, be on pins and needles, wince, fret, chafe, worry oneself, be in a taking, fret and fume, take -on, – to heart.

grieve; mourn &c. (*lament*) 839; yearn, repine, pine, droop, languish, sink; give way; despair &c. 859; break one's heart; weigh upon the heart &c. (*inflict pain*) 830.

Adj. in –, in a state of –, full of- pain &c. *n.*; suffering &c. *v.*; pained, afflicted, worried, displeased &c. 830; aching, griped, sore &c. (*physical pain*) 378; on the rack, in limbo; between hawk and buzzard.

un-comfortable, -easy; ill at ease; in a -taking, – way; disturbed; discontented &c. 832; out of humour &c. 901*a*; weary &c. 841.

heavy laden, stricken, crushed, a prey to, victimized, ill-used.

unfortunate &c. (*hapless*) 735; to be pitied, doomed, devoted, accursed, undone, lost, stranded.

unhappy, infelicitous, poor, wretched, miserable, woe-begone; cheerless &c. (*dejected*) 837; careworn.

concerned, sorry; sorrow-ing, -ful; cut up, chagrined, horrified, horror-stricken; in –, plunged in –, a prey to- grief &c. *n.*; in tears &c. (*lamenting*) 839; steeped to the lips in misery; heart-stricken, -broken, -scalded; broken-hearted; in despair &c. 859.

Phr. 'the iron entered into the soul'; '*hæret lateri lethalis arundo*'; one's heart bleeding.

829. [Capability of giving pleasure; cause or source of pleasure.] **Pleasurableness.**—**N.** pleasurable-, pleasant-, agreeable-ness &c. *adj.*; pleasure giving, jocundity, delectability; amusement &c. 840.

attraction &c. (*motive*) 615; attractiveness, -ability; invitingness &c. *adj.*; charm, fascination, captivation, en-

830. [Capability of giving pain; cause or source of pain.] **Painfulness.**—**N.** painfulness &c. *adj.*; trouble, care &c. (*pain*) 828; trial; af-, in-fliction; cross, blow, stroke, burden, load, curse; bitter -pill, – draught, – cup; waters of bitterness.

annoyance, grievance, nuisance, vexation, mortification, sickener; bore,

chantment, witchery, seduction, winsomeness, winning ways, amenity, amiability, sweetness.

loveliness &c. (*beauty*) 845; sunny –, bright- side; sweets &c. (*sugar*) 396; goodness &c. 648; manna in the wilderness, land flowing with milk and honey.

treat; regale &c. (*physical pleasure*) 377; dainty; tit-, tid-bit; nuts, *sauce piquante.*

V. cause –, produce –, create –, give –, afford –, procure –, offer –, present –, yield- pleasure &c. 827.

please, charm, delight; gladden &c. (*make cheerful*) 836; take, captivate, fascinate; enchant, entrance, enrapture, transport, bewitch; en-, ravish.

bless, beatify; satisfy; gratify, – desire &c. 865; slake, satiate, quench; indulge, humour, flatter, tickle; tickle the palate &c. (*savoury*) 394; regale, refresh; enliven; treat; amuse &c. 840; take –, tickle –, hit- one's fancy; meet one's wishes; win –, gladden –, rejoice –, warm the cockles of- the heart; do one's heart good.

attract, allure &c. (*move*) 615; stimulate &c. (*excite*) 824; interest, intrigue.

make things pleasant, popularize, gild the pill, sweeten.

Adj. causing pleasure &c. v.; pleasure-giving; pleas-ing, -ant, -urable; agreeable, cushy; grat-eful, -ifying; leef, lief, acceptable; welcome, – as the roses in May; welcomed; favourite; to one's -taste, – mind, – liking, – heart's content; satisfactory &c. (*good*) 648.

refreshing; comfortable; cordial; genial; glad, -some; sweet, delectable, nice, dainty; delic-ate, -ious; dulcet; luscious &c. 396; palatable &c. 394; luxurious, voluptuous; sensual &c. 377.

attractive &c. 615; inviting, prepossessing, engaging; win-ning, -some; taking, fascinating, captivating, killing; seduc-ing, -tive; alluring, enticing; appetizing &c. (*exciting*) 824; cheering &c. 836; bewitching; interesting, absorbing, enchanting, entrancing, enravishing.

charming; delightful, felicitous, exquisite; lovely &c. (*beautiful*) 845;

bother, pother, hot water, sea of troubles, hornet's nest, plague, pest.

cancer, ulcer, sting, thorn; canker &c. (*bane*) 663; scorpion &c. (*evil-doer*) 913; dagger &c. (*arms*) 727; scourge &c. (*instrument of punishment*) 975; carking –, canker worm of- care.

mishap, misfortune &c. (*adversity*) 735; désagrément, esclandre, rub.

source of -irritation, – annoyance; wound, sore subject, skeleton in the closet; thorn in -the flesh, – one's side; where the shoe pinches, gall and wormwood.

sorry sight, heavy news, provocation; affront &c. 929; head and front of one's offending.

infestation, molestation; malignity &c. (*malevolence*) 907; acrimony.

V. cause –, occasion –, give –, bring –, induce –, produce –, create –, inflict- pain &c. 828; pain, hurt, wound.

pinch, prick, gripe &c. (*physical pain*) 378; pierce, lancinate, cut.

hurt –, wound –, grate upon –, jar upon- the feelings; wring –, pierce –, lacerate –, break –, rend- the heart; make the heart bleed; tear –, rend- the heart-strings; draw tears from the eyes.

sadden; make -unhappy &c. 828; plunge into sorrow, grieve, fash, afflict, distress; cut -up, – to the heart.

displease, annoy, incommode, discommode, discompose, trouble, disquiet, disturb, thwart, cross, perplex, molest, tease, rag, tire, irk, vex, mortify, wherret, worry, plague, bother, pester, bore, pother, harass, harry, badger, heckle, bait, beset, infest, persecute, importune, be troublesome.

wring, harrow, torment, torture; put to the -rack, – question; break on the wheel, rack, scarify; cruci-ate, -fy; convulse, agonize; barb the dart; plant a -dagger in the breast, – thorn in one's side.

irritate, provoke, sting, nettle, try the patience, pique, fret, rile, tweak the nose, chafe, gall; sting –, wound –, cut- to the quick; aggrieve, affront, enchafe, enrage, ruffle, sour the temper; give offence &c. (*resentment*) 900.

ravishing, rapturous; heartfelt, thrilling, ecstatic; beat-ic, -ific; seraphic; empyrean; elysian &c. (*heavenly*) 981. palmy, halcyon, Saturnian.

Phr. *decies repetita placebit.*

---

maltreat, bite, snap at, assail, bully; smite &c. (*punish*) 972.

sicken, disgust, revolt, nauseate, disenchant, repel, offend, shock, stink in the nostrils; go against –, turn- the stomach; make one sick, set the teeth on edge, go against the grain, grate on the ear; stick in one's -throat, – gizzard; rankle, gnaw, corrode, horrify, appal, freeze the blood; chill the spine; make the -flesh creep, – hair stand on end; make the blood -curdle, – run cold; make one shudder.

haunt, – the memory; weigh –, prey- on the -heart, – mind, – spirits; bring one's grey hairs with sorrow to the grave; add a nail to one's coffin.

Adj. causing pain, hurting &c. *v.*; hurtful &c. (*bad*) 649; painful; dolor-ific, -ous; unpleasant; un-, dis-pleasing; disagreeable, unpalatable, bitter, distasteful; uninviting; unwelcome; undesir-able, -ed; obnoxious; unacceptable, unpopular, thankless.

unsatisfactory, untoward, unlucky, uncomfortable.

distressing; afflict-ing, -ive; joy-, cheer-, comfort-less; dismal, disheartening; depress-ing, -ive; dreary, melancholy, grievous, piteous; woeful, rueful, mournful, deplorable, pitiable, lamentable; sad, affecting, touching, pathetic.

irritating, provoking, stinging, annoying, aggravating, mortifying, galling; unaccommodating, invidious, vexatious; trouble-, tire-, irk-, weari-some; plagu-ing, -y; awkward.

importunate; teas-, pester-, bother-, harass-, worry-, torment-, cark-ing.

in-toler-, -suffer-, -support-able; un-bear-, -endur-able; past bearing; not to be -borne, – endured; more than flesh and blood can bear; enough to -drive one mad, – provoke a saint, – make a parson swear, – try the patience of Job.

shocking, terrific, grim, appalling, crushing; dreadful, fearful, frightful; thrilling, tremendous, dire; heart-breaking, -rending, -wounding, -corroding, -sickening; harrowing, rending.

odious, hateful, execrable, repulsive, repellent, abhorrent; horri-d, -ble, -fic, -fying; offensive; nause-ous, -ating; disgust-, sicken-, revolt-ing; nasty; loath-some, -ful; fulsome; vile &c. (*bad*) 649; hideous &c. 846.

sharp, acute, sore, severe, grave, hard, harsh, cruel, biting, acrimonious, caustic; cutting, corroding, consuming, racking, excruciating, searching, searing, grinding, grating, agonizing; envenomed.

ruinous, disastrous, calamitous, tragical; desolating, withering; burdensome, onerous, oppressive; cumb-rous, -ersome.

Adv. painfully &c. *adj.*; with -pain &c. 828; deuced.

Int. *hinc illæ lachrymæ!* woe is me!

Phr. *surgit amari aliquid*; the place being too hot to hold one; the iron entering into the soul.

---

831. Content.—**N.** content, -ment, -edness; complacency, satisfaction, entire satisfaction, ease, heart's ease, peace of mind; serenity &c. 826; cheer-

832. Discontent. — **N.** discontent, -ment; dissatisfaction; dissent &c. 489; labour unrest.

disappointment, mortification; cold

fulness &c. 836; ray of comfort; comfort &c. (*well-being*) 827.

re-, conciliation; resignation &c. (*patience*) 826.

waiter on Providence.

V. be -content &c. *adj.*; rest -satisfied, – and be thankful; take the good the gods provide, let well alone, feel oneself at home, hug oneself, lay the flattering unction to one's soul.

take -up with, – in good part; assent &c. 488; be reconciled to, make one's peace with; get over it; take -heart, – comfort; put up with &c. (*bear*) 826.

render -content &c. *adj.*; set at ease, comfort; set one's -heart, – mind- at -ease, – rest; speak peace; conciliate, reconcile, win over, propitiate, disarm, beguile; content, satisfy; gratify &c. 829.

be -tolerated &c. 826; go down, – with; do.

Adj. content, -ed; satisfied &c. *v.*; at -ease, – one's ease, – home; with the mind at ease, *sans souci, sine curâ*, easy-going, not particular; conciliatory; unrepining, of good comfort; resigned &c. (*patient*) 826; cheerful &c. 836.

un-afflicted, -vexed, -molested, -plagued; serene &c. 826; at rest; snug, comfortable; in one's element.

satisfactory, satisfying, ample, sufficient, adequate, tolerable.

Adv. to one's heart's content; *à la bonne heure*; all for the best.

Int. amen &c. (*assent*) 488; very well, so much the better, well and good; it -, that- will do; it cannot be helped.

Phr. nothing comes amiss.

---

comfort; regret &c. 833; repining, taking on &c. *v.*; inquietude, vexation of spirit, soreness; heart-burning, -grief; querulousness &c. (*lamentation*) 839; hypercriticism.

malcontent, grumbler, growler, croaker, *laudator temporis acti*; censurer, complainer, faultfinder, murmurer, Adullamite, Diehard, Bitterender.

the Opposition, cave of Adullam, indignation meeting, 'winter of our discontent.'

V. be -discontented &c. *adj.*; quarrel with one's bread and butter; repine; regret &c. 833; wish one at the bottom of the Red Sea; take -on, – to heart; shrug the shoulders; make a wry -, pull a long- face; knit one's brows; look -blue, – black, – black as thunder, – blank, – glum.

take -in bad part, – ill; fret, chafe, make a piece of work; grumble, croak, grouse; lament &c. 839.

cause -discontent &c. *n.*; dissatisfy, disappoint, mortify, put out, disconcert; cut up; dishearten.

Adj. discontented; dissatisfied &c. *v.*; unsatisfied, ungratified; dissident; dissentient &c. 489; malcontent, exigent, exacting, hypercritical.

repining &c. *v.*; regretful &c. 833; down in the mouth &c. (*dejected*) 837.

in -high dudgeon, – a fume, – the sulks, – the dumps, – bad humour; glum, sulky; sour, – as a crab; soured, sore; out of -humour, – temper.

disappointing &c. *v.*; unsatisfactory.

Int. so much the worse!

Phr. that –, it- will never do.

---

833. Regret.—**N.** regret, repining; home sickness, nostalgia; *mal –, maladie-du pays*; lamentation &c. 839, contrition, compunction, penitence &c. 950.

bitterness, heart-burning.

laudator temporis acti &c. (*discontent*) 832.

V. regret, deplore; bewail &c. (*lament*) 839; repine, cast a longing lingering look behind; rue, – the day; repent &c. 950; *infandum renovare dolorem*.

prey -, weigh -, have a weight- on the mind; leave an aching void.

Adj. regretting &c. *v.*; regretful; home-sick.

regretted &c. *v.*; much to be regretted, regrettable; lamentable &c. (*bad*) 649.

Int. what a pity! hang it!
Phr. 'tis -pity, – too true.

834. Relief.—N. relief; deliverance; refreshment &c. 689; easement, softening, alleviation, mitigation, palliation &c. 174; soothing, lullaby; cradle song, *berceuse.*

solace, consolation, comfort, encouragement.

lenitive, restorative &c. (*remedy*) 662; poultice &c. *v.*; cushion &c. 215; crumb of comfort, balm in Gilead; aspirin.

V. relieve, ease, alleviate, mitigate, palliate, soothe, addulce; salve; soften, – down; foment, stupe, poultice; assuage, allay.

cheer, comfort, console; encourage, bear up, pat on the back, give comfort, set at ease; enliven, gladden –, cheer-the heart.

remedy; cure &c. (*restore*) 660; refresh; pour -balm into, – oil on.

smooth the ruffled brow of care, temper the wind to the shorn lamb, lay the flattering unction to one's soul.

disburden &c. (*free*) 705; take off a load of care.

be relieved; breathe more freely, draw a long breath; take comfort; dry –, wipe- the -tears, – eyes.

Adj. relieving &c. *v.*; consolatory, soothing; assua-ging, -sive; bal-my, -samic; lenitive, palliative; anodyne &c. (*remedial*) 662; curative &c. 660.

835. Aggravation.—N. aggravation, heightening; exacerbation; exasperation; overestimation &c. 482; exaggeration &c. 549.

V. aggravate, render worse, heighten, embitter, sour; ex-, acerbate; exasperate, envenom; tease, provoke, enrage.

add fuel to the -fire, – flame; fan the flame &c. (*excite*) 824; go from bad to worse &c. (*deteriorate*) 659.

Adj. aggravated &c. *v.*; worse, unrelieved; aggravable; aggravating &c. *v.*

Adv. out of the frying pan into the fire, from bad to worse, worse and worse.

Int. so much the worse!

_____

836. Cheerfulness.—N. cheerfulness &c. *adj.*; geniality, gaiety, *l'allegro*, cheer, good humour, spirits; high –, animal –, flow of- spirits; glee, high glee, light heart; sunshine of the -mind, – breast; *gaieté de cœur, bon naturel.*

liveliness &c. *adj.*; life, alacrity, vivacity, animation, *allégresse*; jocundity, joviality, jollity; levity; jocularity &c. (*wit*) 842.

mirth, merriment, hilarity, exhilaration; laughter &c. 838; merry-making &c. (*amusement*) 840; heyday, rejoicing &c. 838; marriage bells.

nepenthe, Euphrosyne.

optimism &c. (*hopefulness*) 858; self-complacency.

V. be -cheerful &c. *adj.*; have the mind at ease, smile, put a good face upon, keep up one's spirits; view -the bright side of the picture, – things *en couleur de rose*; *ridentem dicere verum,*

837. Dejection.—N. dejection; dejectedness &c. *adj.*; depression, prosternation; lowness –, depression- of spirits; weight –, oppression –, damp-on the spirits; low –, bad –, drooping –, depressed- spirits; heart sinking; heaviness –, failure- of heart.

heaviness &c. *adj.*; infestivity, gloom; weariness &c. 841; *tædium vitæ*, disgust of life; *mal du pays* &c. (*regret*) 833.

melancholy; sadness &c. *adj.*; *il penseroso, melancholia*, dismals, mumps, mopes, lachrymals, dumps, blues, blue devils, doldrums, vapours, megrims, spleen, horrors, hypochondriasis, pessimism; despondency, slough of Despond; disconsolateness &c. *adj.*; hope deferred, blank despondency.

prostration, – of soul; broken heart; despair &c. 859; cave of -despair, – Trophonius.

cheer up, brighten up, light up, bear
up; chirp, take heart, cast away care,
drive dull care away, perk up.

rejoice &c. 838; carol, chirrup, lilt;
frisk, rollick, give a loose to mirth.

cheer, enliven, elate, exhilarate, gladden, inspirit, animate, raise the spirits,
inspire; put in good humour; cheer —,
rejoice- the heart; delight &c. (*give
pleasure*) 829.

Adj. cheerful; happy &c. 827; cheer-
y, -ly; of good cheer, smiling; blithe;
in —, in good- spirits; in high -spirits, —
feather; happy as -the day is long, — a
king; gay, — as a lark; *allegro*; light,
-some, -hearted; buoyant, *débonnaire*,
bright, free and easy, airy; janty,
jaunty, canty; spright-ly, -ful; spry;
spirit-ed, -ful; lively; animated, breezy,
vivacious; brisk, — as a bee; sparkling;
sportive; full of -play, — spirit; all alive.

sunny, palmy; hopeful &c. 858.

merry, — as a -cricket, — grig, — marriage bell; joyful, joyous, jocund,
jovial; jolly, — as a thrush, — as a sand-
boy; blithesome; glee-ful, -some; hilari-
ous, rattling.

winsome, bonny, hearty, buxom.

play-ful, -some; *folâtre*, playful as a
kitten, tricksy, frisky, frolicsome;
gamesome; jocose, jocular, waggish;
mirth-, laughter-loving; mirthful, rollicking.

elate, -d; exulting, jubilant, flushed;
rejoicing &c. 838; cock-a-hoop.

cheering, inspiriting, exhilarating;
cardiac, -al; pleasing &c. 829; flourish-
ing, halcyon.

Adv. cheerfully &c. *adj.*

Int. never say die! come! cheer up!
hurrah! &c. 838; 'hence loathed melancholy!' begone dull care! away with
melancholy!

demureness &c. *adj.*; gravity, solemnity; long —, grave- face.

hypochondriac, seek-sorrow, self-tor-
mentor, *heautontimorumenos*, *malade
imaginaire*, *médecin tant pis*; croaker,
pessimist; mope, mopus.

[Cause of dejection] affliction &c.
830; sorry sight; *memento mori*; damper,
wet blanket, Job's comforter; death's
head, skeleton at the feast.

V. be -dejected &c. *adj.*; grieve;
mourn &c. (*lament*) 839; take on, give
way, lose heart, despond, droop, sink.

lower, look downcast, frown, pout;
hang down the head; pull —, make- a
long face; laugh on the wrong side of
the mouth; grin a ghastly smile; look
-blue, — like a drowned man; lay —,
take- to heart.

mope, brood over; fret; sulk; pine,
— away; yearn; repine &c. (*regret*) 833;
despair &c. 859.

refrain from laughter, keep one's
countenance; be —, look- grave &c. *adj.*;
repress a smile, keep a straight face.

depress; dis-courage, -hearten; dispirit; damp, dull, deject, lower, sink,
dash, knock down, unman, prostrate,
break one's heart; frown upon; cast a
-gloom, — shade- on; sadden; damp —,
dash —, wither- one's hopes; weigh —,
lie heavy —, prey- on the -mind, —
spirits; damp —, depress- the spirits.

Adj. cheer-, joy-, spirit-less; uncheer-
ful, -y; unlively; unhappy &c. 828;
melancholy, dismal, sombre, dark,
gloomy, adust, *triste*, clouded, murky,
lowering, frowning, lugubrious, Acherontic, funereal, mournful, lamentable,
dreadful.

dreary, flat; dull, — as -a beetle, -
ditchwater; depressing &c. *v.*

'melancholy as a gib cat'; oppressed
with —, a prey to- melancholy; downcast, -hearted; down -in the mouth, —
on one's luck; heavy-hearted; in the
-dumps, — suds, — sulks, — doldrums; in doleful dumps, in bad
humour; sullen; mumpish, dumpish; mopish, moping; moody, glum;
sulky &c. (*discontented*) 832; out of -sorts, — humour, — heart,
— spirits; ill at ease, low-spirited, in low spirits, a cup too low;
weary &c. 841; dis-couraged, -heartened; desponding; chop-, jaw-,
crest-fallen.

sad, pensive, *penseroso*, tristful; dole-some, -ful; woebegone,
lachrymose, in tears, melancholic, hipped, hypochondriacal, bil-

ious, jaundiced, atrabilious, saturnine, splenetic; lackadaisical.

serious, sedate, staid, stayed; grave, – as -a judge, – an undertaker, – a mustard pot; sober, solemn, demure; grim; grim-faced, -visaged; rueful, wan, long-faced.

disconsolate; un-, in-consolable; forlorn, comfortless, desolate, *désolé*, sick at heart; soul-, heart-sick; *au désespoir*; in despair &c. 859; lost.

overcome; broken-, borne-, bowed-down; heart-stricken &c. (*mental suffering*) 828; cut up, dashed, sunk; unnerved, unmanned; down-fallen, -trodden; broken-hearted; care-worn.

Adv. with -a long face, – tears in one's eyes; sadly &c. *adj.*

Phr. the countenance falling; the heart -failing, – sinking within-one.

838. [Expression of pleasure.] **Rejoicing.—N.** rejoicing, exultation, triumph, jubilation, heyday, flush, revelling; merry-making &c. (*amusement*) 840; jubilee &c. (*celebration*) 883; pæan, *Te Deum* &c. (*thanksgiving*) 990; congratulation &c. 896; applause &c. 931.

smile, simper, smirk, grin; broad –, sardonic- grin.

laughter, giggle, titter, crow, cheer, chuckle, snicker, snigger, shout; Homeric laughter, horse –, hearty- laugh; guffaw; burst –, fit –, shout –, roar –, peal- of laughter; cachinnation.

risibility; derision &c. 856.

Momus; Democritus the Abderite; rollicker; Laughter holding both his sides.

V. rejoice; thank –, bless- one's stars; congratulate –, hug- oneself; rub –, clap- one's hands; smack the lips, fling up one's cap; dance, skip, caleer; sing, carol, chirrup, chirp; hurrah; cry for –, leap with- joy; exult &c. (*boast*) 884; triumph; hold jubilee &c. (*celebrate*) 883; make merry &c. (*sport*) 840; sing a pæan of joy.

smile, simper, smirk; grin, – like a Cheshire cat; mock, laugh in one's sleeve; laugh, – outright; giggle, titter, snigger, crow, smicker, chuckle, snicker, cackle; burst -out, – into a fit of laughter; shout, split, roar.

shake –, split –, hold both- one's sides; roar –, die- with laughter.

raise laughter &c. (*amuse*) 840.

Adj. rejoicing &c. *v.*; jubilant, exultant, triumphant; flushed, elated; laughing &c. *v.*; risible; ready to -burst, – split, – die with laughter; convulsed with laughter.

839. [Expression of pain.] **Lamentation.—N.** lament, -ation; wail, complaint, plaint, murmur, mutter, grumble, groan, moan, whine, whimper, sob, sigh, suspiration, heaving, deep sigh.

cry &c. (*vociferation*) 411; scream, howl; outcry, wail of woe, frown, scowl.

tear; weeping &c. *v.*; flood of tears, fit of crying, lachrymation, melting mood, weeping and gnashing of teeth.

plaintiveness &c. *adj.*; languishment; condolence &c. 915.

mourning, weeds, willow, cypress, crêpe, crape, deep mourning; sackcloth and ashes; knell &c. 363; dump, deathsong, dirge, coronach, keen, *nenia*, requiem, elegy, *epicedium*; threne; mon-, thren-ody; jeremiad; ululation.

mourner, professional mourner, keener; grumbler &c. (*discontent*) 832; Niobe; Heraclitus.

V. lament, mourn, deplore, grieve, weep over; be-wail, -moan; keen; con- dole with &c. 915; fret &c. (*suffer*) 828; wear –, go into –, put on- mourning; wear -the willow, – sackcloth and ashes; *infandum renovare dolorem* &c. (*regret*) 833; give sorrow words.

sigh; give –, heave –, fetch- a sigh; 'waft a sigh from Indus to the pole'; sigh 'like furnace'; wail.

cry, weep, sob, greet, blubber, pipe, snivel, bibber, whimper, pule; pipe one's eye; drop –, shed- -tears, – a tear; melt –, burst- into tears; *fondre en larmes*; cry -oneself blind, – one's eyes out.

scream &c. (*cry out*) 411; mew &c. (*animal sounds*) 412; groan, moan,

laughable &c. (*ludicrous*) 853.
Int. hip, hip, -hurrah! huzza! aha!
hail! tolderolloll! tra-la la! Heaven be
praised! *io triumphe! tant mieux!* so
much the better.
Phr. the heart leaping with joy.

———

cry out before one is hurt, complain without cause.

whine, yammer; roar; roar -, bellow-
like a bull; cry out lustily, rend the
air, yell.

frown, scowl, make a wry face, grimace, gnash one's teeth, wring one's
hands, tear one's hair, beat one's breast,
roll on the ground, burst with grief.

complain, murmur, mutter, grumble,
growl, clamour, make a fuss about,
croak, grunt, maunder; deprecate &c.
(*disapprove*) 932.

Adj. lamenting &c. *v.*; in mourning, in sackcloth and ashes;
crying, sorrowing, -ful &c. (*unhappy*) 828; mourn-, tear-ful; lachrymose; plaint-ive, -ful, quer-ulous, -imonious; in the melting mood.

in tears, with tears in one's eyes; with -moistened, - watery-
eyes; bathed -, dissolved- in tears; 'like Niobe all tears.'

elagiac, epicedial, threnetic.

Adv. *de profundis; les larmes aux yeux.*

Int. heigh-ho! alas! alack! O dear! ah -, woe is- me! lackadaisy!
well -, lack -, alack- a day! well-a-way! alas the day! *O tempora!
O mores!* what a pity! *miserabile dictu!* O lud lud! too true!

Phr. tears -standing in, - starting from- the eyes; eyes -suffused,
- swimming, - brimming -, overflowing- with tears.

---

840. Amusement.—N. amuse-, entertain-ment; diver-sion, -tissement;
recreation, relaxation, solace; pastime,
passetemps, sport; labour of love;
pleasure &c. 827.

fun, frolic, merriment, whoopee,
jollity; jovial-ity, -ness; heyday; laughter &c. 838; jocos-ity, -eness; droll-,
buffoon-, tomfool-ery; mummery, mas-
quing, pleasantry; wit &c. 842; quip,
quirk.

play; game, - at romps; gambol,
romp, prank, antic, rig, lark, spree,
skylarking, vagary, trick, monkey
trick, *gambade, fredaine, escapade,
échappée,* bout, *espièglerie;* practical
joke &c. (*ridicule*) 856.

dance; round -, square -, solo -,
step -, tap -, clog -, skirt -, sand -,
folk -, morris- dance, *pas seul,* step,
turn, *chassé,* cut, shuffle, double shuffle;
hop, reel, rigadoon, saraband, horn-
pipe, bolero, fandango, pavan, tar-
antella, minuet, waltz, polka; galop,
-ade; schottische, *pas de quatre,* Boston,
one-, two-step, rumba, tango, maxixe,
fox-, turkey-trot, shimmy, ragtime,
cakewalk, jazz, blues, Charleston; jig,
breakdown, fling, strathspey; *alle-*

841. Weariness.—N. weariness, defatigation, boredom, *ennui;* lassitude
&c. (*fatigue*) 688; drowsiness &c. 683.

disgust, nausea, loathing, sickness;
satiety &c. 869; *tædium vitæ* &c.
(*dejection*) 837.

wearisome-, tedious-ness &c. *adj.;*
dull work, tedium, monotony, twice
told tale.

bore, button-holer, proser, wet blanket; heavy hours, 'the enemy' [time].

V. weary; tire &c. (*fatigue*) 688;
bore; bore -, weary -, tire- -to death,
- out of one's life, - out of all patience;
set -, send- to sleep; buttonhole.

pall, sicken, nauseate, disgust.

harp on the same string; drag its
-slow, - weary- length along.

never hear the last of; be -tired &c.
adj. -of, - with; yawn; die with *ennui.*

Adj. wearying &c. *v.*; wearing;
weari-, tire-, irk-some; uninteresting,
stupid, bald, devoid of interest, dry,
monotonous, dull, arid, tedious, humdrum, mortal, flat; pros-y, -ing; slow;
soporific, somniferous, dormitive.

disgusting &c. *v.*; unenjoyed.

weary; tired &c. *v.*; drowsy &c.
(*sleepy*) 683; uninterested, flagging,

mande; gavot, -te; mazurka, morisco; quadrille, lancers, country dance, *co- tillon*, polonaise, Sir Roger de Coverley, Swedish dance; *ballet* &c. (*drama*) 599; ball; *bal, – masqué, – costumé*; masquer- ade, fancy dress ball; *thé dansant*; Terpsichore, choreography, Russian ballet, classical dancing; eurythmics; nautch dance, *danse du ventre*, cancan.

festivity, merry-making; party &c. (*social gathering*) 892; *fête*, festival, gala, *ridotto*; revel-s, -ry, -ling; carnival, brawl, saturnalia, high jinks; feast, banquet &c. (*food*) 298; regale, *symposium*, wassail; carous-e, -al; jollification, junket, wake, picnic, *fête champêtre*, garden party, gymkhana, regatta, track meet, field- day, jamboree, treat.

round of pleasures, dissipation, a short life and a merry one, racketing, holiday making, high jinks.

rejoicing &c. 838; jubilee &c. (*celebration*) 883.

bonfire, fireworks, *feu-de-joie*, rocket, Catherine wheel, roman candle &c.

holiday; gala –, red letter –, play- day; high days and holidays; high –, Bank- holiday; May –, Derby- day; Saint –, Easter –, Whit- Monday; King's birthday, Empire Day; *mi-carême*; *Bairam*; wayzgoose, beanfeast, beano.

place of amusement, theatre &c. 599; concert-, ball-, assembly- room; music-hall, cinema, movies, talkies, vaudeville; hippodrome, circus, rodeo; *casino, kursaal*; winter garden; park, pleasance, arbour; garden &c. 371; pleasure-, play-, cricket-, football-, polo-, croquet-, archery-, hunting-ground; golf links, race course, stadium, gridiron, bowl, speedway, racing track, ring; gymnasium, swimming pool; shooting gallery; tennis-, racket-court; bowling-green, -alley; croquet-lawn, rink, skating rink; roller-coaster, roundabout, carousel, merry-go-round; swing; *montagne russe*; switchback, scenic railway &c.

game, – of -chance, – skill; athletic sports, gymnastics; fencing; archery, rifle-shooting; tournament, pugilism &c. (*contention*) 720; sporting &c. 622; horse-racing, the turf; aquatics &c. 267; skating, roller skating; ski-running, -joring, -jumping, bobsleighing, luging, tobogganing, winter sports; sliding; cricket, tennis, lawn –, table –, deck- tennis, rackets, fives, squash, ping-pong, trap bat and ball, battledore and shuttlecock, badminton, *la grâce*; pall mall, tip-cat, croquet, golf, curling, hockey, basketball, soccer, football, Rugby, Association, *pallone*, polo; tent-pegging, tilting at the ring, quintain, greasy pole; quoits, *discus*; throwing the hammer, putting the -weight, – shot, tossing the caber; knurr and spell; leap-frog, hop, skip and jump; French and English, tug of war; blind man's buff, hunt the slipper, hide-and-seek, kiss in the ring; snapdragon; cross questions and crooked answers; jig-saw puzzle; rounders, base-ball, lacrosse &c.; angling; swimming, diving, water-polo.

billiards, pool, pyramids, snooker, bagatelle; bowls, skittles, ninepins, kail, American bowls.

cards; bridge, auction, contract, whist, rubber; round game, coon-can, loo, cribbage, *bésique*, pinocle, euchre, drole, *écarté*, skat, picquet, all-fours, quadrille, ombre, reverse, Pope Joan, commit;

used up, worn out, *blasé*, life-weary, weary of life; sick of.

Adv. wearily &c. *adj.*; *usque ad nauseam*.

Phr. time hanging heavily on one's hands; *toujours perdrix*; *crambe repetita*.

———

bo-, boa-ston; *vingt-et-un; quinze,* thirty-one, put-and-take, speculation, connections, brag, cassino, lottery, commerce, snip-snap-snorem,
lift smoke, blind hookey, Polish bank, poker, banker; faro; Earl of
Coventry, Napoleon, nap, patience, pairs; old maid, fright, beggar-
my-neighbour; *baccarat, chemin de fer, monte;* craps.

chess, draughts, backgammon, dominoes, checkers, mah jong,
merelles, nine men's morris, go-bang, solitaire; game of –, fox and-
geese; lotto; &c.*

morra; gambling &c. (*chance*) 621; roulette.

toy, plaything, bauble; doll &c. (*puppet*) 554; teetotum; knick-
knack &c. (*trifle*) 643; magic lantern &c. (*show*) 448; peep-, puppet-,
raree-, gallanty-show; marionnettes, Punch and Judy; toy-shop;
'quips and cranks and wanton wiles, nods and becks and wreathèd
smiles.'

sportsman, gamester, gambler &c. 621; reveller, master of the
-ceremonies, – revels; *arbiter elegantiarum.*

V. amuse, entertain, divert, enliven; tickle, – the fancy; titillate,
raise a smile, put in good humour; cause –, create –, occasion –,
raise –, excite –, produce –, convulse with- laughter; set the table
in a roar, be the death of one.

recreate, solace, cheer, rejoice; please &c. 829; interest; treat,
regale.

amuse oneself; game; play, – a game, – pranks, – tricks; sport,
disport, toy, wanton, revel, junket, feast, carouse, banquet, make
merry; drown care; drive dull care away; frolic, gambol, frisk,
romp; caper; dance &c. (*leap*) 309; keep up the ball; run a rig,
sow one's wild oats, have one's fling, paint the town red, take
one's pleasure; see life; *desipere in loco,* play the fool.

make –, keep- holiday; go a Maying.

while away –, beguile- the time; kill time, dally.

Adj. amusing, entertaining, diverting &c. *v.;* recreative, lusory;
pleasant &c. (*pleasing*) 829; laughable &c. (*ludicrous*) 853; witty
&c. 842; fest-ive, -al; jovial, jolly, jocund, roguish, rompish; sporting; playful, – as a kitten; sportive, ludibrious.

amused &c. *v.;* 'pleased with a feather, tickled with a straw.'

Adv. 'on the light fantastic toe,' at play, in sport.

Int. *vive la bagatelle! vogue la galère!*

Phr. *Deus nobis hæc otia fecit; dum vivimus vivamus.*

---

842. Wit.—N. wit, -tiness; attic
-wit, – salt; atticism; salt, *esprit,* point,
fancy, whim, humour, drollery, pleasantry.

farce, buffoonery, fooling, tomfoolery; harlequinade &c. 599; broad
-farce, – humour; fun, *espièglerie; vis
comica.*

jocularity; jocos-ity, -eness; face-
tiousness; wagg-ery, -ishness; whim-
sicality; comicality &c. 853.

smartness, ready wit, banter, *badi-*

843. Dulness.—N. dulness, heaviness, flatness; infestivity &c. 837;
stupidity &c. 499; want of originality,
dearth of ideas.

prose, matter of fact; heavy book,
conte à dormir debout; platitude.

V. be -dull &c. *adj.;* prose, plati-
tudinize, take *au sérieux,* be caught
napping.

render -dull &c. *adj.;* damp, depress,
throw cold water on, lay a wet blanket
on; fall flat upon the ear; hang fire.

---

* A curious list of games is given in Sir Thomas Urquhart's translation of Rabelais'
Life of Gargantua, book i. chapter 22.

nage, persiflage, retort, repartee, *quid pro quo;* ridicule &c. 856.

·*facetiæ,* quips and cranks; jest, joke, capital joke; standing -jest, – joke; conceit, quip, quirk, crank, quiddity, *concetto, plaisanterie,* brilliant idea; merry –, bright –, happy- thought; sally; flash, – of wit, – of merriment; scintillation; *mot, – pour rire;* witticism, smart saying, *bon mot, jeu d'esprit,* epigram; jest book; dry joke, *quodlibet,* cream of the jest.

word-play, *jeu de mots;* play -of, – upon- words; pun, -ning; *double entendre* &c. (*ambiguity*) 520; quibble, verbal quibble; conundrum &c. (*riddle*) 533; anagram, acrostic, double acrostic, *nugæ canoræ,* trifling, idle conceit, *turlupinade.*

old joke, Joe Miller, chestnut, hoary-headed jest.

V. joke, jest, cut jokes; crack a joke; perpetrate a -joke, – pun; make -fun of, – merry with; set the table in a roar &c. (*amuse*) 840; scintillate.

retort, flash back; banter &c. (*ridicule*) 856; *ridentem dicere verum;* joke at one's expense,

Adj. witty, attic, salty; quick-, nimble-witted; keen, clever, smart, brilliant, pungent, jocular, jocose, funny, waggish, facetious, whimsical, humorous, Gilbertian; playful &c. 840; merry and wise; pleasant, sprightly, *spirituel,* sparkling, epigrammatic, full of point, *ben trovato;* comic &c. 853.

Adv. in joke, in jest, in sport, in play.

Adj. dull, – as ditch water; dry, insipid, jejune; unentertaining, uninteresting, unlively, unimaginative; heavisome, heavy-gaited; insulse; dry as dust; pros-y, -ing, -aic; matter of fact, commonplace, banal, pointless; 'weary. flat, stale and unprofitable.'

stupid, slow, flat, sluggish, ponderous, humdrum, monotonous; melancholic &c. 837; stolid &c. 499; plodding.

Phr. *Davus sum non Œdipus.*

---

844. Humorist.—N. humorist, wag, wit, reparteeist, epigrammatist, gag-man, punster; *bel esprit,* life of the party; wit-snapper, -cracker, -worm; joker, jester, jokesmith, Joe Miller, *drôle de corps, gaillard,* spark, *persifleur,* banterer.

buffoon, *farceur,* ·merry-andrew, mime, tumbler, acrobat, mountebank, charlatan, posturemaster, harlequin, punch, *pulcinella,* scaramouch, clown; wearer of the -cap and bells, – motley; motley fool; pantaloon, gipsy; jack -pudding, – in the green, – a dandy; zany; mad-cap, pickle-herring, witling, caricaturist, *grimacier.*

2°. DISCRIMINATE AFFECTIONS

845. Beauty.—N. beauty, the beautiful, *le beau idéal,* loveliness.

[Science of the perception of beauty] Callæsthetics.*

form, elegance, grace, beauty unadorned; symmetry &c. 242; comeliness, fairness &c. *adj.;* pulchritude, polish, gloss; good -effect, – looks; *belle tournure;* bloom, brilliancy, radiance, splendour, gorgeousness, magnificence; sublimi-ty, -fication.

846. Ugliness.—N. ugliness &c. *adj.;* deformity, inelegance; disfigurement &c. (*blemish*) 848; want of symmetry, inconcinnity; distortion &c. 243; squalor &c. (*uncleanness*) 653.

forbidding countenance, vinegar aspect, hanging look, wry face, '*spretæ injuria formæ.*'

eyesore, object, figure, sight, fright, spectre, scarecrow, hag, harridan, satyr, witch, toad, baboon, monster.

* Whewell, 'Philosophy of the Inductive Sciences.'

concinnity, delicacy, refinement; charm, *je ne sais quoi*, style, *chic*, swank.

Venus, – of Milo; Aphrodite, Hebe, the Graces, Peri, Houri, Cupid, Apollo, Hyperion, Adonis, Antinous, Narcissus; Helen of Troy.

peacock, butterfly; flower, flow'ret gay, rose, lily, asphodel; garden; flower of, pink of; *bijou*; jewel &c. (*ornament*) 847; work of art.

pleasurableness &c. 829.

beautifying; landscape gardening; decoration &c. 847; calisthenics.

V. be -beautiful &c. *adj.*; shine, beam, bloom; become one &c. (*accord*) 23; set off, grace, flatter one.

render -beautiful &c. *adj.*; beautify; polish, burnish; gild &c. (*decorate*) 847; set out.

'snatch a grace beyond the reach of art.'

Adj. beaut-iful, -eous; handsome; pretty; lovely, graceful, elegant; delicate, dainty, refined, exquisite; fair, personable, comely, seemly; bonny; good-looking; well-favoured, -made, -formed, -proportioned; proper, shapely; symmetrical &c. (*regular*) 242; harmonious &c. (*colour*) 428; sightly.

fit to be seen, passable, not amiss.

goodly, dapper, tight, jimp; gimp; janty, jaunty; natty, quaint, trim, tidy, neat, spruce, smart, tricksy.

bright, -eyed; rosy-, cherry-cheeked; rosy, ruddy; blooming, in full bloom.

brilliant, shining; beam-y, -ing; sparkling, swanky, splendid, resplendent, dazzling, glowing; glossy, sleek.

showy, specious; rich, gorgeous, superb, magnificent, grand, fine, sublime, imposing; majestic 873.

artistic, -al; æsthetic; pict-uresque, -orial; *fait à peindre*, paintable; well-composed, -grouped, -varied; curious.

enchanting &c. (*pleasure-giving*) 829; attractive &c. (*inviting*) 615; becoming &c. (*accordant*) 23; ornamental &c. 847.

undeformed, undefaced, unspotted; spotless &c. (*perfect*) 650.

Caliban, Æsop, '*monstrum horrendum informe ingens cui lumen ademptum.*'

V. be -ugly &c. *adj.*; look ill, grin horribly a ghastly smile, make faces.

render -ugly &c. *adj.*; deface; dis-, de-figure; deform, spoil, distort &c. 243; blemish &c. (*injure*) 659; soil &c. (*render unclean*) 653.

Adj. ugly, – as -sin, – a toad, – a scarecrow, – a dead monkey; plain, bald &c. 226; homely &c. (*unadorned*) 849; ordinary, unornamental, inartistic; unsightly, unseemly, uncomely, unshapely, unlovely; sightless, seemless; not fit to be seen; unbeaut-eous, -iful; beautiless; shapeless &c. (*amorphous*) 241; course; garish, over-decorated &c. 882.

mis-shapen, -proportioned; monstrous; gaunt &c. (*thin*) 203; dumpy &c. (*short*) 201; curtailed of its fair proportions; ill-made, -shaped, -proportioned; crooked &c. (*distorted*) 243; hard-featured, -visaged; ill-, hard-, evil-favoured; ill-looking; unprepossessing.

graceless, inelegant; ungraceful, ungainly, uncouth; stiff; rugged, rough, gross, rude, awkward, clumsy, slouching, rickety; gawky; lump-ing, -ish; lumbering; hulk-y, -ing; unwieldy.

squalid, haggard; grim, -faced, -visaged; grisly, ghastly; ghost-, deathlike; cadaverous, gruesome.

frightful, hideous, odious, uncanny, forbidding, repellant, repulsive; horri-d, -ble; shocking &c. (*painful*) 830.

foul &c. (*dirty*) 653; dingy &c. (*colourless*) 429; gaudy &c. (*colour*) 428; disfigured &c. *v.*; discoloured (*blemished*) &c. 848.

---

847. Ornament. — N. ornament, -ation, -al art; ornat-ure, -eness; adorn-ment, decoration, embellishment; architecture.

garnish, polish, varnish, French pol-

848. Blemish.—N. blemish, disfigurement, deformity; defect &c. (*imperfection*) 651; flaw; injury &c. (*deterioration*) 659; spots on the sun; eyesore.

ish, gilding, japanning, lacquer, ormolu, enamel.

cosmetics, rouge, powder, lipstick, lip salve, mascara; manicure, nail polish; permanent –, Marcel –, finger-wave.

pattern, diaper, powdering, panelling, graining, pargeting, inlay, detail; texture &c. 329; richness; tracery, moulding, beading, reeding, fillet, listel, strapwork, *coquillage*, flourish, *fleur-de-lis*, arabesque, fret, *anthemion*; egg and -tongue, – dart; *astragal*, zigzag, *acanthus*, *cartouche*; pilaster &c. (*projection*) 250; cyma, ogee.

em-, broidery, needlework; knitting, crochet, tatting, brocade, *brocatelle*, beads, bugles; galloon, lace, gimp, *guipure*, fringe, trapping, border, edging, insertion, *motif*, trimming; *passementerie*; drapery, hanging, tapestry, arras; millinery, ermine.

wreath, festoon, garland, lei, chaplet, flower, nosegay, *bouquet*, posy, 'daisies pied and violets blue.'

tassel, knot; shoulder-knot, *épaulette*, epaulet, aigulet, *aiguillette*, frog; star, rosette, bow; feather, plume, *panache*, *aigrette*.

jewel, -ry, -lery; bijoutry; *bijou*, *-terie*; diadem, tiara; pendant, trinket, locket, necklace, armilla, bracelet, bangle, armlet, anklet, ear-, nose- ring, carcanet, chain, *châtelaine*, albert, brooch, torque.

gem, precious stone; diamond, brilliant, beryl, aquamarine, alexandrite, cat's eye, emerald, calcedony, chrysoprase, cornelian, jasper, bloodstone, agate, heliotrope; girasol, -e; onyx, plasma; sard, -onyx; garnet, lapis-lazuli, opal, peridot, chrysolite, sapphire, ruby; spinel, -le; balais; oriental –, topaz; turquois, -e; zircon, jacinth, hyacinth, carbuncle, amethyst; moonstone; pearl, coral.

finery, frippery, gewgaw, gimcrack, knick-knack, tinsel, spangle, sequin, *clinquant*, pinch-beck, paste; excess of ornament &c. (*vulgarity*) 851; gaud, pride, ostentation; frills and furbelows.

illustration, illumination, *vignette*; *fleuron*; head-, tail-piece; *cul-de-lampe*; flowers of rhetoric &c. 577; work of art, article of vertu, *bric-à-brac*, curio, *bibelot*.

V. ornament, embellish, enrich, decorate, adorn, beautify, adonize.

smarten, furbish, polish, gild, varnish, whitewash, enamel, japan, lacquer, paint, grain.

garnish, trim, dizen, bedizen, prink, prank; trick –, fig- out; deck, bedeck, dight, bedight, array; dress, – up, preen, spruce up,

stain, blot, slur; spot, -tiness; speck, -le; blur, freckle, mole, *macula*, patch, blotch, birthmark, blain, maculation, tarnish, smudge, smear; dirt &c. 653; bruise, black eye, scar, wem; pustule; excrescence, pimple &c. (*protuberance*) 250.

V. disfigure &c. (*injure*) 659; speckle; render ugly &c. 846.

Adj. pitted, freckled, discoloured, bloodshot, bruised, disfigured; stained &c. *n*.; imperfect &c. 651; injured &c. (*deteriorated*) 659.

849. Simplicity. — N. simplicity; plain-, homeli-ness; undress, nudity, nakedness, beauty unadorned, chastity, chasteness.

V. be -simple &c. *adj.*

render -simple &c. *adj.*; simplify, chasten, strip of ornament.

Adj. simple, plain; home-ly, -spun: ordinary, household.

natural, unaffected; free from -affectation, – ornament; *simplex munditiis*; *sans façon*, *en déshabillé*, nude, naked.

chaste, inornate, severe.

un-adorned, -ornamented, -decked, -garnished, -arranged, -trimmed, -varnished.

bald, flat, dull, blank.

titivate; spangle, bespangle, powder; embroider, work; chase, tool, emboss, fret; emblazon, blazon, illuminate; illustrate.

become &c. (*accord with*) 23.

Adj. ornamented, beautified &c. *v.*; ornate, rich, gilt, begilt, tesselated, enamelled, inlaid; festooned; topiary.

smart, gay, tricksy, flowery, glittering; new-gilt, -spangled; fine, – as -a Mayday queen, – fivepence, – a carrot fresh scraped; pranked out, bedight, well-groomed.

in full dress &c. (*fashion*) 852; *en grande -tenue*, – *toilette*; in best bib and tucker, in Sunday best, *endimanché*; dressed to advantage.

showy, flashy; gaudy &c. (*vulgar*) 851; garish; gorgeous.

ornamental, decorative; becoming &c. (*accordant*) 23.

---

850. [Good taste.] **Taste.—N.** taste; good –, refined –, cultivated- taste; delicacy, refinement, fine feeling, gust, *gusto*, tact, *finesse*; nicety &c. (*discrimination*) 465; polish, elegance, grace.

virtu; dilettanteism, virtuosity; fine art; cul-ture, -ivation.

[Science of taste] æsthetics.

man of -taste &c.; *connoisseur*, judge, critic, *conoscente*, *virtuoso*, *amateur*, *dilettante*, Aristarchus, Corinthian, *arbiter elegantiarum*, stagirite, euphemist.

'caviare to the general.'

V. appreciate, judge, criticize, discriminate &c. 465.

Adj. in good taste; tasteful, tasty; unaffected, pure, chaste, classical, attic; cultivated, refined; dainty; æsthetic, artistic; elegant &c. 578; euphemistic.

to one's -taste, – mind; after one's fancy; *comme il faut*; *tiré à quatre épingles*.

Adv. elegantly &c. *adj.*

Phr. *nihil tetigit quod non ornavit.*

852. Fashion.—N. fashion, style, *ton*, *bon ton*, society; good –, polite-society; drawing room, civilized life, civilization, town, *beau monde*, high life, court; world; fashionable -, gay-world; Vanity Fair; show &c. (*ostentation*) 822.

manners, breeding &c. (*politeness*) 894; air, demeanour &c. (*appearance*) 448; *savoir-faire*; gentlemanliness, gentility, decorum, propriety, *bienséance*; conventions -, dictates- of society; Mrs. Grundy; convention, -ality; punctilio; form, -ality; etiquette, point of

851. [Bad taste.] **Vulgarity.—N.** vulgar-ity, -ism; barbar-, Vandal-, Gothic-ism; *mauvais goût*, bad taste; Babbittry; *gaucherie*, awkwardness, want of tact; ill-breeding &c. (*discourtesy*) 895; ungentlemanly behaviour.

coarseness &c. *adj.*; indecorum, misbehaviour.

low-, homeli-ness; low life, *mauvais ton*, rusticity; boorishness &c. *adj.*; brutality; rowdy-, ruffian-, blackguardism; ribaldry; slang &c. (*neology*) 563.

bad joke, *mauvaise plaisanterie*.

[Excess of ornament] gaudi-, tawdriness; false ornament; finery, frippery, trickery, tinsel, gewgaw, *clinquant*.

rough diamond, tomboy, hoyden, cub, unlicked cub; clown &c. (*commonalty*) 876; Hun, Goth, Vandal, Bœotian; vulgarian; snob, cad, bounder, gent; *parvenu* &c. 876; frump, dowdy; slattern &c. 653.

V. be -vulgar &c. *adj.*; misbehave; talk -, smell of the- shop.

Adj. in bad taste, vulgar, unrefined, gutter.

coarse, indecorous, ribald, gross; unseemly, unbeseeming, unpresentable; *contra bonos mores*; ungraceful &c. (*ugly*) 846.

dowdy; slovenly &c. (*dirty*) 653; ungenteel, shabby genteel; low &c. (*plebeian*) 876; uncourtly; uncivil &c. (*discourteous*) 895; ill-bred, -mannered; underbred; ungentleman-ly, -like; unladylike, unfeminine; wild, – as an unbacked colt.

unkempt, uncombed, untamed, unlicked, unpolished, uncouth, plebeian;

etiquette; custom &c. 613; mode, vogue, style, go; rage &c. (*desire*) 865; prevailing taste, *dernier cri*, dress &c. 225.

man –, woman- of -fashion, – the world; height –, pink –, star –, glass –, leader- of fashion; *arbiter elegantiarum* &c. (*taste*) 850; upper ten thousand &c. (*nobility*) 875; *élite* &c. (*distinction*) 873.

V. be -fashionable &c. *adj.*, – the rage &c. *n.*; have a run, pass current.

follow –, conform to –, fall in with- the fashion &c. *n.*; go with the stream &c. (*conform*) 82; *savoir -vivre*, – *faire*; keep up appearances, behave oneself.

set the –, bring into- fashion; give a tone to –, cut a figure in- society, rub shoulders with nobility, keep one's carriage.

incondite; heavy, rude, awkward; home-ly, -spun, -bred; provincial, hick, countrified, rustic, uncultivated, fresh-water; boorish, clownish; savage, brut-ish, blackguard, rowdy, snobbish; barbar-ous, -ic; Gothic, unclassical, doggerel, heathenish, tramontane, out-landish; Bohemian.

obsolete &c. (*antiquated*) 124; un-fashionable, old-fashioned, out of date; new-fangled &c. (*unfamiliar*) 83; fan-tastic, odd &c. (*ridiculous*) 853.

particular; affected &c. 855; mere-tricious; extravagant, monstrous, hor-rid; shocking &c. (*painful*) 830.

gaudy, tawdry, bedizened, tricked out, gingerbread; obtrusive, flaunting, loud, flashy, garish, showy.

Adj. fashionable; in -fashion &c. *n.*; *à la mode, comme il faut*; admitted –, admissible- in.-society &c. *n.*; presentable, decorous, punctilious, conventional &c. (*customary*) 613; genteel; well-bred, -mannered, -behaved, -spoken; gentleman-like, -ly; ladylike; civil, polite &c. (*courteous*) 894.

polished, refined, thoroughbred, courtly; *distingué*, aristocratic, unembarrassed, poised, *dégagé*; ja-, jau-nty; dashing, fast, showy, high toned, toney.

modish, stylish, in the latest style, *recherché*; new-fangled &c. (*unfamiliar*) 83.

in -court, – full, – evening- dress; *en grande tenue* &c. (*ornament*) 847.

Adv. fashionably &c. *adj.*; for fashion's sake.

---

853. Ridiculousness.—N. ridiculousness &c. *adj.*; comical-, odd-ity &c. *adj.*; extravagance, drollery.

farce, comedy; burlesque &c. (*ridicule*) 856; buffoonery &c. (*fun*) 840; frippery; doggerel verses; Irish bull, Hibernianism, Hibernicism; Spoonerism; absurdity &c. 497; bombast &c. (*unmeaning*) 517; anti-climax, bathos; monstrosity &c. (*unconformity*) 83; laughing stock &c. 857.

V. be -ridiculous &c. *adj.*; pass from the sublime to the ridiculous; make one laugh; play the fool, make a fool of oneself, commit an absurdity.

play a joke on, make a -fool of, – sucker of, – monkey of.

Adj. ridiculous, ludicrous; comic, -al; droll, funny, laughable, *pour rire*, grotesque, farcical, odd; whimsical, – as a dancing bear; fanciful, fantastic, queer, rum, quizzical, waggish, quaint, *bizarre*; eccentric &c. (*unconformable*) 83; strange, outlandish, out of the way, *baroque*, *rocaille*, rococo; awkward &c. (*ugly*) 846.

absurd, extravagant, *outré*, monstrous, preposterous, bombastic, inflated, stilted, burlesque, mock heroic.

drollish; serio-, tragic-comic; gimcrack, contemptible &c. (*unimportant*) 643; doggerel; ironical &c. (*derisive*) 856; risible.

.Phr. *'risum teneatis amici?'* *rideret Heraclitus.*

854. Fop.—N. fop, fine gentleman; swell; dand-y, -iprat; exquisite, coxcomb, toff, beau, macaroni, blade, blood, buck, man about town, fast man; fribble, jemmy, spark, popinjay, puppy, prig, *petit maître*; jacka-napes, -dandy; man milliner; Jemmy Jessamy, carpet-knight, masher, Dundreary, Johnnie, dude.

belle, fine lady, *coquette*, flirt.

855. Affectation.—N. affectation; affectedness &c. *adj.*; acting a part &c. *v.*; pretence &c. (*falsehood*) 544, (*ostentation*) 882; boasting &c. 884.

charlatanism, quackery, shallow profundity, humbug, pretension, airs, pedantry, purism, precisianism, euphuism, prunes and prisms; teratology &c. (*altiloquence*) 577.

mannerism, *simagrée*, grimace.

conceit, foppery, dandyism, man millinery, coxcombry, puppyism.

stiffness, formality, buckram; prudery, demureness, coquetry, mock modesty, *minauderie*, sentimentalism; *mauvaise honte*, false shame.

affector, performer, actor; pedant, pedagogue, *doctrinaire*, purist, euphuist, mannerist; shoneen; *grimacier*; lump of affectation, *précieuse ridicule*, *bas bleu*, blue stocking, poetaster; prig, hypocrite; charlatan &c. (*deceiver*) 548; *petit maître* &c. (*fop*) 854; flatterer &c. 935; *coquette*, prude, puritan; precisian, formalist.

V. affect, act a part, put on; give oneself airs &c. (*arrogance*) 885; boast &c. 884; coquet; simper, mince, attitudinize, strike a pose, pose; flirt a fan; over-act, -play, -do.

Adj. affected, full of affectation, pretentious, pedantic, stilted, stagey, theatrical, big-sounding, *ad captandum*, canting, insincere.

not natural, unnatural; self-conscious; *maniéré*; artificial; over-wrought, -done, -acted; euphuistic &c. 577.

stiff, starch, formal, prim, smug, demure, *tiré à quatre épingles*, quakerish, puritanical, prudish, pragmatical, priggish, conceited, coxcomical, foppish, dandified; fini-cal, -kin, -cky, mincing, simpering, namby-pamby, sentimental, languishing.

856. Ridicule.—N. ridicule, derision; sardonic -smile, – grin; irrision; snigger; scoffing &c. (*disrespect*) 929; mockery, quiz, banter, irony, *persiflage*, raillery, chaff, *badinage*; quizzing &c. *v.*

squib, satire, skit, quip, quib, grin.

parody, burlesque, travesty; farce &c. (*drama*) 599; caricature, take-off.

buffoonery &c. (*fun*) 840; practical joke, horseplay.

V. ridicule, deride; laugh at, grin at, smile at; snigger; laugh in one's sleeve; banter, rally, chaff, joke, twit, quiz, poke fun at, jolly, roast, rag; fleer; play –, play tricks- upon; fool, – to the top of one's bent; show up.

satirize, parody, caricature, burlesque, travesty.

turn into ridicule; make merry with; make -fun, – game, – a fool, – an April fool- of; rally; scoff &c. (*disrespect*) 929.

raise a laugh &c. (*amuse*) 840; play the fool, make a fool of oneself. be ridiculous &c. 853.

Adj. deris-ory, -ive; mock; sarcastic, ironical, quizzical, burlesque, Hudibrastic; scurrilous &c. (*disrespectful*) 929.

Adv. in -ridicule &c. *n.*

857. [Object and cause of ridicule.] **Laughing-stock.—N.** laughing-, jesting-, gazing-stock; butt, game, fair game; April fool &c. (*dupe*) 547.

original, oddity; queer –, odd- fish; quiz, square-toes; old –, fogey *or* fogy.

monkey; buffoon &c. (*jester*) 844; pantomimist &c. (*actor*) 599.

jest &c. (*wit*) 842.

3°. PROSPECTIVE AFFECTIONS

858. Hope.—N. hope, -s; desire &c. 865; fervent hope, sanguine expectation, trust, confidence, reliance; faith &c. (*belief*) 484; affiance, assurance; secur-eness, -ity; reassurance.

good -omen, – auspices; promise, well-grounded hopes; good –, bright-prospect; clear sky.

as-, pre-sumption; anticipation &c. (*expectation*) 507.

hopefulness, buoyancy, optimism, enthusiasm, heart of grace, aspiration; optimist, utop-ian, -ist; Pollyanna.

castles in the air, *châteaux en Espagne*, hope chest, *le pot au lait*, Utopia, millennium; day '-, golden-dream; dream of Alnaschar; airy hopes, fool's paradise; *mirage* &c. (*fallacies of vision*) 443; fond hope.

beam –, ray –, gleam –, glimmer –, dawn –, flash –, star- of hope; cheer; bit of blue sky, silver lining of the cloud, bottom of Pandora's box, balm in Gilead.

anchor, sheet-anchor, main-stay; staff &c. (*support*) 215; heaven &c. 981.

V. hope, trust, confide, rely on, put one's trust in, lean upon; pin one's -hope, – faith- upon &c. (*believe*) 484.

feel –, entertain –, harbour –, in-dulge –, cherish –, feed –, foster –, nourish –, encourage –, cling to –, live in- hope &c. *n.*; see land; feel –, rest- -assured, – confident &c. *adj.*

presume; promise oneself; expect &c. (*look forward to*) 507.

hope for &c. (*desire*) 865; anticipate.

be -hopeful &c. *adj.*; look on the bright side of, view on the sunny side, make the best of it, hope for the best; put -a good, – a bold, – the best- face upon; keep one's spirits up; take heart, – of grace; be of good -heart, – cheer; flatter oneself, lay the flattering unction to one's soul.

859. [Absence, want, or loss of hope.] **Hopelessness.—N.** hopelessness &c. *adj.*; despair, desperation; despondency &c. (*dejection*) 837; pessimism.

hope deferred, dashed hopes; vain expectation &c. (*disappointment*) 509.

airy hopes &c. 858; forlorn hope; bad -job, – business; *enfant perdu*; gloomy –, black spots in the- horizon; slough of Despond, cave of Despair.

Job's comforter; bird of -bad, – ill-omen.

V. despair; lose –, give up –, aban-don –, relinquish- -all hope, – the hope of; give -up, – over; yield to despair; falter; despond &c. (*be dejected*) 837; *jeter le manche après la cognée*.

inspire –, drive to- despair &c. *n.*; disconcert; dash –, crush –, shatter –, destroy- one's hopes; hope against hope.

Adj. hopeless, desperate, despairing, in despair, *au désespoir*, forlorn; in-consolable &c. (*dejected*) 837; broken-hearted.

out of the question, not to be thought of; impracticable &c. 471; past -hope, – cure, – mending, – recall; at one's last gasp &c. (*death*) 360; given -up, – over.

incurable, cureless, immedicable, re-mediless, beyond remedy; incorrigible; irre-parable, -mediable, -coverable, -versible, -trievable, -claimable, -deem-able, -vocable; ruined, undone; im-mitigable.

unpromising, unpropitious; inauspi-cious, ill-omened, threatening, clouded over, lowering, ominous.

Phr. '*lasciate ogni speranza voi ch' entrate*'; its days are numbered; the worst come to the worst.

860. Fear.—N. fear, timidity, diffi-dence, want of confidence; apprehen-sive-, fearful-ness &c. *adj.*; solicitude,

catch at a straw, hope against hope, count one's chickens before they are hatched.

give –, inspire –, raise –, hold out-hope &c. *n.*; raise expectations; en-courage, hearten, cheer, assure, re-assure, buoy up, embolden; promise, bid fair, augur well, be in a fair way, look up, flatter, tell a flattering tale.

Adj. hoping &c. *v.*; in -hopes &c. *n.*; hopeful, confident; secure &c. (*certain*) 484; sanguine, in good heart, buoyed up, buoyant, elated, flushed, exultant, enthusiastic; utopian.

unsus-pecting, -picious; fearless, free –, exempt from- -fear, – suspicion, – distrust, – despair; undespairing, self-reliant.

probable, on the high road to; within sight of -shore, – land; promising, propitious; of –, full of- promise; of good omen; auspicious, *de bon augure*; reassuring; encouraging, cheering, in-spiriting, looking up, bright, roseate, *couleur de rose*, rose-coloured.

Adv. hopefully &c. *adj.*

Int. God speed! good luck!

Phr. *nil desperandum*; never say die, *dum spiro spero, latet scintillula forsan,* all is for the best, *spero meliora;* the wish being father to the thought; 'hope told a flattering tale'; *rusticus expectat dum defluat amnis.*

anxiety, care, apprehension, misgiving; mistrust &c. (*doubt*) 485; suspicion, qualm; hesitation &c. (*irresolution*) 605.

nervous-, restless-ness &c. *adj.*; in-, dis-quietude; flutter, trepidation, fear and trembling, perturbation, tremor, quivering, shaking, trembling, throb-bing heart, palpitation, ague fit, cold sweat; abject fear &c. (*cowardice*) 862; mortal funk, heart-sinking, despond-ency; despair &c. 859.

fright; affright, -ment; alarm, pavor, dread, awe, terror, horror, dismay, consternation, panic, scare, stampede [of horses].

intimidation, terrorism, reign of terror.

[Object of fear] bug-bear, -aboo; scarecrow; hobgoblin &c. (*demon*) 980; daymare, nightmare, Gorgon, Medusa, mormo, ogre, Hurlothrumbo, raw head and bloody bones, fee faw fum, *bête noire, enfant terrible.*

alarmist &c. (*coward*) 862.

V. fear, stand in awe of; be -afraid &c. *adj.*; have -qualms &c. *n.*; appre-hend, sit upon thorns, eye askance; distrust &c. (*disbelieve*) 485.

hesitate &c. (*be irresolute*) 605; falter, funk, cower, crouch; skulk &c. (*coward-ice*) 862; let 'I dare not' wait upon 'I would'; take -fright, – alarm; start, wince, flinch, shy, shrink; fly &c. (*avoid*) 623.

tremble, shake; shiver, – in one's shoes; shudder, flutter; shake –, tremble- -like an aspen leaf, – all over; quake, quaver, quiver, quail; get the wind up.

grow –, turn- pale; blench, stand aghast; not dare to say one's soul is one's own.

inspire –, excite- -fear, – awe; raise apprehensions; give –, raise –, sound- an alarm; alarm, startle, scare, cry 'wolf,' disquiet, dismay; fright, -en; affright, terrify; astound; frighten from one's propriety; frighten out of one's -wits, – senses, – seven senses; awe; strike -all of a heap, – an awe into, – terror; harrow up the soul, appal, unman, petrify, horrify.

make one's -flesh creep, – hair stand on end, – blood run cold, – teeth chatter; chill one's spine; take away –, stop- one's breath; make one -tremble &c.

haunt, obsess, beset; prey –, weigh- on the mind.

put in -fear, – bodily fear; terrorize, intimidate, cow, daunt, over-awe, abash, deter, discourage; browbeat, bully; threaten &c. 909

Adj. fearing &c. *v.*; frightened &c. *v.*; in -fear, – a fright &c. *n.*; haunted with the -fear &c. *n.*- of.

afraid, fearful; tim-id, -orous; nervous, diffident, coy, faint-hearted, tremulous, shaky, afraid of one's shadow, apprehensive, restless, fidgety; more frightened than hurt.

aghast; awe-, horror-, terror-, panic- -struck, -stricken; frightened to death, white as a sheet; pale, – as -death, – ashes, – a ghost; breathless, in hysterics.

inspiring fear &c. *v.*; alarming; formidable, redoubtable; perilous &c. (*danger*) 665; portentous; fear-ful, -some; dread, -ful; fell; dire, -ful; shocking; terri-ble, -fic; tremendous; horri-d, -ble, -fic; ghastly; awful, awe-inspiring, eerie, weird; revolting &c. (*painful*) 830.

Adv. *in terrorem.*

Int. 'angels and ministers of grace defend us!'

Phr. *ante tubam trepidat; horresco referens,* one's heart failing one, *obstupui steteruntque comæ et vox faucibus hæsit.*

---

861. [Absence of fear.] **Courage.**—**N.** courage, bravery, valour; resolute-, bold-ness &c. *adj.*; spirit, daring, gallantry, intrepidity; contempt –, defiance- of danger; derring-do; audacity; rashness &c. 863; dash; defiance &c. 715; confidence, self-reliance.

man-liness, -hood; nerve, pluck, mettle, game; heart, – of grace; spunk, gameness, grit, face, virtue, hardihood, fortitude; firmness &c. (*stability*) 150; heart of oak; bottom, backbone &c. (*perseverance*) 604a.

resolution &c. (*determination*) 604; tenacity, bull-dog courage.

prowess, heroism, chivalry.

exploit, feat, achievement; heroic -deed, – act; bold stroke.

man, – of mettle; hero, demigod, paladin, heroine, Amazon, Hector, Joan of Arc; lion, tiger, panther, bull-dog; game-, fighting-cock; bully, fire-eater &c. 863; dare-devil.

V. be -courageous &c. *adj.*; dare, venture, make bold; face –, front –, affront –, confront –, brave –, defy –, despise –, mock- danger; look in the face; look -full, – boldly, – danger- in the face; face; meet, – in front; brave, beard; defy &c. 715.

take –, muster –, summon up –, pluck up- courage; nerve oneself, take heart; take –, pluck up- heart of grace; hold up one's head, screw one's courage to the sticking place; come -to, – up to- the scratch; stand, – to one's guns, – fire, – against; bear up, – against; hold out &c. (*persevere*) 604a.

put a bold face upon; show –,

862. [Excess of fear.] **Cowardice.**—**N.** cowardice, pusillanimity; cowardliness &c. *adj.*; timidity, effeminacy.

poltroonery, baseness; dastard-ness, -y; abject fear, funk; Dutch courage; fear &c. 860; white feather, faint heart.

coward, poltroon, dastard, sneak, recreant; shy –, dunghill- cock; coistril, milksop, white-liver, nidget, cur, craven, one that cannot say 'Bo' to a goose; Bob Acres, Jerry Sneak.

alarm-, terror-, pessim-ist; runagate &c. (*fugitive*) 623; shirker.

V. quail &c. (*fear*) 860; be -cowardly &c. *adj.*, – a coward &c. *n.*; funk; cower, skulk, sneak; flinch, shy, fight shy, slink, turn tail; run away &c. (*avoid*) 623; show the white feather, have cold feet, show a yellow streak.

Adj. coward, -ly; fearful, shy; tim-id, -orous; skittish; poor-spirited, spiritless, soft, effeminate.

weak-minded; infirm of purpose &c. 605; weak-, faint-, chicken-, lily-, pigeon-hearted; yellow; white-, lily-, milk-livered; milksop, smock-faced; unable to say 'Bo' to a goose.

dastard, -ly; base, craven, sneaking, dunghill, recreant; unwar-, unsoldier-like.

'in face a lion but in heart a deer.' unmanned; frightened &c. 860.

Int. *sauve qui peut!* devil take the hindmost!

Adv. in fear and trembling, in fear of one's life, in a blue funk.

Phr. *ante tubam trepidat,* one's courage oozing out.

present- a bold front, face the music; envisage; show fight.

bell the cat, take the bull by the horns, beard the lion in his den, march up to the cannon's mouth, go through fire and water, run the gauntlet, go over the top.

give –, infuse –, inspire- courage; reassure, encourage, embolden, inspirit, cheer, hearten, nerve, put upon one's mettle, rally, raise a rallying cry; pat on the back, make a man of, keep in countenance.

Adj. courageous, brave; val-iant, -orous; gallant, intrepid; spirit-ed, -ful; high-spirited, -mettled; mettlesome, game, plucky; man-ly, -ful; resolute; stout, -hearted; iron-, lion-hearted; heart of oak; Penthesilean.

bold, – spirited; daring, audacious; fear-, daunt-, dread-, awe-less; un-daunted, -appalled, -dismayed, -awed, -blenched, -abashed, -alarmed, -flinching, -shrinking, -blenching, -apprehensive; confident, self-reliant; bold as -a lion, – brass.

enterprising, adventurous; ventur-ous, -esome; dashing, chival-rous; soldierly &c. (*warlike*) 722; heroic.

fierce, savage; pugnacious &c. (*bellicose*) 720.

strong-minded, hardy, doughty; firm &c. (*stable*) 150; determined &c. (*resolved*) 604; dogged, indomitable &c. (*persevering*) 604a.

up to, – the scratch; upon one's mettle; reassured &c. *v.*; un-feared, undreaded.

Phr. one's blood being up.

---

863. Rashness.—N. rashness &c. *adj.*; temerity, want of caution, imprudence, indiscretion; over-confidence, presumption, audacity.

precipit-ancy, -ation; impetuosity; levity; foolhardi-hood, -ness; heed-, thought-lessness &c. (*inattention*) 458; carelessness &c. (*neglect*) 460; desperation; Quixotism, knight-errantry; fire-eating.

gam-ing, -bling; blind bargain, leap in the dark, fool's paradise; too many eggs in one basket.

desperado, rashling, mad-cap, dare-devil, Hotspur, fire-eater, bully, *bravo*, Hector, scapegrace, *enfant perdu*; Don Quixote, knight-errant, Icarus; adventurer; gam-bler, -ester; dynamitard.

V. be -rash &c. *adj.*; stick at nothing, play a desperate game; run into danger &c. 665; play with -fire, – edge tools.

carry too much sail, sail too near the wind, ride at single anchor, go out of one's depth.

take a leap in the dark, buy a pig in a poke.

donner tête baissée; knock one's head against a wall &c. (*be unskilful*) 699; rush on destruction; kick against the

864. Caution.—N. caution; cautious-ness &c. *adj.*; discretion, prudence, cautel, heed, circumspection, calculation, deliberation; safety first.

foresight &c. 510; vigilance &c. 459; warning &c. 668.

coolness &c. *adj.*; self-possession, -command; presence of mind, *sang-froid*; well-regulated mind; worldly wisdom, Fabian policy.

V. be -cautious &c. *adj.*; take -care, – heed, – good care; have a care; mind, – what one is about; be on one's guard &c. (*keep watch*) 459; make assurance double sure; ca' canny.

bespeak &c. (*be early*) 132.

think twice, look before one leaps, keep one's weather eye open, count the cost, look to the main chance, cut one's coat according to one's cloth; feel one's -ground, – way; see how the land lies &c. (*foresight*) 510; wait to see how the cat jumps; bridle one's tongue; *reculer pour mieux sauter* &c. (*prepare*) 673; let well alone, let sleeping dogs lie, *ne pas réveiller le chat qui dort*.

keep out of -harm's way, – troubled waters; keep at a respectful distance, stand aloof; keep –, be- on the safe side,

pricks, tempt Providence, go on a forlorn hope.

count one's chickens before they are hatched; reckon without one's host; catch at straws; trust to –, lean on– a broken reed.

Adj. rash, incautious, indiscreet, injudicious; imprudent, improvident, temerarious; uncalculating; heedless; careless &c. (*neglectful*) 460; without ballast, heels over head; giddy &c. (*inattentive*) 458; wanton, reckless, wild, madcap; desperate, devil-may-care.

hot-blooded, -headed, -brained; head-long, -strong; break-neck; foolhardy; hare-brained; precipitate, impulsive.

over-confident, -weening; ventur-esome, -ous; adventurous, Quixotic; fire-eating, cavalier; free-and-easy.

off one's guard &c. (*inexpectant*) 508.

Adv. post haste, *à corps perdu*, hand over head, *tête baissée*, head-foremost; happen what may.

Phr. neck or nothing, the devil being in one.

husband one's resources &c. 636.

caution &c. (*warn*) 668.

Adj. cautious, wary, guarded; on one's guard &c. (*watchful*) 459; *cavendo tutus*; *in medio tutissimus*.

care-, heed-ful; cautelous, stealthy, chary, shy of, circumspect, prudent, canny, safe, non-committal, discreet, politic; sure-footed &c. (*skilful*) 698.

unenterprising, unadventurous, cool, steady, self-possessed; over-cautious.

suspicious, leery, vigilant.

Adv. cautiously, gingerly &c. *adj.*

Int. have a care! look out! *cave canem!*

Phr. *timeo Danaos; festina lente.*

---

865. Desire.—N. desire, wish, fancy, fantasy; want, need, exigency.

mind, inclination, leaning, bent, *animus*, partiality, *penchant*, predilection; propensity &c. 820; willingness &c. 602; liking, love, fondness, relish.

longing, hankering; solicitude, anxiety; yearning, coveting; aspiration, ambition, vaulting ambition; eagerness, zeal, ardour, *empressement*, breathless impatience, over-anxiety; solicitude, impetuosity &c. 825.

appet-ite, -ition, -ence, -ency; sharp appetite, keenness, hunger, stomach, twist; thirst, -iness; drouth, mouth-watering; itch, -ing; prurience, *cacoëthes*, cupidity, lust, concupiscence.

edge of -appetite, – hunger; torment of Tantalus; sweet –, lickerish- tooth; itching palm; longing –, wistful –, sheep's- eye.

avidity; greed, -iness; covetous-, ravenous-ness &c. *adj.*; grasping, craving, canine appetite, rapacity; voracity &c. (*gluttony*) 957.

passion, rage, *furore*, mania, *manie*; inextinguishable desire; dips-, klept-, mon-omania.

[Person desiring] desirer, lover, *ama-*

866. Indifference.—N. indifference neutrality; coldness &c. *adj.*; uncon-cern, *insouciance, nonchalance*; want of -interest, – earnestness; anorexy, in-appetency; apathy &c. (*insensibility*) 823; supineness &c. (*inactivity*) 683; disdain &c. 930; recklessness &c. 863; inattention &c. 458.

V. be -indifferent &c. *adj.*; stand neuter; take no interest in &c. (*insensibility*) 823; have no -desire &c. 865, – taste, – relish- for; not care for; care nothing -for, – about; not care a -straw &c. (*unimportance*) 643 -about, – for; not mind.

set at naught &c. (*make light of*) 483; spurn &c. (*disdain*) 930.

Adj. indifferent, cold, frigid, luke-warm; cool, – as a cucumber; uncon-cerned, *insouciant*, phlegmatic, *pococu-rante*, easy-going, devil-may-care, care-less, listless, lackadaisical, feckless; half-hearted; un-ambitious, -aspiring, -desirous, -solicitous, -attracted.

un-attractive, -alluring, -desired, -de-sirable, -cared for, -wished, -valued, all one to.

insipid &c. 391; vain.

Adv. for aught one cares.

teur, votary, devotee, aspirant, solicitant, candidate; cormorant &c. 957; sycophant.

[Object of desire] *desideratum*; want &c. (*requirement*) 630; 'consummation devoutly to be wished'; attraction, magnet, allurement, fancy, temptation, seduction, lure, fascination, *prestige*, height of one's ambition, idol; whim, -sey; maggot; hobby, -horse.

Fortunatus's cap, wishing cap, love potion.

V. desire; wish, – for; be -desirous &c. *adj.*; have a -longing &c. *n.*; hope &c. 858.

care for, affect, like, list; take to, cling to, take a fancy to; fancy; prefer &c. (*choose*) 609.

have -an eye, – a mind- to; find it in one's heart &c. (*be willing*) 602; have a fancy for, set one's eyes upon; cast a sheep's eye –, look sweet- upon; take into one's head, have at heart, be bent upon; set one's -cap at, – heart upon, – mind upon; covet.

want, miss, need, lack, desiderate, feel the want of; would fain -have, – do; would be glad of.

be -hungry &c. *adj.*; have a good appetite, play a good knife and fork; hunger –, thirst –, crave –, lust –, itch –, hanker –, run mad- after; raven –, die- for; burn to.

desiderate; sigh –, cry –, gape –, gasp –, pine –, pant –, languish –, yearn –, long –, be on thorns –, hope- for; aspire after; catch at, grasp at, jump at.

woo, court, solicit; fish –, spell –, whistle –, put up- for; ogle.

cause –, create –, raise –, excite –, provoke- desire; whet the appetite; appetize, titillate, allure, attract, take one's fancy, tempt; hold out -temptation, – allurement; tantalize, make one's mouth water, *faire venir l'eau à la bouche*.

gratify desire &c. (*give pleasure*) 829.

Adj. desirous; desiring &c. *v.*; orectic, appetitive; inclined &c. (*willing*) 602; partial to; fain, wishful, optative; anxious, wistful, curious; at a loss for, sedulous, solicitous.

craving, hungry, sharp-set, peckish,

Int. never mind.

867. Dislike.—N. dis-like, -taste, -relish, -inclination, -placency.

reluctance; backwardness &c. (*unwillingness*) 603.

repugnance, disgust, queasiness, turn, nausea, loathing; avers-eness, -ation, -ion; abomination, antipathy, abhorrence, horror; mortal –, rooted- -antipathy, – horror; hatred, detestation; hate &c. 898; animosity &c. 900; hydrophobia.

sickener; gall and wormwood &c. (*unsavoury*) 395; shuddering, cold sweat.

V. dis-, mis-like, -relish; mind, object to; have rather not, not care for; have –, conceive –, entertain –, take- -a dislike, – an aversion- to; have no -taste, – stomach- for.

shun, avoid &c. 623; eschew; withdraw –, shrink –, recoil- from; not be able to -bear, – abide, – endure; shrug the shoulders at, shudder at, turn up the nose at, look askance at; make a -mouth, – wry face, – grimace; make faces.

loathe, nauseate, abominate, detest, abhor; hate &c. 898; take amiss &c. 900; have enough of &c. (*be satiated*) 869.

cause –, excite- dislike; disincline, repel, sicken; make –, render- sick; turn one's stomach, nauseate, wamble, disgust, shock, stink in the nostrils; go against the -grain, – stomach; stick in the throat; make one's blood run cold &c. (*give pain*) 830; pall.

Adj. disliking &c. *v.*; averse to, loth, adverse; shy of, sick of, out of conceit with; disinclined; heart-, dog-sick; queasy.

disliked &c. *v.*; uncared for, unpopular; out of favour; repulsive, repugnant, repellent; abhorrent, insufferable, fulsome, nauseous; loath-some, -ful; offensive; disgusting &c. *v.*; disagreeable &c. (*painful*) 830; unsavoury &c. 395.

Adv. *usque ad nauseam.*

Int. faugh! foh! ugh!

868. Fastidiousness.—N. fastidiousness &c. *adj.*; nicety, meticulosity,

ravening, with an empty stomach, esurient, lickerish, thirsty, athirst, parched with thirst, pinched with hunger, famished, dry, drouthy; hungry as a -hunter, – hawk, – horse, – church mouse.

greedy, – as a hog; over-eager, voracious; ravenous, – as a wolf; openmouthed, covetous, rapacious, grasping, extortionate, exacting, sordid, *alieni appetens*; insati-able, -ate; unquenchable, quenchless; omnivorous.

unsatisfied, unsated, unslaked.

eager, avid, keen; burning, fervent, ardent; agog; all agog; breathless; impatient &c. (*impetuous*) 825; bent –, intent –, set- -on, – upon; mad after, *enragé*, rabid, dying for, devoured by desire.

aspiring, ambitious, vaulting, sky-aspiring.

desirable; popular; desired &c. *v.*; in demand; pleasing &c. (*giving pleasure*) 829; appeti-zing, -ble; tantalizing.

Adv. wistfully &c. *adj.*; fain.

Int. would -that, – it were! O for! *esto perpetua!* if only!

Phr. the wish being father to the thought; *sua cuique voluptas*; *hoc erat in votis*, the mouth watering, the fingers itching; *aut Cæsar aut nullus.*

hypercriticism, difficulty in being pleased, *friandise*, epicurism, *omnia suspendens naso.*

discrimination, discernment, good taste, perspicacity.

epicure, gourmet.

[Excess of delicacy] prudery, prudishness, primness.

V. be -fastidious &c. *adj.*; split hairs, discriminate, have a sweet tooth.

mince the matter; turn up one's nose at &c. (*disdain*) 930; look a gift horse in the mouth, see spots on the sun.

Adj. fastidious, meticulous, exacting, nice, delicate, *délicat*, finical, finicky, difficult, dainty, lickerish, squeamish, thin-skinned; s-, queasy; hard –, difficult- to please; querulous, particular, over-particular, straitlaced, prudish, prim, scrupulous; censorious &c. 932; hypercritical, discriminating, discerning, perspicacious.

Phr. *noli me tangere.*

869. Satiety.—N. satiety, satisfaction, saturation, repletion, glut, surfeit; weariness &c. 841.

spoiled child; *enfant gâté*; too much of a good thing, *toujours perdrix*; *crambe repetita.*

V. sate, satiate, satisfy, saturate; cloy, quench, slake, pall, glut, gorge, surfeit; bore &c. (*weary*) 841; tire &c. (*fatigue*) 688; spoil.

have -enough of, – quite enough of, – one's fill, – too much of; be -satiated &c. *adj.*

Adj. satiated &c. *v.*; overgorged; *blasé*, used up, sick of, heart-sick.

Int. enough! hold! *eheu jam satis!*

4°. Contemplative Affections

870. Wonder.—N. wonder, marvel; astonish-, amaze-, wonder-, bewilderment; amazedness &c. *adj.*; admiration, awe; stup-or, -efaction; stound, fascination; sensation; surprise &c. (*inexpectation*) 508; cynosure.

note of admiration; thaumaturgy &c. (*sorcery*) 992.

V. wonder, marvel, admire; be -surprised &c. *adj.*; start; stare; open –, rub –, turn up- one's eyes; gloar; gape, open one's mouth, hold one's breath;

871. [Absence of wonder.] **Expectance.—N.** expectan-ce, -cy &c. (*expectation*) 507; calmness, composure, tranquillity, serenity, coolness, imperturbability &c. 826.

nine days' wonder.

V. expect &c. 507; not -be surprised, – wonder &c. 870; *nil admirari*, make nothing of.

Adj. expecting &c. *v.*; unamazed, astonished at nothing; *blasé* &c. (*weary*) 841; unimaginative, calm, serene, im-

look –, stand- -aghast, – agog; look blank &c. (*disappointment*) 509; *tomber des nues*; not believe one's -eyes, – ears, – senses.

not be able to account for &c. (*unintelligible*) 519; not know whether one stands on one's head or one's heels.

surprise, astonish, amaze, astound; dumbfound, -er; startle, dazzle; strike, – with -wonder, – awe; electrify; stun, stupefy, petrify, confound, bewilder, flabbergast; stagger, throw on one's beam ends, fascinate, turn the head, take away one's breath, strike dumb; make one's -hair stand on end, – tongue cleave to the roof of one's mouth; make one stare.

take by surprise &c. (*be unexpected*) 508.

be -wonderful &c. *adj.*; beggar –, baffle- description; stagger belief.

Adj. surprised &c. *v.*; aghast, all agog, breathless, agape; open-mouthed; awe-, thunder-, moon-, planet-struck; spell-bound; lost in -amazement, – wonder, – astonishment; struck all of a heap, unable to believe one's senses, like a duck in thunder.

wonderful, wondrous; surprising &c. *v.*; unexpected &c. 508; un-heard of; mysterious &c. (*inexplicable*) 519; miraculous; *foudroyant*.

in-describable, -expressible, -effable; un-utterable, -speakable.

monstrous, prodigious, stupendous, marvellous; in-conceivable, -credible; in-, un-imaginable; strange &c. (*uncommon*) 83; passing strange.

striking &c. *v.*; over-whelming; wonder-working.

Adv. wonderfully &c. *adj.*; fearfully; for a –, in the name of-wonder; strange to say; *mirabile -dictu, – visu*; to one's great surprise.

with -wonder &c. *n.*, – gaping mouth, – open eyes, – upturned eyes; eyes starting out of one's head.

Int. lo, – and behold! O! hey-day! halloo! what! indeed! really! surely! humph! hem! good -lack, – heavens, – gracious! – lord! by jove! gad so! well a day! dear me! only think! lack-a-daisy! my -stars, – goodness! gracious goodness! goodness gracious! mercy on us! heavens and earth! God bless me! bless -us, – my heart! odzookens! *O gemini!* adzooks! hoity-toity! strong! Heaven save –, bless- the mark! can such things be! zounds! 'sdeath! what -on earth, – in the world! who would have thought it! &c. (*inexpectation*) 508; fancy! did you ever? you don't say so! what do you say to that! how now! where am I? well I'm blowed! &c.

Phr. *vox faucibus hæsit*; one's hair standing on end.

perturbable &c. 826; expected &c. *v.*; foreseen.

common, ordinary &c. (*habitual*) 613.

Int. no wonder; of course; why not?

————

872. Prodigy.—N. prodigy, phenomenon; wonder, -ment; genius, marvel, miracle; freak, monster &c. (*unconformity*) 83; curiosity, lion, infant prodigy, sight, spectacle; *jeu –, coup- de théâtre*; gazing-stock; sign; portent &c. 512.

bursting of a -shell, – bomb; volcanic eruption, peal of thunder; thunder-clap, -bolt.

what no words can paint; wonders of the world; *annus mirabilis*; *dignus vindice nodus*.

5°. INTRINSIC AFFECTIONS*

873. Repute.—N. distinction, mark, name, figure; repute, reputation, char-

874. Disrepute.—N. disrepute, dis-credit; ill-, bad- -repute, -name, -odour,

* Or personal affections derived from the opinions or feelings of others.

acter; good –, high- repute; note, notability, notoriety, *éclat*, 'the bubble reputation,' vogue, celebrity; fame, famousness; renown; popularity, *aura popularis*; esteem, approval, approbation &c. 931; credit, *succès d'estime*, *prestige*, talk of the town; name to conjure with.

glory, honour; lustre &c. (*light*) 420; illustriousness &c. *adj.*,

account, regard, respect; reputableness &c. *adj.*; respectability &c. (*probity*) 939; good -name, – report; fair name.

dignity; stateliness &c. *adj.*; solemnity, grandeur, splendour, nobility, majesty, sublimity.

rank, standing, brevet rank, precedence, *pas*, station, place, *status*; position, – in society; order, degree, *locus standi*, caste, condition.

greatness &c. *adj.*; eminence; height &c. 206; importance &c. 642; pre-, super-eminence; high mightiness, primacy; top of the -ladder, – tree.

elevation; ascent &c. 305; super-, ex-altation; dignification, aggrandizement.

dedication, consecration, enthronement, canonization, apotheosis, deification, celebration, enshrinement, glorification.

hero, man of mark, great card, celebrity, champion, worthy, lion, *rara avis*, notability, somebody; man of rank &c. (*nobleman*) 875; pillar of the -state, – society, – church.

chief &c. (*master*) 745; first fiddle &c. (*proficient*) 700; scholar &c. 492; cynosure, mirror; flower, pink, pearl; paragon &c. (*perfection*) 650; choice and master spirits of the age; *élite*; star, sun, constellation, galaxy.

ornament, honour, feather in one's cap, halo, aureole, nimbus; halo –, blaze- of glory; blushing honours; laurels &c. (*trophy*) 733.

memory, posthumous fame, niche in the temple of fame; immor-tality, -tal name; *magni nominis umbra*.

V. be conscious of glory; be proud of &c. (*pride*) 878; exult &c. (*boast*) 884; be vain of &c. (*vanity*) 880.

be -distinguished &c. *adj.*; shine &c.

-favour; disapprobation &c. 932; ingloriousness, derogation; a-, de-basement; abjectness &c. *adj.*; degradation, dedecoration; 'a long farewell to all one's greatness'; odium, obloquy, opprobrium, ignominy.

dishonour, disgrace; shame, humiliation; scandal, baseness, vileness; perfidy, turpitude &c. (*improbity*) 940; infamy.

tarnish, taint, defilement, pollution.

stain, blot, spot, blur, stigma, brand, reproach, imputation, slur.

crying –, burning- shame; *scandalum magnatum*, badge of infamy, blot in one's escutcheon; bend –, bar- sinister; champain, point champain; by-word of reproach; Ichabod.

argumentum ad verecundiam; sense of shame &c. 879.

V. be -inglorious &c. *adj.*; incur -disgrace &c. *n.*; have –, earn- a bad name; put –, wear- a halter round one's neck; disgrace –, expose- oneself.

play second fiddle; lose caste; pale one's ineffectual fire; recede into the shade; fall from one's high estate; keep in the background &c. (*modesty*) 881; be conscious of disgrace &c. (*humility*) 879; look -blue, – foolish, – like a fool; cut a -poor, – sorry- figure; laugh on the wrong side of the mouth; make a sorry face, go away with a flea in one's ear, slink away.

cause -shame &c. *n.*; shame, disgrace, put to shame, dishonour; throw –, cast –, fling –, reflect- dishonour &c. *n.* upon; be a -reproach &c. *n.* to; derogate from.

tarnish, stain, blot, sully, taint; discredit; degrade, debase, defile; beggar; expel &c. (*punish*) 972.

impute shame to, brand, post, stigmatize, vilify, defame, slur, cast a slur upon, hold up to shame, send to Coventry; tread –, trample- under foot; show up, drag through the mire, heap dirt upon; reprehend &c. 932.

bring low, put down, snub; take down a peg, – lower, – or two.

obscure, eclipse, outshine, take the shine out of; throw –, cast- into the shade; overshadow; leave –, put- in the background; push into a corner,

(*light*) 420; shine forth, figure; make –, cut- a -figure, – dash, – splash.

rival, surpass; out-shine, -rival, -vie, -jump; emulate, vie with, eclipse; throw –, cast- into the shade; overshadow.

live, flourish, glitter, scintillate, flaunt; gain –, acquire- honour &c. *n*.; play first fiddle &c. (*be of importance*) 642; bear the -palm, – bell; lead the way; take -precedence, – the wall of; gain –, win- -laurels, – spurs, – golden opinions &c. (*approbation*) 931; graduate, take one's degree, pass one's examination, win a -scholarship, – fellowship.

make -a, – some- -noise, – noise in the world; leave one's mark, exalt one's horn, star, have a run, be run after; enjoy popularity, come -into vogue, – to the front; raise one's head.

enthrone, signalize, immortalize, deify, exalt to the skies; hand one's name down to posterity.

consecrate; dedicate to, devote to; enshrine, inscribe, blazon, lionize, blow the trumpet, crown with laurel.

confer –, reflect- honour &c. *n*. on; shed a lustre on; redound to one's honour, ennoble.

give –, do –, pay –, render- honour to; honour, accredit, pay regard to, dignify, glorify; sing praises to &c. (*approve*) 931; look up to; exalt, aggrandize, elevate, nobilitate.

Adj. distinguished, *distingué*, noted; of -note &c. *n*.; honoured &c. *v*.; popular; fashionable &c. 852.

put one's nose out of joint; put out, – of countenance.

upset, throw off one's centre; discompose, disconcert; put to the blush &c. (*humble*) 879.

Adj. disgraced &c. *v*.; blown upon; shorn of -its beams, - one's glory; overcome, down-trodden; loaded with -shame &c. *n*.; in -bad repute &c. *n*.; out of -repute, – favour, – fashion, – countenance; at a discount; under -a cloud, – an eclipse; unable to show one's face; in the -shade, – background; out at elbows, down in the world, down and out.

inglorious; nameless, renownless, obscure, unknown to fame; un-noticed, -noted, -honoured, -glorified.

shameful; dis-graceful, -creditable, -reputable; despicable; questionable; unbecoming, unworthy; derogatory; degrading, humiliating, *infra dignitatem*, dedecorous; scandalous, infamous, too bad, unmentionable; ribald, opprobrious; arrant, shocking, outrageous, notorious, shady.

ignominious, scrubby, dirty, abject, vile, beggarly, pitiful, low, mean, shabby; base &c. (*dishonourable*) 940.

Adv. to one's shame be it spoken.

Int. fie! shame! for shame! *pro pudor! O tempora! O mores!* ough! *sic transit gloria mundi!*

---

in good odour; in –, in high- favour; reput-, respect-, credit-able.

remarkable &c. (*important*) 642; notable, notorious; celebrated. renowned, in every one's mouth, talked of; fam-ous, -ed; far-famed; conspicuous, to the front; foremost; in the -front rank, – ascendant.

imperishable, deathless, immortal, never fading, *ære perennius*; time-honoured.

illustrious, glorious, splendid, brilliant, radiant; bright &c. 420; full-blown; honorific.

eminent, prominent; high &c. 206; in the zenith; at the -head of, – top of the tree; peerless, of the first water; superior &c. 33; super-, pre-eminent.

great, dignified, proud, noble, honourable, worshipful, lordly, grand, stately, august, princely, imposing, solemn, transcendent, majestic, sacred, sublime, heaven-born, heroic, *sans peur et sans reproche*; sacrosanct.

Int. hail! all hail! *ave! viva! vive!* long life to! glory –, honour- be to!

Phr. one's name -being in every mouth, – living for ever; *sic itur ad astra, fama volat, aut Cæsar aut nullus*; not to know him argues oneself unknown; none but himself could be his parallel, *palmam qui meruit ferat.*

875. Nobility.—N.

nobility, rank, condition, distinction, optimacy, blood, *pur sang*, birth, high descent, order; quality, gentility; blue blood of Castile; *ancien régime.*

high life, *haut monde*; upper -classes, – ten thousand; *élite*, aristocracy, great folks; fashionable world &c. (*fashion*) 852; salariat.

peer, -age; House of -Lords, – peers; lords, – temporal and spiritual; *noblesse*; baronage, knightage; noble, -man; lord, -ling; grandee, *magnifico*, *hidalgo*; don, -ship; aristocrat, swell, three-tailed bashaw; gentleman, squire, squireen, patrician, laureate.

gentry, gentlefolk; squirarchy, better sort, *magnates*, *primates*, *optimates.*

king &c. (*master*) 745; prince, crown prince, *Dauphin*; duke; marquis, -ate; earl, viscount, baron, thane, banneret; baronet, -cy; knight, -hood; count, armiger, laird; sig-, seig-nior; esquire, boyar, margrave, vavasour, sheik, emir, ameer, scherif, *pasha*, effendi, sahib.

queen &c. 745; princess, begum, duchess, marchioness; countess &c.; lady, dame.

personage –, man- of -distinction, – mark, – rank; nota-bles, -bilities; celebrity, big-wig, magnate, great man, star; *magni nominis umbra*; 'every inch a king'; grand Panjandrum.

V. be -noble &c. *adj.*

Adj. noble, exalted; of -rank &c. *n.*; princely, titled, patrician, aristocratic; high-, well-born; of gentle blood; genteel, *comme il faut*, gentlemanlike, courtly &c. (*fashionable*) 852; highly respectable.

Adv. in high quarters.

877. Title.—N.

title, honour; knighthood &c. (*nobility*) 875.

royal –, serene- highness, excellency, grace; lordship, worship, Rt. Hon., rever-ence, -end; esquire, sir; madam, *madame*; master, mistress, Mr., Mrs., *signor*, *señor*, *Mein Herr*, *mynheer*;

876. Commonalty.—N.

commonalty, democracy; obscurity; low -condition, – life, – society, – company; *bourgeoisie*; mass of -the people, – society; Brown, Jones, and Robinson; Tom, Dick, and Harry; lower –, humbler- -classes, – orders; vulgar –, common- herd; rank and file, *hoc genus omne*; the -many, – general, – crowd, – people, – populace, – multitude, – million, – masses, – mobility, – peasantry; king Mob; proletariat, *fruges consumere nati*, great unwashed; man in the street.

mob; rabble, – rout; chaff, rout, horde, *canaille*; scum –, *residuum* –, dregs- of -the people, – society; swinish multitude, *fæx populi*; *profanum* –, *ignobile- vulgus*; vermin, riff-raff, tag-rag and bobtail; small fry.

commoner, one of the people, democrat, plebeian, republican, proletary, *prolétaire*, *roturier*, Mr. Snooks, *bourgeois*, *épicier*, Philistine, cockney; *grisette*, *demi-mondaine.*

peasant, countryman, boor, carle, churl; vill-ain, -ein; serf, kern, tyke, tike, chuff, ryot, fellah; long-shore-man; swain, clown, hind; clod, -hopper; hobnail, yokel, hick, rube, cider squeezer, bog-trotter, bumpkin; plough-man, -boy; rustic, chawbacon, tiller of the soil; hewers of wood and drawers of water, groundling; gaffer, loon, put, cub, Tony Lumpkin, looby, lout, underling; *gamin*, guttersnipe, street arab, mudlark; rough, rowdy, ruffian, roughneck; pot-walloper, slubberde-gullion; vulgar –, low- fellow; cad, curmudgeon.

upstart, *parvenu*, *nouveau-riche*, skip-jack; nobody, – one knows; *hesterni quirites*, *pessoribus orti*; *bourgeois gentil-homme*, *novus homo*, snob, gent, mush-room, no one knows who, adventurer; man of straw.

beggar, panhandler, gaberlunzie, muckworm, mudlark, *sans-culotte*, raff, tatterdemalion, caitiff, ragamuffin, Pariah, outcast of society, tramp, weary Willie, bum, vagabond, *chiffon-*

your –, his- honour; handle to one's name.

decoration, laurel, palm, wreath, garland, bays, medal, ribbon, riband, blue ribbon, *cordon*, cross, crown, coronet, star, garter; feather, – in one's cap; chevron, epaulet, *épaulette*, colours, cockade; livery; order, arms, armorial bearings, shield, scutcheon, crest, reward &c. 973.

nier, rag-picker, Cinderella, cinder-wench, scrub, jade; boots, gosscon.

Goth, Vandal, Hottentot, savage, barbarian, Yahoo; unlicked cub, rough diamond.

barbar-ousness, -ism; Bœotia.

V. be -ignoble &c. *adj.*, – nobody &c. *n.*

Adj. ignoble, common, mean, low, base, vile, sorry, scrubby, beggarly, below par; no great shakes &c. (*unimportant*) 643; home-ly, -spun; vulgar, low-minded; snobbish, *parvenu*.

plebeian, proletarian; of -low, – mean- -parentage, – origin, extraction; low-, base-, earth-born, low bred; mushroom, dunghill, risen from the ranks; unknown to fame, obscure, untitled.

rustic, uncivilized; lout-, boor-, clown-, churl-, brut-, raff-ish; rude, unlicked, unpolished.

barbar-ous, -ian, -ic, -esque; cockney, born within sound of Bow bells.

underling, menial, servile, subaltern.

Adv. below the salt.

---

878. Pride.—N. dignity, self-respect, *mens sibi conscia recti.*

pride; haughtiness &c. *adj.*; high notions, *hauteur*; vainglory, crest; arrogance &c. (*assumption*) 885; pomposity &c. 882.

proud man, highflier; fine -gentleman, – lady; *grande dame.*

V. be -proud &c. *adj.*; put a good face on; look one in the face; stalk abroad, perk oneself up; presume, swagger, strut; rear –, lift up –, hold up- one's head; hold one's head high, look big, take the wall, 'bear like the Turk no rival near the throne,' carry with a high hand; ride the –, mount on one's- high horse; set one's back up, bridle, toss the head; give oneself airs &c. (*assume*) 885; boast &c. 884.

pride oneself on; glory in, take a pride in; pique –, plume –, hug- oneself; stand upon, be proud of; put a good face on; not -hide one's light under a bushel, – put one's talent in a napkin; not think small beer of oneself &c. (*vanity*) 880.

Adj. dignified; stately; proud, -crested; lordly, baronial; lofty-minded; high-souled, -minded, -mettled, -handed, -plumed, -flown, -toned.

879. Humility.—N. hum-ility, -bleness; meek-, low-ness; lowli-ness, -hood; abasement, self-abasement, -effacement; submission &c. 725; resignation.

condescension; affability &c. (*courtesy*) 894.

modesty &c. 881; verecundity, blush, suffusion, confusion; sense of -shame, – disgrace; humiliation, mortification; let –, set- down.

V. be -humble &c. *adj.*; deign, vouchsafe, condescend; humble –, demean- oneself; stoop, – to conquer; carry coals; submit &c. 725; submit with a good grace &c. (*brook*) 826; yield the palm.

lower one's -tone, – note; sing small, draw in one's horns, sober down; hide one's -face, – diminished head; not dare to show one's face, take shame to oneself, not have a word to say for oneself; feel –, be conscious of- -shame, – disgrace; drink the cup of humiliation to the dregs; eat -humble pie, – one's words, – dirt; be humiliated, receive a snub.

blush -for, – up to the eyes; redden, change colour; colour up; hang one's head, look foolish, feel small.

render humble; humble, humiliate;

haughty, paughty, insolent, lofty, high, mighty, swollen, puffed up, flushed, blown; vain-glorious; purse-proud, fine; proud as -a peacock, Lucifer; bloated with pride.

supercilious, disdainful, bumptious, magisterial, imperious; high -handed, – and mighty; overweening, consequential; arrogant &c. 885; unblushing &c. 880.

stiff, -necked; starch; perked –, stuck- up; in buckram, straitlaced; prim &c. (*affected*) 855.

on one's -high horses, – tight ropes, – high ropes; on stilts; *en grand seigneur*.

Adv. with head erect, with one's nose in the air.

Phr. *odi profanum vulgus et arceo.*

---

let –, set –, take –, tread –, frown-down; snub, abash, abase, make one sing small, strike dumb; teach one -his distance, – his place; take down a peg, – lower; throw –, cast- into the shade &c. 874; stare –, put- out of countenance; put to the blush; confuse, ashame, mortify, disgrace, crush; send away with a flea in one's ear.

get a set down.

Adj. humble, lowly, meek; modest &c. 881; humble-, sober-minded; unoffended; submissive &c. 725; servile &c. 886.

condescending; affable &c. (*courteous*) 894.

humbled &c. *v.*; bowed down, resigned; abashed, ashamed, dashed; out of countenance; down in the mouth; down on one's -knees, – marrow-bones; humbled in the dust, brow-beaten; chap-, crest-fallen; dumbfoundered, flabbergasted, struck all of a heap.

shorn of one's glory &c. (*disrepute*) 874.

Adv. with -downcast eyes, – bated breath, – bended knee; on all fours, on one's feet.

under correction, with due deference.

Phr. I am your -obedient, – very humble- servant; my service to you.

---

880. Vanity.—N. vanity; conceit, -edness; self-conceit, -complacency, -confidence, -sufficiency, -esteem, -love, -approbation, -praise, -glorification, -laudation, -gratulation, -applause, -admiration; *amour-propre*; selfishness &c. 943.

airs, pretensions, mannerism; egotism; prigg-ism, -ishness; coxcombry, gaudery, vainglory, elation; pride &c. 878; ostentation &c. 882; assurance &c. 885.

vox et præterea nihil; *cheval de bataille.*

ego-ist, -tist; peacock, coxcomb &c. 854; Sir Oracle &c. 887.

V. be -vain &c. *adj.*, – vain of; pique oneself &c. (*pride*) 878; lay the flattering unction to one's soul.

have -too high, – an overweening-opinion of -oneself, – one's talents; blind oneself as to one's own merit; not think -small beer, – *vin ordinaire*- of oneself; put oneself forward; fish

---

881. Modesty.—N. modesty; humility &c. 879; diffidence, timidity; retiring disposition, unobtrusiveness, bashfulness &c. *adj.*; *mauvaise honte*; blush, -ing; verecundity; self-knowledge.

reserve, constraint; demureness &c. *adj.*; blushing honours.

V. be -modest &c. *adj.*; retire, reserve oneself; give way to; draw in one's horns &c. 879; hide one's face.

keep -private, – in the background, – one's distance; pursue the noiseless tenor of one's way, 'do good by stealth and blush to find it fame,' hide one's light under a bushel, cast a sheep's eye.

Adj. modest, diffident; humble &c. 879; timid, timorous, bashful; shy, nervous, skittish, coy, sheepish, shame-faced, blushing, over-modest.

unpreten-ding, -tious; un-obtrusive, -assuming, -ostentatious, -boastful, -aspiring; poor in spirit.

for compliments; give oneself airs &c. (*assume*) 885; boast &c. 884.

render -vain &c. *adj.*; inspire with -vanity &c. *n.*; inflate, puff up, turn up, turn one's head.

Adj. vain, – as a peacock; conceited, assured, overweening, pert, forward, perky; vain-glorious, high-flown; ostentatious &c. 882; puffed up, inflated, flushed.

self-satisfied, -confident, -sufficient, -flattering, -admiring, -applauding, -glorious, -opinionated; *entêté* &c. (*wrong-headed*) 481; wise in one's own conceit, pragmatical, overwise, pretentious, priggish; egotistic, -al; *soi-disant* &c. (*boastful*) 884; arrogant &c. 885.

un-abashed, -blushing; un-constrained, -ceremonious; free and easy.

Adv. vainly &c. *adj.*

Phr. how we apples swim!

out of countenance &c. (*humbled*) 879.

reserved, constrained, demure.

Adv. humbly &c. *adj.*; quietly, privately; without -ceremony, – beat of drum; *sans façon*.

---

882. Ostentation.—N. ostentation, display, show, flourish, parade, *étalage*, pomp, array, state, solemnity; dash, splash, glitter, strut, swank, side, swagger, pomposity; preten-se, -sions; showing off; fuss.

magnificence, splendour; *coup d'œil*; grand doings.

coup de théâtre; stage -effect, – trick; clap-trap; *mise en scène*; *tour de force*; *chic*.

demonstration, flying colours; tomfoolery; flourish of trumpets &c. (*celebration*) 883; pageant, -ry; spectacle, exhibition, procession; turn -, set- out; grand function; *fête*, gala, field-day, review, march past, promenade, insubstantial pageant.

dress; court -, full -, evening -, ball -, fancy- dress; tailoring, millinery, man-millinery, frippery; foppery, equipage.

ceremon-y, -ial; ritual; form, -ality; etiquette; punct-o, -ilio, -iliousness; starched-, stateli-ness.

mummery, solemn mockery, mouth honour.

attitudinarian; fop &c. 854.

V. be -ostentatious &c. *adj.*; come -, put oneself- forward; attract attention, star it.

make -, cut- a -figure, – dash, – splash; strut, blow one's own trumpet; figure, – away; make a show, – display; glitter.

show -off, – one's paces; parade, march past; display, exhibit, put forward, hold up; trot -, hang- out; sport, brandish, blazon forth; dangle, – before the eyes.

cry up &c. (*praise*) 931; *prôner*, flaunt, emblazon, prink, set off, mount, have framed and glazed.

put a good, – smiling- face upon; clean the outside of the platter &c. (*disguise*) 544.

Adj. ostentatious, showy, dashing, pretentious; ja-, jau-nty; grand, pompous, palatial; high-sounding; turgid &c. (*big-sounding*) 577; garish, gorgeous; gaudy, – as a -peacock, – butterfly, – tulip; flaunting, flashing, flaming, glittering; gay &c. (*ornate*) 847; colourful.

splendid, magnificent, sumptuous.

theatrical, dramatic, spectacular, scenic, ceremonial, ritual, -istic.

solemn, stately, majestic, formal, stiff, ceremonious, punctilious, starch-ed, -y.

en grande tenue, in best bib and tucker, in Sunday best, *endimanché*.

Adv. with -flourish of trumpet, – beat of drum, – flying colours, – a brass band.

ad captandum vulgus.

883. Celebration.—N. celebration, solemnization, jubilee, diamond jubilee, commemoration, ovation, pæan, triumph, jubilation.

triumphal arch, bonfire, salute; salvo, – of artillery; *feu de joie*, flourish of trumpets, *fanfare*, colours flying, illuminations, fireworks.

inauguration, installation, presentation; *début*, coming out, birthday anniversary, bi-, ter-, centenary; silver –, golden –, diamond-wedding, -day; coronation; Lord Mayor's show; harvest home, red letter day, festival; trophy &c. 733; *Te Deum* &c. (*thanksgiving*) 990; fête &c. 882; holiday &c. 840.

V. celebrate, keep, signalize, do honour to, commemorate, solemnize, hallow, mark with a red letter, hold high festival, maffick.

pledge, drink to, toast, hob and nob.

inaugurate, install, instate, induct, chair.

rejoice &c. 838; kill the fatted calf, hold jubilee, roast an ox, fire a salute.

Adj. celebrating &c. *v.*; commemorative, celebrated, immortal.

Adv. in -honour, – commemoration, – celebration of.

Int. hail! all hail! *io -pæan, – triumphe!* 'see the conquering hero comes!'

884. Boasting.—N. boasting &c. *v.*; boast, vaunt, crake; preten-ce, -sions; puff, -ery; flourish, *fanfaronnade*; gasconade; bluff, swank, brag, -gardism; bravado, bunkum, Buncombe; highfalutin; jact-itation, -ancy; bounce, rant, bluster; venditation, vapouring, rodomontade, bombast, fine talking, tall talk, magniloquence, teratology, heroics; jingoism, Chauvinism; exaggeration &c. 549; gas, hot air.

vanity &c. 880; *vox et præterea nihil*; much cry and little wool, *brutum fulmen*.

exultation; glorification; flourish of trumpets; triumph &c. 883.

boaster; bragg-art, -adocio; hot air merchant; Gascon, *fanfaron*, pretender, fourflusher, *soi-disant*; windbag, blowhard, bluffer; chauvinist; blusterer &c. 887; charlatan, jack-pudding, trumpeter; puppy &c. (*fop*) 854.

V. boast, make a boast of, brag, vaunt, puff, show off, flourish, crake, crack, trumpet, strut, swagger, vapour, bluff; draw the long bow.

exult, crow over, neigh, chuckle, triumph; glory, gloat, jubilate; throw up one's cap; talk big, *se faire valoir, faire claquer son fouet*, take merit to oneself, make a merit of, sing *Io triumphe*, holloa before one is out of the wood.

Adj. boasting &c. *v.*; magniloquent, flaming, Thrasonic, stilted, gasconading, braggart, boastful, pretentious, *soi-disant*; vain-glorious &c. (*conceited*) 880.

elate, -d; jubilant, triumphant, exultant; in high feather; flushed, – with victory; cock-a-hoop; on stilts.

vaunted &c. *v.*

Adv. vauntingly &c. *adj.*; with a brass band.

Phr. 'let the galled jade wince.'

885. [Undue assumption of superiority.] Insolence.—**N.** insolence; haughtiness &c. *adj.*; arrogance, airs; overbearance, brashness, bumptiousness, contumely, disdain; domineering &c. *v.*; tyranny &c. 739.

impertinence; cheek, nerve, sauce; sauciness &c. *adj.*; flippancy, dicacity, petulance, procacity, bluster; swagger, -ing &c. *v.*; bounce; terrorism; jingoism, chauvinism.

as-, pre-sumption; beggar on horseback; usurpation.

impudence, assurance, audacity, self-assertion, hardihood, front, face, brass; shamelessness &c. *adj.*; effrontery, hardened front, face of brass.

assumption of infallibility.

malapert, saucebox &c. (*blusterer*) 887.

V. be -insolent &c. *adj.*; bluster, vapour, swagger, swell, give oneself airs, snap one's fingers, kick up a dust; swear &c. (*affirm*) 535; rap out oaths; roister.

arrogate; as- pre-sume; make -bold, - free; take a liberty, give an inch and take an ell.

domineer, bully, dictate, hector; lord it over, bulldoze; *traiter de haut, regarder de haut en bas*; exact; snub, huff, beard, fly in the face of; put to the blush; bear -, beat- down; browbeat, intimidate; trample -, tread- -down, - under foot; dragoon, ride roughshod over, terrorize.

out-face, -look, -stare, -brazen, -brave; stare out of countenance; brazen out; lay down the law; teach one's grandmother to suck eggs; assume a lofty bearing; talk -, look- big; put on big looks, act the *grand seigneur*; mount -, ride- the high horse; toss the head, carry with a high hand.

tempt Providence, want snuffing.

Adj. insolent, haughty, arrogant, imperious, magisterial, dictatorial, arbitrary; high-handed, high and mighty; contumelious, supercilious, overbearing, intolerant, domineering; overweening, high-flown.

flippant, pert, cavalier, saucy, forward, impertinent, fresh, malapert.

precocious, assuming, would-be, bumptious.

bluff; brazen-, -browed, -faced, shameless, aweless, unblushing, unabashed; bold-, bare-faced; dead -, lost- to shame.

886. Servility.—**N.** servility; slavery &c. (*subjection*) 749; obsequiousness &c. *adj.*; subserviency; abasement; pros-tration, -ternation; genuflexion &c. (*worship*) 990; fawning &c. *v.*; tuft-hunting, time-serving, flunkeyism; sycophancy &c. (*flattery*) 933; humility &c. 879.

sycophant, parasite, yes-man; toad, -y, -eater; tuft-hunter; snob, flunkey, lap-dog, spaniel, lickspittle, smell-feast, *Græculus esuriens*, hanger on, stooge, *cavaliere servente*, led captain, carpet knight; time-server, fortune-hunter, Vicar of Bray, Sir Pertinax Mac Sycophant, pick-thank; flatterer &c. 935; doer of dirty work; *âme damnée*, tool; reptile; slave &c. (*servant*) 746; courtier; sponge, jackal; truckler.

V. cringe, bow, stoop, kneel, bend the knee; fall on one's knees, prostrate oneself; worship &c. 990.

sneak, crawl, crouch, cower, truckle to, grovel, fawn, toady, lick the feet of, kiss the hem of one's garment.

pay court to; feed -, fatten -, batten on; dance attendance on, pin oneself upon, hang on the sleeve of, *avaler des couleuvres*, keep time to, fetch and carry, do the dirty work of.

go with the stream, follow the crowd, worship the rising sun, hold with the hare and run with the hounds.

Adj. servile, obsequious; supple, - as a glove; soapy, oily, pliant, cringing, fawning, slavish, grovelling, snivelling, mealy-mouthed; beggarly, sycophantic, parasitical; abased, abject, prostrate, down on one's marrow-bones; base, mean, sneaking; crouching &c. *v.*

Adv. hat -, cap- in hand.

---

impudent, audacious, presumptuous, free and easy, devil-may-
care, rollicking; janty, jaunty; roistering, blustering, hectoring,
swaggering, vapouring; thrasonic, fire-eating, 'full of sound and
fury.'

Adv. insolently, with a high hand; *ex cathedrâ*.

Phr. one's bark being worse than his bite.

887. Blusterer.—N. bluster-, swagger-, vapour-, roister-, brawl-er;
brazen-face; *fanfaron*; braggart &c. (*boaster*) 884; bully, terrorist,
rough, rough-neck; hooligan, hoodlum, larrikin, ruffian; Mo-hock,
-hawk; drawcansir, swashbuckler, Captain Boabdil, Sir Lucius
O'Trigger, Thraso, Pistol, Parolles, Bombastes Furioso, Hector,
Chrononhotonthologos; jingo; desperado, dare-devil, fire-eater; fury
&c. (*violent person*) 173; rowdy.

puppy &c. (*fop*) 854; prig; Sir Oracle, dogmatist, *doctrinaire*, stump
orator, jack-in-office; saucebox, malapert, jackanapes, minx; bantam-
cock.

Section III. SYMPATHETIC AFFECTIONS

1°. Social Affections

888. Friendship. — N. friendship,
amity; friendliness &c. *adj.*; brotherhood, fraternity, sodality, confrater-
nity, sorosis, sisterhood; harmony &c.
(*concord*) 714; peace &c. 721.

firm -, staunch -, intimate -, familiar -, bosom -, cordial -, tried -,
devoted -, lasting -, fast -, sincere -,
warm -, ardent- friendship.

cordiality, fraternization, *entente cordiale*, good understanding, *rapprochement*, sympathy, fellow-feeling, response, welcomeness; *camaraderie*.

affection &c. (*love*) 897; favouritism;
goodwill &c. (*benevolence*) 906; partiality.

acquaintance, familiarity, intimacy,
intercourse, fellowship, knowledge of;
introduction.

V. be -friendly &c. *adj.*, – friends &c.
890, – acquainted with &c. *adj.*; know;
have the ear of; keep company with &c. (*sociality*) 892; hold communication -, have dealings -·, sympathize- with; have a leaning
to; bear good will &c. (*benevolence*) 906; love &c. 897; make much
of; befriend &c. (*aid*) 707; introduce to.

set one's horses together; hold out -, extend- the right hand of
·friendship, – fellowship; become -friendly &c. *adj.*; make -friends
&c. 892 with; break the ice, be introduced to; make -, pick -,
scrape- acquaintance with; get into favour, gain the friendship of.

shake hands with, fraternize, embrace; receive with open arms,
throw oneself into the arms of; meet half way, take in good part.

Adj. friendly; amic-able, -al; well affected, unhostile, neighbourly,
brotherly, fraternal, sisterly, sympathetic, harmonious, hearty,
cordial, warm-hearted, devoted.

889. Enmity.—N. enmity, hostility,
unfriendliness &c. *adj.*; discord &c. 713.

alienation, estrangement; dislike &c.
867; hate &c. 898; antagonism.

heartburning; animosity &c. 900;
malevolence &c. 907.

V. be -inimical &c. *adj.*; keep -, hold-
at arm's length; be at loggerheads;
bear malice &c. 907; fall out; take
umbrage &c. 900; harden the heart,
alienate, estrange.

Adj. inimical, unfriendly, hostile; at
-enmity, – variance, – swords points,
– daggers drawn, – open war with; up
in arms against; in bad odour with.

on bad -, not on speaking- terms;
cool; cold, -hearted; estranged, alien-
ated, disaffected, irreconcilable.

friends –, well –, at home –, hand in hand- with; on -good, – friendly, – amicable, – cordial, – familiar, – intimate- -terms, – footing; on -speaking, – visiting- terms; in one's good -graces, – books.

acquainted, familiar, intimate, thick, hand and glove, hail fellow well met, free and easy; welcome.

Adv. amicably &c. *adj.*; with open arms; *sans cérémonie*; arm in arm.

890. Friend.—N. friend, – of one's bosom, intimate acquaintance, neighbour, well-wisher; *alter ego*; best –, bosom –, fast- friend; *amicus usque ad aras*; *fidus Achates*; *persona grata*.

favourer, *fautor*, patron, backer, Mæcenas; tutelary saint, good genius, advocate, partisan, sympathiser; ally; friend in need &c. (*auxiliary*) 711.

891. Enemy.—N. enemy; antagonist, foeman; open –, bitter- enemy; opponent &c. 710; back friend.

public enemy, enemy to society, traitor, anarchist &c. 742; *persona non grata*.

Phr. every hand being against one.

_____

associate, compeer, comrade, mate, companion, *confrère*, *camarade*, *confidante*, colleague; old –, crony; side-kick; chum, buddy, bunkie, roommate, pal; play-fellow, -mate; classmate, schoolfellow; bed-fellow, -mate; maid of honour.

compatriot; fellow –, countryman, – townsman.

shop-, ship-, mess-mate; fellow –, boon –, pot- companion; co-partner.

Arcades ambo, Pylades and Orestes, Castor and Pollux, Nisus and Euryalus, Damon and Pythias, *par nobile fratrum*.

host, Amphitryon, Boniface; guest, visitor, frequenter, *habitué*; *protégé*.

892. Sociality.—N. soci-ality, -ability, -ableness &c. *adj.*; social intercourse; consociation; inter-course, -community; consort-, companion-, fellow-, comrade-ship; clubbism; *esprit de corps*.

conviviality; good -fellowship, – company, *camaraderie*; joviality, jollity, *savoir-vivre*, festivity, festive board, merry-making; loving cup; hospitality, heartiness; cheer.

welcome, -ness; greeting; hearty –, warm –, welcome- reception; urbanity &c. (*courtesy*) 894; intimacy, familiarity.

good –, jolly- fellow, good mixer, Rotarian; *bon enfant*.

social –, family- circle; circle of acquaintance, *coterie*, society, company.

social -gathering, – *réunion*; assembly &c. (*assemblage*) 72; party, entertainment, reception, *levée*, at home, *conversazione*, *soirée*, *matinée*, evening –, morning –, afternoon –, garden –, dinner –, tea –, cocktail- party; symposium, sing-song; kettle-, drum; *partie carrée*, dish of tea, *ridotto*, rout, house-

893. Seclusion. Exclusion.—N. seclusion, privacy; retirement; concealment; reclusion, recess; snugness &c. *adj.*; delitescence; rustication, *rus in urbe*; solitude; solitariness &c. (*single-ness*) 87; isolation; loneliness &c. *adj.*; estrangement from the world, anchoritism, voluntary exile; aloofness.

cell, hermitage; convent &c. 1000; *sanctum sanctorum*; study, library, den; hide-out.

depopulation, desertion, desolation; wilderness &c. (*unproductive*) 169; howling wilderness; rotten borough, Old Sarum.

exclusion, excommunication, banishment, exile, ostracism, proscription; cut, – direct; dead cut.

inhospit-ality, -ableness &c. *adj.*; un-, dis-sociability; domesticity, Darby and Joan.

recluse, hermit, eremite, cenobite; anchor-et, -ite; Simon Stylites; Troglodyte, Timon of Athens, Santon, *solitaire*, ruralist, disciple of Zimmermann, closet cynic, Diogenes; outcast, pariah.

warming; ball, prom, hop, dance, *thé dansant*; festival &c. (*amusement*) 840; wedding breakfast; 'the feast of reason and the flow of soul.'

visit, -ing; round of visits; call, morning call; interview &c. (*interlocution*) 588; assignation; tryst, -ing place; appointment.

club &c. (*association*) 712.

V. be -sociable &c. *adj.*; know; be -acquainted &c. *adj.*; associate -, sort -, keep company -, walk hand in hand -with; eat off the same trencher, club together, consort, bear one company, join; make acquaintance with &c. (*friendship*) 888; make advances, fraternize, embrace; intercommunicate.

be -, feel -, make oneself- at home with; make free with; crack a bottle with; take pot luck with, receive hospitality, live at free quarters.

visit, pay a visit; interchange -visits, - cards; call -at, - upon; leave a card; drop in, look in; look one up, beat up one's quarters.

entertain; give a -party &c. *n.*; be at home, see one's friends, hang out, keep open house, do the honours; receive, - with open arms; welcome; give a warm reception &c. *n.* to; kill the fatted calf.

Adj. sociable, companionable, clubbable, clubby, conversable, cosy, cosey, chatty, conversational; homiletical.

convivial; fest-ive, -al; jovial, jolly, hospitable.

welcome, - as the roses in May; *fêté*, entertained.

free and easy, hail fellow well met, familiar, on visiting terms, acquainted.

social, neighbourly; international, cosmopolitan, gregarious.

Adv. *en famille*, in the family circle; *sans -façon*, - *cérémonie*, arm in arm.

castaway, outsider, pilgarlic; wastrel, foundling, orphan.

V. be -, live- secluded &c. *adj.*; keep -, stand -, hold oneself- -aloof, - in the background; keep snug; shut oneself up; deny -, seclude- oneself; creep into a corner, rusticate, *aller planter ses choux*; retire, - from the world; hermetize, take the veil; abandon &c. 624.

cut, - dead; refuse to -associate with, - acknowledge; look cool -, turn one's back -, shut the door- upon; repel, blackball, excommunicate, exclude, exile, expatriate; banish, outlaw, maroon, ostracize, proscribe, cut off from, send to Coventry, keep at arm's length, draw a cordon round; boycott, blockade, lay an embargo on, isolate.

depopulate; dis-, un-people.

Adj. secluded, sequestered, retired, delitescent, private, bye; out of the -world, -way; in a backwater; 'the world forgetting by the world forgot.'

snug, domestic, stay-at-home.

unsociable; un-, dis-social; inhospitable, cynical, inconversable, unclubbable, *sauvage*, eremetic.

solitary; lone-ly, -some; isolated, single.

excluded, estranged; unfrequented; uninhabit-able, -ed; tenantless; un-tenanted, -occupied; abandoned; deserted, - in one's utmost need; unfriended; kith-, friend-, home-less; lorn, forlorn, desolate.

un-visited, -introduced, -invited, -welcome; under a cloud, left to shift for oneself, derelict, outcast, outside the gates.

banished &c. *v.*; under an embargo.

Phr. *noli me tangere*.

---

894. Courtesy.—N. courtesy; respect &c. 928; good -manners, - behaviour, - breeding; manners; politeness &c. *adj.*; *bienséance*, urbanity, comity, gentility; gentle -, breeding; polish, presence, cultivation, culture; civili-ty, -zation; amenity, suavity; good -temper, - humour; amiability, easy temper, complacency, soft tongue,

895. Discourtesy.—N. discourtesy; ill-breeding; ill -, bad -, ungainly- manners; insuavity; grouchiness; uncourteousness &c. *adj.*, tactlessness; rusticity, inurbanity; illiberality, in- civility, displacency.

disrespect &c. 929; procacity, impudence; barbar-ism, -ity; misbehaviour, brutality, blackguardism, conduct un-

mansuetude; condescension &c. (*humility*) 879; affability, complaisance, *prévenance*, amiability, gallantry, chivalry; pink of -politeness, – courtesy.

compliment; fair -, soft -, sweet-words; honeyed phrases, flattering remarks, ceremonial; salutation, reception, presentation, introduction, *accueil*, greeting, recognition; welcome, *abord*, respects, *devoir*, regards, remembrances; kind -regards, – remembrances; love, best love, duty; deference.

obeisance &c. (*reverence*) 928; bow, courtesy, curtsy, scrape, *salaam*, *kowtow*, bowing and scraping; kneeling; genuflexion &c. (*worship*) 990; obsequiousness &c. 886; capping, shaking hands &c. *v.*; grip of the hand, embrace, hug, squeeze, *accolade*, loving cup, *vin d'honneur*, pledge; love token &c. (*endearment*) 902; kiss, buss, salute.

mark of recognition, nod; 'nods and becks and wreathed smiles'; valediction &c. 293; condolence &c. 915.

V. be -courteous &c. *adj.*; show -courtesy &c. *n.*

mind one's P's and Q's, behave oneself, be all things to all men, conciliate, speak one fair, take in good part; make -, do- the amiable; look as if butter would not melt in one's mouth; mend one's manners.

receive, do the honours, usher, greet, hail, bid welcome; welcome, – with open arms; shake hands; hold out -, press -, squeeze- the hand; bid God speed; speed the parting guest; cheer, serenade.

salute; embrace &c. (*endearment*) 902; kiss, – hands; drink to, pledge, hob and nob; move to, nod to; smile upon.

uncover, cap; touch -, take off- the hat; doff the cap; pull the forelock; present arms; make way for; bow; make one's bow; scrape, curtsy, courtesy; bob a -curtsy, – courtesy; kneel; bow -, bend- the knee; salaam, *kowtow*.

visit, wait upon, present oneself, pay one's respects, pay a visit &c. (*sociability*) 892; dance attendance on &c. (*servility*) 886; pay attentions to; do homage to &c. (*respect*) 928.

becoming a gentleman, *grossièreté, brusquerie*; vulgarity &c. 851.

churlishness &c. *adj.*; spinosity, perversity; moroseness &c. (*sullenness*) 901a.

bad-, ill-temper; sternness &c. *adj.*; austerity; moodishness, captiousness &c. 901; cynicism; tartness &c. *adj.*; acrimony, acerbity, virulence, asperity.

scowl, black looks, frown; short answer, rebuff; hard words, contumely; unparliamentary language, personality.

bear, bruin, brute, grouch, blackguard, beast; unlicked cub; frump, cross-patch; saucebox &c. 887.

V. be -rude &c. *adj.*; insult &c. 929; treat with discourtesy; take a name in vain; make -bold, – free- with; take a liberty; stare out of countenance, ogle, point at, put to the blush.

cut; turn -one's back upon, – on one's heel; give the cold shoulder; keep at -a distance, – arm's length; look -cool, – coldly, – black- upon; show the door to, send away with a flea in the ear.

lose one's temper &c. (*resentment*) 900; sulk &c. 901a; frown, scowl, glower, pout; snap, snarl, growl.

render -rude &c. *adj.*; brut-alize, -ify.

Adj. dis-, un-courteous; uncourtly; ill-bred, -mannered, -behaved, -conditioned; unbred; unmanner-ly, ed; im-, un-polite; un-polished, -civilized, -genteel; ungentleman-like, -ly; unladylike; blackguard; vulgar &c. 851; dedecorous; foul-mouthed, -spoken; abusive.

un-civil, -gracious, -ceremonious; cool; pert, forward, obtrusive, impudent, rude, saucy, precocious; insolent &c. 885.

repulsive; un-complaisant, -accommodating, -neighbourly, -gallant; inaffable; un-gentle, -gainly; rough, rugged, bluff, blunt, gruff; churl-, boor-, bear-ish; brutal, *brusque*; stern, harsh, austere; cavalier.

tart, sour, crabbed, sharp, short, trenchant, sarcastic, crusty, biting, caustic, virulent, bitter, acrimonious, venomous, contumelious; snarling &c, *v.*; surly, – as a bear; perverse; grim.

prostrate oneself &c. (*worship*) 990. give –, send- one's duty &c. *n.* to.

render -polite &c. *adj.*; polish, civilize, humanize.

Adj. courteous, polite, civil, mannerly, urbane; well-behaved, -mannered, -bred, -brought up, gently bred, of gentle -breeding, – manners, good-mannered, polished, civilized, cultivated; refined &c. (*taste*) 850; gentlemanlike &c. (*fashion*) 852; gallant, chivalrous, on one's good behaviour.

fine –, fair –, soft- spoken; honey-mouthed, -tongued; oily, unctuous, bland, suave; obliging, conciliatory, complaisant, complacent; obsequious &c. 886.

ingratiating, winning; gentle, mild; good-humoured, cordial, gracious, amiable, tactful, addressful, affable, genial, friendly, familiar; neighbourly.

Adv. courteously &c. *adj.*; with a good grace; with -open, – outstretched- arms; *à bras ouverts*; *suaviter in modo*, in good humour.

Int. hail! welcome! well met! *ave!* all hail! good -day, – morning &c., – morrow! God speed! *pax vobiscum!* may your shadow never be less! *chin-chin!*

sullen &c. 901*a*; peevish &c. (*irascible*) 901.

Adv. discourteously &c. *adj.*; with -discourtesy &c. *n.*, – a bad grace.

---

896. Congratulations.—N. con-, gratulation; felicitation; salute &c. 894; condolence &c. 915; compliments of the season; good –, best-wishes.

V. con-, gratulate; felicitate, compliment; give –, wish one- joy; tender –, offer- one's congratulations; wish -many happy returns of the day, – a merry Christmas and a happy new year.

congratulate oneself &c. (*rejoice*) 838.

Adj. con-, gratulatory.

---

897. Love.—N. love; fondness &c. *adj.*; liking; inclination &c. (*desire*) 865; regard, dilection, admiration, fancy.

affection, sympathy, fellow-feeling; tenderness &c. *adj.*; heart, brotherly love; benevolence &c. 906; attachment.

yearning, tender passion, *affaire de cœur*, *amour* gallantry, passion, flame, devotion, fervour, enthusiasm, transport of love, rapture, enchantment, infatuation, adoration, idolatry.

narcissism, Œdipus complex, Electra complex.

Cupid, Venus, Eros; myrtle; true lover's knot; love -token, – suit, – affair, – tale, – story; the old story, plighted love; courtship &c. 902; *amourette*.

maternal love.

attractiveness, charm; popularity; favourite &c. 899.

lover, suitor, follower, admirer, adorer, wooer, amoret, beau, sweet-

898. Hate.—N. hate, hatred, vials of hate; Hymn of Hate.

dis-affection, -favour; alienation, estrangement, coolness; enmity &c. 889; animosity &c. 900.

umbrage, pique, grudge; dudgeon, spleen; bitterness, – of feeling; ill –, bad- blood; acrimony; malice &c. 907; implacability &c. (*revenge*) 919.

repugnance &c. (*dislike*) 867; odium, unpopularity; loathing, detestation, antipathy; object of -hatred, – execration; abomination, aversion, *bête noire*; enemy &c. 891; bitter pill; source of annoyance &c. 830.

V. hate, detest, abominate, abhor, loathe; recoil –, shudder- at; shrink from, view with horror, hold in abomination, revolt against, execrate; scowl &c. 895; disrelish &c. (*dislike*) 867.

owe a grudge; bear -spleen, – a grudge, – malice &c. (*malevolence*) 907; conceive an aversion to.

heart, inamorato, swain, young man, flame, love, truelove; leman, Lothario, gallant, paramour, *amoroso, cavaliere servente*, captive, *cicisbeo; caro sposo*, Don Juan, sheik, ladies' man, squire of dames, Knave of Hearts.

inamorata, lady-love, idol, darling, duck, Dulcinea, angel, goddess, *cara sposa*; mistress.

betrothed, affianced, *fiancée*.

flirt, *coquette*; amorette; pair of turtle doves; abode of love, *agapemone*.

V. love, like, affect, fancy, care for, take an interest in, be partial to, sympathize with; be -in love &c. *adj.*-with; have -, entertain -, harbour -, cherish- a -love &c. *n.* for; regard, revere; take to, bear love to, be wedded to; set one's affections on; make much of, feast one's eyes on; hold dear, prize, treasure; hug, cling to, cherish, pet, caress &c. 902.

burn; adore, idolize, love to distraction, *aimer éperdument*; dote -on, - upon.

take a fancy to, fall for, be stuck on, look sweet upon; become -enamoured &c. *adj.*; fall in love with, lose one's heart; desire &c. 865.

excite love; win -, gain -, secure -, engage- the -love, - affections, - heart; take the fancy of; have a place in -, wind round- the heart; attract, attach, endear, charm, fascinate, captivate, bewitch, seduce, enamour, enrapture, turn the head.

get into favour; ingratiate -, insinuate -, worm- oneself; propitiate, curry favour with, pay one's court to, make a date with, *faire l'aimable*, set one's cap at, flirt, coquet.

Adj. loving &c. *v.*; fond of; taken -, struck- with; smitten, bitten; attached to, wedded to; enamoured; charmed &c. *v.*; in love; love-sick; over head and ears in love.

affectionate, tender, sweet upon, sympathetic, loving, fond, amorous, amatory; erotic, uxurious, ardent, passionate, rapturous, devoted, motherly.

loved &c. *v.*; beloved; well -, dearly- beloved; dear, precious, darling, pet, little; favourite, popular.

congenial; to -, after- one's -mind, - taste, - fancy, - own heart.

in one's good -graces &c. (*friendly*) 888; dear as the apple of one's eye, nearest to one's heart.

lovable, adorable; lovely, sweet; attractive, seductive, winning; charming, engaging, interesting, enchanting, captivating, fascinating, intriguing, bewitching; amiable, like an angel, angelic, seraphic.

excite -, provoke- hatred &c. *n.*; be -hateful &c. *adj.*; stink in the nostrils; estrange, alienate, repel, set against, sow dissension, set by the ears, envenom, incense, irritate, rile, ruffle, vex; horrify &c. 830.

Adj. hating &c. *v.*; abhorrent; averse from &c. (*disliking*) 867; set against.

bitter &c. (*acrimonious*) 895; implacable &c. (*revengeful*) 919.

un-loved, -beloved, -lamented, -deplored, -mourned, -cared for, -endured, -valued; disliked &c. 867.

crossed in love, forsaken, rejected, love-lorn, jilted.

obnoxious, hateful, odious, abominable, repulsive, offensive, shocking; disgusting &c. (*disagreeable*) 830.

invidious, spiteful; malicious &c. 907; insulting, irritating, provoking.

[Mutual hate] at -daggers drawn, - swords points; not on speaking terms &c. (*enmity*) 889.

Phr. no love lost between.

---

899. Favourite.—**N.** favourite, pet, cosset, minion, idol, jewel, spoiled child, *enfant gâté*; led captain; crony; fondling; apple of one's eye, man after one's own heart; *persona grata*.

love, dear, darling, duck, honey, jewel; mopsey, moppet; sweetheart &c. (*love*) 897.

general –, universal- favourite; idol of the people; matinée idol, movie –, radio- star.

900. Resentment.—N. resentment, displeasure, animosity, anger, wrath, indignation; vexation, exasperation, bitter resentment, wrathful indignation.

pique, umbrage, huff, miff, soreness, dudgeon, acerbity, virulence, bitterness, acrimony, asperity, spleen, gall; heart-burning, -swelling; rankling.

ill –, bad- -humour, – temper; irascibility &c. 901; ill blood &c. (*hate*) 898; revenge &c. 919.

excitement, irritation; warmth, bile, choler, ire, fume, pucker, dander, ferment, ebullition; towering -passion, – rage, *acharnement,* angry mood, taking, pet, tiff, passion, fit, tantrums.

burst, explosion, paroxysm, storm, rage, fury, desperation; violence &c. 173; fire and fury; vials of wrath; gnashing of teeth, hot blood, high words.

scowl &c. 895; sulks &c. 901*a.*

[Cause of umbrage] affront, provocation, offence; indignity &c. (*insult*) 929; grudge, crow to pluck, sore subject; red rag to a bull; *casus belli.*

Furies, Erinys, Eumenides, Alecto, Megæra, Tisiphone.

buffet, slap in the face, box on the ear, rap on the knuckles.

V. resent; take -amiss, – ill, – to heart, – offence, – umbrage, – huff, – exception; take in -ill part, – bad part, – dudgeon; *ne pas entendre raillerie*; breathe revenge, cut up rough.

fly –, fall –, get- into a -rage, – passion; bridle –, bristle –, froth –, fire –, flare- up; open –, pour out- the vials of one's wrath.

pout, knit the brow, frown, scowl, lower, snarl, growl, gnarl, gnash, snap; redden, colour; look -black, – black as thunder, – daggers; bite one's thumb; show –, grind- one's teeth; champ the bit.

chafe, mantle, fume, kindle, fly out, take fire; boil, – over; boil with -indignation, – rage; rage, storm, foam; vent one's -rage, – spleen; lose one's temper, stand on one's hind legs, stamp the foot, kick up a row, fly off the handle, cut up rough; stamp –, quiver –, swell –, foam- with rage; burst with anger; raise Cain, breathe fire and fury.

have a fling at; bear malice &c. (*revenge*) 919.

cause –, raise- anger; affront, offend; give -offence, – umbrage; anger; hurt the feelings; insult, discompose, fret, ruffle, nettle, heckle, huff, pique; excite &c. 824; irritate, stir the blood, stir up bile; sting, – to the quick; rile, provoke, chafe, wound, incense, inflame, enrage, aggravate, add fuel to the flame, fan into a flame, widen the breach, envenom, embitter, exasperate, infuriate, kindle wrath; stick in one's gizzard; rankle &c. 919.

put out of humour; put one's -monkey, – back- up; set –, get- one's back up; raise one's -gorge, – dander, – choler; work up into a passion; make -one's blood boil, – the ears tingle; throw into a ferment, madden, drive one mad; lash into -fury, – madness; fool to the top of one's bent; set by the ears.

bring a hornet's nest about one's ears.

Adj. angry, wrath, irate; ire-, wrath-ful; cross &c. (*irascible*) 901; sulky &c. 901*a*; bitter, virulent; acrimonious &c. (*discourteous*) &c. 895; violent &c. 173.

warm, burning; boiling, – – over; fuming, raging; foaming, – at the mouth; convulsed with rage.

offended &c. *v.*; waxy, *acharné*; wrought, worked up; indignant, hurt, sore, peeved; set against.

fierce, wild, rageful, furious, mad with rage, fiery, infuriate, rabid, savage; relentless &c. 919.

flushed with -anger, – rage; in a -huff, – stew. – fume, – pucker, – passion, – rage, – fury; on one's high ropes. up in arms; in high dudgeon.

Adv. angrily &c. *adj.*; in the height of passion; in the heat of -passion, – the moment.

Int. *tantæne animis cœlestibus iræ!* marry come up! zounds! 'sdeath!

Phr. one's -blood, – back, – monkey- being up; *fervens difficili bile jecur*; the gorge rising, eyes flashing fire; the blood -rising, – boiling; *hæret lateri lethalis arundo.*

901. Irascibility.—N. irascibility, temper; crossness &c. *adj.*; susceptibility, procacity, petulance, irritability, tartness, acerbity, protervity; pugnacity &c. (*contentiousness*) 720.

excitability &c. 825; bad –, fiery –, crooked –, irritable &c. *adj.*; temper; *genus irritabile*, hot blood.

ill humour &c. (*sullenness*) 901a; asperity &c., churlishness &c. (*discourtesy*) 895.

huff &c. (resentment) 900; a word and a blow.

Sir Fretful Plagiary; brabbler, Tartar; shrew, vixen, virago, termagant, dragon, scold, Xanthippe; porcupine; spit-fire; fire-eater &c.; (*blusterer*) 887; fury &c. (*violent person*) 173.

V. be -irascible &c. *adj.*; have a -temper &c. *n.*, – devil in one; fire up &c. (*be angry*) 900.

Adj. irascible; bad-, ill-tempered; irritable, susceptible; excitable &c. 825; thin-skinned &c. (*sensitive*) 822; fretful, fidgety; on the fret.

hasty, over-hasty, quick, warm, hot, testy, touchy, techy, tetchy; like -touchwood, – tinder; huffy; pet-tish, -ulant; waspish, snapp-y, -ish, peppery, fiery, passionate, choleric, shrewish, 'sudden and quick in quarrel.'

querulous, captious, mood-y, -ish; quarrelsome, contentious, disputatious; pugnacious &c. (*bellicose*) 720; cantankerous, exceptious; restive &c. (*perverse*) 901a; churlish &c. (*discourteous*) 895.

cross, – as -crabs, – two sticks, – a cat, – a dog, – the tongs; like a bear with a sore head; fractious, peevish, *acariâtre*.

in a bad temper; sulky &c. 901a; angry &c. 900.

resent-ful, -ive; vindictive &c. 919.

Int. pish!

901a. Sullenness.—N. sullenness &c. *adj.*; morosity, spleen; churlishness &c. (*discourtesy*) 895; irascibility &c. 901.

moodiness &c. *adj.*; perversity; obstinacy &c. 606; torvity, spinosity; crabbedness &c. *adj.*

ill –, bad- -temper, – humour; sulks, dudgeon, mumps, doleful dumps, doldrums, fit of the sulks, *bouderie*, black looks, scowl; huff &c. (*resentment*) 900.

V. be -sullen &c. *adj.*; sulk; frown, scowl, lower, glower, grouse, grouch, crab, gloam, pout, have a hang-dog look, glout.

Adj. sullen, sulky; ill-tempered, -humoured, -affected, -disposed; in -an ill. – a bad, – a shocking- -temper, – humour; out of -temper, –

humour; knaggy, **torvous**, crusty, crabbed; sore as a boil; surly &c. (*discourteous*) 895.

moody; spleen-ish, -ly; splenetic, cankered.

cross, -grained; perverse, wayward, humoursome; restive; cantankerous, refractory, intractable, exceptious, sinistrous, deaf to reason, unaccommodating, rusty, crusty, froward.

dogged &c. (*stubborn*) 606.

grumpy, glum, grim, grum, morose, frumpish; in the -sulks &c. *n.*; out of sorts; scowl-, glower-, growl-ing.

peevish &c. (*irascible*) 901.

902. [Expression of affection or love.] Endearment.—N. endearment, caress; blandish-, blandi-ment; *épanchement*, fondling, billing and cooing, dalliance.

embrace, salute, kiss, buss, smack, osculation, deosculation; amorous glances; ogle, side glance, sheep's eyes.

courtship, wooing, suit, addresses, the soft impeachment; lovemaking; an affair; serenading; caterwauling.

flirting &c. *v.*; flirtation, gallantry; coquetry, spooning.

true lover's knot, plighted love, engagement, betrothal; love -tale, – token, – letter; *billet-doux*, valentine.

honeymoon; Strephon and Chloe, 'Arry and 'Arriet.

V. caress, fondle, pet, dandle, nurse; pat, – on the -head, – cheek; chuck under the chin, smile upon, coax, wheedle, cosset, coddle, cocker; make -of, – much of, pamper; cherish, foster, kill with kindness.

clasp, hug, cuddle; fold –, strain- in one's arms; nestle, nuzzle, neck, embrace, kiss, buss, smack, blow a kiss; salute &c. (*courtesy*) 894.

bill and coo, spoon, toy, dally, flirt, coquet; galli-, gala-vant; philander; make love; pay one's -court, – addresses, – attentions- to; serenade; court, woo; set one's cap at; be –, look- sweet upon; ogle, cast sheep's eyes upon; *faire les yeux doux*.

fall in love with, win the affections &c. (*love*) 897; die for.

propose; make –, have- an offer; pop the question; plight one's -troth, – faith; become -engaged, – betrothed.

Adj. caressing &c. *v.*; 'sighing like furnace'; love-sick, spoony.

caressed &c. *v.*

903. Marriage.—N. marriage, matrimony, wedlock, union, intermarriage, *vinculum matrimonii*, nuptial tie, knot.

married state, coverture. bed, cohabitation.

match; betrothment &c. (*promise*) 768; wedding, nuptials, Hymen, bridal; e-, spousals; leading to the altar &c. *v.*; nuptial benediction, *epithalamium*.

torch –, temple- of Hymen; hymeneal altar; honeymoon.

bride, bridegroom; brides-maid, -man.

best –, grooms-man, page, usher.

married -man, – woman, – couple; neogamist, Benedick, partner, spouse, mate, yokemate; husband, man, con-

904. Celibacy.—N. celibacy, singleness, single blessedness; bachelor-hood, -ship; miso-gamy, -gyny.

virginity, *pucelage*; maiden-hood, -head.

unmarried man, bachelor, Cœlebs, agamist, old bachelor; miso-gamist, -gynist; celibate.

unmarried woman, spinster; maid, -en; virgin, *femme sole*, old maid; bachelor girl; nun &c.

V. live single; keep bachelor hall.

Adj. un-married, -wedded; wife-, spouse-less; single, virgin, celibate.

905. Divorce.—N. divorce, -ment; separation; judicial separation, separ-

sort, baron; old –, good- man; wife
of one's bosom; help-meet, -mate,
rib, better half, grey mare, old woman,
good wife; *femme couverte*; squaw,
lady; matron, -age, -hood; man and
wife; wedded pair, Darby and Joan.

affinity, soul-mate.

mono-, bi-, di-, deutero-, tri-, polygamy; mormonism; poly-andry; Turk,
Bluebeard.

unlawful –, left-handed –, companionate –, morganatic –, ill-
assorted- marriage; *mésalliance; mariage de convenance;* an affair.

match-maker, marriage broker, matrimonial agent.

V. marry, wive, take to oneself a wife; be -married, – spliced;
go –, pair- off; wed, espouse, lead to the hymeneal altar, take 'for
better, for worse,' give one's hand to, bestow one's hand upon;
remarry; intermarry.

marry, join, handfast; couple &c. (*unite*) 43; tie the nuptial knot;
give -away, – in marriage; affy, affiance; betroth &c. (*promise*) 768;
publish –, bid- the banns; be asked in church.

Adj. married &c. *v.*; one, – bone and one flesh.

marriageable, nubile.

engaged, betrothed, affianced.

matrimonial, marital, conjugal, connubial, wedded; nuptial, hymeneal, spousal, bridal.

Phr. the grey mare the better horse.

ate maintenance; *separatio a -mensâ
et thoro, – vinculo matrimonii.*

widowhood, viduage, viduity, weeds.

widow, -er; relict; dowager; *divorcée;*
cuckold.

V. live -separately, – apart; separate,
divorce, disespouse, put away; wear
the horns.

2°. Diffusive Sympathetic Affections

906. Benevolence.—N. benevolence,
Christian charity; God's -love, – grace;
good-will; philanthropy &c. 910; un-
selfishness &c. 942.

good -nature, – feeling, – wishes;
kind-, kindli-ness &c. *adj.*; lovingkind-
ness, benignity, brotherly love, charity,
humanity, fellow-feeling, sympathy;
goodness –, warmth- of heart; *bonhomie;* kind-heartedness; amiability,
milk of human kindness, tenderness;
love &c. 897; friendship &c. 888.

toleration, consideration, generosity;
mercy &c. (*pity*) 914.

charitableness &c. *adj.*; bounty,
alms-giving; good works, beneficence,
the luxury of doing good.

acts of kindness, a good turn; good
–, kind- -offices, – treatment.

good Samaritan, sympathizer, well-
wisher, philanthropist, *bon enfant;*
altruist.

V. be -benevolent &c. *adj.*; have
one's heart in the right place, bear
good will; wish -well, – God speed;

907. Malevolence.—N. malevolence;
bad intent, -ion; un-, dis-kindness; ill
-nature, – will, – blood; acrimony; bad
blood; enmity &c. 889; hate &c. 898;
malignity; malice, – aforethought, –
prepense; maliciousness &c. *adj.*; spite,
despite; resentment &c. 900.

uncharitableness &c. *adj.*; incom-
passionateness &c. 914*a*; gall, venom,
rancour, rankling, virulence, mordac-
ity, acerbity; churlishness &c. (*discourtesy*) 895.

hardness of heart, heart of stone,
obduracy; cruelty; cruelness &c. *adj.*;
brutality, savagery; fer-ity, -ocity;
barbarity, inhumanity, immanity, truc-
ulence, ruffianism; evil eye, cloven
-foot, – hoof; inquisition; torture.

ill –, bad- turn; affront &c. (*disrespect*) 929; outrage, atrocity; ill usage;
intolerance, bigotry, persecution; tender mercies [ironical]; 'unkindest cut
of all.'

V. be -malevolent &c. *adj.*; bear –,
harbour- -spleen, – a grudge, – mal-

view -, regard- with an eye of favour; take in good part; take -, feel- an interest in; be -, feel- interested- in; sympathize with, feel for; fraternize &c. (*be friendly*) 888.

enter into the feelings of others, do as you would be done by, meet halfway.

treat well; give comfort, smooth the bed of death; do -good, – a good turn; benefit &c. (*goodness*) 648; render a service, be of use; aid &c. 707.

Adj. benevolent; kind, -ly; wellmeaning; amiable; obliging, accommodating, indulgent, considerate, gracious, complacent, good-humoured.

warm-, soft-, kind-, tender-, large-, broad-hearted; merciful &c. 914; philanthropic &c. 910; charitable, beneficent, humane, benign, benignant; bount-eous, -iful &c. 816.

good-, well-natured; spleenless; sympath-izing, -etic; complaisant &c. (*courteous*) 894; kindly, well-meant, -intentioned.

fatherly, motherly, brotherly, sisterly; pat-, mat-, frat-ernal; friendly &c. 888.

Adv. with -a good intention, – the best intentions.

Int. God speed! much good may it do!

---

ice; betray -, show- the cloven foot.

hurt &c. (*physical pain*) 378; annoy &c. 830; injure, harm, wrong; do -harm, – an ill office- to; outrage; disoblige, malign, plant a thorn in the breast.

molest, worry, harass, haunt, harry, bait, tease, throw stones at; play the devil with; hunt down, dragoon, hound; persecute, oppress, grind; maltreat; ill-treat, -use.

wreak one's malice on, do one's worst, break a butterfly on the wheel; dip -, imbrue- one's hands in blood; have no mercy &c. 914a.

Adj. male-, unbene-volent; unbenign; ill-disposed, -intentioned, -natured, -conditioned, -contrived; evil-minded, -disposed.

malicious; malign, -ant; rancorous; de-, spiteful; mordacious, caustic, bitter, envenomed, acrimonious, virulent; un-amiable, -charitable; maleficent, venomous, grinding, galling.

harsh, disobliging; un-kind, -friendly, -gracious; treacherous; inofficious; invidious; uncandid; churlish &c. (*uncourteous*) 895; surly, sullen &c. 901a.

cold, -blooded, -hearted; hard-, flintmarble-, stony-hearted; hard of heart; unnatural; ruthless &c. (*unmerciful*) 914a; relentless &c. (*revengeful*) 919.

cruel; brut-al, -ish; savage, – as a -bear, – tiger; ferine, feral, ferocious; inhuman; barbarous, fell, untamed, tameless, truculent, incendiary; bloodthirsty &c. (*murderous*) 361; atrocious.

fiend-ish, -like; demoniacal; diabolic, -al; devilish, infernal, hellish, Satanic.

Adv. malevolently &c. *adj.*; with -bad intent &c. *n.*

---

908. Malediction.—N. malediction, malison, curse, imprecation, denunciation, execration, anathema, ban, proscription, excommunication, commination, thunders of the Vatican, fulmination, aspersion, vilification, vituperation, scurrility.

abuse; foul -, bad -, strong -, unparliamentary- language, Limehouse; Billingsgate, sauce, evil speaking; cursing &c. *v.*; profane swearing, oath.

threat &c. 909; more bark than bite; invective &c. (*disapprobation*) 932.

V. curse, accurse, imprecate, damn, swear at; slang; curse with bell, book and candle; invoke -, call down- curses on the head of; devote to destruction.

execrate, beshrew, scold; anathematize &c. (*censure*) 932; hold up to execration, denounce, proscribe, excommunicate, fulminate, thunder against; threaten &c. 909; curse up hill and down dale.

curse and swear; swear, – like a trooper; fall a cursing, rap out an oath, damn, cuss.

Adj. curs-ing, -ed &c. *v.*; maledictory.

Int. woe to! beshrew! *ruat cœlum!* ill –, woe- betide! confusion seize! damn! confound! blast! curse! devil take! hang! out with! a plague –, out- upon! aroynt! *honi soit!*

Phr. *delenda est Carthago.*

909. Threat.—N. threat, menace; defiance &c. 715; abuse, minacity, intimidation; fulmination; commination &c. *(curse)* 908; gathering clouds &c. *(warning)* 668.

V. threat, -en; menace; snarl, growl, gnarl, mutter, bark, bully. defy &c. 715; intimidate &c. 860; keep –, hold up –, hold out- *in terrorem*; shake –, double –, clinch- the fist at; thunder, talk big, fulminate, use big words, bluster, look daggers.

Adj. threatening, menacing; mina-tory, -cious; comminatory, abusive; *in terrorem*; ominous &c. *(predicting)* 511; defiant &c. 715; under the ban.

Int. *vœ victis!* at your peril! do your worst!

910. Philanthropy. — N. philan-thropy; altruism, humanit-y, -arian-ism; universal benevolence; *deliciæ humani generis*; cosmopolitanism, utilitarianism, the greatest happiness of the greatest number, social science, sociology.

common weal, public welfare, social-ism, communism.

patriotism, civism, nationality, love of country, *amor patriæ*, public spirit.

chivalry, knight errantry; generosity &c. 942.

911. Misanthropy.—N. misanthropy. incivism; egotism &c. *(selfishness)* 943: moroseness &c. 901a; cynicism; defeat-ism.

misanthrope, misanthropist, egotist, cynic, man-hater, Timon, Diogenes.

woman-hater, misogynist.

Adj. misanthropic, antisocial, unpa-triotic; egotistical &c. *(selfish)* 943; morose &c. 901a.

philanthropist, altruist &c. 906; utilitarian, Benthamite, socialist, communist, cosmopolite, citizen of the world, *amicus humani generis*; knight errant; patriot.

Adj. philanthropic, altruistic, humanitarian, utilitarian, cos-mopolitan; public-spirited, patriotic; humane, large-hearted &c. *(benevolent)* 906; chival-ric, -rous, generous &c. 942.

Adv. *pro -bono publico, – aris et focis.*

Phr. *'humani nihil a me alienum puto.'*

912. Benefactor. — N. benefactor, saviour, good genius, tutelary saint, patron, guardian angel, fairy god-mother, good Samaritan; *pater patriæ*; salt of the earth &c. *(good man)* 948; auxiliary &c. 711.

913. [Maleficent being.] Evil-doer. —N. evil- -doer, – worker; wrong doer &c. 949; mischief maker, marplot; oppressor, tyrant; firebrand, incen-diary, pyromaniac, anarchist, destroyer, Hun, *Boche*, Vandal, iconoclast; com-munist; terrorist, *apache*, gunman, gangster, racketeer.

savage, brute, ruffian, barbarian, semi-barbarian, caitiff, desper-ado; Mo-hock, -hawk; bludgeon man, bully, rough, hooligan, larrikin, dangerous classes, ugly customer; thief &c. 792.

cockatrice, scorpion, hornet; viper, adder; snake, – in the grass;

serpent, cobra, asp, rattlesnake, anaconda; canker-, wire-worm; locust, Colorado beetle; torpedo; bane &c. 663.

cannibal; Anthropophag-us, -ist; bloodsucker, vampire, ogre, ghoul, gorilla; vulture; gyr-, ger-falcon.

wild beast, tiger, hyæna, butcher, hangman; cut-throat &c.; (*killer*) 361; blood-, sleuth-, hell-hound.

hag, hellhag, beldam, Jezebel.

monster; fiend &c. (*demon*) 980; homicidal maniac, devil incarnate, demon in human shape; Frankenstein's monster.

harpy, siren, vampire; Furies, Eumenides &c. 900.

Attila, scourge of the human race.

Phr. *fœnum habet in cornu.*

3°. SPECIAL SYMPATHETIC AFFECTIONS

914. Pity.—N. pity, compassion, commiseration; bowels, – of compassion; condolence &c. 915; sympathy, fellow-feeling, tenderness, yearning, forbearance, humanity, mercy, clemency, exorability; leniency &c. (*lenity*) 740; charity, ruth, long-suffering.

melting mood; *argumentum ad misericordiam*; quarter, grace, *locus pœnitentiæ*.

sympathizer, champion, partisan.

V. pity; have –, show –, take- pity &c. *n.*; commiserate, compassionate; condole &c. 915; sympathize; feel –, be sorry –, yearn- for; weep, melt, thaw, enter into the feelings of.

forbear, relent, relax, give quarter, wipe the tears, *parcere subjectis*, give a *coup de grâce*, put out of one's misery; be cruel to be kind.

raise –, excite- pity &c. *n.*; touch, soften; melt, – the heart; appeal to one's better feelings; propitiate, disarm.

ask for -mercy &c. *n.*; supplicate &c. (*request*) 765; cry for quarter, beg one's life, kneel; deprecate.

Adj. pitying &c. *v.*; pitiful, compassionate, sympathetic, touched.

merciful, clement, ruthful; humane; humanitarian &c. (*philanthropic*) 910; tender. – hearted, – as a chicken; soft, – hearted; unhardened; lenient &c. 740; exorable, forbearing; melting &c. *v.*; weak.

Int. for pity's sake! mercy! have –, cry you- mercy! God help you! poor -thing, – dear, – fellow! woe betide! *quis talia fando temperet a lachrymis!*

Phr. one's heart bleeding for; *haud ignara mali miseris succurrere disco.*

914a. Pitilessness.—N. pitilessness &c. *adj.*; inclemency; inexorability. hardness of heart; inflexibility; severity &c. 739; malevolence &c. 907.

V. have no –, shut the gates of- mercy &c. 914; give no quarter.

Adj. piti-, merci-, ruth-, bowel-less; unpitying, unmerciful, inclement; in-, un-compassionate; inexorable, inflexible; harsh &c. 739; cruel &c. 907; unrelenting &c. 919.

----

915. Condolence.—N. condolence; lamentation &c. 839; sympathy, consolation.

V. condole with, console, sympathize &c. 914, share one's misery; feel for; express –, testify- pity; afford –, supply- consolation; lament &c. 839- with; send one's condolences.

4°. Retrospective Sympathetic Affections

916. Gratitude. — N. gratitude, thankfulness, gratefulness, feeling of obligation.

acknowledgment, recognition thanksgiving, giving thanks.

thanks, praise, benediction; pæan; *Te Deum* &c. (*worship*) 990; grace, – before, – after- meat; thank-offering. requital.

V. be -grateful &c. *adj.*; thank; give –, render –, return –, offer –, tender-thanks &c. *n.*; acknowledge, requite.

feel –, be –, lie- under an obligation; *savoir gré*; not look a gift horse in the mouth; never forget, overflow with gratitude; thank –, bless- one's stars; fall on one's knees.

Adj. grateful, thankful, obliged, beholden, indebted to, under obligation.

Int. thanks! many thanks! gramercy! much obliged! thank you! thank Heaven! Heaven be praised!

917. Ingratitude.—N. ingratitude, thanklessness, oblivion of benefits; unthankfulness.

'benefits forgot'; thankless -task, – office.

V. be -ungrateful &c. *adj.*; forget benefits; look a gift horse in the mouth.

Adj. un-grateful, -mindful, -thankful; thankless, ingrate, wanting in gratitude, insensible of benefits.

forgotten; un-acknowledged, -thanked, -requited, -rewarded; ill-requited.

Int. thank you for nothing! '*et tu Brute !*'

---

918. Forgiveness.—N. forgiveness, pardon, condonation, grace, remission, absolution, amnesty, oblivion; indulgence; reprieve.

conciliation; reconciliation &c. (*pacification*) 723; propitiation.

excuse, exoneration, quittance, release, indemnity; bill –, act –, covenant –, deed- of indemnity; exculpation &c. (*acquittal*) 970.

longanimity, placability, forbearance; *amantium iræ*; *locus pœnitentiæ*.

V. forgive, – and forget; pardon, condone, think no more of, let bygones be bygones, shake hands; forget an injury, bury the hatchet; clean the slate.

excuse, pass over, overlook; wink at &c. (*neglect*) 460; bear with; allow –, make allowances- for; let one down easily, not be too hard upon, pocket the affront; blot out one's transgression.

let off, remit, absolve, give absolution, reprieve; acquit &c. 970.

beg –, ask –, implore- pardon &c. *n.*; conciliate, propitiate, placate; make up a quarrel &c. (*pacify*) 723; let the wound heal.

919. Revenge.—N. revenge, -ment; vengeance; avenge-ment, -ance; sweet revenge, *vendetta*, death-feud, eye for an eye, blood for blood, a Roland for an Oliver; retaliation &c. 718; day of reckoning.

rancour, vindictiveness, implacability; malevolence &c. 907; ruthlessness &c. 914a.

avenger, vindicator, Nemesis, Eumenides.

V. re-, a-venge; take –, have one's-revenge; breathe -revenge, – vengeance; wreak one's -vengeance, – anger; give no quarter.

have -accounts to settle, – a crow to pluck, – a rod in pickle; pay off old scores.

keep the wound green; harbour -revenge, – vindictive feeling; bear malice; rankle, – in the breast; have at one's mercy.

Adj. revenge-, venge-ful; vindictive, rancorous; pitiless &c. 914a; ruthless, rigorous, avenging, retaliative.

unforgiving, unrelenting; inexorable, stony-hearted, implacable; relent-, remorse-less.

æternum servans sub pectore vulnus; rankling, immitigable.

Adj. forgiving, placable, conciliatory. forgiven &c. *v.*; un-resented, -avenged, -revenged.

Adv. cry you mercy.

Phr. *veniam petimusque damusque vicissim*; more in sorrow than in anger.

Phr. *manet -cicatrix, – altâ mente repostum.*

revenge is sweet.

---

920. Jealousy.—N. jealous-y, -ness; jaundiced eye, heartburning; green-eyed monster; yellows; Juno.

V. be -jealous &c. *adj.*; view with -jealousy, – a jealous eye.

Adj. jealous, – as a Barbary pigeon; jaundiced, yellow-eyed, horn-mad.

921. Envy.—N. envy; enviousness &c. *adj.*; rivalry; *jalousie de métier.*

V. envy, covet, lust after, crave, burst with envy, regard with envious eyes.

Adj. envious, invidious, covetous; *alieni appetens.*

Section IV. MORAL AFFECTIONS
1°. Moral Obligations

922. Right.—N. right; what -ought to, – should- be; fitness &c. *adj.*; *summum jus.*

justice, equity; equitableness &c. *adj.*; propriety; fair play, impartiality, measure for measure, give and take, *lex talionis*, square deal.

Astræa, Nemesis, Themis.

scales of justice, even-handed justice, retributive justice, *suum cuique*; clear stage –, fair field- and no favour; Queensberry rules.

morals &c. (*duty*) 926; law &c. 963; honour &c. (*probity*) 939; virtue &c. 944.

V. be -right &c. *adj.*; stand to reason.

see -justice done, – one righted, – fair play; do justice to; recompense &c. (*reward*) 973; hold the scales even, give and take; serve one right, put the saddle on the right horse; give -every one, – the devil- his due; *audire alteram partem.*

deserve &c. (*be entitled to*) 924.

Adj. right, good; just, reasonable; fit &c. 924; equ-al, -able, -itable; even-handed, fair, – and square.

legitimate, justifiable, rightful; as it -should, – ought to- be; lawful &c. (*permitted*) 760, (*legal*) 963.

deserved &c. 924.

Adv. rightly &c. *adj.*; in -justice, – equity, – reason.

without -distinction of, – regard to, – respect to- persons; upon even terms.

Int. all right!

923. Wrong. — N. wrong; what -ought not to, – should not- be; *malum in se*; unreasonableness, grievance; shame.

injustice; unfairness &c. *adj.*; iniquity, foul play, partiality, leaning; favour, -itism; nepotism, party spirit, partisanship; undueness &c. 925; unlawfulness &c. 964.

robbing Peter to pay Paul &c. *v.*; the wolf and the lamb; vice &c. 945.

a custom more honoured in the breach than the observance.

V. be -wrong &c. *adj.*; cry to heaven for vengeance.

do -wrong &c. *n.*; be -inequitable &c. *adj.*; favour, lean towards; encroach; impose upon; reap where one has not sown; give an inch and take an ell; rob Peter to pay Paul.

Adj. wrong, -ful; bad, too bad; unjust, -fair; in-, un-equitable; unequal, partial, one-sided.

objectionable; un-reasonable, -allowable, -warrantable, -justifiable; not cricket, not playing the game; improper, unfit; unjustified &c. 925; illegal &c. 964; iniquitous, criminal; immoral &c. 945; injurious &c. 649.

in the wrong, – box.

Adv. wrongly &c. *adj.*

Phr. it will not do; this is too bad.

---

924. Dueness.—N. due, -ness; right, privilege, prerogative, prescription, title, claim, pretension, demand, birthright.

immunity, licence, liberty, franchise; vested -interest, – right; licitness.

sanction, authority, warranty, charter; warrant &c. (*permission*) 760; constitution &c. (*law*) 963; tenure; bond &c. (*security*) 771.

deserts, merits, dues.

claimant, appellant; plaintiff &c. 938.

V. be -due &c. *adj.* to, – the due &c. *n.* of; have -right, – title, – claim- to; be entitled to; have a claim upon; belong to &c. (*property*) 780.

deserve, merit, be worthy of, richly deserve.

demand, claim; call upon –, come upon –, appeal to- for; re-vendicate, -claim; exact; insist -on, – upon; challenge; take one's stand, make a point of, require, lay claim to, assert, assume, arrogate, make good; substantiate; vindicate a -claim, – right; make out a case.

give –, confer- a right; sanction, entitle; authorize &c. 760; sanctify, legalize, ordain, prescribe, allot.

give every one his due &c. 922; pay one's dues; have one's -due, – rights; stand upon one's rights.

use a right, assert, enforce, put in force, lay under contribution.

Adj. having a right to &c. *v.*; entitled to; claiming; deserving, meriting, worthy of.

privileged, allowed, sanctioned, warranted, authorized; ordained, prescribed, constitutional, chartered, enfranchised.

925. [Absence of right.] **Undueness —N.** unueness &c. *adj.*; *malum prohibitum*; impropriety; illegality &c. 964.

falseness &c. *adj.*; emptiness –, invalidity- of title; illegitimacy.

loss of right, disfranchisement, forfeiture.

usurpation, assumption, tort, violation, breach, encroachment, presumption, seizure, stretch, exaction, imposition, lion's share.

usurper, pretender, Carlist; impostor.

V. be -undue &c. *adj.*; not be -due &c. 924.

infringe, encroach, trench on, exact; arrogate, – to oneself; give an inch and take an ell; stretch –, strain- a point; usurp, violate, do violence to; sail under false colours.

dis-franchise, -entitle, -qualify; invalidate.

relax &c. (*be lax*) 738; misbehave &c. (*vice*) 945; misbecome.

Adj. undue; unlawful &c. (*illegal*) 964; unconstitutional, *ultra vires*; illicit; un-authorized, -warranted, -allowed, -sanctioned, -justified; un-, dis-entitled, -qualified; un-privileged, -chartered.

illegitimate, bastard, spurious, false; usurped, tortious.

un-deserved, -merited, -earned; unfulfilled.

forfeited, disfranchised.

improper; un-meet, -fit, -befitting, -seemly; un-, mis-becoming; seemless; *contra bonos mores*; not the thing, out of the question, not to be thought of; preposterous, pretentious, would- be.

---

prescriptive, presumptive; absolute, indefeasible; un-, in-alienable; imprescriptible, inviolable, unimpeachable, unchallenged; sacrosanct.

due to, merited, deserved, condign, richly deserved, *emeritus*.

allowable &c. (*permitted*) 760; lawful, licit, legitimate, legal; legalized &c. (*law*) 963.

square, unexceptionable, right; equitable &c. 922; due, *en règle*; fit, -ting; correct, proper, meet, befitting, becoming, seemly; decorous; creditable, up to the mark, right as a trivet; just –, quite- the thing; *selon les règles*.

Adv. duly, *ex officio*, *de jure*; by -right, – divine right; as is -fitting, – proper, – fitting and proper; *jure divino*, *Dei gratiâ*, in the name of.

Phr. *civis Romanus sum.*

926. Duty.

N. duty, what ought to be done, moral obligation, accountableness, liability, *onus*, responsibility; bounden –, imperative- duty; call, – of duty.

allegiance, fealty, tie; engagement &c. (*promise*) 768; part; function, calling &c. (*business*) 625.

morality, morals, decalogue; case of conscience; conscientiousness &c. (*probity*) 939; conscience, inward monitor, still small voice within, sense of duty, tender conscience.

dueness &c. 924; propriety, fitness, seemliness, amenableness, decorum; the -thing, – proper thing; the -right, – proper- thing to do.

[Science of morals] eth-ics, -ology; deon-, are-tology; moral –, ethical-philosophy; casuistry, polity.

observance, fulfilment, discharge, performance, acquittal, satisfaction, redemption; good behaviour.

V. be -the duty of, – incumbent &c. *adj.* on, – responsible &c. *adj.*; behoove, become, befit, beseem; belong –, pertain- to; fall to one's lot; devolve on; lie -upon, – on one's head, – at one's door; rest -with, – on the shoulders of.

take upon oneself &c. (*promise*) 768; be –, become- -bound to, – sponsor for; be responsible for; incur a -responsibility &c. *n.*; be –, stand –, lie- under an obligation; have to answer for, owe it to oneself.

impose a -duty &c. *n.*; enjoin, require, exact; bind, – over; saddle with, prescribe, assign, call upon, look to, oblige.

927. Dereliction of Duty.

N. dereliction of duty; fault &c. (*guilt*) 947- sin &c. (*vice*) 945; non-observance, -performance, -co-operation; neglect, carelessness, laziness, incompetence, eye-service, relaxation, infraction, violation, transgression, failure, evasion, indolence; dead letter.

slacker, loafer, striker, non-co-operator.

V. violate; break, – through; infringe; set -aside, – at naught; trample -on, – under foot; slight, neglect, evade, renounce, forswear, repudiate; wash one's hands of; escape, transgress, fail.

call to account &c. (*disapprobation*) 932.

927a. Exemption.

N. exemption, freedom, irresponsibility, immunity, liberty, licence, release, exoneration, excuse, dispensation, absolution, franchise, renunciation, discharge; exculpation &c. 970; *ægrotat*.

V. be -exempt &c. *adj.*

exempt, release, acquit, discharge, quit-claim, remise, remit; free, set at liberty, let off, pass over, spare, excuse, dispense with, give dispensation, license; stretch a point; absolve &c. (*forgive*) 918; exonerate &c. (*exculpate*) 970; save the necessity.

Adj. exempt, free, immune, at liberty, scot free; released &c. *v.*; unbound, unencumbered; irresponsible, unaccountable, not answerable; excusable.

————

enter upon –, perform –, observe –, fulfil –, discharge –, adhere to –, acquit oneself of –, satisfy- -a duty, – an obligation; act one's part, redeem one's pledge, do justice to, be at one's post; do duty; do one's duty &c. (*be virtuous*) 944.

be on one's good behaviour, mind one's P's and Q's.

Adj. obligatory, binding; imperative, peremptory; stringent &c. (*severe*) 739; behooving &c. *v.*; incumbent –, chargeable- on; under obligation; obliged –, bound –, tied- by; saddled with.

due –, beholden –, bound –, indebted- to; tied down; compromised &c. (*promised*) 768; in duty bound.

amenable, liable, accountable, responsible, answerable.

right, meet &c. (*due*) 924; moral, ethical, casuistical, consciensious, ethological.

Adv. with a safe conscience, as in duty bound, on one's own responsibility, at one's own risk, *suo periculo*; *in foro conscientiæ*; *quamdiu se bene gesserit*; at one's post, on duty.

Phr. *dura lex sed lex.*

2°. MORAL SENTIMENTS

928. Respect.—N. respect, regard, consideration; courtesy &c. 894; attention, deference, reverence, honour, esteem, estimation, veneration, admiration; approbation &c. 931.

homage, fealty, obeisance, genuflexion, kneeling, prostration; obsequiousness &c. 886; salaam, *kowtow*, bow, presenting arms, salute.

respects, regards, duty, *devoirs*, *égards*.

devotion &c. (*piety*) 987.

V. respect, regard; revere, -nce; hold in reverence, honour, venerate, hallow; esteem &c. (*approve of*) 931; think much of; entertain -, bear-respect for; have a high opinion of; look up to, defer to; pay -attention, - respect &c. *n.*- to; do -, render- honour to; do the honours, hail; show courtesy &c. 894; salute, present arms; do -, pay- homage to; pay tribute to, kneel to, bow to, bend the knee to; fall down before, prostrate oneself, kiss the hem of one's garment; worship &c. 990.

keep one's distance, make room, observe due decorum, stand upon ceremony.

command -, inspire- respect; awe, impose, overawe, dazzle.

Adj. respecting &c. *v.*; respectful, deferential, decorous, reverential, obsequious, ceremonious, bare-headed, cap in hand, on one's knees; prostrate &c. (*servile*) 886.

respected &c. *v.*; in high -esteem, - estimation; time-honoured, venerable, *emeritus*.

Adv. in deference to; with -all, - due, - the highest- respect; with submission.

saving your -grace, - presence; *salva sit reverentia*; *pace tanti nominis*.

Int. hail! all hail! *esto perpetua!* may your shadow never be less!

---

929. Disrespect. — N. dis-respect, -esteem, -estimation, -favour, -repute; low estimation; disparagement &c. (*dispraise*) 932, (*detraction*) 934.

irreverence; slight; neglect; *spretæ injuria formæ*; superciliousness &c. (*contempt*) 930.

vilipendency, contumely, affront, dishonour, insult, indignity, outrage, discourtesy &c. 895; practical joking; scurrility, scoffing, sibilation; ir-, derision; mockery; irony &c. (*ridicule*) 856; sarcasm.

hiss, hoot, gibe, flout, jeer, scoff, gleek, taunt, sneer, quip, fling, wipe, slap in the face.

V. hold in disrespect &c. (*despise*) 930; misprize, disregard, slight, undervalue, depreciate, trifle with, set at naught, pass by, push aside, overlook, turn one's back upon, laugh in one's sleeve; be -disrespectful &c. *adj.*, - discourteous &c. 895; treat with -disrespect &c. *n.*; set down, browbeat.

dishonour, desecrate; insult, affront, outrage.

speak slightingly of; disparage &c. (*dispraise*) 932; vilipend, call names; throw -, fling- dirt; drag through the mud, point at, indulge in personalities; make -mouths, - faces; bite the thumb; take -, pluck- by the beard; toss in a blanket, tar and feather.

have -, hold- in derision; deride, scoff, sneer, laugh at, snigger, ridicule, gibe, mock, jeer, taunt, twit, niggle, gleek, gird, flout, fleer; roast, turn into ridicule; guy, burlesque &c. 856; laugh to scorn &c. (*contempt*) 930; smoke; fool; make -game, - a fool, - an April fool- of; play a practical joke; rag; lead one a dance, run the rig upon, have a fling at, scout, hiss, hoot, mob.

Adj. disrespectful; aweless, irreverent; disparaging &c. 934; insulting &c. *v.*; supercilious &c. (*scornful*) 930; rude, derisive, contemptuous, sarcastic; scurri-le, -lous; contumelious.

un-respected, -worshipped, -envied, -saluted; un-, dis-regarded.
Adv. disrespectfully &c. *adj.*

930. Contempt.—N. contempt, disdain, scorn, sovereign contempt; despi-sal, -ciency; vilipendency, contumely; slight, sneer, spurn, by-word.

contemptuousness &c. *adj.*; scornful eye; smile of contempt; deri-sion &c. (*disrespect*) 929.

[State of being despised] despisedness.

V. despise, contemn, scorn, disdain, feel contempt for, view with a scornful eye, disregard, slight, not mind; pass by &c. (*neglect*) 460.

look down upon; hold -cheap, – in contempt, – in disrespect; think -nothing, – small beer- of; make light of; underestimate &c. 483; esteem -slightly, – of small or no account; take no account of, care nothing for; set no store by; not care a -straw &c. (*unimportance*) 643; set at naught, laugh in one's sleeve, snap one's fingers at, shrug one's shoulders, turn up one's nose at, pooh-pooh, damn with faint praise; sneeze –, whistle –, sneer- at; curl up one's lip, toss the head, *traiter de haut*; laugh at &c. (*be disrespectful*) 929.

point the finger of –, hold up to –, laugh to- scorn; scout, hoot, flout, hiss, scoff at.

turn -one's back, – a cold shoulder- upon; tread –, trample- -upon, – under foot; spurn, kick; fling to the winds &c. (*repudiate*) 610; send away with a flea in the ear.

Adj. contemptuous; disdain-, scorn-ful; withering, contumelious, supercilious, cynical, haughty, bumptious, cavalier; derisive.

contemptible, despicable; pitiable; pitiful &c. (*unimportant*) 643; despised &c. *v.*; down-trodden; unenvied.

Adv. contemptuously &c. *adj.*

Int. a fig for &c. (*unimportant*) 643; bah! never mind! away with! hang it! fiddle-de-dee!

---

931. Approbation.—N. approbation; approv-al, -ement; sanction, advocacy; nod of approbation; esteem, estimation, good opinion, golden opinions, admira-tion; love &c. 897; appreciation, regard, account, popularity, *kudos*, credit; re-pute &c. 873.

commendation, praise; laud, -ation; good word; meed –, tribute- of praise; encomium; eulog-y, -ium; *éloge*, pane-gyric; homage, hero worship; benedic-tion, blessing, benison.

applause, plaudit, clap; clapping, – of hands; accl-aim, -amation; cheer; pæan, hosannah; shout –, peal –, chorus –, thunders- of -applause &c.; Kentish fire; Prytaneum; blurb.

V. approve; think -good, – much of, – well of, – highly of; esteem, value, prize; set great store -by, – on.

do justice to, appreciate; honour, hold in esteem, look up to, admire; like &c. 897; be in favour of, wish God speed; hail, – with satisfaction.

stand –, stick- up for; uphold, hold

932. Disapprobation.—N. disappro-bation, -val; improbation; dis-esteem, -valuation, -placency; odium; dislike &c. 867; dissent &c. 489.

dis-praise, -commendation; blame, censure, obloquy; detraction &c. 934; disparagement, depreciation; denuncia-tion; condemnation &c. 971; ostracism; boycott; black-list, -ball; *index -expur-gatorius, – librorum prohibitorum.*

animadversion, reflection, stricture, objection, exception, criticism; sar-donic -grin, – laugh; sarcasm, insinua-tion, innuendo; bad –, poor –, left-handed- compliment.

satire; sneer &c. (*contempt*) 930; taunt &c. (*disrespect*) 929; cavil, carp-ing, censoriousness; hypercriticism &c. (*fastidiousness*) 868.

reprehension, remonstrance, expost-ulation, reproof, reprobation, admoni-tion, increpation, reproach; rebuke, reprimand, castigation, jobation, lec-ture, curtain lecture, blow up, wigging, dressing, – down; rating, scolding, trim-

up, countenance, sanction; clap -, pat-on the back; keep in countenance, en-dorse, give credit, recommend; mark with a white -mark, - stone.

commend, praise; be-, laud; com-pliment, pay a tribute, bepraise; clap, - the hands; applaud, cheer, acclaim, acclamate, encore; panegyrize, eulo-gize, cry up, *prôner*, puff; extol, - to the skies; magnify, glorify, exalt, boost, swell, make much of; flatter &c. 933; bless, give a blessing to; have -, say- a good word for; speak -well, - highly, - in high terms- of; sing -, sound -, chaunt -, resound- the praises of; sing praises to; cheer -, applaud- to the -echo, - very echo.

redound to the -honour, - praise, - credit- of; do credit to; deserve -praise &c. *n.*; recommend itself; pass muster.

be -praised &c.; receive honourable mention; be in -favour, - high favour-with; ring with the praises of, win golden opinions, gain credit, find favour with, stand well in the opinion of; *laudari a laudato viro*.

Adj. approving &c. *v.*; in favour of; lost in admiration.

commendatory, complimentary, ben-edictory, laudatory, panegyrical, eulo-gistic, encomiastic, acclamatory, lavish of praise, uncritical.

approved, praised &c. *v.*; un-cen-sured, -impeached; popular, in good odour; in high esteem &c. (*respected*) 928; in -, in high- favour.

deserving -, worthy of- praise &c. *n.*; praiseworthy, commendable, of estima-tion; good &c. 648; meritorious, estim-able, creditable, plausible, unimpeach-able; beyond all praise.

Adv. commendably, with credit, to admiration; well &c.-618; with three times three.

Int. hear, hear! well done! *brav-o! -a! -i! bravissimo! euge! macte virtute!* so far so good, that's right, quite right; *op-time!* one cheer more; may your shad-ow never be less! *esto perpetua!* long life to! *viva! evviva!* God speed! *valete et plaudite! encore! bis!*

Phr. *probatum est.*

---

ming; correction, set down, rap on the knuckles, *coup de bec*, rebuff; slap, - on the face; home thrust, hit; frown, scowl, black look.

diatribe; jeremiad; *tirade*, philippic.

clamour, outcry, hue and cry; hiss, -ing; sibilation, cat-call; execration &c. 908.

chiding, upbraiding &c. *v.*; expro-bration, abuse, vituperation, invective, objurgation, contumely, personal re-marks; hard -, cutting -, bitter- words.

evil-speaking; bad language &c. 908; personality.

V. disapprove; dislike &c. 867; la-ment &c. 839; object to, take excep-tion to; be scandalized at, think ill of; view with -disfavour, - dark eyes, - jaundiced eyes; *nil admirari*, dis-value, improbate.

frown upon, look grave; bend -, knit- the brows; shake the head at, shrug the shoulders; turn up the nose &c. (*contempt*) 930; look -askance, - black upon; look with an evil eye; make a wry -face, - mouth- at; set one's face against.

dis-praise, -commend, -parage; de-precate, speak ill of, not speak well of, slate, condemn &c. (*find guilty*) 971.

blame; lay -, cast- blame upon; censure, *fronder*, reproach, pass censure on, reprobate, impugn.

remonstrate, expostulate, recrimin-ate.

reprehend, chide, admonish; bring -, call- -to account, - over the coals, - to order; take to task, reprove, lecture, bring to book; read a -lesson, - lecture-to; rebuke, correct.

reprimand, chastise, castigate, lash, blow up, trounce, trim, *laver la tête*, overhaul; give it one, - finely; gibbet.

accuse &c. 938; impeach, denounce; hold up to -reprobation, - execration; expose, brand, gibbet, stigmatize; show -, pull -, take- up; cry 'shame' upon; be outspoken; raise a hue and cry against.

execrate &c. 908; exprobrate, speak daggers, vituperate; abuse, - like a pickpocket; scold, rate, objurgate, up-braid, fall foul of; jaw; rail, - at, - in good set terms; bark at; anathematize, call names; call by -hard, – ugly- names; a-, re-vile; vili-fy, -pend; bespatter; backbite; clapperclaw; rave –, thunder –, fulminate-against; load with reproaches; lash with the tongue.

exclaim –, protest –, inveigh –, declaim –, cry out –, raise one's voice- against.

decry; cry –, run –, frown- down; clamour, hiss, hoot, mob, ostracize; draw up –, sign- a round robin; black-ball, -list.

animadvert –, reflect- upon; glance at; cast -reflection, – re-proach, – a slur- upon; insinuate, damn with faint praise; 'hint a fault and hesitate dislike'; not to be able to say much for.

scoff at, point at; twit, taunt &c. (*disrespect*) 929; sneer at &c, (*despise*) 930; satirize, lampoon; defame &c. (*detract*) 934; depre-ciate, find fault with, criticize, cut up; pull –, pick- to pieces; take exception; cavil; peck –, nibble –, carp- at; be -censorious &c. *adj.*; pick -holes, – a hole, – a hole in one's coat; make a fuss about.

take –, set- down; snub, snap one up, give a rap on the knuckles; throw a stone -at, – in one's garden; have a -fling, – snap- at; have words with, pluck a crow with; give one a -wipe, – lick with the rough side of the tongue.

incur blame, excite disapprobation, scandalize, shock, revolt; get a bad name, forfeit one's good opinion, be under a cloud, come under the ferule, bring a hornet's nest about one's ears.

take blame, stand corrected; have to answer for.

Adj. disapproving &c. *v.*; scandalized.

disparaging, condemnatory, damnatory, denunciatory, reproach-ful, abusive, objurgatory, clamorous, vituperative; defamatory &c. 934.

satirical, sarcastic, sardonic, cynical, dry, sharp, cutting, biting, severe, virulent, withering, trenchant, hard upon; censorious, criti-cal, captious, carping, hypercritical; fastidious &c. 868; sparing of –, grudging- praise.

disapproved, chid &c. *v.*; in bad odour, blown upon, unapproved; unblest; at a discount, exploded; weighed in the balance and found wanting.

blameworthy, reprehensible &c. (*guilt*) 947; to –, worthy of-blame, answerable, uncommendable, exceptionable, not to be thought of, bad &c. 649; vicious &c. 945.

un-lamented, -bewailed, -pitied.

Adv. with a wry face; reproachfully &c. *adj.*

Int. it is too bad! it -won't, – will never- do! marry come up! Oh! come! 'sdeath!

forbid it Heaven! God –, Heaven- forbid! out –, fie- upon it! away with! tut! *O tempora! O mores!* shame! fie, – for shame! out on you!

tell it not in Gath!

933. Flattery.—N. flattery, adula-tion, gloze; bland-ishment, -iloquence; cajolery; fawning, wheedling &c. *v.*; captation, coquetry, sycophancy, ob-sequiousness, flunkeyism, toad-eating, tuft-hunting; snobbishness.

incense, honeyed words, flummery; bun-kum, -combe; blarney, *placebo*, but-

934. Detraction.—N. detraction, dis-paragement, depreciation, vilification, obloquy, scurrility, scandal, defama-tion, aspersion, traducement, slander, calumny, obtrectation, evil-speaking, backbiting, *scandalum magnatum.*

personality, libel, squib, lampoon, skit, pasquinade; *chronique scandaleuse.*

ter; soft -soap, – sawder; rose water.

voice of the charmer, mouth honour; lip-homage; euphemism; unctuousness &c. *adj.*

V. flatter, praise to the skies, puff; wheedle, cajole, glaver, coax; fawn, – upon; humour, gloze, soothe, pet, coquet, slaver, butter; be-spatter, -slubber, -plaster, -slaver; lay it on thick, overpraise; earwig, cog, col- logue; truckle –, pander *or* pandar –, pay court- to; court; creep into the good graces of; curry favour with, hang on the sleeve of; fool to the top of one's bent; lick the dust.

lay the flattering unction to one's soul, gild the pill, make things pleasant.

overestimate &c. 482; exaggerate &c. 549.

Adj. flattering &c. *v.*; adulatory; mealy-, honey-mouthed; honeyed; smooth, – tongued; soapy, oily, unc- tuous, blandiloquent, specious; fine-, fair-spoken; plausible, servile, syco- phantic, fulsome; courtier-ly, -like.

Adv. *ad captandum.*

---

935. Flatterer.—N. flatterer, adula- tor; eu-logist, -phemist; optimist, en- comiast, *laudator*, whitewasher, booster.

toad-y, -eater; sycophant, courtier, pickthank, Sir Pertinax MacSycophant; *flâneur*, *prôneur*; puffer, touter, *cla- queur*; claw-back, ear-wig, doer of dirty work; parasite, hanger on &c. (*servility*) 886.

---

937. Vindication.—N. vindication, justification, warrant; exoneration, ex- culpation; acquittal &c. 970; white- washing.

extenuation; pallia-tion, -tive; soft- ening, mitigation.

reply, defence; recrimination &c. 938.

apology, gloss, varnish; plea &c. 617; salvo; excuse, extenuating circum- stances; allowance, – to be made; *locus pœnitentiæ.*

apologist, vindicator, justifier; de- fendant &c. 938.

justifiable charge, true bill.

sarcasm, cynicism; criticism (*disap- probation*) 932; invective &c. 932; en- venomed tongue; *spretæ injuria formæ.* detractor &c. 936.

V. detract, derogate, decry, depre- ciate, disparage; run –, cry- down; minimize, make light of; belittle, sneer at &c. (*contemn*) 930; criticize, pull to pieces, pick a hole in one's coat, asperse, cast aspersions, blow upon, bespatter, blacken; vili-fy, -pend; avile; give a dog a bad name, brand, malign, back- bite, libel, lampoon, traduce, slander, defame, calumniate, bear false witness against; speak ill of behind one's back.

'damn with faint praise, assent with civil leer; and without sneering, others teach to sneer.'

fling dirt &c. (*disrespect*) 929; ana- thematize &c. 932; dip the pen in gall, view in a bad light.

Adj. detracting &c. *v.*; defamatory, detractory, derogatory; disparaging, libellous; scurril-e, -ous; abusive; foul- spoken, -tongued, -mouthed; slander- ous; calumni-ous, -atory; sar-castic, -donic; satirical, cynical.

---

936. Detractor.—N. detractor, re- prover; cens-or, -urer; cynic, critic, caviller, carper, wordcatcher.

defamer, backbiter, slanderer, knock- er, Sir Benjamin Backbite, lampooner, satirist, traducer, libeller, calumniator, dearest foe, dawplucker, Thersites; Zoilus; good-natured –, candid- friend [satirically]; reviler, vituperator, casti- gator; shrew &c. 901.

disapprover, *laudator temporis acti.*

---

938. Accusation. — N. accusation, charge, imputation, slur, inculpation; exprobration, delation; crimination; in-, ac-, re-crimination; *tu quoque* argu- ment; invective &c. 932.

de-nunciation, -nouncement; libel, challenge, citation, arraignment; im-, ap-peachment; indictment, bill of in- dictment, true bill; lawsuit &c. 969; condemnation &c. 971.

gravamen of a charge, head and front of one's offending, *argumentum ad hominem*; scandal &c. (*detraction*) 934; *scandalum magnatum.*

V. justify, warrant; be an -excuse &c. *n.*- for; lend a colour, furnish a handle; vindicate; ex-, dis-culpate; acquit &c. 970; clear, set right, exonerate, whitewash.

extenuate, palliate, excuse, soften, apologize, varnish, slur, gloze; put a -gloss, – good face- upon; mince; gloss over, bolster up, help a lame dog over a stile.

advocate, defend, plead one's cause; stand –, stick –, speak- up for; contend –, speak- for; bear out, keep in countenance, support; plead &c. 617; say in defence; plead ignorance; confess and avoid, propugn, put in a good word for.

take the will for the deed, make allowance for, do justice to; give -one, – the Devil- his due.

make good; prove -the truth of, – one's case; be justified by the event.

Adj. vindicat-ed, -ing &c. *v.*; vindicat-ive, -ory; palliative; exculpatory; apologetic.

excusable, defensible, pardonable; veni-al, -able; specious, plausible, justifiable.

Phr. *'honi soit qui mal y pense.'*

accuser, prosecutor, plaintiff, complainant, petitioner; relator, informer; appellant.

accused, defendant, prisoner, panel, co-, respondent; litigant.

V. accuse, charge, tax, impute, twit, taunt with, reproach.

brand with reproach; stigmatize, slur; cast a -stone at, – slur on; incriminate; inculpate, implicate; call to account &c. (*censure*) 932; take to -blame, – task; put in the black book.

inform against, indict, denounce, arraign; im-, ap-peach; have up, show up, pull up; challenge, cite, lodge a complaint; prosecute, bring an action against &c. 969.

charge –, saddle- with; lay to one's -door, – charge; lay the blame on, bring home to; cast –, throw- in one's teeth; cast the first stone at.

have –, keep- a rod in pickle for; have a crow to pluck with.

trump up a charge.

Adj. accusing &c. *v.*; accusat-ory, -ive; imputative, denunciatory; re-, criminatory.

accused &c. *v.*; suspected; under -suspicion, – a cloud, – *surveillance*; in -custody, – detention; in the -lock up, – watch house, – house of detention.

accusable, imputable; in-defensible, -excusable; un-pardonable, -justifiable; vicious &c. 945.

Int. look at home; *tu quoque* &c. (*retaliation*) 718.

3°. MORAL CONDITIONS

939. Probity.—**N.** probity, integrity, rectitude; uprightness &c. *adj.*; honesty, faith; honour; good faith, *bona fides*; purity, clean hands.

fairness &c. *adj.*; fair play, justice, equity, impartiality, principle; grace.

constancy; faithfulness &c. *adj.*; fidelity, loyalty; incorrupt-ion, -ibility.

trustworthiness &c. *adj.*; truth, candour, singleness of heart; veracity &c. 543; tender conscience &c. (*sense of duty*) 926.

punctil-iousness, -io; delicacy, nicety; scrupul-osity, -ousness &c. *adj.*; scruple; point, – of honour; punctuality.

dignity &c. (*repute*) 873; respectability, -bleness &c. *adj.*; gentleman; **man** of -honour, – his word; *fidus*

940. Improbity. N. improbity; dishon-esty, -our; deviation from rectitude; disgrace &c. (*disrepute*) 874; fraud &c. (*deception*) 545; lying &c. 544; bad –, Punic- faith; *mala –, Punica- fides*; infidelity; faithlessness &c. *adj.*; Judas kiss, betrayal; scrap of paper.

breach of -promise, – trust, – faith; prodition, disloyalty, divided allegiance, treason, high treason; apostasy &c. (*tergiversation*) 607; non-observance &c. 773.

shabbiness &c. *adj.*; villainy; baseness &c. *adj.*; abjection, debasement, turpitude, moral turpitude, laxity, trimming, shuffling.

perfidy; perfidiousness &c. *adj.*;

Achates, preux chevalier, galantuomo; truepenny, trump, brick; true Briton, white man, sportsman.

court of honour, a fair field and no favour; *argumentum ad verecundiam*.

V. be -honourable &c. *adj.*; deal -honourably, – squarely, – impartially, – fairly; speak the truth &c. (*veracity*) 543; tell the truth and shame the devil, *vitam impendere vero*; show a proper spirit, make a point of; do one's duty &c. 944; play the game.

redeem one's pledge &c. 926; keep –, be as good as- one's -promise, – word; keep faith with, not fail

give and take, *audire alteram partem*, give the devil his due, put the saddle on the right horse.

redound to one's honour.

Adj. upright; honest, – as daylight; veracious &c. 543; virtuous &c. 944; honourable; fair, right, just, equitable, impartial, even-handed, square; fair –, open- and aboveboard.

constant, – as the northern star; faithful, loyal, staunch; true, – blue, – to one's colours, – to the core, – as the needle to the pole; true-hearted, trust-y, -worthy; as good as one's word, to be depended on, incorruptible.

manly, straightforward &c. (*ingenuous*) 703; frank, candid, open-hearted.

conscientious, tender - conscienced, right-minded; high-principled, -minded; scrupulous, religious, strict; nice, punctilious, correct, punctual; respect-, reput-able; gentlemanlike.

inviol - able, - ate; un - violated, -broken, -betrayed; un-bought, -bribed.

innocent &c. 946; pure; stainless; un-stained, -tarnished, -sullied, -tainted, -perjured; uncorrupt, -ed; unde-filed, -praved, -bauched; *integer vitæ scelerisque purus*; *justus et tenax propositi*.

chivalrous, jealous of honour, *sans peur et sans reproche*; high-spirited.

supra-mundane, unworldly, over-scrupulous.

Adv. honourably &c. *adj.*; *bona fide*; on the square, in good faith, honour bright, *foro conscientiæ*, with clean hands; by fair means.

treachery, double-dealing; unfairness &c. *adj.*; knavery, roguery, rascality, foul-play; jobb-ing, -ery; Tammany, graft; venality, nepotism; corruption, job, shuffle, fishy transaction, barratry; sharp practice, heads I win, tails you lose; mouth-honour &c. (*flattery*) 933.

V. be -dishonest &c. *adj.*; play false; break one's -word, – faith, – promise; jilt, betray, forswear; shuffle &c. (*lie*) 544; live by one's wits, sail near the wind; play with marked cards.

disgrace –, dishonour –, demean –, degrade- oneself; derogate, stoop, grovel, sneak, lose caste; sell oneself, go over to the enemy; seal one's infamy..

Adj. dishon-est, -ourable; un-conscientious, -scrupulous; fraudulent &c. 545; knavish; disgraceful &c. (*disreputable*) 874; wicked &c. 945.

false-hearted, disingenuous; unfair, one-sided; double, -tongued. -faced; time-serving, crooked, tortuous, insidious, Machiavellian, dark, slippery; questionable; fishy; perfidious, treacherous, perjured.

infamous, arrant, foul, base, vile, low, ignominious, blackguard.

contemptible, abject, mean, shabby, little, paltry, dirty, scurvy, scabby, sneaking, grovelling, scrubby, rascally, pettifogging; beneath one; not cricket.

low-minded, -thoughted; base-minded.

undignified, indign; unbe-coming, -seeming, -fitting; de-rogatory, -grading; *infra dignitatem*; ungentleman-ly, -like; un-knightly, -chivalric, -manly, -handsome; recreant, inglorious.

corrupt, venal; debased, mongrel.

faithless, of bad faith, false, unfaithful, disloyal; untrustworthy; trust-, troth-less; lost to shame, dead to honour.

Adv. dishonestly &c. *adj.*; *malâ fide*, like a thief in the night, by crooked paths; by foul means.

Int. *O tempora! O mores!*

---

941. Knave.—N. knave, rogue, villain; Scapin, rascal; Lazarillo de Tormes; bad man &c. 949; blackguard &c. 949.

traitor, betrayer, arch-traitor, conspirator, stool pigeon, Judas, Catiline; reptile, serpent, snake in the grass, wolf in sheep's clothing, sneak, Jerry Sneak, tell-tale, squealer, mischief-maker, trimmer; renegade &c. (*tergiversation*) 607; truant, recreant; sycophant &c. (*servility*) 886.

942. Disinterestedness.—N. disinterestedness &c. *adj.*; generosity; liberal-ity, -ism; altruism; benevolence &c. 906; elevation, loftiness of purpose, exaltation, magnanimity; chival-ry, -rous spirit; heroism, sublimity.

self-denial, -abnegation, -effacement, -sacrifice, -immolation, -control &c. (*resolution*) 604; stoicism, devotion, martyrdom, *suttee*.

labour of love.

V. be -disinterested &c. *adj.*; make a sacrifice, lay one's head on the block; put oneself in the place of others, do as one would be done by, do unto others as we would men should do unto us.

Adj. disinterested; unselfish; self-denying, -sacrificing, -devoted; generous.

handsome, liberal, noble; noble-, high-minded; princely, great, high, elevated, lofty, exalted, spirited, stoical, magnanimous; great-, large-hearted, chivalrous, heroic, sublime.

un-bought, -bribed; uncorrupted &c. (*upright*) 939.

---

943. Selfishness.—N. selfishness &c. *adj.*; self-love, -indulgence, -worship, -interest; ego-tism, -ism; egocentrism, narcissism; *amour propre* &c. (*vanity*) 880; nepotism.

worldliness &c. *adj.*; world wisdom. illiberality; meanness &c. *adj.*

time-server; tuft-, fortune-hunter; self-seeker; jobber, worldling; egotist, egoist, monopolist, nepotist, profiteer; temporizer, trimmer; dog in the manger, charity that begins at home.

V. be -selfish &c. *adj.*; please -, indulge -, coddle- oneself; consult one's own -wishes, - pleasure; look after one's own interest; feather one's nest; take care of number one, have an eye to the main chance, know on which side one's bread is buttered; give an inch and take an ell; wangle.

Adj. selfish; self-seeking, -indulgent, -interested; wrapped up -, centred- in self; egotistic, -al; egoistical; egocentric.

illiberal, mean, ungenerous, narrow-minded; mercenary, venal; covetous &c. 819.

unspiritual; earthly, -minded; mundane; worldly, -minded, -wise; time-serving.

interested; *alieni appetens sui profusus.*

Adv. ungenerously &c. *adj.*; to gain some private ends; from selfish -, interested- motives.

Phr. *après nous le déluge.*

---

944. Virtue.—N. virtue; virtuousness &c. *adj.*; morality; moral rectitude; integrity &c. (*probity*) 939; nobleness &c. 873.

morals; ethics &c. (*duty*) 926; cardinal virtues.

merit, worth, desert, excellence, credit; self-control &c. (*resolution*) 604; self-denial &c. (*temperance*) 953.

well-doing; good -actions, - behaviour; discharge -, fulfilment -, performance- of duty; well-spent life; innocence &c. 946.

V. be -virtuous &c. *adj.*; practise -virtue &c. *n.*; do -, fulfil -, perform -,

945. Vice. — N. vice; evil -doing, - courses; wrong doing; wickedness, viciousness &c. *adj.*; iniquity, peccability, demerit; sin, Adam; old -, offending- Adam.

immorality, impropriety, indecorum, scandal, laxity, looseness of morals; want of -principle, - ballast; obliquity, backsliding, infamy, demoralization, pravity, depravity, pollution; hardness of heart; brutality &c. (*malevolence*) 907; corruption &c. (*debasement*) 659; knavery &c. (*improbity*) 940; profligacy; lust &c. 961; flagrancy, atrocity; cannibalism.

discharge- one's duty; redeem one's pledge &c. 926; act well, – one's part; fight the good fight; acquit oneself well; command –, master- one's passions; keep -straight, – in the right path.

set -an, – a good- example; be on one's -good, – best- behaviour.

Adj. virtuous, good; innocent &c. 946; meritorious, deserving, worthy, desertful, correct; dut-iful, -eous; moral; right, -eous, -minded; well-intentioned, creditable, laudable, commendable, praiseworthy; above –, beyond- all praise; excellent, admirable; sterling, pure, noble.

exemplary; match-, peer-less; saintly, -like; heaven-born, angelic, seraphic, godlike.

Adv. virtuously &c. *adj.*; *e merito*.

---

infirmity; weakness &c. *adj.*; weakness of the flesh, frailty, imperfection; error; weak side; foible; fail-ing, -ure; crying –, besetting- sin; defect, deficiency, shortcoming; cloven foot.

lowest dregs of vice, sink of iniquity, Alsatian den; *gusto picaresco*.

fault, crime; criminality &c. (*guilt*) 947.

sinner &c. 949.

V. be -vicious &c. *adj.*; sin, commit sin, do amiss, err, transgress; misdemean –, forget –, misconduct- oneself; mis-do, -behave; fall, lapse, slip, trip, offend, trespass; deviate from the -line of duty, – path of virtue &c. 944; take a wrong course, go astray; hug a -sin, – fault; sow one's wild oats.

render -vicious &c. *adj.*; demoralize, brutalize; corrupt &c. (*degrade*) 659.

Adj.* vicious; sinful; sinning &c. *v.*; wicked, iniquitous, bad, immoral, unrighteous, wrong, criminal; naughty, incorrect; undut-eous, -iful.

unprincipled, lawless, disorderly, *contra bonos mores*, indecorous, unseemly, improper; dissolute, profligate, scampish; unworthy; worth-, desert-less; disgraceful, recreant; reprehensible, blameworthy, uncommendable; dis-creditable, -reputable.

base, sinister, scurvy, foul, gross, vile, black, grave, facinorous, felonious, nefarious, shameful, scandalous, infamous, villainous, of a deep dye, heinous; flag-rant, -itious; atrocious, incarnate, accursed.

Mephistophelian, satanic, diabolic, hellish, infernal, stygian, fiend-ish, -like, hell-born, demoniacal, devilish.

mis-created, -begotten; demoralized, corrupt, depraved.

evil-minded, -disposed; ill-conditioned; malevolent &c. 907; heart-, grace-, shame-, virtue-less; abandoned, lost to virtue; unconscionable; sunk –, lost –, deep –, steeped- in iniquity.

incorrigible, irreclaimable, obdurate, reprobate, past praying for; culpable, reprehensible &c. (*guilty*) 947.

unjustifiable; in-defensible, -excusable; inexpiable, unpardonable, irremissible.

weak, frail, lax, infirm, imperfect, indiscreet; demoralizing, degrading.

Adv. wrong; sinfully &c. *adj.*; without excuse.

Int. *O tempora! O mores!*

---

946. Innocence. — N. innocence; guiltlessness &c. *adj.*; incorruption, impeccability.

clean hands, clear conscience, *mens sibi conscia recti*.

innocent, new born babe, lamb, dove.

V. be -innocent &c. *adj.*; *nil conscire sibi nullâ pallescere culpâ*.

947. Guilt.—N. guilt, -iness; culpability; crimin-ality, -ousness; deviation from rectitude &c. (*improbity*) 940; sinfulness &c. (*vice*) 945; peccability.

mis-conduct, -behaviour, -doing, -deed; malpractice, fault, sin, error, transgression; dereliction, delinquency; indiscretion, lapse, slip, trip, *faux pas*,

---

* Most of these adjectives are applicable both to the act and to the agent.

acquit &c. 970; exculpate &c. (*vindicate*) 937.

Adj. innocent, not guilty; unguilty; guilt-, fault-, sin-, stain-, blood-, spotless; clear, immaculate; *rectus in curiâ*; un-spotted, -blemished, -erring; undefiled &c. 939; unhardened, Saturnian; Arcadian &c. (*artless*) 703.

in-, un-culpable; unblam-ed, -able; blameless, inerrable, above suspicion; irrepr-oachable, -ovable, -ehensible; un-exceptionable, -objectionable, -impeachable; salvable; venial &c. 937.

harmless; in-offensive, -noxious, -nocuous; dove-, lamb-like; pure, harmless as doves; innocent as -a lamb, – the babe unborn; more sinned against than sinning.

virtuous &c. 944; un-reproved, -impeached, -reproached.

Adv. innocently &c. *adj.*; with clean hands; with a -clear, – safe- conscience.

948. Good Man. — **N.** good man, worthy.

good woman, goddess, *madonna*, virgin.

model, paragon &c. (*perfection*) 650; good example; hero, demigod, seraph, angel; innocent &c. 946; saint &c. (*piety*) 987; benefactor &c. 912; philanthropist &c. 910; Aristides.

brick, trump, rough diamond, ugly duckling.

salt of the earth; one in ten thousand; one of the best.

Phr. *si sic omnes!*

peccadillo; flaw, blot, omission; failing, -ure.

offence, trespass; mis-demeanour, -feasance, -prision; tort; mal-efaction, -feasance, -versation; crime, felony.

enormity, atrocity, outrage; deadly –, mortal –, unpardonable- sin; died without a name.

corpus delicti.

Adj. guilty, to blame, culpable, peccable, in fault, censurable, reprehensible, blameworthy, uncommendable, illaudable; weighed in the balance and found wanting; exceptionable, objectionable.

Adv. *in flagrante delicto*; red-handed, in the very act.

949. Bad Man.—**N.** bad man, wrong-doer, worker of iniquity; evil-doer &c. 913; sinner; the -wicked &c. 945; bad example.

rascal, scoundrel, villain, miscreant, caitiff; wretch, reptile, viper, serpent, cockatrice, basilisk, urchin; tiger, monster; devil &c. (*demon*) 980; devil incarnate; demon in human shape, Nana Sahib; hell-hound, -cat; rake-hell.

bad woman, jade, Jezebel, adultress. &c. 962.

scamp, scapegrace, rip, runagate, ne'er-do-well, reprobate, *roué*, rake; limb; one who has sold himself to the devil, fallen angel, *âme damnée, vaurien,* mauvais sujet, loose fish, sad dog; lost –, black- sheep; castaway, recreant, defaulter; prodigal &c. 818; libertine &c. 962.

rough, rowdy, ugly customer, ruffian, hoodlum, bully; Jonathan Wild; hangman; incendiary; thief &c. 792; murderer &c. 361.

culprit, delinquent, criminal, malefactor, misdemeanant; felon; convict, jail-bird, ticket-of-leave man; outlaw.

blackguard, *polisson,* loafer, sneak; raps-, ras-callion; cullion, mean wretch, varlet, kern, *âme-de-boue, drôle*; cur, dog, hound, whelp, mongrel; lown, loon, runnion, outcast, vagabond; rogue &c. (*knave*) 941; scum of the earth, riff-raff; *Arcades ambo.*

Int. sirrah!

950. Penitence.—**N.** penitence, contrition, compunction, repentance, remorse; regret &c. 833.

self-reproach, -reproof, -accusation,

951. Impenitence.—**N.** impenitence, irrepentance, recusance.

hardness of heart, seared conscience, induration, obduracy.

-condemnation, -humiliation; stings -, pangs -, qualms -, prickings -, twinge -, twitch -, touch -, voice- of conscience; compunctious visitings of nature.

acknowledgment, confession &c. (*disclosure*) 529; apology &c. 952; recantation &c. 607; penance &c. 952; resipiscence.

awakened conscience, deathbed repentance, *locus pœnitentiæ*, stool of repentance, cutty stool.

penitent, Magdalen, prodigal son, returned prodigal, a sadder and a wiser man.

V. repent, be sorry for; be -penitent &c. *adj.*; rue; regret &c. 833; think better of; recant &c. 607; knock under &c. (*submit*) 725; plead guilty; sing -*miserere*, - *de profundis*; cry *peccavi*; own oneself in the wrong; acknowledge, confess &c. (*disclose*) 529; humble oneself; beg pardon &c. (*apologize*) 952; turn over a new leaf, put on the new man, turn from sin; reclaim; repent in sackcloth and ashes &c. (*do penance*) 952; learn by experience.

Adj. penitent; repenting &c. *v.*; repentant, contrite; conscience-smitten, -stricken; self-accusing, -convicted.

penitenti-al, -ary; chastened, reclaimed; not hardened; unhardened.

Adv. meâ culpâ.

Phr. *peccavi; erubuit; salva res est; vous l'avez voulu, Georges Dandin.*

V. be -impenitent &c. *adj.*; steel -, harden- the heart; die -game, - and make no sign.

Adj. impenitent, uncontrite, obdurate; hard, -ened; seared, recusant; unrepentant; relent-, remorse-, grace-, shrift-less.

lost, incorrigible, irreclaimable.

unre-claimed, -formed; unrepented, unatoned.

---

952. Atonement.—N. atonement, reparation; compromise, composition; compensation &c. 30; quittance, quits; indemni-ty, -fication; expiation, redemption, reclamation, conciliation, propitiation.

amends, apology, *amende honorable*, satisfaction; peace -, sin -, burnt- offering; scapegoat, sacrifice.

penance, fasting, maceration, sackcloth and ashes, white sheet, shrift, flagellation, lustration; purga-tion, -tory.

V. atone, - for; expiate; propitiate; make -amends, - good; reclaim, redeem, repair, ransom, absolve, purge, shrive, do penance, stand in a white sheet, repent in sackcloth and ashes.

set one's house in order, wipe off old scores, make matters up; pay the -forfeit, - penalty.

apologize, beg pardon, express regret, *faire amende honorable*, give satisfaction; come -, fall- down on one's -knees, - marrow bones.

Adj. propitiatory, expiatory; sacrific, -ial, -atory; piacul-ar, -ous.

4°. MORAL PRACTICE

953. Temperance.—N. temperance moderation, sobriety, soberness.

forbearance, abnegation; self-denial, -restraint, -control &c. (*resolution*) 604.

frugality; vegetarianism, teetotalism, total abstinence, prohibition; abst-inence, -emiousness, asceticism &c. 955; system of -Pythagoras, - Cornaro; Pythagorism, Stoicism.

954. Intemperance.—N. intemperance; sensuality, animalism, carnality; pleasure; effeminacy, silkiness; luxur-y, -iousness; lap of -pleasure, - luxury.

indulgence; high-, free- living, inabstinence, self-indulgence; voluptuousness &c. *adj.*; epicur-ism, -eanism; sybaritism.

vegetarian; Pythagorean, gymnosophist; teetotaler &c. 958; abstainer.

V. be -temperate &c. adj.; abstain, forbear, refrain, deny oneself, spare; know when one has had enough; take the pledge; look not upon the wine when it is red.

Adj. temperate, moderate, sober, frugal, sparing; abst-emious, -inent; within compass; measured &c. (sufficient) 639.

Pythagorean; vegetarian; teetotal, pussy-foot.

dissipation; licentiousness &c. adj., debauchery; crapulence.

revel-s, -ry; debauch, carousal, jollification, drinking bout, wassail, Saturnalia, orgies; excess, too much; intoxication &c. 959.

Circean cup; drug habit &c. 663.

V. be -intemperate &c. adj.; indulge, exceed; live -well, – high, – on the fat of the land; give a loose to -indulgence &c. n.; dine not wisely but too well; wallow in -voluptuousness &c. n.; plunge into dissipation.

revel, rake, live hard, run riot, sow one's wild oats; slake one's -appetite, – thirst; swill; pamper.

Adj. intemperate, inabstinent, intoxicated &c. 959; sensual, self-indulgent; voluptuous, luxurious, licentious, wild, dissolute, rakish, fast, debauched.

brutish, crapulous, swinish, piggish, porcine, hoggish, bestial.

Paphian, Epicurean, Sybaritical; bred –, nursed- in the lap of luxury; indulged, pampered, full-fed.

954a. Sensualist.—N. Sybarite, voluptuary, Sardanapalus, man of pleasure, carpet knight; epicure, -an; gourm-et, -and; gormandizer, gutling, glutton, pig, hog; votary –, swine- of Epicurus; sensualist; Heliogabalus; free –, hard- liver; libertine &c. 962; hedonist.

955. Asceticism.—N. asceticism, puritanism, sabbatarianism; cynicism, austerity; total abstinence.

mortification, maceration, sackcloth and ashes, flagellation; penance &c. 952; fasting &c. 956; martyrdom.

ascetic; anchor-et, -ite; martyr; Heautontimorumenos; hermit &c. (recluse) 893; puritan, sabbatarian, cynic.

Adj. ascetic, austere, puritanical; cynical; over-religious.

956. Fasting. — N. fasting; xerophagy; famishment, starvation; banting.

fast, jour maigre; fast –, banyan-day; Lent, quadragesima; Rama-dan, -zan; spare –, meagre- diet; lenten -diet, – entertainment; soupe maigre, short -rations, – commons; Barmecide feast; hunger strike.

V. fast, starve, clem, famish, perish with hunger; dine with Duke Humphrey; make two bites of a cherry.

Adj. lenten, quadragesimal; unfed; starved &c. v.; half-starved; fasting &c. v.; hungry &c. 865.

957. Gluttony.—N. gluttony; greed; greediness &c. adj.; voracity.

epicurism; good –, high- living; edacity, gulosity, crapulence; gutt-, guzz-ling; over-indulgence.

good cheer, blow out; feast &c. (food) 298; gastronomy.

epicure, bon vivant, gourmand; glutton, cormorant, hog, belly-god, Apicius, gastronome, gormandizer.

V. gormandize, gorge; over-gorge, -eat- oneself; engorge, eat one's fill, cram, stuff, stodge, glut, satiate; gutt-le, guzz-le; bolt, devour, gobble up; gulp &c. (swallow food) 298; raven, eat out of house and home.

have the stomach of an ostrich; play a good knife and fork &c. (appetite) 865. pamper, indulge.

Adj. gluttonous, greedy; gormandizing &c. v.; edacious, omnivorous, crapulent, swinish, voracious, devouring.
pampered; over-fed, -gorged.

958. Sobriety.—N. sobriety; teetotalism, temperance &c. 953.

water-drinker; teetotal-er, -ist; abstainer, Good Templar, Rechabite, band of hope; prohibitionist, pussyfoot.
V. take the pledge.
Adj. sober, – as a judge; dry, on the water wagon.

959. Drunkenness.—N. drunkenness &c. adj.; intemperance; drinking &c. v.; inebri-ety, -ation; ebri-ety, -osity; befuddlement; insobriety; intoxication; temulency, bibacity, wine-bibbing; com-, potation; deep potations, bacchanals, *bacchanalia*, libations.

oino-, dipso-mania; *delirium tremens*, d.t.; alcohol, -ism.

drink; alcoholic drinks, alcohol, booze; gin, blue ruin, grog, brandy, port wine; punch, -bowl; cup, rosy wine, flowing bowl; drop, – too much; dram; beer, wine, spirits &c. (*beverage*) 298; cocktail, nip, peg; stirrup cup.

drunkard, sot, toper, tippler, bibber, wine-bibber; hard –, gin –, dram- drinker; soak, soaker, sponge, tun; love-, toss-pot; thirsty soul, reveller, carouser; Bacchanal, -ian; Bacch-al, -ante; devotee to Bacchus, dipsomaniac.

V. get –, be- drunk &c. adj.; see double; take a -drop, – glass- too much; drink, tipple, tope, booze, bouse, guzzle, swill, soak, sot, lush, bib, swig, carouse; sacrifice at the shrine of Bacchus; take to drinking; drink -hard, – deep, – like a fish; have one's swill, drain the cup, splice the main brace, take a hair of the dog that bit you.

liquor, – up; wet one's whistle, take a whet; lift one's elbow; crack a –, pass the- bottle; toss off &c. (*drink up*) 298; go to the -ale, – public-house.

make one -drunk &c. adj.; inebriate, fuddle, fuzzle, get into one's head.

Adj. drunk, tipsy; intoxicated; inebri-ous, -ate, -ated; in one's cups; in a state of -intoxication &c. n.; temulent, -ive; fuddled, mellow, cut, boosy, fou, fresh, merry, elevated, squiffy; plastered, befuddled, sozzled; flush, -ed; flustered, disguised, groggy, beery; topheavy; pot-valiant, glorious; potulent; over-come, -taken; whittled, screwed, tight, primed, oiled, corned, raddled, sewed up, lushy, nappy, muddled, muzzy, bosky, obfuscated, maudlin; crapulous, dead –, blind- drunk.

inter pocula; in –, the worse for- liquor, having had a drop too much, half seas over, three sheets in the wind; under the table, blind to the world, one over the eight.

drunk as -a piper, – a fiddler, – a lord, – Chloe, – an owl, – David's sow, – a wheelbarrow.

drunken, bibacious, bibulous, sottish; given –, addicted- to -drink, – the bottle; toping &c. v.; wet.
Phr. *nunc est bibendum.*

960. Purity.—N. purity; decency, decorum, delicacy; continence, chastity, honesty, virtue, modesty, shame; pudicity, *pucelage*, virginity.

vestal, virgin, Joseph, Hippolytus; Lucretia, Diana; prude.

961. Impurity.—N. impurity; uncleanness &c. (*filth*) 653; immodesty; grossness &c. adj.; indelicacy, indecency; impudicity; obscenity, ribaldry, smut, bawdry, *double entendre*, *équivoque*; Aretinism; pornography.

Adj. pure, undefiled, modest, delicate, decent, decorous; *virginibus puerisque*; chaste, continent, virtuous, honest, Platonic.

———————

concupiscence, lust, carnality, flesh, salacity; pruriency, lechery, lasciviency, lubricity, lewdness.

incontinence, intrigue, *faux pas*; *amour, -ette*; gallantry; debauchery, libertinism, *libertinage*, fornication; *liaison*; wenching, venery, dissipation.

seduction; defloration, defilement, abuse, violation, rape; incest.

social evil, harlotry, stupration, whoredom, concubinage, cuckoldom, adultery, advoutry, *crim. con.*; free love.

seraglio, harem, zenana; brothel, bagnio, stew, bawdy-house, *lupanar*, house of ill fame, *bordel*, kip.

V. be -impure &c. *adj.*; intrigue; debauch, defile, assault, attack, seduce; prostitute; abuse, violate, deflower; commit -adultery &c. *n.*

Adj. impure; unclean &c. *(dirty)* 653; not to be mentioned to ears polite; immodest, shameless; in-decorous, -delicate, -decent; loose, suggestive, *risqué*, coarse, gross, broad, free, equivocal, smutty, fulsome, ribald, obscene, bawdy, pornographic.

concupiscent, prurient, lickerish, rampant, lustful; carnal, -minded; lewd, lascivious, lecherous, libidinous, erotic, ruttish, salacious; Paphian; voluptuous; incestuous.

unchaste, light, wanton, licentious, adulterous, debauched, dissolute; of -loose character, - easy virtue; frail, gay, riggish, incontinent, meretricious, rakish, gallant, dissipated; no better than she should be; on the -town, - streets, - *pavé*, - loose.

adulterous, incestuous, bestial.

---

962. Libertine.—N. libertine; voluptuary &c. 954*a*; rake, debauchee, loose fish, rip, rake-hell, fast man; *intrigant*, gallant, seducer, fornicator, lecher, satyr, goat, whoremonger, *paillard*, adulterer, gay deceiver, Lothario, Don Juan, Bluebeard.

adulteress, advoutress, courtesan, prostitute, strumpet, tart, hustler, chippy, broad, harlot, whore, punk, *fille de joie*; woman, - of the town; street-walker, Cyprian, miss, piece; frail sisterhood, fallen woman; demirep, wench, trollop, trull, baggage, hussy, drab, bitch, jade, skit, rig, quean, mopsy, slut, minx, harridan; woman -of easy virtue &c. *(unchaste)* 961; wanton, fornicatress; Jezebel, Messalina, Delilah, Thaïs, Phryne, Aspasia, Lais, *lorette, cocotte, petite dame, grisette; demimondaine*; white slave.

concubine, mistress, fancy woman, kept woman, doxy, *chère amie, bona roba.*

pimp; pand-er, -ar; bawd, *conciliatrix*, procuress, mackerel; wittol.

5°. INSTITUTIONS

963. Legality.—N. legality; legitimacy, -teness, legitimization.

legislature; law, code, *corpus juris*, constitution, pandect, charter, act, enactment, statute, rule; canon &c. *(precept)* 697; ordinance, institution, regulation; by-, bye-law, rescript; decree &c. *(order)* 741; *ordonnance*;

964. [Absence or violation of law.] **Illegality.—N.** lawlessness; breach -, violation- of law; disobedience &c. 742; unconformity &c. 83.

arbitrariness &c. *adj.*; antinomy, violence, brute force, despotism, outlawry.

mob -, lynch -, club -, Lydford -,

standing order; *plébiscite* &c. (*choice*) 609.

legal process; form, -ula, -ality; rite; arm of the law; *habeas corpus*.

[Science of law] jurisprudence, nomology; legislation, codification.

equity, common law; *lex* –, *lex non-scripta*, unwritten law; law of nations, international law, *jus gentium*; *jus civile*; civil –, criminal –, canon –, statute –, ecclesiastical- law; *lex mercatoria*.

constitutional-ism, -ity; justice &c. 922.

V. legalize, legitimize; enact, ordain; decree &c. (*order*) 741; pass a law; legislate; codify, formulate; authorize.

Adj. legal, legitimate; according to law; vested, constitutional, chartered, legalized; lawful &c. (*permitted*) 760; statut-able, -ory; legislat-orial, -ive.

Adv. legally &c. *adj.*; in the eye of the law; *de jure*.

martial –, drumhead- law; *coup d'état*; *le droit du plus fort*; *argumentum ad baculum*.

illegality, informality, unlawfulness, illegitimacy, bar sinister.

trover and conversion; smuggling, boot-legging, rum-running, poaching; simony.

speakeasy, speakie, blind pig.

V. offend against –, violate- the law; set the law at defiance, ride rough-shod over, drive a coach and six through a statute; make the law a dead letter, take the law into one's own hands.

smuggle, run, poach.

Adj. illegal; prohibited &c. 761; not allowed, unlawful, illegitimate, illicit, contraband, actionable.

unchartered, unconstitutional; unwarrant-ed, -able; unauthorized; informal, unofficial; in-, extra-judicial.

lawless, arbitrary; despotic, -al; summary, irresponsible; un-answerable, -accountable.

null and void; a dead letter.

Adv. illegally &c. *adj.*; with a high hand, in violation of law.

965. Jurisdiction. [Executive.]—N. jurisdiction, judicature, administration of justice, soc; executive, commission of the peace; magistracy &c. (*authority*) 737.

judge &c. 967; tribunal &c. 966; municipality, corporation, bailiwick, shrievalty; lord lieutenant; lord –, mayor, city manager, alderman &c. 745; sheriff, bailie, shrieve, chief –, constable; police, – force; constabulary, bumbledom.

officer; proctor, high –, commissioner; bailiff, tipstaff, bum-bailiff, catchpoll, beadle; police-man, -constable, -sergeant; *sbirro, alguazil, gendarme*, kavass, *lictor*, macebearer, *huissier*, bedel.

press-gang; exciseman, gauger, custom-house officer, *douanier*.

coroner, edile, ædile, portreeve, paritor; *posse comitatus*.

V. judge, sit in judgment.

Adj. executive, administrative, municipal; inquisitorial, causidical; judic-atory, -iary, -ial; juridical.

Adv. *coram judice*.

966. Tribunal.—N. tribunal, court, board, bench, judicatory, curia; court of -justice, – law, – arbitration; inquisition; guild.

justice –, judgement –, mercy- seat; woolsack; bar, – of justice; dock; forum, hustings, *bureau*, drum-head; jury-, witness-box.

senate-house, town-hall, theatre; House of -Lords, – Commons.

assize, eyre; ward-, burgh-mote; superior courts of Westminster; court of -record, – oyer and terminer, – assize, – appeal, – error; High court of -Judicature, – Appeal; Judicial Committee of the Privy Council; Star-Chamber; Court of -Chancery, – King's *or* Queen's Bench, – Exchequer, – Common Pleas, – Probate, – Arches, – Admiralty, – Criminal Appeal; Lords Justices' –, Rolls –, Vice-Chancellor's –,

Stannary –, Divorce –, Palatine –, ecclesiastical –, county –, police-court; sessions; quarter –, petty- sessions; court -leet, – baron, – of pie poudre, – of common council; board of green cloth.

court-martial; drum-head court-martial; *durbar*, divan; Areopagus; *rota*.

Adj. judicial &c. 965; appellate; curial.

967. Judge.—**N.** judge; justi-ce, -ciar, -ciary; chancellor; justice –, judge- of assize; recorder, common serjeant; puisne –, assistant –, county court- judge; conservator –, justice- of the peace, J.P.; court &c. (*tribunal*) 966; grand –, petty –, coroner's- jury; panel, juror, juryman; twelve men in a box; magistrate, police magistrate, stipendiary, the great unpaid, beak; his -worship, – honour, – lordship; deemster, moderator.

Lord -Chancellor, – Justice; Master of the Rolls, Vice-Chancellor; Lord Chief -Justice, – Baron; Mr. Justice; Baron, – of the Exchequer.

jurat, assessor; arbi-ter, -trator; umpire; refer-ee, -endary; revising barrister; domesman; censor &c. (*critic*) 480; official –, receiver.

archon, tribune, prætor, *ephor*, syndic, *podestà*, mullah, ulema, mufti, cadi, kadi; Rhadamanthus.

litigant &c. (*accusation*) 938.

V. adjudge &c. (*determine*) 480; try a -case, – prisoner.

Adj. judicial &c. 965. **Phr.** 'a Daniel come to judgment.'

968. Lawyer.—**N.** lawyer, jurist, legist, civilian, pundit, publicist, jurisconsult, legal adviser, advocate; barrister, – at law; counsel, -lor; King's *or* Queen's counsel; K.C.; Q.C.; silk gown, leader; junior, – counsel; stuff gown, serjeant-at-law, bencher; tubman; judge &c. 967.

bar, legal profession, gentleman of the long robe; junior –, outer –, inner- bar; Inns of Court; equity draftsman, conveyancer, pleader, special pleader.

solicitor, attorney, proctor; notary, – public; scrivener, cursitor; writer, – to the signet; S.S.C.; limb of the law; pettifogger.

V. practise -at, – within- the bar; plead; call –, be called- -to, – within- the bar; take silk.

Adj. learned in the law; at the bar; forensic.

969. Lawsuit.—**N.** lawsuit, suit, action, cause, petition; litigation; dispute &c. 713.

citation, arraignment, prosecution, impeachment; accusation &c. 938; presentment, true bill, indictment.

apprehension, arrest; committal; imprisonment &c. (*restraint*) 751.

writ, summons, subpœna, *-duces tecum, latitat, nisi prius; habeas corpus*.

pleadings; declaration, bill, claim; *procès-verbal*, bill of right, information, *corpus delicti*; affidavit, state of facts; answer, replication, plea, demurrer, rebutter, rejoinder; surre-butter, -joinder.

suitor, party to a suit; litigant &c. 938; libellant.

hearing, trial; verdict &c. (*judgment*) 480; appeal, – motion; writ of error; *certiorari*.

case, decision, precedent, ruling; decided case, reports.

V. go to –, appeal to the- law; bring to -justice, – trial, – the bar; put on trial, pull up; accuse &c. 938; prefer –, file- a claim &c. n.; take the law of, inform against.

serve with a writ, cite, apprehend, arraign, sue, prosecute, bring an action against, indict, impeach, attach, distrain, commit; arrest; summon, -s; give in charge &c. (*restrain*) 751.

empanel a jury, implead, join issue; close the pleadings; set down for hearing.

try, hear a cause; sit in judgment; adjudicate &c. 480.

Adj. litigious &c. (*quarrelsome*) 713; *qui tam*; *coram* –, *sub*- *judice*.

Adv. *pendente lite*.

Phr. *adhuc sub judice lis est*.

---

970. Acquittal. — **N.** acquit-tal, -ment; clearance, exculpation, exoneration; discharge &c. (*release*) 750; *quietus*, absolution, compurgation, reprieve, respite; pardon &c. (*forgiveness*) 918.

[Exemption from punishment] impunity, immunity.

V. acquit, exculpate, exonerate, clear; absolve, whitewash, assoil, discharge, release; liberate &c. 750.

reprieve, respite; pardon &c. (*forgive*) 918; let off, – scot free.

Adj. acquitted &c. *v.*; un-condemned, -punished, -chastised; recommended to mercy.

971. Condemnation.—**N.** condemnation, conviction, proscription, damnation; death warrant; penalty &c. 974.

attain-der, -ture, -tment.

V. condemn, convict, cast, bring home to, find guilty, damn, doom, sign the death warrant, sentence pass sentence on, attaint, confiscate, proscribe, sequestrate; non-suit.

disapprove &c. 932; accuse &c. 938.

stand condemned.

Adj. condem-, dam-natory; condemned &c. *v.*; non-suited &c. (*failure*) 732; self-convicted.

Phr. *mutato nomine de te fabula narratur.*

---

972. Punishment. — **N.** punishment, punition; chast-isement, -ening; correction, castigation.

discipline, infliction, trial; judgement; penalty &c. 974; retribution; thunderbolt, Nemesis; requital &c. (*reward*) 973; penology; retributive justice.

lash, scaffold &c. (*instrument of punishment*) 975; imprisonment &c. (*restraint*) 751; chain gang; transportation, banishment, expulsion, deportation, exile, involuntary exile, ostracism; penal servitude, hard labour; galleys &c. 975; beating &c. *v.*; flagellation, fustigation, ga-ntlet, *strappado*, *estrapade*, *bastinado*, *argumentum ad baculum*, stick law, rap on the knuckles, box on the ear; blow &c. (*impulse*) 276; stripe, cuff, kick, buffet, pummel; slap, – in the face; wipe, douse; *coup de grâce*; torture, rack; picket, -ing; *dragonnade*; capital punishment, extreme penalty; execution; hanging &c. *v.*; de-capitation, -collation; *garrotte*; electrocution, lethal chamber; crucifixion, impalement; martyrdom, *auto-da-fé*; *noyade*; hara-kiri, happy despatch.

V. punish; chast-ise, -en; castigate, correct, inflict punishment, administer correction, deal retributive justice.

visit upon, pay; pay –, serve- out; settle with, get even with, get one's own back; do for; make short work of, give a lesson to, strafe, serve one right, make an example of; have a rod in pickle for; give it one.

strike &c. 276; deal a blow to, administer the lash, smite; slap, – the face; smack, cuff, box the ears, spank, thwack, thump, beat, lay on, swinge, buffet; thresh, thrash, pummel, drub, leather, trounce, baste, belabour; lace, – one's jacket; dress, give a -dressing, – down; trim, warm, wipe, tund, cob, bang, strap, comb, lash, lick, larrup, whallop, whop, flog, scourge, whip, birch, cane, give the stick, switch, flagellate, horsewhip, *bastinado*, towel, rub down with an oaken towel, rib roast, dust one's jacket, fustigate, pitch into, lay about one, beat black and blue; beat to a -mummy, – jelly; give a black eye; hit on the head; sandbag.

tar and feather; pelt, stone, lapidate; mast-head, keelhaul.

execute; bring to the -block, – gallows; behead; de-capitate, -collate; guillotine; hang, turn off, gibbet, bowstring, hang, draw and quarter; shoot; decimate; burn; electrocute; break on the wheel, crucify; em-, im-pale; flay; lynch; put to death.

torture; put -on, – to- the rack; picket.

banish, exile; trans-, de-port; expel, ostracize; rusticate; drum out; dismiss, -bar, -bench; strike off the roll, unfrock; post.

suffer, – for, – punishment; be -flogged, – hanged &c.; come to the gallows, dance upon nothing, die in one's shoes; be rightly served.

Adj. punishing &c. *v.*; penal; puni-tory, -tive; inflictive, castigatory; punished &c. *v.*

Int. *à la lanterne!*

973. Reward.—N. reward, recompense, remuneration, prize, meed, guerdon, reguerdon; indemni-ty, -fication, price; quittance; compensation; reparation, *ersatz*, assythment, redress; retribution, reckoning, acknowledgment, requital, amends, sop; atonement; consideration, return, *quid pro quo*; salvage, perquisite; vail &c. (*donation*) 784; *douceur*, bribe, bait, baksheesh, tip; hush-, smart-money; blackmail; carcelage; *solatium*.

allowance, salary, stipend, wages; pay, -ment; emolument; tribute; batta, shot, scot; premium, fee, *honorarium*; hire.

crown &c. (*decoration of honour*) 877.

V. re-ward, -compense, -pay, -quite; re-, munerate; compensate; fee, tip, bribe; pay one's footing &c. (*pay*) 807; make amends, indemnify, atone; satisfy, acknowledge.

get for one's pains, reap the fruits of.

Adj. remunerat-ive, -ory; munerary, compensatory, retributive, reparatory.

974. Penalty.—N. penalty; retribution &c. (*punishment*) 972; pain, pains and penalties; *peine forte et dure*; penance &c. (*atonement*) 952; the devil to pay.

fine, mulct, amercement; forfeit, -ure; escheat, damages, deodand, sequestration, confiscation, *premunire*.

V. penalize, fine, mulct, amerce, sconce, confiscate; sequest-rate, -er; escheat; estreat, forfeit.

975. [Instrument of punishment.] Scourge.—N. scourge, rod, cane, stick; ra-, rat-tan; birch, – rod; rod in pickle; switch, ferule, cudgel, truncheon; rubber hose.

whip, lash, strap, thong, cowhide, knout; cat, – o'-nine-tails, *sjambok*; quirt; rope's end.

pillory, stocks, whipping-post; cuck-, duck-ing stool; brank; triangle, wooden horse, maiden, thumbscrew, boot, rack, wheel, iron heel; treadmill, crank, galleys.

scaffold; block, axe, *guillotine*; stake; cross; gallows, gibbet, Tyburn tree; drop, noose, rope, halter, bowstring; electric chair, lethal chamber.

house of correction &c. (*prison*) 752.

gaol-, jail-er; executioner; hang-, heads-man; Jack Ketch; lyncher.

Section V. RELIGIOUS AFFECTIONS

1°. Superhuman Beings and Regions

976. Deity.—N. Deity, Divinity; God-head, -ship; Omnipotence, Providence.

[Quality of being divine] divin-eness, -ity.

God, Lord, Jehovah, *Deus*; The -Almighty, – Supreme Being, – First Cause; *Ens Entium*; Author –, Creator- of all things; Author of our being; The -Infinite, – Eternal; The All-powerful, -wise, -merciful, -holy; The Omni-potent, -scient.

[Attributes and perfections] infinite -power, – wisdom, – goodness, – justice, – truth, – love, – mercy; omni-potence, -science, -presence; unity, immutability, holiness, glory, majesty, sovereignty, infinity, eternity.

The -Trinity, – Holy Trinity, – Trinity in Unity, – Triune God; Three in One and One in Three.

God the Father; The -Maker, – Creator, – Preserver.

[Functions] creation, preservation, divine government; The-ocracy, -archy; providence; ways –, dealings –, dispensations –, visitations- of Providence.

God the Son, Jesus, Christ; The -Messiah, – Anointed, – Saviour, – Redeemer, – Mediator, – Intercessor, – Advocate, – Judge; The Son of -God, – Man, – David; The Only Begotten; The Lamb of God, The Word; Em-, Im-manuel; The -King of Kings and Lord of Lords, – King of Glory, – Prince of Peace, – Good Shepherd, – Way, – Truth, – Life, – Bread of Life, – Light of the World; The -Lord our, – Sun of- Righteousness.

The -Incarnation, – Hypostatic Union, – Word made Flesh.

[Functions] salvation, redemption, atonement, propitiation, mediation, intercession, judgment.

God the Holy Ghost, The Holy Spirit, Paraclete; The -Comforter, – Consoler, – Spirit of Truth, – Dove.

[Functions] inspiration, unction, regeneration, sanctification, consolation.

eon, æon, special providence, *Deus ex machinâ*; *Avatar*.

V. create, uphold, preserve, govern &c.

atone, redeem, save, propitiate, mediate &c.

predestinate, elect, call, ordain, bless, justify, sanctify, glorify &c.

Adj. almighty, holy, hallowed, sacred, divine, heavenly, celestial; messianic; sacrosanct; all-powerful, -wise, -seeing, -knowing; omnipotent, omniscient; supreme.

super-human, -natural; ghostly, spiritual, hyperphysical, unearthly; the-istic, -ocratic, deistic; anointed.

Adv. *jure divino*, by divine right; *Deo volente*, D.V.

977. [Beneficent spirits.] Angel.—N. angel, archangel; heavenly host, choir invisible, host of heaven, sons of God; Michael, Gabriel &c.; seraph, -im; cherub, -im; ministering spirit, morn-

978. [Maleficent spirits.] Satan.—N. Satan, the Devil, Lucifer, Ahrimanes, Belial; Sammael, Zamiel, Beelzebub, the Prince of the Devils; Mephistopheles, his satanic majesty.*

* The slang expressions 'the -deuce, – dickens, – old Gentleman; old -Nick, – Scratch, – Horny, – Harry, – Gooseberry,' have not been inserted in the text.

ing star; saint, *Madonna*; Our Lady, the Blessed Virgin, the Virgin Mary. **Adj.** angelic, seraphic, cherubic.

the tempter; the evil -one, - spirit; the -author of evil, - wicked one, - old Serpent; the Prince of -darkness, - this world, - the power of the air: the -foul, - arch- fiend; the devil incarnate; the -common enemy, - angel of the bottomless pit; Abaddon, Apollyon, Mammon.

fallen angels, unclean spirits, devils; the -rulers, - powers- of darkness; inhabitants of Pandemonium; demon &c. 980.

diabolism; devil-ism, -ship, -dom, -ry, -worship; *diablerie*; satanism, manicheism; the cloven foot; black magic &c. 992.

Adj. satanic, diabolic, devilish, infernal, hell-born.

Heathen, Mythological and other fabulous Deities and Powers*

979. Jupiter.—N. god, -dess; heathen gods and goddesses; Pantheon; Jupiter, Jove, Zeus, Apollo, Mars, Mercury, Neptune, Vulcan, Bacchus, Pluto, Saturn, Cupid, Eros, Pan; Juno, Ceres, Proserpina, Diana, Minerva, Pallas Athene, Venus, Aphrodite, Vesta; The Fates &c. 601.

Allah, Brahma, Vishnu, Siva, Shiva, Krishna, Juggernaut, Buddha; Ra, Isis, Osiris; Belus, Bel, Baal, Asteroth &c.; Thor, Odin; Mumbo Jumbo; good -, tutelary- genius; demiurge, familiar, - spirit; Sibyl; fairy, fay; sylph, -id; Ariel, peri, nymph, nereid, dryad, oread, sea-maid, Banshee, Benshie, Ormuzd; Oberon, Titania, Mab, hamadryad, naiad, mermaid, kelpie, Ondine, nix, nixie, sprite; denizens of the air; pixy &c. (*bad spirit*) 980.

mythology; heathen -, fairy- mythology; Lemprière, folklore.

Adj. fairy-, sylph-like; sylphic.

980. Demon.—N. demon, -ry, -ism, -ology; evil genius, fiend, familiar, - spirit, devil; bad -, unclean- spirit; cacodemon, incubus, Frankenstein's monster, succubus and succuba, Titan, Shedim, Mephistopheles, Asmodeus, Moloch, Belial, Ahriman, fury, The Furies &c. 900; harpy; Friar Rush.

vampire, ghoul; af-, ef-freet; afrite; ogre, -ss; gnome, gin, djinn, imp, deev, *lamia*; bo-gie, -gle; nis, kobold, flibbertigibbet, fairy, brownie, pixy, elf, dwarf, urchin, Puck, Robin Goodfellow; lepre-, cluri-chaune; troll, dwerger, sprite, oaf, changeling, bad fairy, nixe, pigwidgeon, Will-o'-thewisp; Erl King.

[Supernatural appearance] ghost, spectre, apparition, genie, spirit, shade, shadow, vision, phantom &c. 443; materialization (*spiritualism*) 992; hob-, goblin; wraith, spook, werwolf, boggart, banshee, *loup-garou, lemures*; evil eye.

nisse, necks; mer-man, -maid, -folk; siren, Lorelei; satyr, faun.

Adj. supernatural, weird, uncanny, unearthly, spectral; ghost-ly, -like; elf-in, -like; fiend-ish, -like; impish, demoniacal; haunted.

981. Heaven.—N. heaven; kingdom of -heaven, - God; heavenly kingdom; throne -, presence- of God; inheritance of the saints in light.

Paradise, Eden, abode of the blessed; Holy City, New Jerusalem; celestial bliss, glory.

[Mythological -heaven] Olympus; [- paradise] Elysium, Elysian fields, Arcadia, bowers of bliss, garden of the Hesperides, Islands of the Blessed;

982. Hell.—N. hell, bottomless pit, place of torment; habitation of fallen angels; Pandemonium, Abaddon, Domdaniel.

hell fire; everlasting -fire, - torment; lake of fire and brimstone; fire that is never quenched, worm that never dies.

purgatory, limbo, gehenna, abyss.

[Mythological hell] Tartarus, Hades, Avernus, Styx, Stygian creek, pit of Acheron, Cocytus, Phlegethon, Lethe

* Only a selection of those best known to literature is included.

happy hunting-ground; third –, seventh- heaven; Valhalla (Scandinavian); Nirvana (Buddhist).

future state, eternity, eternal life, life after death, eternal home, resurrection, translation; resuscitation &c. 660; apotheosis, deification.

Adj. heavenly, celestial, supernal, unearthly, from on high, paradisiacal, beatific, elysian, Olympian, Arcadian.

infernal regions, *inferno*, shades below, realms of Pluto.

Pluto, Rhadamanthus, Erebus, Charon, Cerberus; Tophet.

Adj. hellish, infernal, stygian.

2°. RELIGIOUS DOCTRINES

983. [Religious Knowledge.] **Theology.—N.** Theology (natural and revealed); Theo-gony, -sophy; Divinity; Hagio-logy, -graphy; Caucasian mystery; monotheism; religion; religious -persuasion, – sect, – denomination; cult; creed &c. (*belief*) 484; articles –, declaration –, profession –, confession- of faith.

theolog-ue, -ian; divine, schoolman, canonist, monotheist.

Adj. theological, religious; canonical; denominational; sectarian &c. 984.

983a. Orthodoxy.—N. orthodoxy; strictness, soundness, religious truth, true faith; truth &c. 494.

Christian-ity, -ism; Catholic-ism, -ity; 'the faith once delivered to the saints'; hyperorthodoxy &c. 984; iconoclasm.

the Holy –, the Orthodox- Church; Catholic –, Universal –, Apostolic –, Established- Church; temple of the Holy Ghost; Church –, body –, members –, disciples –, followers- of Christ; Christian, – community; true believer; canonist &c. (*theologian*) 983; Christendom, collective body of Christians, the Church Militant.

canons &c. (*belief*) 484; thirty-nine articles; Apostles' –, Nicene –, Athanasian- Creed; Church Catechism; textuary.

Adj. orthodox, sound, literal, strict, faithful, catholic, schismless, Christian, evangelical, scriptural, divine, monotheistic; true &c. 494.

High –, Low –, Broad –, Free-Church; ultramontanism; monasticism; pap-ism, -istry; papacy; Anglican-, Catholic-, Roman-ism; popery; Scarlet Lady, Church of Rome, Greek Church; Christian Science, The Church of Christ Scientist.

984. Heterodoxy. [Sectarianism.]— **N.** heterodoxy; error &c. 495; false doctrine, heresy, schism; schismaticism, -alness; recusancy, backsliding, apostasy; atheism &c. (*irreligion*) 989.

bigotry &c. (*obstinacy*) 606; fanaticism, iconoclasm; hyperorthodoxy, precisianism, bibliolatry, hagiolatry, sabbatarianism, puritanism; idolatry &c. 991; superstition &c. (*credulity*) 486; dissent &c. 489.

sectar-ism, -ianism; nonconformity; secularism; syncretism, religious sects; the clash of creeds.

protestant-, advent-, Arian-, Erastian-, Calvin-, quaker-, method-, anabapt-, Pusey-, tractarian-, ritual-, Origen-, Sabellian-, Socinian-, De-, The-, mon-, material-, positiv-, latitudinarian-ism &c.

pagan-, heathen-, ethic-ism; mythology; animism; poly-, di-, tri-, pantheism; dualism; heathendom.

Juda-, Gentil-, Mahometan-, Islam-, Turc-, Brahmin-, Hindoo-, Buddh-, Lama-, Confucian-, Shinto-, Sabian-, Gnostic-, Soofee-, Hylothe-, Mormonism.

Theosophy; Spiritualism, Occultism.

heretic, antichrist; pagan, heathen; pai-, pay-nim; *giaour*; gentile; pan-, poly-theist; idolator; misbeliever, apostate, backslider.

bigot &c. (*obstinacy*) 606; fanatic, dervish, abdal, iconoclast.

latitudinarian, limitarian, Deist, Theist, Unitarian; positivist, materialist; agnostic, skeptic &c. 989.

schismatic; sectar-y, -ian, -ist; seceder, separatist, recusant, dissenter; non-conformist, -juror; Huguenot, Protestant; orthodox dissenter, Congregationalist, Independent; Episcopalian, Presbyterian; Lutheran, Calvinist, Quaker, Methodist, Wesleyan; Ana-, Baptist; Dunker; Mormon, Latter-day Saint, Irvingite, Sandemanian, Glassite, Erastian; Sub-, Supra-lapsarian; Gentoo, Antinomian, Swedenborgian, Adventist, Plymouth Brother; Theosophist &c.

Catholic, Roman Catholic, Romanist, papist, ultramontane; Old Catholic, tractarian, Anglican, Puseyite, ritualist; Puritan.

Jew, Hebrew, Rabbist; Mahometan, Mohammedan, Mussulman, Moslem, Islamite, Osmanli; Brahm-in, -an; Parsee, Sofi, Soofee; Buddhist; Zoroastrian, Magi, Gymnosophist, fire-worshipper, Sabian, Gnostic, Sadducee, &c.

Adj. heterodox, heretical; un-orthodox, -scriptural, -canonical; antiscriptural, apocryphal; un-, anti-christian; schismatic, recusant, iconoclastic; sectarian; dis-senting, -sident; secular &c. (*lay*) 997.

pagan; heathen, -ish; ethnic, -al; gentile, painim; pan-, poly-theistic; agnostic, skeptic.

Judaical, Mohammedan, Moslem, Brahminical, Buddhist &c. *n.* Romish, Protestant &c. *n.*

bigoted &c. (*prejudiced*) 481, (*obstinate*) 606; superstitious &c. (*credulous*) 486; fanatical; idolatrous &c. 991; visionary &c. (*imaginative*) 515.

985. Revelation.—N. revelation, inspiration, *afflatus.*

Word, - of God; Scripture; the -Scriptures, - Bible, - Book of Books; Holy -Writ, - Scriptures; inspired writings, Gospel.

Old Testament, Septuagint, Vulgate, Pentateuch; Octateuch; the -Law, - Jewish Law, - Prophets; major -, minor- Prophets; Hagio-grapha, -logy; Hierographa; Apocrypha.

New Testament; Gospels, Evangelists, Acts, Epistles, Apocalypse, Revelations.

Talmud; Mishna, Masorah.

986. Pseudo-Revelation.*—N. the -Koran, - Alcoran; Ly-king, Shaster Vedas, Zendavesta, Vedidad, Purana, Edda; Go-, Gau-tama; Book of Mormon.

[False prophets and religious founders] Buddha, Zoroaster, Zerdhusht, Confucius, Mahomet.

[Idols] golden calf &c. 991; Baal, Moloch, Dagon.

prophet &c. (*seer*) 513; evangelist, apostle, disciple, saint; the -, the Apostolical- fathers; Holy Men of old, inspired -writers, - penmen.

Adj. scriptural, biblical, sacred, prophetic; evangel-ical, -istic; apostolic, -al; inspired, theopneustic, apocalyptic, ecclesiastical, canonical, textuary.

* See note on page 378.

3°. Religious Sentiments

987. Piety.—N. piety, religion, theism, faith; religiousness, holiness &c. *adj.*; saintship; religionism; sanctimony &c. (*assumed piety*) 988; reverence &c. (*respect*) 928; humility, veneration, devotion; prostration &c. (*worship*) 990; grace, unction, edification; sancti-ty, -tude; consecration.

spiritual existence, odour of sanctity, beauty of holiness.

theopathy, beatification, adoption, regeneration, conversion, justification, sanctification, salvation, inspiration, bread of life; Body and Blood of Christ.

believer, convert, theist, Christian, devotee, pietist; the -good, – righteous, – just, – believing, – elect; Saint, *Madonna*.

the children of -God, – the kingdom, – *l*ight.

V. be -pious &c. *adj.*; have -faith &c. *n.*; believe, receive Christ; revere &c. 928; worship &c. 990; be -converted &c.

convert, edify, sanctify, hallow, keep holy, beatify, regenerate, inspire, consecrate, enshrine.

Adj. pious, religious, devout, devoted, reverent, godly, heavenly minded, humble; pure, – in heart; holy, spiritual, pietistic; saint-ly, -like; seraphic, sacred, solemn.

believing, faithful, Christian, Catholic.

elected, adopted, justified, sanctified, regenerated, inspired, consecrated, converted, unearthly, not of the earth.

988. Impiety.—N. impiety; sin &c. 945; irreverence; profan-eness &c. *adj.*, -ity, -ation; blasphemy, desecration, sacrilege; scoffing &c. *v.*

[Assumed piety] hypocrisy &c. (*falsehood*) 544; pietism, cant, pious fraud; lip-devotion, -service, -reverence; misdevotion, formalism, austerity; sanctimon-y, -iousness &c. *adj.*; pharisaism, precisianism; sabbat-ism, -arianism; *odium theologicum*, sacerdotalism; bigotry &c. (*obstinacy*) 606, (*prejudice*) 481.

hardening, backsliding, declension, perversion, reprobation, apostasy, recusancy.

sinner &c. 949; scoffer, blasphemer; sacrilegist; worldling; hypocrite &c. (*dissembler*) 548; Scribes and Pharisees; Tartufe, Maw-worm.

bigot; saint [ironically]; Pharisee, sabbatarian, formalist, methodist, puritan, pietist, precisian, religionist, devotee, ranter, fanatic, wowser.

the -wicked, – evil, – unjust, – reprobate; son of -men, – Belial, , – the wicked one; children of darkness.

V. be -impious &c. *adj.*; profane, desecrate, blaspheme, revile, scoff; swear &c. (*malediction*) 908; commit sacrilege.

snuffle; turn up the whites of the eyes; idolize.

Adj. impious; irreligious &c. 989; desecrating &c. *v.*; profane, irreverent, sacrilegious, blasphemous.

un-hallowed, -sanctified, -regenerate; hardened, perverted, reprobate.

hypocritical &c. (*false*) 544; canting, pietistical, sanctimonious, unctuous, pharisaical, over-righteous, righteous over much.

bigoted, fanatical &c. 481 & 606; priest-ridden.

Adv. under the -mask, cloak, – pretence, – form, – guise- of religion.

989. Irreligion.—N. irreligion, indevotion; ungodliness &c. *adj.*; laxity, quietism, apathy, indifference, passivity.

scepticism, doubt; un-, dis-belief; incredul-ity, -ousness &c. *adj.*; want of -faith, – belief; pyrrhonism; doubt &c. 485; agnosticism. atheism, deism; hylotheism; materialism; positivism; nihilism. infidelity, freethinking, antichristianity, rationalism.

atheist, anti-christian, sceptic, unbeliever, deist, infidel, pyr-rhonist; *giaour*, heathen, alien, gentile, Nazarene; *esprit fort*, free-thinker, latitudinarian, rationalist; materialist, positivist, nihilist, agnostic.

V. be -irreligious &c. *adj.*; disbelieve, lack faith; doubt, question &c. 485.

dechristianize; serve Mammon, love darkness better than light.

Adj. irreligious; in-, un-devout; devout-, god-, grace-less; un-godly, -holy, -sanctified, -hallowed; atheistic, without God.

sceptical, free-thinking; un-believing, -converted; incredulous, faithless, lacking faith; deistical; un-, anti-christian.

worldly, mundane, earthly, carnal, unspiritual; worldly &c.-minded.

Adv. irreligiously &c. *adj.*

4°. Acts of Religion

990. Worship.—N. worship, adoration, devotion, aspiration, latria, homage, service, humiliation; kneeling, genuflexion, prostration.

prayer, invocation, supplication, rogation, intercession, orison, holy breathing; petition &c. (*request*) 765; collect, litany, Lord's prayer, paternoster, *Ave Maria*, rosary; bead-roll; latria, dulia, hyperdulia, vigils; revival; cult.

thanksgiving; giving –, returning- thanks; grace, praise, glorifica-tion, benediction, doxology, hosanna; h-, allelujah; *Te Deum, non nobis Domine, nunc dimittis*; pæan.

psalm, -ody; hymn, plainsong, chant, chaunt, response, anthem, motet; antiphon, -y.

oblation, sacrifice, incense, libation; burnt –, votive –, thank-offering; offertory, collection.

discipline; self-discipline, -examination, -denial; fasting.

divine service, office, duty; morning prayer; mass, matins, evensong, vespers, compline; holy day &c. (*rites*) 998.

worshipper, congregation, communicant, celebrant.

V. worship, lift up the heart, aspire; revere &c. 928; adore, do serv-ice, pay homage; humble oneself, kneel; bow –, bend- the knee; fall -down, – on one's knees; prostrate oneself, bow down and worship, recite the rosary.

pray, invoke, supplicate; put –, offer- up -prayers, – petitions; beseech &c. (*ask*) 765; say one's prayers, tell one's beads.

return –, give- thanks; say grace, bless, praise, laud, glorify, magnify, sing praises; give benediction, lead the choir, intone, chant, sing.

propitiate, offer sacrifice, fast, deny oneself; vow, offer vows, give alms.

work out one's salvation; go to church; attend -service, – mass; communicate &c. (*rite*) 998.

Adj. worshipping &c. *v.*; devout, devotional, reverent, pure, solemn; fervid &c. (*heartfelt*) 821.

Int. h-, allelujah! hosanna! glory be to God! O Lord! pray God that! God -grant, – bless, – save, – forbid! *sursum corda*.

991. Idolatry.—N. idol-atry, -ism; demon-ism, -olatry; idol –, demon –, devil –, fire- worship; zoolatry, fetishism, Mari-, Bibli-, ecclesi-, heli-olatry.

deification, apotheosis, canonization; hero worship.

sacrifices, hecatomb, holocaust; human sacrifices, immolation, mactation, infanticide, self-immolation, *suttee*.

idol, golden calf, graven image, fetish, *avatar*, Juggernaut, joss, *lares et penates*; Baal &c. 986.

idolater &c. *n.*

V. worship -idols, – pictures, – relics; put on a pedestal, bow down to, prostrate oneself before, make sacrifice to; deify, canonize, idolize.

Adj. idolatrous.

992. Sorcery.—N. sorcery; superstition; occult -art, – sciences; black –, magic; the black art, necromancy, theurgy, thaumaturgy; demon-ology, -omy, -ship; *diablerie*, bedevilment; witch-craft, -ery; glamour; fetis-hism, -ism; ghost dance; hoodoo, voodoo; Shamanism [Esquimaux], vampirism; conjuration; bewitchery, exorcism, enchantment, incantation, obsession, possession, mysticism, second sight, mesmerism, animal magnetism; od –, odylic- force; electro-biology, *clairvoyance*; spiritualism, spirit-rapping, table-turning; thought reading, telepathy, thought transference, automatic writing, *planchette*, ouija board; crystal gazing; spirit manifestation, materialization, astral body, ectoplasm &c.

divination &c. (*prediction*) 511; sortilege, ordeal, *sortes Virgilianæ*, -*biblicæ*, hocus-pocus &c. (*deception*) 545; oracle &c. 513.

V. practice -sorcery &c. *n.*; cast a -horoscope, – nativity; conjure, exorcise, charm, enchant; be-witch, -devil; overlook, look on with the evil eye; entrance, mesmerize, magnetize; fascinate &c. (*influence*) 615; taboo; wave a wand; rub the -ring, – lamp; cast a spell; call up spirits, – from the vasty deep; raise spirits from the dead; raise –, lay- ghosts; command genii.

Adj. magic, -al; mystic, weird, cabalistic, talismanic, phylacteric, incantatory; charmed &c. *v.*

993. Spell.—N. spell, charm, incantation, exorcism, weird, cabala, exsufflation, cantrap, runes, abracadabra, hocus-pocus, open *sesame*, counter-charm, Ephesian letters, bell, book and candle, Mumbo Jumbo, evil-eye, fee-faw-fum.

talisman, amulet, periapt, telesm, phylactery, philtre, wish-bone, merry-thought, mascot, scarab, swastika; fetish; *agnus Dei*.

wand, caduceus, rod, divining rod, lamp of Aladdin, magic carpet, seven-league boots; magic ring; wishing –, Fortunatus's- cap.

994. Sorcerer.—N. sorcerer, magician; thaumat-, the-urgist; conjuror, necromancer, seer, wizard, witch; fairy &c. 980; *lamia*, hag, warlock, charmer, exorcist, voodoo, mage, diviner, dowser; cunning –, medicine- man, witch doctor; Shaman, figure-flinger, ecstatica, medium, *clairvoyant*, mesmerist, hypnotist; *deus ex machinâ*; astrologer; soothsayer &c. 513.

Katerfelto, Cagliostro, Merlin, Comus, Mesmer; Hecate, Circe, Lilith, siren, weird sisters; witch of Endor.

5°. RELIGIOUS INSTITUTIONS

995. Churchdom.—N. church, -dom; ministry, apostleship, priesthood, prelacy, hierarchy, church government, christendom, pale of the church.

clerical-, sacerdotal-, episcopalian-, ultramontan-ism; Theocracy; ecclesiolog-y, -ist; priestcraft, *odium theologicum*.

monach-ism, -y; monasticism, monkhood.

[Ecclesiastical offices and dignities] pontificate, primacy, archbishopric, archiepiscopacy; prelacy; bishop-ric, -dom; episcop-ate, -acy; see, diocese; deanery, stall; canon-ry, -icate; prebend, -aryship; benefice, incumbency, glebe, advowson, living, cure, – of souls; rectorship; vicar-iate, -ship; pastor-ate, -ship; deacon-ry, -ship; -curacy; chaplain, -cy, -ship; cardinal-ate, -ship; abbacy, presbytery.

holy orders, ordination, institution, consecration, induction, reading in, preferment, translation, presentation.

popedom, papacy; the -Vatican, – apostolic see, – see of Rome; religious sects &c. 984.

council &c. 696; conclave, college of cardinals, convocation, synod, consistory, chapter, vestry, presbytery; sanhedrim, *congé d'élire*; ecclesiastical courts, consistorial court, court of Arches.

V. call, ordain, induct, prefer, translate, consecrate, present, elect, bestow.

take -orders, – the veil, – vows.

Adj. ecclesi-astical, -ological; clerical, sacerdotal, priestly, prelatical, pastoral, ministerial, capitular, theocratic; hierarchical, archiepiscopal; episcopal, -ian; canonical; mon-astic, -achal; monkish; abbati-al, -cal;. pontifical, papal, apostolic; ultramontane, priest-ridden.

996. Clergy.—N. clergy, clericals, ministry, priesthood, presbytery, the cloth, the pulpit.

clergyman, divine, ecclesiastic, churchman, priest, presbyter, hierophant, pastor, shepherd, minister, clerk in holy orders; father, – in Christ; *padre, abbé, curé*; patriarch; reverend; black coat; confessor; sky pilot.

dignitaries of the church; ecclesi-, hier-arch; eminence, reverence, elder, primate, metropolitan, archimandrite, archbishop, bishop, prelate, diocesan, suffragan, dean, subdean, archdeacon, prebendary, canon, rural dean, rector, parson, vicar, perpetual curate, residentiary, beneficiary, incumbent, chaplain, curate, – in charge; deacon, -ess; preacher; lay reader, lecturer; capitular; missionary, propagandist, Jesuit, revivalist, field preacher.

churchwarden, sidesman; clerk, precentor, choir; almoner, *suisse*, verger, beadle, sexton, sacristan; acol-yth, -othyst, -yte; thurifer; chorister, choir boy.

[Roman Catholic priesthood] Pope, *Papa*, Holy Father, pontiff, high priest, cardinal; ancient –, flamen; confessor, penitentiary; spiritual director.

cenobite, conventual, abbot, prior, monk, friar, lay brother, beadsman, mendicant, pilgrim, palmer; canon-regular, -secular; Jesuit, Franciscan, Friars minor, Minorites; Observant, Capuchin, Dominican, Carmelite; Augustinian; Gilbertine; Austin-, Black-, White-, Grey-, Crossed-, Crutched-Friars; Bonhomme, Carthusian, Benedictine, Cistercian, Trappist, Cluniac, Premonstratensian, Maturine; Templar. Hospitaller.

997. Laity.—N. laity, flock, fold, congregation, assembly, brethren, people.

temporality, secularization.

layman, civilian; parishioner, catechumen; secularist.

V. secularize.

Adj. secular, lay, laical, civil, temporal, profane.

abb-, prior-, canon-ess; mother superior; *religieuse*, nun, sister, *béguine*, novice, postulant.

[Under the Jewish dispensation] prophet, priest, high priest, Levite; Rabbi, -n; scribe.

[Mohammedan &c.] mullah, ulema, imaum, sheik; so-fi, -phi; mufti, hadji, muezzin, dervish; fa-kir, -quir; brahmin, gooroo, druid, bonze, santon, abdal, Lama, talapoin, caloyer &c.

V. take orders &c. 995.

Adj. the –, the very –, the Right- Reverend; ordained, in orders, called to the ministry.

998. Rite.—**N.** rite; ceremon-y, -ial; ordinance, observance, function, duty; form, -ulary; solemnity, sacrament; incantation &c. (*spell*) 993; service, psalmody &c. (*worship*) 990; liturgies.

ministration; preach-ing, -ment; predication, sermon, homily, exhortation, lecture, discourse, pastoral.

baptism, christening, chrism, immersion; baptismal regeneration; font; circumcision.

confirmation; imposition –, laying on- of hands; churching, purification, ordination &c. (*churchdom*) 995; excommunication.

Eucharist, Lord's supper, communion; the –, the holy- sacrament; celebration, high celebration; *missa cantata*; offertory; introit; consecration; con-, tran-substantiation; real presence; elements, bread and wine; mass; high –, low –, dry- mass.

matrimony &c. 903; burial &c. 363; visitation of the sick.

seven sacraments, impanation, extreme unction, last rites. *viaticum*, invocation of saints, canonization, transfiguration, auricular confession; fasting; maceration, flagellation, sackcloth and ashes; penance &c. (*atonement*) 952; absolution; telling of beads, reciting the rosary, processional; thurification, incense, holy water, aspersion.

relics, rosary, beads, reliquary, host, cross, rood, crucifix, pax, pix, pyx, *agnus Dei*, censer, thurible, patera, urceole; chalice, patten, Holy Grail, sangrail; seven-branch candle stick, monstrance, sacring bell

ritual, rubric, canon, ordinal; liturgy, prayer-book, book of common prayer, pietas, euchology, litany, lectionary; missal, breviary, massbook, bead-roll.

psalter; psalm –, hymn- book; hymn-al, -ology; psalmody.

ritual-, ceremonial-ism; sabbat-ism, -arianism; ritualist, sabbatarian.

holyday, feast, fast; Sabbath, Passover, Pentecost; Advent, Christmas, Noël, Epiphany, Lent, Shrove Tuesday, Ash Wednesday, Maundy Thursday; Passion –, Holy- week; Good Friday, Easter, Ascension Day, Whitsuntide; Trinity Sunday, Corpus Christi; All-Saints' –, – Souls'- Day; Candle-, Lam-, Martin-, Michael-mas; hogmanay; Rama-dan, -zan; Bairam &c. &c.

V. perform service, do duty, minister, officiate, baptize, dip, sprinkle; confirm. lay hands on; give –, administer –, take –, receive –. attend –, partake of- the -sacrament, – communion; communicate; celebrate mass; administer –, receive- extreme unction, anele, shrive, absolve, confess; do penance; genuflect; cross oneself, make the sign of the cross.

excommunicate, ban with bell, book and candle.

preach, sermonize, predicate, lecture.

Adj. ritual, -istic; ceremonial, liturgic; baptismal, eucharistical; paschal.

999. Canonicals.—**N.** canonicals, vestments; robe, gown, Geneva gown, frock, pallium, surplice, cassock, dalmatic, scapulary, cope. scarf, tunicle, chasuble, alb, *alba*, stole;˙fan-on, -nel; tonsure, cowl, hood; calo-te, -tte; bands; capouch, amice, orarium, ephod; apron, lawn sleeves, pontificals, pall; mitre, tiara, triple crown; shovel –, cardinal's-hat; biretta; crosier; pastoral staff; costume &c. 225.

1000. Temple.—N. place of worship; house of -God, – prayer.

temple, cathedral, minster, church, kirk, chapel, meeting-house, bethel, tabernacle, conventicle, *basilica*, fane, holy place, chantry, oratory.

synagogue; mosque; marabout; pantheon; pagoda; joss-house; dagobah, tope; kiosk.

parsonage, rectory, vicarage, manse, deanery, glebe, church house; Vatican; bishop's palace; Lambeth.

altar, shrine, sanctuary, Holy of Holies, *sanctum sanctorum*, sacrarium, -isty; communion –, holy –, Lord's- table; table of the Lord; pyx; baptistery, font; piscina, stoup; aumbry; sedile; reredos; rood -loft, – screen; jube.

chancel, quire, choir, nave, aisle, transept, lady chapel, vestry, crypt, cloisters, porch; triforum, clerestory, churchyard, *golgotha*, calvary, Easter sepulchre; stall, pew, sitting; pulpit, ambo, lectern, reading-desk, confessional, prothesis, credence, baldachin, *baldacchino*; jesse, apse, belfry; chapter-house; presbytery.

monastery, priory, abbey, friary, convent, nunnery, cloister.

Adj. claustral, cloistered; monast-ic, -erial; conventual.

INDEX

N.B.: The numbers refer to the headings under which the words or phrases occur. When the same word or phrase may be used in various senses, the several headings under which it, or its synonyms, will be found, according to those meanings, are indicated by the words printed in Italics. These words in Italics are not intended to explain the meaning of the word or phrase to which they are annexed, but only to assist in the required reference.

When the word given in the Index is itself the title or heading of a category, the number of reference is printed in blacker type, thus: **abode 189.**

---

accipient 785
acclamation
  assent 488
  approbation 931
acclimatize 370, 613
acclivity 217
accloy 641
accolade 894
accommodate
  suit 23
  adjust 27
  aid 707
  reconcile 723
  give 784
  lend 787
  – oneself to 82
accommodation
  space 180
accommodating
  kind 906
accompaniment
  adjunct 39
  coexistence **88**
  musical 415
accompany
  add 37
  coexist 88
  concur 120
  music 416
accompli, fait – 729
accomplice 711
accomplish
  execute 161
  complete 729
  succeed 731
accomplishment
  490, 698
accompts 811
accord
  uniform 16
  agree 23
  music 413
  assent 488
  concord 714
  grant 760
  give 784
  of one's own – 602
according
  – as *qualification* 469
  – to *evidence* 467
  – to circumstances 8
  – to law 963
  – to rule
  conformably 82
  – rumour 527
accordingly
  logically 476
accordion 417
accost 586

accoucheur 631, 662
accouchement 161
account *list* 86
  adjudge 480
  description 594
  credit 805
  money - 811
  fame 873
  approbation 931
  call to – 932
  find one's – in
  useful 644
  success 731
  make no – of 483, 930
  not – for 519
  on – of *motive* 615
  behalf 707
  on no – 536
  send to one's – 361
  take into – 457, 469
  small – 643
  to one's – 780
  turn to –
  improve 658
  use 677
  success 731
  gain 775
  – as *deem* 484
  – book 551
  – for 155, 522
  – with 794, 807
accountable
  liable 177
  debit 811
  duty 926
accountant 801, 811
  certified public – 811
accounts **811**
accouple 43
accoutred
  armed 717
accoutrement
  dress 225
  appliance 633
  equipment 673
accoy 174
accredit
  commission 755, 759
  money 805
  honour 873
accredited 484, 613
  – to 755, 759
accretion 35, 46
accrimination 938
accroach 789
accrue *add* 37
  result 154

acquire 775
  be received 785, 810
accubation 213
accueil 894
accultural 658
accumbent 213
accumulate
  collect 72
  store 636
  redundance 641
accurate 494
  – *knowledge* 490
accurse 908
accursed
  disastrous 649
  undone 828
  vicious 945
accusation **938**
accuse
  disapprove 932
  charge 938
  lawsuit 969
accustom 613
ace *small* 32
  unit 87
  within an – 197
aceldama *kill* 361
  arena 728
acephalous 59
acerbate 659, 835
acerbity
  acrimony 395
  sourness 397
  rudeness 895
  spleen 900, 901
  malevolence 907
acervate 72
acetous 397
acetylene 388
acharné 900
Achates, fidus – 890, 939
ache *physical* 378
  mental 828
Acheron
  pit of – 982
Acherontic
  moribund 360
  gloomy 837
achievable 470
achieve *end* 67
  produce 161
  do 680
  accomplish 729
achievement 551, 861
Achilles, heel of –
  vulnerable 665
achromatism **429**
acicular 253

acid 397
acid test 463
acknowledge
  answer 462
  assent 488
  disclose 529
  avow 535
  consent 762
  observe 772
  pay 807
  thank 916
  repent 950
  reward 973
acknowledged
  custom 613
acme 210
  – of perfection 650
Acology 662
acolyte 996
acomous 226
aconite 663
acoustic 418
  – organs 418
acoustics 402
acquaint
  – oneself with 539
  – with 527
acquaintance
  knowledge 490
  information 527
  friend 890
  make – with 888
acquiesce
  assent 488
  willing 488
  consent 762
  tolerate 826
acquire
  develop 161
  get 775
  receive 785
  – a habit 613
  – learning 539
acquirement
  knowledge 490
  learning 539
  talent 698
  receipt 810
acquisition
  knowledge 490
  gain 775
acquit
  liberate 750
  exempt 927a
  vindicate 937
  innocent 946
  absolve 970
acquit oneself
  behave 692
  – of a debt 807
  – of a duty 926

– of an obligation
    772
acquittal 506, 970
acquittance 771
acres *space* 180
    land 342
    property 780
Acres, Bob 862
acrid 392, 395
acridity 171
acrimony
    physical 171
    caustic 830
    discourtesy 895
    hatred 898
    anger 900
    malevolence 907
acroamatics 490
acrobat
    strength 159
    actor 599
    proficient 700
    mountebank 844
Acropolis 210
across 219, 708
acrostic 533, 561,
    842
act *imitate* 19
    physical 170
    – *of a play* 599
    personate 599
    voluntary 680
    statute 697
    in the – 680, 947
    – a part *feign* 544
    – one's part 625,
    926
    – upon
    physical 170
    mental 615
    take steps 680
    – up to 772
    – well one's part
    944
    – without author-
    ity 738
acting *deputy* 759
actinic 420
actinometer 445
action *physical* 170
    voluntary **680**
    battle 720
    law 969
    line of – 692
    put in – 677
    suit the – to the
    word 550
    thick of the – 682
activate 171
actionable 964
active *physical* 171

voluntary 682
– service 722
– thought 457
activity 682
actor
    impostor 548
    player 599
    agent 690
    affectation 855
Acts *record* 551
    Apostolic 985
actual *existing* 1
    present 118
    real 494
actuary 85, 811
actuate 175, 615
actum est 729
acu tetigisti, rem
    465, 494
acuity 253
aculeate 253
acumen 498
acuminate 253
acupuncture 260
acustics 402
acute *energetic* 171
    physically violent
    173
    pointed 253
    physically sensible
    375
    musical tone 410
    perspicacious 498
    cunning 702
    strong feeling 821
    morally painful
    830
    – angle 244
    – ear 418
    – note 410
acutely 31
acuteness 465
ad
    – eundem 27
    – hominem 79
    – infinitum 105
    – instar 82
    – interim 106
    – lib 705
    –·rem 23
A.D. 106
adage 496
adagio *music* 415
    slow 275
Adam *sin* 945
    – 's apple 250
adamant 159, 323
adapt 23, 27
    – oneself to 82
adaptable
    conformable 82

useful 644
add *increase* 35
    join 37
    numerically 85
    – up 811
addendum 39
adder 913
addict *habit* 613
adding machine 85
additament 39
addition
    extrinsical 6
    increase 35
    adjunction **37**
    thing added 39
    arithmetical 85
addle *barren* 169
    incomplete 730
    abortive 732
    – the wits, 475, 503
addlehead 501
addleheaded 499
address
    residence 189
    direction 550
    speech 582
    speak to 586
    skill 698
    request 765
    – oneself to 673
addresses
    courtship 902
addressful 894
adduce
    bring to 288
    evidence 467
adulce 834
ademption 789
adenoid 250
adenology 329
adept 700
adequate *power* 157
    sufficient 639
    for a purpose 644
adhere *stick* 46
    – to 604a, 613
    – to an obligation
    772
    – to a duty 926
adherent
    follower 711
adhesive, 46, 327,
    352
adhibit 677
adhortation 695
adieu *departure* 293
    loss 776
adipocere 356
adipose 355
adit *orifice* 260
    conduit 350

passage 627
adjacent 197
adjection 37
adjective 39
adjoin 197, 199
adjourn 133
adjudge 480
adjudicate 480
adjunct
    thing added **39**
    accompaniment 88
    aid 707
    auxiliary 711
adjuration 535
adjure 765, 768
adjust *adapt* 23
    equalize 27
    order 58
    prepare 673
    settle 723, 762
    – differences 774
adjutage 260, 350
adjutant
    auxiliary 711
    military 745
adjuvant *helping*
    707
    auxiliary 711
admeasurement
    466
adminicle 467
administer
    utilize 677
    conduct 693
    exercise authority
    737
    distribute 786
    – correction 972
    – oath 768
    – sacrament 998
    – to *aid* 707
    give 784
administration of
    justice 965
administrative 737,
    965
administrator 694
admirable 648, 944
admiral 745
Admiralty, court of
    – 966
admirari, nil – 871,
    932
admiration
    wonder 870
    love 897
    respect 928
    approval 931
admired disorder 59
admirer 897
admissible

relevant 23
receivable 296
tolerable 651
– in society 852
admit
  composition 54
  include 76
  let in 296
  assent 488
  acknowledge 529
  permit 760
  concede 762
  accept 785
  – exceptions 469
  – of 470
admitted
  customary 613
  – maxim &c. 496
admixture 41
admonish
  warn 668
  advise 695
  reprove 932
ado *activity* 682
  exertion 686
  difficulty 704
  make much –
    about 642
  much – about
    nothing
  overestimate 482
  unimportant 643
  unskilful 699
adolescence 131
Adonis 845
adonize 847
adopt
  naturalize 184
  choose 609
  – a cause *aid* 707
  – a course 692
  – an opinion 484
adoption
  religious 987
adore 897, 990
adorn 847
adown 207
adrift *unrelated* 10
  disjoined 44
  dispersed 73
  uncertain 475
  unapt 699
  free 750
  go – *deviate* 279
  turn – *disperse* 73
  liberate 750
  dismiss 756
adroit 698
adscititious
  extrinsic 6
  added 37

redundant 641
adscriptus glebæ
  746
adulation 933
adulator 935
Adullam, cave of –
  624, 832
Adullamite 832
adult 131
adulterate *mix* 41
  deteriorate 659
adulterated 545
adulterer 962
adultery 961
adumbrate
  darkness 421
  allegorize 521
  represent 554
adumbration
  semblance 21
  allusion 526
aduncity 244, 245
adust
  colour 433
  gloomy 837
adustion 384
advance *increase* 35
  course 109
  progress 282
  assert 535
  improve 658
  aid 707
  succeed 731
  lend 787
  in – *precedence* 62
  front 234
  precession 280
  in – of 33
  in – of one's age
    498
  – against 716
  – of learning &c.
    490
advanced 282
  – in life 128
  – guard 234
  – student 541
  – work 717
advances, make –
  offer 763
  social 892
advantage
  superiority 33
  influence 175
  good 618
  expedience 646
  mechanical – 633
  dressed to – 847
  find one's – in 644
  gain an – 775
  set off to – **658**

take – of 677, 698
– over *success* 731
advantageous
  beneficial 648
  profitable 775
advene 37
advent
  futurity 121
  event 151
  approach 286
  arrival 292
Advent 998
adventism 984
adventitious 6, 156
adventive 156
adventure *event* 151
  chance 156
  pursuit 622
  danger 665
  trial 675
  the great – 360
adventurer
  traveller 268
  deceiver 548
  experimenter 463
  gambler 621
  rash 863
  ignoble 876
adventures 594
adventurous
  undertaking 676
  bold 861
  rash 863
adversaria 551
adversary 710
adverse
  contrary 14
  opposed 708
  unprosperous 735
  disliking 867
  – party 710
adversity 735
advert 457
advertise 531
advice *notice* 527
  news 532
  counsel **695**
advisable 646
advise *predict* 511
  inform 527
  counsel 695
  – with one's pillow
    451
advised *predeter-*
  mined 611
  intended 620
  better – 658
adviser 540, 695
advocacy 931
advocate
  prompt 615

recommend 695
aid 707
auxiliary 711
friend 890
vindicate 937
counsellor 968
Advocate, the – 976
advocation 617
advoutress 962
advoutry 961
advowson 995
adynamic 160
adytum *room* 191
  prediction 511
  secret place 530
adze 253
adzooks 870
ædile 965
ægis 717
ægrescit medendo
  659
ægrotat 927*a*
æolian 349
  – harp 417
æon 976
æquam servare
  mentem 826
æquo animo 823,
  826
aerate 334, 353
ære perennius 873
aerial 273
  elevated 206
  flying 267
  gas 334
  air 338
  – navigation 267
  – navigator 269
  – mail 534
  – patrol 726
  – perspective 428
  – warfare 722
aerie 189
aerify 334
aerodonetics 267
aerodrome 728
aerodynamics 267
  334, 349
aerolite 318
aerology 338
aeromancy 511
aeromechanics 267
aerometer 338
aeronaut 269
aeronautical 273
aeronautics 267,
  338
aeroplane 273
aerostat *balloon* 273
aerostatics 267, 334
aerostation 338

aery 317
Æsculapius 662
Æsop 846
æsthetic
 sensibility 375
 beauty 845
 taste 850
æstival 125
æternum servans
 sub pectore vul-
 nus 919
ætiology [*see* etiol-
 ogy]
afar 196
affable 879, 894
affair *event* 151
 topic 454
 business 625
 battle 720
 love 902, 903
 – *of honour* 720
affaires, chargé d' –
 758
affaire de cœur 897
affect *relate to* 9
 tend to 176
 qualify 469
 feign 544
 touch 824
 desire 865
 love 897
affectation **855**
affected with
 feeling 821
 disease 655
affectibility 822
affecting 830
affection 821, 897
affections **820**
affettuoso 415
affiance 768, 858
affianced 897, 903
affiche 531
affidation 769
affidavit
 affirmation 535
 record 551
 lawsuit 969
affiliation
 relation 9
 kindred 11
 attribution 155
affine 11
affinitive 9
affinity 9, 17
 mate 903
affirmation **535**, 488
affix *add* 37
 sequel 39
 fasten 43
 letter 561

afflation 349
afflatus 349, 597,
 985
afflict 830
 – with illness 655
affliction *pain* 828
 infliction 830
 adversity 735
affluence
 sufficiency 639
 prosperity 734
 wealth 803
affluent *river* 348
afflux 286
afford *supply* 784
 wealth 803
 yield 810
 sell for 812
 – *aid* &c. 707
afforestation 371
affranchise
 make free of 748
 liberate 750
affray 720
affreet 980
affriction 331
affright 860
affront *molest* 830
 provocation 900
 insult 929
 – *danger* 861
affuse 337
afield 186
afire 382
afloat *extant* 1
 unstable 149
 going on 151
 ship 273
 navigation 267
 ocean 341
 news 532
 preparing 673
 keep oneself – 734
 set – *publish* 531
afoot *on hand* 625
 preparing 673
 astir 682
afore 116
aforementioned 116
aforesaid
 preceding 62
 repeated 104
 prior 116
aforethought 611
aforetime 116
afraid 860
 be – *irresolute* 605
 – to say *uncertain*
 475
afresh 104, 123
Afric heat 382

Afrikander 57
afrite 980
aft 235
after *in order* 63
 in time 117
 too late 135
 rear 235
 pursuit 622
 be – *intention* 620
 pursuit 622
 go – *follow* 281
 – all *for all that* 30
 qualification 469
 on the whole 476
 – time 133
after acceptation
 516
after-age 124
after-clap 509
after-crop 65, 168
after-dinner 117
after-glow 40, 65,
 420
after-growth 65
after-life 152
aftermath
 sequel 65
 fertile 168
 profit 775
aftermost 235
afternoon 126
 – farmer 683
after-part 65, 235
after-piece 599
after-taste 65, 390
after-thought
 thought 451
 memory 505
 change of mind
 607
after-time 121
afterwards 117
aga 745
agacerie 615
again 90, 104
 – and again 136
 come – *periodic* 138
 fall off – 661
 live – 660
against
 counteraction 179
 anteposition 237
 provision 673
 *voluntary opposi-
 tion* 708
 chances – 473
 declaim – 932
 false witness – 934
 go – 708
 set – *actively* 898
 set one's face –

 764, 932
 stand up – *resist*
 719
 raise &c. one's
  voice – 489
 – one's will 744
 – one's expecta-
  tion 508
 – the grain *difficult*
  704
 painful 830
 dislike 867
 – the stream 704
 – the time when
  510
 – one's will 744
 – one's wishes 603
agamist 904
agape *open* 260
 curious 455
 expectant 507
 wonder 870
Agapemone 827,
 897
agate 847
age *time* 106
 period 108
 long time 110
 era 114
 present time 118
 oldness 124
 advanced life **128**
 of – 131
 from age to – 112
age quod agis! 682
agency
 physical **170**
 instrumentality
  631
 means 632
 employment 677
 voluntary action
  680
 direction 693
 commission 755
agenda 625, 626
agent *physical* 153
 intermediary 228
 voluntary **690**
 consignee 758
 – *provocateur* 615
agentship 755
ages: for – 110
 – ago 122
agglomerate 46, 72
agglutinate 46
aggrandize
 in degree 35
 in bulk 194
 honour 873
aggravate

increase 35
vehemence 173
exaggerate 549
render worse 659
distress 835
exasperate 900
aggravating 830
aggravation 835
aggregate 50, 72, 84
aggregation 46
aggression 716
aggressor 726
aggrieve 649, 830
aggroup 72
aghast
  disappointed 509
  fear 860
  wonder 870
agile 274, 682
agio 813
agiotage 794
agitate *move* 315
  inquire 461
  activity 682
  excite the feelings
    824
– a question 476
agitation [*see* agi-
  tate]
  changeableness
    149
  energy 171
  motion **315**
  in – *preparing* 673
agitator *leader* 694
aglet 554
agley, gang – 732
aglow 382, 420
agnate 11
agnition 762
agnomen 564
agnostic 487
agnosticism 984,
  989
agnus Dei 993, 998
ago 122
  not long – 123
agog *expectant* 507
  desire 865
  wonder 870
agoing 682
  set – 707
agonism 720
agonizing 824, 830
agony 378, 828
  – of death 360
  – of excitement
    825
agrarian 371
agree *accord* 23
  concur 178

assent 488
concord 714
consent 762
compact 769
compromise 774
– in opinion 488
– with *salubrity*
  656
agreeable
  comfortable 82
  physically 377
  mentally 829
agreeably to 82
agreement 23 [*see*
  agree]
  compact 769
agrestic 371
agriculture 371
agronomy 371
aground *fixed* 150
  in difficulty 704
  failure 732
ague-fit 860
aguets, aux –
  expectation 507
  ambush 530
aguish *cold* 383
ah me! 839
aha! *rejoicing* 838
ahead 234, 280
  go – *progression*
    282
  shoot – *transcur-*
    sion 303
  activity 682
  rock – 665, 667
Ahrimanes 978, 980
aid 707, 906
  by the – of 631,
    632
aide-de-camp 711,
  745
aidless 160
aigrette 847
aiguille 253
aiguillette 747, 847
aigulet 847
ail 655, 828
aileron 267, 273
ailment 655
aim 278, 620, 675
  – a blow at 716
aimable 894
  faire l' – 897
aimer éperdument
  897
aimless *without*
  motive 615a
  chance 621
air *unsubstantial* 4
  broach 66

lightness 320
gas 334
atmospheric **338**
wind 349
tune 415
appearance 448
refresh 689
demeanour 692
fashionable 852
beat the – 645
fill the – 404
fine – *salubrity* 656
fish in the – 645
fowls of the – 366
in the – 527
rend the – 404
take – 531
air-balloon 273
air base 728
air-commodore 745
aircraft 273, 726
air-drawn 515
airdrome 273
air-force 726
air-gun 727
airing 266
air-mail 273
airman 269
airmanship 698
air-marshal 745
air-passage 351
air-pipe 351
airport 273, 292,
  728
air-pump 349
air-raid 716
airs *affectation* 855
  pride 878
  vanity 880
  arrogance 885
air-shaft 351
air service 267
airship 273, 726
air-tight 261
airways 267
airworthy 273, 664
airy [*see* air]
  windy 349
  unimportant 643
  gay 836
– hopes 858, 859
give to – nothing
  a local habita-
  tion &c. 515
aisle *passage* 260
  way 627
  in a church 1000
ait 346
ajar *open* 260
  discordant 713
ajee 217

ajutage 260, 350
akimbo *angular* 24
  stand – 715
akin *related* 9
  consanguineous 11
  similar 17
al fresco 220
alabaster *white* 430
alack! 839
alacrity *willing* 602
  active 682
  cheerful 836
Aladdin's lamp 993
alar 267
alarm *warning* 668
  notice of danger
    669
  fear 860
  cause for – 665
  give an – *indicate*
    550
alarmist 862
alarum 114, 550, 669
alas! 839
alate 267
alb 999
albeit 30
albert
  chain 847
albification 430
albinescence 430
albinism 430
albino 443
album 593, 596
albumen
  semi-liquid 352
  protein 357
Alcaic 597
alcaid 745
alcalde 745
alcazar 189
alchemy 144
alcohol 959
Alcoran 986
alcove 191, 252
Aldebaran 423
alderman 745
ale 298
alea, jacta est – 601
aleatory 665
Alecto 173
alectryomancy 511
alehouse 189
  go to the – 959
alembic
  conversion 144
  vessel 191
  furnace 386
  laboratory 691
alentours 197
alert *watchful* 457,

459
active 682
alerte 669
aleuromancy 511
Alexandrine
  ornate style 577
  verse 597
alexandrite 847
alexipharmic 662
alexiteric 662
algebra 85
algid 383
algology 369
algorithm 85
alguazil 965
alias
  otherwise 18
  pseudonym 565
alibi 187
alien *irrelevant* 10
  foreign 57
  transfer 783
  gentile 989
alienable 783
alienate
  transfer 783
  estrange 44, 889
  set against 898
alienation
  mental – 503
alieni appetens
  grasping 865
  envious 921
  selfish 943
alienism 57
alight *stop* 265
  arrive 292
  descend 306
  on fire 382
align 278
alike 17
  share and share –
    778
aliment *food* 298
alimentary 662
  – canal 350
alimentation
  aid 707
alimony
  property 780
  provision 803
  income 810
aliquot 51, 84
aliter visum, dis –
    601
alive
  living 359
  intelligent 498
  active 682
  cheerful 836
  be – with 102

keep – *continue*
  143
keep the memory
  – 505
look – 684
  – to *attention* 457
  cognizant 490
  informed 527
  able 698
  sensible 822
alkahest 335
all *whole* 50
  complete 52
  generality 78
  – absorbing 642
in – ages 112
  – abroad 495
  – agog 865
  – in all 50
  – along 106
  – along of 154
  – but 32
  – colours 440
  – considered 451,
    480
  – day long 110
  – devouring 789
in – directions 278
  – engulfing 789
at – events *com-*
  pensation 30
  qualification 469
  true 494
  resolve 604
  – fours *easy* 705
  cards 840
  – in good time 152
  – hail! *welcome* 292
  honour to 873
  celebration 883
  courtesy 894
  – hands *everybody*
    78
on – hands 488
  – of a dither 824
  – of a heap 72
  – knowing 976
  – manner of *differ-*
    ence 15
  multiform 81
with – one's might
  686
  – at once 113
  – one 27, 866
  – out 52
  – over *end* 67
  universal 78
  destruction 162
  space 180
at – points 52
  – in one's power

686
  – powerful
  mighty 159
  God 976
in – quarters 180
with – respect 928
in – respects 52,
    494
  – right! 922
  – Saints' day 998
  – searching 461
  – seeing 976
on – sides 227
  – sorts *diverse* 16a
  mixed 41
  multiform 81
  – talk 4
  – things to all
    men 894
  – the time 106
at – times 136
  – together 50
  – ways 243, 279
  – wise 976
  – the world and
    his wife 78
of – work
  useful 644
  maid - 746
Allah 979
allay
  moderate 174
  pacify 723
  relieve 834
  – excitability 826
allective 615
allege *evidence* 467
  assert 535
  plea 617
allegiance 743, 926
allegory 464, 521,
    594
allegro *music* 415
  cheerful 836
allelujah 990
allemande 840
all-embracing 76
alleviate 174, 834
alley *court* 189
  passage 260
  way 627
alliance *relation* 9
  kindred 11
  physical co-opera-
    tion 178
  voluntary co-oper-
    ation 709
  party 712
  union 714
allied to *like* 17
alligation 43

allign 278
alliteration
  similarity 17
  style in writing
    577
  poetry 597
allocation 60, 786
allocution 586
allodium *free* 748
  property 780
allopathy 662
alloquy 586
allot *arrange* 60
  distribute 786
  due 924
allow *assent* 488
  admit 529
  permit 760
  consent 762
  give 784
  – to have one's
    own way 740
allowable 760, 924
allowance
  qualification 469
  gift 784
  allotment 786
  discount 813
  salary 973
  with grains of –
    485
  make – for *forgive*
    918
  vindicate 937
alloy *mixture* 41
  combination 48
  debase 659
allude *hint* 514
  mean 516
  refer to 521
  latent 526
  inform 527
allure *move* 615
  create desire 865
alluring 829
allusive
  relative 9
alluvial *level* 213
  land 342
  plain 344
alluvium
  deposit 40
  land 342
  soil 653
ally *combine* 48
  auxiliary 711
  friend 890
alma mater 542
almanac
  list 86
  chronometry 114

record 551
almighty 157
Almighty, the – 976
almoner
　treasurer 801
　giver 784
　church officer 996
almonry 802
almost *nearly* 32
　not quite 651
　– all 50
　– *immediately* 132
alms *gift* 784
　benevolence 906
　worship 990
almshouse 189, 666
almsman 785
Alnaschar's dream
　515, 858
aloes 395
aloft 206
alogy 497
alone *single* 87
　unaided 706
　let – *not use* 678
　not restrain 748
along 200
　get – *progress* 282
　go – *depart* 293
　go – with *concur*
　178
　assent 488
　co-operate 709
　– of *caused by* 154
　– with *added* 37
　together 88
　by means of 631
alongside *near* 197
　parallel 216
　laterally 236
aloof *distant* 196
　high 206
　secluded 893
　stand – *inaction*
　681
　refuse 764
　cautious 864
alopecia 226
aloud 404
　think – 589
　naïveté 703
Alp 206
alpenstock 215
Alpha 66
　– and Omega 50
alphabet
　beginning 66
　letters 561
alphabetarian 541
alphabeticize 60
Alphitomancy 511

alpine *high* 206
Alpine Club 268, 305
already
　antecedently 116
　even now 118
　past time 122
Alsatia 791, 945
also 37
altar 903, 1000
alter 140
　– the case 468
　– one's course 279
alter ego *similar* 17
　auxiliary 711
　deputy 759
　friend 890
alterable 149
alteram partem,
　audire–468, 922
alterative
　substitute 634
　remedy 662
altercation 713
altered *worn* 688
　– for the worse 659
alternate
　reciprocal 12
　sequence 63
　discontinuous 70
　periodic 138
　changeable 149
　oscillate 314
alternative
　substitute 147
　choice 609
　plan 626
although
　compensation 30
　counteraction 179
　unless 469
altiloquence 577
altimetry
　height 206
　angle 244
　measurement 466
altitude *height* 206
　– and azimuth 466
alto 410, 416
　– part 415
alto-rilievo 250, 557
altogether 50, 52
　nude 226
altruism 910, 942
altruist 906
alum 397
alumnus 541
alveolus 252
always
　uniformly 16
　generally 78
　during 106

perpetually 112
　habitually 613
a.m. 114, 125
amah 753
amain 173, 684
amalgam, -ate 41,
　48
amalgamation 709
Amalthæa's horn
　639
amantium iræ 918
amanuensis 553,
　590
amaranthine 112
amari aliquid
　bad 649
　imperfect 651
　painful 830
amaritude 395
amass *whole* 50
　collect 72
　store 636
amateur *volunteer*
　602
　layman 699
　taste 850
　votary 865
amatory 897
amaurosis 442
amaze 870
amazingly 31
Amazon
　woman 374
　warrior 726
　courage 861
ambages
　convolutions 248
　circumlocution
　573
　circuit 629
ambagious 573
ambassador
　messenger 534
　representative 758
　recall of –s 713
amber 356a
　– colour 436
ambidexter
　right and left 238
　fickle 607
　clever 698
ambient 227
ambigu 41
ambiguas spargere
　voces
　uncertain 475
　misteach 538
　false 544
　cunning 702
ambiguous
　uncertain 475

unintelligible 519
　equivocal 520
　obscure 571
ambiloquy 520
ambit 230
ambition 620, 865
ambivalence 605,
　708
amble 266
ambo *school* 542
　pulpit 1000
ambo, Arcades –
　alike 17
　friends 890
　bad men 949
ambrosia 298
ambrosial 394, 490
ambulance
　vehicle 272
　hospital 662
ambulation 266
ambuscade 530
ambush 530, 667
　lie in – 528
âme – de boue 949
　– damnée
　catspaw 711
　servant 746
　servile 886
　bad man 949
　– qui vive 101, 187
ameer 875
ameliorate 658
amen *assent* 488
　submission 725
　content 831
amenable 177, 602,
　926
　not – to reason 608
amend 658
amendatory 20
amende honorable
　952
amends
　compensation 50
　atonement 952
　reward 973
amenity 829, 894
amentia 503
amerce 974
American organ 417
Americanism 563
amethyst
　purple 437
　jewel 847
amiable
　courteous 894
　loving 897
　kind 906
amiability 829, 894
amicable 707, 888

amice 999
amicus – curiæ 527
 – humani generis 910
 – usque ad aras 890
amidships 68
amidst 41, 228
amiss 619
 come – *disagree* 24
 mistime 135
 inexpedient 647
 do – 945
 nothing comes – 823
 take – 867, 900
amity *concord* 714
 peace 721
 friendship 888
ammunition 635, 727
amnesia 506
amnesty 506, 723, 918
amnis, rusticus expectat dum defluat – *hope* 858
amœbæan 63
amok 503
among 41, 228
amor patriæ 910
amore, con – 602, 821
amoroso 599
amorous 897
 – glances 902
amorphous 83, 241
amorphism 241
amortization 784
amotion 270
amount
 quantity 25
 degree 26
 sum of money 800
 price 812
 gross – 50
 – to 27, 85
amour 897, 961
 – propre 880
ampere 466
amphibian 366
amphibious 83
amphibology 520
Amphictyonic council 696
amphigouri 497
amphitheatre
 prospect 441
 school 542
 theatre 599
 arena 728

Amphitryon 890
amphora 191
ample *much* 31
 spacious 180
 large 192
 broad 202
 copious 639
amplify
 expand 194
 exaggerate 549
 diffuse style 573
amplitude
 quantity 25
 degree 26
 size 192
 breadth 202
 enough 639
ampoule 191
ampulla 191
amputate 38
amuck 173, 361, 503, 716, 825
amulet 247, 993
amusare la bocca, per – 394
amuse 829, 840
amusement **840**
 place of – 840
amussim ad – 494
amylaceous 352
an *if* 514
ana 594
Anabaptist 984
anabasis 35
anachronism
 false time **115**
 inopportune 135
 error 495
anacoluthon 70
anaconda 913
anacreontic 597
anæmia 160
anæsthesia 376, 381, 683
anaglyph 554, 557
anagoge 521, 526
anagram
 double sense 520
 secret 533
 letter 561
 wit 842
analecta 596
analeptic 662
analgesia 376
analogy 9, 17
analogous 12
analysis
 decomposition 49
 arrangement 60
 algebra 85

inquiry 461
experiment 463
reasoning 476
grammar 567
compendium 596
analyst 461, 463
anamorphosis
 distortion 243
 optical 443
 misrepresentation 555
anápæst 597
anaphylaxis 375
anarchist
 destroyer 165
 disobedient 742
 evil-doer 913
anarchy 59, 738
anastatic printing 558
anastomosis 43, 219
anastrophe 218
anathema 908
anathematize 908
 censure 932
 detract 934
anatomize *dissect* 44
 investigate 461
anatomy
 dissection 44
 leanness 203
 texture 329
 science 357
 comparative – 368
anatriptic 331
ancestral
 bygone 122
 old 124
 aged 128
ancestry 166
anchor
 connection 45
 stop 265
 safeguard 666
 badge 747
 hope 858
 at – *fixed* 150
 stationed 184
 safe 664
 cast – *settle* 184
 arrive 292
 have an – to windward 664
 sheet – *means* 632
anchorage
 location 184
 roadstead 189
 refuge 666
anchored 150

anchorite 893, 955
ancien régime 875
ancient *old* 124
 flag 550
 – times 122
ancientness 122
ancillary 707
and 37, 88
andante 415
andiron 386
androgynous 83
anecdote 594
anele 998
anemography 349
anemometer
 wind 349
 measure 466
anent 9
aneroid 338
anew *again* 104
 newly 123
anfractuosity 248
angel
 object of love 897
 good person 948
 supernatural being **977**
 fallen –
  bad man 949
  devil 978
 guardian –
  safety 664
  auxiliary 711
  benefactor 912
 – of Death 360
 – 's visits 137
angelic 944
angels and ministers of grace defend us! 860
angelus 550
anger 900
 more in sorrow than in – 826, 918
angiology 329
angle 244
 try 463
 at an – 217
Anglicanism 984
angling 622, 840
anguille au genou, rompre l' – 158, 471
anguilliform 205, 248
anguis in herbâ 667
anguish
 physical 378
 moral 828

angular 244
 – velocity 264
angularity **244**
angusta domi, res
 – 804
angustation 203
anhelation 688
anhydrate 340
anhydrous 340
aniline dyes 437
anility 128, 499
animadvert
 consider 451
 attend to 457
 reprehend 932
animal **366**
 female – 374
 – cries 412
 – economy 359
 – gratification 377
 – life 364
 – physiology 368
 – spirits 836
 – and vegetable
  kingdom 357
animalcule 193, 366
animalism
 sensuality 954
animality **364**
animate
 induce 615
 excite 824
 enliven 836
animation
 life 359
 animality 364
 activity 682
 vivacity 836
 suspended – 823
animism 984
animo, ex – 602
 quo – 620
animosity
 dislike 867
 enmity 889
 hatred 898
 anger 900
animus
 willingness 602
 intention 620
 desire 865
ankle 244
 – deep 208, 209
anklet 847
ankylosis 150
annalist 114, 553
annals
 chronology 114
 record 551
 account 594

anneal 673
annex
 addition 37
 adjunct 39
 junction 43
 acquire 775
Annie Oakley 815
annihilate 2, 162
anniversary 138
anno 106
Anno Domini
 era 106
 old age 124
annotation 522, 550
annotator 524
 scholar 492
 interpreter 524
 editor 595
annotto 434
announce
 predict 511
 inform 527
 publish 531
 assert 535
announcer 527
annoy
 molest 649, 907
 disquiet 830
annoyance 828
 source of – 830
annual *periodic* 138
 plant 367
 book 593
annuity 810
annul 162, 756
annular 247
annunciate 527
annus magnus 108
anodyne
 lenitive 174
 remedial 662
 relief 834
anoint *coat* 223
 lubricate 332
 oil 355
anointed
 deity 976
 king 745
anomaly
 disorder 59
 irregularity 83
anon 132
anonymous 565
anopsia 442
anorexy 866
another
 different 15
 repetition 104
 – story 468, 526
 go upon – tack 607
 – time 119

answer
 to an inquiry **462**
 confute 479
 solution 522
 succeed 731
 pecuniary profit
  775
 pleadings 969
 require an – 461
 – for *deputy* 759
 promise 768
 go bail 806
 I'll – for it 535
 – the helm 743
 – the purpose 731
 – to *correspond* 9
 – one's turn 644
answerable
 agreement 23
 liable 177
 bail 806
 duty 926
 censurable 932
ant 690
Antæus 159, 192
antagonism
 difference 14
 physical 179
 voluntary 708
 enmity 889
antagonist 710, 891
antagonistic 24
antarctic 237
antecedence 62, 116
antecedent 64
antechamber 191
ante Christum 106
antedate 115
antediluvian 124
antelope 274
antemundane 124
antenna 379
anteposition 62
anterior
 in order 62
 in time 116
 in place 234
 – to reason 477
anteroom 191
antevert 706
anthem 990
anthemion 847
anthology
 book 593
 collection 596
 poem 597
anthracite 388
anthropoid 372
anthropology
 zoology 368
 mankind 372

anthropomancy 511
anthropophagi 913
anthroposcopy 511
anthroposophy 372
anti-aircraft gun
 564, 727
antic 840
antichambre,
 faire – 133
antichristian 984,
 989
antichronism 115
anticipate
 anachronism 115
 priority 116
 future 121
 early 132
 expect 507
 foresee 510
 prepare 673
 hope 858
 in – 116
anticlimax
 decrease 36
 bathos 497, 853
anticlinal 217
anticyclone 265
antidote 662
antigropelos 225
antilogarithm 84
antilogy 477
antimony 663
Antinomian 984
antinomy 964
Antinous 845
antiparallel 217
antipathy 867, 898
antiphon *music* 415
 answer 462
 worship 990
antiphrasis 563
antipodes
 difference 14
 distance 196
 contraposition
  237
antipoison 662
antiquary
 past times 122
 scholar 492
 historian 553
antiquas vias,
 stare super –
 613, 670
antiquated 128
antique 124
antiquity 122
antiscriptural 984
antiseptic 652, 662
antisocial 911
antistrophe 597

antithesis
contrast 14
difference 15
opposite 237
style 574, 577
antitoxin 662
antitype 22
antler 253
antonomasia
metaphor 521
nomenclature 564
antonym 14
antrum 252
anvil *support* 215
on the –
intended 620
in hand 625
preparing 673
anxiety *pain* 828
fear 860
desire 865
anxious expectation
507
any *some* 25
part 51
no choice 609a
at – *price* 604a
at – *rate*
certain 474
true 494
at all hazards 604
anybody 78
anyhow 460, 627
anything one
knows, for – 491
aorist 109, 119
aorta 350
apace *early* 132
swift 274
apache 913
apart 44, 87
set – 636
wide – 196
apartment 191
–s 189
–s to let
imbecile 499
apathetic 275
apathy
indifference 456
insensibility 823
irreligion 989
ape *imitate* 19
Apelles 559
aperçu 596
aperture 260
apex 210
aphasia 583
aphelion 196
aphonic 403
aphony 581

[398]

aphorism 496
Aphrodite 845, 979
apiary 370
apiculture 370
Apicius 957
apiece 79
apish 19, 499
aplanatic 429
aplomb
stability 150
self-possession
498
resolution 604
Apocalypse 985
Apocrypha 985
apocryphal
uncertain 475
erroneous 495
heterodox 984
apodictic 478
apodosis 67
apogee 210
apograph 21
Apollo *sun* 318
music 416
luminary 423
beauty 845
god 979
magnus – 500, 695
Apollyon 978
apologue
metaphor 521
teaching 537
description 594
apology *excuse* 617
vindication 937
penitence 950
atonement 952
apophthegm 496
apophysis 250
apoplexy 158, 655
aporetic 487
aposiopesis 585
apostasy
recantation 607
dishonour 940
heterodoxy 984
apostate
convert 144
turncoat 607
impiety 988
apostle *teacher* 540
disciple 541
inspired 985
–'s creed 983a
apostolic 985
– *church* 983a
– *see* 995
apostrophe
address 586
soliloquy 589

appeal 765
apothecary 662
–'s weight 319
apothegm 496
apotheosis
resuscitation 163
canonization 873
heaven 981
hero worship 991
apozem 335, 384
appal 830, 860
appanage
property 780
gift 784
apparatus 633
apparel 225
apparent
visible 446
appearing 448
probable 472
manifest 525
heir – 779
apparition
fallacy of vision
443
spirit 980
apparitor 534
appeach 938
appeal 586, 765
court of – 966
– to arms 722
– motion 969
– from Philip
drunk to Philip
sober 658
– to *call to witness*
467
– to for (*claim*) 924
appear 446, 525
– for 759
– in print 591
appearance 448
make one's – 292
to all – 448
probable 472
appearances
keep up – 852
appease 174
appellant 924, 938
appellate 966
appellation 564
append *add* 37
sequence 63
hang 214
appendage 39
appendectomy 662
appendix
adjunct 39
sequel 65
end 67
book 593

appertain
related to 9
component 56
belong 777
property 780
appetite 865
tickle the –
savoury 394
appetizing 865
exciting 824
applaud 931
apple – *of discord*
713
golden –
allurement 615
– *of one's eye good*
648
love 897
favorite 899
– off another tree
15
how we –s swim!
880
apple-green 435
apple-pie order 58
appliance *use* 677
–s *means* 632
machinery 633
applicable *relevant*
23
useful 644
expedient 646
applicability 9
applicant 767
application *study*
457
metaphor 521
use 677
request 765
apply, *use* 677
– a match 384
– the match to
train 66
– the mind 457
– a remedy 662
appoggiatura 413
appointment
employment 625
order 741
charge 755
assignment 786
interview 892
appointments
gear 633
apportion *arrange*
60
disperse 73
allot 786
apportionment 786
appositeness 9
apposition

ment 24
topic 454
discussion 476
meaning 516
have the best of
an – 478
argumentum
– ad baculum
compel 744
lawless 964
punish 972
– ad crumenam
800
– ad hominem
reasoning 476
accuse 938
– ad verecundiam
939
Argus-eyed 441, 459
argute 498
aria 415
arianism 984
arid 340
unproductive 169
uninteresting 841
Ariel *courier* 268
swift 274
messenger 534
spirit 979
arietation 276
arietta 415
aright *well* 618
Ariman [*see* Ahrimanes*]
ariolation 511
arioso 415
aris et focis, pro –
defence 717
philanthropy 910
arise *exist* 1
begin 66
happen 151
mount 305
appear 446
– *from* 154
Aristarchus 850
Aristides
good man 948
aristocracy
power 737
fashion 852
nobility 875
Arithmancy 511
arithmetic 85
ark *abode* 189
asylum 666
arm *part* 51
power 157
instrument 633
provide 637

prepare 673
war 722
weapon 727
make a long – 200
– *chair* 215
– *in arm*
together 88
friends 888
sociable 892
– of the law 963
– of the sea 343
armada 726
Armageddon 720,
722
armament 673, 727
armed 717
– at all points 673
– *force* 726
– *guard* 664
armet 717
armful 25
armiger 875
armigerent 726
armigerous 722
armilla 247, 847
armillary sphere
466
armipotent 157
armistice
cessation 142
respite 672
pacification 723
armless 158
armlet *ring* 247
gulf 343
ornament 847
armorial bearings
550, 877
armour *cover* 223
defence 717
arms 727
buckle on one's –
673
– plated 223
armoured
– *car* 726
– *cruiser* 726
– *train* 726
armoury *store* 636
workshop 691
arm's length
at – 196
keep at –
repel 289
defence 717
enmity 889
seclusion 893
discourtesy 895
arms 727 [*see* arm]
heraldry 550
war 722

honours 877
clash of – 720
deeds of – 720
with folded – 681
in – *infant* 129
throw oneself into
the – of 666, 888
under – 722
up in – *active* 682
discord 713
resistance 719
resentment 900
enmity 889
Armstrong gun 727
army *collection* 72
multitude 102
troops 726
aroma 400
around 227
lie – 220
arouse *move* 615
excite 824
– oneself 682
aroynt *begone* 297
malediction 908
arquebusade 662
arquebuse 727
arraign 938, 969
arrange
set in order 60
plan 626
compromise 774
– with creditors
807
– itself 58
arrange – matters
pacify 723
– *music* 413, 416
– in a series 69
– under 76
arrangement 23, **60**
[*see* arrange]
order 58
temporary – 111
arrant *identical* 31
manifest 525
notorious 531
bad 649
disreputable 874
base 940
arras 847
array *order* 58, 60
series 69
assemblage 72
multitude 102
dress 225
prepare 673
adorn 847
ostentation 882
battle – 722
arrear, in – 53, 808

arrears *debt* 806
arrectis auribus
hear 418
expect 507
arrest *stop* 142
restrain 751
in law 969
– the attention 457
arrière-pensée
after-thought 65
mental reservation
528
motive 615
set purpose 620
arrival 292
arrive *happen* 151
reach 292
complete 729
– at a conclusion
480
– at the truth 480*a*
arrogant *severe* 739
proud 878
insolent 885
arrogate 885, 924
– to oneself
undue 925
arrondissement 181
arrosion 331
arrow *swift* 274
missile 284
arms 727
broad – 550
arrow-head
form 253
writing 590
'Arry and 'Arriet
902
ars celare artem
698
arsenal *store* 636
workshop 691
arsenic 663
arson 384
art *representation*
554
business 625
skill 698
cunning 702
fine – 850
work of – 845, 847
– gallery 556
artery 350, 627
**artes, hæ tibi
erunt** – 627
artesian well 343
artful 544, 702
– dodge 545, 702
article *thing* 3
part 51
matter 316

chapter 593
review 595
goods 798
articled clerk 541
articles
 thirty-nine – 983*a*
 – of agreement
  770
 – of faith 484, 983
articulate 366
articulation
 junction 43
 speech 580
articulo, in –
 transient 111
 dying 360
artifice 626, 702
artificer 690
artificial
 fictitious 545
 cunning 702
 affected 855
 – language 579
artillery
 explosion 404
 arms 727
artilleryman 726
artisan 690
artist *painter* &c.
 559
 contriver 626
 agent 690
artiste *music* 416
 drama 599
artistic *skilful* 698
 beautiful 845
 taste 850
 – language 578
artlessness **703**
arundo, hæret
 lateri lethalis –
 828
aruspex 513
aruspicy 511
as *motive* 615
 – broad as long 27
 – can be 52
 – good as 27
 – if *similar* 17
 suppose 514
 – little as may be
  32
 – it may be
 circumstance 8
 event 151
 chance 156
 – much again 90
 – soon as 120
 – they say 496, 532
 – things are 7
 – things go 151,

613
– to 9
– usual 82
– it were 17, 521
– you were 141,
 283
– well as 37
– the world wags
 151
ascend *be great* 31
 increase 35
 rise 305
 improve 658
ascendancy
 power 157
 influence 175
 success 731
ascendant
 lord of the – 745
 in the –
 influence 175
 important 642
 success 731
 authority 737
 repute 873
 one's star in the –
 prosperity 734
ascension
 [see ascend]
 calefaction 384
 – Day 998
ascent
 [see ascend]
 gradient 217
 rise **305**
 glory 873
ascertain *fix* 150
 determine 480
ascertained 474,
 490
ascertainment 480*a*
asceticism **955**
ascititious
 intrinsic 6
 additional 37
 supplementary 52
ascribe 155
aseptic 652
ash 384
 – coloured 432
 – blond 430
 Ash Wednesday
 998
ashamed 879
ashen 429
ashes *corpse* 362
 dirt 653
 lay in – 162
 pale as – 429, 860
 rise from one's –
 660

ashore 342
 go – *arrive* 292
ashy 429
Asian mystery 533
aside *laterally* 236
 whisper 405
 private 528
 say – 589
 set &c. – *displace*
 185
 neglect 460
 negative 536
 reject 610
 disuse 678
 abrogate 756
 discard 782
 step – 279
asinine *ass* 271
 fool 499
ask *inquire* 461
 request 765
 for sale 794
 price 812
 – leave 760
askance 217
 eye – *fear* 860
 look – *vision* 441,
 443
 dissent 489
 dislike 867
 disapproval 932
askari 726
asked in church 903
askew 217, 243
aslant 217
asleep 683
aslope 217
Asmodeus 980
asomatous 317
asp *animal* 366
 evil-doer 913
Aspasia 962
aspect *feature* 5
 state 7
 situation 183
 appearance 448
aspen leaf
 shake like an –
 315, 860
asperity
 roughness 256
 discourtesy 895
 anger 900
 irascibility 901
asperse 934
aspersion
 malediction 908
 rite 998
asphalt
 smooth 255
 resin 356*a*

material 635
asphodel 845
asphyxia 360
asphyxiate 361
aspic 352
aspirant 767, 865
aspirate 580
aspirator 349
aspire *rise* 305
 hope 858
 desire 865
 worship 990
aspirin 834
asportation 270
asquint 217
ass *beast of burden*
 271
 fool 501
 make an – of
 delude 545
 – between two
 bundles of
 hay 605
 –'s bridge 519
 – in lion's skin
 cheat 548
 bungler 701
assafœtida 401
assagai 727
assail 716, 830
assailant 710, 726
assassin, –ate 361
assault 716, 961
 take by – 789
assay 463
asseguay 727
assemblage **72**
assembly
 council 696
 society 892
 religious 997
assembly hall 588
assembly room 189
assent *belief* 484
 agree **488**
 willing 602
 consent 762
 content 831
assert 535, 924
assess *measure* 46*a*
 determine 480
 tax 812
assessor
 judge 967
assets 780, 800
asseverate 535
assiduity 110
assiduous 682
assign
 commission 755
 transfer 270, **783**

give 784
allot 786
– as cause 155
– a duty 926
– places 60
assignat 800
assignation 892
 place of – 74
assignee *donee* 785
assimilate
 uniform 16
 resemble 17
 imitate 19
 agree 23
 transmute 144
assist 707
– at 186
assistant 711
assister *be present*
 186
assize *measure* 466
 tribunal 966
 justice of – 967
associate *mix* 41
 unite 43
 collect 72
 accompany 88
 colleague 690
 auxiliary 711
 friend 890
– with 892
association
 [*see* associate]
 relation 9
 combination 48
 co-operation 709
 partnership 712
– of ideas
 intellect 450
 thought 451
 intuition 477
 hint 514
– football 840
assoil *acquit* 970
assonance
 music 413
 poetry 597
assort *arrange* 60
assortment 72, 75
assuage 174, 834
assuetude 613
assume *believe* 484
 suppose 514
 falsehood 544
 take 789
 insolent 885
 right 924
– authority 737
– a character 554
– command 741
– a form 144

– the offensive 716
assumed name 565
assumption
 [*see* assume]
 severity 739
 hope 858
 usurpation 925
assurance
 speculation 156
 certainty 474
 belief 484
 assertion 535
 promise 768
 security 771
 hope 858
 vanity 880
 insolence 885
 make – double
  sure *safe* 664
 caution 864
assuredly
 assent 488
assythment 973
astatic 320
asterisk 550
astern 235
 put the engines –
  275
 fall – 283
asteroid 318
Asteroth 979
asthenia 160
astigmatism 443
astir 682
 set – 824
astonish 870
astonished
– at nothing 871
astonishing
 great 31
astound *excite* 824
 fear 860
 surprise 870
astra, sic itur ad –
 360, 873
Astræa 922
astraddle 215
astragal 847
astral 318
– body 317, 992
– influence 601
– plane 317
astray 475, 495
 go – *deviate* 279
 sin 945
astriction 43
astride 215
astringent 195
astrolabe 466
astrologer 994

astrology 511
astromancy 511
astronomy 318
astute 498, 702
asunder 44, 196
 as poles – 237
asylum *hospital* 663
 retreat 666
 defence 717
asymptote 290
at, be – 620
 up and – them!
  716
ataghan 727
atavism 145, 163
ataxia 158
atelier 556, 691
athanasia 112
Athanasian creed
 983a
athanor 386
atheism 989
atheist 487
Athenae 979
Athens, owls to –
 641
athirst 865
athlete *strong* 159
 gladiator 726
athletic *strong* 159
 strenuous 686
– sports
 contest 720
 games 840
athwart
 oblique 217
 crossing 219
 opposing 708
Atkins, Tommy 726
Atlantis 515
Atlas *arrangement*
 60
 list 86
 strength 159
 support 215
 maps 554
atmosphere
 circumambience
  227
 air 338
 painting 556
atmospheric blue
 438
atoll 346
atom *small* 32, 193
atomic energy 157
atomizer 336
atoms
 crush to – 162
atomy 193

atonement
 restitution 790
 expiation **952**
 amends 973
 religious 976
atony 160
atrabilious 837
atramentous 431
atrium 191
atrocity
 malevolence **907**
 vice 945
 guilt 947
atrophy
 shrinking 195
 disease 655
 decay 659
Atropos 601
attach *join* 43
 love 897
 legal 969
– importance to
 642
attaché
 employé 746
 diplomatic 758
– case 191
attack *singing* 580
 disease 655
 assault **716**
 debauch 961
attaghan 727
attain *arrive* 292
 succeed 731
– majority 131
attainable 470
attainder
 taint 651
 at law 971
attainment
 knowledge 490
 learning 539
 skill 698
attar 400
attemper 41, 174
attempered 820
attempt 675
 vain – 732
– impossibilities
 471
attend
 accompany 88
 be present 186
 follow 281
 apply the mind
  457
 medically 662
 aid 707
 serve 746
– to business 625
– to orders 743

balanced 150, 242
balbucinate 583
balbutiate 583
balcony 250
  theatre 599
bald *bare* 226
  style 575
  uninteresting 841
  ugly 846
  plain 849
baldachin 223, 1000
balderdash 517, 577
baldric 230, 247
bale *bundle* 72
  load 190
  ladle 270
  evil 619
  – *out* 297
baleful 649
balister 727
balize 550
balk *disappoint* 509
  deceive 545
  hinder 706
Balkanize 713
ball *globe* 249
  missile 284
  shot 727
  dance 840
  party 892
  – *at one's feet* 731, 737
  keep up the – 143, 682
ballad 415, 597
  – *monger* 597
ballast
  compensation 30
  weight 319
  wisdom 498
  safety 666
  without – *rash* 863
  vicious 945
ballerina 599
ballet 599, 840
ballet-dancer 599
ballistics
  projectiles 284
  war 722
  arms 727
ballon d'essai 463
balloon 273, 726
balloonist 269
balloonry 267
ballot 535, 609
ball-room 840
balm *moderate* 174
  fragrance 400
  remedy 662
  relief 834
Balmoral *boot* 225

balmy
  sleep 683
balneal 337
balourdise 699
balsam 662
balsamic
  salubrious 834
balustrade
  support 215
  inclosure 232
bam 544
bambino 129
bamboozle 545
ban *exclude* 55
  prohibit 761
  denounce 908
  under the – 909
  – *with bell, book, and candle* 998
banal 613, 843
band *ligature* 45
  assemblage 72
  filament 205
  belt 230
  ring 247
  music 415, 416, 417
  party 712
  shackle 752
  – *of hope* 958
  – *together* 709
  – *with* 720
bandage 43, 45
  support 215
  cover 223
  remedy 662
  restraint 752
  the eyes -d 442
bandana 225
bandbox 191
banded together 178, 713
bandit 792
bandog 664, 668
bandolier 636
bandore 417
bandrol 550
bands 999
bandurria 417
bandy
  exchange 148
  agitate 315
  – *about* 531
  – *legged* 243
  – *words* 476, 588
bane 619, **663**
baneful 649
bang *impel* 276
  sound 406
  beat 972
bangle 847

banish *eject* 297
  seclude 893
  punish 972
banister 215
banjo 417
bank *acclivity* 217
  side of lake 342
  store 636
  sand 667
  fence 717
  money 802
  sea – 342
  – *of elegance* 800
  – *holiday* 840
  – *up* 670
banker 797, 801
  game 840
bank-note 800
bankruptcy 732, 808
banlieue 197, 227
banner 550
  enlist under the -s *of* 707
  raise one's – 722
banneret 875
banns
  forbid the – 761
  publish the –
  ask 765
  marriage 903
banquet 298, 840
banquette 717
banshee 979, 980
bantam cock 887
banter 842, 856
banterer 844
banting 956
bantling 129, 167
banyan *stint* 640
  fast 956
baptism *name* 564
  rite 998
Baptist 984
baptistery 1000
bar *except* 38
  exclude 55
  hotel 189
  line 200
  support 215
  inclosure 232
  close 261
  music 413
  hindrance 706
  insignia 747
  prison 752
  prohibit 761
  ingot 800
  tribunal 966
  legal profession 968
  – *sinister flaw* 651

  disrepute 874
  illegal 964
  crossing the – 360
Barabbas 792
baragouin 517
barb *spike* 253
  nag 271
  – *the dart pain* 830
barbacan 717
barbarian
  uncivilized 876
  evil-doer 913
barbaric 851, 876
barbarism
  neology 563
  bad style 579
  vulgarity 851
  discourtesy 895
barbarous
  unformed 241
  plebeian 876
  maleficent 907
barbette 717
barbican 717
barbouillage 590
barcarolle 415
bard 416, 597
bare *mere* 32
  nude 226
  manifest 525
  disclose 529
  scanty 640
  – *back* 226
  – *bone* 203
  – *faced deceitful* 544, *insolent* 885
  – *foot* 226, 804
  – *headed* 928
  scud under - *poles* 704
  – *possibility* 473
  – *supposition* 514
bargain
  compact 769
  barter 794
  cheap 815
  into the - 37
  - *for* 507
  - *and sale transfer of property* 783
barge 273
bargee 269
baritone 408
bark *rind* 223
  strip 226
  ship 273
  yelp 412
  - *at threaten* 909
  censure 932
  more - *than bite* 908

bazaar 799
B.C. 106
be 1
– **all and end all**
  whole 50
  intention 620
  importance 642
– **off** *depart* 293
  eject 297
  retract 773
– **it so** 488
– **that as it may** 30
beach 231, 342
beach comber 268
beacon 550, 663
bead 249
beadle *janitor* 263
  law officer 965
  church 996
beadledom 737
beadroll *list* 86
  prayers 990
  ritual 998
beads
  ornament 847
  tell one's – 990, 998
beadsman
  servant 746
  clergy 996
beagle 366
beak *face* 234
  nose 250
  magistrate 967
beaker 191
beam *support* 215
  side 236
  weigh 319
  light 420
on – ends
  powerless 158
  horizontal 213
  side 236
  fail 732
  wonder 870
beaming
  beautiful 845
bean 276
beanfeast 840
bear *produce* 161
  sustain 215
  carry 270
  admit of 470
  suffer 821
  endure 826
bring to – 677
more than flesh and blood can – 824
unable to –
  excited 825

dislike 867
– away 789
– away the bell 648, 731
– the brunt 704, 717
– the burden 625
– the cross 828
– company 88
– down 173, 885
– down upon 716
– false witness 544
– fruit *produce* 161
  useful 644
  success 731
  prosper 734
– a hand 680
– hard upon 649
– harmless 717
– ill 825
– off *deviate* 279
– on 215
– oneself 692
– out *evidence* 467
  vindicate 937
– pain 828
– the palm 33
– a sense 516
– through 707
– up *approach* 286
  persevere 604a
  relieve 834
  cheerful 836
– up against 719, 861
– upon
  relevant 9, 23
  influence 175
– with
  tolerate 740
  permit 760
  take coolly 826
  forgive 918
bear
  savage 907
  surly 895
had it been a – it would have bitten you 458
– garden
  disorder 59
  discord 713
  arena 728
– leader 540
– pit 370
– skin *cap* 225
  helmet 717
– with a sore back 901
bearable 651
beard *hair* 205

  prickles 253
  rough 256
  defy 715
  brave 861
  insolence 885
pluck by the –
  disrespect 929
– the lion 604
beardless 127, 226
bearer 271, 363
bearing *relation* 9
  support 215
  direction 278
  meaning 516
  demeanour 692
– rein 706, 752
bearings
  circumstances 8
  situation 183
  armorial – 550
beast *animal* 366
  unclean 653
  discourteous 895
– of burden 271, 690
beat *be superior* 33
  periodic 138
  region 181
  impulse 276
  surpass 303
  oscillate 314
  agitation 315
  crush 330
  sound 407
  line of pursuit 625
  path 627
  overcome 731
  strike 972
– about
  circuit 629
– the air 645
– against 708
– one's breast 839
– about the bush
  try for 463
  evade the point 477
  prevaricate 544
  diffuse style 573
– down *destroy* 162
  cheapen 794, 819
  insolent 885
– of drum
  music 416
  publish 531
  alarm 669
  war 722
  command 741
  pomp 882
without – of
  drum 528
– into *teach* 537

– off 717
– a retreat
  retire 283
  avoid 623
  submit 725
– time *clock* 114
  music 416
– up *churn* 352
– up against
  oppose 708
– up for *cater* 637
– up one's quarters
  seek 461
  visit 892
– up for recruits
  prepare 673
  aid 797
beaten track
  habit 613
  way 627
leave the – 83
tread the – 82
beatic 827
beatific 829, 981
beatification 827, 987
beating high
  the heart – 824
beatitude 827
beau *man* 373
  fop 854
  admirer 897
– idéal 650, 845
– monde 852
beautify 845, 847
beautiless 846
beauty 845
beaver *hat* 225
becalm 265
because *cause* 153
  attribution 155
  answer 462
  reasoning 476
  motive 615
bechance 151
beck *rill* 348
  sign 550
  mandate 741
at one's – *aid* 707
  obey 743
beckon *sign* 550
  motive 615
  call 741
becloud *dark* 421
  hide 528
become
  accord with 23
  change to 144
  behove 926
– of 151
becoming

accordant 23
proper 646
beautiful 845, 847
due 924
becripple 158
bed *lodgment* 191
layer 204
support 215
garden 371
marriage 903
brought to – 161
death – 360
smooth the – of death 707
go to – 265, 683
keep one's – 655
– of down 687
– gown 255
– maker 746
– out 371
– ridden 655
– room 191
– of roses 377, 734
put to – with a shovel 363
– time 126
bedarken 421
bedaub 223
bedazzle 420
bedding 215
bedeck 847
bedel 965
bedesman
[*see* beadsman]
bedevil *derange* 61
sorcery 992
bedew 339
bedight 847
bedim 421, 422
bedizen *clothe* 225
ornament 847
vulgar 851
Bedlam
– broke loose 59
candidate for – 504
be-dog 281
Bedouin 792
bedraggled 59
bedwarf 195
bee 690
busy – 682
swarm like –s 102
– in one's bonnet 503
– in a bottle 407
– line 246, 278
–'s wax 352
beef-eater 726
beef-headed 499
beehive 250

Beelzebub 978
beer 298
beery 959
beetle *overhang* 206, 214
project 250
blind as a – 442
Colorado – 913
– head 501
befall 151
befit *agree* 23
expedient 646
due 924, 926
befog 353, 528
befool *mad* 503
deceive 545
befooled
victimized 732
before *in order* 62
in time 116
presence 186
in space 234
precession 280
preference 609
set – one 525
– Christ 106
– long 132
– mentioned 62, 116
– now 122
– one's eyes 446, 525
– one's time 132
– you could –turn round, – say Jack Robinson 113
beforehand
prior 116
early 132
foresight 510
resolve – 611
befoul 653
befriend 707, 888
befuddlement 959
beg *Turk* 745
ask 765
– one's bread 765
poor 804
– leave 760
– one's life 914
– pardon 952
– the question 477
beget 161
begetter 166
beggar *idler* 683
petitioner 767
poor 804
degrade 874
low person 876
sturdy – 792

– description 83, 870
– my neighbour 840
– on horseback 885
beggared
bankrupt 808
beggarly *mean* 643
vile 874
vulgar 876
servile 886
– account of empty boxes 640, 804
begging
go a –
too much 641
useless 645
offered 763
free 748
– letter 765
begilt 847
begin 66
– again 104
beginner 541
beginning 66
begird 227, 229
beglerbeg 745
begone
depart 293
ejection 297
abrogate 756
– dull care 836
Begotten, the only – 976
begrime 653
begrudge
unwilling 603
refuse 764
stingy 819
beguile *mislead* 495
deceive 545
reconcile 831
– the time
inaction 681
amusement 840
béguine 996
begum 745, 875
behalf 618, 707
in – of 759
behave oneself
conduct 692
fashion 852
courtesy 894
behaviour 692
on one's good – 894, 944
behead 361, 972
behemoth 192
behest 741
behind

in order 63
in space 235
sequence 281
– the age 124, 491
– one's back 187
speak ill of – one's back 934
– the bars 751
– the scenes
cause 153
unseen 447
cognizant 490
latent 526
hidden 528
playhouse 599
– time 133
behindhand
late 133
shortcoming 304
adversity 735
insolvent 808
behold 441, 457
beholden 916, 926
beholder 444
behoof 618
behoove 926
being 1, 3
created – 366
human – 372
time – 106
Bel 979
belabour 276, 972
belated *late* 133
ignorant 491
belaud 931
belay *join* 43
restrain 706
belch 297
beldam 130, 913
beldame 173
beleaguer 716
bel esprit 844
belfry 206, 1000
Belial 978, 980
son of – 988
belie *deny* 536
falsify 544
contradict 708
belief 484, 488
easy of – 472
hug a – 606
believe
[*see* belief]
suppose 514
reason to – 472
– who may 485
not – one's senses 870
believer
religious 987
true – 983*a*

bespeak *early* 132
  evidence 467
  indicate 516
  engage 755
  ask for 765
bespeckle 440
bespot 440
besprinkle 41, 440
best 648, 650
  all for the –
  good 618
  prosper 734
  content 831
  hope 858
  bad is the – 649
  do one's –
  care 459
  try 675
  activity 682
  exertion 686
  have the – of it 731
  make the – of it
  over-estimate 482
  use 677
  submit 725
  compromise 774
  take easily 826
  hope 858
  the – 800
  to the – of one's
  belief 484
  – bib and tucker
  prepared 673
  ornament 847
  ostentation 882
  – friends 890
  – intentions 906
  – man 903
  – part 31, 50
  – seller 731
  make the – of
  one's time 684
bestead 644
bestial 954, 961
bestir oneself
  activity 682
  haste 684
  exertion 686
bestow 784
  – one's hand 903
  – thought 451
bestraddle 215
bestrew 73
bestride 206, 215
bet 621
betake oneself to
  journey 266
  business 625
  use 677
bête, pas si – 498
bête noire *bane* 663

fear 860
hate 898
bethel 1000
bethink 451, 505
bethral 749, 751
betide 151
betimes 132
betoken
  evidence 467
  predict 511
  indicate 550
betray *disclose* 529
  deceive 545
  dishonour 940
  – itself *visible* 446
betrayer 941
betrim 673
betroth 768, 903
betrothed 897
better *good* 648
  improve 658
  appeal to one's –
  feelings 914
  get – *health* 654
  improve 658
  refreshment 689
  restoration 660
  get the – of, 479,
  702, 731
  think – of 658, 950
  seen – days
  deteriorate 659
  adversity 735
  poor 804
  – half 903
  only – than noth-
  ing 651
  – sort 875
  for – for worse
  choice 609
  marriage 903
between 228
  – cup and lip 111
  far – 198
  lie – 228
  – the lines 526
  vibrate – two ex-
  tremes 149
  – ourselves 528
  – two fires 665
  – maid 746
betwixt 228
bevel 217
  – gearing 633
bever 298
beverage 298
bévue 732
bevy 72, 102
bewail *regret* 833
  lament 839
beware 665, 668

bewilder
  put out 458
  uncertainty 475
  astonish 870
bewitch .
  fascinate 615
  please 829
  excite love 897
  exorcise 992
bey 745
beyond *superior* 33
  distance 196
  go – 303
  – compare 31, 33
  – control 471
  – one's depth 208,
  519
  – expression 31
  – one's grasp 471
  – hope 731, 534
  – the mark 303,
  641
  – measure 641
  – possibility 471
  – praise
  perfect 650
  approbation 931
  virtue 944
  – price 814
  – question 474, 494
  – reason 471
  – remedy 859
  – seas 57
bezel 217 ¦
bhang 663
bias *influence* 175
  tendency 176
  slope 217
  prepossession 481
  disposition 820
bib *pinafore* 225
  drink 959
bibber *weep* 839
  toper 959
bibble-babble 584
bibelot 847
bibendum, nunc
  est – 959
Bible 985
  – oath 535
biblioclasm 162
bibliography 593
bibliolatry
  learning 490
  heterodoxy 984
  idolatry 991
bibliomancy 511
bibliomania 490
bibliomaniac 492
bibliophile 492
bibliopole 593

bibliotheca 593
bibulous 298, 959
bicameral 90
bicapital 90
bice 435, 438
bicentenary 98,
  138, 883
bicker *flutter* 315
  quarrel 713
biconjugate 91
bicuspid 91
bicycle 272
bid *order* 741
  offer 763
  – the banns 903
  – defiance 715
  – fair *tend* 176
  probable 472
  promise 511
  hope 858
  – a long farewell
  624
  – for *intend* 620
  offer 763
  request 765
  bargain 794
bidder 767
bide *wait* 133
  remain 141
  take coolly 826
  – one's time 133
  watch 507
  inactive 681
bidet 271
biennial
  periodic 138
  plant 367
bienséance 852, 894
bier 363
bifacial 90
bifarious 90
bifid 91
bifold 90
biform 90
bifurcate 91, 244
big *in degree* 31
  in size 192
  wide 194
  look – *defy* 715
  proud 878
  insolent 885
  talk – 885, 909
  – sounding
  loud 404
  words 577
  affected 855
  – swollen 194
  – with 161
  – with the fate of
  511

bigamy 903
biggin 191
bight 343
bigot *positive* 474
   prejudice 481
   obstinate 606
   heterodox 984
   impious 988
bigotry 907
bigwig *scholar* 492
   sage 500
   nobility 875
bijou *goodness* 648
   beauty 845
   ornament 847
bilander 273
bilateral 90, 236
bilbo 727
bilboes 752
   put into – 751
bile 900
bilge *base* 211
   convex 250
   yawn 260
   – water 653
bilingual 560
bilious 837
bilk
   disappoint 509
   cheat 545
   steal 791
bill *list* 86
   hatchet 253
   placard 531
   ticket 550
   paper 593
   plan 626
   weapon 727
   money order 800
   money account
     811
   charge 812
   in law 969
   true – 969
   – and coo 902
   – of exchange 771
   – of fare *food* 298
   plan 626
   – of indictment
     938
   –s of mortality 360
   – of sale 771
billet *locate* 184
   ticket 550
   apportion 786
billet *epistle* 592
   – doux 902
billfold 191
billhook 253
billiard – ball 249
   – room 191

– table *flat* 213
billiards 840
Billingsgate 563,
   908
billion 98 .
billow *sea* 348
   river 341
billy-cock 225
billy-goat 373
bimetallism 800
bin 191
binary 89
bind *connect* 43
   cover 223
   compel 744
   condition 770
   obligation 926
   – hand and foot
     751
   – oneself 768
   – over 744
   – up wounds 660
binding 744
bine 367
binnacle 693
binocular 445
binomial 89
biogenesis 161
biograph 448
biography 594
biology 357, 359
bioscope 448
biota 357
biparous 89
bipartite 44, 91
biplane 273
biplicity 89
biquadrate 96
birch *flog* 972
   – rod 975
bird 366
   kill two –s with
     one stone 682
   –'s eye view 441,
     448
   –s of a feather 17
   the – has flown
     187, 671
   – in hand 777, 781
   – of ill omen
     omen 512
     warning 668
     hopeless 859
   – of passage 268
   – of prey 739
   a little – told me
     527
birdcage 370
birdlime *glue* 45
   trap 545
biretta 999

birth *beginning* 66
   production 161
   paternity 166
   nobility 875
   – place 153
   – right 924
birthday 138, 883
   – suit 226
birthmark 848
bis *repeat* 104
   approval 931
biscuits, s'embar-
   quer sans – 674
bise 349
bisection 68, **91**
bishop *punch* 298
   clergy 996
   –'s palace 1000
   –'s purple 437
bishopric 995
bisque 33
bissextile 138
bistoury 253
bistre 433
bisulcate 259
bit
   small quantity 32
   part 51
   interval 106
   curb 752
   just a – 26
   – by bit
   by degrees 26
   by instalments 51
   in detail 79
   slowly 275
   – between the
     teeth 600, 719
bitch *animal* 366
   female 374
   clumsy 699
   fail 732
   impure 962
bite *eat* 298
   physical pain 378
   cold 385
   cheat 545
   dupe 547
   etch 558
   mental pain 830
   – the dust 725
   – in 259
   – the thumb 900,
     929
   – the tongue 392
biter bit 718
biting *pain* 378
   cold 383
   pungent 392
   painful 830
   discourteous 895

   censorious 932
bitten 897
bitter *beer* 298
   cold 383
   taste 392, 395
   painful 830
   acrimonious 895
   hate 898
   angry 900
   malevolent 907
   – end 67
   – ender 606, 710,
     832
   – pill 735
   – words 932
bitterly *greatly* 31
bitterness
   [see bitter]
   pain 828
   regret 833
bitumen 356a
bituminous coal
   388
bivouac
   encamp 184
   camp 189
   repose 265
   watch 668
bi-weekly 138
bizarre 83, 853
blab 529
blabber 584
black *colour* 431
   crime 945
   look – *feeling* 821
   discontent 832
   angry 900
   – art 992
   – and blue
    beat 972
   – board 590
   – book 938
   – eye 848, 972
   – in the face
    swear 535
    excitement 821,
     824
   – flag 722
   – hole *crowd* 72
    prison 752
   – lead 556
   – letter *old* 124
    barbarism 563
    print 591
   – list 932
   – looks
    discourteous 895
    sullen 901a
    disapprove 932
    magic 992
   – mail *theft* 791

booty 793
bribe 973
– sheep 949
– spots in the horizon 859
– swan 83
– and white
  chiaroscuro 420
  colourless 429
  record 551
  writing 590
prove that – is white 477
blackamoor 431
wash a – white 471
blackball 55, 893, 932
blackcoat 996
blacken [*see* black]
  defame 934
blackguard
  vulgar 851
  rude 895
  base 940
  vagabond 949
blackleg 792
black Maria 727
blackness 431
blacksmith 690
bladder 191
blade *edge tool* 253
  man 373
  instrument 633
  sharp fellow 682
  proficient 700
  sword 727
  fop 854
blague 545
blain 250, 848
blame 155, 932
lay – on 938
take – 932
blameless 946
blameworthy
  disapprove 932
  vice 945
  guilt 947
blanc-bec 701
blanch 429, 430
blancmange 298
bland 174, 894
blandiloquence 933
blandishment
  inducement 615
  endearment 902
  flattery 933
blank 2, 4
  empty 187
  simple 849
look –
  disappointed 509

discontent 832
  wonder 870
point – 576
– cartridge 158
– verse 597
blanket 223, 384
wet – 174
toss in a – 929
blare 404, 412
blarney 933
blasé 841, 869
blasphemy 988
blast
  destroy 162
  explosion 173
  wind 349
  sound 404
  adversity 735
  curse 908
– furnace 386
blatant *loud* 404
  cry 412
  silly 499
blather 584
blatter 412
blaze *heat* 382
  light 420
  mark 550
  excitement 824
– abroad 531
blazer 225
blazing
  luminary 423
blazon *publish* 531
  repute 873
  ornament 847
  ostentation 882
blé: manger son – en herbe 818
bleach 429, 430
bleak 383
blear-eyed 443
bleary 422
bleat 412
bleed
  physical pain 378
  remedy 662
  spend money 809
  extort money 814
  moral pain 828
make the heart – 830
– freely *liberal* 816
bleeding
  hemorrhage 299
  remedy 662
– heart 828
blemish
  imperfection 651
  injure 659

ugly 846
defect **848**
blench *avoid* 623
  whiten 821
  fear 860
blend 41, 48
– with 714
bless
  give pleasure 829
  approve 931
  divine function 976
  worship 990
– my heart 870
– one's stars 838, 916
blessed 827
abode of the – 981
blessedness
single – 904
blessing *good* 618
  approval 931
blessings 734
blest 827
– with 177
bletonism 511
blight
  deteriorate 659
  adversity 735
– hope 509
blighty 189
blimp 273
blind 223
  shade 424
  cecily 442
  inattentive 458
  ignorant 491
  conceal 528
  screen 530
  deception 545
  instinctive 601
  pretext 617
  insensible 823
  drunk 959
– alley 261
– bargain
  uncertain 475
  purposeless 621
  rash 863
– the eyes *hide* 528
  deceive 545
– hookey 840
– lead the blind 538
– man's buff 840
– man's holiday *evening* 126
  dark 421, 422
– to one's own merit 880

– to the world 959
– of one eye 443
– reasoning 486
– side *prejudice* 481
  credulity 486
  obstinacy 606
blinders 424, 443
blindness **442**
blind pig 964
blink *wink* 443
  neglect 460
  falter 605
  avoid 623
– at *blind to* 442, 458
blinkard 443
blinker 424, 530
bliss 827
  celestial 981
blister 250
blithe 836
blizzard 349
bloat 194
bloated
  expanded 194
  misshapen 243
  convex 250
– with pride 878
blob 250
block *mass* 192
  support 215
  dense 321
  hard 323
  fool 501
  engraving 558
  writing 590
  hinder 706
  execution 975
bring to the – 972
wood – 558
– of buildings 189
– out 230, 240, 673
– printing 591
– up 261, 706
blockade
  surround 227
  close 261
  restrain 751
  exclude 893
blockhead 501
blockhouse 717
blockish 499
blond 429, 430
blood
  consanguinity 11
  fluid 333
  kill 361
  fop 854
  nobility 875
dye with –

fragrant 400
beauty 847
bourdon 215
bourgeois
 middle class 29
 type 591
 commoner 876
bourgeon 194
bourn 233
bourse 621, 799
bouse 959
bout *turn* 138
 job 680
 fight 720
 prank 840
 drinking – 954
bout
 au – du compte
  476
 au – de son latin
  sophistry 477
  ignorance 491
  difficulty 704
boutade 497, 608
boutonnière 400
bovine 366, 499
bow *be inferior* 34
 fore part 234
 curve 245
 projection 250
 stoop 308
 fiddlestick 417
 weapon 727
 ornament 847
 servility 886
 reverence 894
 respect 928
 bend the – 686
 draw the long –
  884
 – down *worship*
  990, 991
 – out 297
 – submission 725
 – window 260
Bow bells
 born within sound
  of – 876
Bowdlerize 652
bowed down 837,
 879
bowelless 914*a*
bowels *inside* 221
 – of compassion
  914
 – of the earth 208
bower 189, 191
 –s of bliss 981
bowery 424
bowie knife 727
bowl *vessel* 191

rotate 312
stadium 840
flowing – 959
 – along *walk* 266
 swift 274
bowlder 249
bowline 45
bowler *hat* 225
bow-legged 243
bowling-green 213,
 840
bowls 840
bowman 726
bowshot 197
bowsprit 234
bowstring *execution*
 972, 975
box *house* 189
 chest 191
 seat 215
 theatre 599
 fight 720
 horse – 272
 musical – 417
 wrong – *error* 495
 unskilful 699
 dilemma 704
 – the compass
  direction 278
  rotation 312
  change of mind
  607
 – the ear 900, 972
 – up 751
boxer 726
boy 129
 – scout 534
boyar 875
boycott 55, 297, 893
boyhood 127
brabble 713, 720
brabbler 901
brace *tie* 43
 fasten 45
 two 89
 strengthen 159
 support 215
 music 413
 refresh 689
bracelet *circle* 247
 handcuff 752
 ornament 847
bracer 392
braces 45
brachial 633
Brachygraphy 590
bracing 656
bracken 367
bracket *tie* 43, 45
 couple 89
 support 215

brackish 392
brad 45
bradawl 262
Bradbury 800
Bradshaw 266
brae 206
brag *cards* 840
 boast 884
Braggadocio 884
braggart 884
Brahma 979
Brahmin 984, 996
braid *tie* 43
 ligature 45
 net 219
 variegate 440
brain *kill* 361
 intellect 450
 skill 498
 blow one's –s out
  361
 coinage of the –
  515
 suck one's –s 461
 rack one's –s 451,
  515
brainless 499
brainpan 450
brainsick 458
brain-storm 503,
 825
brainwork 451
brainy 498
brake *carriage* 272
 copse 367
 hindrance 706
 curb 752
 apply the – 275
brakeman 268
bramble *thorn* 253
 bane 663
bran 330
brancard 272
branch *member* 51
 class 75
 posterity 167
 fork 244
 tree 367
 – off 91, 291
 – out *ramify* 91
 diffuse style 573
branching
 symmetry 242
brand *burn* 384
 fuel 388
 torch 423
 mark 550
 sword 727
 disrepute 874
 censure 932
 stigmatize 934

 – of discord 713
 – new 123
 – with reproach
  938
brandish
 oscillate 314
 flourish 315
 display 882
brandy 959
brangle 713
brangler 710
brank 975
bras
 les – croisés 681
 à – ouverts 894
brashness 885
brasier 386
brass *alloy* 41
 money 800
 insolence 885
 bold as – 861
 – band 417, 884
 with a – 884
 – coloured 439
 – hat 747
 – farthing 643
brassard 550, 747
brat 129
brattice 224, 228
bravado 884
brave *confront* 234
 healthy 654
 defy 715
 warrior 726
 bear 821, 826
 courage 861
 – a thousand
  years 110
bravo
 assassin 361
 desperado 863
 applause 931
bravura 415
brawl *cry* 411
 discord 713
 revel 840
brawler
 disputant 710
 rioter 742
 blusterer 887
brawny 159, 192
bray *grind* 330
 cry 412
Bray, Vicar of –
 607, 886
braze 43
brazen 525, 885
 – browed 885
 – faced 885
brazier
 [*see* brasier]

breach *crack* 44
  gap 198
  quarrel 713
  violation 925
  custom honoured
    in the – 614
  – of faith 940
  – of law 83, 964
  – of the peace 713
bread 298
  beg – 765
  selfish 943
  quarrel with –
    and butter 699
  – of idleness 683
  – of life *Christ* 976
  piety 987
  – upon the waters
    638
  – and wine 998
breadbasket 191
breadth 202
  chiaroscuro 420
break
  fracture 44
  discontinuity 70
  change 140
  gap 198
  carriage 272
  crumble 328
  disclose 529
  cashier 756
  violate 773, 927
  bankrupt 808
  – away 623
  – bread 298
  – bulk 297
  – camp 293
  – of day *morning*
    125
  twilight 422
  – down *destroy*
    162
  fall short 304
  decay 659
  fail 732
  dance 840
  – one's fetters 614
  – forth 295
  – ground 66
  – a habit 614
  – the heart *pain*
    828, 830
  dejection 837
  – the ice 888
  – in *ingress* 294
  domesticate 370
  teach 537
  tame 749
  – in upon *derange*
    61

inopportune 135
  hinder 706
  – a lance 716, 722
  – a law 83
  – loose 671, 750
  – one's neck
  powerless 158
  die 360
  – the neck of
  task 676
  success 731
  – the news 529
  – no bones 648
  – of 660
  – off *cease* 142
  relinquish 624
  abrogate 756
  – out *begin* 66
  violent 173
  disease 655
  excited 825
  – the peace 173,
    720
  – Priscian's head
    568
  – prison 750
  – the ranks 61
  – short 328
  – silence 582
  – the teeth 579
  – the thread 70
  – through the
    clouds *visible*
    446
  disclose 529
  – through a cus-
    tom 614
  – up *disjoin* 44
  decompose 49
  end 67
  revolution 146
  destroy 162
  – up of the system,
    360, 655
  – on the wheel
  physical pain 378
  mental pain 830
  punishment 972
  – with 713
  – with the past
    146
  – word *deceive* 545
  improbity 940
breaker
  of horses 268
  reef 346
  wave 348
breakers 348, 667
  surrounded by –
    704
  – ahead 665

breakfast 298
breakneck
  precipice 217
  rash 863
breakwater
  refuge 666
  obstruction 706
breast *interior* 221
  confront 234
  convex 250
  mind 450
  oppose 708
  soul 820
  at the – 129
  in the – of 620
  – the current 719
  – high 206
breastplate 717
breastwork 717
breath *instant* 113
  breeze 349
  life 359
  animality 364
  faint sound 405
  with bated – 581
  hold – *quiet* 265
  expect 507
  wonder 870
  not a – of air 265,
    382
  out of – 688
  in the same – 120
  shortness of – 688
  take – 265, 689
  take away one's –
  unexpected 508
  fear 860
  wonder 870
breathe *exist* 1
  blow 349
  live 359
  faint sound 405
  evince 467
  mean 516
  inform 527
  disclose 529
  utter 580
  speak 582
  refresh 689
  – freely 827, 834
  – one's last 360
  not – a word 528
breathing time 687,
  723
breathless
  voiceless 581
  out of breath 688
  feeling 821
  fear 860
  eager 865
  wonder 870

  – attention 457
  – expectation 507
  – impatience 865
  – speed 684
bred in the bone 820
breech 235
  – loader 727
breeches 225
  wear the – 737
  – buoy 666
  – maker 225
  – pocket
  money 800, 802
breed *kind* 75
  multiply 161
  progeny 167
  animals 370
  rear 537
breeding 161, 852,
  894
breeze *wind* 349
  discord 713
breezy 836
brethren 997
breve 413
brevet
  warrant 741
  commission 755
  permit 760
  – rank 873
breviary 998
brevier 591
brevity 201, 572
brew 41, 673
brewing
  impending 152
  storm – 665
bribe *equivalent* 30
  tempt 615
  offer 763
  gift 784
  buy 795
  expenditure 809
  reward 973
bric-à-brac 847
brick *hard* 323
  pottery 384
  material 635
  trump 939, 948
  make -s without
    straw 471
  – colour 434
brickbat 727
bricklayer 690
bride 903
bridewell 752
bridge 45, 627
  – over *join* 43
  facilitate 705
  make peace 723
  compromise 774

cards 840
bridle *restrain* 751
   rein 752
– road 627
– one's tongue
   585, 864
– up 900
brief *time* 111
   space 201
   concise 572
   compendium 596
hold a – for 759
– case 191
briefly *anon* 132
brier
   sharp 253
   pipe 392
   bane 663
brig 273
brigade 726
brigadier 745
brigand 792
brigandage 791
brigandine 717
brigantine 273
bright *shine* 420
   colour 428
   intelligent 498
   cheery 836
   beauty 845
   glory 873
– days 734
– eyed 845
– prospect 858
– side 829
look at the – side
   836, 858
– thought
   sharp 498
   good stroke 626
   wit 842
brighten up
   furbish 658
brigue 712, 720
brilliant
   shining 420
   good 648
   wit 842
   beautiful 845
   gem 847
   glorious 873
– idea 842
brilliantine 356
brim 231
– over 641
brimful 52
brimstone 388
brindled 440
brine 341, 392
bring 270
– about 153, 729

– back 790
– back to the
   memory 505
– to bear upon
   relation 9
   action 170
– into being 161
– to a crisis 604
– forth 161
– forward
   evidence 467
   manifest 525
   teach 537
   improve 658
– grey hairs to the
   grave 735, 830
– grist to the mill
   644
– home 775
– home to 155
– in *receive* 296
   income 810
   price 812
– to life 359
– to light 480*a*
– low 874
– to maturity 673,
   729
– to mind 505
– under one's
   notice 457
– off 672
– out
   discover 480*a*
   manifest 525
   publish 591
– over
   persuade 484
– to perfection
   650, 729
– into play 677
– to a point 74
– in question 461
– up the rear 235
– round
   persuade 615
   restore 660
– to terms 723
– to *convert* 144
   halt 265
– together 72
– in its train 88
– to trial 969
– up *develop* 161
   vomit 297
   educate 537
– in a verdict 480
– word 527
brink 231
on the –
   almost 32

coming 121
   near 197
– of the grave 360
briny 392
– ocean 341
brio *music* 415
   active 682
brisk *prompt* 111
   energetic 171
   active 682
   cheery 836
bristle 253
– up *stick up* 250
   angry 900
– with 639, 641
– with arms 722
bristly 256
Britannia metal
   545
Briticism 563
British 188
– lion 604
Briton, true – 939
   work like a – 686
brittleness 328
britzska 272
broach *begin* 66
   found 153
   reamer 262
   tap 297
   publish 531
   assert 535
broad *general* 78
   space 202
   lake 343
   emphatic 535
   indelicate 961,
   962
– accent 580
– awake 459, 682
– daylight 420,
   525
– farce 842
– grin 838
– highway 627
– hint 527
– meaning 516
– minded 498
broadcast
   disperse 73
   spread 78
   publish 531
   sow – 818
broadcloth 219
broadhearted 906
broadsheet 593
broad-shouldered
   159
broadside 236
   publication 531
   cannonade 716

broadsword 727
Brobdingnagian
   192
brocade 847
brochure 593
Brocken, spectre of
   the 443
broder 549
brogue *boot* 225
   dialect 563
broidery 847
broil *heat* 382
   fry 384
   fray 713, 720
broke *poor* 804
broken
   discontinuous 70
   weak 160
– colour 428
– down
   decrepit 659
   failing 732
   dejected 837
– English 563
– fortune 735, 804
– heart 828, 837
   hopeless 859
– reed 160, 665
– meat 645
– voice 581, 583
– winded
   disease 655
   fatigue 688
broker 758, 797
brokerage *pay* 812
brokery 794
bromidic 613
bronchia 351
bronze *alloy* 41
   brown 433
   sculpture 557
brooch 847
brood 102, 167
– over 451, 847
brooding
   preparing 673
brook *stream* 348
   bear 821, 826
broom 652
broth 298
brothel 961
brother *kin* 11
   similar 17
   equal 27
brotherhood 712
brotherly
   friendship 888
   love 897
   benevolence 906
brougham 272
brought to bed 161

cartes sur table 525, 543
Carthago, delenda est – 908
Carthusian 996
cartilage
dense 321
hard 323
tough 327
cartography 466, 554
cartoon 21, 556
cartoonist 559
cartouche
ammunition 727
ornament 847
cartridge 727
cartulary 86, 551
caruncle 250
carve *cut* 44
make 161
form 240
sculpture 557
apportion 786
– one's way 282
carvel 273
carver 559
caryatides 215
Cary's chickens, Mother – 668
cascade 348
case *state* 7
box 191
sheath 223
topic 454
argument 476
specification 527
grammar 567
affair 625
patient 655
law-suit 969
be the – 1, 494
in good – 654, 734
in –
circumstance 8
event 151
supposition 514
make out a – 467, 924
– in point 23, 82
caseation 321
caseharden
strengthen 159
habituate 613
case-hardened
callous 376, 823
obstinate 606
casemate 189, 717
casement 260
casern 189
cash *money* 800

pay 807
in – 803
pay – for 795
– account 811
– book 551
– box 802
– down 807
– register 85, 553, 802
cashier *dismiss* 756
treasurer 801
casing 223
casino 712; 840
cask 191
casket 191
casque 717
Cassandra 513, 668
cassation 552
casserole 191
Cassiopeia's chair 318
cassock 999
cast *mould* 21
small quantity 32
spread 73
tendency 176
form 240
throw 284
tinge 428
aspect 448
drama 599
reject 610
plan 626
company 712
give 784
allot 786
condemn 971
give one a – 707
set on a – 621
– about for 463
– accounts 811
– adrift *disperse* 73
eject 297
liberate 750
dismiss 756
– anchor 265, 292
– aside 460
– aspersions 934
– away 610, 638
lost 732
– behind one
forget 506
refuse 764
relinquish 782
– away care 836
– off clothes 645
– of countenance 448
– of the dice 156
– in a different

mould 18
– dishonour &c. upon 874
– to the dogs 162
– down 308, 837
– in the eye 443
– the eyes back 122
– eyes on 441
– the eyes over 457
– a gloom 837
– off a habit 614
– iron 323
resolute 604
– in one's lot with 609
– lots 621
– lustre upon 420
– of mind 820
– a nativity 511, 992
– one's net 463
– off *divest* 226
disused 678
dismiss 756
relinquish 782
– over-board 678
– the parts 60
– reflection upon 932
– in the same mould 17
– a shade 421
– the skin 226
– a slur 874
accuse 938
– a spell 992
– off trammels 750
– up *add* 85
happen 151
eject 297
castanet 417
castaway *exile* 893
reprobate 949
caste 75, 873
lose – 940
castellan 746, 753
castellated 717
caster *cruet* 191
wheel 312
castigate 932, 972
castigator 936
casting 21
casting – *vote* 480
– weight 28, 30
castle *at chess* 148
abode 189
defence 717
– in the air *impossible* 471

imagination 515
hope 858
Castle of Indolence 683
castor *hat* 225
Castor and Pollux 89, 890
castrametation 189, 722
castrate *subduct* 38
impotent 158
casual *extrinsic* 6
chance 156
uncertain 475
lax 773
casualty *event* 151
killed 361
evil 619
misfortune 735
casuist 476
casuistry
sophistry 477
falsehood 544
duty 926
casus belli
quarrel 713
irritation 824, 900
casus fœderis 770
cat *nine lives* 359
animal 366
keen sight 441
fall on one's feet 734
cross 901
gib –, tom – *male* 373
rain –s and dogs 348
let – out of bag 529
– boat 273
– burglar 792
– call *whistle* 417
disapproval 932
–'s cradle 219
– and dog life 713
as the – jumps
event 151
see how the – jumps 510
fickleness 607
caution 864
– o' nine tails 975
– in pattens 652
–'s paw *dupe* 547
instrumental 631
use 677
auxiliary 711
catabasis 36
catachresis 521, 523

cataclysm
convulsion 146
destruction 162
deluge 348
catacomb 363
catacoustics 402
catadupe 348
catafalque 363
catalectic 597
catalepsy 265, 376, 683
catalogue 60, 86
catalysis 49, 140
catamaran 273, 726
catamenial 138, 299
cataphonics 402
cataplasm 662
catapult 284, 726, 727
cataract
waterfall 348
blindness 442, 443
catarrh 299
catastrophe
disaster 619
finish 729
misfortune 735
end 67
catch *imitate* 19
fastening 45
song 415
detect 480a
joke 497
gather the meaning 518
cheat 545
receive 785
take 789
by –es 70
no great – 651
– at *willing* 602
desire 865
– the attention 457
– one's death 360
– a disease 655
– the ear 418
– the eye 446
– fire 384
– a glimpse of 441
– an idea 498
– the infection *excitation* 824
– a likeness 554
– a sound 418
– at straws *overrate* 482
credulous 486
unskilful 699
rash 863

– by surprise 508
– a Tartar *dupe* 547
retaliate 718
– in a trap 545
– tripping 480a
– up 789
catching
infectious 657
catchpenny
deceiving 545
trumpery 643
cheap 815
catchpoll 965
catchword 550
catechism 461, 484
church – 983a
catechize 461
catechumen 541, 997
categorical
positive 474
demonstrative 478
affirmative 535
categorically true 494
category 7, 75
in the same – 9
catena 69
catenary 245
catenation 69
cater 298, 637
caterpillar tractor 271
caterwaul
cat-cry 412
discord 414
courting 902
cates 298
catgut 417
– scraper 416
cathartic 652
cathedrâ, ex –
affirm 535
school 542
authority 737
audacity 885
cathedral 1000
Catherine wheel 840
catholic
universal 78
religious 987
– church 983a
Roman – 984
catholicon 662
Catiline 941
catopsis 441
catoptrics 420
catoptromancy 511
cattle 271, 366

– truck 272
catwalk 273, 627
Caucasian mystery 983
caucus 696
caudal 67, 235
caudate 214
caudex 215
Caudine forks 162
cauf 370
caught tripping 491
caulk 660
cause *source* **153**
law-suit 969
final – 620
take up the – of 707
tell the – of 522
–d by 154
causeless
casual 156
aimless 621
causerie 588
causeway 627
causidical 965
caustic
energetic 171
feeling 821
painful 830
gruff 895
malevolent 907
– curve 245
cautel 864
cautelâ, ex abundanti – 664
cautery 384
caution *warn* 668
prudence 864
security 771
want of – 863
cavalcade 69, 266
cavalier
horseman 268
rash 863
insolent 885
discourteous 895
contemptuous 930
cavaliere servente
servile 886
lover 897
cavalry 726
cavatina 415
cave *dwelling* 189
cell 191
cavity 252
– canem 864
– of Adullam 624, 832
– in *hollow* 252
submit 725
caveat

warning 668
command 741
– emptor 769
cavendo tutus 664, 864
cavern [*see* cave]
cavernous 252
caviare 392, 393
– to the general 850
cavil *sophistry* 477
dissent 489
censure 932
caviller 936
cavity 252
caw 412
cayak 273
cayenne 392, 393
cazique 745
cease 142
– to breathe 360
– to exist 2
ceaseless 112
cecity 442
cede *submit* 725
relinquish 782
give 784
ceiling 206, 210, 223
celare artem, ars – 698
cela va sans dire
conformity 82
consequence 154
celebrant 990
celebration **883**, 998
celebrity 873, 875
celerity 274
celeste 417
celestial
physical 318
religious 976
heaven 981
celibacy **904**
cell *abode* 189
receptacle 191
cavity 221, 252
prison 752
hermitage 893
cellar 191
cellaret 191
cello 417
cellular 191, 252
cement
medium 45
unite 43, 46, 48
covering 223
hard 323
material 635
– a party 712
cemented
concord 714

unanimity 488
poetry 597
opera 599
concord 714
– *girl* 599
chose
– in action 780
– in possession 777
chouse 545
choux gras, faire ses – 377
chrestomathy 560
chrism 998
Christ 976
   Church of – 893*a*
   receive – 987
Christ-cross-row 561
christen 564, 998
Christendom 983*a*, 995
Christian 983*a*, 987
– charity 906
– *science* 662, 984
Christmas 138, 998
Christmas-box 784
chromatic
   colour 428
– *scale music* 413
chromato-pseudo-blepsis 443
chromatrope 445
chrome 436
chromolithograph 558
chromosphere 318
chronic 110
chronicle
   measure time 114
   annals 551
chronicler 553
chronography
   measure time 114
   description 594
chronology 114
chronometry 114
Chrononhotontho-logos 887
chrysalis 129
chrysoprase 847
chrysolite 847
   perfection 650
chrysology 800
chubby 192
chuck *throw* 284
   animal cry 412
– it 142
– under chin 902
chuck-farthing 621
chuckle

animal cry 412
laugh 838
exult 884
chuff 876
chum 711, 890
chunk 51
Church
   infallible 474
   orthodox 983*a*
   Christendom 995
   temple 1000
   dignitaries of – 996
   go to – 990
   High –, Low – &c. 984
– of Christ 983*a*
– bell 550
– house 1000
churchdom **995**
churching 998
churchman 996
churchwarden 996
   pipe 392
churchyard 363, 1000
– cough 655
churl *boor* 876
churlish
   niggard 819
   rude 895
   sulky 901*a*
   malevolent 907
churn 315, 352
chut! *silent* 403
   taciturn 585
chute 348
chutney 393
chypre 400
cibarious 298
cicatrix 551
   manet – 919
cicatrize 660
Cicero 582
cicerone 524, 527
ciceronian 578
cicisbeo 897
cicuration **370**
cider 298
cider squeezer 876
ci-devant 122
cigar 392
ci-gît 363
cilia 205, 256
cimeter 727
Cimmerian 421
cinch 45
cincture 247
cinder
   combustion 384
   dirt 653

Cinderella
   servant 746
   commonalty 876
cinema 448, 599, 840
cinematograph 448
cinematographer 553
cinerary 363
cineration 384
cinereous 432
cingle 230
cinnabar 434
cinnamon 393, 433
cinque 98
cipher
   unsubstantial 4
   number 84
   compute 85
   zero 101
   concealment 528
   mark 550
   letter 561
   unimportant 643
   writing in – 590
Circe 615, 994
–an cup 377, 954
circination 312
circle *region* 181
   embrace 227
   form 247
   party 712
   describe a – 311
   great – sailing 628
– of acquaintance 892
– of the sciences 490
circlet 247
circling 248
circuit *region* 181
   outline 230
   winding 248
   tour 266
   indirect path 311
   indirect course **629**
circuition **311**
circuitous 279, 311
– method 629
circular *round* 247
   publication 531
   letter 592
   pamphlet 593
– note 805
circularity **247**
circularize 592
circulate
   circuit 311
   rotate 312
   publish 531

circulating medium 800
circulation
   [*see* circulate]
   in – *news* 532
– of money 809
circumambient 227, 229, 311, 629
circumambulate
   travel 266
   go round 311, 629
circumaviate 311
circumbendibus 248, 629
circumcision 44, 998
circumduction 552
circumference 230
circumferential 227
circumflex 311
circumfluent
   lie round 227
   move round 311
circumforaneous
   travelling 266
   circuition 311
circumfuse 73
circumgyration 312
circumjacence **227**
circumlocution 573
circumnavigate
   navigation 267
   circuition 311
circumrotation 312
circumscribe
   surround 229
   limit 233, 761
circumscription **229**
circumspection
   attention 457
   care 459
   caution 459
circumstance
   phase 8
   event 151
circumstances
   property 780
   bad – 804
   depend on – 475
   good – 803
   under the – 8
circumstantial 8
– account 594
– evidence 467
   probability 472
circumstantiality 459
circumstantiate 467
circumvallation
   enclosure 229, 232

lofty 206
inattentive 458
dreaming 515
under a –
insane 503
adversity 735
disrepute 874
secluded 893
censured 932
accused 938
– burst 348
–capt 206
– of dust 330, 353
–s gathering
dark 421
danger 665
warning 668
– no bigger than a
man's hand 668
– of skirmishers
726
– of smoke 353
– of words 573
clouded
variegated 440
dejected 837
hopeless 859
– perception 499
cloudiness 571
cloudland 515
cloudless
light 420
happy 827
cloudy *dim* 422,
426
clough 206
clout 276
cloven 91
cloven foot
mark 550
malevolence 907
vice 945
Satan 978
see the – 480*a*
show the – 907
clover
luxury 377
prosperity 734
comfort 827
clown
pantomime 599
bungler 702
buffoon 844
vulgar 851
rustic 876
cloy 641, 869
club
place of meeting
74
house 189
association 712

weapon 727
sociality 892
– law
compulsion 744
lawless 964
– together
co-operate 709
clubby 892
club car 272
clubfooted 243
cluck 412
clue 550
seek a – 461
clump
assemblage 72
projecting mass
250
– of trees 367
clumsy
unfit 647
awkward 699
ugly 846
Cluniac 996
clurichaune 980
cluster 72
clutch *retain* 781
seize 789
clutches 737
in the – of 749
clutter 407
coacervation 72
coach
carriage 272
teach 537
tutor 540, 673
– painter 540
– road 627
drive a – and six
through 964
– up 539
coachhouse 191
coachman 268, 694
coaction 744
coadjutant 709
coadjutor 711
coadjuvancy 709
coagency 178, 709
coagmentation 72
coagulate
cohere 46
density 321
semi-liquid 352
coal 388
call over the –s
932
carry –s 879
– black 431
carry –s to New-
castle 641
coalesce
identity 13

combine 48
coalheaver
work like a – 686
coalition 43, 709,
712
coaming 232
coaptation 23
coarctation
decrease 36
contraction 195
narrow 203
impede 706
restraint 751
coarse *harsh* 410
dirty 653
unpolished 674
garish 846
vulgar 851
impure 961
– grain 329
coast *border* 231
slide 266
navigate 267
land 342
– defence 717
– line 230
coaster 273
coastguard 753
coat *layer* 204
paint 223
habit 225
cut – according to
cloth 698
– of arms 550
– of mail 717
coating, inner –
224
coax *persuade* 615
endearment 902
flatter 933
cob *horse* 271
punish 972
cobalt 438
cobble *mend* 660
cobbler 225
cobbles 635
coble 273
cobra 913
cobweb *light* 320
fiction 545
flimsy 643
dirt 653
–s of antiquity
124
–s of sophistry
477
cocaine 376, 381,
663
cochineal 434
cock *bird* 366
male 373

game – 861
– boat 273
– and bull story
546
– the eye 441
– of the roost
best 648
master 745
– up *vertical* 212
convex 250
cockade *badge* 550
title 877
cock-a-hoop
gay 836
exulting 884
Cockaigne 827
cockatrice
monster 83
piercing eye 548
evil-doer 913
miscreant 949
cockcrow 125
cocked hat 225, 745
cocker *fold* 258
caress 902
Cocker
school book 542
according to – 82
cockle *fold* 258
– of one's heart
820
cockleshell 273
cockloft 191
cockney
Londoner 188
plebeian 876
cockpit *hold* 191
council 696
arena 728
cockshut
morning 125
evening 126
dusk 422
cock-sparrow 193
cocksure 484
cockswain 269
cocktail 298, 959
– party 892
cocoa 298
cocotte 962
coction 384
Cocytus 982
cod *shell* 223
coddle 902
– oneself 943
code *conceal* 528
precept 697
law 963
codex 593
codger 819
codicil *sequel* 65

comfit 396
comfort
  pleasure 377
  delight 827
  content 831
  relief 834
  give – 906
comfortable
  pleasing 829
comforter
  covering 223
Comforter 976
comfortless
  painful 830
  dejected 837
comic *wit* 842
  ridiculous 853
  – opera 599
  – strips 531
coming [*see* come]
  impending 152
  – events
  prediction 511
  – out 883
  – time 121
comitia 696
comity 894
comma 142
  inverted –s 550
command *high* 206
  requisition 630
  authority 737
  order **741**
  possess 777
  at one's –
  obedient 743
  – belief 484
  – of language
  writing 574
  speaking 582
  – of money 803
  – one's passions
  944
  – respect 928
  – one's temper
  826
  – a view of 441
commandant 745
commandeer 744,
  789
commander 269
commanding
  [*see* command]
  important 642
commando 726
commandment 697
comme deux
  gouttes d'eau 17
comme il faut
  taste 850
  fashion 852

genteel 875
commemorate 883
commence 66
commencement de
  la fin *end* 67
  destruction 162
commend 931
  – the poisoned
  chalice 544
commendable 944
commensurate
  accordant 23
  numeral 85
  adequate 639
comment
  reason 476
  judgment 480
  interpretation 522
  criticize 595
commentary 595
commentator 492,
  524, 527
commerce
  conversation 588
  barter 794
  cards 840
commercial 811
  – arithmetic 811
  – traveller 758
commère 599
commination 908,
  909
commingle 41
comminute 330
commiserate 914
commissariat 637
commissary
  provisions 637
  consignee 758
commission
  task 625
  delegate **755,** 759
  Royal – 696
  – of the peace 965
commissioner 758
commissionaire
  doorkeeper 263
  messenger 534
  consignee 758
commissure 43
commis-voyageur
  758
commit *do* 680
  delegate 755
  cards 840
  arrest 969
  – an absurdity 853
  – oneself to a
  course 609
  – to the flames
  384

– to memory 505
– oneself
  clumsy 699
  promise 768
– to prison 751
– sin 945
– to writing 551
committee
  council 696
  consignee 758
  (*director* 694)
commix 41
commode 191
commodious 644
commodity 798
commodore 745
common
  general 78
  ordinary 82
  plain 344
  habitual 613
  trifling 643
  base 876
  in – *related* 9
  participate 778
  right of – 780
  short –s 640
  tenant in – 778
  make – cause 709
  – consent 488
  – council 966
  – course 613
  – herd 876
  – law *old* 124
  law 697, 963
  – measure 84
  – origin 153
  – parlance 576
  – place 82
  – place book
  record 551
  compendium 596
  – saying 496
  – sense 498
  – sewer 653
  – stock 778
  – weal
  mankind 372
  good 618
  utility 644
  philanthropy 910
Common Pleas
  Court of – 966
commonalty **876**
commoner 876
commonplace
  usual 82
  known 490
  plain 576
  habit 613
  unimportant 643

dull 843
commons 298
commonwealth
  territory 181
  community 372
  authority 737
commorant 188
commotion 315
communalism 778
commune
  township 181
commune with 588
  – oneself 451
communibus annis
  29
communicant 990
communicate
  join 43
  tell 527
  correspond 592
  give 784
  sacrament 998
communication
  news 532
  of disease 657
  oral – 582, 588
communion
  discourse 588
  society 712
  participation 778
  sacrament 998
  hold – with 888
  – table 1000
communiqué 527
communism 737
communist
  party 712
  rebel 742
  participation 778
  philanthropy 910
  evil doer 913
community
  party 712
  – at large 372
  – of goods 778
commutation
  compensation 30
  substitution 147
  interchange 148
  compromise 774
  barter 794
commutual 12
compact
  joined 43
  united 87
  receptacle 191
  small 193
  compressed 195
  compendious 201
  dense 321
  bargain **769**

compages
whole 50
structure 329
compagination 43
companion *match* 17
accompaniment 88
ladder 305
friend 890
companionable 892
companionship 892
companionway 305
company
assembly 72
actors 599
party, partnership 712
troop 726
sociality 892
bear – 88
in – *with* 88
comparable 9
comparative 464
degree 26
– *anatomy* 368
comparatively 32
compare 464
– *notes* 695
comparison **464**
compartition 44
compartment
part 51
region 181
place 182
cell 191
carriage 272
compass
degree 26
space 180
surround 227
measure 466
intend 620
guidance 693
achieve 729
box the –
direction 278
rotation 312
keep within –
moderation 174
fall short 304
economy 817
points of the – 236
in a small – 193
– *about* 229
– *of thought* 498
compassion 914
object of – 828
compatible
consentaneous 23
possible 470

compatriot
inhabitant 188
friend 890
compeer *equal* 27
friend 890
compel 744
compellation 564
compendency 43
compendious 201
compendium **596**
book 593
compensate
make up for 30
requite 973
compensation **30**
compère 599
competence
power 157
sufficiency 639
skill 698
wealth 803
competition
opposition 708
contention 720
competitor
opponent 710
combatant 726
candidate 767
compilation
collect 72
book 593
compendium 596
compile 54
complacent
pleased 827
content 831
courteous 894
kind 906
complain 839
complainant 938
complaint
illness 655
murmur 839
lodge a – 938
– *without cause* 839
complaisant
lenient 740
courteous 894
kind 906
complement
adjunct 39
remainder 40
part 52
arithmetic 84
complementary
correlation 12
colour 428
complete
entire 52
accomplish 729

compact 769
– *answer* 479
– *circle* 311
in a – *degree* 31
completeness **52**
completion **729**
complex 59
complexion
state 7
colour 428
appearance 448
compliance
conformity 82
obedience 743
consent 762
observance 772
complicate
derange 61
complicated
disorder 59
convolution 248
complice 711
complicity 709
compliment
courtesy 894, 896
praise 931
poor – 932
–*s of season* 896
complimentary
free 815
complot 626
comply [*see* compliance]
compo *coating* 223
material 635
component **56**
componere lites 723, 724
comport
– *oneself* 692
– *with* 23
compos mentis 502
compose
make up 54, 56
produce 161
moderate 174
music 416
write 590
printing 591
pacify 723
assuage 826
composed
self-possessed 826
composer
music 413
composite 41
composition **54**
[*see* compose]
combination 48
piece of music 415
picture 556

style 569
writing 590
building material 635
compromise 774
barter 794
atonement 952
compositor
printer 591
compost 653
composure 826, 871
compotation 959
compote 298
compound
mix 41
combination 48
limited space 182
enclosure 232
compromise 774
– *arithmetic* 466
– *for substitute* 147
barter 794
comprador 637
comprehend
compose 54
include 76
know 490
understand 518
comprehension [*see* comprehend]
intelligence 498
comprehensive 76
complete 50
general 78
wide 192
– *argument* 476
compress
contract 195
curtail 201
condense 321
remedy 662
compressible 322
comprise 76
comprobation
evidence 467
demonstration 478
compromise
dally with 605
mid-course 628
taint 659
danger 665
pacify 723
compact 769
compound **774**
atone 952
compromised
promised 768
compter 799
compte rendu
record 551
accounts 811

comptroller 694
compulsion 744
compunction 833, 950
compurgation
  evidence 467
  acquittal 970
compute 85
comrade 890
comradeship 892
con *think* 451
  get by heart 505
  learn 539
conation 600
conatu magnas
  nugas, magno –
  waste 638
  unimportance 643
conatus 176
concamerate 245
concatenation
  junction 43
  continuity 69
concavity 252
conceal
  invisible 447
  hide 528
  cunning 702
concealment 528,
  893
concede
  assent 488
  admit 529
  permit 760
  consent 762
  give 784
conceit *idea* 453
  folly 499
  supposition 514
  imagination 515
  wit 842
  affectation 855
  vanity 880
conceited
  dogmatic 481
conceivable 470
conceive *begin* 66
  beget 161
  teem 168
  believe 484
  understand 490
  imagine 515
  plan 626
concent 413
concentrate
  assemble 72
  centrality 222
  converge 290
concentric 216, 222
conception
  [*see* conceive]

intellect 450
idea 453
concern
  relation 9
  event 151
  business 625
  importance 642
  firm 797
  grief 828
  – oneself with 625
concert
  agreement 23
  synchronism 120
  music 415
  act in – 709
  in – *musical* 413
  concord 714
  – measures 626
concertina 417
concerto 415
concert-room 840
concession
  permission 760
  consent 762
  compromise 774
  giving 784
  discount 813
concesso, ex –
  reasoning 476
  assent 488
concetto 842
conchoid 245
conchology 223
concierge 263, 753
conciliate
  talk over 615
  pacify 723
  satisfy 831
  courtesy 894
  atonement 952
conciliatory [*see*
  conciliate]
  concord 714
  forgiving 918
conciliatrix 962
concinnity
  agreement 23
  style 578
  beauty 845
conciseness 572
concision 201
conclave
  assembly 72
  council 696
  church 995
conclude
  end 67
  infer 480
  resolve 604
  complete 729
  compact 769

conclusion
  [*see* conclude]
  sequel 65
  germination 161
  judgment 480
  try –s 476
  forgone – 611
  hasty – 481
conclusive
  [*see* conclude]
  answer 462
  evidence 467
  certain 474
  proof 478
  – reasoning 476
concoct *lie* 544
  write 590
  plan 626
  prepare 673
concomitant
  accompany 88
  same time 120
  concurrent 178
concord *agree* 23
  music **413**
  assent 488
  harmony **714**
concordance 562
  book 593
concordant 173
concordat 769
concordia discors
  24, 59
concours 720
concourse
  assemblage 72
  convergence 290
concremation 384
concrete *existent* 3
  mass 46
  definite 79
  density 321
  hardness 323
  materials 635
concubinage 961
concubine 926
concupiscence 865,
  961
concur
  co-exist 120
  causation 178
  converge 290
  assent 488
  concert 709
concurrence 178,
  216
concussion 276
condemnation 932,
  971
condemned cell 752
condense

compress 195
dense 321
condensed
  concise 572
condescend 879
condign 924
condiment 393
condisciple 541
condition *state* 7
  modification 469
  supposition 514
  term 770
  repute 873
  rank 875
  in – *plump* 192
  in good – 648
  on – 770
  in perfect – 650
  physical – 316
conditional 8
conditions 770
condolence 914, **915**
condone 918
condottiere
  traveller 268
  fighter 726
conduce
  contribute 153
  tend 176
  concur 178
  avail 644
conducive 631
conduct
  transfer 270
  music 416
  procedure **692**
  lead 693
  safe –
  passport 631
  safety 664
  – a funeral 363
  – an inquiry 461
  – to 278
conduction 264
conductor 268
  conveyer 271
  director 694
  lightning – 666
conduit 350
conduplicate 89
condyle 250
cone *round* 249
  pointed 253
confabulation 588
confection 396
  confectionery 396
confectioner 637
confederacy
  co-operation 709
  party 712
confederate 711

conquer 731
conquered
 (*failure* 732)
conquering hero
 comes 883
conqueror 731
consanguinity **11**
consciarecti, mens–
 pride 878
 innocence 946
conscience
 knowledge 490
 moral sense 926
 in all – *great* 31
 affirmation 535
 awakened – 950
 qualms of – 603
 clear – 946
 stricken – 950
 tender – 926
 honour 939
conscientious 926
 scrupulous 939
 – objector 489
conscious
 intuitive 450
 knowledge 490
 – of disgrace 874
 – of glory 873
conscript 726
conscription 744
consecrate *use* 677
 dedicate 873
 sanctify 987
 holy orders 995
consecration
 rite 998
consectary 478
 – reasoning 476
consecution 63
consecutive
 following 63
 continuous 69
 – fifth 414
consecutively
 slowly 275
consensus 488
 – of opinion 23
consent *assent* 488
 compliance **762**
 with one – 178
consentaneous
 agreeing 23
 (*expedient* 646)
consequence
 event 151
 effect 154
 importance 642
 in – 478
 of no – 643
 take the –s 154

consequent 63
consequential
 deducible 478
 arrogant 878
consequently
 reasoning 476
 effect 154
conservation
 permanence 141
 storage 636
 preservation 670
conservatism 141,
 670
conservative 141,
 712
 – policy 681
conservatoire 542
conservator
 of the peace 967
conservatory
 receptacle 191
 floriculture 371
 furnace 386
 store 636
conserve 396, 636
consider *think* 451
 attend to 457
 examine 461
 adjudge 480
 believe 484
considerable
 in degree 31
 in size 192
 important 642
considerate
 careful 459
 judicious 498
 benevolent 906
consideration
 purchase money
  147
 thought 451
 idea 453
 attention 457
 qualification 469
 inducement 615
 importance 642
 gift 784
 benevolence 906
 respect 928
 requital 973
 deserve – 642
 in – of
  compensation 30
  reasoning 476
 on – 658
 take into –
  thought 451
  attention 457
 under –
  topic 454

inquiry 461
plan 626
considered, all
 things –
 collectively 50
 judgment 480
 premeditation 611
 imperfection 651
consign
 transfer 270
 commission 755
 property 783
 give 784
 – to the flames 384
 – to oblivion 506
 – to the tomb 363
consignee **758**
consignor 796
consignment
 commission 755
 gift 784
 apportionment
  786
consilience 178
consist
 – in 1
 – of 54
consistence
 density 321
consistency
 uniformity 16
 agreement 23
consistently with
 82
consistory
 council 696
 church 995
consolation
 relief 834
 condole 915
 religious 976
console
 table 215
Consoler
 the – 976
consolidate
 unite 46, 48
 condense 321
consols 802
consommé 298
consonant
 agreeing 23
 musical 413
 letter 561
consort
 accompany 88
 associate 892
 spouse 903
 – with 23
consortium 23
consortship 892

conspection 441
conspectus 596
conspicuous
 visible 446
 famous 873
conspiracy 626
conspirator 626
 traitor 941
conspire
 concur 178
 co-operate 709
constable
 policeman 664
 governor 745
 officer 965
constant
 fixed 5
 uniform 16
 continuous 69
 regular 80
 continual 112
 frequent 136
 regular 138
 immutable 150
 exact 494
 persevering 604a
 obey 743
 faithful 939
 – flow 69
constellation
 stars 318
 luminary 423
 glory 873
consternation 860
constipation
 closure 261
 density 321
constituency 181,
 737
constituent 51, 56
constitute
 compose 54, 56
 produce 161
constitution
 nature 5
 state 7
 composition 54
 structure 329
 charter 924
 law 963
constitutional
 walk 266
 – government 737
constrain
 compel 744
 restrain 751
 abash 881
constraint 195
constrict 195, 706
constringe 195
construct 161

acrid 171
destructive 649
– *sublimate* 663
corrugate
  derange 61
  constrict 195
  roughen 256
  rumple 258
  furrow 259
corruption
  decomposition 49
  neology 563
  foulness 653
  disease 655
  deterioration 659
  improbity 940
  vice 945
corrupting
  noxious 649
corsage 225
corsair 273, 792
corse 362
corselet 225
corset 225
corso 728
cortège
  adjunct 39
  continuity 69
  accompaniment 88
  journey 266
  suite 746
cortes 696
cortex
  cortical 223
coruscate 420
corvette 273, 726
corybantic 503
coryphée 599
Corypheus
  teacher 540
  director 694
coscinomancy 511
cosey 892
cosignificative 522
cosine 217
cosmetic
  remedy 662
  ornament 847
cosmic 318
cosmogony &c. 318
cosmopolitan
  abode 189
  mankind 372
  philanthropic 910
  sociality 892
cosmorama 448
cosmos 60, 318
Cossack 726
cosset
  darling 899

caress 902
cost 812
  pay –s 807
  to one's –
    evil 619
    badness 649
  – *what it may* 604
  – *price* 815
costermonger 797
costless 815
costly 814
costive
  taciturn 585
costume 225
  theatrical – 599
costumé 225
  bal – 840
costumier 225
  theatrical 599
cosy *snug* 377
  sociable 892
cot *abode* 189
  bed 215
cote 189
cotenancy 778
coterie *class* 75
  junto 712
  society 892
coterminous 120
cothurnus 599
cotillon 840
cottage 189
  – *piano* 417
cottager 188
cotter 188
cotton 205
  – *seed oil* 356
couch *lie* 213
  bed 215
  stoop 308
  lurk 528
  – *one's lance* 720
  – *in terms* 566
couchant 213
couci-couci 651
cough 349
  churchyard – 655
couleur de rose
  good 648
  prosperity 734
  view en – 836
coulisses 599
coulter 253
council
  senate **696**
  church 995
  hold a – 695
  – *of education* 542
  – *school* 542
councillor 696
counsel

advice 695
lawyer 968
keep one's own –
  528
take – *think* 451
  inquire 461
  be advised 695
count *clause* 51
  item 79
  compute 85
  estimate 480
  lord 875
  – one's chickens
    before they are
    hatched 858,
    863
  – the cost 864
  – upon
    believe 484
    expect 507
  to be –ed on one's
    fingers 103
countenance
  face 234
  appearance 448
  favour 707
  approve 931
  keep in –
    conform 82
    induce 615
    encourage 861
    vindicate 937
  keep one's –
    brook 826
    not laugh 837
  out of –
    abashed 879
  put out of – 874
  stare out of – 885
  – falling
    disappointment 509
    dejection 837
counter *contrary* 14
  number 84
  table 215
  stern 235
  token 550
  shop-board 799
  over the –
    barter 794
    buy 795
    sell 796
  run – 179
  – to 708
counteract
  compensate 30
  physically 179
  hinder 706
  voluntarily 708
counteraction 14,

179
counterbalance 30
counterblast
  counteract 179
  retaliate 718
countercharge 462
counterchange
  correlation 12
  interchange 148
countercharm 993
countercheck
  mark 550
  hindrance 706
counterclaim 30
counter-evidence
  468
counterfeit
  imitate 19
  copy 21
  simulate 544
  sham 545
  coinage 792
counterfoil 550
countermand 756
countermarch 266,
  283
countermark 550
countermine
  plan 626
  oppose 708
countermotion 283
counterorder 756
counterpane 223
counterpart
  match 17
  copy 21
  reverse 237
counterplot
  plan 626
  oppose 708
  retaliate 718
counterpoint 415
counterpoise
  compensate 30
  weight 319
  hinder 706
counter-poison 662
counterpole 14
counter-project 718
counter-protest 468
counter-revolution
  146
counterscarp 717
countersign
  evidence 467
  assent 488
  mark 550
counterstroke 718
countervail
  outweigh 28
  compensate 30

[447]

creditable *right* 924
creditor 805
credo quia
impossibile 486
credulity **486**
credulous person
dupe 547
creed *belief* 484
theology 983
Apostles' – 983a
creek *interval* 198
water 343
creel 191
creep *crawl* 275
tingle 380
(*inactivity* 683)
– in 294
– into a corner 893
– into the good
graces of 933
– out 529
– upon one 508
– with
multitude 102
redundance 641
creeper 367
creeping
sensation 380
– thing 366
creese 727
cremation
of corpses 363
burning 384
crematorium 363,
386
crematory 386
crème de la crème
648
Cremona 417
crenate 257
crenelle 257
crenulate 257
creole 57
crêpe 248, 839
crepidam, ultra –
471
crepitation 406
crepuscule
dawn 125
dusk 422
crescendo
increase 35
musical 415
crescent
growing 35
street 189
curve 245
cresset 423, 550
crest *supremacy* 33
summit 210
pointed 253

tuft 256
sign 550
armorial 877
pride 878
on the – 33
crest-fallen
dejected 837
humble 879
crevasse 198, 667
crevice 198
crew *assemblage* 72
inhabitants 188
mariners 269
party 712
crib *bed* 215
key 522
granary 636
steal 791
parsimony 819
cribbage 840
cribbed, confined,
cabined – 751
cribble 260
cribriform 260
Crichton,
Admirable –
scholar 492
perfect 650
proficient 700
crick *pain* 378
cricket *game* 840
not – 940
– *ground* 213
crier 534
send round the –
531
crim. con. 961
crime 945, 947
criminal 923, 945
culprit 949
– *law* 963
court of – appeal
966
criminality 947
criminate 938
crimp *crinkle* 248
notch 257
brittle 328
deceiver 548
take 789
steal 791
crimple 258
crimson 434, 821
cringe *submit* 725
subject 749
servility 886
crinite 256
crinkle *angle* 244
convolution 248
roughen 256
fold 258

crinoline 225
cripple *disable* 158
weaken 160
injure 659
crippled
disease 655
crisis
conjuncture 8
present time 118
opportunity 134
event 151
strait 704
excitement 824
bring to a – 604
come to a – 729
crisp *rumpled* 248
rough 256
brittle 328
style 572
Crispin 225
criss-cross 219
cristallomantia 511
criterion *test* 463
evidence 467
indication 550
crithomancy 511
critic *judge* 480
taste 850
detractor 936
critical
contingent 8
opportune 134
discriminating
465
important 642
dangerous 665
difficult 704
censorious 932
criticism
judgment 480
dissertation 595
disapprobation
932
detraction 934
critique
[*see* criticism]
croak *cry* 412
hoarseness 581
stammer 583
warning 668
discontent 832
lament 839
croaker 832, 837
Croat 726
crochet 847
crock 191
crockery 384
crocodile tears 544
crocus *yellow* 436
Crœsus 803
croft 189, 232

Croix de Guerre 733
cromlech 363, 551
crone *veteran* 130
fool 501
crony *friend* 890
favourite 899
crook *curve* 245
deviation 279
thief 792
crooked
sloping 217
distorted 243
angular 244
latent 526
crafty 702
ugly 846
dishonourable 940
– *path* 704
– *temper* 901
– *ways* 279
croon 580
crop
stomach 191
harvest 154
shorten 201
eat 298
vegetable 367
store 636
gather 775
take 789
second – 167, 775
– out *visible* 446
disclose 529
– up *begin* 66
take place 151
reproduction 163
cropper *fall* 306
croquet *game* 840
– ground *level* 213
croquette 298
crosier 747, 999
cross *mix* 41
across 219
pass 302
grave 363
oppose 708
failure 732
disaster 735
refuse 764
pain 830
decoration 877
fretful 901
punishment 975
rites 998
fiery – 722
proclaim at the –
roads 531
red – 662
-ed bayonets 708
– breed 83
– cut 628

CRO

– fire *interchange* 148
difficulty 704
opposition 708
attack 716
–ed in love 898
– the mind 451
– the path of 706
– and pile 621
– purposes 14
disorder 59
error 495
misinterpret 523
unskilful 699
difficulty 704
opposition 708
discord 713
– oneself 998
– questions
inquiry 461
discord 713
game 840
– road 627
– the Rubicon 609
– sea 348
– swords 722
crossbow 727
cross-examine 461
cross-grained 256
obstinate 606
sulky 901a
crossing 219
– sweeper 652
crosspatch 895
crossroads 8
cross-word puzzle 533
crotch 244
crotchet
eccentric 83
music 413
misjudgment 481
obstinacy 606
caprice 608
crouch *lower* 207
stoop 308
fear 860
servile 886
– before 725
croup 235
croupier 694
crow *cry* 412
black 431
rejoice 838
boast 884
pluck a – with 932
as the – flies 278
–'s foot (*age*) 128
–'s nest 210
– to pluck
discord 713

CRU

anger 900
accuse 938
crowbar 633
crowd 72
multitude 102
close 197
redundance 641
party 712
vulgar 876
in the – *mixed* 41
madding – 682
crown *top* 210
circle 247
complete 729
trophy 733
sceptre 747
install 755
decoration 877
reward 973
to – all 33, 642
–ed head 745
– with laurel 873
– with success 731
crowning
[*see* crown]
superior 33
end 67
– point 210
cruche à l'eau &c.
tant va la – 735
crucial
crossing 219
proof 478
– test 463
cruciate
physical pain 378
mental pain 830
crucible
dish 191
conversion 144
furnace 386
experiment 463
laboratory 691
put into the – 163
crucifix 219, 998
crucifixion 828
cruciform 219
crucify
physical torture 378
mental agony 830
execution 972
crucis, experimen-
tum – 463
crude *colour* 428
- *style* 579
unprepared 674
cruel
painful 830
inhuman 907
– to be kind 914

CRY

cruelly *much* 31
cruet 191
cruise
vessel 191
navigation 267
cruiser 726
cruising 267
crumb *small* 32
powder 330
– of comfort 834
crumble
decrease 36
weak 160
destruction 162
brittle 328
pulverize 330
spoil 659
– into dust
decompose 49
– under one's feet 735
crumbling
[*see* crumble]
dangerous 665
crumenal 800
crump
distorted 243
curved 245
crumple
ruffle 256
fold 258
– up *destroy* 162
crush 195
crunch
shatter 44
chew 298
pulverize 330
crupper 235
crusade 722
crush *crowd* 72
destroy 162
compress 195
pulverize 330
humble 879
– under an iron
heel 739
– one's hopes
disappoint 509
hopeless 859
crushed 828
crushing 830
crust 223
crustacean 366
crusty 895, 901a
crutch
support 215
angle 244
–ed Friars 996
crux 219, 704
– criticorum 533
cry *human* **411**

CSA

animal 412
publish 531, 532
call 550
voice 580
vogue 613
weep 839
far – to 196
full – *loud* 404
raise a – 550
– aloud
implore 765
– out against
dissuade 616
censure 932
– down 932, 934
– for 865
– before hurt 839
– for joy 838
– you mercy
deprecate 766
pity 914
forgive 918
– shame 932
– to *beseech* 765
– up 931
– for vengeance 923
– wolf *false* 544
alarm 669
– and little wool
overrate 482
boast 884
disappoint 509
crying [*see* cry]
urgent 630
weary 841
– evil 619
– shame 874
– sin 945
crypt *cell* 191
grave 363
ambush 530
altar 1000
cryptic 475, 528
cryptography
hidden 528
writing 590
crystal *hard* 323
transparent 425
snow – 383
– gazer 513
– gazing 511, 992
– oil 356
clear as – 518
crystalline
dense 321
hard 323
transparent 425
crystallization 321, 323
csako 225, 717

cub *young* 129
  vulgar 851
  clown 876
  unlicked – 241
cubby-hole 191
cube
  three dimensions 92, 93
  form 244
cubicle 191
cubist 556
cubit 200
cucking stool 975
cuckold 905
cuckoldom 961
cuckoo
  imitation 19
  repetition 104
  sound 407
  cry 412
cuddle 197, 902
cudgel *beat* 276
  weapon 727
  punish 975
  take up the –s
  aid 707
  attack 716
  contention 720
  – one's brains
  think 451
  imagine 515
cue *hint* 527
  watchword 550
  plea 617
  rôle 625
  take one's – from 695
  in proper – 698
cuff *sleeve* 225
  blow 276
  punishment 972
cui bono 644, 645
cuique voluptas sui – 865
cuirass 717
cuirassier 726
cuisine 298
  batterie de – 957
culbute
  inversion 218
  fall 306
cul-de-lampe
  engraving 558
  ornament 847
cul-de-sac
  concave 252
  closed 261
  difficulty 704
culinary 298
  – art 673
cull *dupe* 547

choose 609
  take 789
cullender 260
cullibility 486
cullion 949
cully *deceive* 545, 547
culm 388
culminate
  maximum 33
  height 206
  top 210
  complete 729
culpability *vice* 945
  guilt 947
culprit 949
cult 983
cultivate *till* 365, 371
  sharpen 375
  improve 658
  prepare 673
  aid 707
cultivated
  courteous 894
  – *taste* 850
cultivator 371
culture
  knowledge 490
  improvement 658
  taste 850
  politeness 894
culverin 727
culvert 350
cum multis aliis 37, 102
cumber *load* 319
  obstruct 706
cumbersome
  incommodious 647
  disagreeable 830
cummerbund 225
cumulative 72
  increasing 35
  assembled 72
  – *evidence* 467
  – *vote* 609
cumulus 353
cunctando restituit rem 681
cunctation 133
cuneiform 244
  – *character* 590
cunning
  prepense 611
  sagacious 698
  artful **702**
  – *fellow* 700
  – *man* 994
cup *vessel* 191

hollow 252
  beverage 298
  remedy 662
  trophy 733
  tipple 959
  between – and lip 111
  in one's –s 959
  – that cheers &c. 298
  – of humiliation 879
  dash the – from one's lips 509
  – too low 837
cupbearer 746
cupboard 191
cupellation 384
Cupid *beauty* 845
  love 897
  gods 979
cupidity
  avarice 819
  desire 865
cupola *height* 206
  roof 223
  dome 250
cup-tossing 621
cur *dog* 366
  coward 862
  sneak 949
curable 658, 660, 662
curacy 995
curare 663
curate 996
curative 660
curator 694, 758
curb *moderate* 174
  slacken 275
  dissuade 616
  restrain 751
  shackle 752
curb exchange 621
curbstone 233
curd *density* 321
  pulp 354
  (*cohere* 46)
curdle *condense* 321
  (*cohere* 46)
  make the blood – 830
curdled 352
cure *reinstate* 660
  remedy 662
  preserve 670
  benefice 995
curé 996
cureless 859
curfew 126
curia 966

curio 847
curiosa felicitas 698
curiosity
  unconformity 83
  inquiring **455**
  phenomenon 872
curious
  exceptional 83
  inquisitive 455
  true 494
  beautiful 845
  desirous 865
curiously *very* 31
curl *bend* 245
  convolution 248
  hair 256
  cockle up 258
  badge 747
  – up one's lip 930
curling *game* 840
curmudgeon
  miser 819
  plebeian 876
currency
  publicity 531
  money 800
current *existing* 1
  usual 78
  present 118
  happening 151
  flow 264
  of water 348
  of air 349
  rife 531, 532
  language 560
  habit 613
  danger 667
  account – 811
  against the – 708
  go with the – 82
  pass –
  believed 484
  fashion 852
  stem the – 708
  – belief 488
  – of events 151
  – of ideas 451
  – of time 109
currente calamo 590
curricle 272
curriculum 537
curry *food* 298
  rub 331
  condiment 392, 393
  – favour with
  love 897
  flatter 933
curry-comb 370
curse *bane* 663

Darby and Joan
secluded 893
married 903
dare *defy* 715
face danger 861
– *not* 860
– *say probable* 472
believe 484
suppose 514
dare-devil
courage 861
rash 863
bluster 887
daring 861
unreserved 525
– *imagination* 515
dark
obscure 421
dim 422
black 431
blind 442
invisible 447
unintelligible 519
latent 526
joyless 837
insidious 940
in the –
ignorant 491
leap in the –
experiment 463
chance 621
rash 863
keep – *hide* 528
– *ages* 491
– *cloud* 735
view with – eyes
932
– *lantern* 423
darkly
see through a
glass – 443
darkness [*see* dark]
421
children of – 988
love – better than
light 989
powers of – 978
darky 431
darling *beloved* 897
favourite 899
darn 660
dart *swift* 274
propel 284
missile 727
– to and fro 684
Dartmoor 752
Darwinism 357
dash
small quantity 32
mix 41
swift 276

fling 284
mark 550
courage 861
cut a – *repute* 873
display 882
– *at resolution* 604
attack 716
– *board* 666
– *cup from lips* 761
– *down* 308
– *hopes*
disappoint 509
fail 732
dejected 837
despair 859
– *on* 274
– *off paint* 556
write 590
active 682
haste 684
– *of the pen* 590
dashed [*see* dash]
humbled 879
dashing
fashionable 852
brave 861
ostentatious 882
dastard 862
data *evidence* 467
reasoning 476
supposition 514
date *time* 106
chronology 114
datum 673
daub *cover* 223
paint 428
misrepresent 555
dirt 653
daughter 167
daunt 860
dauntless 861
Dauphin 875
davenport 191, 215
davit 214
Davus sum non
Œdipus
unintelligent 499
artless 703
dull 843
Davy Jones' locker
310
dawdle *tardy* 133
slow 275
inactive 683
dawk 534
dawn
precursor 64
begin 66
priority 116
morning 125
light 420

dim 422
glimpse 490
dawplucker 936
day
period 108
present time 118
light 420
all – 110
clear as –
certain 474
intelligible 518
manifest 525
close of – 126
decline of – 126
denizens of the –
366
good old –'s 122
have had its – 124
one fine – 119
open as – 703
order of the – 613
red letter – 642
see the light of –
446
– after day
diuturnal 110
frequent 136
– by day
repeatedly 104
time 106
periodic 138
– after the fair
135
–s gone by 122
– of judgment 121
happy as the – is
long 827, 836
– and night
frequent 136
labour – and night
686
–s numbered
transient 111
death 360
– one's own 731
– of rest 687
– star 423
– after to-morrow
121
– before yesterday
122
–s of week 138
all in –'s work 625
daybed 215
daybook *record* 551
accounts 811
daybreak
morning 125
dim 422
day-dream
fancy 515

hope 858
day-labourer 690
daylight 125, 420
see – *intelligible*
518
– *saving* 114
daymare 859
daze 420
dazed 376
dazzle
light 420
blind 422, 443
put out 458
astonish 870
awe 928
dazzling
[*see* dazzle]
beautiful 845
de: – *die in diem*
time 106
periodic 138
– *facto* 1
– *fond en comble*
52
– *novo* 104
– *omnibus rebus*
81
– *profundis* 821
deacon 996
deaconry 995
dead *complete* 52
inert 172
colourless 429
lifeless 360
insensible 376
– *against*
contrary 14
oppose 708
more – than alive
688
– *asleep* 683
– *beat*
powerless 158
– *certainty* 474
– *colour* 556
– *cut* 893
– *drunk* 959
– *failure* 732
– *flat* 213
– *heat* 27
– *languages* 560
– *letter*
impotent 158
unmeaning 517
useless 645
laxity 738
exempt 927
illegal 964
– *level* 16
– *lift exertion* 686
difficulty 704, 706

kill 361
play havoc 659
punish 972
decipher 522
decision
  judgment 480
  resolution 604
  intention 620
  law case 969
decisive
  certain 474
  proof 478
  commanding 741
  take a – step 609
deck *floor* 211
  beautify 847
declaim 531, 582
  – against 932
declamatory
  style 577
  speech 582
declaration
  affirmation 535
  law pleadings 969
  – of faith
  belief 484
  theology 983
  – of war 713
declaratory
  meaning 516
  inform 527
declare
  publish 531
declension
  [*see* decline]
  grammar 567
  backsliding 988
declensions 5
declination
  [*see* decline]
  deviation 279
  measurement 466
  rejection 610
decline *decrease* 36
  old 124
  weaken 160
  descent 306
  grammar 567
  be unwilling 603
  reject 610
  disease 655
  become worse 659
  adversity 735
  refuse 764
  – of day 126
  – of life 128
declivity *slope* 217
  descent 306
decoction 335, 384
decode 522
decollate 972

décolleté 226
decoloration 429
decomposition 49
deconsecrate 756
decontrol 158
décor 448, 599
decoration
  insignia 747
  ornament 847
  title 877
decorative 556
decorous
  [*see* decorum]
  fashionable 862
  proper 924
  respectful 928
decorticate 226
decorum
  fashion 852
  duty 926
  purity 960
décousu
  discontinuous 70
  failure 732
decoy *attract* 288
  deceive 545
  deceiver 548
  entice 615
decrease 36, 195
decree
  judgment 480
  order 741
  law 963, 969
decrement
  decrease 36
  thing deducted 40a
  contraction 195
decrepit *old* 128
  weak 158, 160
  disease 655
  decayed 659
decrepitate 406
decrescendo 36
decretal 741
decry *underrate* 483
  censure 932
  detract 934
decumbent 213
decuple 98
decursive 306
decurtation 201
decussation 219
dedecorous
  disreputable 874
  discourteous 895
dedicate *use* 677
  inscribe 873
deduce *deduct* 38
  infer 480
deducible
  evidence 467

proof 478
deduct *retrench* 38
  deprive 789
  subtract 813
deduction
  [*see* deduce]
  decrement 40a
  reasoning 476
deed *evidence* 467
  record 551
  act 680
  security 771
  –s of arms 720
  – without a name
  947
deem 484
deemster 967
deep *great* 31
  profound 208
  sea 341
  sonorous 404
  cunning 702
  plough the – 267
  – colour 428
  – in debt 806
  – game 702
  – knowledge 490
  – mourning 839
  – note 408
  – potations 959
  – reflection 451
  – sense 821
  – sigh 839
  – study 457
  in – water 704
deepen 35
deep-dyed
  intense 171
  black 431
  vicious 945
deep-felt 821
deep-laid *plan* 626
deep-mouthed
  resonant 408
  bark 412
  thrilling 821
deep-musing 458
deep-read 490
deep-rooted
  stable 150
  strong 159
  belief 484
  habit 613
  affections 820
deep-sea 208
deep-seated 208,
  221
deer 366
  in heart a – 862
deev 980
deface

destroy form 241
  obliterate 552
  injure 659
  render ugly 846
defalcation
  incomplete 53
  contraction 195
  shortcoming 304
  non-payment 808
defame *shame* 874
  censure 932
  detract 934
defamer 936
defatigation 841
default
  incomplete 53
  shortcoming 304
  neglect 460
  insufficiency 640
  debt 806
  non-payment 808
  in – of 187
  judgment by – 725
defaulter *thief* 792
  non-payer 808
  rogue 949
defeasance 756
defeat
  confute 479
  succeed 731
  failure 732
  – one's hope 509
defeatism 911
defecate 652
defecation 299
defect
  decrement 40a
  incomplete 53
  imperfect 651
  failing 945
defection
  relinquishment
  624
  disobedience 742
defective
  incomplete 53
  insufficient 640
  imperfect 651
defence
  plea 462
  resist **717**
  vindication 937
  first line of – 726
defenceless
  impotent 158
  weak 160
  exposed 665
defendant 938
defensible *safe* 664
  excusable 937
defensive alliance

712

defer 133
 – to *assent* 488
    submit 725
    respect 928
deference
    obedience 743
    humility 879
    courtesy 894
    respect 928
defiance **715**, 909
    threat 909
in – *opposition* 708
set at – *disobey* 742
 – of danger 861
deficiency
    [see deficient]
    vice 945
deficient
    inferior 34
    incomplete 53
    shortcoming 304
    insufficient 640
    imperfect 651
deficit
    incompleteness 53
    debt 806
defigure 846
defile
    interval 198
    march 266
    dirt 653
    spoil 659
    shame 874
    impure 961
define
    specify 79
    limit 233
    explain 522
    name 564
definite
    [see define]
    visible 446
    certain 474
    exact 494
    intelligible 518
    manifest 525
    perspicuous 570
definition
    interpretation 522
definitive *final* 67
    affirmative 535
    decided 604
deflagration 384
deflate 195
deflation
    currency 800
deflect
    curve 245
    deviate 279
deflower

spoil 659
violate 961
defluxion
    egress 295
    flowing 348
defœdation 653,
    659
deform 241
deformity
    distortion 243
    ugliness 846
    blemish 848
defraud *cheat* 545
    swindle 791
defray 807
deft *suitable* 23
    clever 698
defunct 360, 362
defy 715
    disobey 742
    threaten 909
 – danger 861
dégagé *free* 748
    fashion 852
degenerate 659
deglutition 298
degradation
    deterioration 659
    shame 874
    dishonour 940
degree **26**
    term 71
    honour 873
by –s 26
by slow –s 275
degustation 390
dehiscence 260
dehort
    dissuade 616
    advise 695
dehydrate 340
Dei gratiâ 924
deification 873, 981
deify
    honour 873
    idolatry 991
deign
    condescend 762
    consent 879
Deism
    heterodoxy 984
    irreligion 989
Deity **976**
    tutelary – 664
dejection
    excretion 299
    melancholy **837**
déjeuner 298
délabrement 162
delaceration 659
delation 938

delator 527
delay 133
dele 552
delectable
    savoury 394
    agreeable 829
delectation 827
delectus 562
delegate
    transfer 270
    commission 755
    consignee 758
    deputy 759
delenda est
    Carthago
    destroy 162
    curse 908
delete 162
deleterious
    pernicious 649
    unwholesome 657
deletion 552
deletory
    destructive 162
deliberate
    slow 275
    think 451
    attentive 457
    leisure 685
    advise 695
    cautious 864
deliberately
    [see deliberate]
    late 133
    with premedi-
        tation 611
delicacy *weak* 160
    slender 203
    dainty 298
    brittleness 328
    texture 329
    savoury 394
    colour 428
    exact 494
    scruple 603
    ill health 655
    difficult 704
    pleasing 829
    beauty 845
    taste 850
    fastidious 868
    honour 939
    pure 960
    delicate ear 418
délice 377
delicious *taste* 394
    pleasing 829
delicti, corpus –
    guilt 947
    lawsuit 969
delicto, in

flagrante – 947
delight
    pleasure 827
    pleasing 829
Delilah 962
delimit 233
delineate
    outline 230
    represent 554
    describe 594
delineator 559
delineavit 556
delinquency 304,
    947
delinquent 949
deliquation 335
deliquesce 36
deliquescence 335
deliquium
    paralysis 158
    fatigue 688
delirant reges
    plectuntur
    Achivi 739
delirium
    raving 503
    passion 825
 – tremens 503,
    959
delitescence
    invisible 447
    latency 526
    seclusion 893
deliver
    transfer 270
    utter 580, 582
    birth 662
    rescue 672
    liberate 750
    give 784
    relieve 834
 – as one's act and
    deed 467
 – the goods 729
 – judgment 480
 – a speech 582
deliverance **672**
delivery
    [see deliver]
    bring forth 161
cash on – 807
dell 252
Delphic oracle
    prophetic 513
    equivocal 520
    latent 526
delta 342
delude *error* 495
    deceive 545
deluge *crowd* 72
    water 337

agree to – 489
beg to – 489
– in opinion 489
– toto cœlo
  contrary 14
  dissimilar 18
  dissent 489
difference 15
  [*see* differ]
  numerical 84
  perception of –
    465
  split the – 774
  – engine 85
different 15
  multiform 81
  – time **119**
differentia 15
differential 15, 84
  – calculus 85
differentiate 79, 465
differentiation
  calculation 85
  discrimination
    465
difficult 704
  – to please 868
difficulties
  poverty 804
  in – 806
difficulty 704
  question 461
diffide 485
diffident 860, 881
diffluent 348
diffraction 420
  – grating 445
diffuse *mix* 41
  disperse 73
  publish 531
  style 573
diffuseness 104, **573**
dig *deepen* 208
  excavate 252
  till 371
  – out 461
  – the foundations
    673
  – up 455, 480*a*
digamy 903
digest *arrange* 60
  boil 384
  think 451
  compendium 596
  plan 626
  prepare 673
  brook 826
diggings 189
dight *dress* 225
  ornament 847
digit 84

digitate 44
digitated 253
digladiation 720
dignify 873
dignitary
  clergy 996
dignity
  glory 873
  pride 878
  honour 939
dignus vindice
    nodus
  unintelligible 519
  difficulty 704
  prodigy 872
digress
  deviate 279
  style 573
digression
  circuit 629
dihedral 89
  – angle 244
dijudication 480
dike *gap* 198
  fence 232
  furrow 259
  gulf 343
  conduit 350
  defence 717
dilaceration 44
dilapidation 659
dilate
  increase 35
  swell 194
  widen 202
  rarefy 322
  expatiate 573
dilatory
  slow 275
  inactive 683
dilection 897
dilemma
  uncertain 475
  logic 476
  choice 609
  difficulty 704
dilettante 492, 850
dilettantism
  knowledge 490
diligence
  coach 272
diligent
  active 682
  – thought 457
dilly-dally
  irresolution 605
  inactivity 683
dilucidation 522
diluent 335
dilute *weaken* 160
  water 337

diluvian 124
dim *dark* 421
  faint 422
  invisible 447
  unintelligible 519
dime 800
dimension 192
dimidiate 91
diminish
  lessen 36
  contract 195
  – the number 103
diminutive 32, 193
diminuendo
  decreasingly 36
  music 415
dimness 422
dimple 252, 257
dimsightedness 443
  unwise 499
din 404
  – in the ear
  repeat 104
  drum 407
  loquacity 584
dine 298
  – with Duke
    Humphrey 87
ding 408
ding-dong
  repeat 104
  chime 407
dining-car 272
dining-room 191
dingle 252
dingy *boat* 273
  dark 421, 422
  colourless 429
  black 431
  gray 432
dinner 298
  – jacket 225
  – party 892
dint *power* 157
  concavity 252
  blow 276
  by – of
  instrumentality
    631
dio, sub – 220, 338
diocesan 996
diocese 181, 995
Diogenes
  recluse 893
  cynic 911
  lantern of –
  inquiry 461
dioptrics 420
diorama *view* 448
  painting 556
diorism 465

dip *slope* 217
  concavity 252
  ladle 270
  direction 278
  insert 300
  descent 306
  plunge 310
  water 337
  candle 423
  baptize 998
  – one's hands into
  take 789
  – into
  glance at 457
  inquire 461
  learn 539
diphthong 561
diploma
  evidence 467
  commission 755
diplomacy
  artfulness 702
  mediation 724
  negotiation 769
diplomatist
  messenger 534
  expert 700
  consignee 758
dipper 191
dipsomania
  insanity 503
  desire 865
  drunkenness 959
dipsomaniac 504
diptych 86, 551
dire *hateful* 649
  disastrous 735
  grievous 830
  fearful 860
direct
  straight 246
  teach 537
  artless 703
  command 741
  – attention to 457
  – one's course
  motion 278
  pursuit 622
  – the eyes to 441
direction
  [*see* direct]
  tendency **278**
  indication 550
  management **693**
  precept 697
directly *soon* 132
director
  teacher 540
  theatre 599
  manager **694**
  master 745

- of the budget
  801
directorship 737
directory *list* 86
  council 696
diremption 44
direption 791
dirge
  funeral 363
  song 415
  lament 839
dirigible balloon
  273, 726
dirk 727
dirt 653
  throw –
  defame 874
  disrespect 929
  – cheap 815
  like – under one's
  feet 749
dirty *dim* 422
  opaque 426
  unclean 653
  disreputable 874
  dishonourable 940
  – end of stick 699
  – sky 353
  – weather 349
  do – work
  servile 886
  flatterer 935
diruption 162
dis aliter visum
  disappointment
  509
  necessity 601
disability
  impotence 158
disable 158
  weaken 160
disabuse 527, 529
disaccord 713
disadvantage
  evil 619
  inexpedience 647
  at a – 34
  lie under a – 651
disadvantageous
  647, 649
disaffection
  dissent 489
  enmity 889
  hate 898
disaffirm 536
disagreeable 830,
  867
disagreement
  difference 15
  incongruity **24**
  dissent 489

discord 713
disallow 761
disannul 756
disappearance 449
disappointment
  balk **509**
  fail 732
  discontent 832
disapprobation 706,
  932
disapprover 936
disarm *disable* 158
  weaken 160
  reconcile 831
  propitiate 914
disarrange 61
disarray
  disorder 59
  undress 226
disaster *evil* 619
  failure 732
  adversity 735
  calamity 830
disastrous *bad* 649
disavow 536
disband
  separate 44
  disperse 73
  liberate 750
disbar
  abrogate 756
  punish 972
disbarment 55
disbelief 485, 487
  religious 989
disbench 756, 972
disbowel 297
disbranch 44
disburden
  facilitate 705
  – one's mind 529
  – oneself of 782
disburse 809
disc 220, 234
discard *eject* 297
  relinquish 624
  disuse 678
  abrogate 756
  refuse 764
  repudiate 773
  surrender 782
  – from one's
  thoughts 458
discarded 495
disceptation 476
discern *see* 441
  know 490
discernible 446
discernment 498,
  868
discerption 44

discharge
  violence 173
  propel 284
  emit 297
  excrete 299
  sound 406
  acquit oneself 692
  complete 729
  liberate 750
  abrogate 756
  pay 807
  exempt 927a
  acquit 970
  – a duty 926, 944
  – a function
  business 625
  utility 644
  – itself *egress* 295
  river 348
  – from the mem-
  ory 506
  – from the mind
  458
  – an obligation
  772
discind 44
disciple *pupil* 541
  votary 711
  Christian 985
disciplinarian
  master 540
  martinet 739
discipline
  order 58
  teaching 537
  training 673
  restraint 751
  punishment 972
  religious 990
disclaim *deny* 536
  repudiate 756
  abjure 757
  refuse 764
disclosure 480a, **529**
discoid *layer* 204
  frontal 220
  flat 251
discoloration 429
discoloured
  shabby 659
  ugly 846
  blemish 848
discomfit 731
discomfiture 732
discomfort
  physical 378
  mental 828
discommend 932
discommode
  hinder 706
  annoy 830

discommodious
  645, 647
discompose
  derange 61
  put out 458
  hinder 706
  pain 830
  disconcert 874
  anger 900
discomposure 828
disconcert
  derange 61
  distract 458
  disappoint 509
  hinder 706
  discontent 832
  confuse 879
disconcerted
  hopeless 859
disconformity 83
discongruity 24
disconnected
  style 575
disconnection
  irrelation 10
  disjunction 44
  discontinuity 70
disconsolate 837
discontent **832**
discontinuance
  cessation 142
  relinquishment
  624
discontinuity **70**
discord
  difference 15
  disagreement 24
  of sound **414**
  of colour 428
  dissension **713**
discount
  decrease 36
  decrement 40a
  money **813**
  at a –
  disrepute 874
  disapproved 932
discountenance
  disfavour 706
  refuse 764
discourage
  dissuade 616
  sadden 837
  frighten 860
discourse
  teach 537
  speech 582
  talk 588
  dissert 595
  sermon 998
discourtesy **895**

discous 202
discover
perceive 441
solve 462
find 480*a*
disclose 529
– *itself*
be seen 446
discovery 480*a*
discredit
disbelief 485
dishonour 874
discreditable
vicious 945
discreet *careful* 459
cautious 864
discrepancy 15
discrepant 24, 713
discrete
separate 44, 70
single 87
discretion *will* 600
choice 609
skill 698
caution 864
surrender at – 725
use – 609
years of – 131
discrétion à – 600
discrimination
difference 15
nice perception
465
wisdom 498
taste 850
fastidiousness 868
disculpate 937
discumbency 213
discursion 266
discursive
moving 264
migratory 266
wandering 279
argumentative 476
diffuse style 573
conversable 588
disserting 595
discus 840
discuss *eat* 298
reflect 451
inquire 461
reason 476
dissert 595
discussion
[see discuss]
open to – 475
under – 461
disdain
indifference 866
fastidious 868
arrogance 885

pride 878
contempt 930
disease **655**
occupational – 655
–d mind 503
disembark 292
disembarrass 705
disembody
decompose 49
disperse 73
spiritualize 317
disembogue
emit 295
eject 297
flow out 348
disembowel 297,
301
disembroil 60
disenable 158
disenchant
discover 480*a*
dissuade 616
displease 830
disencumber 705
disendow 756
disengage
detach 44
facilitate 705
liberate 750
disengaged
to let 763
disentangle
separate 44
arrange 60
unroll 313
decipher 522
facilitate 705
liberate 750
disenthral 750
disenthrone 756
disentitle 925
disespouse 905
disestablish
displace 185
abrogate 756
disesteem 929, 932
disfavour
oppose 708
hate 898
disrespect 929
view with – 932
disfigure
deface 241
injure 659
deform 846
blemish 848
disfranchise 925
disgorge *emit* 297
flow out 348
restore 790
pay 807

disgrace
shame 874
dishonour 940
sense of – 879
disgraceful
vice 945
disgruntle 509
disguise
unlikeness 18
conceal 528
mask 530
falsify 544
untruth 546
disguised in drink
959
disgust *taste* 395
offensive 830
weary 841
dislike 867
hatred 898
– of life 837
dish *destroy* 162
plate 191
food 298
– of tea 892
dishabille
undress 226
unprepared 674
dishearten
dissuade 616
pain 830
discontent 832
deject 837
dished 252, 732
disherison 789
dishevel
loose 47
untidy 59
disorder 61
disperse 73
intermix 219
dishonest *false* 544
base 940
dishonour
disrepute 874
disrespect 929
baseness 940
– bills 808
dish-water 653
disillusion 509
disincline
dissuade 616
dislike 867
disinclined 603
disinfect
purify 652
restore 660
disinfectant 662
disingenuous
false 544
dishonourable 940

disinherit
relinquish 782
transfer 783
deprive 789
disintegrate
separate 44
decompose 49
pulverize 330
disinter *exhume* 363
discover 480*a*
disinterested **942**
disjecta membra
separate 44
disorder 59
dispersed 73
– poetæ 597
disjoin 44
disjointed
disorder 59
powerless 158
style 575
disjunction **44**
disjunctive 70
diskindness 907
dislike **867**
reluctance 603
hate 898
dislocate
separate 44
put out of joint 61
dislocated
disorder 59
dislodge
displace 185
eject 297
disloyal 940
dismal
depressing 830
dejected 837
dismantle
destroy 162
divest 226
render useless 645
injure 659
disuse 678
dismask 529
dismast
render useless 645
injure 659
disuse 678
dismay 860
dismember
separate 44
disperse 73
dismiss
send away 289
discharge 297
discard 678
liberate 750
abrogate 756
relinquish 782

punish 972
– from the mind
452, 458
dismount
arrive 292
descend 306
render useless 645
disnest 185
disobedience 742
non-observance
773
disoblige 907
disorder
confusion **59**
derange 61
turbulent 173
disease 655
–ed intellect 503
disorderly
unprincipled 945
disorganize
derange 61
destroy 162
spoil 659
disorganized 59
disown 536
dispair 44
disparage
underrate 483
disrespect 929
dispraise 932
detract 934
disparity
different 15
dissimilar 18
disagreeing 24
unequal 28
isolated 44
dispart 44
dispassionate 826
– opinion 484
dispatch
[*see* despatch]
dispel *scatter* 73
destroy 162
displace 185
repel 289
dispensable
useless 645
dispensary 662
dispensation
[*see* dispense]
command 741
licence 760
relinquishment
782
exemption 927a
–s of Providence
976
dispense
disperse 73

give 784
apportion 786
retail 796
– with
disuse 678
permit 760
exempt 927a
cannot be –d with
630
dispeople
eject 297
expatriate 893
disperse
separate 44
scatter 73
diverge 291
waste 638
dispersion 73
– of light 420
chromatic – 428
dispirit
discourage 616
sadden 837
displacement
derange 61
remove **185**
transfer 270
displacency
dislike 867
incivility 895
disapprobation
932
displant 185
display *appear* 448
show 525
parade 882
displease 830
displeasure 828
anger 900
displosion 173
displume 789
disport 840
disposal
[*see* dispose]
at one's – 763, 777
dispose
arrange 60
tend 176
induce 615
– of *use* 677
complete 729
relinquish 782
give 784
sell 796
disposed 620
disposition
nature 5
order 58
arrangement 60
inclination 602
mind 820

dispossess
transfer 783
take away 789
– oneself of 782
dispraise 932
dispread 73
disprize 483
disproof
counter-evidence
468
confutation 479
disproportion
irrelation 10
disagreement 24
disprove 479
disputable 475, 485
disputant 710, 726
disputatious 901
dispute
discuss 476
doubt 485
deny 536
discord 713
in – 461
disqualification
incapacitate 158
useless 645
unprepared 674
unskilful 699
disentitle 925
disquiet
changeable 149
agitation 315
excitement 825
uneasiness 828
give pain 830
disquietude
apprehension 860
disquisition 539,
595
disregard
overlook 458
neglect 460
make light of 483
insensible to 823,
826
disrespect **929**
contempt 930
– of time 115
disrelish 867, 898
disreputable 874
vicious 945
disrepute **874,** 929
disrespect **929**
despise 930
disrobe 226
disruption
disjunction 44
destruction 162
discord 713
dissatisfaction

disappointment
509
sorrow 828
discontent 832
dissect
anatomize 44, 49
investigate 461
dissemblance 18
dissemble 544
dissembler 548
disseminate
scatter 73
pervade 186
publish 531
teach 537
dissension 713
sow – 898
dissent
disagree **489**
refuse 764
heterodoxy 984
dissentient 15
dissentious 24
dissertation **595**
disservice
disadvantage 619
useless 645
disserviceable 649
dissever 44
dissidence
disagreement 24
dissent 489
discord 713
discontent 832
heterodoxy 984
dissilience 173
dissimilarity **18**
dissimulate 544
dissipate *scatter* 73
destroy 162
pleasure 377
prodigality 818
amusement 840
intemperance 954
dissolute 961
dissocial 893
dissociate 44
dissociation
irrelation 10
separation 44
dissolute 961
profligate 945
intemperate 954
dissolution
[*see* dissolve]
decomposition 49
destruction 162
death 360
dissolve *vanish* 2, 4
liquefy 335
disappear 449

abrogate 756
dissolving views
448, 449
dissonance
disagreement 24
unmusical 414
discord 713
dissuasion 616
dissyllable 561
distaff
– side 374
distain *dirty* 653
ugly 846
distal 196
distance 196
overtake 282
go beyond 303
defeat 731
angular – 244
keep at a –
discourtesy 895
keep one's –
avoid 623
modest 881
respect 928
teach one his – 879
– of time
long time 110
past 122
distaste 867
distasteful 830
distemper 299, 428
colour 428
painting 556
disease 655
distend 194
distended 192
distich 89, 597
distil *come out* 295
extract 301
evaporate 336
drop 348
distinct
disjoined 44
audible 402
visible 446
intelligible 518
manifest 525
express 535
articulate 580
distinction
difference 15
discrimination
465
style 578
fame 873
rank 875
– without a differ-
ence 27
distinctive 15
– feature 79

distinctness 15
distingué 852, 873
distinguish
perceive 441
discriminate 465
– by the name of
564
distinguishable 15
distinguished
superior 33
repute 873
Distinguished
Service Cross
733
distortion
obliquity 217
twist **243**
of vision 443
misinterpret 523
falsehood 544
misrepresent 555
ugly 846
distract 458
distracted
confused 475
insane 503
excited 824
distraction
passion 825
love to – 897
distrain *take* 789
appraise 812
attach 969
distrait 458
distraught 824
distress
distraint 789
poverty 804
affliction 828
cause pain 830
signal of – 669
distressingly
excessively 31
distribute
arrange 60
disperse 44, 73
allot 786
district 181
– council 696
distrust
disbelief 485
fear 860
distrustful 487
disturb
derange 61
change 140
agitate 315
excite 824
distress 828, 830
disturbance 59
disunion

discord 24
separation 44
disorder 59
discord 713
disuse
desuetude 614
relinquish 624
unemploy **678**
disused
old 124
disvalue 932
ditch
inclosure 232
trench 259
water 343
conduit 350
defence 717
to the last – 606
ditch-water 653
ditheism 984
dither 315
dithyramb
music 415
poetry 597
dithyrambic 503
ditto 13, 104
say – to 488
ditty 415
– box 191
diurnal 138
diuturnity 110
diva 416
divagate 279, 629
divan *sofa* 215
council 696
throne 747
tribunal 966
divaricate *differ* 15
bifurcate 91
diverge 291
dive *swim* 267
fly 267
plunge 306, 310
– into *inquire* 461
divellicate 44
diver 208
divergence
difference 15
variation 20a
disagreement 24
deviation 279
separation **291**
divers *different* 15
multiform 81
many 102
– coloured 440
diverse 15
diversify
very 20a
change 140
diversion

change 140
deviation 279
pleasure 377
amusement 840
diversity
difference 15
irregular 16a
dissimilar 18
multiform 81
– of opinion 489
divert *turn* 279
deceive 545
amuse 840
– the mind 452,
458
divertissement
diversion 377
drama 599
amusement 840
Dives 803
divest *denude* 226
take 789
– oneself of
abrogate 756
relinquish 782
divestment 226
divide *differ* 15
separate 44
part 51
arrange 60
arithmetic 85
bisect 91
vote 609
apportion 786
dividend *part* 51
number 84
portion 786
divina particula
auræ 450
divination
prediction 511
sorcery 992
divine *predict* 511
guess 514
perfect 650
of God 976, 983,
983a
clergyman 996
divine afflatus 515
– right
authority 737
due 924
– service 990
diving 840
diving-bell 208
divining-rod 550,
993
Divinity *God* 976
theology 983
divisible
number 84

division
[*see* divide]
part 51
class 75
arithmetic 85
discord 713
military 726
divisor 84
divorce
separation 44
relinquish 782
matrimonial **905**
Divorce Court 966
divulge 529
divulsion 44
divvy 786
dixi 535
dizen 847
dizzard 501
dizzy
dimsighted 443
confused 458
vertigo 503
– height 206
– round 312
djerrid 727
djinn 980
do *fare* 7
suit 23
produce 161
cheat 545
act 680
complete 729
succeed 731
I beg 765
all one can – 686
plenty to – 682
thing to – 625
– away with
destroy 162
eject 297
abrogate 756
– battle 722
– one's bidding
743
– business 625
– to death 361
– as done by 906,
942
– for *destroy* 162
kill 361
conquer 731
serve 746
punish 972
– good 906
– harm 907
– honour 873
– into
translate 522
– justice to 595
– like 19

– little 683
– no harm 648
– nothing 681
– nothing but 136
– one's office 772
– as others do 82
– over 223
– as one pleases
748
– a service
useful 644
aid 707
– up 660
have to – with
680, 692
– without 678
– the work 686
– wrong 923
docere, pisces na-
tare – 641
docile *domesticated*
370
learning 539
willing 602
docimastic 463
dock *diminish* 36
cut off 38
port 189
shorten 201
edge 231
store 636
tribunal 966
docked
incomplete 53
docker 690
docket
list 86
evidence 467
note 550
record 551
security 771
dockyard 691
doctor
learned man 492
restore 660
remedy 662
after death the –
135
– accounts 811
when –s disagree
475
doctrinaire
positive 474
pedant 492
affectation 855
blusterer 887
doctrinal 537
doctrinarian 514
doctrine *tenet* 484
knowledge 490
document 551

documentary
evidence 467
dodder 315
doddering 128
dodecahedron 244
dodge *change* 140
shift 264
deviate 279
oscillate 314
pursue 461
avoid 623
stratagem 702
dodger, artful – 792
dodo 366
extinct as the –
122
Doe, John 4
doe *swift* 274
deer 366
female 374
doer
originator 164
agent 690
doff 226
– the cap 894
dog *follow* 281
animal 366
male 373
pursue 622
wretch 949
cast to the –s
reject 610
disuse 678
abrogate 756
relinquish 782
fire – 386
go to the –s
destruction 162
fail 732
adversity 735
poverty 804
sea – 269
watch –
safety 664
warning 668
keeper 753
hair of – that bit
you 959
let sleeping –s lie
141
– in manger 706,
943
–tired 688
–s of war 722
dog-cart 272
dog-cheap 815
dog-days 382
doge 745
dogged
obstinate 606
valour 861

sullen 901a
dogger 273
doggerel
verse 597
ridiculous 851,
853
dog-hole 189
dog Latin 563
dogma *tenet* 484
theology 983
dogmatic
certain 474
positive 481
assertion 535
obstinate 606
dogmatist 887
dog's ear 258
dog robber 746
dog-sick 867
dog-star 423
dog-trot 275
dog-weary 688
doily 652
doing
up and – 682
what one is – 625
doings
events 151
actions 680
conduct 692
doit *trifle* 643
coin 800
dolce far niente 681
doldrums
dejection 837
sulks 901a
dole
small quantity 32
scant 640
give 784
allot 786
parsimony 819
grief 828
doleful 837
– dumps 901a
doll *small* 193
image 554
dollar 800
dolman 225
dolmen 363, 551
dolorem, infandum
renovare – 833
dolorous 830
dolour
physical 378
moral 828
dolphin 341
dolt 501
doltish 499
domain
class 75

region 181
property 780
Domdaniel 982
dome *high* 206
  roof 223
  curvature 245
  convex 250
Domesday book
  list 86
  record 551
domesman 967
domestic
  inhabitant 188
  home 189
  interior 221
  servant 746
  secluded 893
  – *animals* 366
domesticate
  locate 184
  acclimatize 613
  – *animals* 370
domicile 189
domiciled 186
domiciliary 188
  – *visit* 461
dominant 175
  note in music 413
domination 737
dominical 998
domineer
  tyrannize 739
  insolence 885
Domini, anno – 106
Dominican 996
Dominie 540
dominion 181, 737
domino *dress* 225
  mask 530
  game 840
domn 745
don *put on* 225
  scholar 492
  teacher 540
  noble 875
Don Juan 897
donation 784
done *finished* 729
  work – 729
  – for *spoilt* 659
  failure 732
  – up
    impotent 158
    tired 688
  have – with
    cease 142
    relinquish 624
    disuse 678
donee 785
donjon 717, 752
donkey *ass* 271

fool 501
  talk a –'s hind leg
    off 584
donna 374
Donnybrook Fair
  disorder 59
  discord 713
donor 784
donzel 746
doodle 501
doom *end* 67
  fate 152
  destruction 162
  death 360
  judgment 480
  necessity 601
  sentence 971
  – sealed
    death 360
    adversity 735
doomed 735, 828
doomsday
  end 67
  future 121
  till – 112
door *entrance* 66
  cover 223
  brink 231
  barrier 232
  opening 260
  passage 627
  at one's – 197
  beg from door to –
    765
  bolt the – 666
  close the – upon
    751
  death's – 360
  keep within –s 265
  lie at one's – 926
  lock the – 666
  open a – to
    liable 177
  open the – to
    receive 296
    facilitate 705
    permit 760
  show the – to
    eject 297
    discourtesy 895
  – mat 652
doorkeeper 263
doorway 260
dope 376, 545, 663
doquet
  security 771
Dorado, El – 803
Doric mode 413
dormant
  inert 172
  latent 526

asleep 683
dormer 260
dormeuse 272
dormir debout,
  conte à – 843
dormitive 841
dormitory 191
dormouse 683
dorp 189
dorsal 235
dorser 191
dorsum 235, 250
dory 273
dose *quantity* 25
  part 51
  medicine 662
  apportion 786
dosser 191
dossier *bundle* 72
  record 551
dossil 223, 263
dot *small* 32
  place 182
  little 193
  variegate 440
  mark 550
  dowry 780
  on the – 113
dotage 128, 499
dotard 130, 501
dotation 784
dottle 40, 645
dote *drivel* 499, 503
  – upon 897
douanier 965
double
  similar 17
  increase 35
  duplex 90
  substitute 147
  fold 258
  turn 283
  finesse 702
  march at the – 274
  see –
    dim sight 443
    drunk 959
  – acrostic
    letters 561
    wit 842
  – dutch 519
  – entry 811
  – the fist 909
  – march 684
  – meaning 520
  – a point 311
  in – quick time
    274
  – reef topsails 664
  – sure 474
  work – tides 686

– up
  render powerless
  158
double bar 747
double-bass 417
doublecross 545
double-dealing
  lie 544
  cunning 940
double-distilled 171
double-dyed 428
double-eagle 800
double-edged 90,
  171
double entendre
  ambiguity 520
  impure 961
double-faced
  lie 544
  cunning 702, 940
double-headed 90
double-minded 605
double-shotted 171
doublet 225
double-tongued
  lie 544
  cunning 702, 940
doubt
  uncertain 475
  disbelieve **485**
  sceptic 989
doubtful 475
  more than – 473
  – meaning
    unintelligible 519
doubtless
  certain 474
  belief 484
  assent 488
douceur 784, 973
douche 337
dough 324, 354, 800
doughty 861
dour 739
douse
  immerse 310
  splash 337
  blow 972
Dove
  Holy Ghost 976
dove
  innocent 946
  roar like sucking –
    174
dovecote 189
dovetail
  agree 23
  join 43
  intersect 219
  intervene 228
  angle 244

write 590
- up a statement 594
- upon *money* 800
- the veil 528
drawback *evil* 619
  imperfection 651
  hindrance 706
  discount 813
drawbar 45
drawbridge
  way 627
  escape 671
  raise the – 666
drawcansir 887
drawee 800
drawer
  receptacle 191
  artist 559
  – of water 690
drawers
  dress 225
drawhead 45
drawing
  delineation 554, 556
  prize 810
drawing-room
  assembly 72
  room 191
  fashion 852
drawl *prolong* 200
  creep 275
  in speech 583
  sluggish 683
drawn *equated* 27
  – battle
  – irresistibly 601
  pacification 723
  incomplete 730
dray 272
  – horse 271
drayman 268
dread 860
dreadful *great* 31
  bad 649
  dire 830
  depressing 837
  fearful 860
dreadless 861
dreadnought
  warship 726
dream
  unsubstantial 4
  error 495
  fancy 515
  sleep 683
  golden – 858
  – of *think* 451
  intend 620
  – on other things

458
dreamer
  madman 504
  imaginative 515
dreamy
  unsubstantial 4
  inattentive 458
  sleepy 683
dreary
  monotonous 16
  solitary 87
  melancholy 830, 837
dredge *collect* 72
  extract 301
  raise 307
dregs
  remainder 40
  refuse 645
  dirt 653
  – of the people 876
  – of vice 945
drench *drink* 298
  water 337
  redundance 641
  – with physic 662
drencher 248
drenching rain 348
dress
  uniformity 16
  agree 23
  equalize 27
  clothes 225
  prepare 673
  ornament 847
  ostentation 882
  full – 852
  – circle 599
  – the ground 371
  – up *falsehood* 544
  represent 554
  – wounds 662
  – to advantage 847
dress-coat 225
dresser
  sideboard 215
  surgeon 662
dressing 932, 972
  – room 191, 599
dressing-gown 225
dressmaker 225
dribble 295, 348
driblet 25, 32
drift
  accumulate 72
  distance 196
  motion 264
  flying 267
  float 267
  transfer 270

  direction 278
  deviation 279
  approach 286
  wind 349
  meaning 516
  intention 620
  snow – 383
drifter 273
drifting 605
driftless 621
drill *fabric* 219
  bore 260
  auger 262
  teach 537
  prepare 673
  – hall 191
drink
  swallow 296
  liquor 298
  tipple 959
  – one's fill
  enough 639
  – in *imbibe* 296, 298
  – in learning 539
  – to *celebrate* 883
  courtesy 894
drinking-bout 954
drink-money 784
drip 295, 348
dripping *wet* 339
  fat 356
drive *airing* 266
  impel 276
  propel 284
  break in 370
  urge 615
  haste 684
  direct 693
  attack 716
  compel 744
  – at *mean* 516
  intend 620
  – a bargain
  barter 794
  parsimony 819
  – care away 836
  – a coach and six
  through 83
  – into a corner
  difficult 704
  hinder 706
  defeat 731
  subjection 749
  – to despair 859
  – matters to an extremity 604
  – from *repel* 289
  – one hard 716
  – home 729
  – in 300

  – to the last 133
  – out 297
  – trade
  business 625
  barter 794
drivel *slobber* 297
  imbecile 499
  mad 503
  rubbish 517
driveller 501, 584
driver 268
  director 694
driving rain 348
drizzle 348
droil 683
droit du plus fort 744
drôle *cards* 840
drôle 949
  – de corps 844
drollery
  amusement 840
  wit 842
  ridiculous 853
dromedary 271
drone *slow* 275
  sound 407, 412, 413
  inactive 683
drool 297
droop
  weak 160
  hang 214
  sink 306
  disease 655
  decline 659
  flag 688
  sorrow 828
  dejection 837
drop *small quantity* 32
  discontinue 142
  powerless 158
  bring forth 161
  spherule 249
  emerge 295
  fall 306
  trickle 348
  relinquish 624
  discard 782
  gallows 975
  let – 308
  ready to –
  fatigue 688
  – asleep 683
  – astern 283
  – from the clouds 508
  – dead 360
  – by drop
  by degrees 26

in parts 51
– in the bucket 32
– in upon 674
– into a good
   thing 734
– into the grave
   360
– a hint 527
– all idea of 624
– in *arrive* 292
immerse 300
sociality 892
– the mask 529
– off *decrease* 36
die 360
sleep 683
– in the ocean
trifling 643
– the subject 458
– too much 959
dropping fire 70
drop-scene 599
dropsical 194, 641
droshki 272
dross
remainder 40
slag 384
trash 643, 645
dirt 653
drought
dryness 340
insufficiency 640
drouth *desire* 865
drove
assemblage 72
multitude 102
drover 370
drown
affusion 337
kill 361
ruin 731, 732
– *care* 840
– the voice 581
drowsy *slow* 275
sleepy 683
weary 841
drub
defeat 731, 732
punish 972
drudge *labour* 686
worker 682, 690
drug
render insensible
   376
superfluity 641
trash 643
remedy 662
bane 663
– in the market
   815
drugget

cover 223
clean 652
preserve 670
druggist 662
druid 996
drum
repeat 104
cylinder 249
sound 407
music 417
party 892
beat of –
signal 550
alarm 669
war 722
command 741
parade 882
ear – 418
muffled –
funeral 363
non-resonance
   408a
– and fife band 417
– fire 407
– out 972
drum-head 964,
   966
drum-major 745
drummer 416
drunken 959
reel like a – man
   315
drunkenness 959
dry *arid* 340
style 575, 576, 579
hoarse 581
scanty 640
preserve 670
exhaust 789
tedious 841
dull 842
thirsty 865
cynical 932
teetotal 958
run – 640
with – eyes 823
– dock 189
– joke 842
– land 342
– the tears 834
– up 340, 638
dryad 979
dry-as-dust
antiquarian 122
dull 843
dryness 340
dry-nurse
teach 537
teacher 540
aid 707
dry-point 558

dry-rot
dirt 653
decay 659
bane 663
dualism 984
duality 89
duarchy 737
dub 564
dubious 475
ducat 800
duce 745
duchess 745, 875
duchy 181
duck *stoop* 308
plunge 310
water 337
darling 897, 899
play –s and
   drakes
recoil 277
prodigality 818
–'s egg
zero 101
– in thunder 870
ducking-stool 975
duckling 129
duck-pond 370
duct 350
ductile
elastic 325
flexible 324
trimming 607
easy 705
docile 743
dud 158, 727
dude 854
duds 225
dudgeon
dagger 727
discontent 832
churlishness 895
hate 898
anger 900
sullenness 901a
due
expedient 646
owing 806
proper 924, 926
give his – to
right 922
vindication 937
fair 939
in – course 109
occasion 134
– respect 928
– sense of 498
– time
soon 132
– to
cause and effect
   154, 155

give – weight 465
duel 720
duellist 726
dueness 924
duenna
teacher 540
guardian 664
keeper 753
dues 812
duet 415
duff 298
duffer
bungler 701
smuggler 792
dug 250
dug-out
old man 130
boat 273
defence 717
duke *ruler* 745
noble 875
dulce domum 189
dulcet
sweet 396
sound 405
melodious 413
agreeable 829
dulcify 174, 396
dulcimer 417
Dulcinea 897
dulcorate 396
dulia 990
dull *weak* 160
inert 172
moderate 174
blunt 254
insensible 376,
   381
sound 405
dim 422
colourless 429
ignorant 493
stolid 499
style 575
inactive 683
unapt 699
callous 823
dejected 837
weary 841
prosing 843
simple 849
– of hearing 419
– sight 443
dullard 501
dullness 843
duly 924
duma 696
dumb 581
– animal 366
– show 550
– waiter 307

strike –
ignorant 493
astonish 870
humble 879
dumbfounder
disappoint 509
silence 581
astonish 870
humble 879
dummy
substitute 147
impotent 158
speechless 581
inactive 683
dump *music* 415
store 636
lament 839
undersell 796
dumpling 298
dumps
discontent 832
dejection 837
sulk 901a
dumpy *little* 193
short 201
thick 202
dun *dim* 422
colourless 429
grey 432
importune 765
creditor 805
dunce
ignoramus 493
fool 501
dunderhead 501
dune 206
dung 653
dungeon 752
dunghill
dirt 653
cowardly 862
baseborn 876
– cock 366
Dunker 984
dunt 716
duo 415
duodecimal 99
duodecimo
little 193
book 593
duodenary 98
duologue
interlocution 588
drama 599
dupe
credulous 486
deceive 545
deceived **547**
duplex 90, 189
duplicate
imitate 19

copy 21
double 90
tally 550
record 551
redundant 641
pawn 805
duplication
imitation 19
doubling **90**
repetition 104
duplicature
fold 258
duplicity
duality 89
falsehood 544
dura lex sed lex 926
durable
long time 110
stable 150
durance 141, 751
in – 754
duration 106
contingent – **108a**
infinite – 112
durbar
conference 588
council 696
tribunal 966
duress
compulsion 744
restraint 751
during 106
– *pleasure &c.*
108a
durity 323
dusk
evening 126
half-light 422
dusky
dark 421
black 431
dust *levity* 320
powder 330
corpse 362
trash 643
dirt 653
money 800
come to –
die 360
come down with
the – 807
humbled in the –
879
kick up a – 885
level with the –
162
lick the –
submit 725
fail 732
make to bite the –
731

turn to –
deorganized 358
die 360
– in the balance
643
throw – in the
eyes
blind 442
deceive 545
plead 617
– one's jacket 972
duster 652
dust-bin, dust-hole
191, 645
fit for the –
useless 645
dirty 653
spoilt 659
dustman 653
cleaner 652
dust-storm 330
dusty
powder 330
dirt 653
Dutch
double – 519
high – 519
– auction 796
– courage 862
Dutchman, flying
515
dutiful 944
duty
business 625
work 686
tax 812
courtesy 894
obligation **926**
respect 928
worship 990
rite 998
do one's –
virtue 944
on – 680, 682
duumvirate 737
Duval, Claude –
792
D.V. 470, 976
dwarf
lessen 36
small 193
elf 980
dwell
reside 186
abide 265
– upon
descant 573
dweller 188
dwelling 184, 189
dwindle *lessen* 36
shrink 195

dyad 89
dye 428
dying 360
dyke [*see* dike]
dynamic energy
157
dynamics 276
dynamitard 863
dynamite 727
dynamo 153
dynasty 737
dysentery 299
dyspepsia 655
dysphony 581

E

each 79
– to each 786
– other 12
– in his turn 148
eager
willing 602
active 682
ardent 821
desirous 865
– *expectation* 507
eagle
standard 550
money 800
– boat 726
– eye *sight* 441
intelligence 498
– winged *swift* 274
insignia 747
eagre 348
ean 161
ear 418
corn 154
come to one's –s
527
din in the –
loud 404
drum 407
all – 418
have the – of
belief 484
friendship 888
lend an –
hear 418
attend 457
meet the – 418
nice – 418
no – 419
offend the – 410
pick up the –s
attention 457
expectation 507
put about one's –s
308

quick – 418
reach one's –s 527
ring in the – 408
set by the –s
  discord 713
  hate 898
  resentment 900
split the –s 404
together by the –s
  discord 713
  contention 720
up to one's –s
  redundance 641
  active 680, 682
willing – 602
word in the – 586
– for music 416,
  418
in at one – out at
  the other
  inattention 458
  forget 506
not for –s polite
  961
make the –s tingle
  anger 900
– ache 378
ear-drum 418
earl 875
earless 419
earliness 132
early 132
get up – 682
earmark 550
earn 775
earnest *willing* 602
  determined 604
  emphatic 642
  pledge 771
  pay in advance
  809
  eager 821
in –
  affirmation 535
  veracious 543
  strenuous 682
ear-piercing 410
ear-ring 847
ear-shot 197
out of – 405
ear-splitting 404
earth *ground* 211
  world 318
  land 342
  corpse 362
what on –
  inquiry 461
  wonder 870
– closet 653
earthenware
  baked 384

sculpture 557
earthling 372
earthly 318
end of one's –
  career 360
of no – use 645
earthly-minded
  943, 989
earthquake 146,
  173
earthwork 717
earwig *flatter* 933,
  935
ear-witness 467
ease *bodily* 377
  style 578
  leisure 685
  facility 705
  mental 827
  content 831
at one's –
  prosperous 734
mind at –
  cheerful 836
set at – *relief* 834
take one's – 687
– off *deviate* 297
– one of *take* 789
easel *support* 215
  painting 556
– picture 556
easement
  property 780
  relief 834
easily
  [*see easy*]
let one down – 918
– accomplished
  705
– deceived 486
– persuaded 602
East 236, 278
Easter *period* 138
  rite 998
– Monday
  holiday 840
– offering
  gift 784
– sepulchre 1000
easy *gentle* 275
  style 578
  facile 705
make oneself –
  about 484
take it –
  inactive 683
  inexcitable 826
– ascent 217
– of belief 472
– chair
  support 215

repose 687
– circumstances
  803
– going
  willing 602
  irresolute 605
  lenient 740
  inexcitable 826
  contented 831
  indifferent 866
– sail
  moderate 174
  slow 275
– temper 894
– terms 705
– to understand
  518
– virtue 961
eat *food* 298
  tolerate 826
– dirt 725, 879
– one's fill
  enough 639
  gorge 957
– heartily 298
– one's words 879
– out of house and
  home *take* 789
  prodigal 818
  gluttony 957
– of the same
  trencher 892
– one's words 607
eatables 298
eaten up with 820
eau, battre l' – 645
faire venir l' – à la
  bouche 865
mettre de l' – dans
  son vin 174
eaves 250
eavesdropper 455,
  527
eavesdropping 418,
  532
ébauche 626
ebb *decrease* 36
  contract 195
  regress 283
  recede 287
  waste 638
  spoil 659
low – 36
  low 207
  depression 308
  insufficient 640
– and flow 314
– of life 360
ebb-tide *low* 207
  dry 340
ebony 431

ebriety 959
ebullient
  violent 173
  hot 382
  excited 824
ebullition
  energy 171
  violence 173
  agitation 315
  heating 384
  excitation 825
  anger 900
écarté 840
ecce
  – iterum Crispinus
  104
  – signum 550
eccentric 220
  irregular 83
  foolish 499
  crazed 503, 504
  capricious 608
ecchymosis 299
ecclesiastic
  church 995
  clergy 996
ecclesiastical
  canonical 985
  – court 966
  – law 963
ecclesiolatry 991
écervelé 458
échafaudage 673
échappée 840
échapper belle 671
échelon 279
echo *imitate* 19
  copy 21
  repeat 104
  reflection 277
  resonance 408
  answer 462
  assent 488
  applaud to the –
  931
awake –es 404
éclaircissement 522
éclat 873
eclectic 609
eclipse *surpass* 33
  disappearance
  449
  hide 528
  outshine 873, 874
partial – *dim* 422
total – *dark* 421
under an –
  invisible 447
  out of repute 874
ecliptic 318
eclogue 597

Column 1 (ELB)

drink 959
out at –s
  undress 226
  poor 804
  disrepute 874
– one's way
  progress 282
  pursuit 622
  active 682
elbow-chair 215
elbow-grease 331
elbow-room 180,
  748
elder *older* 124
  aged 128
  veteran 130
  clergy 996
elect *choose* 609
  good 648
  predestinate 976
  pious 987
  clergy 996
election
  numerical 84
  necessity 601
electioneering 609
elector 745
electorate 737
Electra complex
  897
electric
  swift 274
  sensation 821
  excitable 825
  car 272
– blue 438
– chair 974
– light 423
– piano 417
electrician 599, 690
electricity 157, 388
electrify
  unexpected 508
  excite 824
  astonish 870
electro-biology 992
electrocution 972
electrolier 214, 423
electrolyze 49
electro-magnetism
  157
electromobile 272
electron 32
electroplate 223
electrotype 21, 591
electuary 662
eleemosynary 784
elegance
  in style 578
  beauty 845
  taste 850

Column 2 (ELI)

Bank of – 800
elegy *interment* 363
  poetry 597
  lament 839
element
  component 56
  beginning 66
  cause 153
  matter 316
  in one's –
  facility 705
  content 831
  devouring – 382
  out of its – 195
elementary 42
– education 537
– school 542
elements
  Eucharist 998
elench 477
elephant
  large 192
  carrier 271
  white – *bane* 663
elevated
  tipsy 959
elevation
  height 206
  vertical 212
  raising **307**
  plan 554
– of style 574
  improvement 658
  glory 873
– of mind 942
  angular – 244
élève 541
eleven 98
  representative 759
eleventh hour
  evening 126
  late 133
  opportune 134
elf *infant* 129
  little 193
  imp 980
elicit *cause* 153
  draw out 301
  discover 480a
  manifest 525
eligible 646
Elijah's mantle 63
eliminant 299
eliminate
  subduct 38
  simplify 42
  exclude 55
  weed 103
  extract 301
  reject 610
elision 44, 201

Column 3 (EMB)

élite *best* 648
  distinguished 873
  aristocratic 875
elixation 384
elixir 662
– of life 471
elk 223
ell 200
  take an –
  take 789
  insolence 885
  wrong 923
  undue 925
  selfish 943
ellipse 247
ellipsis *shorten* 201
  style 572
ellipsoid 247, 249
elocation 185, 270
elocution 582
éloge 931
elongation 196, 200
elopement 623, 671
eloquence 574, 582
else 37
elsewhere 187
elucidate 522
elude
  sophistry 477
  avoid 623
  escape 671
  succeed 731
  palter 773
elusive 545
elusory 546
elutriate 652
elysian 829, 981
Elysium 827, 981
elytron 223
Elzevir edition 193
emaciation 195,
  203, 640
emanate 151
  go out of 295
  excrete 299
– from 544
emanation 398
emancipate
  facilitate 705
  free 748, 750
emasculate
  impotent 158
embalm
  interment 363
  perfume 400
  preserve 670
– in the memory
  505
embankment
  esplanade 189
  refuge 666

Column 4 (EMB)

fence 717
embar 229
embargo
  stoppage 265
  prohibition 761
  exclusion 893
embark
  transfer 270
  depart 293
– in *begin* 66
  engage in 676
embarquer sans
  biscuits, s' – 674
embarras de
– choix 609
embarrass 641,
  704, 706
embarrassed 804,
  806
embarrassing 475
embase 659
embassy
  errand 532
  commission 755
  consignee 758
embattled
  arranged 60
  leagued 712
  war array 722
embed
  locate 184
  base 215
  enclose 221
  insert 300
embellish 847
embers 384
embezzle 791
embitter
  deteriorate 659
  aggravate 835
  acerbate 900
emblazon
  colour 428
  ornament 847
  display 882
emblem 550, 747
embody
  join 43
  combine 48
  form a whole 50
  compose 54
embolden
  hope 858
  encourage 861
embolism 228, 261,
  300
embonpoint 192
embosomed
  lodged 184
  interjacent 228
  circumscribed 229

emboss *convex* 250
　ornament 847
embouchure 260
embowel 297
embrace
　cohere 46
　compose 54
　include 76
　enclose 227
　choose 609
　take 789
　friendship 888
　sociality 892
　courtesy 894
　endearment 902
　– *an offer* 762
embrangle 61
embranglement 713
embrasure 257, 260
embrocation 662
embroider
　variegate 440
　lie 544
　ornament 847
embroidery
　adjunct 39
　exaggeration 549
embroil *derange* 61
　discord 713
embroilment 59
embrown 433
embryo
　beginning 66
　cause 153
　in – *destined* 152
　preparing 673
embryology 357
embryonic 193, 674
embus 293
embusqué 603
emendation 658
emerald *green* 435
　jewel 847
emerge 295, 446
emergency
　circumstance 8
　event 151
　difficulty 704
emeritus 500, 928
emersion 295, 446
emery
　sharpener 253
　– *paper*
　smooth 255
emetic *remedy* 662
émeute 742
emication 420
emigrant 57, 268
emigrate 266, 295
emigré 268, 295
eminence

height 206
　fame 873
　church dignitary
　　996
eminent domain
　744
eminently 33
emir 745, 875
emissary
　messenger 534
　consignee 758
emission 297
emit *eject* 297
　publish 531
　voice 580
　– *vapour* 336
Emmanuel 976
emmet 193
emollient 662
emolument
　acquisition 775
　receipt 810
　remuneration 973
emotion 821
　–al *appeal* 824
　–al *drama* 599
empale 260, 972
empanel 86, 969
empathy 515
emperor 745
emphasis 580
emphatic 535, 642
emphatically 31
empierce
　perforate 260
　insert 300
empire 737, 789
　– *day* 840
empiric 548
empirical 463, 675
empiricism 463
emplane 293
employ
　business 625
　use 677
　servitude 749
　commission 755
　in one's – 746
　– *one's capital in*
　　794
　– *oneself* 680
　– *one's time in*
　　625
employé
　servant 746
　agent 758
employer 795
empoison 659
emporium 799
empower
　power 157

commission 755
　accredit 759
　permit 760
empress 745
empressement
　activity 682
　emotion 821
　desire 865
emprise 676
emption 795
emptor 795
　caveat – 769
empty *clear* 185
　vacant 187
　deflate 195
　drain 297
　ignorant 491
　waste 638
　deficient 640
　useless 645
　beggarly account
　　of – boxes
　poverty 804
　– one's glass 298
　– *purse* 804
　– *sound* 517
　– *stomach* 865
　– *title name* 564
　undue 925
　– *words* 546
empty-handed 640
empty-headed
　491
empurple 437
empyrean *sky* 318
　blissful 829
empyreuma 41
empyrosis 384
emulate *imitate* 19
　goodness 648
　rival 708
　compete 720
　glory 873
emulsion 352
emunctory 350
en – bloc 50
　– masse 50
　– passant
　　parenthetical 10
　　transient 111
　à *propos* 134
　– rapport 9
　– règle *order* 58
　　conformity 82
　– route
　　journey 266
　　progress 282
enable 157
enact *drama* 599
　action 680
　conduct 692

complete 729
　order 741
　law 963
enallage 521
enamel *coating* 223
　painting 556
　ornament 847
enameller 559
enamour 897
encage 751
encamp 184, 189
encampment 184
encaustic 556
enceinte
　with child 161
　region 181
　inclosure 232
enchafe 830
enchain 751
enchant *please* 829
enchanted 827
enchanting 845,
　897
enchantment
　sorcery 992
enchase 43, 259
enchiridion 593
enchorial 188
encincture 229
encircle 76, 227,
　311
enclave *close* 181
　boundary 233
enclose 227, 229
enclosure
　region 181
　envelope 232
　fence 752
encomiast 935
encomium 931
encompass 227, 233
　–ed with difficul-
　　ties 704
encore 104, 931
encounter
　undergo 151
　clash 276
　meet 292
　withstand 708
　contest 720
　– *danger* 665
　– *risk* 621
encourage
　animate 615
　aid 707
　comfort 834
　hope 858
　embolden 861
encroach
　transcursion 303
　do wrong 923

under the ban-
ners of 707
- into the service
677
enliven
delight 829
cheer 836
amuse 840
enmity 889
ennoble 873
ennui 841
enormity
crime 947
enormous *great* 31
big 192
- *number* 102
enough *much* 31
no more! 142
sufficient 639
moderately 651
satiety 869
know when one
has had - 953
- in all conscience
641
- to drive one
mad 830
- and to spare 639
enounce 535, 580
enrage 830, 900
enragé 865
enrapture
excite 824
beatify 829
love 897
enraptured 827
enravish 829
enravished 827
enravishment 824
enrich
improve 658
wealth 803
ornament 847
enrobe 225
enroll *list* 86
record 551
- *troops* 722
commission 755
ens *essence* 1
Ens Entium 976
ensample 22
ensanguined 361
ensconce
conceal 528
safety 664
ensconced
located 184
ensemble 50
enshrine
circumscribe 229
repute 873

sanctify 987
- in the memory
505
ensiform 253
ensign
standard 550
officer 726
master 745
- of authority 747
ensilage 637
enslave 749
ensnare 545
ensue *follow* 63, 117
happen 151
ensure 474
entablature 210
entail *cause* 153
tie up property
781
entangle
interlink 43
derange 61
ravel 219
entrap 545
embroil 713
entangled
disorder 59
- by difficulties
704
entend, cela s' - 613
entente
agreement 23
alliance 714
friendship 888
enter *go in* 294
appear 446
note 551
accounts 811
- into the compo-
sition of 56
- into details
special 79
describe 594
- into an engage-
ment 768
- into the feelings
of 914
- into the ideas of
understand 518
concord 714
- in *converge* 290
- the lists
attack 716
contention 720
- the mind 451
- a profession 625
- into the spirit of
feel 821
delight 827
- upon 66
- into one's views

488
enterprise
pursuit 622
undertaking 676
commercial - 794
enterprising
active 171, 682
courageous 861
entertain
bear in mind 457
support 707
amuse 840
sociality 892
- doubts 485
- feeling 821
- an idea 451
- an opinion 484
entertainment 840
pleasure 377
repast 298
entêté 481, 606
enthral
subjection 749
restraint 751
enthrone 873
enthronement 755
enthusiasm
language 574
willingness 602
feeling 821
hope 858
love 897
enthusiast
madman 504
obstinate 606
active 682
enthusiastic
imaginative 515
sensitive 822
excitable 825
sanguine 858
enthymeme 476
entice 615
enticing 829
entire *whole* 50
complete 52
continuous 69
- horse 373
entirely *much* 31
entitle *name* 564
give a right 924
entity 1
entoil 545
entomb *inter* 363
imprison 751
Entomology 368
**entourage 88, 183,
227**
entozoon 193
entrails 221
entrain 293

entrammel 751
entrance
beginning 66
ingress 294
way 627
enrapture 827,
829
magic 992
give - to 296
entranced 515
entrancement 824
entrap 545
entre nous 528
entreat 765
entrée
reception 296
dish 298
give the - 296
have the - 294
- dish 191
entremet 298
entrepôt 636, 799
entrepreneur 599
entresol 191
entrust
commission 755
give 784
credit 805
entry *beginning* 66
ingress 294
record 551
entwine *join* 43
intersect 219
convolve 248
enucleate 522
enumerate 85
- among 76
enumeration 86
enunciate
inform 527
affirm 535
voice 580
envelop 225
envelope 223, 232
envenom
deprave 659
excsperate 835
hate 898
anger 900
envenomed
bad 649
insalubrious 657
painful 830
malevolent 907
- tongue 934
environ 227
environment 183
environs 197
in such and such -
183
envisage 515, 861

prank 840
escape 671
  liberate 750
  evade 927
  means of – 664,
  666
  – the lips
  disclosure 529
  speech 582
  – the memory 506
  – notice &c.
  invisible 447
  inattention 458
escarp 717
escarpment
  stratum 204
  height 206
  oblique 217
escharotic
  caustic 171
  pungent 392
eschatology 67
escheat 145, 974
eschew
  avoid 623
  dislike 867
esclandre 828, 830
escort
  accompany 88
  safeguard 664
  keeper 753
escritoire 191
esculent 298
escutcheon 550
esoteric
  private 79
  concealed 528
Espagne, château
  en – *fancy* 515
  hope 858
espalier 232
especial 79
especially 33
Esperanto 560
espial 441
espièglerie
  cunning 702
  fun 840
  wit 842
espionnage 441,
  461
esplanade
  houses 189
  flat 213
espouse
  choose 609
  marriage 903
  – a cause *aid* 707
  co-operate 709
esprit

shrewdness 498
  wit 842
  bel – 844
  – de corps
  bias 481
  co-operation 709
  sociality 892
  (*party* 712)
  – fort
  thinker 500
  irreligious 989
espy 441
esquire 875, 877
essay
  experiment 463
  dissertation 595
  endeavour **675**
essayist 593, 595
esse 1
essence
  nature 5
  scent 398
essential
  intrinsic 5
  great 31
  required 630
  important 642
essentially
  intrinsically 5
  substantially 3
essential stuff 5
establish
  settle 150
  create 161
  place 184
  evidence 467
  demonstrate 478
  – *equilibrium* 27
established
  permanent 141
  habit 613
  – *church* 983*a*
establishment
  party 712
  shop 799
estafette 534
estaminet 189
estate *condition* 7
  property 780
  come to man's –
  131
esteem
  believe 484
  repute 873
  approve 931
  in high – 928
estimable 648
estimate
  measure 466
  adjudge 480
  information 527

– too highly 482
estimation
  [*see* esteem,
  estimate]
estime
  succès d' – 873
estival 382
esto perpetua!
  perpetuity 112
  permanence 141
  desire 865
estop 706
estrade 213
estrange
  alienate 44, 889
  discord 713
  hate 898
estranged
  secluded 893
estrapade
  attack 716
  punishment 972
estreat 974
estuary 343
estuation 384
esurient 865
et – cætera
  add 37
  include 76
  plural 100
  – hoc genus omne
  similar 17
  include 76
  multiform 81
étalage 882
état major 745
etch *furrow* 259
  engraving 558
eternal 112
  – home 981
Eternal, the – 976
eterne 112
eternify 112
eternity 112
  an – 110
  launch into – 360,
  361
ether
  lightness 320
  rarity 322
  vapour 334
  anæsthetic 376
ethereal 4
ethicism 984
ethics 926
Ethiopian 431
  –'s skin 150
Ethiopian's skin
  unchangeable 150
ethnology 372
ethnic 984

ethology 926
ethos 5
etiolate 429, 430
etiology *causes* 155,
  359
  knowledge 490
  disease 655
etiquette
  custom 613
  fashion 852
  ceremony 882
étoile, à la belle –
  out of doors 220
  in the air 338
Eton jacket 225
étourderie
  inattention 458
  unskilfulness 699
etymological 560
etymology 562
etymon *origin* 153
  verbal 562
Eucharist 998
euchology 998
euchre 840
eudiometer
  air 338
  salubrity 656
euge! 931
eugenics 658
eulogist 935
eulogize 482
eulogy 931
Eumenides *fury*
  900
  evil-doers 913
  revenge 919
eunuch 158
eupepsia 654
euphemism
  metaphor 521
  style 577, 578
  flattery 933
euphemist
  man of taste 850
  flatterer 935
euphony 413, 578
euphuism
  metaphor 521
  elegant style 577
  affected style 579
  affectation 855
Eurasian 41
eureka! 462, 480*a*
Euripus 343
Eurus 349
eurythmics 537,
  840
eurythmy 242
Euterpe 416

faintness 405
fair *in degree* 31
  pale 429
  white 430
  wise 498
  important 643
  good 648
  moderate 651
  mart 799
  beautiful 845
  just 922
  honourable 939
  – chance 472
  – copy *copy* 21
  writing 590
  – field
  occasion 134
  – game 857
  by – means 631,
    939
  – name 873
  – play 922, 923
  – question 461
  – sex 374
  in a – way
  tending 176
  probable 472
  convalescent 660
  prosperous 734
  hopeful 858
  – weather 734
  – weather sailor
    701
  – wind 705
  – words 894
fairing 784
fairly
  intrinsically 5
  get on – 736
  – well 643
fair-spoken
  courtesy 894
  flattery 933
fairy *fanciful* 515
  fay 979
  imp 980
  – godmother 711,
    784, 912
  – tale 546, 594
fairy-land 515
fait: au –
  knowledge 490
  skilful 698
  – accompli
  certain 474
  complete 729
faith *belief* 484
  hope 858
  honour 939
  piety 987

declaration of –
  983
bad – 544
i' – 535
keep – with
  observe 772
plight –
  promise 768
  love 902
true –
  orthodox 983a
want of –
  incredulity 487
  irreligious 989
– healing 662
faithful [*see* faith]
  like 17
  copy 21
  exact 494
  obedient 743
  – memory 505
  – to 772
faithless *false* 544
  dishonourable 940
  sceptical 989
fake 544, 545
fakir 996
falcate 244, 245
falchion 727
falciform
  [*see* falcate]
falcon 792
falconet 727
faldstool 215
fall *autumn* 126
  happen 151
  perish 162
  slope 217
  regression 283
  descend 306
  die 360
  fail 732
  adversity 735
  vice 945
  let – *lower* 308
  inform 527
  water– 348
  – asleep 683
  – astern 235, 283
  – away 105
  – back *return* 283
  recede 287
  relapse 661
  – back upon 677,
    717
  have to – back
    upon 637
  – a cursing 908
  – of the curtain 67
  – into a custom 82
  – of day 125

– dead 360
– into decay 659
– down 990
– down before 928
– upon the ear 418
– flat on the ear
  843
– at one's feet 725
– foul of *blow* 276
  hinder 706
  oppose 708
  discord 713
  attack 716
  contention 720
  censure 932
– for 897
– to the ground
  be confuted 479
  fail 732
– into a habit 613
– from one's high
  estate
  adversity 735
  disrepute 874
– in *order* 58
  continuity 69
  event 151
– into
  conversion 144
  river 348
– in with *agree* 23
  conform 82
  converge 2
  discover 480a
  concord 714
  consent 762
– on one's knees
  submit 725
  servile 886
  gratitude 916
  worship 990
– of the leaf 126
– from the lips 582
– in love with 897
– to one's lot
  event 151
  chance 156
  receive 785
  duty 926
– under one's
  notice 457
– into oblivion 506
– off *decrease* 36
  deteriorate 659
– off again 661
– out *happen* 151
  quarrel 713
  enmity 889
– into a passion
  900
– to pieces

disjunction 44
destruction 162
brittle 328
– a prey to 732,
  749
– in price 815
– into raptures
  827
– short *inferior* 32
  contract 195
  shortcoming 304
– of snow 383
– through 304
– to *eat* 298
  take in hand 676
  do battle 722
– into a trap 547
– under
  inclusion 76
  subjection 749
– upon
  discover 480a
  unexpected 508
  devise 626
  attack 716
– in the way of 186
– to work 686
fallacy *sophistry*
  477
  error 495
show the – of 479
fallen angel 949,
978
fallible 475, 477
falling-out 24
falling star 318, 423
fallow
  unproductive 169
  yellow 436
  unready 674
  inactive 681
false *imitation* 19
  sophistry 477
  error 495
  untrue 544, 546
  spurious 925
  dishonourable 940
– alarm 669
– colouring
  misinterpretation
  523
  falsehood 544
– construction
  523, 544
– doctrine 984
– expectation 509
– hearted 940
– impression 495
– light *vision* 443
– money 800
– ornament 851

s

celebration 883
festivity 840, 892
festoon 245, 847
fetch *bring* 270
  arrive 292
  evasion 545
  sell for 812
  – one a blow
    strike 276
    attack 716
  – and carry
    servile 886
  – a sigh 839
fête 840, 882
fêté 892
fetishism 992
fetid 401
fetish 991, 993
fetter 751, 752
fettle 673
  state 5
  prepare 673
  in fine – 159, 654
feu
  – d'enfer 716
  – de joie
    amusement 840
    celebration 883
feud *discord* 713
  possess 777
  property 780
  death – 919
feudal 737, 780
feudatory 749
feuilleton 593
fever *heat* 382
  disease 655
  excitement 825
feverish *hurry* 684
  animated 821
  excited 824
few
  a – 100
  – and far between
    70
  – words
    concise 572
    taciturn 585
    compendium 596
fewness 103
fey 360
fez 225
fiancée 897
fiasco 732
fiat 741
  – money 800
fib *falsehood* 544,
  546
  thump 720
fibre *link* 45
  filament 205

moral – 60
fickle 149, 605
fictile 240
fiction *untruth* 546
  work of – 594
  fictitious 515, 546
fiddle 416, 417
fiddle-de-dee
  absurd 497
  unimportant 643
  contempt 930
fiddlefaddle
  unmeaning 517
  trifle 643
  dawdle 683
fiddler 416
fiddlestick 417
  – end 643
fidelity
  veracity 543
  obedience 743
  observance 772
  honour 939
fidgets *changes* 149
  activity 682
  hurry 684
  excitability 825
fidgety
  irresolute 605
  fearful 860
  irascible 901
fiducial 156
fiduciary 484
fidus Achates
  auxiliary 711
  associate 743
  friend 890
fie *disreputable* 874
  – upon it
  censure 932
fief 777
field *opportunity*
  134
  scope 180
  region 181
  plain 344
  agriculture 371
  business 625
  arena 728
  property 780
  the – *hunting* 622
  beasts of the – 366
  playing –s 728
  the potter's – 361
  take the – 722
  – artillery 726
  the – of blood 361
  – of inquiry
    topic 454
    inquiry 461
  – of view

vista 441
idea 453
field-day
  contention 720
  amusement 840
  display 882
field-glass 445
field-marshal 745
field-piece 727
field-preacher 996
field-work 717
fiend 913, 980
fiend-like
  malevolent 907
  wicked 945
  fiend 980
fierce *violent* 173
  passion 825
  daring 861
  angry 900
fiery *violent* 173
  hot 382
  strong feeling 821
  excitable 825
  angry 900
  irascible 901
  – cross 550, 722
  – furnace 386
  – imagination 515
  – ordeal 828
fife 417
fifer 416
fifth 98, 99
fifty 98
fig
  unimportance 643
  in the name of the
    prophet –s! 497
  – out 847
fight
  contention 720
  warfare 722
  show –
    defence 717
    courage 861
  – one's battles
    again 594
  – against destiny
    606
  – the good fight
    944
  – it out 722
  – shy *avoid* 603,
    623
    coward 862
  – one's way
    pursue 622
    active 682
    exertion 686
fighter 726
fighting-cock 726,

  861
fighting-man 726
figment 515
figurante 599
figurate number 84
figuration 240
figurative
  metaphorical 521
  representing 554
  – *style* 577
figure
  number 84
  form 240
  appearance 448
  metaphor 521
  indicate 550
  represent 554
  price 812
  ugly 846
  cut a –
    repute 873
    display 882
  poor – 874
  – to oneself 515
  – of speech 521
  – out 522
    exaggeration 549
figure-flinger 994
figure-head 4, 550,
  554, 643
figurine 554
figuriste 559
filaceous 205
filament 205
filamentous 256
filch 791
filcher 762
file *subduct* 38
  arrange 60
  row 69
  assemblage 72
  list 86
  reduce 195
  smooth 255
  pulverize 330
  record 551
  store 636
  soldiers 726
  – a claim &c. 969
  – off *march* 266
    diverge 291
file-fire 716
filial 167
filiation
  consanguinity 11
  attribution 155
  posterity 167
filibuster 133, 706,
  792
filibustering 791
filiform 205

smoothness 255
slow 275
leaf 367
sign 550
path 627
infirm 655
inactive 683
tired 688
weary 841
lower one's – 725
red – *alarm* 669
yellow –
　warning 668
　alarm 669
– man 668
– ship 726
– of truce 723
flag-bearer 534
flagellation
　penance 952
　asceticism 955
　flogging 972
　rite 998
flagelliform 205
flageolet 417
flagitious 945
flagon 191
flagrant
　great 31
　manifest 525
　notorious 531
　atrocious 945
flagrante
　– *bello* 722
　– *delicto*
　sure enough 474
　act 680
　guilt 947
flagration 384
flagstaff *tall* 206
　signal 550
flail 276
flair 450, 698
flake 204
　snow – 383
　– white 430
flam 544
flambé 732
flambeau 423
flamboyant 577
flame *fire* 382
　light 420
　luminary 423
　passion 824, 825
　love 897
　catch the –
　emotion 821
　consign to the –s
　　384
　add fuel to the –
　　173

[492]

in –s 382
– up 825
–coloured
　red 434
　orange 439
flame-projector 727
flamen 996
flaming *violent* 173
　feeling 821
　excited 824
　ostentatious 882
　boasting 884
flâneur 935
flange *support* 215
　rim 231
　projection 250
flank *side* 236
　protect 664
flannel 384
flap *adjunct* 39
　hanging 214
　move to and fro
　　315
　– the memory 505
flapdoodle 517
flapper *girl* 129
flapping *loose* 47
flare *violent* 173
　glare 420
　light 423
　– up
　excited 824, 825
　angry 900
flaring *colour* 428
flash *instant* 113
　violent 173
　fire 382
　light 420
　eyes – fire 900
　– lamp 550
　– light 423
　– across the mem-
　　ory 505
　– on the mind
　thought 451
　disclose 529
　impulse 612
　– note 800
　– in the pan
　unsubstantial 4
　transientness 111
　impotent 158
　unproductive 169
　failure 732
　– tongue 563
　– up *excited* 824
　– upon
　unexpected 508
　– of wit 842
flashing
　ostentatious 882

flashy
　gaudy colour 428
　style 577
　ornament 847
　vulgar 851
flask 191
flat *inert* 172
　abode 189
　story 191
　low 207
　horizontal 213
　vapid 391
　low tone 408
　musical note 413
　positive 535
　dupe 547
　back-scene 599
　shoal 667
　bungler 701
　poor 804
　insensible 823
　dejected 837
　weary 841
　dull 843
　simple 849
　fall – 732
　– contradiction
　　536
　– iron 255
　– refusal 764
flatfoot 664
flatness **251**
flatter *deceive* 545
　cunning 702
　please 829
　grace 845
　encourage 858
　approbation 931
　adulation 933
　– oneself
　probable 472
　hope 858
　– the palate 394
flatterer **935**
flattering
　– remarks 894
　– tale
　hope 858
　– unction to one's
　　soul
　content 831
　vain 880
　flattery 933
flattery 544, **933**
flatulent
　gaseous 334
　air 338
　wind 349
　- *style* 573, 575
flatus 334, 349
flaunt 873, 882

flaunting *vulgar* 851
　gaudy 428
　unreserved 525
flautist 416
**Flavian amphi-
　theatre** 728
flavour 390
flavouring 393
flavous 436
flaw *break* 70
　crack 198
　error 495
　imperfection 651
　blemish 848
　fault 947
　– in an argument
　　477
flaxen 436
flay *divest* 226
　punish 972
flea *jumper* 309
　dirt 653
　– in one's ear
　repel 289
　eject 297
　refuse 764
　disrepute 874
　abashed 879
　discourteous 895
　contempt 930
flea-bite 643
flea-bitten 440
fleck 32
flecked 440
flection 279
fled *escaped* 671
fledge 673
fledgling 123
flee *avoid* 623
fleece *tegument* 223
　strip 789
　rob 791
　impoverish 804
　surcharge 814
fleet *ridicule* 856
　insult 929
fleet *ships* 273
　swift 274
　navy 726
Fleet *prison* 752
fleeting 4, 111
flesh *bulk* 192
　animal 364
　mankind 372
　carnal 961
　gain – 194
　ills that – is heir
　　to *evil* 619
　disease 655
　in the – 359
　one – 903

– majeure 744
– open 173
– one's way
  progression 282
  passage 302
forced *irrelative* 10
  - *style* 579
  be – to 601
  – labor 603
  – march 274
forcefully 601
forceps
  extraction 301
  grip 781
forces 726
forcible [*see* force]
ford 302, 627
fore 234
fore and aft
  complete 52
  lengthwise 200
  – *schooner* 273
forearm 673
forebears 166
forebode 511
forecast
  foresight 510
  prediction 511
  plan 626
foreclose 706
foredoom 152, 601
forefathers 166
forefend
  prohibit 761
forefinger 379
forego
  relinquish 624
  renounce 757
  surrender 782
foregoing 62, 116
foregone
  past 122
  – conclusion
  prejudged 481
  predetermined
    611
foreground 234
  in the –
  manifest 525
forehead 234
foreign
  alien 10
  extraneous 57
  – *accent* 580
  – *parts* 196
foreigner 57
forejudge
  prejudge 481
  foresight 510
foreknow 510
foreland 206, 254

forelay 545
forelock
  pull the – 894
  take time by the –
  early 132
  occasion 134
foreman 694
foremost
  superior 33
  beginning 66
  front 234
  in advance 280
  important 642
  reputed 873
forenoon 125
forensic 968
foreordain 152
foreordination 601,
  611
fore part 234
forerun 62, 116, 280
forerunner 64, 512
foresee 507, 510
foreseen 871
foreshadow 152,
  511
foreshorten 201
foreshow 511
foresight 116, **510**
  caution 864
forest 367
forestage 599
forestall
  prior 116
  early 132
  possession 777
forestry 371
foretaste 510
foretell 511
forethought 459,
  510
foretoken 511
forewarn 511, 668
foreword 64
forfeit *fail* 773
  lose 776
  penalty 974
  – one's good
    opinion 932
forfeiture
  disfranchisement
    925
forfend 706, 717
forgather 72
forge *imitate* 19
  produce 161
  furnace 386
  trump up 544
  workshop 691
  – *fetters* 751
forged

  false 546
forger
  maker 690
  thief 792
forgery
  deception 545
forget 506
  hand – cunning
    699
  – benefits 917
  – injury 918
  – oneself 945
forgive 918
forgo
  relinquish 624
  renounce 757
  surrender 782
forgotten
  past 122
  ingratitude 917
  not to be – 505
  – by the world
    893
fork *bifid* 91
  pointed 244
  – *lightning* 423
  – out
  give 784
  pay 807
  expenditure 809
forlorn
  dejected 837
  hopeless 859
  deserted 893
  – hope
  danger 665
  rashness 863
form *state* 7
  likeness 21
  make up 54
  order 58
  arrange 60
  convert 144
  produce 161
  bench 215
  shape **240**
  educate 537
  pupils 541
  manner 627
  beauty 845
  fashion 852
  etiquette 882
  law 963
  rite 998
  – letter 592
  – part of 56
  – a party 712
  – a resolution 604
formal [*see* form]
  regular 82
  definitive 535

  - *style* 579
  affected 855
  stately 882
  – speech 582
formalism 739, 988
formalist 82
formality [*see*
  formal]
  ceremony 852
  affectation 855
  law 963
formation
  composition 54
  production 161
  shape 240
formative 153
formed [*see* form]
  attempered 820
former
  in order 62
  prior in time 116
  past 122
formication 380
formidable 704, 860
formless 241
formula *rule* 80
  arithmetic 84
  maxim 496
  precept 697
  law 963
formulary 998
formulate 590
fornication 961
fornicator 962
foro conscientiæ
  veracity 543
  duty 926
  probity 939
forsake 624
forsaken 898
forsooth 535
forspent 688
forswear *lie* 544
  tergiversation 607
  refuse 764
  transgress 927
  improbity 940
fort 666, 717
fort
  le droit du plus –
  compulsion 744
  illegality 964
  un peu – 641
fortalice 717
forte 415, 698
fortelage 717
forth 282
  come –
  egress 295
  visible 446
  go – *depart* 293

the decree has
 gone – 741
forthcoming 152,
 673
forthwith 132
fortification 717
fortify 159
fortiori, a – 467, 476
fortissimo 404
fortiter in re 171
fortitude 826, 861
fortnightly 138
fortress 717, 752
fortuitous
 extrinsic 6
 chance 156
 undesigned 621
 – *concourse of*
  atoms 59
fortunate
 opportune 134
 successful 731
 prosperous 734
Fortunatus's – cap
 wish 865
 spell 993
 – *purse* 803
fortune *chance* 156
 fate 601
 wealth 803
 be one's – 151
 clean up a – 803
 evil – 621, 735
 good – 734
 make one's –
 succeed 731
 wealth 803
 tempt –
 hazard 621
 essay 675
 trick of – 509
 try one's – 675
 wheel of – 601, 621
fortune-hunter 886,
 943
fortuneless 804
fortune-teller 513
fortune-telling 511
fortunes of
 narrative 594
forty 98
 – winks 683
forum 799
 school 542
 tribunal 966
forward *early* 132
 transmit 270
 advance 282
 willing 602
 improve 658
 active 682

help 707
vain 880
insolent 885
uncourteous 895
bend – 234
come –
 in sight 446
 offer 763
 display 882
 look – to 507
 move – 282
 press – *haste* 684
 put – *aid* 507
 offer 763
 put oneself – 880
 set – 676
 – in *knowledge* 490
foss 348
fosse
 inclosure 232
 ditch 259
 defence 717
fossil
 ancient 124
 hard 323
 organic 357
 dry bones 362
foster *aid* 707
 excite 824
 caress 902
 – a *belief* 484
fou 959
foudroyant 870
foul
 collide 276
 bad 649
 dirty 653
 unhealthy 657
 ugly 846
 base 940
 vicious 945
 fall – of
 oppose 708
 quarrel 713
 attack 716
 fight 720
 censure 932
 run – of
 impede 706
 – fiend 978
 – means 940
 – language
 malediction 908
 – odour 401
 – play *evil* 619
 cunning 702
 wrong 923
 improbity 940
foul-mouthed 895
foul-spoken 934
found 153, 215

foundation
 beginning 66
 stability 150
 base 211
 support 215
 lay the –s 673
 sandy – 667
 shake to its –s 315
founded
 well – 472
 – on *base* 211
 evidence 467
founder
 originator 164
 sink 310
 fail 732
 religious –s 986
foundery 691
founding 22
foundling
 trover 775
 derelict 782
 outcast 893
fount *type* 591
fountain
 source 153
 river 348
 store 636
 – head 210
 – pen 590
four 95
 on all –s 13, 23
 horizontal 213
 easy 705
 prosperous 734
 humble 879
 – in hand 272
 – score &c. 98
 – square 244
 – times 96
 from the – winds
  278
fourflusher 884
fourfold 96
four-oar 273
four-poster 215
fourth 96, 97
 musical 413
 – estate 531
four-wheeler 272
fowl 366
fowling-piece 727
fox *animal* 366
 cunning 702
 – chase 622
fox-trot 840
foxy *colour* 433, 434
 cunning 702
foyer 191, 599
fracas
 disorder 59

noise 404
discord 713
contention 720
fraction *part* 51
 numerical 84
 less than one **100a**
fractious 901
fracture
 disjunction 44
 discontinuity 70
 fissure 198
fragile 160, 328
fragment
 small 32, 193
 part 51, 100*a*
fragrance **400**
fragrant weed 392
frail *weak* 160
 brittle 328
 feeble 575
 irresolute 605
 imperfect 651
 failing 945
 impure 961
 – *sisterhood* 962
frais, à grands –
 481
frame
 condition 7
 make 161
 support 215
 border 231
 form 240
 substance 316
 structure 329
 contrive 626
 cucumber – 371
 have –d and
  glazed 822
 – of mind
 inclination 602
 disposition 820
frame-up 626
framework
 support 215
 structure 329
franchise
 voting 609
 freedom 748
 right 924
 exemption 927*a*
Franciscan 996
franc-tireur 726
frangible 160, 328
frank *open* 525
 sincere 543
 artless 703
 honourable 939
frankalmoigne 748
Frankenstein 913,
 980

frankincense 400
frantic
violent 173
delirious 503
excited 824
fraternal
brother 11
concord 714
friendly 888
fraternity
[*see* fraternal]
party 712
fraternize
co-operate 48, 709
agree 714
sympathize 888
associate 892
fratricide 361
Frau 374
fraud
falsehood 544
deception 545
pretender 548
dishonour 940
pious – 988
fraught *full* 52
pregnant 161
possessing 777
– *with danger* 665
fray *rub* 331
battle 720
in the thick of
the – 722
frayed 659
frazzle
beaten to a – 732
freak 608, 872
– of Nature 83
freckle 848
freckled 440
fredaine 840
free
detached 44
unconditional 52
liberate 672
unobstructed 705
at liberty 748, 750
gratis 815
liberal 816
insolent 885
exempt 927a
impure 961
– balloon 273
– and easy
cheerful 836
adventurous 863
vain 880
insolent 885
friendly 888
sociable 892
– fight 720

– **from**
simple 42
never – from 613
– gift 784
– from imperfec-
tion 650
– lance 726
– land 748
– liver 954a
– love 961
make – of 748
– play 170, 748
– quarters
cheap 815
hospitality 892
– space 180
– stage 748
– trade
commerce 794
– translation 522
– will 600
make – with
frank 703
take 789
sociable 892
uncourteous 895
freebooter 792
freeborn 748
freedman 748
freedom **748**
free-handed 816
freehold 780
freely
willingly 602
freeman 748
freemasonry
unintelligible 519
secret 528
sign 550
co-operation 709
party 712
free-spoken 703
freethinker 989
freeze
benumb 381
cold 385
– the blood 830
freezing 383
– mixture 387
freight *lade* 184
cargo 190
transfer 270
freightage 812
freighter 273
freight train 272
French
peddler's – 563
– and English 840
– horn 417
– leave *avoid* 623
freedom 748

– polish 847
frenetic 503
frenzy
madness 503
imagination 515
excitement 825
frequency **136**
frequent
in number 104
in time 136
in space 186
habitual 613
visit 892
fresco *cold* 383
painting 556
al –
out of doors 220
in the air 338
fresh *additional* 37
new 123
flood 348
cold 383
colour 428
remembered 505
unaccustomed 614
good 648
healthy 654
impertinent 885
tipsy 959
– breeze 349
– colour 434
– news 532
freshen 658, 689
freshet 348
freshman 541
freshwater 851
freshwater sailor
701
fret *suffer* 378
grieve 828
gall 830
discontent 832
sad 837
ornament 847
irritate 900
– and fume 828
fretful 901
fret-work 219
friable 328, 330
friandise 868
friar 996
–'s lantern 423
– Rush 980
Black –s 996
friary 1000
fribble
slur over 460
trifle 643
dawdle 683
fop 854
fricassee 298

frication 331
friction *force* 157
obstacle 179
rubbing **331**
on – wheels 705
friend 711, **890**
candid – 936
next – 759
friendless 893
friendly 714, **894**
friends, be – 888
see one's – 892
friendship 9, **888**
frieze 210
frigate 726
fright
cards 840
alarm 860
frightful 31, 830,
846
frightfully 31
frightfulness 860
frigid
cold 383
– *style* 575
callous 823
indifferent 866
frigidarium 387
frigorific 385
frill 231, 248
frills and furbe-
lows 847
fringe
border 231
lace 256
exaggeration 549
ornament 847
frippery
trifle 643
ornament 847
finery 851
ridiculous 853
ostentation 882
frisk *prance* 266
leap 309
search 461
gay 836
amusement 840
frisky 682, 836
frith *chasm* 198
strait 343
forest 367
fritinancy 412
fritter *small* 32
– away *lessen* 36
waste 638
– away time 683
fritters 298
frivolous
unreasonable 477
foolish 499

fetid 401
  bad 649
  abhorrent 867
  adulatory 933
  impure 961
fulvid 436
fulvous 436
fumble
  derange 61
  handle 379
  grope 463
  awkward 699
fumbler 701
fume
  violent 173
  exhalation 334, 336
  froth 353
  heat 382
  odour 398
  excitement 824, 825
  anger 900
  in a –
  discontented 832
  –s of fancy 515
fumid 426
fumigate
  vaporize 336
  cleanse 652
fumigator 388
fumo, dare pondus – 481
fun 827, 840, 842
  make – of 856
funambulist 700
function
  algebra 84
  office 170
  business 625
  utility 644
  pomp 882
  rite 998
  duty 926
functionary
  director 694
  consignee 758
functus officio 756
fund *store* 636
  sinking – 802
fundamental
  intrinsic 5
  base 211
  support 215
  – bass 413
  – note 413
fundamentally 31
funds 800
  in – 803
  public – 802
funebrial 363

funeral 363
  – pace 275
  – march 415
funereal
  interment 363
  dismal 837
fungiform 249
fungology 369
fungosity 250
fungus
  projection 250
  vegetable 367
  fœtor 401
  bane 663
funicle 205
funicular 627
funk 860, 862
  – hole 530
funnel *opening* 260
  conduit 350
  air-pipe 351
funnel-shaped 252
funny *odd* 83
  boat 273
  humorous 842
  comic 853
fur *covering* 223
  hair 256
  warm 384
  dirt 653
furacious 791
furbelow 231
furbish
  improve 658
  prepare 673
  adorn 847
furcated 244
furcation 91
furcular 244
furfur 653
furfuraceous 330
Furies *anger* 900
  evil-doers 913
  demons 980
furious *violent* 173
  haste 684
  passion 825
  anger 900
furiously 31
furl 312
furlong 200
furlough 760
furnace **386**
  workshop 691
  like a – *hot* 382
  sighing like –
  lament 839
  in love 902
furnish
  provide 637
  prepare 673

give 784
  – aid 707
  – a handle 617
  – its quota 784
furniture 633
  – van 272
furor
  insanity 503
  passion 825
furore
  emotion 820, 821
  passion 825
  desire 865
furrow **259**
further
  added 37
  distant 196
  aid 707
  go – and fare worse
  worse 659
  bungle 699
  not let it go – 528
furthermore 37
furtive
  clandestine 528
  stealing 791
furuncle 250
fury *violence* 173
  excitation 825
  anger 900
  demon 980
furze 367
fuscous 433
fuse *join* 43
  combine 48
  heat 382, 384
  torch 388
fuselage 215
fusel oil 356
fusiform 244, 253
fusil 727
fusileer 726
fusillade 361, 716
fusion *union* 48
  heat 384
  co-operation 709
fuss *agitation* 315
  activity 682
  haste 684
  difficulty 704
  excitement 825
  ostentation 882
  kick up a – 173
  make a – about
  importance 642
  lament 839
  disapprove 932
fussy *crotchety* 481
  bustling 682
  excitable 825

fustian
  absurd 497
  unmeaning 517
  - *style* 577, 579
fustigate 972
fusty 124, 401, 653
futhorc 590
futile 497, 645
future 121
  eye to the – 510
  – possession 777
  – state
  destiny 152
  heaven 981
futurity **121**
fuzzle 959
fuzzy 447

G

gab 584
  gift of the – 582
gabardine 225
gabble 517, 583
gabelle 812
gaberlunzie 876
gabion 717
gable *side* 236
  – end 67
Gabriel 977
gaby 501
gad
  about 266, 268
gadget 626
gad-so 870
gaff 727
gaffer *old* 130
  man 373
  clown 876
gag
  closure 261
  render mute 403, 581
  dramatic 599
  muzzle 751
  imprison 752
gage *measure* 466
  security 771
  throw down the – 715
gaggle 412
gag-man 844
gaieté de cœur 836
gaiety
  [*see* gay] 836
gaillard 844
gain
  increase 35
  advantage 618
  skilful 698

occupant 188
safety 664
defence 717
soldiers 726
garrotte
  render powerless
  158
  kill 361
  punishment 972
garrulity 584
garter
  fastening 45
  decoration 877
  – blue 438
garth 181
gas 334
  talk 482
  fuel 388
  boasting 884
  – balloon 273
  – stove 386
  – bomb 727
  – fitter 690
  – mask 717
  – projector 727
gasconade 884
gaseity **334**
gaselier 214
gash *cut* 44
  interval 198
  wound 619
gasification 334,
  336
gaskins 225
gas-light 423
gasoline 388
gasometer 636
gasp *blow* 349
  droop 655
  fatigue 688
  at the last – 360
  – for *desire* 865
gasper 392
gastriloquism 580
Gastromancy 511
gastronomy 298,
  957
gate *beginning* 66
  inclosure 232
  mouth 260
  barrier 706
  water – 350
  –way *way* 627
  – keeper 263
gâté, enfant – 734
Gath, tell it not in –
  conceal 528
  disapprove 932
gather *collect* 72
  expand 194
  fold 258

conclude 480
acquire 775
take 789
– breath 689
– flesh 194
– from one
  information 527
– fruits 731
gathered
– to one's fathers
  360
gathering
  assemblage 72
  abscess 655
  – clouds *dark* 421
  shade 424
  omen 512
  danger 665
  warning 668
  adversity 735
gathering-place 74
gauche *clumsy* 699
gaucherie 699, 851
gaud 847
gaudery 880
gaudy *colour* 428
  vulgar 851
  showy 882
gauge 466
  rain– 348
  wind– 349
gauger 965
gaunt *bulky* 192
  lean 203
  ugly 846
gauntlet *glove* 225
  armour 717
  fling down 715
  run the – 665, 972
  take up the – 720
gauntry 627
Gautama 986
gauze *shade* 424
  semitransparent
  427
gavel 72, 812
gavelkind 778
gavelock 633
gavot 840
gawky
  awkward 699
  ugly 846
  (*ridiculous* 853)
gay *colour* 428
  cheerful 836
  adorned 847
  showy 882
  dissipated 961
  – deceiver 962
  – world 852
gaze 441

gazebo 441
gazelle *swift* 274
gazette
  publication 531
  record 551
  in the –
  bankrupt 808
gazetteer
  list 86
  information 527
  record 551
gazing-stock
  ridiculous 857
  wondrous 872
géant, à pas de –
  274
gear *clothes* 225
  harness 633
  high – 274
  in – 673
  low – 275
  out of –
  disjoin 44
  derange 61
  useless 645
  unprepared 674
  – wheel 633
geese are swans,
  all his – 482
gehenna 982
geisha 599
Geist 498
gel 352
gelatin 352
gelatinify 352
geld 38, 158
gelding 271, 373
gelid 383
Geloscopy 511
gem 648, 847
geminate 90
Gemini *twins* 89
  O – ! 870
gemote 72
gendarme 726, 965
gender 75
genealogy 69, 166
general
  generic 78
  habitual 613
  officer 745
  the –
  commonalty 876
  things in – 151
  – breaking up 655
  – favourite 899
  – information 490
  – meaning 516
  – public 372
  – run 613
  – servant 690, 746

generalissimo 745
generality
  mean 29
  universal **78**
generalize 476
generally speaking
  613
generalship 692,
  722
generate 161, 168
generation
  consanguinity 11
  period 108
  production 161
  mankind 372
  rising – 167
  spontaneous – 161
  wise in one's – 498
generator 164
generic 78
generosity
  giving 784
  liberality 816
  benevolence 906
  disinterestedness
  942
genesis
  beginning 66
  production 161
genet 271
Genethliacs 511
genetic 161
Geneva gown 999
genial
  productive 161
  sensuous 377
  warm 382
  willing 602
  delightful 829
  affable 894
geniality 836
geniculated 244
genie 980
genital 161
genitor 166
geniture 161
genius
  intellect 450
  talent 498
  skill 698
  proficient 700
  prodigy 872
  evil – 980
  good –
  friend 898
  benefactor 912
  spirit 979
  tutelary – 711
  – for 698
  – of a language
  560

906
– morrow 292
– name 873
– nature 906
– night 293
– for nothing
impotence 158
useless 645
in – odour
repute 873
approbation 931
– offices
mediation 724
kind 906
– old time 122
– omen 858
– opinion 931
take in – part
pleased 827
courteous 894
kind 906
– pennyworth 815
– at the price 815
to – purpose 731
– repute 873
– sense 498
– society 852
– taste 578, 850
– temper 894
– thing 648
– time *early* 132
opportune 134
prosperous 734
– turn
kindness 906
– understanding
714
– wife
woman 374
spouse 903
– will
willingness 602
benevolence 906
– word
approval 931
vindication 937
– as one's word
veracity 543
observance 772
probity 939
– works 906
goodie 652, 746
goodly
great 31
large 192
handsome 845
good mixer 892
goodness
[see good] **648**
virtue 944
have the –

request 765
– gracious! 870
– of heart 906
goods *effects* 270,
780
merchandise 798
good taste 868
Goodwin sands 667
goody 374, 652, 746
gooroo 996
goose *hiss* 409
game of – 840
giddy as a – 458
tailor's – 255
kill the – with
golden eggs
699, 818
a wild – chase 545
gooseberry
old – 978
play – 459
– eyes 441, 443
goosecap 501
goose egg 101
gooseflesh 383
goosequill 590
goose-skin 383
Gordian knot 59,
704
gore *stab* 260
blood 361
gorge *ravine* 198
conduit 350
fill 641
satiety 869
gluttony 957
raise one's – 900
– the hook 602
gorge de pigeon 440
gorgeous
colour 428
beauty 845
ornament 847
ostentation 882
Gorgon 860
gorilla 913
gormandize 298,
954*a*, 957
gorse 367
gory *red* 434
murderous 361
unclean 653
gospel
certainty 474
truth 494
take for – 484
Gospels 985
gossamer
filament 205
light 320
texture 329

gossip *news* 532
babbler 584
conversation 588
gossoon 876
Gotama 986
Goth 851, 876
Gotham, wise men
of – 501
gothic
amorphous 241
gouache 556
gouge *concave* 252
perforator 262
goulash 298
gourd 191
gourmand 954*a*,
957
gourmet 868, 954*a*
gout 378
goût, haut – 392
goutte d'eau, il se
noyerait dans
une – 699
govern 693, 737
[see govern]
ruling power 745
divine – 976
petticoat – 737
governess 540
governor
tutor 540
director 694
ruler 745
keeper 753
gowk 501
gown *dress* 225
canonicals 999
gownsman 492
grab *take* 789
miser 819
grabble 379
grace *style* 578
permission 760
concession 784
elegance 845
polish 850
title 877
pity 914
forgiveness 918
honour 939
piety 987
worship 990
act of – 784
God's – 906
with a bad – 603
with a good –
willing 602
courteous 894
in one's good –s
888
heart of – 861

say – 990
submit with a
good – 826
– before meat 916
grâce: coup de –
914
la – 840
graceless
inelegant 579
ugly 846
vicious 945
impenitent 951
irreligious 989
Graces 845
gracile 203
gracious
willing 602
courteous 894
kind 906
good – 870
grade *degree* 26
arrange 60
term 71
ascent 217
on the down – 658
on the up – 659
gradatim
gradually 26
in order 58
continuous 69
slow 275
gradation
degree 26
order 58
continuity 69
gradient 217
gradual *degree* 26
continuous 69
slow 275
graduate
adjust 23
calibrate 26
arrange 60
series 69
measure 466
scholar 492, 873
graduated scale 466
gradus 86, 562
Græculus esuriens
886
graft *join* 43
locate 184
insert 300
trees 371
teach 537
booty 794
corruption 940
Grail
holy – 998
grain *essence* 5
small 32

tendency 176
little 193
rough 256
weight 319
texture 329
powder 330
paint 428
temper 820
ornament 847
against the –
　rough 256
　unwilling 603
　opposing 708
in the – 820
–s of allowance
　qualification 469
　doubt 485
like –s of sand
　incoherent 47
gramercy 916
graminivorous 298
grammar
　beginning 66
　teaching 537
　school 542
　language **567**
bad – 568
comparative – 560
grammarian 492
gramme 319
gramophone 417,
　418, 553
granary 636
grand
　great 31
　style 574
　important 642
　money 800
　handsome 845
　glorious 873
　ostentatious 882
　– climacteric 128
　– doings 882
　– duchy 181
　– jury 967
　en – seigneur
　　proud 878
　　insolent 885
　en –e tenue
　　ornament 847
　　show 882
　– piano 417
　– style 556
　– tour 266
　– Turk 745
　– vizier 694
grandam 130
grandchildren 167
grandee 875
grande dame 878
grandeur 873

grandfather 130,
　166
grandiloquent 577
grandiose 577
grandmother 166
　simple 501
　teach – 538
grandsire 130, 166
grange 189
granite 323
granivorous 298
grano salis, cum
　469, 485
grant *admit* 529
　permit 760
　consent 762
　confer 784
　God – 990
　– a lease 771
granted 488
　take for –
　　believe 484
　　suppose 514
grantee
　possessor 779
　receiver 785
granular 330
granulate 330
granule 32
grapes, sour –
　unattainable 471
　falsehood 544
　excuse 617
grape-shot
　attack 716
　arms 727
graph 554
graphic
　intelligible 518
　painting 556
　descriptive 594
graphite 332
graphito 556
graphology 590
graphometer 244
graphotype 558
grapnel 666
grapple
　fasten 43
　clutch 789
　– with
　　- *a question* 461
　　- *difficulties* 704
　　oppose 708
　　resist 719
　　contention 720
grappling-iron
　fastening 45
　safety 666
grasp
　comprehend 518

power 737
retain 781
seize 789
in one's – 737
　possess 777
tight – *severe* 739
　– at 865
　– of intellect 498
grasping
　miserly 819
　covetous 865
grass 344, 367
let the – grow
　under one's feet
　neglect 460
　inactive 683
not let the – &c.
　active 682
grasshopper 309
grass-plat 371
grate *rub* 330
　physical pain 378
　stove 386
　– on the ear
　　harsh sound 410
　– on the feelings
　　830
grated
　barred 219
grateful
　*physically pleas-
　　ant* 377
　agreeable 829
　thankful 916
grater 260, 330
gratification
　animal – 377
　moral – 827
gratify 829
　permit 760
　please 829
grating [*see* grate]
　lattice 219
　harsh 713
gratis 815
gratitude **916**
gratuitous
　inconsequent 477
　suppositious
　　514
　voluntary 602
　payless 815
gratuity
　gift 784
　gratis 815
gratulate 896
gravaman 642
　– of a charge 938
grave *great* 31
　engrave 259, 558
　tomb 363

important 642
composed 826
distressing 830
sad 837
heinous 945
beyond the – 360
look –
　disapprove 932
rise from the – 660
silent as the – 403
sink into the – 360
on this side of the
　– 359
– in the memory
　505
– note 408
– trap 599
gravel
　earth 342
　material 635
　puzzle 704
graven image 991
graveolent 398
graver 558
graving dock 189
gravitate
　descend 306
　weigh 319
　– towards 176
gravity *force* 157
　weight **319**
　vigour 574
　importance 642
　sedateness 826
　seriousness 837
centre of – 222
specific –
　weight 319
　density 321
gravy 333
　– boat 191
gray **432** [and *see*
　grey]
graze *touch* 199
　browse 298
　rub 331
　brush 379
grazier 370
gré, savoir – 916
grease
　lubricate 332
　oil 356
　– the palm
　　tempt 615
　　give 784
　　pay 807
greasy 355
great *much* 31
　big 192
　glorious 873
　magnanimous

land 342
plain 344
evidence 467
teach 537
motive 615
plea 617
above – 359
down to the – 52
dress the – 371
fall to the – 732
get over the – 274
go over the – 302
level with the –
  162
maintain one's –
  persevere 604*a*
play– 840
prepare the – 673
stand one's –
  defend 717
  resist 719
– bait 784
– cut from under
  one 732
– floor
  chamber 191
  low 207
  base 211
– on
  attribute 155
– plan 554
– of quarrel 713
– sliding from
  under one 665
– swell
  agitation 315
  waves 348
grounded
  stranded 732
well– 490
– on *basis* 211
  evidence 467
groundless
  unsubstantial 4
  illogical 477
  erroneous 495
groundling 876
grounds
  dregs 653
groundwork
  precursor 64
  cause 153
  basis 211
  support 215
  preparation 673
group
  marshal 60
  cluster 72
– *captain* 745
grouping 60
grouse 832, 901*a*

grout 45
grove
  street 189
  glade 252
  wood 367
grovel
  below 207
  move slowly 275
  cringe 886
  base 940
grow
  increase 35
  become 144
  expand 194
– from
  effect 154
– into 144
– less 195
– taller 206
– together 46
– up 194
– upon one 613
grower 164
growl *cry* 412
  complain 839
  discourtesy 895
  anger 900
  threat 909
growler *cab* 272
  discontented 832
  sulky 901*a*
grown up 131
growth [*see* grow]
  development 161
  - *in size* 194
  tumour 250
  vegetation 367
groyne 706
grub
  small animal 193
  food 298
– up
  eradicate 301
  discover 480*a*
Grub-street writer
  593
grudge
  unwilling 603
  refuse 764
  stingy 819
  hate 898
  anger 900
bear a – 907
owe a – 898
grudging 603
– *praise* 932
gruel 298
gruesome 846
gruff
  harsh sound 410
  discourteous 895

grum
  harsh sound 410
  morose 901*a*
grumble
  cry 411
  complain 832,
  839
grume 321, 354
grumous 321, 354
grumpy 901*a*
Grundy, Mrs. 852
grunt 412
  complain 839
guano 653
guarantee 768, 771
guard
  travelling 268
  safety 664
  defence 717
  soldier 726
  sentry 753
advanced – 668
mount –
  care 459
  safety 664
off one's –
  inexpectant 508
throw off one's –
  cunning 702
on one's –
  careful 459
  cautious 864
rear – 668
– against
  prepare 673
  defence 717
– ship 664, 726
guarda costa 753
guarded
  conditions 770
guardian
  safety 664
  defence 717
  keeper 753
– *angel*
  helper 711
  benefactor 912
guardless 665
guard-room 752
gubernation 693
gubernatorial 737
gudgeon 547
guerdon 973
guernsey 225
guerre:
nom de – 565
– à outrance &c.
  722
guerilla 726
– *warfare* 720
guess 514

guesswork 514
guest 890
paying – 188
guet:
mot de – 550
–à-pens 545
guffaw 838
guggle
  gush 348
  bubble 353
  resound 408
  cry 412
guide
  pattern 22
  courier 524
  teach 537
  teacher 540
  indicate 550
  direct 693
  director 694
  advise 695
guide-book 527
guided by, be – 82
guideless 665
guide-post 550
guiding star 693
guild 712, 966
guildhall 799
guile
  deceit 544, 545
  cunning 702
guileless 543, 703
guillotine 972, 975
guilt 947
guiltless 946
guilty:
find – 971
plead – 950
guindé 579
guinea 800
guipure 847
guisard 599
guise
  state 7
  dress 225
  appearance 448
  plea 617
  mode 627
  conduct 692
guiser 599
guitar 417
gulch 198
gules 434
gulf
  interval 198
  deep 208
  lake 343
gull 545, 547
gullet *throat* 260
  rivulet 348
gullible 486

– a gale 349
– and half
 equal 27
 mixed 41
 incomplete 53
– a hundred 98
– light 422
– measures
 incomplete 53
 vacillating 605
 mid-course 628
– moon 245
– price 815
– rations 640
– scholar 493
– seas over 959
– sight 443
– speed
 moderate 174
 slow 275
– truth 546
half-blind 443
half-blood
 mixture 41
 unconformity 83
 imperfect 651
half-frozen 352
half-hearted
 irresolute 605
 insensible 823
 indifferent 866
half-learned 491
half-melted 352
halfpenny
 trifle 643
half-starved
 insufficient 640
 fasting 956
half-way
 small 32
 middle 68
 between 228
 go – *irresolute* 605
 mid-course 628
 meet –
 willing 602
 compromise 774
half-witted 499, 501
hall *house* 189
 lobby 191
 mart 799
 music – 599
 – of audience 588
 – mark 550
hallelujah 990
halliard 45
halloo *cry* 411
 look here! 457
 call 586
 wonder 870
hallow

celebrate 883
respect 928
hallowed 976
hallucination
 error 495
 insanity 503
halo *light* 420
 glory 873
Halomancy 511
halser 45
halt *cease* 142
 weak 160
 rest 265
 go slowly 275
 lame 655
 fail 732
 at the – 265
halter *rope* 45
 restraint 752
 punishment 975
 wear a – 874
 with a – round
 one's neck 665
halting
 style 579
 – place 292
halve [see half]
halves
 do by –
 neglect 460
 not complete 730
 not do by – 729
 go – 778
ham *house* 189
hamadryad 979
hamlet 189
hammam 386, 652
hammer
 repeat 104
 knock 276
 stammer 583
 under the –
 auction 796
 between the – and
 the anvil 665
 – at *think* 451
 work 686
 – out *form* 240
 prepare 673
 complete 729
hammock 215
hamper *basket* 191
 obstruct 706
hamstring 158, 659
hanaper 802
hand
 measure of
 length 200
 side 236
 transfer 270
 man 372

organ of touch
 379
indicator 550
writing 590
medium 631
agent 690
grasp 781
transfer 783
at – *future* 121
 destined 152
 near 197
 useful 644
bad – 590
bird in – 781
come to – 292, 785
fold one's –s 681
give one's – to
 marry 903
good –
 writing 590
 skill 698
 proficiency 700
helping – 707, 711
hold in – 737
hold out the – 894
hold up the –
 vote 609
in –
 incomplete 53
 business 625
 preparing 673
 not finished 730
 possessed 777
 money 800
in the –s of
 authority 737
 subjection 749
lay – s on
 discover 480a
 use 677
 take 789
 rite 998
much on one's –s
 682
on one's –s
 business 625
 redundant 641
 not finished 730
 for sale 796
on the other – 468
no – in 623
poor – 701
put into one's –s
 784
put one's – to 676
ready to one's –
 673
shake –s 918
stretch forth one's
 – 680
take by the – 707

take in –
 teach 537
 undertake 676
time hanging on
 one's –s
 inaction 681
 leisure 685
 weary 841
try one's – 675
turn one's – 675
turn one's – to 625
under one's –
 in writing 590
 promise 768
 compact 769
– back 683
– cart 272
– of death 360
– down
 record 551
 transfer 783
have one's –s full
 682
– gallop 274
– glass 445
– and glove 709,
 888
– in hand
 joined 43
 accompanying 88
 same time 120
 concur 178
 co-operate 709
 party 712
 concord 714
 friend 888
 social 892
– to hand
 touching 199
 transfer 270
 fight 720, 722
– over head
 inattention 458
 neglect 460
 reckless 863
have a – in
 cause 153
 act 680
 co-operate 709
have one's – in
 skill 698
keep one's – in
 613
live from – to
 mouth
 insufficient 640
 unprepared 674
 poor 804
–s off! *avoid* 623
 leave alone 681
 prohibition 761

– over
transfer 783
give 784
win –s down 731
with the –s in the
pockets 681
hand-bag 191
hand-barrow 272
handbook
travel 266
information 527
book 593
handcuff 751, 752
handfast 903
handful
quantity 25
small 32
few 103
handicap
equalize 27
inferiority 34
encumber 706
race 720
handicraft 625, 680
handicraftsman 690
effect 154
doing 680
handkerchief
clothes 225
cleaner 652
handle
feel, touch 379
name 565
dissert 595
plea 617
instrument 633
use 677
manage 693
furnish a – 937
make a – of 677
– a case 693
– to one's name
name 564
honour 877
handmaid
instrumentality
631
auxiliary 711
servant 746
handpost 550
handsel
begin 66
security 771
gift 784
pay 809
handsome
liberal 816
beautiful 845
disinterested 942
– fortune 803
handspike 633

handstaff 727
handwriting
signature 550
autograph 590
– on the wall
warning 668
handy
near 197
useful 644, 646
ready 673
dexterous 698
hang
pendency 214
kill 361
curse 908
execute 972
– about 133, 197
– back 133, 623
– in the balance
133
– in doubt 485
– fire *late* 133
cease 142
unproductive 169
inert 172
slow 275
reluctance 603
inactive 683
not finish 730
fail 732
refuse 764
dullness 843
– on hand 641
– down the head
837
– over the head
152
– it! *regret* 833
contempt 930
– out a light 420
– upon the lips of
418
– on
accompany 88
– out
display 882
entertain 892
– over
destiny 152
height 206
project 250
– out a signal 550
– on the sleeve of
servant 746
servility 886
flattery 933
– in suspense 605
– by a thread 665
– together
joined 43
cohere 46

concur 178
co-operate 709
– upon
effect 154
dependency 749
hangar 191, 273
hang-dog look 901a
hanged if, I'll be –
489
hanger
weapon 727
suspender 45, 214
pothooks and –s
590
– on
accompaniment
88
servant 746
servile 886
hanging [*see* hang]
elevated 307
ornament 847
– look 846
hangman
evil-doer 913
bad man 949
executioner 975
hank *tie* 45
hanker 865
hanky-panky 545
Hansard 551
hansom 272
hap 156
haphazard
chance 156, 621
hapless
unfortunate 735
(*miserable* 828)
(*hopeless* 859)
haply
possibly 470
(*by chance* 156)
happen 151
– as it may
chance 621
– what may
certain 474
reckless 863
happening 151
happiness
[*see* happy]
the greatest – of
the greatest
number 910
happy *fit* 23
opportune 134
style 578
glad 827
cheerful 836
– despatch 972
– go lucky 674

– hunting grounds
981
– returns of the
day 896
– thought 842
– valley
imagination 515
delight 827
harangue 582
hara-kiri 972
harass
fatigue 688
vex 830
worry 907
harbinger
precursor 64
omen 512
informant 527
harbour
abode 189
haven 292
refuge 666
cherish 821
natural – 343
– a design 620
in – 664
– an idea 451
– revenge 919
harbourless 665
hard *strong* 159
dense 323
physically insen-
sible 376
sour 397
difficult 704
severe 739
morally insen-
sible 823
grievous 830
impenitent 951
blow – 349
go –
difficult 704
failure 732
adversity 735
pain 828
hit – 276
look – at 441
not be too – upon
918
strike –
energy 171
impulse 276
try – 675
work – 686
– at it 682
– bargain 819
– of belief 487
– to believe 485
– by 197
– case 735

– cash 800
– earned 704
– and fast rule 80
– fought 704
– frost 383
– of hearing 419
– heart
　malevolent 907
　vicious 945
　impenitent 951
– hit 732
– knocks 720
– life 735
– lines
　adversity 735
　severity 739
– liver 954*a*
– lot 735
– master 739
– measure 739
– names 932
– necessity 601
– nut to crack 704
– to please 868
– pressed
　haste 684
　difficulty 704
　hindrance 706
– put to it 704
– set 704
– tack 298
– task 703
– time 704
– up 704, 804
– upon
　attack 716
　severe 739
　censure 932
– winter 383
– words
　obscure 571
　rude 895
　censure 932
– work 686
– at work 682
harden [*see* hard]
　strengthen 159
　accustom 613
– the heart
　insensible 823
　enmity 889
　impenitence 951
hardened
　impious 988
– front
　insolent 885
hardening
　habit 613
hard-featured 846
hard-fisted 819
hard-headed 498,

739
hardihood 861, 885
hardly
　scarcely 32
deal – with 739
– any *few* 103
– anything
　small 32
　unimportant 643
– ever 137
ha̅rd-mouthed 606
hardness 323
– of heart 914*a*
hardship 735
hardy
　strong 159
　healthy 654
　brave 861
hare 274
hold with the –
and run with
the hounds
　fickle 607
　servile 886
hare-brained 458,
863
harem 961
hariolation 511
hark 418, 457
– back 283
harl 205
harlequin
　changeable 149
　nimble 274
　motley 440
　pantomimic 599
　humorist 844
harlequinade 599
harlot 962
harlotry 961
harm
　evil 619
　badness 649
　malevolence 907
harmattan 349
harmless
　impotent 158
　good 648
　perfect 650
　salubrious 656
　safe 664
　innocent 946
bear – 717
harmonica 417
harmonics 413
harmonist 413
harmonium 417
harmonize 178, 416
harmony
　agreement 23
　order 58

music 413
colour 428
concord 714
peace 721
friendship 888
harness
　fasten 43
　fastening 45
　accoutrement 225
　yoke 370
　instrument 633
　restraint 752
in –
　prepared 673
　in action 680
　active 682
　subjection 749
– up 293
harp
　repeat 104
　*musical instru-
　　ment* 417
　weary 841
Harpagon 819
harper 416
harpist 416
harpoon 727
harpsichord 417
harpy
　relentless 739
　thief 792
　miser 819
　evil-doer 913
　demon 980
harquebuss 727
harridan 846, 962
harrier 366
harrow
　agriculture 371
– up the soul 860
harrowing 830
harry *pain* 830
　attack 716
　persecute 907
Harry, old – 978
harsh
　acrid 171
　sound 410
　style 579
　discordant 713
　severe 739
　disagreeable 830
　morose 895
　malevolent 907
– voice 581
hart 366, 373
hartal 142, 489
harum-scarum 59,
458
haruspice 513
Haruspicy 511

harvest
　effect 154
　profit 618
　store 636
　acquisition 775
get in the –
　complete 729
　succeed 731
– home
　celebration 883
– time
　autumn 126
　exertion 686
has been 122
hash *mix* 41
　cut 44
　confusion 59
　food 298
make a – 699
hashish 663
hasp 43, 45
hassock 215
hastate 253
haste
　velocity 274
　activity 682
　hurry **684**
hasten
　promote 707
hasty
　transient 113
　hurried 684
　impatient 825
　irritable 901
– pudding 298
hat 225
cardinal's – 999
send round the –
　765
shovel – 999
– in hand 886
hatch
　produce 161
　gate 232
　opening 260
　chickens 370
　fabricate 544
　shading 556
　plan 626
　prepare 673
– a plot 626
hatches, under –
　restraint 751
　prisoner 754
　poor 804
hatchet
　cutting 253
bury the – 918
dig up the – 722
throw the helve
　after the – 818

height 206
projection 250
headlong
hurry 684
rush 863
rush –
violence 173
headman 694
headmost
front 234
precession 280
head-piece
summit 210
intellect 450
helmet 717
ornament 847
headquarters
focus 74
abode 189
authority 737
head-race 350
heads
compendium 596
– or tails 156, 621
lay – together
advice 695
co-operate 709
– I win tails you
lose
unfair 940
headship 737
headsman 975
head-stone 363
headstrong
violent 173
obstinate 606
rash 863
headway *space* 180
navigation 267
progression 282
headwind 708
headwork 451
heady 606
heal *restore* 660
remedy 662
let the wound –
forgive 918
– the breach
pacify 723
healing art 662
health 654
picture of – 654
healthiness 655
health resort 189
healthy 656
heap *quantity* 31
collection 72
store 636
too many 641
heaps 102
rubbish – 645

hear
audition 418
be informed 527
not – of (refuse)
764
– a cause
adjudge 480
lawsuit 969
– hear! 931
– and obey 743
– out 457
hearer 418
hearing 418, 696
[*see* hear]
gain a – 175
give a – 418
hard of – 419
out of – 196
within – 197
hearken 457
hearsay 532
– evidence 467
hearse 363
heart
intrinsicality 5
interior 221
centre 222
mind 450
willingness 602
essential 642
affections 820
courage 861
love 897
man after one's
own – 899
with all one's –
438, 602
at – 820, 821
from bottom of –
543
beating – 821, 824
break the – 830
by –
memory 505
go to one's – 824
in good – 858
with a heavy –
603
know by – 490
lay to – 837
learn by – 539
lift up the – 990
lose – 837
lose one's – 897
nearest to one's –
897
not find it in one's
– 603
have a place in
the – 897
put one's – into

604
set one's – upon
604
take –
content 831
hope 858
courage 861
take to –
sensibility 822
discontent 832
dejection 837
anger 900
warm – 822
wind round the –
897
– bleeding for 914
to one's –'s con-
tent
willing 602
enough 639
success 731
pleasure 829
–'s core
mind 450
affections 820
– expanding 821
– failing one 837,
860
do one's – good
829
– of grace 858
– in hand 602
– leaping with joy
827, 838
– leaping into
one's mouth 824
– of oak
strong 159
hard 323
– in right place
906
– sinking *fear* 860
– and soul
completely 52
willing 602
resolute 604
exertion 686
feeling 821
– of stone 823, 907
– swelling 824
heartache 828
heart-breaking 821,
830
heart-broken 828
heartburning
discontent 832
regret 833
enmity 889
anger 900
jealousy 920
hearten 858, 861

heartfelt 821, 829
hearth
home 189
fireplace 386
heartless 823, 945
heart-rending 830
heartsease 831
heart-shaped 245
heart-sick
dejection 837
dislike 867
satiety 869
heart-stricken 828
**heart-strings, tear
the** – 830
hearty
willing 602
healthy 654
feeling 821
cheerful 836
friendly 888
social 892
– laugh 838
– meal 298
– reception 892
heat *warmth* **382**
make hot 384
contest 720
excitement 824,
825
dead – 27
– of passion 900
– wave 382
heated imagination
515
heater 386
heath *moor* 344
plant 367
heathen 984, 989
– mythology 979
heathenish 851
heather *moor* 344
plant 367
heaume 717
**heautontimoru-
menos** 837, 955
heave *raise* 307
emotion 821
– the lead 208,
466
– a sigh 839
– in sight 446
– to 265
heaven 827, **981**
call – to witness
535
in the face of –
525
light of – 420
move – and earth
686

will of – 601
– forfend! 766
– knows 475, 491
– be praised 838, 916
for –'s sake 765
heaven-born
wise 498
repute 873
virtue 944
heaven-directed
498
heaven-kissing 206
heavenly
celestial 318
rapturous 829
divine 976
of heaven 981
– bodies 318
– host 977
– kingdom 981
heavenly-minded
987
heavens 318
– and earth! 870
Heaviside layer
338
heavisome 843
heavy *great* 31
inert 172
weighty 319
stupid 499
actor 599
sleepy 683
dull 843
brutish 851
– affliction 828
– artillery 726
– cost 814
– dragoon 726
– father 599
– gaited 843
– gun 727
– hand
clumsy 699
severe 739
– on hand 641
– heart *loth* 603
pain 828
dejection 837
– hours 841
– on the mind 837
– news 830
– sea
agitation 315
waves 348
– sleep 683
– type 591
– wet 298
heavy-laden 706,
828

hebdomadal 138
Hebe 845
hebetate 823, 826
hebetude
imbecile 499
insensible 823
inexcitable 826
Hebrew
unintelligible 519
Jew 984
Hecate 994
hecatomb
number 98
sacrifice 991
heckle 830, 900
hectic 382, 821
Hector *brave* 861
rash 863
bully 885, 887
hedge
compensate 30
inclosure 232
– in
circumscribe 229
hinder 706
conditions 770
hedgehog 253
hedonism 377, 827
hedonist 954a
heed *attend* 457
care 459
beware 668
caution 864
heedful 457
heedless
inattentive 458
neglectful 460
oblivious 506
rash 863
heel *support* 215
lean 217
deviate 279
go round 311
iron – 975
lay by the –s 162
turn on one's –
go back 283
go round 311
avoid 623
– of Achilles 665
heel-piece
sequel 65
back 235
repair 660
heel-tap
remainder 40
dress 653
heels *lowness* 207
at the – of
near 197
behind 235

cool one's – 681
follow on the – of
281
laid by the – 751
lay by the – 789
show a light pair
of – 623
take to one's –
623
tread on the – of
near 197
follow 281
approach 286
– over head
inverted 218
hasty 684
rash 863
heft *handle* 633
exertion 686
hegemony
influence 175
direction 693
authority 737
hegira [*see* hejira]
heifer 366
heigho! 839
height *degree* 26
altitude 206
summit 210
at its –
great 31
supreme 33
draw oneself up to
his full – 307
– finder 206
heighten
increase 35
elevate 307
exaggerate 549
aggravate 835
heinous 945
heir *futurity* 121
posterity 167
inheritor 779
heirloom 780
heirship 777
hejira 293
Helen of Troy 845
heliacal 318
helical 248
Helicon 597
helicon-horn 417
helicopter 273
Heliogabalus 954a
heliograph
signal 550
picture 554
heliography 550
light 420
painting 556
Helios 423

heliotrope 847
heliotype 558
helix 248
hell *abyss* 208
gaming-house 621
gehenna **982**
– upon earth
misfortune 735
pain 828
– broke loose 59
hell-born 945, 978
hellebore 663
hell-hound 913, 949
hellish
malevolent 907
vicious 945
hell 982
helluo librorum 492
helm *handle* 633
sceptre 747
(*authority* 737)
answer the – 743
at the – 693
obey the – 705
take the – 693
helmet 225, 717
helminthology 368
helmsman 269, 694
helot 746
help *benefit* 618
utility 644
remedy 662
aid 707
servant 746
give 784
it can't be –ed
submission 725
never mind 823
content 831
God – you 914
so – me God 535
– oneself to 789
helper 711
helpless 158, 665
helpmate
auxiliary 711
wife 903
helter-skelter 59,
684
helve
throw the – after
the hatchet 818
hem *edge* 231
fold 258
indeed! 870
kiss the – of one's
garment 886
– in *enclose* 227
restrain 751
hemi- 91
hemisphere 181

hemispheric 250
hemlock 663
hemorrhage 299
hemp 205
hen 366
  female 374
  – with one chicken
    busy 682
henbane 663
hence
  arising from 155
  departure 293
  deduction 476
  – loathed mel-
    ancholy 836
henceforth 121
henchman 746
hencoop 370
hendiadys 91
henna 433
henpecked 743, 749
heptagon 244
heptarchy 98
Heraclitus 839
  rideret – 853
herald
  precursor 64
  precession 280
  predict 511
  forerunner 512
  proclaim 531
  messenger 534
heraldry 550
herb 367
herbage 365
herbal 369
herbivorous 298
herborize 369
herculean
  strong 159
  exertion 686
  difficult 704
Herculem, ex pede
  – 550
Hercules 159, 215
  pillars of – 233,
    550
herd 72, 102
herdsman 746
here
  situation 183
  presence 186
  arrival 292
  come –! 286
  – below 318
  – goes 676
  – and there
    dispersed 73
    few 103
    place 182, 183
  – there and

everywhere
  diversity 16a
  space 180
  omnipresence 186
  – to-day and gone
    to-morrow 111
hereabouts 183,
  197
hereafter 121, 152
hereby 631
hereditament 780
hereditary
  intrinsic 5
  derivative 154,
    167
heredity 167
herein 221
heresy 495, 984
heretic 984
heretofore 122
hereupon 106
herewith 88, 632
heritage
  futurity 121
  possession 777
  property 780
heritor 779
hermaphrodite 83
  – brig 273
hermeneutics 522
Hermes 534, 582
hermetically 261
hermit 893, 955
hermitage
  house 189
  cell 191
  seclusion 893
hero *brave* 861
  glory 873
  good man 948
  – worship 931, 991
Herod, out-Herod
  – 549
heroic [*see* hero]
  magnanimous
    942
  mock – 853
heroics 884
heroin 663
heroine 861
herpetology 368
Herr 373
herring
  pungent 392
  – pond 341
  draw a – across
    the trail 545
  trail of a red –
    615, 706
herring-gutted 203
hesitate

uncertain 475
sceptical 485
stammer 583
reluctant 603
irresolute 605
fearful 860
Hesperian 236
Hesperides, garden
  of the – 981
Hesperus 423
Hessian boot 225
hest 741
hesterni quirites
  876
heterarchy 737
heteroclite 83
heterodoxy 489,
  984
heterogeneous
  unrelated 10
  different 15
  mixed 41
  multiform 81
  exceptional 83
heterogeneity 15,
  16a
heteromorphism
  16a
hetman 745
hew *cut* 44
  shorten 201
  fashion 240
  – down 308
hewers of wood
  workers 690
  commonalty 876
hexagon 98, 244
hexahedron 244
hexameter 98, 597
hey! 586
heyday
  exultation 838
  festivity 840
  wonder 870
  – of the blood 820
  – of youth 127
hiation 260
hiatus 198
hibernal 383
hibernate 683
Hibernicism 497,
  563
hic:
  – jacet 363
  – labor hoc opus
    704
hick 701, 851, 876
hiccup 349
hid under a bushel
  460

hidalgo 875
hidden 528
  – meaning 526
hide *skin* 223
  conceal 528
  – diminished head
    inferior 34
    decrease 36
    humility 879
  – one's face
    modesty 881
  – and seek
    deception 545
    avoid 623
    game 840
hide-bound 751,
  819
hideous 846
hide-out 893
hiding-place
  abode 189
  ambush 530
  refuge 666
hie 264, 274
  – to 266
hiemal 126
hierarch 996
hierarchy 995
hieratic 590
hieroglyphic
  representation
    554
  letter 561
  writing 590
hierographa 985
hieromancy 511
hierophant 996
hieroscopy 511
higgle 794
higgledy piggledy
  59
higgler 797
high *much* 31
  lofty 206
  fetid 401
  treble 410
  foul 653
  noted 873
  proud 878
  from on – 981
  on – 206
  think –ly of 931
  – art 556
  – celebration 998
  – colour
    colour 428
    red 434
    exaggerate 549
  – commissioner
    745
  – days and holi-

days 840
in a – degree 31
– descent 875
– and dry
 stable 150
 safe 664
in – esteem 928
in – feather
 strong 159
 health 654
 cheerful 836
 boasting 884
– glee 836
– hand
 violent 173
 resolved 604
 authority 737
 severe 739
 pride 878
 insolence 885
 lawless 964
– jinks 840
ride the – horse
 878
– hat 225
– life *fashion* 852
 rank 875
– living
 intemperance 954
 gluttony 957
– mass 998
– mightiness 873
– and mighty
 pride 878
 insolence 885
– note 410
– notions 878
– places 210
– pressure
 energy 171
 excitation of
  feeling 824
– price 814
– priest 996
in – quarters 875
– relief 448
– repute 873
–ly respectable
 875
on the – road to
 way 627
 hope 858
on one's – ropes
 excitation 824
 pride 878
 anger 900
– seas 341
in – spirits 836
– tide *wave* 348
 prosperity 734
– time *late* 133

occasion 134
– in tone
 white 430
– treason
 disobedience 742
 dishonour 940
– words
 quarrel 713
 anger 900
high-ball 298
high-born 875
high-brow 492
higher 33
highest 210
highfalutin 884
high-flavoured 392
high-flier
 madman 504
 proud 878
high-flown
 imaginative 515
 style 577
 proud 878
 vain 880
 insolent 885
high-flying
 inattentive 458
 exaggerated 549
 ostentatious 822
highlands 206
high-low 225
high-mettled
 excitable 825
 brave 861
high-minded
 honourable 939
 magnanimous
  942
highness *title* 877
high-pitched 410
high-seasoned 392
high-souled 878
high-sounding
 loud 404
 words 577
 display 882
high-spirited 861,
 939
hight 564
high-toned 852
high-water
 completeness 52
 height 206
 water 337
– mark
 measure 466
highway 627
–s and byways
 627
– robbery 791
highwayman 792

high-wrought
 good 648
 prepared 673
 excited 824
hike 266
hilarity 836
hill *height* 206
 convexity 250
 ascent 305
 descent 306
 take to the –s 666
 –dwelling 206
hillock 206
hilt 633
hinc illæ lachrymæ
 155
hind *back* 235
 clown 876
 on one's – legs
 elevation 307
 anger 900
– quarters 235
hinder 706
hindermost 67, 235
Hindooism 984
hindrance 706
hinge *fasten* 43
 fastening 45
 cause 153
 depend upon 154
 rotate 312
hinny 271
hint *reminder* 505
 suppose 514
 inform 527
 take a – 498
– a fault &c. 932
hinterland 235
hip 236
 have on the –
 confute 479
 success 731
 authority 737
 subjection 749
– hip, hurrah! 838
hipped [*see* hypped]
hippocentaur 83
Hippocrates 662
hippocratic 360
hippodrome
 drama 599
 arena 728
 amusement 840
hippogriff 83
Hippolytus 960
hippophagy 298
hippopotamus 192
hirdie-girdie 218
hire
 commission 755
 borrowing 788

 price 812
 reward 973
 on – 763
hireling 746
hirsute 256
hispid 256
hiss *sound* 409
 animal cry 412
 disrespect 929
 contempt 930
 disapprobation
  932
hist! 585, 586
histology 329
historian 553
historic 594
historiette 594
historical:
– painter 559
– painting 556
historiographer 553
historiography 594
history *past* 122
 record 551
 narrative 594
History, Natural –
 357
histrionic 599
hit *chance* 156
 strike 276
 reach 292
 succeed 731
 censure 932
 (*punish* 972)
 good – 626
make a – 731
– one's fancy 829
– the mark 731
– off 554
– upon
 discover 480*a*
 plan 626
hitch
 fasten 43
 knot 45
 stoppage 142
 hang 214
 jerk 315
 harness 370
 difficulty 704
 hindrance 706
– up 293
hither 278, 292
 come – 286
hitherto 122
hive
 multitude 102
 location 184
 abode 189
 bees 370
 workshop 691

H.M.S. 726
hoar *aged* 128
  white 430
  – frost 383
hoard 636
hoarse
  husky 405
  harsh 410
  voiceless 581
  talk oneself – 584
hoary [*see* hoar]
hoax 545
hob *support* 215
  stove 386
  – and nob
  celebration 883
  courtesy 894
hobble
  limp 275
  awkward 699
  difficulty 704
  fail 732
  shackle 751
  – skirt 225
hobbledehoy 129
hobby
  crotchet 481
  pursuit 622
  desire 865
hobby-horse 272
hobgoblin
  fearful 860
  demon 980
hobo 268
hobnail 876
Hobson's choice
  necessity 601
  no choice 609a
  compulsion 744
hoc genus omne
  876
hock 771
hock shop 787
hockey 840
hockey rink 213
hocus 545
hocus-pocus
  interchange 148
  unmeaning 517
  cheat 545
  conjuration 992
  spell 993
hod
  receptacle 191
  support 215
  vehicle 272
hoddy-doddy 501
hodge-podge 41
hoe 272, 371
hog *animal* 366
  sensualist 954a

  glutton 957
  greedy as a – 865
  go the whole – 604
hog's back 206
hogmanay 998
hogshead 191
hog-wash 653
hoist 307
  – the black flag
   722
  – a flag 550
  – on one's own
   petard
  retaliation 718
  failure 732
hoity-toity! 815,
  870
hold *cohere* 46
  contain 54
  remain 141
  cease 142
  go on 143
  happen 151
  receptacle 191
  cellar 207
  base 211
  support 215
  halt 265
  believe 484
  be passive 681
  defend 717
  power 737
  restrain 751
  prison 752
  prohibit 761
  possess 777
  retain 781
  enough! 869
  have a firm – 781
  have a – upon 175
  gain a – upon 737
  get – of 789
  quit one's – 782
  take – 175
  – aloof
  stay away 187
  distrust 487
  avoid 623
  – an argument
   476
  – authority 737
  – back *avoid* 623
  store 636
  hinder 706
  restrain 751
  retain 781
  miserly 819
  – one's breath
  wonder 870
  – converse 588
  – a council 695

  – fast 751, 781
  – forth *teach* 537
  speak 582
  – good 478, 494
  – one's ground
   141
  – in hand 737
  – one's hand
  cease 142
  relinquish 624
  – hard 265
  – up one's head
   861
  – a lease 771
  – a meeting 72
  – off 623
  – office 693
  – on
  continue 141, 143
  persevere 604a
  – out [*see below*]
  – one's own
  preserve 670
  defend 717
  resist 719
  – oneself in readi-
   ness 673
  – in remembrance
   505
  – both one's sides
   838
  – a situation 625
  – in solution 335
  – to 602
  – together 43, 709
  – one's tongue
   403, 585
  – up [*see below*]
  – oneself up 307
hold out
  endure 106
  affirm 535
  persevere 604a
  resist 719
  offer 763
  brave 861
  – expectation
  predict 511
  promise 768
  – temptation 865
hold up
  continue 143
  support 215
  not rain 340
  aid 707
  rob 791
  display 882
  extol 931
  – one's hand
  sign 550
  threat 609

  – to execration
  cures 908
  censure 932
  – the mirror 525
  – to scorn 930
  – to shame 874
  – to view 525
holder 779
holdfast 45
holding
  tenancy 777
  property 780
hole *place* 182
  hovel 189
  receptacle 191
  opening 260
  ambush 530
  – in one's coat 651
  – and corner
  place 182
  peer into – 461
  hiding 528, 530
  – to creep out of
  plea 617
  escape 671
  facility 705
holiday *leisure* 685
  repose 687
  amusement 840
  – task *easy* 705
holiness *God* 976
  piety 987
holloa 411
  – before one is out
   of the wood 884
hollow
  unsubstantial 4
  completely 52
  incomplete 53
  depth 208
  concavity 252
  channel 350
  - sound 408
  specious 477
  false 544
  voiceless 581
  beat – 731
  – truce 723
holm 346
holocaust
  kill 361
  sacrifice 991
  (*destruction* 162)
holograph 590
holster 191
holt 367
holus bolus 684
Holy *of God* 976
  pious 987
  keep – 987
  – breathing 990

– Church 983*a*
– City 981
– day 998
– Ghost 976
temple of the –
    Ghost 983*a*
– men of old 985
– orders 995
– place 1000
– Scriptures 985
– Spirit 976
– water 998
– week 998
holystone 652
homage
    submission 725
    fealty 743
    reverence 928
    approbation 931
    worship 990
home *focus* 74
    habitation 189
    near 197
    interior 221
    arrival 292
    refuge 666
at – *party* 72
    present 186
    within 221
    at ease 705
    social gathering
        892
be at –
    - *to visitors* 892
feel at –
    freedom 748
    pleasure 827
    content 831
look at –
    accusation 938
make oneself at –
    free 748
    sociable 892
not be at – 764
stay at – 265
at – in
    knowledge 490
    skill 698
at – with
    friendship 888
bring – to
    evidence 467
    belief 484
    accuse 938
    condemn 971
come – 292
eternal – 981
from – 187
get – 292
go – 283
go from – 293

long – 363
strike –
    energy 171
    attack 716
    – stroke 170
    – thrust
    attack 716
    censure 932
home-bred 851
home-felt 821
home-rule 737, 748
homeless
    unhoused 185
    banished 893
homely
    language 576
    unadorned 849
    common 851, 876
Homeric
    – laughter 838
home-sick 833
home-spun
    texture 329
home-stall 189
homestead 189
homeward bound
    292
homicidal maniac
    913
homicide 361
homiletical 892
homily
    teaching 537
    advice 595
    sermon 998
hominem, argu-
    mentum ad –
    938
homœopathic
    small 32
    little 193
Homœopathy 662
homogeneity
    relation 9
    identity 13
    uniformity 16
    simplicity 42
homogenesis 161
homologous 23
homology
    relation 9
    uniformity 16
    equality 27
    concord 714
homonym
    equivocal 520
    vocal sound 580
homophony 413
homunculus 193
Hon. 817
hone 253

honest
    veracious 543
    honourable 939
    pure 960
    – meaning 516
turn an – penny
    775
    – truth 494
honey
    sweet 396
    favourite 899
milk and – 734
honeycomb
    concave 252
    opening 260
    deterioration 659
honeyed
    – phrases 894
    – words
    allurement 615
    flattery 933
honeymoon
    pleasure 827
    endearment 902
    marriage 903
honey-mouthed
    894, 933
honeysuckle 396
honorarium 784, 973
honorary 815
honour
    demesne 780
    glory 873
    title 877
    respect 928
    approbation 931
    probity 939
affair of – 720
do – to 883
do the –s
    sociality 892
    courtesy 894
    respect 928
his – *judge* 967
in – of 883
man of – 939
upon my – 535,
    768
word of – 768
    – be to 873
    – a bill 807
    – in the breach
        923
    – bright
    veracity 543
    probity 939
honte, mauvaise –
    881
hood 225, 999
hooded 223
hoodlum 887

hoodoo 649
hoodwink
    ignore 491
    blind 442
    hide 528
    deceive 545
hoof 211
    cloven – 907
hook *fasten* 43
    fastening 45
    hang 214
    curve 245
    deceive 545
    retain 781
    take 789
by – or by crook
    631
hookah 392
hooker *ship* 273
hookey, blind – 840
hooks, go off the
    360
hooligan 887, 913
hoop *circle* 247
    cry 411
hoot *cry* 411, 412
    deride 929
    contempt 930
    censure 932
hop *leap* 309
    dance 840, 892
    – off 293
    – skip and jump
    leap 309
    agitation 315
    haste 684
    game 840
    – the twig 360
hope 858
    band of – 958
    beyond – 658, 734
    dash one's –s 837
    excite – 511
    foster – 858
    well-grounded –
        472
    – against hope 859
    – for the best 858
    – deferred
    dejection 837
    lamentation 859
    – for *expect* 507
    desire 865
    hope chest 858
hopeful *infant* 129
    probable 472
    hope 858
hopelessness 471,
    859
Hop-o'-my-thumb
    193

identification
  identity 13
  comparison 464
  discovery 480a
identity **13**
  – book 206
Ideology 450
Ides of **March** 601
idiocrasy
  essence 5
  tendency 176
idiocy 499
idiom 560, 566
idiomatic 79
idiosyncrasy
  essence 5
  speciality 79
  unconformity 83
  tendency 176
  temperament 820
idiot 501
  tale told by an –
    517
idiotic
  foolish 499
idiotism
  folly 499
  phrase 566
idle *foolish* 499
  trivial 643
  slothful 683
  lie – *inaction* 681
  – conceit 842
  – hours 681
  be an – man
    leisure 685
  – talk 588
  – time away 683
idler 683
Ido 560
idol *desire* 865
  favourite 899
  fetich 991
  – of the people
    899
idolater 984
idolatry 897, **991**
idolize *love* 897
  impiety 988
idoneous 23
idyl 597
if *circumstance* 8
  qualification 469
  supposition 514
  – you please 765
  – possible 470
igloo 189
igneous 382
ignis fatuus
  luminary 423
  phantom 443

ignite 384
ignoble 876
ignominy 874, 940
ignoramus **493**
ignorance **491**
  keep in – 528
  plead – 937
ignoratio elenchi
  477
ignore
  neglect 460
  incredulity 487
  not known 491
  repudiate 756,
    773
ignotum per
    ignotius 477
ilk 13
ill *evil* 619
  badness 649
  sick 655
  go on – *fail* 732
  adversity 735
  look – 846
  take –
    discontent 832
    anger 900
  – betide 908
  – blood *hate* 898
    malevolence 907
  – at ease *pain* 828
    dejection 837
  house of – *fame*
    961
  –s that flesh is
    heir to *evil* 619
    disease 655
  – humour
    anger 900
    sullenness 901a
  – luck 735
  as – luck would
    have it 135
  – off
    insufficient 640
    adversity 735
    poor 804
  do an – office to
    907
  bird of – omen
    668
  – repute 874
  – turn *evil* 619
    spiteful 907
  – usage 907
  – will 907
  wind *bad* 649
    hindrance 706
    adversity 735
ill-adapted 24
ill-advised

foolish 499
  inexpedient 647
  unskilful 699
ill-affected 901a
illapse
  conversion 144
  ingress 294
illaqueate 545
ill-assorted 24
illation 480
illaudable 947
ill-balanced 28
ill-bred 851, 895
ill-conditioned
  bad 649 ·
  difficult 704
  discourteous 895
  malevolent 907
  vicious 945
ill-conducted 699
ill-contrived
  inexpedient 647
  bad 649
  unskilful 699
  malevolent 907
ill-defined 447
ill-devised 499, 699
ill-digested 674
ill-disposed 901a,
  907
illegality **964**
illegible 519
  render – 552
  –' hand 590
illegitimate
  deceitful 545
  undue 925
  illegal 964
ill-fated 735
ill-flavoured 395
ill-furnished 640
illiberal
  narrow-minded
    481
  stingy 819
  uncourteous 895
  selfish 943
illicit 925, 964
ill-imagined 499,
  699
illimited 105
ill-intentioned 907
illiterate 491, 493
ill-judged 499, 699
ill-judging 481
ill-made 243, 846
ill-mannered 851,
  895
ill-marked 447
ill-matched 24
ill-mated 24

ill-natured 907
illogical 477, 495
ill-omened 605, 859
ill-proportioned 243
ill-provided 640
ill-qualified 699
ill-requited 917
ill-spent 645
ill-tempered 901
ill-timed 135
ill-treat *bad* 649
  severe 739
  malevolent 907
illuminant 388
illuminate
  enlighten 420
  colour 428
  excite 824
  ornament 847
illuminati 492
illumination
  [see illuminate]
  book-illustration
    558
  celebration 883
ill-use 907
ill-used 828
illusion
  fallacy of vision
    443
  error 495
illusive, illusory
  sophistical 477
  erroneous 495
  deceitful 545, 546
illustrate
  exemplify 82
  interpret 522
  represent 554
  engravings 558
  ornament 847
illustrious 873
image
  likeness 17
  copy 21
  appearance 448
  idea 453
  metaphor 521
  representation
    554
  graven – *idol* 991
imagery *fancy* 515
  metaphor 521
  representation
    554
imaginable 470
imaginary
  non-existing 2
  fancied 515
  – quantity 84
imagination **515**

character 820
ingrate 917
ingratiate 897
ingratiating 894
ingratitude **917**
ingredient 51, 56
ingress **294**
  forcible – 300
ingurgitate 296
ingustible 391
inhabile 699
inhabit 186
inhabitant **188**
inhale *receive* 296
  breathe 349
  smell 398
inharmonious
  discord 713
  – colour 428
  – sound 414
inhere 1
inherent 5, 820
inherit 775, 777
inheritance 780
  – of the saints 981
inherited
  intrinsic 5
inheritor 779
inhesion 5
inhibit *hinder* 706
  restrain 751
  prohibit 761
inhospitable 893
inhuman 907
inhume 363
inimaginable
  impossible 471
  improbable 473
  wonderful 870
inimical 708, 889
inimitable
  non-imitation 20
  supreme 33
  very good 648
  perfect 650
iniquity 923, 945
  worker of – 949
inirritability 826
initial 66
  – letter 558
initiate *begin* 66
  admit 296
  teach 537
initiated *skilful* 698
initiative 66
inject 300, 337
injection 662
injudicial 964
injudicious 499,
  863
injunction

acquirement 630
advice 695
command 741
prohibition 761
injure *evil* 619
  damage 659
  spite 907
injuria formæ,
  spretæ – 846,
  930
injury *evil* 619
  badness 649
  damage 659
injustice 923
ink 431
  pen and – 590
  before the – is dry
  132
  – slinging 720
inkle 45
inkling
  knowledge 490
  supposition 514
  information 527
inkstand 590
inland 221
inlay 440, 847
inlet *beginning* 66
  interval 198
  opening 260
  ingress 294
  - *of the sea* 343
inly 221
inmate 188
inmost 221
  to the – core 822
  – soul 820
  – thoughts 451
inn 189
  – s of Court 968
innate 5, 601
innavigable 471
inner 221
  – coating 224
  – man *intellect* 450
  affections 820
innermost recesses
  221
innings *land* 342
  acquisition 775
  receipt 810
innkeeper 601
innocence **946**
innocent *fool* 501
  good 648
  healthy 656
  artless 703
  guiltless 946
innocuous *good* 648
  healthy 656
  innocent 946

innominate 565
innovation
  variation 20a
  new 123
  change 140
innoxious
  salubrious 656
  innocent 946
innuendo *hint* 527
  censure 932
innumerable 105
innutritious 657
inobservance 773
inoccupation 681
inoculate
  insert 300
  teach 537
  influence 615
inodorous **399**
inoffensive 648, 946
inofficious 907
inoperative
  powerless 158
  unproductive 169
  useless 645
inopportune
  untimely 135
  inexpedient 647
inordinate 31, 641
inorganization **358**
inornate 849
inosculate *join* 43
  intersect 219
  convoluted 248
inquest 461
inquietude
  changeable 149
  uneasy 828
  discontent 832
  apprehension 860
inquinate 659
inquire 461
  – into 595
inquirer 461
inquiring mind 455
inquiry **461**
inquisition
  inquiry 461
  severity 739
  torture 907
  tribunal 966
inquisitive 455
inquisitorial
  prying 455
  inquiry 461
  severe 739
  jurisdiction 965
inroad *ingress* 294
  devastation 659
  invasion 716
inrolment 551

insalubrity **657**
insanity **503**
insatiable 865
inscribe 590, 873
inscription 551
inscroll 551
inscrutable 519
insculpture 557
insculptured 558
insecable 43, 87
insect *minute* 193
  animal 366
  – cry 412
insecure
  uncertain 475
  danger 665
insensate
  foolish 499
  insane 503
insensibility
  slow 275
  physical **376**
  moral **823**
  – of benefits 917
  – to the past 506
inseparable 43, 46
insert *locate* 184
  interpose 228
  enter 294
  put in 300
  record 551
  – itself 300
insertion **300**
  adjunct 39
  ornament 847
inservient 645
inseverable 43, 87
inside 221
  – out 218
  turn – out 529
insidious
  deceitful 545
  cunning 702
  dishonourable 940
insight 465, 490
insignia 550
  – of authority 747
insignificant
  unmeaning 517
  unimportant 643
insincere 544, 855
insinuate
  intervene 228
  ingress 294
  insert 300
  latency 526
  hint 527
  ingratiate 897
  blame 932
insipid
  style 575

dull 840
insipidity
  tasteless **391**
  indifferent 866
insist *argue* 476
  command 741
  – upon *affirm* 535
  dwell on 573
  be determined 604
  contend 720
  compel 744
  conditions 770
  due 924
insnare 545
insobriety 959
insolation 382, 384
insolence 878, 885
insoluble *dense* 321
  unintelligible 519
insolvable 519
insolvent
  poverty 804
  debt 806
  non-payment 808
insomnia 682
insouciance
  thoughtlessness
    458
  supineness 823
  indifference 866
inspan 293
inspect 441, 457
inspector 444
  inquisitor 461
  judge 480
  director 694
inspiration
  wisdom 498
  imagination 515
  poetry 597
  impulse 612
  motive 615
  feeling 821
  Deity 976
  revelation 985
  religious - 987
inspire *improve* 658
  prompt 615
  animate 824
  cheer 836
  – *courage* 861
  – *hope* 858
  – *respect* 928
inspirit *incite* 615
  animate 824
  encourage 861
inspiriting
  hopeful 858
inspissate 321, 352
instability 149
install *locate* 184

commission 755
  celebrate 883
instalment
  portion 51
  payment 807, 809
instance
  example 82
  motive 615
  solicitation 765
instant *moment* 113
  present 118
  destiny 152
  required 630
  importance 642
  active 682
  lose not an – 684
  on the – 132
instantaneity 113
instanter 113, 132
instar omnium 17,
    82
instate 883
instauration 660
instead 147
instep 245
instigate 615
instil *extrinsic* 6
  mix 41
  insert 300
  teach 537
instinct
  intellect 450
  intuition 477
  impulse 601
  – *with motive* 615
  possession 777
  brute – 450a
instinctive
  inborn 5
institute *begin* 66
  cause 153
  produce 161
  academy 542
  society 712
  – *an inquiry* 461
institution
  academy 542
  society 712
  political - 963
  church 995
institutor 540
instruct *teach* 537
  advise 695
  precept 697
  order 741
instructed 490
instructor 540
instrument
  implement **633**
  security 771
  musical – 417

optical – 445
  recording – 553
instrumental 631
  – *music* 415
instrumentalist 416
instrumentality 631
insuavity 895
insubordinate 742
insubstantial 4
  – *pageant* 882
insufferable
  painful 830
  dislike 867
insufficiency 640
insufflation 349
insular *unrelated* 10
  detached 44
  single 87
  local 181
  island 346
  prejudice 481
insulate 44
insulse 499, 843
insult *rudeness* 895
  offence 900
  disrespect 929
insulting 898
insuperable 471
  – *obstacle* 706
insupportable 830
insuppressible 173
insurance 768, 771
insure
  make sure 474
  obtain security
    771
insurgent 742
insurmountable
    471
insurrection 719,
    742
insusceptible 823
  – *of change* 150
inswept 195
intact
  permanent 141
  perfect 650
  preserved 670
intaglio *mould* 22
  concave 252
  sculpture 557
  engraving 558
intangible *little* 193
  numb 381
integer 50, 84
integer vitæ scele-
    risque purus 939
integral 50
  – *calculus* 85
  – *part* 56
integrate 50

integrity *whole* 50
  probity 939
  virtue 944
integument 223
intellect 450
  absence of – **450a**
  exercise of the –
    451
intellectual 450
intelligence
  mind 450
  capacity **498**
  news 532
intelligencer 527
intelligentsia 492
intelligibility 518
intemperance 954
  drunkenness 959
intempestivity 135
intend 620
intendant 694
intended *will* 600
  predetermined
    611
intense *great* 31
  energetic 171
  – *colour* 428
  – *thought* 457
intensification 35
intensify
  increase 35
  stimulate 171
intensity *degree* 26
  greatness 31
  energy 171
intensive culture
    371
intent *attention* 457
  will 600
  design 620
  active 682
  – upon *desire* 865
  resolved 604
intention 620
  bad – 907
  good – 906
intently, look – 441
intents and pur-
    poses, to all –
    27, 52
inter 363
interact 12
inter: – alia 82
  – nos 528
interaction 170
interbreeding 41
intercalate 228
intercalation 300
intercede
  mediate 724
  deprecate 766

INT INT INT INT

intercept
 hinder 706
 take 789
intercession
 [*see* intercede]
 worship 990
Intercessor 976
interchange 148
 barter 794
 – *visits &c.* 892
interchangeable 12
intercipient 706
interclude 706
intercommunication 527
intercommunity 892
interconnection 9
intercourse
 copulation 43
 friendship 888
 sociality 892
 verbal – 582, 588
intercurrence
 interchange 148
 interjacence 228
 passage 302
interdependence 12
interdict 761
interdictive 55
interdigitate 219, 228
interest *concern* 9
 influence 175
 curiosity 455
 advantage 618
 importance 642
 property 780
 debt 806
 excite 824
 please 829
 amuse 840
 devoid of – 841
 feel an – in 906
 not know one's
  own – 699
 make – for 707
 place out at –
  lend 787
 economy 817
 take an – in
  curiosity 455
  love 897
 take no – in
  insensibility 823
  indifference 866
 want of – 866
interested
 selfish 943
 – *in* 457
interesting

lovable 897
interfere *disagree* 24
 counteract 179
 intervene 228
 activity 682
 thwart 706
 mediate 724
interference
 light 420
interfretted 219
interfusion 41
interim 106, 120
interior 221
 painting 556
interjacence 68, **228**
interject 228, 300
interlace *join* 43
 twine 219
interlacing 41
interlard 41, 228
interleave 228
interline
 interpolate 228
 write 590
interlineation 39
interlink 43, 219
interlocation 228
**interlocking director-
 torate** 709
interlocution 588
interlocutor 582
interloper
 extraneous 57
 intervene 228
 obstruct 706
interlude
 time 106
 dramatic 599
intermarriage 903
intermeddle 682, 706
intermeddling 724
intermediary 534
intermediate
 mean 29
 middle 68
 intervening 228
 ministerial 631
 – *time* 106
intermedium
 mean 29
 link 45
 intervention 228
 instrument 631
interment 363
 insertion 300
intermezzo 415
intermigration 266
interminable

infinite 105
 eternal 112
 long 200
intermingle 41
intermission 106, 142
intermit
 interrupt 70
 recur 138
 discontinue 142
intermittence
 time 106
intermix 41, 48
intermutation 148
intermural 278
intern 221
internal 5, 221
 – *evidence* 467
international
 reciprocal 12
 sociality 892
 – *law* 963
internecine 361
 – *war* 722
internuncio 534, 758
interpel 142
interpellation
 inquiry 461
 address 586
 summons 741
 appeal 765
interpenetration
 interjacence 228
 ingress 294
 passage 302
interpolation
 adjunct 39
 analytical 85
 interpose 228
 insertion 300
interpose
 intervene 228
 act 682
 hinder 706
 mediate 724
interposit 799
interplanetary 228
interpretation 522
interpreter 524
interrelation 9, 12
interregnum
 intermission 106
 transient 111
 discontinuance 142
 interval 198
 laxity 738
interrogate 461
interrupt
 discontinuity 70

cessation 142
 hinder 706
interruption
 derangement 61
 interval 198
intersect 219
interspace 198, 221
intersperse 73, 228
interstellar 228
interstice 198
interstitial 221, 228
intertexture
 intersection 219
 tissue 329
inter-twine, -twist
 unite 43
 cross 219
interval
 – *of time* 106
 – *of space* **198**
 – *in music* 413
 at –s
  discontinuously 70
 at regular –s 138
intervene
 – *in order* 70
 – *in time* 106
 – *in space* 228
 be instrumental 631
 mediate 724
intervert 140, 279
interview 588, 892
intervolved 43
interweave *join* 43
 cross 219
 interjacence 228
interworking 170
intestate 552
intestine 221
inthral 749, 751
intimacy 9
intimate
 personal 79
 close 197
 inside 221
 tell 527
 friendly 888, 892
intimately
 joined 43
intimidate
 frighten 860
 insolence 885
 threat 909
intitule 564
into: go – 294
 put – 300
 run – 300
intolerable 830
intolerance

itinerary 266, 527
itur ad astra, sic –
   360
ivory 430
Ixion 312

J

jab 276
jabber
   unmeaning 517
   stammer 583
   chatter 584
jacent 213
jacet, hic – 363
jacinth 847
jack
   rotation 312
   ensign 550
   instrument 633
   money 800
Jack – Cade 742
  – Ketch 975
  – o' lantern 423
  – in office
   director 694
   bully 887
  – at a pinch 711
  – Pudding
   actor 599
   humorist 844
   boaster 884
  before one can say
   ' – Robinson'
   132
  – tar 269
  – of all trades 700
jack-a-dandy 844,
  854
jackal
   auxiliary 711
   servility 886
jackanapes 854,
  887
Jackass 271
jack-boot 225
jackdaw in pea-
  cock's feathers
  701
jacket 225
  cork – 666
Jacobin 710
Jacquerie 716, 719
jacta est alea 601
jactitation
   tossing 315
   boasting 884
jaculation 284
jade *horse* 271
   fatigue 688

low woman 876
  scamp 949
  drab 962
jag 257
jagged 244
jail 752
  – bird
   prisoner 754
   bad man 949
jailer 753, 975
jakes 653
jalousie de métier
  921
jam *squeeze* 43
  crowd 72
  food 298
  pulp 354
  sweet 396
  scrape 732
  – in *interpose* 228
jamb 215
jamboree 840
jammed in 751
jangle
   harsh sound 410
   quarrel 713
janissary 726
janitor 263
janty *gay* 836
   pretty 845
   stylish 852
   showy 882
   insolent 885
January 138
januis clausis 528
Janus *deceiver* 607
   tergiversation 607
  close the temple
  of – 723
Janus-faced 544
japan *coat* 223
  resin 356a
  ornament 847
jar *clash* 24
  vessel 191
  agitation 315
  stridor 410
  discord 713
  – upon the feel-
   ings 830
jardinière 191
jargon
   absurdity 497
   no meaning 517
   unintelligible 519
   neology 563
jarvey 694
jasper 847
jaundiced
   yellow 436
   prejudiced 481

dejected 837
jealous 920
view with – eyes
  disapprove 932
jaunt 266
jaunting car 272
jaunty [*see* janty]
javelin 727
jaw *chatter* 584
  scold 932
jaw-fallen 837
jaws *mouth* 231
  eating 298
  – of death 360
jay 584
jaywalker 701
jazz 415, 840
  – band 417
jealous of honour
  939
jealousy 920
  suspicion 485
jecur, difficili bile –
  900
jeer 929
Jehovah 976
Jehu 268, 694
jejune *insipid* 391
  style 575
  scanty 640
  dull 843
jell 352
jelly 298, 352
  beat to a – 972
jemidar 745
jemmy *lever* 633
  dandy 854
je ne sais quoi
  exceptional 83
  what d'ye call 'em
  563
  beauty 845
jennet 271
jeopardy 665
jerboa 309
jeremiad
   lament 839
   invective 932
Jericho, send to –
  297
jerk *start* 146
   throw 284
   pull 285
   agitate 315
jerkin 225
jerks, by – 70
Jerry Sneak 862,
  941
jersey 225
Jerusalem
  the new – 981

Jessamy, Jemmy
  854
jesse 1000
jest *trifle* 643
  wit 842
jest-book 842
jester 844
jesting-stock 857
Jesuit *deceiver* 548
  priest 996
jesuitical 477, 544
Jesus 976
jet *stream* 348
  – black 431
jetsam 73, 782
jettison 782
jetty *protection* 250
  harbour 666
jeu
  le – n'en vaut pas
   la chandelle
   waste 638
   unimportant 643
   dear 814
  – d'esprit 842
  – de mots 842
  – de théâtre 599
jeune
  – premier 599
  – veuve 599
Jew *cunning* 702
  lender 787
  rich 803
  extortioner 819
  heretic 984
  worth a –'s eye
   648, 814
  –'s harp 417
jewel *gem* 648
  ornament 847
  favourite 899
jewellery, false –
  545
Jezebel *wicked* 913
  wretch 949
  courtesan 962
jib *front* 234
  regression 283
  cut of one's –
   form 240
   appearance 448
jibe 140
jiffy 113
jig 840
jig-saw puzzle 840
jilt *disappoint* 509
  deceive 545
  deceiver 548
  cast off 756
  dishonour 940
jilted 898

KEE

- one's promise 772
- quiet 265
- a secret 528
- a shop 625
- in sight 459
- silence 585
- straight 944
- in suspense
uncertainty 475
irresolution 605
- in the thoughts 505
- time
punctual 132
music 416
- to 604a
- together 709
- under
authority 737
subjection 749
restraint 751
- up [*see below*]
- in view
attend to 457
remember 505
expect 507
- waiting 133
- watch 459
- one's word 939
keep up
continue 143
preserve 670
stimulate 824
- appearances 852
- the ball 682, 840
- a correspondence 592
- the memory of 505
- one's spirits 836
- with 274
keeper 370, **753**
keeping
congruity 23
in – 82
safe – *safety* 664
preservation 670
keepsake 505
keg 191
kelpie 979
kelson 211
kempt 652
ken 441, 490
beyond mortal – 360
kennel
assemblage 72
hovel 189
ditch 259
conduit 350

KIC

Kentish fire 931
képi 225
kerb-stone 233
kerchief 225
wave a – 550
kern *quern* 330
low fellow 876
varlet 949
kernel *heart* 5
cause 153
central 222
important 642
kerosene 356
ketch
ship 273
Ketch, Jack – 975
kettle *vessel* 191
caldron 386
- drum *music* 417
tea-party 892
- of fish
disorder 59
difficulty 704
key *cause* 153
opener 260
music 413
colour 428
interpretation 522
indication 550
instrument 631, 633
emblem of authority 747
deliver the –s of the city 725
key-hole 260
key-note *model* 22
rule 80
music 413
key-stone
support 215
motive 615
importance 642
completion 729
khaki 225, 433
khan *inn* 189
governor 745
khedive 745
kibitka 272
kibitzer 682
kick *impulse* 276
recoil 277
assault 716
thrill 821
spurn 930
punish 972
- against
oppose 708
resist 719
- against the pricks

KIN

useless 645
rash 863
unequal 28
superior 33
- up a dust
active 682
discord 713
insolent 885
- a row 900
- one's heels
kept waiting 133
nothing to do 681
- off 62
- up a row
violent 173
- over the traces 742
kicking, alive and – 359
kickshaw *food* 298
trifle 643
kid *child* 129
progeny 167
leather 223
not to be handled with – gloves
dirty 653
difficult 704
kidnap
deceive 545
take 789
steal 791
kidney *class* 75
kilderkin 191
Kilkenny cats 713
kill 361
- or cure 662
- the fatted calf 883
- the goose with golden eggs 699
- with kindness 902
- the slain 641
- time 106
inactivity 683
amusement 840
- two birds with one stone 682
killing 361
delightful 829
kill-joy 706
kiln 386
kilowatt 466
kilt 225
kimbo 244
kimono 225
kin 75
kind *class* 75
benevolent 906

KIT

- regards 894
kinder-garten 542
kindle *cause* 153
produce 161
quicken 171
inflame 173
set fire to 384
excite 824
incense 900
kindling wood 388
kindred 9, 11
kine 366
kinematics 264
kinetic energy 157
king 745
every inch a –
authority 737
rank 875
-maker 694
King –'s Bench 752, 966
-'s birthday 268
-'s counsel 968
- Death 360
-'s English 560
-'s evidence 529
-'s highway 627
-'s ransom 648
- of Kings 976
kingcraft 693
kingdom
region 181
property 780
- of heaven 981
kingly 737
king-post 215
kink 248, 378, 608
kiosk 189, 1000
kip 961
kirk 1000
kirtle 225
kismet 601
kiss *touch* 199
courtesy 894
endearment 902
- the book 535
- the hem of one's garment 928
- in the ring 840
- the rod 725
kit *class* 75
equipment 191
fiddle 417
-bag 191
kitcat 556
kitchen 191, 691
- maid 746
- range 386
kitchener 386
kitchenette 691
kite *fly* 273

tion 625
- unrest 832
laboured - *style* 579
prepared 673
- study 457
labourer 690
labouring
- man 690
- oar 686
labyrinth
disorder 59
convolution 248
secret 533
lac *number* 98
resin 356a
- of rupees 800
lace *stitch* 43
netting 219
ornament 847
- one's jacket 972
lacerable 328
lacerate 44
- the heart 830
laches 460, 773
Lachesis 601
lachrymæ, hinc
illæ - 830
lachrymatory gas
727
lachrymis, quis
temperet a - 914
lachrymose 837
lack *require* 630
insufficient 640
destitute 804
desire 865
- faith 989
- harmony 708
- preparation 674
- wit 501
lackadaisical
inactive 683
melancholy 837
indifferent 866
lackadaisy! 839,
870
lack-brain 499, 501
lacker [*see* lacquer]
lackey 746
lack-lustre 422, 429
laconic 572
lacquer
covering 223
resin 356a
adorn 847
lacrosse 840
lacteal 352
lacuna 198, 252
lacustrine 343
lad 129
ladder 305, 627

kick down the -
604
lade *load* 184
transfer 185
contents 190
dip 270
- out 297
laden 52
heavy - 828
- with 777
ladies' man 897
lading 190, 780
bill of - *list* 86
ladle *receptacle* 191
transfer 270
vehicle 272
lady *woman* 374
rank 875
wife 903
our - 977
- day 138
- help 746
-'s maid 746
lady chapel 1000
ladylike
womanly 374
fashionable 852
lady-love 897
lag *linger* 275
follow 281
dawdle 683
- behind 133
laggard 603, 683
lager *beer* 298
lagoon 343
laical 997
laid: - on one's
back 158
- by the heels 751
- low 160
- up 655
lair 189, 653
laird *master* 745
proprietor 779
nobility 875
Lais 962
laisse manger, cela
se - 394
laisser: - aller,
- faire
permanence 141
neglect 460
inaction 681
laxity 738
freedom 748
inexcitable 826
laity 997
lake *water* 343
pink 434
- of fire and brim-
stone 982

Lama 745, 996
Lamaism 984
Lamarkism 357
lamb *infant* 129
animal 366
gentle 826
innocent 946
go out like a - 174
lion lies down
with - 721
Lamb of God 976
lambent
touching 379
- flame *heat* 382
light 420
Lambeth 1000
lame *incomplete* 53
impotent 158
weak 160
imperfect 651
disease 655
injury 659
failing 732
- conclusion
illogical 477
failure 732
help a - dog over
a stile *aid* 707
vindicate 937
- duck 808
- excuse 617
lamellar 204
lamentable *bad* 649
painful 830
sad 837
lamentably *very* 31
lamentation 839
lamia 980, 994
lamina 51, 204
lamination 204
Lammas 998
lamp 423
rub the - 992
safety - 666
smell of the -
style 577
prepared 673
lamplighter
quick 682
lampoon 932, 934
lampooner 936
lanâ caprinâ, de -
643
lanary 636
lanate 255, 256
lance *pierce* 260
throw 284
spear 727
break a - with
attack 716
warfare 722

couch one's - 720
- corporal 745
lancer 726
-'s *dance* 840
lancet 253, 262
lancinate 378, 830
land *arrive* 292
ground **342**
estate 780
gone to a better -
360
hug the - 286
make the - 286
on - 342
see - 858
- covered with
water 343
- flowing with
milk and honey
168
how the - lies
circumstances 8
experiment 463
foresight 510
in the - of the
living 359
landamman 745
landau 272
landed
- gentry 779
- estate 780
landgrave 745
landholder 779
landing field 273
landing-place 215,
292
landlady 779
land-locked 229,
343
landloper 268
landlord 779
land-lubber 343,
701
landmark
limit 233
indication 550
land-mine 727
landreeve 694
landscape
prospect 448
- gardening
agriculture 371
beauty 845
- painting 556
- painter 559
land-shark 792
land-slip 306
landsman 342
Landsturm 726
land-surveying 466
Landwehr 726

pioneer 64
influence 175
tend 176
soundings 208
- *in motion* 280
heavy 319
rôle 599
induce 615
direct 693
authority 737
heave the - 466
red - 434
take the -
influence 175
importance 642
authority 737
white - 430
- to the altar 903
- astray 495
- captive
subject 749
restraint 751
- a merry chase
623
- the choir 990
- a dance
run away 623
circuit 629
difficulty 704
disrespect 929
- the dance 280
- one to expect
511
- a life 692
- on 693
- to no end 645
- by the nose 737
- off 62
- the way
precedence 62
begin 66
precession 280
importance 642
direction 693
repute 873
leaden *dim* 422
colourless 429
grey 432
inactive 683
leader
precursor 64
dissertation 595
director 694
counsel 968
- writer 595
leading
beginning 66
important 642
- article 595
- lady 599
- note *music* 413

- part 175
- question 461
- seaman 745
- strings
childhood 127
child 129
pupil 541
subject 749
restraint 751, 752
leads 223
leaf *part* 51
layer 204
plant 367
- *of a book* 593
turn over a new -
658
- green 435
leafless 226
leaflet 531
leafy 256
league *length* 200
co-operation 709
party 712
- of Nations 696
leak *crack* 198
dribble 295
waste 638
spring a -
injury 659
- out
disclosure 529
leaky *imperfect* 651
leal 743
lean *thin* 203
oblique 217
- on 215
- to *shed* 191
willing 602
- towards 923
- upon *belief* 484
subjection 749
hope 858
leaning
tendency 176
willingness 602
desire 865
friendship 888
favouritism 923
leap
sudden change
146
ascent 305
jump **309**
-s and bounds 274
make a - at 622
- in the dark
experiment 463
uncertain 475
chance 621
rash 863
- with joy 838

- year 138
leap-frog 840
learn 490, 539
- by experience
950
- by heart 505
learned 490
learner **541**
learning 490, **539**
lease *property* 780
lending 787
grant a - 771
take a new - of
life 654
- and release 783
leasehold 780
leash *lie* 43
three 92
hold in - 751
least
- *in quantity* 34
- *in size* 193
at the - 32
leather *skin* 223
tough 327
beat 972
nothing like - 481
- bottle 191
- or prunello 643
leave *remainder* 40
part company 44
relinquish 624
permission 760
bequeathe 784
French - 623
take - *depart* 293
freedom 748
- alone
inaction 681
freedom 748
permit 760
- the beaten track
83
- to chance 621
- an inference 526
- a loophole 705
- in the lurch
pass 303
decisive 545
- no trace
be no more 2
disappear 449
obliterate 552
- it to one 760
- to oneself 748
- off *cease* 142
desuetude 614
relinquish 624
disuse 678
- out 55
- out of one's cal-

culation 460
- a place 293
- ad referendum
605
give me - to say
535
- undecided 609a
- undone 730
- a void *regret* 833
- word 527
leaven
component 56
cause 153
lighten 320
qualify 469
unclean 653
deterioration 659
bane 663
leavings
remainder 40
useless 645
lecher 962
lechery 961
lectern 1000
lection *special* 79
interpretation 522
lectionary 998
lecture *teach* 537
speak 582
dissertation 595
censure 932
sermon 998
- room 542
lecturer
teacher 540
preacher 996
lectureship 542
led - *captain*
follower 746
servile 886
favourite 899
- by the nose **749**
ledge *height* 206
horizontal 213
shelf 215
projection 250
ledger *list* 86
record 551
accounts 811
lee 236
leech 662, 695
leef 829
leek eat the -
recant 607
submit 725
Lee-Metford
rifle 727
leer *stare* 441
dumb-show 550
leery 702, 864
lees 653

lee-shore 665, 667
leet, court – 966
lee-wall 666
leeward 236
lee-way *space* 180
  tardy 133
  navigation 267
  deviation 279
  progression 282
  shortcoming 304
left *residuary* 40
  sinistral 239
  over the – 545
  – alone 748
  – in the lurch 732
  – to shift for one-
    self 893
  pay over the –
    shoulder 808
left-handed
  clumsy 699
  – compliment 932
  – marriage 903
leg *support* 215
  walker 266
  thief 792
  best – foremost
    686
  fast as –s will
    carry 274
  have a – to stand
    on 470
  keep on one's –s
    654
  last –s *spoiled* 659
  fatigue 688
  light on one's –s
    734
  make a – 894
  not a – to stand on
  illogical 477
  confuted 479
  failure 732
  off one's –s
  propulsion 284
  on one's –s
  upright 212
  elevation 307
  speaking 582
  in health 654
  active 682
  free 748
  set on one's –s 660
  – bail 623
legacy 270, 780, 784
legal *permitted* 760
  legitimate 924
  relating to law
    963
  – adviser 968
  – estate 780

legality 963
legate 534
legatee 779, 785
legation 755
legato 415
legend 551, 594
legendary
  imaginary 515
legerdemain 146,
  545
légèreté 605
leggings 225
leghorn hat 225
legible 518
  – hand 590
legion
  multitude 102
  army 726
legionary 726
legislation 693, 963
legislative assem-
  bly 696
legislator 694
legislature 693, 696
legist 968
legitimate *true* 494
  permitted 760
  right 922
  due 924
  legal 963
legume 367
lei 847
leisure 685
  at one's – *late* 133
leisurely 275
leman 897
lemma 476
lemon *colour* 436
Lemprière 979
lemures 980
lend 787
  – aid 707
  – countenance 707
  – a hand 680
  – oneself to
  assent 488
  co-operate 709
  – on security 789
  – wings to 707
lender *creditor* 805
lending 787
length 200
  go all –s
  resolution 604
  activity 682
  exertion 686
  at – *in time* 133
  full – *portrait* 556
  go great –s 549
  – and breadth of
    50

– and breadth of
  the land
  space 180
  publication 531
  – of time 110
lengthen 35, 200
  – out
  diuturnity 110
  late 133
lengthwise 200
lengthy *long* 200
  diffuse 573
lenient
  moderate 174
  mild 740
  compassionate
    914
lenify 174
lenitive
  moderating 174
  remedy 662
  relieving 834
lenity 740
lens 445
Lent 956, 998
lenten 956
lenticular 245, 250
lentor *slowness* 275
  spissitude 352
  inactivity 683
lentous 352
leonem, ex ungue –
  550
leonine verses 597
leopard
  variegated 440
  –'s spots
  unchanging 150
leprechaune 980
leprosy 655
lerret 273
lèse-majesté 742
less *inferior* 34
  subduction 38
  – than no time
    113
lessee
  possessor 779
  receiver 785
lessen
  – in quantity or
    degree 36
  – in size 195
  – an evil 658
lesson *teaching* 537
  warning 668
  give a – to
  punish 972
  read a – to
  censure 932
  say one's –

  memory 505
lessor 805
lest 623
let *hindrance* 706
  permit 760
  lease 771
  lend 787
  sell 796
  apartments to –
  fool 499
  to – 763
  – alone *besides* 37
  permanence 141
  quiescence 265
  avoid 623
  disuse 678
  inaction 681
  not complete 730
  free 748
  – be
  permanence 141
  continuance 143
  inaction 681
  – blood 297
  – 'I dare not' wait
    upon 'I would'
    605
  – down
  depress 308
  humble 879
  – down easily
  forgive 918
  – fall *drop* 308
  inform 527
  speak 582
  – fly *violence* 173
  propel 284
  – fly at 716
  – go *neglect* 460
  liberate 750
  relinquish 782
  restitution 790
  – in *interpose* 228
  admit 296
  trick 545
  – into *inform* 490
  disclose 529
  – one know 527
  – off *violent* 173
  propel 284
  permit 760
  forgive 918
  exempt 927a
  acquit 970
  – out *disperse* 73
  lengthen 200
  eject 297
  disclose 529
  liberate 750
  – out at 716
  – pass 460

put – into 359
recall to – 660
see – 840
support – 359
take away – 361
tenant for – 779
– to come 152
– after death 981
– or death
  need 630
  important 642
  contention 720
– and spirit 682
Life, the 976
life-blood 5, 359
life-boat 273, 666
life-giving 168
lifeguards 726
lifeless 172, 360
lifelike 17
lifelong 110
life-preserver 666,
  727
life-size 192
lifetime 108
life-weary 841
lift *raise* 307
  aid 707
  steal 791
– cattle 791
– up the eyes 441
– a finger 680
– hand against
  716
– one's head 734
– up the heart 990
– the mask 529
– the voice
  shout 411
  speak 582
lift-smoke 840
ligament 45
ligation 43
ligature 45
light *state* 7
  small 32
  window 260
  velocity 274
  arrive 292
  descend 306
  levity 320
  kindle 384
  match 388
  luminosity **420**
  luminary 423
  - in colour 429
  white 430
  aspect 448
  knowledge 490
  interpretation 522
  unimportant 643

easy 705
gay 836
loose 961
blue – *signal* 550
bring to –
  discover 480a
  manifest 525
  disclose 529
children of – 987
come to – 529
false – 443
foot –s 599
half – 422
make – of
  underrate 483
  easy 705
  inexcitable 826
  despise 930
in one's own – 699
obstruct the – 426
side – 490
see the – *life* 359
  publication 531
transmit – 425
throw – upon 522
a – breaks in upon
  one 529
– under a bushel
  hide 528
  not hide 878
  modesty 881
– comedy 599
– cruiser 726
– fantastic toe 309
– upon one's feet
  664
– heart 836
– of heel 274
– horse 726
– infantry 726
– purse 804
– and shade 420
– of truth 543
– up *illumine* 420
  excite 824
  cheer 836
– upon *chance* 156
  arrive at 292
  discover 480a
  acquire 775
Light of the World
  976
lighten
  make light 320
  illume 420
  facilitate 705
lighter *boat* 273
lighterage 812
lighterman 269
light-fingered 791,
  792

light-footed 274,
  682
light-headed 503
lighthouse 550
lightless 421
light-minded 605
lightning
  velocity 274
  flash 420
  spark 423
like greased – 113
lightsome
  luminous 420
  irresolute 605
  cheerful 836
ligneous 367
lignite 388
lignography 558
ligulate 205
like *similar* 17
  relish 394
  enjoy 377, 827
  wish 865
  love 897
do what one –s
  748
look – 448
we shall not look
  upon his – again
  33
– master like man
  19
– a pin in paper 58
likely 472
  think – 507
likeness 21, 554
  bad – 555
likewise 37
liking 865, 897
  have a – for 827
  to one's – 829
lilac *colour* 437
Liliputian 193
Lillith 994
lilt 416, 836
lily *white* 430
  beauty 845
  paint the – 641
lily-livered 862
limæ labor
  improve 658
  toil 686
limature 330, 331
limb *member* 51
  instrument 633
  scamp 949
– of the law 968
limber 272, 324
limbo *prison* 751,
  752
  pain 828

purgatory 982
lime *entrap* 545
– light 423, 531,
  599
Limehouse 908
limine, in – 66
limit *complete* 52
  end 67
  circumscribe 229
  boundary **233**
  qualify 469
  restrain 751
  prohibit 761
limitarian 984
limitation [*see*
  limit]
  estate 780, 783
limited
  - *in quantity* 32
  - *in size* 193
  to a – extent
  imperfect 651
limitless 105
limitrophe 197
limn 556
limner 559
limousine 272
limp. *weak* 160
  slow 275
  supple 324
  fail 732
limpid 425
lin 343, 348
lincture 662
line *fastening* 45
  continuous 69
  ancestors 166
  descendants 167
  length 200
  no breadth 203
  string 205
  lining 224
  outline 230
  straight 246
  of steamers 273
  direction 278
  music 413
  appearance 448
  measure 466
  mark 550
  writing 590
  verse 597
  vocation 625
  army and navy
  726
  boundary – 233
  draw the – 465
  drop a – to 526
  in a –
  continuous 69
  straight 246

in a – with 278	linstock 388	liquidate 807, 812	lithograph 558
read between the	lint 223	liquidator 801	lithology 358
–s 522	lintel 215	liquor *potable* 298	lithomancy 511
sounding – 208	lion	*fluid* 333	lithotint 558
straight – 246	*courage* 861	in – 959	litigant
troops of the – 726	*prodigy* 872	– up 959	*litigious* 713
– of action 692	*repute* 873	liquorice 396	*combatant* 726
– of battle 69	come in like a –	liquorish [*see*	*accusation* 938
– of battle ship	173	lickerish]	litigation
726	as dewdrops from	lisp 583	*quarrel* 713
– engraving 558	the –'s mane	lissom 324	*contention* 720
– of march 278	483	list *catalogue* **86**	*lawsuit* 969
– of road 627	in the –'s den 665	*strip* 205	litigious 713
lineage *kindred* 11	– lies down with	*leaning* 217	litter *disorder* 59
series 69	the lamb 721	*fringe* 231	*derange* 61
ancestry 166	put one's head in	*hear* 418	*multitude* 102
posterity 167	the –'s mouth	*record* 551	*brood* 167
lineament	665	*will* 600	*support* 215
outline 230	– in the path 706	*choose* 609	*vehicle* 272
feature 240	–'s share *more* 33	*arena* 728	*useless* 645
appearance 448	*chief part* 50	*desire* 865	littéraire, la
mark 550	*too much* 641	enter the –s	morgue – 569
linear	*undue* 925	*attack* 716	littérateur 492, 593
continuity 69	lioness 374	*contend* 720	little
pedigree 166	lion-hearted 861	listed 440	– *in degree* 32
length 200	lionize 455, 873	listel 847	– *in size* 193
linen 225	lip *beginning* 66	listen 418	*darling* 897
liner 273	*edge* 231	– in 457	*mean* 940
lines	*side* 236	– to 457	*cost* – 815
fortification 717	*prominence* 250	be –ed to 175	*do* – 683
hard –	between cup and	– to reason 498	make – of 483
adversity 735	– 111	listless	signify – 643
severity 739	finger on the –s	*inattentive* 458	think – of 458
reins 752	*silent* 581	*inactive* 683	– did one think
linger *protract* 110	*speechless* 585	*indifferent* 866	508
delay 133	hang on the –s of	litany 990, 998	– by little
loiter 275	418	lite, pendente – 969	*degree* 26
lingerie 225	open one's –s	literæ scriptæ 590	*slowly* 275
lingo 560, 563	*speak* 582	literal	– Mary 191
lingua franca 563	seal the –s 585	*imitated* 19	– one 129
linguacious 584	smack the –	*exact* 494	to – purpose
lingual 560, 582	*taste* 390	*manifest* 525	*useless* 645
linguist 492	*savoury* 394	*letter* 561	*failure* 732
linguistics 560	– homage	*word* 562	littleness **193**
liniment 356, 662	*flattery* 933	*orthodox* 983a	littoral 342
lining **224**	– service	– meaning 516	liturgy 998
link *relation* 9	*falsehood* 544	– translation 522	live *exist* 1
connect 43	*hypocrisy* 988	literarum	*continue* 141
connecting - 45	– wisdom 499	homo multarum –	*energetic* 171
part 51	lip salve 847	492	*dwell* 186
term 71	lipstick 847	homo trium – 792	*life* 359
crossing 219	lipothymy 688	literary 560	*repute* 873
torch 423	lippitude 443	– hack 593	– apart 905
golf –s 840	liquefaction **335,**	– man 492	– to fight again
missing – 53, 729	384	– power 569	110
linked together	liquescence 335	literati 492	– from hand to
party 712	liqueur 298, 396	literatim [*see*	mouth 674
linoleum 223	liquid	literal]	– hard 954
linotype 591	*fluid* 333	literature 490, 560	– in hope 858
linseed oil 356	*sound* 405	lithe 324	– and let live
linsey-wolsey 41	*letter* 561	lithic 323	*inaction* 681

freedom 748
inexcitability 826
– in the memory 505
– upon nothing 819
– on 298
– separately 905
– by one's wits 545
livelihood 803
livelong 110
lively *keen* 375
 - *style* 574
 active 682
 acute 821
 sensitive 822
 sprightly 836
 – *imagination* 515
 – *pace* 274
liver 83; hard – 954a
 white – 862
liver-coloured 433
livery *suit* 225
 colour 428
 badge 550
 decoration 877
 – *servant* 746
liveryman 748
live wire 171
livid *dark* 431
 grey 432
 purple 437
living *life* 359
 business 625
 benefice 995
 good – 957
 – *beings* 357
 –room 191
 – *soul* 372
 – *thing* 366
livraison 593
livret 593
lixiviate 335, 652
lixivium 335
llama 271
lo! 457, 870
load *quantity* 31
 fill 52
 lade 184
 cargo 190
 weight 319
 store 636
 redundance 641
 hindrance 706
 adversity 735
 anxiety 828
 oppress 830
 prime and – 673
 take off a – of care

834
– the memory 505
– with 706
– with reproaches 932
loads 102
loadstar 288, 350, 693
loadstone 288, 615
loaf *mass* 192
 do nothing 681
 dawdle 683
loafer
 stroller 268
 inactive 683
 neglect 927
 bad man 949
loam 342
loan 787
loathe 867, 898
loathing
 [see loathe]
 weariness 841
 hate 898
loathsome
 unsavoury 395
 painful 830
 dislike 867
loaves and fishes
 prosperity 734
 acquisition 775
 wealth 803
Lob's pound, in – 751
lobby 191, 615, 627
lobbying 615
lobe 51
local
 – *habitation* 184, 189
 – *board* 966
locale 183
locality 182, 183
localize 184
location **184**
loch 343
loci, genius – 664
lock *fasten* 43
 fastening 45
 tuft 256
 canal 350
 hindrance 706
 prison 752
 dead – 265
 in the –up 938
 under – and key
 safe 664
 restraint 751
 prisoner 754
 – *hospital* 662
 –out 55, 719
 - the stable door

too late 135
useless 645
unskilful 699
–, stock and barrel 50
– up *hide* 528
 imprison 751
locker 191
locket 847
lock-up *prison* 752
loco, in –
 agreeing 23
 situation 183
 expedience 646
locofoco 388
locomotion 264
 – by air 267
 – by land 266
 – by water 267
locomotive 266, 271
locular 191
locum tenens
 substitute 147
 inhabitant 188
 deputy 759
locus:
 – *pœnitentiæ* 937
 – *standi*
 support 215
 plea 617
 social rank 873
locust *prodigal* 818
 evil-doer 913
 swarm like –s 102
locution 582
lode 636
lodestar
 attraction 288
 indication 550
 direction 693
lodestone 288, 615
lodge *place* 184
 presence 186
 dwelling 189
 – a complaint 938
lodgement 184
lodger
 inhabitant 188
 possessor 779
lodging 189
loft 191, 210
lofty *high* 206
 - *style* 574
 proud 878
 insolent 885
 magnanimous 942
log *velocity* 274
 fuel 388
 record 551
 heave the – 466

sleep like a – 683
logarithm 84
loggerhead 501
 at –s *discord* 713
 contention 720
 enmity 889
loggia 191
logic 476
 – of facts 467
logician 476
logical acuteness 570
logography 590
logogryph 533
logolept 562
logomachy
 discussion 476
 words 588
 dispute 720
logometer 85
logometric 84
log-rolling 709
loin 235, 236
 gird up one's –s
 strong 159
 prepare 673
 – *cloth* 225
loisir, impromptu fait à – 673
loiter *tardy* 133
 slow 275
 inactive 683
loll *sprawl* 213
 recline 215
 inactive 683
lollipop 396
lollop 683
Lombard Street to a China orange 472
lone 87
lonesome 893
long - *in time* 110
 - *in space* 200
 diffuse 573
 go to one's – account 360
 – ago 122
 make a – arm
 exertion 686
 seize 789
 –boat 273
 draw the – bow 549
 take a – breath
 refreshment 689
 relief 834
 – clothes 129
 – drawn out 573
 – duration 110
 –expected 507

- face 832, 837
- for 865
-headed *wise* 498
- life to *glory* 873
  approval 931
-lived 110
- odds *chance* 156
  improbability 473
  difficulty 704
- pending 110
- primer 591
- pull and strong
  pull 285
- range 196
- robe 968
- run *average* 29
  whole 50
  destiny 152
- sea 348
- and the short
  whole 50
  concise 572
-sighted
  dim-sighted 443
  wise 498
  foresight 510
- since 122
- spun 573
- standing
  diuturnal 110
  old 124
-suffering
  lenient 740
  inexcitable 826
  pity 914
- time 110
-winded 573
longanimity
  inexcitable 826
  forgiving 918
longevity 110, 128
longhead 500
longing 865
- lingering look
  behind 833
longinquity 196
longitude
  situation 183
  length 200
  measurement 466
longitudinal 200
longo intervallo
  discontinuity 70
  diuturnity 110
  distance 196
  interval 198
longshore-man
  waterman 269
  plebeian 876
longways 217
loo 840

looby *fool* 501
  bungler 701
  clown 876
look *small degree* 32
  see 441
  appearance 448
  attend to 457
- about 459, 461
- after 459, 693
- ahead 510
- alive 457, 684
- another way 442
- back 122
- beyond 510
- black *or* blue
  feeling 821
  discontent 832
  dejection 837
- down upon 930
- in the face
  sincerity 703
  courage 861
  pride 878
- foolish 874
- for 461, 507
- forwards 121,
  510
- here 457
- into 457, 461
- before one leaps
  864
- like 17, 448
- on 186
- out *view* 448
  attention 457
  care 459
  seek 461
  expect 507
  intention 620
  business 625
  danger 665
  warning 668
  caution 864
- over *examine*
  461
- round *seek* 461
- sharp 682
- to 459, 926
- through 461
- up *prosper* 734
  high price 814
  hope 858
  visit 892
- up to *repute* 873
  respect 928
  approbation 931
- upon as 480, 484
looker-on 444
looking-glass 445
loom *destiny* 152
  dim 422

  dim sight 443
  come in sight 446
  weave 691
- of the land 342
- up 31
loon *fool* 501
  clown 876
  rascal 949
loop 245, 247, 629
- the loop 245
loop-hole
  opening 260
  vista 441
  plea 617
  device 626
  escape 671
  fortification 717
loose *detach* 44
  incoherent 47
  pendent 214
  desultory 279
  illogical 477
  vague 519
- *style* 575
  lax 738
  free 748
  liberate 750
  debauched 961
give a - to
- *imagination* 515
  laxity 738
  permit 760
  indulgence 954
let - 750
on the - 961
screw - 713
- character 961
at a - end 685
- fish 949, 962
- morals 945
- rein 738
- suggestion 514
- thread 495
  leave a - 460
  take up a - 664
loosen 47, 750
loot 791, 793
lop 201
- and top 371
lopped
  incomplete 53
loppet 699
lop-eared 53
lop-sided 28
loquacity **584**
loquendi
  cacoëthes - 584
  jus et norma - 567
  usus - 582
lorcha 273
Lord, lord

  ruler 745
  nobleman 875
  God 976
O - *worship* 990
- Chancellor 967
- of the creation
  372
-'s day 687
-s Justices 966,
  967
the - knows 491
- lieutenant 965
- of Lords 976
- of the manor
  779
- it over 737, 885
-'s prayer 990
-'s supper 998
-'s table 1000
lordling 875
lordly 873, 878
Lord Mayor 745,
  965
-'s show 883
lordship
  authority 737
  property 780
  title 877
  judge 967
lore 490, 539
Lorelei 980
lorette 962
lorgnette 445
lorication
  armour 717
loricated
  clothed 223
lorn 893
lorry 272
lose *forget* 506
  unintelligible 519
  fail 732
  loss 776
no time to - 684
- one's balance
  732
- breath 688
- caste 874, 940
- the clew 475,
  519
- colour 429
- one's cunning
  699
- the day 732
- flesh 195
- ground
  slow 275
  regression 283
  shortcoming 304
- one's head
  bewildered 475

Column 1 (MAG):

store 636
– rifle 727
Magdalen 950, 962
mage 994
magenta 434
maggot *little* 193
  fancy 515
  caprice 608
  desire 865
maggoty
  capricious 608
  unclean 653
  – headed
  silly 499
  excitable 825
Magi *sage* 500
  sect 984
magic 175, 992
  – lantern
  instrument 445
  show 448
magician 548, 994
magilp 356*a*
magisterial 878,
  885
magistery 330
magistracy 737, 965
magistrate 745, 967
magistrature 737
magistri, jurare in
  verba – 481
  nullius – 487
magma 41
Magna Charta 769
magna pars fui,
  quorum – 690
magnanimity 942
magnate 875
magnet *attract* 288
  desire 865
magnetism
  power 157
  influence 175
  attraction 288
  motive 615
  animal – 992
magnetize
  influence 175
  motive 615
  conjure 992
magni nominis
  umbra
  wreck 659
  repute 873
  rank 875
magnificent
  large 192
  fine 845
  grand 882
magnifico 875
magnifier 445

Column 2 (MAI):

magnifique et pas
  cher 815
magnify
  increase 35
  enlarge 194
  over-rate 482
  exaggerate 549
  approve 931
  praise 990
magniloquent 577,
  884
magnitude 25, 31,
  192
magno conatu
  magnas nugas
  638, 643
Magnus Apollo 500
magpie 584
magsman 792
maharajah 745
maharani 745
mah jong 840
mahl-stick [*see*
  maulstick]
mahogany
  colour 433
Mahomet 986
Mahometan 984
maid *girl* 129
  servant 631, 746
  spinster 374, 904
  – of all work 690
  – of honour 890
maiden *first* 66
  girl 129
  punishment 975
  – speech 66
maidenhood 904
maidenly 374
maigre 956
mail *post* 270, 534
  armour 717
  – coach 272, 534
  – steamer 273
  – van 272, 534
maim 158, 659
main *tunnel* 260
  ocean 341
  conduit 350
  principal 642
  coup de – 680
  in the –
  intrinsically 5
  greatly 31
  on the whole 50
  principally 642
  with might and –
  686
  plough the – 267
main-chance 156
  good 618

Column 3 (MAJ):

important 642
profit 775
look to the –
foresight 510
skill 698
economy 817
caution 864
selfish 943
main-force
  strength 159
  violence 173
  compulsion 744
mainland 342
main-part 31, 50
mainpernor 771
main-spring 153,
  633
mainstay
  support 215
  refuge 666
  hope 858
maintain
  permanence 141
  continue 143
  sustain 170
  support 215
  assert 535
  preserve 670
  – one's course
  persevere 604*a*
  – the even tenor of
  one's way 623
  – one's ground 717
maintenance
  [*see* maintain]
  assistance 707
  wealth 803
maintien 692
maison de santé
  662
maisonette 189
maître: coup de –
  goodness 648
  skill 698
  l'œil de – 459
majesté, lèse– 742
majestic 873, 882
majesty *king* 745
  rank 873
  deity 976
major *greater* 33
  officer 745
  –domo
  director 694
  retainer 746
  –general 745
  – key 413
  – part *great* 31
  all 50
majority
  superiority 33

Column 4 (MAK):

multitude 102
age 131
join the – 360
majuscule 561
make
  constitute 54, 56
  render 144
  produce 161
  form 240
  arrive at 292
  complete 729
  compel 744
  – acquainted with
  527, 539
  – after 622
  – its appearance
  446
  – away with 162,
  361
  – believe 544, 545,
  546
  – the best of 725
  – bold to differ 489
  – a date with 897
  – choice of 609
  – fast 43
  – a fool of 853
  – for 278
  – one's fortune 734
  – fun of 842, 856
  – a fuss 642, 682
  – good
  compensation 30
  complete 52, 729
  establish 150
  evidence 467
  demonstrate 478
  provide 637
  restore 660
  - one's escape 671
  - one's word 772
  – a go of 731
  – haste 684
  – hay while the
  sun shines 134
  – interest 765
  – known 527
  – the land 292
  – light of 483, 705,
  934
  – oneself master
  of 539
  – money 775
  – a monkey of 853
  – much of 549, 642
  – no doubt 484
  – no secret of 525
  – no sign 526, 528
  – nothing of
  unintelligible 519
  not wonder 871

- of 902
- off 623, 671
- off with 791
- out *see* 441
  evidence 467
  demonstrate 478
  discover 480a
  know 490
  intelligible 518
  interpret 522
  due 924
- over 658, 783, 784
- peace 723, 724
- a piece of work 832
- things pleasant 702
- a present 784
- public 531
- a push 682
- ready 673
- a requisition 741, 765
- a speech 582
- a sucker of 853
- sure 150, 673
- terms 769
- time 110
- tracks 293
- towards 278
- up [*see below*]
- use of 677
- way 282
- one's way 302, 734
- way for 147, 623
- a wry face 867
make up
  complete 52
  compose 54
- accounts 811
- for 30
- matters 952
- one's mind
  judgment 480
  belief 484
  resolve 604
- a quarrel 723
- a sum 809
- to *approach* 286
  address 586
maker *artificer* 690
Maker, the - 976
makeshift 147, 617
make-weight
  inequality 28
  compensation 30
  completeness 52
making of, be the -
  utility 644

goodness 648
aid 707
mal du pays 833
maia fides 940
malachite 435
malacology 368
malade imaginaire 837
maladie du pays 833
maladministration 699
maladroit 699
malady 655
malaise 378, 828
malapert 885, 887
Malaprop, Mrs. - 565
malapropism 495
mal à propos 24, 135
malaria 657, 663
malconformation 243
malcontent 710, 832
male 159, 373
- animal 373
malediction 908
malefaction 947
malefactor 949
malefic 649
maleficent 907
- being 913
malevolence 907
malfeasance 647
malformed 241
malformation 243
malgré 179
- soi 603
malice *hate* 898
  spite 907
bear - *revenge* 919
- aforethought 907
- prepense 907
malign *bad* 649
  malevolent 907
  detract 934
malignant 649, 907
malignity
  violence 173
malinger 544, 655
malison 908
malkin 653
mall *walk* 189
  club 276
malleable 324
mallet 276
malnutrition 655
mal-odour 401

malpractice 947
malt liquor 298
maltreat
  injure 649
  aggrieve 830
  molest 907
malum
- prohibitum 925
- in se 923
malversation 818, 947
Mameluke 726
mamelon 250
mamma 166
mammal 366
mammiform 250
mammilla 250
Mammon 803, 978
serve - 989
mammoth 192
man *adult* 131
  mankind 372
  male 373
  prepare 673
  workman 690
  servant 746
  courage 861
  husband 903
make a - of 648, 861
Son of - 976
straight - 599
to a - 488
-at-arms 726
one's - of business 758
-'s estate 131
- in office 745
- in the street 876
-of-war 273, 726
-of-war's man 269
- at the wheel 694
- and wife 903
manacle 751, 752
manage 693
- to *succeed* 731
manageable 705
management
  conduct 692
  skill 698
manager
  stage - 599
  director 694
managery 693
manche après la cognée, jeter le - 859
manciple 637
mancipation 751
mandamus 741
mandarin 745

mandate 630, 741
mandible 298
mandolin 417
mandragora 174
mandrel 312
manducation 298
mane 256
man-eater 361
manège 266, 370
manes 362
manet: altâ mente repostum 505
- cicatrix 919
manful *strong* 159
  resolute 604
  brave 861
manger 191
manger:
  cela se laisse - 394
- son blé en herbe 818
mangle
  separate 44
  smooth 255
  injure 659
mangled 53
mangy 655
man-hater 911
manhood 131, 861
mania *insanity* 503
  desire 865
maniac 504
manibus pedibus-que 686
manic 503
manic-depressive 503
manicure 847
manicheism 978
manichord 417
manie 865
maniéré 855
manifest
  list 86
  visible 446
  obvious 525
  disclose 529
manifestation 525
manifesto 531
manifold 81, 102
manikin *dwarf* 193
  image 554
maniple 103
manipulate
  handle 379
  use 677
  conduct 692
manipulator 621
mankind 372
manly
  adolescent 131

marquetry 440
marquis 875
marriage 903
  companionate –
    903
  ill-assorted – 903
  – bells 836
  – portion 780
marriageable 131,
  903
marrow *essence* 5
  interior 221
  central 222
  chill to the – 385
marrow-bones, on
  one's –
  submit 725
  beg 765
  humble 879
  servile 886
  atonement 952
marrowless 158
marry *combine* 48
  assertion 535
  wed 903
  – come up
  defiance 715
  anger 900
  censure 932
Mars 722, 979
  – orange 439
marsh 345
marshal
  arrange 60
  messenger 534
  auxiliary 711
  officer 745
Marshalsea 752
marsupial 191, 366
mart 799
Marte, suo –
  exertion 686
  skill 698
martello tower 717
martial 722
  court– 966
  – law 737, 739
  compulsory 744
  illegal 964
  – music 415
martinet 739
martingale 752
Martinmas 998
martyr
  bodily pain 378
  mental pain 828
  ascetic 955
  – to disease 655
martyrdom
  killing 361
  agony 378, 828

  unselfish 942
  punishment 972
marvel 870, 872
  – whether 514
marvellous 31, 870
  deal in the – 549
Masaniello 742
mascaro 847
mascot 993
masculine 159, 373
mash *mix* 41
  disorder 59
  soft 324
  semiliquid 352
  pulpify 354
masher 854
mask *dress* 225
  shade 424
  concealment 528
  ambush 530
  deceit 545
  shield 717
  put on the – 544
mason 690
Masorah 985
masque 599
masqué, bal – 840
masquerade
  dress 225
  concealment 528
  disguise 530
  frolic 840
mass *quantity* 25
  much 31
  whole 50
  heap 72
  size 192
  gravity 319
  density 321
  worship 990
  rite 998
  attend – 990
  in the – 50
  – book 998
  – of society 876
massacre 361
massage 324, 331,
  379
masse, en – 712
masses, the – 876
massive *large* 31
  huge 192
  heavy 319
  dense 321
mast 206
master
  boy 129
  influence 175
  man 373
  know 490
  understand 518

  learn 539
  teacher 540
  director 694
  proficient 698,
    700
  succeed, conquer
    731
  ruler **745**
  possession 777
  possessor 779
  title 877
  eye of the – 693
  hard – 739
  past – 700
  – of Arts 492
  – one's feelings
    826
  – hand 700
  – key *open* 260
  instrument 631
  – mariner 269
  – mind *sage* 500
  proficient 700
  – passion 820
  – one's passions
    944
  – of the position
    731
  – of the revels 840
  – of the Rolls 553,
    967
  – of self 604
  – of the situation
    731, 737
  – spirit of the age
    500, 873
  – of one's time 685
masterdom 737
masterpiece
  good 648
  perfect 650
  skill 698
master-stroke 626,
  731
mastery 731, 737
  get the – over 175
masthead
  punish 972
mastic *viscid* 352
  resin 356a
masticate 298
mastiff 366
mat *support* 215
  woven 219
  misty 427
  cover 652
matador 361
match *coincide* 13
  similar 17
  copy 19
  equal 27

  fuel 388
  contest 720
  marriage 903
matchless
  supreme 33
  excellent 648
  virtuous 944
matchlock 727
mate *similar* 17
  equal 27
  duplicate 89
  mariner 269
  auxiliary 711
  master 745
  friend 890
  wife 903
  check– 732
maté 298
mater alma – 542
  –familias 166
materia medica 662
material
  substance 316
  stuff 635
  important 642
  – for thought 454
  – point 32
materialism
  matter 316
  heterodoxy 984
  irreligion 989
materiality 316
materialize 446
materials 635
matériel 633
maternal
  parental 166
  benevolent 906
  – love 897
maternity 166
mathematical
  precise 494
  – point 193
mathematics 25
mathesis 25
matin 125
matinée 892
matins 990
matrass 191
matriarch 11, 166
matriarchate 737
matriculate 86
matriculation 539
matrilinear 11, 166
matrimony
  mixture 41
  wedlock 903
matrix *mould* 22
  workshop 691
matron 374, 903
matronly 128, 131

matross 726
matter *substance* 3
  material world 316
  topic 454
  meaning 516
  type 591
  business 625
  importance 642
  pus 653
  no – 460
  what – 643
  what's the – 455, 461
  – of course
  conformity 82
  certain 474
  habitual 613
  – in dispute 461
  – of fact *event* 151
  certainty 474
  truth 494
  language 576
  artless 703
  dull 843
  – in hand 454, 625
  – of indifference 866
  – nothing 643
mattock 253
mattress 215
mature *old* 124
  adolescent 131
  conversion 144
  scheme 626
  perfect 650
  improve 658
  prepare 673
  complete 729
  – thought 451
**maturely consid-
  ered** 611
maturine 996
maturity [*see*
  mature]
  bring to – 729
matutinal 125
matzoon 298
maudlin
  inactive 683
  drunk 959
maugre 30
maukin 652
maul *hammer* 276
  hurt 649
maulstick 215
maund *basket* 191
  mumble 583
maunder
  diffuse style 573
  mumble 583

talk 584
lament 839
maundy
  – money 784
  – Thursday 988
Mauser rifle 727
mausoleum 363
mauvais
  – goût 851
  – quart d'heure 828
  – sujet 949
  – ton 851
mauvaise:
  – honte
  affectation 855
  modesty 881
  – plaisanterie 851
mauve 437
maw 191
mawkish 391
Mawworm
  deceiver 548
  sham piety 988
maxim 80, **496**
Maxim gun 727
maximal 33
maximalist 742
maximum 33, 210
maxixe 840
may be 470
  as it – 156
May-day 138, 840
May-fly 111
mayhap 470
mayonnaise 298
mayor 745, 965
maypole 206
May-queen 847
mazard 298
maze
  disorder 59
  convolution 248
  enigma 533
  difficulty 704
  in a –
  uncertain 475
mazed 503
mazurka 840
me 317
me judice 484
meâ culpâ 950
mead *plain* 344
  sweet 396
meadow *plain* 344
  grass 367
  – land 371
meagre *small* 32
  incomplete 53
  thin 203
  - *style* 575

scanty 640
poor 643
– diet 956
meal *repast* 298
  powder 330
mealy-mouthed
  falsehood 544
  servile 886
  flattering 933
mean *average* **29**
  small 32
  middle 68, 228
  signify 516
  intend 620
  contemptible 643
  stingy 819
  shabby 874
  ignoble 876
  sneaking 886
  base 940
  selfish 943
  golden – 174
  take the – 774
  – nothing 517
  – parentage 876
  – time 114
  – wretch 949
meander
  convolution 248
  deviate 279
  circuition 311
  river 348
  – around Robin
  Hood's barn 279
meandering
  diffuse 573
meanest capacity 499
  intelligible to the – 518
meaning **516**
meaningless 517
means
  appliances **632**
  property 780
  wealth 803
  by all – 602
  by any – 632
  by no – 536
  – of access 627
meantime 106
meanwhile 106
measurable 466
  within – distance 470
measure *extent* 25
  degree 26
  moderation 174
  music 413
  compute 466
  verse 597

proceeding 626
action 680
apportion 786
angular – 244
full – 639
out of – 641
without – 641
– of inclination 217
measured
  moderate 174
  sufficient 639
  temperate 953
measureless 105
measurement 25, **466**
measures
  have no – with 713
  take – *plan* 626
  prepare 673
  conduct 692
  – of length 200
meat 298
  broken – 645
  one man's – is
  another man's
  poison 15
mechanic 690
mechanical 601, 633
  – warfare 722
  – powers 633
mechanician 690
mechanism 633
medal
  record 551
  sculpture 557
  palm 733
  decoration 877
  – of Honor 733
medallion 557
medallist 700
meddle 682
médecin tant pis 837
**médecine expec-
  tante** 133, 662
**Medes and Per-
  sians, law of the**
  – 80, 141
mediæval 124
mediævalism 122
medial 29, 68
median 228
mediant 413
medias res, in – 68
  plunge – 300, 576
mediation—*instru-
  mentality* 631
  intercession **724**
  deprecation 766

above –ed 104
not worth –ing 643
mentis gratissimus
   error 481
mentor *sage* 500
   teacher 540
   adviser 695
menu 86, 298
Mephistopheles
   980
Mephistophelian
   945
mephitic 401, 657
mephitis 663
meracious 392
mercantile 794
mercatoria, lex –
   963
mercature 794
mercenary
   soldier 726
   servant 746
   price 812
   parsimonious 819
   selfish 943
mercer 225
merchandise **798**
merchant **797**
merchantman 273
merciful 914
merciless 914*a*
mercurial
   changeable 149
   mobile 264
   quick 274
   excitable 825
Mercury 979
   traveller 268
   quick 274
   messenger 534
mercy *lenity* 740
   pity 914
at the – of
   liable 177
   subject 749
cry you – 766
have at one's –
   919
have no – 914*a*
– on us! 870
for –'s sake 765
– seat 966
mere *simple* 32
   lake 343
   trifling 643
– nothing
   small 32
   trifle 643
buy for a – noth-
   ing 815
– pretext 617

– words 477
– wreck 659
merelles 840
meretricious
   false 495
   vulgar 851
   licentious 961
merfolk 980
merge *combine* 48
   include 76
   insert 300
   plunge 337
– in 56
– into *become* 144
merged 228
meridian
   region 181
   room 125
   summit 210
   light 420
– of life 131
merit
   goodness 648
   due 924
   virtue 944
make a – of 884
– notice 642
merito, e – 944
meritorious 931
Merlin 994
mermaid 341
   monster 83
   mythology 979,
   980
merman 341
mero motu, ex –
   600
merriment
   cheerful 836
   amusement 840
merry *cheerful* 836
   drunk 959
make – *sport* 840
make – with
   wit 842
   ridicule 856
wish a – Christmas
   &c. 896
– and wise 842
merry-andrew 844
merry-go-round
   312, 840
merry-making 827,
   840, 892
merry-thought 842
mersion 337
meruit ferat, pal-
   mam qui – 873
merveille, à – 731
mesa 344
mésalliance 24, 903

meseems 484
mesh 198, 219
meshes *trap* 545
   difficulty 704
– of sophistry 477
meshwork 219
mesial
   middle 68
mesmerism 992
mesmerist 994
mesne lord 779
mess *mixture* 41
   disorder 59
   barracks 191
   meal 298
   difficulty 704
   portion 786
make a –
   unskilful 699
   fail 732
message
   intelligence 532
   command 741
Messalina 962
messenger 271
   envoy **534**
   servant 746
– balloon 463
Messiah 976
messianic 976
messmate 890
messuage 189
messy 59
metabolism 140
metacentre 222
metachronism 115
metage 466
metagenesis 140
metagrammatism
   561
metal 635
   Brittania – 545
metallic *sound* 410
metalepsis 521
metallurgy 358
metamorphosis 140
metaphor
   comparison 464
   figure **521**
   (*analogy* 17)
metaphrase 522
metaphrast 524
metaphrastic 516
metaphysics 450
metastasis, meta-
   thesis
   change 140
   inversion 218
   displacement 270
mete *measure* 466
   distribute 786

– out *give* 784
metempsychosis
   140
meteor 318, 423
meteoric 173, 420
meteorology 338
meteoromancy 511
meter 466
metheglin 396
methinks 484
method *order* 58
   way **627**
want of – 59
methodical 60
Methodist 984
methodist
   journalist 988
methodize 60
Methuselah 130
old as – 124
since the days of –
   124
methylated spirit
   388
meticulous 772
métier 625
métis 83
metonymy 521
metoposcopy
   front 234
   appearance 448
   interpret 522
metre
   length 200
   poetry 597
metrical
   measured 466
   verse 597
metrology 466
   moderation 174
   mid-course 628
metropolis 189
metropolitan
   archbishop 996
mettle *spirit* 820
   courage 861
man of – 861
on one's –
   resolved 604
put on one's –
   excite 824
   encourage 861
mettlesome
   energetic 171
   sensitive 822
   excitable 825
   brave 861
mettre de l'eau
   dans son vin 160
meum et tuum 780

misfit 24
misfortune
adversity 735
unhappiness 830
misgiving 485, 860
misgovern 699
misguide 495, 538
misguided 699
mishap *evil* 619
failure 732
misfortune 735
painful 830
Mishna 985
misinform 538
misinformed 491
misinstruct 538
misintelligence 538
misinterpretation
523
misjoined 24
misjudgment
sophistry 477
misjudge **481**
misinterpretation
523
mislay *derange* 61
lose 776
mislead *error* 495
misteach 538
deceive 545
mislike 867
mismanage 699
mismatch 15, 24
misname 565
misnomer **565**
misogamist 904
misogynist 911
misogyny 904
mispersuasion 538
misplace
derange 61
misplaced
intrusive 24
unconformable 83
displaced 185
misprint 495
misprision
concealment 528
guilt 947
– of treason 742
misprize 483, 929
mispronounce 583
misproportioned
243, 846
misquote 544
misreckon 481, 495
misrelish 867
misreport 495, 544
misrepresent
misinterpret 523
misteach 538

lie 544
misrepresentation
555
untruth 544, 546
misrule
misconduct 699
laxity 738
Lord of – 701
miss *girl* 129
neglect 460
error 495
unintelligible 519
fail 732
lose 776
want 865
courtesan 962
– one's aim 732
– fire 732
– stays 304
– one's way
uncertain 475
unskilful 699
missa cantata 998
missal 998
missay 563, 583
missend 699
misshapen 243, 846
missile 727
missing
non-existent 2
absent 187
disappear 449
– link 53, 83, 729
mission 625, 755
missionary 540, 996
missive 592
misspell 523
misspend 818
misstate 495, 544
misstatement 495,
546
mist 353, 424
in a – 528
seen through a –
519
–s of error 495
– before the eyes
443
mistake *error* 495
misconstrue 523
mismanage 699
failure 732
never was a
greater – 536
misteaching **538**
mister 373
misterm 565
misthink 481
mistime 135
mistral 349
mistranslate 523

mistress *lady* 374
master 745
possessor 779
title 877
love 897
concubine 962
mistrust 485
misty [see mist]
semi-transparent
427
misunderstand
misinterpret 523
misunderstanding
495, 713
misuse **679**
mite *bit* 32
small 193
insufficiency 640
money 800
little – 129
Mithridate 662
mitigate *abate* 174
improve 658
relieve 834
mitigation
[see mitigate]
extenuation 937
mitraille 727
mitrailleur 727
mitre *junction* 43
angle 244
crown 747, 999
mitten 225
mittimus 741
mix 41
– oneself up with
meddle 682
co-operate 709
– with 720
mixen 653
mixture **41**
mere – 59
mix-up 59
mizzen 235
mizzle 348
mnemonics 505
Mnemosyne 505
moa 366
moan 405
cry 411
lament 839
moat *enclosure* 232
ditch 259
canal 350
defence 717
mob *crowd* 72
multitude 102
vulgar 876
hustle 929
scold 932
king – 876

– cap 225
– law
authority 737
illegality 964
mobile
inconstant 149
movable 264
sensitive 822
mobility, the – 876
mobilize
assemblage 72
render movable
264
– troops 722
mobocracy 737
mobster 361
moccasin 225
mock *imitate* 17, 19
repeat 104
erroneous 495
deceptive 545
chuckle 838
ridicule 856
disrespect 929
– danger 861
– modesty 855
– sun 423
mockery
[see mock]
unsubstantial 4
solemn – 882
– delusion and
snare
sophistry 477
deception 545
mocking-bird 19
modal 6, 7, 8
mode *state* 7
music 413
habit 613
method 627
fashion 852
– of expression 561
mode, à la – 852
model *copy* 21
prototype 22
rule 80
form 240
representation
554
sculpture 557
perfection 650
good man 948
new – 658
– after 19
– condition 80
modeller 559
moderate
average 29
small 32
allay **174**

slow 275
sufficient 639
cheap 815
temperate 953
– circumstances
  mediocrity 736
moderately
  imperfect 651
moderation [*see*
  moderate] **174**
  mid-course 628
  inexcitability 826
moderato *music*
  415
moderator 174
  lamp 423
  director 694
  mediator 724
  judge 967
modern 123
  music 415
  art 556
modest *small* 32
modesty
  humility **881**
  purity 960
  mock – 855
modicum *little* 32
  allotment 786
modification
  difference 15
  variation 20a
  change 140
  qualification 469
modish 852
modulation
  variation 20a
  change 140
  music 413
module 22
modulus 84
modus: – operandi
  method 627
  conduct 692
  – in rebus 174
  – vivendi 723
mogul 745
Mohammedan 984
Mohawk
  swaggerer 887
  evil-doer 913
moider 458, 475
moiety 51, 91
moil *active* 682, 686
  exertion 686
moisture *wet* 337
  humid **339**
mokes 219
molar 330
molasses 396
mole *mound* 206

prominence 250
colour 432
refuge 666
defence 717
spot 848
molecular 32
molecule 193
molehill *little* 193
  low 207
  trifling 643
molest *trouble* 830
molestation
  damage 649
  malevolence 907
mollia tempora 134
  – fandi 588
mollify *allay* 174
  soften 324
mollusk 366
mollycoddle 158
Molly Maguire 548
Moloch
  slaughter 361
  demon 980
  heathen deity 986
molten 384
moment
  – *of time* 113
  importance 642
  for the – 111
  lose not a – 684
  not have a – 682
  on the spur of the
  – 612
momentous 152
momentum 276
Momus 838
monachism 995
monad 193
monarch 745
monarchy 737
monastery 1000
monastic 995
monasticism 984
monetary 800
  – arithmetic 11
money 800
  wealth 803
  bad – 800
  command of – 803
  for one's – 609
  made of – 803
  make – 775
  raise – 788
  save – 817
  throw away one's
  – 818
  – to burn 641, 803
  – burning one's
  pocket 818
  – coming in 810

– down 807
– going out 809
– market 800
– matters 811
– paid 809
–'s worth
  useful 644
  price 812
  cheap 815
money-bag 800,
  802
money-belt 802
money-broker 797
money-changer
  797, 801
moneyed 803
moneyer 797
money-grubbing
  775
moneyless 804
monger 797
mongrel
  mixture 41
  anomalous 83
  dog 366
  base 949
moniker 565
moniliform 249
monism 984
monition 527, 668
  information 527
  warning 668
monitor *hear* 418
  oracle 513
  pupil-teacher 540
  director 694
  adviser 695
  war-ship 726
  inward – 926
monitory
  prediction 511
  dissuasion 616
  warning 668
monk 996
monkey
  imitative 19
  support 215
  catapult 276
  ridiculous 857
  play the – 499
  –jacket 225
  – trick
  absurdity 497
  sport 840
  – up 900
monkhood 995
monkish Latin 563
monochord 417
monochrome 429,
  556
monocracy 737

monoculous 443
monode 445
monodrame 599
monody 597, 839
monogamist 904
monogamy 903
monogram
  sign 550
  cipher 533
  diagram 554
  letter 561
monograph
  publication 531
  writing 590
  book 593
  description 594
monolith 551
monolithic 983a
monologue
  soliloquy 589
  drama 599
monomachy 720
monomania 503
  obstinacy 606
  fanaticism 825
monomaniac 504
monomark 550
monoplane 273
monopolist 943
monopoly
  restraint 751
  possession 777
monostich 572
monosyllable 561
monotheism 983
monotonous
  uniform 16
  equal 27
  repetition 104
  permanent 141
  – *style* 575
  weary 841
  dull 843
monotype 591
monsoon 349
monsieur 373
monster
  exception 83
  large 192
  ugly 846
  prodigy 872
  evil-doer 913
  ruffian 949
monstrance 998
monstrosity
  [*see* monster]
  distortion 243
monstrous
  excessive 31
  exceptional 83
  huge 192

at – 32
make the – of
  over-estimate 482
  exaggerate 549
  improve 658
  use 677
  skill 698
the – 33
– often 136
for the – part 78,
  613
make the – of
  one's time 682
mot 496
– de l'énigme 522
– du guet 550
– à mot 19
– d'ordre 741
– de passe 550
– pour rire 842
mote *small* 32
  light 320
– in the eye
  dim-sighted 443
  misjudging 481
motet 990
moth *bane* 663
moth-eaten 124,
  653, 659
mother *parent* 166
  mould 653
– country 189
– of-pearl 440
– superior 996
– tongue 560
– wit 498
motherly *love* 897
  kind 906
motif 415, 847
motile 264
motion
  change of place
  264
  topic 454
  plan 626
  proposal 763
  request 765
  make a – 763
  put in – 284
  put oneself in –
  680
  set in – 677
– downwards 306
– from
  recession 287
  repulsion 289
– into *ingress* 294
  reception 296
– out of 295
– through 302
– towards

approach 286
attraction 288
– upwards 305
motionless 265
motive 615
  absence of – **615a**
– power 264
  motivity 264
motley 81, 440
  wearer of the – 844
motor 153, 266
  vehicle 271, 272
  instrument 633
– boat 273
– car &c. 272
– driver 268
– man 694
motorist 268
motory 264
mottled 440
motto *maxim* 496
  device 550
  phrase 566
motu: ex mero –
  737
  suo – 600
mouchard 527
mould *condition* 7
  matrix 22
  convert 144
  form 240
  structure 329
  earth 342
  vegetation 367
  model 554
  carve 557
  decay 653
  turn to account
  677
moulded 820
– on 19
moulder 653, 659
moulding 847
mouldy 653, 659
moulin:
  se battre contre
  des –s 645
– à paroles 584
moult 226
mound *large* 192
  hill 206
  defence 717
mount *increase* 35
  hill 206
  horse 271
  ascend 305
  raise 307
  display 882
– guard *care* 459
  safety 664
– up to *money* 800

price 812
mountain *large* 192
  hill 206
  weight 319
– artillery 726
– in labour
  waste 638
  make –s of mole-
  hills 482
– brought forth
  mouse
  disappoint 509
mountaineer 268
mountainous 206
mountebank
  quack 548
  drama 599
  buffoon 844
mounted *rifles* 726
mourn 828, 839
mourner 363
mournful
  afflicting 830
  sad 837
  lamentable 839
mourning *dress* 225
  in – *black* 431
  lament 839
mouse *little* 193
  search 461
  mountain brought
  forth – 509
  not a – stirring
  265
mouse-coloured
  432
mousehole 260
mouser 366
mousetrap 545
mousseux 353
moustache 256
mouth *entrance* 66
  receptacle 191
  brink 231
  opening 260
  eat 298
  estuary 343
  enunciate 580
  drawl 583
  deep –ed
  resonant 408
  bark 412
  down in the – 879
  make –s 929
  open one's – 582
  stop one's – 581
  word of – 582
– honour
  falsehood 544
  show 882
  flattery 933

pass from – to
  mouth 531
– wash 652
– watering 865
mouthful
  quantity 25
  small 32
  food 298
mouthpiece
  speaker 524
  information 527
  speech 582
mouthy *style* 577
moutonné 250
moutons, revenons
  à nos – 660
movable 264, 270
movables 780
move *begin* 66
  motion 264
  propose 514
  induce 615
  undertake 676
  act 680
  offer 763
  excite 824
  get a – on 684
  good – 626
  on the – 293
– forward 282
– from 287
– in a groove 82
– heaven and
  earth 686
– off 293
– on *progress* 282
  activity 682
– out of 295
– quickly 274
– slowly 275
– to 894
moveless 265
movement
  motion 264
  music 415
  action 680
  activity 682
moved with 821
mover 164
movies 448, 599,
  840
movie star 899
moving
  keep – 682
  self – 266
– pictures 448
mow *shorten* 201
  smooth 255
  agriculture 371
  store 636
– down

destroy 162	*colour* 429	multifold 81	mundivagant 266
moxa 384	*stupid* 499	multiformity **81**	munerary 973
M.P. 696	mudlark *dirty* 653	multigenerous 81	munerate 973
Mr. 373, 877	*commonly* 876	multilateral 236,	municipal 965
Mrs. 374	muezzin 550, 996	244	municipality 737
MS. 22, 590	muff *incapable* 158	multilocular 191	munificent 816
much 31	*dress* 225	multiloquence 582,	muniment
make – of	*bungle* 699	584	*evidence* 467
importance 642	*bungler* 701	multinomial 102	*record* 551
friends 888	muffettee 225	multiparous 168	*defence* 717
love 897	muffle *wrap* 225	multipartite 44	*security* 771
endearment 902	*silent* 403	multiple 84, 102	munition
approval 931	*deaden* 408a	multiplex 81	*materials* 635
not say – for 932	*conceal* 528	multiplicand 84	*defence* 717
think – of 928, 931	*voiceless* 581	multiplicate 81	mural 717
– ado *exertion* 686	*stammer* 583	multiplication	murder 361
difficulty 704	muffled *faint* 405	*increase* 35	– the King's Eng
– ado about noth-	*latent* 526	*arithmetic* 85	lish
ing	– drums	*multitude* 102	*solecism* 568
over-estimate 482	*funeral* 363	*reproduction* 163	*stammering* 583
exaggerate 549	*non-resonance*	*productiveness*	the – is out 529
unimportant 643	408a	168	murderer 361
unskilful 699	muffler 225, 384	multiplicator 84	muricated 253
– cry and little	mufti *undress* 225	multiplicity 102	murky *dark* 421
wool 884	*judge* 967	multiplier 84	*opaque* 426
– the same	*priest* 996	multiply 35	*black* 431
identity 13	mug *cup* 191	multipotent 157	*gloomy* 837
similarity 17	*face* 234, 448	multisonous 404	murmur *purl* 348
equality 27	*pottery* 384	multitude 72, **102**	*sound* 405
– speaking 584	*dupe* 547	the – 876	*voice* 580
mucid 352, 653	muggy *moist* 339	multum in parvo	*complain* 839
mucilage 352	*dim* 422	596	murmurer 832
muck 653	*opaque* 426	multure 330	murrain 655
run a – *kill* 361	mug-house 189	mum 581, 585	Murray *travel* 266
attack 716	mugient 412	–'s the word 403	Lindley – 542
excitement 825	mugwump 607	mumble *chew* 298	murrey 434
muckle 31	mulatto	*mutter* 583	murrion 717
muckworm 819,	*mixture* 41	Mumbo Jumbo	mus, nascitur ridi-
876	*exception* 83	979, 993	culus – 509, 643
mucor 653	mulct *steal* 791	mummer 599	muscadine 400
mucosity 352	*fine* 974	mummery	muscle 159
mucronate 253	mule *mongrel* 83	*absurdity* 497	muscular 159
muculent 352	*beast of burden*	*imposture* 545	muse 451
mud *marsh* 345	271	*masquerade* 840	[*and see* musing]
semiliquid 352	*obstinate* 606	*parade* 882	Muse *poetry* 597
dirt 653	muleteer 694	mummify 363	historic – 594
clear as – 519	muliebrity 374	mummy *dry* 340	unlettered – 579
stick in the – 704	mull	*corpse* 362	musette 417
– guard 666	*prominence* 250	beat to a – 972	Muses, the – 416
muddle *disorder* 59	*sweeten* 396	mump *mutter* 583	museum
derange 61	mullah 967, 996	*beg* 765	*collection* 72
inattention 458	muller 330	mumper 767, 804	*store* 636
absurd 497	mullion 215	mumpish *sad* 837	mush 354
difficulty 704	mullioned 219	mumps 837, 901a	mushroom
failure 732	multifarious	munch 298	*new* 123
– one's brains 475	*irrelevant* 10	Munchausen 549	*fungus* 367
muddled 959	*diverse* 16a	mundane	*upstart* 734
muddle-headed 499	*multiform* 81	*world* 318	*low-born* 876
muddy *moist* 339	multiferous 102	*selfish* 943	spring up like –s
dim 422	multifid	*irreligious* 989	163
opaque 426	*divided* 51	mundation 652	– anchor 666

next
following 63
later 117
future 121
near 197
– friend 759
– of kin 11
– to nothing 32
– world 152
nexus 45
Niagara 348
niais 501
niaiserie 517
nib *cut* 44
end 67
summit 210
point 253
nibble *eat* 298
– at *censure* 932
– at the bait
dupe 547
willing 602
nice
savoury 394
discriminative 465
exact 494
good 648
pleasing 829
fastidious 868
honourable 939
– ear 418
– hand 700
– perception 465
– point 704
nicely
completely 52
Nicene Creed 983a
nicety 465
niche *recess* 182
receptacle 191
angle 244
– in the temple of fame 873
nicher, se – 184
nick *notch* 257
deceive 545
mark 550
– it 731
– of time 134
Nick, Old – 978
nickel
money 800
nicknack 643
nickname 565
nicotine 392, 663
nictitate 443
nidget 862
nidification 189
nidor 398
nidorous 401

nidus 153, 189
niece 11
niggard 819
nigger 431
– in the woodpile 702
niggle *mock* 929
niggling 643
nigh 197
night 421
labour day and – 686
orb of – 318
– and day 136
– school 542
night-cap 225
nightfall 126
nightingale 416
night-gown 225
nightmare
bodily pain 378
dream 515
incubus 706
mental pain 828
alarm 860
nightshade 663
nigrescent 431
nigrification 431
nihil – ad rem 10
– tetigit quod non ornavit 850
nihilism 989
nihilist 165
nihility 2, 4
nil 2, 4
– admirari
insensible 823
no wonder 871
disapproval 932
– conscire sibi nullâ pallescere culpâ 946
– desperandum 858
nill *unwilling* 603
refuse 764
nim 791
nimble 274, 682
nimble-witted 498, 842
nimbus
cloud 353
halo 420
glory 873
nimiety 641
nimis, ne quid – 817
nimium ne crede colori 485
n'importe 643
Nimrod 361, 622

nincompoop 501
nine 98
tuneful –
music 416
poetry 597
– days' wonder
transient 111
unimportant 643
no wonder 871
– lives 359
– men's morris 840
– points of the law 777
ninefold 98
ninepins 840
ninety 98
ninny 501
Niobe 839
nip *cut* 44
destroy 162
shorten 201
dram 298
freeze 385
pungent 392
drink 959
– in the bud
check 201
kill 361
hinder 706
– up 789
nipperkin 191
nippers 781
nipple 250
Nirvana 981
nis 980
nisi prius 741, 969
Nisus and Euryalus 890
nisus formativus 161
nitid 420
nitor in adversum 708
nitre 392
nitrous oxide 376
nit-wit 499, 501
niveous *cold* 383
white 430
nixe *demon* 980
nixie *fairy* 979
nizam 745
nizy 501
N or M 78
no
dissent 489
negation 536
refusal 764
unable to say – 605
on – account 761
have – business

there 83
– chicken 128, **131**
– choice 601, 609a
– conjuror 501, 701
– consequence 643
in – degree 32
at – great distance 197
– doubt 474, 488
have – end 112
– end of *great* 31
multitude 102
length 200
– fear 473
– go 304, 732
at – hand 32
matter of – import 4
with – interval 199
– one knows who 876
– less 639
– longer 122
– love lost between them 898
– man's land 187
– matter
neglect 460
unimportant 643
and – mistake **474**
– more
inexistent 2
past 122
dead 360
– more than 32
have – notion of 489
– object 643
– one 4, 187
– other 13, 87
to – purpose
shortcoming 304
useless 645
failure 732
give – quarter 361
– scholar 493
make – scruple of 602
– great shakes
small 32
trifling 643
imperfect 651
– sooner said than done 113, 132
– stranger to 490
– such thing
non-existent 2
unsubstantial 4

contrary 14
dissimilar 18
– surrender 606, 717
– thank you 764
at – time 107
– wonder 871
Noah's ark 41, 72
nob 210
nobilitate 873
nobility 875
noble *great* 31
  important 642
  rank 873
  peer 875
  disinterested 942
  virtuous 944
noblesse 875
nobody
  unsubstantial 4
  zero 101
  absence 187
  low-born 876
– knows
  ignorance 491
– knows where
  distance 196
– present 187
– would think 508
noctambulation 266
noctivagant
  travel 266
  dark 421
noctograph 421
noctuary 421, 551
nocturnal
  night 126
  dark 421
  black 431
nocturne 415
nocuous 649
nod *wag* 314
  assent 488
  signal 550
  sleep 683
  command 741
  bow 894
– of approbation 931
– of assent 488
nodding to its fall 162, 306
noddle 210, 450
noddy 501
node 250
nodosity 250, 256
nods and becks and wreathed smiles 894
nodule 250
nodular 256

nodus, dignus vindice – 704
Noel 998
noggin 191
noise 402, 404
– abroad 531
make a – in the world 873
noiseless 403
noisome
  fetid 401
  bad 649
  unhealthy 657
nolens volens 601
noli me tangere
  defiance 715
  excitable 825
  fastidious 868
nolition 603
nolle prosequi 624
nolumus leges
  Angliæ mutari
  permanence 141
  continuance 143
  preservation 670
nom de: – guerre 565
– plume 565
nomad 268
nomadic 266
Nomancy 511
nomenclature 564
nominal
  unsubstantial 4
  word 562
  name 564
– price 815
nomination 564, 755
nominee 758
nominis umbra 4
Nomology 963
non:
– compos mentis 503
– constat 477
– deficit alter 100
– est inventus 187
– hæc in fœdera 536, 610
– nobis Domine 990
– obstante 707
– placet 489
– possumus
  impossible 471
  obstinate 606
  refusal 764
– nostrum tantas componere lites 471, 713

lex – scripta 963
– semper erit æstas 111
– sequitur 70, 477, 495
– sum qualis eram 140, 160
non-addition 38
non-admission 55
nonage 127
nonagenarian 98
non-appearance 447
non-assemblage 73
non-attendance 187
nonce 118
for the – 118, 134
nonchalance
  neglect 460
  insensibility 823
  indifference 866
non-coincidence 14
non-cohesive 47
non-com. 726
non-commissioned officer 745
non-committal 528, 864
non-completion 730
non-compliance 742, 764
nonconformity
  difference 15
  exception 83
  dissent 489
  sectarianism 984
non-content 489
non-cooperation 489, 927
nondescript 83
none 101
– else 87
– to spare 640
– such
  superior 33
  exceptional 83
  very good 648
– in the world 4
– the worse 660
non-endurance 825
nonentity
  inexistence 2
  unsubstantial 4
  unimportant 643
non-essential 6, 643
non-existence 2
non-expectance 508
non-extension 180a
non-fulfilment 730, 732

– of one's hopes 509
non-imitation 20
non-interference
  inaction 681
  freedom 748
nonius 466
non-juror 489, 984
non-naturals 657
nonny 501
non-observance
  inattention 458
  desuetude 614
  infraction **773**
  dereliction 927
nonpareil 648
  type 591
non-payment 808
non-performance
  non-completion 730
  dereliction 927
non-plus
  uncertain 475
  difficulty 704
  conquer 731
non-preparation 674
non-prevalence 614
non-residence 187
non-resistance 725, 743
non-resonance 408a
nonsense
  absurdity 497
  unmeaning 517
  trash 643
  talk – *folly* 499
non-subsistence 2
non-success 732
nonsuch [*see* none]
nonsuit *defeat* 731
  fail 732
  condemn 971
nonum prematur in annum 133
non-uniformity 16a
noodle 501
nook *place* 182
  receptacle 191
  corner 244
noology 450
noon *mid-day* 125
noon-day *light* 420
clear as –
  intelligible 518
  manifest 525
nooscopic 450
noose *ligature* 45
  loop 247

snare 545
gallows 975
norma loquendi 567
normal
  intrinsic 5
  mean 29
  regular 82
  perpendicular 212
  – condition
  rule 80
normality 80, 502
Normand, répon-
  dre en – 544
Norns 601
North 278
  – and South 237
Northern 237
  – light 423
  – star 939
North-west
  passage 311
noscitur a sociis 82
nose *prominence*
  250
  smell 398
  with one's – in
    the air 878
  lead by the – 615,
    737
  led by the – 749
  not see beyond
    one's –
  misjudge 481
  folly 499
  unskilful 699
  speak through
    the – 583
  thrust one's – in
  interjacence 228
  busy 682
  under one's –
  present 186
  near 197
  manifest 525
  defy 715
  put one's – out of
    joint *defeat* 731
  disrepute 874
  – ring 847
nose-dive 306
nosegay 400, 847
nosey 455
nosology 655
nostalgia 833
nostril 351
  breath of one's –s
    359
  stink in the –s 401
nostrum 626, 662
not *negation* 536
  what is – 546

what ought – 923
– at all 32
– allowed 964
– amiss 618, 651,
  845
– any 101
– bad 651
– bargain for 508
– a bit 536
– to be borne 830
– a Chinaman's
  chance 471
– come up to 34
– cricket 923
– to be despised
  642
it will – do 923
– of the earth 987
– expect 508
– fail 939
– far from 197
– a few 102
– fit to be seen 846
– following 477
– grant 764
– guilty 946
– to be had 471,
  640
– having 187, 777a
– hardened 950
– hear of 764
– included 55
– know what to
  make of 519
– a leg to stand
  on 158
– likely 473
– a little 31
– matter 643
– to mention 37
– mind 823, 930
– often 137
– on your life 489
– one 101
– a particle 4
– particular 831
– pay 808
– a pin to choose
  27
– playing the
  game 923
– within previous
  experience 137
– to be put down
  604
– quite 32
– reach 304
– right 503
– sorry 827
– a soul 101
– on speaking

terms 889
– the thing 925
– to be thought of
  incogitancy 452
  impossible 471
  refusal 764
  hopeless 859
  undue 925
  disapprobation
    932
– trouble oneself
  about 460
– understand 519
– vote 609a
– wonder 871
– for the world
  603, 764
– worth
  trifling 643
  useless 645
nota bene 457
notabilia 642
notabilities 875
notable
  manifest 525
  important 642
  active 682
  distinguished 873
notables 875
notably 31
notary 553, 968
notation 85
notch 198, **257**, 550
note *cry* 412
  music 413
  take cognizance
    450
  remark 457
  explanation 522
  sign 550
  record 551
  printing 591
  epistle 592
  minute 596
  money 800
  fame 873
  change one's – 607
  make a – of 551
  of – 873
  take – of 457
  – of admiration
    870
  – of alarm 669
  – of preparation
    673
note-book
  memorandum 505
  record 551
  compendium 569
  writing 590
noted 490, 873

noteworthy
  great 31
  exceptional 83
  important 642
nothing *nihility* 4
  zero 101
  trifle 643
  come to – 304, 732
  do – 681
  for – 815
  go for – 643
  good for – 646
  make – of
  under-estimate
    483
  fail 732
  take – by 732
  think of – 930
  worse than – 808
  – comes amiss 831
  – to do 681
  – to do with 764
  – doing 681
  – to go upon 471
  – in it 4
  – of the kind 18,
    536
  – loth 602
  – on 226
  – more to be said
    478
  – to signify 643
nothingness 2
notice *intellect* 450
  observe 457
  review 480
  information 527
  warning 668
  bring into – 525
  deserve – 642
  give –
  manifest 525
  inform 527
  indicate 550
  short – 111
  take – of 450
  this is to give –
    457
  worthy of – 642
  – is hereby given
  publication 531
  – to quit 782
noticeable 31
notification 527
notion *idea* 453
notional 515
notoriety 531, 873
notorious
  known 490
  public 531
  famous 873

occupancy 186, 777
occupant 188, 779
occupation
  business 625
  in the – of 188
  – road 627
occupied 682
  – by 188
  – with 457, 625
occupier 188, 779
occupy 186, 777
  – the chair 693
  – oneself with 457, 625
  – the mind 451, 457
  – a post 737
  – time 106
occur 1, 151
  – to the mind 451
  – in a place 186
occurrence 151
  of daily – 613
occursion 276
ocean 341
  plough the – 267
oceanography 341
ochlocracy 737
ochre 433, 439
  yellow – 436
o'clock 114
  know what's – 698
octagon 244
octahedron 244
Octateuch 985
octave
  eight 98
  music 413
  period 108
octavo 593
octet 98
octifid 99
octodecimo 593
octogenarian 98, 130
octoroon 41
octroi 812
octuple 98
ocular 441
  – demonstration *see* 441
  visible 446
  – inspection 441
oculis subjecta fidelibus 446
oculist 662
od force 992
odalisque 746
odd *remaining* 40
  exception 83

single 87
  insane 503
  vulgar 851
  ridiculous 853
  – fellows 712
  – fish 857
oddity 857
oddments 51
odds *inequality* 28
  superiority 33
  chance 156
  discord 713
  at – 24, 713
  long – 704
  what's the – 643
  – against one 665
  the – are 472
  – and ends
    remainder 40
    mixture 41
    part 51
    useless 645
ode 597
odi profanum
  vulgus 878
Odin 979
odious
  disagreeable 830
  ugly 846
  hateful 898
odium *disgrace* 874
  hatred 898
  blame 932
odium theologicum 481, 988
  church 995
odograph 200
odometer 200
odontoid 250, 253
odour **398**
  in bad – 932
  – of sanctity 897
odylic force 992
odzookens 870
œcumenical 78
œdematous 194, 324
Œdipus 462, 524
  – complex 897
Davus sum non – 703
œil de maître 459
o'er [*see* over]
œsophagus 260
œuvre 161
of: – all things 33
  – course 82, 154
  – late 123
  – one mind 23
  – no effect 169
  – old 122

– a piece
  uniform 16
  similar 17
  agreeing 23
off 196
  be – 623
  keep – 623
  make – with 791
  move – 287
  sheer – 287
  stand – 287
  start – 293
  – one's balance 605
  throw – one's centre 874
  – one's guard 260, 508
  – one's hands 776
  take – one's hands 785
  – one's head 503
  – one's legs 284, 309
  – one's mind 452
  – and on
    periodical 138
    changeable 149
    irresolute 605
  throw – the scent
    uncertain 475
    avoid 623
  – side 238
  – with you 297
offal 653
offence *attack* 716
  anger 900
  guilt 947
offend 830, 945
  – against the law 964
offensive
  unsavoury 395
  fetid 401
  foul 653
  aggressive 716
  displeasing 830
  distasteful 867
  obnoxious 898
  – and defensive alliance 712
  – to ears polite 579
offer *proposal* **763**
  – the alternative 609
  – a choice 609
  – of marriage 902
  – oneself 763
  – up prayers 990
  – sacrifice 990
  – for sale 796

offering *gift* 784
  burnt – 990
  sin – 952
offertory *gift* 784
  worship 990
  rite 998
off-hand *soon* 132
  inattentive 458
  careless 460
  spontaneous 612
office *doing* 170
  room 191
  business 625
  mart 799
  worship 900
  do one's – 772
  good –s 724, 906
  hold – 693
  kind –s 906
  do an ill – 907
  man in – 694
officer *director* 694
  commander 745
  constable 965
offices
  kitchen &c. 191
official *certain* 474
  true 494
  business 625
  man in *office* 694
  authoritative 737
  master 745
  servant 746
officialism 739
officiate
  business 625
  act 680
  conduct 692
  religious 998
officio, ex –
  officer 694
  authority 737
  duly 924
officinal 613
officious 682
offing 196, 341
offscourings 645, 653
offset
  compensation 30
  offspring 167
offshoot *adjunct* 39
  part 51
  effect 154
  offspring 167
offspring *effect* 154
  posterity 167
offuscate 421, 426
often *repeated* 104
  frequent 136
  most – 613

– to be met with 136
ogee 847
Ogham 590
ogive 215
ogle *look* 441
  desire 865
  rude 895
  endearment 902
ogpu 696
ogre *bugbear* 860
  evil-doer 913
  demon 980
oil *lubricate* 332
  grease 355, **356**
  pour – on
  relieve 834
  – on the troubled
    waters 174, 714
  – lamp 423
  – stove 386
oilcloth 223
oiled *drunk* 959
oilskin 386
oil-painting 556
oily *smooth* 255
  greasy 355
  servile 886
  courteous 894
  flattery 933
oinomania 959
ointment
  grease 356
  remedy 662
O.K. 488
old 124
  of – 122
  – age 128
  die of – age 729
  – bachelor 904
  – clothes 225
  – fashioned 851
  – fogey 501, 857
  – joke 842
  – maid *cards* 840
  spinster 904
  – man *veteran* 130
  husband 903
  – man of the sea
    706
  – Nick 978
  – school 124
  obstinate 606
  habit 613
  pay off – scores
    718
  – song
  repetition 104
  trifle 643
  cheap 815
  – stager

veteran 130
  actor 599
  proficient 700
  – story
  repetition 104
  stale news 532
  love 897
  – times 122
  one's – way 613
  – woman *fool* 501
  wife 903
Oldbuck 122
olden 124
older 128
oldest inhabitant
  not in memory of
  – 137
old-fashioned 124,
  851
oldness 124
oleagine 356
oleaginous 355
oleomargarine 356
oleum addere
  camino 35, 173
olfactory 398
olid 401
oligarch 745
oligarchy 737
olio 41
olive-branch
  infant 129
  offspring 167
  pacification 723
olive-green 435
olla podrida 41
Olympiad 720
Olympus 981
ombre 840
ombres chinoises
  448
omega *end* 67
omelet 298
omen **512**
ominate 511
ominous
  predicting 511
  indicating 550
  danger 665
  hopeless 859
omission
  incomplete 53
  exclusion 55
  neglect 460
  failure 732
  non-observance
    773
  guilt 947
omitted 2, 187
omne tulit
  punctum 731

omnibus 272
omnifarious 81
omnific 168
omniform 81
omnigenous 81
omnipotence 157,
  976
omnipresence 186,
  976
omniscience 490,
  976
omnium gatherum
  mixture 41
  confusion 59
  assemblage 72
omnivorous
  eating 298
  desire 865
  gluttony 957
omphalos 68
on *forwards* 282
  – account of 155
  – all accounts 52
  – that account 155
  – approval 463
  – an average 29
  – the brink of 32
  – the cards 152
  – foot *duration* 106
  event 151
  doing 170
  – the fire 730
  – all fours 13, 23
  – the other hand
    30
  – one's head 218
  – the increase 35
  – a large scale 31
  – these lines 627
  – the move 264
  – the nail 118
  – no account 32
  – no occasion 107
  – a par 27
  – the part of 9
  – the point of 111
  – the present oc-
    casion 118
  – trial 463
  – the whole 50
on dit 532, 588
once *past* 119, 122
  seldom 137
  at – 113, 132
  – for all *final* 67
  infrequency 137
  tell one – 527
  determine – 604
  choose 609
  – in a blue moon
    137

– more 90, 104
– over 457
– upon a time
  time 106
  different time 119
  formerly 122
– in a way 137
Ondine 979
one *identical* 13
  whole 50
  unity 87
  somebody 372
  married 903
  all – to 823
  at – with *agree* 23
  concur 178
  concord 714
  make – of 186
  neither – nor the
    other 610
  of – *accord* 488
  – and all
  whole 50
  general 78
  unanimous 488
  from – to another
  transfer 783
  – thing with
    another 476
  – of the best 948
  – bone and one
    flesh 903
  – consent 178, 488
  – of these days 121
  – fell swoop 113,
    173
  – fine morning 106
  – and a half 87
  – horse 643
  – idea 481
  – jump 113
  – leg in the grave
    160
  as – man 488, 709
  – mind 178, **488**
  – by one
  separately 44
  respectively 79
  unity 87
  both the – and
    the other 89
  the – or the other
    609
  – over the eight
    959
  – and the same 13
  on – side 217, 236
  – step 840
  – in ten thousand
    648, 948
  – at a time 87

below – *low* 207
imperfect 651
– excellence 33
– nobile fratrum
alike 17
friends 890
de – le roi 737
– parenthèse 134
– pari refero 718
– value 812
parable
metaphor 521
teaching 537
description 594
parabola *curve* 245
parabolic
metaphorical 521
paracentesis 297
parachronism 115
parachute
balloon 273
means of safety 666
– light 423
Paraclete 976
parade *procession* 69, 266
walk 189
ostentation 882
paradigm 22, 567
Paradise *bliss* 827
heaven 981
in – 827
parados 717
paradox
absurdity 497
obscurity 519
difficulty 704
paradoxical 475, 519
paraffin 356
paragon
perfect 650
glory 873
good man 948
paragram
ambiguous 520
neology 563
paragraph *part* 51
phrase 566
article 593
paraleipsis 460
parallax 196
parallel
similarity 17
imitate 19
harmonious 178
– *position* 216
symmetry 242
draw a – 464
none but himself

can be his – 873
run – 178
parallelism **216**
agreement 23
parallelogram 244
parallelopiped 244
paralogism 477
paralogize 477
paralysis
impotence 158
physical insensibility 376
disease 655
moral insensibility 823
paralyse 158, 376, 823
paramount
supreme 33
important 642
authority 737
lord – *master* 745
possessor 779
– estate 780
paramour 897
paranoia 503, 504
parapet 717
paraph 550
paraphernalia
machinery 633
belonging 780
paraphrase
imitation 19
copy 21
synonym 522
phrase 566
paraphrast 524
paraphrastic 19, 522
parasite *auxiliary* 711
servile 886
flatterer 935
parasitic
subjection 749
grasping 789
servile 886
parasol *covering* 223
shade 424
paratus:
in utrumque –
resolved 604
ready 673
semper – 673
parboil 384
parbuckle 633
Parcæ 601
parcel *part* 51
group 72
part and – 56
– out *arrange* 60

allot 786
parcels
property 780
parcere subjectis 740, 914
parch *dry* 340
heat 382
bake 384
parched with thirst 865
parchment
writing 590
security 771
parcity 819
pardi 535
pardon 506, 918
beg – 952
– me 489
pardonable 937
pare *cut* 38
reduce 195
peel 204
divest 226
– down
shorten 201
paregoric 662
parenchyma 316, 329
parent 166
– ship 726
parentage 11, 166
parenthesis
discontinuity 70
inversion 218
interjacence 228
by way of – 134
parenthetical
irrelative 10
pargeting 847
parhelion 423
pari passu 27, 120
Pariah
outlaw 83
commonalty 876
outcast 893
parian
sculpture 557
parietal 236
parietes 224
paring 32
parish 181
bring to the – 804
come upon the – 804
– council 696
parishioner 997
paritor 965
parity 17, 27
park *house* 189
plain 344
trees 367

artillery 727
pleasure ground 840
– paling 232
parkway 627
parlance 582
in common – 576
parlante 415
parlementaire 534, 723
parler:
facon de – 521
– à tort et à travers
illogical 477
nonsense 497
parley *talk* 588
conference 695
mediation 724
parliament 696
parliamentary
securities 802
parlour 191
parlour-maid 746
parlous 665
Parnassus 597
parochial 181, 189
prejudiced 481
parody
imitation 19
copy 21
misinterpret 523
misrepresent 555
travesty 856
parole *speech* 582
on – *restraint* 751
prisoner 754
promise 768
Parolles 887
paronomasia
neology 563
ornament 577
paronymous 562
paroxysm
violence 173
agitation 315
emotion 825
anger 900
parquetry 440
Parr, Old – 130
parricide 361
parrot
imitation 19
repetition 104
loquacity 584
repeat as a – 505
parry *confute* 479
avert 623
defend 717
pars magna fui,
quorum – 690

PAR   PAR   PAS   PAS

Paul Pry
curious 455
prattle 588
paulo post futurum
121
paunch 191, 250
pauper 804
pause
discontinue 70
cease 142
quiescence 265
doubt 485
irresolution 605
repose 687
pauvre diable 804
pavanne 840
pave 223
– the way 705
pavé, on the – 961
pavement *base* 211
covering 223
path 627
pavilion 189
paving 211
paviour 673
pavor 860
paw *touch* 379
retention 781
– the ivories 416
pawky 702
pawl 45
pawn 771
pawnbroker 787
pax *hush!* 403
– in bello 723
– vobiscum 894
pay *paint* 223
profitable 775
defray 807
expend 809
income 810
punish 972
remunerate 973
in one's –
servant 746
hired 795
– in advance 809
– attention to 457
– back 718
– down 807
– dues 924
– in full 807
– homage
submission 725
worship 990
– the debt of
nature 360
– no attention &c.
to 458, 460
– through the

nose 814
– off 718
– off old scores 919
– old debts 807
– out 200, 972
– in one's own
coin 718
– the penalty 952
– the piper 707
– regard to 484
– one's respects
894
– too much 814
– a visit 892, 894
– one's way
defray 807
economy 817
paymaster 801
payment 807
remuneration 973
paynim 984
pays, mal du –
regret 833
sociality 892
pea 249
peace
silence 403
concord 714
amity **721**
at – 714
commission of
the – 965
justice of the –
967
keep the –
moderation 174
concord 714
make – 723
make – with 831
Prince of – 976
speak – 831
peaceable
moderate 174
peaceably, get on –
736
peaceful
inexcitable 826
peace-maker 714
mediator 724
contented 831
peace-offering
pacification 723
mediation 724
gift 784
atonement 952
peach 529
peach-coloured 434
peacock
variegation 440
beauty 845
proud 878

vain 880
gaudy 882
jackdaw in –'s
feathers 701
pea-green 435
pea-jacket 225
peak *height* 206
summit 210
sharp 253
sicken 655
peaked 253
peaky 203
peal *loud* 404
roll 407
music 415
– of bells 407, 417
– of laughter 838
pearl *type* 591
goodness 648
ornament 847
glory 873
mother-of- 440
cast –s before
swine 638
pearly
semitransparent
427
colour 428
white 430
grey 432
variegated 440
pear-shape 249
peasant 876
peat 388
pebble *little* 193
hard 323
– dash 223
peccability 945
peccable 947
peccadillo 947
peccant *bad* 649
unclean 653
diseased 655
– humour 653, 655
peccavi 950
peck *much* 31
multitude 102
eat 298
– at *censure* 932
– of troubles
difficulty 704
adversity 735
pain 828
peckish 865
Pecksniff 548
pectinated 253
peculate 791
peculator 792
peculiar 79, 83
peculiarly 31, 33
pecuniary 800

pecunious 803
pedagogic 537
pedagogue
scholar 492
teacher 540
pedantic 855
pedagogy 537
pedal 633
– note 408
– point 416
pedant *scholar* 492
pedantic
half-learned 491
- *style* 577
affected 855
pedantry 481
peddle *meddle* 683
hawk 796
peddler 796, 797
peddling
trifling 643
miserly 819
pederero 727
pedestal 215
place on a – 307,
931
pedestrian 268
pedicel 215
pedicle 215
pedigree 69, 166
pediment 210, 215
pedlar 797
–'s French 563
pedometer 200
peduncle 214
peek 441
peel *layer* 204
skin 223
uncover 226
– off *separate* 44
peeler 664
peel-house 717
peep 441
– behind the cur-
tain 461
– of day 125
– into the future
510
– out 446, 529
peep-hole 260
peep-show 448, 840
peer *equal* 27
pry 441
inquire 461
lord 875
– out 446
peerless *supreme* 33
first rate 648
glorious 873
virtuous 944
peeved 900

firm 604
  authoritative 737
  rigorous 739
  compulsory 744
  duty 926
  – denial 536
  – refusal 764
perennial
  continuous 69
  diuturnal 110
  – *plants* 367
perennius, ære –
  873
pererration 266
perfect
  great 31
  entire 52
  excellent 650
  complete 729
perfection 650
  bring to – 729
**perfervidum in-
  genium** 682
perfidy 874, 940
perflate 349
perforate 260
perforator 262
perforce 601, 744
perform
  produce 161
  do 170
  – *music* 416
  action 680
  achieve 729
  fulfil 772
  – a circuit 629
  – a duty 926
  – the duties of 625
  – a function 644
  – an obligation
    772
  – a part 599, 680
  – a service 998
performable 470
performance
  [*see* perform]
  effect 154
performer
  musician 416
  stage-player 599
  agent 690
  affectation 855
perfume 400
perfunctory 53, 460
pergola 191
perhaps 470, 514
peri 845, 979
periapt 993
pericranium 450
periculous 665
peridot 847

perihelion 197
peril 665
  at your – 909
  take heed at
    one's – 668
perilepsis 476
perimeter 230
period *end* 67
  point 71
  – *of time* 106, **108**
  recurrence 138
  at fixed –s 138
  well rounded –s
    577, 578
periodical
  recurring 138
  book 593
periodicity 138
peripatetic 266, 268
periphery 230
periphrase 566, 573
periplus 267
periscope 441, 445
periscopic 446
  – *lens* 445
perish
  cease to exist 2
  be destroyed 162
  die 360
  decay 659
  – with cold 383
  – with hunger 956
perishable 111
perissology 573
peristaltic 248
peristyle 189
periwig 225
perjured 940
perjurer 548
perjury 544
perk *dress* 225
  – up *elevate* 307
  revive 689
perked up
  proud 878
perky 880
perlustration 441
permanence
  durability 110
  unchanging **141**
  unchangeable 150
permanent
  habitual 613
permeable 260
permeate
  insinuate 228
  pervade 186
  pass through 302
  –d with 613
permissible 760
permission 760

permissive 760
permit 760
permitting
  weather &c. – 469,
    470
permutation
  numerical – 84
  change 140
  interchange 148
pernicious 649
pernicity 274
perorate
  diffuse style 573
peroration
  sequel 65
  end 67
  speech 582
perpend *think* 451
perpendicular 212
perpension
  attention 457
perpetrate 680
  – a pun &c. 842
perpetrator 690
perpetua, esto –
  928, 931
perpetual 112
  frequent 136
  – *curate* 996
  – *motion* 467
perpetuate 112
  continue 143
  establish 150
perpetuity 69, **112**
perplex *derange* 61
  distract 458
  uncertainty 475
  bother 830
perplexed 59, 248
perplexity
  disorder 59
  uncertainty 475
  unintelligibility
    519
  difficulty 704
perquisite 775, 973
perquisition 461
perron 627
perscrutation 461
persecute
  oppress 649
  annoy 830
  malevolence 907
perseverance 143,
  604a
Persides 215
persiflage 842, 856
persifleur 844
persist *duration* 106
  permanence 141
  continue 143

persevere 604a
persistence
  diuturnity 110
person 3, 372
  without distinc-
    tion of –s 922
persona grata 890,
  899
personable 845
personæ, dramatis
  – 599, 690
personage 372
personal
  [*see* person]
  special 79
  subjective 317
  – *narrative* 594
  – *property* 780
  – *remarks* 932
  – *security* 771
personality
  [*see* personal]
  discourtesy 895
  disrespect 929
  censure 932
  detraction 934
personalty 780
personate 19, 554
personify 521, 554
personnel 56, 590
perspective
  view 448
  expectation 507
  painting 556
  aerial – 428
  in – 200
perspicacity
  sight 441
  intelligence 498
  fastidiousness 868
perspicuity
  intelligibility 518
  style **570**
perspiration 295,
  299
  in a – 382
perstringe 457
persuadable 602
persuade *belief* 484
  induce 615
persuasibility
  willingness 602
persuasion
  class 75
  opinion 484
  teaching 537
  inducement 615
  religious – 983
persuasive
  reasoning 476
pert

[591]

pointless 843
poise 27, 319, 852
  mental – 498
poison 659, 663
  – gas 722, 727
poisoned 655
  commend the –
    chalice 544
poisonous 657, 665
poke
  pocket 191
  pig in a –
    uncertain 475
    chance 621
    dawdle 683
    rash 863
  – at 276, 716
  – the fire 384
  – fun at 856
  – one's nose in
    682
  – out *project* 250
poker 386
  cards 840
polacca 273
polacre 273
polar 210
  cold 383
  – co-ordinates 466
polarization 420
polariscope 445
polarity
  duality 89
  counteraction 179
  contraposition
    237
pole *measure of*
    length 200
  tall 206
  summit 210
  axis 222
  punt 267
  rotation 312
  greasy – 840
  opposite –s 237
  from – to pole 180
pole-axe 727
polecat 401
pole-star 550, 693
polemic
  discussion 476
  discord 713
  contention 720
  combatant 726
polemoscope 445
police 965
  – court 966
  – magistrate 967
policeman 664, 965
policy 626, 692
polish *smooth* 255

rub 331
furbish 658
beauty 845
ornament 847
taste 850
politeness 894
– off *finish* 729
Polish bank 840
polished
  – *language* 578
  fashionable 852
  polite 894
polisson 949
polite 894
  offensive to ears –
    579
  – literature 560
  – society 852
politic *wise* 498
  cunning 702
  cautious 864
  body –
    mankind 372
    government 737
political economy
    692
politician
  director 694
  proficient 700
politics 702
polity *conduct* 692
  authority 737
  duty 926
polka 840
poll 85, 609
  – tax 812
pollard 193, 201
  tree 367
Poll-parrot 584
pollute *soil* 653
  corrupt 659
  disgrace 874
pollution
  disease 655
  vice 945
Pollyanna 858
polo 840
polonaise 840
poltroon 862
polyandry 903
polychord 417
polychromatic 428,
    440
polychrome 440,
    556
polygamy 903
polygastric 191
polyglot 522, 560
polygon
  buildings 189
  figure 244

polygraphy 590
polyiogy 573
polymorphic 81
polyphonism 580
polypus 250
polyscope 445
polysyllable 561
polytheism 984
pomade 356
pomatum 356
pommel
  support 215
  round 249
  beat 972
Pomona 369
pomp 882
pom-pom 727
pomposity 882
pompous
  language 577
poncho 225
pond 343, 636
  fish – 370
ponder 451
ponderable 316,
    319
ponderation 319,
    480
ponderous 319
  – *style* 574, 579
  dull 843
pondus fumo, dare
  – 481
poniard 727
pons asinorum 519,
    704
pontifical 995
pontificals 999
pontificate 995
pontiff 996
pontoon
  vehicle 272
  boat 273
  way 627
pony 271
poodle 366
pooh, pooh!
  unimportance 643
  contempt 930
pool *lake* 343
  combination 709
  prize 775
  billiards 840
poop 235
poor *weak* 160
  – *reasoning* 477
  – *style* 575
  insufficient 640
  trifling 643
  indigent 804
  unhappy 828

cut a – figure 874
  – hand 701
  – head 499
  – house 189
  – man 804
  – in spirit 881
  – stick 501
  – thing 914
poorly 160, 655
  – off 804
poor-spirited 862
pop *noise* 406
  unexpected 508
  – at 716
  – in *ingress* 294
  insertion 300
  – off *die* 360
  – a question 461
  – the question
    request 765
    endearment 902
  – upon *arrive* 29
    discover 480a
Pope
  infallibility 474
  priest 996
Popedom 995
Pope Joan 840
Popery 984
pop-gun *trifle* 643
popinjay 854
poplar *tall* 206
poppy *sedative* 174
populace 876
popular
  in demand 865
  celebrated 873
  favourite 897
  approved 931
  – opinion 488
popularis, aura –
    873
popularize
  render intelligible
    518
  facilitate 705
  make pleasant
    829
populate 184
population 188, 372
populi, vox –
  publication 531
  election 609
  authority 737
populous
  crowded 72
  multitude 102
  presence 186
porcelain
  baked 384
  sculpture 557

hope 858
potable 298
potage 298
potager 191
potation 298, 959
pot-bellied 194
pot-companion 890
potency 157
potent 157, 159
potentate 745
potential
  inexistent 2
potentiality 157,
  470
pother *disorder* 59
  feeling 821
  excitement 825
  annoyance 830
pot-herbs 393
pot-hooks 590
pot-house 189
pot-hunter 767
potion
  beverage 298
  medicine 662
  cordial 392
pot-luck *eating* 298
  chance 621
  non-preparation
  674
  take – with 892
Potosi 803
pot-pourri
  mixture 41
  fragrance 400
  music 415
pottage 298
pottering 682, 683
pottery *baked* 384
  art 557
pottle 191
potulent 298, 959
pot-valiant 959
potwalloper 876
pouch 191
poudre:
  qui n'a pas
   inventé la –
   501, 701
  jeter de la – aux
   yeux 442
poultice *pulp* 354
  remedy 662
  relief 834
poultry 298, 366
pounce upon
  unexpected 508
  attack 716
  seize 789
pound *inclose* 232
  weight 319

bruise 330
imprison 752
– together 41
poundage 813
pounds, shillings,
  and pence 800
pour *emerge* 295
  stream 348
  sufficient 639
  it never rains but
   it –s 641
– out blood like
  water 361
– a broadside into
  716
– forth *eject* 297
  speak 582
  loquacity 584
– forth like water
  818
– in *converge* 290
  ingress 294
  sufficiency 639
– on *lavish* 784
– with rain 348
– water into a
  sieve 638, 818
– out 295, 297
pourboire 784
pourparler
  interlocution 588
  advice 695
  council 696
pout *project* 250
  sad 837
  discourteous 895
  irate 900
  sulky 901a
poverty
  insufficiency 640
  unimportance 643
  indigence 804
– of intellect 499
powder 330
  cosmetics 847
  food for – 726
  gun– 727
  smell – 722
  keep one's – dry
   673
– and shot 727
  waste – 638
  not worth – 645
powdered
  variegated 440
powdering
  ornament 847
power
  much 31, 102
  numerical 84
  efficacy **157**

loud 404
– *of style* 574
  authority 737
  do all in one's –
  686
  give – 760
  in the – of
  authority 737
  subjection 749
  literary – 569
– of attorney 755
– behind the
  throne 694
– of money 800
powerful 159, 171
– voice 580
powerless 158, 160
powers that be 745
pow-wow 588, 696
pox 655
praam 273
practicable 470, 644
practical
  acting 170
  expedient 646
  executive 692
– joke
  absurdity 497
  deception 545
  ridicule 856
  disrespect 929
– knowledge 698
practically
  intrinsically 5
practice
  arithmetic 85
  training 537
  habit 613
  conduct 692
  in – *prepared* 673
  skilled 698
  put in – *use* 677
  action 680
  conduct 692
  complete 729
  out of – 699
– of medicine 662
practise *train* 537
  use 677
  act 680
– at the bar 968
– on one's credu-
  lity 545
– upon
  experiment 463
  deceive 545
practised
  skilled 698
– eye 700
– hand 700
practitioner

medical - 662
  doer 690
præcognita 467
prænomen 564
prætor 967
Pragmatic
  Sanction 769
pragmatical 855,
  880
pragmatism 677
prahu 273
prairie *space* 180
  plain 344
  vegetation 367
praise *thanks* 916
  commendation
  931
  worship 990
praiseworthy 931,
  944
prame 273
prance 266, 315
prandial 298
prank *caprice* 608
  amusement 840
  adorn 847
prate 584
prattle 582, 584
pravity 945
praxis
  grammar 567
  action 680
Praxiteles 559
pray 765, 990
prayer 765, 990
  house of – 1000
prayer-book 998
preach *teach* 537
  speak 582
  predication 998
– to the winds 645
– to the wise 538
preacher
  teacher 540
  priest 996
preachment 998
preadamite 124,
  130
preamble 64
preapprehension
  481
prebend 995
prebendary 996
precarious
  transient 111
  uncertain 475
  dangerous 665
precatory 765
precaution
  care 459
  expedient 626

safety 664
preparation 673
precede
superior 33
- *in order* 62
- *in time* 116
- *in motion* 280
precedence 873
precedent
[*see* precede]
prototype 22
precursor 64
habit 613
legal decision 969
follow –s 82
precentor 694, 996
precept *adage* 496
maxim **697**
order 741
permit 760
preceptor 540
precession 62, **280**
précieuse ridicule
855
precinct *region* 181
place 182
environs 227
boundary 233
precious *great* 31
excellent 648
valuable 814
beloved 897
– metals 800
– stone 648, 847
precipice
vertical 212
slope 217
dangerous 667
on the verge of
a – 665
precipitancy 684,
863
precipitate
early 132
sink 308
consolidate 321
refuse 653
haste 684
rash 863
– oneself 306
precipitous 217
précis 596
precise *exact* 494
preciosity 578
precisely
literally 19
assent 488
precisianism
affectation 855
heterodoxy 984
***over**-religious* 988

preclude 55, 706
precocious
early 132
immature 674
pert 885
rude 895
precognition
forethought 490
knowledge 510
preconceived idea
481
preconception 481
preconcert 611, 626
preconcertation 673
precursor
- *in order* 62, **64**
- *in time* 116
predict 511
predatory 789, 791
predecessor 64
predeliberation
510, 611
predella 215
predesigned 611
predestination
fate 152
necessity 601
predetermination
611
Deity 976
predetermination
611
predial
land 342
agriculture 371
manorial 780
predicament 8, 75
predicate
affirm 535
preach 998
prediction **511**
predilection
bias 481
affection 820
desire 865
predispose 615, 673
predisposed
willing 602
predisposition 176,
820
predominant 175,
737
predominate 33
pre-eminent 33, 873
pre-emption 795
preen 847
pre-engage 132
pre-engagement
768
pre-establish 626
pre-examine 461

pre-exist 1, 116
preface 62, 64
prefect 745, 759
prefecture 737
prefer *choose* 609
– a claim 969
– a petition 765
preference 62
preferment
improvement 658
ecclesiastical –
995
prefigure 511
prefix 62, 64
letter 561
pre-glacial 124
pregnable 158
pregnant
producing 161
productive 168
predicting 511
- *style* 572
important 642
– with meaning
516
prehensile 789
prehension 789
pre-historic 124
pre-instruct 537
prejudge 481
prejudicate 481
prejudice
misjudge 481
evil 619
detriment 659
prejudicial 481, 649
prelacy 995
prelate 996
prelation 609
prelection 537, 582
prelector 540
preliminaries:
settle – 673
- of peace 723
preliminary 62, 64
prelude 62, 64
beginning 66
music 415
premature 132, 674
premeditate 611,
620
prémices 154
premier 694, 759
– pas 66
premiership 693
premise *prefix* 62
precede 116
announce 511
premises
precursor 64
prior 116

ground 182
evidence 467
logic 476
premium
debt 806
receipt 810
reward 973
at a – 814
premonish 668
premonitory 511,
668
Premonstratensian
996
premonstration
appearance 448
prediction 511
manifestation 525
premunire 742, 974
prendre la balle au
bond 134
prenotion
misjudgment 481
foresight 510
prensation 789
prentice 541
prenticeship 539
preoccupancy
possession 777
preoccupation
inattention 458
preoption 609
preordain 152, 601
preparation **673**
music 413
instruction 537
in – 730
in course of – 626
preparatory
preceding 62
prepare the way
facilitate 705
prepared *expectant*
507
ready 698
preparing
destined 152
prepense
spontaneous 600
predetermined
611
intended 620
malice – 907
prepollence 157
preponderance
superiority 33
influence 175
dominance 737
prepossessed
obstinate 606

prepossessing 829
prepossession
prejudice 481
possession 777
preposterous
great 31
absurd 497
exaggerated 549
ridiculous 853
undue 925
prepotency 157
pre-Raphaelite 122,
124, 556
pre-require 630
pre-resolve 611
prerogative 737,
924
presage 511, 512
presbyopia 443
presbyter 996
Presbyterian 984
presbytery 995,
996, 1000
prescience 510
prescious 511
prescribe *direct* 693
advice 695
order 741
entitle 924
enjoin 926
prescript 697, 741
prescription
remedy 662
prescriptive *old* 124
unchanged 141
habitual 613
due 924
presence
in space **186**
appearance 448
breeding 894
in the – of
near 197
real – 998
saving one's – 928
– of God 981
– of mind 826,
864
presence-chamber
191
present
– *in time* 118
– *in space* 186
offer 763
give 784
church prefer-
ment 995
at – 118
these –s 590, 592
– arms 894, 928
– a bold front 861

– a front 719
– itself *event* 151
visible 446
thought 451
– oneself
presence 186
offer 763
courtesy 894
– to the mind
457, 505
– time **118**
instant 113
– to the view 448
presentable 852
presentation 883,
894
presentiment
instinct 477
prejudgment 481
foresight 510
presently 132
presentment
information 527
law proceeding
969
preservation
continuance 141
conservation **670**
Divine attributes
976
preserve *sweets* 396
preserver 664
preshow 511
preside 693, 737
presidency 737
president 694, 745
press *crowd* 72
closet 191
weight 319
public - 531
printing 591
book 593
move 615
compel 744
offer 763
solicit 765
go to – 591
under – of 744
writer for the –
593
– of business 682
– one hard 716
– in 300
– on *course* 109
progression 282
haste 684
– into the service
677, 707
– out 301
press-agent 599
pressed: hard – 704

– for time 684
press-gang 965
pressing *need* 630
urgent 642
pressure *power* 157
influence 175
weight 319
urgency 642
exertion 686
adversity 735
centre of – 222
high – 824
work under – 684
Prester John 515
prestidigitation 545
prestidigitator 548
prestige *bias* 481
authority 737
fascination 865
fame 873
prestigiation 545
prestissimo 415
presto
instantly 113
music 415
prestriction 442
presumable 472
presume
misjudge 481
believe 484
suppose 514
hope 858
pride 878
presumption
[*see* presume]
probability 472
expectation 507
rashness 863
arrogance 885
unlawfulness 925
presumptive
probable 472
supposed 514
due 924
heir – 779
– evidence
evidence 467
probability 472
presumptuous 885
presuppose
misjudge 481
suppose 514
presurmise 510,
514
pretence
imitation 19
falsehood 544
untruth 546
excuse 617
ostentation 882
boast 884

pretend *assert* 535
simulate 544, 546
pretended 545
pretender
deceiver 548
braggart 884
unentitled 925
pretending 544
pretension
ornament 577
affectation 855
due 924
pretentious
affected 855
vain 880
ostentatious 882
boasting 884
undue 925
preterite 122
preterition **122**
preterlapsed 122
pretermit 460
preternatural 83
preterperfect 122
pretext 546, 617
pretty
much 31
imperfectly 651
beautiful 845
– fellow 501
– good 651
– kettle of fish,
pass &c. 59, 704
– well *much* 31
little 32
trifling 643
preux chevalier 939
prevail *exist* 1
superior 33
general 78
influence 175
habit 613
succeed 731
– upon 615
prevailing 78
– taste 852
prevalence
[*see* prevail]
prevaricate 544
prévenance 894
prevenient 62, 132
prevention
prejudice 481
hindrance 706
– of waste 817
preventive 55
preventorium 656
previous 116
move the –
question 624
not within –

experience 137
prevision 510
pre-war 116
prewarn 668
prey *food* 298
quarry 620
booty 793
victim 732, 828
fall a – to
be defeated 732
subjection 749
– to grief 828
– to melancholy
837
– on the mind
excite 824
regret 833
fear 860
– on the spirits
837
price
consideration 147
value 648
money **812**
reward 973
at any – 604*a*
beyond – 814
cheap at the – 815
of great –
good 648
dear 814
have one's – 812
price-current 812
priceless
valueless 645
dear 814
prick *sharp* 253
hole 260
sting 378
sensation of touch
380
incite 615
mental suffering
830
kick against the –s
useless 645
resistance 719
– up one's ears
hear 418
curiosity 455
attention 457
expect 707
prickle 253, 380
pride
ornament 847
loftiness **878**
take a – in 878
prie-dieu 215
priest 996
priestcraft 995
priesthood 995, 996

priest-ridden 988,
995
prig *steal* 791
puppy 854
affected 855
blusterer 887
priggish 855, 880
prim *affected* 855
fastidious 868
proud 878
prima: – donna
actress 599
important 642
proficient 700
– facie *sight* 441
appearance 448
probable 472
- *meaning* 516
manifest 525
primacy
superiority 33
celebrity 873
church 995
primary
original 20
cause 153
important 642
– colour 428
– education 537
primarily 66
primate 996
primates 875
prime
primeval 124
early 132
teach 537
important 642
excellent 648
prepare 673
in one's – 131
in the – of man-
hood 159
– cost *price* 812
cheap 815
– of life *youth* 127
adolescence 131
– and load 673
– minister 694
– of the morning
125
– mover 153
– number 84
prime constituent 1
primed
skilled 698
tipsy 959
primer 542
primeval 124
– forest 367
primigenous 124
primitive 124, 153

– colour 428
primogenial 66
primogeniture
old 124
age 128
posterity 167
primordial 20, 124,
153
primordinate 124
primrose-coloured
436
primum:
– mobile 153, 615
primus inter pares
33
prince
perfection 650
master 745
nobility 875
– of darkness 978
princely
authoritative 737
liberal 816
famous 873
noble 875
generous 942
princeps
facile – 33
princess 745, 875
principal
important 642
director 694
– part 31, 50
principality 181,
780
principally 33
principia 66, 496
principiis obstare
673
principle
intrinsic 5
rule 80
cause 153
element 316
idea 453
reasoning 476
tenet 484
maxim 496
motive 615
probity 939
on – 615
want of – 945
principled, high-
939
prink 847, 882
print *copy* 21
mark 550
engraving 558
letter-press 591
out of – 552
printer 591

printing 531, **591**
– telegraph 553
prior
- *in order* 62
- *in time* 116
clergy 996
priori reasoning,
a – 476
priority 116, 234
priory 1000
Priscian's head,
break – 568
prism
angularity 244
optical 445
see through a –
443
prismatic
colour 428
variegated 440
prison **752**
cast into – 751
in – 754
prisoner **754**, 938
take – 751, 789
prison-house
secrets of the –
529, 533
pristine 20, 122
prithee 765
prittle-prattle 588
private *special* 79
hidden 528
secluded 893
to gain some –
ends 943
in – 528
keep – 881
talk to in – 586,
588
– road 627
– soldier 726
privateer 726, 792
privateering 791
privately 881
privation 776, 804
privative 789
privilege
freedom 748
permission 760
exemption 777*a*
due 924
privity 490
privy *hidden* 528
latrines 653
– to 490
Privy Council 696
prize *good* 618
palm 733
gain 775
booty 793

receipt 810
love 897
approve 931
reward 973
win the – 731
– open 173
prizer 767
prize-fighter 726
prize-fighting 720
prizeman 700
pro: – and con
476, 615
– formâ 82
– hâc vice
special 79
present time 118
occasion 134
seldom 137
– rata 23
– re natâ
circumstances 8
relation 9
special 79
occasion 134
conditions 770
– tanto 26, 32
– tempore 111
proa 273
probability 156, **472**
probable 858
probate 771
Probate Court 966
probation
trial 463
demonstration
478
probationary 463,
675
probationer 541
probative 478
probatum est 478,
931
probe *depth* 208
perforator 262
investigate 461
measure 466
probity **939**
problem *topic* 454
question 461
enigma 533
problematical 475
proboscis 250
procacity
insolence 885
rudeness 895
irascibility 901
procedure
method 627
action 680
conduct 692
proceed *time* 109

advance 282
– from 154
– with 692
proceeding
incomplete 53
event 151
action 680
not finished 730
course of – 692
proceedings 551
proceeds *gain* 775
money 800
receipts 810
procerity 206
procès-verbal
record 551
law proceeding
969
process
projection 250
conduct 692
legal – 963
– engraving 558
– of time 109
in – of time 117
procession
continuity 69
march 266
ceremony 882
processional
rite 998
prochronism 115
proclaim 531
proclivity 176, 820
proconsul 759
proconsulship 737
procrastination 133,
460, 683
procreant 168
procreate 161, 168
procreator 166
procrustean 82
– law 80
Procrustes:
stretch on the bed
of – 27
proctor *teacher* 540
officer 694, 965
consignee 758
lawyer 968
proctorship 693
procumbent 213
procurator 694
procuration 170,
755
procure *cause* 153
induce 615
get 775
buy 795
procuress 962
procurement 170

prod 276
prodigal 641, 818
prodigality **818**
prodigious 31, 870
prodigy 83, **872**
– of learning 700
prodition 940
prodrome 64
produce
increase 35
cause 153
effect 154
create 161
prolong 200
show 525
stage 599
fruit 775
merchandise 798
– itself 446
producer **164**
product
multiple 84
effect 154
harvest 636
gain 775
finished – 154
production 54, **161**
[*and see* pro-
duce]
productive
cause 153
power 157
inventive 515
profitable 775
productiveness **168**
proem 64
proemial
preceding in order
62
beginning 66
profane
desecrate 679
impious 988
laical 997
– swearing 908
profanum vulgus
876
profession
assertion 535
pretence 546
business 625
promise 768
enter a – 625
– of faith 484, 983
professional 700
– mourner 363,
839
professor 492, 540,
700
professorship 542
proffer 763

proficient
knowledge 490
skill 698
adept **700**
proficuous 644
profile
outline 230
side 236
appearance 448
portraiture 556
profit
increase 35
advantage 618
utility 644
acquisition 775
– by *use* 677
– sharing 778
profitable
useful 644
good 648
gainful 775
profitless 645
profligacy 945
profligate 818
profluent
progressive 282
stream 348
profound
great 31
deep 208
learned 490
wise 498
sagacious 702
feeling 821
– attention 457
– knowledge 490
– secret 533
profundis, de –
839, 950
profuse
diffuse style 573
redundant 641
prodigal 818
profusion 102, 639
prog 298
progenerate 161
progenitive 163
progenitor 166
progeny 167
prognosis 510, 511,
522, 655
prognostic 511, 512
prognosticate 511
prognostication 507
programme
catalogue 86
publication 531
plan 626
progress
growth 144
motion 264
advance 282

in – *incomplete*
53, 730
make – 282
in mid – 270
– of science 490
– of time 109
progression
gradation 58
series 69
numerical – 84
motion **282**
progressive
continuous 69
course 109
advancing 282
improving 658
prohibition 761
exclusion 55
stoppage 706
teetotalism 953,
958
project *bulge* 250
impel 284
intend 620
plan 626
projectile 727
projection *map* 554
projector
lantern 423
film 445
designer 626
prolation 580, 582
prole, sine – 169
prolegomena 64
prolepsis 64, 115
proletarian 876
prolific 168
prolix 573
prolocutor
interpreter 524
teacher 540
speaker 582
prologue
precursor 64
drama 599
prolong
protract 110
late 133
continue 143
lengthen 200
prolongation 63,
143
prolusion 64
prom 892
promenade 266
display 882
on pier 189
Promethean 359
prominent
convex 250
manifest 525

important 642
eminent 873
prominently 31, 33
promiscuous
mixed 41
irregular 59
indiscriminate
465a
casual 621
promise
predict 511
engage **768**
hope 858
keep one's – 939
keep – to ear and
break to hope
545
– oneself 507, 858
promissory 768
– note 771, 800
promontory
height 206
projection 250
land 342
promote 153, 658,
707
promoter 626
promotion 658
prompt *early* 132
remind 505
tell 527
induce 615
active 682
advise 695
– memory 505
prompter
drama 599
motive 615
adviser 695
promptuary 636
promulgate 531
– a decree 741
pronation and
supination 218
prone
horizontal 213
proneness
tendency 176
disposition 820
prôner 882, 931
prôneur 935
prong 91
pronounce
judge 480
assert 535
voice 580
speak 582
pronounced 525
pronouncement 531
pronunciamento
531

pronunciation 580
pronunciative 535
proof *hard* 323
insensible 376
test 463
demonstration
478
printing 591
draft 626
ocular – 446
– against
strong 159
resolute 604
safe 664
defence 717
resistance 719
insensible 823
prop 215, 707
propædeutics 537
propagable 168
propaganda 537,
542
propagandism 537
propagandist 540,
996
propagate
produce 161
be productive 168
publish 531
propel 284
propellant 727
propeller 267, 312
propend 602
propendency
predetermination
611
inclination 820
propense 602
propension 820
propensity 176, 820
proper *special* 79
expedient 646
handsome 845
due 924
– name 564
in its – place 58
show a – spirit
939
the – thing 926
– time 134
properties
theatrical – 225,
599
property *power* 157
possessions **780**
wealth 803
property-man 599
prophecy 511
prophet 513, 996
false –s 986
in the name of the

– figs! 497
prophetic 511, 985
Prophets, the – 985
prophylactic
healthful 656
remedy 662
preservative 670
hindrance 706
prophylaxis 670
propinquity 197
propitiate
pacify 723, 724
calm 826
content 831
love 897
pity 914
forgive 918
atone 952
worship 990
propitious
timely 134
beneficial 648
helping 707
prosperous 734
auspicious 858
proplasm 22
proportion
relation 9
degree 26
mathematical 84
symmetry 242
style 578
allotment 786
proportionate
agreeing 23
proportions 180,
192
proposal *plan* 626
propose
suggest 514
broach 535
intend 620
offer 763
offer marriage
902
– a question 461
proposition
supposition 454
reasoning 476
project 626
suggestion 514
offer 763
propound 514, 535
– a question 461
propriâ personâ
in – *speciality* 79
presence 186
proprietary 779
proprietor 779
proprietorship 780
propriety

agreement 23
elegance 578
expedience 646
fashion 852
right 922
duty 926
proprio motu 600
props 599
propter hoc 155
propugn
resist 717
vindicate 937
propulsion 284
propylon 66
prore 234
prorogue 133
proruption 295
prosaic *usual* 82
- *style* 575, 576
dull 843
prosaism *prose* 598
proscenium
front 234
theatre 599
proscribe
interdict 761
banish 893
curse 908
condemn 971
prose
diffuse style 573
prate 584
not verse **598**
- run mad 577, 597
- writer 598
prosecute
pursue 622
act 680
accuse 938
arraign 969
- an inquiry 461
prosecutor 938
proselyte
convert 144, 607
learner 541
proselytism 537
proser 841
prosody 597
prosopopœia 521
prospect
futurity 121
view 448
probability 472
expectation 507
*landscape paint-
ing* 556
good - 858
in - *intended* 620
prospective 121
prospector 463
prospectus *list* 86

foresight 510
compendium 596
scheme 626
prosper 618
prosperity 734
prospicience 510
prosternation
dejection 837
servility 886
prostitute
corrupt 659
misuse 679
impure 961
courtesan 962
prostrate
powerless 158
destroyed 162
low 207
horizontal 213
depress 308
laid up 655
exhausted 688
dejected 837
servile 886
fall - 306
- oneself
servile 886
obeisance 928
worship 990, 991
prostration
[see prostrate]
submission 725
pain 828
prosy 841, 843
prosyllogism 476
protagonist
actor 599
proficient 700
protasis
precursor 64
beginning 66
maxim 496
protean 149
protect *safe* 664
protected cruiser
726
protective 717
protection
influence 175
defence 717
restrain 751
protector 664, 717
master 745
keeper 753
**protectorate 737,
780**
protégé *servant* 746
friend 890
proteiform 149
protein 298
semiliquid 352

organic 357
protervity 901
protest *dissent* 489
assert 535
deny 536
refuse 764
deprecate 766
not observe 773
not pay 808
counter - 468
enter a - 766
under - 603, 744
- against 708, 932
protestant 489, 764
Protestant 984
protested bills 808
Proteus 149
prothesis 1000
prothonotary 553
protocol *scheme* 626
compact 769
protogram 572
protoplasm
prototype 22
material 316
organization 357
protoplast 22
prototype 22
prediction 511
prototypal 20
protozoon 366
protract *time* 110
late 133
lengthen 200
diffuse style 573
protreptical 615
protrude 250
protuberance 250
protypify 511
proud 873, 878
- flesh 250
prove
arithmetic 85
turn out 151
try 463
demonstrate 478
affect 821
- one's case
vindication 937
- true 494
provender 298, 637
proverb 496
proverbe *acting* 599
proverbial 490
provide
furnish 637
- against
prepare 673
- against a rainy
day 817
provided

conditionally 8
qualification 469
supposition 514
well - 639
- for 803
providence
foresight 510
preparation 673
*divine govern-
ment* 976
Providence 976
special - 711
waiter on - 683,
831
provident
careful 459
wise 498
prepared 673
providential
opportune 134
fortunate 734
province
department 75
region 181
abode 189
office 625
provincial
[see province]
prejudiced 481
vulgar 851
provincialism
neology 563
provision *food* 298
supply **637**
preparation 673
wealth 803
- merchant 637
provisional
uncertain 475
circumstances 8
temporary 111
preparing 673
provisions
conditions 770
proviso 469, 770
provisory 111
provoke *cause* 153
incite 615
excite 824
vex 830
anger 900
- desire 865
- hatred 898
provoquant 824
provost *master* 745
deputy 759
prow 234
prowess 861
prowl *walk* 266
lurk 528
- after 622

[607]

wrath 900
the battle –s 722
ragged 226
ragoût 41, 298
rag-picker 876
rags *clothes* 225
   useless 645
   do to – 384
   tear to – 162
   worn to – 659
ragtime 415, 473
raid 716, 791
rail *inclosure* 232
   prison 752
   – at 932
   – in
   circumscribe 229
   restrain 751
railing 232
raillerie, ne pas en-
   tendre – 900
raillery 856
railway 627
   – speed 274
   – station 292
raiment 225
rain *stream* 348
   sufficient 639
   – or shine 474,
   604
rainbow 440
raincoat 225
rainless 340
rains but it pours,
   never – 641
rainy day 735
   provide against
   a – 673, 817
rainy season 348
raise *increase* 35
   produce 161
   erect 212
   elevate 307
   excite 824
   – alarm 860
   – anger 900
   – one's banner
   722
   – a cry 531
   – a dust 682
   – expectations 858
   – the finger 550
   – funds 775
   – one's head
   improve 658
   refresh 689
   prosperity 734
   repute 873
   – ghosts 992
   – hope 511
   – a hue and cry

against 932
– a laugh 840
– the mask 529
– money 788
– a question 461,
   485
– a report 531
– a siege 723
– the spirits 836
– spirits from the
   dead 992
– a storm 173
– troops 722
– up 212, 824
– the voice 411
– one's voice 535,
   932
– the wind 775,
   788
raised *convex* 250
raison:
   – d'être 620
   – de plus 467
raj 737
rajah 745
rajpoot 726
rake *drag* 285
   gardening 371
   clean 652
   profligate 949
   intemperance 954
   libertine 962
   – out 301
   – up *collect* 72
   extract 301
   recall 505
   excite 824
   – up evidence 467
rake-hell 949, 962
raking-fire 716
rakish
   intemperate 954
   licentious 961
rallentando 415
rally *arrange* 60
   improve 658
   restore 660
   ridicule 856
   encourage 861
   – round *order* 58
   co-operate 709
rallying: – cry 550,
   861
   – point 74
ram *impulse* 276
   sheep 366
   male 373
   man-of-war 726
   milk the – 645
   – down 261, 321
   – in 300

Ramadan 956, 998
ramage 367
ramble *stroll* 266
   wander 279
   folly 499
   delirium 503
   digress 573
rambler 268
rambling 139
ramification *part* 51
   bisection 91
   posterity 167
   filament 205
   symmetry 242
   divergence 291
rammer 263, 276
ramose 242
ramp *slope* 217
   climb 305
   leap 309
rampage 173
rampant
   violent 173
   prevalent 175
   vertical 212
   raised 307
   free 748
   vehement 825
   licentious 961
rampart 717
ramrod 263
ramshackle 665
ranch 780
rancid 401, 653
rancour 907, 919
randan 273
random *casual* 156
   carriage 272
   uncertain 475
   aimless 621
   talk at –
   sophistry 477
   exaggerate 549
   loquacity 584
   - *experiment* 463
   chance 621
range *extent* 26
   collocate 60
   series 69
   term 71
   class 75
   space 180
   distance 196
   roam 266
   direction 278
   stove 386
   freedom 748
   out– 196
   long – 196
   within – 197
   –finder 200

– itself 58
– under, – with 76
ranger
   director 694
   keeper 753
   thief 792
rank *have place* 1
   degree 26
   thorough 31
   collocate 60
   row 69
   term 71
   vegetation 365
   fetid 401
   estimate 480
   bad 649
   soldiers 726
   glory 873
   nobility 875
   man of – 875
   – and file
   continuity 69
   soldiers 726
   commonalty 876
   – marks 747
rankle *unclean* 653
   corrupt 659
   painful 830
   animosity 900
   malevolence 907
   revenge 919
ranks
   fill up the – 660
   risen from the –
   876
ransack *seek* 461
   deliver 672
   plunder 791
   price 812
   atonement 952
   – one's brains
   451, 515
ransom 672
rant
   unmeaning 517
   exaggeration 549
   diffuse style 573
   turgescence 577
   speech 582
   acting 599
   excitement 825
   boasting 884
ranter *talker* 584
   false piety 988
rantipole 458
rap *blow* 276
   sound 406
   trifle 643
   money 800
   not worth a – 804
   – on the knuckles

repeat 104
– one's efforts 686
redoubt 717
redoubtable 860
redound to
   conduce 176
– one's honour
   glory 873
   approbation 931
   honour 939
redress *restore* 660
   remedy 662
   reward 973
red-tape 694, 739
reduce *lessen* 36
   - *in number* 103
   weaken 160
   contract 195
   shorten 201
   lower 308
   subdue 731
   discount 813
   – to ashes 384
   – to demonstra-
     tion 478
   – to a mean 29
   – to order 60
   – to poverty 804
   – to powder 330
   – the speed 275
   – in strength 160
   – to subjection 749
   – to *convert* 144
   – to writing 551
reduced [*see* reduce]
   impoverished 804
   – to the last ex-
     tremity 665
   – to a skeleton 659
   – to straits 704
reductio ad absur-
   dum 476, 479
reduction
   [*see* reduce]
   arithmetical 85
   conversion 144
   at a – 815
   – of temperature
     385
redundance
   diffuseness 573
   too much **641**
redundancy 104
reduplication 19, 90
re-echo *imitate* 19
   repeat 104
   resonance 408
reechy 653
reed *weak* 160
   pan 590
   arrow 727

trust to a broken –
   699
   – instrument 417
reef *slacken* 275
   shoal 346
   danger 667
   take in a – 664
   double – topsails
     664
reefer 269
reek *gas* 334
   vaporize 336
   liquid 337
   hot 382
   fester 653
reeking 339, 653
reel *rock* 314
   agitate 315, 851
   dance 840
   – back *yield* 725
re-embody
   junction 43
   combination 48
re-enter 245
re-entrant angle
   244
re-establish 660
re-estate 660
refashion 163
refect
   strengthen 159
refection
   meal 298
   refreshment 689
   (*restoration* 660)
refectory 191
refer to *relate* 9
   include 76
   attribute 155
   cite 467
   allude 521
   take advice 695
referable 9, 155
referee
   judgment 480
   judge 967
reference
   [*see* refer]
referendary 967
referendum 480,
   609
   ad – 461, 605
referrible 9, 155
refine *clean* 652
   – upon 658
refined *colour* 428
   fashionable 852
refinement
   discrimination
     465
   wisdom 498

elegance 578, 845
improvement 658
taste 850
over– 477
refit 660
reflect *imitate* 19
   think 451
   – dishonour 874
   – *light* 420
   – upon *censure* 932
reflecting 498
reflection 408, 453
   light 420
reflector *mirror* 445
reflex *copy* 21
   recoil 277
   regressive 283
reflexion 21, 277
refluence *recoil* 277
   regress 283
reflux *decrease* 36
   recoil 277
   regress 283
   current 348
refocillate
   strengthen 159
   refresh 689
reform *convert* 144
   improve 658
reformatory 542,
   752
reformer 658
refound 144
refraction
   deviation 279
   light 420
   fallacy of vision
     443
refractory
   obstinate 606
   difficult 704
   mutinous 742
   ill-tempered 901a
refrain *poetry* 597
   avoid 623
   do nothing 681
   temperate 953
   – from laughter
     837
   – from voting
     609a
   repetition 104
refresh
   strengthen 159
   cool 385
   refit 658
   restore 660
   recruit 689
   relieve 834
   – the memory 505

refreshing 377, 829
refreshment
   food 298
   recruiting **689**
   delight 827
refrigeration
   anæsthetic 376
   making cold **385**
refrigerator **387**
reft 44
refuge **666**
refugee 268, 623
refulgence 420
refund 807
refurbish 673
refusal **764**
   pre-emption 795
refuse *remains* 40
   useless 645
   not consent 764
   – *assent* 489
   – to associate with
     893
   – to believe 487
   – to hear 460
refute 479
refuted 495
regain 775
   – breath 689
regal 737
regale *feast* 298
   physical pleasure
     377
   refresh 689
   pleasing 829
   amusement 840
regalia 747
regality 737
regard
   relation 9
   view 441
   attention 457
   judge 480
   credit 873
   love 897
   respect 928
   approbation 931
   have – to 457
   merit – 642
   pay – to
     believe 484
     honour 873
   – as 484
regardful 457, 459
regardless 458, 823
regards 894, 928
regatta 720, 840
regency 755
regenerate
   reproduce 163
   restore 660

choose 609
store 636
disuse 678
retain 781
shyness 881
in − *destined* 152
prepared 673
− forces 726
− oneself 881
reservoir 636
re-shape 140
resiance 189
resiant 186
reside 1, 186
residence 189
resident
  consignee 758
  present 186
  inhabitant 188
residentiary 186,
  188
  clergy 996
residue 40
residuum
  remainder 40
  dregs 653
  commonalty 876
resign 757, 782
− one's being 364
− one's breath 360
− oneself 725, 826
resignation [*see*
  resign]
  submission 725
  obedience 743
  abdication **757**
  renunciation 782
  endurance 826
  humility 879
resile 277
resilience
  regression 283
  elasticity 325
resin **356a**
resipiscence 950
resist *oppose* 179
  withstand 719
  disobey 742
  refuse 764
resistance 719
résistance, pièce de
  − 298
resister
  passive − 710
resisting
  tenacious 327
resistless 159, 601
resolute 604, 861
resolution
  decomposition 49
  conversion 144

music 413
topic 454
investigation 461
mental energy **604**
intention 620
scheme 626
courage 861
resolvable into 27,
  144
resolve *change* 140
  liquefy 335
  investigate 461
  discover 480a
  interpret 522
  determine 604
  predetermine 611
  intend 620
− into elements 49
− into *convert* 144
resonance 402, **408**
resorb 296
resort *assemble* 72
  focus 74
  dwelling 189
  converge 290
last − 601
− to *be present* 186
  travel 266
  employ 677
resound *loud* 404
  ring 408
− *praises* 931
resourceful 698
resources
  means 632
  property 780
  wealth 803
respect *relation* 9
  observe 772
  fame 873
  salutation 894
  deference **928**
have − to 9
in no − 536
with − to 9
respectability
  mediocrity 736
  repute 873
  probity 939
respectable
  unimportant 643
respectful 928
− *distance* 623,
  864
respective 79, 786
respectless 458
respects 894, 928
resperse 73
respicere finem 510
respire *breathe* 349
  live 359

refresh 689
respite
  intermission 106
  defer 133
  pause 142
  deliver 672
  repose 687
  reprieve 970
resplendent
  luminous 420
  splendid 845
respond *accord* 23
  answer 462
  feel 821
respondent 462
  accused 938
response
  answer 462, **587**
  concord 714
  feeling 821
  friendship 888
  worship 990
responsible 177,
  926
responsibility
  upon one's own −
  600
responsive 375
rest *remainder* 40
  pause 141
  cessation 142
  support 215
  quiescence 265
  death 360
  silence 403
  music 413
  inaction 681
  repose 687
at − *repose* 687
  content 831
home of − 189
set at −
  answer 462
  ascertain 474
  complete 729
  compact 769
set one's mind at −
  calm 826
set the question
  at − 478, 480
− assured 484, 858
− on *support* 215
− on one's oars
  142, 687
− satisfied 831
− and be thankful
  681, 687
− upon
  evidence 467
  confide 484
− with *duty* 926

restaurant 189
− car 272
restaurateur **637**
restful 265
resting place
  support 215
  quiet 265
  arrival 292
restitution **790**, 660
restive *averse* 603
  obstinate 606
  disobedient 742
  refusal 764
  perverse 901a
restless
  changeable 149
  moving 264
  agitated 315
  active 682
  excited 825
  fearful 860
restoration **660**
restorative
  salubrious 656
  remedial 662
  relieving 834
restore *reinstate*
  660
  refresh 689
  return 790
− equilibrium 27
− harmony 723
− to health 654
restrain 616, 706,
  751
restrainable 743
restrained 751
restraint 578, **751**
  self − 826, 953
restrict *hinder* 706
  restrain 751
  prohibit 761
restringency 751
result *remainder* 40
  follow 117
  effect 154
  conclusion 480
  completion 729
resultant 48, 154
resume *begin* 66
  repeat 104
  change 140
  restore 660
  take 789
résumé 596
resupination 213
resurgence 163, 660
resurrection
  reproduction 163
  restoration 660
  heaven 981

resuscitate
  reproduce 163
  reinstate 660
retable 215
retail *distribute* 73
  inform 527
  barter 794
  sell 796
retailer 797
retain *stand* 150
  keep 781
  – the memory of
  505
  – one's reason 502
retainer 746
retake 789
retaliation **718**, 919
retard *later* 133
  slower 275
  hinder 706
retch 297
retection 529
retention **781**
retentive 781
  – memory 505
reticence 528
reticle 219
reticulation 219,
  248
reticule 191
retiform 219
retina 441
retinue *followers* 65
  series 69
  servants 746
retire *move back* 283
  recede 287
  resign 757
  modest 881
  seclusion 893
  – into the shade
  inferior 34
  decrease 36
  – from sight
  disappear 449
  hide 528
retiring
  concave 252
  – *colour* 438
retold 104
retort
  receptacle 191
  vaporizer 336
  boiler 386
  answer 462
  confutation 479
  retaliation 718
  wit 842
retouch *restore* 660
retoucher 559
retrace 505

– one's steps 607
retract
  recant 607
  annul 756
  abjure 757
  violate 773
retreat
  resort 74
  withdraw 187
  abode 189
  regression 283
  recede 287
  ambush 530
  refuge 666
  escape 671
  give way 725
  beat a – 623
retreating
  concave 252
retrench *subduct* 38
  shorten 201
  lose 789
  economize 817
retribution
  retaliation 718
  payment 807
  punishment 972
  reward 973
retrieve *restore* 660
  acquire 775
retriever *dog* 366
retroaction
  counteraction 179
  recoil 277
  regression 283
retroactive
  past 122
retrocession
  regression 283
  recession 287
retrograde
  moving back 283
  deteriorated 659
  relapsing 661
retrogression
  regression 283
  deterioration 659
  relapse 661
retrospection
  past 122
  thought 451
  memory 505
retroussé 245
retroversion 218
retrude 289
return *list* 86
  repeat 104
  periodic 138
  reverse 145
  recoil 277
  regression 283

arrival 292
answer 462
report 551
relapse 661
appoint 755
profit 775
restore 790
proceeds 810
reward 973
in –
  compensation 30
  – the compliment
  interchange 148
  retaliate 718
  – to the original
  state 660
  –ed prodigal 950
  – thanks 916, 990
return game 104
return match 104
reunion *junction* 43
réunion
  assemblage 72
  concord 714
lieu de – 74
point de – 74
social – 892
revamp 140
revanche, en – 718
reveal 529
  – itself 446
reveille 550
réveiller le chat qui
  dort, ne pas –
  668, 864
revel 840, 954
  – in *enjoy* 377
revelation
  disclosure 480a,
  529
  theological 985
Revelations 985
reveller 840
  drunkard 959
revelling 59, 838
revendicate
  claim 741
  acquisition 775
  due 924
revenge **919**
  breathe – 900
revenons à nos
  moutons 283,
  660
revenue 632, 810
reverberate 277,
  408
reverberatory 386
revere *love* 897
  respect 928
  piety 987

reverence *title* 877
  respect 928
  piety 987
  clergy 996
reverenced 500
reverend 877, 996
reverent 987, 990
reverential 928
reverie
  train of thought
  451
  inattention 458
  imagination 515
reversal 218, 607
reverse *contrary* 14
  inversion 218
  – *of a medal* 235
  contraposition 237
  adversity 735
  abrogate 756
  cards 840
  – of the shield 468
reverseless 150
reversible 605
reversion
  [see reverse]
  posterity 117
  return **145**
  possession 777
  property 780
  succession 783
  remitter 790
reversioner 779
revert *repeat* 104
  return 145
  turn back 283
  revest 790
  – to 457
revest 790
revet 223
reviction 660
review *consider* 457
  inquiry 461
  judge 480
  recall 505
  periodical 531
  dissertation 595
  compendium 596
  entertainment 599
  revise 658
  parade 882
reviewer 480, 595
revile 932, 988
reviler 936
revise *copy* 21
  consider 457
  printing 591
  plan 626
  improve 658
revising barrister
  967

revision, under – 673
revisit 186
revival
  reproduction 163
  restoration 660
  worship 990
revivalist 996
revive
  reproduce 163
  improve 658
  resuscitate 660
  excite 824
revivify
  reproduce 163
  life 359
  improve 658
  resuscitate 660
revocable 605
revoir, au – 293
revoke 607, 756
revolt *resist* 719
  disobey 742
  shock 830
  disapproval 932
  – against *hate* 898
  – at the idea
  dissent 489
revolting
  painful 830
revolution
  periodicity 138
  change **146**
  rotation 312
  disobedience 742
revolutionize 140, 146
revolve
  [*see* revolution]
  – in the mind 451
revolver 727
revue 599
  intimate – 599
revulsion
  reversion 145
  revolution 146
  inversion 218
  recoil 277
reward **973**
reword 104
Reynard
  animal 366
  cunning 702
rez-de-chaussée 191, 207 .
rhabdology 85
rhabdomancy 511
Rhadamanthus 967, 982
rhapsodical
  irregular 139

imaginary 515
rhapsodist
  fanatic 504
rhapsody
  discontinuity 70
  music 415
  nonsense 497
  fancy 515
  poetry 597
rhetoric *speech* 582
  flowers of – 577
rheum
  excretion 299
  fluidity 333
  water 337
rhino 800
rhinoceros *hide* 376, 823
rhomb 244
rhumb 278
rhyme
  similarity 17
  verse 597
  without – or
  reason
  absurd 497
  caprice 608
  motiveless 615*a*
rhymeless 598
rhymester 597
rhythm
  periodicity 138
  melody 413
  elegance 578
  verse 597
rhythmical
  - *style* 578
Rialto 799
rib *support* 215
  ridge 250
  wife 903
ribald *vulgar* 851
  disreputable 874
  impure 961
riband
  [*see* ribbon]
ribbed 259
ribbon *tie* 45
  filament 205
  record 551
  decoration 877
  –s *reins* 752
  handle the – 693
ribroast 972
rich *savoury* 394
  colour 428
  language 577
  abundant 639
  wealthy 803
  beautiful 845
  ornament 847

– man 803
riches 803
richesses, embarras de – 641, 803
richly *much* 31
  – deserve 924
rick 72, 636
rickety *weak* 160
  ugly 846
  imperfect 651
rickshaw 272
ricochet 277
ricordo, non mi – 506
rid *deliver* 672
  get – of *eject* 297
  liberation 750
  loose 776
  relinquish 782
riddance 672, 776, 782
  good – 776
riddle *arrange* 60
  sieve 260
  secret 533
  clean 652
ride *get above* 206
  move 266
  break in 370
  – at anchor 265
  – full tilt at 622, 716
  – hard 274
  – one's hobby 622
  – rough shod
  violence 173
  severity 739
  insolence 885
  illegality 964
  – out the storm 664
  – and tie
  periodicity 138
  journey 266
  – the whirlwind 604, 737
rideau, lever de – 599
ridentem dicere verum 836, 842
rider *appendix* 39
  equestrian 268
rideret Heraclitus 853
ridge *narrow* 203
  height 206
  prominence 250
ridicule **856**, 929
ridiculous
  absurd 497
  foolish 499

trifling 643
  grotesque 853
ridiculousness **853**
riding *district* 181
  journey 266
ridotto 840, 892
rifacimento 104, 660
rife *existence* 1
  general 78
  influence 175
riff-raff *dirt* 653
  commonalty 876
  bad folk 949
rifle *musket* 727
  plunder 791
  – shot 406
rifled cannon 727
rifleman 726
rifler 792
rifles 726
rifle-shooting 840
rift 44, 198
  – within the lute 651, 713
rig *dress* 225
  prepare 673
  frolic 840
  strumpet 962
  – the market 794
  run the – upon 929
rigadoon 840
rigging *ropes* 45
  gear 225
  instrument 633
riggish 961
right *dextral* 238
  straight 246
  true 494
  property 780
  just **922**
  privilege 924
  duty 926
  honour 939
  virtuous 944
  bill of – 969
  by – 924
  have a – to 924
  set – *inform* 527
  disclose 529
  that's – 931
  – about
  [*see below*]
  – ahead 234
  – angle 212
  – ascension 466
  – away 133
  step in the – direction 644
  – hand [*see below*]
  – itself 660

roseate *red* 434	*pungent* 392	*periodic* 138	*overcome* 731
hopeful 858	*unsavoury* 395	*recant* 607	*discomfit* 732
rose-coloured	*sour* 397	*persuade* 615	*rabble* 876
hope 858	*sound* 410	dizzy – 312	*assembly* 892
Rosetta stone 522	*unprepared* 674	get – 660	put to the – 731
rosette 847	*fighter* 726	go – 311	– out 652
rose-water	*ugly* 846	go one's –s 266	route 627
moderation 174	*low fellow* 876	go the –	en – 270
flattery 933	*bully* 887	*publication* 531	en – for 282
not made with –	*churlish* 895	make the – of 311	routine
704	*evil-doer* 913	run the – of 682	*uniform* 16
Rosicrucian	*bad man* 949	go the same – 104	*order* 58
order or *party*	cut up – 900	turn – *invert* 218	*rule* 80
712	– copy *writing* 590	*retreat* 283	*periodic* 138
rosin *rub* 331	*unprepared* 674	*revolve* 311	*custom* 613
resin 356*a*	– diamond	– assertion 535	*business* 625
Rosinante 271	*uncouth* 241	– a corner 311	rove *travel* 266
roster 86	*unprepared* 674	– dance 840	*deviate* 279
rostrum *beak* 234	*artless* 703	– game 840	rover *traveller* 268
pulpit 542	*vulgar* 851	– hand 590	*pirate* 792
rosy 434	*commonalty* 876	– like a horse in a	roving commission
– wine 959	*good man* 948	mill 613	475
rosy-cheeked 845	– draft 626	– of the ladder 71	row *disorder* 59
rot *decompose* 49	– guess 514	– number 84, 102	*series* 69
absurdity 497	– it 686	in – numbers 29,	*violence* 173
rubbish 517	– sea 348	197	*street* 189
putrefy 653	– side of the	– pace 274	*navigate* 267
disease 655	tongue 932	– of pleasures	*discord* 713
decay 659	– and tumble 59	377, 840	– in the same
rota 86, 138	– weather 173, 349	– robin	boat 88
Rotarian 892	rough-cast 256	*information* 527	rowdy *vulgar* 851,
rotate 138	*covering* 223	*petition* 765	876
rotation 312	*shape* 240	*censure* 932	*blusterer* 887
periodicity 138	*scheme* 626	– and round 138,	*bad man* 949
rote, by – 505	*unpolished* 674	312	rowel 253, 615
know – 490	rough-hew 240, 673	– sum 800	rower 269
learn – 539	roughly	– terms 566	rowlock 215
rôti 298	*nearly* 197	– trot 274	royal 737
rôtisserie 189	rough-neck 876,	– up 370	– blue 438
rotogravure 531,	887	– of visits 892	– highness 877
558	roughness 256	round about	– road 627, 705
rotten *weak* 160	rough-rider 268	*circumjacent* 227	Royal Academician
bad 649	roughshod over,	*deviation* 279	559
foul 653	ride – 739	*circuit* 311	royalist 737
decayed 659	roulade 415	*amusement* 840	royaliste que le roi,
– at the core	rouleau	– phrases 573	plus 33
deceptive 545	*assemblage* 72	– way 279	royalty 737
diseased 655	*cylinder* 249	rounded periods	Rt. Hon. 877
– borough 893	*money* 800	577, 578	ruade *impulse* 276
rotulorum, custos –	roulette 621, 840	roundelay 597	*attack* 716
553	round *series* 69	rounders 840	ruat cœlum 908
rotund 249	*revolution* 138	round-house 752	rub *friction* 331
rotunda 189	– of a ladder 215	roundlet 247	*touch* 379
rotundity 249	*curve* 245	round-shouldered	*difficulty* 704
roturier 876	*circle* 247	243	*adversity* 735
roué 949	*rotund* 249	roup 796	*painful* 830
rouge 434, 847	*music* 415	rouse 615, 824	– off corners 82
rouge-et-noir 621	*fight* 720	– oneself 682	– down *lessen* 195
rough *violent* 173	all – 227	rousing 171	*powder* 330
shapeless 241	bring – 660	rout *crowd* 72	– down with an
uneven 256	come –	*agitation* 315	oaken towel 972

saddle 215
in the – 673
– on 37, 43
– on the right
horse
discovery 480*a*
skill 698
right 922
fair 939
– with *add* 37
attribute 155
quarter on 184
clog 706
impose a duty
926
accuse 938
– on the wrong
horse 495, 699
– up 293
saddle-bags 191
Sadducee 984
sadness, in – 535
safe *cupboard* 191
hiding place 530
secure 664
treasury 802
cautious 864
– conduct 631
– conscience 926,
946
– deposit 636
– keeping 670
– and sound 654
on the – side 864
safety 664
– bicycle 272
– curtain 599
– first 664, 864
– match 388
– valve 666
saffron *colour* 436
sag 214, 217, 245
saga 594
sagacious 498, 510
sage 498, **500**
– *maxim* 496
saggar 386
sagittal 253
sagittary 83
sagum 225
Sahara 169
sahib 373, 745, 875
saick 273
said *preceding* 62
repeated 104
prior 116
it is – 532
thou hast – 488
more easily – than
done 704
sail *navigate* 267

ship 273
set out 293
easy – 174
full – 274
press of – 274
shorten – 275
take in – 174
take the wind out
of one's –s 706
too much – 863
under – 267
– before the wind
734
– near the wind
698
– too near the
wind 863
sailing: plain – 705
– vessel 273
sailor 269
fair weather – 701
saint *angel* 977
revelation 985
piety 987
false piety 988
tutelary – 664
Saint Monday 840
saintly 944, 987
sais quoi, je ne –
563
sake:
for the – of 615,
707
for goodness – 765
salaam
bow 308
submit 725
courtesy 894
respect 928
salacity 961
salad 41
– oil 356
salade 717
salamander 386
salariat 875
salary 973
sale 796
bill of – 771
for – *offer* 763
barter 794
saleable 796
salebrosity 256
salesman 797
salient
projecting 250
sharp 253
manifest 525
important 642
– angle 244
– points 642
saline 392

saliva 299, 332
salivate 297
salle-à-manger 191
sallet 717
sallow
colourless 429
yellow 436
sally *issue* 293
attack 716
wit 842
sally-port 295, 717
salmagundi 41
salmi 298
salmon-coloured
434
saloon 189, 191
salt *sailor* 269
pungent 392
condiment 393
importance 642
preserve 670
money 800
wit 842
below the – 876
worth one's – 644
– of the earth
648, 948
– water 341
saltation 309
saltatory 315
saltimbanco 548
saltpetre 392, 727
saltum, per – 315
salubrity 656
salutary 656
salutatory 582
salute
allocution 586
celebration 883
courtesy 894
kiss 902
respect 928
salutiferous
[*see* salutary]
salva:
– res est 664
– sit reverentia
928
salvable 946
salvage
acquisition 775
tax 812
discount 813
reward 973
salvation
preservation 670
deliverance 672
religious 976
piety 987
work out one's –
990

salve *unguent* 356
remedy 662
relieve 834
salver 191
salvo *exception* 83
explosion 406
qualification 469
plea 617
attack 716
excuse 937
– of artillery
celebration 883
Samaritan, good –
906, 912
same 13
all the – to 823
in the – boat 709
in the – breath
113, 120
go over the –
ground 104
of the – mind 488
on the – tack 709
adds up to the –
thing 27
at the – time 30,
120
sameness 16
samiel 349
samisen 417
Sammael 978
samovar 191
sampan 273
sample 82, 463
Samson 159
sana, mens – 502
– in corpore sano
827
sanation 660
sanative 662
sanatorium 662
sanctification 976
sanctify 926, 987
sanctimony 988
sanction
permission 760
dueness 924
approbation 931
sanctitude 987
sanctity 987
sanctuary 666, 100.
sanctum 191
– sanctorum
abode 189
privacy 893
temple 1000
sand *powder* 330
–bag 727
built upon – 665
–dance 840
sow the – 645

scroll 86, 551
scrub *rub* 331
  bush 367
  clean 652
  dirty person 653
  commonalty 876
scrubby *small* 193
  trifling 643
  stingy 819
  disreputable 874
  vulgar 876
  shabby 940
scruff 235
scruple
  small quantity 32
  weight 319
  doubt 485
  reluctance 603
  probity 939
scrupulous
  careful 459
  incredulous 487
  exact 494
  reluctant 603
  fastidious 868
  punctilious 939
scrutator 461
scrutiny 457, 461
scrutoire 191
scud *sail* 267
  speed 274
  shower 348
  cloud 353
  – under bare
    poles 704
scuffle 720
scull *row* 267
  brain 450
scull-cap 225
scullery 191
scullion 746
sculpsit 558
sculptor 559
sculpture 240, **557**
scum *dirt* 653
  – of the earth 949
  – of society 876
scupper 350
scurf 653
scurrilous
  ridicule 856
  malediction 908
  disrespect 929
  detraction 934
scurry 274, 684
scurvy.
  insufficient 640
  unimportant 643
  base 940
  wicked 945
scut 235

scutcheon
  standard 550
  honour 877
scutiform 251
scuttle *destroy* 162
  receptacle 191
  speed 274
  – along *haste* 684
Scylla and Charyb-
  dis, between –
  danger 665
  difficulty 704
Scyllam, incidit
  in – 699
scythe *pointed* 244
  sharp 253
'sdeath! *wonder* 870
  anger 900
  disapprobation
    932
se non è vero è ben
  trovato 546
sea *multitude* 102
  ocean 341
  at – 341
  uncertain 475
  erroneous 495
  go to – 293
  on the high –s 341
  heavy – 315
  the seven –s 341
  – of doubt 475
  – of troubles
  difficulty 704
  adversity 735
seaboard 342
seafarer 269
seafaring 267, 273
sea-fight 720
sea-girt 346
sea-going 267, 341
sea-green 435
seal
  matrix 22
  close 261
  evidence 467
  mark 550
  resolve 604
  complete 729
  compact 769
  security 771
  break the – 529
  under – 769
  – the doom of 162
  – one's infamy 940
  – the lips 585
  – of secrecy 528
  – up *restrain* 751
sealed:
  one's fate is – 601
  hermetically – 261

– book
  ignorance 491
  unintelligible 519
  secret 533
sealing-wax 356
seals *insignia* 747
sealskin 223
seam 43
sea-maid 979
sea-man 269
seamanship 692,
  698
sea-mark 550
seamless 50
seamstress 225,
  690
seamy side 651
séance 525, 696
sea-piece 556
seaplane 273, 726
sea-port 666
sear *dry* 340
  burn 384
  deaden 823
  – and yellow leaf
    128, 659
search *inquire* 461
searching
  severe 739
  painful 830
searchless 519
searchlight 423,
  726
seared conscience
  951
searing 830
seascape 556
sea-serpent 83
seaside 342
season *mix* 41
  time 106
  pungent 392
  accustom 613
  preserve 670
  prepare 673
seasonable 23, 134
seasoning 393
seasons 138
seat *place* 183
  locate 184
  abode 189
  support 215
  posterior 235
  parliament 693
  country – 189
  judgment – 966
  – of government
    737
  – of war 728
seated, firmly – 150
seaway 180

seaweed 367
seaworthy 273, 664
sebaceous 355
secant 219
secede *dissent* 489
  relinquish 624
  disobey 742
seceder
  heterodox 984
secern 297
seclusion **893**
second
  duplication 90
  – *of time* 108
  instant 113
  – *in music* 413,
    415
  abet 707
  play or sing a –
    416
  – best 651, 732
  – childhood 128,
    499
  – crop 168, **775**
  – edition 104
  play – fiddle
  obey 743
  subject 749
  disrepute 874
  – nature 613
  – to none 33
  one's – self 17
  – rate 659
  – sight
  foresight 510
  sorcery 992
  – thoughts
  sequel 65
  thought 451
  improvement 658
  – youth 660
secondary
  inferior 34
  following 63
  imperfect 651
  deputy 759
  – education 537
  – evidence 467
  – school 542
seconder 711
second-hand
  imitation 19
  old 124
  deteriorated 659
  received 785
secondly 90
second-rate 651
secret *key* 522
  latent 526
  hidden 528
  riddle **533**

in the – 490
keep a – 585
– motive 615
– passage 627, 671
– place 530
– writing 590
secrétaire 191
secretary
  recorder 553
  writer 590
  director 694
  auxiliary 711
  servant 746
  consignee 758
– of state 694
– of the treasury
  801
secrete *excrete* 297
  conceal 528
secretion 299
secretive 528
sect 75
religious – 983,
  984
sectarian
  dissent 489
  ally 711
  heterodox 984
sectary 489
section *division* 44
  part 51
  class 75
  chapter 593
  troops 726
sector *part* 51
  circle 247
secula seculorum,
  in – 112
secular
  centenary 98
  periodic 138
  laity 997
– education 537
secularism 984
secundum artem
  82, 698
secure *fasten* 43
  bespeak 132
  belief 484
  safe 664
  restrain 751
  engage 768
  gain 775
  confident 858
– an object 731
securities 802–805
security *safety* 664
  pledge **771**
  hope 858
lend on – 787
Sedan

disaster 162
sedan chair 272
sedate
  thoughtful 451
  calm 826
  grave 837
sedative 174, 662
sedentary 265
sedge 367
sedile 1000
sediment *dregs* 653
sedimentary 40
sedition 742
seduce *entice* 615
  love 897
  debauch 961
seducer 962
seduction 829, 865
sedulous 682, 865
see *view* 441
  look 457
  believe 484
  know 490
  bishopric 995
we shall – 507
– after 459
– daylight 480*a*
– double 959
– fit 600, 602
– at a glance 498
– justice done 922
– life 840
– the light
  born 359
  published 531
– service 722
– sights 455
– through 480*a*,
  498
– to *attention* 457
  care 459
  direction 693
– one's way
  foresight 510
  intelligible 518
  skill 698
  easy 705
seed *small* 32
  cause 153
  posterity 167
  grain 330
run to – *age* 128
  lose health 659
sow the – 673
seedling 129
seed-plot 168, 371
seed-time of life
  127
seedy *weak* 160
  disease 655
  deteriorated 659

exhausted 688
  needy 804
seeing that 8, 476
seek *inquire* 461
  pursue 622
  offer 763
  request 765
– safety 664
seek-sorrow 837
seel 217
seem 448
as it –s good to
  600
seeming 448
seemingly 472
seemless 846, 925
seemliness 926
seemly
  expedient 646
  handsome 845
  due 924
seep 295
seer *veteran* 130
  madman 504
  oracle 513
  sorcerer 994
see-saw 12, 314
seethe *wet* 339
  hot 382
  make hot 384
  excitement 824
seething caldron
  386
segar 392
segment 44, 51
segnitude 683
s'égosiller 411
segregate
  not related 10
  separate 44
  exclude 55
segregated
  incoherent 47
seigneur, grand –
  pride 878
  insolence 885
seignior 745, 875
seigniority
  authority 737
  possession 777
  property 780
seigniory 737
seine net 232
seisin 777, 780
seismic 314
seismograph 553
seismometer 276,
  314
seize 789, 791
– an opportunity
  134

seized with
  disease 655
  feeling 821
seizure 925
sejunction 44
seldom 137
select *choose* 609
  good 648
self 13, 79
–abasement 879
–accusing 950
–admiration 880
–applause 880
–appointed task
  602
–assertion 885
–called 565
–command 604,
  864
–communing 451
–complacency
  836, 880
–confidence 880
–conquest 604
–conscious 855
–consultation 451
–contained 52
–control 604
–conviction
  belief 484
  penitent 950
  condemned 971
–counsel 451
–deceit *error* 495
–deception 486
–defence 717
–delusion 486
–denial
  disinterested 942
  temperance 953
  penance 990
–discipline 990
–effacement 879,
  942
–esteem 880
–evident 474, 525
–examination 990
–existing 1
–government 748
–help 698
–immolation 991
–indulgence
  selfishness 943
  intemperance 954
–interest 943
–knowledge 881
–love 943
–luminous 423
–mastery 604
–opinioned 481
–possession

sanity 502
resolution 604
inexcitability 826
caution 864
−praise 880
−preservation 717
−reliance
resolution 604
hope 858
courage 861
−reproach 950
−respect 878
−restraint 953
−sacrifice 942
−satisfied 880
−seeking 943
−styled 565
−sufficient 880
−taught 490
−tormentor 837
−will 606
selfishness **943**
self-same 13
sell *convince* 484
absurdity 497
deception 545
untruth 546
sale 796
− for 812
− one's life dearly
719, 722
− off 796
− oneself 940
− out 796
seller 796
selon les règles 82
selvedge 231
semaphore 550
semblance
similarity 17
imitation 19
copy 21
probability 472
wear the − of
appearance 448
semeiology 522
semeiotics 550
semester 108
semi- 91
semi-barbarian 913
semibreve 413
semicircle 247
semicircular 245
semicolon 142
semi-diaphanous
427
semi-fluid 352
semi-liquidity **352**
semi-lunar 245
seminal 153
seminary 542

semination 673
semi-opaque 427
semi-pellucid 427
semiquaver 413
semitone 413
semi-transparency
427
sempervirent 110
sempiternal 112
sempstress 225, 690
senary 98
senate 696
senate-house 966
senator 695, 696
senatorship 693
senatus consultum
741
send 270, 284
− adrift 597
− away
repel 289
eject 297
refuse 764
− for 741
− forth 284, 531
− a letter to 592
− off 284
− out *eject* 297
− packing 289
commission 755
− word 527
senescence 128
seneschal
director 694
master 745
servant 746
seneschalship 737
senile 128
senility 158, 659
senior *age* 128
student 541
master 745
seniores priores 62,
280
seniority 124, 128
sennight 108
señor 373, 877
señora 374
sensation
*physical sensi-
bility* 375
emotion 821
wonder 870
sensational 574,
824
sensation drama
599
sensations of touch
380
sense 498, 516
deep − 821

horse − 498
in no − 565
accept in a par-
ticular − 522
− of duty 926
senseless
insensible 376
absurd 497
foolish 499
unmeaning 517
senses
external - 375
intellect 450
sanity 502
sensibility **375, 822**
sensible
material 316
wise 498
sensitive 375, 822
sensorial 821
sensorium 450
sensual 377, 954
sensualist 954a
sensuous
sensibility 375
pleasure 377
feeling 821
sentence
decision 480
maxim 496
affirmation 535
phrase 566
condemnation 971
sententious 572,
574
sentient 375, 821
sentiment 453
sentimental
sensitive 822
affected 855
sentinel ⎫
           ⎬ 263
sentry ⎭
guardian 664
watch 668
keeper 753
separate *disjoin* 44
exclude 55
bisect 91
diverge 291
divorce 905
− the chaff from
the wheat
discriminate 465
select 609
− into elements 49
− maintenance 905
separation 44
separatist 489, 984
sepia 433
seposition 44, 55
sepoy 726

sept *kin* 11
class 75
clan 166
Septentrional 237
septet 415
septic 655, 657
septicæmia 655
septuagenarian 98
Septuagint 985
septum 228
sepulchral
interment 363
resonance 408
stridor 410
hoarse 581
sepulchre 363
whited − 545
sepulture 363
sequacious 63
sequacity *soft* 324
tenacity 327
sequel **65**, 117
sequela 65, 154
sequence
- *in order* **63**
- *in time* 117
motion **281**
logical − 476
sequent 63
sequester 789, **974**
sequestered 893
sequestrate
seize 789
condemn 971
confiscate 974
sequin 847
serac 383
seraglio 961
seraph 948, 977
seraphic
blissful 829
virtuous 944
pious 987
seraphina 417
seraskier 745
sere and yellow
leaf 128
serein 339, 348
serenade *music* 415
compliment 894
endearment 902
serene
pellucid 425
calm 826
content 831
imperturbable **871**
− highness 877
serf *slave* 746
clown 876
serfdom 749
sergeant 745

serial
continuous 69
periodic 138
book 593
seriatim
in order 58
continuously 69
each to each 79
slowly 275
series 69, 84
sérieux, take au –
843
serio-comic 853
serious *great* 31
resolved 604
important 642
dejected 837
seriously 535
serjeant:
common – 967
–at-law 968
sermon *lesson* 537
speech 582
dissertation 595
pastoral 998
funeral – 363
sermonizer 584
seroon 72
serosity 333, 337
serpent
tortuous 248
snake 366
hiss 409
wind instrument
417
wise 498
deceiver 548
cunning 702
evil-doer 913
knave 941
demon 949
the old – 978
great sea – 515
serpentine 248
serrated 244, 257
serried 72, 321
serum 333, 337
servant *instrumentality* 631
help 711
retainer **746**
– of all work 690
serve *benefit* 618
business 625
utility 644
aid 707
warfare 722
obey 743
servant 746
– an apprenticeship 539

– faithfully 743
– loyally 743
– notice 527
– out 972
– one right
retaliation 718
right 922
punish 972
– as a substitute
147
– one's turn 644
– with a writ 969
service *good* 618
utility 644
use 677
warfare 722
servitude 749
worship 990
rite 998
hold – 363
at one's – 763
press into the –
677
render a – 644,
906
serviceable 644, 648
serviette 652
servile 749, 876, **886**
servitor 746
servitorship 749
servitude 749
penal – 972
sesame, open – 260
watchword 550
spell 993
sesqui- 87
sesquipedalia verba
577
sesquipedalian 200
sess 812
sessile 46
session *council* 696
sessions *law* 966
sestet 597
set
condition **7**
join 43
coherence 46
group 72
class 75
firm 150
tendency 176
place 184
form 240
sharpen 253
direction 278
go down 306
dense 321
stage 599
habit 613
prepare 673

gang 712
impose 741
make a dead – at
716
– about 66, 676
– abroach 73
– one's affections
on 897
– afloat 153, 531
– against
oppose 708
quarrel 713
hate 898
angry 900
– against one
another 464
– agoing
impulse 276
propulsion 284
aid 707
– apart
separate 44
exclude 55
select 609
– aside
displace 185
disregard 458
neglect 460
negative 536
reject 610
disuse 678
annul 756
refuse 764
not observe 773
relinquish 782
dereliction 927
– one's back up
878
– before
inform 527
choice 609
– before oneself
620
– by 636
– one's cap at
897, 902
– on a cast 621
– down [see below]
– by the ears 898
– at ease 831
– an example
model 22
motive 615
– the eyes on 441
– one's face
against
oppose 708
refuse 764
disapprove 932
– the fashion
influence 175

authority 737
fashion 852
– fast 704
– on fire
ignite 384
excite 824
– on foot 66
– foot on 294
– forth *show* 525
assert 535
describe 594
– forward 293
– free 750
– going
[see – agoing]
– one's hand to
467
– one's heart upon
604, 865
– at hazard 665
– in *begin* 66
rain 348
– on its legs 150
– on one's legs 159,
660
– in motion 264,
677
– to music 416
– at naught
make light of 483
reject 610
oppose 708
defy 715
disobey 742
not observe 773
dereliction 927
– no store by 483,
930
– off
compensation 30
depart 293
improve 658
discount 813
adorn 845
display 882
– on 615
– in order 60
– out *arrange* 60
begin 66
depart 293
decorate 845
display 882
– over 755
– phrase 566
– a price 85, 812
– purpose 620
– at rest *end* 67
answer 462
adjudge 480
complete 729
compact 769

Column 1 (SET)

– right
inform 527
disclose 529
teach 537
reinstate 660
vindicate 937
– to rights 60
– sail 293
– the seal on 729
– one's seal to 467
– store by 642
– straight 246, 723
– the table in a
   roar 840
– one's teeth 604
– terms
manifest 525
phrase 566
style 574
– a trap for 545
– to 720, 722
– in towards 286
– up
printing 54
originate 153
strengthen 159
produce 161
upright 212
raise 307
successful 731
prosperous 734
– up shop 676
– upon
resolved 604
attack 716
desirous 865
– too high a value
   upon 482
– watch 459
– one's wits to
   work *think* 451
imagine 515
plan 626
– to work
undertake 676
impose 741
set-back 735
set down
record 551
unseat 756
humiliate 879
slight 929
censure 932
give one a –
confute 479
– as 484
– for 484
– a cause for
   hearing 969
– to 155
– in writing 551

Column 2 (SEV)

setaceous 256
seton 662
setose 256
sett *lease* 771, 787
settee 215
setter 366
settle *regulate* 60
establish 150
be located 184
bench 215
come to rest 265
subside 306
kill 361
decide 480
choose 609
vanquish 731
consent 762
compact 769
pay 807
– accounts 807,
   811
– down 131
stability 150
moderate 174
locate oneself 184
– into 144
– matters 723
– preliminaries
   673
– property 781
– the question 478
– to sleep 683
– upon *give* 784
– with 807, 972
settled [*see* settle]
characteristic 5
ended 67
account – 811
– opinion 484
– purpose 620
settlement [*see*
   settle]
location 184
colony 188
dregs 653
compact 769
deed 771
property 780
strict – 781
settler 188
settlor 784
seven 98
–league boots 274,
   992
wake the –
   sleepers 404
seventy 98
sever 38, 44
several *special* 79
plural 100
many 102

Column 3 (SHA)

– times 104
severalize 465
severally 44, 79
severalty 44
severance 38
severe
energetic 171
symmetry 242
exact 494
- *style* 576
harsh 739
painful 830
simple 849
critical 932
severely *very* 31
severity **739**
sew 43
sewage 299, 653
sewed up
drunk 959
sewer 350, 653
sewerage 652, 653
sewer-gas 663
sewing-silk 205
sex *kind* 75
women 374
fair – 374
sexagenarian 98,
   130
sexagenary 99
sextant 217, 244,
   247
sextet 98
sextodecimo 593
sexton 363, 996
sextuple 98
seyyid 745
sforzando 415
shabbiness 34
shabby *trifling* 643
deteriorated 659
stingy 819
mean 874
disgraceful 940
shabby-genteel 851
shack 189
shackle
fastening 45
hinder 706
restrain 751
fetter 752
shade *degree* 26
small quantity 32
manes 362
darkness 421
shadow **424**
colour 428
conceal 528
screen 530
paint 556
ghost 980

Column 4 (SHA)

eye – 443
in the – 528, 874
shadow of a – 32,
   422
throw into the –
surpass 303
conceal 528
glory 873
throw all else into
   the – 642
thrown into the –
   34, 874
under the – of 664
without a – of
   doubt 474
shades:
– below 982
– of death 360
– of difference 15
– of evening 422
shading 421
– off 26
shadow
unsubstantial 4
copy 21
small 32
accompaniment
   88
thin 203
be behind 235
sequence 281
dark 421
shade 424
pursue 461, 622
dream 515
demon 980
fight with a – 699
follow as a – 281
partial – 422
without a – of
   turning 141
worn to a –
thin 203
worse for wear
   659
– of coming
   events 511
– forth *dim* 422
predict 511
metaphor 521
represent 554
may your – never
   be less
courtesy 894
respect 928
approbation 931
take the – for the
   substance
credulous 486
mistake 495
unskilful 699

under the – of
  one's wing 664
shadowy 4, 447
shady 874
shaft *deep* 208
  frame 215
  pit 260
  missile 284
  axis 312
  air-pipe 351
  handle 633
  weapon 727
shaggy 256
shagreen 223
shah 745
shake *totter* 149
  weak 160
  vibrate 314
  agitation 315
  shiver 383
  trill 407
  music 416
  dissuade 616
  injure 659
  impress 821
  excited 824
  fear 860
– one's faith 485
– hands
  pacification 723
  friendship 888
  courtesy 894
  forgive 918
– the head
  dissent 489
  deny 536
  refuse 764
  disapprove 932
– off 297
– off the yoke 750
– to pieces 162
– one's sides 838
– up 315
shakedown *bed* 215
shakes, no great –
  643, 651
shako 225, 717
shaky *weak* 160
  in danger 665
  fearful 860
shallop 273
shallow
  not deep 32, 209
  ignorant 491
  ignoramus 493
  foolish 499
  trifling 643
– *pretext* 617
– *profundity* 855
shallow-brain 501
shallowness 209

shallow-pated 499
shallows
  danger 667
sham *imitation* 19
  falsehood 544
  deception 545,
  546
– *fight* 720
shaman 994
shamanism 992
shamble 275, 315
shambles 361
shame
  disrepute 874
  wrong 923
  censure 932
  chastity 960
  cry – upon 932
  false – 855
  for – 874
  sense of – 879
– the devil 939
  to one's – be it
  spoken 874
shamefaced 881
shameful
  disgraceful 874
  profligate 945
shameless
  bold 525
  impudent 885
  profligate 945
  indecent 961
shampoo 652
shandredhan 272
shanghai 791
shank *support* 215
  instrument 633
Shanks's mare 266
shanty 189
shape 240, 448
– one's course
  direction 278
  pursuit 622
  conduct 692
– out a course 626
shapeless 241, 846
shapely 242, 845
shard 51
share
  part 51
  participate 778
  allotted portion
  786
– and share alike
  778
shareholder 778
shark 792
sharp
  energetic 171
  violent 173

acute 253
sensible 375
pungent 392
– *sound* 410
musical tone 413
intelligent 498
active 682
clever 698
cunning 702
feeling 821
painful 830
rude 895
censorious 932
look – 459, 682
– appetite 865
– contest 720
– ear 418
– eye 441
– fellow 682, 700
– frost 383
– look-out 459,
  507
– pain 378
– practice
  cunning 702
  severity 739
  improbity 940
– set 865
sharpen
  [*see* sharp]
  excite 824
– one's tools 673
– one's wits 537
sharpener 253
sharper 792
sharpness 253
sharpshooter 726
sharpshooting 716
Shaster 986
shatter *disjoin* 44
  disperse 73
  render powerless
  158
  destroy 162
shatter-brained 503
shattered 160, 688
shave *reduce* 195
  shorten 201
  layer 204
  smooth 255
  cut 44
  lie 546
  close – 671
shaved 226
shaving *small* 32
  layer 204
  filament 205
shave-tail 726, 745
shawl 225
shawm 417
shay 272

she 374
sheaf 72
shear *reduce* 195
  shorten 201
  sheep 370
  take 789
shears 253
sheath 191, 223
sheathe 225
  moderate 174
– the sword 723
sheathing 223
sheave 633
shed *scatter* 73
  building 189
  divest 226
  emit 297
  give 784
– blood 361
– light upon 420
– a lustre on 873
– tears 839
Shedim 980
sheen 420
sheep 366
sheep-dog 366
sheep-fold 232
sheepish 881
sheep's eye, cast a –
  desire 865
  modest 881
  endearment 902
sheer *simple* 42
  complete 52
  deviate 279
– off *avoid* 623
sheet *layer* 204
  covering 223
  paper 593
  come down in –s
  rain 348
  white – 952
  winding – 363
– of fire 382
– of water 343
sheet-anchor
  safety 664, 666
  hope 858
sheet-lightning 423
sheik *ruler* 745, 875
  lover 897
  priest 996
shelf 215, 667
  on the –
  powerless 158
  disused 678
  inaction 681
shell *cover* 223
  coffin 363
  bombard 716
  bomb 727

–burst 404
–shock 655
– out 784, 807, 809
shellac 356*a*
shellback 269
shell-fish 366
shelter 664, 666
– oneself under plea of 617
sheltie 271
shelve *defer* 133
 locate 184
 slope 217
 neglect 460
 disuse 678
shelving beach 217
shend 659
shepherd *tender of sheep* 370
 director 694
 pastor 996
Shepherd, the Good – 976
shepherd's dog 366
Sheppard, Jack – 792
shere 32
sheriff 745, 965
Shetland pony 271
shew [*see* show]
shibboleth 550
shield
 heraldry 550
 safety 664
 buckler 666
 defend 717
 scutcheon 877
 look only at one side of the – 481
 reverse of the – 235, 468
 under the – of 664
shift *change* 140
 convert 144
 substitute 147
 changeable 149
 chemise 225
 move 264
 transfer 270
 deviate 279
 prevaricate 546
 plea 617
 cunning 702
 last – 601
 make a – with 147, 677
 put to one's –s 704, 804
 – one's ground 607

– off *defer* 133
– for oneself 692, 748
left to – for oneself 893
– one's quarters 264
– the scene 140
– to and fro 149
shifting [*see* shift]
 transient 111
 – sands 149
 – trust or use 783
shiftless 674, 699
shillelagh 727
shilling 800
 cut off with a – 789
– shocker 594
shilly-shally 605
shimmer 420
shimmy
 dance 840
shindy 720
shine *light* 420
 beauty 845
 glory 873
 take the – out of 874
 – in conversation 588
 – forth 873
 – upon *illumine* 420
 aid 707
shingle 330
shingled
 hair 53
shingles 223
shining [*see* shine]
 – light *sage* 500
Shintoism 984
shiny 420
ship *lade* 190
 transfer 270
 vessel **273**
 take – 267, 293
 one's – coming in 803
 – of the line 726
shipboard, on – 273
ship-load 31, 190
shipman 269
shipmate 890
shipment
 contents 190
 transfer 270
shippen 189
shipping 273
shipshape *order* 58
 conformity 82

 skill 698
shipwreck
 destruction 162
 vanquish 731
 failure 732
shire 181
shirk 603, 623, 742
shirker 862
shirt 225
Shiva 979
shive 32, 204
shiver
 small piece 32
 divide 44
 destroy 162
 filament 205
 shake 315
 brittle 328
 cold 383
 fear 860
 go to –s 162
 – in one's shoes 860
shivery *brittle* 328
 powdery 330
shoal
 assemblage 72
 multitude 102
 shallow 209
shoals *danger* 667
surrounded by –
 difficulty 704
shoat 366
shock *sheaf* 72
 violence 173
 concussion 276
 agitation 315
 unexpected 508
 disease 655
 discord 713
 affect 821
 move 824
 pain 828
 give pain 830
 dislike 867
 scandalize 932
shocking *bad* 649
 painful 830
 ugly 846
 vulgar 851
 fearful 860
 disreputable 874
 hateful 898
in a – temper 901*a*
shockingly *much* 31
shod 225
shoddy 645
shoe *support* 215
 dress 225
 hindrance 706
 stand in the –s of

 commission **755**
 deputy 759
where the –
 pinches
 badness 649
 difficulty 704
 opposition 708
 sensibility 822
 painful 830
shoemaker 225
shofle 272
shoful 792
shog 173
shoneen 855
shoot
 offspring 167
 expand 194
 dart 274
 propel 284
 kill 361
 sprout 365, 367
 pain 378
 execute 972
 teach the young idea to – 537
 – ahead 282
 – ahead of 303
 – at 716
 – out beams 420
 – up *increase* 35
 prominent 250
shooting
 [*see* shoot]
 chase 622
 – pain 378
 – star 318, 423
shooting-coat 225
shop 795, 799
 keep a – 625, 794
 shut up – *end* 67
 cease 142
 relinquish 624
 rest 687
 smell of the – 851
shopkeeper 797
shoplifter 792
shoplifting 791
shopman 797
shopmate 890
shopping 794, 795
shore
 support 215
 border 231
 land 342
 buttress 717
 hug the – 286
 on – 342
 – up 215, 670
shoreless 180
shorn *cut short* **201**
 deprived 776

plantation 371
shrug *sign* 550
– the shoulders
  dissent 489
  submit 725
  discontent 832
  dislike 867
  contempt 930
  disapprobation
   932
shrunk 193, 195
shudder *cold* 383
  fear 860
  make one –
  painful 830
  – at *aversion* 867
  hate 898
shuffle *mix* 41
  derange 61
  change 140
  interchange 148
  changeable 149
  move slowly 275
  agitate 315
  falsehood 544
  untruth 546
  irresolute 605
  recant 607
  dance 840
  improbity 940
  – the cards
  begin again 66
  change 140
  chance 621
  prepare 673
  patience and –
   the cards 826
  – off *run away* 623
  – off this mortal
   coil 360
  – on 266
shuffler 548
shun 623, 867
shunt 270, 279
shunted
  shelved 460
shut 261
  – the door 761
  – the door in one's
   face 764
  – the door upon
   893
  – one's ears 419,
   487
  – the eyes 442
  – one's eyes to
  not attend to 458
  neglect 460
  not believe 487
  permit 760
  not observe 773

– the gates of
  mercy 914*a*
– in 751
– oneself up 893
– out 55, 761
– up shop *end* 67
  cease 142
  silence 403
  relinquish 624
  repose 687
– up *close* 261
  confute 479
  imprison 751
shutter 424
shuttle 314
shuttlecock 605
shy *deviate* 279
  draw back 283
  propel 284
  avoid 623
  fearful 860
  cowardly 862
  modest 881
  fight – of 623
  have a – at 716
  – of belief 487
  – cock 862
  – of *doubtful* 485
  unwilling 603
  cautious 864
  dislike 867
Shylock 787
Siamese twins 89
sib 11
Siberia 383
sibi gladio hunc
  jugulo, suo – 718
sibilation *hiss* 409
  disrespect 929
  disapprobation
   932
Sibyl *oracle* 513
  ugly 846
Sibylline 511
  – leaves 513
sic *imitation* 19
  exact 494
  si – omnes! 948
  – transit gloria
   mundi 111
  – volo sic jubeo
   600
  – vos non vobis
   791
siccity 340
sick *ill* 655
  make one – 830,
   867
  visitation of the –
   998
  – at heart 837

– of *weary* 841
  dislike 867
  satiated 869
  in –ness and in
   health 604
sick-chamber 655
sicken *nauseate* 395
  disease 655
  pain 830
  weary 841
  disgust 867
sickener
  too much 641
sickle 244, 253
sickly *weak* 160
sick-room 655
side
  consanguinity 11
  edge 231
  laterality 236
  party 712
  ostentation 882
  at one's – 197
  on every – 227
  on one – 243
  on one's – 714
  look only at one –
   of the shield 481
  pass from one – to
   another 607
  take up a – 476
  wrong – up 218
  – by side
  accompaniment
   88
  near 197
  laterality 236
  party 712
  from – to side 314
  – with *aid* 707
  co-operate 709
  concord 714
side-arms 727
side-blow 702
sideboard 191
side-car 272
side-dish 298
side-drum 417
side-kick 890
side issue 643
sideling 279
sidelong 236
sideration 158
sidereal 318
  – time 114
siderite 288
Sideromancy 511
side-saddle 215
side-scene 599
sideslip 267
sidesman 996

side-track 287
sidewalk 627
sideways 217, 236
side-wind
  oblique 217
  circuit 629
  cunning 702
sidle *oblique* 217
  lateral 236
  deviate 279
siege 716
  lay – to 716
  state of – 722
siege-train 727
siesta 683
sieve *sort* 60
  perforate 260
  clean 652
  memory like a –
   506
  pour water into
   a – 638, 818
  stop one hole in
   a – 819
sift *simplify* 42
  sort 60
  inquire 461
  discriminate 465
  clean 652
  – the chaff from
   the wheat 609
sigh 405, 839
  – for 865
sighing like
  furnace 902
sight *much* 31
  multitude 102
  vision 441
  appearance 448
  ugly 846
  prodigy 872
  at – 132, 441
  dim – 443
  in – 446
  in – of 197, 441
  in plain – 525
  keep in – 457
  within – of shore
   858
sightless
  blind 442
  invisible 447
  ugly 846
sightly 845
sights, see – 455
sightseeing 441
sightseer 444, 455
sigil *seal* 550
  evidence 769
sigmoidal 248
sign *attest* 467

left-handed 239
sullen 901a
sink *disappear* 4
  destroy 162
  descend 306
  lower 308
  submerge 310
  neglect 460
  conceal 528
  cloaca 653
  fatigue 688
  vanquish 731
  fail 732
  adversity 735
  invest 787
  pain 828
  depressed 837
  – back 661
  – of corruption
    653
  – into the grave
    360
  – of iniquity 945
  – in the mind
  thought 451
  memory 505
  excite 824
  – money 809
  – into oblivion 506
  – or swim
  certainty 474
  perseverance 604a
sinking
  heart – 837
  – fund 802
sinless 946
**sinned against than
  sinning, more –**
  946
sinner 949
Sinn Fein 742
sin-offering 952
sinuous 243, 248
sinus 252
sip *small* 32
  drink 298
siphon 350
sippet 298
sir *man* 373
  title 877
  – Oracle 887
sirdar 745
sire 166
siren
  sea-nymph 341
  loud sound 404
  musician 416
  seducing 615
  warning 668
  alarm 669
  evil-doer 913

demon 980
  sorcerer 994
  song of the –s 615
  – strains 415
sirene *musical
    instrument* 417
siriasis 503
sirius 423
sirocco *wind* 349
  heat 382
sirrah! 949
sister *kin* 11
  likeness 17
  nurse 662
  nun 996
sisterhood
  party 712
  frail – 962
sisterly 906
sisters:
  weird – 994
  – three 601
sistrum 417
Sisyphus, task of –
  useless 645
  difficult 704
sit 308
  – down *settle* 184
  lie 213
  stoop 308
  – in judgment
  adjudge 480
  jurisdiction 965
  lawsuit 969
  – on 215
  – on thorns
  annoyance 828
  fear 860
site 183, 780
sith 476
sitting [*see* sit]
  incubation 673
  convocation 696
  – up *late* 133
  work 686
sitting-room 191
situ, in – 183, 265
situation
  circumstances 8
  place **183**
  location 184
  business 625
  out of a – 185
Siva 979
six 98
  – of one and half-
    a-dozen of the
    other 27
**sixes and sevens,
  at** – 59, 713
sixty 98

sizar 746
size *degree* 26
  magnitude 31
  glue 45
  arrange 60
  dimensions **192**
  viscid 352
  – up 480
sizzle 409
sjambok 975
skat 840
skate
  locomotion 266
  vehicle 272
skating 840
skean 727
skedaddle 623
skeel 191
skein 219
  tangled – 59
skeleton
  remains 40
  essential part 50
  thin 203
  support 215
  corpse 362
  plan 626
  reduced to a – 659
  – in the closet
    649, 830
  – at the feast 837
skelter 276
skepticism
  doubt 485
  incredulity 487
  irreligion 989
sketch
  form 240
  represent 554
  paint 556
  describe 594
  plan 626
sketcher 559
sketchy
  incomplete 53
  feeble 575
  unfinished 730
skew 217
  –bald 440
skewer 45
ski 266, 272
  –running 840
  –joring 840
  –jumping 840
skiagraphy 421,
  554, 556
skid *support* 215
  hindrance 706
skies:
  exalt to the – 873
  praise to the – 933

skiff 273
skill **698**
  acquisition of –
    539
  game of – 840
skillet 191
skilly 298
skim *move* 266
  navigate 267
  rapid 274
  neglect 460
  summarize 596
skimp 460, 819
skimpy 640
skin *outside* 220
  tegument 223
  peel 226
  swindle 791
  fleece 814
  wet to the – 339
  with a whole – 670
  without – 822
  mere – and bone
    203
  – a flint 471, 819
  – over 660
skin-deep
  shallow 32, 209
  external 220
skinned: thick– 376
  thin– 375
skinny 203, 223
skip *jump* 309
  neglect 460
  rejoice 838
skipjack
  prosperous 734
  low-born 876
skipper
  sea captain 269
  captain 745
skippingly 70
skips, by – 70
skirmish 720
skirmisher 726
skirt
  appendix 39
  pendent 214
  dress 225
  surrounding 227
  edge 231
  side 236
  – dance 840
skirting 231
skirts of:
  hang upon the –
  sequence 281
  on the –
  near 197
skit *ridicule* 856
  detraction 934

z

song *music* 415
  poem 597
  death – 360, 839
  love– 597
  for a mere – 815
  no – no supper 812
  old – 643
songster 416
soniferous 402
sonnet 597
sonneteer 597
sonorous *sound* 402
  loud 404
  language 577
sons of:
  – Belial 988
  – God 977
Soofeeism 984
soon *transient* 111
  future 121
  early 132
  too – for 135
sooner: – or later
  another time 119
  future 121
  – said than done
  704
soot 431, 653
sooth 511
  in good – 543
soothe
  allay 174
  relieve 834
  flatter 933
soothing
  faint sound 405
  – syrup 174
soothsay 511
soothsayer 513, 994
soothsaying 511
sop
  small quantity 32
  food 298
  fool 501
  inducement 615
  reward 973
  – to Cerberus 458
  – in the pan 615
soph 492, 541
Sophi 745, 996
sophism 477, 497
sophist *scholar* 492
  dissembler 548
sophister 492
  student 541
sophistical 477
sophisticate *mix* 41
  debase 659
sophisticated
  spurious 545
sophistry 477

sophomore 541
soporific 683, 841
soporous 683
soprano 410, 416
sorbet 298
sorcerer 994
sorcery 992
sordes 653
sordet 417
sordid *stingy* 819
  covetous 865
sordine 417
sore
  bodily pain 378
  disease 655
  mental suffering
  828, 830
  discontent 832
  anger 900
  – as a boil 901*a*
  – place 822
  – subject 830, 900
sorely *very* 31
s'orienter 278
sorites 476
sorority 712
sorrel 433, 434
sorrow 828
  give – words 839
sorry *trifling* 643
  grieved 828
  mean 876
  make a – face 874
  cut a – figure 874
  be – for 750, 914
  in a – plight 732
  – sight 830, 837
sort *degree* 26
  arrange 60
  kind 75
  – with
  sociality 892
sortable }
sortance }
  agreement 23
sortes
  chance 156, 621
  – Virgilianæ
  sorcery 992
sortie 716
sortilege
  prediction 511
  sorcery 992
sortilegy 621
sortition 621
sorts, out of –
  ill-health 655
  sulky 901*a*
S.O.S. 669, 707
so-so *small* 32
  trifling 643

  imperfect 651
sostenuto 415
sot *fool* 501
  drunkard 959
sot à triple étage
  501
sotto voce
  faint sound 405
  conceal 528
  voiceless 581
sou *money* 800
  qui n'a pas le –
  804
soubrette 599, 746
sough *conduit* 350
  noise 405
  cloaca 653
soul *essence* 5
  person 372
  intellect 450
  genius 498
  affections 820
  cure of –s 995
  flow of – 588
  not a – 187
  not dare to say
  one's – is his
  own *subjection*
  749
  fear 860
  – of wit 572
  have one's whole
  – in his work
  686
soulless 683, 823
soul-mate 903
soul-sick 837
soul-stirring 821,
  824
sound *great* 31
  conformable 82
  stable 150
  strong 159
  fathom 208
  bay 343
  noise **402**
  investigate 461
  measure 466
  true 494
  wise 498
  sane 502
  good 648
  perfect 650
  healthy 654
  solvent 803
  orthodox 983*a*
  catch a – 418
  safe and – 654,
  670
  – the alarm
  indication 550

  warning 668
  alarm 669
  fear 860
  – asleep 683
  full of – and fury
  unmeaning 517
  insolent 885
  – the horn 416
  – of limb 654
  – locator 726
  – mind 502
  – the praises of
  931
  – the note of prep-
  aration 673
  – reasoning 476
  – a retreat 283
  – sleep 683
  – a trumpet
  publish 531
  alarm 669
  – of wind 654
sounding: big –
  577
  – brass 517
sounding-board 417
soundings 208
soundless
  unfathomable 208
  silent 403
soup 298, 352
soupçon 32, 41
soufflé 298
sour *acid* 397
  discontented 832
  embitter 835
  uncivil 895
  sulky 901
  – grapes
  impossible 471
  excuse 617
  – the temper 830
source *beginning* 66
  cause 153
sourdet 417
sourdine 417
  à la – *noiseless* 405
  concealed 528
sourdough 463
soured 832
sourness **397**
sous tous les
  rapports 52
souse 310, 337
South *direction* 278
  North and –
  opposite 237
Southern
  antipodes 237
  – Cross 318
souvenir 505

spring balance 319
springe 545
spring-gun 545
spring tide
 greatness 31
 increase 35
 completeness 52
 youth 127
 high 206
 low 207
 wave 348
 water 337
springy 325
sprinkle *add* 37
 mix 41
 scatter 73
 wet 337
 rain 348
 variegate 440
 baptize 998
sprinkler 348, 385
sprinkling
 small quantity 32
sprint 274
sprit *sprout* 167
 support 215
sprite 979, 980
sprout *grow* 35
 germinate 161
 offspring 167
 expand 194
 – *from result* 154
spruce 652, 845
 – *up* 847
sprue 653
sprung 651, 659
spry 682, 836
spud 272
spume 353
spun out 110, 573
spunk 861
spur
 pointed 250
 sharp 253
 incite 615
 hasten 684
 win –s *succeed* 731
 glory 873
 on the – of the
  moment
 instantly 113
 now 118
 soon 132
 opportune 134
 impulse 612
 – *gearing* 633
 the – of necessity
  745
spurious
 erroneous 495
 false 544

 deceptive 545
 illegitimate 925
spurlos versenkt 2,
 449
spurn *reject* 55
 disdain 930
spurred 253
spurt
 transient 111
 swift 274
 gush 348
 impulse 612
 haste 684
 exertion 686
sputa 299
sputter *emit* 297
 splash 348
 stammer 583
spy *see* 441
 spectator 444
 inquire 461
 informer 527
 emissary 534
 watcher 664
 warning 668
spy-glass 445
squab *large* 192
 short 201
 broad 202
 bench 215
squabble 713
squad 72, 726
squadron 726
 – *leader* 745
squalid 653, 846
squall *violent* 173
 wind 349
 cry 411
 quarrel 713
squalor 653
squamous 204, 223
squander *waste* 638
 misuse 679
 lose 776
 prodigal 818
square
 congruous 23
 compensate 30
 four 95
 limited space 182
 houses 189
 perpendicular 212
 form 244
 sparring 720
 justice 924
 honourable 939
 make all – 660
 on the – 939
 – accounts
 pay 807
 account 811

 – dance 840
 – deal 922
 – the circle 471
 – inches 180
 – peg into a round
  hole 699
 – up 556
 – with 23
 – yards 180
square-toes 857
squash *destroy* 162
 flatten 251
 blow 276
 soft 324
 marsh 345
 semiliquid 352
 hiss 409
 game 840
squashy 345, 352
squat 308
 locate oneself 184
 little 193
 short 201
 thick 202
 low 207
squatter 188
squaw *woman* 374
 wife 903
squeak⎫ 411, 412
squeal⎭
squeamish 655
 unwilling 603
 fastidious 868
squeasy 868
squeezable 762
squeeze
 contract 195
 condense 321
 embrace 894
squeeze out 301,
 784
squelch 162
squib *sound* 406
 lampoon 856, 934
squiffy 959
squilgee 652
squint
 peephole 260
 look 441
 defective sight 443
squirarchy 875
squire *aid* 707
 attendant 746
 gentry 875
 – of Dames 897
squirm 315
squirrel 274, 682
squirt 297, 348
S.S.C. 968
stab *pierce* 260
 kill 361

 pain 378, 649,
  828
 injure 659
stabilimetre 150
stabilizator 150
stability 16, **150**
stable *firm* 150
 house 189
 lock the – door
  when the steed
  is stolen
 too late 135
 useless 645
 bungling 699
 – equilibrium 150
staccato 415
stack 72, 636
staddle 215
stade 252
stadium 728, 840
stadtholder 745
staff *support* 215
 music 413
 measure 466
 signal 550
 council 696
 party 712
 weapon 727
 chief 745
 retinue 746
 pastoral – 999
 – of life 298
 – of office 747
 – officer 745
stag *deer* 366
 male 373
 defaulter 808
stage *degree* 26
 term 71
 time 106
 position 183
 layer 204
 platform 215
 forum 542
 drama 599
 arena 728
 come upon the –
  446
 on the – 525, 599
 go off the – 293
 revolving – 599
 – business 599
 – coach 272
 – craft 599
 – direction 697
 – effect 882
 – hand 599
 – manager 599
 – name 565
 – play 599
 – player 599

[653]

silent 403
– less 467
– life *matter* 316
painting 556
– more
superior 33
evidence 467
– small voice 405
in – water 714
still-born 360, 732
stillroom 636
stillicidium 348
stilted
elevated 307
- *style* 577
ridiculous 853
affected 855
boasting 884
stilts *support* 215
on – *high* 206
elevated 307
hyperbolical 549
proud 878
boasting 884
stimulant 662
stimulate
energy 171
violence 173
incite 615
excite 824
stimulating
suggestive 514
stimulus 615
sting *pain* 378
tingle 380
poison 663
excite 824
mental suffering 830
anger 900
stinging
pungent 392
stingo 298
stingy 819
stink 401
– in the nostrils
unpleasant 830
dislike 867
hate 898
stink-bomb 727
stink-pot 401
stint *degree* 26
limit 233
scanty 640
begrudge 819
stintless 639
stipend *salary* 973
stipendiary
subject 749
receiving 785
magistrate 967

stipple
variegate 440
painting 556
engraving 558
stipulate 769, 770
– for 720
stipule 51
stir *energy* 171
move 264
agitation 315
excite 375
activity 682
jail 752
emotion 824
make a – 642, 682
– about 682
– the blood 824, 900
– up dissension 713
– the embers 163, 824
– the feelings 824
– the fire 384
– a question 461, 476
– one's stumps 266, 682
– up *mix* 41
violent 173
excite 824
stirps *kin* 11
source 153
paternity 166
stirring *events* 151
important 642
active 682
– news 532
stirrup
support 215
with a foot in the – 293
stirrup-cup 293, 959
stitch *junction* 43
pain 378
work 680
– in time 132
– of work 686
stive 384
stiver 800
stoat 401
stoccado 717
stock *kinship* 11
quantity 25
origin 153
paternity 166
collar 225
soup 298
fool 501
habitual 613
materials 635

store 636
property 780
merchandise 798
money 800
in – 777
laughing – 857
lay in a – 637
take – *inspect* 457
accounts 811
– exchange 799
– still 265
– in trade
means 632
store 636
property 780
merchandise 798
– with 637
stockade 717
stocked, well – 639
stock exchange 621
stock-farm 370
stocking 225
hoard 800
stock-jobbing 794
stock operator 621
stocks *prison* 752
funds 802
punishment 975
on the –
business 625
preparation 673
incomplete 730
– and stones 316, 823
stocky 201
stodge 957
stoicism
insensibility 823
inexcitability 826
disinterested 942
temperance 953
stoke 388
stoker 268
stole 999
stolen: – away 671
– goods 793
stolid 499, 843
stomach *pouch* 191
taste 390
brook 826
desire 865
not have the – to 603
turn the – 830
– of an ostrich 957
stomacher 225
stone *heavy* 319
dense 321
hard 323
kill 361
lithography 558

material 635
attack 716
weapon 727
punish 972
corner – 642
go down like a – 310
cast the first – at 938
heart of – 823, 907
key– 642
musical –s 417
no – unturned 461, 686
philosopher's – 662
precious – 648
stepping – 627
throw a – at
attack 716
censure 932
accuse 938
throw –s at 907
tomb– 363
mark with a white – 642
throw a – in one's own garden 699
– dead 360
– of Sisyphus 645
stone-blind 442
stone-coloured 432
stone-deaf 419
stone's throw 197
stoneware 384
stony 323
stony-hearted 907, 919
stooge 711, 746, 886
stook 72
stool 215
between two –s 704
– of repentance 950
– pigeon 527, 548
stoop *slope* 217
lower 308
humble 879
servile 886
dishonourable 940
– to conquer 702
stop *end* 67
cease 142
close 261
rest 265
silent 403
danger 665
inaction 681
hinder 706
prohibit 761

put a – to 142
– the breath 361
– the ears 419
– a flow 348
– a gap 660
– the mouth 479,
   581
– payment 808
– press news 532
– short 142, 265
– short of 304
– the sound 408*a*
– up 261
– the way 706
stopcock 263
stopgap
   substitute 147
   stopper 263
stoppage
   cessation 142
   hindrance 706
stopper 263
stopping place 292
store *store* 184
   stock **636**
   shop 799
   in – *destiny* 152
   preparing 673
   lay in a – 637
   set – by 642, 931
   set no – 483
   – of knowledge
     490
   – in the memory
     505
store-house 636
store-keeper 636
store-ship 273, 726
storied 594
storm *crowd* 72
   convulsion 146
   violence 173
   agitation 315
   wind 349
   danger 667
   attack 716
   passion 825
   anger 900
   ride the – 267
   take by –
   conquer 731
   seize 789
   – brewing 665
   – in a teacup
   overrate 482
   exaggerate 549
   unimportance 643
storthing 696
story *rooms* 191
   layer 204
   news 532

lie 546
history 594
the old – 897
as the – goes 532
story-teller 548, 594
stot 366
stound 870
stoup *cup* 191
   altar 1000
stour 59
stout *strong* 159
   large 192
   drink 298
stout-hearted 861
stove *fireplace* 386
   – in 252
stow *locate* 184
   pack close 195
   store 636
stowage 180, 184
stowaway 528, 673
strabism 443
straddle 266, 607
Stradivarius 417
strafe 972
straggle 266, 279
straggler 268
straggling 44, 59
straight
   vertical 212
   rectilinear 246
   direction 278
   all – *rich* 803
   solvent 807
   – course 628
   – descent 167
   – face 837
   – sailing 705
straighten 246
   – up 60
straightforward 278
   truthful 543
   artless 703
   honourable 939
straightness 246
straight shot 278
straightway 132
strain *race* 11
   weaken 160
   operation 170
   violence 173
   percolate 295
   transgress 303
   sound 402
   melody 415
   overrate 482
   exaggerate 549
   style 569
   poetry 597
   voice 580
   clean 652

effort 686
fatigue 688
– in the arms 902
– one's eyes 441,
   507
– at a gnat and
   swallow a camel
   608
– one's invention
   515
– the meaning 523
– every nerve 686
– a point
   go beyond 303
   exaggerate 549
   not observe 773
   undue 925
– the throat 411
strait
   interval 198
   water 343
   difficulty 704
straitened
   poor 804
strait-handed 819
strait-jacket 752
strait-laced
   severe 739
   restraint 751
   fastidious 868
   haughty 878
strait-waistcoat
   751, 752
strake 205
stramash 720
strand *thread* 205
   shore 231, 342
stranded
   stuck fast 150
   in difficulty 704
   failure 732
   pain 828
strange
   unrelated 10
   exceptional 83
   ridiculous 853
   wonderful 870
   – bedfellows 713
   – to say 870
strangely *much* 31
stranger 57
   a – to 491
strangle
   render powerless
     158
   contract 195
   kill 361
strap *fasten* 43
   fastening 45
   restraint 752
   punish 972

instrument of
   punishment 975
strappado 972
strapping
   mighty 31
   strong 159
   pace 274
   big 192
strapwork 847
stratagem
   deception 545
   plan 626
   artifice 702
strategic *plan* 626
   artifice 702
strategist
   planner 626
   director 694
   proficient 700
strategy 692, 722
strath 252
strathspey 840
stratification 204,
   329
stratocracy 737
stratosphere 338
stratum 204
stratus 353
straw *scatter* 73
   light 320
   unimportant 643
   care not a – 866,
     930
   catch at –s
   overrate 482
   credulous 486
   misuse 679
   unskilful 699
   hope 858
   rash 863
   the eyes drawing
   –s 683
   in the – 161
   man of –
   unsubstantial 4
   cheat 545
   insolvent 808
   low person 876
   not worth a –
     643, 645
   – to show the
     wind 463
straw-coloured 436
straw-hat 225
stray *dispersion* 73
   exceptional 83
   random 156
   wanderer 268
   deviate 279
streak *intrinsicality*
   5

long 200
narrow 203
furrow 259
light 420
stripe 440
mark 550
streaked 219, 440
stream *assemble* 72
move 264
– *of fluid* **347**
– *of water* 348
– *of air* 349
– *of light* 420
abundance 639
against the – 708
with the –
conformity 82
progression 282
assent 488
facility 705
concord 714
fashion 852
servility 886
– of events 151
– of time 109
streamer *flag* 550
streaming 47, 73
streamlet 348
street 189, 627
man in the – 876
streets:
in the open – 525
on the – 961
street-walker 962
strength
quantity 25
degree 26
greatness 31
vigour **159**
energy 171
tenacity 327
animality 364
put all one's –
into 686
lose – 655
tower of – 717
– of mind 604
strengthen 35
strengthless 160
strenuous
persevering 604*a*
active 682
exertion 686
Strephon and Chloe
902
stress *emphasis* 580
requirement 630
importance 642
strain 686
difficulty 704
by – of 601

lay – on 476
– of circumstances
compulsion 744
– of weather 349
stretch *expanse* 180
expand 194
extend 200
exaggerate 549
exertion 686
encroach 925
at a – 69
mind on the – 451
on the – 686
upon the – 457
– away to 196
– forth one's hand
680, 789
– of the imagina-
tion 515, 549
– the meaning 523
– a point 83, 303
exaggerate 549
severity 739
permit 760
not observe 773
undue 925
exempt 927*a*
– to *distance* 196
length 200
stretcher 215, 272
strew 73
striæ, striated 259,
440
stricken *pain* 828
terror– 860
be – by 655
– in years 128
strict
in conformity 82
exact 494
severe 739
conscientious 939
orthodox 983*a*
– inquiry 461
– interpretation
522
– search 461
– settlement 780
strictly speaking
literally 19
exact 494
interpreted 522
stricture
constriction 203
hindrance 706
censure 932
stride *distance* 196
motion 264
walk 266
strident 410
strides: make – 282

rapid – 274
stridor **410**
strife 713, 720
strigil 652
strike *operate* 170
hit 276
resist 719
disobey 742
impress 824
beat 972
– at 716
– a balance
equalize 27
mean 29
pay 807
– a bargain 769,
794
– a blow *act* 680
– dumb *dumb* 581
excitement 824
wonder 870
humble 879
– the eye 457
– the first blow
716
– one's flag 725
– hard 171
– all of a heap
824, 860
– home 171
– in with
imitate 19
assent 488
cooperate 709
– the iron while it
is hot 134
– a light 384, 420
– the lyre 416
– the mind 457
– out something
new 146, 515
– off *exclude* 55
– one 451
– out *exclude* 55
destroy 162
invent 515
obliterate 552
scheme 626
– off the roll 756,
972
– at the root of
162
– root 150
– sail 275
– tents 293
– terror 860
– up 416
– with wonder 870
striker 927
striking 525
– likeness 554

strikingly
greatly 31
string *tie* 43
ligature 45
continuity 69
filament 205
musical note 413
– together 60, 69
stringed instru-
ments 417
stringent
energetic 171
authoritative 737
strict 739
compulsory 744
strings: *music* 417
leading – 541
pull the – 175, 693
two – to one's bow
632
stringy 205, 327
strip *adjunct* 39
narrow 203
filament 205
divest 226
take 789
rob 791
stripe *length* 200
variegation 440
mark 550
badge 747
blow 972
stripling 129
stripped *poor* 804
strive *endeavour*
675
exert 686
contend 720
– against 720
stroke *impulse* 276
touch 379
mark 550
evil 619
expedient 626
disease 655
action 680
success 731
painful 830
at a – 113
good – 626
– of death 360
– of the pen
writing 590
command 741
– of policy 626
– of time 113
– of work 686
– the wrong way
256
stroll 266
strolling player 599

strong *great* 31	hour upon a	– in 300	*astonish* 870
powerful 159	stage 359, 599	– the memory	**stupendous**
energetic 171	**strychnine** 663	with 505	*great* 31
tough 327	**stub** 40, 550	– and nonsense	*large* 192
taste 390	**stubbed** 201	*unsubstantial* 4	*wonderful* 870
pungent 392	**stubble** *remains* 40	*absurdity* 497	**stupid**
fetid 401	*useless* 645	*unmeaning* 517	*unsubstantial* 4
healthy 654	**stubborn**	– *up* *close* 261	*misjudging* 481
feeling 821	*strong* 159	*hoax* 545	*credulous* 486
wonderful! 870	*hard* 323	**stuffed**	*unintelligent* 499
smell – of 398	*obstinate* 606	*redundancy* 641	*tiresome* 841
– accent 580	*resistance* 719	**stuffing** *contents* 190	*dull* 843
– argument 476	**stubby** 201	*lining* 224	**stupor**
by a – arm 744	**stucco** 45, 223	*stopper* 263	*insensibility* 823
– box 802	**stuck** [*see* stick]	**stuffy** 321, 382	*wonder* 870
with a – hand	– *fast* 150, 704	**stultified** 732	**stupration** 961
resolution 604	be – *on* 897	**stultify oneself** 699	**sturdy** *strong* 159
exertion 686	**stuck-up** 878	**stultiloquy** 497	*persevering* 604a
severity 739	**stud** *hanging-peg*	**stumble** *fall* 306	– *beggar* 767, 792
– language 574	214	*flounder* 315	**stutter** 583
– pull 686	*knob* 250	*error* 495	**sty** *house* 189
– point 476	*horses* 271	*unskilful* 699	*enclosure* 232
strong-headed 498	**studded** *many* 102	*failure* 732	*dirt* 653
stronghold	*spiked* 253	– *on chance* 156	**Stygian** *dark* 421
refuge 666	*variegated* 440	*discover* 480a	*diabolic* 945
defence 717	**student** 541	**stumbling-block**	*infernal* 982
prison 752	**stud-farm** 370	*difficulty* 704	cross the – ferry
strong-minded 498,	**studied**	*hindrance* 706	*die* 360
861	*predetermined*	**stump**	– *shore*
strong-scented 398	611	*remainder* 40	*death* 360
strong-willed 604	**studio** *room* 191	*trunk* 51	**style** *state* 7
strop 253	*painting* 556	*walk* 266	*time* 114
strophe 597	*workshop* 691	*drawing* 556	*painting* 556
strow 73	**studious**	*speak* 582	*graver* 558
struck [*see*	*thoughtful* 451	stir your –s	*name* 564
stricken, strike]	*docile* 539	*active* 682	*diction* 569
awe– 860	*intending* 620	worn to the – 659	*writing* 590
– down 732	**study** *copy* 21	– *along slow* 275	*beauty* 845
– all of a heap	*room* 191	**stump** *orator* 582,	*fashion* 852
emotion 821	*thought* 451	887	**stylet**
wonder 870	*attention* 457	**stumpy** *short* 201	*awl* 262
humbled 879	*research* 461	**stun** *physically*	*dagger* 727
– with *love* 897	*learning* 539	*insensible* 376	**stylist** 578
structural *state* 7	*painting* 556	*loud* 404	**Stylites, Simon** –
structure	*intention* 620	*deafen* 419	893
production 161	*retreat* 893	*unexpected* 508	**stylographic pen**
form 240	brown – 515	*morally insen-*	590
texture 329	**stuff** *substance* 3	*sible* 823	**stylography** 590
organization 357	*contents* 190	*affect* 824	**stylus** 590
struggle *exert* 686	*expand* 194	*astonish* 870	**styptic** 397
difficulty 704	*line* 224	**stung** [*see* sting]	**Styx** 982
contend 720	*matter* 316	– to the quick 824	**suasible** 602
strum 416, 517	*texture* 329	**stunt** *shorten* 201	**suasion** 615
strumpet 962	*absurdity* 497	*performance* 680	**suave mari magno**
strung	*unmeaning* 517	**stunted** 193, 195	664
highly – 825	*material* 635	*insufficient* 640	**suaviter in modo**
strut *walk* 266	*trifle* 643	**stupe** 834	826, 894
pride 878	*overeat* 957	**stupefaction** 826	**suavity** 894
parade 882	such – as dreams	**stupefy**	**sub** 34
boast 884	are made of 515	- *physically* 376	– spe rati 475
– and fret one's	– gown 968	- *morally* 823	**subacid** 397

suo: – .periculo 926
– sibi gladio hunc
jugulo
absurdity 479
retaliation 718
sup *small quantity*
32
feed 298
– full of horrors
828
super *theatrical* 599
superable 470
superabound 641
superadd 37
superannuated 128
superb 845
supercargo 694
supercherie 545
supercilious
proud 878
insolent 885
disrespectful 929
scornful 930
superdreadnought
726
supereminence
648, 873
supererogation 641,
645
superexaltation 873
superexcellence
648
superfetation 37,
168
superficial
shallow 209
outside 220
misjudging 481
ignorant 491
– extent 180
superficies 220
superfine 648
superfluitant 305
superfluity 40, 641
superfluous 645
superhuman 650,
976
superimpose 223
superimposed 206
superincumbent
206, 319
superinduce
change 140
cause 153
produce 161
superintend 693
superintendent 694
superior *greater* 33
– *in size* 194
important 642
good 648

director 694
superiority 33
superjunction 37
superlative 33
superlatively good
·648
superman 33
supernal 206, 210,
981
supernatant 206,
305
supernatural 976,
980
– aid 707
supernumerary
adjunct 39
theatrical 599
reserve 636
redundant 641
superpose 37, 223
supersaturate 641
superscription 550,
590
supersede
substitute 147
disuse 678
relinquish 782
supersensible 317
superstition
credulity 486
error 495
religion 984
superstratum 220
superstructure 729
supertax 812
supertonic 413
supervacaneous
641
supervene
extrinsic 6
be added 37
succeed 117
happen 151
supervise 693
supervisor 694
supination 213
supine
horizontal 213
inverted 218
sluggish 683
mentally torpid
823
suppeditate 637
supper 298
supplant 147
supple *soft* 324
servile 886
supplement
addition 37
adjunct 39
completion 52

publication 531
book 593
suppletory 37
suppliant 765, 767
supplicate *beg* 765
pity 914
worship 990
supplies
materials 635
aid 707
money 800
supply *store* 636
provide 637
give 784
– aid 707
– deficiencies 52
– the place of 147
– and transport
726
support *perform* 170
sustain **215**
evidence 467
preserve 670
aid 707
feel 821
endure 826
vindicate 937
– life 359
supporter 711
–s *heraldic* 550
suppose 514
supposing 469
supposition 514
supposititious 546
suppress
destroy 162
conceal 528
silent 581
restrain 751
suppression of
truth 544
suppuration 653
suppute 85
supralapsarian 984
supramundane 939
supremacy 33, 737
supreme 33
summit 210
authority 737
in a – degree 31
Supreme Being 976
surbate 659
surbated 688
surcease 142
surcharge 641
– and falsify 811
surcingle 45
surcoat 225
surd *number* 84
deaf 419
silent letter 561

sure *certain* 474
belief 484
safe 664
make – against
673
make – of
inquire 461
take 789
you may be – 535
to be – *assent* 488
on – ground 664
security 771
sure-footed
careful 459
skilful 698
cautious 864
surely 488, 602, 870
sureness 474
surety 474, 664
surf 348, 353
surface *outside* 220
texture 329
below the – 526
lie on the – 518,
525
skim the – 460
Surface, Joseph –
548
surfeit 641, 869
surge *swarm* 72
swell 305
rotation 312
wave 348
surgeon 662
surgery 662
surgit amari
aliquid 651
surly *gruff* 895
sullen 901a
unkind 907
surmise 514
surmount *be*
superior 33
tower 206
transcursion 303
ascent 305
– a difficulty
overcome 731
surmountable 470
surname 564
surpass
be superior 33
grow 194
go beyond 303
outshine 873
surplice 999
surplus 40, 641
surplusage 641
surprint 550
surprise
non-expectation

508
unprepared 674
wonder 870
surprisingly 31
surrebutter &c.
    answer 462
    pleadings 969
surrender 725, 782
– one's life 360
surreptitious
    furtive 528
    deceptive 545
    untrue 546
surrogate 759
surround 227, 229
surroundings 227
    amidst such and
    such – 183
sursum corda 990
surtax 812
surtout *coat* 225
surveillance
    care 459
    direction 693
    under – 938
survene 151
survey 441, 466
surveyor 85, 694
survive *remain* 40
    long time 110
    permanent 141
susceptibility
    power 157
    tendency 176
    liability 177
    sensibility 375
    motive 615
    impressibility 822
    irascibility 901
suscipient 785
suscitate *cause* 153
    produce 161
    stir up 173
    excite 824
suspect *doubt* 485
    suppose 514
suspected 938
suspectless 484
suspend *defer* 133
    discontinue 142
    hang 214
suspended anima-
    tion 823
suspender 45, 214
suspense
    cessation 142
    uncertainty 475
    expectation 507
    irresolution 605
    in – *inert* 172
suspension

cessation 142
hanging 214
music 413
– of arms 723
suspicion *doubt* 485
    incredulity 487
    knowledge 490
    supposition 514
    fear 860
    under – 938
suspiration 839
sustain
    continue 143
    strength 159
    perform 170
    support 215
    preserve 670
    aid 707
    endure 821
sustained note 413
sustenance 298
sustentation
    [*see* sustain]
    food 298
susurration 405
sutler 637, 797
suttee *killing* 361
    arson 384
    unselfishness 942
    idolatry 991
suture 43
suum cuique 780,
    922
suzerain 745
suzerainty 737
swab *dry* 340
    clean 652
    lubber 701
swaddle *clothe* 225
    restrain 751
swaddling clothes,
    in – *infant* 129
    subjection 749
swag *hang* 214
    lean 217
    curve 245
    drop 306
    oscillate 314
    booty 793
    ostentation 887
swag-bellied 194
swage 174
swagger
    pride 878
    boast 884
    bluster 885
swaggerer 887
swain *man* 373
    rustic 876
    lover 897
swale 659

swallow *gulp* 296
    eat 298
    believe 484
    credulous 486
    brook 826
– the bait 547,
    602
– flight 274
– the leek 607,
    725
– up *destroy* 162
    use 677
    take 789
– hook, line and
    sinker 602
– whole 465a, 484
    swallow-tail coat
    225
swamp *destroy* 162
    marsh 345
    defeat 731
swamped
    failure 732
swampy *moist* 339
swank 845, 882, 884
swan-pan 85
swan-song 360
swap *exchange* 148
    blow 276
sward 344
swarm *crowd* 72
    multitude 102
    climb 305
    sufficiency 639
    redundance 641
swarthy 431
swash *affuse* 337
    spurt 348
swashbuckler 726,
    887
swashy 339
swastika 621, 993
swat 276
swath 72
swathe *fasten* 43
    clothe 225
    restrain 751
sway *power* 157
    influence 175
    lean 217
    oscillate 314
    agitation 315
    induce 615
    authority 737
– to and fro 149
sweal 659
swear *affirm* 535
    promise 768
    curse 908
    just enough to –

by 32
– at 908
– by *believe* 484
– false 544
– a witness 768
sweat *exude* 295
    excretion 299
    heat 382
    exertion 686
    fatigue 688
    cold – 860
    in a – 382
– of one's brow
    686
sweater 225
Swedenborgian 984
Swedish dance 840
sweep *space* 180
    curve 245
    oar 267
    rapid 274
    bend 279
    clean 652
    dirty fellow 653
    steal 791
    make a clean – of
    297
– along 264
– away
    destroy 162
    eject 297
    abrogate 756
    relinquish 782
– the chords 416
– off 297
– out 297, 652
– of time 109
sweeper 652
    mine– 726
sweeping *whole* 50
    complete 52
    general 78
– change 146
sweepings
    useless 645
    dirt 653
sweepstakes 775,
    810
sweet
    saccharine 396
    melodious 413
    colour 428
    clean 652
    agreeable 829
    lovely 897
    look – upon
    desire 865
    love 897
    endearment 902
– smell 400
– tooth 865, 868

[661]

830

tee 66

teetotalism 953, 958

teetotum 312, 840

teg 366

tegument 223

teind 99

teinoscope 445

tekel upharsin 668

telautograph 553

telegram 532

telegraph
velocity 274
messenger 534
signal 550
– boy 534
by – *haste* 684

telegraphone 553

telegraphy
publication 531

teleology 620

telemeter 200

telepathy 992

telephone 418
inform 527
messenger 534

telescope 445
– word 572

telescopic 196

telesis 658

telesm 993

tell *count* 85
influence 175
evidence 467
inform 527
speak 582
describe 594
succeed 731
let me – you 535
who can – 475
– one's beads 990, 998
– the cause of 522
– fortunes 511
– how 155
– a lie 544
– a piece of one's mind 529
– of 467
– off 85
– one plainly 527
– its own tale 518
– tales
disclose 529
– the truth 543

teller *treasurer* 801
– of tales 594

telling 175
graphic 518
important 642

exciting 824
with – effect 171, 175

telltale *news* 532
indicator 550
knave 941

telluric 318

telum imbelle 158

temerity 863

temper *nature* 5
state 7
moderate 174
elasticity 323
pliability 324
modify 469
prepare 673
affections 820
irascibility 901
command of – 826
lose one's – 900
out of – 901a
trial of – 824
– the wind to the shorn lamb 834

tempera 556

temperament
nature 5
tendency 176
musical 413
affections 820

temperance 174, **953**

temperate
[*see* temperance]
mild 826

temperature 382
increase of – 384
reduction of – 385

tempest
violence 173
agitation 315
wind 349
excitement 825

tempestivity 134

tempest-tossed 824

tempestuous 59

Templar 996
Good – 958

temple *house* 189
side 236
church **1000**
– of the Holy Ghost 983a

templet 22

tempora:
O –! O mores!
lament 839
disreputable 874
disapprobation 932
improbity 940

vice 945
– mutantur 140

temporal
transient 111
laical 997
lords – and spiritual 875

temporality 997

temporary 111

temporize
protract 110
defer 133
cunning 702

temporizer 943

tempt *entice* 615
attempt 675
desire 865
– fortune 621, 675
– Providence 863, 885

tempter 615
Satan 978
voice of the – 615

temulency 959

ten 98
– to one 472
– thousand 98

tenable 664

tenacity
coherence 46
toughness **327**
memory 505
resolution 604
obstinacy 606
retention 781
avarice 819
courage 861
– of life 359
– of purpose 604a

tenaculum 781

tenancy 777

tenant
present 186
occupier 188
possessor 779

tenantless
absence 187
seclusion 893

tenax propositi 204, 939

tend *conduce* 176
- *animals* 370
aid 707
serve 631, 746
– towards 278

tendence 749

tendency 176

tender *slight* 32
ship 273
soft 324
painful 378

colour 428
war vessel 726
offer 763
susceptible 822
affectionate 897
compassionate 914
– age 127
– conscience 926
– heart
susceptible 822
kind 906
compassionate 914
– mercies [ironical]
badness 649
severity 739
cruelty 907
– passion 897
– one's resignation 757
– to 707

tenderfoot 57, 541

tendon 45

tendril *fastening* 45
offshoot 51
infant 129
filament 205
convoluted 248
plant 367

tenebrious 421

tenebrosity 421

tenement 189, 780
– of clay 362

tenet *belief* 484

tenner 800

tennis 840
– ground 213

tenor *course* 7
degree 26
direction 278
high note 410
singer 416
violin 417
meaning 516
pursue the noiseless – of one's way 881

tense *hard* 323

tensile 325

tension 159, 200

tensure 200

tent *abode* 189
covering 223
pitch one's –
locate 184
arrive 292

tentacle 781

tentative 463, 675

tente d'abri 223

tented field 722

tenter-hook 214
on –s 507
tenth 99
tenths
  tithe 812
tent-pegging 840
tents, O Israel, to
  your – 722
tenue, en grande –
  847, 882
tenuity
  smallness 32
  thinness 203
  rarity 322
tenuous
  shadowy 4
tenure
  possession 777
  property 780
  due 924
tepee 189
tepefaction 384
Tephramancy 511
tepid 382
tepidarium 386
ter quaterque
  beatus 827
teratology
  unconformity 83
  distortion 243
  altiloquence 577
  boasting 884
tercentenary 98,
  138, 883
terceron 41
terebration 260
teres atque rotun-
  dus 249
in seipso – 650
tergiversation 283,
  607
term *end* 67
  place in series **71**
  period of time 106
  limit 233
  word 562
  name 564
  lease 780
termagant 901
terminal 67, 233,
  292
terminate 67, 292
  limit 233
termination 154
termine, mezzo –
  628
terminology 562
terminus *end* 67
  limit 233
  arrival 292
termless 105

terms [*see* term]
  circumstances **8**
  reasoning 476
  pacification 723
  conditions 770
bring to – 723
come to –
  assent 488
  pacify 723
  submit 725
  consent 762
  compact 769
couch in – 566
on friendly – 888
in no measured –
  574
ternary 93
ternion 92
Terpsichore 416,
  840
terra: – cotta
  baked 384
  sculpture 557
– firma
  support 215
  land 342
  safety 664
– incognita 491
terrace *houses* 189
  level 213
terrain 181
terraqueous 318
terre verte 435
terrene 318, 342
terrine 191
terrestrial 318
terrible 860
terribly *greatly* 31
terrier *list* 86
  auger 262
  dog 366
terrific 31, 830, 860
terrify 860
territorial *land* 342
  soldier 726
territory 181, 780
terror 860
  King of –s 360
  reign of – 739, 828
terrorem, in – 860,
  909
terrorism 860
  insolence 885
terrorist
  coward 862
  blusterer 887
  evil-doer 913
terse 572
tertian *periodic* 138
tertiary *three* 92
tertium quid

  dissimilar 18
  mixture 41
  combination 48
  unconformable 83
tesselated 440, 847
tesseræ
  mosaic 440
  counters 550
test 463
testa, voce di – 410
testament 771
Testament 985
tester *bedstead* 215
  sixpence 800
testify 467, 550
testimonial 551
testimony 467
testy 901
tetanus 315
tetchy 901
tête: – baissée 863
– exaltée 503
– montée 503, 825
–à-tête *two* 89
  near 197
  confer 588
tether *fasten* 43
  locate 184
  restrain 751
  means of restraint
  752
go beyond the
  length of one's
  – 738
tethered *firm* 150
tetrachord 413
tetractic 95
tetrad 95
tetrahedral 95
tetrahedron 244
tetrarch 745
text *prototype* 22
  topic 454
  meaning 516
  printing 591
  –book 542, 596
textile 219, 329
textuary 983a, 985
texture *mixture* 41
  roughness 256
  fabric **329**
Thais 962
Thalia 599
Thalmud 985
Thames on fire
set the – 471
never set the –
  501, 701
thane *nobility* 875
thank 916
no – you 764

– one's stars 838
– you for nothing
  917
thankful 916
rest and be – 265,
  831
thankless
  painful 830
  ungrateful 917
thank-offering 916,
  990
thanks to 155
thanksgiving
  gratitude 916
  worship 990
that 79
– is 118
– is to say 79
– being so 8
at – time 119
thatch *roof* 223
thaumatrope 445
thaumaturgist 994
thaumaturgy 992
thaw *melt* 335
  heart 382
  heating 384
  calm the mind 826
  pity 914
Thearchy
  authority 737
  Deity 976
theatre
  spectacle 441
  school 542
  drama 599
  arena 728
  amusement 840
  tribunal 966
théâtre: coup de –
  appearance 448
  prodigy 872
  display 882
jeu de – 448, 872
nom de – 565
theatrical 599
  affected 855
  ostentatious 882
Theban, learned –
  492
theca 223
thé dansant 840
theft 775, 791
theism 984, 987
theistic *of God* 976
theme *topic* 454
  dissertation 595
Themis 922
then *time* 106
  therefore 476
thence

627

thorough-going 52
thoroughly, do –
  729
thorough-paced 31
thorp 189
though
  compensation 30
  qualification 469
  opposition 708
thought *little* 32
  reflection **451**
  idea 453
  give a – to 457
  not to be – of
   610, 761
  organ of – 450
  quick as – 274
  seat of – 450
  subject of – 454
  want of – 458
  who would have –
   it? 508
  – of 454
thoughtful 451, 498
thoughtless
  incogitant 452
  inattentive 458
  careless 460
  improvident 674
thoughts:
  – that breathe 574
  – elsewhere 458
thousand 98, 102
  one in a – 648,
   948
thralldom 749, 751
thrash 972
Thraso 887
Thrasonic 884, 885
thread
  arrange 60
  series 69
  weak 160
  filament 205
  pass through 302
  not have a dry –
   339
  hang by a – 665
  life hangs by a –
   360
  worn to a – 659
  – one's way 266,
   302
threadbare 226, 659
threadpaper 203
threat **909**
threaten
  future 121
  destiny 152
  danger 665

threatening
  warning 668
  unhopeful 859
three 93
  – in one and one
   in – 976
  sisters – 601
  go through – hun-
   dred and sixty
   degrees 311
  – sheets in the
   wind 959
  times three
   number 98
  approbation 931
threefold 93
three-score 98
  – years and ten
   128
three-tailed
  bashaw
  master 745
  nobility 875
threne 839
threnody 839
thresh 972
  – out 461
threshold
  beginning 66
  edge 231
  at the – *near* 197
  – of an inquiry 461
thrice 93
  – happy 827
  –told tale 573
thrid 302
thrift
  prosperity 734
  gain 775
  economy 817
thriftless 818
thrill
  physical pain 378
  touch 380
  feeling 821
  excitation 824
thrilling
  pleasing 829
  painful 830
thrive 734
throat *opening* 260
  pipe 350, 351
  cut the – 361
  force down the –
   739
  stick in one's –
   581, 585
  take by the – 789
throb 315, 821
throbbing: – heart
  860

– pain 378
throe
  revolution 146
  violence 173
  agitation 315
  physical pain 378
  agony 828
  birth– 161
throne *abode* 189
  seat 215
  emblem of au-
   thority 747
  ascend the – 737
  occupy the – 737
  power behind
   the – 526
  – of God 981
throng 72
throttle
  render powerless
   158
  close 261
  kill 361
  seize 789
  – down 275
through
  owing to 154
  viâ 278
  by means of 631
  get – 729
  go – one 824
  wet – 339
  – thick and thin
  complete 52
  violence 173
  perseverance 604a
throughout 50, 52
  – the world 180
throw *impel* 276
  propel 284
  exertion 686
  – oneself into the
   arms of 666
  – away *reject* 610
  waste 638
  relinquish 782
  – back 145
  – cold water on
   616
  – of the dice 156
  – doubt upon 485
  – down 162, 308
  – oneself at the
   feet of 725
  – good money
   after bad 818
  – in 228
  – off [*see below*]
  – open 260, 296
  – out [*see below*]
  – over *destroy* 162

– overboard
  exclude 55
  destroy 162
  eject 297
  abrogate 756
  – on paper 590
  – away the scab-
   bard 722
  – into the shade
  superior 33
  lessen 36
  surpass 303
  important 642
  – a tub to catch a
   whale 545
  – up [*see below*]
  – a veil over 528
throw off 297
  – all disguise 529
  – one's guard 508
  – the mask 529
  – the scent
  misdirect 538
  avoid 623
throw out 284, 297
  eject 297
  – a feeler 379
  – of gear
  disjoin 44
  derange 61
  – a hint 527
  – a suggestion 514
throw up *eject* 297
  resign 757
  – one's cap 884
  – the game 624
throwing stick 727
thrown out 704
thrum 416
thrush 416
thrust *push* 276
  attack 716
  – in *insert* 300
  (*interpose*) 228
  – one's nose in 682
  – out 55
  – down one's
   throat 744
  – upon 784
thud 406, 408a
thug *murderer* 361
  thief 792
thumb *touch* 379
  bite the – 929
  one's fingers all –s
   699
  rule of –
  experiment 463
  unreasoning 477
  essay 675
twiddle one's –

inaction 681
leisure 685
weariness 841
– immemorial 122
– of life
   duration 106
   now 118
   age 128
– out of mind 122
– to spare 685
– after time 104
– up 111, 134
– was 122
there being –s
   when 136
timeful 134
time-honoured
   old 124
   repute 873
   respected 928
time-keeper 114
time-recorder 553
timeless 135
timelessness 112
timely 132, 134
timeo Danaos 485, 864
timeous 134
time-piece 114
time-pleaser 607
timetable 266
times *present* 118
   events 151
   hard - 735
   many – 136
   – out of number 104
time-serving
   tergiversation 607
   cunning 702
   servility 886
   improbity 940
   selfishness 943
time-worn *old* 124
   age 128
   deteriorated 659
timid *fearful* 860
   cowardly 862
   humble 881
timist 607
Timocracy 803
Timon of Athens
   wealth 803
   seclusion 893
   misanthrope 911
timorous [*see* timid]
tin *preserve* 670
   money 800
   – hat 717
tinct 428
tinctorial 428

tincture
   small quantity 32
   mixture 41
   colour 428
tinctured
   disposition 820
tinder *fuel* 388
   irascible 901
tine 253
tinge
   small quantity 32
   mix 41
   colour 428
tingent 428
tingle *pain* 378
   touch 380
   emotion 821
   make the ears – 900
tink 408
tinker
   repair 660
tinkle
   faint sound 405
   resonance 408
tinkling cymbal 517
tinnient 408
tinsel *glitter* 420
   sham 545
   ornament 847
   frippery 851
tinsmith 690
tint 428
tintamarre 404
tintinnabulary 408
tiny 32, 193
   – bit 32
tip *end* 67
   summit 210
   cover 223
   give 784
   reward 973
   on –toe *high* 206
   expect 507
   – off 527
   – the wink 550
tip-cat 840
tippet 214, 225
tipple 298, 959
tippler 959
tipstaff 965
tipsy 959
tip-top 210, 648
tirade 582, 932
tire *dress* 225
   fatigue 688
   worry 830
   weary 841
tiré à quatre épin-
   gles 850
tirer d'affaire 672

se – 731
Tiresias 513
tiresome [*see* tire]
Tisiphone 173, 900
tissue *whole* 50
   assemblage 72
   matted 219
   texture 329
tit *small* 193
   pony 271
tit for tat 718
Titan 159, 980
Titania 979
titanic 192
titbit 298, 394, 829
tithe *tenth* 99
   tax 812
tithing 181
titillate 840, 865
titillation 377, 380
titivate 847
title
   indication 550
   name 564
   printing 591
   right to property 780
   distinction **877**
   right 924
titled 875
title-deed 771
title-page 66
titter 838
tittle 32
   to a – 494
tittle-tattle 532, 588
titubancy 583
titubate 306, 732
titular 562, 564
tmesis 218
T.N.T. 727
to *direction* 278
   lie – 681
   – all intents and purposes 27, 52
   – a certain degree 32
   – come 121, 152
   – the credit of 805
   – crown all 33, 642
   – do 59
   – the end of the chapter 52
   – the end of time 112
   – and fro 12, 314
   – the full 52
   – a great extent 31
   – the letter 19
   – a man 78

– the point 23
– the purpose 23
– a small extent 32
– some extent 26
– be sure 488
– this day 118
– wit 79
toad 649, 846
   – under a harrow 378
toad-eater 886, 935
toad-eating
   flattery 933
toadstool 367
toady 886
toast *roast* 384
   celebrate 883
tobacco 392
toboggan 272, 840
toby *jug* 191
toccata 415
tocsin 669
tod 319
to-day 118
toddle 266, 275
toddy 298
toe 211
   on the light fan-
   tastic 309, 840
toes turn up the –
   die 360
toff 854
toffee 396
toga 225, 747
   assume the –
   virilis 131
together 88, 120
   come – 290
   get – 72
   hang – 709
   lay heads – 695
   – with 37, 88
toggery 225
toil
   activity 682
   exertion 686
   – of a pleasure 682
   –s *trap* 545
toilet 225
   – water 400
toilette 225
   en grande – 847
toilsome 686, 704
toilworn 688
token 550
   give – 525
   – of remembrance 505
told, do what one
   is – 743
tolderolloll 838

Toledo 727
tolerable
  a little 32
  trifling 643
  pretty good 648
  not perfect 651
  satisfactory 831
tolerably, get on –
  736
toleration
  laxity 738
  lenity 740
  permission 760
  feeling 821
  calmness 826
  benevolence 906
toll *sound* 407
  tax 812
  – the knell 363
tollbooth
  prison 752
  market 799
tomahawk 727
tomb 363
  lay in the – 363
  – of the Capulets
    506
tombé des nues 83,
  870
tombola 156
tomboy 129, 851
tombstone 363
tom-cat 373
tome 593
tomentous 256
tomfool 501
tomfoolery
  absurdity 497
  amusement 840
  wit 842
  ostentation 882
Tom Noddy 501
Tommy Atkins 726
tommy-gun 727
to-morrow 121
  – and to-morrow
    104, 109
tompion 263
tomtit 193
Tom Thumb 193
tom-tom 417, 722
ton *weight* 319
  fashion 852
  –s of money 800
tonality 413, 420
tone *state* 7
  strength 159
  tendency 176
  sound 402
  music 413
  colour 428

blackness 431
  painting 556
  method 627
  disposition 820
  give a – to 852
  – down
  moderate 174
  darken 421
  discolour 429
  – in with 714
  – of voice 580
tone poem 415
toney 852
tongs
  fire-irons 386
  retention 781
tongue
  projection 250
  taste 390
  language 560
  bite the – 392
  bridle one's – 585
  give – 404, 580
  hold one's – 403
  slip of the –
  error 495
  solecism 568
  stammering 583
  on the tip of
    one's –
  near 197
  forget 506
  latent 526
  speech 582
  wag the – 582
  – cleave to the
    roof of one's
    mouth 870
  have a – in one's
    head 582
  – of land 342
  – running loose
    584
  keep one's – be-
    tween one's
    teeth 585
tongueless 581
tongue-tied 581
tonic
  musical note 413
  healthy 656
  medicine 662
  – sol fa 415
tonicity 159
tonnage 192
tonsillectomy 662
tonsils 351
tonsure 999
tonsured 226
tontine 810
tony 501

Tony Lumpkin 876
too
  also 37
  excess 641
  – bad
  disreputable 874
  wrong 923
  censure 932
  – clever by half
    702
  in a – great degree
    31
  – far 641
  – hot to hold one
    830
  – late 133
  – late for 135
  – little 640
  – many 641
  – much [*see below*]
  – soon 132
  – soon for 135
  – true 833, 839
too much
  redundance 641
  intemperance 954
  have – of 869
  make – of 482
  – for 471
  – of a good thing
    869
tool *instrument* 633
  steer 693
  catspaw 711
  ornament 847
  servile 886
  edge – 253
  mere – 690
toot 406
tooth *fastening* 45
  projection 250
  sharp 253
  roughness 256
  notch 257
  texture 329
  taste 390
  sweet –
  desire 865
  fastidious 868
  – and nail
  violence 173
  exertion 686
  attack 716
  – paste &c. 652
toothache 378
toothed 253
toothsome 394
top *supreme* 33
  summit 210
  roof 223
  spin 312

sleep like a – 683
  fool to the – of
    one's bent 545
  go over the – 861
  – to bottom 52
  – coat 225
  – hat 225
  at the – of the
    heap 210
  – of the ladder 873
  at the – of one's
    speed 274
  from – to toe 200
  at the – of the
    tree 210, 873
  at the – of one's
    voice 404, 411
toparchy 737
topaz 436, 847
top-boot 225
tope *tomb* 363
  trees 367
  drink 959
  temple 1000
topee 225
toper 959
top-full 52
top-gallant mast,
  206, 210
top-heavy
  unbalanced 28
  inverted 218
  dangerous 665
  tipsy 959
Tophet 982
topiary 847
topic 454
  – of the day 532
topical 183
top-mast 206
topmost 210
topography 183
topographer 466
topple
  unbalanced 28
  perish 162
  decay 659
  – down *fall* 306
  – over 28, 306
topsail schooner
  273
topsawyer 642, 700
top sergeant 745
topsy-turvy 14, 218
toque 225
tor 206
torch 388, 423
  apply the – 824
  light the – of war
    722
  – of Hymen 903

Tories 712
torment
  physical 378
  moral 828, 830
  place of – 982
Tormes, Lazarillo
  de – 941
torn [*see* tear]
  discord 713
tornado 312, 349
torpedo *bane* 663
  sluggish 683
  weapon 727
  evil-doer 913
  – boat 726
  – boat destroyer
    726
  – plane 276
torpid, torpor
  inert 172
  inactive 683
  insensible 823
torque 847
  torrefy 384
torrent
  violence 173
  rapid 274
  flow 348
  rain in –s 348
torrid 382
torsion 248
torso 50
tort 925, 947
tort et à travers, à –
  disagreement 24
  absurdity 497
  resolution 604
tortious 925
tortile 248
tortive 248
tortoise 275
tortoise-shell 440
tortuous
  twisted 248
  dishonourable 940
torture
  physical 378
  moral 828, 830
  cruelty 907
  punishment 972
  – a question 476
torvity 901*a*
toss *derange* 61
  throw 284
  oscillate 314
  agitate 315
  – in a blanket 929
  – the caber 840
  – the head
    pride 878
    insolence 885

contempt 930
  – off *drink* 298
  – overboard 610
  – on one's pillow
    825
  – up 156, 621
tosspot 959
tot *child* 129
tot homines, tot
  sententiæ 15
total 50, 84
  sum – 800
  – abstinence 953,
    955
  – eclipse 421
totalisator 621
totality 52
totally 52
totidem verbis 19,
  494
totient 84
toties quoties 136
totis viribus 686
totitive 84
toto: in – 52
  – cœlo 52
totter
  changeable 149
  weak 160
  limp 275
  oscillate 314
  agitate 315
  decay 659
  danger 665
  – to its fall 162
touch *relate to* 9
  small quantity 32
  mixture 41
  contact 199
  sensation 379,
    380
  music 416
  test 463
  indication 550
  act 680
  receive 785
  excite 824
  pity 914
  – and go
    instant 113
    soon 132
    changeable 149
    easy 705
  – the guitar 416
  – the hat 894
  – the heart 824
  – on 516
  – to the quick 822
  – up 658
  – upon 595
  in – with 9

touched *crazy* 503
  tainted 653
  compassion 914
  – in the wind 655
  – with *feeling* 821
touching 830
touchstone 463
touchwood
  fuel 388
  irascible 901
touchy 901
tough *coherent* 46
  tenacious 327
  difficult 704
toujours perdrix
  repetition 104
  weary 841
  satiety 869
toupee 256
tour 266
tour de force
  skill 698
  stratagem 702
  display 882
touring car 272
tourist 268
tournament 720
tourniquet 263
tournure 230, 448
  belle – 845
tous les rapports,
  sous – 494
tousle 61
tout *solicit* 765
tout: – au contraire
  14
  – court 265
  – ensemble 50
  – le monde 78
touter *agent* 758
  solicitor 767
  eulogist 935
tow 285
  take in – *aid* 707
towage 812
towardly 705
towards 278
  draw – 288
  move – 286
towel *clean* 652
  flog 972
tower
  stability 150
  edifice 161
  abode 189
  height 206
  soar 305
  defence 717
  – of strength
    strong 159
    influential 175

  safety 664
towering *great* 31
  furious 173
  large 192
  high 206
  – passion 900
  – rage 900
town *city* 189
  fashion 852
  man about – 854
  on the – 961
  all over the – 532
  talk of the – 873
  – council 696
town-hall 189, 966
township 181
townsman 188
  fellow – 892
town-talk 532, 588
toxic 657
toxicology 663
toxophilite 284
toy *trifle* 643
  amusement 840
  fondle 902
toy-dog 366
toy-shop 840
trabant 717
tracasserie 713
trace *inquire* 461
  discover 480*a*
  mark 550
  record 551
  delineate 554
  – back 122
  – out 480*a*
  – to 155
  – up 461
tracery
  lattice 219
  curve 245
  ornament 847
traces *harness* 45
trachea 351
tracing 21
track *trace* 461
  record 551
  way 627
  cover up one's –s
    528
  in one's –s 113
  racing – 840
  – meet 840
  – racing 728
trackless
  space 180
  difficult 704
  – trolley 272
tract *region* 181
  book 593
  dissertation 595

– of time 109
tractable
  malleable 324
  willing 602
  easy 705
tractarian 984
tractile
  traction **285**
  soft 324
traction 285
tractor 271
trade *exchange* 148
  business 625
  traffic 794
  drive a – 625
  learn one's – 539
  tricks of the – 702
  two of a – 708
  – with 794
trader 797
trade-mark 550
tradesman 797
trade-publication
  531
trade-union 712
trade-wind 349
tradition *old* 124
  description 594
  custom 613
traduce 934
traducer 936
traffic 794
tragedian 599
tragedy
  drama 599
  evil 619
tragic *drama* 599
tragical 830
tragi-comedy 599
tragi-comic 853
trail *sequel* 65
  pendent 214
  slow 275
  follow 281
  traction 285
  odour 398
  inquiry 461
  record 551
  highway 627
  follow in the – of
  281
  – of a red herring
  615, 706
train *sequel* 65
  series 69
  pendent 214
  vehicle 272
  sequence 281
  traction 285
  - *animals* 370
  teach 537

accustom 613
  prepare 673
  bring in its – 615
  in – 673
  in the – of 281,
  746
  lay a – 626, 673
  put in – 673
  siege – 727
  – de luxe 272
  – of reasoning 476
  – of thought 451
train-band 726
train-bearer 746
train-ferry 273
trained 698
trainer 673
  - *of horses* 268
  - *of animals* 370
  teacher 540
training
  education 537
  – *college* 542
train-oil 356
traipse 275
trait *speciality* 79
  appearance 448
  mark 550
  description 594
traitor
  disobedient 742
  knave 941
  enemy 891
trajection 297
trajectory 627
tra-la-la 838
tralatitious 521
tralineate 279
tralucent 425
tram 272
trammel *hinder* 706
  restrain 751
  fetter 752
  cast –s off 750
tramontane
  foreign 57
  distant 196
  wind 349
  outlandish 851
tramp *stroll* 266
  stroller 268
  idler 683
  vagabond 876
  on the – 264
trample
  – in the dust
  destroy 162
  prostrate 308
  – out 162
  – under foot
  vanquish 731

not observe **773**
  disrepute 874
  insolence 885
  dereliction 927
  contempt 930
  – upon 649, 739
tramway 627
trance *insensibility*
  376
  dream 515
  sleep 683
  lethargy 823
tranquil *calm* 174
  quiet 265
  peaceful 721
  calmness 871
  – *mind* 826
tranquillize
  moderate 174
  pacify 723
  soothe 826
transact *act* 680
  conduct 692
  – *business* 625
  – *business with*
  794
transaction 151,
  625, 680, 769
transactions 551
transalpine 196
transanimation 140
transatlantic 196
transcalency 384
transcend *great* 31
  superior 33
  go beyond 303
transcendency 641
transcendent 33,
  873
transcendental 78,
  519
transcendentalism
  450
transcolate 295
transcribe 19, 590
transcript 21, 590
transcursion **303**
transept 1000
transfer
  copy 21
  displace 185
  - *of things* 270
  - *of property* **783**
transference **270**
transfiguration
  change 140
  divine - 998
transfix 260
transfixed *firm* 150
transform 140
transformation

scene 599
transfuse 41, 270
  – the sense of 522
transgress
  go beyond 303
  infringe 773
  violate 927
  sin 945
transgression 947
transi de froid 383
transient 111, 149
transientness 111
transilience 146,
  303
transit
  conversion 144
  motion 264
  transference 270
  - *circle* 244
transit gloria
  mundi, sic –
  735, 874
transition 144, 270
transitional 140
transitory 111
transitu, in –
  transient 111
  journey 266
  transference 270
translate
  interpret 522
  promote 995
translator 524
translation
  transference 270
  resurrection 981
translocation 270
translucence 425
transmarine 196
transmigration 140,
  144
transmission
  moving 270
  passage 302
  - *of property* 783
transmit *light* 425
transmogrify 140
transmutation 140,
  144
transom 215
transparency **425**
transparent
  transmitting
  light 425
  obvious 518
transpicuous
  transmitting
  light 425
  obvious 518
transpierce 260
transpire

[676]

adversity 735
pain 828
painful 830
bring into – 649
get into – 649, 732
in – 619, 735
take – 686
– one's head
about 682
– one for 765
– oneself 686
troubled waters,
fish in – 704
troublesome 686,
704, 830
troublous 59, 173
– times 713
trough hollow 252
trench 259
conduit 350
trounce 932, 972
troupe 72
trousers 225
trousseau 225
trouvaille 775
trouvère 597
trover 775, 964
trow think 451
believe 484
know 490
trowel 191
troy-weight 319
truant absent 187
runaway 623
idle 682
apostate 941
truce cessation 142
deliverance 672
peace 721
pacification 723
flag of – 724
trucidation 361
truck summit 210
vehicle 272
barter 794
truck driver 268
truck farm 371
truckle to
submit 725
servile 886
flatter 933
truckle-bed 215
truck-load 31
truckman 268
truculent 907
trudge 266, 275
truditur dies die
109
true real 1
straight 246
assent 488

accurate 494
veracious 543
faithful 772
honourable 939
orthodox 983a
– bill
vindicate 937
accuse 938
lawsuit 969
see in its –
colours 480a
– meaning 516
– to nature 17
– to oneself 604a
– saying 496
– to scale 494
true-hearted 543,
939
true-love 897
true-lover's knot
897, 902
true-penny 939
truism axiom 496
unmeaning 517
trull 962
truly very 31
assent 488
really 494
indeed 535
trump perfect 650
honourable 939
good man 948
turn up –s 731
– card device 626
success 731
– up falsehood 544
accuse 938
trumped up 468,
545, 546
trumpery 517, 643
trumpet music 417
war cry 722
boast 884
flourish of –s
ostentation 882
celebration 883
boasting 884
ear– 418
penny –
skill 410
sound of –
alarm 669
speaking – 418
– blast 404
– call 550, 741
– forth 531
trumpeter
musician 416
messenger 534
boaster 884
trumpet-toned 410

trumpet-tongued
404, 531
truncate 201, 241
truncated 53
truncheon
weapon 727
staff of office 747
instrument of
punishment 975
trundle 284, 312
trunk whole 50
origin 153
paternity 166
box 191
trunk-hose 225
trunnion
support 215
projection 250
truss tie 43
pack, packet 72
support 215
trust
belief 484
combination 709
property 780
credit 805
hope 858
– to a broken reed
699
– to the chapter of
accidents 621
trustee
consignee 758
possessor 779
treasurer 801
trustful 484
trustless 940
trustworthy
certain 474
belief 484
- memory 505
veracious 543
honourable 939
truth
exactness 494
veracity 543
probity 939
arrive at the –
480a
in – certainly 474
love of – 543
of a – 535, 543
prove the – of 937
religious – 983a
speak the – 529,
543
in very – 543
Truth, Spirit of –
976
truthless 544
trutination 319

try experiment 463
adjudge 480
endeavour 675
use 677
lawsuit 969
– a case 967
– a cause 480
– conclusions
discuss 476
quarrel 713
contend 720
– one's hand 675
– one's luck 621
– one 704
– out 463
– the patience 830
– a prisoner 967
– one's temper 824
– one's utmost 686
trying 688, 704
tryst 892
trysting-place 74
tsar [see czar]
tu quoque 718
– argument
counter-evidence
468
confutation 479
accuse 938
tub 191
– thumper 582
– to a whale 545,
617
tuba 417
tubam trepidat,
ante – 860, 862
tubby 202
tube 260
test – 144
tubercle 250
tuberculous 655
tuberosity 250
tubman 968
tubular 260
tubulated 260
tubule 260
tuck fold 258
dagger 727
– in locate 184
eat 298
insert 300
tucker 225
tuft collection 72
rough 256
tufted 256
tuft-hunter 886,
943
tuft-hunting 886,
933
tug ship 273
pull 285

unforfeited 781
unforgettable 505
unforgiving 919
unforgotten 505
unformed 241, 674
unfortified
   pure 42
   powerless 158
unfortunate
   ill-timed 135
   failure 732
   adversity 735
   unhappy 828
   – woman 962
unfounded 546
unfrequent 137
unfrequented 893
unfriended
   powerless 158
   secluded 893
unfriendly
   opposed 708
   hostile 889
   malevolent 907
unfrock 756, 972
unfrozen 382
unfruitful 169
unfulfilled 773, 925
unfurl
   unfold 313
   – a flag 525, 550
unfurnished 640,
   674
ungainly 846, 895
ungallant 895
ungarnished 849
ungathered 678
ungenerous 819,
   943
ungenial 657
ungenteel 851, 895
ungentle 173, 895
ungentlemanly
   vulgar 851
   rude 895
   dishonourable 940
ungifted 499
unglorified 874
unglue 47
ungodly 989
ungovernable
   violent 173
   disobedient 742
   passionate 825
ungoverned 748
ungraceful
   – *language* 579
   ugly 846
   vulgar 851
ungracious 895, 907
ungrammatical 568

ungranted 764
ungrateful 917
ungratified 832
ungrounded
   unsubstantial 4
   erroneous 495
ungrudging 816
unguarded
   neglected 460
   spontaneous 612
   unprepared 674
   in an – *moment*
   unexpectedly 508
unguem, ad – 494,
   650
unguent 356
unguibus et rostro
   686
unguided
   ignorant 491
   impulsive 612
   unskilled 699
unguilty 946
unhabitable 187
unhabituated 614
unhackneyed 614
unhallowed 988,
   989
unhand 750
unhandseled 123
unhandsome 940
unhandy 699
unhappy
   adversity 735
   pain 828
   dejected 837
   make – 830
unharbored 185
unhardened
   tender 914
   innocent 946
   penitent 950
unharmonious 24,
   414
unharness 750
unhatched 674
unhazarded 664
unhealthy 655, 657
unheard of
   exceptional 83
   improbable 473
   ignorant 491
   wonderful 870
unheated 383
unheed, -ed 460
unheeding 458
unhesitating
   belief 484
   resolved 604
unhewn 241, 674
unhindered 748

unhinge 61, 158
unhinged
   impotent 158
   insane 503
   failure 732
unhitch 44
unholy 989
unhonoured 874
unhook (44)
unhoped 508
unhorsed 732
unhostile 888
unhouse 297
unhoused 185
unhurt 670
unicorn
   monster 83
   carriage 272
unideal *existing* 1
   no thought 452
   true 494
unification 48, 87
uniform
   homogeneous 16
   simple 42
   orderly 58
   regular 80
   dress 225
   symmetry 242
   livery 550
uniformity 16
unilluminated 421
unimaginable 471,
   473
   wonderful 870
unimaginative 576,
   843, 871
unimagined 1, 494
unimitated 20
unimpaired 670
unimpassioned 826
unimpeachable
   certain 474
   true 494
   due 924
   approved 931
   innocent 946
unimpeached 931,
   946
unimpeded 705, 748
unimportance 643
unimpressed 838
unimpressible 823
unimproved 659
unincreased 36
unincumbered
   easy 705
   exempt 927a
uninduced 616
uninfected 652
uninfectious 656

uninflammable 385
uninfluenced
   obstinate 606
   unactuated 616
   free 748
uninfluential 172,
   175a
uninformed 491
uningenuous 544
uninhabit, -able,
   -ed 187, 893
uninitiated 491, 699
uninjured
   perfect 650
   healthy 654
   preserved 670
uninjurious 656
uninquisitive 456
uninspired 823
uninstructed 491
unintellectual 452,
   499
unintelligent 499
unintelligibility 519
unintelligible 519
   - *style* 571
   render – 538
unintentional
   necessary 601
   undesigned 621
uninterested 456,
   841, 843
unintermitting
   unbroken 69
   durable 110
   continuing 143
   persevering 604a
uninterrupted
   continuous 69
   perpetual 112
   unremitting 143
unintroduced 893
uninured 614
uninvented 526
uninvestigated 491
uninvited 893
uninviting 830
union
   agreement 23
   junction 43
   combination 48
   concurrence 178
   workhouse 189
   party 712
   concord 714
   marriage 903
unionist 712
union-jack 550
union-pipes 417
unique
   dissimilar 18

unopened 261
unopposed 709
unorganized 674
– matter 358
unornamental 846
unornamented
– style 576
simple 849
unorthodox 984
unostentatious 881
unowed 807
unowned 782
unpacific 713, 722
unpacified 713
unpack
unfasten 44
take out 297
unpaid *debt* 806
honorary 815
the great –
magistracy 967
– worker 602
unpalatable 395, 830
unparagoned
supreme 33
best 648
perfect 650
unparalleled
unimitated 20
supreme 33
exceptional 83
unpardonable 938, 945
unparliamentary
language 895, 908
unpassable 261
unpassionate 826
unpatriotic 911
unpeaceful 720, 722
unpeople
emigration 297
banishment 893
unperceived
neglected 460
unknown 491
unperformed 730
unperjured 543, 939
unperplexed 498
unpersuadable 606
unpersuaded 616
unperturbed 826
unphilosophical 499
unpierced 261
unpin (44)
unpitied 932
unpitying 914a
unplaced 185
unplagued 831

unpleasant 830
unpleasing 830
unpoetical 598, 703
unpolished
rough 256
inelegant 579
unprepared 674
vulgar 851, 876
rude 895
unpolite 895
unpolluted
good 648
perfect 650
unpopular 830, 867
unpopularity 898
unportioned 804
unpossessed 777a
unpractical 699
unprecedented 83, 137
unprejudiced 498, 748
unpremeditated
impulsive 612
undesigned 621
unprepared 674
unprepared 508, 674
unprepossessed 498
unprepossessing 846
unpresentable 851
unpretending 881
unprevented 748
unprincipled 945
unprivileged 925
unprized 483
unproclaimed 526
unproduced 2
unproductive 645
unproductiveness 169
unproficiency 699
unprofitable
unproductive 169
useless 645
inexpedient 647
bad 649
unprolific 169
unpromising 859
unprompted 612
unpronounceable 519
unpronounced 526
unpropitious
ill-timed 135
opposed 708
hopeless 859
unproportioned 24
unprosperous 735
unprotected 665

unproved 477
unprovided
scanty 640
unprepared 674
unprovoked (616)
unpublished 526
unpunctual
tardy 133
untimely 135
irregular 139
unpunished 970
unpurchased 796
unpurified 653
unpurposed 621
unpursued 624
unqualified
incomplete 52
impotent 158
certain 474
unprepared 674
inexpert 699
unentitled 925
– *truth* 494
unquelled 173
unquenchable
strong 159
desire 865
unquenched
violence 173
heat 382
unquestionable 474
unquestionably 488
unquestioned 474, 488
unquiet
motion 264
agitation 315
excitable 825
unravel *untie* 44
arrange 60
straighten 246
evolve 313
discover 480a
interpret 522
disembarrass 705
unreached 304
unread 491
unready 674
unreal
not existing 2
erroneous 495
imaginary 515
unreasonable
impossible 471
illogical 477
misjudging 481
foolish 499
exorbitant 814
unjust 923
unreclaimed 951
unrecognizable 146

unreconciled 713
unrecorded 552
unrecounted 55
unreduced 31
unrefined 851
unreflecting 458
unreformed 951
unrefreshed 688
unrefuted 478, 494
unregarded
neglected 460
unrespected 929
unregenerate 988
unregistered 552
unreined 748
unrelated 10
unrelenting 914a, 919
unreliable
uncertain 475
irresolute 605
dangerous 665
unrelieved 835
unremarked 460
unremembered 506
unremitting
continuous 69
continuing 110
unvarying 143
persevering 604a
unremoved 184
unremunerated 808
unrenewed 141
unrepealed 141
unrepeated 87, 103
unrepentant 951
unrepining 831
unreplenished 640
unrepressed 173
unreproached 946
unreproved 946
unrequited 806, 917
unresented 918
unresenting 826
unreserved
manifest 525
veracious 543
artless 703
unresisted 743
unresisting 725
unresolved 605
unrespected 929
unrest 149, 264
unrestored 688
unrestrained
capricious 608
unencumbered 705
free 748
unrestricted
undiminished 31

free 748
unretracted 535
unrevenged 918
unreversed 143
unrevoked 143
unrewarded 806, 917
unrhymed 598
unriddle 480a, 529
unrig 645
unrighteous 945
unrip 260
unripe
  young 127
  sour 397
  immature 674
unrivalled 33
unroll *evolve* 313
  display 525
unromantic 494
unroot 301
unruffled
  calm 174
  quiet 265
  unaffected 823
  placid 826
unruly *violent* 173
  obstinate 606
  disobedient 742
unsaddle 756
unsafe 665
unsaid 526
unsaleable
  useless 645
  selling 796
  cheap 815
unsaluted 929
unsanctified 988, 989
unsanctioned 925
unsated 865
unsatisfactory
  inexpedient 647
  bad 649
  displeasing 830
  discontent 832
unsatisfied 832, 865
unsavouriness **395**
unsay *recant* 607
unscanned 460
unscathed 654
unschooled 491
unscientific 477
unscoured 653
unscriptural 984
unscrupulous 940
unseal 529
unsearched 460
unseasonable 24, 135
unseasoned 614,

674
unseat 756
unseemly
  inexpedient 647
  ugly 846
  vulgar 851
  undue 925
  vicious 945
unseen
  invisible 447
  neglected 460
  latent 526
unseldom 136
unselfish 942
unseparated 46
unserviceable 645
unsettle *derange* 61
unsettled
  mutable 149
  displaced 185
  uncertain 475
  – in one's mind 503
unsevered 50
unsex 146
unshaded 525
unshaken 159
  – *belief* 484
unshapely 846
unshapen 241
unshared 777
unsheathe
  – the sword 722
unsheltered 665
unshielded 665
unshifting 143
unship 185, 297
unshocked 823
unshorn 50
unshortened 200
unshrinking 604, 861
unsifted 460
unsightly 846
unsinged 670
unskilfulness **699**
unslaked 865
unsleeping 604a, 682
unsmooth 256
unsociable 893
unsocial 893
unsoiled 652
unsold 777
unsoldierlike 862
unsolicitous 866
unsolved 526
unsophisticated
  simple 42
  genuine 494
  artless 703

unsorted 59
unsought
  avoided 623
  unrequested 766
unsound
  illogical 477
  erroneous 495
  deceptive 545
  imperfect 651
  – mind 503
unsown 674
unsparing
  abundant 639
  severe 739
  liberal 816
  with an – hand 818
unspeakable 31, 870
unspecified 78
unspent 678
unspied 526
unspiritual 316, 989
unspoiled 648
unspotted
  clean 652
  beautiful 845
  innocent 946
unstable 218
  changeable 149
  uncertain 475
  irresolute 605
  precarious 665
  – equilibrium 149
unstaid 149
unstained
  clean 652
  honourable 939
unstatesmanlike 699
unsteadfast 605
unsteady
  mutable 149
  irresolute 605
  in danger 665
unstinted 639
unstinting 816
unstirred 823, 826
unstopped
  continuing 143
  open 260
unstored 640
unstrained
  turbid 653
  relaxed 687
  – *meaning* 516
unstrengthened 160
unstruck 823
unstrung 160
unstudied 460
unsubject 748

unsubmissive 742
unsubservient
  useless 645
  inexpedient 647
unsubstantial 4
  weak 160
  rare 322
  erroneous 495
  imaginary 515
unsubstantiality **4**
unsuccessful 732
unsuccessive 70
unsuitable
  incongruous 24
  (*inexpedient* 647)
  – time 135
unsullied *clean* 652
  honourable 939
  (*guiltless* 946)
unsung 526
unsupplied 640
unsupported
  weak 160
  (*unassisted* 706)
  – by evidence 468
unsuppressed 141
unsurmountable 471
unsurpassed 33
unsusceptible 823
unsuspected
  latent 526
unsuspecting
  belief 484
  hopeful 858
unsuspicious
  belief 484
  artless 703
  hope 858
unsustainable 495
unsweet 395
unswept 653
unswerving
  straight 246
  direct 278
  persevering 604a
unsymmetric 83
unsymmetrical 59, 243
unsystematic 59
untainted *pure* 652
  healthy 654
  honourable 939
untalked of 526
untamed 851, 907
untarnished 939
untasted 391
untaught 491, 674
untaxed 815
unteach 538
unteachable 499,

699
untenable
powerless 158
illogical 477
undefended 725
untenanted 187, 893
unthanked 917
unthankful 917
unthawed 321, 383
unthinkable 471
unthinking
unconsidered 452
involuntary 601
unthought of 452, 460
unthreatened 664
unthrifty
unprepared 674
prodigal 818
unthrone 756
untidy 59, 653
untie 44, 750
– the knot 705
until 106
– now 118
untilled 674
untimely 135
– end 360
untinged 42
untired 689
untiring 604a
untitled 876
untold
countless 105
uncertain 475
latent 526
secret 528
untouched
disused 678
insensible 823
untoward
ill-timed 135
bad 649
unprosperous 735
unpleasant 830
untraced 526
untracked 526
untractable 606, 699
untrained
unaccustomed 614
unprepared 674
unskilled 699
untrammelled 705, 748
untranslatable 523
untranslated 523
untravelled 265
untreasured 640
untried *new* 123

not decided 461
untrimmed 674, 849
untrodden *new* 123
impervious 261
not used 678
untroubled 174, 721
untrue 495, 546
untrustworthy
uncertain 475
erroneous 495
danger 665
dishonourable 940
untruth 544, **546**
untunable 414
unturned 246
untutored
ignorant 491
unprepared 674
artless 703
untwine 313
untwist 313
unused
new 123
unaccustomed 614
unskilful 699
unusual 83
unusually *very* 31
unutterable 31, 519, 870
unvalued
underrated 483
undesired 866
disliked 898
unvanquished 748
unvaried
continuing 143
- *style* 575, 576
unvarnished
true 494
- *style* 576
unreserved 703
simple 849
- *tale* 494, 543
unvarying 16, 143
unveil 525, 529
unventilated 261
unveracious 544
unversed 491
unvexed 831
unviolated 939
unvisited 893
unwakened 683
unwarlike 862
unwarmed 383
unwarned 508, 665
unwarped judg-ment 498
unwarrantable 923
unwarranted
illogical 477

undue 925
illegal 964
unwary 460
unwashed 653
great – 876
unwatchful 460
unwavering 604a
unweakened 159
unwearied
persevering 604a
indefatigable 682
refreshed 689
unwedded 904
unweeded garden 674
unweeting 491
unweighed 460
unwelcome 830, 893
unwell 655
unwept 831
unwholesome 657
unwieldy
large 192
heavy 319
cumbersome 647
difficult 704
ugly 846
unwilling 489
unwillingness **603**
unwind *evolve* 313
unwiped 653
unwise 499
unwished 866
unwithered 159
unwitting
ignorant 491
involuntary 601
unwittingly 621
unwomanly 373
unwonted 83, 614
unworldly 939
unworn 159
unworshipped 929
unworthy
shameful 874
vicious 945
– of belief 485
– of notice 643
unwrap 246
unwrinkled 255
unwritten
latent 526
obliterated 552
spoken 582
– *law* 697, 963
unwrought 674
unyielding
tough 323
resolute 604
obstinate 606

resisting 719
up
aloft 206
vertical 212
effervescing 353
excited 824
the game is – 735
prices looking – 814
time – 111
– in arms
prepared 673
active 682
opposition 708
attack 716
resistance 719
warfare 722
– and at them 716
– and doing 682
– and down 314
– on end 212
– in 698
– to [*see below*]
all – with
destruction 162
failure 732
adversity 735
up to
time 106
power 157
knowing 490
skilful 698
brave 861
– the brim 52
– date 123
– one's ears 641
– one's eyes 641
– the mark
equal 27
sufficient 639
good 648
due 924
– snuff 702
– this time
time 106
past 122
Upas tree 663
upbear 215, 307
upbraid 932
upcast 307
upgrow 206
upgrowth 194, 305
upheaval 146
upheave 307
uphill
acclivity 217
ascent 305
laborious 686
difficult 704
uphoist 307
uphold

continue 143
support 215
evidence 467
aid 707
praise 931
upholder 488, 711
upholstery 633
uplands 180, 206, 344
uplift 307, 658
upon:
　– my honour 535
　– oath 535
　– which 117, 121
upper 206
　– boxes, – circle 599
　– classes 875
　– hand
　　influence 175
　　success 731
　　sway 737
　– story
　　summit 210
　　intellect 450
　　wisdom 498
　– ten thousand 875
　be on one's –'s 804
uppermost 210
　say what comes – 612
　– in the mind
　　thought 451
　　topic 454
　　attention 457
　– in one's thoughts
　　memory 505
upraise 307
uprear 307
upright
　vertical 212
　honest 939
uprise 305
uprising 742
uproar
　disorder 59
　violence 173
　noise 404
uproarious 825
uproot 301
ups and downs of life 151, 735
upset *destroy* 162
　invert 218
　throw down 308
　defeat 731
　excite 824
　disconcert 874
　– the apple cart 732

upshot *result* 154
　judgment 480
　completion 729
upside down 218
upstairs 206
upstart
　new 123
　prosperous 734
　plebeian 876
upturn 218
upwards 206
　– of 33, 100
uranology 318
urban 189
urbane 894
urbis conditæ, anno – 106
urceole 998
urchin
　child 129
　small 193
　wretch 949
　imp 980
urge *violence* 173
　impel 276
　incite 615
　hasten 684
　beg 765
urgent
　required 630
　important 642
　haste 684
　request 765
urn *vase* 191
　funereal 363
　heater 386
　cinerary – 363
usage 613, 677
usance 806
use *habit* 613
　waste 638
　utility 644
　employ **677**
　property 780
　make good – of 658
　in – 677
　be of – to *aid* 707
　benevolence 906
　– one's discretion 600
　– one's endeavour 675
　– a right 924
　– up 677
used to 613
used up
　deteriorated 659
　disuse 678
　fatigue 688
　weary 841

satiated 869
useful 644
　render – 677
useless 645
user,
　right of – 780
usher
　guard 263
　receive 296
　teacher 540
　servant 746
　courtesy 894
　wedding 903
　– in *precedence* 62
　begin 66
　precession 280
　announce 511
　– into the world 161
usque ad nauseam 841
U.S.S. 726
ustulation 384
usual
　general 78
　ordinary 82
　customary 613
usufruct 677
usurer
　lender 787
　merchant 797
　credit 805
　miser 819
usurious 819
usurp *assume* 739
　seize 789
　illegal 925
　– authority 738
usurpation
　insolence 885
usurper 737
usury 806
utensil 191, 633
uti possidetis
　permanence 141
　possession 777
　retention 781
utilitarian 677, 910
utility 644
　general –
　　actor 599
utilize 677
utmost 33
　do one's – 686
　– height 210
　in one's – need 735
　deserted in one's – need 893
Utopia 515, 858
utricle 191

utter *extreme* 31
　distribute 73
　disclose 529
　publish 531
　speak 580, 582
　money 800
utterly 52
uttermost 31
　to the – parts of the earth 180, 196
uxorious 897

V

va sans dire, cela – 474, 525
vacant *void* 4
　absent 187
　thoughtless 452
　unmeaning 517
　scanty 640
　– hour 685
　– mind *folly* 499
vacate *displace* 185
　absent 187
　depart 293
　resign 757
vacation 687
vaccine 366
vache 191
vacillate
　changeable 149
　undulate 314
　waver 605
vacuity 187
vacuous
　unsubstantial 4
　absent 187
vacuum 187
　– cleaner 652
vade mecum 527, 542
vadium 771
væ victis! *war* 722
　threat 909
vagabond
　wanderer 268
　low person 876
　rogue 949
vagabondage 266
vagary
　absurdity 497
　imagination **515**
　whim 608
　antic 840
vagrant
　changeable 149
　roving 266
　traveller 268

concealment 526, 527
conceal 528
ambush 530
behind the – 360
draw aside the – 529
take the – 893, 995
veiled
  uncertain 475
  invisible 447
  concealed 528
vein temper 5
  tendency 176
  thin 203
  thread 205
  channel 350
  humour 602
  mine 636
  affections 820
  in the – 602
  not in the – 603
veined 440
veldt 344
velis et remis 274
velitation 720
velleity 600
vellicate 315
vellicating 392
vellum 590
veloce music 415
velocipede 272
velocity 264, **274**
  angular – 244
veluti in speculum 17
velvet 255, 256
  pleasure 377
  on – easy 705
venal price 812
  stingy 819
  dishonest 940
  selfish 943
venation 622
vend 796
vendee 795
vender 796
vendetta 919
vendible 796
venditation 884
vendor 796
veneer 204, 223
venenation 659
venerable old 124
  aged 128
  sage 500
  respected 928
veneration
  respect 928
  piety 987

venereal disease 655
venery killing 361
  hunting 622
  impurity 961
venesection
  ejection 297
  remedy 662
Venetian blinds 351
vengeance 919
  cry to heaven for – 923
  with a – 31, 173
vengeful 919
veni vidi vici 731
venial 937
veniam petimusque damusque vicissim 918
venienti occurrere morbo 673
venison 394
venom 663, 907
venomous bad 649
  poisonous 657
  rude 895
  maleficent 907
vent opening 260
  egress 295
  air-pipe 351
  disclose 529
  escape 671
  sale 796
  find – egress 295
  passage 302
  publish 531
  escape 671
  give – to 297, 529
  – one's rage 900
  – one's spleen 900
venter 191
ventiduct 351
ventilate
  begin 66
  air 338
  wind 349
  discuss 595
  – a question 461, 476
ventilator 349, 351
ventosity 349
vent-peg
  stopper 263
  safety 666
  escape 671
ventre
  – à terre 274
  danse du – 840
ventricle 191
ventriloquism 580

venture
  chance 621
  danger 665
  try 675
  courage 861
  I'll – to say 535
venturesome
  undertaking 677
  brave 861
  rash 863
venue 74, 183
Venus woman 374
  planet 423
  beauty 845
  love 897
  goddess 979
veracity **543**
verandah 191
verbal 562
  – intercourse 582, 588
  – quibble 497, 842
verbatim
  imitation 19
  exact 494
  words 562
verbiage
  unmeaning 517
  words 562
  diffuse 573
verbis:
  totidem – 494
  – ad verbera 720
verborum, copia –
  diffuse 573
  eloquence 582
  loquacious 584
verbosity
  words 562
  diffuse 573
  loquacity 584
verboten 761
verbum sapienti 527
verdant 367, 435
verd-antique 435
verdict
  opinion 480
  lawsuit 969
  snatch a – 545, 702
verdigris 435
verditer 435
verdure 367, 435
verecundiam, argumentum ad – 874, 939
verecundity 879, 881
veredical 543
Verein 712

verge
  tendency 176
  near 197
  edge 231
  limit 233
  direction 278
verger 996
veriest 31
verification 463, 771
verify 463
  evidence 467
  demonstrate 478
  find out 480a
verily truly 494
verisimilitude 472
veritable 494
veritas, nuda – 494
vérité, palais de – 703
verity 494
verjuice 397
vermicular
  convoluted 248
  worm 366
vermiform 248
vermilion 434
vermin
  animal 366
  unclean 653
  base 876
vernacular
  native 188
  internal 221
  language 560
  habitual 613
vernal 123, 125
vernier
  minuteness 193
  - scale 466
vero, vitam impendere – 535, 939
verrons, nous – 507
versatile 149
verse division 51
  poetry 597
versed in 490
versicolour 440
versify 597
version change 140
  special 79
  interpretation 522
versus 278, 708
vert 435
vertebral 222
vertebrate 366
vertex 210
verticality **212**
verticity 312
vertigo
  rotation 312

delirium 503
verve
  imagination 515
  vigorous language
    574
  energy 682
  feeling 821
very 31
  – best 648
  – image 554
  – many. 102
  – minute 113
  – much 31
  – picture 17
  – small 32
  – thing
  identity 13
  agreement 23
  exact 494
  – true 488
  – well 831
Véry light 423
vesicle *cell* 191
  covering 223
  globe 249
vesicular 191, 260
vespers 126, 990
vespertine 126
vessel
  receptacle 191
  tube 260
  ship 273
vest *place* 184
  dress 225
  – in *belong to* 777
  give 784
Vesta 979
vesta *match* 388
vestal 960
vested *fixed* 150
  legal 963
  – in *located* 184
  – interest
  given 780
  due 924
vestibule 66, 191
vestige 551
vestigia:
  veteris – flammæ
    505, 613
  – nulla retrorsum
    282, 604*a*
vestment 225, 999
vestry *council* 696
  churchdom 995
  church 1000
vesture 225
vesuvian
  match 388
veteran *old* **130**
  adept 700

[692]

warrior 726
veterinary art 370
veteris vestigia
  flammæ 505,
  613
veto 761
vetturino 694
vex 830, 898
vexata quæstio 704,
  713
vexation 828, 830
  – of spirit 828
  discontent 832
  resentment 900
vexatious 830
vexed question
  704, 713
vi et armis
  violence 173
  exertion 686
  compulsion 744
viâ 278, 627
viable 359
via lactea 318
viaduct 627
vial 191
vials:
  – of hate 898
  – of wrath 900
viands 298
viaticum
  provision 637
  rite 998
vibrate 314
  – between two
    extremes 149
vibrato 415
vibratory 149
vibroscope 314
vicar *deputy* 759
  clergyman 996
  – of Bray 607, 886
vicarage 1000
vicariate 995
vicarious 147
vicarship 995
vice *deputy* 759
  holder 781
  wickedness **945**
vice versâ
  reciprocal 12
  contrary 14
  interchange 148
vice-admiral 745
Vice-Chancellor
  967
–'s Court 966
vicegerency 755
vicegerent 758, 759
vice-president 694
vice-regal 759

viceroy
  governor 745
  deputy 759
vicesimal 98
vicinage 197
vicinism 145
vicinity 197, 227
vicious 173, 945
  render – 659
  – reasoning 477
vicissitude 149
Vickers gun 727
victim *dupe* 547
  defeated 732
  sufferer 828
victimize *kill* 361
  deceive 545
  injure 649
  baffle 731
victis, væ – 722, 909
victor 731
victoria
  carriage 272
Victoria Cross 733
victory 731
victual *provide* 637
victuals 298
videlicet 79, 522
viduage 905
viduity 905
vie *good* 648
  – with 720
vielle 417
view
  sight 441
  appearance 448
  attend to 457
  opinion 484
  landscape paint-
    ing 556
  intention 620
  bring into – 525
  come into – 446
  commanding – 441
  in – *visible* 446
  intended 620
  expected 507
  keep in – 457
  on – 448
  present to the –
    448
  with a – to 620
  – as 484
  – in a new light
    658
viewer 444
viewless 447
view-point 441
vigesimal 98
vigil *care* 459
vigilance *care* 459

wisdom 498
  activity 682
  caution 864
vigils *worship* 990
vignette 558, 594,
  847
vigour *strength* 159
  energy 171
  style **574**
  resolution 604
  health 654
  activity 682
viking 792
vile *valueless* 643
  bad 649
  painful 830
  disgraceful 874
  plebeian 876
  dishonourable 940
  vicious 945
vilify *shame* 874
  malediction 908
  censure 932
  detract 934
vilipend
  disrespect 929
  censure 932
  detract 934
vilipendency 930
villa 189
village 189
  – talk 588
villager 188
villain
  servant 746
  serf 876
  knave 941
  rascal 949
villainous 649, 945
  – saltpetre 727
villainy 940
villein [*see* villain]
villenage 749, 777
villi 256
villous 256
vim 171
vin: – d'honneur
  292, 894
  not think – ordi-
    naire of oneself
    880
vinaigrette 400
vincible 158
vincture 43
vinculo matrimonii,
  separatio a – 905
vinculum 45
  – matrimonii 903
vindicate 467, 937.
  – a right 924
vindication **937**

wait 133, 681
lie in – for 530
– for 507
– impatiently 133
– on *accompany* 88
   aid 707
– to see how the
   wind blows 607
– upon *serve* 746
   call on 894
waiter *servant* 746
– on Providence
   neglect 460
   inactive 683
   content 831
waiting 507
be kept – 133
waiting-maid 746
waitress 746
waits 416
waive *defer* 133
   not choose 609a
   not use 678
waivode 745
wake *sequel* 65
   rear 235
   funeral 363
   trace 551
   excite 824
   amusement 840
in the – of 281
enough to – the
   dead 404
– the thoughts
   457
– up 824
wakeful
   careful 459
   active 682
Walhalla 981
walk *region* 181
   lane 189
   move 266
   business 625
   way 627
   conduct 692
   arena 728
– one's chalks
   293, 623
– the earth 359
– of life 625
–ed off one's legs
   688
– off with 791
– over the course
   705, 731
– in the shoes of
   19
walker 268
walking gentleman
   599

wall *vertical* 212
   parietes 224
   inclosure 232
   refuge 666
   obstacle 706
   defence 717
   prison 752
driven to the –
   704
go to the –
   destruction 162
   die 360
   fail 732
pushed to the –
   601
take the – 873,
   878
wooden –s 726
–eyed 442
– in 229, 751
wallah 746
wallet 191
wallop 315
wallow *low* 207
   plunge 310
   rotate 312
– in 377, 641
– in the mire 653
– in riches 803
– in voluptuous-
   ness 954
wallsend 388
Wall-street 799
– *slang* 563
waltz 415, 840
wamble
   vacillate 149
   oscillate 314
   dislike 867
wampum 800
wan 429, 837
wand *sceptre* 747
   magic 993
wave a – 992
wander *move* 264
   journey 266
   deviate 279
   delirium 503
the attention –s
   458
wanderer 268
wandering
   exceptional 83
– Jew 268
wane
   decrease 36
   age 128
   contract 195
   decay 659
one's star on the –
   735

wax and – 140
wangle 943
want
   inferiority 34
   shortcoming 304
   requirement 630
   insufficiency 640
   poverty 804
   desire 865
wanted 187
wanting
   incomplete 53
   absent 187
   imbecile 499
found –
   imperfect 651
   disapproval 932
   guilt 947
wantless 639
wanton
   unconformable 83
   capricious 608
   unrestrained 748
   amusement 840
   rash 863
   impure 961
wapentake 181
war 722
at – 24, 720
at – with 708, 722
declare – 713
man of – 726
seat of – 728
– correspondent
   534, 593
– of words 588,
   720
warble 416
war-cry *alarm* 669
   defiance 715
   war 722
ward *part* 51
   parish 181
   safety 664
   asylum 666
   dependent 746
   restraint 751
watch and – 459,
   753
– off 706, 717
war-dance 715
warden
   guardian 664
   master 745
   deputy 759
warder
   perforator 262
   porter 263
   guardian 664
   keeper 753
wardmote 966

wardrobe 191, 225
ward-room 191
war-drum 417
wardship 664
ware
   warning 668
   merchandise 798
warehouse 636, 799
warfare 722
   discord 713
war-horse 726
warlike 722
warlock 994
warm
   violent 173
   hot 382
   make hot 384
   red 434
   orange 439
   wealthy 803
   ardent 821
   excited 824
   angry 900
   irascible 901
   flog 972
– bath 386
– the blood 824
– the cockles of
   the heart 829
– imagination 515
– man 803
– reception
   repel 717
   welcome 892
– up 658, 660
– work 686
warm-hearted
   feeling 821
   sensibility 822
   friendship 888
   benevolence 906
warming 384
warming-pan
   locum tenens 147
   heater 386
   preparation 673
warmth
   vigorous language
   574
warn *dissuade* 616
   caution 668
– off 761
warning *omen* 512
   dissuasion 616
   caution **668**
give – *dismiss* 678
   relinquish 782
– voice *alarm* 668
warp *change* 140
   tend 176
   contract 195

find its – 302
gather – 267
get into the – of
   613
go one's – 293
go your – 297
let it have its –
   681
it must have its –
   601
have one's own –
   748
in a – 828, 900
in the – *near* 197
in the – of 706,
   708
make – 302
make one's –
   journey 266
   progression 282
   passage 302
   prosperity 734
make – for
   substitution 147
   opening 260
   turn aside 279
   avoid 623
   facilitate 705
   courtesy 894
on the – 282
place in one's –
   763
put in the – of
   470, 537
see one's – 490
show the – 693
under – *move* 264
   sail 267
   progression 282
   depart 293
wing one's – 267
– in 294
long – off 196
have – on 267
– out 295
– of speaking 521
– of thinking 484
not know which –
   to turn 475
Way, the – 976
wayfarer 268
wayfaring 266
waylay 545, 702
wayless 261
ways 692
   in all manner of –
      278
   – and means 632,
      800
wayward
   changeable 149

obstinate 606
capricious 608
sullen 901a
waywode 745
wayworn 266, 688
wayzgoose 840
weak *feeble* 160
   water 337
   insipid 391
   illogical 477
   foolish 499
   – *style* 575
   irresolute 605
   trifling 643
   lax 738
   compassionate
      914
   vicious 945
   – point 477, 651
   expose one's –
      point 479
   – side 499, 945
weaken
   decrease 36, 38
   enfeeble 160
   refute 468
weaker vessel 374
weak-headed 499
weak-hearted 862
weak-kneed 725
weakness 160
   – of the flesh 945
weal 618
   common – 644
weald 367
wealth 780, **803**
wean 484, 614
   – from 616
   – one's thoughts
      from 506
weanling 129
weapon 727
weaponless 158
wear *decrease* 36
   clothes 225
   deflect 279
   use 677
   – away *cease* 142
   deteriorate 659
   – the breeches 737
   – off 142, 614
   – on 109
   – out 659, 688
   – and tear
      decrease 36
   waste 638
   injury 659
   exertion 686
weariness **841**
wearing 841
   – apparel 225

wearisome
   laborious 686
   fatiguing 688
   painful 830
weary *fatigue* 688
   painful 828
   sad 837
   ennuyant 841
   – flat, stale, and
      unprofitable 843
   – waste 344
   – Willie 876
weasand 260, 351
weasel asleep,
   catch a – 471, 682
weather 338
   keep one's – eye
      open 864
   rough – 173, 349
   – the storm
   stability 150
   recover 660
   safe 664
   succeed 731
weather permitting
   469, 470
weather-beaten
   weak 160
   damaged 659
   fatigue 688
weather-bound 751
weathercock
   changeable 149
   wind 349
   indication 550
   fickle 607
weathered 659
weather-gauge 338
weather-glass 338
weather-proof 654,
   664
weatherwise 338
   foresight 510
weave *produce* 161
   interlace 219
   – a tangled web
      704
weazen 193
web
   complexity 59
   intersection 219
   texture 329
wed 48, 903
wedded: – pair 903
   – to *belief* 484
   habit 613
   loving 897
   – to an opinion
   misjudgment 481
   obstinacy 606
wedding 903

– breakfast 892
– day 883
wedge *join* 43
   angular 244
   sharp 253
   instrument 633
   thin edge of the
   begin 66
   insinuate 228
   cunning 702
   – in 228
wedged in 751
wedlock 903
wee 193
weed *exclude* 55
   few 103
   plant 367
   agriculture 371
   cigar 392
   trifle 643
   clean 652
   – out 297, 301
weeds *dress* 225
   useless 645
   mourning 839
   widowhood 905
weedy 203, 643
week 108
weekly 138
   – paper 531
ween *judge* 480
   believe 484
   know 490
weeny 32
weep 839, 914
weet 480, 490
weetless 491
weft, warp and –
   329
weigh *influence* 175
   lift 307
   heavy 319
   ponder 451
   under – [see way]
   – anchor 293
   – carefully 465
   – down 649, 749
   – on the heart 830
   – heavy on 649
   – on the mind
   regret 833
   dejection 837
   fear 860
   – with 615
weighed and found
   wanting 34, 932
weighing machine
   319
weight
   influence **175**
   gravity 319

wide 202
- apart 15
- awake *hat* 225
 intelligent 498
- away 196
- berth 748
- of the mark
 distance 196
 deviation 279
 error 495
- of *distant* 196
- open 194, 260
- of the truth 495
- world 180, 318
 in the - world 180
widen 194
- the breach 713,
 900
wide-spread
 great 31
 dispersed 73
 space 180
 expanded 194
widow 905
widowhood 905
width 202
wield
 brandish 315
 handle 379
 use 677
- authority 737
- the sword 722
wieldy 705
wife 903
wig 225
wigging 932
wiggle 315
wight 373
wigwam 189
wild 851
 unproductive 169
 violent 173
 plain 344
 inattentive 458
 mad 503
 shy 623
 unskilled 699
 excited 824, 825
 untamed 851
 rash 863
 angry 900
 licentious 954
 run - 825
- animals 366
- beast *fierce* 173
 evil-doer 913
- goose chase
 caprice 608
 useless 645
 unskilful 699
- imagination 515

sow one's - oats
 grow up 131
 improve 658
 amusement 840
 vice 945
 intemperance 954
Wild, Jonathan -
 thief 792
 bad man 949
wilderness
 disorder 59
 unproductive 169
 space 180
 solitude 893
wild-fire 382
 spread like -
 violence 173
 influence 175
 expand 194
 publication 531
wile 545, 702
wilful
 voluntary 600
 obstinate 606
will ·
 volition **600**
 resolution 604
 testament 771
 gift 784
 at - 600
 at one's own
 sweet - 608
 have one's own -
 600, 748
 make one's - 360
 tenant at - 779
- be 152
- for the deed
 774, 937
- of Heaven 601
- he nil he 601
- power 600
- and will not 605
- you 765
 Will o' the wisp
 luminary 423
 imp 980
willing or unwilling
 601
willingness **602**
willow 839
willy-nilly 601, 744
wilted 659
wily 702
wimble 262
wimple 225
win 731, 775
- the affections
 897
- golden opinions
 931

- the heart 829
- laurels 873
- out 33
- over *belief* 484
 induce 615
 content 831
wince
 bodily pain 378
 emotion 821
 excitement 825
 mental pain 828
 flinch 860
winch 307, 633
wind *convolution*
 [*see below*]
 velocity 274
 blast **349**
 life 359
 against the - 278,
 708
 before the - 278,
 734
 cast to the -s
 repudiate 610
 disuse 678
 not observe 773
 relinquish 782
 close to the - 278
 fair - 705
 to the four -s 180
 get - 531
 get the - up 860
 see how the -
 blows
 direction 278
 experiment 463
 foresight 510
 fickle 607
 in the - 151, 152
 lose - 688
 sail near the -
 direction 278
 skill 698
 sharp practice 940
 outstrip the - 274
 preach to the -s
 645
 raise the - 775
 scatter to the -s
 756
 see where the -
 lies 698
 short -ed 688
 sport of -s and
 waves 315
 sound of - and
 limb 654
 take the - out of
 one's sails
 render powerless
 158

 hinder 706
 defeat 731
 touched in the -
 655
 what's in the - ?
 461
- ahead 708
- bag 584
 in the -'s eye 278
- the horn 416
 hit between - and
 water 659
- and weather
 permitting
 qualification 469
 possibility 470
wind *blast* [*see
 above*]
 convolution 248
 deviate 279
 circuition 311
- round the heart
 897
- up *strengthen* 159
 prepare 673
 complete 729
- accounts 811
windbag 884
wind instruments
 417
wind-bound 706
windfall 618
wind-gauge 349
wind-gun 727
winding 248, 311
winding-sheet 363
**windings and turn-
 ings** 248
wind-jammer 273
windlass 307, 633
windless 688
windmill 312
 tilt at -s 638
window 260
 make the -s shake
 loud noise 404
- dressing 544
wind-pipe 351
wind-up 67
windward, to - 236,
 278
windy 349
wine 298, 959
 put new - into old
 bottles 699
 look upon the -
 when it is red
 953
wine-bibbing 959
wine-cooler 387
wineglass 191